CASES AND MATERIALS ON
SEXUAL ORIENTATION AND THE LAW

Fifth Edition

■ ■ ■

by

William B. Rubenstein
Sidley Austin Professor of Law
Harvard Law School

Carlos A. Ball
Distinguished Professor of Law & Judge Frederick Lacey Scholar
Rutgers University School of Law (Newark)

Jane S. Schacter
William Nelson Cromwell Professor of Law
Stanford Law School

Douglas NeJaime
Professor of Law
University of California, Irvine School of Law

AMERICAN CASEBOOK SERIES®

Mat #41552215

For Richard. And for our sons, Emmanuel and Sebastian.

C.A.B.

For Juliet, Gabe and Zoe.

J.S.S.

For Shaun. And for my parents, Julie and Michael.

D.N.

PREFACE TO THE FIFTH EDITION

As readers of this casebook undoubtedly know, the legal frameworks surrounding sexual orientation and gender identity are among the most dynamic and rapidly evolving in all of law. Since the last edition of this casebook, there have been significant developments at every level—federal and state; judicial, legislative and executive; constitutional and statutory. And the U.S. Supreme Court has weighed in with a historic decision on the federal Defense of Marriage Act. Of course, change has not been confined to legal arenas. Social and cultural change is happening even more rapidly. And in November 2012, for the first time voters approved marriage equality at the ballot box. The intense pace of all of this activity makes it not only impossible for a casebook to stay fully current, but misguided to try. This edition, then, undertakes to be as current as possible as of its publication, but its more fundamental aim remains the one that inspired its creation nearly two decades ago: to provide an engaging, interdisciplinary basis for studying the movement for LGBT equality and the law's complex regulation of sexual orientation and gender identity. We hope that the book provides a solid foundation, recognizing that it can and should be supplemented by current developments as they arise.

We are grateful to Harvard Law School, Stanford Law School, Rutgers School of Law—Newark, and the University of California, Irvine School of Law for supporting our work on this casebook. We are indebted to colleagues who have consistently provided critical and thoughtful comments and suggestions over multiple editions of this casebook. We owe special thanks to Clifford Rosky at the University of Utah, Steven Homer at the University of New Mexico, and Brad Sears at the Williams Institute at UCLA School of Law. We would also like to thank the many students we have had the privilege of teaching—and learning from—over the years; their contributions are reflected throughout these pages. They include students at nearly a dozen law schools scattered throughout the United States—Harvard, Yale, Stanford, UCLA, Wisconsin, Michigan, Illinois, Rutgers, Penn State, Loyola–Los Angeles, and UC Irvine. For their help with this edition, we especially want to thank Stanford Law students Christina Black, Lydia Gray and Matthew Higgins, and UC Irvine Law student David Bethea.

Acknowledgements

We are indebted to the copyright holders identified below for permission to reprint excerpts from the following copyrighted materials (listed in the order they appear in the book):

Carlos A. Ball, Martha Nussbaum, Essentialism, and Sexuality, 19 Columbia Journal of Gender & the Law 3 (2010). Copyright © 2008 by the Columbia Journal of Gender and the Law. Reprinted by permission of the Columbia Journal of Gender and the Law.

Sonia Katyal, Exporting Identity, 14 Yale Journal of Law & Feminism 97 (2006). Copyright © 2006 by the Yale Journal of Law & Feminism. Reprinted with Permission of the Yale Journal of Law & Feminism.

Polyamory as a Sexual Orientation, by Ann Tweedy, from 79 Univeristy of Cincinnati Law Review 1461 (2011). Copyright © 2011. Reprinted by permission of the University of Cincinnati Law Review.

The Epistemic Contract of Bisexual Erasure, by Kenji Yoshino, from 52 Stanford Law Review 353 (2002). Copyright © 2002 by the Board of Trustees of the Leland Stanford Junior University. Reprinted with permission.

Terry S. Kogan, Transsexuals and Critical Gender Theory: The Possibility of a Restroom Labeled "Other", 48 Hastings Law Journal 1223 (1997). © 1997 by University of California, Hastings College of the Law. Reprinted from Hastings Law Journal, Volume 48, Number 6, August 1997 (1223), by permission, and by permission of Terry S. Kogan.

Resisting Medicine, Re/modeling Gender, by Dean Spade, from 18 Berkeley Women's Law Journal 15 (2003). Copyright © 2003. Reprinted by permission of the Regents of the University of California.

Documenting Gender, by Dean Spade, from 59 Hastings Law Journal 731 (2008). Copyright © 2008. Reprinted by permission of the University of California, Hastings.

Defining Male and Female: Intersexuality and the Collision Between Law and Biology, by Julie A. Greenberg, from 41 Arizona Law Review 265 (1999). Copyright © 1999 by the Arizona Law Review. Reprinted with permission.

The Enforcement of Morals, by Patrick Devlin, reprinted in Criminal Law and Its Processes: Cases and Materials 45–49 (Sanford H. Kadish and Monrad G. Paulsen eds.). Copyright © 1975 by Little, Brown & Company. Reprinted with permission.

Immorality and Treason, by H.L.A. Hart, reprinted in Criminal Law and Its Processes: Cases and Materials (Sanford H. Kadish and Monrad G. Paulsen eds.). Copyright © 1975 by Little, Brown & Company. Reprinted with permission.

Model Penal Code. Copyright © 1985 by The American Law Institute. Reprinted with permission of the American Law Institute.

Private Experiences in the Public Domain: Lesbians in Organizations, by Marny Hall. Copyright © 1989, by Marny Hall. Reprinted by permission of Marny Hall.

Allen Grant Richards, Out at Work: A Trans Perspective, Bay Windows, June 27, 2003. Reprinted by permission of author.

M.V. Lee Badgett, Brad Sears, Holning Lau, Deborah Ho, Bias in the Workplace: Consistent Evidence of Sexual Orientation and Gender Identity Discrimination 1998–2008, 84 Chicago-Kent Law Review 559 (2009). Copyright © 2009 by Chicago-Kent Law Review. Reprinted by permission of the Chicago-Kent Law Review.

Kenji Yoshino, Covering, 111 Yale Law Journal 769 (2002). Copyright © 2002 by the Yale Law Journal. Reprinted by permission of the Yale Law Journal.

At Least Me and Rafael Tried, by Paul Butler, from Aurora: A Feminist Magazine (Winter 1982). Copyright © 1982 by Paul Butler. Reprinted by permission of Paul Butler.

Marriage and the Struggle for Gay, Lesbian and Black Liberation, by Randall Kennedy, from 2005 Utah Law Review 781. Copyright © 2005 by the Utah Law Review. Reprinted with permission.

The Positive in the Fundamental Right to Marry: Same–Sex Marriage in the Aftermath of Lawrence v. Texas, by Carlos A. Ball, from 88 Minnesota Law Review 1184 (2004). Copyright © 2004 by the Minnesota Law Review. Reprinted with permission.

Interstate Recognition of Same–Sex Marriages and Civil Unions: A Handbook for Judges, by Andrew Koppelman, from 153 University of Pennsylvanian Law Review 2143 (2005). Copyright © 2005 by the University of Pennsylvania Law Review. Reprinted by permission of the University of Pennsylvania Law Review and William S. Hein & Co., Inc.

Brown and Lawrence (and Goodridge), by Michael Klarman. Reprinted from Michigan Law Review, December 2005, vol. 104, no. 3. Copyright © 2005 by the Michigan Law Review Association. Reprinted by permission of the Michigan Law Review and Michael Klarman.

Mary L. Bonauto, Goodridge in Context, 40 Harvard Civil Rights-Civil Liberties Law Review 1 (2005). © 2005 by the President and Fellows of Harvard College and the Harvard Civil Rights–Civil Liberties Law Review.

Gabriel Arana, Gay on Trial, *The American Prospect*: December 2009, Volume 20, Issue 10. http.www.prospect.org. *The American Prospect*,

1710 Rhode Island Avenue, NW, Washington, DC 20036. All rights reserved.

Beyond DOMA: Choice of State Law in Federal Statutes, by William Baude, from 64 Stanford Law Review 1371 (2012). Copyright © 2012. Reprinted by permission of the Board of Trustees of the Leland Stanford Junior University, from the Stanford Law Review at Vol. 64 Stan. L. Rev. 1371 (2012).

Marriage Inequality: Same-Sex Relationships, Religious Exemptions, and the Production of Sexual Orientation Discrimination, by Douglas NeJaime, from 100 California Law Review 1169 (2012). Copyright © 2012 by the California Law Review, Inc. Reprinted by permission of the California Law Review.

Why Gay People Should Seek the Right to Marry, by Thomas Stoddard, from Out/Look: National Lesbian and Gay Quarterly (Fall 1989). Copyright © 1989 by the Out/Look Foundation. Reprinted by permission of Out/Look.

Since When is Marriage a Path to Liberation?, by Paula Ettelbrick, from Out/Look: National Lesbian and Gay Quarterly (Fall 1989). Copyright © 1989 by the Out/Look Foundation. Reprinted by permission of Out/Look.

(How) Does the Sexual Orientation of Parents Matter?, by Judith Stacey and Timothy J. Biblarz, from American Sociological Review, vol. 66, p. 159 (2001). Copyright © 2001 by the American Sociological Review. Reprinted by permission of the American Sociological Review and the authors.

Sexual Orientation and Adoptive Matching, by Joseph Evall, from 25 Family Law Quarterly 347 (1991). Copyright © 1992 by the American Bar Association. Reprinted by permission.

Nancy D. Polikoff, Resisting "Don't Ask, Don't Tell" in the Licensing of Lesbian and Gay Foster Parents: Why Openness Will Benefit Lesbian and Gay Youth, 48 Hastings Law Journal 1183 (1997). © 1997 by University of California, Hastings College of the Law. Reprinted from Hastings Law Journal, Volume 48, Number 6, August 1997 (1183), by permission, and by permission of Nancy D. Polikoff.

Protecting Families: Standards for Child Custody in Same–Sex Relationships, by Gay & Lesbian Advocates & Defenders, from 10 UCLA Women's Law Journal 151 (1999). Copyright © 1999 by the UCLA Women's Law Journal. Reprinted with permission.

Carlos A. Ball, The Right to be Parents: LGBT Families and the Transformation of Parenthood (2010). Copyright © 2010 by the New York University Press. Reprinted with permission.

* * *

We have made every effort to obtain permission to reproduce copyrighted material in this volume. If permission has inadvertently been missed or proper acknowledgment has not been made, please contact the authors c/o West Publishing Company.

WILLIAM B. RUBENSTEIN
CARLOS A. BALL
JANE S. SCHACTER
DOUGLAS NEJAIME

March, 2014

SUMMARY OF CONTENTS

TABLE OF CONTENTS

TABLE OF CASES

The principal cases are in bold type.

CASES AND MATERIALS ON
SEXUAL ORIENTATION AND THE LAW

Fifth Edition

CHAPTER 1

BASIC DOCUMENTS

▪ ▪ ▪

I. SEXUALITY, GENDER, AND IDENTITY

SEXUALITY AND GLOBAL FORCES: DR. ALFRED KINSEY AND THE SUPREME COURT OF THE UNITED STATES*
Michael Kirby

Dr. Alfred Kinsey [began teaching as an assistant professor of biology at Indiana University in Bloomington in 1920.] His research on gall wasps . . . effectively [made him] a world expert on that subject.

Kinsey's obscure but worthy scholarly life might have continued in Bloomington in this way but for one of those shifts of the mind that mark out the greatest of scientists. By the mid-1930s, Kinsey became very interested in great scientists, participating in an undergraduate course, "Life Views of Great Men of Science." Perhaps it was reflecting upon such scientists, and their breakthroughs, that led Kinsey's mind into a new field of biology concerning what he sometimes called "the human animal." He later claimed that published research of Dr. Robert Dickinson, an American leader in sex education, maternal health, and birth control, led him to become interested in sex research in humans. In 1938 he began a marriage course for undergraduates and others at Indiana University. Predictably enough, this attracted opposition from conservative circles, but it was supported by the University Trustees. By the late 1930s, Kinsey was working on a "biometric treatment of data," applying the same meticulous scientific methodologies he had developed in studying gall wasps, so far as that was possible, to the study of human sexual behavior.

Books have been written, plays have been staged, and documentaries and films have been screened concerning the way Kinsey began his program of research involving human sexual experience in prisons and elsewhere. One of the early ideas that evolved from his thousands of interviews was that the previous assumption of a strict binary division between "homosexuals" and "heterosexuals" was factually inaccurate. Kinsey was beginning to postulate a rating scale by which individuals

---

*   MICHAEL KIRBY, *Sexuality and Global Forces: Dr. Alfred Kinsey and the Supreme Court of the United States*, 14 IND. J. GLOBAL LEGAL STUD. 485, 491–500 (2007).

1

could be ranked at different points in relation to their sexual behavior, inclinations, and interests. His was not an enterprise to collect erotic stories for the titillation of particular audiences. It was a case of a "taxonomist working with a taxonomic problem. The methods remain the same; only the material is changed."

Kinsey's questionnaire format was refined during the 1940s. From the beginning, it covered questions on the major sexual outlets of the human subjects: masturbation, sex dreams, petting, and coitus. The last was subdivided into categories based on the identity of the sexual partner. This allowed for sub-classifications including pre-marital, marital, extra-marital, and post-marital coitus as well as intercourse with prostitutes. Kinsey added two almost unexplored areas of sexual activity, namely homosexual relations and sexual contacts with animals. His research was quite unique. No one, with such methodological precision, had ever before attempted such a systematic study of human sexual experience. * * *

[There was] fierce opposition to Kinsey's research from churches, politicians, fellow academics, civic groups, and others. His work on human sexuality survived only because of the strength of his personality, the support of his wife and of his immediate colleagues, and the unwavering insistence of the President of Indiana University, Dr. Herman Wells, that the University existed both for teaching and for the search for truth. . . .

Kinsey's first major report, published in 1948, was titled *Sexual Behavior in the Human Male*. The second report, published in 1953, was *Sexual Behavior in the Human Female*. Each report, but especially the first, burst upon the world as an intellectual bombshell of new ideas. Each report challenged assumptions that were generally accepted throughout the world concerning human sexual experience. Each undermined the strict binary notions of sexual orientation. Each demonstrated widespread human inclination to sexual variety, experimentation, and sexual experience of various kinds throughout life. . . .

The research of Kinsey and his colleagues helped revolutionize thinking about sexual behavior both in the United States and far beyond. The Kinsey approach had eschewed fixed or preordained categories and hypotheses. Instead, it focused on comprehensive fact-gathering from a large but non-random sample of college students, prisoners, and Indianans swept into the giant study at Kinsey's Institute for Sex Research.

The study of male respondents concluded:

Males do not represent two discrete populations, heterosexual and homosexual. The world is not to be divided into sheep and goats. . . . It is a fundamental of taxonomy that nature rarely deals with discrete categories. Only the human mind invents categories and tries to force facts into separated pigeon-holes. The living world is a continuum in each and every one of its aspects. The sooner we learn this concerning human sexual behavior the sooner we shall reach a sound understanding of the realities of sex.

Amongst the most surprising findings recorded in the 1948 Kinsey Report concerned homosexuality. Until that time, American psychologists, Freudian and otherwise, and their counterparts world-wide, had depicted homosexuality as biologically abnormal and psychologically poisonous. The Kinsey findings cast doubt at least on the rarity and abnormality of homosexual orientation.

- 37% of the male population had at least one overt homosexual experience to orgasm between the ages of 16 and 45, while another 13% react erotically to other males without having an experience to orgasm. This means that 50% of the male population had experienced significant homosexual erotic attraction during adulthood.

- 30% of the male population had had at least incidental homosexual experience or reactions (rating one or above on the Kinsey scale) over at least a three-year period between ages 16 and 55.

- 25% of the male population had had more than incidental experience (rating two or above). . . .

- 18% of the male population had had at least as much homosexual as heterosexual experience (rating three or above) over at least a three-year period. . . .

- 10% of the male population had been more or less exclusively homosexual (rating five or six) for at least a three-year period, with 8% being completely homosexual (rating six) for at least that period.

- 4% of the white male population was exclusively homosexual (rating six) for their entire adult lives.

The findings in the 1948 Kinsey Report concerning heterosexual activity were almost as surprising. Contrary to the then accepted mores, Kinsey and his colleagues found that virtually all men masturbated, even after they were married; that many husbands had sexual affairs during their marriage, many of them without guilt (or discovery); and that married couples engaged in a range of sexual activities, including oral and anal sex as well as vaginal sex.

The 1953 study on *Sexual Behavior in the Human Female* reported significant, but much lower, homosexual attraction and activity among women. It found that 28 percent of the women sampled had experienced significant erotic attraction to other women (compared with 50 percent of the male sample), and 13 percent had homosexual experiences to orgasm (compared with 37 percent of the male sample). But Kinsey's great contribution to the study of women's sexuality was to establish beyond reasonable doubt that women are sexually active rather than passive "by nature":

- "Nearly 50% of the sample had engaged in premarital intercourse, a considerable portion with their fiances in the year or two before marriage." This discovery, unremarkable in today's society, came as a great shock to many in 1953.

- "Among married couples, women tended to be more interested in intercourse later in the marriage, whereas men tended to be most interested early in the marriage."

- "26% of women (in contrast to 50% of the male sample) had engaged in extramarital coitus by the age of forty. Incidence of extramarital inter-course in women was affected by religious background more than any other factor."

- "By age twenty, only 33% of women had masturbated compared with 92% of their male contemporaries."

Kinsey's findings confronted social assumptions that were the foundation of much religious and other moral instruction. They challenged the beliefs about fellow citizens and human beings held by most people and the laws that gave effect to the social postulates about sexual experience. Those laws concerned matters such as the woman's role in marriage and her subordination to the rights of her husband with very limited entitlements to divorce, the woman's access to forms of contraception to control reproduction and to prevent unwanted pregnancies, and the operation of anti-sodomy laws and laws against the so-called unnatural offenses designed to stamp out such "abominable crimes" which one judge in Georgia, in 1904, had declared to be " 'the abominable crime not fit to be named amongst Christians.' " * * *

[B]ig changes in the law and in society have undoubtedly been made in the fifty years since Dr. Kinsey's death [in 1956]. He is not alone responsible for the changes. But his research encouraged other investigations casting doubt on the previously accepted generalizations about homosexuals. One of the foremost followers of Kinsey was Evelyn Hooker, a psychologist who, like Kinsey, was drawn into sex research as a second career. Eventually, this scientific work caused the American Psychological Association to move away from the earlier assumptions and, in 1975, to declare that "[h]omosexuality, per se, implies no impairment in judgment, stability, reliability or general social or vocational capabilities [and mental health professionals should] take the lead in removing the stigma of mental illness that has long been associated with homosexual orientations."

THE SOCIAL ORGANIZATION OF SEXUALITY*
Edward O. Laumann et al.

THE MYTH OF 10 PERCENT AND THE KINSEY RESEARCH

* * *

Kinsey's figures are much higher than those found in all the recent population surveys, including ours. There are a number of reasons for this. . . . the major difference between Kinsey and recent research is that Kinsey did not use probability sampling. Kinsey's respondents were all purposefully recruited rather than sampled with known probabilities of inclusion. This means both that they were volunteers who may have differed in systematic ways from those who did not participate (e.g., by being more open and comfortable about their sex lives and perhaps more sexually active) and that there is no statistically sound way to generalize from his sample to a population. In fact, Kinsey roamed far and wide in selecting his subjects. He was not averse to using institutional settings, including prisons and reform schools, from which to recruit his subjects. Kinsey also purposely recruited subjects for his research from homosexual friendship and acquaintance networks in big cities. Kinsey combined fantasy, masturbation, and sexual activity with partners in some of his calculations (e.g., the 50 percent figure). Experiences were collected retrospectively over the whole lifetime and almost as a matter of course were reported to include activity since puberty or since age sixteen. These devices would all tend to bias Kinsey's results toward higher estimates of homosexuality (and other rarer sexual practices) than those that he would have obtained using probability sampling. Almost all the recent sexual behavior research, largely prompted by AIDS and the sexual transmission of disease, has focused on behavior, primarily penetrative sexual practices.

* * *

DIMENSIONS OF HOMOSEXUALITY

To quantify or count something requires unambiguous definition of the phenomenon in question. And we lack this in speaking of homosexuality. When people ask how many gays there are, they assume that everyone knows exactly what is meant. Historians and

---

*   EDWARD O. LAUMANN, JOHN H. GAGNON, ROBERT T. MICHAEL & STUART MICHAELS, *Homosexuality*, in THE SOCIAL ORGANIZATION OF SEXUALITY 283, 289–301 (1994).

anthropologists have shown that homosexuality as a category describing same-gender sexual desire and behavior is a relatively recent phenomenon (only about 100 years old) peculiar to the West. But, even within contemporary Western societies, one must ask whether this question refers to same-gender behavior, desire, self-definition, or identification or some combination of these elements. In asking the question, most people treat homosexuality as such a distinctive category that it is as if all these elements must go together. On reflection, it is obvious that this is not true. One can easily think of cases where any one of these elements would be present without the others and that combinations of these attributes, taken two or three at a time, are also possible.

Examples abound. Some people have fantasies or thoughts about sex with someone of their own gender without ever acting on these thoughts or wishes. And the holder of such thoughts may be pleased, excited, or upset and made to feel guilty by them. They may occur as a passing phase, only sporadically, or even as a persisting feature of a person's fantasy life. They may or may not have any effect at all on whether a person thinks of himself or herself as a homosexual in any sense. Clearly, there are people who experience erotic interest in people of both genders and sustain sexual relationships over time with both men and women. Some engage in sex with same-gender partners without any erotic or psychological desire because they have been forced or enticed into doing so. A classic example is sex in prison. Deprived of the opportunity to have sex with opposite-gender partners gives rise to same-gender sex, by volition or as the result of force. Surely this is to be distinguished phenomenally from situations in which people who, given access to both genders, actively seek out and choose to have sex with same-gender partners. Development of self-identification as homosexual or gay is a psychologically and socially complex state, something which, in this society, is achieved only over time, often with considerable personal struggle and self-doubt, not to mention social discomfort. All these motives, attractions, identifications, and behaviors vary over time and circumstances with respect to one another—that is, are dynamically changing features of an individual's sexual expression.

* * *

MEASUREMENT AND PREVALENCE OF SAME-GENDER BEHAVIOR, DESIRE, AND IDENTITY

[Thus,] for the purpose of this analysis, we have divided the questions that relate to homosexual experiences and feelings into three basic dimensions: behavior, desire, and identity. The questions that we asked about behavior always refer to partners or practices in specific time frames. Desire and identity are measured by questions about the respondents' current states of mind. * * *

THE INTERRELATION OF SAME-GENDER SEXUAL BEHAVIOR, DESIRE, AND IDENTITY

How are these three aspects of homosexuality interrelated? To answer this question, we first need to define a simple dichotomous variable denoting the presence or absence of each dimension. We sought relatively broad and inclusive summary measures for this analysis. However, we have excluded people who report their only same-gender sex partners before they turned eighteen. Thus, we have defined *behavior* in terms of a composite measure intended to tap the presence of any same-gender partner after age eighteen. *Desire* combines the *appeal* and *attraction* measures defined above. For this purpose, any respondent who reported either being attracted to people of his or her own gender or finding same-gender sex appealing is considered to have some same-gender desire. Same-gender identity includes people who said that they considered themselves to be either homosexual or bisexual (or an equivalent).

Figure 8.2 displays the overlap among these three conceptually separable dimensions of homosexuality using Venn diagrams. These diagrams make use of overlapping circles to display all the logically possible intersections among different categories. While a Venn diagram distinguishes all possible combinations, it does not attempt to scale the areas in the circles to reflect the relative numbers of respondents in each category because of technical constraints in the geometry of representation. The latter is indicated by the numbers and percentages attached to each area.

The three circles each represent a dimension or component of same-gender sexuality. The totals of 150 women and 143 men, respectively, who report any same-gender behavior, desire, or identity are distributed across all the possible mutually exclusive combinations of the three categories. For example, the area of the circle labeled *desire* that does not overlap with either of the other circles includes only those respondents who reported some same-gender desire but reported neither same-gender partners since eighteen nor self-identification as a homosexual or bisexual. Desire with no corresponding adult behavior or identity is the largest category for both men and women, with about 59 percent of the women and 44 percent of the men in this cell. About 13 percent of the women and 22 percent of the men report a same-gender partner since turning eighteen, but no current desire or identity.

A.   Women

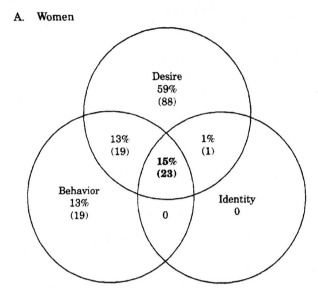

B.   Men

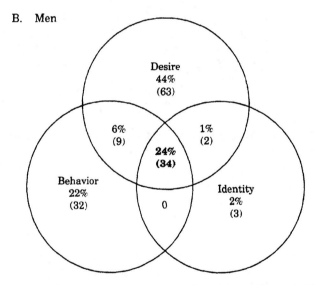

Fig. 8.2 Interrelation of components of homosexuality. A, For 150 women (8.6 percent of the total 1,749) who report any adult same-gender sexuality. B, For 143 men (10.1 percent of the total 1,410) who report any adult same-gender sexuality.

No women reported homosexual identity alone. But there were three men who said that they considered themselves homosexual or bisexual even though they did not report desire or partners. This being an unlikely status, it is possible that these men simply misunderstood the categories of self-identification since none of them reported any same-gender experience or interest.

About 15 percent of the women and 24 percent of the men are found in the intersection of all three circles. This is practically all the women (twenty-three out of twenty-four) and the vast majority of the men (thirty-four out of thirty-nine) who identify as homosexual or bisexual. In order to see the relative proportions in each set of categories more clearly, pie charts based on the same data and categories are displayed in figure 8.3.

As it is measured here, sexual identity does not appear to represent an analytically separate dimension because it logically entails the existence of both desire and action. Desire, behavior, and the combination of desire and behavior seem to exist in at least a substantial minority of the cases, but identity independent of the other two is quite rare. It is thus not surprising that no men or women reported behavior and identity without desire. Some sort of homosexual desire seems at the heart of most notions of homosexual identity. To report same-gender partners, *and* to say that one considers oneself to be homosexual or bisexual, *but* to deny any attraction or appeal of homosexuality, seems illogical. On the other hand, the idea of someone reporting desire and identity but no (adult) behavior does not seem so implausible since homosexuality is often thought of as an underlying sexual orientation understood in a psychological sense of fantasy or desire. One can at least imagine people who consider themselves to be homosexual (or bisexual) without necessarily having had any sex partners. In fact, this state appears to be quite rare, with only one woman and two men found in this category.

This analysis demonstrates the high degree of variability in the way that differing elements of homosexuality are distributed in the population. This variability relates to the way that homosexuality is both organized as a set of behaviors and practices and experienced subjectively. It raises quite provocative questions about the definition of *homosexuality*. While there is a core group (about 2.4 percent of the total men and about 1.3 percent of the total women) in our survey who define themselves as homosexual or bisexual, have same-gender partners, and express homosexual desires, there are also sizable groups who do not consider themselves to be either homosexual or bisexual but have had adult homosexual experiences or express some degree of desire. Despite pervasive social disapproval, about 5 percent of the men and women in our sample express some same-gender desire, but no other indicators of adult activity or self-identification. A sizable number have had same-gender partners, but consider themselves neither as bisexual or homosexual nor as experiencing any current homosexual desire. While the measurement of same-gender practices and attitudes is crude at best, with unknown levels of underreporting for each, this preliminary analysis provides unambiguous evidence that no single number can be used to provide an accurate and valid characterization of the incidence and prevalence of homosexuality in the population at large. In sum, homosexuality is fundamentally a multidimensional phenomenon that has manifold meanings and interpretations, depending on context and purpose.

A. Women

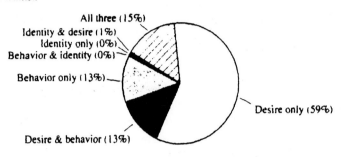

B. Men

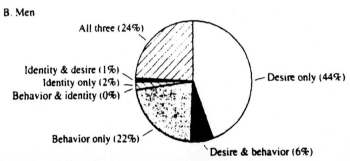

Fig. 8.3   Interrelation of different aspects of same-gender sexuality. A, For 150 women (8.6 percent of the total 1,749) who report any adult same-gender sexuality. B, For 143 men (10.1 percent of the total 1,410) who report any adult same-gender sexuality.

HOW MANY PEOPLE ARE LESBIAN, GAY, BISEXUAL, AND TRANSGENDER?*

Gary J. Gates

INTRODUCTION

Increasing numbers of population-based surveys in the United States and across the world include questions designed to measure sexual orientation and gender identity. Understanding the size of the lesbian, gay, bisexual, and transgender (LGBT) population is a critical first step to informing a host of public policy and research topics. . . .

---

*   Gary Gates, *How Many People are Lesbian, Gay, Bisexual, and Transgender?*, WILLIAMS INSTITUTE (2011).

CHALLENGES IN MEASURING THE LGBT COMMUNITY

Estimates of the size of the LGBT community vary for a variety of reasons. These include differences in the definitions of who is included in the LGBT population, differences in survey methods, and a lack of consistent questions asked in a particular survey over time.

In measuring sexual orientation, lesbian, gay, and bisexual individuals may be identified strictly based on their self-identity or it may be possible to consider same-sex sexual behavior or sexual attraction. Some surveys (not considered in this brief) also assess household relationships and provide a mechanism of identifying those who are in same-sex relationships. Identity, behavior, attraction, and relationships all capture related dimensions of sexual orientation but none of these measures completely addresses the concept.

Defining the transgender population can also be challenging. Definitions of who may be considered part of the transgender community include aspects of both gender identities and varying forms of gender expression or non-conformity. Similar to sexual orientation, one way to measure the transgender community is to simply consider self-identity. Measures of identity could include consideration of terms like transgender, queer, or genderqueer. The latter two identities are used by some to capture aspects of both sexual orientation and gender identity.

Similar to using sexual behaviors and attraction to capture elements of sexual orientation, questions may also be devised that consider gender expression and non-conformity regardless of the terms individuals may use to describe themselves. An example of these types of questions would be consideration of the relationship between the sex that individuals are assigned at birth and the degree to which that assignment conforms with how they express their gender. Like the counterpart of measuring sexual orientation through identity, behavior, and attraction measures, these varying approaches capture related dimensions of who might be classified as transgender but may not individually address all aspects of assessing gender identity and expression.

Another factor that can create variation among estimates of the LGBT community is survey methodology. Survey methods can affect the willingness of respondents to report stigmatizing identities and behaviors. Feelings of confidentiality and anonymity increase the likelihood that respondents will be more accurate in reporting sensitive information. Survey methods that include face-to-face interviews may underestimate the size of the LGBT community while those that include methods that allow respondents to complete questions on a computer or via the internet may increase the likelihood of LGBT respondents identifying themselves. Varied sample sizes of surveys can also increase variation. Population-based surveys with a larger sample can produce more precise estimates.

A final challenge in making population-based estimates of the LGBT community is the lack of questions asked over time on a single large survey. One way of assessing the reliability of estimates is to repeat questions over time using a consistent method and sampling strategy. Adding questions to more large-scale surveys that are repeated over time would substantially improve our ability to make better estimates of the size of the LGBT population.

[Gates then analyzes and compares estimates of the LGBT population from eleven recent United States and international surveys.] * * *

HOW MANY LESBIAN, GAY, BISEXUAL AND TRANSGENDER PEOPLE ARE THERE IN THE UNITED STATES?

Federal data sources designed to provide population estimates in the United States (e.g., the Decennial Census or the American Community Survey) do not include direct questions regarding sexual orientation or gender identity. . . . [N]o single survey offers a definitive estimate for the size of the LGBT community in the United States.

However, combining information from the population-based surveys considered in this brief offers a mechanism to produce credible estimates for the size of the LGBT community. Specifically, estimates for sexual orientation identity will be derived by averaging results from . . . five US surveys. . . .

Separate averages are calculated for lesbian and bisexual women along with gay and bisexual men. An estimate for the transgender population is derived by averaging the findings from . . . Massachusetts and California surveys. . . .

It should be noted that some transgender individuals may identify as lesbian, gay, or bisexual. So it is not possible to make a precise combined LGBT estimate. Instead, Figure 5 presents separate estimates for the number of LGB adults and the number of transgender adults.

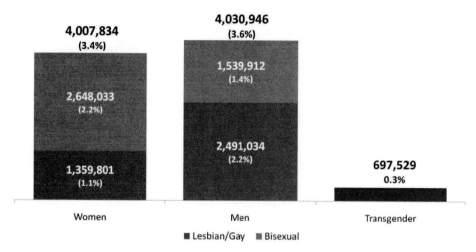

Figure 5. Percent and number of adults who identify as LGBT in the United States.

The analyses suggest that there are more than 8 million adults in the US who are LGB, comprising 3.5% of the adult population. This is split nearly evenly between lesbian/gay and bisexual identified individuals, 1.7% and 1.8%, respectively. There are also nearly 700,000 transgender individuals in the US. Given these findings, it seems reasonable to assert that approximately 9 million Americans identify as LGBT.

Averaging measures of same-sex sexual behavior yields an estimate of nearly 19 million Americans (8.2%) who have engaged in same- sex sexual behavior. The National Survey of Family Growth is the only source of US data on attraction and suggests that 11% or nearly 25.6 million Americans acknowledge at least some same-sex sexual attraction.

SPECIAL REPORT: 3.4% OF U.S. ADULTS IDENTIFY AS LGBT*

Gary J. Gates and Frank Newport

The inaugural results of a new Gallup question—posed to more than 120,000 U.S. adults thus far—shows that 3.4% say "yes" when asked if they identify as lesbian, gay, bisexual, or transgender.

Do you, personally, identify as lesbian, gay, bisexual, or transgender?

	Yes	No	DK/Refused
All Americans	3.4%	92.2%	4.4%

Gallup Daily tracking
June 1-Sept. 30, 2012

GALLUP

These results are based on responses to the question, "Do you, personally, identify as lesbian, gay, bisexual, or transgender?" included in 121,290 Gallup Daily tracking interviews conducted between June 1 and Sept. 30, 2012. This is the largest single study of the distribution of the lesbian, gay, bisexual, and transgender (LGBT) population in the U.S. on record. . . . The 3.4% figure is similar to a 3.8% estimate made by one of the authors of this study (Gates), averaging a group of smaller U.S. surveys conducted from 2004 to 2008. . . .

Gallup chose the broad measure of personal identification as LGBT because this grouping of four statuses is commonly used in current American discourse, and as a result has important cultural and political significance. One obvious limitation of this approach is that it is not possible to separately consider differences among lesbians, gay men, bisexuals, or transgender individuals. A second limitation is that this approach measures broad self-identity, and does not measure sexual or other behavior, either past or present.

The following sections review the percentage identifying as LGBT across specific subgroups of the U.S. population. Overall, the results from this analysis run counter to some media stereotypes that portray the LGBT community as predominantly white, highly educated, and very wealthy.

Nonwhite Individuals More Likely to Identify as LGBT

Nonwhites are more likely than white segments of the U.S. population to identify as LGBT. The survey results show that 4.6% of African-Americans identify as LGBT, along with 4.0% of Hispanics and 4.3% of Asians. The disproportionately higher representation of LGBT status among nonwhite population segments corresponds to the slightly below-average 3.2% of white Americans who identified as LGBT.

*Do you, personally, identify as lesbian, gay, bisexual, or
transgender?*

	Yes	No	DK/Ref
	%	%	%
Non-Hispanic white	3.2	93.9	2.8
Black	4.6	90.1	5.3
Hispanic	4.0	90.2	5.8
Asian	4.3	92.0	3.7

Gallup Daily tracking
June 1-Sept. 30, 2012

GALLUP

Overall, a third of LGBT-identifiers are nonwhite (33%), compared
with 27% of non-LGBT individuals.

Women Are More Likely to Identify as LGBT Than Are Men

Although the difference is not large, women are slightly more likely
to identify as LGBT than are men (3.6% vs. 3.3%)—a finding that is
consistent with other surveys. Put differently, more than 53% of LGBT
individuals are women.

*Do you, personally, identify as lesbian, gay, bisexual, or
transgender?*

	Yes	No	DK/Ref
	%	%	%
Men	3.3	92.5	4.2
Women	3.6	91.8	4.6

Gallup Daily tracking
June 1-Sept. 30, 2012

GALLUP

Younger Americans More Likely to Identify as LGBT

Adults aged 18 to 29 (6.4%) are more than three times as likely as
seniors aged 65 and older (1.9%) to identify as LGBT. Among those aged
30 to 64, LGBT identity declines with age—at 3.2% for 30- to 49-year-olds
and 2.6% for 50- to 64-year-olds.

Consistent with other recent studies and with the gender gap identified earlier in this report, younger women are more likely to identify as LGBT than are younger men. Among 18- to 29-year-olds, 8.3% of women identify as LGBT, compared with 4.6% of men the same age.

Do you, personally, identify as lesbian, gay, bisexual, or transgender?

	Yes	No	DK/Ref
	%	%	%
18 to 29	6.4	90.1	3.5
30 to 49	3.2	93.6	3.2
50 to 64	2.6	93.1	4.3
65+	1.9	91.5	6.5
18 to 29 Women	8.3	88.0	3.8
18 to 29 Men	4.6	92.1	3.3

Gallup Daily tracking
 June 1-Sept. 30, 2012

GALLUP

It is possible that some of these age differences are due to a greater reluctance on the part of older Americans who may be LGBT to identify as such. In general, younger Americans are more accepting of equal rights and opportunities for gay men and lesbians.

LGBT Americans Tend to Have Lower Levels of Education and Income

Gallup's analysis shows that identification as LGBT is highest among Americans with the lowest levels of education—contrary to what other, more limited, studies have shown. Among those with a high school education or less, 3.5% identify as LGBT, compared with 2.8% of those with a college degree and 3.2% of those with postgraduate education. LGBT identification is highest among those with some college education but not a college degree, at 4.0%.

Do you, personally, identify as lesbian, gay, bisexual, or transgender?

	Yes	No	DK/Ref
	%	%	%
High school or less	3.5	90.3	6.3
Some college	4.0	93.2	2.8
College graduate	2.8	94.7	2.6
Postgraduate education	3.2	94.5	2.3

Gallup Daily tracking
June 1-Sept. 30, 2012

GALLUP

A similar pattern is found across income groups. More than 5% of those with incomes of less than $24,000 a year identify as LGBT, a higher proportion than among those with higher incomes—including 2.8% of those making $60,000 a year or more.

Do you, personally, identify as lesbian, gay, bisexual, or transgender?

	Yes	No	DK/Ref
	%	%	%
Under $24,000	5.1	92.2	2.7
$24,000 to <$60,000	3.6	95.1	1.3
$60,000 to <$90,000	2.8	96.5	0.7
$90,000+	2.8	96.4	0.8

Gallup Daily tracking
June 1-Sept. 30, 2012

GALLUP

Among those who report income, about 16% of LGBT-identified individuals have incomes above $90,000 per year, compared with 21% of the overall adult population. Additionally, 35% of those who identify as LGBT report incomes of less than $24,000 a year, significantly higher than the 24% for the population in general. These findings are consistent with research showing that LGBT people are at a higher risk of poverty.
* * *

THE SCIENCE OF GAYDAR*

David France

. . . A small constellation of researchers is specifically analyzing the traits and characteristics that, though more pronounced in some than in others, not only make us gay but also make us *appear* gay.

At first read, their findings seem like a string of unlinked, esoteric observations. Statistically, for instance, gay men and lesbians have about a 50 percent greater chance of being left-handed or ambidextrous than straight men or women. The relative lengths of our fingers offer another hint: The index fingers of most straight men are shorter than their ring fingers, while for most women they are closer in length, or even reversed in ratio. But some researchers have noted that gay men are likely to have finger-length ratios more in line with those of straight women, and a study of self-described "butch" lesbians showed significantly masculinized ratios. The same goes for the way we hear, the way we process spatial reasoning, and even the ring of our voices. One study, involving tape-recordings of gay and straight men, found that 75 percent of gay men *sounded* gay to a general audience. It's unclear what the listeners responded to, whether there is a recognized gay "accent" or vocal quality. And there is no hint as to whether this idiosyncrasy is owed to biology or cultural influences—only that it's unmistakable. . . .

"These are all part and parcel of the idea that being gay is different—that we are different animals to some extent," says Simon LeVay, the British-born neuroscientist who has dedicated himself to studying these issues. ". . . I support the idea that we're a third sex—or a third sex and a fourth sex, gay men and lesbians. Today, there's scientific documentation behind this." . . .

A string of . . . studies, most of them conducted quietly and with small budgets, has offered up a number of other biological indicators. . . . Some of this work has been derided as modern-day phrenology, and obviously possessing one trait or another—a counterclockwise hair whorl here, an elongated ring finger there—doesn't necessarily make a person gay or straight. But researchers point out that these are statistical averages from the community as a whole. And the cumulative findings support the belief now widely held in the scientific community that sexual orientation—perhaps along with the characteristics we typically associate with gayness—is biological. . . .

Because many of these newly identified "gay" traits and characteristics are known to be influenced in utero, researchers think they may be narrowing in on when gayness is set—and identifying its

---

* David France, *The Science of Gaydar*, NEW YORK MAGAZINE (June 17, 2007), *at* http://nymag.com/news/features/33520/.

possible triggers. They believe that homosexuality may be the result of some interaction between a pregnant mother and her fetus. Several hypothetical mechanisms have been identified, most pointing to an alteration in the flow of male hormones in the formation of boys and female hormones in the gestation of girls. What causes this? Nobody has any direct evidence one way or another, but a list of suspects includes germs, genes, maternal stress, and even allergy—maybe the mother mounts some immunological response to the fetal hormones. . . .

Some of this research may prove to be significant; some will ultimately get chalked up to coincidence. But the thrust of these developing findings puts activists in a bind and brings gay rights to a major crossroads. . . . If sexual orientation is biological, and we are learning to identify how it happens inside the uterus, doesn't it suggest a future in which gay people can be *prevented*? . . .

That in part is why gay people have not hungered for this breakthrough. Late last year, Martina Navratilova joined activists from PETA to speak out against an experiment that sought to intentionally turn sheep gay (it failed, but another experiment successfully turned ferrets into homosexuals, and the sexual orientations of fruit flies have been switched in laboratories). Some 20,000 angry e-mails clogged the researchers' inboxes, comparing the work to Nazi eugenics and arguing that it held no promise of any kind to gay people. "There are positives, but many negatives" to this kind of research, says Matt Foreman, executive director of the National Gay and Lesbian Task Force. "I will bet my life that if a quote-unquote cure was found, that the religious right would have no problem with genetic or other kind of prenatal manipulations. People who don't think that's a clear and present danger are simply not living in reality."

At the dawn of gay politics a half-century ago, the government treated gay people as a menace to national security, and much of the public, kept from any ordinary depictions of gay life, lived in terror of encountering one of us. . . . The groundwork for change began when Evelyn Hooker, a UCLA psychologist, was approached by a gay former student in the fifties. He had noticed that all research on homosexuals looked at men and women who were imprisoned or institutionalized, thereby advancing the belief that homosexuals were abnormal. He proposed that she study men like him as a counterpoint. Over the next two decades, she did just that, proving that none of the known psychological screens could detect a healthy gay person—that there was no clinical pathology to sexual orientation. Of necessity, research at the time was focused on demonstrating how unremarkable gay men and lesbians are: indistinguishable on all personality inventories, equally good at all jobs, benign as parents, unthreatening as neighbors, and so on. On the strength of Hooker's findings, and a Gandhian effort by activists, the APA [American Psychiatric Association] changed its view on homosexuals 34 years ago.

Thereafter, the field of sexual-orientation research fell dormant until 1991, when Simon LeVay conducted the very first study of homosexual biological uniqueness. He had been a researcher at the Salk Institute in La Jolla, California, when his lover fell ill with AIDS. He took a year off to care for him, but his partner ultimately died. Returning to work, LeVay decided he wanted to concentrate on gay themes. "Just like a lot of gay people who'd been directly affected by the epidemic, I felt a desire to do something more relevant to my identity as a gay man," says LeVay. "Some people have said I was out to try and prove that it wasn't my fault that I was gay. I reject that. In my case, since neuroscience was my work, that just seemed like the way to go."

Ironically, AIDS had also given LeVay opportunity. Before the epidemic, cadavers available for dissecting came with scant personal background besides age and cause of death. But because AIDS was still largely a gay disease, it was possible for the first time to do detailed neuroanatomical studies on the bodies of known gay men. (Being lucky enough to have no proprietary cause of death, lesbians were excluded from the study.)

LeVay decided to make the first detailed comparison of the brain's hypothalamus. . . . It was already known that in (presumably straight) men, a cell cluster in the hypothalamus called INAH3 is more than twice the size of the cluster in (presumably straight) women. . . . LeVay designed a study to see if there were any size differences inside gay brains. His results were startling and unexpected. In gay men, INAH3 is similar in size to straight women's. . . .

At the time, LeVay presented his findings with caution, acknowledging that HIV or AIDS medications might have been responsible for altering brain structure. But more recently, an important study of sheep brains has replicated his findings. . . . A second study in humans also found size differences, though less dramatic, in the hypothalamus cluster identified by LeVay. . . .

If LeVay's research suggested that biology—not environment, vice, or sinfulness—was likely responsible for male homosexuality, the geneticist Dean Hamer, an author and molecular biologist at the National Institutes of Health, hoped to pinpoint the exact biological mechanism responsible. He scanned gene groups in pairs of gay siblings looking for sites where the relatives had inherited the same DNA more frequently than would be expected on the basis of chance. In 1993, he located a region in the human genome, called Xq28, that appeared to be associated with gayness, a finding that has generated some controversy among researchers who have not fully confirmed the results. . . .

Fewer studies have focused specifically on lesbians, perhaps because AIDS didn't provide the same urgent impetus for studying female sexuality. But the research that has been conducted has yielded some interesting, though decidedly cloudy, results. According to some studies, lesbians are more likely to have homosexual relatives than nonlesbians. They also have notably longer bone growth in their arms, legs, and hands, hinting that they had greater androgen exposure during development, according to James Martin, a physiologist with Western University of Health Sciences in Pomona, California. Another indicator comes in a 2003 study in the journal *Behavioral Neuroscience* that measured something called "prepulse inhibition," which is the part of our startle mechanism that's believed to defy practice or training—something hardwired, in other words. Men tend to blink less than women in such experiments; gay and heterosexual men had similar responses, but lesbians, it turns out, were more like men than not.

In many other studies, though, lesbians have appeared less unique than gay men, leading some people to wonder if their sexual orientation is innate. [Northwestern University psychologist] Michael Bailey—who, as a heterosexual researcher, is a minority in this field—even doubts the existence of female sexual orientation, if by orientation we mean a fundamental drive that defies our conscious choices. He bases this provocative gambit on a sexual-arousal study he and his students conducted. When shown pornographic videos, men have an undeniable response either to gay or straight images but not both, according to sensitive gauges attached to their genitals—it's that binary. Female sexual response is more democratic, opaque, and unpredictable: Arousal itself is harder to track, and there is evidence that it defies easy categorization. "I don't yet understand female partner choices very well, and neither does anyone else," Bailey wrote me in an e-mail. "What I do think it's time to do is admit that female sexuality looks in some ways very different from male sexuality, and that there is no clear analog in women of men's directed sexual-arousal pattern, which I think is their sexual orientation. I am not sure that women don't have a sexual orientation, but it is certainly unclear that they do."

He contends that what they have instead is sexual preference—they might prefer sex with women, but something in their brains can still sizzle at the thought of men. Many feminist scholars agree with this assessment, and consider sexuality more of a fluid than an either-or proposition, but some don't. "I think women do have orientations, but they don't circumscribe the range of desires that women can experience to the same degree as men," says Lisa Diamond, a psychology professor at the University of Utah, who is writing a book on the subject. "For women, there's more wiggle room. You can think of orientation as defining a range of possible responses, and for women, it's much broader." . . .

I suppose the main upside to this kind of work, besides any impact it might have on securing gay rights, is the comfort of self-knowledge. The secrets lurking in the hypothalamus (and the ring finger and the hair whorl) aren't just about who we desire but about a more fundamental organization of our personalities, individually and collectively. Still, some have dismissed all this field-guide work as wrongheaded. Gaydar can no more be proved than a sixth sense, they say. What's being classified as fundamentally gay is nothing more than cultural signals that vary so much from one part of the world to another that they're worthless as clues to anything. . . .

Still, Dr. [Richard] Lippa, [a psychologist at California State University at Fullerton], is publishing a paper in the *Archives of Sexual Behavior* later this year that seems to prove the existence of gay-typical behavior across the globe. . . . "It probably comes as no shock to you that on average men say they're interested in being mechanics, or electrical engineers, or construction workers, whereas on average women are more interested in, say, being an interior decorator or a social worker or an artist," he tells me. "Similarly, the differences between gay men and straight men are pretty large. On average, gay men are interested more in what you would consider female-typical occupations and hobbies than straight men. Same with women. It's not universal. Some gay men like football games and like working on cars and are electrical engineers. But a large majority answer this way."

It could be that his study says more about the limited number of vocations where gay men feel comfortable expressing themselves, and we might be equally drawn to construction sites if we thought we might be accepted there. It could be that the study says as much about the globalization of culture as the biological nature of gayness.

Even Lippa hesitates to say that gay people are *essentially* different from straight. "Essentialism," he explains, "is the enemy of a lot of academics," because it shuts down inquiry into all the possible influences. Perhaps there are a dozen possible routes to homosexuality, any combination of which might produce a number of the traits being catalogued now. It might be that there is no single thing called homosexuality—that there are instead dozens of homosexualities, scores of potential outcomes in terms of personality, and endless potentials for describing them. "For example, do gay men who have older brothers show more or less feminine? Do gay men with counterclockwise hair have more masculine traits? One cause might create a more feminine homosexuality than another."

Of course, biology doesn't determine everything. And some critics of sexual-orientation researchers blame them for minimizing the role of experience in determining our affectional course in life. The feminist biologist Anne Fausto-Sterling has waged a constant battle against their research, which she calls "a big house of cards" that ignores the power of environment in creating personality. Nurture, she argues, can and should be studied as a link to sexual orientation. The baby penguin raised by her two dads is a potential case study—though genetically unrelated to either parent, in the last few mating seasons she has mated with another female.

The rush to declare a biological mandate is motivated by a political agenda, says Fausto-Sterling, the author of *Sexing the Body,* who is married to a woman after a marriage to a man. "For me and for any feminist, I think it's a pretty fragile way to argue for human rights. I want to see the claims for gay rights made on moral, ethical, legal, and constitutional bases that don't rely on a particular scientific view of sexual development."

Especially if that view invites the opponents of gay people to consider dramatic interventions meant to stop the development of homosexual orientation in a fetus. What if prenatal tests were able to show a predisposition to gayness? How long would it be before some pharmaceutical company develops a patch to regulate hormone flow and direct the baby's orientation? Michael Bailey, for one, isn't troubled by the moral implications any more than he would oppose fetal screens for potential birth defects, though he quickly adds his personal belief that homosexuality is "a good" on par with heterosexuality. "There's no reason to ban, or become hysterical about, selecting for heterosexuality," he says. "That's precisely what parenting is about: shaping the children to have traits the parents value."

It's bizarre to think some value systems might lump gayness in with—say—sickle-cell anemia or Down syndrome. As Matt Foreman from the Task Force put it, "It's not playing with the number of toes you have; it's really manipulating your very essence. So many people see gay people only in terms of sexual behavior, as opposed to what sexual orientation is really about, which is how you fit into the world. I don't want to get mushy, but it's about your soul."

II.   SEXUALITY, GENDER, AND IDENTITY
IN HISTORICAL CONTEXT

A.   TRANSHISTORICAL ANALYSIS

REVOLUTIONS, UNIVERSALS, AND SEXUAL CATEGORIES*
John Boswell

Do categories exist because humans recognize real distinctions in the world around them, or are categories arbitrary conventions, simply names for things that have categorical force because humans agree to use them in certain ways? The two traditional sides in this controversy, which is called "the problem of universals," are "realists" and "nominalists." Realists consider categories to be the footprints of reality ("universals"): They exist because humans perceive a real order in the universe and name it. The order is present without human observation, according to realists; the human contribution is simply the naming and describing of it. Most scientists operate—tacitly—in a realist mode, on the assumption that they are discovering, not inventing, the relationships within the physical world. The scientific method is, in fact, predicated on realist attitudes. On the other hand, the philosophical structure of the modern West is closer to nominalism: the belief that categories are only the names (Latin: *nomina*) of things agreed upon by humans, and that the "order" people see is their creation rather than their perception. Most modern philosophy and language theory is essentially nominalist, and even the more theoretical sciences are nominalist to some degree: In biology, for example, taxonomists disagree strongly about whether they are discovering (realists) or inventing (nominalists) distinctions among phyla, genera, species, etc. (When, for example, a biologist announces that bats, being mammals, are "more closely related to" humans than to birds, is he expressing some real relationship, present in nature and detected by humans, or is he employing an arbitrary convention, something that helps humans organize and sort information but that bears no "truth" or significance beyond this utility?)

This seemingly arcane struggle now underlies an epistemological controversy raging among those studying the history of gay people. The "universals" in this case are categories of sexual preference or orientation (the difference is crucial). Nominalists ("social constructionists" in the current debate) in the matter aver that categories of sexual preference and behavior are created by humans and human societies. Whatever reality they have is the consequence of the power they exert in those

---

    *   John Boswell, *Revolutions, Universals, and Sexual Categories, in* HIDDEN FROM HISTORY: RECLAIMING THE GAY AND LESBIAN PAST 17, 18–23, 34–36 (Martin Bauml Duberman et al. eds., 1989).

societies and the socialization processes that make them seem real to persons influenced by them. People consider themselves "homosexual" or "heterosexual" because they are induced to believe that humans are either "homosexual" or "heterosexual." Left to their own devices, without such processes or socialization, people would simply be sexual. The category "heterosexuality," in other words, does not so much describe a pattern of behavior inherent in human beings as it creates and establishes it.

Realists ("essentialists") hold that this is not the case. Humans are, they insist, differentiated sexually. Many categories might be devised to characterize human sexual taxonomy, some more or less apt than others, but the accuracy of human perceptions does not affect reality. The heterosexual/homosexual dichotomy exists in speech and thought because it exists in reality: It was not invented by sexual taxonomists, but observed by them.

Neither of these positions is usually held absolutely: Most nominalists would be willing to admit that some aspects of sexuality are present, and might be distinguished, without direction from society. And most realists are happy to admit that the same real phenomenon might be described by various systems of categorization, some more accurate and helpful than others. One might suppose that "moderate nominalists" and "moderate realists" could therefore engage in a useful dialogue on those areas where they agree and, by careful analysis of their differences, promote discussion and understanding of these issues.

Political ramifications hinder this. Realism has historically been viewed by the nominalist camp as conservative, if not reactionary, in its implicit recognition of the value and/or immutability of the status quo; and nominalism has generally been regarded by realists as an obscurantist radical ideology designed more to undercut and subvert human values than to clarify them. Precisely these political overtones can be seen to operate today in scholarly debate over issues of sexuality. The efforts of sociobiology to demonstrate an evolutionary etiology of homosexuality have been vehemently denounced by many who regard the enterprise as reactionary realism, an effort to persuade people that social categories are fixed and unchangeable, while on the other side, psychiatric "cures" of homosexuality are bitterly resented by many as the cynical folly of nominalist pseudoscience: Convince someone he shouldn't want to be a homosexual, persuade him to think of himself as a "heterosexual," and—presto!—he is a heterosexual. The category is the person.

Whether or not there are "homosexual" and "heterosexual" persons, as opposed to persons called "homosexual" or "heterosexual" by society, is obviously a matter of substantial import to the gay community, since it brings into question the nature and even the existence of such a community. It is, moreover, of substantial epistemological urgency to nearly all of society, and the gravity and extent of this can be seen in the case of the problems it creates for history and historians.

The history of minorities poses ferocious difficulties: censorship and distortion, absence or destruction of records, the difficulty of writing about essentially personal and private aspects of human feelings and behavior, problems of definition, political dangers attendant on choosing certain subjects, etc. But if the nominalists are correct and the realists wrong, the problems in regard to the history of gay people are of an entirely different order: If the categories "homosexual/heterosexual" and "gay/straight" are the inventions of particular societies rather than real aspects of the human psyche, there is no gay history. If "homosexuality" exists only when and where people are persuaded to believe in it, "homosexual" persons will have a "history" only in those particular societies and cultures.

In its most extreme form, this nominalist view has argued that only early modern and contemporary industrial societies have produced "homosexuality," and it is futile and misguided to look for "homosexuality" in earlier human history.

> What we call "homosexuality" (in the sense of the distinguishing traits of "homosexuals"), for example, was not considered a unified set of acts, much less a set of qualities defining particular persons, in pre-capitalist societies ... Heterosexuals and homosexuals are involved in social "roles" and attitudes which pertain to a particular society, modern capitalism.[2]

If this position is sustained, it will permanently alter, for better or worse, the nature and extent of minority history.

Clearly it has much to recommend it. No characteristics interact with the society around them uniformly through time. Perceptions of, reactions to, and social response regarding blackness, blindness, left-handedness, Jewishness, or any other distinguishing (or distinguished) aspect of persons or peoples must necessarily vary as widely as the social circumstance in which they occur, and for this reason alone it could be reasonably argued that being Jewish, black, blind, left-handed, etc., is essentially different from one age and place to another. In some cultures, for example, Jews are categorized chiefly as an ethnic minority; in others they are not or are not perceived to be ethnically distinct from the peoples around them, and are distinguished solely by their religious beliefs. Similarly, in some societies anyone darker than average is considered

---

[2] Robert Padgug, *Sexual Matters: On Conceptualizing Sexuality in History, in* HIDDEN FROM HISTORY: RECLAIMING THE GAY AND LESBIAN PAST 54, 59 (Martin Bauml Duberman et al. eds., 1989).

"black"; in others, a complex and highly technical system of racial categorization classes some persons as black even when they are lighter in color than many "whites." In both cases, moreover, the differences in attitudes held by the majority must affect profoundly the self-perception of the minority itself, and its patterns of life and behavior are in all probability notably different from those of "black" or "Jewish" people in other circumstances.

There can be no question that if minority history is to merit respect it must carefully weigh such fundamental subtleties of context: Merely cataloguing references to "Jews" or to "Blacks" may distort more than it reveals of human history if due attention is not paid to the meaning, in their historical setting, of such words and the concepts to which they apply. Do such reservations, on the other hand, uphold the claim that categories such as "Jew," "black," or "gay" are not diachronic and can not, even with apposite qualification, be applied to ages and times other than those in which the terms themselves were used in precisely their modern sense? Extreme realists, without posing the question, have assumed the answer was no; extreme nominalists seem to be saying yes.

The question can not be addressed intelligently without first noting three points. First, the positions are not in fact as clearly separable as this schema implies. It could be well argued, for example, that Padgug, Weeks, et al., are in fact extreme *realists* in assuming that *modern* homosexuality is not simply one of a series of conventions designated under the same rubric, but is instead a "real" phenomenon that has no "real" antecedent in human history. Demonstrate to us the "reality" of this homosexuality, their opponents might legitimately demand, and prove to us that it has a unity and cohesiveness that justifies your considering it a single, unparalleled entity rather than a loose congeries of behaviors. Modern scientific literature increasingly assumes that what is at issue is not "homosexuality" but "homosexualities"; if these disparate patterns of sexuality can be grouped together under a single heading in the present, why make such a fuss about a diachronic grouping?

Second, adherents of both schools fall prey to anachronism. Nearly all of the most prominent nominalists are historians of the modern U.S., modern Britain, or modern Europe, and it is difficult to eschew the suspicion that they are concentrating their search where the light is best rather than where the answers are to be found, and formulating a theoretical position to justify their approach. On the other hand, nominalist objections are in part a response to an extreme realist position that has been predicated on the unquestioned, unproven, and overwhelmingly unlikely assumption that exactly the same categories and patterns of sexuality have always existed, pure and unchanged by the systems of thought and behavior in which they were enmeshed.

Third, both extremes appear to be paralyzed by words. The nominalists are determined that the same word can not apply to a wide range of meaning and still be used productively in scholarly discourse: In order to have a meaning, "gay," for example, must be applied only as the speaker would apply it, with all the precise ramifications he associates with it. This insistence follows understandably from the implicit assumption that the speaker is generating the category himself, or in concert with certain contemporaries, rather than receiving it from a human experience of great longevity and adjusting it to fit his own understanding. Realist extremists, conversely, assume that lexical equivalence betokens experiential equality, and that the occurrence of a word that "means" "homosexual" demonstrates the existence of "homosexuality," as the modern realist understands it, at the time the text was composed.

It is my aim to circumvent these difficulties as far as possible in the following remarks, and my hope that in so doing I may reduce the rhetorical struggle over "universals" in these matters and promote thereby more useful dialogue among the partisans. Let it be agreed at the outset that something can be discussed, by modern historians or ancient writers, without being named or defined. (Ten people in a room might argue endlessly about proper definitions of "blue" and "red," but could probably agree instantly whether a given object was one or the other [or a combination of both].) "Gravity" offers a useful historical example. A nominalist position would be that gravity did not exist before Newton invented it, and a nominalist historian might be able to mount a convincing case that there is no mention of gravity in any texts before Newton. "Nonsense," realists would object. "The Latin *gravitas*, which is common in Roman literature, describes the very properties of matter Newton called 'gravity.' Of course gravity existed before Newton discovered it."

Both, of course, are wrong. Lack of attention to something in historical sources can in no wise be taken as evidence of its nonexistence, and discovery can not be equated with creation or invention. But *gravitas* does not mean "gravity"; it means "heaviness," and the two are not at all the same thing. Noting that objects have heaviness is entirely different from understanding the nature and operations of gravity. For adherents of these two positions to understand each other each would have to abandon specific nomenclature, and agree instead on questions to be asked of the sources. If the proper questions were addressed, the nominalist could easily be persuaded that the sources prove that gravity existed before Newton, in the sense that the operations of the force now designated gravity are well chronicled in nearly all ancient literature. And the realist could be persuaded that despite this fact the nature of gravity was not clearly articulated—whether or not it was apprehended—before Newton.

The problem is rendered more difficult in the present case by the fact that the equivalent of gravity has not yet been discovered: There is still no essential agreement in the scientific community about the nature of human sexuality. Whether humans are "homosexual" or "heterosexual" or "bisexual" by birth, by training, by choice, or at all is still an open question. Neither realists nor nominalists can, therefore, establish any clear correlation—positive or negative—between modern sexuality and its ancient counterparts. But it is still possible to discuss whether modern conceptualizations of sexuality are novel and completely socially relative, or correspond to constants of human epistemology which can be documented in the past.

POSTSCRIPT

This essay was written five years ago, and several of the points it raises now require clarification or revision. I would no longer characterize the constructionist-essentialist controversy as a "debate" in any strict sense: One of its ironies is that no one involved in it actually identifies him- or herself as an "essentialist," although constructionists (of whom, in contrast, there are many) sometimes so label other writers. Even when applied by its opponents the label seems to fit extremely few contemporary scholars. This fact is revealing, and provides a basis for understanding the controversy more accurately not as a dialogue between two schools of thought, but as a revisionist (and largely one-sided) critique of assumptions believed to underlie traditional historiography. This understanding is not unrelated to my nominalist/realist analogy: One might describe constructionism (with some oversimplification) as a nominalist rejection of a tendency to "realism" in the traditional historiography of sexuality. The latter treated "homosexuality" as a diachronic, empirical entity (not quite a "universal," but "real" apart from social structures bearing on it); constructionists regard it as a culturally dependent phenomenon or, as some would have it, not a "real" phenomenon at all. It is not, nonetheless, a debate, since no current historians consciously defend an essentialist point of view.

Second, although it is probably still accurate to say that "most" constructionists are historians of the nineteenth and twentieth centuries, a number of classicists have now added their perspective to constructionist theory. This has broadened and deepened the discussion, although, strikingly, few if any historians of periods between Periclean Athens and the late nineteenth century articulate constructionist views.

Third, my own position, perhaps never well understood, has changed. In my book *Christianity, Social Tolerance and Homosexuality* I defined "gay persons" as those "conscious of erotic inclination toward their own gender as a distinguishing characteristic." It was the supposition of the book that such persons have been widely and identifiably present in Western society at least since Greco-Roman times, and this prompted many constructionists to label the work "essentialist." I would now define "gay persons" more simply as those whose erotic interest is predominantly directed toward their own gender (i.e., regardless of how conscious they are of this as a distinguishing characteristic). This is the sense in which, I believe, it is used by most American speakers, and although experts in a field may well wish to employ specialized language, when communicating with the public it seems to me counterproductive to use common words in senses different from or opposed to their ordinary meanings.

In this sense, I would still argue that there have been "gay persons" in most Western societies. It is not clear to me that this is an "essentialist" position. Even if societies formulate or create "sexualities" that are highly particular in some ways, it might happen that different societies would construct similar ones, as they often construct political or class structures similar enough to be subsumed under the same rubric (democracy, oligarchy, proletariat, aristocracy, etc.—all of which are both particular and general).

Most constructionist arguments assume that essentialist positions necessarily entail a further supposition: that society does not create erotic feelings, but only acts on them. Some other force—genes, psychological forces, etc.—creates "sexuality," which is essentially independent of culture. This was not a working hypothesis of *Christianity, Social Tolerance and Homosexuality*. I was and remain agnostic about the origins and etiology of human sexuality.

COMPULSORY HETEROSEXUALITY AND LESBIAN EXISTENCE*
Adrienne Rich

Biologically men have only one innate orientation—a sexual one that draws them to women—while women have two innate orientations, sexual toward men and reproductive toward their young.[1]

I was a woman terribly vulnerable, critical, using femaleness as a sort of standard or yardstick to measure and discard men. Yes—something like that. I was an Anna who invited defeat from men without ever being conscious of it. (But I

---

* Adrienne Rich, *Compulsory Heterosexuality and Lesbian Existence*, in POWERS OF DESIRE: THE POLITICS OF SEXUALITY 177–78, 182–83, 192–202 (Ann Snitow et al. eds., 1983).

[1] Alice Rossi, "Children and Work in the Lives of Women," paper delivered at the University of Arizona, Tucson, February, 1976.

am conscious of it. And being conscious of it means I shall leave it all behind me and become—but what?) I was stuck fast in an emotion common to women of our time, that can turn them bitter, or Lesbian, or solitary. Yes, that Anna during that time was . . .

[Another blank line across the page:][2]

I

The bias of compulsory heterosexuality through which lesbian experience is perceived on a scale ranging from deviant to abhorrent, or simply rendered invisible, could be illustrated from many other texts than the two just preceding. The assumption made by Rossi, that women are "innately sexually oriented" toward men, or by Lessing, that the lesbian choice is simply an acting-out of bitterness toward men, are by no means theirs alone; they are widely current in literature and in the social sciences.

I am concerned here with two other matters as well: first, how and why women's choice of women as passionate comrades, life partners, co-workers, lovers, tribe, has been crushed, invalidated, forced into hiding and disguise; and second, the virtual or total neglect of lesbian existence in a wide range of writings, including feminist scholarship. Obviously there is a connection here. I believe that much feminist theory and criticism is stranded on this shoal.

My organizing impulse is the belief that it is not enough for feminist thought that specifically lesbian texts exist. Any theory or cultural/political creation that treats lesbian existence as a marginal or less "natural" phenomenon, as mere "sexual preference," or as the mirror image of either heterosexual or male homosexual relations is profoundly weakened thereby, whatever its other contributions. Feminist theory can no longer afford merely to voice a toleration of "lesbianism" as an "alternative life style," or make token allusion to lesbians. A feminist critique of compulsory heterosexual orientation for women is long overdue. In this exploratory paper, I shall try to show why.

* * *

II

If women are the earliest sources of emotional caring and physical nurture for both female and male children, it would seem logical, from a feminist perspective at least, to pose the following questions: whether the search for love and tenderness in both sexes does not originally lead toward women; *why in fact women would ever redirect that search;* why species-survival, the means of impregnation, and emotional/erotic

---

[2]   Doris Lessing, *The Golden Notebook* (1962; New York: Bantam Books, 1977), p. 480.

relationships should ever have become so rigidly identified with each other; and why such violent strictures should be found necessary to enforce women's total emotional, erotic loyalty and subservience to men. I doubt that enough feminist scholars and theorists have taken the pains to acknowledge the societal forces that wrench women's emotional and erotic energies away from themselves and other women and from woman-identified values. These forces, as I shall try to show, range from literal physical enslavement to the disguising and distorting of possible options.

I do not, myself, assume that mothering-by-women is a "sufficient cause" of lesbian existence. But the issue of mothering-by-women has been much in the air of late, usually accompanied by the view that increased parenting by men would minimize antagonism between the sexes and equalize the sexual imbalance of power of males over females. These discussions are carried on without reference to compulsory heterosexuality as a phenomenon let alone as an ideology. I do not wish to psychologize here, but rather to identify sources of male power. I believe large numbers of men could, in fact, undertake child care on a large scale without radically altering the balance of male power in a male-identified society.

* * *

III

I have chosen to use the terms *lesbian existence* and *lesbian continuum* because the word *lesbianism* has a clinical and limiting ring. *Lesbian existence* suggests both the fact of the historical presence of lesbians and our continuing creation of the meaning of that existence. I mean the term *lesbian continuum* to include a range—through each woman's life and throughout history—of woman-identified experience; not simply the fact that a woman has had or consciously desired genital sexual experience with another woman. If we expand it to embrace many more forms of primary intensity between and among women, including the sharing of a rich inner life, the bonding against male tyranny, the giving and receiving of practical and political support; if we can also hear in it such associations as *marriage resistance* and the "haggard" behavior identified by Mary Daly (obsolete meanings . . . include "intractable," "willful," "wanton," and "unchaste." . . . "[A] woman reluctant to yield to wooing. . . .")[45]—we begin to grasp breadths of female history and psychology that have lain out of reach as a consequence of limited, mostly clinical, definitions of "lesbianism."

Lesbian existence comprises both the breaking of a taboo and the rejection of a compulsory way of life. It is also a direct or indirect attack

---

[45] Mary Daly, *Gyn/Ecology: The Meta–Ethics of Radical Feminism* (Boston: Beacon Press, 1978), p. 15.

on male right of access to women. But it is more than these, although we may first begin to perceive it as a form of nay-saying to patriarchy, an act of resistance. It has of course included role-playing, self-hatred, breakdown, alcoholism, suicide, and intrawoman violence; we romanticize at our peril what it means to love and act against the grain, and under heavy penalties; and lesbian existence has been lived (unlike, say, Jewish or Catholic existence) without access to any knowledge of a tradition, a continuity, a social underpinning. The destruction of records and memorabilia and letters documenting the realities of lesbian existence must be taken very seriously as a means of keeping heterosexuality compulsory for women, since what has been kept from our knowledge is joy, sensuality, courage, and community, as well as guilt, self-betrayal, and pain.

Lesbians have historically been deprived of a political existence through "inclusion" as female versions of male homosexuality. To equate lesbian existence with male homosexuality because each is stigmatized is to deny and erase female reality once again. To separate those women stigmatized as "homosexual" or "gay" from the complex continuum of female resistance to enslavement, and attach them to a male pattern, is to falsify our history. Part of the history of lesbian existence is, obviously, to be found where lesbians, lacking a coherent female community, have shared a kind of social life and common cause with homosexual men. But this has to be seen against the differences: women's lack of economic and cultural privilege relative to men; qualitative differences in female and male relationships, for example, the prevalence of anonymous sex and the justification of pederasty among male homosexuals, the pronounced ageism in male homosexual standards of sexual attractiveness, and so forth. In defining and describing lesbian existence I would hope to move toward a dissociation of lesbian from male homosexual values and allegiances. I perceive the lesbian experience as being, like motherhood, a profoundly *female* experience, with particular oppressions, meanings, and potentialities we cannot comprehend as long as we simply bracket it with other sexually stigmatized existences. Just as the term *parenting* serves to conceal the particular and significant reality of being a parent who is actually a mother, the term *gay* serves the purpose of blurring the very outlines we need to discern, which are of crucial value for feminism and for the freedom of women as a group.

As the term lesbian has been held to limiting, clinical associations in its patriarchal definition, female friendship and comradeship have been set apart from the erotic, thus limiting the erotic itself. But as we deepen and broaden the range of what we define as lesbian existence, as we delineate a lesbian continuum, we begin to discover the erotic in female terms: as that which is unconfined to any single part of the body or solely to the body itself, as an energy not only diffuse but, as Audre Lorde has described it, omnipresent in "the sharing of joy, whether physical, emotional, psychic," and in the sharing of work; as the empowering joy which "makes us less willing to accept powerlessness, or those other supplied states of being which are not native to me, such as resignation, despair, self-effacement, depression, self-denial."[46]

* * *

IV

Woman-identification is a source of energy, a potential springhead of female power, violently curtailed and wasted under the institution of heterosexuality. The denial of reality and visibility to women's passion for women, women's choice of women as allies, life companions, and community; the forcing of such relationships into dissimulation and their disintegration under intense pressure, have meant an incalculable loss to the power of all women *to change the social relations of the sexes, to liberate ourselves and each other.* The lie of compulsory female heterosexuality today afflicts not just feminist scholarship, but every profession, every reference work, every curriculum, every organizing attempt, every relationship or conversation over which it hovers. It creates, specifically, a profound falseness, hypocrisy, and hysteria in the heterosexual dialogue, for every heterosexual relationship is lived in the queasy strobelight of that lie. However we choose to identify ourselves, however we find ourselves labeled, it flickers across and distorts our lives.

The lie keeps numberless women psychologically trapped, trying to fit mind, spirit, and sexuality into a prescribed script because they cannot look beyond the parameters of the acceptable. It pulls on the energy of such women even as it drains the energy of "closeted" lesbians—the energy exhausted in the double-life. The lesbian trapped in the "closet," the woman imprisoned in prescriptive ideas of the "normal," share the pain of blocked options, broken connections, lost access to self-definition freely and powerfully assumed.

The lie is many-layered. In Western tradition, one layer—the romantic—asserts that women are inevitably, even if rashly and tragically, drawn to men, that even when that attraction is suicidal (e.g., *Tristan und Isolde,* Kate Chopin's *The Awakening*) it is still an organic imperative. In the tradition of the social sciences it asserts that primary love between the sexes is "normal," that women *need* men as social and economic protectors, for adult sexuality, and for psychological completion; that the heterosexually constituted family is the basic social unit; that women who do not attach their primary intensity to men must be, in functional terms, condemned to an even more devastating outsiderhood

---

[46] Audre Lorde, *Uses of the Erotic: The Erotic as Power,* Out & Out Books Pamphlet No. 3 (New York: Out & Out Books [476 2d Street, Brooklyn, New York 11215], 1979).

than their outsiderhood as women. Small wonder that lesbians are reported to be a more hidden population than male homosexuals. The black lesbian/feminist critic, Lorraine Bethel, writing on Zora Neale Hurston, remarks that for a black woman—already twice an outsider—to choose to assume still another "hated identity" is problematic indeed. Yet the lesbian continuum has been a lifeline for black women both in Africa and the United States.

> Black women have a long tradition of bonding together . . . in a Black/women's community that has been a source of vital survival information, psychic and emotional support for us. We have a distinct Black women-identified folk culture based on our experiences as Black women in this society; symbols, language and modes of expression that are specific to the realities of our lives. . . . Because Black women were rarely among those Blacks and females who gained access to literary and other acknowledged forms of artistic expression, this Black female bonding and Black woman-identification has often been hidden and unrecorded except in the individual lives of Black women through our own memories of our particular Black female tradition.

Another layer of the lie is the frequently encountered implication that women turn to women out of hatred for men. Profound skepticism, caution, and righteous paranoia about men may indeed be part of any healthy woman's response to the woman-hatred embedded in male-dominated culture, to the forms assumed by "normal" male sexuality, and to *the failure even of "sensitive" or "political" men to perceive or find these troubling.* Yet woman-hatred is so embedded in culture, so "normal" does it seem, so profoundly is it neglected as a social phenomenon, that many women, even feminists and lesbians, fail to identify it until it takes, in their own lives, some permanently unmistakable and shattering form. Lesbian existence is also represented as mere refuge from male abuses, rather than as an electric and empowering charge between women. I find it interesting that one of the most frequently quoted literary passages on lesbian relationship is that in which Colette's Renee, in *The Vagabond*, describes "the melancholy and touching image of two weak creatures who have perhaps found shelter in each other's arms, there to sleep and weep, safe from man who is often cruel, and there to taste *better than any pleasure, the bitter happiness of feeling themselves akin, frail and forgotten*" [emphasis added]. Colette is often considered a lesbian writer; her popular reputation has, I think, much to do with the fact that she writes about lesbian existence as if for a male audience; her earliest "lesbian" novels, the Claudine series, were written under compulsion for her husband and published under both their names. At all events, except for her writings on her mother, Colette is a far less reliable source on lesbian than, I would think, Charlotte Brontë, who understood that while women may, indeed must, be one another's allies, mentors, and comforters in the female struggle for survival, there is quite extraneous delight in each other's company and attraction to each others' minds and character, which proceeds from a recognition of each others' strengths.

By the same token, we can say that there is a *nascent* feminist political content in the act of choosing a woman lover or life partner in the face of institutionalized heterosexuality. But for lesbian existence to realize this political content in an ultimately liberating form, the erotic choice must deepen and expand into conscious woman-identification—into lesbian/feminism.

The work that lies ahead, of unearthing and describing what I call here lesbian existence, is potentially liberating for all women. It is work that must assuredly move beyond the limits of white and middle-class Western women's studies to examine women's lives, work, and groupings within every racial, ethnic, and political structure. There are differences, moreover, between lesbian existence and the lesbian continuum— differences we can discern even in the movement of our own lives. The lesbian continuum, I suggest, needs delineation in light of the double-life of women, not only women self-described as heterosexual but also of self-described lesbians. We need a far more exhaustive account of the forms the double-life has assumed. Historians need to ask at every point how heterosexuality as institution has been organized and maintained through the female wage scale, the enforcement of middle-class women's "leisure," the glamorization of so-called sexual liberation, the withholding of education from women, the imagery of "high art" and popular culture, the mystification of the "personal" sphere, and much else. We need an economics that comprehends the institution of heterosexuality, with its doubled workload for women and its sexual divisions of labor, as the most idealized of economic relations.

The question inevitably will arise: Are we then to condemn all heterosexual relationships, including those that are least oppressive? I believe this question, though often heartfelt, is the wrong question here. We have been stalled in a maze of false dichotomies that prevents our apprehending the institution as a whole: "good" versus "bad" marriages; "marriage for love" versus arranged marriage; "liberated" sex versus prostitution; heterosexual intercourse versus rape; Liebeschmerz versus humiliation and dependency. Within the institution exist, of course, qualitative differences of experience; but the absence of choice remains the great unacknowledged reality, and in the absence of choice, women will remain dependent on the chance or luck of particular relationships and will have no collective power to determine the meaning and place of sexuality in their lives. As we address the institution itself, moreover, we begin to perceive a history of female resistance that has never fully understood itself because it has been so fragmented, miscalled, erased. It will require a courageous grasp of the politics and economics, as well as the cultural propaganda, of heterosexuality to carry us beyond individual cases or diversified group situations into the complex kind of overview needed to undo the power men everywhere wield over women, power that has become a model for every other form of exploitation and illegitimate control.

B. EARLIER LGBT MOBILIZATION

According to historian Martin Duberman:

"Stonewall" is *the* emblematic event in modern lesbian and gay history. The site of a series of riots in late June-early July 1969 that resulted from a police raid on a Greenwich Village gay bar, "Stonewall" has become synonymous over the years with gay resistance to oppression. Today, the word resonates with images of insurgency and self-realization and occupies a central place in the iconography of lesbian and gay awareness. The 1969 riots are generally taken to mark the birth of a modern gay and lesbian political movement—that moment in time when gays and lesbians recognized all at once their mistreatment and solidarity. As such, "Stonewall" has become an empowering symbol of global proportions.[1]

The following contemporaneous account provides further context for understanding the meaning of Stonewall.

HOMO NEST RAIDED, QUEEN BEES ARE STINGING MAD[*]
New York Daily News

She sat there with her legs crossed, the lashes of her mascara-coated eyes beating like the wings of a hummingbird. She was angry. She was so upset she hadn't bothered to shave. A day old stubble was beginning to push through the pancake makeup. She was a he. A queen of Christopher Street.

Last weekend the queens had turned commandos and stood bra strap to bra strap against an invasion of the helmeted Tactical Patrol Force. The elite police squad had shut down one of their private gay clubs, the Stonewall Inn at 57 Christopher St., in the heart of a three-block homosexual community in Greenwich Village. Queen Power reared its bleached blonde head in revolt. New York City experienced its first homosexual riot. "We may have lost the battle, sweets, but the war is far

---

[1] MARTIN DUBERMAN, STONEWALL xv (1994).

[*] Jerry Lisker, *Homo Nest Raided, Queen Bees Are Stinging Mad*, N.Y. DAILY NEWS, July 6, 1969, at 2.

from over," lisped an unofficial lady-in-waiting from the court of the Queens.

"We've had all we can take from the Gestapo," the spokesman, or spokeswoman, continued. "We're putting our foot down once and for all." The foot wore a spiked heel. According to reports, the Stonewall Inn, a two-story structure with a sand painted brick and opaque glass facade, was a mecca for the homosexual element in the village who wanted nothing but a private little place where they could congregate, drink, dance and do whatever little girls do when they get together.

The thick glass shut out the outside world of the street. Inside, the Stonewall bathed in wild, bright psychedelic lights, while the patrons writhed to the sounds of a juke box on a square dance floor surrounded by booths and table. The bar did a good business and the waiters, or waitresses, were always kept busy, as they snaked their way around the dancing customers to the booths and tables. For nearly two years, peace and tranquility reigned supreme for the Alice in Wonderland clientele.

THE RAID LAST FRIDAY

Last Friday the privacy of the Stonewall was invaded by police from the First Division. It was a raid. They had a warrant. After two years, police said they had been informed that liquor was being served on the premises. Since the Stonewall was without a license, the place was being closed. It was the law. All hell broke loose when the police entered the Stonewall. The girls instinctively reached for each other. Others stood frozen, locked in an embrace of fear.

Only a handful of police were on hand for the initial landing in the homosexual beachhead. They ushered the patrons out onto Christopher Street, just off Sheridan Square. A crowd had formed in front of the Stonewall and the customers were greeted with cheers of encouragement from the gallery.

The whole proceeding took on the aura of a homosexual Academy Awards Night. The Queens pranced out to the street blowing kisses and waving to the crowd. A beauty of a specimen named Stella wailed uncontrollably while being led to the sidewalk in front of the Stonewall by a cop. She later confessed that she didn't protest the manhandling by the officer, it was just that her hair was in curlers and she was afraid her new beau might be in the crowd and spot her. She didn't want him to see her this way, she wept.

QUEEN POWER

The crowd began to get out of hand, eye witnesses said. Then, without warning, Queen Power exploded with all the fury of a gay atomic bomb. Queens, princesses and ladies-in-waiting began hurling anything they could get their polished, manicured fingernails on. Bobby pins, compacts, curlers, lipstick tubes and other femme fatale missiles were flying in the direction of the cops. The war was on. The lilies of the valley had become carnivorous jungle plants.

Urged on by cries of "C'mon girls, let[']s go get'em," the defenders of Stonewall launched an attack. The cops called for assistance. To the rescue came the Tactical Patrol Force. Flushed with the excitement of battle, a fellow called Gloria pranced around like Wonder Woman, while several Florence Nightingales administered first aid to the fallen warriors. There were some assorted scratches and bruises, but nothing serious was suffered by the honeys turned Madwoman of Chaillot.

Official reports listed four injured policemen with 13 arrests. The War of the Roses lasted about 2 hours from about midnight to 2 a.m. There was a return bout Wednesday night. Two veterans recently recalled the battle and issued a warning to the cops. "If they close up all the gay joints in this area, there is going to be all out war."

BRUCE AND NAN

Both said they were refugees from Indiana and had come to New York where they could live together happily ever after. They were in their early 20's. They preferred to be called by their married names, Bruce and Nan. "I don't like your paper," Nan lisped matter-of-factly. "It's anti-fag and pro-cop." "I'll bet you didn't see what they did to the Stonewall. Did the pigs tell you that they smashed everything in sight? Did you ask them why they stole money out of the cash register and then smashed it with a sledge hammer? Did you ask them why it took them two years to discover that the Stonewall didn't have a liquor license."

Bruce nodded in agreement and reached over for Nan's trembling hands. "Calm down, doll," he said. "Your face is getting all flushed." Nan wiped her face with a tissue. "This would have to happen right before the wedding. The reception was going to be held at the Stonewall, too," Nan said, tossing her ashen-tinted hair over her shoulder.

"What wedding?," the bystander asked. Nan frowned with a how-could-anybody-be-so-stupid look. "Eric and Jack's wedding, of course. They're finally tieing the knot. I thought they'd never get together."

MEET SHIRLEY

"We'll have to find another place, that's all there is to it," Bruce sighed. "But every time we start a place, the cops break it up sooner or later." "They let us operate just as long as the payoff is regular," Nan said bitterly. "I believe they closed up the Stonewall because there was some trouble with the payoff to the cops. I think that's the real reason. It's a shame. It was such a lovely place. We never bothered anybody. Why couldn't they leave us alone?"

Shirley Evans, a neighbor with two children, agrees that the Stonewall was not a rowdy place and the persons who frequented the club were never troublesome. She lives at 45 Christopher St. "Up until the night of the police raid there was never any trouble there," she said. "The homosexuals minded their own business and never bothered a soul. There were never any fights or hollering, or anything like that. They just wanted to be left alone. I don't know what they did inside, but that's their business. I was never in there myself. It was just awful when the police came. It was like a swarm of hornets attacking a bunch of butterflies."

A reporter visited the now closed Stonewall and it indeed looked like a cyclone had struck the premises. Police said there were over 200 people in the Stonewall when they entered with a warrant. The crowd outside was estimated at 500 to 1,000. According to police, the Stonewall had been under observation for some time. Being a private club plain clothesmen were refused entrance to the inside when they periodically tried to check the place. "They had the tightest security in the Village," a First Division officer said, "We could never get near the place without a warrant."

POLICE TALK

The men of the First Division were unable to find any humor in the situation, despite the comical overtones of the raid. "They were throwing more than lace hankies," one inspector said. "I was almost decapitated by a slab of thick glass. It was thrown like a discus and just missed my throat by inches." The beer can didn't miss, though, "it hit me right above the temple."

Police also believe the club was operated by Mafia connected owners. The police did confiscate the Stonewall's cash register as proceeds from an illegal operation. The receipts were counted and are on file at the division headquarters. The warrant was served and the establishment closed on the grounds it was an illegal membership club with no license, and no license to serve liquor.

The police are sure of one thing. They haven't heard the last from the Girls of Christopher Street.

NOTES

1.   Stonewall proved to be a major turning point, and it helped to inaugurate a new era of gay advocacy. According to historian John D'Emilio:

> After the second night of disturbances, the anger that had erupted into street fighting was channeled into intense discussion of what many had begun to memorialize as the first gay riot in history. Allen Ginsberg's stature in the 1960s had risen almost to that of guru for many counterculture youth. When he arrived at the

Stonewall on Sunday evening, he commented on the change that had already taken place. "You know, the guys there were so beautiful," he told a reporter. "They've lost that wounded look that fags all had ten years ago." The New York Mattachine Society hastily assembled a special riot edition of its newsletter that characterized the events, with camp humor, as "The Hairpin Drop Heard Round the World." It scarcely exaggerated. Before the end of July, women and men in New York had formed the Gay Liberation Front, a self-proclaimed revolutionary organization in the style of the New Left. Word of the Stonewall riot and GLF spread rapidly among the networks of young radicals scattered across the country, and within a year gay liberation groups had sprung into existence on college campuses and in cities around the nation.

John D'Emilio, *A New Beginning: The Birth of Gay Liberation, in* SEXUAL POLITICS: THE MAKING OF A HOMOSEXUAL MINORITY IN THE UNITED STATES, 1940–1970, 231–33 (1983). *See also* PATRICIA CAIN, RAINBOW RIGHTS: THE ROLE OF LAWYERS AND COURTS IN THE LESBIAN AND GAY RIGHTS CIVIL RIGHTS MOVEMENT 91 (2000) (noting that "it is fitting that the event occurred at a gay bar, a place that symbolized the center of the gay community," and that "what the Stonewall riots of June 1969 accomplished was the politicization of the social community").

2.   As D'Emilio's historical work has shown, the fact that Stonewall marked a major turning point should not obscure the history of activism that preceded it. Early organizations like the Mattachine Society and the Daughters of Bilitis formed well before Stonewall. For historical analysis tracing the activities of early groups like these, see D'EMILIO, SEXUAL POLITICS, *supra*; MARCIA M. GALLO, DIFFERENT DAUGHTERS: A HISTORY OF THE DAUGHTERS OF BILITIS AND THE RISE OF THE LESBIAN RIGHTS MOVEMENT (2007); Martin Meeker, *Behind the Mask of Respectability: Reconsidering the Mattachine Society and Male Homophile Practice, 1950s and 1960s*, 10 JOURNAL OF THE HISTORY OF SEXUALITY 78 (2001).

3.   In addition to early political activism, there were social practices that brought gay people together well before Stonewall. According to historian George Chauncey's study of New York:

In the half-century between 1890 and the beginning of the Second World War, a highly visible, remarkably complex, and continually changing gay male world took shape in New York City. That world involved several gay neighborhood enclaves, widely publicized dances and other social events, and a host of commercial establishments where gay men gathered, ranging from saloons, speakeasies, and bars to cheap cafeterias and elegant restaurants. The men who participated in that world forged a distinctive culture with its own language and customs, its own traditions and folk histories, its own heroes and heroines. They organized male beauty contests at Coney Island and drag balls in Harlem; they performed at gay clubs in the Village and at tourist traps in Times Square. Gay writers and performers produced a flurry of gay literature and theater in the 1920's and early 1930's; gay impresarios organized cultural events that sustained and enhanced gay men's communal ties and group identity. Some gay men were involved in long-term monogamous relationships they called marriages; others participated in an extensive sexual underground. . . . The gay male world that flourished before World War II has been almost entirely forgotten in popular memory and overlooked by professional historians; it was not supposed to have existed.

GEORGE CHAUNCEY, GAY NEW YORK: GENDER, URBAN CULTURE, AND THE MAKING OF THE GAY WORLD 1890–1940 1 (1994). For a variety of additional historical perspectives on pre-Stonewall lesbian and gay life in the twentieth century, see HIDDEN FROM HISTORY: RECLAIMING THE GAY AND LESBIAN PAST 233–476 (Martin Bauml Duberman et al. eds., 1989); LILLIAN FADERMAN, ODD GIRLS AND TWILIGHT LOVERS: A HISTORY OF LESBIAN LIFE IN TWENTIETH-CENTURY AMERICA (1991); LILLIAN FADERMAN & STUART TIMMONS, GAY L.A.: A HISTORY OF SEXUAL OUTLAWS, POWER POLITICS, AND LIPSTICK LESBIANS (2006); DAVID K. JOHNSON, THE LAVENDER SCARE: THE COLD WAR PERSECUTION OF GAYS AND LESBIANS IN THE FEDERAL GOVERNMENT (2004); JONATHAN NED KATZ, GAY AMERICAN HISTORY (1976); MAKING HISTORY: THE STRUGGLE FOR GAY AND LESBIAN EQUAL RIGHTS, 1945–1990: AN ORAL HISTORY (Eric Marcus ed., 1992).

In addition to mobilization against harsh legal rules and a hostile political and cultural environment, LGBT activists in the second half of the twentieth century confronted the medical profession. Consider the following excerpt:

TREATMENT[*]
Jonathan Katz

INTRODUCTION

Lesbians and Gay men have long been subjected to a varied, often horrifying list of "cures" at the hands of psychiatric-psychological professionals, treatments usually aimed at asexualization or heterosexual reorientation. This treatment has almost invariably involved a negative value judgment concerning the inherent character of homosexuality. The treatment of Lesbians and Gay men by psychiatrists and psychologists constitutes one of the more lethal forms of homosexual oppression.

---

[*] JONATHAN KATZ, GAY AMERICAN HISTORY: LESBIANS AND GAY MEN IN THE U.S.A. 197–205 (1976).

Among the treatments are surgical measures: castration, hysterectomy, and vasectomy. In the 1800s, surgical removal of the ovaries and of the clitoris are discussed as a "cure" for various forms of female "erotomania," including, it seems, Lesbianism. Lobotomy was performed as late as 1951. A variety of drug therapies have been employed, including the administration of hormones, LSD, sexual stimulants, and sexual depressants. Hypnosis, used on Gay people in America as early as 1899, was still being used to treat such "deviant behavior" in 1967. Other documented "cures" are shock treatment, both electric and chemical; aversion therapy, employing nausea-inducing drugs, electric shock, and/or negative verbal suggestion; and a type of behavior called "sensitization," intended to increase heterosexual arousal, making ingenious use of pornographic photos. Often homosexuals have been the subjects of Freudian psychoanalysis and other varieties of individual and group psychotherapy. Some practitioners (a Catholic one is quoted) have treated homosexuals by urging an effort of the will directed toward the goal of sexual abstinence. Primal therapists, vegetotherapists, and the leaders of each new psychological fad have had their say about treating homosexuals. Even musical analysis has reportedly assisted a doctor in such a "cure." Astrologers, Scientologists, Aesthetic Realists, and other quack philosophers have followed the medical profession's lead with their own suggestions for treatment.

* * *

The treatment of homosexuality by medical practitioners is of relatively recent origin, and is closely tied to the conceptualization of homosexuality as a medical-psychological phenomenon, a "mental illness." This conceptualization is itself a fairly recent invention: European discussion of homosexuality as a medical phenomenon dates to the early 1800s. Before that time, ecclesiastical authorities conceived of homosexuality as essentially a theological-moral phenomenon, a sin. Next, legislative bodies declared it a legal matter, a crime. The historical change in the conception of homosexuality from sin to crime to sickness is intimately associated with the rise to power of a class of petit bourgeois medical professionals, a group of individual medical entrepreneurs, whose stock in trade is their alleged "expert" understanding of homosexuality, a special-interest group whose facade of scientific objectivity covers their own emotional, economic, and career investments in their status as such authorities. At its time of origin, the medical practitioners' concept of homosexuality as a sickness may have been a liberal and humane advance over the conception and punishment of homosexuality as a crime. In 1976, psychiatrists and psychologists are among the major ideologues of homosexual oppression.

Research is now starting to trace the exact historical process by which these medical businessmen (for they are mostly males) acquired the power to define the character of homosexuals—and to trace that political movement by which Gay people are beginning to redefine themselves, struggling for power over that society which affects their lives. Today, Gay liberationists are challenging the long-accepted, medically derived notion that homosexuality is essentially a psychological phenomenon—any more than it is a political, economic, or historical one. They are disputing that view by which the complex human phenomena of homosexual behavior, emotion, lifestyle, culture, and history are reduced to mere psychology. Neither homosexuality nor heterosexuality, they argue, is encompassed by the psychological. Calling for the reconceptualization of homosexuality in broad, humanistic, and social terms, Gay people are today beginning the work of reconceptualizing themselves.

NOTES

1. When the American Psychiatric Association issued its first official listing of mental disorders (known as the *Diagnostic and Statistical Manual, Mental Disorders (DSM-I)*) in 1952,

> homosexuality and the other sexual deviations were included among the sociopathic personality disturbances. These disorders were characterized by the absence of subjectively experienced distress or anxiety despite the presence of profound pathology. Thus it was possible to include homosexuality in the nosology despite the apparent lack of discomfort or disease on the part of some homosexuals. It was the pattern of behavior that established the pathology. Explicitly acknowledging the centrality of dominant social values in defining such conditions, *DSM-I* asserted that individuals so diagnosed were "ill primarily in terms of society and of conformity with the prevailing cultural milieu."

RONALD BEYER, HOMOSEXUALITY AND AMERICAN PSYCHIATRY: THE POLITICS OF DIAGNOSIS 39 (1981). But in

> the revised *Diagnostic and Statistical Manual of Psychiatric Disorders (DSM-II)* [published in 1968] homosexuality was removed from the category of sociopathic personality disturbances and listed together with the other sexual deviations—fetishism, pedophilia, transvestitism, exhibitionism, voyeurism, sadism and masochism— among the "other non-psychotic mental disorders." Despite the existence of a very well-developed homophile movement at the time *DSM-II* was issued, homosexual activists appear to have been unconcerned with its publication. Two years later the classification of homosexuality in the *Manual* was to become the central focus of the Gay Liberation movement's attack on psychiatry.

Id. Indeed, "in 1973, as the result of three years of challenge on the part of gay activists and their allies within the American Psychiatric Association, homosexuality was [deemed to be no longer a psychiatric disorder]. That decision marked the culmination of two decades of struggle that had shattered the fundamental moral and professional consensus on homosexuality." *Id.* at 40.

2.   As late as 1967, a majority of the Supreme Court held that a gay Canadian could be deported from the United States under a section of the Immigration and Nationality Act of 1952 that excluded persons "afflicted with psychopathic personality." *Boutilier v. INS*, 387 U.S. 118, 122, 87 S.Ct. 1563, 1566, 18 L.Ed.2d 661 (1967). The dissent objected to the breadth and vagueness of the statutory provision, putting special emphasis on Kinsey's findings about the relative prevalence of homosexual experiences. Nevertheless, the dissent wrote that "[t]he homosexual is one who, by some freak, is the product of an arrested development. . . ." *Id.* at 127, 87 S.Ct. at 1568 (Douglas, J., dissenting). In 1990, Congress amended the immigration laws to lift the ban on gay applicants. *See* Immigration Act of 1990, Pub. L. No. 101–649, 104 Stat. 4978 (codified as amended in scattered sections of 8 U.S.C.). Ironically, the psychiatric treatment that constituted grounds for deportation in *Boutilier* may now be a reason that bars the United States government from deporting a foreigner; in 1997, the Ninth Circuit held that forced psychiatric treatment in Russia constituted "persecution" enabling a Russian national to claim refugee status in the United States. *Pitcherskaia v. INS*, 118 F.3d 641, 647 (9th Cir. 1997).

3.   Contrast the understandings of homosexuality reflected in the *Boutilier* opinions with the positions taken by the American Psychological Association, the American Psychiatric Association, and associated professional groups in an amicus brief filed in *Lawrence v. Texas*. That brief asserted categorically that "the sexual orientation known as homosexuality— which is based on an enduring pattern of sexual or romantic attraction exclusively or primarily to others of one's own sex—is a normal variant of human sexual expression; it is not a mental or psychological disorder; and it is highly resistant to change." Brief of the American Psychological Association et al. as Amici Curiae Supporting Petitioners, *Lawrence v. Texas*, 539 U.S. 558, 123 S.Ct. 2472, 156 L.Ed.2d 508 (2003) (No. 02–102) 2003 WL 152338 (footnote omitted). The brief also went on to address and rebut at some length the idea that sexual orientation can be changed through clinical intervention:

> Some groups and individuals continue to offer interventions— sometimes called "conversion" or "reparative" therapies—that purport to change sexual orientation from homosexual to heterosexual. To date, however, there has been no scientifically adequate research to show that interventions aimed at changing sexual orientation are effective or safe. Moreover, critical examinations of reports of the effectiveness of these therapies have highlighted numerous problems with such claims. . . .

In addition to the lack of scientific evidence for the effectiveness of efforts to change sexual orientation, there is reason to believe such efforts can be harmful to the psychological well-being of those who attempt them. Clinical observations and self-reports indicate that many individuals who unsuccessfully attempt to change their sexual orientation undergo considerable psychological distress. In fact, the potential psychological risks to some patients undergoing conversion therapies are sufficiently significant that treatment protocols have been developed to assist them in overcoming a wide range of psychological and relational problems. . . .

Accordingly, the mainstream view in the mental health professions is that the most appropriate response of a therapist treating an individual who is troubled about his or her homosexual feelings is to help that person cope with social prejudices against homosexuality and lead a happy and satisfying life as a lesbian or gay man. Reflecting that view, all major national mental health organizations—including *amici* American Psychological Association, American Psychiatric Association, and NASW, as well as the American Academy of Pediatrics and the American Counseling Association—have adopted policy statements cautioning the profession and the public about treatments that purport to change sexual orientation.

Id. at 4, 13–15 (footnotes omitted). More recently, LGBT advocates have convinced some state lawmakers to prohibit the use of "sexual orientation change efforts" on minors. *See* CAL. BUS. & PROF. CODE § 865 (2013); N.J. STAT. ANN. § 45:1–55 (2013).

Largely responding to the HIV/AIDS epidemic that emerged in the 1980s, queer protest activity has played a powerful role in LGBT mobilization. Consider the range of voices captured in the following pamphlet:

QUEERS READ THIS*
Anonymous Queers

Being queer is not about a right to privacy; it is about the freedom to be public, to just be who we are. It means everyday fighting oppression; homophobia, racism, misogyny, the bigotry of religious hypocrites and our own self-hatred. (We have been carefully taught to hate ourselves.) And now of course it means fighting a virus as well, and all those homo-haters who are using AIDS to wipe us off the face of the earth.

---

* ANONYMOUS QUEERS, QUEERS READ THIS; I HATE STRAIGHTS (1990) (pamphlet distributed at New York City's Gay Pride Parade, June 1990).

Being queer means leading a different sort of life. It's not about the mainstream, profit margins, patriotism, patriarchy or being assimilated. It's not about executive directors, privilege and elitism. It's about being on the margins, defining ourselves; it's about gender-fuck and secrets, what's beneath the belt and deep inside the heart; it's about the night. Being queer is "grass roots" because we know that everyone of us, every body, every cunt, every heart and ass and dick is a world of pleasure waiting to be explored. Everyone of us is a world of infinite possibility.

We are an army because we have to be. We are an army because we are so powerful. (We have so much to fight for; we are the most precious of endangered species.) And we are an army of lovers because it is we who know what love is. Desire and lust, too. We invented them. We come out of the closet, face the rejection of society, face firing squads, just to love each other! Every time we fuck, we win.

We must fight for ourselves (no one else is going to do it) and if in that process we bring greater freedom to the world at large then great. (We've given so much to that world: democracy, all the arts, the concepts of love, philosophy and the soul, to name just a few gifts from our ancient Greek Dykes, Fags.) Let's make every space a lesbian and gay space. Every street a part of our sexual geography. A city of yearning and then total satisfaction. A city and a country where we can be safe and free and more. We must look at our lives and see what's best in them, see what is queer and what is straight and let that straight chaff fall away! Remember there is so, so little time. And I want to be a lover of each and every one of you. Next year, we march naked.

* * *

I hate straight people who think they have anything intelligent to say about "outing." I hate straight people who think stories about themselves are "universal" but stories about us are only about homosexuality. I hate straight recording artists who make their careers off of queer people, then attack us, then act hurt when we get angry and then deny having wronged us rather than apologize for it. I hate straight people who say, "I don't see why you feel the need to wear those buttons and t-shirts. I don't go around telling the whole world I'm straight."

I hate that in twelve years of public education I was never taught about queer people. I hate that I grew up thinking I was the only queer in the world, and I hate even more that most queer kids still grow up the same way. I hate that I was tormented by other kids for being a faggot, but more that I was taught to feel ashamed for being the object of their cruelty, taught to feel it was my fault. I hate that the Supreme Court of this country says it's okay to criminalize me because of how I make love. I hate that so many straight people are so concerned about my goddamned sex life. I hate that so many twisted straight people become parents, while I have to fight like hell to be *allowed* to be a father. I hate straights.

* * *

I wear my pink triangle everywhere. I do not lower my voice in public when talking about lesbian love or sex. I always tell people I'm a lesbian. I don't wait to be asked about my "boyfriend." I don't say it's "no one's business."

I don't do this for straight people. Most of them don't know what the pink triangle even means. Most of them couldn't care less that my girlfriend and I are totally in love or having a fight on the street. Most of them don't notice us no matter what we do. I do what I do to reach other lesbians. I do what I do because I don't want lesbians to assume I'm a straight girl. I am out all the time, everywhere, because I WANT TO REACH YOU. Maybe you'll notice me, maybe we'll start talking, maybe we'll exchange numbers, maybe we'll become friends. Maybe we won't say a word but our eyes will meet and I will imagine you naked, sweating, open-mouthed, your back arched as I am fucking you. And we'll be happy to show we aren't the only ones in the world. We'll be happy because we found each other, without saying a word, maybe just for a moment.

But no.

You won't wear a pink triangle on that linen lapel. You won't meet my eyes if I flirt with you on the street. You avoid me on the job because I'm "too" out. You chastise me in bars because I'm "too political." You ignore me in public because I bring "too much" attention to "my" lesbianism. But then you want me to be your lover, you want me to be your friend, you want me to love you, support you, fight for "OUR" right to exist.

* * *

Queer!

Ah, do we really have to use that word? It's trouble. Every gay person has his or her own take on it. For some it means strange and eccentric and kind of mysterious. That's okay, we like that. But some gay girls and boys don't. They think they're more normal than strange. And for others "queer" conjures up those awful memories of adolescent suffering. Queer. It's forcibly bittersweet and quaint at best—weakening and painful at worst. Couldn't we just use "gay" instead. It's a much brighter word. And isn't it synonymous with "happy"? When will you militants grow up and get over the novelty of being different?

WHY QUEER

Well, yes, "gay" is great. It has its place. But when a lot of lesbians and gay men wake up in the morning we feel angry and disgusted, not gay. So we've chosen to call ourselves queer. Using "queer" is a way of reminding us how we are perceived by the rest of the world. It's a way of telling ourselves we don't have to be witty and charming people who keep our lives discreet and marginalized in the straight world. We use queer as gay men loving lesbians and lesbians loving being queer. Queer, unlike GAY, doesn't mean MALE.

And when spoken to other gays and lesbians it's a way of suggesting we close ranks, and forget (temporarily) our individual differences because we face a more insidious common enemy. Yeah, QUEER can be a rough word but it is also a sly and ironic weapon we can steal from the homophobe's hands and use against him.

III.   RELIGION

Religious bodies have taken a range of perspectives on homosexuality, LGBT rights, and marriage for same-sex couples. While some religious groups have opposed advances on LGBT issues, others have embraced LGBT individuals and their families. And just as the broader culture has shifted toward greater acceptance of LGBT people, many religious communities have moved toward more affirmative stances on LGBT issues. After reviewing the U.S. Conference of Catholic Bishops' position on same-sex marriage, consider the following excerpts from *amicus curiae* briefs filed by religious groups, including the U.S. Conference of Catholic Bishops, in *Hollingsworth v. Perry*. In that case, discussed at greater length in Chapter 6, the U.S. Supreme Court considered a challenge to California's Proposition 8, which eliminated same-sex couples' right to marry.

BETWEEN MAN AND WOMAN: QUESTIONS AND ANSWERS ABOUT MARRIAGE AND SAME-SEX UNIONS*

We, the Catholic bishops of the United States, offer here some basic truths to assist people in understanding Catholic teaching about marriage and to enable them to promote marriage and its sacredness.

1. What is marriage?

Marriage, as instituted by God, is a faithful, exclusive, lifelong union of a man and a woman joined in an intimate community of life and love. They commit themselves completely to each other and to the wondrous

---

   *   *Between Man and Woman: Questions and Answers About Marriage and Same-Sex Unions* was developed by the Committee on Marriage and Family Life of the U.S. Conference of Catholic Bishops and was approved for publication by the full body of bishops in November 2003.

responsibility of bringing children into the world and caring for them. The call to marriage is woven deeply into the human spirit. Man and woman are equal. However, as created, they are different from but made for each other. This complementarity, including sexual difference, draws them together in a mutually loving union that should be always open to the procreation of children (see *Catechism of the Catholic Church* [CCC], nos. 1602–1605). These truths about marriage are present in the order of nature and can be perceived by the light of human reason. They have been confirmed by divine Revelation in Sacred Scripture. * * *

3. Why can marriage exist only between a man and a woman?

The natural structure of human sexuality makes man and woman complementary partners for the transmission of human life. Only a union of male and female can express the sexual complementarity willed by God for marriage. The permanent and exclusive commitment of marriage is the necessary context for the expression of sexual love intended by God both to serve the transmission of human life and to build up the bond between husband and wife (see CCC, nos. 1639–1640).

In marriage, husband and wife give themselves totally to each other in their masculinity and femininity (see CCC, no. 1643). They are equal as human beings but different as man and woman, fulfilling each other through this natural difference. This unique complementarity makes possible the conjugal bond that is the core of marriage.

4. Why is a same-sex union not equivalent to a marriage?

For several reasons a same-sex union contradicts the nature of marriage: It is not based on the natural complementarity of male and female; it cannot cooperate with God to create new life; and the natural purpose of sexual union cannot be achieved by a same-sex union. Persons in same-sex unions cannot enter into a true conjugal union. Therefore, it is wrong to equate their relationship to a marriage. * * *

6. Does denying marriage to homosexual persons demonstrate unjust discrimination and a lack of respect for them as persons?

It is not unjust to deny legal status to same-sex unions because marriage and same-sex unions are essentially different realities. In fact, justice requires society to do so. To uphold God's intent for marriage, in which sexual relations have their proper and exclusive place, is not to offend the dignity of homosexual persons. Christians must give witness to the whole moral truth and oppose as immoral both homosexual acts and unjust discrimination against homosexual persons. The *Catechism of the Catholic Church* urges that homosexual persons "be accepted with respect, compassion, and sensitivity" (no. 2358). It also encourages chaste friendships. "Chastity is expressed notably in *friendship with one's* *neighbor*. Whether it develops between persons of the same or opposite sex, friendship represents a great good for all" (no. 2347). * * *

[In the two briefs that follow, religious groups argued in support of the proponents of Proposition 8.]

BRIEF *AMICUS CURIAE* OF UNITED STATES CONFERENCE OF CATHOLIC BISHOPS IN SUPPORT OF PETITIONERS AND SUPPORTING REVERSAL*

Hollingsworth v. Perry

INTEREST OF AMICUS

The United States Conference of Catholic Bishops ("USCCB" or "Conference") is a nonprofit corporation, the members of which are the Catholic Bishops in the United States. The USCCB advocates and promotes the pastoral teaching of the U.S. Catholic Bishops in such diverse areas of the nation's life as the free expression of ideas, fair employment and equal opportunity for the underprivileged, protection of the rights of parents and children, the sanctity of life, and the nature of marriage. Values of particular importance to the Conference include the promotion and defense of marriage, the protection of the First Amendment rights of religious organizations and their adherents, and the proper development of the nation's jurisprudence on these issues.

We submit this brief in support of Petitioners, and urge this Court to uphold Proposition 8. * * *

ARGUMENT

I. Proposition 8 Is Rationally Related to Legitimate State Interests.

* * *

A. Two Unique Features of Opposite-Sex Unions Supply Two of Many Rational Bases for Distinguishing Those Unions from Other Relationships.

* * *

1. Recognizing the Unique Capacity of Opposite-Sex Couples to Procreate. As a matter of simple biology, only sexual relationships between men and women can lead to the birth of children by natural means. As these relationships alone may generate new life, the state has an interest in

---

*   Brief *Amicus Curiae* of United States Conference of Catholic Bishops in Support of Petitioners and Supporting Reversal, *Hollingsworth v. Perry*, 570 U.S. ___, 133 S.Ct. 2652, 186 L.Ed.2d 768 (2013) (No. 12–144).

channeling the sexual and reproductive faculties of men and women into the kind of sexual union where responsible childbearing will take place and children's interests will be protected. . . .

2. Recognizing the Unique Value to Children of Being Raised by Their Mother and Father Together. It is reasonable to conclude that the optimal environment for the raising of children is a family structure in which both a mother and a father are present and bonded together. Only marriage, understood as the union of one man and one woman, assures that children will have the opportunity to be raised by both a mother and a father. A mother and father each bring something unique and irreplaceable to child-rearing that the other cannot. It is precisely such unions, which house the unique and irreplaceable gifts of mother and father, to which the people of California have exclusively conferred the name "marriage."

> In short, marriage
>
> "reinforces the idea that the union of husband and wife is (as a rule and ideal) the most appropriate environment for the bearing and rearing of children. . . . If same-sex partnerships were recognized as marriages, however, that ideal would be abolished from our law: no civil institution would any longer reinforce the notion that children need both a mother and father; that men and women on average bring different gifts to the parenting enterprise; and that boys and girls need and tend to benefit from fathers and mothers in different ways."

Sherif Girgis, Robert P. George, & Ryan T. Anderson, *What is Marriage?*, 34 HARV. J.L. & PUB. POL'Y 245, 262–63 (Winter 2011). . . .

It bears emphasizing that a government preference for husband-wife unions as the optimal environment in which to raise children is a judgment about marriage as the only institution that serves to connect children with their father and mother together in a stable home. It is not a judgment about the dignity or worth of any person, married or not. *See, e.g., Lawrence v. Texas*, 539 U.S. 558, 585 (2003) (O'Connor, J., concurring in the judgment) ("[R]easons exist to promote the institution of marriage beyond mere moral disapproval of an excluded group.").[10] It also is not a

---

[10] Some advocates and even some lower courts (including the lower courts in this case) have caricatured a moral preference for marital unions as disapproval of persons with same-sex attractions. This is as misleading and inaccurate as saying that the current marriage laws of 50 states disparage or undermine the dignity of single persons, or of persons who practice polygamy, as opposed to simply representing a moral preference for marriage. First, the current debate specifically concerns the meaning of marriage and the proposal to redefine marriage, not the phenomenon of same-sex attraction and the persons who experience such attraction. For this reason, the suggestion that opposition to the redefinition of marriage is equivalent to an animus against people who experience same-sex attraction is particularly offensive and plainly wrong. Second, the Church's pastoral care of persons who are sexually attracted solely or predominantly to persons of the same sex is informed not only by its teaching about the proper use of the sexual faculty, but by its conviction that each and every human person, regardless of sexual inclination,

judgment about the parental competency of any one person over another. * * *

II. Proposition 8 Is Not Rendered Invalid Because It Was Informed by Religious and Moral Viewpoints.

It is hard to recall any significant legal reform movement in American history that has not been informed by religious and moral viewpoints, against which different or opposing religious and moral viewpoints are often arrayed. As this Court has insisted, "[w]e are a religious people." *Lynch v. Donnelly*, 465 U.S. 668, 675 (1984), quoting *Zorach v. Clauson*, 343 U.S. 306, 313 (1952). If the religious viewpoints of the people were deemed "out of bounds" in public policy—falling below even a minimum standard of rationality—then the history of our Nation would have been much different (and worse). . . .

Moreover, the arguments made in favor of redefining marriage to include same-sex relationships are themselves shaped by religious and moral arguments and viewpoints, albeit (in our view) erroneous ones. Thus, if the policy arguments made by those favoring marriage are ruled "out of bounds" simply because they are religiously and morally motivated, then those religious and moral claims favoring the redefinition of marriage are equally impermissible. In short, religious and moral considerations—sometimes explicit, sometimes implicit—are interwoven into the fabric of the current and unfolding debate about marriage, on all sides of the debate.

. . . It is therefore a mistake to characterize laws defining marriage as the union of one man and one woman as somehow embodying a purely religious viewpoint over against [sic] a purely secular one. * * *

BRIEF *AMICUS CURIAE* OF CATHOLIC ANSWERS, CHRISTIAN LEGAL SOCIETY, AND CATHOLIC VOTE EDUCATION FUND*
Hollingsworth v. Perry; United States v. Windsor

INTEREST OF THE *AMICI CURIAE*

The **Christian Legal Society** ("CLS") . . . is an association of Christian attorneys, law students, and law professors, with student chapters at approximately ninety public and private law schools. As

---

has a dignity and worth that derives from his or her Creator. Thus, the further suggestion that opposition to homosexual conduct is simply animus against persons who engage in such conduct is also erroneous and offensive.

    *   Brief *Amicus Curiae* of Catholic Answers, Christian Legal Society, and Catholic Vote Education Fund in Support of Petitioner Hollingsworth and Respondent Bipartisan Legal Advisory Group Addressing the Merits and Supporting Reversal, *Hollingsworth v. Perry*, 570 U.S. ___, 133 S.Ct. 2652, 186 L.Ed.2d 768 (2013) (No. 12–144); *United States v. Windsor*, 570 U.S. ___, 133 S.Ct. 2675, 186 L.Ed.2d 808 (2013) (No. 12–307). *United States v. Windsor*, considered at the same time as *Hollingsworth* and excerpted at length in Chapter 6, involved a challenge to Section 3 of the Defense of Marriage Act (DOMA).

Christian groups have done for nearly two millennia, CLS requires its leaders to agree with a statement of central, traditional Christian beliefs, by which CLS has defined itself for over fifty years. CLS law student chapters typically are small groups of students who meet for weekly prayer, Bible study, and worship at a time and place convenient to the students. CLS meetings are open to all students. . . .

Catholic Answers is America's largest lay-run organization dedicated to Catholic apologetics and evangelization. It began in 1979 and uses a wide variety of media to explain and defend the teachings of the Catholic Church. . . .

The **CatholicVote Education Fund** is a non-partisan voter education program devoted to building a culture that embodies respect for the sanctity of life, religious liberty, marriage, and the family. . . .

Members of CatholicVote.org believe there is no institution more important to the continued vitality of our illustrious nation, and its great tradition of ordered liberty and respect for the common good, than the institution of the family, properly understood in light of the natural law tradition as the union of one man and one woman in marriage.

SUMMARY OF ARGUMENT

. . . There is already a broad and intense conflict between the gay rights movement and religious liberty regarding marriage, family, and sexual behavior. If the Court creates a new suspect classification for sexual orientation, it will take sides in that conflict and place millions of religious believers and organizations at a potentially irreversible disadvantage in their efforts to consistently live out their faith.

. . . In sum, if this Court declares that religious judgments about marriage, family, and sexual behavior are the legal equivalent of racism, it will diminish the religious liberty of millions of religious believers and religious communities.

* * *

II. A Broad And Fundamental Conflict Exists Between Religious Liberty And Sexual Orientation Protections.

. . . [M]any traditional religious believers approach issues regarding sexual orientation as primarily religious questions about sexual behavior, rather than personal identity. Moreover, many traditional religious believers experience religion as a matter of personal identity and, thus, deem religious liberty to be a fundamental right necessary to allow them to fulfill that identity by living out their duty to obey God. To these people, all sexual behavior outside the bond of marriage between a man and a woman is sinful and, out of obedience to God, should be avoided on both a personal and societal level. Indeed, Christian Scripture identifies marriage as the sole proper context for sex, and family as inseparably fundamental to the purpose of sex. This understanding forms the foundation of traditional Christian belief on sexuality. . . .

III. Recognizing Sexual Orientation As A Suspect Class Will Legally Undermine The Ability Of Many Religious People To Live Their Faiths.

* * *

C. Defining Millions of Religious Believers as Bigots

In essence, Respondents ask this Court to declare that the traditional religious beliefs of many Americans are completely wrong on a subject of singular societal importance. And not merely wrong in the way that we may consider those who disagree with us to be wrong about one of the myriad issues of electoral politics, but wrong about a fundamental commitment enshrined in our nation's Constitution. To be a devout Catholic, Protestant, Mormon, Muslim, or Orthodox Jew will become the effective equivalent of being a member of a racist organization.

In short, respondents seek affirmation of their own preferences, and corresponding condemnation of contrary religious faiths in many ways, and one of the most potent is in obtaining suspect class status for sexual orientation. Suspect class status has been historically reserved for morally neutral categories, categories upon which people could discriminate only for reasons that our history and traditions decisively condemn as "evil." By elevating sexual orientation to suspect class status, the Court would correspondingly consign traditional religious beliefs regarding marriage and the family to the same circle of constitutional purgatory as racism. Thus, simply by virtue of affirming the traditional faith that their churches, synagogues, or mosques have publicly supported for centuries, tens of millions of religious believers in the United States would be branded as the legal equivalent of racists.

Religious believers will then face harsh dilemmas, rarely faced in a country founded as a refuge for those seeking religious liberty. While the treatment of race as a suspect category broadly accords with their religious beliefs, privileging sexual orientation and its related conduct as a new suspect category will deepen and provoke further widespread tensions. The faith communities that, for millennia, have been committed to the belief that sexual conduct should occur only within the marital union of a man and a woman are unlikely to change those beliefs or otherwise fade away. . . .

[In the following brief, religious groups argued in support of the same-sex couples who challenged Proposition 8.]

BRIEF OF *AMICI CURIAE* BISHOPS OF THE EPISCOPAL CHURCH IN THE STATE OF CALIFORNIA *ET AL.**

Hollingsworth v. Perry

INTERESTS OF THE *AMICI CURIAE*

Amici curiae ("*Amici*") represent a broad range of religious groups, organizations, and leaders who support equal treatment for same-sex couples with respect to state-regulated civil marriage. While *Amici* come from faiths that have approached issues affecting lesbian and gay people and their families in different ways over the years, they are united in the belief that, in our vastly diverse and pluralistic society, particular religious views or definitions of marriage should not be permitted to influence who the state permits to marry or how legally married couples are treated by the federal government. Such rights must be determined by religiously neutral principles of equal protection under the law. . . .

INTRODUCTION AND SUMMARY OF ARGUMENT

. . . The American religious panorama embraces a multitude of theological perspectives on lesbian and gay people and same-sex relationships. A vast range of religious perspectives affirms the inherent dignity of lesbian and gay people, their relationships, and their families. This affirmation reflects the deeply rooted belief, common to many faiths, in the essential worth of all individuals and, more particularly, the growing respect accorded within theological traditions to same-sex couples. Thus, some faiths celebrate same-sex couples' marriages identically to those of different-sex couples. Others solemnize same-sex relationships in ways other than marriage.

Faiths embracing same-sex couples—both theologically and with respect to the distinct issue of equality under civil law—participate in the mainstream of American religious observance. They include Mainline Protestant denominations such as the United Church of Christ and the Episcopal Church; the Unitarian Universalist Church; portions of the Religious Society of Friends (Quakers); and Judaism's Reform, Reconstructionist, and Conservative movements. Millions of religious individuals from other faiths also embrace and celebrate same-sex couples, including members of many other Protestant denominations,

---

* Brief of *Amici Curiae* Bishops of the Episcopal Church in the State of California; Manhattan Conference of the Metropolitan New York Synod of the Evangelical Lutheran Church in America; The Rabbinical Assembly; The Reconstructionist Rabbinical Association; Reconstructionist Rabbinical College; Rabbi Akiva Herzfeld of Shaarey Tphiloh; The Union for Reform Judaism; Unitarian Universalist Association; United Church of Christ; The United Synagogue of Conservative Judaism; Affirmation; Covenant Network of Presbyterians; Friends for Lesbian, Gay, Bisexual, Transgender, and Queer Concerns; Methodist Federation for Social Action; More Light Presbyterians; Presbyterian Welcome; Reconciling Ministries Network; ReconcilingWorks; Lutherans for Full Participation; and Religious Institute, Inc. in Support of Affirmance in Favor of Respondents, *Hollingsworth v. Perry*, 570 U.S. __, 133 S.Ct. 2652, 186 L.Ed.2d 768 (2013) (No. 12–144).

Roman Catholics, Orthodox Jews, and Muslims. These citizens comprise a major part of the American religious landscape.

Eliminating discrimination in civil marriage will not impinge upon religious doctrine or practice. All religions would remain free . . . to define *religious* marriage in any way they choose. Nor would affirmance interfere with religious institutions' constitutionally protected speech or operations. The types of conflicts forecast by certain other *amici* already can and sometimes do arise under public accommodation laws whenever religiously affiliated organizations operate in the commercial or governmental spheres. Courts know how to respond if enforcement of civil rights laws overreaches to infringe First Amendment rights. It appears that what those other *amici* want is not protection for their own free speech and free exercise rights, but rather immunity from disapproval they may face by those who affirm the rights and relationships of lesbian and gay people.

Certain *amici* supporting reversal have argued that permitting civil marriages of same-sex couples would alter a longstanding "Christian" definition of "marriage." But this and other religiously based arguments for limiting civil marriage to different-sex couples cannot constitutionally be given weight by this Court. Crediting such arguments would improperly both enshrine a particular religious belief in the law—itself prohibited under the Establishment Clause—and implicitly privilege religious viewpoints that oppose marriage equality over those that favor it.

For these and other reasons, civil recognition of same-sex relationships, including through marriage, is fundamentally consistent with the religious pluralism woven into the fabric of American law, culture, and society. An affirmance here would not amount to "taking sides" with one religious view against another or constitute an attack on religion. Nor would it signal a judicial imprimatur on changing social mores. Rather, an affirmance would recognize the creative tension inherent in religions' interface with our pluralistic, changing society while confirming that all, regardless of faith, are entitled to equal protection under the law.

ARGUMENT

* * *

I. A Wide Cross-Section Of American Religious Traditions Recognizes The Dignity Of Lesbian And Gay People And Their Relationships

* * *

A. The Inherent Dignity Of Lesbian And Gay Individuals Informs The Theology Of Numerous Religious Believers And Bodies

Nearly three decades ago, the United Church of Christ, with 1.1 million members today, adopted a policy of membership nondiscrimination with regard to sexual orientation. In 1989, the 45th General Assembly for the Union of Reform Judaism, which represents 1.5 million Reform Jews, resolved to "urge [its] member congregations to welcome gay and lesbian Jews to membership, as singles, couples, and families" and to "embark upon a movement-wide program of heightened awareness and education to achieve the fuller acceptance of gay and lesbian Jews in our midst." These are but two examples—views on this subject abound, and common to them is the foundational theological belief in the dignity of lesbian and gay Americans *as persons*:

- The Episcopal Church, with more than 2.1 million members, has "reaffirm[ed] that gay and lesbian persons are by Baptism full members of the Body of Christ and of The Episcopal Church as 'children of God who have a full and equal claim with all other persons upon the love, acceptance, and pastoral concern and care of the Church.'"

- The United Methodist Church, with 7.8 million members in the United States, has affirmed that "homosexual persons no less than heterosexual persons are individuals of sacred worth" and that "all persons are equally valuable in the sight of God."

- The Evangelical Lutheran Church in America, composed of nearly 4.8 million members, has articulated its "commit[ment] to welcoming all people, regardless of sexual orientation, and their families into our congregations."

- The Presbyterian Church (U.S.A.), with 1.9 million members, has concluded that it would be "grave error to deny baptism or church membership to gay and lesbian persons or to withhold pastoral care to them and their families."

- The Unitarian Universalist Church, with over 1,000 congregations, likewise has affirmed the "inherent worth and dignity of every human being, including lesbian, gay, bisexual, and transgender individuals."

- Reconstructionist Judaism, with nearly 100 congregations in the United States, also has enunciated acceptance of gay and lesbian members, avowing that "the inherent dignity, integrity and equality of human beings" has "primacy over historically conditioned attitudes."

Religious individuals, too, have demonstrated an increasingly positive view of lesbian and gay Americans. According to a Public Religion Research Institute study, *the majority of Americans from most major religious groups* have positive moral and theological views of gay and lesbian people, including 62% of Roman Catholics, 63% of white Mainline Protestants, and 69% of non-Christian, religiously affiliated Americans. While individual liberties should not be subject to public opinion polls, these figures put into perspective the statement of *amicus* Becket Fund for Religious Liberty that most religious adherents belong to bodies that oppose marriage equality. Many of the faiths counted in that total (including Roman Catholics and many major Protestant denominations) have a *majority* of adherents who disagree with church leaders on this question.

Meanwhile, 57% of white Mainline Protestants and 50% of American Roman Catholics support the ordination of gay and lesbian clergy. Unsurprisingly, therefore, some denominations—both Christian and Jewish—long have permitted openly lesbian and gay clergy. Others more recently have amended their practices to admit openly lesbian and gay people to various forms of ministry. Such changes have extended to top leadership eligibility as well, as in the election of the first openly gay bishop in the Episcopal Church in 2003.

Whether it be the ordination of lesbian and gay clergy, the express welcome to lesbian and gay congregants and their families, or the affirmation that lesbian and gay individuals possess the same inherent dignity as any other person, the American religious landscape is one that includes same-sex couples and their families and that affirms their role in the faith community.

B. A Vast Spectrum Of American Faith Groups And Religious Observers Affirms Same-Sex Couples' Relationships In A Multitude Of Ways, Including By Celebrating And Solemnizing Their Marriages

Loving, committed relationships that same-sex couples have elected to enter also have been accorded doctrinal and theological affirmation in many faiths—unsurprisingly, in ways as diverse as America's religious families. For example, having witnessed "[f]or many years ... the blessings of having same-sex couples and marriages in [their] midst," and ascribing these blessings to "the work of the Spirit," the New England Yearly Meeting of Friends (Quakers) reached a formal consensus in 2009 to rejoice in same-sex couples' marriages. The Evangelical Lutheran Church in America has described the manner in which same-sex unions are, and are expected to be, like different-sex unions in several constitutive dimensions: "[T]he neighbor and community are best served when same-gender relationships are lived out with lifelong and monogamous commitments that are held to the same rigorous standards, sexual ethics, and status as heterosexual marriage. [We] surround such couples and their lifelong commitments with prayer to live in ways that glorify God, find strength for the challenges that will be faced, and serve others."

Support for same-sex relationships in religious doctrine and practice likewise has informed a diverse array of formal marriage rituals. The Unitarian Universalist Association began celebrating the unions of same-sex couples as it would any other consenting adult couple's union in 1979 and formally affirmed this practice in 1984. The Conservative, Reform, and Reconstructionist Jewish movements allow their rabbis to perform religious wedding ceremonies for same-sex couples. Indeed, this practice was approved by a unanimous vote of the Rabbinical Assembly's Committee on Jewish Law and Standards. The United Church of Christ promulgated a new Order for Marriage—a template for marriage ceremonies—so that it could be used in any marriage ceremony regardless of gender. The Episcopal Church acknowledged in 2000 that its membership includes same-sex couples living in "lifelong committed relationships ... characterized by fidelity, monogamy, mutual affection and respect, careful, honest communication and the holy love which enables those in such relationships to see in each other the image of God," and in 2012 approved a provisional liturgy for the blessing of same-sex unions that may be used with the permission of the local bishop. And some faiths that do not celebrate or solemnize marriages of same-sex couples per se accord recognition to them in various other ways.

In short, even limited to the sphere of *religious* marriage, organized religion in the United States exhibits a tremendous diversity of views and practices regarding unions of same-sex couples.

II. Recognizing The Necessary Distinction Between Civil And Religious Marriage, A Growing Number Of Faiths Support Civil Marriage Equality

. . . Two Christian denominations that trace their history directly to the Puritans of New England support civil marriage for gay and lesbian couples. Almost seventeen years ago, in 1996, the Unitarian Universalist

Association . . . formally resolved to support equal civil marriage rights in part because the marriage equality debate "ha[d] focused on the objections of certain religious communities" to equal access to marriage. In 2004, the Association further affirmed that "Civil Marriage is a Civil Right," and opposed any amendment of the United States Constitution to bar same-sex couples from marrying. The following year, in 2005, the United Church of Christ "affirm[ed] equal marriage rights for couples regardless of gender and declar[ed] that the government should not interfere with couples regardless of gender who choose to marry and share fully and equally in the rights, responsibilities and commitment of legally recognized marriage."

In addition, the Reform, Reconstructionist, and Conservative movements of Judaism all support equal civil marriage rights for same-sex couples, as does the American Friends Service Committee of the Religious Society of Friends (Quakers). More than three thousand clergy from numerous faiths have endorsed an open letter by the Religious Institute, Inc. calling for marriage equality. *Amici* also note that the very church founded by the Pilgrims who sailed on the Mayflower in 1620— First Parish in Plymouth, now a Unitarian Universalist congregation— has issued a proclamation invoking its historical pursuit of religious freedom, recounting its long history of openness to lesbian and gay congregants, and calling for full civil marriage equality for same-sex couples. Given its historical pedigree, the First Parish proclamation underscores the resonance of today's marriage equality debate with the nation's founding ideal of liberty.

In 2006, the Episcopal Church likewise called on federal, state, and local governments to provide same-sex couples protections equivalent to those "enjoyed by non-gay married couples" and "oppose[d] any state or federal constitutional amendment that prohibits same-sex civil marriage or civil unions," a stance growing out of its "historical support of gay and lesbian persons as children of God and entitled to full civil rights." In 2012, the Episcopal Church called on Congress "to repeal federal laws that have a discriminatory effect on same-gender civilly married couples, and to pass legislation to allow the U.S. federal government to provide benefits to those couples."

Even within faiths that do not believe the government should issue marriage licenses to same-sex couples—a position their leaders remain free to express—many adherents (in some cases, a majority) nonetheless have come to support equal access to civil marriage. For example, the Roman Catholic Church hierarchy is strongly opposed to both civil and religious marriage for same-sex couples. Yet Catholic teaching joins other mainstream religions in affirming the fundamental human dignity of lesbian and gay individuals and calling for an end to "any forms of injustice, oppression, or violence against them." Consistent with the latter teaching, many individual American Catholics have come to favor marriage equality: polling conducted by the Pew Forum in late 2011 showed that "[a]mong Catholics as a whole, supporters" of marriage for same-sex couples had come to "outnumber opponents (52% vs. 37%)," whereas just one year before, 46% had favored same-sex marriage while 42% expressed opposition. There are American Muslims, too, who believe that their religious faith is not contravened when the government affords marriage rights to same-sex couples.

The preceding survey belies the claim of certain *amici* favoring reversal that American religions speak uniformly or overwhelmingly in opposition to marriage equality for same-sex couples. To the contrary, American religious thought and practice embrace a rich diversity. No one view speaks for "religion"—even if, contrary to the Establishment Clause, it were appropriate to give weight to religious views in evaluating and applying the Constitution's secular promise of equal protection. * * *

NOTES

1.   How did the religious groups opposing same-sex marriage articulate their arguments to the Supreme Court? What differences did you notice between the two briefs supporting the proponents of Proposition 8? Why do you think these briefs focused more on legal arguments while the brief opposed to Proposition 8 extensively covered various religions' treatment of same-sex relationships?

2.   The brief submitted by the Christian Legal Society, Catholic Answers, and CatholicVote Education Fund distinguished race, as both a legal and religious matter, from sexual orientation. Why? For an analysis of the legacy of religious opposition to antidiscrimination protections, see William N. Eskridge, Jr., *Noah's Curse: How Religion Often Conflates Status, Belief, and Conduct to Resist Antidiscrimination Norms*, 45 GA. L. REV. 657 (2011).

3.   As religious groups have helped to shape the public policy debate about sexual orientation equality and marriage for same-sex couples, many religions have been engaged in fierce internal struggles of their own about the role of gays, lesbians, and bisexuals within their institutions and traditions. *See, e.g.*, Sharon Otterman, *Caught in Methodism's Split Over Same-Sex Marriage*, N.Y. TIMES, May 6, 2013, at A16; Charles A. Radin, *Debate Over Gay Clergy is Testing Many Faiths*, BOSTON GLOBE, Nov. 29, 2005, at A1; Jane Lampman, *Gay-Union Debate Intensifies in Churches*, CHRISTIAN SCIENCE MONITOR, Aug. 1, 2003, at 1.

IV.   PHILOSOPHY

The editors of *The New Republic* extracted and edited the following documents from legal depositions in the case challenging the constitutionality of Colorado's Amendment 2, *Romer v. Evans*.

DISINTEGRITY*

John Finnis

The underlying thought is on the following lines. In masturbating, as in being masturbated or sodomized, one's body is treated as instrumental for the securing of the experiential satisfaction of the conscious self. Thus one disintegrates oneself in two ways, (1) by treating one's body as a mere instrument of the consciously operating self, and (2) by making one's choosing self the quasi-slave of the experiencing self which is demanding gratification. The worthlessness of the gratification, and the disintegration of oneself, are both the result of the fact that, in these sorts of behavior, one's conduct is not the actualizing and experiencing of a real common good. Marriage, with its double blessing—procreation and friendship—is a real common good. Moreover, it is a common good that can be both actualized and experienced in the orgasmic union of the reproductive organs of a man and a woman united in commitment to that good. Conjugal sexual activity, and—as Plato and Aristotle and Plutarch and Kant all argue—*only* conjugal activity is free from the shamefulness of instrumentalization that is found in masturbating and in being masturbated or sodomized.

At the very heart of the reflections of Plato, Xenophon, Aristotle, Musonius Rufus and Plutarch on the homoerotic culture around them is the very deliberate and careful judgment that homosexual *conduct* (and indeed all extramarital sexual gratification) is radically incapable of participating in, or actualizing, the common good of friendship. Friends who engage in such conduct are following a natural impulse and doubtless often wish their genital conduct to be an intimate expression of their mutual affection. But they are deceiving themselves. The attempt to express affection by orgasmic nonmarital sex is the pursuit of an illusion. The orgasmic union of the reproductive organs of husband and wife really unites them biologically (and their biological reality is part of, not merely an instrument of, their *personal* reality); that orgasmic union therefore can actualize and allow them to experience their real common good—their marriage with the two goods, children and friendship, which are the parts of its wholeness as an intelligible common good. But the common good of friends who are not and cannot be married (man and man, man and boy, woman and woman) has nothing to do with their having children by each other, and their reproductive organs cannot make them a biological (and therefore a personal) unit. So their genital acts together cannot do what they may hope and imagine.

In giving their considered judgment that homosexual conduct cannot actualize the good of friendship, Plato and the many philosophers who

---

* John Finnis, *Disintegrity, reprinted in Is Homosexual Conduct Wrong? A Philosophical Exchange*, THE NEW REPUBLIC, Nov. 15, 1993, at 12.

followed him intimate an answer to the questions why it should be considered shameful to use, or allow another to use, one's body to give pleasure, and why this use of one's body differs from one's bodily participation in countless other activities (e.g., games) in which one takes and/or gets pleasure. Their response is that pleasure is indeed a good, when it is the experienced aspect of one's participation in some intelligible good, such as a task going well, or a game or a dance or a meal or a reunion. Of course, the activation of sexual organs with a view to the pleasures of orgasm is sometimes spoken of as if it were a game. But it differs from real games in that its point is not the exercise of skill; rather, this activation of reproductive organs is focused upon the body precisely as a source of pleasure for one's consciousness. So this is a "use of the body" in a strongly different sense of "use." The body now is functioning not in the way one, as a bodily person, acts to instantiate some other intelligible good, but precisely as providing a service to one's consciousness, to satisfy one's desire for satisfaction.

This disintegrity is much more obvious when masturbation is solitary. Friends are tempted to think that pleasuring each other by some forms of mutual masturbation could be an instantiation or actualization or promotion of their friendship. But that line of thought overlooks the fact that if their friendship is not marital ... activation of their reproductive organs cannot be, in reality, an instantiation or actualization of their friendship's common good. In reality, whatever generous hopes and dreams with which the loving partners surround their use of their genitals, *that use* cannot express more than is expressed if two strangers engage in genital activity to give each other orgasm, or a prostitute pleasures a client, or a man pleasures himself. Hence, Plato's judgment, at the decisive moment of the *Gorgias*, that there is no important distinction in essential moral worthlessness between solitary masturbation, being sodomized as a prostitute and being sodomized for the pleasure of it. . . .

Societies such as classical Athens and contemporary England (and virtually every other) draw a distinction between behavior found merely (perhaps extremely) offensive (such as eating excrement) and behavior to be repudiated as destructive of human character and relationships. Copulation of humans with animals is repudiated because it treats human sexual activity and satisfaction as something appropriately sought in a manner that, like the coupling of animals, is divorced from the expressing of an intelligible common good—and so treats human bodily life, in one of its most intense activities, as merely animal. The deliberate genital coupling of persons of the same sex is repudiated for a very similar reason. It is not simply that it is sterile and disposes the participants to an abdication of responsibility for the future of humankind. Nor is it simply that it cannot *really* actualize the mutual devotion that some homosexual persons hope to manifest and experience by it; nor merely that it harms the personalities of its participants by its disintegrative manipulation of different parts of their one personal reality. It is also that it treats human sexual capacities in a way that is deeply hostile to the self-understanding of those members of the community who are willing to commit themselves to real marriage even one that happens to be sterile in the understanding that its sexual joys are not mere instruments or accompaniments to, or mere compensation for, the accomplishments of marriage's responsibilities, but rather are the actualizing and experiencing of the intelligent commitment to share in those responsibilities. . . .

This pattern of judgment, both widespread and sound, concludes as follows. Homosexual orientation—the deliberate willingness to promote and engage in homosexual acts—is a standing denial of the intrinsic aptness of sexual intercourse to actualize and give expression to the exclusiveness and open-ended commitment of marriage as something good in itself. All who accept that homosexual acts can be a humanly appropriate use of sexual capacities must, if consistent, regard sexual capacities, organs and acts as instruments to be put to whatever suits the purposes of the individual "self" who has them. Such an acceptance is commonly (and in my opinion rightly) judged to be an active threat to the stability of existing and future marriages; it makes nonsense, for example, of the view that adultery is per se (and not merely because it may involve deception), and in an important way, inconsistent with conjugal love. A political community that judges that the stability and educative generosity of family life is of fundamental importance to the community's present and future can rightly judge that it has a compelling interest in denying that homosexual conduct is a valid, humanly acceptable choice and form of life, and in doing whatever it properly can, as a community with uniquely wide but still subsidiary functions, to discourage such conduct.

INTEGRITY[*]

Martha Nussbaum

Finnis's arguments against homosexuality set themselves in a tradition of "natural law" argumentation that derives from ancient Greek traditions. The term "law of nature" was first used by Plato in his *Gorgias*. The approach is further developed by Aristotle, and, above all, by the Greek and Roman Stoics, who are usually considered to be the founders of natural law argumentation in the modern legal tradition, through their influence on Roman law. This being so, it is worth looking

---

[*] Martha Nussbaum, *Integrity, reprinted in Is Homosexual Conduct Wrong? A Philosophical Exchange*, THE NEW REPUBLIC, Nov. 15, 1993, at 13.

to see whether those traditions did in fact use "natural law" arguments to rule homosexual conduct morally or legally substandard.

Plato's dialogues contain several extremely moving celebrations of male-male love, and judge this form of love to be, on the whole, superior to male-female love because of its potential for spirituality and friendship. The *Symposium* contains a series of speeches, each expressing conventional views about this subject that Plato depicts in an appealing light. The speech by Phaedrus points to the military advantages derived by including homosexual couples in a fighting force: because of their intense love, each will fight better, wishing to show himself in the best light before his lover. The speech of Pausanias criticizes males who seek physical pleasure alone in their homosexual relationships, and praises those who seek in sex deeper spiritual communication. Pausanias mentions that tyrants will sometimes promulgate the view that same-sex relations are shameful in order to discourage the kind of community of dedication to political liberty that such relations foster. The speech of Aristophanes holds that all human beings are divided halves of formerly whole beings, and that sexual desire is the pursuit of one's lost other half; he points out that the superior people in any society are those whose lost "other half" is of the same sex—especially the male-male pairs—since these are likely to be the strongest and most warlike and civically minded people. Finally, Socrates's speech recounts a process of religious-mystical education in which male-male love plays a central guiding role and is a primary source of insight and inspiration into the nature of the good and beautiful.

Plato's Phaedrus contains a closely related praise of the intellectual, political and spiritual benefits of a life centered around male-male love. Plato says that the highest form of human life is one in which a male pursues "the love of a young man along with philosophy," and is transported by passionate desire. He describes the experience of falling in love with another male in moving terms, and defends relationships that are mutual and reciprocal over relationships that are one-sided. He depicts his pairs of lovers as spending their life together in the pursuit of intellectual and spiritual activities, combined with political participation. (Although no marriages for these lovers are mentioned, it was the view of the time that this form of life does not prevent its participants from having a wife at home, whom they saw only rarely and for procreative purposes.)

Aristotle speaks far less about sexual love than does Plato, but it is evident that he too finds in male-male relationships the potential for the highest form of friendship, a friendship based on mutual well-wishing and mutual awareness of good character and good aims. He does not find this potential in male-female relationships, since he holds that females are incapable of good character. Like Pausanias in Plato's Symposium,

Aristotle is critical of relationships that are superficial and concerned only with bodily pleasure; but he finds in male-male relationships—including many that begin in this way—the potential for much richer developments.

The ideal city of the Greek Stoics was built around the idea of pairs of male lovers whose bonds gave the city rich sources of motivation for virtue. Although the Stoics wished their "wise man" to eliminate most passions from his life, they encouraged him to foster a type of erotic love that they defined as "the attempt to form a friendship inspired by the perceived beauty of young men in their prime." They held that this love, unlike other passions, was supportive of virtue and philosophical activity.

Furthermore, Finnis's argument, in his article against homosexuality, is a bad moral argument by any standard, secular or theological. First of all, it assumes that the purpose of a homosexual act is always or usually casual bodily pleasure and the instrumental use of another person for one's own gratification. But this is a false premise, easily disproved by the long historical tradition I have described and by the contemporary lives of real men and women. Finnis offers no evidence for this premise, or for the equally false idea that procreative relations cannot be selfish and manipulative. Second, having argued that a relationship is better if it seeks not casual pleasure but the creation of a community, he then assumes without argument that the only sort of community a sexual relationship can create is a "procreative community." This is, of course, plainly false. A sexual relationship may create, quite apart from the possibility of procreation, a community of love and friendship, which no religious tradition would deny to be important human goods. Indeed, in many moral traditions, including those of Plato and Aristotle, the procreative community is ranked beneath other communities created by sex, since it is thought that the procreative community will probably not be based on the best sort of friendship and the deepest spiritual concerns. That may not be true in a culture that values women more highly than ancient Greek culture did; but the possibility of love and friendship between individuals of the same sex has not been removed by these historical changes.

V. QUEER THEORY

MARTHA NUSSBAUM, ESSENTIALISM, AND HUMAN SEXUALITY

Carlos A. Ball[*]

As far as we can tell from the historical record, "erotic and sexual interactions between persons of the same sex are attested in almost all cultures known to us across time and across the globe." Some scholars have looked at this consistency through time and place and concluded that "gay people," that is, individuals who have a distinct identity based on their same-sex erotic preferences, have always existed. These writers, in other words, believe that there are "objective, intrinsic, culture-independent facts about what a person's sexual orientation is."

This so-called essentialist position in matters of sexuality is usually associated with the late historian John Boswell. As he made clear in the title of his 1980 book, *Christianity, Social Tolerance and Homosexuality: Gay People in Western Europe from the Beginning of the Christian Era to the Fourteenth Century*, Boswell believed that "gay people," as a distinct category of individuals, have existed in all Western societies. Although Boswell, like almost everyone else, eschewed the label of "essentialist," he believed that there have always been people whose "erotic inclination toward their own gender [is] a distinguishing characteristic."

Boswell's position . . . was inconsistent with that of Michel Foucault as set forth in his highly influential book *The History of Sexuality, Volume I*. In that book, Foucault famously contended that there is nothing intrinsic or fixed about human sexuality; instead, what we think of as sexuality is a byproduct of the work of systems of knowledge and power as represented, most specifically, by scientific, medical, and psychiatric disciplines. According to Foucault, one of the defining characteristics of the modern era is the extent to which these disciplines have grabbed hold of sexuality by studying, analyzing, and schematizing it through an endless discussion and cataloging of sexual desires, tendencies, and acts. It is from these discursive processes that what had before been viewed simply as the sexual act of sodomy became the basis for a social identity. As Foucault quipped, "[t]he sodomite had been a temporary aberration; the homosexual was now a species." He added that while under

> ancient civil or canonical codes, sodomy was a category of forbidden acts, . . . [in the] nineteenth-century [the] homosexual became a personage, a past, a case history, and a childhood, in

---

[*] Carlos A. Ball, *Martha Nussbaum, Essentialism, and Human Sexuality*, 19 COLUM. J. GENDER & L. 3, 6–9 (2010).

addition to being a type of life, a life form, and a morphology. . . . Nothing that went into his total composition was unaffected by his sexuality.

Foucault's work has served as the foundation for that of many sexuality scholars who have both embraced and elaborated on a socially constructed understanding of sexual identity categories. These writers have in part supported their position linguistically by noting that the word 'homosexual' did not exist before scientific discourses first put it to use in the second half of the nineteenth century. The absence of such a term through most of history strongly suggests to the social constructionists that homosexuality—though not necessarily homosexual sex—is a modern invention. As Robert Padgug puts it, " '[h]omosexual' and 'heterosexual' behavior may be universal; homosexual and heterosexual *identity and consciousness* are modern realities. . . . To 'commit' a homosexual act is one thing; to *be* a homosexual is something entirely different."

In addition, social constructionists point to historical evidence from before the second half of the nineteenth century, which suggests that many societies failed to problematize sexuality along the (for us) familiar homosexual/heterosexual axis. For example, David Halperin . . . points out that the scientific and medical professions in Western countries during the first half of the nineteenth century viewed same-sex sexual acts as a manifestation of "sexual inversion," a categorization of sexual deviance without a clear correlation to what we today consider to constitute homosexuality. . . . Halperin also argues that Aristophanes's famous myth in Plato's *Symposium* shows that the Greeks did not classify or distinguish individuals according to the gender of their sexual partners.

NOTE

In *The History of Sexuality, Volume I*, Michel Foucault described how Western societies in the second half of the nineteenth century—at around the time that "homosexuality" began to be understood as a distinct form of identity—simultaneously silenced and incited sexuality. In the Victorian bourgeoisie home, for example, "silence [was] the rule. The legitimate and procreative couple laid down the law. The couple imposed itself as model, enforced the norm, safeguarded the truth, and reserved the right to speak while retaining the principle of secrecy." MICHEL FOUCAULT, THE HISTORY OF SEXUALITY: AN INTRODUCTION 3 (1978). At the same time, however, well-established institutional discourses regarding sexuality represented "a political, economic, and technical incitement to talk about sex. And not so much in the form of a general theory of sexuality as in the form of analysis, stocktaking, classification, and specification, and of quantitative or causal studies." *Id.* at 23–24. Studies of populations, of birthrates and the appropriate age to marry, of fertility and infertility, of childhood sexuality, of sexual normality and abnormality, of sexual crimes and other infractions against nature, and of debilitating and frustrating sexual desires, all created a discourse on sexuality that was extensive and multifaceted. "What is peculiar to modern societies," Foucault explained, "is not that they consigned sex to a shadow existence, but that they dedicated themselves to speaking of it ad infinitum, while exploiting it as the secret." *Id.* at 35. For essays on Foucault and the theorizing of law, see FOUCAULT AND LAW (Ben Golden & Peter Fitzpatrick eds., 2010).

EXPORTING IDENTITY*

Sonya Katyal

[T]he predominant gay civil rights movement in the United States has displayed a yearning tendency to substitute a discernible sexual orientation and identity for same-sex sexual conduct; and then to attach a categorical imperative to "coming out." Just as gay and lesbian activists in the United States have successfully sought to transform the social meaning of homosexuality in a legal context, they have also asserted significant leadership over the global constitution of that identity, exerting enormous power in determining the manner by which individuals define their sexual identities. Gay pride parades have become a global phenomenon; and gay and lesbian activists have made their way around the globe to assist the formation of nascent movements.

Yet this monopoly power over sexual self-definition can also be deeply problematic. Categories of gay, lesbian, heterosexual, or bisexual identity, as a basis for individual and collective identity, often obscure a deeper question of whether such categories of sexual orientation can—or should—serve as universal categories for everyone. Moreover, imposing a gay, lesbian, or bisexual identity on individuals who may engage in same-sex sexual behavior, but who do not fit a substitutive paradigm between identity and conduct, can be unduly confining, exclusionary, and inappropriate.

These insights draw much of their power from the social construction movement, which has flourished almost entirely outside of—and yet parallel to—the global gay civil rights movement. In the last twenty years, even though gay legal activists continued to focus on emphasizing the importance of identity-based claims to gay civil rights, scholars in other fields—historians, anthropologists, sociologists, and others—have actively deconstructed the presumed equation between identity, desire, and sexual conduct that animates a gay or lesbian sexual identity. For example, a proliferation of studies on the social construction of identity have argued that gay personhood, or gay essentialism, is utterly

---

* Sonya Katyal, *Exporting Identity*, 14 YALE J.L. & FEMINISM 97, 114–19 (2002).

incapable of capturing an emerging divide between act and identity. Many of these scholars are sympathetic to the work of Michel Foucault, who critiqued the centrality of sexuality to personhood in Western society. Under a social constructionist perspective, sexual acts, in and of themselves, lack an inherent meaning. Rather, culture, society, and history assign particular meanings to sexual behavior, desire and experiences. Thus, social constructionists argue that notions of sexuality and sexual identity can only be understood in terms of their sociohistorical and political contexts.

According to this view, the presumed substitutive relationship between sexual acts and identity that characterizes gay personhood is instead a semiotic conflation that obscures the growing complexities of sexuality, modernity, and socialization. Since sexual acts carry different meanings in different cultural and temporal contexts, it is largely impossible to universalize clear definitions of identity, and the relationship between act and identity is not nearly as "fixed" as the model of gay personhood presupposes. Instead, constructionists argue that sexual identity is rarely a matter of sexual practice, and rarely a matter of the gender of one's object choice. Jeffrey Weeks, for example, argued that an important distinction must be made between homosexual behavior (which is universal) and a homosexual identity (which emerged only at the end of the nineteenth century). * * *

Such perspectives brought to the table of gay civil rights an unyielding commitment to reexamine—and openly challenge—the foundational categories upon which much of the movement was based upon. As Joshua Gamson has eloquently pointed out, the social constructionist movement, "shakes the ground on which gay and lesbian politics have been built," by taking apart concepts like "'sexual minority,' 'gay community,' indeed of 'gay' and 'lesbian' and even 'man' and 'woman.'" Instead of viewing homosexuality as a natural, biologically driven, psychological condition, social constructionists approached homosexuality as a social role, rather than a discrete identity. "If we focus only on the 'subculture' of homosexuality, and if we never interrogate the conditions which engender its marginalization, we shall remain trapped within a theoretical framework which refuses to acknowledge its own complicity in constructing its object (or subjects) of study," one author, Ki Namaste, explained.

Such observations built upon important early work by Mary McIntosh, who argued in the late 1960s that the category of "homosexual" was created largely as a means to deflect contagion because homosexual practices are so widespread. Instead of exploring the cause of homosexuality, she inquired about the social conditions that produced the notion that homosexuality constituted a distinctive, discrete human identity. By singling out a particular group as "homosexuals" on the basis of conflating act and identity, she argued that the rest of society remains facially "pure" and unmarred by sexual ambiguity. McIntosh's work contributed an important insight: that homosexuals are not born, but created in order to sustain a division between gay and straight.

Following these insights, many scholars rejected the necessity of a natural, essential, or universal gay identity to mobilize and to legitimate minority-based claims to civil rights in the United States. Drawing on French poststructuralist theorists like Jacques Lacan, various scholars and activists embraced an alternative paradigm, labeled queer theory, that loosely referred to gay, lesbian, bisexual, and transgendered individuals in terms of their resistance to heteronormative structures, and to essentialist claims to identity itself. This form of "anti-identity" politics argued powerfully against the idea that one's identity or sexuality should be fixed, stable, or nameable. Instead, queer theorists noted that specific identity constructs are arbitrary, unstable, and ultimately exclusionary. Their function, it is thought, is to discipline, regulate, and silence the multiplicity of different ways one can identify oneself.

Judith Butler, perhaps the most influential queer theorist of this period, argued that gender categories were similarly problematic in her book *Gender Trouble: Feminism and the Subversion of Identity*. In *Gender Trouble*, Butler argued that there was no natural core or essential nature of gender categories, that "gender" instead constituted a series of performative acts that, taken together, created the appearance of an authentic "core" of gender identity. Gay rights advocates, she argued, subverted many of the interests of their movement by relying on clearly demarcated categories of gender, sex, or sexuality. A commitment to such delineated categories, Butler argued, erases certain kinds of identities— that is, those in which gender does not follow from sex and those in which the practices of desire do not follow from either sex or gender. Thus, instead of normalizing or essentializing same-sex sexual desires or conduct, which is the traditional strategy of lesbian and gay rights activists, Butler argued that gay rights advocates should seek to challenge, rather than replicate, gender categories.

Others who embraced queer theory also pointed out that vast numbers of individuals who engaged in same-sex sexual activity were routinely excluded from the frameworks that ostensibly protected "sexual orientation" as a category. For example, bisexual and transgendered activists found a welcome place at the table of queer theory—quite unlike their experiences under the mainstream gay civil rights model, where their concerns were often dismissed or alienated.

The rift between gay civil rights activists and queer theorists is startling and compelling. While gay rights activists sought to use the language of minoritization and sexual identity in order to protect gays and lesbians from discrimination in the wake of [*Bowers v.*] *Hardwick*, queer theorists powerfully argued that such categories were entirely arbitrary, simplistic, and assimilationist; and that they failed to take into account the importance of challenging categorization itself. Indeed, perhaps because of the polarization that such theories produced between queer theorists and gay rights activists, queer theory has remained a predominantly academic, rather than a legal, enterprise. * * *

POLYAMORY AS A SEXUAL ORIENTATION*

Ann Tweedy

[T]his Article asks whether polyamory—a preference for having multiple romantic relationships simultaneously—should be defined as a type of sexual orientation for purposes of anti-discrimination law. . . .

Today, sexual orientation is almost universally understood to signify whether a person is attracted to members of the same sex, the opposite sex, or both sexes. Thus, of the twenty-one states that had statewide statutes in place as of July 2010 prohibiting discrimination in employment based on sexual orientation, the eighteen states that statutorily defined sexual orientation defined it in terms of heterosexuality, homosexuality, and bisexuality. . . .**

The salience of the term in our culture in turn implies that the sex of the objects of each person's attraction says something important about her or him. . . . Although this basic definition of sexual orientation, with its attendant implications, is so common as to be taken for granted as correct, there is nothing intrinsic about either the noun "orientation" or the adjective "sexual" that would tie the term specifically to the sex of those to whom a person is attracted. Instead, as scholars such as Dr. Ruth Hubbard have explained, in the abstract, the limited use of the term employed in common usage appears to be somewhat arbitrary: "the use of the phrase 'sexual orientation' to describe only a person's having sex with members of their own, or the other, sex obscures the fact that many of us have other strong and consistent sexual orientations—toward certain hair colors, body shapes, and racial types." Indeed, as Michel Foucault argued, it appears that our contemporary cultural understanding of the concept of sexual orientation is rooted in the late 1800s, when, as regulation of sexuality increased, those who practiced sodomy began to be imputed with certain essential (and societally undesirable) characteristics[.]

---

* Ann Tweedy, *Polyamory as a Sexual Orientation*, 79 U. CIN. L. REV. 1461, 1462–66, 1474–76, 1479–81, 1514 (2011).

** *Editor's Note*: Tweedy explains that some of these states also include gender identity as part of sexual orientation. She notes that the remaining three states do not statutorily define "sexual orientation."

. . . [A] person's sexual orientation may, in actual application, be both broader and narrower than the common use of the term. . . . The facts that the current usage of the term "sexual orientation" is artificially limited and that it poses problems for those whom it is most often invoked to describe, however, do not necessarily lead to the conclusion that, as a matter of anti-discrimination law, the definition should be opened up to include any and all sexual preferences that are either sufficiently strong and consistent or sufficiently settled to technically qualify as a sexual orientation. Rather, it could well be argued that only those sexual preferences that are likely to be the basis for discrimination should be protected by anti-discrimination law.

Polyamory, which is commonly shortened to "poly," "in general describes the practice, state or ability of having more than one sexual [or, for some, romantic] loving relationships at the same time, with the full knowledge and consent of all partners involved." Thus, polyamory, which literally means having more than one lover, is relationship-based and should be distinguished from more casual types of non-monogamy such as swinging. It "is a lifestyle embraced by a minority of individuals who exhibit a wide variety of relationship models and who articulate an ethical vision that . . . encompass[es] five main principles: self-knowledge, radical honesty, consent, self-possession, and privileging love and sex over other emotions and activities such as jealousy." As suggested by these principles, polyamory is not only "a practice," but is also, at least for some of its adherents, "a theory of relationships." . . .

It is estimated that there are more than half a million "openly polyamorous families in the United States . . . with thriving contingents in nearly every major city." . . .

Finally, some polyamorists see themselves as "hardwired" that way, while others do not necessarily see polyamory as an identity or, alternatively, see it as a constructed identity.

. . . Because polyamory appears to be at least moderately embedded as an identity, because polyamorists face considerable discrimination, and because non-monogamy is an organizing principle of inequality in American culture, anti-discrimination protections for polyamorists are warranted. Moreover, polyamory shares some of the important attributes of sexual orientation as traditionally understood, so it makes conceptual sense for polyamory to be viewed as part of sexual orientation. On the other hand, however, some of our culture's cherished myths about sexual orientation, especially its unchangeableness, would have to be given up to make such a change. In the short-term, this could well be very risky for existing sexual orientation protections and it could make some legal strategies in sexual orientation cases, such as analogizing sexual orientation to race, obsolete. In the long run, however, it would arguably be better culturally to come to a deeper and more nuanced understanding of sexual orientation that is not based on its similarity to other identities.

NOTES

1.   Why do we define sexual orientation merely in terms of the sex of the individuals to whom someone is attracted? Even if we continue to view sexual orientation as a primary identity category, can we understand it in more expansive and multidimensional terms?

2.   As the excerpts above illustrate, queer theoretical work in legal scholarship draws heavily on scholarship from non-legal disciplines. For foundational work from a queer perspective, see LEO BERSANI, HOMOS (1996); Gayle Rubin, *Thinking Sex: Notes for a Radical Theory of the Politics of Sexuality*, *in* PLEASURE AND DANGER: EXPLORING FEMALE SEXUALITY (Carole S. Vance ed., 1984); and MICHAEL WARNER, THE TROUBLE WITH NORMAL: SEX, POLITICS, AND THE ETHICS OF QUEER LIFE (1999).

VI.   BEYOND DICHOTOMY

A.   SEXUALITY

THE EPISTEMIC CONTRACT OF BISEXUAL ERASURE[*]
Kenji Yoshino

Teaching a seminar on Sexual Orientation and the Law, I faced an old inconsistency so frontally that it became difficult to avoid giving it sustained attention. I began the course in what appears to be a common way, by posing basic questions about sexual orientation. I asked why contemporary American society organizes people according to their sexualities; why we do so on the basis of sexual orientation in particular; and why, when classifying by sexual orientation, we insist on doing so with the binary system of heterosexual and homosexual. In discussing the last question, I adduced the view—powerful in modern American culture from at least the publication of the Kinsey studies onward—that sexual orientation arrays itself along a continuum from exclusive heterosexuality to exclusive homosexuality. I noted that this view encouraged us to think of the straight/gay binary as defining the ends of a continuum that could be stretched, accordion-like, to accommodate ever finer gradations of cross-sex and same-sex desire. This meant recognizing a group—often called bisexuals—on the intermediate stretch of the continuum, as well as the possibility of a group—sometimes called asexuals—not represented on the continuum at all. Indeed, I argued that sexual orientation

---

[*]   Kenji Yoshino, *The Epistemic Contract of Bisexual Erasure*, 52 STAN. L. REV. 353, 356–429 (2000).

classifications that only used the two "monosexual" terms "heterosexual" and "homosexual" were unstable and naive.

As soon as the introductory unit was over, however, the inconsistency occurred. I found myself and the class falling back into the very "unstable" usages I had worked hard to retire—specifically the usages of the words "heterosexual" and "homosexual" as mutually exclusive, cumulatively exhaustive terms. While we sometimes rallied by using the word "queer" instead of "gay," or by adding the rider "or bisexual" to "gay," these efforts were token and fitful. In the face of legal discussions and academic commentary that were relentless in reifying the straight/gay binary, it was difficult to hold the bisexual steadily visible, even as a spectral possibility. And while this failure to resist what I had criticized as a distortion was striking in a class that sought to treat the issue of sexual orientation with sophistication, it was simultaneously all too recognizable as an inconsistency that riddles more quotidian discourse. Many who would not deny that bisexuals exist when the subject of bisexuality arises can nonetheless revert to the straight/gay dichotomy when the topic shifts. I myself can speak at length about bisexuals at one moment and then, in the next, field a question such as "Is X straight or gay?" without instinctively feeling as if an important possibility—the bisexual possibility—has been elided.

What is happening here? Why is bisexuality so invisible? If we interpret that invisibility as the product of erasure, why does that erasure occur? Why is bisexuality now becoming sufficiently visible that commentators have begun to theorize its invisibility as the result of erasure? How might contemporary sexual orientation politics and law look different if this trend toward visibility continues?

I.   THE ERASURE OF BISEXUALS

* * * Bisexual invisibility manifests itself in the studied omission of bisexuality in discussions of sexual orientation. . . .

On-line searches for the words "homosexuality" and "bisexuality" in mainstream newspapers, newsmagazines, and academic abstracts reveal a striking discrepancy in the incidence of the two terms. In the period from January 1, 1990 to November 30, 1999, the *Los Angeles Times* had 2790 documents mentioning homosexuality and 121 documents mentioning bisexuality; *USA Today* had 1768 documents mentioning homosexuality and 29 documents mentioning bisexuality; and *The Wall Street Journal* had 396 documents mentioning homosexuality and nine documents mentioning bisexuality. In the same time period, *Time* magazine had 240 documents mentioning homosexuality and fifteen documents mentioning bisexuality; *U.S. News and World Report* had 120 documents mentioning homosexuality and three documents mentioning bisexuality; and *The New Republic* had 144 documents mentioning homosexuality and three documents mentioning bisexuality. While I expected much less of a discrepancy in moving from popular to academic sources, this proved not to be the case. In the same time period, the Social Sciences Abstract Database on Wilson Web had 1122 documents mentioning homosexuality and 87 documents mentioning bisexuality; the General Sciences Abstracts had 221 documents mentioning homosexuality and six documents mentioning bisexuality; the Humanities Abstracts had 962 documents mentioning homosexuality and 26 documents mentioning bisexuality.

The discrepancy between the relative visibility of homosexuality and bisexuality can be described sociologically as well as statistically. Robin Ochs has argued that bisexuals are invisible not only relative to straights, but also relative to gays. She points out that while we sometimes suspend the general presumption that all individuals are straight, the presumption that replaces it is that all individuals within that context are gay. Thus, "[i]n most families, for example, members are presumed to be heterosexual; conversely, at a women's bar all the women present are presumed lesbians." There are few contexts, however, in which an individual is presumed bisexual. In a similar vein, Marjorie Garber has observed that bisexuals have few recognizable symbols of their identity— the pink and blue "biangle" is one of the few symbols specifically denoting bisexuality and is much less culturally visible than the gay symbols of the pink triangle or the rainbow. Thus, even when the heterosexual presumption that all individuals are straight is suspended, it is replaced by the monosexual presumption that all individuals are straight or gay.

[Yet studies of sexuality suggest that bisexual desire is quite widespread. In Laumann's study] [s]ubjects were asked to complete the phrase "In general are you sexually attracted to . . ." with one of five responses: "(1) only men; (2) mostly men; (3) both men and women; (4) mostly women; and (5) only women." . . . For men, 0.6 percent (narrow definition) to 3.9 percent (broad definition) were attracted to both men and women, while 2.4 percent (narrow definition) to 3.1 percent (broad definition) reported attraction to men only. For women, 0.8 percent (narrow definition) to 4.1 percent (broad definition) reported attraction to both men and women, while 0.3 percent (narrow definition) to 0.9 percent (broad definition) reported attraction to women only. Taking the narrow and broad definitions as setting the endpoints of a range, the percentages of "bisexuals" are again greater than or comparable to those of "homosexuals." * * *

I conclude that bisexuals are invisible in modern American society and that this invisibility arises from erasure rather than from nonexistence. I now turn to the reasons for this erasure.

II. THE EPISTEMIC CONTRACT OF BISEXUAL ERASURE

* * * My hypothesis is that bisexuals remain invisible because both self-identified straights and self-identified gays have overlapping political interests in bisexual erasure. It is as if self-identified straights and self-identified gays have concluded that whatever their other disagreements, they will agree that bisexuals do not exist. Put another way, the sexual orientation continuum that runs from straight through bisexual to gay is a "loopified" one, in which straights and gays are actually closer to each other on this issue than either group is to bisexuals. Because of this, self-identified straights and self-identified gays enter into what I will call an epistemic contract of bisexual erasure. * * *

. . . [S]traights and gays have entered into [this] contract . . . because of three different investments: (1) an investment in stabilizing sexual orientation; (2) an investment in retaining the primacy of sex; and (3) an investment in preserving norms of monogamy.

Straights and gays have an investment in stabilizing sexual orientation categories. The shared aspect of this investment is the security that all individuals draw from rigid social orderings. The distinctively straight investment is the retention of heterosexual privilege. And the distinctively gay investment relates to the perception that bisexuality endangers the immutability defense and effective political mobilization.

Both straights and gays may also wish to erase bisexuals because bisexuality has disturbing consequences for the current sex regime. All monosexuals are created through a regime that privileges sex, and they thus have an investment in bisexual erasure that relates to their own constitution. Straights have a specific investment in bisexual erasure because bisexuality disrupts the power heterosexuality has to determine sex performance. And gays have a specific investment because bisexuality interferes with complete sex separatism.

Finally, both straights and gays are disquieted by bisexuals insofar as bisexuals are thought to represent nonmonogamy. Straights and gays have a shared investment in decreasing sexual jealousy. Straights are peculiarly threatened insofar as they believe that bisexual nonmonogamy bridges the gap between the HIV-infected gay population and the uninfected straight population. And gays are distinctively threatened by bisexual nonmonogamy to the extent that they wish to retire the stereotype of gays as nonmonogamous.

These multiple and overlapping investments in bisexual erasure explain the longevity of the epistemic contract. But they are not insurmountable. The very fact that bisexual erasure has been recognized indicates this, for the paradox of status hierarchy is that the oppressed category must have some power to be recognized as such. But this means that even as there are investments in bisexual invisibility, there are simultaneous and countervailing investments in bisexual visibility.

NOTE

Yoshino published his article in 2000. Is bisexuality still subject to erasure? For an updated perspective arguing that bisexuality has become hypervisible, see Elizabeth M. Glazer, *Sexual Reorientation*, 100 GEO. L.J. 997 (2012).

B. GENDER

LITTLETON V. PRANGE
Court of Appeals of Texas, 1999
9 S.W.3d 223

HARDBERGER, C.J.

This case involves the most basic of questions. When is a man a man, and when is a woman a woman? Every schoolchild, even of tender years, is confident he or she can tell the difference, especially if the person is wearing no clothes. These are observations that each of us makes early in life and, in most cases, continue to have more than a passing interest in for the rest of our lives. It is one of the more pleasant mysteries.

The deeper philosophical (and now legal) question is: can a physician change the gender of a person with a scalpel, drugs and counseling, or is a person's gender immutably fixed by our Creator at birth? The answer to that question has definite legal implications that present themselves in this case involving a person named Christie Lee Littleton.

FACTUAL BACKGROUND

A complete stipulation of the facts was made by the parties in this case.

Christie is a transsexual. She was born in San Antonio in 1952, a physically healthy male, and named after her father, Lee Cavazos. At birth, she was named Lee Cavazos, Jr. (Throughout this opinion Christie will be referred to as "She." This is for grammatical simplicity's sake, and out of respect for the litigant, who wishes to be called "Christie," and referred to as "she." It has no legal implications.)

At birth, Christie had the normal male genitalia: penis, scrotum and testicles. Problems with her sexual identity developed early though. Christie testified that she considered herself female from the time she was three or four years old, the contrary physical evidence notwithstanding. Her distressed parents took her to a physician, who prescribed male hormones. These were taken, but were ineffective. Christie sought successfully to be excused from sports and physical education because of her embarrassment over changing clothes in front of the other boys.

By the time she was 17 years old, Christie was searching for a physician who would perform sex reassignment surgery. At 23, she enrolled in a program at the University of Texas Health Science Center that would lead to a sex reassignment operation. For four years Christie underwent psychological and psychiatric treatment by a number of physicians, some of whom testified in this case.

On August 31, 1977, Christie's name was legally changed to Christie Lee Cavazos. Under doctor's orders, Christie also began receiving various treatments and female hormones. Between November of 1979 and February of 1980, Christie underwent three surgical procedures, which culminated in a complete sex reassignment. Christie's penis, scrotum and testicles were surgically removed, and a vagina and labia were constructed. Christie additionally underwent breast construction surgery.

Dr. Donald Greer, a board certified plastic surgeon, served as a member of the gender dysphoria team at UTHSC in San Antonio, Texas during the time in question. Dr. Paul Mohl, a board certified psychiatrist, also served as a member of the same gender dysphoria team. Both participated in the evaluation and treatment of Christie. The gender dysphoria team was a mutli-disciplinary team that met regularly to interview and care for transsexual patients.

. . . Dr. Greer and Dr. Mohl would testify that the definition of a transsexual is someone whose physical anatomy does not correspond to their sense of being or their sense of gender, and that medical science has not been able to identify the exact cause of this condition, but it is in medical probability a combination of neuro-biological, genetic and neonatal environmental factors. Dr. Greer and Dr. Mohl would further testify that in arriving at a diagnosis of transsexualism in Christie, the program at UTHSC was guided by the guidelines established by the Johns Hopkins Group and that, based on these guidelines, Christie was diagnosed psychologically and psychiatrically as a genuine male to female transsexual. Dr. Greer and Dr. Mohl also would testify that true male to female transsexuals are, in their opinion, psychologically and psychiatrically female before and after the sex reassignment surgery, and that Christie is a true male to female transsexual.

On or about November 5, 1979, Dr. Greer served as a principal member of the surgical team that performed the sex reassignment surgery on Christie. In Dr. Greer's opinion, the anatomical and genital features of Christie, following that surgery, are such that she has the capacity to function sexually as a female. Both Dr. Greer and Dr. Mohl would testify that, in their opinions, following the successful completion of

Christie's participation in UTHSC's gender dysphoria program, Christie is medically a woman.

Christie married a man by the name of Jonathon Mark Littleton in Kentucky in 1989, and she lived with him until his death in 1996. Christie filed a medical malpractice suit under the Texas Wrongful Death and Survival Statute in her capacity as Jonathon's surviving spouse. The sued doctor, appellee here, filed a motion for summary judgment. The motion challenged Christie's status as a proper wrongful death beneficiary, asserting that Christie is a man and cannot be the surviving spouse of another man.

The trial court agreed and granted the summary judgment. The summary judgment notes that the trial court considered the summary judgment evidence, the stipulation, and the argument of counsel. In addition to the stipulation, Christie's affidavit was attached to her response to the motion for summary judgment. In her affidavit, Christie states that Jonathon was fully aware of her background and the fact that she had undergone sex reassignment surgery.

THE LEGAL ISSUE

Can there be a valid marriage between a man and a person born as a man, but surgically altered to have the physical characteristics of a woman?

OVERVIEW OF ISSUE

This is a case of first impression in Texas. The underlying statutory law is simple enough. Texas (and Kentucky, for that matter), like most other states, does not permit marriages between persons of the same sex. In order to have standing to sue under the wrongful death and survival statu[t]es, Christie must be Jonathon's surviving spouse. The defendant's summary judgment burden was to prove she is not the surviving spouse. Referring to the statutory law, though, does not resolve the issue. This court, as did the trial court below, must answer this question: Is Christie a man or a woman? There is no dispute that Christie and Jonathon went through a ceremonial marriage ritual. If Christie is a woman, she may bring this action. If Christie is a man, she may not.

Christie is medically termed a transsexual, a term not often heard on the streets of Texas, nor in its courtrooms. If we look at other states or even other countries to see how they treat marriages of transsexuals, we get little help. Only a handful of other states, or foreign countries, have even considered the case of the transsexual. The opposition to same-sex marriages, on the other hand, is very wide spread. . . . Marriage is tightly defined in the United States: "a legal union between one man and one woman."

Public antipathy toward same-sex marriages notwithstanding, the question remains: is a transsexual still the same sex after a sex-reassignment operation as before the operation? A transsexual, such as Christie, does not consider herself a homosexual because she does not consider herself a man. Her self-identity, from childhood, has been as a woman. Since her various operations, she does not have the outward physical characteristics of a man either. Through the intervention of surgery and drugs, Christie appears to be a woman. In her mind, she has corrected her physical features to line up with her true gender.

"Although transgenderism is often conflated with homosexuality, the characteristic, which defines transgenderism, is not sexual orientation, but sexual identity. Transgenderism describes people who experience a separation between their gender and their biological/anatomical sex." Mary Coombs, *Sexual Dis-Orientation: Transgendered People and Same-Sex Marriage*, 8 UCLA WOMEN'S L.J. 219, 237 (1998).

Nor should a transsexual be confused with a transvestite, who is simply a man who attains some sexual satisfaction from wearing women's clothes. Christie does not consider herself a man wearing women's clothes; she considers herself a woman wearing women's clothes. She has been surgically and chemically altered to be a woman. She has officially changed her name and her birth certificate to reflect her new status. But the question remains whether the law will take note of these changes and treat her as if she had been born a female. To answer this question, we consider the law of those jurisdictions who have previously decided it.

CASE LAW

The English case of *Corbett v. Corbett* appears to be the first case to consider the issue, and is routinely cited in later cases, including those cases from the United States. April Ashley, like Christie Littleton, was born a male, and like Christie, had undergone a sex-reassignment operation. April later married Arthur Corbett. Arthur subsequently asked for a nullification of the marriage based upon the fact that April was a man, and the marriage had never been consummated. April resisted the nullification of her marriage, asserting that the reason the marriage had not been consummated was the fault of her husband, not her. She said she was ready, willing, and able to consummate the marriage.

Arthur testified that he was "mesmerised" by April upon meeting her, and he dated her for three years before their marriage. He said that she "looked like a woman, dressed like a woman and acted like a woman." Arthur and April eventually married, but they were never successful in having sexual relations. Several doctors testified in the case, as they did in the current case.

Based upon the doctors' testimony, the court came up with four criteria for assessing the sexual identity of an individual. These are:

(1) Chromosomal factors;

(2) Gonadal factors (i.e., presence or absence of testes or ovaries);

(3) Genital factors (including internal sex organs); and

(4) Psychological factors.

Chromosomes are the structures on which the genes are carried which, in turn, are the mechanism by which hereditary characteristics are transmitted from parents to off-spring. An individual normally has 23 pairs of chromosomes in his or her body cells; one of each pair being derived from each parent. One pair of chromosomes is known to determine an individual's sex. The English court stated that "[T]he biological sexual constitution of an individual is fixed at birth (at the latest), and cannot be changed, either by the natural development of organs of the opposite sex, or by medical or surgical means. The respondent's operation, therefore, cannot affect her true sex." The court then reasoned that since marriage is essentially a relationship between man and woman, the validity of the marriage depends on whether April is, or is not, a woman. The court held that the criteria for answering this question must be biological and, having so held, found that April, a transsexual, "is not a woman for the purposes of marriage but is a biological male and has been so since birth," and, therefore, the marriage between Arthur and April was void. The court specifically rejected the contention that individuals could "assign" their own sex by their own volition, or by means of an operation. In short, once a man, always a man.

The year after *Corbett* was decided in England, a case involving the validity of a marriage in which one of the partners was transsexual appeared in a United States court. This was the case of *Anonymous v. Anonymous*, 325 N.Y.S.2d 499 (Sup.Ct.1971).

This New York case had a connection with Texas. The marriage ceremony of the transsexual occurred in Belton, while the plaintiff was stationed at Fort Hood. The purpose of the suit was to declare that no marriage could legally have taken place. The court pointed out that this was not an annulment of a marriage because a marriage contract must be between a man and a woman. If the ceremony itself was a nullity, there would be no marriage to annul, but the court would simply declare that no marriage could legally have taken place. The court had no difficulty in doing so, holding: "The law makes no provision for a 'marriage' between persons of the same sex. Marriage is and always has been a contract between a man and a woman."

Factually, the New York case was less complicated than Corbett, and the instant case, because there had been no sexual change operation, and the "wife" still had normal male organs. The plaintiff made this unpleasant discovery on his wedding night. The husband in Anonymous was unaware that he was marrying a transsexual. In both Corbett and the instant case, the husband was fully aware of the true state of affairs, and accepted it. In fact, in the instant case, Christie and her husband were married for seven years, and, according to the testimony, had normal sexual relations. This is a much longer period of time than any of the other reported cases.

The next reported transsexual case came from New Jersey. This is the only United States case to uphold the validity of a transsexual marriage. In *M.T. v. J.T.*, 140 N.J.Super. 77, 355 A.2d 204, 205 (1976), a transsexual wife brought an action for support and maintenance growing out of her marriage. The husband interposed a defense that his wife was male, and that their marriage was void (and therefore he owed nothing). M.T., the wife, testified she was born a male, but she always considered herself a female. M.T. dated men all her life. After M.T. met her husband-to-be, J.T., they decided that M.T. would have an operation so she could "be physically a woman."

In 1971, M.T. had an operation where her male organs were removed and a vagina was constructed. J.T. paid for the operation, and the couple were married the next year. M.T. and J.T. lived as husband and wife and had sexual intercourse. J.T. supported M.T. for over two years; however, in 1974, J.T. left the home, and his support of M.T. ceased. The lawsuit for maintenance and support followed.

The doctor who had performed the sex-reassignment operation testified. He described a transsexual as a person who has "a great discrepancy between the physical genital anatomy and the person's sense of self-identity as a male or as a female." The doctor defined gender identity as "a sense, a total sense of self as being masculine or female; it pervades one's entire concept of one's place in life, of one's place in society and in point of fact the actual facts of the anatomy are really secondary." The doctor said that after the operation his patient had no uterus or cervix, but her vagina had a "good cosmetic appearance" and was "the same as a normal female vagina after a hysterectomy."

The trial court, in ruling for M.T. by finding the marriage valid, stated:

> It is the opinion of the court that if the psychological choice of a person is medically sound, not a mere whim, and irreversible sex reassignment surgery has been performed, society has no right to prohibit the transsexual from leading a normal life. Are we to look upon this person as an exhibit in a circus side show? What harm has said person done to society? The entire area of transsexualism is repugnant to the nature of many persons within our society. However, this should not govern the legal acceptance of a fact.

The appellate court affirmed, holding:

> If such sex reassignment surgery is successful and the postoperative transsexual is, by virtue of medical treatment, thereby possessed of the full capacity to function sexually as male or female, as the case may be, we perceive no legal barrier, cognizable social taboo, or reason grounded in public policy to prevent the persons' identification at least for purposes of marriage to the sex finally indicated.

* * *

DISCUSSION

... In our system of government it is for the legislature, should it choose to do so, to determine what guidelines should govern the recognition of marriages involving transsexuals. The need for legislative guidelines is particularly important in this case, where the claim being asserted is statutorily-based. The statute defines who may bring the cause of action: a surviving spouse, and if the legislature intends to recognize transsexuals as surviving spouses, the statute needs to address the guidelines by which such recognition is governed. When or whether the legislature will choose to address this issue is not within the judiciary's control.

It would be intellectually possible for this court to write a protocol for when transsexuals would be recognized as having successfully changed their sex. Littleton has suggested we do so, perhaps using the surgical removal of the male genitalia as the test. As was pointed out by Littleton's counsel, "amputation is a pretty important step." Indeed it is. But this court has no authority to fashion a new law on transsexuals, or anything else. We cannot make law when no law exists: we can only interpret the written word of our sister branch of government, the legislature. Our responsibility in this case is to determine whether, in the absence of legislatively-established guidelines, a jury can be called upon to decide the legality of such marriages. We hold they cannot. In the absence of any guidelines, it would be improper to launch a jury forth on these untested and unknown waters.

There are no significant facts that need to be decided. The parties have supplied them for us. We find the case, at this stage, presents a pure question of law and must be decided by this court.

Based on the facts of this case, and the law and studies of previous cases, we conclude:

> (1) Medical science recognizes that there are individuals whose sexual self-identity is in conflict with their biological and anatomical sex. Such people are termed transsexuals.

(2) A transsexual is not a homosexual in the traditional sense of the word, in that transsexuals believe and feel they are members of the opposite sex. Nor is a transsexual a transvestite. Transsexuals do not believe they are dressing in the opposite sex's clothes. They believe they are dressing in their own sex's clothes.

(3) Christie Littleton is a transsexual.

(4) Through surgery and hormones, a transsexual male can be made to look like a woman, including female genitalia and breasts. Transsexual medical treatment, however, does not create the internal sexual organs of a women (except for the vaginal canal). There is no womb, cervix or ovaries in the post-operative transsexual female.

(5) The male chromosomes do not change with either hormonal treatment or sex reassignment surgery. Biologically a post-operative female transsexual is still a male.

(6) The evidence fully supports that Christie Littleton, born male, wants and believes herself to be a woman. She has made every conceivable effort to make herself a female, including a surgery that would make most males pale and perspire to contemplate.

(7) Some physicians would consider Christie a female; other physicians would consider her still a male. Her female anatomy, however, is all man-made. The body that Christie inhabits is a male body in all aspects other than what the physicians have supplied.

We recognize that there are many fine metaphysical arguments lurking about here involving desire and being, the essence of life and the power of mind over physics. But courts are wise not to wander too far into the misty fields of sociological philosophy. Matters of the heart do not always fit neatly within the narrowly defined perimeters of statutes, or even existing social mores. Such matters though are beyond this court's consideration. Our mandate is . . . to interpret the statutes of the state and prior judicial decisions. This mandate is deceptively simplistic in this case: Texas statutes do not allow same-sex marriages, and prior judicial decisions are few.

Christie was created and born a male. Her original birth certificate, an official document of Texas, clearly so states. During the pendency of this suit, Christie amended the original birth certificate to change the sex and name. Under section 191.028 of the Texas Health and Safety Code she was entitled to seek such an amendment if the record was "incomplete or proved by satisfactory evidence to be inaccurate." The trial court that granted the petition to amend the birth certificate necessarily construed the term "inaccurate" to relate to the present, and having been presented with the uncontroverted affidavit of an expert stating that Christie is a female, the trial court deemed this satisfactory to prove an inaccuracy. However, the trial court's role in considering the petition was a ministerial one. It involved no fact-finding or consideration of the deeper public policy concerns presented. No one claims the information contained in Christie's original birth certificate was based on fraud or error. We believe the legislature intended the term "inaccurate" in section 191.028 to mean inaccurate as of the time the certificate was recorded; that is, at the time of birth. At the time of birth, Christie was a male, both anatomically and genetically. The facts contained in the original birth certificate were true and accurate, and the words contained in the amended certificate are not binding on this court.

There are some things we cannot will into being. They just are.

CONCLUSION

We hold, as a matter of law, that Christie Littleton is a male. As a male, Christie cannot be married to another male. Her marriage to Jonathon was invalid, and she cannot bring a cause of action as his surviving spouse.

We affirm the summary judgment granted by the trial court.

ANGELINI, J., concurring.

I concur in the judgment. . . . I note, however, that "real difficulties . . . will occur if these three criteria [chromosomal, gonadal and genital tests] are not congruent." *Corbett v. Corbett*. We must recognize the fact that, even when biological factors are considered, there are those individuals whose sex may be ambiguous. *See* Julie A. Greenberg, *Defining Male and Female: Intersexuality and the Collision Between Law and Biology*, 41 ARIZ. L. REV. 265 (1999). Having recognized this fact, I express no opinion as to how the law would view such individuals with regard to marriage. We are, however, not presented with such a case at this time. . . . [I]n the case of Christie Lee Littleton, it appears that all biological and physical factors were congruent and were consistent with those of a typical male at birth. The only pre-operative distinction between Christie Lee Littleton and a typical male was her psychological sense of being a female. Under these facts, I agree that Texas law will not recognize her marriage to a male.

LOPEZ, J., dissenting.

On its surface, the question of whether a person is male or female seems simple enough. Complicated with the issues of surgical alteration, sexual identity, and same-sex marriage, the answer is not so simple. To answer the question, the majority assumes that gender is accurately determined at birth. Consider the basis for such a determination. Traditionally, an attending physician or mid-wife determines a newborn's gender at birth after a visual inspection of the newborn's genitalia. If the child has a penis, scrotum, and testicles, the attendant declares the child to be male. If the child does not have a penis, scrotum, and testicles, the attendant declares the child to be female. This declaration is then memorialized by a certificate of birth, without an examination of the child's chromosomes or an inquiry about how the child feels about its sexual identity. Despite this simplistic approach, the traditional method of determining gender does not always result in an accurate record of gender.

Texas law recognizes that inaccuracies occur in determining, or at least recording, gender. By permitting the amendment of an original birth certificate upon satisfactory evidence, Texas law allows these inaccuracies to be corrected. Indeed, Christie's gender was lawfully corrected by an amended birth certificate months before the trial court ruled on Dr. Prange's motion for summary judgment. Notably, the amended birth certificate reflects the original filing date of April 10, 1952, the original date of birth, and an issuance date of August, 14, 1998. Retention of the original filing date indicates that the amended birth certificate has been substituted for the original birth certificate in the same way an amended pleading is substituted for an original pleading in a civil lawsuit.

Under the rules of civil procedure, a document that has been replaced by an amended document is considered a nullity. Rule 65 provides that the substituted instrument takes the place of the original. Tex.R. Civ. P. 65. Although neither a state statute nor case law address the specific effect of an amended birth certificate, many cases address the effect of an amended pleading. Under this authority, an amended instrument changes the original and is substituted for the original. Although a birth certificate is not a legal pleading, the document is an official state document. Amendment of the state document is certainly analogous to an amended legal pleading. In this case, Christie's amended birth certificate replaced her original birth certificate. In effect, the amended birth certificate nullified the original birth certificate. As a result, summary judgment was issued based on a nullified document. How then can the majority conclude that Christie is a male? If Christie's evidence that she was female was satisfactory enough for the trial court to issue an order to amend her original birth certificate to change both her name and her gender, why is it not satisfactory enough to raise a genuine question of material fact on a motion for summary judgment?

Granted the issues raised by this case are best addressed by the legislature. In the absence of law addressing those issues, however, this court is bound to rely on the standard of review and the evidence presented by the parties. Here, the stipulated evidence alone raises a genuine question about whether Christie is Jonathon's surviving spouse. Every case need not be precedential. In this case, the court is required to determine as a matter of law whether Christie is Jonathon's surviving spouse, not to speculate on the legalities of public policies not yet addressed by our legislature. Under a focused review of this case, a birth certificate reflecting the birth of a male child named Lee Cavazos does not prove that Christie Littleton is not the surviving spouse of Jonathan Littleton. Having failed to prove that Christie was not Jonathon's surviving spouse, Dr. Prange was not entitled to summary judgment. Because Christie's summary judgment evidence raises a genuine question of material fact about whether she is the surviving spouse of Jonathon Littleton, I respectfully dissent.

NOTE

In a recent decision, the Texas Court of Appeals held that "Texas law recognizes that an individual who has had a 'sex change' is eligible to marry a person of the opposite sex." *In re Estate of Araguz III*, ___ S.W.3d ___, 2014 WL 576085, at *9 (Tex. App. Feb. 13, 2014). In so holding, the court found that "*Littleton* has been legislatively overruled" based on a 2009 family code amendment. *Id*. That amendment provides that "a court order related to an applicant's 'sex change' [is] a form of acceptable proof to establish an applicant's identity and age, and thus, eligibility, to obtain a marriage license." *Id*. at *8 (citing TEX. FAM. CODE. ANN. § 2.005(b)(8)).

––––––––––––

Littleton provides a window into how some judges have approached issues of gender identity. Now consider the following scholarly treatments.

TRANSSEXUALS AND CRITICAL GENDER THEORY: THE POSSIBILITY OF A RESTROOM LABELED "OTHER"*

Terry S. Kogan

An MTF [Male-to-Female] transsexual often describes herself as a person locked, trapped or imprisoned in the wrong body. Thus, an MTF transsexual's self-perceived gender identity as female does not match her male genitals. Many transsexuals report that their sense of being a member of the opposite sex began very early in childhood. They often describe themselves as having sensed that they were supposed to have been born as girls.

A transsexual's early sense of dissonance between her biological sex and her gender identity (referred to as "gender dysphoria" in the

––––––––––––

* Terry S. Kogan, *Transsexuals and Critical Gender Theory: The Possibility of a Restroom Labeled "Other"*, 48 HASTINGS L.J. 1223, 1225–47 (1997).

psychological literature[8]) was centered on her physical body and the meaning that she gave to her body. Not only did she want to present herself in everyday life as feminine; equally important, she experienced extreme discomfort with her male genitals. This discomfort was exacerbated when she reached puberty and began experiencing muscle and genital development and the growth of body hair.

This extreme discomfort ultimately leads most transsexuals to a lifelong desire to conform their bodies, in some way, to their perceived gender identity. Their self-interpretation of their gender identity as female is intimately bound up with their public presentation as a woman. Accordingly, most transsexuals wear clothing and hairstyles culturally identified as female. Virtually all transsexuals cross-dress and remove facial and body hair. Most transsexuals also take female hormones, at least for some period during their lives, in order to further feminize their male bodies by softening skin, reducing growth of body hair, broadening the hips, and enlarging the breasts. Some transsexuals undergo plastic surgery to feminize their facial features, while others undergo vocal cord surgery to raise the pitch of the voice.

The ultimate step is sex reassignment surgery, a top priority for many transsexuals who perceive a driving need to align their genitals with their gender identity. Generally, gender clinics require an individual to undergo extensive counseling and to live full-time as a woman (the so-called "real life test") before undertaking such surgery. Many transsexuals who do not undergo such surgery lack not the desire but rather the financial resources for this extremely expensive operation.

Attitudes of post-operative transsexuals are revealing in understanding the self-interpretation of transsexual gender identity. Many post-operative transsexuals choose to leave the transgendered community after surgery because they no longer consider themselves to be transgendered. They now consider themselves to be women. In

---

[8]   The term "gender dysphoria" was coined by Norman Fisk in the early 1970s to refer to individuals who "were intensely and abidingly uncomfortable in their anatomic and genetic sex and their assigned gender." Norman Fisk, *Gender Dysphoria Syndrome (The How, What and Why of a Disease)*, in PROCEEDINGS OF THE SECOND INTERDISCIPLINARY SYMPOSIUM ON GENDER DYSPHORIA SYNDROME 10 (Donald R. Laub & Patrick Gandy eds., 1973).

The American Psychiatric Association now refers to gender dysphoria as "Gender Identity Disorder," which is defined as follows:

> There are two components of Gender Identity Disorder, both of which must be present to make the diagnosis. There must be evidence of a strong and persistent cross-gender identification, which is the desire to be, or the insistence that one is, of the other sex (Criterion A). This cross-gender identification must not merely be a desire for any perceived cultural advantages of being the other sex. There must also be evidence of persistent discomfort about one's assigned sex or a sense of inappropriateness in the gender role of that sex (Criterion B). The diagnosis is not made if the individual has a concurrent physical intersex condition . . . (Criterion C). To make the diagnosis, there must be evidence of clinically significant distress or impairment in social, occupational, or other important areas of functioning (Criterion D).

DIAGNOSTIC AND STATISTICAL MANUAL OF MENTAL DISORDERS, DSM–IV 532, 533 (1994).

contrast to female impersonators, whom transsexuals tend to view as men engaging in gender parody and play, transsexuals do not view themselves as engaging in illusion or impersonation. Rather, they view themselves as expressing their true feminine gender identity. Anne Bolin explains that from "the transsexual's standpoint, being a male-to-female transsexual was only a temporary condition. Transsexualism was an identity to be outgrown as one eventually became a 'whole' woman. Physical feminization was an important part of this process of personal and social identity transformation." Moreover, because they identify so deeply with the female gender from an early age, MTF transsexuals (irrespective of whether they are pre-operative or post-operative) tend to regard themselves as heterosexual if erotically attracted to males, lesbian if attracted to women, and bisexual if attracted to both.

Metamor- phosis

The autobiographical literature makes clear that transsexuals have a much greater awareness of the intricacies of human gender presentation than do people who have never experienced gender dysphoria. Transsexuals are keenly aware of what it means to present oneself as a woman, an issue far more complex than simply wearing women's clothing. Gender presentation is intimately bound up with one's posture, gait, gestures, and perhaps most importantly, interactions with others in the culture. The ideal towards which most MTF transsexuals aim is the feminine female. Frank Lewin notes that transsexuals want "a body that corresponds to some notion of an ideal image of femininity or . . . an 'exaggerated view of womanliness.' "

An overview of these autobiographies suggests that, in terms of personal identity, a transsexual's sense of her female gender and its presentation—her gender identity—takes precedence over the individual's biological sexual identity. This state of affairs is perceived as an impossibility by critical gender theorists.

A. THE CONSTRAINTS ON GENDER IDENTITY IMPOSED BY A SEXUALLY DIMORPHIC CULTURE

* * * [A]ccepting the reality of a child's sense of gender dysphoria, what is it for a biological male to "know" that she actually was meant to be a female? It is doubtful that one is born with some innate sense that "though I have a penis, I was meant to have a vagina." Instead, a transgendered person's dysphoria is self-interpreted in terms and concepts learned from the surrounding culture. In Euro-American culture, which is highly sexually dimorphic, the dysphoric individual will be inclined to self-interpret her experience in terms that are bipolar—male or female. If the individual experiences discomfort with male identity, the only alternative is to conclude that she must be the opposite—female. This is reinforced by Western culture's essentializing a necessary tie between, on the one hand, those somatic features which

serve as the basis for ascribing sex, and on the other hand, the gendered ways in which we are taught to present ourselves in everyday life.

Given this cultural setting, it is not surprising that individuals experiencing dysphoria conclude that it is not enough to present themselves in gendered ways culturally understood as belonging to the opposite sex. One is not truly a woman unless one is morphologically a woman. Thus, many transsexuals believe that they must "go all the way" and change their bodies by undergoing sex reassignment surgery. In a culturally dimorphic society, if you are not one sex (which is what a transsexual's dysphoria tells him/her), you must be the other. Gender identity is experienced as immutable. Accordingly, one must change that which is mutable given modern technology—one's biological morphology.

Western culture's dimorphic vision of sex and gender has proven destructive to transgendered people, in particular to transsexuals. As critical gender theory has suggested, that vision has made it extremely difficult for transsexual persons to conceptualize their own identities in any way other than as cross-gendered. If a transsexual biological male does not perceive him/herself to be a man, she/he must be a woman.

Dimorphism is not, however, the only vision of sex and gender available. There are cultures which conceptualize three or more sex/genders. Moreover, among certain of these cultures, sex/gender is not necessarily equated with biology. Within such a cultural setting, the response to gender dysphoria might be very different. Though one experiences severe discomfort with the way in which one is gendered by society, if the social understandings of sex/gender are less closely tied to one's biological features, then one might have available ways to alleviate one's dysphoria without turning to genital surgery. The possibility of viewing transsexuals as a third sex/gender is considered in greater detail below.

B. SEXUAL CONTINUISM

In searching for an alternative to sexual dimorphism, let's begin with Martine Rothblatt's vision of "sexual continuism." According to Rothblatt, dividing persons into dimorphic categories of "male" and "female" is as arbitrary a way to distinguish among people as dividing persons into racial categories. She describes this division of people into two sexes as the "apartheid of sex." Rothblatt sees the apartheid of sex as based on the dimorphic gender paradigm because

[i]t claims that this absolute division [of male and female] arises from sex-differentiated levels of hormones released prenatally, which in turn create not only two different reproductive systems, but also two different mental natures. From its ancient genesis, the old gender paradigm has been used to enforce the superiority

of one apparent sex over the other and as a framework for research to prove one sex has a different nature from the other.

Rothblatt proposes an alternative vision of sex which she calls "sexual continuism." This vision "posits that humanity is composed of a continuous blend of sexual identity, far beyond any simplistic male or female categorization." Sexual continuism "predicts that sexual identity, like other aspects of personality, arises from a confluence of factors not solely hormonal or environmental in origin."

Rothblatt bases sexual continuism on a review of research in sociology, psychology, and neurology. She asserts that what seems to be a natural biological distinction between male and female is not so clear. Rothblatt looks to the fact that approximately four percent of the population displays intersexed attributes, either genitally, gonadally, or chromosomally. Moreover, she looks to the fact that all individuals are hormonally a mix of what have been viewed traditionally as male hormones (testosterone) and female hormones (estrogen). In addition, Rothblatt challenges evidence suggesting that there is any difference between men's brains and women's brains (either structurally or functionally). In terms of physical and mental performance, Rothblatt points out that there is a tremendous overlap between persons viewed as men and women. Finally, as technology begins to free human reproduction from the highly specific requirements of a male parent and a female parent, she claims that human reproduction can no longer serve as a justification for distinguishing males from females. "The new paradigm [of sexual continuism] claims that reproductive systems are not strictly personal, but are sociotechnical and are accessible by all persons regardless of genitalia."

Given her vision of a continuum of sex, Rothblatt urges that biological sex should no longer have any tie to the social, economic, or legal spheres of life. Instead, she states that

> [l]abeling people as male or female, upon birth, exalts biology over sociology. Instead, the new feminist principles inspire us to permit all people to self-identify their sexual status along a broad continuum of possibilities and to create such cultures of gender as human ingenuity may develop.

Thus, Rothblatt believes that a range of gender presentations should be available to all persons. She argues that there is in fact a "continuous blend of sexual identity, far beyond any simplistic male or female categorization." According to Rothblatt's vision, genitals become irrelevant as a mode of determining either sex or gender.

Rothblatt's critique of the dimorphic paradigm of sex is directly intended to support the transgendered movement. "Transgenderism makes manifest the continuum nature of sex types because even if a sex type was real at birth, it can now be changed at will during one's life." She believes that rather than being assigned to one of two sexes at birth, and in turn being tracked toward one set of expected gender behaviors, individuals should be allowed to freely find their place on the continuum of sex as they move through life.

C. THE THIRD SEX/THIRD GENDER

Unlike Rothblatt's theory, which posits a unity of human sexuality along a single continuum, a different alternative to sexual dimorphism posits a multiplicity of sexuality—the notion of a third sex/gender. * * *

. . . I propose that we begin to conceptualize a third sex/gender category for Euro-American culture, which I will tentatively term "Other." . . . [T]he category "Other" is . . . meant to provoke a category crisis. It is not meant to describe any "natural" type, and thus does not refer to any specific biological, psychological, or social attributes of an individual. Rather, it is a classification, freely assumed by an individual, which brings to the fore the ambiguities inherent in the dimorphic division of humans into the seemingly natural categories of male and female. . . .

Let me make clear what I am not proposing by the vision of a new sex/gender category, "Other." I am not suggesting that we view all transsexual persons, or transgendered persons, or any other group of persons, as the unique membership of a third sex/gender. The last thing I wish to advocate is a simplistic replacement of our society's rigid dimorphic vision of sex/gender with an equally rigid trimorphic vision.

Rather, the category "Other" is broadly and inclusively conceived, as potentially excluding no one. So who exactly is a member of the sex/gender category, "Other"? The determination as to whether one is a member of the category has nothing to do with biology, desire, or gender presentation. It is a matter of personal choice. It is an identity category which an individual can assume to challenge the destructive history caused by our culture's adoption of a dimorphic sex/gender division. Identifying oneself as "Other" is a conscious choice by an individual to oppose the male/female, masculine/feminine dichotomies, and the oppressions that result from those dichotomies.

Accordingly, irrespective of one's genitals, chromosomes, sexual orientation, gender presentation, or gender identity, any individual may opt to self-identify as "Other." By so doing, that individual makes a statement of solidarity with other persons who object to the insidious nature of Euro-American sexual dimorphism. "Other," rather than recognizing a new "natural" third sex/gender category, serves as a queer sex, gender-blending sex, transgendered-sex category.

RESISTING MEDICINE, RE/MODELING GENDER*

Dean Spade

[S]ex reassignment-related procedures are regulated through a mental health model which promotes regulatory, binary gender expression and denies access to medical procedures to those who fail to perform normative binary gender for their health care providers.

. . .

[Professor Spade provides excerpts from writing he did while seeking sex reassignment surgery.]

. . . I was experiencing acutely the gulf between trans community understandings of our bodies, our experiences, and our liberation, and the medical interpretations of our lives. The medical model, ultimately, was what I had to contend with in order to achieve the embodiment I was seeking. I learned quickly that to achieve that embodiment, I needed to perform a desire for gender normativity, to convince the doctors that I suffered from GID and wanted to "be" a "man" in a narrow sense of both words. My quest for body alteration had to be legitimized by a medical reference to, and pretended belief in, a binary gender system that I had been working to dismantle since adolescence. Later, as I contended with my own legal gender status and that of my clients, I would learn that not only medical treatment, but also legal rights and social services for trans people are dependent upon successful navigation of that medical system.

Symptoms of GID [Gender Identity Disorder] in the Diagnostic and Statistical Manual (DSM-IV) describe at length the symptom of childhood participation in stereotypically gender inappropriate behavior. Boys with GID "particularly enjoy playing house, drawing pictures of beautiful girls and princesses, and watching television or videos of their favorite female characters. . . . They avoid rough-and-tumble play and competitive sports and have little interest in cars and trucks." Girls with GID do not want to wear dresses, "prefer boys' clothing and short hair," are interested in "contact sports, [and] rough-and-tumble play." Despite the disclaimer in the diagnosis description that this is not to be confused with normal gender non-conformity found in tomboys and sissies, no real line is drawn between "normal" gender non-conformity and gender non-conformity which constitutes GID. The effect is two-fold. First, normative childhood gender is produced by creating and pathologizing a category of deviants: normal kids are simply those who do the opposite of what kids with GID are doing. Non-GID kids can be expected to: play with children of their own sex, play with gender appropriate toys (trucks for boys, dolls for girls), enjoy fictional characters of their own sex (girls, specifically, might

---

    *   Dean Spade, *Resisting Medicine, Re/modeling Gender*, 18 BERKELEY WOMEN'S L.J. 15, 18–29 (2003). © 2003 by Regents of the University of California. Reprinted by permission of the Regents of the University of California.

have GID if they like Batman or Superman), play gender appropriate characters in games of "house," etc. Secondly, a regulatory mechanism is put into place. Because gender nonconformity is established as a basis for illness, parents now have a "mill of speech," speculation, and diagnosis to feed their children's gender through should it cross the line. As Foucault describes, the invention of a category of deviation, the description of the "ill" behavior that need be resisted or cured, creates not a prohibitive silence about such behavior but an opportunity for increased surveillance and speculation, what he would call "informal-governance."

Another immediate error and danger of the medical model of transsexuality is its separation of gender from cultural forces. The Diagnostic Criteria for Gender Identity Disorder names, as a general category of symptom, "[a] strong and persistent cross-gender identification (not merely a desire for any perceived cultural advantages of being the other sex)." This criterion suggests the possibility of a gender categorization not read through the cultural gender hierarchy. This requires one to imagine a child wanting to be a gender transgressive from the one assigned to hir* without having that desire stem from a cultural understanding of gender difference defined by the "advantaging" of certain gender behaviors and identities over others. But gender behavior is learned, and children are not born with some innate sense that girls should wear dresses and boys shouldn't like anything pink. So how can a desire to transgress an assigned gender category be read outside of cultural meaning? Such a standard naturalizes and depoliticizes gender and gender role distress. It creates a fictional transsexual who just knows in hir gut what man is and what woman is, and knows that sie is trapped in the wrong body.

The diagnostic criteria for GID produces a fiction of natural gender in which normal, non-transsexual people grow up with minimal to no gender trouble or exploration, do not crossdress as children, do not play with the wrong-gendered kids, and do not like the wrong kinds of toys or characters. This story is not believable. Yet, it survives because medicine produces it not through a description of the norm, but through a generalized account of the norm's transgression by gender deviants. By instructing the doctor/parent/teacher to focus on the transgressive behavior, the diagnostic criteria for GID establishes surveillance and regulation effective for keeping both non-transsexuals and transsexuals in adherence to their roles. In order to get authorization for body alteration, the scripted transsexual childhood narrative must be performed, and the GID diagnosis accepted, maintaining an idea of two discrete gender categories that normally contain everyone but

---

* *Editor's Note*: Spade uses "the gender-neutral pronouns 'sie' (pronounced 'see') and 'hir' (pronounced 'here') to promote the recognition of such pronouns, which resist the need to categorize all subjects neatly into male and female categories."

occasionally are wrongly assigned, requiring correction to reestablish the norm.

In addition to performing a certain narrative of a gender troubled childhood, the most overt requirement for GID diagnosis is the ability to inhabit and perform the new gender category "successfully." Through my own interactions with medical professionals, accounts of other trans people, and medical scholarship on transsexuality, I have gathered that the favored indication of such "success" seems to be the intelligibility of one's new gender in the eyes of non-trans people. Because the ability to be perceived by non-trans people as a non-trans person is valorized, normative expressions of gender within a singular category are mandated.

. . .

What if the propriety of SRS [sex reassignment surgery] was not determined by trans patients' deviations from (non-trans) normative definitions of femininity and masculinity? What if the "success" of transition was not measured by trans people's adherence to (non-trans) normative definitions of femininity and masculinity? I imagine that, like me, some people have a multitude of goals when they seek gender-related body alteration, such as access to different sexual practices, ability to look different in clothing, enhancement of a self-understanding about one's gender that is not entirely reliant on public recognition, public disruption of female and male codes, or any number of other things. Some birth-assigned "men" might want to embody "woman" as butch lesbians in a way that meant they enjoyed occasionally being "sirred" and only sometimes "corrected" the speaker. Some birth-assigned "women" might want to take hormones and become sexy "bearded ladies" who are interpreted a variety of ways but feel great about how they look. When the gatekeepers employ dichotomous gender standards, they foreclose such norm-resistant possibilities.

Many of the trans people I have talked to do not imagine themselves entering a realm of "real manness" or "real womanness," even if they pass as non-trans all the time. Rather, they recognize the absence of meaning in such terms. They regard their transformations as freeing them to express more of themselves, and enabling more comfortable and exciting self understandings and images. While some do rely on passing as non-trans women or men in various aspects of their lives, and some embrace non-trans male or female identity, I think that all are disserved by the requirement that trans people exhibit hyper-masculine or hyper-feminine characteristics to get through medical gatekeeping.

For most of us, negotiating medical standards—whether we are seeking to change our bodies or identity documents, or seeking to enforce our rights—is fraught with difficulty. The medical approach to our gender identities forces us to rigidly conform ourselves to medical providers' opinions about what "real masculinity" and "real femininity" mean, and to produce narratives of struggle around those identities that mirror the diagnostic criteria of GID. For those of us seeking to disrupt the very definitions and categories upon which the medical model of transsexuality relies, the gender-regulating processes of this medical treatment can be dehumanizing, traumatic, or impossible to complete.

NOTE

The latest version of the American Psychiatric Association's Diagnostic and Statistical Manual, DSM-5, addresses some of the critiques of "gender identity disorder" in DSM-IV. DSM-5 replaces the diagnostic term "gender identity disorder" with "gender dysphoria," attempting to shift the focus from "identity per se" to "distress that may accompany the incongruence between one's experienced or expressed gender and one's assigned gender." AMERICAN PSYCHOLOGICAL ASSOCIATION, DIAGNOSTIC AND STATISTICAL MANUAL 451 (5th ed. 2013). DSM-5 also includes a separate diagnosis for children with criteria that attempt to ratchet up the required showing. In addition to a "strong desire to be of the other gender or an insistence that one is the other gender (or some alternative gender different from one's assigned gender)," the child must show at least five of the following:

- In boys (assigned gender), a strong preference for cross-dressing or simulating female attire; or in girls (assigned gender), a strong preference for wearing only typical masculine clothing and a strong resistance to the wearing of typical feminine clothing.

- A strong preference for cross-gender roles in make-believe or fantasy play.

- A strong preference for the toys, games, or activities stereotypically used or engaged in by the other gender.

- A strong preference for playmates of the other gender.

- In boys (assigned gender), a strong rejection of typically masculine toys, games, and activities and a strong avoidance of rough-and-tumble play; or in girls (assigned gender), a strong rejection of typically feminine toys, games, and activities.

- A strong dislike of one's sexual anatomy.

- A strong desire for the primary and/or secondary sex characteristics that match one's experienced gender.

Id. at 451–52.

A member of the subgroup that formulated the criteria explained, "It's really a narrowing of the criteria because you have to want the diagnosis. It takes psychiatrists out of the business of labeling children or others simply because they show gender-atypical behavior." Mark Moran, *New Gender Dysphoria Criteria Replace GID*, PSYCHIATRIC NEWS, Apr. 5, 2013, at 9 (quoting Dr. Jack Drescher). Do you agree? Does Professor Spade's critique of DSM-IV apply with equal force to the diagnostic criteria for children in DSM-5?

DOCUMENTING GENDER[*]
Dean Spade

Over the past forty years, increasing numbers of identity document issuing agencies, such as departments of health, DMVs [Departments of Motor Vehicles], and the SSA [Social Security Administration], have created policies or practices allowing individuals to change the gender marker on their documents and records from "M" to "F" (male to female) or "F" to "M" (female to male). These policies emerged from a growing awareness of the existence of a population of people, currently labeled "transgender," who live their lives identifying as and expressing a different gender than the one assigned to them at birth. Recognizing the social and economic difficulties faced by those whose lived expression of gender does not match their identity documentation, state and federal agencies have over time created a variety of policies aimed at allowing gender marker change on documents commonly used to verify identity.

Many people are under the impression that everyone has a clear "legal gender" on record with the government, and that changing "legal gender" involves presenting some kind of evidence to a specific agency or institution in order to make a decisive and clear change to the new category. Because of the long history linking transgender identity with medical authority and popular cultural beliefs that changing gender involves surgical procedures, some may assume that achieving gender reclassification requires presenting medical evidence to an appropriate administrative or judicial decisionmaker. As it turns out, the reality of the rules that govern gender reclassification in the United States is far more complex.

The rules of gender reclassification . . . differ across jurisdictions and "expert" agencies responsible for creating and enforcing these policies, producing bureaucratic confusion and serious consequences for those directly regulated. [Spade then explains that a variety of policies exist, ranging from those that completely refuse reclassification to those that use medical authority to determine whether reclassification is allowed to those that reclassify based on self-identification.] . . .

Two examples where gender can never be changed from birth-assigned gender are Tennessee's birth certificate policy and prison placement policies across the United States. Tennessee has a statute

---

[*]   Dean Spade, *Documenting Gender*, 59 HASTINGS L.J. 731, 733–38 (2008).

explicitly forbidding the changing of gender markers on birth certificates, so that transgender people born in that state can never obtain a certificate indicating a gender other than that assigned at birth. Similarly, placement policies in prisons across the United States generally use a "never" rule. Transgender women are placed in men's prisons and transgender men are placed in women's prisons. Of the nine jurisdictions that have written policies regarding treatment of transgender prisoners, none allow placement of transgender prisoners according to current gender identity.

In contrast to those policies, a large subset of gender reclassification policies require medical intervention for reclassification. The type of medical intervention, however, differs significantly from policy to policy. Three different birth certificate policies can be used as examples to show a range of requirements. California's birth certificate gender change policy requires the applicant show that he or she has undergone any of a variety of gender confirmation surgeries, which could include chest surgery (breast enhancement for transwomen or mastectomy and reconstruction for trans men), tracheal shave ("Adam's Apple" reduction), penectomy (removal of the penis), orchiectomy (removal of the testicles), vaginoplasty (creation of a vagina), phalloplasty (creation of a penis), hysterectomy (removal of internal pelvic organs), or any one of a range of other gender-related surgeries. New York City and New York State, however, each require genital surgery, and, interestingly, have differing requirements. People born in New York City are required to provide evidence that they have undergone phalloplasty or vaginoplasty, while people born in New York State must provide evidence that they have undergone penectomy or hysterectomy and mastectomy. The fact that two jurisdictions issuing birth certificates in the same state have come up with entirely different requirements for recognition of gender change, alone, attests to the inconsistency in this area. The Massachusetts DMV gender reclassification policy requires that an applicant prove that he or she has undergone some kind of surgery, which is not specified, as well as provide a birth certificate that indicates the new gender. Further, ... gender reclassification policies often include requirements of recognition by other agencies or institutions.

The SSA's policy requires genital surgery but is non-specific as to which surgeries will be accepted. Some DMV gender reclassification policies, such as those of Colorado, New York, and the District of Columbia do not require evidence of surgery, but still require medical documentation in the form of a doctor's letter attesting that the person is transgender and is living in the new gender.

Still other policies require no medical evidence at all. The homeless shelter placement policies of Boston, San Francisco, and New York City are examples of policies that allow individuals to be recognized according to their current gender identity based solely on self-identity. These policies require that homeless transgender people be placed in the shelter associated with their gender identity without being required to provide any medical documentation or ID as verification of that identity.

. . . Because multiple policies with conflicting criteria for gender reclassification operate within single jurisdictions and upon individuals, the conflicts cause a number of problems. For one, similarly situated people are often treated differently under these policies, because of the ways the differing criteria for gender reclassification interrelate. One brief example will illustrate. Two transgender men living in Massachusetts, one born in California and the other in New York City, seek to obtain drivers' licenses indicating their male gender. Both have undergone mastectomy and no other surgical procedures. The California-born man will be able to obtain the reclassification he seeks, because California will amend his birth certificate and Massachusetts will accept this, and evidence of his surgery, as sufficient to change the document. The New York City-born man will be unable to obtain a corrected document, because he will not be able to provide an amended birth certificate. This man will have to carry an ID with a gender marker that does not match his identity, possibly leading to difficulty and exposure to discrimination in every context in which he might have to present ID, such as police interactions, employment, and travel.

Additionally, as new initiatives from the Department of Homeland Security, primarily focused on the enforcement of immigration laws, have increasingly led to comparisons of records between agencies with differing gender reclassification policies, the conflicts between these policies ha[ve] created a new range of problems. For example, in New York, Maryland, and other states, DMV records were compared with Social Security records in order to find mismatching information that might indicate the misuse of a Social Security Number (SSN) to falsely obtain a DMV ID. People whose identities came up with "no match" information were sent letters warning that their licenses would be revoked, and hundreds of thousands of people lost their licenses. Many transgender people came up as "no matches" because the gender designation on their DMV records did not match that on their SSA records, especially in states where DMV gender reclassification requirements did not require genital surgery, which is required for such reclassification by the SSA. Similar record comparisons have been used to find people misusing SSNs to obtain employment, and employers across the United States have received "no match" letters indicating that their employees have a different gender marker on their SSA records than on their employee records. For transgender employees, this has led to being outed as transgender to their employers.

───────────

Professors Kogan and Spade both critique dichotomous notions of gender from the perspective of transgender individuals. In the following excerpt, Professor Julie Greenberg's analysis of intersexuality further problematizes the gender binary. Given the relationship between transgender individuals and the medical profession that Spade exposes, consider what role medical regulation plays in the context of intersexuality.

DEFINING MALE AND FEMALE: INTERSEXUALITY AND THE COLLISION BETWEEN LAW AND BIOLOGY*
Julie A. Greenberg

"He was a boy, became a girl, and then a boy again." This provocative headline sounds like it should have appeared in a supermarket tabloid. This headline actually appeared in the Los Angeles Times and cited a critical study that had just been reported in the Archives of Pediatric & Adolescent Medicine.

For many decades, the medical and psychological communities have attempted to resolve the issue of how one's sex (whether an individual is a male or female) should be determined for medical purposes. Until recently, however, legal authorities generally have been blind to the need to define the terms "male" and "female" for legal purposes. The law typically has operated under the assumption that the terms "male" and "female" are fixed and unambiguous despite medical literature demonstrating that these assumptions are not true.

Although the law generally presumes these terms are unambiguous, courts and administrative agencies have been forced to determine an individual's legal sex under some limited circumstances. These cases typically have involved transsexuals—individuals whose biological sex does not conform with their self-identified sex.

The law has largely ignored other medical conditions in which an individual's sex may be ambiguous. Recent medical literature indicates that approximately one to four percent of the world's population may be intersexed and have either ambiguous or noncongruent sex features. Thus, the manner in which the law defines "male," "female," and "sex" will have a profound impact on at least 2.7 million persons in the United States. If, as some experts believe, the number of intersexed people is four percent, approximately ten million people in the United States will be affected. . . .

. . . [S]ome individuals with an XY chromosomal pattern (male genotype) and testes (male gonads) have a female phenotype (external

---

*   Julie A. Greenberg, *Defining Male and Female: Intersexuality and the Collision Between Law and Biology*, 41 ARIZ. L. REV. 265, 266–79 (1999).

appearance) and female genitalia. In all senses, these XY women look, feel, and are viewed by society as female. Many of these women are unaware that they carry a Y chromosome and are unaware of their undescended testes. The issue that must be resolved is whether the law will view them as female, based upon their sexual identity and external appearance, or will instead rely on seemingly objective criteria, such as a chromosomal or gonadal analysis, to define them as male. If the law defines sex based on a chromosomal or gonadal analysis, these women would be prohibited from marrying males. Ironically, these same women would be permitted to marry females—a result directly contrary to the legislative intent to prohibit gay and lesbian marriages.

Regardless of the legal, moral, and societal implications of prohibiting same-sex marriages, [the federal Defense of Marriage Act] highlights the difficulty of using objective laboratory tests to effectuate its prohibitions. A variety of factors could contribute to the determination of whether an individual should be considered male or female for legal purposes. These factors include: chromosomal sex, gonadal sex, external morphologic sex, internal morphologic sex, hormonal patterns, phenotype, assigned sex, and sexual identity. In most individuals, these factors are all congruent. For millions of individuals, however, these factors are incongruent or ambiguous. For these individuals, DOMA and its state equivalents must establish which factor(s) will control.

The manner in which legal institutions define the terms "sex," "male," and "female" will also have a significant impact on a variety of areas other than marriage. How the terms "sex," "male," and "female" are defined will also affect the ability to control one's sex designation on official documents such as birth certificates, driver's licenses, and passports, as well as the ability to claim sex discrimination under employment discrimination statutes . . .

II.   A BINARY SEX AND GENDER PARADIGM

A variety of federal and state statutes and regulations differentiate between individuals based upon their sex and gender, or their status as males and females or men and women. Given the prevalence of such regulations, one might assume that these terms have clear legal meanings. In reality, the law defines these terms inconsistently or frequently fails to define them at all. The definition of these terms is critical, however, to the proper enforcement of legislation that seeks to regulate behavior based upon one's status as a male or female. Legal scholars and scholars in other disciplines, such as medicine, sociology, psychology, and gender studies, are investigating and redefining the meanings of these terms.

A. Sex

Sex is commonly used to denote one's status as a man or woman based upon biological factors. Although sex is a reflection of one's biology, as opposed to gender, which is generally considered to be socially constructed, the biological aspect of one's body that determines one's sex has not been legally or medically resolved.

An individual's sex is established for legal purposes on a person's birth certificate. The sex designation on the birth certificate is determined by the birth attendant. If external genitalia appear unambiguous, the external genitalia typically determine the sex designated on the birth certificate.

If the genitalia appear ambiguous, sex is assigned in part based on sex-role stereotypes. The presence of an "adequate" penis in an XY infant leads to the label male, while the absence of an adequate penis leads to the label female. A genetic male with an "inadequate" penis (one that is incapable of penetrating a female's vagina) is "turned into" a female even if it means destroying his reproductive capacity. A genetic female who may be capable of reproducing, however, is generally assigned the female sex to preserve her reproductive capability regardless of the appearance of her external genitalia. If her "phallus" is considered to be "too large" to meet the guidelines for a typical clitoris, it is surgically reduced even if it means that her capacity for satisfactory sex may be reduced or destroyed. In other words, men are defined based upon their ability to penetrate females and females are defined based upon their ability to procreate. Sex, therefore, can be viewed as a social construct rather than a biological fact.

In the presence of ambiguous genitalia, medical professionals generally suggest that surgery be performed to "fix" the genitalia so that they appear clearly male or female. Because one's birth certificate will often be used to obtain other legal documents, an individual's legal sex is generally fixed based upon the appearance of the person's external genitalia at birth.

Although the appearance of the external genitalia generally establishes an individual's sex at birth, other criteria may be used later to determine an individual's sex for other purposes. For instance, before 1968, athletic organizations examined a female athlete's external genitalia to determine her right to participate as a female in athletic competitions. In recent years, however, some athletic organizations, including the International Olympic Organizing Committee, have been using a chromosomal test instead. Individuals with XY chromosomes are defined as males and individuals with XX chromosomes are defined as females.

The absurdity of using a test that defines an individual as a woman based on the presence of two X chromosomes is best illustrated by the story of Maria Patino, a Spanish hurdler. Ms. Patino planned to compete in the World University Games in 1985. She knew that she would be subjected to a sex verification test, but she had no reason to believe that the test would indicate that she was anything other than a female. Although Ms. Patino was not aware of it, she had Androgen Insensitivity Syndrome ("AIS"). Therefore, she had the chromosomal make-up of a male (XY) even though her external morphologic sex, phenotype, and self-identification were clearly female.

Ms. Patino failed the sex chromatin test and was banned from the 1985 competition. She was later barred from further competition by the Spanish national team. The irony of using the sex chromatin test to deter unfair competition is that Ms. Patino's condition may have put her at a competitive disadvantage compared to the typical XX female athlete.

Therefore, although sex is typically defined according to biological factors, the biological factor(s) that control sex determination may vary depending upon the purpose for which sex is being defined. At birth, the appearance of the external genitalia typically determine the sex assigned while the right to participate in some athletic competitions as a female may be controlled by the chromosomal structure.

B. Gender

Gender is generally used to refer to the cultural or attitudinal qualities that are characteristic of a particular sex. Gender, as used in this sense, is socially constructed. Individuals with characteristics that are typically associated with men have a masculine gender while individuals with characteristics that are typically associated with women have a feminine gender. Most legislation utilizes the word "sex," yet courts, legislators, and administrative agencies often substitute the word "gender" for "sex" when they interpret these statutes. Despite the different meanings of the terms "sex" and "gender," they are often used interchangeably.

C. Binary Assumptions

Implicit in legislation utilizing the terms "sex" and "gender" are the assumptions that only two biological sexes exist and that all people fit neatly into either the category male or female. In other words, despite medical and anthropological studies to the contrary, the law presumes a binary sex and gender model. The law ignores the millions of people who are intersexed.

A binary sex paradigm does not reflect reality. Instead, sex and gender range across a spectrum. Male and female occupy the two ends of the poles, and a number of intersexed conditions exist between the two poles. Millions of individuals are intersexed and have some sexual characteristics that are typically associated with males and some sexual characteristics that are typically associated with females.

Although the American legal system blindly clings to a binary sex and gender paradigm, anthropologists who have studied other societies have found cultures that reject binary sex and gender systems. These societies formally recognize that more than two sexes and/or two genders exist.

. . . [R]ules governing intersexuals have existed throughout history in a variety of cultures and religions. Although the United States, other modern societies, and some religions utilize a binary sex paradigm in which intersexuals are classified as either male or female for legal purposes, other societies have recognized a multi-sexual and multi-gender model.

The currently accepted binary model that determines an individual's sex based primarily on the appearance of his/her external genitalia at birth is an inadequate system. . . .

III. INTERSEXED MEDICAL CONDITIONS

Medical experts recognize that many factors contribute to the determination of an individual's sex. According to medical professionals, the typical criteria of sex include:

1.   Genetic or chromosomal sex—XY or XX;

2.   Gonadal sex (reproductive sex glands)—testes or ovaries;

3.   Internal morphologic sex (determined after three months gestation)—seminal vesicles/prostrate or vagina/uterus/fallopian tubes;

4.   External morphologic sex (genitalia)—penis/scrotum or clitoris/labia;

5.   Hormonal sex—androgens or estrogens;

6.   Phenotypic sex (secondary sexual features)—facial and chest hair or breasts;

7.   Assigned sex and gender of rearing; and

8.   Sexual identity.

For most people, these factors are all congruent, and one's status as a man or woman is uncontroversial. For intersexuals, some of these factors may be incongruent, or an ambiguity within a factor may exist.

The assumption is that there are two separate roads, one leading from XY chromosomes at conception to manhood, the other from XX chromosomes at conception to womanhood. The fact is that there are not two roads, but one road with a number of forks that turn in the male or female direction. Most of us turn in the same direction at each fork.

The bodies of the millions of intersexed people have taken a combination of male and female forks and have followed the road less traveled. These individuals have noncongruent sexual attributes. For these individuals, the law must determine which of the eight sexual factors will determine their sex and whether any one factor should be dispositive for all legal purposes.

CHAPTER 2

SEXUALITY & LIBERTY

■ ■ ■

Can you imagine being denied the right to love?

—LARRY KRAMER[1]

A primary means for society's regulation of sexuality, especially same-sex sexuality, has been the criminal law. Various forms of sexual relationships have been proscribed throughout history and some remain illegal today. These include prostitution (sex for money), fornication (sex between unmarried persons), adultery (sex by a married person with someone other than his or her spouse), bestiality (sex with an animal), incest (sex between persons closely related to one another), rape and molestation (sex without consent or with a person, such as a minor, who is said to lack the capacity to consent), and sodomy (defined in various ways, as discussed below). Society has also directly regulated sexuality through, for example, penal restrictions on the use of contraception and abortion.

The first part of this Chapter focuses on sodomy laws. For most of the twentieth century, sodomy laws in the United States were used to provide a legal basis for the regulation of lesbian and gay sexuality, and of lesbian, gay, and bisexual life generally. In fact, some of the cases included later in this book illustrate the ways in which discrimination against lesbians, gay men, and bisexuals—in the workplace, regarding their relationships, and regarding custody and visitation rights to their children—was justified by the existence of laws prohibiting certain sexual practices.

Sodomy laws were not always understood in this way. The first Section of this Chapter sets forth a brief historical overview of sodomy laws. The second Section explores the efforts to eradicate sodomy statutes through legislative repeal (particularly the adoption by states of the Model Penal Code). The third Section examines constitutional litigation challenging sodomy laws, including the unsuccessful challenge in *Bowers v. Hardwick*,[2] and the later successful challenge in *Lawrence v. Texas*.[3]

---

[1] LARRY KRAMER, *Whose Constitution Is It, Anyway?*, *in* REPORTS FROM THE HOLOCAUST: THE MAKING OF AN AIDS ACTIVIST 177, 178 (1989).

[2] 478 U.S. 186, 106 S.Ct. 2841, 92 L.Ed.2d 140 (1986).

[3] 539 U.S. 558, 123 S.Ct. 2472, 156 L.Ed.2d 508 (2003).

The third Section also includes materials on the impact of *Lawrence* on the ability of the state to regulate sexuality more generally, including the sale and distribution of sex toys, solicitation of sexual acts, and sex in semi-public and public places.

I. WHAT WERE SODOMY LAWS?

A. BACKGROUND

AMICI CURIAE BRIEF OF PROFESSORS OF HISTORY*
Lawrence v. Texas

Prohibitions against sodomy are rooted in the teachings of Western Christianity, but those teachings have always been strikingly inconsistent in their definition of the acts encompassed by the term. When the term "sodomy" was first emphasized by medieval Christian theologians in the eleventh century, they applied it inconsistently to a diverse group of non-procreative sexual practices. In subsequent Latin theology, canon law, and confessional practice, the term was notoriously confused with "unnatural acts," which had a very different origin and ranged even more widely (to include, for example, procreative sexual acts in the wrong position or with contraceptive intent). "Unnatural acts" is the older category, because it comes directly from Paul in Romans 1, but Paul does not associate such acts with (or even mention) the story of Sodom (Genesis 19) and appears not to have considered that story to be concerned with same-sex activity.

Later Christian authors did combine Romans 1 with Genesis 19, but they could not agree on what sexual practices were meant by either "unnatural acts" or "sodomy." For example, in Peter Damian, who around 1050 championed the term "sodomy" as an analogy to "blasphemy," the "sins of the Sodomites" include solitary masturbation. In Thomas Aquinas, about two centuries later, "unnatural acts" cover every genital contact intended to produce orgasm except penile-vaginal intercourse in an approved position. Many later Christian writers denied that women could commit sodomy at all; others believed that the defining characteristic of unnatural or sodomitic sex was that it could not result in procreation, regardless of the genders involved. In none of these authors does the term "sodomy" refer systematically and exclusively to same-sex conduct. Certainly it was not used consistently through the centuries to condemn that conduct. * * *

---

* Brief of Professors of History George Chauncey, Nancy F. Cott, John D'Emilio, Estelle B. Freedman, Thomas C. Holt, John Howard, Lynn Hunt, Mark D. Jordan, Elizabeth Lapovsky Kennedy, and Linda P. Kerber as Amici Curiae Supporting Petitioners, *Lawrence v. Texas*, 539 U.S. 558, 123 S. Ct. 2472, 156 L.Ed.2d 508 (2003).

The English Reformation Parliament of 1533 turned the religious injunction against sodomy into the secular crime of buggery when it made "the detestable and abominable vice of buggery committed with mankind or beast" punishable by death. The English courts interpreted this to apply to sexual intercourse between a human and animal and anal intercourse between a man and woman as well as anal intercourse between two men.

Colonial American statutes variously drew on the religious and secular traditions and shared their imprecision in the definition of the offense. Variously defining the crime as (the religious) sodomy or (the secular) buggery, they generally proscribed anal sex between men and men, men and women, and humans and animals, but their details and their rationale varied, and the New England colonies penalized a wider range of "carnall knowledge," including (but by no means limited to) "men lying with men." Puritan leaders in the New England colonies were especially vigorous in their denunciation of sodomitical sins as contrary to God's will, but their condemnation was also motivated by the pressing need to increase the population and to secure the stability of the family. Thus John Winthrop mused that the main offense of one man hanged in New Haven in 1646 for having engaged in masturbation with numerous youths—not, in other words, for "sodomy" as it is usually understood today—was his "frustratinge of the Ordinance of marriage & the hindringe the generation of mankinde."

Another indication that the sodomy statutes were not the equivalent of a statute against "homosexual conduct" is that with one brief exception they applied exclusively to acts performed by men, whether with women, girls, men, boys, or animals, and not to acts committed by two women. Only the New Haven colony penalized "women lying with women," and this for only ten years. For the entire colonial period we have reports of only two cases involving two women engaged in acts with one another. . . .

Statutes enacted in the early decades after independence followed the English authorities, but by the mid-nineteenth century most statutes defined the offense as a crime against nature rather than as a crime against God. Such statutes were still not the equivalent of a statute proscribing "homosexual conduct." In 1868, no statute criminalized oral sex, whether between two men, two women, or a man and woman. * * *

. . . [T]hroughout American history, the authorities have rarely enforced statutes prohibiting sodomy, however defined. Even in periods when enforcement increased, it was rare for people to be prosecuted for consensual sexual relations conducted in private, even when the parties were of the same sex. Indeed, records of only about twenty prosecutions and four or five executions have surfaced for the entire colonial period. Even in the New England colonies, whose leaders denounced "sodomy" with far greater regularity and severity than did other colonial leaders and where the offense carried severe sanctions, it was rarely prosecuted. The trial of Nicholas Sension, a married man living in Westhersfield, Connecticut, in 1677, revealed that he had been widely known for soliciting sexual contacts with the town's men and youth for almost forty years but remained widely liked. Likewise, a Baptist minister in New London, Connecticut, was temporarily suspended from the pulpit in 1757 because of his repeatedly soliciting sex with men, but the congregation voted to restore him to the ministry after he publicly repented. They understood his sexual transgressions to be a form of sinful behavior in which anyone could engage and from which anyone could repent, not as a sin worthy of death or the condition of a particular class of people.

The relative indifference of the public and the authorities to the crime of sodomy continued in the first century of independence. For instance, only twenty-two men were indicted for sodomy in New York City in the nearly eight decades from 1796 to 1873. The number of sodomy prosecutions increased sharply in the last two decades of the nineteenth century and in the twentieth century. This was made possible by the decision of many States to criminalize oral intercourse for the first time. But it resulted in large measure from the pressure applied on district attorneys by privately organized and usually religiously inspired anti-vice societies, whose leaders feared that the growing size and complexity of cities had loosened the constraints on sexual conduct and increased the vulnerability of youth and the disadvantaged. The increase in sodomy prosecutions was only one aspect of a general escalation in the policing of sexual activity, which also included stepped-up campaigns against prostitution, venereal disease, and contraception use. Although in this context a growing number of sodomy prosecutions involved adult males who had engaged in consensual relations, most such relations had taken place in semi-public spaces rather than in the privacy of the home, and the great majority of cases continued to involve coercion and/or minor boys or girls. * * *

Over the generations, sodomy legislation proscribed a diverse and inconsistent set of sexual acts engaged in by various combinations of partners. Above all, it regulated conduct in which anyone (or, at certain times and in certain places, any male person) could engage. Only in the late nineteenth century did the idea of the homosexual as a distinct category of person emerge, and only in the twentieth century did the state begin to classify and penalize citizens on the basis of their identity or status as homosexuals. The States began to enact discriminatory measures in the 1920s and 1930s, but such measures and other forms of anti-gay harassment reached a peak in the twenty years following the Second World War, when government agencies systematically discriminated against homosexuals.

The unprecedented decision of Texas and several other states, primarily in the 1970s, to enact sodomy laws singling out "homosexual sodomy" for penalty, is best understood historically in the context of these discriminatory measures. The new sodomy laws essentially recast the historic purpose of such laws, which had been to regulate conduct generally, by adding them to the array of discriminatory measures directed specifically against homosexuals. Such discriminatory measures against homosexuals, although popularly imagined to be longstanding, are in fact not ancient but a unique and relatively short-lived product of the twentieth century.

It was only in the late nineteenth century that the very concept of the homosexual as a distinct category of person developed. The word "homosexual" appeared for the first time in a German pamphlet in 1868, and was introduced to the American lexicon only in 1892. As Michel Foucault has famously described this evolution, "the sodomite had been a temporary aberration; the homosexual was now a species." 1 Michel Foucault, The History of Sexuality 43 (Robert Hurley trans. 1978).

B. SAMPLE STATUTES

upheld:
Bowers v. Hardwick

Ga. Code Ann. § 16–6–2 (1994)

§ 16–6–2. Sodomy; aggravated sodomy.

(a) A person commits the offense of sodomy when he performs or submits to any sexual act involving the sex organs of one person and the mouth or anus of another. A person commits the offense of aggravated sodomy when he commits sodomy with force and against the will of the other person.

(b) A person convicted of the offense of sodomy shall be punished by imprisonment for not less than one nor more than 20 years. A person convicted of the offense of aggravated sodomy shall be punished by imprisonment for life or by imprisonment for not less than one nor more than 20 years.

Tex. Penal Code Ann. § 21.06 (2003)

§ 21.01. Definitions

In this chapter:

(1) "Deviate sexual intercourse" means:

(A) any contact between any part of the genitals of one person and the mouth or anus of another person; or

(B) the penetration of the genitals or the anus of another person with an object.

§ 21.06   Homosexual Conduct

(a) A person commits an offense if he engages in deviate sexual intercourse with another individual of the same sex.

(b) An offense under this section is a Class C misdemeanor.

II.   LEGISLATIVE DEBATE AND THE MODEL PENAL CODE

As of 1961, all 50 states in the United States had some sort of sodomy law on their books. During the following four decades, many jurisdictions repealed their sodomy laws, particularly as state legislatures adopted the Model Penal Code. Drafted in the 1950s by the American Law Institute (ALI)—an influential body of lawyers and law professors—the Model Penal Code was meant to update and unify American criminal law. A critical development in the Code was the de-criminalization of sexual behavior, including same-sex sexual conduct, between consenting adults in private. The drafters of the Model Penal Code were influenced by a 1957 report to the British Parliament by England's Committee on Homosexual Offenses and Prostitution (the Wolfenden Report) that recommended that consensual same-sex sexual conduct be de-criminalized. The report stated that "[u]nless a deliberate attempt is to be made by society, acting through the agency of the law, to equate the sphere of crime with that of sin, there must remain a realm of private morality and immorality which is, in brief and crude terms, not the law's business. To say this is not to condone or encourage private immorality."[4]

The issuance of the Wolfenden Report led to a spirited debate between two leading figures in British legal circles: Patrick Devlin, a prominent conservative judge who sat on Britain's High Court, and H.L.A. Hart, one of the most influential Anglo-American legal philosophers of the twentieth century.[5] The materials that follow include excerpts from the debate between Devlin and Hart, as well as from the Model Penal Code.

---

[4] DEPARTMENTAL COMMITTEE ON HOMOSEXUAL OFFENSES AND PROSTITUTION, REPORT TO THE SECRETARY OF STATE FOR THE HOME DEPARTMENT ("THE WOLFENDEN REPORT") 24, ¶ 61 (1957).

[5] A recent biography of Hart has revealed that he was sexually attracted to men, despite the fact that he was married to a woman for over fifty years. *See* NICOLA LACEY, A LIFE OF H.L.A. HART: THE NIGHTMARE AND THE NOBLE DREAM 73–75, 110–11, 203–05 (2004).

THE ENFORCEMENT OF MORALS*

Patrick Devlin

What is the connection between crime and sin and to what extent, if at all, should the criminal law of England concern itself with the enforcement of morals and punish sin or immorality as such? * * *

... I must admit that I begin with a feeling that a complete separation of crime from sin (I use the term throughout this lecture in the wider meaning) would not be good for the moral law and might be disastrous for the criminal. But can this sort of feeling be justified as a matter of jurisprudence? And if it be a right feeling how should the relationship between the criminal and the moral law be stated? Is there a good theoretical basis for it, or is it just a practical working alliance, or is it a bit of both? That is the problem which I want to examine. . . .

... Why not define the function of the criminal law in simple terms as the preservation of order and decency and the protection of the lives and property of citizens and elaborate those terms in relation to any particular subject in the way in which it is done in the Wolfenden Report? The criminal law in carrying out these objects will undoubtedly overlap the moral law. Crimes of violence are morally wrong and they are also offences against good order; therefore they offend against both laws. But this is simply because the two laws in pursuit of different objectives happen to cover the same area. Such is the argument.

Is the argument consistent or inconsistent with the fundamental principles of English criminal law as it exists today? That is the first way of testing it, though by no means a conclusive one. . . . The criminal law of England has from the very first concerned itself with moral principles. A simple way of testing this point is to consider the attitude which the criminal law adopts towards consent.

Subject to certain exceptions inherent in the nature of particular crimes, the criminal law has never permitted consent of the victim to be used as a defence. In rape, for example, consent negatives an essential element. But consent of the victim is no defence to a charge of murder. It is not a defence to any form of assault that the victim thought his punishment well deserved and submitted to it; to make a good defence the accused must prove that the law gave him the right to chastise and that he exercised it reasonably. * * *

The reason why a man may not consent to the commission of an offence against himself beforehand or forgive it afterwards is because it is an offence against society. It is not that society is physically injured; that

---

* PATRICK DEVLIN, THE ENFORCEMENT OF MORALS, *reprinted in* CRIMINAL LAW AND ITS PROCESSES: CASES AND MATERIALS 45–49 (Sanford H. Kadish & Monrad G. Paulsen eds., 3rd ed. 1975) (1969).

would be impossible. Nor need any individual be shocked, corrupted, or exploited; everything may be done in private. Nor can it be explained on the practical ground that a violent man is a potential danger to others in the community who have therefore a direct interest in his apprehension and punishment as being necessary to their own protection. That would be true of a man whom the victim is prepared to forgive but not of one who gets his consent first; a murderer who acts only upon the consent, and maybe the request of his victim is no menace to others, but he does threaten one of the great moral principles upon which society is based, that is, the sanctity of human life. There is only one explanation of what has hitherto been accepted as the basis of the criminal law and that is that there are certain standards of behaviour or moral principles which society requires to be observed; and the breach of them is an offence not merely against the person who is injured but against society as a whole.

Thus, if the criminal law were to be reformed so as to eliminate from it everything that was not designed to preserve order and decency or to protect citizens (including the protection of youth from corruption), it would overturn a fundamental principle. It would also end a number of specific crimes. Euthanasia, or the killing of another at his own request, suicide, attempted suicide and suicide pacts, duelling, abortion, incest between brother and sister, are all acts which can be done in private and without offence to others and need not involve the corruption or exploitation of others. . . .

I think it is clear that the criminal law as we know it is based upon moral principle. In a number of crimes its function is simply to enforce a moral principle and nothing else. * * *

The language used in . . . the Wolfenden Report suggest[s] the view that there ought not to be a collective judgment about immorality per se. Is this what is meant by "private morality" and "individual freedom of choice and action"? Some people sincerely believe that homosexuality is neither immoral nor unnatural. Is the "freedom of choice and action" that is offered to the individual freedom to decide for himself what is moral or immoral, society remaining neutral; or is it freedom to be immoral if he wants to be? The language of the Report may be open to question, but the conclusions at which the Committee arrives answer this question unambiguously. If society is not prepared to say that homosexuality is morally wrong, there would be no basis for a law protecting youth from "corruption" or punishing a man for living on the "immoral" earnings of a homosexual prostitute, as the Report recommends. This attitude the Committee makes even clearer when it comes to deal with prostitution. In truth, the Report takes it for granted that there is in existence a public morality which condemns homosexuality and prostitution. What the Report seems to mean by private morality might perhaps be better described as private behaviour in matters of morals.

This view—that there is such a thing as public morality—can also be justified by a prior argument. What makes a society of any sort is community of ideas, not only political ideas but also ideas about the way its members should behave and govern their lives; these latter ideas are its morals. Every society has a moral structure as well as a political one: or rather, since that might suggest two independent systems, I should say that the structure of every society is made up both of politics and morals. * * *

The law of treason is directed against aiding the king's enemies and against sedition from within. The justification for this is that established government is necessary for the existence of society and therefore its safety against violent overthrow must be secured. But an established morality is as necessary as good government to the welfare of society. Societies disintegrate from within more frequently than they are broken up by external pressures. There is disintegration when no common morality is observed and history shows that the loosening of moral bonds is often the first state of disintegration, so that society is justified in taking the same steps to preserve its moral code as it does to preserve its government and other essential institutions. The suppression of vice is as much the law's business as the suppression of subversive activities; it is no more possible to define a sphere of private morality than it is to define one of private subversive activity. * * *

The fact that adultery, fornication, and lesbianism are untouched by the criminal law does not prove that homosexuality ought not to be touched. The error of jurisprudence in the Wolfenden Report is caused by the search for some single principle to explain the division between crime and sin. The Report finds it in the principle that the criminal law exists for the protection of individuals; on this principle fornication in private between consenting adults is outside the law and thus it becomes logically indefensible to bring homosexuality between consenting adults in private within it. But the true principle is that the law exists for the protection of society. It does not discharge its function by protecting the individual from injury, annoyance, corruption, and exploitation; the law must protect also the institutions and the community of ideas, political and moral, without which people cannot live together. Society cannot ignore the morality of the individual any more than it can his loyalty; it flourishes on both and without either it dies.

IMMORALITY AND TREASON*
H.L.A. Hart

The Wolfenden Committee on Homosexual Offences and Prostitution recommended by a majority of 12 to 1 that homosexual behaviour between consenting adults in private should no longer be a criminal offence. One of the Committee's principal grounds for this recommendation was expressed in its report in this way: "There must remain a realm of private morality and immorality which in brief and crude terms is not the law's business." I shall call this the liberal point of view: for it is a special application of those wider principles of liberal thought which John Stuart Mill formulated in his essay on Liberty. Mill's most famous words, less cautious perhaps than the Wolfenden Committee's were:

> The only purpose for which power can be rightfully exercised over any member of a civilized community against his will is to prevent harm to others. His own good, either physical or moral, is not a sufficient warrant. He cannot rightfully be compelled to do or forbear . . . because in the opinion of others to do so would be wise or even right.

The liberal point of view has often been attacked, both before and after Mill. I shall discuss here the repudiation of it made by Sir Patrick Devlin, in his recent lecture, which has now been published. . . .

. . . Mill's formulation of the liberal point of view may well be too simple. The grounds for interfering with human liberty are more various than the single criterion of "harm to others" suggests: cruelty to animals or organizing prostitution for gain do not, as Mill himself saw, fall easily under the description of harm to others. Conversely, even where there is harm to others in the most literal sense, there may well be other principles limiting the extent to which harmful activities should be repressed by law. So there are multiple criteria, not a single criterion, determining when human liberty may be restricted. Perhaps this is what Sir Patrick means by a curious distinction which he often stresses between theoretical and practical limits. But with all its simplicities the liberal point of view is a better guide than Sir Patrick to clear thought in the proper relation of morality to the criminal law: for it stresses what he obscures—namely, the points at which thought is needed before we turn popular morality into criminal law.

No doubt we would all agree that a consensus of moral opinion on certain matters is essential if society is to be worth living in. Laws against murder, theft, and much else would be of little use if they were

---

*   H.L.A. Hart, *Immorality and Treason*, 62 LISTENER 162–63 (1959), *reprinted in* CRIMINAL LAW AND ITS PROCESSES: CASES AND MATERIALS 51–53 (Sanford H. Kadish & Monrad G. Paulsen eds., 3rd ed. 1975) (1969).

not supported by a widely diffused conviction that what these laws forbid is also immoral. So much is obvious. But it does not follow that everything to which the moral vetoes of accepted morality attach is of equal importance to society; nor is there the slightest reason for thinking of morality as a seamless web: one which will fall to pieces carrying society with it, unless all its emphatic vetoes are enforced by law. Surely even in the face of the moral feeling that is up to concert pitch—the trio of intolerance, indignation, and disgust—we must pause to think. We must ask a question at two different levels which Sir Patrick never clearly enough identifies or separates. First, we must ask whether a practice which offends moral feeling is harmful, independently of its repercussion on the general moral code. Secondly, what about repercussion on the moral code? Is it really true that failure to translate this item of general morality into criminal law will jeopardize the whole fabric of morality and so society?

We cannot escape thinking about these two different questions merely by repeating to ourselves the vague nostrum: "This is part of public morality and public morality must be preserved if society is to exist." Sometimes Sir Patrick seems to admit this, for he says in words which both Mill and the Wolfenden Report might have used, that there must be the maximum respect for individual liberty consistent with the integrity of society. Yet this, as his contrasting examples of fornication and homosexuality show, turns out to mean only that the immorality which the law may punish must be generally felt to be intolerable. This plainly is no adequate substitute for a reasoned estimate of the damage to the fabric of society likely to ensue if it is not suppressed.

Nothing perhaps shows more clearly the inadequacy of Sir Patrick's approach to this problem than his comparison between the suppression of sexual immorality and the suppression of treason or subversive activity. Private subversive activity is, of course, a contradiction in terms because "subversion" means overthrowing government, which is a public thing. But it is grotesque, even where moral feeling against homosexuality is up to concert pitch, to think of the homosexual behavior of two adults in private as in any way like treason or sedition either in intention or effect. We can make it seem like treason only if we assume that deviation from a general moral code is bound to affect that code, and to lead not merely to its modification but to its destruction. The analogy could begin to be plausible only if it was clear that offending against this item of morality was likely to jeopardize the whole structure. But we have ample evidence for believing that people will not abandon morality, will not think any better of murder, cruelty, and dishonesty, merely because some private sexual practice which they abominate is not punished by the law. . . .

Sir Patrick's doctrine is also open to a wider, perhaps a deeper, criticism. In his reaction against a rationalist's morality and his stress on feeling, he has I think thrown out the baby and kept the bath water; and the bath water may turn out to be very dirty indeed. When Sir Patrick's lecture was first delivered The Times greeted it with these words: "There is a moving welcome humility in the conception that society should not be asked to give its reason for refusing to tolerate what in its heart it feels intolerable." This drew from a correspondent in Cambridge the retort: "I am afraid that we are less humble than we used to be. We once burnt old women because, without giving our reasons, we felt in our hearts that witchcraft was intolerable."

This retort is a bitter one, yet its bitterness is salutary. We are not, I suppose, likely, in England, to take again to the burning of old women for witchcraft or to punishing people for associating with those of a different race or colour, or to punishing people again for adultery. Yet if these things were viewed with intolerance, indignation, and disgust, as the second of them still is in some countries, it seems that on Sir Patrick's principles no rational criticism could be opposed to the claim that they should be punished by law. We could only pray, in his words, that the limits of tolerance might shift.

It is impossible to see what curious logic has led Sir Patrick to this result. For him a practice is immoral if the thought of it makes the man on the Clapham omnibus sick. So be it. Still, why should we not summon all the resources of our reason, sympathetic understanding, as well as critical intelligence, and insist that before general moral feeling is turned into criminal law it is submitted to scrutiny of a different kind from Sir Patrick's? Surely, the legislator should ask whether the general morality is based on ignorance, superstition, or misunderstanding; whether there is a false conception that those who practise what it condemns are in other ways dangerous or hostile to society; and whether the misery to many parties, the blackmail and the other evil consequences of criminal punishment, especially for sexual offences, are well understood. It is surely extraordinary that among the things which Sir Patrick says are to be considered before we legislate against immorality these appear nowhere; not even as "practical considerations," let alone "theoretical limits." To any theory which, like this one, asserts that the criminal law may be used on the vague ground that the preservation of morality is essential to society and yet omits to stress the need for critical scrutiny, our reply should be: "Morality, what crimes may be committed in thy name!"

MODEL PENAL CODE § 213.2 CMT. 2*

(1962, Comments Revised 1980)

DEVIATE SEXUAL INTERCOURSE BETWEEN CONSENTING ADULTS

Section 231.2 of the Model Code makes a fundamental departure from prior law in excepting from criminal sanctions deviate sexual intercourse between consenting adults. This policy applies to the various styles of sexual intimacy between man and wife and to sexual relations between unmarried persons, regardless of gender. Of course, the exclusion from liability does not extend to sexual relations with a person who is underage or otherwise incapable of giving meaningful consent. Such conduct is proscribed in terms by this section. Additionally, the exclusion does not reach open display, which is covered by Section 251.1 of the Model Code, nor does the exclusion reach prostitution, which constitutes an offense under Section 251.2, nor public solicitation, which is proscribed by Section 251.3. But under the Model Code deviate sexual intercourse is not criminal where both participants consent, where each is of sufficient age and mental capacity to render consent effective, and where they conduct their relations in private and create no public nuisance.

Decriminalization of consensual sodomy reaches three situations commonly covered by pre-Model Code statutes. First, it excludes the prospect of penal sanctions for untraditional sexual practices between husband and wife. This is the weakest case for continuing criminal penalties. So-called deviate sexual intercourse between spouses may contravene an ethical or religious notion but there is nothing approaching societal consensus on this point. Both the popular literature and available empirical data reveal that such practices are anything but uncommon. * * *

The second situation excluded from coverage is consensual sodomy between male and female outside the marital relationship. This is distinguished from the first case only in that sexual intimacy out of wedlock is not affirmatively sanctioned by law. Acceptance of the proposition that the state has no good reason to try to suppress non-standard sexual practices between married persons puts this second situation in its proper perspective. Criminal punishment of so-called deviate sexual intercourse between a man and a woman who are not married to one another presents the same issues of social policy that are raised by laws against genital copulation by such persons. The wrong, if one exists, arises from the fact of sexual intimacy out of wedlock and not from the kind of conduct with which gratification is achieved. In other

---

* *Comment on § 213.2 Deviate Sexual Intercourse by Force or Imposition*, MODEL PENAL CODE AND COMMENTARIES: PART II DEFINITION OF SPECIFIC CRIMES §§ 210.0 TO 213.6, at 357, 362–72 (The American Law Institute 1980) (1962).

words, application of sodomy statutes in this context really involves only a variant of adultery or fornication. The Model Code includes no penal provision against adultery or fornication, for reasons which are explained in some detail in the Note on Adultery and Fornication following the commentary to Section 213.6. The point here is only to emphasize that there is no reason to distinguish among styles of sexual intimacy for the purpose of imposing criminal sanctions on relations out of wedlock. Whatever policy governs traditional heterosexual intercourse between unmarried persons should also extend to other forms of sexual gratification by those same persons.

The third and most controversial case of consensual sodomy is homosexual relations. Here articulation of a legitimate state interest in suppression of such conduct is arguably more plausible. Because ordinary genital copulation is not possible between persons of the same gender, homosexual relations typically involve some sort of deviate sexual intercourse as that term is defined in Section 213.0. The popular aversion to such conduct arises not so much from the physical characteristics of sexuality as from the fact of sexual gratification with a person of one's own gender. This type of sexual preference constitutes a far more dramatic contravention of societal norms and prevailing moral attitudes than is involved in either of the first two situations discussed above. Continued criminal punishment of homosexual relations may be advocated on the ground that such conduct threatens the moral fabric of society by undermining the viability of the family or on the supposition that permitting such behavior between consenting adults leads inevitably to the corruption of youth. Arguments of the former sort raise the broad issue of the proper relation of the criminal law to community morality—a matter that is discussed more fully below. The view that activity between consenting adults should be proscribed in order to protect young persons flounders on the absence of either empirical data or reasoned analysis to suggest that one leads to the other. Perhaps more important than either of these factors is the simple truth that homosexuality excites widespread and often violent emotional hostility. Its manifestation in sexual conduct is viewed by many persons with a deep antipathy. The origin of this reaction is as much aesthetic as moral, and its force is not diminished by the difficulty of specifying exactly what harm is occasioned thereby. The conviction that homosexual conduct is "bad" quickly translates into the conclusion that it therefore should be punished, and there is a corresponding fear that removing criminal sanctions would amount to implied endorsement of a kind of behavior that majoritarian sentiment finds abhorrent.

While these concerns may be dispositive to some, the Model Code takes the view that private homosexual conduct between consenting adults should not be punished as a crime. In part, this conclusion stems from uncertainty about the morality of such conduct. Without delving into the question of the causes of homosexuality, one can identify at least three ways of looking at the phenomenon. First, of course, it may be regarded as a sin. Most orthodox theologies take this position, though there are increasing challenges to this view even from sources within organized religion.

Second, homosexuality may be viewed as a disease. There are two lines of thought in the disease model of homosexuality. Some theorists have posited that homosexuality is a pathological condition, the result of abnormal genetic or hormonal influence. To date, however, studies designed to show a biological basis have been inconclusive at best. Modern authorities have abandoned the position that homosexuality is an inherited genetic trait. On the other hand, many scientists today have adopted a psychological theory of homosexuality, thus viewing it as an emotional or mental disorder. The common theory is that the homosexual's emotional disturbance is caused by childhood environment. Even if this view is correct, however, homosexuality is subject to no known cure, save perhaps as psychiatry or behavior modification may attempt restructuring of the individual personality. For purposes of the criminal law, the real significance of viewing homosexuality as an illness lies not in the realms of medicine and science, but rather in the normative implications conveyed by labeling the homosexual as "sick." On the other hand, the disease model conceded that homosexual behavior is deviate, abnormal, unwelcome, and unattractive. It postulates that homosexuality should not be encouraged and that a "cure" would be desirable if one could be found. On the other hand, describing homosexuality as a kind of illness avoids imputation of moral failing to the individual so afflicted. In other words, the individual who finds himself sexually attracted to persons of his own gender is not blameworthy in the sense with which the criminal law is concerned.

The third view of homosexuality is that it is neither a sin nor an abnormality but only a difference. The notion here is that homosexual conduct is simply a matter of personal preference and is devoid of any normative content whatever. This is the position of the gay rights movement, and it may be gaining support in the community at large.

No doubt this statement of three distinct points of view is simplistic. They are not cleanly different as described above but exist in an infinite variety of gradations and emphases. To the extent, however, that these positions may be taken as paradigms of broadly differing attitudes toward the subject, they suggest an important point. Only one of the three conceptions—i.e. the view that homosexual conduct is a sin—provides an appropriate starting point for imposition of penal sanctions. No principle is more broadly accepted than that the criminal law, involving as it does both punishment and condemnation should be concerned with conduct that is morally reprehensible or culpable. To the extent that it seems inappropriate to regard homosexual relations as blameworthy—that is, as representative of moral failing by the actor—the essential premise for assigning criminal punishment is vitiated. Of course, many in the community view homosexual conduct as morally reprehensible, but it is equally clear that many do not. Given the absence of harm to the secular interests of the community occasioned by atypical sexuality between consenting adults, the problematical nature of the underlying ethical issue should suggest the need for caution in continuing criminal proscription of this kind of behavior.

The foregoing reasoning is supportive of the Model Code position on consensual sodomy, but not essential to its acceptance. Even if one starts from the proposition that homosexual conduct is a moral default for which the actor may justifiably be condemned, there are still sufficient reasons to withhold penal sanctions. The criminal law cannot encompass all behavior that the average citizen may regard as immoral or deviate. In every field of activity the ethical precepts of the community set standards higher than the law can expediently enforce. Verbal cruelty, lying, racial and religious biases in private relationships, and the kiss that betrays a marriage are but a few examples of reprehensible conduct that no sensible legislator would make into a crime. Some of the reasons why the penal law must stop well short of encompassing all immoral conduct are eminently practical. Economic resources are finite. The amount of money that may be spent on law enforcement is limited by the wealth of the community and by the competing demands of other social interests. It seems sensible, therefore, that the criminal justice system should concentrate on repressing murder, robbery, rape, theft, and other crimes that directly threaten security of person and property. Authorization of penalties for consensual sodomy suggests not only that such conduct is wrongful, but also that it is sufficiently important to warrant diversion of resources from other areas. Furthermore, any genuine effort to enforce such prohibitions will be extremely costly and difficult. Private sexual behavior between consenting adults has no victim. There is no one who can be counted on to complain to the police or to provide evidence against suspected offenders. The resulting difficulty of identifying and convicting violators usually leads police to forego any attempt to enforce laws against consensual sodomy except in the rare case that happens to come to their attention. Cases that do surface commonly involve violence, corruption of minors, public solicitation, or some other aggravating factor that would continue to be punished under the Model Code. To the extent, however, that laws against deviate sexual behavior are enforced against private conduct between consenting adults, the result is episodic and capricious selection of an infinitesimal fraction of offenders for severe punishment. This invitation to arbitrary enforcement not only offends notions of fairness and horizontal equity, but it also creates unwarranted opportunity for private blackmail and official extortion. There is also the point that the methods available to the police for enforcing such laws involve tactics which are often unseemly and which, by their very nature, stretch the limits of constitutionality. Moreover, these costs may be incurred without gaining any corresponding benefit, for there is every reason to believe that continued criminal proscription of private sexual relations would prove largely ineffective to deter or inhibit such conduct.

To these practical concerns must be added a broader objection to criminal punishment of atypical behavior between consenting adults. Any exercise of the coercive power of the state against individual citizens diminishes freedom. Nowhere is this curtailment of liberty more pronounced than where the state, acting through the penal law, punishes by incarceration. No doubt such action is necessary to prevent injury to other individuals, to guard them in the secure possession of their property, and to further the interest of all citizens in the unobstructed workings of their government. Less clearly, criminal penalties may also be appropriate in some instances where the actor's behavior does not threaten directly to impair any of these interests. The usual justification for laws against such conduct is that, even though it does not injure any identifiable victim, it contributes to moral deterioration of society. One need not endorse wholesale repeal of all "victimless" crimes in order to recognize that legislating penal sanctions solely to maintain widely held concepts of morality and aesthetics is a costly enterprise. It sacrifices personal liberty, not because the actor's conduct results in harm to another citizen but only because it is inconsistent with the majoritarian notion of acceptable behavior. In the words of the Wolfenden Report, the decisive factor favoring decriminalization of laws against private homosexual relations between consenting adults is "the importance which society and the law ought to give individual freedom of choice and action in matters of private morality."

NOTES

1. Legislative repeal was the route by which most states rid themselves of sodomy statutes. By the time the U.S. Supreme Court decided *Lawrence v. Texas* in 2003, 28 state legislatures (AK, AZ, CA, CO, CT, DE, FL, HA, IL, IN, IA, ME, NB, ND, NH, NJ, NM, NV, NY, OH, OR, RI, SD, VT, WA, WI, WV, and WY) and the District of Columbia City Council had repealed their sodomy laws. (By the time *Lawrence* was decided, courts in nine additional states had questioned the constitutionality of sodomy statutes: AR, GA, KY, MA, MD, MI, MT, PA, and TN.) The first legislative repeal was Illinois's in 1961; no state followed for a decade until Connecticut did so in 1971. Twenty of the legislative repeals took place during the 1970s. The number of repeals fell considerably after that, with only two in the 1980s (Alaska and Wisconsin) and three in the 1990s (Nevada, Rhode Island, and

the District of Columbia). The last two legislative repeals before *Lawrence* occurred in 2001 (Arizona and New York).

2.   While many states were repealing their sodomy statutes, a handful of others amended their laws so as to criminalize same-sex sodomy only. This process of "specification" occurred in eight states: Kansas (1969); Montana and Texas (1973); Kentucky (1974); Arkansas, Missouri and Nevada (1977); and Tennessee (1989). Nan Hunter has noted that

> [t]he specification trend coincided with the emergence of the contemporary versions of both the lesbian and gay rights movement and a renewed movement for religious fundamentalism in American politics. In 1973, . . . two critical events occurred: The American Psychiatric Association removed homosexuality from its list of mental diseases and the United States Civil Service Commission forbade personnel supervisors from finding a person unsuitable for a federal government job based solely on homosexuality. By 1985, anti-discrimination laws had been adopted by the District of Columbia, San Francisco, Los Angeles, Minneapolis, Philadelphia and several smaller cities. Anti-equality forces mobilized during the 1970s also, securing repeal of a civil rights law in Dade County, Florida, and conducting two electoral campaigns to enact laws mandating the firing of state schools systems employees who advocated homosexuality—one unsuccessfully (California) and the other successfully (Oklahoma). For states revising their criminal codes, the specification of homosexual acts as a crime marked both the greater visibility of homosexuality in a positive sense and the tremendous social anxiety which that visibly generated.

Nan D. Hunter, *Life After* Hardwick, 27 HARV. C.R.-C.L. L. REV. 531, 539–40 (1992).

III.   CONSTITUTIONAL LITIGATION

The first constitutional challenges to sodomy statutes were grounded on the idea that they violated due process because they were unduly vague, thus giving citizens insufficient notice as to what conduct would result in criminal liability. Most of those challenges were unsuccessful. For example, the U.S. Supreme Court in 1973 concluded that Florida's "abominable and detestable crime against nature statute" was not unconstitutionally vague.[6] The Court reached the same conclusion two years later when assessing Tennessee's crime against nature statute.[7]

---

[6]   *See Wainwright v. Stone*, 414 U.S. 21, 22–23, 94 S.Ct. 190, 192–93, 38 L.Ed.2d 179, 181–82 (1973) (per curiam).

[7]   *See Rose v. Locke*, 423 U.S. 48, 96 S.Ct. 243, 46 L.Ed.2d 185 (1975) (per curiam). *See also Balthazar v. Superior Court*, 573 F.2d 698, 702 (1st Cir. 1978) (finding that at the time it was applied, the Massachusetts "unnatural and lascivious" acts statute was unconstitutionally vague for acts of fellatio and oral/anal contact, but that subsequent decisions of the state's courts

Those interested in challenging sodomy statutes next turned to the due process right to privacy. The contours of this right were first recognized in a 1965 U.S. Supreme Court decision, *Griswold v. Connecticut*,[8] striking down a Connecticut law that prohibited married couples from using contraceptive devices. For the next decade, the Court further elaborated on the right to privacy in a series of related cases, as described below:

> The Court first announced the new privacy doctrine . . . in *Griswold v. Connecticut*. In *Griswold* the Court invalidated statutes prohibiting the use and distribution of contraceptive devices. Eschewing an approach explicitly grounded in Lochnerian substantive due process, the Court stated that a "right to privacy" could be discerned in the "penumbras" of the first, third, fourth, fifth, and ninth amendments.[47] This right included the freedom of married couples to decide for themselves what to do in the "privacy" of their bedrooms.
>
> Two years later, in *Loving v. Virginia*, the Court struck down a law criminalizing interracial marriage. The Court ruled that states could not interfere in that manner with an individual's choice of whom to marry.[50] On similar grounds, the Court also invalidated laws restricting the ability of poor persons to marry or to divorce.[51]
>
> Although it remained possible after *Loving* to understand the new privacy doctrine as limited (for some unelaborated reason) to marital decisions, in *Eisenstadt v. Baird* the Court extended its *Griswold* holding to protect the distribution of contraceptives to unmarried persons as well. "If the right to privacy means anything," the Court stated, "it is the right of the *individual*, married or single, to be free from unwarranted governmental intrusion into matters so fundamentally affecting a person as the decision whether to bear or beget a child."[53]

"render the statute sufficiently precise to survive a constitutional vagueness attack as applied today to the same conduct").

[8]   381 U.S. 479, 85 S.Ct. 1678, 14 L.Ed.2d 510 (1965).

[47]   . . . The *Griswold* Court used the ideal of "privacy" both in its more intelligible, informational sense—an interest in keeping certain matters out of public view—and in its relatively more obscure, substantive sense—an interest in making one's own decisions about certain "private" matters. . . .

[50]   Although the Court relied in part on the holding that the statute violated the Equal Protection Clause, the opinion rested on a privacy rationale as well.

[51]   *See Zablocki v. Redhail*, 434 U.S. 374 (1978); *Boddie v. Connecticut*, 401 U.S. 371 (1971).

[53]   . . . [S]*ee also Carey v. Population Servs. Int'l*, 431 U.S. 678 (1977) (holding unconstitutional a state statute strictly limiting distribution and advertisement of contraceptive devices); *Skinner v. Oklahoma*, 316 U.S. 535 (1942) (holding, on equal protection grounds, that a statute authorizing forced sterilization of certain convicted felons was unconstitutional).

The next year, the Court took a further step from the confines of marriage and delivered its most controversial opinion since *Brown v. Board of Education*. Justice Blackmun, with only two Justices dissenting, wrote in *Roe v. Wade* that the right to privacy was "broad enough to encompass a woman's decision whether or not to terminate her pregnancy." . . .

The right to privacy was further expanded in the 1977 case of *Moore v. City of East Cleveland*, in which the Court struck down a zoning ordinance that limited occupancy of dwelling units to members of a nuclear family—the "nominal head of a household," his or her spouse, and their parents and children. Although there was no majority opinion, the four-Justice plurality expressly relied on the *Griswold* line of cases . . . emphasizing the "'private realm of family life which the state cannot enter.'"

Jed Rubenfeld, *The Right of Privacy*, 102 HARV. L. REV. 737, 744–46 (1989).

The right to privacy generally, and these cases in particular, lay the jurisprudential ground for challenges to state sodomy laws.

A. PRE-*HARDWICK*

The first privacy-based challenge to a sodomy statute to reach the U.S. Supreme Court was *Doe v. Commonwealth's Attorney*.[9] The lower court in *Doe* determined that the Supreme Court's privacy cases only "condemn[ ] State legislation that trespasses upon the privacy of the incidents of marriage, upon the sanctity of the home, or upon the nurture of family life."[10] The court concluded that there is "no authoritative judicial bar to the proscription of homosexuality . . . since it is obviously no part of marriage, home or family life. . . ."[11] The *Doe* case was appealed to the Supreme Court, which summarily affirmed, over a dissent by Justices William Brennan, Thurgood Marshall, and John Paul Stevens.[12]

Notwithstanding *Doe*, a federal district court in Texas struck down that state's sodomy law as violating the federal Constitution in 1982.[13] Relying on *Doe v. Commonwealth's Attorney*, the U.S. Court of Appeals for the Fifth Circuit reversed.[14]

---

[9]   403 F.Supp. 1199 (D. Va. 1975), *aff'd*, 425 U.S. 901, 96 S.Ct. 1489, 47 L.Ed.2d 751 (1976).

[10]   403 F.Supp. at 1200.

[11]   *Id.* at 1202.

[12]   *See Doe v. Commonwealth's Attorney*, 425 U.S. 901, 96 S.Ct. 1489, 47 L.Ed.2d 751 (1976).

[13]   *Baker v. Wade*, 553 F.Supp. 1121 (D. Tex. 1982), *rev'd*, 769 F.2d 289, 292 (5th Cir. 1985) (en banc).

[14]   *Baker v. Wade*, 769 F.2d 289, 292 (5th Cir. 1985) (en banc).

Although pre-*Hardwick* challenges to sodomy statutes were unsuccessful in the federal courts, progress was made in some state courts. In 1980, the highest courts in New York and Pennsylvania struck down their state's sodomy laws on both federal and state constitutional grounds.[15]

B. *BOWERS v. HARDWICK*

In 1986, the U.S. Supreme Court ruled in *Bowers v. Hardwick*[16] that the constitutional right to privacy did not protect same-sex sexual conduct; thus, the Court affirmed the constitutionality of state statutes criminalizing that behavior. The incident discussed in the case arose when an Atlanta police officer entered Michael Hardwick's bedroom while Hardwick was engaged in oral sex with another man.

BOWERS V. HARDWICK

Supreme Court of the United States, 1986
478 U.S. 186, 106 S.Ct. 2841, 92 L.Ed.2d 140

JUSTICE WHITE.

In August 1982, respondent Hardwick (hereafter respondent) was charged with violating the Georgia statute criminalizing sodomy[1] by committing that act with another adult male in the bedroom of respondent's home. After a preliminary hearing, the District Attorney decided not to present the matter to the grand jury unless further evidence developed. * * *

Respondent then brought suit in the Federal District Court, challenging the constitutionality of the statute insofar as it criminalized consensual sodomy[2]. . . . The District Court granted the defendants' motion to dismiss for failure to state a claim, relying on *Doe v.*

---

[15] *New York v. Onofre*, 415 N.E.2d 936, 51 N.Y.2d 476, 434 N.Y.S.2d 947 (1980); *Commonwealth v. Bonadio*, 415 A.2d 47, 490 Pa. 91 (1980).

[16] 478 U.S. 186, 106 S. Ct. 2841, 92 L. Ed. 2d 140 (1986).

[1] Georgia Code Ann., § 16–6–2 (1984) provides, in pertinent part, as follows:

"(a) A person commits the offense of sodomy when he performs or submits to any sexual act involving the sex organs of one person and the mouth or anus of another. . . .

"(b) A person convicted of the offense of sodomy shall be punished by imprisonment for not less than one nor more than 20 years. . . ."

[2] John and Mary Doe were also plaintiffs in the action. They alleged that they wished to engage in sexual activity proscribed by § 16–6–2 in the privacy of their home, and that they had been "chilled and deterred" from engaging in such activity by both the existence of the statute and Hardwick's arrest. The District Court held, however, that because they had neither sustained, nor were in immediate danger of sustaining, any direct injury from the enforcement of the statute, they did not have proper standing to maintain the action. The Court of Appeals affirmed the District Court's judgment dismissing the Does' claim for lack of standing, 760 F.2d 1202, 1206–1207 (11th Cir. 1985), and the Does do not challenge that holding in this Court.

The only claim properly before the Court, therefore, is Hardwick's challenge to the Georgia statute as applied to consensual homosexual sodomy. We express no opinion on the constitutionality of the Georgia statute as applied to other acts of sodomy.

Commonwealth's Attorney for the City of Richmond, 403 F.Supp. 1199 (E.D.Va.1975), which this Court summarily affirmed, 425 U.S. 901 (1976).

A divided panel of the Court of Appeals for the Eleventh Circuit reversed. 760 F.2d 1202 (1985). * * *

This case does not require a judgment on whether laws against sodomy between consenting adults in general, or between homosexuals in particular, are wise or desirable. It raises no question about the right or propriety of state legislative decisions to repeal their laws that criminalize homosexual sodomy, or of state-court decisions invalidating those laws on state constitutional grounds. The issue presented is whether the Federal Constitution confers a fundamental right upon homosexuals to engage in sodomy and hence invalidates the laws of the many States that still make such conduct illegal and have done so for a very long time. The case also calls for some judgment about the limits of the Court's role in carrying out its constitutional mandate.

We first register our disagreement with the Court of Appeals and with respondent that the Court's prior cases have construed the Constitution to confer a right of privacy that extends to homosexual sodomy and for all intents and purposes have decided this case. The reach of this line of cases was sketched in *Carey v. Population Services International*, 431 U.S. 678, 685 (1977). *Pierce v. Society of Sisters*, 268 U.S. 510 (1925), and *Meyer v. Nebraska*, 262 U.S. 390 (1923), were described as dealing with child rearing and education; *Prince v. Massachusetts*, 321 U.S. 158 (1944), with family relationships; *Skinner v. Oklahoma ex rel. Williamson*, 316 U.S. 535 (1942), with procreation; *Loving v. Virginia*, 388 U.S. 1 (1967), with marriage; *Griswold v. Connecticut, supra*, and *Eisenstadt v. Baird, supra*, with contraception; and *Roe v. Wade*, 410 U.S. 113 (1973), with abortion. The latter three cases were interpreted as construing the due process clause of the Fourteenth Amendment to confer a fundamental individual right to decide whether or not to beget or bear a child. *Carey v. Population Services International, supra*, at 688–689.

Accepting the decisions in these cases and the above description of them, we think it evident that none of the rights announced in those cases bears any resemblance to the claimed constitutional right of homosexuals to engage in acts of sodomy that is asserted in this case. No connection between family, marriage, or procreation on the one hand and homosexual activity on the other has been demonstrated, either by the Court of Appeals or by respondent. Moreover, any claim that these cases nevertheless stand for the proposition that any kind of private sexual conduct between consenting adults is constitutionally insulated from state proscription is unsupportable. Indeed, the Court's opinion in *Carey* twice asserted that the privacy right, which the *Griswold* line of cases found to be one of the protections provided by the due process clause, did not reach so far.

Precedent aside, however, respondent would have us announce, as the Court of Appeals did, a fundamental right to engage in homosexual sodomy. This we are quite unwilling to do. It is true that despite the language of the due process clauses of the Fifth and Fourteenth Amendments, which appears to focus only on the processes by which life, liberty, or property is taken, the cases are legion in which those clauses have been interpreted to have substantive content, subsuming rights that to a great extent are immune from federal or state regulation or proscription. Among such cases are those recognizing rights that have little or no textual support in the constitutional language. *Meyer*, *Prince*, and *Pierce* fall in this category, as do the privacy cases from *Griswold* to *Carey*.

Striving to assure itself and the public that announcing rights not readily identifiable in the Constitution's text involves much more than the imposition of the Justices' own choice of values on the States and the Federal Government, the Court has sought to identify the nature of the rights qualifying for heightened judicial protection. In *Palko v. Connecticut*, 302 U.S. 319, 325, 326 (1937), it was said that this category includes those fundamental liberties that are "implicit in the concept of ordered liberty," such that "neither liberty nor justice would exist if [they] were sacrificed." A different description of fundamental liberties appeared in *Moore v. East Cleveland*, 431 U.S. 494, 503 (1977) (opinion of Powell, J.), where they are characterized as those liberties that are "deeply rooted in this Nation's history and tradition." *Id.*, at 503 (Powell, J.).

It is obvious to us that neither of these formulations would extend a fundamental right to homosexuals to engage in acts of consensual sodomy. Proscriptions against that conduct have ancient roots. *See generally*, Survey on the Constitutional Right to Privacy in the Context of Homosexual Activity, 40 U. Miami L. Rev. 521, 525 (1986). Sodomy was a criminal offense at common law and was forbidden by the laws of the original thirteen states when they ratified the Bill of Rights. In 1868, when the Fourteenth Amendment was ratified, all but 5 of the 37 States in the Union had criminal sodomy laws. In fact, until 1961, all 50 States outlawed sodomy, and today, 24 states and the District of Columbia continue to provide criminal penalties for sodomy performed in private and between consenting adults. *See* Survey, U. Miami L. Rev., *supra*, at 524, n. 9. Against this background, to claim that a right to engage in such conduct is "deeply rooted in this nation's history and tradition" or "implicit in the concept of ordered liberty" is, at best, facetious.

Nor are we inclined to take a more expansive view of our authority to discover new fundamental rights imbedded in the due process clause. The

Court is most vulnerable and comes nearest to illegitimacy when it deals with judge-made constitutional law having little or no cognizable roots in the language or design of the Constitution. That this is so was painfully demonstrated by the face-off between the Executive and the Court in the 1930s, which resulted in the repudiation of much of the substantive gloss that the Court had placed on the Due Process Clauses of the Fifth and Fourteenth Amendments. There should be, therefore, great resistance to expand the substantive reach of those Clauses, particularly if it requires redefining the category of rights deemed to be fundamental. Otherwise, the Judiciary necessarily takes to itself further authority to govern the country without express constitutional authority. The claimed right pressed on us today falls far short of overcoming this resistance.

Respondent, however, asserts that the result should be different where the homosexual conduct occurs in the privacy of the home. He relies on *Stanley v. Georgia*, 394 U.S. 557 (1969), where the Court held that the First Amendment prevents conviction for possessing and reading obscene material in the privacy of one's home: "If the First Amendment means anything, it means that a State has no business telling a man, sitting alone in his house, what books he may read or what films he may watch." *Id.*, at 565.

Stanley did protect conduct that would not have been protected outside the home, and it partially prevented the enforcement of state obscenity laws; but the decision was firmly grounded in the First Amendment. The right pressed upon us here has no similar support in the text of the Constitution, and it does not qualify for recognition under the prevailing principles for construing the Fourteenth Amendment. Its limits are also difficult to discern. Plainly enough, otherwise illegal conduct is not always immunized whenever it occurs in the home. Victimless crimes, such as the possession and use of illegal drugs, do not escape the law where they are committed at home. *Stanley* itself recognized that its holding offered no protection for the possession in the home of drugs, firearms, or stolen goods. *Id.*, at 568, n. 11. And if respondent's submission is limited to the voluntary sexual conduct between consenting adults, it would be difficult, except by fiat, to limit the claimed right to homosexual conduct while leaving exposed to prosecution adultery, incest, and other sexual crimes even though they are committed in the home. We are unwilling to start down that road.

Even if the conduct at issue here is not a fundamental right, respondent asserts that there must be a rational basis for the law and that there is none in this case other than the presumed belief of a majority of the electorate in Georgia that homosexual sodomy is immoral and unacceptable. This is said to be an inadequate rationale to support the law. The law, however, is constantly based on notions of morality, and if all laws representing essentially moral choices are to be invalidated under the Due Process Clause, the courts will be very busy indeed. Even respondent makes no such claim, but insists that majority sentiments about the morality of homosexuality should be declared inadequate. We do not agree, and are unpersuaded that the sodomy laws of some 25 States should be invalidated on this basis.

Accordingly, the judgment of the Court of Appeals is *Reversed.*

CHIEF JUSTICE BURGER, concurring.

I join the Court's opinion, but I write separately to underscore my view that in constitutional terms there is no such thing as a fundamental right to commit homosexual sodomy.

As the Court notes, the proscriptions against sodomy have very "ancient roots." Decisions of individuals relating to homosexual conduct have been subject to state intervention throughout the history of Western civilization. Condemnation of those practices is firmly rooted in Judeao-Christian moral and ethical standards. Homosexual sodomy was a capital crime under Roman law. See Code Theod. 9.7.6; Code Just. 9.9.31. See also D. Bailey, Homosexuality and the Western Christian Tradition, 70–81 (1975). During the English Reformation when powers of the ecclesiastical courts were transferred to the King's Courts, the first English statute criminalizing sodomy was passed. 25 Hen. VIII, ch. 6. Blackstone described "the infamous *crime against nature*" as an offense of "deeper malignity" than rape, a heinous act "the very mention of which is a disgrace to human nature," and "a crime not fit to be named." 4 W. Blackstone, Commentaries *215. The common law of England, including its prohibition of sodomy, became the received law of Georgia and the other Colonies. In 1816 the Georgia Legislature passed the statute at issue here, and that statute has been continuously in force in one form or another since that time. To hold that the act of homosexual sodomy is somehow protected as a fundamental right would be to cast aside millennia of moral teaching.

This is essentially not a question of personal "preferences" but rather of the legislative authority of the State. I find nothing in the Constitution depriving a State of the power to enact the statute challenged here.

JUSTICE POWELL, concurring.

I join the opinion of the Court. I agree with the Court that there is no fundamental right—*i.e.*, no substantive right under the due process clause—such as that claimed by respondent Hardwick, and found to exist by the Court of Appeals. This is not to suggest, however, that respondent may not be protected by the Eighth Amendment of the Constitution. The Georgia statute at issue in this case, Ga. Code Ann., § 16–6–2 (1984), authorizes a court to imprison a person for up to 20 years for a single private, consensual act of sodomy. In my view, a prison sentence for such conduct—certainly a sentence of long duration—would create a serious Eighth Amendment issue. Under the Georgia statute a single act of sodomy, even in the private setting of a home, is a felony comparable in terms of the possible sentence imposed to serious felonies such as aggravated battery, § 16–5–24, first-degree arson, § 16–7–60, and robbery, § 16–8–40.

In this case, however, respondent has not been tried, much less convicted and sentenced. Moreover, respondent has not raised the Eighth Amendment issue below. For these reasons this constitutional argument is not before us.

JUSTICE BLACKMUN, with whom JUSTICE BRENNAN, JUSTICE MARSHALL, and JUSTICE STEVENS join, dissenting.

This case is no more about "a fundamental right to engage in homosexual sodomy," as the Court purports to declare, than *Stanley v. Georgia*, 394 U.S. 557 (1969), was about a fundamental right to watch obscene movies, or *Katz v. United States*, 389 U.S. 347 (1967), was about a fundamental right to place interstate bets from a telephone booth. Rather, this case is about "the most comprehensive of rights and the right most valued by civilized men," namely, "the right to be let alone." *Olmstead v. United States*, 277 U.S. 438, 478 (1928) (Brandeis, J., dissenting).

The statute at issue, Ga.Code Ann. § 16–6–2 (1984), denies individuals the right to decide for themselves whether to engage in particular forms of private, consensual sexual activity. The Court concludes that § 16–6–2 is valid essentially because "the laws of . . . many States . . . still make such conduct illegal and have done so for a very long time." But the fact that the moral judgments expressed by statutes like § 16–6–2 may be " 'natural and familiar . . . ought not to conclude our judgment upon the question whether statutes embodying them conflict with the Constitution of the United States.' " *Roe v. Wade*, 410 U.S. 113, 117 (1973), quoting *Lochner v. New York*, 198 U.S. 45, 76 (1905) (Holmes, J., dissenting). Like Justice Holmes, I believe that "[it] is revolting to have no better reason for a rule of law than that so it was laid down in the time of Henry IV. It is still more revolting if the grounds upon which it was laid down have vanished long since, and the rule simply persists from blind imitation of the past." Holmes, "The Path of the Law," 10 Harv. L. Rev. 457, 469 (1897). I believe we must analyze respondent Hardwick's claim in the light of the values that underlie the constitutional right to privacy. If that right means anything, it means that, before Georgia can prosecute its citizens for making choices about the most intimate aspects of their lives, it must do more than assert that the choice they have made is an " 'abominable crime not fit to be named among Christians.' " *Herring v. State*, 46 S.E. 876, 882 (Ga. 1904). * * *

Only the most willful blindness could obscure the fact that sexual intimacy is "a sensitive, key relationship of human existence, central to family life, community welfare, and the development of human personality," *Paris Adult Theatre I v. Slaton*, 413 U.S. 49, 63 (1973); *see also Carey v. Population Services International*, 431 U.S. 678, 685 (1977). The fact that individuals define themselves in a significant way through their intimate sexual relationships with others suggests, in a nation as diverse as ours, that there may be many "right" ways of conducting those relationships, and that much of the richness of a relationship will come from the freedom an individual has to *choose* the form and nature of these intensely personal bonds. * * *

The behavior for which Hardwick faces prosecution occurred in his own home, a place to which the Fourth Amendment attaches special significance. The Court's treatment of this aspect of the case is symptomatic of its overall refusal to consider the broad principles that have informed our treatment of privacy in specific cases. Just as the right to privacy is more than the mere aggregation of a number of entitlements to engage in specific behavior, so too, protecting the physical integrity of the home is more than merely a means of protecting specific activities that often take place there. Even when our understanding of the contours of the right to privacy depends on "reference to a 'place,'" *Katz v. United States*, 389 U.S., at 361 (Harlan, J., concurring), "the essence of a Fourth Amendment violation is 'not the breaking of [a person's] doors, and the rummaging of his drawers,' but rather is 'the invasion of his indefeasible right of personal security, personal liberty and private property.'" *California v. Ciraolo*, 476 U.S. 207, 226 (1986) (Powell, J., dissenting), quoting *Boyd v. United States*, 116 U.S. 616, 630 (1886).

JUSTICE STEVENS, with whom JUSTICE BRENNAN and JUSTICE MARSHALL join, dissenting.

Our prior cases make two propositions abundantly clear. First, the fact that the governing majority in a State has traditionally viewed a particular practice as immoral is not a sufficient reason for upholding a law prohibiting the practice; neither history nor tradition could save a law prohibiting miscegenation from constitutional attack. Second, individual decisions by married persons, concerning the intimacies of their physical relationship, even when not intended to produce offspring, are a form of "liberty" protected by the due process clause of the Fourteenth Amendment. *Griswold v. Connecticut*, 381 U.S. 479 (1965). Moreover, this protection extends to intimate choices by unmarried as well as married persons. *Carey v. Population Services International*, 431 U.S. 678 (1977); *Eisenstadt v. Baird*, 405 U.S. 438 (1972). * * *

If the Georgia statute cannot be enforced as it is written—if the conduct it seeks to prohibit is a protected form of liberty for the vast majority of Georgia's citizens—the State must assume the burden of justifying a selective application of its law. Either the persons to whom Georgia seeks to apply its statute do not have the same interest in "liberty" that others have, or there must be a reason why the State may be permitted to apply a generally applicable law to certain persons that it does not apply to others.

The first possibility is plainly unacceptable. Although the meaning of the principle that "all men are created equal" is not always clear, it surely must mean that every free citizen has the same interest in "liberty" that the members of the majority share. From the standpoint of the individual, the homosexual and the heterosexual have the same interest in deciding how he will live his own life, and, more narrowly, how he will conduct himself in his personal and voluntary associations with his companions. State intrusion into the private conduct of either is equally burdensome.

The second possibility is similarly unacceptable. A policy of selective application must be supported by a neutral and legitimate interest—something more substantial than a habitual dislike for, or ignorance about, the disfavored group. Neither the State nor the Court has identified any such interest in this case. The Court has posited as a justification for the Georgia statute "the presumed belief of a majority of the electorate in Georgia that homosexual sodomy is immoral and unacceptable." But the Georgia electorate has expressed no such belief—instead, its representatives enacted a law that presumably reflects the belief that *all sodomy* is immoral and unacceptable. Unless the Court is prepared to conclude that such a law is constitutional, it may not rely on the work product of the Georgia legislature to support its holding. For the Georgia statute does not single out homosexuals as a separate class meriting special disfavored treatment.

Nor, indeed, does the Georgia prosecutor even believe that all homosexuals who violate this statute should be punished. This conclusion is evident from the fact that the respondent in this very case has formally acknowledged in his complaint and in court that he has engaged, and intends to continue to engage, in the prohibited conduct, yet the State has elected not to process criminal charges against him. As Justice Powell points out, moreover, Georgia's prohibition on private, consensual sodomy has not been enforced for decades. The record of nonenforcement, in this case and in the last several decades, belies the Attorney General's representations about the importance of the State's selective application of its generally applicable law.

Both the Georgia statute and the Georgia prosecutor thus completely fail to provide the Court with any support for the conclusion that homosexual sodomy, *simpliciter*, is considered unacceptable conduct in that State, and that the burden of justifying a selective application of the generally applicable law has been met.

NOTES

1. Justice Powell's concurrence provided the fifth vote for the *Hardwick* majority. Unknown to the Justice, one of his clerks that year was a gay man. *See* JOHN C. JEFFRIES, JR., JUSTICE LEWIS F. POWELL, JR. 521 (1994). As the two discussed the case and how Powell should vote, the Justice confided in his clerk that "I don't believe I've ever met a homosexual." *Id.* When the clerk explained that he likely had without knowing it, Powell remained unsure. The Justice then asked the clerk whether he thought gay men were at all attracted to women. The clerk explained that some men were gay because they found men, and not women, sexually attractive. Powell seemed confused by this, unable "to grasp . . . that homosexuality was not an act of desperation, not the last resort of men deprived of women, but a logical expression of the desire and affection that gay men felt for other men." *Id.* at 522.

> A few days before the oral argument in *Hardwick*, Powell had

> [u]ncharacteristically . . . not decided how he would vote. In great distress, the clerk debated whether to tell Powell of his sexual orientation. Perhaps if Powell could put a familiar face to these incomprehensible urges, they would seem less bizarre and threatening. He came to the edge of an outright declaration but ultimately drew back, settling for a "very emotional" speech urging Powell to support sexual freedom as a fundamental right. "The right to love the person of my choice," he argued, "would be far more important to me than the right to vote in elections." "That may be," Powell answered, "but that doesn't mean it's in the Constitution."

Id. The Justices met to discuss the case on April 2, 1986. Justice Powell at first voted against the sodomy law, believing it to violate the Eighth Amendment. After a few days, however, Powell reversed himself and decided to uphold the statute, albeit by writing separately. *See id.* at 522–25. Four years later, after giving a lecture at New York University Law School, a law student asked Powell how he could reconcile *Bowers v. Hardwick* with *Roe v. Wade.* He answered as follows: " 'I think I probably made a mistake in that one,' Powell said of *Hardwick.* When a reporter called to confirm the remark, Powell repeated the recantation: 'I do think it was inconsistent in a general way with *Roe.* When I had the opportunity to reread the opinions a few months later, I thought the dissent had the better of the arguments.' " *Id.* at 530.

2. After *Hardwick*, states remained free, as a matter of federal constitutional law, to criminalize same-sex sexual activity. The reality, however, was that by the time *Hardwick* was decided, law enforcement officials were rarely bringing sodomy prosecutions. *Hardwick*, therefore, had a greater practical impact on civil cases than it did on criminal cases. The

fact that states could, if they so chose, impose criminal liability for consensual same-sex sexual conduct was used to justify the continued discrimination against lesbians, gay men, and bisexuals in matters as diverse as those affecting public employment, family law, and immigration. *See generally* Diana Hassel, *The Use of Criminal Sodomy Laws in Civil Litigation*, 79 TEX. L. REV. 813 (2001); Christopher R. Leslie, *Creating Criminals: The Injuries Inflicted by "Unenforced" Sodomy Laws*, 35 HARV. C.R.-C.L. L. REV. 103 (2000).

3.   Even though *Hardwick* was a due process case, the ruling had important repercussions on questions of equal protection as several courts used the case to justify denying suspect class status to lesbians and gay men. If the state could criminalize the conduct that defines the class, the argument went, then the class should not receive heightened scrutiny under the Equal Protection Clause. *See, e.g., High Tech Gays v. Defense Indus. Sec. Clearance Office*, 895 F.2d 563, 571 (9th Cir. 1990) (noting that "if there is no fundamental right to engage in homosexual sodomy . . . , it would be incongruous to expand the reach of equal protection to find a fundamental right of homosexual conduct under the equal protection component of the Due Process Clause of the Fifth Amendment"); *Woodward v. United States*, 871 F.2d 1068, 1076 (Fed. Cir. 1989) (arguing that "[a]fter *Hardwick* it cannot logically be asserted that discrimination against homosexuals is constitutionally infirm"). The issue of sexual orientation and suspect classification is explored further below, in Chapter 3, Section II.B.

4.   Once the question of the federal constitutionality of sodomy statutes was answered by the U.S. Supreme Court in *Hardwick*, parties interested in challenging the statutes turned their attention more specifically to state courts, where, as already noted, there were some pre-*Hardwick* litigation successes. *E.g., New York v. Onofre*, 415 N.E.2d 936, 51 N.Y.2d 476, 434 N.Y.S.2d 947 (1980); *Commonwealth v. Bonadio*, 415 A.2d 47, 490 Pa. 91 (1980). This shift was consistent with a growing body of commentary embracing the use of state constitutions to try to expand civil rights and liberties protections. *See generally* William J. Brennan, Jr., *State Constitutions and the Protection of Individual Rights*, 90 HARV. L. REV. 489 (1977). Six years after *Hardwick*, the Kentucky Supreme Court became the first highest court of a state to strike down a sodomy statute on state constitutional grounds. *See Commonwealth v. Wasson*, 842 S.W.2d 487 (Ky. 1992) (violation of privacy and equal protection). Other state supreme courts followed with similar rulings, *see Gryczan v. State*, 942 P.2d 112, 283 Mont. 433 (1997); *Jegley v. Picado*, 80 S.W.3d 332, 349 Ark. 600 (2002), including the Georgia Supreme Court in a case involving the same statute at issue in *Hardwick. Powell v. State*, 510 S.E.2d 18, 270 Ga. 327 (1998). *Contra State v. Smith*, 766 So.2d 501 (La. 2000) (upholding constitutionality of "crime against nature" statute).

C. POST-*HARDWICK* SCHOLARSHIP

Few members of the legal academy defended either the reasoning or outcome in *Hardwick*. In fact, the opinion quickly became one of the most frequently criticized decisions in the history of the Supreme Court. An important early critique of *Hardwick* was presented by Professor Ann Goldstein, who criticized the Court for assuming

> that "homosexuality" has been an invariant reality, outside of history. In fact, however, like most ways of describing aspects of the human condition, "homosexuality" is a cultural and historical artifact. No attitude toward "homosexuals" or "homosexuality" can really be identified before the mid-nineteenth century because the concept did not exist until then. Before the late 1800s, sexuality—whether tolerated or condemned—was something a person did, not what he or she was. Although both the behavior and the desires we now call "homosexual" existed in earlier eras, our currently common assumption that persons who make love with others of their own sex are fundamentally different from the rest of humanity is only about one hundred years old.[17]

The understanding of "homosexuality" as a relatively recent social construction is important because it belies the notion that it has been the subject of opprobrium and regulation for centuries. As Goldstein noted, "by referring to 'homosexual sodomy' in ancient times, in 1791, and even in 1868, White and Burger were inserting their modern understanding of 'homosexuality' anachronistically into systems of values organized on other principles, obscuring the relative novelty of the distinction between 'homosexuality' and 'heterosexuality' with a myth about its antiquity."[18]

Goldstein and others also pointed out that oral sex, the conduct for which Hardwick was arrested, was not considered illegal in any American jurisdiction at the time the Fourteenth Amendment was ratified. Instead, oral sex was not prohibited until states, at the end of the nineteenth century and early part of the twentieth century, expanded the scope of their sodomy statutes.[19] In short, the historical record was not as simple as the *Hardwick* Court contended, a point that the Supreme Court itself would recognize years later in *Lawrence v. Texas*. *See infra* Section III.D.

The opinions by Justice White and Chief Justice Burger were not the only ones that were subjected to criticism by commentators. As the two excerpts below show, scholars also criticized the understandings of

---

[17] Ann Goldstein, *History, Homosexuality and Public Values: Searching for the Hidden Determinants of* Bowers v. Hardwick, 97 YALE L.J. 1073, 1087–88 (1988).

[18] *Id.* at 1088–89.

[19] *See id.* at 1088. *See also* WILLIAM N. ESKRIDGE JR., GAYLAW: CHALLENGING THE APARTHEID OF THE CLOSET 24–26 (1999).

privacy and liberty set forth in the dissenting opinions in *Hardwick*. The first reading, by Michael Sandel, critiques the philosophical underpinnings of liberal jurisprudence as seen in the substantive due process cases relied on by the Justices Blackmun and Stevens. The second reading, by Jed Rubenfeld, offers an understanding of the right of privacy—and its application to same-sex sexuality—distinct from that articulated by Justice Blackmun.

MORAL ARGUMENT AND LIBERAL TOLERATION*
Michael Sandel

The dissenters' argument for toleration in *Bowers v. Hardwick* illustrates the difficulties with the version of liberalism that ties toleration to autonomy rights alone. In refusing to extend the right of privacy to homosexuals, the majority in *Bowers* declared that none of the rights announced in earlier privacy cases resembled the rights homosexuals were seeking: "No connection between family, marriage, or procreation on the one hand and homosexual activity on the other has been demonstrated. . . ." Any reply to the Court's position would have to show some connection between the practices already subject to privacy protection and the homosexual practices not yet protected. What then is the resemblance between heterosexual intimacies on the one hand, and homosexual intimacies on the other, such that both are entitled to a constitutional right of privacy?

This question might be answered in at least two different ways—one voluntarist, the other substantive. The first argues from the autonomy the practices reflect, whereas the second appeals to the human goods the practices realize. The voluntarist answer holds that people should be free to choose their intimate associations for themselves, regardless of the virtue or popularity of the practices they choose so long as they do not harm others. In this view, homosexual relationships resemble the heterosexual relationships the Court has already protected in that all reflect the choices of autonomous selves.

By contrast, the substantive answer claims that much that is valuable in conventional marriage is also present in homosexual unions. In this view, the connection between heterosexual and homosexual relations is not that both result from individual choice but that both realize important human goods. Rather than rely on autonomy alone, this second line of reply articulates the virtues homosexual intimacy may share with heterosexual intimacy, along with any distinctive virtues of its own. It defends homosexual privacy the way *Griswold* defended marital privacy, by arguing that, like marriage, homosexual union may also be

---

*   Michael Sandel, *Moral Argument and Liberal Toleration: Abortion and Homosexuality*, 77 CAL. L. REV. 521, 533–37 (1989).

"intimate to the degree of being sacred . . . a harm
bilateral loyalty," an association for a "noble . . . purpo

Of these two possible replies, the dissenters in *B*
on the first. Rather than protect homosexual intima
goods they share with intimacies the Court alread
Blackmun cast the Court's earlier cases in individuali
their reading applied equally to homosexuality bec
richness of a relationship will come from the freedom an inuiviuuai has to
choose the form and nature of these intensely personal bonds." At issue
was not homosexuality as such but respect for the fact that "different
individuals will make different choices" in deciding how to conduct their
lives.

Justice Stevens, in a separate dissent, also avoided referring to the
values of homosexual intimacy may share with heterosexual love.
Instead, he wrote broadly of " 'the individual's right to make certain
unusually important decisions' " and " 'respect for the dignity of
individual choice,' " rejecting the notion that such liberty belongs to
heterosexuals alone. "From the standpoint of the individual, the
homosexual and the heterosexual have the same interest in deciding how
he will live his own life, and, more narrowly, how he will conduct himself
in his personal and voluntary associations with his companions." * * *

The case for toleration that brackets the morality of homosexuality
has a powerful appeal. In the face of deep disagreement about values, it
seems to ask the least of the contending parties. It offers social peace and
respect for rights without the need for moral conversion. Those who view
sodomy as sin need not be persuaded to change their minds, only to
tolerate those who practice it in private. By insisting only that each
respect the freedom of others to live the lives they choose, this toleration
promises a basis for political agreement that does not await shared
conceptions of morality.

Despite its promise, however, the neutral case for toleration is
subject to two related difficulties. First, as a practical matter, it is by no
means clear that social cooperation can be secured on the strength of
autonomy rights alone, absent some measure of agreement on the moral
permissibility of the practices at issue. It may not be accidental that the
first practices subject to the right of privacy were accorded constitutional
protection in cases that spoke of the sanctity of marriage and procreation.
Only later did the Court abstract privacy rights from these practices and
protect them without reference to the human goods they were once
thought to make possible. This suggests that the voluntarist justification
of privacy rights is dependent—politically as well as philosophically—on
some measure of agreement that the practices protected are morally
permissible.

A second difficulty with the voluntarist case for toleration concerns the quality of respect it secures. As the New York case [*People v. Onofre*] suggests, the analogy with *Stanley* tolerates homosexuality at the price of demeaning it; it puts homosexual intimacy on a par with obscenity—a base thing that should nonetheless be tolerated so long as it takes place in private. If *Stanley* rather than *Griswold* is the relevant analogy, the interest at stake is bound to be reduced, as the New York court reduced it, to "sexual gratification." (The only intimate relationship at stake in *Stanley* was between a man and his pornography.)

The majority in *Bowers* exploited this assumption by ridiculing the notion of a "fundamental right to engage in homosexual sodomy." The obvious reply is that *Bowers* is no more about a right to homosexual sodomy than *Griswold* was about a right to heterosexual intercourse. But by refusing to articulate the human goods that homosexual intimacy may share with heterosexual unions, the voluntarist case for toleration forfeits the analogy with *Griswold* and makes the ridicule difficult to refute.

The problem with the neutral case for toleration is the opposite side of its appeal; it leaves wholly unchallenged the adverse views of homosexuality itself. Unless those views can be plausibly addressed, even a court ruling in their favor is unlikely to win for homosexuals more than a thin and fragile toleration. A fuller respect would require, if not admiration, at least some appreciation of the lives homosexuals live. Such appreciation, however, is unlikely to be cultivated by a legal and political discourse conducted in terms of autonomy rights alone.

THE RIGHT OF PRIVACY[*]
Jed Rubenfeld

Hardwick has exposed deep flaws in the prevailing jurisprudence and ideology of privacy. The constitutional ground has shifted; perhaps it is dissolving altogether. The changing membership of the High Court raises the possibility of a wholesale reconsideration of the privacy doctrine's propriety. Yet even when the doctrine was first ascendant, the Court never hazarded a definitive statement of what it was supposed to protect. At the heart of the right to privacy, there has always been a conceptual vacuum.

The reason for this, I will try to show, is that the operative analysis in privacy cases has invariably missed the real point. Past privacy analysis has taken the act proscribed by the law at issue—for example, abortion, interracial marriage, or homosexual sex—and asked whether there is a "fundamental right" to perform it. But the fundament of the right to privacy is not to be found in the supposed fundamentality of what

---

[*]   Jed Rubenfeld, *The Right of Privacy*, 102 HARV. L. REV. 737, 739–802 (1989).

the law proscribes. It is to be found in what the law imposes. The question, for example, of whether the state should be permitted to compel an individual to have a child—with all the pervasive, far-reaching, lifelong consequences that child-bearing ordinarily entails—need not be the same as the question of whether abortion or even child-bearing itself is a "fundamental" act within some normative framework. The distinguishing feature of the laws struck down by the privacy cases has been their profound capacity to direct and to occupy individuals' lives through their affirmative consequences. This affirmative power in the law, lying just below its interdictive surface, must be privacy's focal point. * * *

> [Professor Rubenfeld begins with a comprehensive critique of the personhood principle of privacy doctrine—that "homosexual sex should receive constitutional protection because it is so essential to an individual's self-definition—to his identity."]

There is . . . an ambiguity in the idea that homosexual sex is central to the identity of those who engage in it. Is homosexual sex said to be self-definitive simply because it is sex, or especially because it is *homosexual sex*? In fact, proponents of personhood appear to argue for the second proposition. One reason for this is that the first version of the argument would be quite difficult to sustain. To begin with, it would present personhood with the problem discussed earlier—it would be required to claim that prostitution, for example, is an exercise of one's constitutional rights. (Personhood could, of course, choose to defend this position.) Moreover, it simply seems implausible to assert that the act of sex on any given occasion is necessarily fundamental in defining the identity of the person engaging in it. * * *

Without doubt, personhood's arguments for homosexual rights are intended to show and to seek the highest degree of respect for those on behalf of whom they are made. Nevertheless, in the very concept of a homosexual identity there is something potentially disserving—if not disrespectful—to the cause advocated. There is something not altogether liberating. Those who engage in homosexual sex may or may not perceive themselves as bearing a "homosexual identity." Their homosexual relations may be a pleasure they take or an intimacy they value without constituting—at least qua homosexual relations—something definitive of their identity. At the heart of personhood's analysis is the reliance upon a sharply demarcated "homosexual identity" to which a person is immediately consigned at the moment he seeks to engage in homosexual sex. For personhood, that is, homosexual relations are to be protected to the extent that they fundamentally define a species of person that is, by definition, to be strictly distinguished from the heterosexual. Persons may have homosexual sex only because they have elected to define themselves as "homosexuals"—because homosexuality lies at "the heart of . . . what they are." Thus, even as it argues for homosexual rights, personhood becomes yet another turn of the screw that has pinned those who engage in homosexual sex into a fixed identity specified by their difference from "heterosexuals." * * *

To protect the rights of "the homosexual" would of course be a victory; doing so, however, because homosexuality is essential to a person's identity is no liberation, but simply the flip side of the same rigidification of sexual identities by which our society simultaneously inculcates sexual roles, normalizes sexual conduct, and vilifies "faggots."

Thus personhood, at the instant it proclaims a freedom of self-definition, reproduces the very constraints on identity that it purports to resist. Homosexuality is but one instance of this phenomenon. The same flaw can be shown in the context of interracial marriage: once again, for the parties directly involved, to say that the challenged conduct defines their identity, and therefore should be protected, assumes that marrying out of one's race is in some way the cataclysmic event its opponents pretend; it thus repeats the same impulse toward rigid classification presupposing the discrimination sought to be undone. Interracial marriage should be protected because it is no different from intraracial marriage, not because it is *so* different. . . . We must reject the personhood thesis. * * *

III. AN ALTERNATIVE FOR PRIVACY

* * * The methodology heretofore universal in privacy analysis has begun with the question, "What is the state trying to forbid?" The proscribed conduct is then delineated and its significance tested through a pre-established conceptual apparatus: for its role in "the concept of ordered liberty," its status as a "fundamental" right, its importance to one's identity, or for any other criterion of fundamentality upon which a court can settle. Suppose instead we began by asking not what is being *prohibited*, but what is being *produced*. Suppose we looked not to the negative aspect of the law—the interdiction by which it formally expresses itself—but at its positive aspect: the real effects that conformity with the law produces at the level of everyday lives and social practices. * * *

In [Michel] Foucault's conception, the significance of a law does not reside in the interdiction itself, but in the extent to which the law interjects us in a network of norms and practices that affirmatively shape our lives. The critical methodological step is to look away from what the law would keep us from doing and instead look to what the law would have us do. * * *

[L]et us reconsider *Bowers v. Hardwick* in our new terms. . . . Laws against homosexual sex have an effect that most laws do not. They forcibly channel certain individuals—supposing the law is obeyed—into a network of social institutions and relations that will occupy their lives to a substantial degree.

Most fundamentally, the prohibition against homosexual sex channels individuals' sexual desires into *reproductive* outlets. Although the prohibition does not, like the law against abortions, produce as an imminent consequence compulsory child-bearing, it nonetheless forcibly directs individuals into the pathways of reproductive sexuality, rather than the socially "unproductive" realm of homosexuality. These pathways are further guided, in our society, into particular institutional orbits, chief among which are the nuclear family and the constellation of practices surrounding a heterosexuality that is defined in conscious contradistinction to homosexuality. Indeed, it is difficult to separate our society's inculcation of a heterosexual identity from the simultaneous inculcation of a dichotomized complementarity of roles to be borne by men and women. Homosexual couples by necessity throw into question the allocation of specific functions—whether professional, personal, or emotional—between the sexes. It is this aspect of the ban on homosexuality—its central role in the maintenance of institutionalized sexual identities and normalized reproductive relations—that have made its *affirmative* or *formative* consequences, as well as the reaction against these consequences, so powerful a force in modern society.

The use of sexual practices to define and inculcate social identities dates back to antiquity. In our time, the use of the heterosexual/homosexual axis has achieved a paramount normalizing significance. The proscription is against homosexual sex; the products are lives forced into relations with the opposite sex that substantially direct individuals' roles in society and a large part of their everyday existence.

It is no answer to say that an individual interested in homosexual relations might simply remain celibate. The living force of the law is at issue, not its logical form, and the real force of anti-homosexual laws, if obeyed, is that they enlist and redirect physical and emotional desires that we do not expect people to suppress. Indeed, it is precisely the propensity of such prohibitions to operate on and put to use an individual's most elemental bodily faculties that gives the exertion of power in this area such formative force. We tend to analyze these proscriptions today in terms of the propriety of punishing people for homosexual conduct. We tend, in measuring their morality, to form an image of either the homosexual imprisoned or the homosexual forced to give up his sexual acts. We ought, however, to give up the image of "the homosexual" in the first place and measure the law instead in terms of its creation of heterosexuals (and, in a different way, of homosexuals too) within the standardized parameters of a state-regulated identity.

It should be emphasized that conceiving of the right to privacy as protecting homosexuality for the reasons just discussed is not at all to convert the right to privacy into a general protection of "sexual intimacy," as Justice Blackmun suggested. The point is this: childbearing, marriage, and the assumption of a specific sexual identity are undertakings that go on for years, define roles, direct activities, operate on or even create intense emotional relations, enlist the body, inform values, and in sum substantially shape the totality of a person's daily life and consciousness. Laws that force such undertakings on individuals may properly be called "totalitarian," and the right to privacy exists to protect against them.

D. *LAWRENCE v. TEXAS*

After *Hardwick*, the next important substantive due process opinion issued by the U.S. Supreme Court was *Planned Parenthood of Southeastern Pennsylvania v. Casey*.[20] The Court in *Casey* reaffirmed the central holding of *Roe v. Wade*.[21] In a joint opinion by Justices O'Connor, Kennedy, and Souter, the Court stated that "[i]t is . . . tempting . . . to suppose that the Due Process Clause protects only those practices, defined at the most specific level, that were protected against government interference by other rules of law when the Fourteenth Amendment was ratified. But such a view would be inconsistent with our law. It is a promise of the Constitution that there is a realm of personal liberty which the government may not enter. . . . Neither the Bill of Rights nor the specific practices of States at the time of the adoption of the Fourteenth Amendment marks the outer limits of the substantive sphere of liberty which the Fourteenth Amendment protects."[22] The Court added that "[t]he inescapable fact is that adjudication of substantive due process claims may call upon the Court in interpreting the Constitution to exercise that same capacity which by tradition courts always have exercised: reasoned judgment. Its boundaries are not susceptible of expression as a simple rule. That does not mean we are free to invalidate state policy choices with which we disagree; yet neither does it permit us to shrink from the duties of our office."[23]

The last important substantive due process case prior to *Lawrence v. Texas* was *Washington v. Glucksberg*.[24] The Court in *Glucksberg* held that Washington's prohibition of physician-assisted suicide did not violate the Fourteenth Amendment. The Court stated that

> [o]ur established method of substantive-due-process analysis has two primary features: First, we have regularly observed that the

---

[20] 505 U.S. 833, 112 S. Ct. 2791, 120 L. Ed. 2d 674 (1992).

[21] 410 U.S. 113, 93 S. Ct. 705, 35 L. Ed. 2d 147 (1973).

[22] *Casey*, 505 U.S. at 847–48, 112 S. Ct. at 2805, 120 L. Ed. 2d at 695–96.

[23] *Id*. at 849, 112 S. Ct. at 2806, 120 L. Ed. 2d at 697.

[24] 521 U.S. 702, 117 S. Ct. 2258, 138 L. Ed. 2d 772(1997).

Due Process Clause specially protects those fundamental rights and liberties which are, objectively, "deeply rooted in this Nation's history and tradition," and "implicit in the concept of ordered liberty," such that "neither liberty nor justice would exist if they were sacrificed." Second, we have required in substantive-due-process cases a "careful description" of the asserted fundamental liberty interest. Our Nation's history, legal traditions, and practices thus provide the crucial "guideposts for responsible decisionmaking" that direct and restrain our exposition of the Due Process Clause. * * *

In our view . . . the development of this Court's substantive-due-process jurisprudence . . . has been a process whereby the outlines of the "liberty" specially protected by the Fourteenth Amendment—never fully clarified, to be sure, and perhaps not capable of being fully clarified—have at least been carefully refined by concrete examples involving fundamental rights found to be deeply rooted in our legal tradition. This approach tends to rein in the subjective elements that are necessarily present in due-process judicial review. In addition, by establishing a threshold requirement—that a challenged state action implicate a fundamental right—before requiring more than a reasonable relation to a legitimate state interest to justify the action, it avoids the need for complex balancing of competing interests in every case.[25]

In reviewing the historical record in *Glucksberg*, the Court noted that "we are confronted with a consistent and almost universal tradition that has long rejected the asserted right, and continues explicitly to reject it today, even for terminally ill, mentally competent adults. To hold for respondents, we would have to reverse centuries of legal doctrine and practice, and strike down the considered policy choice of almost every State."[26]

THE UNKNOWN PAST OF *LAWRENCE V. TEXAS*[*]

Dale Carpenter

Below I offer a brief history of the Texas sodomy law, in its various statutory iterations. I do so for two reasons. First, though the law never distinguished between acts committed in broad daylight and acts committed in the home, it was almost never enforced against the latter. That is, it was almost never enforced against the most prevalent

---

[25] *Id.* at 720–22, 117 S. Ct. at 2268, 138 L. Ed. 2d at 787–89.

[26] *Id.* at 723, 117 S. Ct. at 2269, 138 L. Ed. 2d at 793.

[*] Dale Carpenter, *The Unknown Past of* Lawrence v. Texas 102 Mich.L.Rev. 1464, 1468–74 (2004).

instances of sodomy. Thus, the law's concern was not with preventing sodomy. The law was intended to send a symbolic message of disdain about the people thought to commonly engage in sodomy.

Second, the history of the law's development establishes an important point: the Texas law, like other sodomy laws around the country, initially applied to certain acts, regardless of the sex of the people involved in the act. It was only through a process of specification that it came to be aimed at certain people engaged in certain acts. The Texas law, like many such laws, instantiates a particular cultural view of homosexuals as hyper-sexualized and dangerous in some way. * * *

1. THE 1860 STATUTE

The criminal code of the Republic of Texas, in force from 1836 to 1845 while Texas was an independent nation, contained no prohibition on sodomy, although common-law crimes were recognized. In its first fifteen years as a state, Texas had no statutory sodomy law.

The state adopted its first sodomy law in 1860, using the common-law definition for the crime. It provided: "If any person shall commit with mankind or beast the abominable and detestable crime against nature . . . he shall be punished by confinement in the penitentiary for not less than five nor more than fifteen years." Commentators and courts of the era understood this language to prohibit anal sex between a man and a woman or between two men. It did not prohibit oral sex, and it did not prohibit any sex between women. The category "homosexual conduct" would have been literally incomprehensible to Texas legislators of the era since there was no word for "homosexual" at the time. * * *

2. THE 1943 STATUTE

In 1943, the Texas legislature revised the state sodomy law a second time. The new version, which passed by votes of 127–0 and 24–0 in the state house and senate, respectively, made oral sex a crime for the first time in Texas:

> Whoever has carnal copulation with a beast, or in an opening of the body, except sexual parts, with another human being, or whoever shall use his mouth on the sexual parts of another human being for the purpose of having carnal copulation, or who shall voluntarily permit the use of his own sexual parts in a lewd or lascivious manner by any minor, shall be guilty of sodomy, and upon conviction thereof shall be deemed guilty of a felony, and shall be confined in the penitentiary not less than two (2) nor more than fifteen (15) years.

The 1943 revision is bizarre in more ways than one. It suggests that while oral sex for the purpose of "carnal copulation" is illegal, oral sex for some other purpose is just fine. It also suggests that while sexual intercourse with an animal is illegal, oral sex performed on an animal is not a problem since it is only oral sex performed on "another human being" that is criminal. Still, the law on its face applied equally to heterosexual and homosexual sex.

3.   THE 1973 STATUTE

In 1973, during a comprehensive criminal code revision, the Texas legislature changed the sodomy law a third time. Now for the first time calling the law "Homosexual Conduct," the legislature banned oral and anal sex only between persons of the same sex. It first defined "deviate sexual intercourse" as "any contact between any part of the genitals of one person and the mouth or anus of another person." Next, it made deviate sexual intercourse a crime only if performed "with another individual of the same sex." The 1973 revision made homosexual conduct a Class C misdemeanor punishable only by a fine of up to $200. It made lesbian sex criminal for the first time.

Also in 1973, the Texas legislature generally liberalized its sex laws, decriminalizing adultery, fornication, seduction, and even bestiality. And while opposite-sex couples were now free to engage in "deviate sexual intercourse," same-sex couples were not.

Thus, the 1973 Texas Homosexual Conduct law represented an expansion of the types of acts historically prohibited. Both anal and oral sex were now covered, though only anal sex was covered before 1943. At the same time, it also represented a narrowing of the class of people historically covered. Same-sex, but not opposite-sex, couples were now covered. * * *

Enforcement of the Texas Sodomy Law

In the entire 143-year history of the Texas sodomy law, . . . there are no publicly reported court decisions involving the enforcement of the law against consensual sex between adult persons in a private space. In some reported decisions, the facts given by the court are too sketchy to determine whether the prosecution was for private, adult, consensual activity. Especially in early cases, the decisions are very short, often no more than a paragraph or two in length. Courts have often seemed too bashful even to present the facts. In a typical example, affirming a sodomy conviction after a guilty plea, one Kentucky court said simply, "It is not necessary to set out the revolting facts." *Medrano v. State*, 205 S.W. 2d 588, 588 (Ky. 1947)

All of the reported Texas cases detailing the circumstances of an arrest for sodomy involve some element that makes them distinct from *Lawrence.* Many involve charges of sodomy violations in a public or quasi-public place, such as a jail. Some cases involve some element of force or coercion. Others involve sex with minors. Indeed, in litigation challenging the state sodomy law, the state has contended that it has only enforced the law in cases where force was used, cases involving minors, and cases involving public sex. This alone makes the arrest and prosecution of Lawrence and Garner, whose case involved none of these factors, anomalous.

However, the absence of reported decisions does not mean that the Texas sodomy law was never enforced against private activity. Instead, perhaps because of the shame long associated with homosexuality and homosexual acts, defendants arrested and charged with violating the law routinely pleaded guilty to the offense, paid whatever fine was imposed, and hushed up about their convictions. As a result, almost all of the uses and misuses by police of the Texas sodomy law (and of sodomy laws in other states) against private acts will never be known. They are lost to history because of shame and fear.

LAWRENCE V. TEXAS

Supreme Court of the United States, 2003
539 U.S. 558, 123 S.Ct. 2472, 156 L.Ed.2d 508

JUSTICE KENNEDY delivered the opinion of the Court.

Liberty protects the person from unwarranted government intrusions into a dwelling or other private places. In our tradition the State is not omnipresent in the home. And there are other spheres of our lives and existence, outside the home, where the State should not be a dominant presence. Freedom extends beyond spatial bounds. Liberty presumes an autonomy of self that includes freedom of thought, belief, expression, and certain intimate conduct. The instant case involves liberty of the person both in its spatial and in its more transcendent dimensions.

The question before the Court is the validity of a Texas statute making it a crime for two persons of the same sex to engage in certain intimate sexual conduct.

In Houston, Texas, officers of the Harris County Police Department were dispatched to a private residence in response to a reported weapons disturbance. They entered an apartment where one of the petitioners, John Geddes Lawrence, resided. The right of the police to enter does not seem to have been questioned. The officers observed Lawrence and another man, Tyron Garner, engaging in a sexual act. The two petitioners were arrested, held in custody overnight, and charged and convicted before a Justice of the Peace.

The complaints described their crime as "deviate sexual intercourse, namely anal sex, with a member of the same sex (man)." App. to Pet. for Cert. 127a, 139a. The applicable state law is Tex. Penal Code Ann. § 21.06(a) (2003). It provides: "A person commits an offense if he engages in deviate sexual intercourse with another individual of the same sex." The statute defines "[d]eviate sexual intercourse" as follows:

"(A) any contact between any part of the genitals of one person and the mouth or anus of another person; or

"(B) the penetration of the genitals or the anus of another person with an object." § 21.01(1). * * *

The petitioners were adults at the time of the alleged offense. Their conduct was in private and consensual.

We conclude the case should be resolved by determining whether the petitioners were free as adults to engage in the private conduct in the exercise of their liberty under the Due Process Clause of the Fourteenth Amendment to the Constitution. For this inquiry we deem it necessary to reconsider the Court's holding in *Bowers*.

There are broad statements of the substantive reach of liberty under the Due Process Clause in earlier cases . . . but the most pertinent beginning point is our decision in *Griswold v. Connecticut*, 381 U.S. 479 (1965). * * *

In *Griswold* the Court invalidated a state law prohibiting the use of drugs or devices of contraception and counseling or aiding and abetting the use of contraceptives. The Court described the protected interest as a right to privacy and placed emphasis on the marriage relation and the protected space of the marital bedroom. *Id.*, at 485.

After *Griswold* it was established that the right to make certain decisions regarding sexual conduct extends beyond the marital relationship. In *Eisenstadt v. Baird*, 405 U.S. 438 (1972), the Court invalidated a law prohibiting the distribution of contraceptives to unmarried persons. The case was decided under the Equal Protection Clause, *id.*, at 454 . . . ; but with respect to unmarried persons, the Court went on to state the fundamental proposition that the law impaired the exercise of their personal rights, *ibid.* It quoted from the statement of the Court of Appeals finding the law to be in conflict with fundamental human rights, and it followed with this statement of its own: "It is true that in *Griswold* the right of privacy in question inhered in the marital relationship. . . . If the right of privacy means anything, it is the right of the *individual*, married or single, to be free from unwarranted governmental intrusion into matters so fundamentally affecting a person as the decision whether to bear or beget a child." *Id.* at 453.

The opinions in *Griswold* and *Eisenstadt* were part of the background for the decision in *Roe v. Wade*, 410 U.S. 113 (1973). . . . *Roe* recognized the right of a woman to make certain fundamental decisions affecting her destiny and confirmed once more that the protection of liberty under the

Due Process Clause has a substantive dimension of fundamental significance in defining the rights of the person.

In *Carey v. Population Services Int'l*, 431 U.S. 678 (1977), the Court confronted a New York law forbidding sale or distribution of contraceptive devices to persons under 16 years of age. Although there was no single opinion for the Court, the law was invalidated. Both *Eisenstadt* and *Carey*, as well as the holding and rationale in *Roe*, confirmed that the reasoning of *Griswold* could not be confined to the protection of rights of married adults. This was the state of the law with respect to some of the most relevant cases when the Court considered *Bowers v. Hardwick*. * * *

The Court began its substantive discussion in *Bowers* as follows: "The issue presented is whether the Federal Constitution confers a fundamental right upon homosexuals to engage in sodomy and hence invalidates the laws of the many States that still make such conduct illegal and have done so for a very long time." That statement, we now conclude, discloses the Court's own failure to appreciate the extent of the liberty at stake. To say that the issue in *Bowers* was simply the right to engage in certain sexual conduct demeans the claim the individual put forward, just as it would demean a married couple were it to be said marriage is simply about the right to have sexual intercourse. The laws involved in *Bowers* and here are, to be sure, statutes that purport to do no more than prohibit a particular sexual act. Their penalties and purposes, though, have more far-reaching consequences, touching upon the most private human conduct, sexual behavior, and in the most private of places, the home. The statutes do seek to control a personal relationship that, whether or not entitled to formal recognition in the law, is within the liberty of persons to choose without being punished as criminals.

This, as a general rule, should counsel against attempts by the State, or a court, to define the meaning of the relationship or to set its boundaries absent injury to a person or abuse of an institution the law protects. It suffices for us to acknowledge that adults may choose to enter upon this relationship in the confines of their homes and their own private lives and still retain their dignity as free persons. When sexuality finds overt expression in intimate conduct with another person, the conduct can be but one element in a personal bond that is more enduring. The liberty protected by the Constitution allows homosexual persons the right to make this choice.

Having misapprehended the claim of liberty there presented to it, and thus stating the claim to be whether there is a fundamental right to engage in consensual sodomy, the *Bowers* Court said: "Proscriptions against that conduct have ancient roots." . . . [T]he following considerations counsel against adopting the definitive conclusions upon which *Bowers* placed such reliance.

At the outset it should be noted that there is no longstanding history in this country of laws directed at homosexual conduct as a distinct matter. Beginning in colonial times there were prohibitions of sodomy derived from the English criminal laws passed in the first instance by the Reformation Parliament of 1533. The English prohibition was understood to include relations between men and women as well as relations between men and men. Nineteenth-century commentators similarly read American sodomy, buggery, and crime-against-nature statutes as criminalizing certain relations between men and women and between men and men. The absence of legal prohibitions focusing on homosexual conduct may be explained in part by noting that according to some scholars the concept of the homosexual as a distinct category of person did not emerge until the late 19th century. Thus early American sodomy laws were not directed at homosexuals as such but instead sought to prohibit nonprocreative sexual activity more generally. This does not suggest approval of homosexual conduct. It does tend to show that this particular form of conduct was not thought of as a separate category from like conduct between heterosexual persons.

Laws prohibiting sodomy do not seem to have been enforced against consenting adults acting in private. A substantial number of sodomy prosecutions and convictions for which there are surviving records were for predatory acts against those who could not or did not consent, as in the case of a minor or the victim of an assault. As to these, one purpose for the prohibitions was to ensure there would be no lack of coverage if a predator committed a sexual assault that did not constitute rape as defined by the criminal law. Thus the model sodomy indictments presented in a 19th-century treatise addressed the predatory acts of an adult man against a minor girl or minor boy. Instead of targeting relations between consenting adults in private, 19th-century sodomy prosecutions typically involved relations between men and minor girls or minor boys, relations between adults involving force, relations between adults implicating disparity in status, or relations between men and animals.

To the extent that there were any prosecutions for the acts in question, 19th-century evidence rules imposed a burden that would make a conviction more difficult to obtain even taking into account the problems always inherent in prosecuting consensual acts committed in private. Under then-prevailing standards, a man could not be convicted of sodomy based upon testimony of a consenting partner, because the partner was considered an accomplice. A partner's testimony, however, was admissible if he or she had not consented to the act or was a minor, and therefore incapable of consent. The rule may explain in part the infrequency of these prosecutions. In all events that infrequency makes it difficult to say that society approved of a rigorous and systematic punishment of the consensual acts committed in private and by adults. The longstanding criminal prohibition of homosexual sodomy upon which the *Bowers* decision placed such reliance is as consistent with a general condemnation of nonprocreative sex as it is with an established tradition of prosecuting acts because of their homosexual character.

The policy of punishing consenting adults for private acts was not much discussed in the early legal literature. We can infer that one reason for this was the very private nature of the conduct. Despite the absence of prosecutions, there may have been periods in which there was public criticism of homosexuals as such and an insistence that the criminal laws be enforced to discourage their practices. But far from possessing "ancient roots," American laws targeting same-sex couples did not develop until the last third of the 20th century. The reported decisions concerning the prosecution of consensual, homosexual sodomy between adults for the years 1880–1995 are not always clear in the details, but a significant number involved conduct in a public place.

It was not until the 1970's that any State singled out same-sex relations for criminal prosecution, and only nine States have done so. Post-*Bowers* even some of these States did not adhere to the policy of suppressing homosexual conduct. Over the course of the last decades, States with same-sex prohibitions have moved toward abolishing them.

In summary, the historical grounds relied upon in *Bowers* are more complex than the majority opinion and the concurring opinion by Chief Justice Burger indicate. Their historical premises are not without doubt and, at the very least, are overstated.

It must be acknowledged, of course, that the Court in *Bowers* was making the broader point that for centuries there have been powerful voices to condemn homosexual conduct as immoral. The condemnation has been shaped by religious beliefs, conceptions of right and acceptable behavior, and respect for the traditional family. For many persons these are not trivial concerns but profound and deep convictions accepted as ethical and moral principles to which they aspire and which thus determine the course of their lives. These considerations do not answer the question before us, however. The issue is whether the majority may use the power of the State to enforce these views on the whole society through operation of the criminal law. "Our obligation is to define the liberty of all, not to mandate our own moral code." *Planned Parenthood of Southeastern Pa. v. Casey*, 505 U.S. 833 (1992).

* * * In all events we think that our laws and traditions in the past half century are of most relevance here. These references show an emerging awareness that liberty gives substantial protection to adult persons in deciding how to conduct their private lives in matters pertaining to sex. "[H]istory and tradition are the starting point but not in all cases the ending point of the substantive due process inquiry." *County of Sacramento v. Lewis*, 523 U.S. 833, 857 (1998) (Kennedy, J., concurring).

This emerging recognition should have been apparent when *Bowers* was decided. In 1955 the American Law Institute promulgated the Model Penal Code and made clear that it did not recommend or provide for "criminal penalties for consensual sexual relations conducted in private." . . . In 1961 Illinois changed its laws to conform to the Model Penal Code. Other States soon followed. [By the time of the Court's decision in *Bowers*, only] 24 States and the District of Columbia had sodomy laws. Justice Powell pointed out that these prohibitions often were being ignored, however. Georgia, for instance, had not sought to enforce its law for decades. ([Justice Powell stated that:] "The history of nonenforcement suggests the moribund character today of laws criminalizing this type of private, consensual conduct.")

[Moreover, a] committee advising the British Parliament recommended in 1957 repeal of laws punishing homosexual conduct. *The Wolfenden Report: Report of the Committee on Homosexual Offenses and Prostitution* (1963). Parliament enacted the substance of those recommendations 10 years later.

Of even more importance, almost five years before *Bowers* was decided the European Court of Human Rights considered a case with parallels to *Bowers* and to today's case. An adult male resident in Northern Ireland alleged he was a practicing homosexual who desired to engage in consensual homosexual conduct. The laws of Northern Ireland forbade him that right. He alleged that he had been questioned, his home had been searched, and he feared criminal prosecution. The court held that the laws proscribing the conduct were invalid under the European Convention on Human Rights. *Dudgeon v. United Kingdom*, 45 Eur. Ct. H.R. (1981) & ¶ 52. Authoritative in all countries that are members of the Council of Europe (21 nations then, 45 nations now), the decision is at odds with the premise in *Bowers* that the claim put forward was insubstantial in our Western civilization.

In our own constitutional system the deficiencies in *Bowers* became even more apparent in the years following its announcement. The 25 States with laws prohibiting the relevant conduct referenced in the *Bowers* decision are reduced now to 13, of which 4 enforce their laws only against homosexual conduct. In those States where sodomy is still proscribed, whether for same-sex or heterosexual conduct, there is a pattern of nonenforcement with respect to consenting adults acting in private. The State of Texas admitted in 1994 that as of that date it had not prosecuted anyone under those circumstances. *State v. Morales*, 869 S.W.2d 941, 943.

Two principal cases decided after *Bowers* cast its holding into even more doubt. In *Planned Parenthood of Southeastern Pa. v. Casey*, 505 U.S. 833 (1992), the Court reaffirmed the substantive force of the liberty protected by the Due Process Clause. The *Casey* decision again confirmed that our laws and tradition afford constitutional protection to personal decisions relating to marriage, procreation, contraception, family relationships, child rearing, and education. In explaining the respect the Constitution demands for the autonomy of the person in making these choices, we stated as follows:

> These matters, involving the most intimate and personal choices a person may make in a lifetime, choices central to personal dignity and autonomy, are central to the liberty protected by the Fourteenth Amendment. At the heart of liberty is the right to define one's own concept of existence, of meaning, of the universe, and of the mystery of human life. Beliefs about these matters could not define the attributes of personhood were they formed under compulsion of the State.

Persons in a homosexual relationship may seek autonomy for these purposes, just as heterosexual persons do. The decision in *Bowers* would deny them this right.

The second post-*Bowers* case of principal relevance is *Romer v. Evans*, 517 U.S. 620 (1996). There the Court struck down class-based legislation directed at homosexuals as a violation of the Equal Protection Clause. * * *

As an alternative argument in this case, counsel for the petitioners and some *amici* contend that *Romer* provides the basis for declaring the Texas statute invalid under the Equal Protection Clause. That is a tenable argument, but we conclude the instant case requires us to address whether *Bowers* itself has continuing validity. Were we to hold the statute invalid under the Equal Protection Clause some might question whether a prohibition would be valid if drawn differently, say, to prohibit the conduct both between same-sex and different-sex participants.

Equality of treatment and the due process right to demand respect for conduct protected by the substantive guarantee of liberty are linked in important respects, and a decision on the latter point advances both interests. If protected conduct is made criminal and the law which does so remains unexamined for its substantive validity, its stigma might remain even if it were not enforceable as drawn for equal protection reasons. When homosexual conduct is made criminal by the law of the State, that declaration in and of itself is an invitation to subject homosexual persons to discrimination both in the public and in the private spheres. The central holding of *Bowers* has been brought in question by this case, and it should be addressed. Its continuance as precedent demeans the lives of homosexual persons.

The stigma this criminal statute imposes, moreover, is not trivial. The offense, to be sure, is but a class C misdemeanor, a minor offense in the Texas legal system. Still, it remains a criminal offense with all that imports for the dignity of the persons charged. The petitioners will bear on their record the history of their criminal convictions. . . . We are advised that if Texas convicted an adult for private, consensual homosexual conduct under the statute here in question the convicted person would come within the registration laws of a least four States were he or she to be subject to their jurisdiction. This underscores the consequential nature of the punishment and the state-sponsored condemnation attendant to the criminal prohibition. Furthermore, the Texas criminal conviction carries with it the other collateral consequences always following a conviction, such as notations on job application forms, to mention but one example.

The foundations of *Bowers* have sustained serious erosion from our recent decisions in *Casey* and *Romer*. When our precedent has been thus weakened, criticism from other sources is of greater significance. In the United States criticism of *Bowers* has been substantial and continuing, disapproving of its reasoning in all respects, not just as to its historical assumptions. *See, e.g.*, C. Fried, *Order and Law: Arguing the Reagan Revolution—A Firsthand Account* 81–84 (1991); R. Posner, *Sex and Reason* 341–350 (1992). The courts of five different States have declined to follow it in interpreting provisions in their own state constitutions parallel to the Due Process Clause of the Fourteenth Amendment.

To the extent *Bowers* relied on values we share with a wider civilization, it should be noted that the reasoning and holding in *Bowers* have been rejected elsewhere. The European Court of Human Rights has followed not *Bowers* but its own decision in *Dudgeon v. United Kingdom*. Other nations, too, have taken action consistent with an affirmation of the protected right of homosexual adults to engage in intimate, consensual conduct. The right the petitioners seek in this case has been accepted as an integral part of human freedom in many other countries. There has been no showing that in this country the governmental interest in circumscribing personal choice is somehow more legitimate or urgent.

The doctrine of *stare decisis* is essential to the respect accorded to the judgments of the Court and to the stability of the law. It is not, however, an inexorable command. In *Casey* we noted that when a Court is asked to overrule a precedent recognizing a constitutional liberty interest, individual or societal reliance on the existence of that liberty cautions with particular strength against reversing course. The holding in *Bowers*, however, has not induced detrimental reliance comparable to some instances where recognized individual rights are involved. Indeed, there has been no individual or societal reliance on *Bowers* of the sort that could counsel against overturning its holding once there are compelling reasons to do so. *Bowers* itself causes uncertainty, for the precedents before and after its issuance contradict its central holding.

The rationale of *Bowers* does not withstand careful analysis. In his dissenting opinion in *Bowers*, Justice Stevens came to these conclusions:

> Our prior cases make two propositions abundantly clear. First, the fact that the governing majority in a State has traditionally viewed a particular practice as immoral is not a sufficient reason for upholding a law prohibiting the practice; neither history nor tradition could save a law prohibiting miscegenation from constitutional attack. Second, individual decisions by married persons, concerning the intimacies of their physical relationship, even when not intended to produce offspring, are a form of 'liberty' protected by the Due Process Clause of the Fourteenth Amendment. Moreover, this protection extends to intimate choices by unmarried as well as married persons.

Justice Stevens' analysis, in our view, should have been controlling in *Bowers* and should control here.

Bowers was not correct when it was decided, and it is not correct today. It ought not to remain binding precedent. *Bowers v. Hardwick* should be and now is overruled.

The present case does not involve minors. It does not involve persons who might be injured or coerced or who are situated in relationships where consent might not easily be refused. It does not involve public conduct or prostitution. It does not involve whether the government must give formal recognition to any relationship that homosexual persons seek to enter. The case does involve two adults who, with full and mutual consent from each other, engaged in sexual practices common to a homosexual lifestyle. The petitioners are entitled to respect for their private lives. The State cannot demean their existence or control their destiny by making their private sexual conduct a crime. Their right to liberty under the Due Process Clause gives them the full right to engage in their conduct without intervention of the government. "It is a promise of the Constitution that there is a realm of personal liberty which the government may not enter." *Casey*, 505 U.S. at 47. The Texas statute furthers no legitimate state interest which can justify its intrusion into the personal and private life of the individual.

Had those who drew and ratified the Due Process Clauses of the Fifth Amendment or the Fourteenth Amendment known the components of liberty in its manifold possibilities, they might have been more specific. They did not presume to have this insight. They knew times can blind us to certain truths and later generations can see that laws once thought necessary and proper in fact serve only to oppress. As the Constitution endures, persons in every generation can invoke its principles in their own search for greater freedom.

JUSTICE O'CONNOR, concurring in the judgment.

The Court today overrules *Bowers*. I joined *Bowers*, and do not join the Court in overruling it. Nevertheless, I agree with the Court that Texas' statute banning same-sex sodomy is unconstitutional. Rather than relying on the substantive component of the Fourteenth Amendment's Due Process Clause, I base my conclusion on the Fourteenth Amendment's Equal Protection Clause. * * *

The statute at issue here makes sodomy a crime only if a person "engages in deviate sexual intercourse with another individual of the same sex." Sodomy between opposite-sex partners, however, is not a crime in Texas. That is, Texas treats the same conduct differently based solely on the participants. Those harmed by this law are people who have a same-sex sexual orientation and thus are more likely to engage in behavior prohibited by § 21.06.

The Texas statute makes homosexuals unequal in the eyes of the law by making particular conduct—and only that conduct—subject to criminal sanction. It appears that prosecutions under Texas' sodomy law are rare. This case shows, however, that prosecutions under § 21.06 *do* occur. And while the penalty imposed on petitioners in this case was relatively minor, the consequences of conviction are not. As the Court notes, petitioners' convictions, if upheld, would disqualify them from or restrict their ability to engage in a variety of professions, including medicine, athletic training, and interior design. Indeed, were petitioners to move to one of four States, their convictions would require them to register as sex offenders to local law enforcement.

And the effect of Texas' sodomy law is not just limited to the threat of prosecution or consequence of conviction. Texas' sodomy law brands all homosexuals as criminals, thereby making it more difficult for homosexuals to be treated in the same manner as everyone else. Indeed, Texas itself has previously acknowledged the collateral effects of the law, stipulating in a prior challenge to this action that the law "legally sanctions discrimination against [homosexuals] in a variety of ways unrelated to the criminal law," including in the areas of "employment, family issues, and housing." *State v. Morales*, 826 S.W.2d 201, 203 (Tex. App. 1992).

Texas attempts to justify its law, and the effects of the law, by arguing that the statute satisfies rational basis review because it furthers the legitimate governmental interest of the promotion of morality. In *Bowers*, we held that a state law criminalizing sodomy as applied to homosexual couples did not violate substantive due process. We rejected the argument that no rational basis existed to justify the law, pointing to the government's interest in promoting morality. The only question in front of the Court in *Bowers* was whether the substantive component of the Due Process Clause protected a right to engage in homosexual sodomy. *Bowers* did not hold that moral disapproval of a group is a rational basis under the Equal Protection Clause to criminalize homosexual sodomy when heterosexual sodomy is not punished.

This case raises a different issue than *Bowers*: whether, under the Equal Protection Clause, moral disapproval is a legitimate state interest to justify by itself a statute that bans homosexual sodomy, but not heterosexual sodomy. It is not. Moral disapproval of this group, like a bare desire to harm the group, is an interest that is insufficient to satisfy rational basis review under the Equal Protection Clause. *See, e.g., Department of Agriculture v. Moreno*, 413 U.S. 528, 534 (1973)*; Romer v. Evans*, 517 U.S. 620, 634–35 (1996). Indeed, we have never held that moral disapproval, without any other asserted state interest, is a sufficient rationale under the Equal Protection Clause to justify a law that discriminates among groups of persons.

Moral disapproval of a group cannot be a legitimate governmental interest under the Equal Protection Clause because legal classifications must not be "drawn for the purpose of disadvantaging the group burdened by the law." *Id.* at 633. Texas' invocation of moral disapproval as a legitimate state interest proves nothing more than Texas' desire to criminalize homosexual sodomy. But the Equal Protection Clause prevents a State from creating "a classification of persons undertaken for its own sake." *Id.* at 635. And because Texas so rarely enforces its sodomy law as applied to private, consensual acts, the law serves more as a statement of dislike and disapproval against homosexuals than as a tool to stop criminal behavior. The Texas sodomy law "raises the inevitable inference that the disadvantage imposed is born of animosity toward the class of persons affected." *Id.* at 634.

Texas argues, however, that the sodomy law does not discriminate against homosexual persons. Instead, the State maintains that the law discriminates only against homosexual conduct. While it is true that the law applies only to conduct, the conduct targeted by this law is conduct that is closely correlated with being homosexual. Under such circumstances, Texas' sodomy law is targeted at more than conduct. It is instead directed toward gay persons as a class. After all, there can hardly be more palpable discrimination against a class than making the conduct that defines the class criminal. *Id.* at 641 (Scalia, J. dissenting).

Indeed, Texas law confirms that the sodomy statute is directed toward homosexuals as a class. In Texas, calling a person a homosexual is slander *per se* because the word "homosexual" "imputes the commission of a crime." *Plumley v. Landmark Chevrolet, Inc.*, 122 F.3d 308, 310 (5th Cir. 1997) (applying Texas law). The State has admitted that because of the sodomy law, *being* homosexual carries the presumption of being a criminal. *See State v. Morales*, 826 S.W.2d, at 202–203 ("The statute brands lesbians and gay men as criminals and thereby legally sanctions discrimination against them in a variety of ways unrelated to the criminal law."). Texas' sodomy law therefore results in discrimination against homosexuals as a class in an array of areas outside the criminal law. In *Romer v. Evans*, we refused to sanction a law that singled out homosexuals "for disfavored legal status." The same is true here. The Equal Protection Clause " 'neither knows nor tolerates classes among citizens.' " *Id.*, at 623 (quoting *Plessy v. Ferguson*, 163 U.S. 537, 559 (1896) (Harlan, J. dissenting)).

A State can of course assign certain consequences to a violation of its criminal law. But the State cannot single out one identifiable class of citizens for punishment that does not apply to everyone else, with moral disapproval as the only asserted state interest for the law. The Texas sodomy statute subjects homosexuals to "a lifelong penalty and stigma. A legislative classification that threatens the creation of an underclass . . . cannot be reconciled with" the Equal Protection Clause. *Plyler v. Doe*, 457 U.S. 202, 239 (1982) (Powell, J., concurring).

Whether a sodomy law that is neutral both in effect and application would violate the substantive component of the Due Process Clause is an issue that need not be decided today. I am confident, however, that so long as the Equal Protection Clause requires a sodomy law to apply equally to the private consensual conduct of homosexuals and heterosexuals alike, such a law would not long stand in our democratic society. In the words of Justice Jackson:

> The framers of the Constitution knew, and we should not forget today, that there is no more effective practical guaranty against arbitrary and unreasonable government than to require that the principles of law which officials would impose upon a minority be imposed generally. Conversely, nothing opens the door to arbitrary action so effectively as to allow those officials to pick and choose only a few to whom they will apply legislation and thus to escape the political retribution that might be visited upon them if larger numbers were affected. *Railway Express Agency, Inc. v. New York,* 336 U.S. 106, 112–113 (1949) (concurring opinion).

That this law as applied to private, consensual conduct is unconstitutional under the Equal Protection Clause does not mean that other laws distinguishing between heterosexuals and homosexuals would similarly fail under rational basis review. Texas cannot assert any legitimate state interest here, such as national security or preserving the traditional institution of marriage. Unlike the moral disapproval of same-sex relations—the asserted state interest in this case—other reasons exist to promote the institution of marriage beyond mere moral disapproval of an excluded group.

A law branding one class of persons as criminal solely based on the State's moral disapproval of that class and the conduct associated with that class runs contrary to the values of the Constitution and the Equal Protection Clause, under any standard of review. I therefore concur in the Court's judgment that Texas' sodomy law banning "deviate sexual intercourse" between consenting adults of the same sex, but not between consenting adults of different sexes, is unconstitutional.

JUSTICE SCALIA, with whom the CHIEF JUSTICE and JUSTICE THOMAS join, dissenting.

I begin with the Court's surprising readiness to reconsider a decision rendered a mere 17 years ago in *Bowers v. Hardwick.* * * *

Today's approach to *stare decisis* invites us to overrule an erroneously decided precedent (including an "intensely divisive" decision) if: (1) its foundations have been "eroded" by subsequent decisions; (2) it has been subject to "substantial and continuing" criticism; and (3) it has not induced "individual or societal reliance" that counsels against overturning. The problem is that *Roe* itself—which today's majority surely has no disposition to overrule—satisfies these conditions to at least the same degree as *Bowers.* * * *

"[T]here has been," the Court says, "no individual or societal reliance on *Bowers* of the sort that could counsel against overturning its holding. . . ." It seems to me that the "societal reliance" on the principles confirmed in *Bowers* and discarded today has been overwhelming. Countless judicial decisions and legislative enactments have relied on the ancient proposition that a governing majority's belief that certain sexual behavior is "immoral and unacceptable" constitutes a rational basis for regulation. We ourselves relied extensively on *Bowers* when we concluded, in *Barnes v. Glen Theatre, Inc.*, 501 U.S. 560, 569 (1991), that Indiana's public indecency statute furthered "a substantial government interest in protecting order and morality." State laws against bigamy, same-sex marriage, adult incest, prostitution, masturbation, adultery, fornication, bestiality, and obscenity are likewise sustainable only in light of *Bowers*' validation of laws based on moral choices. Every single one of these laws is called into question by today's decision; the Court makes no effort to cabin the scope of its decision to exclude them from its holding. The impossibility of distinguishing homosexuality from other traditional "morals" offenses is precisely why *Bowers* rejected the rational-basis challenge. * * *

What a massive disruption of the current social order, therefore, the overruling of *Bowers* entails. Not so the overruling of *Roe*, which would simply have restored the regime that existed for centuries before 1973, in which the permissibility of, and restrictions upon, abortion were determined legislatively State-by-State. *Casey*, however, chose to base its *stare decisis* determination on a different "sort" of reliance. "People," it said, "have organized intimate relationships and made choices that define their views of themselves and their places in society, in reliance on the availability of abortion in the event that contraception should fail." 505 U.S., at 856 This falsely assumes that the consequence of overruling *Roe* would have been to make abortion unlawful. It would not; it would merely have *permitted* the States to do so. Many States would unquestionably have declined to prohibit abortion, and others would not have prohibited it within six months (after which the most significant reliance interests would have expired). Even for persons in States other than these, the choice would not have been between abortion and childbirth, but between abortion nearby and abortion in a neighboring State.

To tell the truth, it does not surprise me, and should surprise no one, that the Court has chosen today to revise the standards of *stare decisis* set forth in *Casey*. It has thereby exposed *Casey*'s extraordinary deference to precedent for the result-oriented expedient that it is.

Having decided that it need not adhere to *stare decisis*, the Court still must establish that *Bowers* was wrongly decided and that the Texas statute, as applied to petitioners, is unconstitutional. Texas Penal Code Ann. § 21.06(a) (2003) undoubtedly imposes constraints on liberty. So do laws prohibiting prostitution, recreational use of heroin, and, for that matter, working more than 60 hours per week in a bakery. But there is no right to "liberty" under the Due Process Clause, though today's opinion repeatedly makes that claim. The Fourteenth Amendment *expressly allows* States to deprive their citizens of "liberty," *so long as "due process of law" is provided.* Our opinions applying the doctrine known as "substantive due process" hold that the Due Process Clause prohibits States from infringing *fundamental* liberty interests, unless the infringement is narrowly tailored to serve a compelling state interest. We have held repeatedly, in cases the Court today does not overrule, that *only* fundamental rights qualify for this so-called "heightened scrutiny" protection—that is, rights which are "deeply rooted in this Nation's history and tradition." All other liberty interests may be abridged or abrogated pursuant to a validly enacted state law if that law is rationally related to a legitimate state interest.

Bowers held, first, that criminal prohibitions of homosexual sodomy are not subject to heightened scrutiny because they do not implicate a "fundamental right" under the Due Process Clause. Noting that "[p]roscriptions against that conduct have ancient roots," that "[s]odomy was a criminal offense at common law and was forbidden by the laws of the original 13 States when they ratified the Bill of Rights," and that many States had retained their bans on sodomy, *Bowers* concluded that a right to engage in homosexual sodomy was not "deeply rooted in this Nation's history and tradition."

The Court today does not overrule this holding. Not once does it describe homosexual sodomy as a "fundamental right" or a "fundamental liberty interest," nor does it subject the Texas statute to strict scrutiny. Instead, having failed to establish that the right to homosexual sodomy is "deeply rooted in this Nation's history and tradition," the Court concludes that the application of Texas's statute to petitioners' conduct fails the rational-basis test, and overrules *Bowers'* holding to the contrary. * * *

After discussing the history of antisodomy laws, the Court proclaims that, "it should be noted that there is no longstanding history in this country of laws directed at homosexual conduct as a distinct matter." This observation in no way casts into doubt the "definitive [historical] conclusion," on which *Bowers* relied: that our Nation has a longstanding history of laws prohibiting *sodomy in general*—regardless of whether it was performed by same-sex or opposite-sex couples. * * *

It is (as *Bowers* recognized) entirely irrelevant whether the laws in our long national tradition criminalizing homosexual sodomy were "directed at homosexual conduct as a distinct matter." Whether homosexual sodomy was prohibited by a law targeted at same-sex sexual relations or by a more general law prohibiting both homosexual and heterosexual sodomy, the only relevant point is that it *was* criminalized—which suffices to establish that homosexual sodomy is not a right "deeply rooted in our Nation's history and tradition." The Court today agrees that homosexual sodomy was criminalized and thus does not dispute the facts on which *Bowers actually* relied.

Next the Court makes the claim, again unsupported by any citations, that "[l]aws prohibiting sodomy do not seem to have been enforced against consenting adults acting in private." The key qualifier here is "acting in private"—since the Court admits that sodomy laws *were* enforced against consenting adults (although the Court contends that prosecutions were "infrequent"). I do not know what "acting in private" means; surely consensual sodomy, like heterosexual intercourse, is rarely performed on stage. If all the Court means by "acting in private" is "on private premises, with the doors closed and windows covered," it is entirely unsurprising that evidence of enforcement would be hard to come by. (Imagine the circumstances that would enable a search warrant to be obtained for a residence on the ground that there was probable cause to believe that consensual sodomy was then and there occurring.) Surely that lack of evidence would not sustain the proposition that consensual sodomy on private premises with the doors closed and windows covered was regarded as a "fundamental right," even though all other consensual sodomy was criminalized. There are 203 prosecutions for consensual, adult homosexual sodomy reported in the West Reporting system and official state reporters from the years 1880–1995. *See* W. Eskridge, *Gaylaw: Challenging the Apartheid of the Closet* 375 (1999) (hereinafter *Gaylaw*). There are also records of 20 sodomy prosecutions and 4 executions during the colonial period. J. Katz, *Gay/Lesbian Almanac* 29, 58, 663 (1983). *Bowers'* conclusion that homosexual sodomy is not a fundamental right "deeply rooted in this Nation's history and tradition" is utterly unassailable.

Realizing that fact, the Court instead says: "[W]e think that our laws and traditions in the past half century are of most relevance here. These references show *an emerging awareness* that liberty gives substantial protection to adult persons in deciding how to conduct their private lives *in matters pertaining to sex.*" Apart from the fact that such an "emerging awareness" does not establish a "fundamental right," the statement is factually false. States continue to prosecute all sorts of crimes by adults "in matters pertaining to sex": prostitution, adult incest, adultery, obscenity, and child pornography. Sodomy laws, too, have been enforced "in the past half century," in which there have been 134 reported cases involving prosecutions for consensual, adult, homosexual sodomy. *Gaylaw* at 375. In relying, for evidence of an "emerging recognition," upon the American Law Institute's 1955 recommendation not to criminalize " 'consensual sexual relations conducted in private,' " the Court ignores the fact that this recommendation was "a point of resistance in most of the states that considered adopting the Model Penal Code." *Gaylaw* at 159.

In any event, an "emerging awareness" is by definition not "deeply rooted in this Nation's history and tradition[s]," as we have said "fundamental right" status requires. Constitutional entitlements do not spring into existence because some States choose to lessen or eliminate criminal sanctions on certain behavior. Much less do they spring into existence, as the Court seems to believe, because *foreign nations* decriminalize conduct. The *Bowers* majority opinion *never* relied on "values we share with a wider civilization," but rather rejected the claimed right to sodomy on the ground that such a right was not "deeply rooted in *this Nation's* history and tradition." *Bowers'* rational-basis holding is likewise devoid of any reliance on the views of a "wider civilization." The Court's discussion of these foreign views (ignoring, of course, the many countries that have retained criminal prohibitions on sodomy) is therefore meaningless dicta. Dangerous dicta, however, since "this Court . . . should not impose foreign moods, fads, or fashions on Americans." *Foster v. Florida*, 537 U.S. 990 (2002) (Thomas, J., concurring in denial of certiorari).

I turn now to the ground on which the Court squarely rests its holding: the contention that there is no rational basis for the law here under attack. This proposition is so out of accord with our jurisprudence—indeed, with the jurisprudence of *any* society we know— that it requires little discussion.

The Texas statute undeniably seeks to further the belief of its citizens that certain forms of sexual behavior are "immoral and unacceptable"—the same interest furthered by criminal laws against fornication, bigamy, adultery, adult incest, bestiality, and obscenity. *Bowers* held that this *was* a legitimate state interest. The Court today reaches the opposite conclusion. . . . This effectively decrees the end of all morals legislation. If, as the Court asserts, the promotion of majoritarian sexual morality is not even a *legitimate* state interest, none of the above-mentioned laws can survive rational-basis review.

Finally, I turn to petitioners' equal-protection challenge, which no Member of the Court save Justice O'Connor embraces. * * *

No purpose to discriminate against men or women as a class can be gleaned from the Texas law, so rational-basis review applies. That review is readily satisfied here by the same rational basis that satisfied it in *Bowers*—society's belief that certain forms of sexual behavior are "immoral and unacceptable." This is the same justification that supports many other laws regulating sexual behavior that make a distinction based upon the identity of the partner—for example, laws against adultery, fornication, and adult incest, and laws refusing to recognize homosexual marriage. * * *

Even if the Texas law *does* deny equal protection to "homosexuals as a class," that denial *still* does not need to be justified by anything more than a rational basis, which our cases show is satisfied by the enforcement of traditional notions of sexual morality.

* * * [Justice O'Connor's] reasoning leaves on pretty shaky grounds state laws limiting marriage to opposite-sex couples. Justice O'Connor seeks to preserve them by the conclusory statement that "preserving the traditional institution of marriage" is a legitimate state interest. But "preserving the traditional institution of marriage" is just a kinder way of describing the State's *moral disapproval* of same-sex couples. Texas's interest in § 21.06 could be recast in similarly euphemistic terms: "preserving the traditional sexual mores of our society." In the jurisprudence Justice O'Connor has seemingly created, judges can

validate laws by characterizing them as "preserving the traditions of society" (good); or invalidate them by characterizing them as "expressing moral disapproval" (bad).

Today's opinion is the product of a Court, which is the product of a law-profession culture, that has largely signed on to the so-called homosexual agenda, by which I mean the agenda promoted by some homosexual activists directed at eliminating the moral opprobrium that has traditionally attached to homosexual conduct. I noted in an earlier opinion the fact that the American Association of Law Schools (to which any reputable law school *must* seek to belong) excludes from membership any school that refuses to ban from its job-interview facilities a law firm (no matter how small) that does not wish to hire as a prospective partner a person who openly engages in homosexual conduct. See *Romer, supra,* at 653, 116 S. Ct. 1620.

One of the most revealing statements in today's opinion is the Court's grim warning that the criminalization of homosexual conduct is "an invitation to subject homosexual persons to discrimination both in the public and in the private spheres." It is clear from this that the Court has taken sides in the culture war, departing from its role of assuring, as neutral observer, that the democratic rules of engagement are observed. Many Americans do not want persons who openly engage in homosexual conduct as partners in their business, as scoutmasters for their children, as teachers in their children's schools, or as boarders in their home. They view this as protecting themselves and their families from a lifestyle that they believe to be immoral and destructive. The Court views it as "discrimination" which it is the function of our judgments to deter. So imbued is the Court with the law profession's anti-anti-homosexual culture, that it is seemingly unaware that the attitudes of that culture are not obviously "mainstream"; that in most States what the Court calls "discrimination" against those who engage in homosexual acts is perfectly legal; that proposals to ban such "discrimination" under Title VII have repeatedly been rejected by Congress, see Employment Non-Discrimination Act of 1994, S. 2238, 103d Cong., 2d Sess. (1994); Civil Rights Amendments, H.R. 5452, 94th Cong., 1st Sess. (1975); that in some cases such "discrimination" is *mandated* by federal statute, see 10 U.S.C. § 654(b)(1) (mandating discharge from the Armed Forces of any service member who engages in or intends to engage in homosexual acts); and that in some cases such "discrimination" is a constitutional right, *see Boy Scouts of America v. Dale*, 530 U.S. 640, 120 S. Ct. 2446, 147 L. Ed. 2d 554 (2000).

Let me be clear that I have nothing against homosexuals, or any other group, promoting their agenda through normal democratic means. Social perceptions of sexual and other morality change over time, and every group has the right to persuade its fellow citizens that its view of such matters is the best. That homosexuals have achieved some success in that enterprise is attested to by the fact that Texas is one of the few remaining States that criminalize private, consensual homosexual acts. But persuading one's fellow citizens is one thing, and imposing one's views in absence of democratic majority will is something else. I would no more *require* a State to criminalize homosexual acts—or, for that matter, display *any* moral disapprobation of them—than I would *forbid* it to do so. What Texas has chosen to do is well within the range of traditional democratic action, and its hand should not be stayed through the invention of a brand-new "constitutional right" by a Court that is impatient of democratic change. It is indeed true that "later generations can see that laws once thought necessary and proper in fact serve only to oppress;" and when that happens, later generations can repeal those laws. But it is the premise of our system that those judgments are to be made by the people, and not imposed by a governing caste that knows best. * * *

At the end of its opinion—after having laid waste the foundations of our rational-basis jurisprudence—the Court says that the present case "does not involve whether the government must give formal recognition to any relationship that homosexual persons seek to enter." Do not believe it. . . . Today's opinion dismantles the structure of constitutional law that has permitted a distinction to be made between heterosexual and homosexual unions, insofar as formal recognition in marriage is concerned. If moral disapprobation of homosexual conduct is "no legitimate state interest" for purposes of proscribing that conduct, and if, as the Court coos (casting aside all pretense of neutrality), "[w]hen sexuality finds overt expression in intimate conduct with another person, the conduct can be but one element in a personal bond that is more enduring," what justification could there possibly be for denying the benefits of marriage to homosexual couples exercising "[t]he liberty protected by the Constitution"? Surely not the encouragement of procreation, since the sterile and the elderly are allowed to marry. This case "does not involve" the issue of homosexual marriage only if one entertains the belief that principle and logic have nothing to do with the decisions of this Court. Many will hope that, as the Court comfortingly assures us, this is so.

The matters appropriate for this Court's resolution are only three: Texas's prohibition of sodomy neither infringes a "fundamental right" (which the Court does not dispute), nor is unsupported by a rational relation to what the Constitution considers a legitimate state interest, nor denies the equal protection of the laws. I dissent.

JUSTICE THOMAS, dissenting.

I join Justice Scalia's dissenting opinion. I write separately to note that the law before the Court today "is . . . uncommonly silly." *Griswold*, 381 U.S. at 527 (Stewart, J., dissenting). If I were a member of the Texas Legislature, I would vote to repeal it. Punishing someone for expressing his sexual preference through noncommercial consensual conduct with another adult does not appear to be a worthy way to expend valuable law enforcement resources.

Notwithstanding this, I recognize that as a member of this Court I am not empowered to help petitioners and others similarly situated. My duty, rather, is to "decide cases 'agreeably to the Constitution and laws of the United States.'" *Id.* at 530. And, just like Justice Stewart, I "can find [neither in the Bill of Rights nor any other part of the Constitution a] general right of privacy," or as the Court terms it today, the "liberty of the person both in its spatial and more transcendent dimensions."

Professor Dale Carpenter has sought to determine exactly what happened on the night that Lawrence and Garner were arrested. The former was a fifty-five year old white man who worked as a laboratory technician at a Houston hospital. Garner was a thirty-one year old black man who had worked as a cook and a waiter.[27] The two men were introduced by Robert Eubanks, a former roommate of Lawrence who had previously dated Garner. "After Eubanks introduced them in the mid-1990s, Lawrence and Garner never became much more than acquaintances."[28]

On the evening of the arrest, the three men spent several hours in Lawrence's apartment. At some point, Eubanks became upset with the other two men and left the apartment to call the police to report falsely that there was a man with a gun in Lawrence's apartment.

The following version of what happened next is based largely on Professor Carpenter's interviews with the arresting officers:

> Eubanks waited for the deputies at the bottom of the stairs leading to Lawrence's apartment. He didn't have to wait long. Deputy Joseph Quinn was on patrol nearby and arrived within minutes of the call. Quinn was the first deputy on the scene, followed shortly thereafter by deputies William D. Lilly, Donald Tipps, and Kenneth Landry. According to standard procedure, Quinn took the lead on the scene because he was the first deputy to arrive. The deputies, weapons drawn, began looking for the

---

[27] DALE CARPENTER, FLAGRANT CONDUCT: THE STORY OF *LAWRENCE V. TEXAS*: HOW A BEDROOM ARREST DECRIMINALIZED GAY AMERICANS 43–44 (2012).

[28] *Id.* at 45.

man who had called in the report and for the apartment containing the armed suspect. Eubanks saw the deputies and motioned toward them, saying, "Over here! Over here!" The deputies could tell that Eubanks was upset because he was visibly shaking and crying. Quinn asked, "Where is the man with the gun?" Eubanks pointed up the stairs toward Lawrence's apartment, saying, "He is in that apartment up there and he has a gun."

Quinn, Lilly, Tipps and Landry headed up the stairwell in what is known as a "tactical stack," one deputy right behind the other, with Quinn at the front of the stack. When they reached the apartment Quinn saw that the door was mostly closed, but not pulled completely shut. It was resting against the door jam, slightly ajar, as Eubanks had left it. Quinn could not see into the apartment. He turned the door knob and determined it was unlocked. Quinn knocked on the door, which pushed it open slightly and allowed him to get a peek inside. The light was on but no sound could be heard. Seeing no armed suspect or other person, Quinn pushed the door wide open into a standard living room. Still no one could be seen inside. Announcing "Sheriff's Department! Sheriff's Department!" in a loud voice, Quinn and the deputies quickly entered the apartment. * * *

Guns still drawn, Quinn and Lilly moved toward Lawrence's bedroom. Lilly took the lead in approaching the bedroom, with Quinn right behind him. With the aid of the lights from other rooms Lilly made out the moving shapes of two nude men in the bedroom. Startled at the sight, he jumped back. Quinn, who had not yet seen the naked men, guessed that Lilly must have seen the reported gunman. In a crouched position, Quinn came around low on Lilly's right side with his gun pointed ahead. The deputies entered the room, with their fingers on the triggers of their guns, ready to fire. Lilly turned the bedroom light on and the two deputies saw Lawrence and Garner standing there in the nude, shocked looks on their faces. Quinn shouted at the men, "Let me see your hands!" Lawrence and Garner complied, raising their hands.

Hearing this, Tipps and Landry immediately came to see what was happening. The deputies ordered the men to put on their underwear, handcuffed them, and led them into the living room where they sat the . . . men down to figure out what was going on. Lawrence, genuinely upset and bewildered at the deputies' intrusion into his home, asked, "What the fuck are y'all doing here? You don't have any right to be here." Quinn replied that they had every right to enter the apartment under the circumstances.

A deputy fetched Eubanks and brought him up to the apartment. The deputies quickly determined Eubanks had lied about an armed black man because he was jealous of the attention Lawrence and Garner were paying to each other. At one point Eubanks became so angry he stood up, shouted at Garner, and had to be forced to sit back down. When the deputies learned the report had been false, their frustration and anger grew. From their perspective, the prank could easily have resulted in a fatal shooting.

"Do you realize that not once but twice we called out?" Quinn told the men. "You were close to being shot." Lawrence remained angry, calling the deputies "gestapo" and "storm troopers" and "jack-booted thugs."

As the deputies looked around the apartment, they found stacks of gay pornography and explicit images hanging as art on the walls. "The apartment was loaded with pornography," says Quinn. "Everywhere you looked there was some kind." In particular, the deputies noticed "two pencil sketchings of James Dean, naked with an extremely oversized penis on him." The sketches "were hung up like regular pictures," says Quinn. Quinn and Tipps laughed about the Dean etchings, joking, "This is the kind of thing I would have in my house!"

Tipps asked Quinn, "Did you see anyone with a gun?" Quinn, angry about the false report, shocked at seeing two nude men in a bedroom together, offended by the gay pornographic images in the apartment, and frustrated with Lawrence for being uncooperative and name-calling the deputies, glanced at Lilly and made a split-second decision to charge them with homosexual conduct, which Quinn knew was a crime in Texas. "No," he replied. "But you ain't gonna believe this. Those guys were having sex." "Really?" asked Tipps, incredulous. "Yep," responded Quinn, "we caught 'em in the act." Quinn figured he would teach Lawrence and Garner a lesson not to disrespect law enforcement authorities. He also had nothing to lose in citing them. They were obviously not rich or important men. They would probably just pay their fines and move on. Lilly remained quiet, figuring this was Quinn's show, that he (Lilly) would not be filing the charges, and that Lawrence and Garner had probably been having sex at some point anyway. With the men caught naked and now sitting there in their underwear, Tipps and Landry had no reason to doubt Quinn's word.

Lawrence accused the deputies of "harassing" them because they were gay. Quinn responded: "I don't know you. And I don't know your sexual orientation. So how can I be harassing you because you're homosexual other than that I caught you in the act?" Lawrence and Garner understood that they were being charged with "homosexual conduct" which, for all they knew, included any gay sexual activity.

By now, several other deputies had arrived, including Sgt. Kenneth O. Adams. Quinn discussed with Adams what to do about Lawrence and Garner. Because Homosexual Conduct was a Class C misdemeanor (like a traffic ticket), punishable in Texas by fine but not prison, Quinn knew that the deputies had the option to issue no citation, or to issue a citation without actually taking the men to jail. But Quinn recommended that the men not only be charged with violating the Homosexual Conduct law but also be taken to prison. "I think the totality of the circumstances where I think there's a guy with a gun and I almost have to shoot, that it warranted me giving them a citation" and taking them to jail, Quinn says. "It was a lovers' triangle that could have got somebody hurt. I could have killed these guys over having sex. They were stupid enough to let it go that far."

Adams agreed with Quinn and it was decided to call the assistant D.A. on duty (in Harris County, Texas, there is a D.A. available twenty-four-hours a day, offering legal counsel to the deputies in the field) to get approval for the citation and arrest. The D.A. on duty was Ira Jones. Quinn told Jones that he had seen Lawrence and Garner having anal sex and then asked Jones if it mattered, under the Homosexual Conduct law, whether the conduct occurred in a home or in a public place. Jones looked at the statute and confirmed it did not matter where the offense occurred.

Eubanks was charged with filing a false report, a more serious Class B misdemeanor. He later served more than two weeks in prison for it. . . .

Enraged by the deputies' intrusion into his home, their behavior, and the charge, Lawrence engaged in his own form of civil disobedience. He refused to put on more than his underwear for his trip to jail. He demanded to see a lawyer. He also refused to walk out of his home and was physically carried by the deputies down the stairs, in his underwear, to a patrol car. Lawrence's legs dragged on the ground as the deputies carried him down the stairs, resulting in minor cuts and bruises. Quinn says that Lawrence could have been cited for resisting transport while under arrest. But Quinn did not cite him because Lawrence "was doing all this to entice me to do something that could show I hated homosexuals."

As the deputies prepared to leave the scene, Quinn advised them to wash their hands. "You have to wonder," says Quinn, " 'What have we touched? Have we come into contact with any fluids?' " Quinn recalls that, "I made sure I doused myself with sanitizer" that he kept handy in his patrol car.

Lawrence, Garner, and Eubanks were led away to the station in separate patrol cars. Eubanks rode with Quinn. Once they arrived at the station, Lawrence continued to be angry and uncooperative throughout the standard intake procedures. By contrast, Garner was quiet and cooperative. Garner had had enough prior experience with the police to know better than to provoke them. Lawrence and Garner were given orange prisoners' jump-suits and spent the night in jail.

The next evening, September 18, Lawrence and Garner appeared before a hearing officer and pleaded "Not guilty." Lawrence requested a trial by jury; Garner, a trial by judge. They were released on personal recognizance, with bond set at $200, the maximum fine allowed for violating the state sodomy law.[29]

Professor Carpenter reports that, for many years, Lawrence and Garner's attorneys advised them not to talk about whether they actually had been having sex when the police stormed into the apartment. Carpenter notes, however, that there were reasons to believe that Lawrence and Garner may not have had sex on that evening. Although the lawyers claimed that they wanted to protect the men's privacy, Carpenter suggests that the attorneys instead may have wanted to prevent "the disclosure of information—the likelihood that sex had not occurred—that they believed would be unhelpful to the case and larger cause."[30]

In any event, the attorneys eventually relented when Lawrence, several years after the Supreme Court's ruling, insisted that he wanted to set the record straight so that "the police were not allowed to get away with their tall tale of seeing uncontrollable gay sex."[31] (Garner, who died in 2006, abided by his lawyers' recommendation that he not discuss

---

[29] Dale Carpenter, The Unknown Past of *Lawrence v. Texas*, 102 MICH. L. REV. 1464, 1508–13 (2004).

[30] DALE CARPENTER, FLAGRANT CONDUCT: THE STORY OF *LAWRENCE V. TEXAS*: HOW A BEDROOM ARREST DECRIMINALIZED GAY AMERICANS 70 (2012).

[31] *Id.*

whether the two men had been sexually intimate on the night of their arrest.)

In 2011, Lawrence told Professor Carpenter that Garner and he were watching the late-evening news on television in his living room when the police burst in demanding to know the gun's whereabouts. " 'There was no sex,' insisted Lawrence. . . . In fact, he said, Garner and he were not physically touching one another, and were seated as much as fifteen feet apart."[32] Although Lawrence acknowledged that he sometimes flirted with Garner, the two "had never before or since had sex. The police invented the story, he declared. 'They told bald-faced lies.' "[33]

NOTES

1. *Rational Basis v. Heightened Scrutiny.* One of the intriguing, and perhaps frustrating, aspects of *Lawrence* is that much of the Court's lofty language about liberty, when coupled with its use of precedents (such as *Griswold* and *Roe*), makes the opinion sound like a fundamental rights case. The Court, however, did not apply heightened scrutiny. Instead, it assessed the state's interest in enacting the sodomy statute under the rational basis test. *See Lawrence*, 539 U.S. at 578, 123 S.Ct. at 2484. It may be that the Court believed that the state's interest in support of the law was so weak that it could not withstand constitutional scrutiny even under the most deferential form of judicial review, making it unnecessary for it to hold explicitly that a fundamental right was at issue in the case. Or, alternatively, it may be that the Court was unwilling to state explicitly what it seemed to believe implicitly given the rhetoric of the opinion, namely, that it would be skeptical of any purported justification for a law that so significantly compromised the liberty of individuals and the dignity of their relationships. Either way, Justice Scalia in his dissent was quick to deem *Lawrence* a non-fundamental rights case, *see id.* at 594, 123 S. Ct. at 2492 (Scalia, J., dissenting). We will return to the crucial issue of what level of judicial scrutiny is required by *Lawrence* in *infra* Section III.F.

2. *Liberty v. Privacy.* Although the *Lawrence* Court on a few occasions noted the "private" nature of the conduct in question, it relied very little on a right to privacy as such in its interpretation of the Fourteenth Amendment. In this way, *Lawrence* is a departure from the Court's opinions in *Griswold*, *Eisenstadt*, and *Roe* (as well as from Justice Blackmun's dissent in *Hardwick*), all of which relied heavily on a right to privacy in their reasoning. Rather than emphasizing "privacy," the *Lawrence* Court elaborated on the meaning of "liberty," perhaps giving the opinion greater constitutional legitimacy since that is the word used in the Fourteenth Amendment. It remains to be seen whether *Lawrence* represents the beginning of a shift away from the right to privacy in the Court's substantive due process

---

[32] *Id.* at 71.

[33] *Id.*

jurisprudence, or, alternatively, whether the Court in future cases goes back to using privacy as the normative foundation for that jurisprudence.

3. *Due Process vs. Equal Protection.* Justice Kennedy reasoned that it was preferable to decide *Lawrence* on due process grounds because such a decision would address the very authority of the State to enact sodomy laws. To decide the case on equal protection grounds, Justice Kennedy noted, might simply lead the State to enact a broader sodomy law. *See Lawrence*, 539 U.S. at 574–75, 123 S.Ct. at 2481–81, 156 L.Ed.2d at 523. Justice Kennedy, however, reasoned that equal treatment and due process are "linked in important respects, and a decision on the latter point advances both interests." *Id.* at 575, 123 S. Ct. at 2482, 156 L. Ed. 2d at 523. He then proceeded to elaborate at some length on the equality implications of sodomy laws by noting how they can be used to justify both private and public discrimination against lesbians and gay men. *See id.*

Justice O'Connor, who did not wish to overrule *Hardwick*, concluded in her concurring opinion that the sodomy law represented a form of impermissible moral disapproval of lesbians and gay men as a group, and as such, violated the Equal Protection Clause. *See id.* at 582–83, 123 S. Ct. at 2486–87, 156 L. Ed. 2d at 528–29 (O'Connor, J., concurring). Her willingness to leave *Hardwick* in place leads to the question of why moral disapproval is a sufficient justification for a law to pass constitutional muster under the Due Process Clause but not under the Equal Protection Clause.

4. *Sodomy vs. Same-Sex Marriage Part I.* Justice Kennedy distinguished between sodomy laws and bans on same-sex marriage when he noted that the case did "not involve [the question of] whether the government must give formal recognition to any relationships that homosexual persons seek to enter." *Lawrence*, 539 U.S. at 578, 123 S.Ct. at 2484, 156 L.Ed.2d at 525. Justice O'Connor went further by suggesting that while sodomy laws are unconstitutional, same-sex marriage bans are not because "unlike the moral disapproval of same-sex relations—the asserted state interest in this case— other reasons exist to promote the institution of marriage beyond mere moral disapproval of an excluded group." *Id.* at 585, 123 S. Ct. at 2488, 156 L. Ed. 2d at 530 (O'Connor, J., concurring). Justice Scalia, on the other hand, concluded that once sodomy statutes fall, so must the marriage bans. *See id.* at 604–05, 123 S. Ct. at 2498, 156 L. Ed. 2d at 542–43 (Scalia, J., dissenting).

Five months after *Lawrence*, the Massachusetts Supreme Judicial Court struck down that state's same-sex marriage ban in *Goodridge v. Department of Public Health*, 798 N.E.2d 941, 440 Mass. 309 (2003) (discussed below, Chapter 6, Section II). While the *Goodridge* court based its holding on state rather than federal constitutional grounds, it seems to have been influenced by *Lawrence*. The Massachusetts court, for example, noted that the *Lawrence* "Court affirmed that the core concept of common human dignity protected by the Fourteenth Amendment to the United States Constitution precludes government intrusion into the deeply personal realms of consensual adult expressions of intimacy and one's choice of an intimate partner. The Court also reaffirmed the central role that decisions whether to marry or have children bear in shaping one's identity." *Id.* at 948, 440 Mass. at 313.

Other courts, however, have concluded that there is no connection between the State's constitutional inability to criminalize same-sex sexual conduct and its ability to prohibit same-sex marriage. This is what the New York Court of Appeals concluded in *Hernandez v. Robles*, 855 N.E.2d 1, 7 N.Y.3d 338, 821 N.Y.S.2d 770 (2006) (discussed below Chapter 6, Section II). The *Hernandez* court explained that the "[p]laintiffs here do not, as the petitioners in *Lawrence* did, seek protection against state intrusion on intimate, private activity. They seek from the courts access to a state-conferred benefit that the Legislature has rationally limited to opposite-sex couples. We conclude that, by defining marriage as it has, the New York Legislature has not restricted the exercise of a fundamental right." 855 N.E.2d at 10, 7 N.Y.3d at 363, 821 N.Y.S.2d at 779. *See also Standhardt v. Superior Court*, 77 P.3d 451, 457, 206 Ariz. 276, 282 (2003) ("[w]e view [*Lawrence*] as acknowledging a homosexual person's right to define his or her own existence, and achieve the type of individual fulfillment that is a hallmark of a free society, by entering into a homosexual relationship. We do not view [*Lawrence*] as stating that such a right includes the choice to enter a state-sanctioned, same-sex marriage.").

5.   *Sodomy vs. Same-Sex Marriage Part II.* Although Justice Kennedy in *Lawrence* claimed that the case had nothing to do with marriage, he twice turned to its reasoning, a decade later, in writing the majority opinion striking down the federal Defense of Marriage Act. *See United States v. Windsor*, ___ U.S. ___, 133 S.Ct. 2675 (2013). First, Kennedy noted that "the States' interest in defining and regulating the marital relation . . . stems from the understanding that marriage is more than a routine classification for purposes of certain statutory benefits. Private, consensual sexual intimacy between two adult persons of the same sex may not be punished by the State, and it can form 'but one element in a personal bond that is more enduring.' "*Id.* at 2692 (citing *Lawrence*, 539 U.S. at 567). By recognizing same-sex relationships as marital, Kennedy explained, some states had chosen to "give further protection and dignity to that bond." *Id.*

Second, Kennedy turned to *Lawrence* to explain how the Defense of Marriage Act demeaned the marital relationships of same-sex couples: "DOMA undermines both the public and private significance of state-sanctioned same-sex marriages; for it tells those couples, and all the world, that their otherwise valid marriages are unworthy of federal recognition. This places same-sex couples in an unstable position of being in a second-tier marriage. The differentiation demeans the couple, whose moral and sexual choices the Constitution protects, see *Lawrence,* 539 U.S. 558, 123 S.Ct. 2472, and whose relationship the State has sought to dignify." *Windsor*, 133 S.Ct. at 2694. For a detailed exploration of *Windsor*, see *infra* Chapter 6, Section II.D.3.

Does Kennedy's reliance on *Lawrence* in *Windsor* suggest that Justice Scalia was correct when he complained that the majority in *Lawrence* was not being entirely forthright when it claimed that the sodomy ruling had nothing to do with the question of which intimate relationships the state should recognize as marital? *See Lawrence*, 539 U.S. at 605 ("This case 'does not involve' the issue of homosexual marriage only if one entertains the belief that principle and logic have nothing to do with the decisions of this Court.") (Scalia, J., dissenting).

6. *How Would You Vote and Rule?* Consider the activities listed in the first column and then decide whether you would, first, as a legislator vote to criminalize the activity; and, second, as a judge find that *Lawrence* prohibits a state from criminalizing the activity.

	If you were a legislator, would you vote in favor of a law that would criminalize this conduct?	If you were a judge, would *Lawrence* allow you to strike down a law that criminalizes this conduct?
S & M sexual relations in private whereby a 35 year old woman lightly whips a 33 year old man		
S & M sexual relations in private whereby a 35 year old woman badly beats a 33 year old man		
Consensual sexual relations in private between a 35 year old woman and her 33 year old brother		
Consensual sexual relations in private between a 35 year old woman and her 55 year old father		
Consensual sexual relations in private between a 35 year old woman and a 16 year old boy or girl		
A marriage of one man and three women		
A marriage of eight men to one another		
Sexual relations between an unmarried woman and an unmarried man (fornication)		

Sexual relations between a married woman and a man to whom she is not married (adultery)		
Sexual relations between a 35 year old woman and another woman she pays to have sex with her (prostitution)		

E. POST-*LAWRENCE* SCHOLARSHIP

The Supreme Court's opinion in *Lawrence* has already produced an extensive body of academic commentary. We provide excerpts from three of those articles below. In the first excerpt, Katherine Franke criticizes *Lawrence* for "domesticating" sexual liberty, that is, for valuing sexual intimacy as an expression of liberty only when it takes place from within ongoing relationships. The second excerpt, by Nelson Lund and John McGinnis, is a frontal attack on what they call the "ad hoc" due process approach of the *Lawrence* opinion. Finally, Laurence Tribe, in the final excerpt, praises the Court for grounding its due process analysis in considerations of equal dignity, and for moving away from a focus on distinct activities (such as particular sexual acts) and toward a more holistic and comprehensive understanding of liberty.

THE DOMESTICATED LIBERTY OF *LAWRENCE V. TEXAS**
Katherine M. Franke

In this commentary I provide a critical reading of both the *Lawrence* opinion and the gay community's response to it. I argue that in *Lawrence* the Court relies on a narrow version of liberty that is both geographized and domesticated—not a robust conception of sexual freedom or liberty, as is commonly assumed. In this way, *Lawrence* both echoes and reinforces a pull toward domesticity in current gay and lesbian organizing. * * *

Justice Kennedy in *Lawrence* takes it as given that the sex between John Lawrence and Tyron Garner took place within the context of a relationship. With respect to the right to make decisions about intimate affiliations in private settings, Justice Kennedy notes that "[p]ersons in a homosexual relationship may seek autonomy for these purposes, just as heterosexual persons do," and that the statutes at issue in *Lawrence* and in *Bowers* "seek to control a personal relationship that, whether or not entitled to formal recognition in the law, is within the liberty of persons to choose without being punished as criminals." Note that the analogy here

---

*   Katherine M. Franke, *The Domesticated Liberty of* Lawrence v. Texas, 104 COLUM. L. REV. 1399, 1400, 1407–16 (2004).

is between persons in a homosexual *relationship* and heterosexual persons. Thus, the issue in *Lawrence*, as well as in *Bowers*, was not the right to engage in certain sexual conduct—that, says Kennedy, would be demeaning to John Lawrence and Tyron Garner. *They* would be disgraced just as a *married couple* would be if the claim were made that "marriage is simply about the right to have sexual intercourse." Kennedy writes that "[sexual conduct] can be but one element in a personal bond that is more enduring." More enduring than what? Than sex?

In two paragraphs, Justice Kennedy does a thorough job of domesticating John Lawrence and Tyron Garner—Lawrence an older white man, Garner a younger black man, who for all we know from the opinion, might have just been tricking with each other. Did they even know each other's name at the point police entered Lawrence's apartment? Did they plan on seeing each other again? None of these facts is in the record, none of the briefing in the case indicated that they were in a relationship. Nevertheless, the Court took it as given that Lawrence and Garner were in a relationship, and the fact of that relationship does important normative work in the opinion. Remember, sex is but one element in a personal bond that is more enduring.

Just as the Court's earlier *Bowers* decision and the military's "don't ask, don't tell" policy overdetermined gay men and lesbians in sexual terms, we now celebrate a victory that at its heart underdetermines, if not writes out entirely, their sexuality. Previously, when courts considered the legal status of gay men, they approached the specter of homosexual sex with a horror ordinarily reserved for incest cases. Now gay men are portrayed as domesticated creatures, settling down into marital-like relationships in which they can both cultivate and nurture desires for exclusivity, fidelity, and longevity in place of other more explicitly erotic desires. "The instant case involves liberty of the person both in its spatial and more transcendent dimensions," writes Justice Kennedy. We come to learn later in the opinion that by "spatial" he means private, and by "transcendent" he means to refer to relationship-based intimacy. The price of the victory in *Lawrence* has been to trade sexuality for domesticity—a high price indeed, and a difficult spot from which to build a politics of sexuality. * * *

[D]ecriminalization merely disables a form of public regulation of private adult activity. Indeed, it neither sanctions nor suggests any alternative form of legitimization. So too, it does not render viable any particular kind of sexual politics or political legibility. Without more, *Lawrence*-like decriminalization merely signals a public tolerance of the behavior, so long as it takes place in private and between two consenting adults in a relationship. * * *

There is no denying that rights in general, and liberty in particular, are something we cannot not want. . . . But rights, particularly in the form articulated in *Lawrence*, cannot exhaust our political projects. *Lawrence* recognizes, in a manner far more robust than *Romer v. Evans*, that homosexuals are rights-bearing subjects. But the political agenda leveraged by that recognition does not exceed honor of the domesticated private. The most likely project to be launched from this conception of subjectivity is, of course, marriage. And, of course, that's exactly what *Lawrence* has unleashed. Less than six months after the Supreme Court issued the *Lawrence* decision, the Massachusetts Supreme Judicial Court found that Massachusetts's refusal to license same-sex marriage was unconstitutional, and in so finding it relied very heavily upon *Lawrence*. For a short period thereafter, gay and lesbian couples overwhelmed public officials in a handful of cities demanding marriage licenses. The relevant officials in San Francisco, New Paltz, and a couple of other jurisdictions accommodated those demands and married thousands of gay and lesbian couples. As such, the subjects of gay and lesbian political organizing at this moment have become same-sex *couples*, not persons who seek nonnormative kinship formations or individuals who engage in nonnormative sex.

But it is wrong to understand the fight for gay marriage as a fight for sexual freedom or, for that matter, relationship-based freedom. Marriage is not a freedom. Rather, it is a *power* understood in Hohfeldian terms, and as a *power* it is the less interesting *pouvoir*, not *puissance*. The states have created a civil status called marriage, just as the states have created voting criteria and rights to inheritance. One either is or is not the kind of person to whom the state has given the power to enter into a civil marriage, to exercise the vote, or to inherit property. One has the power, not the freedom, to marry, to vote, and to inherit property. . . . The state creates rules and conventions that govern these sorts of powers, and the denial of the ability to participate does not trammel upon a fundamental freedom, understood in traditional liberal terms. To the extent that same-sex couples are denied the ability to marry, that denial best surfaces in law as a problem of equality, of indefensible differential treatment, but not as a matter of freedom. . . .

I fear that *Lawrence* and the gay rights organizing that has taken place in and around it have created a path dependency that privileges privatized and domesticated rights and legal liabilities, while rendering less viable projects that advance nonnormative notions of kinship, intimacy, and sexuality. * * *

Lawrence is a slam-dunk victory for a politics that is exclusively devoted to creating safe zones for homo- and hetero-sex/intimacy, while at the same time rendering all other zones more dangerous for nonnormative sex. It can be used to float political projects that render certain normative heterosexual couples as its primary reference points and ethical paradigms. *Lawrence* and the ethics from which it evolved do little to open up new forms of public and private sexual intelligibility that are not always already domestinormative. The landscape post-*Lawrence* is not one that makes formal legal distinctions between heterosexual and homosexual practices, but rather one that likely renders different legal treatment to those who express their sexuality in domesticated ways and those who don't—regardless of orientation. The world post-*Lawrence* remains invested in forms of social membership and, indeed, citizenship that are structurally identified with domesticated heterosexual marriage and intimacy. *Lawrence* offers us no tools to investigate "kinds of intimacy [and sex] that bear no necessary relation to domestic space, to kinship, to the couple form, to property, or to the nation."[84] In this regard, the opinion's implications are at once modest and quite broad in scope. The legal program that is most easily suggested by *Lawrence* is one undertaken by adult gay couples who seek recognition for their relationships and whose sexuality is not merely backgrounded, but closeted behind the closed doors of the bedroom. This is a project devoted to celebrating our *relationships*; it is not a project of sexual rights or the politics of sexuality. Indeed, against this framing of the "gay agenda," the heterosexual reproductive rights cases start looking pretty darn radical. In this sense, overreliance on *Lawrence* risks domesticating rights, sex, and politics, and charting us down a path of domestinormative sexual citizenship. The political subjects it predetermines are husbands and wives, and the legal projects it maps out do not extend beyond gay marriage. * * *

Lawrence announces that the criminalization of same-sex sodomy is unconstitutional because it interferes with gay people's right to enter into serious domestic relationships, but that should not be taken to define the political dimension of sexuality or sexual citizenship. Sex gets figured, if at all, in *Lawrence* as instrumental to the formation of intimate relationships—it seems not to have a social or legal status in its own right. As a result, sexual rights qua sexual are exiled from the legal struggle on behalf of gay men and lesbians.

LAWRENCE v. TEXAS AND JUDICIAL HUBRIS[*]

Nelson Lund & John O. McGinnis

Lawrence is a paragon of the most anticonstitutional branch of constitutional law: substantive due process. The decision also reflects a breakdown of the Court's most recent attempt to put doctrinal restraints on that intoxicating doctrine. It is a commonplace observation—often

---

[84] Lauren Berlant & Michael Warner, *Sex in Public*, 24 CRITICAL INQUIRY 547, 558 (1998).

[*] Nelson Lund & John O. McGinnis, Lawrence v. Texas *and Judicial Hubris*, 102 MICH. L. REV. 1555, 1557, 1578–80, 1584–85, 1606–07 (2004).

repeated by members of the Court itself—that substantive due process makes judges into unelected and unremovable superlegislators. History has recorded several efforts to tame the doctrine in ways designed to give it a more law-like nature, and thereby to protect the properly judicial function of the Court from its all-too-human members. In *Lawrence*, the latest effort fell apart.

The *Lawrence* opinion is a tissue of sophistries embroidered with a bit of sophomoric philosophizing. It is a serious matter when the Supreme Court descends to the level of analysis displayed in this opinion, especially in a high-visibility case that all but promises future adventurism unconstrained by anything but the will of the judicial majority. This performance deserves to be condemned rather than celebrated, even by those—like us—who have no sympathy for the statute that the Court struck down. Nor does *Lawrence*, which displays a dismissive contempt for both the Constitution and the work of prior Courts, deserve to be preserved by the doctrine of stare decisis. * * *

As an initial matter, *Lawrence* does not bother even to say what standard of review it is purporting to apply. Since *Carolene Products*, the most important threshold question in substantive due process cases has been whether they involve a fundamental right. If such a right is found, the Court demands a strong justification for infringing it, and gives little or no deference to legislative judgments; if no fundamental right has been infringed, rational basis review applies, and the legislature will receive almost unquestioning deference. *Lawrence* refuses to make express use of these categories, leaving its standard of review indeterminate.

Even more significantly, the Court neither analyzes the interests of the government, as heightened scrutiny would require, nor makes any effort to imagine what legitimate purpose the statute might serve, as rational basis review would require. Nor, as we shall see, does the Court supply any alternative rational analysis, legal or otherwise. Inflated and empty pronouncements about more transcendent dimensions and defining one's own concept of meaning do not constitute rational analysis. And without such analysis, we have not been told more than what the Court wants and that it has the power to do what it wants. * * *

. . . [T]he Court could have tried to articulate a logically coherent argument based on existing case law, for *Bowers* is difficult or impossible to reconcile with the *Griswold-Roe* line of cases. But that is not the basis on which *Lawrence* overrules *Bowers*. The Court comes closest to making a legal argument when it contends that the deeply rooted tradition of proscribing sodomy, on which *Bowers* had relied, did not support the holding in that case because sodomy laws traditionally applied to heterosexual conduct as well as homosexual conduct: "[T]here is no longstanding history in this country of laws directed at homosexual conduct *as a distinct matter*." By the *Lawrence* Court's logic, the traditional proscription against prostitution must be quite compatible with a fundamental right to engage in homosexual prostitution, or heterosexual prostitution for that matter, since the law has generally not singled out either of them "as a distinct matter." That is absurd.

Let us assume, furthermore, that *Lawrence* is right to claim that *Bowers* overstated what the Court calls its "historical premises" about anti-sodomy laws. Even if this were true, it would be no more than a red herring. The *Lawrence* Court's perfectly plausible claim that the states have not aggressively and consistently punished homosexual conduct does not advance one whit the argument that a *right* to homosexual sex specifically, or nonprocreative sex in general, is deeply rooted in the Nation's history and tradition. The absence of consistent condemnation does not imply the existence of consistent protection. If it did, there would be deeply rooted traditional rights to incest, prostitution, bestiality, cocaine, gambling, child labor, animal cruelty, and thousands of other practices that have been tolerated at some times but not others. * * *

Nowhere in the *Lawrence* opinion does the Court so much as entertain the possibility that state legislatures could have any valid reason for proscribing sodomy in general or homosexual sodomy in particular. Furthermore, the Court comes very close to implying that one obvious basis for such proscriptions—a desire to discourage behavior considered immoral by the majority—is inherently illegitimate. Even if we leave aside other possible rationales for the statute, such as public health and promoting the institution of marriage, how is the desire to discourage putatively immoral behavior really different in any way marked out by the Constitution from the paternalistic desire to discourage other forms of putatively dangerous or self-destructive behavior? When the government outlaws conduct that it regards as risky or unhealthy—such as the recreational use of drugs, or working long hours in a bakery, or driving a motorcycle without a helmet—it is making a *moral* decision that assigns a higher value to health and physical safety than to the spiritual insights that some people have said they get from LSD, or the moral satisfaction that some people get from following a strict work ethic, or the mystical exhilaration of flirting with danger on the open road. Unless the Court were to distinguish without any constitutional justification between the different moral judgments reflected in different forms of paternalistic legislation, it is hard to see how any regulatory statute could survive unless it is demonstrably necessary to prevent immediate injuries to people other than those who want to engage in the conduct.

We certainly do not believe that the *Lawrence* Court consciously decided to embrace any such radically libertarian interpretation of the Due Process Clauses. Nor do we assume that the apparent sympathy for the more limited Playboy Philosophy actually reflects a conscious adoption of Hugh Hefner's views by all the Justices who joined the majority opinion. In fact, we think that the most salient characteristic of *Lawrence* is the impossibility of determining what it means, other than that five Justices have decided to forbid laws proscribing sodomy. Whatever new rights the Court may find or refuse to find among "the components of liberty in its manifold possibilities," *Lawrence* will stand primarily for the proposition that due process jurisprudence has transcended the bounds of rational discourse. * * *

[T]he ad hoc due process approach that has culminated in *Lawrence* is the more likely alternative to genuine common law reasoning. Judicial behavior becomes indistinguishable from naked political judgments: judges reach their decisions by deciding what they think is just and socially beneficial, what will please the elites who shape their reputations, and what they guess the nation will tolerate.

This openly discretionary mode of judging has long term costs—costs that the Justices can impose on future generations with relative impunity. If constitutional debates about contentious issues of the day become simply politics by other means, the Constitution will have failed in one of its primary purposes—to create a framework by which disputes are authoritatively and predictably settled without simply replicating the strong moral and political disagreements that lead to the need for such rules in the first place. When the Court refuses to resolve such disputes by resorting to settled legal rules, and instead injects its members' personal ideological preferences, it sharply reduces the value of this settlement function. Other politicians, moreover, and occasionally even the people themselves, will come to recognize that the Court is engaging in ordinary politics while exempting itself from the mechanisms of political accountability. Once this extraordinary leverage is widely recognized, it is likely that Justices will be nominated and confirmed on increasingly narrow ideological grounds, which eventually may threaten a general dissolution of the Court's constitutional function.

The Court's increasingly casual imposition of elite—and even foreign—views about the appropriate content of constitutional rights may also have the cost of alienating the people from their Constitution. If the Supreme Court doesn't take the Constitution seriously, why should anybody else? And if the Constitution is not actually our unifying law, why should the people treat the constitutional order with more than benign neglect? One important feature of the American tradition is the bond of affection that citizens have for their founding document, in some measure because it is theirs. Imposing elitist views in general, and citing international or foreign judicial decisions as justification for doing so, exacerbates this danger. Flaunting a cosmopolitan sensibility may be quite chic, but this high style comes with a price. The emphatically

American nature of our Constitution has been a source of affection and pride that have contributed to our social stability.

LAWRENCE V. TEXAS: THE "FUNDAMENTAL RIGHT" THAT DARE NOT SPEAK ITS NAME*

Laurence H. Tribe

There is a certain conventional understanding, largely unexamined and too often uncritically accepted, of what it means for the state to deprive someone of "liberty" without "due process of law" in the substantive sense of that phrase. According to this understanding, courts more or less passively identify a set of personal activities in which individuals may engage free of government regulation. This list derives from American constitutional text and tradition, fixed, if not at the nation's founding, then, at the very latest, at the time of the post-Civil War constitutional upheaval that left its textual mark principally in the Fourteenth Amendment. To name the activities on that list is to know what substantive areas are marked off as presumptively beyond the reach of governmental power, both state and federal. And, according to that understanding, if one is to broaden the vistas of freedom beyond the list, one must turn from the properly conservative and suitably backward-looking domain of substantive due process to the domain of a norm focused more on the present and the future—the more aspirational domain of equal protection. Indeed, proponents of this theory emphasize, it is in the name of equal protection that judges since the late nineteenth century have taken the crucially progressive steps toward first racial and then gender equality, steps that broke sharply with history and tradition precisely because the Equal Protection Clause was understood from the beginning to call for the rejection of certain received ways of doing things.

But this sketch tells at best a half-truth. Trying to make sense of the conclusions judges have reached by attending carefully to the rulings they have actually rendered in the name of substantive due process reveals a very different narrative. It is a narrative in which due process and equal protection, far from having separate missions and entailing different inquiries, are profoundly interlocked in a legal double helix. It is a single, unfolding tale of equal liberty and increasingly universal dignity. This tale centers on a quest for genuine self-government of groups small and large, from the most intimate to the most impersonal. It reflects the fact that within any group, the project of self-government is necessarily a process that extends over time (and, at times, even across generations) as the group's experiences, and typically its membership, evolve. * * *

---

*   Laurence H. Tribe, Lawrence v. Texas: *The "Fundamental Right" That Dare Not Speak Its Name*, 117 HARV. L. REV. 1893, 1897–99, 1902–06, 1934–37 (2004).

Lawrence, more than any other decision in the Supreme Court's history, both presupposed and advanced an explicitly equality-based and relationally situated theory of substantive liberty. The "liberty" of which the Court spoke was as much about equal dignity and respect as it was about freedom of action—more so, in fact. And the Court left no doubt that it was protecting the equal liberty and dignity not of atomistic individuals torn from their social contexts, but of people as they relate to, and interact with, one another. Although this concept of liberty far transcends the enumerated "specifics" of the Bill of Rights, *Lawrence*, when viewed through the lens of the Constitution as a framework for individual and group self-government, has much to teach about what those "specific" provisions represent and protect and about how they operate. To be sure, the broad and bold strokes with which the Court painted in *Lawrence* left a good bit of this picture to the reader's imagination, but this mode of exposition hardly seems inapt for a decision laying down a landmark that opens vistas rather than enclosing them.

In particular, the Court gave short shrift to the notion that it was under some obligation to confine its implementation of substantive due process to the largely mechanical exercise of isolating "fundamental rights" as though they were a historically given set of data points on a two-dimensional grid, with one dimension representing time and the other representing a carefully defined and circumscribed sequence of protected primary activities (speaking, praying, raising children, using contraceptives in the privacy of the marital bedroom, and the like). By implicitly rejecting the notion that its task was simply to name the specific activities textually or historically treated as protected, the Court lifted the discussion to a different and potentially more instructive plane. It treated the substantive due process precedents invoked by one side or the other not as a record of the inclusion of various activities in—and the exclusion of other activities from—a fixed list defined by tradition, but as reflections of a deeper pattern involving the allocation of decisionmaking roles, not always fully understood at the time each precedent was added to the array. The Court, it seems, understood that the unfolding logic of this pattern is constructed as much as it is discovered. Constructing that logic is in some ways akin to deriving a regression line from a scatter diagram, keeping in mind, of course, that the choice of one method of extrapolation over another is, at least in part, a subjective one. As if to demonstrate the inevitable dependence of the diagram upon the diagrammer, the *Lawrence* Court, beyond overruling *Bowers v. Hardwick*, took the *Bowers* Court to task for the very way it had formulated the question posed for decision. In doing so, *Lawrence* significantly altered the historical trajectory of substantive due process and thus of liberty.
* * *

The *Lawrence* Court's blend of equal protection and substantive due process themes was neither unprecedented nor accidental: "Equality of treatment and the due process *right to demand respect* for conduct protected by the substantive guarantee of liberty are linked in important respects," Justice Kennedy wrote for the Court, "and a decision on the latter point advances both interests." How might we unpack this rather cryptic statement to view more vividly what was driving the majority in *Lawrence*? It seems to me that two crucial and interrelated concepts are bound up in Justice Kennedy's thesis:

First. The vice of the Texas prohibition of same-sex sodomy was not principally, as some have argued, the cruelty of punishing some people for the only mode of sexual gratification available to them. Nor was it principally the lack of "fair notice" and the danger of "arbitrary and unpredictable enforcement" in dealing with a law that either had become moribund or never was seriously enforced and that, in either case, was "able to persist only because it [was] enforced so rarely." Rather, the prohibition's principal vice was its stigmatization of intimate personal relationships between people of the same sex: the Court concluded that these relationships deserve to be protected in the same way that nonprocreative intimate relationships between opposite-sex adult couples—whether marital or nonmarital, lifelong or ephemeral—are protected. Focusing on the centrality of the relationship in which intimate conduct occurs rather than on the nature of the intimate conduct itself, the Court emphasized its view that "[t]o say that the issue in *Bowers* was simply the right to engage in certain sexual conduct demeans the claim the individual put forward, just as it would demean a married couple were it to be said marriage is simply about the right to have sexual intercourse." Justice Scalia, dissenting, evidently thought he had scored a major point by parsing the majority opinion and concluding, triumphantly: "Not once does it describe homosexual sodomy as a 'fundamental right' or a 'fundamental liberty interest.' " Of course not! How can one put it more clearly? Try this: "It's not the sodomy. It's the relationship!"

And what kind of relationship was it? Apparently, it was quite fleeting, lasting only one night and lacking any semblance of permanence or exclusivity. The Court nonetheless spoke in relational terms: "when sexuality finds overt expression in intimate conduct with another person," Justice Kennedy wrote, "the conduct can be but one element in a personal bond that is more enduring." The Court clearly proceeded from a strong constitutional presumption against allowing government, including its judicial branch, "to define the meaning of [any given personal] relationship or to set its boundaries absent injury to a person or abuse of an institution the law protects." And in unflinchingly applying that presumption despite the seemingly casual character of the encounter involved, the Court evidently recognized an obligation to extend constitutional protection to some brief interactions that might not ripen into meaningful connections over time—even to some that might be chosen precisely for their fleeting and superficial character and their lack of emotional involvement. Had the Court done otherwise, it would have ceded to the state the power to determine what count as meaningful relationships and to decide when and how individuals might enter into such relationships. Doing so would have drained those relationships of their unique significance as expressions of self-government.

Second. The stigmatization of same-sex relationships is concretized and aggravated by the law's denunciation as criminal of virtually the only ways of consummating sexual intimacy possible in such relationships. For although "sodomy" is by no means a "gays only" act, the term has come to carry a strong cultural association with gay male, and to a much lesser extent lesbian, sexual activities—an association that the *Bowers* Court's conflation of sodomy with gay sex both underscored and helped to perpetuate. Many heterosexuals, even those who regularly engage in one or another form of opposite-sex sodomy, no doubt associate "sodomy" with acts that strike them as perverse and alien. Even worse, in their eyes such acts might uncomfortably resemble their own intimacies, simultaneously caricaturing or demeaning these intimacies and inspiring fear of suppressed homosexual proclivities and desires. It follows that even if the Texas law, like the Georgia law at issue in *Bowers*, had been applied to opposite-sex as well as same-sex sodomy and had been enforced equally against both (or not enforced at all), it would still have been "anti-gay" in terms of both its practical impact and its cultural significance. * * *

The *Lawrence* Court's explicit recognition of the "due process right to demand respect for conduct protected by the substantive guarantee of liberty" and of the way in which that right is linked to "[e]quality of treatment" was an obviously important doctrinal innovation. But the Court developed its substantive due process jurisprudence in a way that connected *Lawrence* with the long line of decisions that described the protected liberties at higher levels of generality than any "protected activities" catalog could plausibly accommodate, and typically did so in temporally extended, relationship-focused terms rather than in strictly solitary, atomistic terms. Thus *Meyer* and *Pierce*, the two sturdiest pillars of the substantive due process temple—both survivors of the largely discredited Lochner era—described what they were protecting from the standardizing hand of the state in language that spoke of the family as a center of value-formation and value-transmission that was not to be commandeered by state power. Their language bespoke the authority of parents to make basic choices directing the upbringing of their children. Those judicial decisions did not describe what they were protecting merely as the personal activities of sending one's child to a religious school (*Pierce v. Society of Sisters*) or . . . of hiring a teacher to educate one's child in the German language (*Meyer*).

In much the same way, *Lawrence* makes clear, if only by conspicuous omission, that any such exercise in enumeration is a fool's errand that misconceives the structure of liberty and of the constitutional doctrines that provide its contents. Indeed, *Lawrence* is likely to endure in large part because it highlights the futility of describing liberty in so one-dimensional a manner. The Court left no doubt about *its* understanding of the fundamental claim to "liberty" being advanced in *Lawrence* and in *Bowers* alike: at stake in both cases were claims that a state may not undertake to "control a personal relationship" in the way that Georgia had in *Bowers* and Texas had in *Lawrence*.

Lawrence's focus on the role of self-regulating relationships in American liberty suggests that the "Trivial Pursuit" version of the due process "name that liberty" game arguably validated by *Glucksberg* has finally given way to a focus on the underlying pattern of self-government (rather than of state micromanagement) defined by the rights enumerated or implicit in the Constitution or recognized by the landmark decisions construing it. It's always possible to persuade oneself that data points lying along a great arc are in fact just so many isolated points—to see the dots but not the path that passes through them. *Bowers* might not seem aberrant to someone of that sort—someone who collects and categorizes the continuous stream of rulings about human freedom as though cataloging so many discrete data points rather than searching for and constructing a regression line that satisfyingly explains the relationship of the points to one another and to liberty as a whole. Count them, if you will: one data point for the right to become a parent (*Skinner*); several more points marking the rights of parents to direct the upbringing of their children (*Meyer, Pierce, Troxel*); a pair of points for the right to keep one's children safe from the distractions and temptations of a too-diverse world, coupled with a right either to inculcate one's religion (*Yoder*) or to transmit one's views of morality (*Boy Scouts*); yet another point for the rights of married couples to have sexual intercourse without risking pregnancy and parenthood (*Griswold*); another pair for the rights of individuals (married or unmarried) not to risk unwanted pregnancy or sexually transmitted disease as penalties inflicted (without trial!) for breaking the state's codes of sexual conduct (*Eisenstadt, Carey*); two points more to mark the rights of pregnant women to end their pregnancies (*Roe, Casey*) or, if they wish, to continue their pregnancies to term (*Casey*); and three last points celebrating the rights of straight couples to marry without restrictions based on race (*Loving*), poverty (*Zablocki*), or imprisonment (*Turner*). So many points, so many disconnected dots!

Lawrence eschewed such isolated point-plotting. The whole of substantive due process, *Lawrence* teaches us, is larger than, and conceptually different from, the sum of its parts. *Lawrence* contrasts with Justice Harlan's justly celebrated "rational continuum" that purported to connect the Bill of Rights with a discourse defined by our society's specific historical experience and that led Justice Harlan, dissenting in *Poe v. Ullman*, to put intimate marital relations on a pedestal and to relegate fornication and homosexuality to a disconnected netherworld. Justice Kennedy's opinion for the Court in *Lawrence* instead suggests the globally unifying theme of shielding from state control *value-forming* and *value-transmitting* relationships, procreative and nonprocreative alike, drawing from *Griswold* a right to decouple sex from conception in an intimate marital relationship and from *Eisenstadt* a right to an intimate sexual relationship distinct from marriage. *Lawrence* also suggests this theme when it looks beyond the American historical experience for insight both contemporary and cross-cultural into the range of relationships through which individuals might seek to transcend the boundaries of the self.

NOTE

For a sampling of additional scholarly commentary on *Lawrence*, see Carlos A. Ball, *The Positive in the Fundamental Right to Marry: Same-Sex Marriage and the Aftermath of* Lawrence v. Texas, 88 MINN. L. REV. 1184 (2004); Thomas P. Crocker, *From Privacy to Liberty: The Fourth Amendment After* Lawrence, 57 UCLA L. Rev. 1 (2009); Mary Anne Case, *Of "This" and "That" in* Lawrence v. Texas, 2003 SUP. CT. REV. 75; William N. Eskridge, Jr., Lawrence*'s Jurisprudence of Tolerance: Judicial Review to Lower the Stakes of Identity Politics*, 88 MINN. L. REV. 1021 (2004); Chai R. Feldblum, *The Right to Define One's Own Concept of Existence: What* Lawrence *Can Mean for Intersex and Transgender People*, 7 GEO. J. GENDER & L. 115 (2006); Suzanne B. Goldberg, *Morals-Based Justifications for Lawmaking: Before and After* Lawrence v. Texas, 88 MINN. L. REV. 1233 (2004); Nan D. Hunter, *Living with* Lawrence, 88 MINN. L. REV. 1103 (2004); Pamela S. Karlan, *Loving* Lawrence, 102 MICH. L. REV. 1447 (2004); Sonya Katyal, *Sexuality and Sovereignty: The Global Limits and Possibilities of* Lawrence, 14 WM. & MARY BILL RTS. J. 1429 (2006); Miranda Oshige McGowan, *From Outlaws to Ingroup:* Romer, Lawrence *and the Inevitable Normativity of Group Recognition*, 88 MINN. L. REV. 1312 (2004); Jane S. Schacter, Lawrence v. Texas *and the Fourteenth Amendment's Democratic Aspirations*, 13 TEMP. POL. & CIV. RTS. L. REV. 733 (2004); Cass R. Sunstein, *What Did* Lawrence *Hold? Of Autonomy, Desuetude, Sexuality, and Marriage*, 2003 SUP. CT. REV. 276; Francisco Valdes, *Anomalies, Warts and All: Four Score of Liberty, Privacy and Equality*, 65 OHIO ST. L.J. 1341 (2004).

F. THE LEVEL OF SCRUTINY DEBATE

Despite Justice Scalia's concerns about how *Lawrence* would lead to the striking down of a panoply of criminal laws grounded on moral concerns,[34] many efforts to use *Lawrence* as a means to limit the ability of the State to regulate sexual conduct and expression have failed. For example, *Lawrence*-based challenges to laws prohibiting sex for compensation have not succeeded.[35] Challenges to bans on incest,[36] polygamy,[37] and obscenity[38] have also failed. However, the Virginia Supreme Court did strike down the state's fornication statute, which prohibited sex between unmarried individuals, because it violated the right of adults, as recognized in *Lawrence*, to engage in private sexual conduct.[39] In addition, the U.S. Court of Appeals for the Fourth Circuit held that Virginia's sodomy statute was facially unconstitutional under *Lawrence* and that it therefore could not be applied to a male defendant who was charged with soliciting a 17-year old female to commit sodomy.[40] The court explained that while it was likely that the state could, consistent with *Lawrence*, enact a statute prohibiting sodomy between adults and minors, its general sodomy statute, which did not take the age of the parties into account, could not be enforced at all, including against someone who had solicited a minor to engage in sodomy.[41]

The most important disagreement among lower courts, as we will see in this Section, has been over the level of judicial scrutiny that *Lawrence* requires when assessing the constitutionality of government regulations that impact on sexuality matters.

---

[34] *Lawrence*, 539 U.S. at 590, 123 S.Ct. at 2490, 156 L.Ed.2d at 533 (Scalia, J., dissenting).

[35] *See State v. Romano,* 155 P.3d 1102, 114 Haw. 1 (2007); *People v. Williams*, 811 N.E.2d 1197, 347 Ill.App.3d 1123, 285 Ill.Dec. 318 (2004); *State v. Thomas*, 891 So.2d 1233 (La. 2005); *State v. Green*, 989 N.E.2d 1088 (Ohio.App. 2013).

[36] *See Muth v. Frank*, 412 F.3d 808 (7th Cir. 2005); *People v. McEvoy*, 215 Cal.App.4th 431, 154 Cal.Rpt.3d 914 (Ca.App. 2013); *People v. Scott*, 157 Cal.App.4th 189, 68 Cal.Rptr.3d 592 (Cal.App. 2007); *State v. Lowe*, 861 N.E.2d 512, 112 Ohio St.3d 507 (2007); State *v. Freeman*, 801 N.E.2d 906, 155 Ohio App.3d 492 (2003).

[37] *See Bronson v. Swensen*, 394 F.Supp.2d 1329 (D.Utah 2005), *vacated on other grounds by* 500 F.3d 1099, 1102 (10th Cir 2007); *State v. Holm*, 137 P.3d 726 (Ut. 2006).

[38] *See United States v. Extreme Assocs., Inc.*, 431 F.3d 150, 161–62 (3d Cir. 2005) (ruling that *Lawrence* did not render federal obscenity laws unconstitutional); *United States v. Stagliano*, 693 F.Supp.2d 25, 37 (D.D.C. 2010) (rejecting "the notion that the liberty interest announced in *Lawrence* somehow includes a right to obtain or distribute obscenity"); *Ex parte Dave*, 220 S.W.3d 154, 159 (Tex. App. 2007) (holding that *Lawrence* does not preclude application of Texas obscenity statute).

[39] *See Martin v. Ziherl*, 607 S.E.2d 367, 370–71, 269 Va. 35, 41–42 (2005).

[40] *See MacDonald* v. *Moose*, 710 F.3d 154, 166 (4th Cir. 2013), *cert. denied*, 134 S.Ct. 200 (2013).

[41] Although Virginia prohibited sexual conduct between adults and minors under the age of 15, it did not have a statute proscribing sexual contact between adults and older minors. *Id.* at 165 n.16.

1. *Lawrence* as a Rational Basis Case

LOFTON V. SECRETARY OF THE DEPARTMENT OF CHILDREN & FAMILY SERVICES*

United States Court of Appeals, Eleventh Circuit, 2004
358 F.3d 804

BIRCH, CIRCUIT JUDGE.

Since 1977, Florida's adoption law has contained a codified prohibition on adoption by any "homosexual" person. 1977 Fla. Laws, ch. 77–140, § 1, Fla. Stat. § 63.042(3) (2002). [The statute provides that "[n]o person eligible to adopt under the statute may adopt if that person is a homosexual." *Id.*] For purposes of this statute, Florida courts have defined the term "homosexual" as being "limited to applicants who are known to engage in current, voluntary homosexual activity," thus drawing "a distinction between homosexual orientation and homosexual activity." *Fla. Dep't of Health & Rehab. Servs. v. Cox*, 627 So.2d 1210, 1215 (Fla. Dist. Ct. App. 1993), *aff'd in relevant part*, 656 So.2d 902, 903 (Fla. 1995). During the past twelve years, several legislative bills have attempted to repeal the statute, and three separate legal challenges to it have been filed in the Florida courts. To date, no attempt to overturn the provision has succeeded. We now consider the most recent challenge to the statute. * * *

Laws that burden the exercise of a fundamental right require strict scrutiny and are sustained only if narrowly tailored to further a compelling government interest. Appellants argue that the Supreme Court's recent decision in *Lawrence v. Texas*, 539 U.S. 558, 123 S.Ct. 2472 (2003), which struck down Texas's sodomy statute, identified a hitherto unarticulated fundamental right to private sexual intimacy. They contend that the Florida statute, by disallowing adoption to any individual who chooses to engage in homosexual conduct, impermissibly burdens the exercise of this right.

We begin with the threshold question of whether *Lawrence* identified a new fundamental right to private sexual intimacy. *Lawrence*'s holding was that substantive due process does not permit a state to impose a criminal prohibition on private consensual homosexual conduct. The effect of this holding was to establish a greater respect than previously existed in the law for the right of consenting adults to engage in private sexual conduct. Nowhere, however, did the Court characterize this right as "fundamental." *Cf. id.* at 2488 (Scalia, J., dissenting) (observing that

---

* *Editors' Note:* In Chapter 7, Section III.A, we provide an extended excerpt from the *Lofton* ruling on the constitutionality of Florida's ban on adoption by lesbians and gay men. Here, we provide the brief section of the opinion that discusses whether *Lawrence* is a fundamental rights case.

"nowhere does the Court's opinion declare that homosexual sodomy is a 'fundamental right' under the Due Process Clause"). Nor did the Court locate this right directly in the Constitution, but instead treated it as the by-product of several different constitutional principles and liberty interests.

We are particularly hesitant to infer a new fundamental liberty interest from an opinion whose language and reasoning are inconsistent with standard fundamental-rights analysis. The Court has noted that it must "exercise the utmost care whenever [it is] asked to break new ground" in the field of fundamental rights, *Washington v. Glucksberg*, 521 U.S. 702, 720 (1997), which is precisely what the *Lawrence* petitioners and their *amici curiae* had asked the Court to do. That the Court declined the invitation is apparent from the absence of the "two primary features" of fundamental-rights analysis in its opinion. First, the *Lawrence* opinion contains virtually no inquiry into the question of whether the petitioners' asserted right is one of those fundamental rights and liberties which are, objectively, deeply rooted in this Nation's history and tradition and implicit in the concept of ordered liberty, such that neither liberty nor justice would exist if they were sacrificed. Second, the opinion notably never provides the careful description of the asserted fundamental liberty interest that is to accompany fundamental-rights analysis. Rather, the constitutional liberty interests on which the Court relied were invoked, not with "careful description," but with sweeping generality. *See, e.g.*, *Lawrence*, 123 S. Ct. at 2475 ("Liberty protects the person from unwarranted government intrusions into a dwelling or other private places."); *id.* ("The instant case involves liberty of the person both in its spatial and more transcendent dimensions."); *id.* at 2484 ("[T]here is a realm of personal liberty which the government may not enter.") (citation omitted). Most significant, however, is the fact that the *Lawrence* Court never applied strict scrutiny, the proper standard when fundamental rights are implicated, but instead invalidated the Texas statute on rational-basis grounds, holding that it "furthers no legitimate state interest which can justify its intrusion into the personal and private life of the individual." * * *

Moreover, the holding of *Lawrence* does not control the present case. Apart from the shared homosexuality component, there are marked differences in the facts of the two cases. The Court itself stressed the limited factual situation it was addressing in *Lawrence*:

> The present case does not involve minors. It does not involve persons who might be injured or coerced or who are situated in relationships where consent might not easily be refused. It does not involve public conduct or prostitution. It does not involve whether the government must give formal recognition to any relationship that homosexual persons seek to enter. The case

does involve two adults who, with full and mutual consent from each other, engaged in sexual practices common to a homosexual lifestyle.

Here, the involved actors are not only consenting adults, but minors as well. The relevant state action is not criminal prohibition, but grant of a statutory privilege. And the asserted liberty interest is not the negative right to engage in private conduct without facing criminal sanctions, but the affirmative right to receive official and public recognition. Hence, we conclude that the *Lawrence* decision cannot be extrapolated to create a right to adopt for homosexual persons. * * *

WILLIAMS V. ATTORNEY GENERAL OF ALABAMA

U.S. Court of Appeals, Eleventh Circuit, 2004
378 F.3d 1232

BIRCH, CIRCUIT JUDGE.

In this case, the American Civil Liberties Union ("ACLU") invites us to add a new right to the current catalogue of fundamental rights under the Constitution: a right to sexual privacy. It further asks us to declare Alabama's statute prohibiting the sale of "sex toys" to be an impermissible burden on this right. Alabama responds that the statute exercises a time-honored use of state police power—restricting the sale of sex. We are compelled to agree with Alabama and must decline the ACLU's invitation.

I.   BACKGROUND

Alabama's Anti-Obscenity Enforcement Act prohibits, among other things, the commercial distribution of "any device designed or marketed as useful primarily for the stimulation of human genital organs for any thing of pecuniary value." Ala.Code § 13A–12–200.2 (Supp.2003).

The Alabama statute proscribes a relatively narrow bandwidth of activity. It prohibits only the sale—but not the use, possession, or gratuitous distribution—of sexual devices (in fact, the users involved in this litigation acknowledge that they already possess multiple sex toys). The law does not affect the distribution of a number of other sexual products such as ribbed condoms or virility drugs. Nor does it prohibit Alabama residents from purchasing sexual devices out of state and bringing them back into Alabama. Moreover, the statute permits the sale of ordinary vibrators and body massagers that, although useful as sexual aids, are not "designed or marketed . . . primarily" for that particular purpose. *Id.* Finally, the statute exempts sales of sexual devices "for a bona fide medical, scientific, educational, legislative, judicial, or law enforcement purpose." *Id.* § 13A–12–200.4.

This case, which is now before us on appeal for the second time, involves a challenge to the constitutionality of the Alabama statute. The ACLU, on behalf of various individual users and vendors of sexual devices, initially filed suit seeking to enjoin the statute on 29 July 1998, a month after the statute took effect. The ACLU argued that the statute burdens and violates sexual-device users' right to privacy and personal autonomy under the Fourteenth Amendment to the United States Constitution.

Following a bench trial, the district court concluded that there was no currently recognized fundamental right to use sexual devices and declined the ACLU's invitation to create such a right. *Williams v. Pryor*, 41 F. Supp. 2d. 1257, 1282–84 (N.D. Ala. 1999) (*Williams I*). The district court then proceeded to scrutinize the statute under rational basis review. *Id.* at 1284. Concluding that the statute lacked any rational basis, the district court permanently enjoined its enforcement. *Id.* at 1293.

On appeal, we reversed in part and affirmed in part. *Williams v. Pryor*, 240 F.3d 944 (11th Cir. 2001) (*Williams II*). We reversed the district court's conclusion that the statute lacked a rational basis and held that the promotion and preservation of public morality provided a rational basis. *Id.* at 952. However, we affirmed the district court's rejection of the ACLU's *facial* fundamental-rights challenge to the statute. *Id.* at 955. We then remanded the action to the district court for further consideration of the *as-applied* fundamental-rights challenge. *Id.* at 955.

On remand, the district court again struck down the statute. *Williams v. Pryor*, 220 F. Supp. 2d 1257 (N.D. Ala. 2002) (*Williams III*). On cross motions for summary judgment, the district court held that the statute unconstitutionally burdened the right to use sexual devices within private adult, consensual sexual relationships. *Id.* After a lengthy discussion of the history of sex in America, the district court announced a fundamental right to "sexual privacy," which, although unrecognized under any existing Supreme Court precedent, the district court found to be deeply rooted in the history and traditions of our nation. *Id.* at 1296. The district court further found that this right "encompass[es] the right to use sexual devices like the vibrators, dildos, anal beads, and artificial vaginas" marketed by the vendors involved in this case. *Id.* The district court accordingly applied strict scrutiny to the statute. *Id.* Finding that the statute failed strict scrutiny, the district court granted summary judgment to the ACLU and once again enjoined the statute's enforcement. *Id.* at 1307.

Alabama now appeals that decision. The only question on this appeal is whether the statute, as applied to the involved users and vendors, violates any fundamental right protected under the Constitution. The proper analysis for evaluating this question turns on whether the right asserted by the ACLU falls within the parameters of any presently recognized fundamental right or whether it instead requires us to recognize a hitherto unarticulated fundamental right.

II.   DISCUSSION

A.   Asserted Right

* * * The ACLU invokes "privacy" and "personal autonomy" as if such phrases were constitutional talismans. In the abstract, however, there is no fundamental right to either. *See, e.g., Glucksberg,* 521 U.S. at 725 (fundamental rights are "not simply deduced from abstract concepts of personal autonomy"). Undoubtedly, many fundamental rights currently recognized under Supreme Court precedent touch on matters of personal autonomy and privacy. However, "[t]hat many of the rights and liberties protected by the Due Process Clause sound in personal autonomy does not warrant the sweeping conclusion that any and all important, intimate, and personal decisions are so protected." *Id.* at 727. Such rights have been denominated "fundamental" not simply because they implicate deeply personal and private considerations, but because they have been identified as "deeply rooted in this Nation's history and tradition and implicit in the concept of ordered liberty, such that neither liberty nor justice would exist if they were sacrificed." *Id.* at 720–21.

Nor, contrary to the ACLU's assertion, have the Supreme Court's substantive-due-process precedents recognized a free-standing "right to sexual privacy." The Court has been presented with repeated opportunities to identify a fundamental right to sexual privacy—and has invariably declined. * * *

The Supreme Court's most recent opportunity to recognize a fundamental right to sexual privacy came in *Lawrence v. Texas,* where petitioners and *amici* expressly invited the court to do so. That the *Lawrence* Court had declined the invitation was this court's conclusion in our recent decision in *Lofton v. Sec. of Dept. of Children & Family Servs.,* 358 F.3d 804, 815–16 (11th Cir. 2004). In *Lofton,* we addressed in some detail the "question of whether *Lawrence* identified a new fundamental right to private sexual intimacy." *Id.* at 815. We concluded that, although *Lawrence* clearly established the unconstitutionality of criminal prohibitions on consensual adult sodomy, "it is a strained and ultimately incorrect reading of *Lawrence* to interpret it to announce a new fundamental right"—whether to homosexual sodomy specifically or, more broadly, to all forms of sexual intimacy. We noted in particular that the *Lawrence* opinion did not employ fundamental-rights analysis and that it ultimately applied rational-basis review, rather than strict scrutiny, to the challenged statute.

The dissent seizes on scattered *dicta* from *Lawrence* to argue that *Lawrence* recognized a *substantive* due process right of consenting adults to engage in private intimate sexual conduct, such that all infringements of this right must be subjected to strict scrutiny. As we noted in *Lofton*, we are not prepared to infer a new fundamental right from an opinion that never employed the usual *Glucksberg* analysis for identifying such rights. Nor are we prepared to assume that *Glucksberg*—a precedent that *Lawrence* never once mentions—is overruled by implication.

The dissent in turn argues that the right recognized in *Lawrence* was a longstanding right that preexisted *Lawrence*, thus obviating the need for any *Glucksberg*-type fundamental rights analysis. But the dissent never identifies the source, textual or precedential, of such a preexisting right to sexual privacy. It does cite *Griswold*, *Eisenstadt*, *Roe*, and *Carey*. However, although these precedents recognize various substantive rights *closely related* to sexual intimacy, none of them recognize the overarching right to sexual privacy asserted here. *Griswold* (marital privacy and contraceptives); *Eisenstadt* (equal protection extension of *Griswold*); *Roe* (abortion); *Carey* (contraceptives)... [I]n the most recent of these decisions, *Carey*, the Court specifically observed that it had not answered the question of whether there is a constitutional right to private sexual conduct. Moreover, nearly two decades later, the *Glucksberg* Court, listing the current catalog of fundamental rights, did not include such a right.

In short, we decline to extrapolate from *Lawrence* and its *dicta* a right to sexual privacy triggering strict scrutiny. To do so would be to impose a fundamental-rights interpretation on a decision that rested on rational-basis grounds, that never engaged in *Glucksberg* analysis, and that never invoked strict scrutiny. Moreover, it would be answering questions that the *Lawrence* Court appears to have left for another day. Of course, the Court may in due course expand *Lawrence*'s precedent in the direction anticipated by the dissent. But for us preemptively to take that step would exceed our mandate as a lower court.

B.   Glucksberg Analysis

1.   Careful Description

* * * In searching for, and ultimately finding, [a] right to sexual privacy, the district court did little to define its scope and bounds. As formulated by the district court, the right potentially encompasses a great universe of sexual activities, including many that historically have been, and continue to be, prohibited. At oral arguments, the ACLU contended that "no responsible counsel" would challenge prohibitions such as those against pederasty and adult incest under a "right to sexual privacy" theory. However, mere faith in the responsibility of the bar scarcely provides a legally cognizable, or constitutionally significant, limiting principle in applying the right in future cases.

The sole limitation provided by the district court's ruling was that the right would extend only to *consenting adults*. The consenting-adult formula, of course, is a corollary to John Stuart Mill's celebrated "harm principle," which would allow the state to proscribe only conduct that causes identifiable harm to another. *See generally* John Stuart Mill, *On Liberty* (Elizabeth Rapaport ed., Hackett Pub. Co. 1978) (1859). Regardless of its force as a policy argument, however, it does not translate *ipse dixit* into a constitutionally cognizable standard.

If we were to accept the invitation to recognize a right to sexual intimacy, this right would theoretically encompass such activities as prostitution, obscenity, and adult incest—even if we were to limit the right to consenting adults. This in turn would require us to subject all infringements on such activities to strict scrutiny. In short, by framing our inquiry so broadly as to look for a general right to sexual intimacy, we would be answering many questions not before us on the present facts.

Indeed, the requirement of a "careful description" is designed to prevent the reviewing court from venturing into vaster constitutional vistas than are called for by the facts of the case at hand. * * *

[T]he scope of the liberty interest at stake here must be defined in reference to the scope of the Alabama statute. We begin by observing that the broad rights to "privacy" and "sexual privacy" invoked by the ACLU are not at issue. The statute invades the privacy of Alabama residents in their bedrooms no more than does any statute restricting the availability of commercial products for use in private quarters as sexual enhancements.[12] Instead, the challenged Alabama statute bans the commercial distribution of sexual devices. At a minimum, therefore, the putative right at issue is the right to sell and purchase sexual devices.

It is more than that, however. For purposes of constitutional analysis, restrictions on the ability to purchase an item are tantamount to restrictions on the use of that item. Thus it was that the *Glucksberg* Court analyzed a ban on *providing* suicide assistance as a burden on the right to *receive* suicide assistance. Similarly, prohibitions on the *sale* of contraceptives have been analyzed as burdens on the *use* of contraceptives. Because a prohibition on the distribution of sexual devices would burden an individual's ability to use the devices, our analysis must be framed not simply in terms of whether the Constitution protects a

---

[12] The mere fact that a product is used within the privacy of the bedroom, or that it enhances intimate conduct, does not in itself bring the use of that article within the right to privacy. If it were otherwise, individuals whose sexual gratification requires other types of material or instrumentalities—perhaps hallucinogenic substances, depictions of child pornography or bestiality, or the services of a willing prostitute—likewise would have a colorable argument that prohibitions on such activities and materials interfere with their privacy in the bedchamber. Under this theory, all such sexual-enhancement paraphernalia (as long as it was used only in consensual encounters between adults) would also be encompassed within the right to privacy—and any burden thereon subject to strict scrutiny.

right to *sell* and *buy* sexual devices, but whether it protects a right to *use* such devices.

2. *"History and Tradition" and "Implicit in the Concept of Ordered Liberty"*

With this "careful description" in mind, we turn now to the second prong of the fundamental-rights inquiry. The crucial inquiry under this prong is whether the right to use sexual devices when engaging in lawful, private sexual activity is (1) "objectively, deeply rooted in this Nation's history and tradition" and (2) "implicit in the concept of ordered liberty, such that neither liberty nor justice would exist if [it] were sacrificed." *Glucksberg*, 521 U.S. at 721.

a. The Scope of the District Court's History and Tradition Analysis

The district court began its *Glucksberg*-mandated history and tradition inquiry by defining its task as one of determining whether to "recognize a fundamental right to sexual privacy." *Williams III*, 220 F.Supp.2d at 1277. After an extensive survey of the history of sex in American culture and law—replete with cites to the Kinsey studies and Michel Foucault—the district court concluded that "there exists a constitutionally inherent right to sexual privacy that firmly encompasses state non-interference with private, adult, consensual sexual relationships." *Id.* at 1296. As examined above, the Supreme Court's own reticence in this area, and its admonition to carefully define the right at stake, convince us that the district court erred in undertaking to find a generalized "right to sexual privacy." Given this over-broad starting point, the district court's subsequent inquiry, predictably, was likewise broader than called for by the facts of the case. The inquiry should have been focused not broadly on the vast topic of sex in American cultural and legal history, but narrowly and more precisely on the treatment of *sexual devices* within that history and tradition.

b. The District Court's Focus on "Contemporary Practice"

In reaching its holding, the district court relied heavily on "contemporary practice," emphasizing the "contemporary trend of legislative and societal liberalization of attitudes toward consensual, adult sexual activity." *Id.* at 1294. * * *

Our first concern is the legal significance, or the lack thereof, of much of the district court's source material for this contemporary practice. In addition to invoking a cluster of Supreme Court precedents touching on matters of procreation and familial integrity, the district court looked to social science data respecting premarital intercourse, marriage and divorce rates, and the like. It further noted the revolutionary impact of the Kinsey studies, the "imagery and implements of adult sexual relationships [that] pervade modern American society," the availability of "pornography of the grossest sort," and the "widespread marketing of Viagra". . . . *Id.* at 1294. While such evidence undoubtedly confirms the district court's discovery of "the specter of a twentieth century sexual liberalism," *id.* at 1291, its relevance under *Glucksberg* is scant. * * *

c.   The District Court's Faulty Equation of Historical Non-Interference with Historical Protection

The district court's central holding—its discovery of a constitutional "right to use sexual devices like . . . vibrators, dildos, anal beads, and artificial vaginas"—was not based on any evidence of a history and tradition of *affirmative protection* of this right. *Williams III*, 220 F.Supp.2d at 1296. The district court's lengthy opinion cites no reference to such a right in the usual repositories of our freedoms, such as federal and state constitutional provisions, constitutional doctrines, statutory provisions, common-law doctrines, and the like. Instead, the critical evidence for the district court was the relative scarcity of statutes explicitly banning sexual devices and the rarity of reported cases of sexual-devices prosecutions—along with various factual assertions from declarations by the ACLU's experts. From this, the district court inferred "that history and contemporary practice demonstrate a conscious avoidance of regulation of [sexual] devices by the states." *Id.* at 1296.

This negative inference essentially inverted *Glucksberg*'s history and tradition inquiry. *Glucksberg*, 521 U.S. at 721. The district court—rather than requiring a showing that the right to use sexual devices is "deeply rooted in this Nation's history and tradition," *id.*—looked for a showing that *proscriptions* against sexual devices are deeply rooted in history and tradition. Under this approach, the freedom to smoke, to pollute, to engage in private discrimination, to commit marital rape—at one time or another—all could have been elevated to fundamental-rights status. Moreover, it would create the perverse incentive for legislatures to regulate every area within their plenary power for fear that their restraint in any area might give rise to a right of constitutional proportions. * * *

[N]othing in *Glucksberg* indicates that an absence of historical *prohibition* is tantamount, for purposes of fundamental-rights analysis, to an historical record of *protection* under the law. . . . Not only does the record before us fail to evidence such a deeply rooted right, but it suggests that, to the extent that sex toys historically have attracted the attention of the law, it has been in the context of proscription, not protection.

The chief example of this proscription is the "Comstock Laws," federal and state legislation adopted in the late 1800s. The federal Comstock Act of 1873 was a criminal statute directed at "the suppression of Trade in and Circulation of obscene Literature and Articles of immoral Use." *See Bolger v. Youngs Drug Prods. Corp.*, 463 U.S. 60, 70 (1983). The

Act prohibited importation of and use of the mails for transporting, among other things, "every article or thing intended or adapted for any indecent or immoral use." *United States v. Chase*, 135 U.S. 255, 257, 10 S. Ct. 756, 756, 34 L. Ed. 117 (1890). Various states also enacted similar statutes prohibiting the sale of such articles. * * *

[T]he negative inference drawn by the district court—that the scarcity of explicit reference to sexual devices in statutory schemes and reported cases reflects a "deliberate non-interference," *id.* at 1286—is too speculative a basis for constitutionalizing a hitherto unrecognized right. This is especially true given the lack of any indicia of affirmative protection under the law. In short, there is no competent evidence in the record before us indicating that the lack of explicit and aggressive proscription of sex toys was, as the district court surmised, "conscious avoidance of regulation of these devices by the states." *Id.* at 1296. * * *

We REVERSE the district court's grant of the ACLU's motion for summary judgment and REMAND to the district court for further proceedings consistent with this opinion.

BARKETT, CIRCUIT JUDGE, dissenting.

The majority's decision rests on the erroneous foundation that there is no substantive due process right to adult consensual sexual intimacy in the home and erroneously assumes that the promotion of public morality provides a rational basis to criminally burden such private intimate activity. These premises directly conflict with the Supreme Court's holding in *Lawrence v. Texas*, 539 U.S. 558 (2003).

This case is not, as the majority's demeaning and dismissive analysis suggests, about sex or about sexual devices. It is about the tradition of American citizens from the inception of our democracy to value the constitutionally protected right to be left alone in the privacy of their bedrooms and personal relationships. As Justice Brandeis stated in the now famous words of his dissent in *Olmstead v. United States*, 277 U.S. 438 (1928), when "[t]he makers of our Constitution undertook to secure conditions favorable to the pursuit of happiness . . . [t]hey conferred, as against the government, the right to be let alone—the most comprehensive of rights and the right most valued by civilized men." [*Id.*] at 478.

The majority claims that *Lawrence*, like *Bowers v. Hardwick*, 478 U.S. 186, 106 S. Ct. 2841, 92 L. Ed. 2d 140 (1986), failed to recognize the substantive due process right of consenting adults to engage in private sexual conduct. Conceding that *Lawrence* must have done *something*, the majority acknowledges that *Lawrence* "established the unconstitutionality of criminal prohibitions on consensual adult sodomy." The majority refuses, however, to acknowledge *why* the Court in *Lawrence* held that criminal prohibitions on consensual sodomy are unconstitutional. This failure underlies the majority's flawed conclusion in this case.

. . . *Lawrence* held that a state may not criminalize sodomy because of the existence of the very right to private sexual intimacy that the majority refuses to acknowledge. *Lawrence* reiterated that its prior fundamental rights cases protected individual choices "concerning the intimacies of [a] physical relationship." *Lawrence*, 123 S. Ct. at 2483. Because of this precedent, the *Lawrence* Court overruled *Bowers*, concluding that *Bowers* had "misapprehended the claim of liberty there presented" as involving a particular sexual act rather than the broader right of adult sexual privacy. *Id.* at 2478. Instead of heeding the Supreme Court's instruction regarding *Bowers*' error, the majority *repeats* it, ignoring *Lawrence*'s teachings about how to correctly frame a liberty interest affecting sexual privacy.

Compounding this error, the majority also ignores *Lawrence*'s holding that although history and tradition may be used as a "starting point," they are not the "ending point" of a substantive due process inquiry. *Id.* at 2480. In cases solely involving adult consensual sexual privacy, the Court has never required that there be a long-standing history of *affirmative* legal protection of *specific conduct* before a right can be recognized under the Due Process Clause. To the contrary, because of the fundamental nature of this liberty interest, this right has been protected by the Court despite historical, legislative *restrictions* on private sexual conduct. Applying the analytical framework of *Lawrence* compels the conclusion that the Due Process Clause protects a right to sexual privacy that encompasses the use of sexual devices.

Finally, even under the majority's own constrained and erroneous interpretation of *Lawrence*, we are, at a bare minimum, obliged to revisit this Court's previous conclusion in *Williams v. Pryor*, 240 F.3d 944 (11th Cir. 2001) ("*Williams II*"), that Alabama's law survives the most basic level of review, that of rational basis. *See* 240 F.3d at 949. That decision explicitly depended upon the finding in *Bowers* that the promotion of public morality provided a rational basis to restrict private sexual activity. While the majority recognizes that *Bowers* has been overruled, it inexplicably fails to offer any explanation whatsoever for why public morality provides a rational basis to criminalize the private sexual activity in this case, when it was clearly not found to be a legitimate state interest in *Lawrence*.

NOTES

1.   The following question can be asked after a ruling like *Williams*: Why is consensual sexual conduct involving body parts (a penis and an anus, for example) constitutionally protected, while consensual sexual conduct

involving a device and a body part (a vibrator and a vagina, for example) is not?

2.   The *Williams* court remanded the case for a determination of whether the Alabama statute survived rational basis review. A federal district court subsequently held that it did, see *Williams v. King*, 420 F.Supp.2d 1224 (N.D.Ala. 2006) (*Williams V*), and the Eleventh Circuit affirmed. *See Williams v. Morgan,* 478 F.3d 1316 (11th Cir. 2007) (*Williams VI*). In affirming, the appellate court explained that "while the statute at issue in *Lawrence* criminalized *private* sexual conduct, the statute at issue in this case forbids *public, commercial* activity. To the extent *Lawrence* rejects public morality as a legitimate government interest, it invalidates only those laws that target conduct that is *both* private *and* non-commercial. Unlike *Lawrence,* the activity regulated here is *neither* private *nor* non-commercial. This statute targets *commerce* in sexual devices, an inherently public activity, whether it occurs on a street corner, in a shopping mall, or in a living room." *Id.* at 1322. (Is this reasoning inconsistent with the same court's statement in the main case that "for purposes of constitutional analysis, restrictions on the ability to purchase an item are tantamount to restrictions on the use of that item?" *Williams v. Attorney General of Alabama,* 378 F.3d 1232, 1242 (11th Cir. 2004).) The *Williams VI* court then went on to make clear that it did "not read *Lawrence* [or] the overruling of *Bowers* . . . to have rendered public morality altogether illegitimate as a rational basis. The principle that '[t]he law . . . is constantly based on notions of morality,' *Bowers,* 478 U.S. at 196, 106 S.Ct. at 2846, was not announced for the first time in *Bowers* and remains in force today." *Williams,* 478 F.3d at 1323.

3.   The U.S. Court of Appeals for the Fifth Circuit disagreed with *Williams* when it held that *Lawrence* required it to strike down Texas's statute prohibiting the sale of sexual devices. *See Reliable Consultants, Inc. v. Earle,* 517 F.3d 738, 745–46 (5th Cir. 2008). The court explained: "Because of *Lawrence,* the issue before us is whether the Texas statute impermissibly burdens the individual's substantive due process right to engage in private intimate conduct of his or her choosing." *Id.* at 744. In finding an impermissible burden, the court did not read *Lawrence* as a fundamental rights case: "*Lawrence* did not categorize the right to sexual privacy as a fundamental right, and we do not purport to do so here. Instead, we simply follow the precise instructions from *Lawrence* and hold that the statute violates the right to sexual privacy, however it is otherwise described." *Id.* at 745 n.32.

The court rejected the government's effort to justify the statute on moral grounds, explaining that "if in *Lawrence* public morality was an insufficient justification for a law that restricted 'adult consensual intimacy in the home,' then public morality also cannot serve as a rational basis for Texas's statute, which also regulates private sexual intimacy." *Id.* at 745 (quoting *Lawrence,* 539 U.S. at 564, 123 S.Ct. at 2476) (footnote omitted).

The *Reliable Consultants* court also rejected a second rationale proffered by the state: that the statute was needed to protect the sensibilities of "unwilling adults from exposure to sexual devices and their advertisement." *Reliable Consultants*, 517 F.3d at 746. In rejecting this government interest, the court noted that it "bears no rational relation to the restriction on sales of sexual devices because an adult cannot buy a sexual device without making the affirmative decision to visit a store and make the purchase." *Id.*

Finally, the court rejected the argument that striking down the statute essentially provides constitutional protection to the "commercial sale of sex." *Id.* at 746. Instead, the court explained that "[t]he sale of a device that an individual may choose to use during intimate conduct with a partner in the home is not the 'sale of sex' (prostitution)." *Id.*

4.   After the almost decade-long *Williams* litigation finally came to an end in 2007, the Alabama Supreme Court added its two cents by upholding the validity of the sexual device statute under both the federal and state constitutions. *See 1568 Montgomery Hwy. Inc. v. City of Hoover*, 45 So.3d 319 (Ala.Sup.Ct. 2010). Prior to *Lawrence*, three state supreme courts had struck down their respective statutes prohibiting the sale, distribution, and promotion of obscene devices. *See Colorado v. Seven Thirty-Five East Colfax, Inc.*, 697 P.2d 348 (Colo. 1985); *Kansas v. Hughes*, 792 P.2d 1023, 246 Kan. 607 (1990); *Louisiana v. Brenan*, 772 So.2d 64 (La. 2000). The U.S. Court of Appeals for the Eleventh Circuit, the same court that upheld Alabama's law in *Williams*, had struck down Georgia's statute, which not only prohibited the sale of sexual devices, but also their advertisement. The court concluded that the latter restriction was a violation of the First Amendment. *See This That and the Other Gift and Tobacco, Inc. v. Cobb County*, 285 F.3d 1319, 1323 (11th Cir. 2002). There remain, in addition to Alabama, only two states with such laws: Mississippi, see MISS. CODE. ANN. § 97–29–105 (2010) and Virginia, see VA. CODE. ANN. § 18.2373 (2010). The Mississippi statute was upheld by the state supreme court in *PHE, Inc. v. State*, 877 So.2d 1244 (Miss. 2004).

5.   *Incest.* Paul Lowe was found guilty of incest for having consensual sexual intercourse with his 22-year-old stepdaughter. After his conviction was upheld by the state's supreme court, see *State v. Lowe*, 861 N.E.2d 512, 112 Ohio St.3d 507 (2007), he filed a habeas corpus petition in federal court. The U.S. Court of Appeals for the Sixth Circuit dismissed the petition after rejecting Lowe's claim that he had a fundamental right under *Lawrence* to engage in consensual sexual conduct with his adult stepdaughter, with whom he was not biologically related. *See Lowe v. Swanson*, 663 F.3d 258, 264–65 (6th Cir. 2011), *cert. denied*, 123 S.Ct. 2383 (2012). The court explained that "[u]nlike sexual relationships between unrelated same-sex adults, the stepparent-stepchild relationship is the kind of relationship in which a person might be injured or coerced or where consent might not easily be refused, regardless of age, because of the inherent influence of the stepparent over the stepchild." *Id.* at 264. The court, citing *Williams*, also rejected Lowe's contention that the incest statute was unconstitutional because it was

"morality-based," concluding that "the *Lawrence* Court did not categorically invalidate criminal laws that are based in part on morality." *Id.*

6.   *Polygamy.* In rejecting a due process challenge to Utah's bigamy statue, which prohibits a married person from cohabiting with or purporting to marry another person, the state supreme court explained that

> the behavior at issue in this case is not confined to personal decisions made about sexual activity, but rather raises important questions about the State's ability to regulate marital relationships and prevent the formation and propagation of marital forms that the citizens of the State deem harmful. "Sexual intercourse . . . is the most intimate behavior in which the citizenry engages. [*Lawrence*] spoke to this discreet, personal activity. Marriage, on the other hand, includes both public and private conduct. Within the privacy of the home, marriage means essentially whatever the married individuals wish it to mean. Nonetheless, marriage extends beyond the confines of the home to our society." (citation omitted). . . . The very "concept of marriage possesses undisputed social value" (citation omitted). Utah's own constitution enshrines a commitment to prevent polygamous behavior. That commitment has undergirded this State's establishment of "a vast and convoluted network of . . . laws . . . based exclusively upon the practice of monogamy as opposed to plural marriage." *Potter v. Murray City,* 760 F.2d 1065, 1070 (10th Cir. 1985). Our State's commitment to monogamous unions is a recognition that decisions made by individuals as to how to structure even the most personal of relationships are capable of dramatically affecting public life.

State v. Holm, 137 P.3d 726, 743 (Ut. 2006). The court added that "marital relationships serve as the building blocks of our society. The State must be able to assert some level of control over those relationships to ensure the smooth operation of laws and further the proliferation of social unions our society deems beneficial while discouraging those deemed harmful. The people of this State have declared monogamy a beneficial marital form and have also declared polygamous relationships harmful." *Id.* at 744.

In contrast, a dissenting opinion disputed the view that the state's interest in protecting marriage provided it with the constitutional authority to criminalize consensual sexual relationships between adults:

> I agree with the majority that marriage, when understood as a legal union, qualifies as "an institution the law protects." *See* [Lawrence 539 U.S.] at 568, 123 S.Ct. 2472. However, the Court's statement in *Lawrence* that a state may interfere when such an institution is "abuse[d]," *id.,* together with its holding that the sodomy statute was unconstitutional, leads me to infer that, in the Court's view, sexual acts between consenting adults and the private personal relationships within which these acts occur, do not "abuse" the institution of marriage simply because they take place outside its

confines. *See id.* at 585, 123 S.Ct. 2472 (O'Connor, J., concurring in the judgment) (indicating that Texas's criminal sodomy law did not implicate the state's interest in "preserving the traditional institution of marriage" but expressed "mere moral disapproval of an excluded group"). In the wake of *Lawrence,* the Virginia Supreme Court has come to the same conclusion, striking down its state law criminalizing fornication. *Martin v. Ziherl,* 269 Va. 35, 607 S.E.2d 367, 371 (2005). In my opinion, these holdings correctly recognize that individuals in today's society may make varied choices regarding the organization of their family and personal relationships without fearing criminal punishment. * * *

I am concerned that the majority's reasoning may give the impression that the state is free to criminalize any and all forms of personal relationships that occur outside the legal union of marriage. While under *Lawrence* laws criminalizing isolated acts of sodomy are void, the majority seems to suggest that the relationships within which these acts occur may still receive criminal sanction. Following such logic, nonmarital cohabitation might also be considered to fall outside the scope of federal constitutional protection. Indeed, the act of living alone and unmarried could as easily be viewed as threatening social norms.

Holm, 137 P.2d at 777–78 (Durham, C.J., dissenting in part). In 2013, a federal district court struck down the section of the Utah statute that prohibits married individuals from cohabiting with others as violating the Free Exercise Clause of the First Amendment and having no rational basis under the Due Process Clause. *See Brown v. Buhman,* 947 F. Supp.2d 1170 (D. Utah 2013).

A BEDROOM OF ONE'S OWN: MORALITY AND SEXUAL PRIVACY AFTER *LAWRENCE V. TEXAS*[*]

Marybeth Herald

In recent opinions such as *Glucksberg* and *Lawrence*, the Supreme Court has made the discussion of history and tradition a mandatory part of any substantive due process conversation. The *Lawrence* opinion spends a great deal of time arguing that private, consensual sodomy was not historically prosecuted, criticizing the opposite conclusion reached by the Court in *Bowers v. Hardwick*, and illustrating the slippery nature of the Court's historical test. It is unclear from the *Lawrence* opinion, however, what the relevant referential timeframe is, and what level of protection or lack thereof needs to be present.

Moreover, even if we set aside the question of whether there is a sound and consistent method to arrive at a decisive statement of history

---

[*]   Marybeth Herald, *A Bedroom of One's Own: Morality and Sexual Privacy after* Lawrence v. Texas, 16 YALE J. L. & FEMINISM 1, 15–26 (2004).

and tradition, an analysis of the history of sex aids supports finding a privacy interest in private adult use of sex aids. First, private adult masturbation traditionally has not been criminalized. Likewise, there is no significant history or tradition of regulating sex aids such a vibrators and genital massage. In fact, there is a tradition of their legal use, although one coupled with a history of medical misunderstanding and ignorance of women's sexuality.

Physicians used genital massage as early as the middle 1600's to treat female "hysteria" or "womb disease." The symptoms of womb disease included fainting, insomnia, headaches, and, of course, the tendency to be very cranky. The invention of electricity sped up the treatment by allowing the rather lengthy hand massage process to be reduced to a ten-minute treatment. Doctors apparently saw the benefits of using faster electrical devices to treat more patients and bring in more fees. Genital massage was lauded as a miracle cure for its ability to alleviate so many different symptoms so quickly. Before the American Psychiatric Association caught on and changed the medical criteria in 1952, "hysteria" was "one of the most frequently diagnosed diseases in history."

Over the centuries, a variety of devices were invented to supplement or replace hand massage. Indirect methods such as horseback riding, train travel, the vibrations of a sewing machine, and bicycles all had their adherents. Other devices, such as vibrating helmets and jolting chairs met with mixed success. Electromechanical vibrators were used in medicine in 1878. Both men and women were treated with these devices.

The at-home version of the cure appeared publicly at the turn of the twentieth century. An advertisement for a home vibrator named "Vibratile" turned up in McClure's magazine in March 1899, promising a cure for "Neuralgia, Headache, and Wrinkles." The "American Vibrator," advertised that the device "may be attached to any electric light socket, can be used by yourself in the privacy of dressing room or boudoir, and furnishes every woman with the very essence of perpetual youth." Vibrating genital massagers were sold in the Sears Roebuck catalog until the 1920s, ranging in price from $5.95 to $28.75 for the deluxe model. As smaller electrical handheld vibrators were developed, the role of the medical profession disappeared with no real resistance from physicians, perhaps because the time required for the treatment was annoying even before the time constraints of managed care.

Despite the use of vibrators and genital massage as a medical therapy to induce orgasm in women, it is far from clear that a woman's sexual pleasure was in itself important, as opposed to an occasional nuisance to be satisfied as a remedy for other ailments. During the nineteenth century, expert opinion was that sexual intercourse was healthy for women, but there was a difference of opinion as to whether orgasm was required. Of course, recognizing the importance of intercourse, without a corresponding role for female orgasm, satisfied male concerns with a minimum of effort. Expert concern centered on the fear that "manipulation of the clitoris by the partner or by the woman herself would lead directly to compulsive masturbation, nymphomania, or an outright rejection of intercourse." The anxiety about the "potential to unsettle heterosexual hierarchies" translated into medical apathy at best and conscious disregard at worst. Medical textbooks ignored the clitoris, although there is some evidence that, in the 1920s and 1930s in the United States, "expert" opinion in marital sex manuals reflected the importance of female orgasm and clitoral stimulation, but placed responsibility for achieving both upon the male partner.

From the 1930s to the 1960s, vibrator advertising disappeared. Concerns were expressed about female addiction to the device and "male dismay at its efficacy compared to their own efforts." The shift in focus from the female orgasm to male orgasm was reflected in the post World War II sex manuals that "emphasized the male's pleasure when defining successful intercourse and made women's sexual technique responsible for male sexual satisfaction." Unlike the earlier sex manuals of the 1920s and 1930s, these later sex manuals did not put much stock in the importance of female orgasm, finding it overemphasized the responsibility of the woman, and even unnecessary—urging women to acquire the art of "faking it."

The popularity of Sigmund Freud's theories of sexuality was apparent. Freud constructed a theory of female sexuality that distinguished between clitoral and vaginal sexuality, referring to the former as the "immature" form and the latter as the "mature." Freud's theory, in summary, was that a young girl's heterosexual identity "would be consolidated only when the girl shifted her libido away from the mother and the clitoris and on to the father and the vagina." Much depended upon this transfer, because if not completed, neurotic discontent, penis envy, hysteria, and hostility toward men could result. Psychoanalyst Helene Deutsch carried the Freudian theory further into "healthy" subordination: "the vagina symbolically brought together women's reproductive and sexual identities, two aspects of women's psychology that psychoanalysis sought to harmonize under the rubric of innate heterosexuality." There was a label for those women who did not renounce their clitoris: "frigid."

Not only did personal psychological problems flow from the clitoris, but broader societal tragedy as well, including the chaos of women overwhelming men and the resultant destruction of the family. Acceptance of the roles of wife and mother, as well as general passivity were considered normal and crucial. Sexuality was male-centered, culturally established, and labeled as science. If women's sexual satisfaction stemmed from the clitoris—and thus could be achieved independently—then the subordinate and dependent role of women intrinsic to the contemporary understandings of both family and sexuality would be challenged.

Freud's theories conveniently maximized male sexual pleasure by redefining female sexual pleasure. Yet other studies of human sexual behavior, such as those by Kinsey and by Masters and Johnson lent support to the notion that the vagina was not the center of female sexual pleasure. Masters and Johnson's famous study of sexuality, however, involved female subjects who were chosen because they reached orgasm through coitus. In 1976, Shere Hite pointed this flaw out in her own study: obtaining a representative sample of women who would openly discuss their sexuality, especially when they often suffer from the stigmatizing condition of a lack of orgasm, would never be easy * * *

The medical establishment has only recently begun a serious exploration of female sexuality. The dearth of clinical trials and resultant data has created a serious information gap. More research is needed in a variety of areas, including the "determinants of sexual desire in women." The clitoris, now believed to be the centerpiece of female sexual response, has received little specific attention. Despite the fact that more than half of all women, as reported in the Kinsey and Hite reports, do not experience orgasm through penetration alone, the reasons behind women's lack of sexual responsiveness have generally been ignored. * * *

To state the obvious, the male and female anatomies differ, but these differences have both more and less importance than our culture has recognized. Medical care, based on different anatomies, may be different in a number of key respects. For instance, the nature of women's sexual drives has not been adequately emphasized or medically explored. Moreover, the inaccurate belief persists that what pleases men sexually pleases women generally. But what is sauce for the goose is not always sauce for the gander. The anatomical and psychological differences between men and women play a critical role in their different sexual responses, as do cultural roles and lack of sex education. Until recently, little attention has been paid to these differences. Ignorance hardly has resulted in bliss in these circumstances.

When states have banned vibrators and other sex aids, litigation strategies challenging these laws have reinforced existing biases involving women's sexuality. Lawyers have framed their arguments in a language that asserts that banning these devices would harm women who need them medically to achieve orgasm. The reality is that many healthy women find their normal sexual needs often are met with sex aids better than through traditional male-female sexual positions.

Use of the terms "dysfunction" and "medical need" in litigation reinforces a view of female sexuality through a male-oriented lens. Instead of fighting for general recognition that the use of vibrators makes achievement of orgasm easier for a broad range of women, past litigation strategies have opted to chip away at the laws by using socially sympathetic plaintiffs. This strategy is understandable: offering plaintiffs who are anorgasmic married women using the sex devices with their husbands, women who began using the devices with their husbands but who now are single (no reason for the split revealed), or disabled women allows the court to acknowledge female sexual needs without challenging the primacy of marriage and the male role. Courts seem more willing to see a constitutional right of women to the private use of these devices as long as they have a legally sanctioned relationship with a man or as long as the use of the device is for medical or therapeutic purposes, suggesting a quasi-prescription requirement. Thus to use a vibrator, women have to be sick or married. Practicing sound litigation strategies, lawyers have chosen plaintiffs who have the best chance of chipping away at the law, given cultural bias, but that also maintain existing legal restrictions on women's sexual fulfillment in general.

Arguing within the quasi-prescription rubric in the Kansas case *State v. Hughes* [792 P.2d 1023 (Kan. 1990)] a psychologist and sex therapist testified on behalf of a defendant (charged with selling various devices) that vibrators and dildos were used in the treatment of anorgasmic and incontinent women. The justifications for use of the prohibited sex toys included: (1) some women are physiologically less responsive and use of the vibrator or dildo lowers the threshold for response; (2) by producing intense stimulation and orgasm, these devices break down the patient's orgasmic inhibitions; and (3) the dildo or vibrator helps the patient perform Kegel exercise to improve pelvic muscles.

The strategy was successful. The Kansas court held that the "statute is impermissibly overbroad when it impinges without justification on the sphere of constitutionally protected privacy which encompasses therapy for medical and psychological disorders." Note that the exception that the Kansas Supreme Court carved out of the statute defines a female pathology. In Louisiana and Colorado, similar laws were struck down as being overbroad because they contained no exception for medical and therapeutic uses. [*Louisiana v. Brenan*, 772 So.2d 64 (La. 2000); *Colorado v. Seven Thirty-Five East Colfax, Inc.*, 697 P.2d 348 (Colo. 1985)].

With regard to sex aids, rather than conceptualizing these devices as necessary to correct sexual dysfunction in women, it would be more accurate to recognize that many women may not necessarily achieve orgasm through the traditional sexual positions that allow a male to achieve orgasm. Because of anatomical differences, the sexual position that is most likely to guarantee procreation and male orgasm may be much less likely to achieve orgasm in females because it does not stimulate the clitoris.

Studies that are more recent indicate that forty-three percent of women experience sexual problems. These numbers are consistent with earlier studies of the "frigidity" rates of women. It is a wonder that the high percentage alone does not alert us to the fact that it may not necessarily be the woman who is sexually dysfunctional. A more logical conclusion to be drawn from the data might be that it is the culture, one that fails to investigate the issues and to educate its citizenry, that is dysfunctional. Rather than claiming this high percentage of sexual problems is a treatable "medical condition," it could be recognized as a "social condition," leading to much-needed research and education of both women and men.

If women are to achieve orgasm on a regular basis, as men do, apparently some method in addition to, or other than, the traditional implantation of the penis into the vagina often has to take place. The idealization of heterosexual sex generally as requiring male erection and vaginal penetration likely arose because it is a good position for procreation and male orgasm. If not satisfied by this model of heterosexual sex, women risked being labeled frigid, or learned the adaptive behavior of "faking it," a talent that Meg Ryan demonstrated to the surprised Billy Crystal in a restaurant in the movie When Harry Met Sally. Like Crystal's character, most college men in a study were almost certain that women never faked orgasm with them, while almost all the college women acknowledged "faking it" some of the time.

In summary, very little research has been done in the area of female sexuality; as a result, almost half of women are labeled sexually dysfunctional (if in fact the other half are even being honest about their sex lives). Furthermore, several states have criminalized the sale of devices that aid female orgasm. Lawyers have smartly noted that the most sympathetic challenges involve those brought by "dysfunctional" females. Consequently, these cases are brought to the attention of the courts. Thus, women currently must be tagged with the medical and legal label of "dysfunctional" in order to gain access to devices that help women achieve orgasm. These laws are unfair, stigmatizing, misguided, and "uncommonly silly." The question that remains is whether these laws are unconstitutional after the Court's decision in *Lawrence*.

2. *Lawrence* as a Heightened Scrutiny Case

In contrast to the ruling by the U.S. Court of Appeals for the Eleventh Circuit in *Williams v. Attorney General of Alabama*,[42] the U.S. Court of Appeals for the Ninth Circuit held in *Witt v. Department of Air*

---

[42] 378 F.3d 1232 (11th Cir. 2004).

the Force, the next case, that *Lawrence* requires the application of heightened scrutiny.[43] As you will see, *Witt* involved a constitutional challenge to the military's "Don't Ask, Don't Tell" policy. We will explore that policy, which has since been repealed by Congress, in more detail below in Chapter 5, Section III.B.3. For now, we are mostly interested in how the *Witt* court interpreted and applied *Lawrence v. Texas*.[44]

WITT V. DEPARTMENT OF THE AIR FORCE

U.S. Court of Appeals, Ninth Circuit, 2008
527 F.3d 806

GOULD, CIRCUIT JUDGE.

Plaintiff-Appellant Major Margaret Witt ("Major Witt") sued the Air Force, the Secretary of Defense, the Secretary of the Air Force, and her Air Force commander ("the Air Force") after she was suspended from duty as an Air Force reservist nurse on account of her sexual relationship with a civilian woman. Major Witt alleges that 10 U.S.C. § 654, commonly known as the "Don't Ask, Don't Tell" policy ("DADT"), violates substantive due process, the Equal Protection Clause, and procedural due process. She seeks to enjoin DADT's enforcement. The district court dismissed the suit under Federal Rule of Civil Procedure 12(b)(6) for failure to state a claim. We reverse and remand in part, and affirm in part. . . .

Major Witt entered the Air Force in 1987. She was commissioned as a Second Lieutenant that same year and promoted to First Lieutenant in 1989, to Captain in 1991, and to Major in 1999. In 1995, she transferred from active to reserve duty and was assigned to McChord Air Force Base in Tacoma, Washington.

By all accounts, Major Witt was an outstanding Air Force officer. She received medals for her service, including the Meritorious Service Medal, the Air Medal, the Aerial Achievement Medal, the Air Force Commendation Medal, and numerous others. Her annual "Officer Performance Reviews" commended her accomplishments and abilities. Major Witt was made an Air Force "poster child" in 1993, when the Air Force featured her in recruitment materials; photos of her appeared in Air Force promotional materials for more than a decade.

Major Witt was in a committed and long-term relationship with another woman from July 1997 through August 2003. Major Witt's partner was never a member nor a civilian employee of any branch of the armed forces, and Major Witt states that she never had sexual relations while on duty or while on the grounds of any Air Force base. During their

---

[43] 527 F.3d 806 (9th Cir. 2008).

[44] 539 U.S. 558, 123 S.Ct. 2472, 156 L.Ed.2d 508 (2003).

relationship, Major Witt and her partner shared a home in Spokane, Washington, about 250 miles away from McChord Air Force Base. While serving in the Air Force, Major Witt never told any member of the military that she was homosexual.

In July 2004, Major Witt was contacted by Major Adam Torem, who told her that he had been assigned to investigate an allegation that she was homosexual. She declined to make any statement to him. An Air Force chaplain contacted her thereafter to discuss her homosexuality, but she declined to speak to him, as well. In November 2004, Major Witt's Air Force superiors told her that they were initiating formal separation proceedings against her on account of her homosexuality. This was confirmed in a memorandum that Major Witt received on November 9, 2004. That memorandum also stated that she could not engage in any "pay or point activity pending resolution" of the separation proceedings. Stated another way, she could not be paid as a reservist, she could not earn points toward promotion, and she could not earn retirement benefits. When she received this memorandum, Major Witt was less than one year short of twenty years of service for the Air Force, at which time she would have earned a right to a full Air Force retirement pension.

Sixteen months later, on March 6, 2006, Major Witt received another memorandum notifying her that a discharge action was being initiated against her on account of her homosexuality. It also advised her of her right to request an administrative hearing, which she promptly did. On April 12, 2006, Major Witt filed this suit in the United States District Court for the Western District of Washington, seeking declaratory and injunctive relief from the discharge proceedings.

A military hearing was held on September 28–29, 2006. The military board found that Major Witt had engaged in homosexual acts and had stated that she was a homosexual in violation of DADT. It recommended that she be honorably discharged from the Air Force Reserve. The Secretary of the Air Force acted on this recommendation on July 10, 2007, ordering that Major Witt receive an honorable discharge.

Major Witt is well regarded in her unit, and she believes that she would continue to be so regarded even if the entire unit was made aware that she is homosexual. She also contends that the proceedings against her have had a negative effect on unit cohesion and morale, and that there is currently a shortage of nurses in the Air Force of her rank and ability. We must presume those facts to be true for the purposes of this appeal. * * *

To evaluate Major Witt's substantive due process claim, we first must determine the proper level of scrutiny to apply. In previous cases, we have applied rational basis review to DADT and predecessor policies. However, Major Witt argues that *Lawrence* effectively overruled those cases by establishing a fundamental right to engage in adult consensual sexual acts. The Air Force disagrees. Having carefully considered *Lawrence* and the arguments of the parties, we hold that *Lawrence* requires something more than traditional rational basis review and that remand is therefore appropriate. * * *

The parties urge us to pick through *Lawrence* with a fine-toothed comb and to give credence to the particular turns of phrase used by the Supreme Court that best support their claims. But given the studied limits of the verbal analysis in *Lawrence,* this approach is not conclusive. Nor does a review of our circuit precedent answer the question; as the Court of Appeals for the Armed Forces stated in *United States v. Marcum,* 60 M.J. 198 (C.A.A.F. 2004), "[a]lthough particular sentences within the Supreme Court's opinion may be culled in support of the Government's argument, other sentences may be extracted to support Appellant's argument." In these ambiguous circumstances, we analyze *Lawrence* by considering what the Court actually *did,* rather than by dissecting isolated pieces of text. In so doing, we conclude that the Supreme Court applied a heightened level of scrutiny in *Lawrence.*

We cannot reconcile what the Supreme Court did in *Lawrence* with the minimal protections afforded by traditional rational basis review. First, the Court overruled *Bowers,* an earlier case in which the Court had upheld a Georgia sodomy law under rational basis review. If the Court was undertaking rational basis review, then *Bowers* must have been wrong because it failed under that standard; namely, it must have lacked "any reasonably conceivable state of facts that could provide a rational basis for the classification." *FCC v. Beach Commc'ns, Inc.,* 508 U.S. 307 (1993). But the Court's criticism of *Bowers* had nothing to do with the basis for the law; instead, the Court rejected *Bowers* because of the "Court's own failure to appreciate the extent of the liberty at stake." *Lawrence,* 539 U.S. at 567, 123 S.Ct. 2472.

The criticism that the Court in *Bowers* had misapprehended "the extent of the liberty at stake" does not sound in rational basis review. Under rational basis review, the Court determines whether governmental action is so arbitrary that a rational basis for the action cannot even be conceived *post hoc.* If the Court was applying that standard—"a paradigm of judicial restraint," *Beach,* 508 U.S. at 314—it had no reason to consider the extent of the liberty involved. Yet it did, ultimately concluding that the ban on homosexual sexual conduct sought to "control a personal relationship that, whether or not entitled to formal recognition in the law, is within the liberty of persons to choose without being punished as criminals." *Lawrence,* 539 U.S. at 567, 123 S.Ct. 2472. This is inconsistent with rational basis review.

Second, the cases on which the Supreme Court explicitly based its decision in *Lawrence* are based on heightened scrutiny. As Major Witt pointed out, those cases include *Griswold, Roe,* and *Carey.* Moreover, the Court stated that *Casey,* a post-*Bowers* decision, cast its holding in *Bowers* into doubt. *Lawrence,* 539 U.S. at 573–74, 123 S.Ct. 2472. Notably, the Court did not mention or apply the post-*Bowers* case of *Romer v. Evans,* 517 U.S. 620, 116 S.Ct. 1620, 134 L.Ed.2d 855 (1996), in which the Court applied rational basis review to a law concerning homosexuals. Instead, the Court overturned *Bowers* because "[i]ts continuance as precedent demeans the lives of homosexual persons." *Lawrence,* 539 U.S. at 575, 123 S.Ct. 2472.

Third, the *Lawrence* Court's rationale for its holding—the inquiry analysis that it was applying—is inconsistent with rational basis review. The Court declared: "The Texas statute furthers no legitimate state interest *which can justify its intrusion into the personal and private life of the individual.*" *Id.* at 578, 123 S.Ct. 2472 (emphasis added). Were the Court applying rational basis review, it would not identify a legitimate state interest to "justify" the particular intrusion of liberty at issue in *Lawrence;* regardless of the liberty involved, any hypothetical rationale for the law would do.

We therefore conclude that *Lawrence* applied something more than traditional rational basis review. This leaves open the question whether the Court applied strict scrutiny, intermediate scrutiny, or another heightened level of scrutiny. Substantive due process cases typically apply strict scrutiny in the case of a fundamental right and rational basis review in all other cases. When a fundamental right is recognized, substantive due process forbids the infringement of that right "at all, no matter what process is provided, unless the infringement is narrowly tailored to serve a compelling state interest." *Reno v. Flores,* 507 U.S. 292, 301–02, 113 S.Ct. 1439, 123 L.Ed.2d 1 (1993) (emphasis omitted). Few laws survive such scrutiny, and DADT most likely would not. However, we hesitate to apply strict scrutiny when the Supreme Court did not discuss narrow tailoring or a compelling state interest in *Lawrence,* and we do not address the issue here.

Instead, we look to another recent Supreme Court case that applied a heightened level of scrutiny to a substantive due process claim—a scrutiny that resembles and expands upon the analysis performed in *Lawrence.*[6] In *Sell v. United States,* 539 U.S. 166, 179, 123 S.Ct. 2174, 156 L.Ed.2d 197 (2003), the Court considered whether the Constitution permits the government to forcibly administer antipsychotic drugs to a

---

[6] Although we agree with the Eleventh Circuit that the *Lawrence* Court did not apply strict scrutiny, *Lofton,* 358 F.3d at 817, in our view, the Eleventh Circuit failed to appreciate both the liberty interest recognized by *Lawrence* and the heightened-scrutiny balancing employed by *Lawrence.*

mentally-ill defendant in order to render that defendant competent to stand trial. The Court held that the defendant has a "significant constitutionally protected liberty interest" at stake, so the drugs could be administered forcibly "only if the treatment is medically appropriate, is substantially unlikely to have side effects that may undermine the fairness of the trial, and, taking account of less intrusive alternatives, is necessary significantly to further important governmental trial-related interests." *Id.* at 178–80, 123 S.Ct. 2174 (internal quotation marks omitted).

Although the Court's holding in *Sell* is specific to the context of forcibly administering medication, the scrutiny employed by the Court to reach that holding is instructive. The Court recognized a "significant" liberty interest—the interest "in avoiding the unwanted administration of antipsychotic drugs"—and balanced that liberty interest against the "legitimate" and "important" state interest "in providing appropriate medical treatment to reduce the danger that an inmate suffering from a serious mental disorder represents to himself or others."[7] *Sell,* 539 U.S. at 178, 123 S.Ct. 2174 (internal quotation marks omitted). To balance those two interests, the Court required the state to justify its intrusion into an individual's recognized liberty interest against forcible medication—just as *Lawrence* determined that the state had failed to "justify its intrusion into the personal and private life of the individual." *Lawrence,* 539 U.S. at 578, 123 S.Ct. 2472.

The heightened scrutiny applied in *Sell* consisted of four factors:

> First, a court must find that *important* governmental interests are at stake. . . . Courts, however, must consider the facts of the individual case in evaluating the Government's interest. . . . Special circumstances may lessen the importance of that interest. . . . Second, the court must conclude that involuntary medication will *significantly further* those concomitant state interests. . . . Third, the court must conclude that involuntary medication is *necessary* to further those interests. The court must find that any alternative, less intrusive treatments are unlikely to achieve substantially the same results. . . . Fourth, . . . the court must conclude that administration of the drugs is *medically appropriate.* . . .

539 U.S. at 180–81. The fourth factor is specific to the medical context of *Sell,* but the first three factors apply equally here. We thus take our direction from the Supreme Court and adopt the first three heightened-scrutiny *Sell* factors as the heightened scrutiny balancing analysis

---

[7] This inquiry is similar to intermediate scrutiny in equal protection cases. *See Craig v. Boren,* 429 U.S. 190, 197, 97 S.Ct. 451, 50 L.Ed.2d 397 (1976) ("To withstand constitutional challenge, . . . classifications by gender must serve important governmental objectives and must be substantially related to achievement of those objectives.").

required under *Lawrence.* We hold that when the government attempts to intrude upon the personal and private lives of homosexuals, in a manner that implicates the rights identified in *Lawrence,* the government must advance an important governmental interest, the intrusion must significantly further that interest, and the intrusion must be necessary to further that interest. In other words, for the third factor, a less intrusive means must be unlikely to achieve substantially the government's interest.

In addition, we hold that this heightened scrutiny analysis is as-applied rather than facial. "This is the preferred course of adjudication since it enables courts to avoid making unnecessarily broad constitutional judgments." *City of Cleburne v. Cleburne Living Ctr. Inc.,* 473 U.S. 432, 447, 105 S.Ct. 3249, 87 L.Ed.2d 313 (1985). In *Cleburne,* the Court employed a "type of 'active' rational basis review," *Pruitt,* 963 F.2d at 1165–66, in requiring the city to justify its zoning ordinance as applied to the specific plaintiffs in that case. And *Sell* required courts to "consider the facts of the individual case in evaluating the Government's interest." 539 U.S. at 180. Under this review, we must determine not whether DADT has some hypothetical, posthoc rationalization in general, but whether a justification exists for the application of the policy as applied to Major Witt. This approach is necessary to give meaning to the Supreme Court's conclusion that "liberty gives substantial protection to adult persons in deciding how to conduct their private lives in matters pertaining to sex." *Lawrence,* 539 U.S. at 572. * * *

Here, applying heightened scrutiny to DADT in light of current Supreme Court precedents, it is clear that the government advances an important governmental interest. DADT concerns the management of the military, and "judicial deference to . . . congressional exercise of authority is at its apogee when legislative action under the congressional authority to raise and support armies and make rules and regulations for their governance is challenged." *Rostker v. Goldberg,* 453 U.S. 57, 70, 101 S.Ct. 2646, 69 L.Ed.2d 478 (1981). Notably, "deference does not mean abdication." *Id.* "Congress, of course, is subject to the requirements of the Due Process Clause when legislating in the area of military affairs. . . ." *Weiss v. United States,* 510 U.S. 163, 176, 114 S.Ct. 752, 127 L.Ed.2d 1 (1994).

However, it is unclear on the record before us whether DADT, as applied to Major Witt, satisfies the second and third factors. The Air Force attempts to justify the policy by relying on congressional findings regarding "unit cohesion" and the like, but that does not go to whether the application of DADT specifically to Major Witt significantly furthers the government's interest and whether less intrusive means would achieve substantially the government's interest. Remand therefore is required for the district court to develop the record on Major Witt's substantive due process claim. Only then can DADT be measured against the appropriate constitutional standard.

[The discussion of the plaintiff's equal protection and procedural due process claims is omitted, as is a concurring and dissenting opinion].

NOTES

1. A few months after *Witt*, the U.S. Court of Appeals for the First Circuit upheld the constitutionality of the DADT policy in *Cook v. Gates*, 528 F.3d 42 (1st Cir. 2008). In discussing the due process claim, the court in *Cook* rejected the government's position that *Lawrence* had applied traditional rational basis review. Instead, the court held that *Lawrence* "recognize[d] a protected liberty interest for adults to engage in private, consensual sexual intimacy and applied a *balancing* of constitutional interests *that defies either the strict scrutiny or rational basis label.*" *Id.* at 52 (emphases added). But the First Circuit then proceeded to deny the plaintiff's challenge to the DADT policy, concluding that the government's interest in "preserv[ing] the military's effectiveness as a fighting force, and thus . . . ensur[ing] national security, outweighed the plaintiff's interest in engaging in consensual and private sexual activity." *Id.* at 60. As we will see in Chapter 5, Section III.B.3, Congress two years later repealed the DADT statute.

2. After remand, and before Congress repealed the policy, the federal district judge hearing the *Witt* case ruled that the plaintiff's dismissal from the military was unconstitutional. *See Witt v. Department of the Air Force*, 739 F.Supp.2d 1308 (W.D. Wash.2010). The judge's ruling stated that "[t]he evidence before the Court is that Major Margaret Witt was an exemplary officer. She was an effective leader, a caring mentor, a skilled clinician, and an integral member of an effective team. Her loss within the squadron resulted in a diminution of the unit's ability to carry out its mission . . . The evidence clearly supports the plaintiff's assertion that the reinstatement of Major Witt would not adversely affect the morale or . . . cohesion of" her unit. *Id.* at 1315.

3. For over a decade after *Lawrence v. Texas*, the Uniform Code of Military Justice continued to criminalize consensual sodomy regardless of the gender of the parties. Whether that provision was constitutional after *Lawrence* was addressed by the Court of Appeals for the Armed Forces in *United States v. Marcum*, 60 M.J. 198 (C.A.A.F. 2004). The *Marcum* court rejected the government's argument that *Lawrence* had no applicability to the military's criminal code. At the same time, however, the court refused to address the facial constitutionality of the military's sodomy statute; instead, it held that the constitutional determination had to be made on an as-applied basis. The court developed a three part test to assess whether a particular defendant could be prosecuted for consensual sodomy: first, whether the conduct in question fell within the range of protected conduct under *Lawrence*; second, whether any of the exceptions noted in *Lawrence* (such as sexual conduct in public or with minors) applied; and third, whether there

were "additional factors relevant solely in the military environment that affect the nature and reach of the *Lawrence* liberty interest[.]" *Id.* at 207. The court upheld Marcum's conviction for consensual sodomy, which occurred in private and off-base, because he engaged in the conduct with another member of the armed forces who was of a lower rank. The court concluded that the difference in rank between the two men was a sufficient justification to uphold the constitutionality of the Uniform Code of Military Justice's sodomy provision as applied to the facts of the case. A few years after it repealed DADT, Congress amended the Uniform Code of Military Justice by limiting its prohibition against "unnatural carnal copulation" to instances of forcible sodomy and bestiality. Article 125, Uniform Code of Military Justice, as amended by section 1707 of the 2014 Defense Authorization Bill.

G. THE CASE OF PUBLIC SEX

The defendants in *Lawrence* were arrested for allegedly engaging in consensual sex in the home. What if they had been arrested for engaging in sex in a less private place, such as a sex club, public bathroom or park? Would the liberty interest recognized in *Lawrence* to engage in consensual sexual conduct apply then? The following materials address that question.

SINGSON V. COMMONWEALTH

Court of Appeals of Virginia, 2005
621 S.E.2d 682, 46 Va.App. 724

ROBERT J. HUMPHREYS, JUDGE.

Appellant Joel Dulay Singson ("Singson") appeals his conviction, following a conditional guilty plea, for solicitation to commit oral sodomy, in violation of Code §§ 18.2–29 (criminal solicitation) and 18.2–361 (crimes against nature). Based on the holding of the United States Supreme Court in *Lawrence v. Texas*, 539 U.S. 558 (2003), Singson contends that Code § 18.2–361 is facially unconstitutional because it prohibits private acts of consensual sodomy, in violation of the Due Process Clause of the Fourteenth Amendment. Thus, Singson argues that he cannot be convicted for attempting, through solicitation, to violate that statute. * * *

The relevant facts are not in dispute. At approximately 4:00 p.m. on March 20, 2003, Singson walked into a men's restroom located in a department store. The restroom is freely accessible to members of the public, including children. Once in the restroom, Singson entered the handicapped bathroom stall and remained in that stall for approximately thirty minutes. Singson then left the handicap bathroom stall and approached a stall occupied by an undercover police officer. Singson "stopped in front of the stall, leaned forward," and "peered into [the] stall through the crack in the stall door." The undercover police officer, who was in "a state of undress," asked Singson "What's up?" and "What are you looking for?" Singson replied, "Cock." The officer then asked "What do you want to do," and Singson replied, "I want to suck cock." The undercover officer asked if Singson wanted to suck his penis, and Singson responded, "Yes." When the officer asked, "Do you want to do it in here," Singson nodded towards the handicap stall. The officer then asked if Singson wanted to suck his penis in the handicap stall, and Singson responded, "Yes."

A grand jury indicted Singson for "command[ing], entreat[ing] or otherwise attempt[ing] to persuade another to commit a felony other than murder," specifically, "Crimes Against Nature," in violation of Code §§ 18.2–29 and 18.2–361. Singson moved to dismiss the indictment, arguing that Code § 18.2–361 "is overbroad and vague, [and] violates the defendant's rights to Due Process under the United States Constitution as outlined in the recent U.S. Supreme Court opinion in [*Lawrence v. Texas*, 539 U.S. 558]."

The trial court overruled the motion to dismiss, reasoning that *Lawrence* did not apply because "the restrooms within [s]tores open to the public are not within the zone of privacy as contemplated by the United States Supreme Court." The court further noted that it could not "imagine too much more [of a] public place than a restroom in a shopping mall." Singson entered a conditional guilty plea, and the trial court, noting Singson's extensive criminal history of prior, similar behavior, imposed a sentence of three years in prison. The court suspended two and one-half years of Singson's sentence, resulting in a total active sentence of six months. * * *

Citing the United States Supreme Court's decision in *Lawrence v. Texas*, Singson . . . contends that Code § 18.2–361 is facially unconstitutional because it encompasses private acts of consensual sodomy, thus offending the Due Process Clause of the Fourteenth Amendment. However, because Singson's conduct occurred in a public place—not a private location—we hold that he lacks standing to challenge the constitutionality of Code § 18.2–361 on this ground. Accordingly, we do not reach the issue of whether, applying *Lawrence*, Code § 18.2–361 is facially unconstitutional under the Fourteenth Amendment because it encompasses private—as well as public—acts of consensual sodomy. And, because application of Code § 18.2–361 under the circumstances of this case neither implicates nor violates Singson's constitutional right to due process of law, we conclude that this assignment of error has no merit. * * *

[A] litigant "has standing to challenge the constitutionality of a statute only insofar as it has an adverse impact on his own rights." *County Court of Ulster County v. Allen*, 442 U.S. 140, 154–55 (1979).

Thus, "[a]s a general rule, if there is no constitutional defect in the application of the statute to the litigant, he does not have standing to argue that it would be unconstitutional if applied to third parties in hypothetical situations." *Id.* at 155. * * *

Accordingly . . . we hold that Singson lacks standing to mount a facial challenge to Code § 18.2–361. Rather, this Court is constrained to deciding whether Code § 18.2–361 is constitutional as applied to the circumstances of this case. And, for the reasons that follow, we hold that application of Code § 18.2–361 to Singson's proposed conduct does not offend the Due Process Clause of the Fourteenth Amendment. * * *

[I]n *Lawrence*, the Supreme Court explicitly noted that the case being decided on appeal did not "involve public conduct or prostitution." *Id.* The Court, therefore, only addressed the constitutionality of criminalizing "adult consensual sexual intimacy in the home," *id.* at 564, leaving undisturbed the states' authority to prohibit sexual conduct that occurs in a public—rather than private—arena. *See, e.g., State v. Thomas*, 891 So.2d 1233, 1236, 1238 (La.2005) (declining to use *Lawrence* to strike down a law criminalizing solicitation of a crime against nature, noting that "the majority opinion in *Lawrence* specifically states the court's decision does not disturb state statutes prohibiting public sexual conduct or prostitution"); *State v. Pope*, 608 S.E.2d 114, 116 (reversing dismissal of indictment based upon the defendant's "encounter with undercover police officers in which she indicated she would perform oral sex in exchange for money," reasoning that, "[a]s the *Lawrence* Court expressly excluded prostitution and public conduct from its holding, the State of North Carolina may properly criminalize the solicitation of a sexual act it deems a crime against nature"), *review denied*, 612 S.E.2d 636 (N.C.2005).

Singson argues, however, that, in *Lawrence*, the Supreme Court effectively declared all sodomy statutes facially unconstitutional. Singson points to the Court's statement that "*Bowers* was not correct when it was decided, and it is not correct today," 539 U.S. at 578, 123 S. Ct. at 2484, as evidencing the Supreme Court's belief that no statute encompassing private acts of sodomy can survive scrutiny under the Due Process Clause. We disagree.

In *Bowers*, the appellant was prosecuted for engaging in homosexual acts of sodomy in the privacy of his own home. *See* 478 U.S. at 187–88. After the indictment was dismissed, the appellant brought a suit in federal district court seeking, in essence, a declaratory judgment that the Georgia statute was unconstitutional "as applied to consensual homosexual sodomy." *Id.* at 188 n. 2. The *Bowers* majority carefully stated that its decision "express[ed] no opinion on the constitutionality of the Georgia statute as applied to other acts of sodomy," *id.*, later noting that the issue being resolved in the appeal involved the continuing imposition of "criminal penalties for sodomy performed in private and between consenting adults," *id.* at 194. Similarly, the principal dissent in *Bowers* noted that the issue being decided concerned "the right of an individual to conduct intimate relationships in the intimacy of his or her own home." *Id.* at 208 (Blackmun, J., dissenting). Thus, despite Singson's argument to the contrary, *Bowers* did not involve a facial challenge to the Georgia sodomy statute. At best, then, the *dicta* in *Lawrence* indicates that the as-applied challenge in *Bowers* should have been upheld, and the statement does not—as Singson contends—announce a *per se* rule that all sodomy statutes are facially unconstitutional.

Singson also argues, however, that the decision of the Virginia Supreme Court in *Martin v. Ziherl*, 607 S.E.2d 367 (2005), effectively declared Code § 18.2–361 facially unconstitutional. In *Martin*, the Virginia Supreme Court held that Code § 18.2–344, which prohibits unmarried individuals from "voluntarily [ ] hav[ing] sexual intercourse with any other person," was unconstitutional in light of the decision in *Lawrence*. However, the Virginia Supreme Court carefully noted that its decision "does not involve minors, non-consensual activity, prostitution, *or public activity*." 607 S.E.2d at 371 (emphasis added). Rather, the Court explicitly restricted its holding to "private, consensual conduct between adults and the respective statutes' impact on such conduct," further noting that its decision "does not affect the Commonwealth's police power regarding regulation of public fornication, prostitution, or other such crimes." *Id.*

Thus, to the extent that Code § 18.2–361 prohibits individuals from engaging in *public* acts of sodomy, the statute survives constitutional scrutiny under the Due Process Clause. And, because Singson's proposed conduct occurred in a public location, application of Code § 18.2–361 under the circumstances of this case does not implicate Singson's constitutionally-protected right to engage in private, consensual acts of sodomy.

Our decision in *DePriest*, 537 S.E.2d 1, is instructive on this point. In *DePriest*, we affirmed the appellants' convictions for solicitation to commit oral sodomy, holding that application of Code § 18.2–361 under the circumstances of that case did not "infringe [ ] [the appellants'] right to privacy" because "the appellants' conduct was not private." [*Id.*] at 5. The appellants in *DePriest* approached "strangers in public parks" and "proposed to commit sodomy in the public parks." *Id.* at 763, 537 S.E.2d at 5. We held that "[t]he appellants' acts and their proposed conduct were clothed with no circumstance giving rise to a supportable claim of privacy," reasoning that, "[w]hatever may be the constitutional privacy rights of one who engages in sodomy in private, those rights do not attach to one who does the same thing in public." *Id.*

Similarly, here, ... Singson approached a stranger in a public restroom in a public department store during business hours, and he proposed to commit sodomy in that restroom. Because Singson's proposed conduct involved a public rather than private location, application of Code § 18.2–361 under the circumstances of this case does not implicate the narrow liberty interest recognized in *Lawrence*. * * * *Affirmed.*

PRIVACY, PROPERTY, AND PUBLIC SEX*
Carlos A. Ball

For the gay rights movement, *Lawrence* represented the culmination of a twenty year effort to convince the courts to include gay sexual intimacy within the scope of constitutional protection afforded to other sexual conduct that takes place in the home. Many queer theorists, however, are troubled by this effort to "domesticate" sexual liberty. From th[eir] perspective, the home, as a sexual site, can serve as an extension of the closet, a place where sex is permitted (or tolerated) precisely because it is hidden from view. The notion that the only gay sex that is permissible is that which takes place in the privacy of the bedroom reinforces the idea that such sex is shameful and debasing. When lesbians and gay men limit their sexuality to sex with their partners in the privacy of their homes, the argument goes, they replicate the traditional sexual practices and mores of heterosexuals. The bedroom, then, acts as a sanitizing site through which gay sex is cleansed and made more acceptable (i.e., made more like heterosexual sex). In contrast, when gay sex takes place outside of the privacy of the home, its publicness transforms it into *queer* sex. It becomes, in other words, a form of transgressive sex that challenges heteronormative values and practices.

Part of the transgressiveness of public (or non-domesticated) sex lies in the fact that it is usually both anonymous and lacking in emotional commitment. Some queer theorists are critical of the efforts by the gay rights movement to "mainstream" gay sexuality by, for example, seeking admission into the institution of marriage. From this queer theory perspective, the struggle to gain marital recognition of same-sex relationships is a misguided effort to normalize gay sexuality by creating the illusion that all gay people want the same thing, in terms of sexual intimacy, that ostensibly most straight people seek, that is, a life-long commitment with one sexual partner. The anonymity and lack of emotional commitment that usually accompany public sex, then, become for some an appealingly transgressive alternative to the assimilationist and conservative goal of encouraging individuals, regardless of sexual orientation, to marry.

---

* Carlos A. Ball, *Privacy, Property, and Public Sex*, 18 COLUM. J. GENDER & L. 1, 6–10, 13–14, 42–45, 21–22, 48–51 (2008).

Queer theorists value public sex not only because of its transgressiveness, but also because of its accessibility. Not everyone has a bedroom to call her own, and [young] gay people in particular may have a hard time finding spaces in their family homes where they can have sex. In contrast to bedrooms, public sex sites are generally accessible by anyone who is interested in the type of sex that takes place therein.

The accessibility of public sex, in turn, plays an important role in transmitting knowledge about gay sexuality. Michael Warner notes that gay people have a limited opportunity to learn about gay sex, and that the ability to observe others engaging in that sex, whether in person or through pornographic materials, helps to educate gay people sexually. Warner points out that "[s]exual knowledges can be made cumulative," so that when queers see others like themselves having sex, they come to realize "that each touch, gesture, or sensation condenses lessons learned not only through one's own experience, but through the experience of others."[34] * * *

A truly radical understanding of sexual liberty . . . could seek to defend the rights of individuals to have sex anywhere, at any time, and in front of anybody. There are, however, at least three reasons why not even the most radical proponents of public sex defend such an expansive understanding of sexual liberty. The first is that those who do not want to observe the sex in question—individuals whom we can refer to as "unwilling gazers"—have a legitimate interest in not having sex thrust upon them. The second reason is that while a *willing* gaze by consenting observers may enhance the pleasurable experience arising from sex for some sexual actors, an *unwilling* gaze by hostile observers is likely to have the opposite effect by creating tension and discomfort, thus inhibiting or constraining the sexual actors. Finally, unwilling gazes can lead to the harassment of sexual actors by hostile gazers or by law enforcement officials. * * *

[It turns out that] privacy is an exceedingly important consideration for those who choose to engage in public sex. In fact, the likelihood of privacy serves as the crucial factor that helps to distinguish the vast number of public places that are not used as public sex sites from the limited number that are. The important point is this: *without privacy, a public place cannot function as a public sex site.* * * *

[I]t is possible to create zones of privacy in public places [where individuals engage in sex]. An expectation of privacy at these sites may be reasonable if the sexual actors have taken the necessary steps to shield their conduct from unwilling gazers. It would seem, for example, that individuals have a reasonable expectation of privacy when they have sex

---

[34] MICHAEL WARNER, THE TROUBLE WITH NORMAL: SEX POLITICS AND THE ETHICS OF QUEER LIFE 178 (2000).

at a commercial [sex] establishment behind the closed doors of a cubicle or booth. The doors serve as physical barriers that, when coupled with a prevailing norm that other patrons will not enter unless invited, make it unlikely that the sex will be observed by unwilling gazers.

Admittedly, not all of the sexual conduct that occurs in commercial sex establishments takes place behind closed doors. Nonetheless, some commercial sex establishments are configured in ways that make it unlikely that sex which takes place outside of booths and cubicles will be observed by unwilling gazers. The use of the backroom in [a] gay adult bookstore [in Washington, D.C.,] is an example of such a configuration. In order to enter that backroom, patrons have to pay a fee, and then go through a set of curtains to enter a dimly lit area. "The important characteristics [of this backroom] are several: the site is marked, explicitly, for erotic activity, and persons who enter the site may freely assume that they share similar erotic interests with persons already on-site."[154] It is reasonable to assume, therefore, that individuals who enter that particular backroom have consented to observe, and to be observed engaging in, sexual conduct.

It is also, however, reasonable to assume that the likelihood that sex will be observed by unwilling gazers increases, and the extent of the reasonableness of the privacy expectations of the sexual actors therefore decreases, when shifting from private commercial sites to open access areas [such as parks and public bathrooms]. Nonetheless, the sociological literature on public sex shows that it is possible, at least under some circumstances, for sexual actors to use open access spaces in ways that go undetected by potential unwilling gazers.

A . . . study by John Hollister of a highway rest stop that functions as a sexual site [shows] how sexual actors go about privatizing open access areas.[79] Hollister explains, for example, that where individuals park their automobiles (far from or near the restroom facility) and where they stroll after they park (away from or toward the facility) communicate sexual intentions, *but only to the initiated*. As Hollister puts it, "[c]ommunication takes place in relation to the space, and the likely possibilities for the use of that space. Participants reach conclusions as to a man's sexual availability based on how he approaches and occupies the space, and they [in turn] use the space in ways that the other man might recognize." He adds that "[t]he communication is rarely so obvious or direct as to expose

---

[154] William L. Leap, *Sex in "Private" Places: Gender, Erotics, and Detachment in Two Urban Locales, in* PUBLIC SEX/GAY SPACE (William L. Leap ed., 1999), at 115, 127. When Leap interviewed the patrons of this particular establishment, they repeatedly "use[d] the term 'private' . . . to identify and describe [the backroom]." *Id.* at 129.

[79] *See* John Hollister, *A Highway Rest Area as a Socially Reproducible Site, in* PUBLIC SEX/GAY SPACE (William L. Leap ed., 1999), at 55, 58.

the situation to someone who is there by accident, or who may respond violently."

... Hollister [found] that the private/sexual and public/nonsexual uses of the highway rest stop coexist with little interference from each other: "Rest area cruisers take great care in camouflaging themselves. The few who don't are as effective in inducing [other cruisers] to leave as a policeman ... [T]he sites I observed were concealed from nonparticipants." * * *

It may be argued that the possibility that sex in open access areas may be observed by a third party renders unreasonable the sexual actors' expectations of privacy. What should ultimately matter in establishing the scope of the right to sexual liberty, however, should not be whether the sex is observed but whether such observation is consensual. The state's interest in regulating sexual conduct is implicated only once it is likely that the sex will be observed by unwilling gazers. There is no harm that justifies the interference with sexual liberty when there is consent on the part of both the observers and the sexual actors. As Richard Mohr argues, "[w]e need to abandon the idea that in order for sex to be considered private, it must be hidden away behind four walls. It is not geography or mere physical enclosure that makes sex private.... If the participants are all consenting to be there with each other for the possibility of sex polymorphic, then they fulfill the criterion of the private in the realm of the sexual." * * *

There can be, of course, no guarantee that sex in open access areas, such as public bathrooms and highway rest stops, will remain undetected. It is always possible that, despite significant precautions taken by sexual actors, unsuspecting individuals may nonetheless stumble across sexual conduct that they will find offensive. The question, however, should not be whether it is possible that an unwilling gazer will observe the sex. It is, after all, possible that an unwilling gazer (such as an unexpected visitor) will stumble across sexual conduct that takes place in the home. The question instead should be whether it is *likely* that a nonconsenting third party will observe the sex. The public sex literature suggests that such an outcome is unlikely in at least some open access sites under some circumstances. * * *

We should, therefore, resist the urge to jump to the conclusion that sex in open access areas should always be constitutionally unprotectable. This is particularly true in cases in which law enforcement officials have to engage in intrusive or deceptive practices to observe the sexual conduct in question. Public sex advocates argue that much of the sex that takes place in open access areas would go undetected *but for* the aggressive investigative tools used by government officials. Pat Califia, for example, notes that "[i]f people are going to see what is going on in these places, they must intrude. They must actively look for things that will offend them either by penetrating physical barriers, by setting up covert surveillance, or by posing as potential participants."[165] The greater the efforts that must be engaged in by law enforcement officials and others to observe public sex, the more likely it is that the sexual actors in question are taking the necessary steps to exclude unwilling gazers and other potential intruders.

UNITED STATES V. LANNING
U.S. Court of Appeals for the Fourth Circuit, 2013
723 F.3d 476

WYNN, CIRCUIT JUDGE.

In the context of a sting operation specifically targeting gay men, an undercover ranger approached Defendant, initiated a sexually suggestive conversation with him, and then expressly agreed to have sex with him. In response, Defendant backed up to the ranger and "[v]ery briefly" touched the ranger's fully-clothed crotch. That conduct gave rise to Defendant's conviction for disorderly conduct under 36 C.F.R. § 2.34, which prohibits conduct that is "obscene," "physically threatening or menacing," or "likely to inflict injury or incite an immediate breach of the peace." 36 C.F.R. § 2.34(a)(2).

Upon review, we hold that the term "obscene" is unconstitutionally vague as applied to Defendant. We further hold that no rational trier of fact could find beyond a reasonable doubt that Defendant's brief touch of the ranger's crotch, done in response to the ranger's deliberate attempt to convince Defendant that he would have sex with him, was "physically threatening or menacing" or "likely to inflict injury or incite an immediate breach of the peace." Accordingly, we reverse and remand for a judgment of acquittal.

After receiving complaints about male-on-male sexual activity around the Sleepy Gap Overlook of the Blue Ridge Parkway in Buncombe County, North Carolina, the National Park Service and the United States Forest Service conducted a joint operation "designed to enable officers to identify and arrest men who were using the area for sexual solicitation and activity with other men." Appellee's Br. at 3. Joseph Darling, a thirty-three-year-old, two-hundred-pound park ranger, participated in the sting operation as an undercover officer. In November 2009, in the course of the sting operation, Darling saw Defendant, a sixty-two-year-old male retiree, on a nearby trail. As Darling walked past Defendant, Defendant grabbed his own groin and kept walking. Darling said hello and also kept walking.

---

[165] PAT CALIFIA, PUBLIC SEX: THE CULTURE OF RADICAL SEX 76 (1994).

Five or ten minutes later, after walking around in the woods and talking to a few other people, Darling went looking for Defendant and found him standing by himself on an unofficial trail. Darling engaged Defendant in a casual conversation about the weather for several minutes. Darling then commented that Asheville was "an open community," accepting of a homosexual lifestyle. Defendant responded that he "wanted to be F'ed." Darling replied "okay or yes, or something to that affirmative[,]" and "gave [Defendant] every reason to believe that [Darling] was good to go." At that point, Defendant—who was facing Darling and standing approximately three to five feet away from him— turned around, took one or two steps backward towards Darling, and, with his left hand, reached back and "[v]ery briefly" touched Darling's fully-clothed crotch. Darling described the touch as "a fairly firm grasp" that lasted "[v]ery briefly[,] [u]ntil I could get the words out: 'Police officer, you're under arrest.'"

Defendant was charged with disorderly conduct in violation of 36 C.F.R. § 2.34(a)(2). Before trial, Defendant unsuccessfully moved to dismiss the case. At trial, Darling was the only witness. And at the close of the government's evidence, Defendant moved for judgment of acquittal. This, too, the magistrate judge denied. The magistrate judge then found Defendant guilty of disorderly conduct, giving no specific reasons for his decision and noting only that he was "convinced beyond a reasonable doubt" that Defendant had violated the statute. The magistrate judge sentenced Defendant to 15 days' imprisonment, a $1000 fine, and a two-year ban on visiting government forests and parks.

Defendant appealed to the district court. The district court affirmed Defendant's conviction, [but] vacated and remanded Defendant's sentence because the magistrate judge lacked the authority to ban Defendant from government parks. The magistrate judge resentenced Defendant to 15 days' imprisonment and a $500 fine, and the district court affirmed. Defendant then appealed to this Court.

Section 2.34 is an enactment of the Secretary of the Interior, who is authorized to promulgate regulations "necessary or proper for the use and management" of parks under the jurisdiction of the National Park Service, including the Blue Ridge Parkway. . . . Section 2.34(a)(2) [states as follows:]

> A person commits disorderly conduct when, with intent to cause public alarm, nuisance, jeopardy or violence, or knowingly or recklessly creating a risk thereof, such person . . . [u]ses language, an utterance, or gesture, or engages in a display or act that is obscene, physically threatening or menacing, or done in a manner that is likely to inflict injury or incite an immediate breach of the peace.

36 C.F.R. § 2.34(a)(2). . . . Defendant argues that the government failed to prove the second element of disorderly conduct under Section 2.34(a)(2). We therefore must analyze each prong of that element—that is, whether the conduct at issue was "obscene," "physically threatening or menacing," or "likely to inflict injury or incite an immediate breach of the peace"—to determine whether the government met its burden. * * *

. . . [T]he provision's legislative history reveals that the rule's promulgator believed "[t]he harms that the regulation seeks to avoid [to be] *commonly understood.*" 48 Fed.Reg. 30252, 30270 (June 30, 1983) (emphasis added). Similarly, in *United States v. Coutchavlis,* the Ninth Circuit declared that "the regulation contained only 'common words,' easily understandable by 'people of ordinary intelligence.' The words of § 2.34 are not so obscure that they require any special skill to interpret." 260 F.3d 1149, 1155 (9th Cir.2001).

We regularly turn to the dictionary for the "ordinary, contemporary, common meaning" of words undefined by statute, as is the case with "obscene" here. *The American Heritage Dictionary* defines "obscene" as "[o]ffensive to accepted standards of decency" and "[m]orally repulsive[.]" *Id.* at 1216 (5th ed.2011). *The Oxford English Dictionary* defines "obscene" as "[o]ffensively or grossly indecent, lewd[.]" *Oxford English Dictionary Online,* http://www.oed.com/view/Entry/129823?redirected From=obscene (last visited April 10, 2013).

The government argues that "the standard dictionary definition" of obscene "appl[ies] in determining whether a defendant is guilty of 'disorderly conduct'" and, when doing so here, "the evidence amply supports the magistrate judge's finding that Defendant's conduct was obscene." Defendant counters that if a dictionary definition of obscene applies, then Section 2.34(a)(2) is "unconstitutionally vague as applied." Under the circumstances of this case, we must agree with Defendant.

It is axiomatic that a law fails to meet the dictates of the Due Process Clause "if it is so vague and standardless that it leaves the public uncertain as to the conduct it prohibits. . . ." *City of Chicago v. Morales,* 527 U.S. 41, 56, 119 S.Ct. 1849, 144 L.Ed.2d 67 (1999). "A statute can be impermissibly vague for either of two independent reasons. First, if it fails to provide people of ordinary intelligence a reasonable opportunity to understand what conduct it prohibits. Second, if it authorizes or even encourages arbitrary and discriminatory enforcement." *Hill v. Colorado,* 530 U.S. 703, 732, 120 S.Ct. 2480, 147 L.Ed.2d 597 (2000). As the Supreme Court has noted, "perhaps the most meaningful aspect of the vagueness doctrine is not actual notice, but the other principal element of the doctrine—the requirement that a legislature establish minimal guidelines to govern law enforcement." *Smith v. Goguen,* 415 U.S. 566, 574, 94 S.Ct. 1242, 39 L.Ed.2d 605 (1974).

Turning first to the notice issue, we agree with Defendant that Section 2.34(a)(2) would not have provided him, or anyone of ordinary intelligence, fair warning that the complained-of conduct was obscene. The evidence, even when viewed in the light most favorable to the government, shows that: Defendant grabbed his own clothed groin once while walking; after being engaged in a flirtatious conversation by an undercover ranger who noted that "Asheville [was] an open community;" Defendant told the undercover ranger that "he wanted to be F'ed[,]"; and, after the ranger accepted Defendant's sexual proposition, Defendant quickly walked backwards toward the ranger and grabbed the ranger's clothed crotch "fairly firm[ly] . . . [v]ery briefly[,] [u]ntil [the ranger] could get the words out: 'Police officer, you're under arrest.'" Under these circumstances, we cannot conclude that anyone "of ordinary intelligence," would understand that such conduct is "[m]orally repulsive," or "[o]ffensively or grossly indecent, lewd[,]" so as to be "obscene" and thus proscribed by Section 2.34(a)(2).[3]

Further, the facts of this case illustrate the real risk that the provision may be "arbitrar[ily] and discriminator[ily] enforce[d]." *Hill,* 530 U.S. at 732, 120 S.Ct. 2480. The sting operation that resulted in Defendant's arrest was aimed not generally at sexual activity in the Blue Ridge Parkway; rather, it specifically targeted gay men. Perhaps not surprisingly, then, the all-male undercover rangers arrested only men on the basis of disorderly homosexual conduct.

The impetus for the sting operation: citizen complaints. Darling testified that "the public was concerned" about "male on male [sexual] activity in that area that was targeted."[4] Darling testified that every single one of the citizen complaints had been about homosexuals.

It may be that gay men engage more frequently in sexual activity in the Blue Ridge Parkway and therefore generate more citizen complaints. Yet it is also entirely plausible that the public in and around the Blue

---

[3]   Perhaps recognizing its weak hand, the government suggests that "the magistrate judge could reasonably *infer* from Defendant's conduct that he, in fact, *intended* to have sexual intercourse in the very location in which he backed into Ranger Darling and grabbed Ranger Darling's [clothed] genitals." Yet Defendant's conviction was for disorderly *conduct*—not disorderly thoughts or desires. And it is undisputed that Defendant's actual conduct never went further than his backing up to Darling and very briefly grabbing Darling's clothed crotch. Moreover, even Darling agreed that, "for all [he] knew, [Defendant] could have very well intended for [the intercourse] to happen at [Defendant's] house." And such private sexual conduct would, of course, have been perfectly legal. As the Supreme Court pronounced a decade ago, "[l]iberty presumes an autonomy of self that includes freedom of thought, belief, expression, and certain intimate conduct" and "allows homosexual persons the right to" engage in consensual intimate conduct in the privacy of their homes. *Lawrence v. Texas,* 539 U.S. 558, 567, 123 S.Ct. 2472, 156 L.Ed.2d 508 (2003).

[4]   One wonders why a sting operation was implemented in the first place. If instead the rangers had, for example, hidden themselves, monitored the area, and arrested individuals who engaged in public sexual conduct, many of the questionable aspects of this case, from the discriminatory targeting to the alleged inchoate conduct the government attempts to inject into this matter would almost surely fall away.

Ridge Parkway subjectively finds homosexual conduct, even relatively innocuous conduct such as that at issue here, particularly "morally repulsive" and "grossly indecent," and therefore complains. If the public is, by contrast, not similarly troubled by a woman propositioning her boyfriend for sex and then briefly touching his clothed crotch, there would exist no citizen complaint and no related sting, even for otherwise identical heterosexual conduct. Simply enforcing the disorderly conduct regulation on the basis of citizen complaints therefore presents a real threat of anti-gay discrimination.

To be sure, in concluding that Section 2.34(a)(2)'s "obscene" is unconstitutionally vague as applied to Defendant, we do not mean to suggest that the statute is impermissibly vague per se. As the Supreme Court has recognized, "there are statutes that by their terms or as authoritatively construed apply without question to certain activities, but whose application to other behavior is uncertain." *Smith,* 415 U.S. at 577–78, 94 S.Ct. 1242.

Section 2.34(a)(2) may be just such a law. For example, we have no doubt that the court [in *United States v. Mather,* 902 F.Supp. 560 (E.D.Pa.1995)] correctly held that the conduct at issue there—i.e., two individuals with their pants down, masturbating in front of one another and engaging in fellatio in a national park—was obscene and disorderly under Section 2.34(a)(2). Unquestionably, it was; and were that conduct before us, this would surely be a radically different opinion.

The conduct at issue here, however, is of a qualitatively different, significantly more benign nature. We do not believe that a reasonable defendant would know that by engaging in such conduct under the circumstances of this case, he would be subjecting himself to criminal liability. That, coupled with our serious concern regarding discriminatory enforcement, leads us to conclude that Section 2.34(a)(2) is unconstitutionally vague as applied and that the "obscene" prong of the regulation therefore cannot serve as a basis for Defendant's conviction.

We also acknowledge the dissenting opinion's assertion that we fail to "accord[ ] the level of deference to the magistrate judge's findings of fact required by our standard of review." But that assertion misses the mark as to the regulation's obscenity prong, because even where a rational trier of fact could find facts sufficient to support a conviction, a statute can still be unconstitutional because it "authorizes or even encourages arbitrary and discriminatory enforcement." *Hill,* 530 U.S. at 732, 120 S.Ct. 2480. Indeed, the sufficiency of the evidence seems irrelevant to such a constitutional analysis.

Turning to the next prong of the regulation's second element, we analyze whether Defendant's conduct was "physically threatening or menacing." 36 C.F.R. § 2.34(a)(2).

Even the government concedes that an objective reasonable person standard applies to this inquiry. Stated differently, a fact finder must focus not on whether a particular victim subjectively felt physically threatened or menaced, but instead must ask whether a reasonable person objectively would have felt so under the circumstances of the case. * * *

. . . [A]lthough Darling testified that Defendant's touch was "firm," the government presented no evidence that Darling experienced any pain or suffered any injury as a consequence. . . . [It is true that] Darling testified that he felt "shocked" and "caught . . . off guard" by Defendant's touch. But the disorderly conduct regulation requires "physically threatening or menacing" conduct, not merely surprising conduct. 36 C.F.R. § 2.34(a)(2). And even if surprise were sufficient to trigger the regulation (it is not), and even if Darling's subjective reaction were relevant to our inquiry (it is not), it defies logic that Darling was shocked by Defendant's touch when it was, in fact, precisely what Darling had been "string[ing Defendant] along" to do—"to cross a certain line."

Facts matter. Had Defendant and Darling engaged in flirtatious conversation that did not involve an agreement to have sex, a reasonable person might well have felt physically threatened or menaced by Defendant's "[v]ery briefly" touching Darling's clothed crotch. Likewise, had Defendant pinned Darling down and attempted to remove Darling's clothing, a reasonable person, even one who had consented to sex, might well have felt physically threatened or menaced by that conduct. But given the totality of the circumstances actually before us, even when viewing the evidence in the light most favorable to the government, no rational fact finder could conclude that a reasonable person would feel physically threatened or menaced by Defendant's conduct. * * *

[Finally], we point to a recent Sixth Circuit decision, *Alman v. Reed,* which we find insightful, even if distinguishable.703 F.3d 887 (6th Cir.2013). In *Alman,* law enforcement arrested a gay man during an undercover sting at a Michigan park. The *Alman* sting, too, resulted from complaints of sexual activity in the park. There as here, an undercover officer approached Alman and initiated conversation. While the two men engaged in apparently flirtatious conversation, unlike in this case, the undercover officer never expressly agreed to engage in anal intercourse, or anything else for that matter. Nevertheless, "Alman leaned forward and reached out and touched the zipper area on the front of [the undercover officer's] crotch." *Id.* at 893. The undercover officer backed away and soon thereafter "pulled out his badge and told Alman that he was under arrest." *Id.* Alman was charged with being a disorderly person, battery, soliciting and accosting, and criminal sexual conduct in the fourth degree. Ultimately, all of the charges were dismissed.

Alman (along with his partner and a gay rights organization) brought a Section 1983 suit alleging that law enforcement violated his constitutional rights. The district court dismissed the case, but the Sixth Circuit resuscitated it, expressly holding that law enforcement, as a matter of law, lacked probable cause as to each offense with which Alman had been charged. The Sixth Circuit held that "there is nothing in the record describing circumstances that would be sufficient to create a reasonable fear of dangerous consequences." *Id.* at 897. The Court expressly refused to make "assumptions about Alman's intentions that the record does not substantiate" and noted that "a reasonable officer would have needed more evidence of Alman's intentions before concluding that he was inviting [the undercover officer] to do a public lewd act." *Id.* at 899. Under the circumstances, the Sixth Circuit concluded that "no reasonable officer" would have thought that Alman committed, or was about to commit, any of the crimes with which he was charged. * * *

REVERSED AND REMANDED

DUNCAN, CIRCUIT JUDGE, dissenting:

I respect the thoughtfulness of the majority opinion and share its distaste for Officer Darling's conduct. I also appreciate the narrowness of its focus and its careful tethering to the specific facts before us. However, the concern that prompts my brief dissent is that I am unable to agree that the majority opinion accords the level of deference to the magistrate judge's findings of fact required by our standard of review. I believe that a rational trier of fact could have found a physical touching such as this implying an immediate intent to engage in sexual activity in public both obscene and physically threatening or menacing within the meaning of 36 C.F.R. § 2.34(a)(2).

NOTES

1.   Notice that although the court in *Lanning* struck down the disorderly conduct regulation on the due process ground that it was impermissibly vague as applied, it was also troubled by the unequal enforcement of the regulation against gay men. Indeed, law enforcement agencies have historically targeted gay men in enforcing disorderly conduct, solicitation, and public lewdness laws. *See* Christopher R. Leslie, *Standing in the Way of Equality: How States use Standing Doctrine to Insulate Sodomy Laws from Constitutional Attack*, 2001 WIS. L. REV. 29, 84 (noting that "[m]any police departments employ undercover operations designed to entrap gay men into offering or requesting oral sex."). *See also* Amber Arellano et al., *Group Says Detroit Cops Target Gays*, DETROIT FREE PRESS, July 6, 2001, at 1B; Matt Lait, *LAPD Officers Target Gays, Police Commission is Told*, L.A. TIMES, May 6, 1998, at B3. The actions of the Detroit police led the city council to approve an award of $170,000 to settle litigation challenging a pattern of entrapment in the enforcement of public lewdness laws against gay

men at a local park. *See* Darren Nichols, *Detroit Settles Lawsuit Over Police Sting on Gays*, DETROIT NEWS, May 16, 2002, at D2. *See also Martinez v. Port Authority of New York & New Jersey*, 2005 WL 2143333 (S.D.N.Y 2005), *aff'd*, 445 F.3d 158 (2nd Cir. 2006) (defendants ordered to pay $464,000 to compensate plaintiff for police policy of arresting men perceived to be gay for public lewdness at a subway station without probable cause).

2.   A few years after *Singer*, the U.S. Court of Appeals for the Fourth Circuit held that Virginia's sodomy statute was *facially* unconstitutional. *See MacDonald v. Moose*, 710 F.3d 154, 166 (4th Cir. 2013), *cert. denied*, 134 S.Ct. 200 (2013). A short time later, the Virginia legislature amended it "crime against nature" provision so that it covered bestiality only and not consensual sex between adults. *See* Virginia Senate Bill 14 (2014).

3.   Although in most instances, the challenges to the enforcement of solicitation and public lewdness statutes relate to laws that are neutral on their face, some laws explicitly targeted lesbians and gay men. Ohio, for example, until 2003 proscribed the crime of "importuning," defined as the "solicit[ation] [of] a person of the same sex to engage in sexual activity with the offender, when the offender knows such solicitation is offensive to the other person." OHIO REV. CODE ANN. § 2907.07B (2007). The Ohio Supreme Court in 1979 upheld the constitutionality of the importuning statute, concluding that same-sex solicitation is "often grossly offensive and emotionally disturbing." *State v. Phipps*, 389 N.E.2d 1128, 1134, 58 Ohio St.2d 271, 279 (1979). The same court struck down the statute in 2002, concluding that it was a content-based restriction on speech, which by extension violated state and federal equal protection guarantees. *See State v. Thompson*, 767 N.E.2d 251, 95 Ohio St.3d 264 (2002). The Ohio legislature repealed the law the following year.

4.   In 1998, the Phoenix city council enacted an ordinance that prohibited "the operation of a business for purposes of providing the opportunity to engage in . . . or view . . . live sex acts." PHOENIX, AZ., CITY CODE ch. 23, art. IV, § 23–54 (1998). Fleck and Associates operated a health club in the city, and as part of their operations, they rented rooms inside the facility to men for the purpose of engaging in sexual activity. The club brought a lawsuit against the city seeking an injunction against the enforcement of the ordinance arguing inter alia that it violated their patrons' constitutional rights after *Lawrence*. The court refused to issue the injunction, concluding that "*Lawrence* does not suggest that sexual activities in a place of public accommodation are Constitutionally protected. Because [the plaintiff's] club is not private, the sexual activities that take place there likewise are not private." *Fleck & Assocs., Inc. v. Phoenix*, 356 F.Supp.2d 1034, 1041 (D.Ariz.2005), *rev'd on other grounds*, 471 F.3d 1100 (9th Cir. 2006). *See also 832 Corp., Inc. v. Gloucester*, 404 F.Supp.2d 614, 623 (D.N.J. 2005) (contrary to argument raised by owners of a nightclub where consensual sex took place, "*Lawrence* did not recognize a broad right to engage in sexual conduct outside of private settings."); *Commonwealth v. Can-Port Amusement Corp.*, 2005 WL 2009672 (Mass.Super.Ct.2005) (holding

that *Lawrence* did not protect same-sex sexual conduct that took place in adult movie theater).

CHAPTER 3

SEXUALITY, GENDER, & EQUALITY

■ ■ ■

I.   INTRODUCTION

The equal protection clause is designed to police group-based discrimination by the government. If a group is excluded from a government program or government employment—for instance, if schools will not hire black teachers because of their race—the equal protection clause is implicated. The U.S. Supreme Court has, over the last several decades, developed an elaborate jurisprudential scheme for adjudicating equal protection claims. According to the type of discrimination being considered, the Court's doctrine states that three levels of review will be used in equal protection cases: strict, intermediate, and what is called "rational basis" review.

Under this doctrine, some classifications made by the government—classifications based on race or national origin, for example—are "suspect" and require "strict" judicial scrutiny to ensure that they are not illegitimate attempts to discriminate on these bases. In these cases, the judge's task is to ensure that the government's classification is supported by a "compelling governmental interest" and is narrowly tailored to serve that purpose. It is usually very difficult for the government to justify a classification under this strict standard.

At the opposite end of the spectrum are governmental distinctions that are considered ordinary, like those routinely made in the realm of economic regulation. The government must justify these types of distinctions by showing only that the classification challenged is "rationally related to a legitimate state interest." This is a standard that the government can almost always meet, although there are significant exceptions to that truism that will be explored below.

A third, intermediate category, has also developed—here classifications, such as those based on sex, are sometimes thought to be based on legitimate differences between the sexes, but are other times found to be discriminatory. Thus, courts are instructed to employ a medium level of scrutiny to ensure that such classifications "serve important governmental objectives and [are] substantially related to achievement of those objectives."

This schema has been severely criticized, both by some members of the Court itself,[1] and by academic commentators.[2] One of the primary criticisms of this method of jurisprudence is that the level of scrutiny a court employs frequently—though not invariably—determines whether a plaintiff prevails.[3] Thus, much of the fight in equal protection cases has traditionally concerned the level of scrutiny applicable to the case. The Supreme Court has articulated a series of principles that determine whether a classification should trigger strict, or "heightened," judicial scrutiny. These include whether there has been a history of discrimination against the group at issue, whether the discrimination is unrelated to the individual group members' abilities, and whether the members of the group are so poorly represented in the political processes such that those processes could not be expected to correct the harm at issue.[4] Some courts have also said that the trait that defines the class must be "immutable" for the group to be deserving of heightened judicial scrutiny.[5]

A second criticism focuses on the inconsistency in the doctrine and notes the ways that the tiers of scrutiny have been breaking down in recent years. Indeed, as the material in this Chapter will show, cases in the sexual orientation area illustrate this breakdown particularly well. There have been significant victories for LGBT equality in cases where the Court—puzzlingly—purports to use the "rational basis" standard that typically guarantees a victory for the government.

This Chapter will focus on the rubrics used by courts to evaluate constitutional claims of both sex discrimination and sexual orientation discrimination. We begin and end the Chapter with ideas about sex discrimination. The first Section lays out the constitutional framework for sex discrimination claims, including the early debate about whether sex should—like race—be a suspect classification, and presents some of the cases settling on intermediate scrutiny as the relevant standard. We then turn to the framework for constitutional claims of sexual orientation discrimination, with special focus on *Romer v. Evans*, the U.S. Supreme Court's first major equal protection decision concerning the rights of sexual minorities. Finally, we circle back to sex discrimination and consider the argument that sexual orientation discrimination should

---

[1] *See, e.g., Adarand Constructors, Inc. v. Pena*, 515 U.S. 200, 247, 115 S.Ct. 2097, 2122, 132 L.Ed.2d 158, 195 (1995) (Stevens, J., dissenting); *San Antonio Indep. Sch. Dist. v. Rodriguez*, 411 U.S. 1, 98–99, 93 S.Ct. 1278, 1330, 36 L.Ed.2d 16, 81–82 (1973) (Marshall, J., dissenting).

[2] *See, e.g.,* Suzanne B. Goldberg, *Equality Without Tiers*, 77 S. CAL. L. REV. 481, 508–18 (2004); Gerald Gunther, *The Supreme Court 1971 Term—Foreword: In Search of Evolving Doctrine on a Changing Court: A Model for a Newer Equal Protection*, 86 HARV. L. REV. 1, 17–18 (1972).

[3] Gunther, 86 HARV. L. REV. at 8.

[4] *Frontiero v. Richardson*, 411 U.S. 677, 684–87, 93 S.Ct. 1764, 1769–71, 36 L.Ed.2d 583, 590–92 (1973).

[5] *See id.* at 686, 93 S. Ct. at 1770.

itself be seen as a form of sex discrimination and, therefore, call for the application of intermediate scrutiny.

II. THE LEVEL OF SCRUTINY DEBATE

A. THE CONSTITUTION AND SEX DISCRIMINATION

The constitutional law of sex discrimination under the equal protection clause began to evolve in earnest in the early 1970s. That body of law has set the conceptual stage in various ways for the unfolding constitutional law of sexual orientation discrimination. Consider the following leading constitutional cases on sex discrimination. Bear in mind some key questions as you read: What ideas of sex and gender underpin the Court's approach? What standard of review does the Court arrive at for sex-based classifications? What is the relevance of the Court's arguments regarding sex-based claims for the question of what standard of review should be applied to sexual orientation-based claims? Do you think that any of the arguments made for heightened scrutiny of sex-based claims apply to sexual orientation-based claims as well?

FRONTIERO V. RICHARDSON

Supreme Court of the United States, 1973
411 U.S. 677, 93 S.Ct. 1764, 36 L.Ed.2d 583

JUSTICE BRENNAN announced the judgment of the Court and an opinion in which JUSTICE DOUGLAS, JUSTICE WHITE, and JUSTICE MARSHALL join.

The question before us concerns the right of a female member of the uniformed services to claim her spouse as a "dependent" for the purposes of obtaining increased quarters allowances and medical and dental benefits under 37 U.S.C. 401, 403, and 10 U.S.C. 1072, 1076, on an equal footing with male members. Under these statutes, a serviceman may claim his wife as a "dependent" without regard to whether she is in fact dependent upon him for any part of her support. 37 U.S.C. 401(1); 10 U.S.C. 1072(2)(A). A servicewoman, on the other hand, may not claim her husband as a "dependent" under these programs unless he is in fact dependent upon her for over one-half of his support. 37 U.S.C. 401; 10 U.S.C. 1072(2)(c). Thus, the question for decision is whether this difference in treatment constitutes an unconstitutional discrimination against servicewomen in violation of the Due Process Clause of the Fifth Amendment. * * *

Appellant Sharron Frontiero, a lieutenant in the United States Air Force, sought increased quarters allowances, and housing and medical benefits for her husband, appellant Joseph Frontiero, on the ground that he was her "dependent." Although such benefits would automatically have been granted with respect to the wife of a male member of the uniformed services, appellant's application was denied because she failed to demonstrate that her husband was dependent on her for more than one-half of his support. * * *

Although the legislative history of these statutes sheds virtually no light on the purposes underlying the differential treatment accorded male and female members, a majority of the three-judge District Court surmised that Congress might reasonably have concluded that, since the husband in our society is generally the "breadwinner" in the family—and the wife typically the "dependent" partner—"it would be more economical to require married female members claiming husbands to prove actual dependency than to extend the presumption of dependency to such members." 341 F. Supp., at 207. Indeed, given the fact that approximately 99% of all members of the uniformed services are male, the District Court speculated that such differential treatment might conceivably lead to a "considerable saving of administrative expense and manpower." *Ibid.*

At the outset, appellants contend that classifications based upon sex, like classifications based upon race, alienage, and national origin, are inherently suspect and must therefore be subjected to close judicial scrutiny. We agree and, indeed, find at least implicit support for such an approach in our unanimous decision only last Term in *Reed v. Reed.* * * *

There can be no doubt that our Nation has had a long and unfortunate history of sex discrimination. Traditionally, such discrimination was rationalized by an attitude of "romantic paternalism" which, in practical effect, put women, not on a pedestal, but in a cage. Indeed, this paternalistic attitude became so firmly rooted in our national consciousness that, 100 years ago, a distinguished Member of this Court was able to proclaim:

> "Man is, or should be, woman's protector and defender. The natural and proper timidity and delicacy which belongs to the female sex evidently unfits it for many of the occupations of civil life. The constitution of the family organization, which is founded in the divine ordinance, as well as in the nature of things, indicates the domestic sphere as that which properly belongs to the domain and functions of womanhood. The harmony, not to say identity, of interests and views which belong, or should belong, to the family institution is repugnant to the idea of a woman adopting a distinct and independent career from that of her husband. . . . The paramount destiny and mission of woman are to fulfil the noble and benign offices of wife and mother. This is the law of the Creator." *Bradwell v. State.*

As a result of notions such as these, our statute books gradually became laden with gross, stereotyped distinctions between the sexes and, indeed, throughout much of the 19th century the position of women in our society was, in many respects, comparable to that of blacks under the pre-Civil War slave codes. Neither slaves nor women could hold office, serve on juries, or bring suit in their own names, and married women traditionally were denied the legal capacity to hold or convey property or to serve as legal guardians of their own children. * * *

And although blacks were guaranteed the right to vote in 1870, women were denied even that right—which is itself "preservative of other basic civil and political rights"—until adoption of the Nineteenth Amendment half a century later.

It is true, of course, that the position of women in America has improved markedly in recent decades. Nevertheless, it can hardly be doubted that, in part because of the high visibility of the sex characteristic, women still face pervasive, although at times more subtle, discrimination in our educational institutions, in the job market and, perhaps most conspicuously, in the political arena. * * *

Moreover, since sex, like race and national origin, is an immutable characteristic determined solely by the accident of birth, the imposition of special disabilities upon the members of a particular sex because of their sex would seem to violate "the basic concept of our system that legal burdens should bear some relationship to individual responsibility. . . ." And what differentiates sex from such nonsuspect statuses as intelligence or physical disability, and aligns it with the recognized suspect criteria, is that the sex characteristic frequently bears no relation to ability to perform or contribute to society. As a result, statutory distinctions between the sexes often have the effect of invidiously relegating the entire class of females to inferior legal status without regard to the actual capabilities of its individual members.

We might also note that, over the past decade, Congress has itself manifested an increasing sensitivity to sex-based classifications. In Tit. VII of the Civil Rights Act of 1964, for example, Congress expressly declared that no employer, labor union, or other organization subject to the provisions of the Act shall discriminate against any individual on the basis of "race, color, religion, sex, or national origin." Similarly, the Equal Pay Act of 1963 provides that no employer covered by the Act "shall discriminate . . . between employees on the basis of sex." And § 1 of the Equal Rights Amendment, passed by Congress on March 22, 1972, and submitted to the legislatures of the States for ratification, declares that "[e]quality of rights under the law shall not be denied or abridged by the United States or by any State on account of sex." Thus, Congress itself has concluded that classifications based upon sex are inherently invidious, and this conclusion of a coequal branch of Government is not without significance to the question presently under consideration.

With these considerations in mind, we can only conclude that classifications based upon sex, like classifications based upon race, alienage, or national origin, are inherently suspect, and must therefore be subjected to strict judicial scrutiny. Applying the analysis mandated by that stricter standard of review, it is clear that the statutory scheme now before us is constitutionally invalid. * * *

Moreover, the Government concedes that the differential treatment accorded men and women under these statutes serves no purpose other than mere "administrative convenience." In essence, the Government maintains that, as an empirical matter, wives in our society frequently are dependent upon their husbands, while husbands rarely are dependent upon their wives. Thus, the Government argues that Congress might reasonably have concluded that it would be both cheaper and easier simply conclusively to presume that wives of male members are financially dependent upon their husbands, while burdening female members with the task of establishing dependency in fact. * * *

[O]ur prior decisions make clear that, although efficacious administration of governmental programs is not without some importance, "the Constitution recognizes higher values than speed and efficiency." *Stanley v. Illinois*, 405 U.S. 645, 656, 92 S.Ct. 1208, 1215, 31 L.Ed.2d 551 (1972). And when we enter the realm of "strict judicial scrutiny," there can be no doubt that "administrative convenience" is not a shibboleth, the mere recitation of which dictates constitutionality. On the contrary, any statutory scheme which draws a sharp line between the sexes, solely for the purpose of achieving administrative convenience, necessarily commands "dissimilar treatment for men and women who are . . . similarly situated," and therefore involves the "very kind of arbitrary legislative choice forbidden by the [Constitution]. . . ." *Reed v. Reed*, 404 U.S., at 77, 76, 92 S.Ct., at 254. We therefore conclude that, by according differential treatment to male and female members of the uniformed services for the sole purpose of achieving administrative convenience, the challenged statutes violate the Due Process Clause of the Fifth Amendment insofar as they require a female member to prove the dependency of her husband.

Reversed.

NOTE

Justice Brennan's argument to apply strict scrutiny to sex-based classifications failed to command a majority on the Supreme Court; only four justices took that view. A few years later, the Court decided *Craig v. Boren*, 429 U.S. 190, 97 S.Ct. 451, 50 L.Ed.2d 397 (1976), a case challenging the constitutionality of prohibiting the sale of "nonintoxicating" beer to males under the age of 21 and to females under the age of 18. The Court struck down the law, rejected the statistical evidence purporting to justify the stricter rule for males, and articulated a standard of review that has come to be known as intermediate scrutiny. The majority opinion said:

> To withstand constitutional challenge, previous cases establish that classifications by gender must serve important governmental objectives and must be substantially related to achievement of those objectives. Thus, in *Reed*, the objectives of "reducing the workload on probate courts," 404 U.S. at 76, and "avoiding intrafamily controversy," *id.*, at 77, were deemed of insufficient importance to sustain use of an overt gender criterion in the appointment of administrators of intestate decedents' estates. Decisions following *Reed* similarly have rejected administrative ease and convenience as sufficiently important objectives to justify gender-based classifications. *See, e. g., Stanley v. Illinois; Frontiero v. Richardson; cf. Schlesinger v. Ballard.* * * *

> *Reed v. Reed* has also provided the underpinning for decisions that have invalidated statutes employing gender as an inaccurate proxy for other, more germane bases of classification. Hence, "archaic and overbroad" generalizations, *Schlesinger v. Ballard*, concerning the financial position of servicewomen, *Frontiero v. Richardson*, and working women, *Weinberger v. Wiesenfeld*, could not justify use of a gender line in determining eligibility for certain governmental entitlements. Similarly, increasingly outdated misconceptions concerning the role of females in the home rather than in the "marketplace and world of ideas" were rejected as loose-fitting characterizations incapable of supporting state statutory schemes that were premised upon their accuracy. *Stanton v. Stanton; Taylor v. Louisiana.* In light of the weak congruence between gender and the characteristic or trait that gender purported to represent, it was necessary that the legislatures choose either to realign their substantive laws in a gender-neutral fashion, or to adopt procedures for identifying those instances where the sex-centered generalization actually comported with fact.

Craig, 429 U.S. at 197–99, 97 S.Ct. 451, 457–58, 50 L.Ed.2d at 407–08.

The next case is a leading decision on the constitutional law of sex discrimination.

UNITED STATES V. VIRGINIA

Supreme Court of the United States, 1996
518 U.S. 515, 116 S.Ct. 2264, 135 L.Ed.2d 735

JUSTICE GINSBURG delivered the opinion of the Court.

Virginia's public institutions of higher learning include an incomparable military college, Virginia Military Institute (VMI). The United States maintains that the Constitution's equal protection guarantee precludes Virginia from reserving exclusively to men the unique educational opportunities VMI affords. We agree.

Founded in 1839, VMI is today the sole single-sex school among Virginia's 15 public institutions of higher learning. VMI's distinctive mission is to produce "citizen-soldiers," men prepared for leadership in civilian life and in military service. VMI pursues this mission through pervasive training of a kind not available anywhere else in Virginia. Assigning prime place to character development, VMI uses an "adversative method" modeled on English public schools and once characteristic of military instruction. VMI constantly endeavors to instill physical and mental discipline in its cadets and impart to them a strong moral code. The school's graduates leave VMI with heightened comprehension of their capacity to deal with duress and stress, and a large sense of accomplishment for completing the hazardous course. * * *

Neither the goal of producing citizen-soldiers nor VMI's implementing methodology is inherently unsuitable to women. And the school's impressive record in producing leaders has made admission desirable to some women. Nevertheless, Virginia has elected to preserve exclusively for men the advantages and opportunities a VMI education affords. * * *

VMI today enrolls about 1,300 men as cadets. Its academic offerings in the liberal arts, sciences, and engineering are also available at other public colleges and universities in Virginia. But VMI's mission is special. It is the mission of the school

> " 'to produce educated and honorable men, prepared for the varied work of civil life, imbued with love of learning, confident in the functions and attitudes of leadership, possessing a high sense of public service, advocates of the American democracy and free enterprise system, and ready as citizen-soldiers to defend their country in *522 time of national peril.' " 766 F. Supp. 1407, 1425 (W.D.Va.1991) (quoting Mission Study Committee of the VMI Board of Visitors, Report, May 16, 1986). * * *

VMI attracts some applicants because of its reputation as an extraordinarily challenging military school, and "because its alumni are exceptionally close to the school." 766 F.Supp., at 1421. * * *

The District Court ruled in favor of VMI . . . * * * The District Court reasoned that education in "a single-gender environment, be it male or female," yields substantial benefits. 766 F.Supp., at 1415. VMI's school for men brought diversity to an otherwise coeducational Virginia system, and that diversity was "enhanced by VMI's unique method of instruction." *Ibid.* If single-gender education for males ranks as an important governmental objective, it becomes obvious, the District Court concluded, that the only means of achieving the objective "is to exclude women from the all-male institution—VMI." *Ibid.*

"Women are [indeed] denied a unique educational opportunity that is available only at VMI," the District Court acknowledged. Id., at 1432. But "[VMI's] single-sex status would be lost, and some aspects of the [school's] distinctive method would be altered," if women were admitted, *id.*, at 1413: "Allowance for personal privacy would have to be made," *id.*, at 1412; "[p]hysical education requirements would have to be altered, at least for the women," *id.*, at 1413; the adversative environment could not survive unmodified, id., at 1412–1413. Thus, "sufficient constitutional justification" had been shown, the District Court held, "for continuing [VMI's] single-sex policy." *Id.*, at 1413. * * *

The Court of Appeals for the Fourth Circuit disagreed and vacated the District Court's judgment. * * * Remanding the case . . . the court suggested these options for the Commonwealth: Admit women to VMI; establish parallel institutions or programs; or abandon state support, leaving VMI free to pursue its policies as a private institution. 976 F.2d 890, 900 (1992). * * *

In response to the Fourth Circuit's ruling, Virginia proposed a parallel program for women: Virginia Women's Institute for Leadership (VWIL). The 4-year, state-sponsored undergraduate program would be located at Mary Baldwin College, a private liberal arts school for women, and would be open, initially, to about 25 to 30 students. Although VWIL would share VMI's mission—to produce "citizen-soldiers"—the VWIL program would differ, as does Mary Baldwin College, from VMI in academic offerings, methods of education, and financial resources. *See* 852 F.Supp. 471, 476–477 (W.D. Va.1994). * * *

[T]his suit present two ultimate issues. First, does Virginia's exclusion of women from the educational opportunities provided by VMI—extraordinary opportunities for military training and civilian leadership development—deny to women "capable of all of the individual activities required of VMI cadets," 766 F.Supp., at 1412, the equal protection of the laws guaranteed by the Fourteenth Amendment? Second, if VMI's "unique" situation, *id.*, at 1413—as Virginia's sole single-sex public institution of higher education—offends the Constitution's equal protection principle, what is the remedial requirement?

We note, once again, the core instruction of this Court's pathmarking decisions in *J.E.B. v. Alabama ex rel. T.B.*, and *Mississippi Univ. for Women*: Parties who seek to defend gender-based government action must demonstrate an "exceedingly persuasive justification" for that action. Today's skeptical scrutiny of official action denying rights or opportunities based on sex responds to volumes of history. As a plurality of this Court acknowledged a generation ago, "our Nation has had a long and unfortunate history of sex discrimination." *Frontiero v. Richardson.* Through a century plus three decades and more of that history, women did not count among voters composing "We the People"; not until 1920 did women gain a constitutional right to the franchise. *Id.*, at 685. And for a half century thereafter, it remained the prevailing doctrine that government, both federal and state, could withhold from women opportunities accorded men so long as any "basis in reason" could be conceived for the discrimination. *See, e.g., Goesaert v. Cleary* (rejecting challenge by female tavern owner and her daughter to Michigan law denying bartender licenses to females—except for wives and daughters of male tavern owners; Court would not "give ear" to the contention that "an unchivalrous desire of male bartenders to . . . monopolize the calling" prompted the legislation).

In 1971, for the first time in our Nation's history, this Court ruled in favor of a woman who complained that her State had denied her the equal protection of its laws. *Reed v. Reed* (holding unconstitutional Idaho Code prescription that, among " 'several persons claiming and equally entitled to administer [a decedent's estate], males must be preferred to females' "). Since *Reed*, the Court has repeatedly recognized that neither federal nor state government acts compatibly with the equal protection principle when a law or official policy denies to women, simply because they are women, full citizenship stature—equal opportunity to aspire, achieve, participate in and contribute to society based on their individual talents and capacities. * * *

Without equating gender classifications, for all purposes, to classifications based on race or national origin, the Court, in post-*Reed* decisions, has carefully inspected official action that closes a door or denies opportunity to women (or to men). *See J.E.B.* (Kennedy, J., concurring in judgment) (case law evolving since 1971 "reveal[s] a strong presumption that gender classifications are invalid"). To summarize the Court's current directions for cases of official classification based on gender: Focusing on the differential treatment or denial of opportunity for which relief is sought, the reviewing court must determine whether the proffered justification is "exceedingly persuasive." The burden of justification is demanding and it rests entirely on the State. *See Mississippi Univ. for Women.* The State must show "at least that the [challenged] classification serves 'important governmental objectives and that the discriminatory means employed' are 'substantially related to the achievement of those objectives.' " * * *

The justification must be genuine, not hypothesized or invented post hoc in response to litigation. And it must not rely on overbroad generalizations about the different talents, capacities, or preferences of males and females. * * *

The heightened review standard our precedent establishes does not make sex a proscribed classification. Supposed "inherent differences" are no longer accepted as a ground for race or national origin classifications. *See Loving v. Virginia.* Physical differences between men and women, however, are enduring: "[T]he two sexes are not fungible; a community made up exclusively of one [sex] is different from a community composed of both." * * *

"Inherent differences" between men and women, we have come to appreciate, remain cause for celebration, but not for denigration of the members of either sex or for artificial constraints on an individual's opportunity. Sex classifications may be used to compensate women "for particular economic disabilities [they have] suffered," *Califano v. Webster,* to "promot[e] equal employment opportunity," *see California Federal Sav. & Loan Assn. v. Guerra,* to advance full development of the talent and capacities of our Nation's people. But such classifications may not be used, as they once were, *see Goesaert,* to create or perpetuate the legal, social, and economic inferiority of women.

Measuring the record in this case against the review standard just described, we conclude that Virginia has shown no "exceedingly persuasive justification" for excluding all women from the citizen-soldier training afforded by VMI. We therefore affirm the Fourth Circuit's initial judgment, which held that Virginia had violated the Fourteenth Amendment's Equal Protection Clause. Because the remedy proffered by Virginia—the Mary Baldwin VWIL program—does not cure the constitutional violation, i.e., it does not provide equal opportunity, we reverse the Fourth Circuit's final judgment in this case.

NOTES

1.   How would you state the standard of review that the Court uses for sex-based classifications? Is there a difference between the principles articulated in *Craig* and those offered in the *Virginia* case?

2.   Recall the materials in Chapter 1, Sections VI & VII, on sex and gender, particularly the material on the performative concept of gender and on transgender issues. How might the evolving constitutional law of sex discrimination and sex-based classifications be consistent or be in tension with the ideas stressed in those accounts?

3.   The terms "sex" and "gender" are sometimes used interchangeably in the cases. Should the terms, properly understood, be given different meanings? Consider, Professor Katherine Franke's perspective:

> Contemporary sex discrimination jurisprudence accepts as one of its foundational premises the notion that sex and gender are two distinct aspects of human identity. That is, it assumes that the identities male and female are different from the characteristics

masculine and feminine. Sex is regarded as a product of nature, while gender is understood as a function of culture. This disaggregation of sex from gender represents a central mistake of equality jurisprudence.

Antidiscrimination law is founded upon the idea that sex, conceived as biological difference, is prior to, less normative than, and more real than gender. Yet in every way that matters, sex bears an epiphenomenal relationship to gender; that is, under close examination, almost every claim with regard to sexual identity or sex discrimination can be shown to be grounded in normative gender rules and roles. Herein lies the mistake. In the name of avoiding "the grossest discrimination," that is, "treating things that are different as though they were exactly alike," sexual equality jurisprudence has uncritically accepted the validity of biological sexual differences. By accepting these biological differences, equality jurisprudence reifies as foundational *fact* that which is really an *effect* of normative gender ideology. This jurisprudential error not only produces obvious absurdities at the margin of gendered identity, but it also explains why sex discrimination laws have been relatively ineffective in dismantling profound sex segregation in the wage-labor market, in shattering "glass ceilings" that obstruct women's entrance into the upper echelons of corporate management, and in increasing women's wages, which remain a fraction of those paid men. The targets of antidiscrimination law, therefore, should not be limited to the "gross, stereotyped distinctions between the sexes" but should also include the social processes that construct and make coherent the categories male and female. In many cases, biology operates as the excuse or cover for social practices that hierarchize individual members of the social category "man" over individual members of the social category "woman." In the end, biology or anatomy serve as metaphors for a kind of inferiority that characterizes society's view of women.

The authority to define particular categories or types of people and to decide to which category a particular person belongs is a profoundly powerful social function. While the state has always performed this role, its actions have rarely been subject to equal protection scrutiny. Given the epiphenomenal relationship between identity and equality, the Fourteenth Amendment and Title VII should apply with equal force to acts of classification as well as to disparate treatment of classes. Rather than accepting sexual differences as the starting point of equality discourse, sex discrimination jurisprudence should consider the role that the ideology of sexual differences plays in perpetuating and ensuring sexual hierarchy.

A reconceptualization of the two most fundamental elements of sexual equality jurisprudence is necessary to correct this foundational error. First, sexual identity—that is, what it means to be a woman and what it means to be a man—must be understood not in deterministic, biological terms, but according to a set of behavioral, performative norms that at once enable and constrain a degree of human agency and create the background conditions for a person to assert, *I am a woman*. To say that someone is a woman demands a complex description of the history and experience of persons so labeled. This conception of sexual identity ultimately provides the basis for a fundamental right to determine gendered identity independent of biological sex.

Second, what it means to be discriminated against *because of one's sex* must be reconceived beyond biological sex as well. To the extent that the wrong of sex discrimination is limited to conduct or treatment which would not have occurred *but for* the plaintiff's biological sex, antidiscrimination law strives for too little. Notwithstanding an occasional gesture to the contrary, courts have not interpreted the wrong of sex discrimination to reach rules and policies that reinforce masculinity as the authentic and natural exercise of male agency and femininity as the authentic and natural exercise of female agency. . . .

Katherine M. Franke, *The Central Mistake of Sex Discrimination Law: The Disaggregation of Sex from Gender*, 144 U. PA. L. REV. 1, 1–4 (1995). For other perspectives on this question and its relationship to sexual orientation, see Mary Ann C. Case, *Disaggregating Gender from Sex and Sexual Orientation: The Effeminate Man in the Law and Feminist Jurisprudence*, 105 YALE L.J. 1 (1995); Francisco Valdes, *Queers, Sissies, Dykes and Tomboys: Deconstructing the Conflation of "Sex," "Gender," and "Sexual Orientation" in Euro-American Law and Society*, 83 CAL. L. REV. 3 (1995).

B.   SEXUAL ORIENTATION: WHAT LEVEL OF REVIEW?

1.   Heightened Scrutiny?

What level of scrutiny should be applied to constitutional claims of sexual orientation-based discrimination? Are LGBT persons a suspect or quasi-suspect class? The following two cases explore that question. As you will see, the Connecticut and Washington state supreme courts reached different conclusions. In each case, plaintiffs, same-sex couples, asserted that a state law preventing them from marrying violated rights protected by a state constitution. In each, the court was called upon to decide what level of scrutiny to apply. (The same-sex marriage debate is explored in detail in Chapter 6). Note that, while the courts analyzed these claims under the provisions of a state constitution, they nevertheless chose to ground their approaches in federal equal protection precedents. As you read the cases, consider what factors seem to be the most important to these justices, and which court's approach better conceptualizes and applies these factors. Are the courts applying the same test, with different interpretations of the facts, or are they applying different tests?

KERRIGAN V. COMMISSIONER OF PUBLIC HEALTH
Connecticut Supreme Court, 2008
289 Conn. 135, 957 A.2d 407

PALMER, JUDGE.

* * *

IV

QUASI-SUSPECT CLASSIFICATIONS UNDER THE STATE CONSTITUTION

Although this court has indicated that a group may be entitled to heightened protection under the state constitution because of its status as a quasi-suspect class, we previously have not articulated the specific criteria to be considered in determining whether recognition as a quasi-suspect class is warranted. The United States Supreme Court, however, consistently has identified two factors that must be met, for purposes of the federal constitution, if a group is to be accorded such status. These two required factors are: (1) the group has suffered a history of invidious discrimination; * * * and (2) the characteristics that distinguish the group's members bear "no relation to [their] ability to perform or contribute to society." * * * The United States Supreme Court also has cited two other considerations that, in a given case, may be relevant in determining whether statutory provisions pertaining to a particular group are subject to heightened scrutiny. These two additional considerations are: (1) the characteristic that defines the members of the class as a discrete group is immutable or otherwise not within their control; * * * and (2) the group is "a minority or politically powerless." (Internal quotation marks omitted.) * * *

Because of the evident correlation between the indicia of suspectness identified by the United States Supreme Court and the issue of whether a class that has been singled out by the state for unequal treatment is entitled to heightened protection under the federal constitution, we conclude that those factors also are pertinent to the determination of whether a group comprises a quasi-suspect class for purposes of the state constitution. * * * It is evident, moreover, that immutability and minority status or political powerlessness are subsidiary to the first two primary factors because, as we explain more fully hereinafter, the United States Supreme Court has granted suspect class status to a group whose distinguishing characteristic is not immutable; see *Nyquist v. Mauclet*, (rejecting immutability requirement in treating group of resident aliens as suspect class despite their ability to opt out of class voluntarily); and has accorded quasi-suspect status to a group that had not been a minority or truly politically powerless. See *Frontiero v. Richardson*, supra, (plurality opinion) (according women heightened protection despite court's acknowledgment that women "do not constitute a small and powerless minority"). * * *

Finally, we note that courts generally have applied the same criteria to determine whether a classification is suspect, quasi-suspect or neither. * * * Just as there is no uniformly applied formula for determining whether a group is entitled to heightened protection under the constitution, there also is no clear test for determining whether a group that deserves such protection is entitled to designation as a suspect class or as a quasi-suspect class. * * * With these principles in mind, we consider the plaintiffs' contention that they are entitled to recognition as a quasi-suspect class.

V

STATUS OF GAY PERSONS AS A QUASI-SUSPECT CLASS

For the reasons that follow, we agree with the plaintiffs' claim that sexual orientation meets all of the requirements of a quasi-suspect classification. Gay persons have been subjected to and stigmatized by a long history of purposeful and invidious discrimination that continues to manifest itself in society. The characteristic that defines the members of this group—attraction to persons of the same sex—bears no logical relationship to their ability to perform in society, either in familial relations or otherwise as productive citizens. Because sexual orientation is such an essential component of personhood, even if there is some possibility that a person's sexual preference can be altered, it would be wholly unacceptable for the state to require anyone to do so. Gay persons also represent a distinct minority of the population. It is true, of course, that gay persons recently have made significant advances in obtaining equal treatment under the law. Nonetheless, we conclude that, as a minority group that continues to suffer the enduring effects of centuries of legally sanctioned discrimination, laws singling them out for disparate treatment are subject to heightened judicial scrutiny to ensure that those laws are not the product of such historical prejudice and stereotyping.

A

History of Discrimination

The defendants do not dispute that gay persons historically have been, and continue to be, the target of purposeful and pernicious discrimination due solely to their sexual orientation. * * * As the United States Supreme Court has recognized, "[p]roscriptions against [homosexual sodomy] have ancient roots." *Bowers v. Hardwick*, 478 U.S. 186, 192 (1986), overruled on other grounds by *Lawrence v. Texas*, 539

U.S. 558 (2003); see also *High Tech Gays v. Defense Industrial Security Clearance Office*, 909 F.2d 375, 382 (9th Cir. 1990) (Canby, J., dissenting) ("mainstream society has mistreated [homosexuals] for centuries"); *Baker v. Wade*, 769 F.2d 289, 292 (5th Cir. 1985) ("the strong objection to homosexual conduct . . . has prevailed in Western culture for the past seven centuries"), cert. denied, 478 U.S. 1022 (1986). . . .

There is no question, therefore, that gay persons historically have been, and continue to be, the target of purposeful and pernicious discrimination due solely to their sexual orientation. We therefore turn to the second required factor, namely, whether the sexual orientation of gay persons has any bearing on their ability to participate in society.

B

Whether Sexual Orientation Is Related to a Person's Ability to Participate in or Contribute to Society

The defendants also concede that sexual orientation bears no relation to a person's ability to participate in or contribute to society, a fact that many courts have acknowledged, as well. See, e.g., *Watkins v. United States Army*, 875 F.2d 699, 725 (9th Cir. 1989) (Norris, J., concurring in the judgment) ("[s]exual orientation plainly has no relevance to a person's ability to perform or contribute to society" [internal quotation marks omitted]), cert. denied, 498 U.S. 957, 111 S. Ct. 384, 112 L. Ed. 2d 395 (1990). In this critical respect, gay persons stand in stark contrast to other groups that have been denied suspect or quasi-suspect class recognition, despite a history of discrimination, because the distinguishing characteristics of those groups adversely affect their ability or capacity to perform certain functions or to discharge certain responsibilities in society. See, e.g., *Cleburne v. Cleburne Living Center, Inc.*, supra, 473 U.S. 442 (for purposes of federal constitution, mental retardation is not quasi-suspect classification because, inter alia, "it is undeniable . . . that those who are mentally retarded have a reduced ability to cope with and function in the everyday world"); *Massachusetts Board of Retirement v. Murgia*, supra, 427 U.S. 315 (age is not suspect classification because, inter alia, "physical ability generally declines with age"). . . .

C

Immutability of the Group's Distinguishing Characteristic

A third factor that courts have considered in determining whether the members of a class are entitled to heightened protection for equal protection purposes is whether the attribute or characteristic that distinguishes them is immutable or otherwise beyond their control. See, e.g., *Bowen v. Gilliard*, supra, 483 U.S. 602. Of course, the characteristic that distinguishes gay persons from others and qualifies them for recognition as a distinct and discrete group is the characteristic that historically has resulted in their social and legal ostracism, namely, their attraction to persons of the same sex. * * *

A number of courts that have considered this factor have rejected the claim that sexual orientation is an immutable characteristic. Other courts, however, as well as many, if not most, scholarly commentators, have reached a contrary conclusion. Although we do not doubt that sexual orientation—heterosexual or homosexual—is highly resistant to change, it is not necessary for us to decide whether sexual orientation is immutable in the same way and to the same extent that race, national origin and gender are immutable, because, even if it is not, the plaintiffs nonetheless have established that they fully satisfy this consideration. * * *

In view of the central role that sexual orientation plays in a person's fundamental right to self-determination, we fully agree with the plaintiffs that their sexual orientation represents the kind of distinguishing characteristic that defines them as a discrete group for purposes of determining whether that group should be afforded heightened protection under the equal protection provisions of the state constitution. This prong of the suspectness inquiry surely is satisfied when, as in the present case, the identifying trait is "so central to a person's identity that it would be abhorrent for government to penalize a person for refusing to change [it]. . . ." *Watkins v. United States Army*, supra, 875 F.2d 726 (Norris, J., concurring in the judgment); * * * In other words, gay persons, because they are characterized by a "central, defining [trait] of personhood, which may be altered [if at all] only at the expense of significant damage to the individual's sense of self" * * *

D

Whether the Group Is a Minority or Lacking in Political Power

* * *

1

We commence our analysis by noting that, in previous cases involving groups seeking heightened protection under the federal equal protection clause, the United States Supreme Court described this factor without reference to the minority status of the subject group, focusing instead on the group's lack of political power. See, e.g., *Massachusetts Board of Retirement v. Murgia*, supra, 427 U.S. 313 (explaining that "a suspect class is one saddled with such disabilities, or subjected to such a history of purposeful unequal treatment, or relegated to such a position of political powerlessness as to command extraordinary protection from the majoritarian political process" [internal quotation marks omitted]); *San Antonio Independent School District v. Rodriguez*, supra, 411 U.S. 28

(same). In its most recent formulation of the test for determining whether a group is entitled to suspect or quasi-suspect classification, however, the Court has indicated that this factor is satisfied upon a showing either that the group is a minority or that it lacks political power. *Bowen v. Gilliard*, supra, 483 U.S. 602; *Lyng v. Castillo*, supra, 477 U.S. 638. Indeed, in characterizing this factor in disjunctive terms, the Court cited to *Murgia*; *Bowen v. Gilliard*, supra, 602–603; *Lyng v. Castillo*, supra, 638; thereby also indicating that, for purposes of this aspect of the inquiry, the test always has involved a determination of whether the group is a "discrete and insular" minority; *United States v. Carolene Products Co.*, 304 U.S. 144, 152–53 n.4, 58 S. Ct. 778, 82 L. Ed. 1234 (1938); or, if not a true minority; see, e.g., *Frontiero v. Richardson*, supra, 411 U.S. 686 n.17, 688 (plurality opinion) (women accorded protected status although not minority); the group nonetheless is lacking in political power. This disjunctive test properly recognizes that a group may warrant heightened protection even though it does not fit the archetype of a discrete and insular minority. The test also properly recognizes that legislation singling out a true minority that meets the first three prongs of the suspectness inquiry must be viewed with skepticism because, under such circumstances, there exists an undue risk that legislation involving the historically disfavored group has been motivated by improper considerations borne of prejudice or animosity.

When this approach is applied to the present case, there is no doubt that gay persons clearly comprise a distinct minority of the population. Consequently, they clearly satisfy the first part of the disjunctive test and, thus, may be deemed to satisfy this prong of the suspectness inquiry on that basis alone.

2

* * * In support of their claim, the defendants rely primarily on this state's enactment of the gay rights and civil union laws, which, of course, were designed to provide equal rights for gay persons, and which undoubtedly reflect a measure of political power. The defendants also rely on the fact that several state legislators in Connecticut are openly gay. From the defendants' standpoint, these significant advances undermine the plaintiffs' claim that gay persons are so lacking in political power that they are entitled to heightened judicial protection. * * *

In this state, no openly gay person ever has been elected to *statewide* office, and only five of the 187 members of the state legislature are openly gay or lesbian. No openly gay man or lesbian ever has been appointed to the state Supreme Court or Appellate Court, and we are aware of only one openly gay or lesbian judge of the Superior Court. By contrast, this state's current governor, comptroller and secretary of the state are women, as are the current chief justice and two associate justices of the state Supreme Court, and other women now hold and previously have held statewide office and positions in the United States House of Representatives. By any standard, therefore, gay persons "remain a political underclass in our [state and] nation." *Andersen v. King County*, supra, 158 Wash.2d at 105, 138 P.3d 963 (Bridge, J., concurring in dissent).

In recent years, our legislature has taken substantial steps to address discrimination against gay persons. These efforts are most notably reflected in this state's gay rights law; see General Statutes §§ 46a–81a through 46a–81r; which broadly prohibits discrimination against a person because of his or her "preference for heterosexuality, homosexuality or bisexuality, having a history of such preference or being identified with such preference. . . ." General Statutes § 46a–81a. This public policy extends to a wide range of activities, including membership in licensed professional associations; see General Statutes § 46a–81b; employment; see General Statutes § 46a–81c; public accommodations; see General Statutes § 46a–81d; housing; see General Statutes § 46a–81e; credit practices; see General Statutes § 46a–81f; employment in state agencies; see General Statutes §§ 46a–81h and 46a–81j; the granting of state licenses; see General Statutes § 46a–81k; educational and vocational programs of state agencies; see General Statutes § 46a–81m; and the allocation of state benefits. See General Statutes § 46a–81n. Other statutes also seek to prohibit discrimination against same sex couples and gay persons. See General Statutes § 45a–724 et seq. (permitting same sex couples to adopt children); General Statutes §§ 53a–181j, 53a–181k and 53a–181 *l* (recognizing crimes of intimidation based on bigotry or bias for conduct directed at another on account of that person's actual or perceived sexual orientation). These antidiscrimination provisions, along with the civil union law, reflect the fact that gay persons are able to exert some degree of political influence in the state.

Notwithstanding these provisions, however, the legislature expressly has stated that the gay rights law shall *not* be "deemed or construed (1) to mean the state of Connecticut condones homosexuality or bisexuality or any equivalent lifestyle, (2) to authorize the promotion of homosexuality or bisexuality in educational institutions or require the teaching in educational institutions of homosexuality or bisexuality as an acceptable lifestyle, (3) to authorize or permit the use of numerical goals or quotas, or other types of affirmative action programs, with respect to homosexuality or bisexuality in the administration or enforcement of the [state's antidiscrimination laws], (4) to authorize the recognition of or the right of marriage between persons of the same sex, or (5) to establish sexual orientation as a specific and separate cultural classification in society." General Statutes § 46a–81r. By singling out same sex relationships in this manner—there is, of course, no such statutory disclaimer for opposite sex relationships—the legislature effectively has proclaimed, as a matter of state policy, that same sex relationships are disfavored. That policy, which is unprecedented among the various antidiscrimination measures enacted in this state, represents a kind of state-sponsored disapproval of same sex relationships and, consequently, serves to undermine the legitimacy of homosexual relationships, to perpetuate feelings of personal inferiority and inadequacy among gay persons, and to diminish the effect of the laws barring discrimination against gay persons. Indeed, the purposeful description of homosexuality as a "lifestyle" not condoned by the state stigmatizes gay persons and equates their identity with conduct that is disfavored by the state. Furthermore, although the legislature eventually enacted the gay rights law, its enactment was preceded by nearly a decade of numerous, failed attempts at passage. In addition, the bill that did become law provides more limited protection than the proposals that had preceded it, all of which would have added sexual orientation to the existing nondiscrimination laws and would have treated the classification in the same manner as other protected classes. Finally, as we have explained, the legislation that ultimately emerged from this process passed only after a compromise was reached that resulted in, inter alia, an unprecedented proviso expressing the position of the legislature that it does not condone homosexuality. Thus, to the extent that those civil rights laws, as well as the civil union law, reflect the fact that gay persons wield a measure of political power, the public policy articulated in § 46a–81r is clear evidence of the limits of that political influence. * * *

4

In sum, the relatively modest political influence that gay persons possess is insufficient to rectify the invidious discrimination to which they have been subjected for so long. Like the political gains that women had made prior to their recognition as a quasi-suspect class, the political advances that gay persons have attained afford them inadequate protection, standing alone, in view of the deep-seated and pernicious nature of the prejudice and antipathy that they continue to face. Today, moreover, women have far greater political power than gay persons, yet they continue to be accorded status as a quasi-suspect class. See Breen v. Carlsbad Municipal Schools, supra, 138 N.M. 338 (explaining that intermediate scrutiny is appropriate with respect to discrimination based on sex "even though the darkest period of discrimination may have passed for [the] historically maligned group" and that "[such] scrutiny should still be applied to protect against more subtle forms of unconstitutional discrimination created by unconscious or disguised prejudice"). We conclude, therefore, that, to the extent that gay persons possess some political power, it does not disqualify them from recognition as a quasi-suspect class under the state constitution in view of the pervasive and invidious discrimination to which they historically have been subjected due to an innate personal characteristic that has absolutely no bearing on their ability to perform in or contribute to society.

ANDERSEN V. KING COUNTY
Supreme Court of Washington, 2006
158 Wash.2d 1, 138 P.3d 963

MADSEN, JUDGE.

* * *

To qualify as a suspect class for purposes of an equal protection analysis, the class must have suffered a history of discrimination, have as the characteristic defining the class an obvious, immutable trait that frequently bears no relation to ability to perform or contribute to society, and show that it is a minority or politically powerless class. *Hanson,* 83 Wash.2d at 199, 517 P.2d 599; *City of Cleburne v. Cleburne Living Ctr., Inc.,* 473 U.S. 432, 440–41, 105 S.Ct. 3249, 87 L.Ed.2d 313 (1985); *High Tech Gays v. Def. Indus. Sec. Clearance Office,* 895 F.2d 563 (9th Cir.1990). Race, alienage, and national origin are examples of suspect classifications. *City of Cleburne,* 473 U.S. at 440, 105 S.Ct. 3249. Suspect classifications require heightened scrutiny because the defining characteristic of the class is "so seldom relevant to the achievement of any legitimate state interest that laws grounded in such considerations are deemed to reflect prejudice and antipathy—a view that those in the burdened class are not as worthy or deserving as others." *Id.* There is no dispute that gay and lesbian persons have been discriminated against in the past.

The parties dispute whether homosexuality is immutable. The State relies on the decision in *High Tech Gays* that homosexuality is behavioral, and thus not immutable. The plaintiffs counter that the Ninth Circuit has since "corrected" *High Tech Gays* and held that gay and lesbian persons constitute a suspect class. They rely on *Hernandez-Montiel v. Immigration & Naturalization Serv.,* 225 F.3d 1084 (9th Cir. 2000), *overruled in part on other grounds by Thomas v. Gonzales,* 409 F.3d 1177 (9th Cir. 2005), where the court determined that asylum should be granted to an immigration applicant, reasoning among other things that as a gay man with a female sexual identity the applicant had a well-grounded fear of persecution as a member of a particular social group. The court concluded the applicant was a member of a particular social group because "[s]exual orientation and sexual identity are immutable; they are so fundamental to one's identity that a person should not be required to abandon them." *Id.* at 1093. This conclusion was drawn from other immigration cases and secondary authority.

Notwithstanding *Hernandez-Montiel,* the Ninth Circuit has since referenced *High Tech Gays* for its holding that gay and lesbian persons do not constitute a suspect class. *Flores v. Morgan Hill Unified Sch. Dist.,* 324 F.3d 1130, 1137 (9th Cir. 2003) (citing *High Tech Gays*).

The plaintiffs do not cite other authority or any secondary authority or studies in support of the conclusion that homosexuality is an immutable characteristic. They focus instead on the lack of any relation between homosexuality and ability to perform or contribute to society. But plaintiffs must make a showing of immutability, and they have not done so in this case.

Finally, with regard to the ability to obtain redress through the legislative process (the political powerless prong), several state statutes and municipal codes provide protection against discrimination based on sexual orientation and also provide economic benefit for same sex couples. Recently, the legislature amended the Washington State Law Against Discrimination to prohibit discrimination on the basis of sexual orientation. Engrossed Substitute H.B. 2661, 59th Leg., Reg. Sess. (Wash.2006). In addition, the Intervenors point to evidence that a number of openly gay candidates were elected to national, state, and local offices in 2004.

The enactment of provisions providing increased protections to gay and lesbian individuals in Washington shows that as a class gay and lesbian persons are not powerless but, instead, exercise increasing political power. Indeed, the recent passage of the amendments to chapter 49.60 RCW is particularly significant given that, as the plaintiffs point out, the legislature had previously declined on numerous occasions to add sexual orientation to the laws against discrimination. We conclude that plaintiffs have not established that they satisfy the third prong of the suspect classification test.

Our conclusion here, that plaintiffs have not established that they are members of a suspect class, accords with the decisions of the overwhelming majority of courts, which find that gay and lesbian persons do not constitute a suspect class. *See Lofton v. Sec'y of the Dep't of Children & Family Servs.,* 358 F.3d 804, 818 & n.4 (11th Cir. 2004), *cert. denied,* 543 U.S. 1081 (2005) (concluding that gay and lesbian persons are not a suspect class and citing cases from the Fourth, Fifth, Sixth, Seventh, Ninth, and Tenth Circuits that have reached the same conclusion). The Second and Eighth Circuits have reached the same conclusion. *Able v. United States,* 155 F.3d 628, 632 (2d Cir. 1998); *Richenberg v. Perry,* 97 F.3d 256, 260 (8th Cir. 1996). The Court of Appeals held in *Singer,* 11 Wn. App. 247, that gay and lesbian persons do not constitute a suspect class. And even two state courts deciding that same-sex couples have a right to a civil union or marriage did not find a suspect class. *Baker v. State,* 170 Vt. 194, 744 A.2d 864 (1999) (under the state constitution's common benefits clause, plaintiffs seeking same-sex marriage are entitled to benefits and obligations like those accompanying marriage); *Goodridge v. Dep't of Pub. Health,* 440 Mass. 309, 798 N.E.2d 941 (2003) (denial of civil marriage to same-sex [*22] couples violates state equal protection principles). And, while the plaintiffs cite cases they say hold that gay and lesbian persons constitute a suspect class, most do not support the proposition or are otherwise distinguishable. * * *

The plaintiffs also suggest that *Miguel v. Guess,* 112 Wash.App. 536, 51 P.3d 89 (2002), *Romer,* 517 U.S. 620, 116 S.Ct. 1620, 134 L.Ed.2d 855, and *Lawrence v. Texas,* 539 U.S. 558, 123 S.Ct. 2472, 156 L.Ed.2d 508 (2003) indicate a trend toward heightened scrutiny where gay and lesbian persons are concerned. *Miguel* and *Romer* are based on another constitutional principle, however. In *Romer,* the Court invalidated on equal protection grounds Colorado's constitutional Amendment 2, which prohibited all legislative, executive, or judicial action designed to protect gay and lesbian persons from discrimination. The Court noted that "if a law neither burdens a fundamental right nor targets a suspect class, we will uphold the legislative classification so long as it bears a rational relation to some legitimate end." *Romer,* 517 U.S. at 631, 116 S.Ct. 1620. The Court said that Amendment 2 "fails, indeed defies" this inquiry. *Id.* at 632, 116 S.Ct. 1620. The court noted that central to equal protection is the principle that "government and each of its parts remain open . . . to all who seek its assistance," and "[a] law declaring that in general it shall be more difficult for one group of citizens than for all others to seek aid from the government is itself a denial of equal protection in the most literal sense." *Id.* at 633, 116 S.Ct. 1620. The Court found that there was no legitimate government purpose of Amendment 2 and held the amendment did not satisfy rational relation review.

Similarly, in *Miguel,* where the plaintiff claimed her civil rights were violated as a result of discrimination based on being a lesbian, the court found that a discriminatory classification based on prejudice or bias is not rationally related to a legitimate governmental purpose as a matter of law. *See also Cleburne Living Ctr.,* 473 U.S. at 448, 105 S.Ct. 3249 (noting that while private biases may be outside the reach the law, the law cannot give them effect). Both *Miguel* and *Romer* rest on the principle that equal protection is denied where the law's purpose is discrimination and it has no legitimate government purpose. Neither case supports the proposition that gay and lesbian persons constitute a suspect class. Indeed, as plaintiffs recognize, neither case addressed suspect classifications; the court in *Miguel* expressly declined to decide whether gay and lesbian persons constitute a suspect class. *Miguel,* 112 Wash.App. at 552 n. 3, 51 P.3d 89.

In *Lawrence,* the Court held that Texas's sodomy law violated equal protection under a rational basis analysis, thus overruling its decision in *Bowers v. Hardwick,* 478 U.S. 186, 106 S.Ct. 2841, 92 L.Ed.2d 140 (1986). *Lawrence* is widely viewed as reflecting changing societal attitudes toward gay and lesbian persons. The Court emphasized "an emerging awareness that liberty gives substantial protection to adult persons in deciding how to conduct their private lives in matters pertaining to sex." *Lawrence,* 539 U.S. at 572, 123 S.Ct. 2472. However, the Court did not address suspect classification and invalidated the challenged law on the basis that it did not satisfy rational basis review, a standard that would not apply if the court had found an inherently suspect class.

In light of the lack of a sufficient showing of immutability and the overwhelming authority finding that gay and lesbian persons are not a suspect class for purposes of the equal protection clause, we decline to conclude that gay and lesbian persons constitute an inherently suspect class for purposes of article I, section 12.

NOTES

1. Note the difference in how the Connecticut and Washington courts treat the issue of immutability. Which court has the better approach? What role—if any—do you think immutability should play in determining a level of scrutiny? As you think about this question, consider Professor Janet Halley's views, set out in the next section.

2. How does the practice of gay "conversion therapy" bear on the immutability of sexual orientation? Such therapy involves controversial treatment designed to change a person's sexual orientation to heterosexual. California and New Jersey have banned this treatment for young persons, and other states are considering similar action. *See* Katie McDonough, *Ohio May Be Next State to Ban Gay Conversion Therapy,* SALON (Oct. 7, 2013, 9:53 AM), http://www.salon.com/2013/10/07/ohio_may_be_next_state_to_ban_gay_conversion_therapy/. Opponents of the therapy argue that it does not work and harms those subject to it. Is the treatment's efficacy relevant to the immutability question? For constitutional analysis, does it matter whether a characteristic is literally immutable versus difficult to change? Should the law require individuals to change a personal characteristic to avoid discrimination? The California ban on conversion therapy was challenged as a violation of the First Amendment. The Ninth Circuit upheld the law in *Pickup v. Brown,* 728 F.3d 1042 (9th Cir. 2013).

3. Note the contrasting discussions of LGBT political power in the Connecticut and Washington opinions. In view of legislative gains made on issues such as repealing sodomy laws and enacting anti-discrimination laws based on sexual orientation, can it be persuasively said that LGBT persons are politically powerless? Does it depend on how "political power" is defined for purposes of heightened scrutiny review? Two political scientists debated

this point at great length in their expert testimony in the federal lawsuit challenging the constitutionality of California's Proposition 8. *See Perry v. Schwarzenegger*, 704 F. Supp. 2d 921, 937, 943–44, 950–52 (N.D. Cal. 2010) (excerpted in Chapter 6, Section II.C.2.c); Jane S. Schacter, *Ely at the Altar: Political Process Theory Through the Lens of the Marriage Debate*, 109 MICH. L. REV. 1363 (2011).

4.   At the time that the Connecticut and Washington courts wrote, judicial action on marriage equality was crucially important because no state legislature had yet enacted marriage equality into law. In recent years, however, it has become more common for legislatures to be the driving force for marriage equality. What significance do these new institutional dynamics have for assessing the political power of the LGBT community?

5.   The Connecticut and Washington courts agreed that, for purposes of the heightened scrutiny inquiry, the LGBT community had suffered a history of discrimination. In *Sevcik v. Sandoval*, 911 F. Supp. 2d 996 (D. Nev. 2012), the district court pursued a contrasting approach. That court upheld Nevada's ban on same-sex marriage and declined to apply heightened scrutiny, relying on *High Tech Gays v. Def. Indus. Sec. Clearance Office*, 895 F.2d 563, 574 (9th Cir. 1990). In so doing, the court said the following about the history-of-discrimination prong of the analysis:

> [H]omosexuals have indeed suffered a history of discrimination, but it is indisputable that public acceptance and legal protection from discrimination has increased enormously for homosexuals, such that this factor is weighted less heavily towards heightened scrutiny than it was [when *High Tech Gays* was decided] in 1990. It is the present state of affairs and any lingering effects of past discrimination that are important to the analysis, not the mere historical facts of discrimination taken in a vacuum. Although historical discrimination taken alone may be relevant to a showing under the second factor, i.e., whether the group is in fact a discretely identifiable group, without a showing of continuing discrimination or lingering effects of past discrimination, the first factor does not tend to support an argument that the group need be protected from majoritarian processes. Unlike members of minority races, for example, homosexuals do not in effect inherit the effects of past discrimination through their parents. That is, members of certain racial minorities are more likely to begin life at a socioeconomic disadvantage because of historical discrimination against their ancestors, the effects of which are passed from parent to child, taking many generations to ameliorate via the later removal of discrimination. On the contrary, homosexuality by its nature, whether chosen or not, is a characteristic particularly unlikely to be passed from parent to child in such a way that the effects of past discrimination against one's ancestors will have effects upon oneself. In the context of a characteristic like homosexuality, where no lingering effects of past discrimination are

inherited, it is contemporary disadvantages that matter for the purposes of assessing disabilities due to discrimination. Any such disabilities with respect to homosexuals have been largely erased since 1990.

6.   The level of scrutiny appropriate for sexual orientation-based classifications figured centrally in a February 2011 letter from Attorney General Eric Holder to the Speaker of the House announcing a new Department of Justice policy about defending the constitutionality of the Defense of Marriage Act. *See* Chapter 6, Section II.D. In that letter, Holder made the case for applying heightened scrutiny to sexual orientation claims and announced that the Department would no longer defend DOMA in any circuit that had not already decided to apply rationality review to such claims.

7.   In 2012, following the Holder letter, the Second Circuit upheld a district court ruling invalidating DOMA. Unlike the district court in that case, however, the Second Circuit employed intermediate scrutiny. *Windsor v. United States*, 699 F.3d 169 (2d Cir. 2012). The opinion acknowledged that the LGBT community has "clearly" achieved some political successes but said the key question is whether the group has "the strength to politically protect [itself] from wrongful discrimination." 699 F.3d at 184. When the decision was affirmed by the Supreme Court, Justice Kennedy's majority opinion applied rational basis in striking down DOMA and made no comment about the appropriateness of heightening scrutiny. *United States v. Windsor*, 133 S. Ct. 2675 (2013). That decision is addressed in Chapter 6. Nevertheless, the approach taken by the Second Circuit reflects the first time a federal court of appeals has embraced intermediate scrutiny for sexual orientation-based equal protection claims.

8.   In a case involving the dismissal of a bisexual public school teacher, Justice Brennan provided an early blueprint for the argument that some form of heightened scrutiny may be appropriate in analyzing claims by LGBT persons:

> First, homosexuals constitute a significant and insular minority of this country's population. Because of the immediate and severe opprobrium often manifested against homosexuals once so identified publicly, members of this group are particularly powerless to pursue their rights openly in the political arena. Moreover, homosexuals have historically been the object of pernicious and sustained hostility, and it is fair to say that discrimination against homosexuals is "likely . . . to reflect deep-seated prejudice rather than . . . rationality." State action taken against members of such groups based simply on their status as members of the group traditionally has been subjected to strict, or at least heightened, scrutiny by this Court.

Rowland v. Mad River Local Sch. Dist., 470 U.S. 1009, 1014, 105 S.Ct. 1373, 1377, 84 L.Ed.2d 392, 396 (1985) (Brennan, J., dissenting from the denial of certiorari). This analysis provides the framework for *Watkins v. United States Army*, 837 F.2d 1428 (9th Cir. 1988), *amended by* 847 F.2d 1329 (9th Cir. 1988), *reh'g granted*, 847 F.2d 1362 (9th Cir. 1988), *different results reached on reh'g*, 875 F.2d 699 (9th Cir. 1989) (en banc), *cert. denied*, 498 U.S. 957, 111 S.Ct. 384, 112 L.Ed.2d 395 (1990), where a three-judge panel of the U.S. Court of Appeals for the Ninth Circuit held that an Army regulation excluding gays and lesbians from military service violated the equal protection clause. This marked the first federal circuit court decision finding heightened scrutiny for lesbians and gay men. Although it was later vacated en banc, the panel decision is notable for its elaboration of the argument for heightened scrutiny.

9.   Recall Professor Kogan's analysis of transgender discrimination in Chapter 1 (*see supra* Chapter 1, Section VII). Is heightened scrutiny appropriate for discrimination based on gender identity?

2.   Scholarly Perspectives on the Level of Scrutiny Debate

A significant body of scholarship has developed around the question of whether classifications based on sexual orientation warrant heightened judicial scrutiny. In an influential book, John Hart Ely built on the famous footnote 4 in the U.S. Supreme Court's decision in *United States v. Carolene Prods. Co.*, 304 U.S. 144, 152 n.4, 58 S.Ct. 778 n.4, 82 L.Ed. 1234 n.4 (1938), which suggested that "prejudice against discrete and insular minorities may be a special condition . . . curtail[ing] the operation of those political processes ordinarily to be relied upon to protect minorities, and [so] may call for a correspondingly more searching judicial inquiry." In Ely's view, judicial review should compensate for malfunctions in the democratic process, which occur when "representatives beholden to an effective majority are systematically disadvantaging some minority out of simple hostility or a prejudiced refusal to recognize commonalities of interest, and thereby denying that minority the protection afforded other groups by a representative system." JOHN HART ELY, DEMOCRACY AND DISTRUST: A THEORY OF JUDICIAL REVIEW 103 (1980). Ely argued that "a combination of the factors of [anti-gay] prejudice and hideability" warranted heightened scrutiny because they impaired the ability of gay persons to advocate effectively in the political process. Id. at 163.

The first two readings that follow challenge aspects of the approach suggested by Ely and footnote 4. The last two consider other dimensions of constitutional equality analysis.

BEYOND *CAROLENE PRODUCTS**

Bruce A. Ackerman

IV. *DISCRETE* AND INSULAR MINORITIES?

[I]t is not obvious whether most constitutional lawyers endow the word "discrete" with independent significance in their understanding of the *Carolene* doctrine. Nonetheless, we can conceive the term in a way that adds something important to the overall formula. I propose to define a minority as "discrete" when its members are marked out in ways that make it relatively easy for others to identify them. For instance, there is nothing a black woman may plausibly do to hide the fact that she is black or female. Like it or not, she will have to deal with the social expectations and stereotypes generated by her evident group characteristics. In contrast, other minorities are socially defined in ways that give individual members the chance to avoid easy identification. A homosexual, for example, can keep her sexual preference a very private affair and thereby avoid much of the public opprobrium attached to her minority status. It is for this reason that I shall call homosexuals, and groups like them, "anonymous" minorities and contrast them with "discrete" minorities of the kind paradigmatically exemplified by blacks.

This way of defining terms allows us to complement our analysis of insularity in a natural way. While the insularity-diffuseness continuum measures the intensity and breadth of intra-group interaction, the discreteness-anonymity continuum measures the ease with which people outside a group can identify group members. It should be plain that these two continua are not invariably associated with one another. Blacks, for example, are both discrete and insular, whereas women are discrete yet diffuse; homosexuals are anonymous but may be somewhat insular,[28] whereas the poor are both relatively anonymous and diffuse. Because there is no necessary correlation between discreteness and insularity, I shall treat discreteness as a distinct subject for analysis and consider how a group's place on the discreteness-anonymity continuum can be expected to add to, or detract from, its probable political influence.

Carolene takes a straightforward position on this question. In its view, discreteness is a political liability. Once again, however, the only thing that is obvious is that this is not obvious. The main reason why has been elegantly developed in Albert Hirschman's modern classic, *Exit,*

---

*   Bruce A. Ackerman, *Beyond* Carolene Products, 98 HARV. L. REV. 713, 728–31 (1985).

[28] At this point the distinction between intensity and breadth may be helpful in refining the text's qualifying "somewhat." Although homosexuals do not characteristically share a broad range of social settings in which they interact as homosexuals, a few social contexts do serve as loci for an intense reaffirmation of homosexual identities—most notably, the network of homosexual bars and restaurants found in major American cities. Predictably, this network provided an important organizational focus for the recent political movement on behalf of homosexual rights. *See* J. D'EMILIO, SEXUAL POLITICS, SEXUAL COMMUNITIES 129–250 (1983).

Voice and Loyalty (1970). The book's title refers to three nonviolent ways of responding to an unsatisfactory situation: if you dislike something, you may try to avoid it (exit), you may complain about it (voice), or you may grin-and-hope-for-improvement (loyalty). Although these three responses may be related to one another in a number of ways, the relationship between two of them—exit and voice—is of special relevance here. People do not respond to a bad situation by engaging in a random pattern of avoidance and protest. Instead, according to Hirschman, an inverse relationship obtains: the more exit, the less voice, and vice versa. The reason for this is straightforward: the easier it is to avoid a bad situation, the less it will seem worthwhile to complain, and vice versa.

This inverse relationship holds significant implications for the relative political strength of minorities at different points on the discreteness-anonymity scale. If you are a black in America today, you know there is no way you can avoid the impact of the larger public's views about the significance of blackness. Because exit is not possible, there is only one way to do something about disadvantageous racial stereotypes: complain about them. Among efficacious forms of complaint, the possibility of organized political action will surely rank high.

This is not to say, of course, that individual blacks, or members of other discrete minorities, will necessarily lend their support to interest-group activity. They may, instead, succumb to the temptations of free-riding and thus deprive the group of vital political resources. But even if discreteness is no cure-all for selfishness, it does free a minority from the organizational problem confronting an anonymous group of comparable size. To see my point, compare the problem faced by black political organizers with the one confronting organizers of the homosexual community. As a member of an anonymous group, each homosexual can seek to minimize the personal harm due to prejudice by keeping his or her sexual preference a tightly held secret. Although this is hardly a fully satisfactory response, secrecy does enable homosexuals to "exit" from prejudice in a way that blacks cannot. This means that a homosexual group must confront an organizational problem that does not arise for its black counterpart: somehow the group must induce each anonymous homosexual to reveal his or her sexual preference to the larger public and to bear the private costs this public declaration may involve.

Although some, perhaps many, homosexuals may be willing to pay this price, the fact that each must individually choose to pay it means that this anonymous group is less likely to be politically efficacious than is an otherwise comparable but discrete minority. For, by definition, discrete groups do not have to convince their constituents to "come out of the closet" before they can engage in effective political activity. So it would seem that *Carolene Products* is wrong again: a court concerned with pluralist bargaining power should be more, not less, attentive to the claims of anonymous minorities than to those of discrete ones.

ELY AT THE ALTER: POLITICAL PROCESS THEORY THROUGH THE LENS OF THE MARRIAGE DEBATE[1]

Jane S. Schacter

In the absence of clearer substantive commitments about what makes a political process fair and how much/what kind of political power a group "should" have, [process] theory offers little to resolve questions of application like those raised in the marriage debate. * * * Process theory essentially asks whether LGBT people—or other disadvantaged groups— have "sufficient" power to be left to their own political devices, rather than receiving solicitous treatment from a court. Answering this question depends not only on how political power is defined, but on how sufficiency is understood. Therein lies the baseline question. To assess meaningfully whether historical prejudice undermines a group's power, we, presumably, need to know something about what the group's political power would look like in a properly functioning political process. * * *

[I]dentifying the relevant baseline begins to get both enigmatic and interesting when we recognize that there is no particular reason to believe that LGBT people would be politically organized and active as LGBT people in the way that has become familiar *but for* the phenomena that called into being the organization of their social movement. The animating goal that gave rise to the gay rights movement was, precisely, to dislodge longstanding structures of discrimination. . . . The dilemma is this: if the need to politically organize is itself generated by long-term historical subordination, it is difficult to conjure the untainted baseline political process against which to measure the current process, because there are good grounds to wonder whether LGBT people would be legislatively active as LGBT people in the absence of that subordination. * * *

A second set of problems with process theory that the marriage debate reveals—and a second way in which process theory is thin— relates to its institutional assumptions. There is a distinctly caricatured quality to the roles that process theory assigns to courts and to legislatures.

Process theory is built on the assumption that, while legislatures will predictably fall prey to—and remain mired in—forms of prejudice that will skew and distort their approach to public policy, courts can and will overcome such prejudice in adjudication. * * *

---

[1] Jane S. Schacter, *Ely at the Altar: Political Process Theory Through the Lens of the Marriage Debate*, 109 MICH. L. REV. 1363, 1390, 1392–93, 1397–99 (2011).

[A] core empirical problem with this view is that, while the vision of courts as consistent countermajoritarian forces has deep and enduring normative appeal, it is not empirically well supported. . . . [C]ourts, across the long march of history, are not often all that far out of step with popular opinion or out front on controversial social issues. * * *

Indeed, in every state whose supreme court issued a judicial decision favorable to same-sex couples, the political process had taken significant strides toward recognizing gay civil rights by the time the court ruled. * * * [C]ontrary to the assumption of process theory, it is strikingly implausible to think that judges in [the states most hostile to LGBT rights] can or will stand apart from prevailing public opinion and take action to compensate for anti-gay bias decades before the political process shows movement on marriage or other issues of concern to LGBT citizens of the state. Such a prospect, indeed, depends in the first instance on the improbable notion that courts in these states would *characterize* as anti-gay bias the resistance of legislators and citizens to gay equality claims. . . .

SEXUAL ORIENTATION AND THE POLITICS OF BIOLOGY*
Janet E. Halley

I.   THE ARGUMENT FROM IMMUTABILITY

Before the Human Genome Project became a household word, gay-rights articles asserted the argument from immutability in dispassionate, even perfunctory, recitations. The first serious reevaluation of equal protection for gay men and lesbians after *Hardwick* embraced the argument from immutability with readily apparent reluctance. As stronger biological claims pointing to a genetic role emerged, that tone changed; indeed, the first strong post-*Hardwick* proposal emphasizing immutability came from the intersection of law and medicine. Bolstered by citations to recent scientific experiments claiming to show that human sexual orientation rests on a biological substrate, the argument from immutability has become the platform on which many gay-rights advocates prefer to contest post-*Hardwick* courts' equation of homosexual identity with criminalizable sodomy.

Although pro-gay advocates often advance the argument from immutability with enthusiasm, it is clear that many judges do not find it persuasive. . . . Strong biological evidence, however, might alter future judicial outcomes. Several courts have noted that the *controversy* over biological causation is a reason to reject the argument from immutability, a rationale that might cut the other way if the scientific community were to reach consensus on the etiology of homosexual orientation. Courts are

---

*   Janet E. Halley, *Sexual Orientation and the Politics of Biology: A Critique of the Argument from Immutability*, 46 STAN. L. REV. 503, 512–16, 567–68 (1994).

increasingly prepared, moreover, to commit the questions raised when pro-gay litigators rely on recent scientific reports to the jury for factfinding.

Not discouraged by this lackluster track record, gay-rights plaintiffs have begun to bolster the argument from immutability by citing the new scientific reports. In at least four recent cases challenging discrimination against gay men, lesbians, and bisexuals, plaintiffs' attorneys have cited the new scientific findings to support their arguments that homosexual orientation is a suspect classification because it is immutable. * * *

The scientific evidence available has not made judges more likely to accept pro-gay advocates' argument from immutability. As the foregoing legal analysis suggests, gay-rights advocates who base their equal protection cases on the argument from immutability do so at their option. . . . It is time to think carefully about whether the pro-gay argument from immutability has any justifiable part to play in pro-gay litigation. . . .

The argument from immutability responds to a particularly contemptuous and dismissive form of anti-gay animus with elegant simplicity and plangent appeal. It also works. Indeed, it often is the *only* effective resource available to gay men, lesbians, and bisexuals seeking to persuade their parents, coworkers, and neighbors that they can love someone of the same sex and remain fully human. Moreover, for most of the gay children, workers, and neighbors who use the argument from immutability in these settings, it is absolutely true: They can't change their sexual orientation.

When the argument from immutability leaves those settings and becomes a legal strategy, however, the terms by which we should judge its plausibility and effectiveness shift. While it may be entirely responsive to the particular form of personal criticism faced by many gay men, lesbians, and bisexuals ("Why don't you just change?"), it is not fully or even coherently responsive to the forms of anti-gay argument used to justify state-sponsored discrimination against all of us. Three new elements need to be taken into account.

First, anti-gay public policy is complex and flexible, and finds ways to justify itself even on the assumption that homosexual orientation in many, most, or all its bearers is immutable. Second, the reasons *why* the state should not discriminate against gay men, lesbians, and bisexuals are different in important ways from the reasons why parents should not think ill of their gay children. Suspect class analysis (when given its best reading) asks whether the resources of the state are being used to enforce, confirm, and validate social hierarchies. The argument from immutability has never attained the preeminence in suspect class analysis that some pro-gay advocates attribute to it because it carries so little water in that analysis. And third, the argument from immutability, when advanced on behalf of a complex movement, many of whose members can change some aspect of their sexuality that is targeted by anti-gay policy, is less directly responsive to the problem we face. Moreover, the argument becomes burdened with an ethical problem it does not have when used privately: When pro-gay advocates use the argument from immutability before a court on behalf of gay men, lesbians, and bisexuals, they misrepresent us.

Even worse, when the pro-gay argument from immutability annexes recent scientific findings to bolster its empirical claim that homosexual orientation is immutable, it becomes simply incoherent. As I have indicated in my summaries of the internal criticism of behavioral genetics and of the particular scientific articles that advocates of the pro-gay argument from immutability have considered most useful, biologically caused traits can change; there is as yet no proof that human sexual orientation has a biological cause; and even if a biological cause of human sexual orientation were eventually identified, the conceptually distinct question whether it causes *homosexuality and heterosexuality* would remain outstanding.

Failure to emphasize that last point is perhaps the most disturbing feature of the way in which pro-gay advocates of the argument from immutability have introduced the scientific findings into the broader culture. Of course, one day science may find that the sexual-orientation categories of our culture are natural, but today their adequacy is a political question—in fact the very same political question that divides pro-gay advocates of the argument from immutability and many of its pro-gay detractors. Proponents of the pro-gay argument from immutability have covertly withdrawn a political question from the political sphere by falsely implying that science has answered it.

Retrieving that political question for social and political debate also provides a better basis for antidiscrimination analysis. A prerequisite for the latter is a representation of homosexuals and heterosexuals, of homosexuality and heterosexuality, that does not divide pro-gay communities (or divides them as little as possible). The controversy over the pro-gay argument from immutability is a controversy between essentialism and constructivism, but it has been conducted with a dangerously thin notion of the complexity of the logical entailments of those theories. It has assumed that an essentialist view of sexual orientation committed one to a claim that homosexuality, as such, is the product of nature; and that a constructivist view committed one to a claim that homosexuality is an entirely contingent social artifact, subject to change at whim. It has assumed that essentialism and constructivism are logical opposites. A more careful explanation of what is involved in essentialism and constructivism indicates that a *weak* form of essentialism—holding that a given entity is subject to consistent conventional definition—actually subtends many forms of constructivism, and that constructivism varies quite widely in the depth of its contingency claims.

Disaggregating the various forms of essentialism and constructivism thus indicates that they are actually intertwined in all but the most extreme ends of their own ranges, and offers the possibility of finding a conceptual location from which pro-gay essentialists and pro-gay constructivists can frame legal arguments that avoid the argument from immutability while not contradicting its empirical predicate. Recent sexuality studies in history, anthropology, and cultural studies vary more or less continuously in the depth of their claim that sexual-orientation categories are socially contingent. All but the most extreme forms of constructivism retain a weak essentialist view of homosexual orientation. And all but the most extreme forms of essentialism permit attention to focus on the social meanings of sexual desire, behavior, and self-description. My proposal is that pro-gay advocates can form litigation strategy at the resulting intersection of essentialism and constructivism. There are distinct legal advantages to this compromise, moreover: Strong essentialism actually supports courts in holding that *Hardwick* forecloses heightened scrutiny; the justifications for heightened scrutiny arise from precisely the social and political elements of sexual-orientation identity that constructivist analysis identifies; and rational basis analysis, because it involves examination of the discriminator's reasons for discriminating, looks not at what gay men, lesbians, and bisexuals really are, but at what we are *thought to be*. Litigating on common ground is thus not only the right thing to do—it is also more likely to work.

THE CONSTITUTION OF STATUS*

J.M. Balkin

Analyzing discrimination in terms of status groups also helps us understand our objections to discrimination more clearly in situations where courts hold that the Constitution already proscribes it. Discrimination against blacks, for example, is not unjust simply because race is an immutable characteristic. Focusing on immutability per se confuses biological with sociological considerations. It confuses the physical existence of the trait with what the trait means in a social system. Racial discrimination is wrong because of the historical creation of a status hierarchy organized around the meaning of skin color. The question to ask is not whether a trait is immutable, but whether there has been a history of using the trait to create a system of social meanings, or define a social hierarchy, that helps dominate and oppress people. Any

---

* J.M. Balkin, *The Constitution of Status*, 106 YALE L.J. 2313, 2365–67 (1997).

conclusions about the importance of immutability already presuppose a view about background social structure.

Indeed, a focus on immutability makes sense only as long as we recognize its relationship to social structure. Social hierarchies often assign differential social meanings to immutable traits because they make exit from low status more difficult. But not all immutable characteristics are or have been the basis for unjust social hierarchies, and not all unjust social hierarchies are founded on immutable characteristics.

Religion is not an immutable trait—many religions are always looking for new converts—but status-based discrimination against religious groups is surely also unjust. Defenders of the immutability criterion can point to the Religion Clauses as an independent justification for protection of religious minorities; but this puts the cart before the horse. The Religion Clauses exist in part because the Framers recognized that religious intolerance was an evil long before they recognized that racial intolerance was.

The importance of immutability as a criterion of judgment is also sometimes defended on the grounds that immutable characteristics—for example, race—are morally irrelevant. But this argument, too, really depends on a view about the justness of a particular status hierarchy. When status distinctions are internalized in a culture, status hierarchies *make* traits morally relevant. They become signs of positive and negative associations. They become permissible proxies for inferences about character, honesty, ability, and judgment. Such traits are morally irrelevant only to persons not in the grip of that particular hierarchy. In the aristocracy of pre-Revolutionary America, for example, high birth was viewed as correlating with many other positive attributes—honesty, sagacity, learning, and good manners—and society was organized to make these positive associations a self-fulfilling prophecy. Generations of whites thought blacks naturally inferior; succeeding generations who learned not to make biological arguments have nevertheless continued to regard blacks as culturally inferior—as displaying negative qualities of sloth, violence, and licentiousness. A characteristic becomes "morally irrelevant" precisely when we understand the status hierarchy it is based on to be unjust. Only then do we become embarrassed to use the trait as a signifier of, or a proxy for, positive or negative associations. Our objection to the moral relevance of the characteristic is really our objection to the system of social meanings and the hierarchy of social status that uses this trait as a criterion for judgment. The real issue is whether society has created an unjust status hierarchy organized around a particular trait or set of traits, whether those traits are immutable, or—like religion—voluntarily chosen or instilled through socialization.

3. *Romer* and Rational Basis

In the landmark case of *Romer v. Evans*, the U.S. Supreme Court struck down a voter initiative hostile to gay civil rights statutes that added sexual orientation to statutory anti-discrimination laws. Initiatives like this one date to the 1970s, but, in the early 1990s, the opponents of gay equality initiated a new round of measures designed to counter advances made by lesbians, gay men, and bisexuals. Initiatives were proposed to ban protections against anti-gay discrimination in two California cities (Riverside and Concord), but both were declared unconstitutional and barred from being placed on the ballot.[6] In 1992, statewide initiatives were promulgated by opponents of sexual orientation laws in Oregon and Colorado. The Oregon measure was defeated at the polls, but the Colorado initiative, known as Amendment 2, was enacted by the voters by a 53.4%-46.6% margin. Amendment 2 repealed existing protections against discrimination based on sexual orientation—including ordinances in the cities of Aspen, Boulder, and Denver; a statewide Executive Order prohibiting discrimination in state employment; and an insurance code provision prohibiting health insurers from determining insurability and premiums based on an applicant's sexual orientation.[7] Amendment 2 also barred state and local governmental units from enacting such protections in the future.

The constitutionality of Amendment 2 was immediately challenged in the Colorado state courts and, due to the issuance of an injunction pending the outcome of the case, Amendment 2 never went into effect. In two decisions, the Colorado Supreme Court found Amendment 2 unconstitutional. In *Evans I*, the court held that the Amendment had the effect of burdening the plaintiffs' fundamental right "to participate equally in the political process" and thus that it could be sustained only if the state could show at trial that it was necessary to serve a compelling governmental interest and that it did so in the least restrictive manner possible. *Evans v. Romer*, 854 P.2d at 1276 (Colo. 1993), *cert. denied*, 510 U.S. 959, 114 S.Ct. 419, 126 L.Ed.2d 365 (1993). The Colorado high court based its decision in *Evans I* on a series of cases involving similar referenda that arose in the race context, *e.g., Hunter v. Erickson*, 393 U.S. 385, 89 S.Ct. 557, 21 L.Ed.2d 616 (1969); the state argued unsuccessfully that the application of heightened scrutiny in these earlier cases was solely a function of the classifications therein being racial, not a result of the presence of a fundamental right. Following a lengthy trial, the lower court rejected all of the reasons the state put forward as compelling state interests; its decision was affirmed by the Colorado Supreme Court in

---

[6] *See Citizens for Responsible Behavior v. Superior Court*, 2 Cal.Rptr.2d 648, 661, 1 Cal.App. 4th 1013, 1036 (1991); *Jester v. City of Concord*, No. C91–05455 (Cal. Super. Ct. 1992).

[7] *See Evans v. Romer*, 854 P.2d 1270, 1284–85 & n.26 (Colo. 1993).

Evans II, Evans v. Romer, 882 P.2d 1335, 1350 (Colo. 1994), *cert. granted*, 513 U.S. 1146, 115 S. Ct. 1092, 130 L. Ed. 2d 1061 (1995).

In May of 1996, the U.S. Supreme Court affirmed the Colorado Supreme Court's conclusion that Amendment 2 violated the federal constitution, but it reached that conclusion through a different route.

ROMER V. EVANS
Supreme Court of the United States, 1996
517 U.S. 620, 116 S.Ct. 1620, 134 L.Ed.2d 855

JUSTICE KENNEDY delivered the opinion of the Court.

One century ago, the first Justice Harlan admonished this Court that the Constitution "neither knows nor tolerates classes among citizens." *Plessy v. Ferguson*, 163 U.S. 537, 559 (1896) (dissenting opinion). Unheeded then, those words now are understood to state a commitment to the law's neutrality where the rights of persons are at stake. The Equal Protection Clause enforces this principle and today requires us to hold invalid a provision of Colorado's Constitution.

I

The enactment challenged in this case is an amendment to the Constitution of the State of Colorado, adopted in a 1992 statewide referendum. The parties and the state courts refer to it as "Amendment 2," its designation when submitted to the voters. The impetus for the amendment and the contentious campaign that preceded its adoption came in large part from ordinances that had been passed in various Colorado municipalities. For example, the cities of Aspen and Boulder and the City and County of Denver each had enacted ordinances which banned discrimination in many transactions and activities, including housing, employment, education, public accommodations, and health and welfare services. What gave rise to the statewide controversy was the protection the ordinances afforded to persons discriminated against by reason of their sexual orientation. See Boulder Rev. Code § 12–1–1 (defining "sexual orientation" as "the choice of sexual partners, i.e., bisexual, homosexual or heterosexual"); Denver Rev. Municipal Code, Art. IV § 28–92 (defining "sexual orientation" as "the status of an individual as to his or her heterosexuality, homosexuality or bisexuality"). Amendment 2 repeals these ordinances to the extent they prohibit discrimination on the basis of "homosexual, lesbian or bisexual orientation, conduct, practices or relationships."

Yet Amendment 2, in explicit terms, does more than repeal or rescind these provisions. It prohibits all legislative, executive or judicial action at any level of state or local government designed to protect the named class, a class we shall refer to as homosexual persons or gays and lesbians. The amendment reads:

"No Protected Status Based on Homosexual, Lesbian, or Bisexual Orientation. Neither the State of Colorado, through any of its branches or departments, nor any of its agencies, political subdivisions, municipalities or school districts, shall enact, adopt or enforce any statute, regulation, ordinance or policy whereby homosexual, lesbian or bisexual orientation, conduct, practices or relationships shall constitute or otherwise be the basis of or entitle any person or class of persons to have or claim any minority status, quota preferences, protected status or claim of discrimination. This Section of the Constitution shall be in all respects self-executing."

Soon after Amendment 2 was adopted, this litigation to declare its invalidity and enjoin its enforcement was commenced in the District Court for the City and County of Denver. Among the plaintiffs (respondents here) were homosexual persons, some of them government employees. They alleged that enforcement of Amendment 2 would subject them to immediate and substantial risk of discrimination on the basis of their sexual orientation. Other plaintiffs (also respondents here) included the three municipalities whose ordinances we have cited and certain other governmental entities which had acted earlier to protect homosexuals from discrimination but would be prevented by Amendment 2 from continuing to do so. Although Governor Romer had been on record opposing the adoption of Amendment 2, he was named in his official capacity as a defendant, together with the Colorado Attorney General and the State of Colorado.

The trial court granted a preliminary injunction to stay enforcement of Amendment 2, and an appeal was taken to the Supreme Court of Colorado. Sustaining the interim injunction and remanding the case for further proceedings, the State Supreme Court held that Amendment 2 was subject to strict scrutiny under the Fourteenth Amendment because it infringed the fundamental right of gays and lesbians to participate in the political process. *Evans v. Romer*, 854 P.2d 1270 (Colo. 1993) (*Evans I*). To reach this conclusion, the state court relied on our voting rights cases, *e.g.*, *Reynolds v. Sims*, 377 U.S. 533 (1964); *Carrington v. Rash*, 380 U.S. 89 (1965); *Harper v. Virginia Bd. of Elections*, 383 U.S. 663 (1966); *Williams v. Rhodes*, 393 U.S. 23 (1968), and on our precedents involving discriminatory restructuring of governmental decisionmaking, *see e.g.*, *Hunter v. Erickson*, 393 U.S. 385 (1969); *Reitman v. Mulkey*, 387 U.S. 369 (1967); *Washington v. Seattle School Dist. No. 1*, 458 U.S. 457 (1982); *Gordon v. Lance*, 403 U.S. 1 (1971). On remand, the State advanced various arguments in an effort to show that Amendment 2 was narrowly tailored to serve compelling interests, but the trial court found none sufficient. It enjoined enforcement of Amendment 2, and the Supreme Court of Colorado, in a second opinion, affirmed the ruling. *Evans v. Romer*, 882 P.2d 1335 (Colo. 1994) (*Evans II*). We granted certiorari and now affirm the judgment, but on a rationale different from that adopted by the State Supreme Court.

II

The State's principal argument in defense of Amendment 2 is that it puts gays and lesbians in the same position as all other persons. So, the State says, the measure does no more than deny homosexuals special rights. This reading of the amendment's language is implausible. We rely not upon our own interpretation of the amendment but upon the authoritative construction of Colorado's Supreme Court. The state court, deeming it unnecessary to determine the full extent of the amendment's reach, found it invalid even on a modest reading of its implications. The critical discussion of the amendment, set out in *Evans I*, is as follows:

> The immediate objective of Amendment 2 is, at a minimum, to repeal existing statutes, regulations, ordinances, and policies of state and local entities that barred discrimination based on sexual orientation. *See* Aspen, Colo., Mun.Code § 13–98 (1977) (prohibiting discrimination in employment, housing and public accommodations on the basis of sexual orientation); Boulder, Colo., Rev. Code §§ 12–1–2 to –4 (1987) (same); Denver, Colo., Rev. Mun. Code art. IV, §§ 28–91 to –116 (1991) (same); Executive Order No. D0035 (December 10, 1990) (prohibiting employment discrimination for "all state employees, classified and exempt" on the basis of sexual orientation); Colorado Insurance Code, § 10–3–1104, 4A C.R.S. (1992 Supp.) (forbidding health insurance providers from determining insurability and premiums based on an applicant's, a beneficiary's, or an insured's sexual orientation); and various provisions prohibiting discrimination based on sexual orientation at state colleges.[26] "The 'ultimate effect' of Amendment 2 is to prohibit any governmental entity from adopting similar, or more protective statutes, regulations, ordinances, or policies in the future unless the state constitution is first amended to permit such measures." 854 P.2d, at 1284–1285, and n. 26.

Sweeping and comprehensive is the change in legal status effected by this law. So much is evident from the ordinances that the Colorado Supreme Court declared would be void by operation of Amendment 2. Homosexuals, by state decree, are put in a solitary class with respect to

---

[26] Metropolitan State College of Denver prohibits college sponsored social clubs from discriminating in membership on the basis of sexual orientation and Colorado State University has an antidiscrimination policy which encompasses sexual orientation.

transactions and relations in both the private and governmental spheres. The amendment withdraws from homosexuals, but no others, specific legal protection from the injuries caused by discrimination, and it forbids reinstatement of these laws and policies.

The change that Amendment 2 works in the legal status of gays and lesbians in the private sphere is far-reaching, both on its own terms and when considered in light of the structure and operation of modern anti-discrimination laws. That structure is well illustrated by contemporary statutes and ordinances prohibiting discrimination by providers of public accommodations. "At common law, innkeepers, smiths, and others who 'made profession of a public employment,' were prohibited from refusing, without good reason, to serve a customer." *Hurley v. Irish-American Gay, Lesbian & Bisexual Group of Boston, Inc.*, 515 U.S. 557, 571 (1995). The duty was a general one and did not specify protection for particular groups. The common law rules, however, proved insufficient in many instances, and it was settled early that the Fourteenth Amendment did not give Congress a general power to prohibit discrimination in public accommodations, *Civil Rights Cases*, 109 U.S. 3, 25 (1883). In consequence, most States have chosen to counter discrimination by enacting detailed statutory schemes.

Colorado's state and municipal laws typify this emerging tradition of statutory protection and follow a consistent pattern. The laws first enumerate the persons or entities subject to a duty not to discriminate. The list goes well beyond the entities covered by the common law. The Boulder ordinance, for example, has a comprehensive definition of entities deemed places of "public accommodation." They include "any place of business engaged in any sales to the general public and any place that offers services, facilities, privileges, or advantages to the general public or that receives financial support through solicitation of the general public or through governmental subsidy of any kind." Boulder Rev. Code § 12–1–1(j) (1987). The Denver ordinance is of similar breadth, applying, for example, to hotels, restaurants, hospitals, dental clinics, theaters, banks, common carriers, travel and insurance agencies, and "shops and stores dealing with goods or services of any kind," Denver Rev. Municipal Code, Art. IV, § 28–92.

These statutes and ordinances also depart from the common law by enumerating the groups or persons within their ambit of protection. Enumeration is the essential device used to make the duty not to discriminate concrete and to provide guidance for those who must comply. In following this approach, Colorado's state and local governments have not limited anti-discrimination laws to groups that have so far been given the protection of heightened equal protection scrutiny under our cases. *See, e.g., J.E.B. v. Alabama ex rel. T.B.*, 511 U.S. 127 (1994) (sex); *Lalli v. Lalli*, 439 U.S. 259, 265 (1978) (illegitimacy); *McLaughlin v. Florida*, 379

U.S. 184, 191–192 (1964) (race); *Oyama v. California*, 332 U.S. 633 (1948) (ancestry). Rather, they set forth an extensive catalogue of traits which cannot be the basis for discrimination, including age, military status, marital status, pregnancy, parenthood, custody of a minor child, political affiliation, physical or mental disability of an individual or of his or her associates and, in recent times, sexual orientation.

Amendment 2 bars homosexuals from securing protection against the injuries that these public accommodations laws address. That in itself is a severe consequence, but there is more. Amendment 2, in addition, nullifies specific legal protections for this targeted class in all transactions in housing, sale of real estate, insurance, health and welfare services, private education, and employment. *See, e.g.*, Aspen Municipal Code §§ 13–98(b), (c) (1977); Boulder Rev. Code §§ 12–1–2, 12–1–3 (1987); Denver Rev. Municipal Code, Art. IV §§ 28–93 to 28–95, § 28–97 (1991).

Not confined to the private sphere, Amendment 2 also operates to repeal and forbid all laws or policies providing specific protection for gays or lesbians from discrimination by every level of Colorado government. The State Supreme Court cited two examples of protections in the governmental sphere that are now rescinded and may not be reintroduced. The first is Colorado Executive Order D0035 (1990), which forbids employment discrimination against " 'all state employees, classified and exempt' on the basis of sexual orientation." 854 P.2d, at 1284. Also repealed, and now forbidden, are "various provisions prohibiting discrimination based on sexual orientation at state colleges." *Id.*, at 1284, 1285. The repeal of these measures and the prohibition against their future reenactment demonstrates that Amendment 2 has the same force and effect in Colorado's governmental sector as it does elsewhere and that it applies to policies as well as ordinary legislation.

Amendment 2's reach may not be limited to specific laws passed for the benefit of gays and lesbians. It is a fair, if not necessary, inference from the broad language of the amendment that it deprives gays and lesbians even of the protection of general laws and policies that prohibit arbitrary discrimination in governmental and private settings. *See, e.g.*, Colo. Rev. Stat. § 24–4–106(7) (1988) (agency action subject to judicial review under arbitrary and capricious standard); § 18–8–405 (making it a criminal offense for a public servant knowingly, arbitrarily or capriciously to refrain from performing a duty imposed on him by law); § 10–3–1104(1)(f) (prohibiting "unfair discrimination" in insurance); 4 Colo. Code of Regulations 801–1, Policy 11–1 (1983) (prohibiting discrimination in state employment on grounds of specified traits or "other non-merit factor"). At some point in the systematic administration of these laws, an official must determine whether homosexuality is an arbitrary and thus forbidden basis for decision. Yet a decision to that effect would itself amount to a policy prohibiting discrimination on the basis of homosexuality, and so would appear to be no more valid under Amendment 2 than the specific prohibitions against discrimination the state court held invalid.

If this consequence follows from Amendment 2, as its broad language suggests, it would compound the constitutional difficulties the law creates. The state court did not decide whether the amendment has this effect, however, and neither need we. In the course of rejecting the argument that Amendment 2 is intended to conserve resources to fight discrimination against suspect classes, the Colorado Supreme Court made the limited observation that the amendment is not intended to affect many anti-discrimination laws protecting non-suspect classes, *Romer II*, 882 P.2d at 1346, n. 9. In our view that does not resolve the issue. In any event, even if, as we doubt, homosexuals could find some safe harbor in laws of general application, we cannot accept the view that Amendment 2's prohibition on specific legal protections does no more than deprive homosexuals of special rights. To the contrary, the amendment imposes a special disability upon those persons alone. Homosexuals are forbidden the safeguards that others enjoy or may seek without constraint. They can obtain specific protection against discrimination only by enlisting the citizenry of Colorado to amend the state constitution or perhaps, on the State's view, by trying to pass helpful laws of general applicability. This is so no matter how local or discrete the harm, no matter how public and widespread the injury. We find nothing special in the protections Amendment 2 withholds. These are protections taken for granted by most people either because they already have them or do not need them; these are protections against exclusion from an almost limitless number of transactions and endeavors that constitute ordinary civic life in a free society.

III

The Fourteenth Amendment's promise that no person shall be denied the equal protection of the laws must co-exist with the practical necessity that most legislation classifies for one purpose or another, with resulting disadvantage to various groups or persons. *Personnel Administrator of Mass. v. Feeney*, 442 U.S. 256, 271–272 (1979); *F.S. Royster Guano Co. v. Virginia*, 253 U.S. 412, 415 (1920). We have attempted to reconcile the principle with the reality by stating that, if a law neither burdens a fundamental right nor targets a suspect class, we will uphold the legislative classification so long as it bears a rational relation to some legitimate end. *See, e.g., Heller v. Doe*, 509 U.S. 312 (1993).

Amendment 2 fails, indeed defies, even this conventional inquiry. First, the amendment has the peculiar property of imposing a broad and undifferentiated disability on a single named group, an exceptional and, as we shall explain, invalid form of legislation. Second, its sheer breadth is so discontinuous with the reasons offered for it that the amendment seems inexplicable by anything but animus toward the class that it affects; it lacks a rational relationship to legitimate state interests.

Taking the first point, even in the ordinary equal protection case calling for the most deferential of standards, we insist on knowing the relation between the classification adopted and the object to be attained. The search for the link between classification and objective gives substance to the Equal Protection Clause; it provides guidance and discipline for the legislature, which is entitled to know what sorts of laws it can pass; and it marks the limits of our own authority. In the ordinary case, a law will be sustained if it can be said to advance a legitimate government interest, even if the law seems unwise or works to the disadvantage of a particular group, or if the rationale for it seems tenuous. *See New Orleans v. Dukes*, 427 U.S. 297 (1976) (tourism benefits justified classification favoring pushcart vendors of certain longevity); *Williamson v. Lee Optical of Okla., Inc.*, 348 U.S. 483 (1955) (assumed health concerns justified law favoring optometrists over opticians); *Railway Express Agency, Inc. v. New York*, 336 U.S. 106 (1949) (potential traffic hazards justified exemption of vehicles advertising the owner's products from general advertising ban); *Kotch v. Board of River Port Pilot Comm'rs for Port of New Orleans*, 330 U.S. 552 (1947) (licensing scheme that disfavored persons unrelated to current river boat pilots justified by possible efficiency and safety benefits of a closely knit pilotage system). The laws challenged in the cases just cited were narrow enough in scope and grounded in a sufficient factual context for us to ascertain that there existed some relation between the classification and the purpose it served. By requiring that the classification bear a rational relationship to an independent and legitimate legislative end, we ensure that classifications are not drawn for the purpose of disadvantaging the group burdened by the law. *See United States Railroad Retirement Bd. v. Fritz*, 449 U.S. 166, 181 (1980) (STEVENS, J., concurring) ("If the adverse impact on the disfavored class is an apparent aim of the legislature, its impartiality would be suspect.").

Amendment 2 confounds this normal process of judicial review. It is at once too narrow and too broad. It identifies persons by a single trait and then denies them protection across the board. The resulting disqualification of a class of persons from the right to seek specific protection from the law is unprecedented in our jurisprudence. The absence of precedent for Amendment 2 is itself instructive; "[d]iscriminations of an unusual character especially suggest careful consideration to determine whether they are obnoxious to the constitutional provision." *Louisville Gas & Elec. Co. v. Coleman*, 277 U.S. 32, 37–38 (1928).

It is not within our constitutional tradition to enact laws of this sort. Central both to the idea of the rule of law and to our own Constitution's guarantee of equal protection is the principle that government and each of its parts remain open on impartial terms to all who seek its assistance. " 'Equal protection of the laws is not achieved through indiscriminate imposition of inequalities.' " *Sweatt v. Painter*, 339 U.S. 629, 635 (1950) (quoting *Shelley v. Kraemer*, 334 U.S. 1, 22 (1948)). Respect for this principle explains why laws singling out a certain class of citizens for disfavored legal status or general hardships are rare. A law declaring that in general it shall be more difficult for one group of citizens than for all others to seek aid from the government is itself a denial of equal protection of the laws in the most literal sense. "The guaranty of 'equal protection of the laws is a pledge of the protection of equal laws.' " *Skinner v. Oklahoma ex rel. Williamson*, 316 U.S. 535, 541 (1942) (quoting *Yick Wo v. Hopkins*, 118 U.S. 356, 369 (1886)).

Davis v. Beason, 133 U.S. 333 (1890), not cited by the parties but relied upon by the dissent, is not evidence that Amendment 2 is within our constitutional tradition, and any reliance upon it as authority for sustaining the amendment is misplaced. In *Davis*, the Court approved an Idaho territorial statute denying Mormons, polygamists, and advocates of polygamy the right to vote and to hold office because, as the Court construed the statute, it "simply excludes from the privilege of voting, or of holding any office of honor, trust or profit, those who have been convicted of certain offences, and those who advocate a practical resistance to the laws of the Territory and justify and approve the commission of crimes forbidden by it." *Id.*, at 347. To the extent *Davis* held that persons advocating a certain practice may be denied the right to vote, it is no longer good law. *Brandenburg v. Ohio*, 395 U.S. 444 (1969) (per curiam). To the extent it held that the groups designated in the statute may be deprived of the right to vote because of their status, its ruling could not stand without surviving strict scrutiny, a most doubtful outcome. *Dunn v. Blumstein*, 405 U.S. 330, 337 (1972); *cf. United States v. Brown*, 381 U.S. 437 (1965); *United States v. Robel*, 389 U.S. 258 (1967). To the extent *Davis* held that a convicted felon may be denied the right to vote, its holding is not implicated by our decision and is unexceptionable. *See Richardson v. Ramirez*, 418 U.S. 24 (1974).

A second and related point is that laws of the kind now before us raise the inevitable inference that the disadvantage imposed is born of animosity toward the class of persons affected. "[I]f the constitutional conception of 'equal protection of the laws' means anything, it must at the very least mean that a bare . . . desire to harm a politically unpopular group cannot constitute a legitimate governmental interest." *Department of Agriculture v. Moreno*, 413 U.S. 528, 534 (1973). Even laws enacted for broad and ambitious purposes often can be explained by reference to legitimate public policies which justify the incidental disadvantages they impose on certain persons. Amendment 2, however, in making a general announcement that gays and lesbians shall not have any particular protections from the law, inflicts on them immediate, continuing, and real injuries that outrun and belie any legitimate justifications that may be claimed for it. We conclude that, in addition to the far-reaching deficiencies of Amendment 2 that we have noted, the principles it offends, in another sense, are conventional and venerable; a law must bear a rational relationship to a legitimate governmental purpose, *Kadrmas v. Dickinson Public Schools*, 487 U.S. 450, 462 (1988), and Amendment 2 does not.

The primary rationale the State offers for Amendment 2 is respect for other citizens' freedom of association, and in particular the liberties of landlords or employers who have personal or religious objections to homosexuality. Colorado also cites its interest in conserving resources to fight discrimination against other groups. The breadth of the Amendment is so far removed from these particular justifications that we find it impossible to credit them. We cannot say that Amendment 2 is directed to any identifiable legitimate purpose or discrete objective. It is a status-based enactment divorced from any factual context from which we could discern a relationship to legitimate state interests; it is a classification of persons undertaken for its own sake, something the Equal Protection Clause does not permit. "[C]lass legislation . . . [is] obnoxious to the prohibitions of the Fourteenth Amendment. . . ." *Civil Rights Cases*, 109 U.S., at 24.

We must conclude that Amendment 2 classifies homosexuals not to further a proper legislative end but to make them unequal to everyone else. This Colorado cannot do. A State cannot so deem a class of persons a stranger to its laws. Amendment 2 violates the Equal Protection Clause, and the judgment of the Supreme Court of Colorado is affirmed. It is so ordered.

JUSTICE SCALIA, with whom THE CHIEF JUSTICE and JUSTICE THOMAS join, dissenting.

The Court has mistaken a Kulturkampf for a fit of spite. The constitutional amendment before us here is not the manifestation of a " 'bare . . . desire to harm' " homosexuals, but is rather a modest attempt by seemingly tolerant Coloradans to preserve traditional sexual mores against the efforts of a politically powerful minority to revise those mores through use of the laws. That objective, and the means chosen to achieve it, are not only unimpeachable under any constitutional doctrine hitherto pronounced (hence the opinion's heavy reliance upon principles of righteousness rather than judicial holdings); they have been specifically approved by the Congress of the United States and by this Court.

In holding that homosexuality cannot be singled out for disfavorable treatment, the Court contradicts a decision, unchallenged here, pronounced only 10 years ago, *see Bowers v. Hardwick*, 478 U.S. 186 (1986), and places the prestige of this institution behind the proposition that opposition to homosexuality is as reprehensible as racial or religious bias. Whether it is or not is precisely the cultural debate that gave rise to the Colorado constitutional amendment (and to the preferential laws against which the amendment was directed). Since the Constitution of the United States says nothing about this subject, it is left to be resolved by normal democratic means, including the democratic adoption of provisions in state constitutions. This Court has no business imposing upon all Americans the resolution favored by the elite class from which the Members of this institution are selected, pronouncing that "animosity" toward homosexuality is evil. I vigorously dissent.

I

Let me first discuss Part II of the Court's opinion, its longest section, which is devoted to rejecting the State's arguments that Amendment 2 "puts gays and lesbians in the same position as all other persons," and "does no more than deny homosexuals special rights." The Court concludes that this reading of Amendment 2's language is "implausible" under the "authoritative construction" given Amendment 2 by the Supreme Court of Colorado.

In reaching this conclusion, the Court considers it unnecessary to decide the validity of the State's argument that Amendment 2 does not deprive homosexuals of the "protection [afforded by] general laws and policies that prohibit arbitrary discrimination in governmental and private settings." I agree that we need not resolve that dispute, because the Supreme Court of Colorado has resolved it for us. In *Evans v. Romer*, 882 P.2d 1335 (1994), the Colorado court stated:

> "It is significant to note that Colorado law currently proscribes discrimination against persons who are not suspect classes, including discrimination based on age; marital or family status; veterans' status; and for any legal, off-duty conduct such as smoking tobacco, § 24–34–402.5, 10A C.R.S. (1994 Supp.). *Of course Amendment 2 is not intended to have any effect on this legislation, but seeks only to prevent the adoption of anti-discrimination laws intended to protect gays, lesbians, and bisexuals.*" *Id.*, at 1346, n. 9 (emphasis added).

The Court utterly fails to distinguish this portion of the Colorado court's opinion. Colorado Rev. Stat. § 24–34–402.5 (Supp. 1995), which this passage authoritatively declares not to be affected by Amendment 2, was respondents' primary example of a generally applicable law whose protections would be unavailable to homosexuals under Amendment 2.

The clear import of the Colorado court's conclusion that it is not affected is that "general laws and policies that prohibit arbitrary discrimination" would continue to prohibit discrimination on the basis of homosexual conduct as well. This analysis, which is fully in accord with (indeed, follows inescapably from) the text of the constitutional provision, lays to rest such horribles, raised in the course of oral argument, as the prospect that assaults upon homosexuals could not be prosecuted. The amendment prohibits *special treatment* of homosexuals, and nothing more. It would not affect, for example, a requirement of state law that pensions be paid to all retiring state employees with a certain length of service; homosexual employees, as well as others, would be entitled to that benefit. But it would prevent the State or any municipality from making death-benefit payments to the "life partner" of a homosexual when it does not make such payments to the long-time roommate of a nonhomosexual employee. Or again, it does not affect the requirement of the State's general insurance laws that customers be afforded coverage without discrimination unrelated to anticipated risk. Thus, homosexuals could not be denied coverage, or charged a greater premium, with respect to auto collision insurance; but neither the State nor any municipality could require that distinctive health insurance risks associated with homosexuality (if there are any) be ignored.

Despite all of its hand-wringing about the potential effect of Amendment 2 on general antidiscrimination laws, the Court's opinion ultimately does not dispute all this, but assumes it to be true. The only denial of equal treatment it contends homosexuals have suffered is this: They may not obtain *preferential* treatment without amending the state constitution. That is to say, the principle underlying the Court's opinion is that one who is accorded equal treatment under the laws, but cannot as readily as others obtain *preferential* treatment under the laws, has been denied equal protection of the laws. If merely stating this alleged "equal protection" violation does not suffice to refute it, our constitutional jurisprudence has achieved terminal silliness.

The central thesis of the Court's reasoning is that any group is denied equal protection when, to obtain advantage (or, presumably, to avoid disadvantage), it must have recourse to a more general and hence more difficult level of political decisionmaking than others. The world has never heard of such a principle, which is why the Court's opinion is so long on emotive utterance and so short on relevant legal citation. And it seems to me most unlikely that any multilevel democracy can function under such a principle. For *whenever* a disadvantage is imposed, or conferral of a benefit is prohibited, at one of the higher levels of democratic decisionmaking (*i.e.*, by the state legislature rather than local government, or by the people at large in the state constitution rather than the legislature), the affected group has (under this theory) been denied equal protection. To take the simplest of examples, consider a state law prohibiting the award of municipal contracts to relatives of mayors or city councilmen. Once such a law is passed, the group composed of such relatives must, in order to get the benefit of city contracts, persuade the state legislature—unlike all other citizens, who need only persuade the municipality. It is ridiculous to consider this a denial of equal protection, which is why the Court's theory is unheard-of.

The Court might reply that the example I have given is not a denial of equal protection only because the same "rational basis" (avoidance of corruption) which renders constitutional the *substantive discrimination* against relatives (i.e., the fact that they alone cannot obtain city contracts) also automatically suffices to sustain what might be called the *electoral-procedural* discrimination against them (*i.e.*, the fact that they must go to the state level to get this changed). This is of course a perfectly reasonable response, and would explain why "electoral-procedural discrimination" has not hitherto been heard of: a law that is valid in its substance is automatically valid in its level of enactment. But the Court cannot afford to make this argument, for as I shall discuss next, there is no doubt of a rational basis for the substance of the prohibition at issue here. The Court's entire novel theory rests upon the proposition that there is something *special*—something that cannot be justified by normal "rational basis" analysis—in making a disadvantaged group (or a nonpreferred group) resort to a higher decisionmaking level. That proposition finds no support in law or logic.

II

I turn next to whether there was a legitimate rational basis for the substance of the constitutional amendment—for the prohibition of special protection for homosexuals.[1] It is unsurprising that the Court avoids discussion of this question, since the answer is so obviously yes. The case most relevant to the issue before us today is not even mentioned in the Court's opinion: In *Bowers v. Hardwick*, 478 U.S. 186 (1986), we held that the Constitution does not prohibit what virtually all States had done from the founding of the Republic until very recent years—making homosexual conduct a crime. That holding is unassailable, except by those who think that the Constitution changes to suit current fashions. But in any event it is a given in the present case: Respondents' briefs did not urge overruling *Bowers*, and at oral argument respondents' counsel expressly disavowed

---

[1]   The Court evidently agrees that "rational basis"—the normal test for compliance with the Equal Protection Clause—is the governing standard. The trial court rejected respondents' argument that homosexuals constitute a "suspect" or "quasi-suspect" class, and respondents elected not to appeal that ruling to the Supreme Court of Colorado. *See Evans v. Romer*, 882 P.2d 1335, 1341, n. 3 (Colo. 1994). And the Court implicitly rejects the Supreme Court of Colorado's holding, see *Evans v. Romer*, 854 P.2d 1270, 1282 (Colo. 1993), that Amendment 2 infringes upon a "fundamental right" of "independently identifiable classes" to "participate equally in the political process."

any intent to seek such overruling. If it is constitutionally permissible for a State to make homosexual conduct criminal, surely it is constitutionally permissible for a State to enact other laws merely disfavoring homosexual conduct. (As the Court of Appeals for the District of Columbia Circuit has aptly put it: "If the Court [in *Bowers*] was unwilling to object to state laws that criminalize the behavior that defines the class, it is hardly open . . . to conclude that state sponsored discrimination against the class is invidious. After all, there can hardly be more palpable discrimination against the class than making the conduct that defines the class criminal." *Padula v. Webster*, 822 F.2d 97, 103 (1987).) And a fortiori it is constitutionally permissible for a State to adopt a provision not even disfavoring homosexual conduct, but merely prohibiting all levels of state government from bestowing special protections upon homosexual conduct. Respondents (who, unlike the Court, cannot afford the luxury of ignoring inconvenient precedent) counter *Bowers* with the argument that a greater-includes-the-lesser rationale cannot justify Amendment 2's application to individuals who do not engage in homosexual acts, but are merely of homosexual "orientation." Some courts of appeals have concluded that, with respect to laws of this sort at least, that is a distinction without a difference. See *Equality Foundation of Greater Cincinnati, Inc. v. Cincinnati*, 54 F.3d 261, 267 (6th Cir.1995) ("[F]or purposes of these proceedings, it is virtually impossible to distinguish or separate individuals of a particular *orientation* which predisposes them toward a particular sexual conduct from those who actually *engage* in that particular type of sexual conduct"); *Steffan v. Perry*, 41 F.3d 677, 689–690 (D.C. Cir. 1994). The Supreme Court of Colorado itself appears to be of this view. See 882 P.2d, at 1349–1350 ("Amendment 2 targets this class of persons based on four characteristics: sexual orientation; conduct; practices; and relationships. Each characteristic provides a potentially different way of identifying that class of persons who are gay, lesbian, or bisexual. These four characteristics are not truly severable from one another because each provides nothing more than a different way of identifying *the same class of persons*") (emphasis added).

But assuming that, in Amendment 2, a person of homosexual "orientation" is someone who does not engage in homosexual conduct but merely has a tendency or desire to do so, *Bowers* still suffices to establish a rational basis for the provision. If it is rational to criminalize the conduct, surely it is rational to deny special favor and protection to those with a self-avowed tendency or desire to engage in the conduct. Indeed, where criminal sanctions are not involved, homosexual "orientation" is an acceptable stand-in for homosexual conduct. A State "does not violate the Equal Protection Clause merely because the classifications made by its laws are imperfect," *Dandridge v. Williams*, 397 U.S. 471, 485 (1970). Just as a policy barring the hiring of methadone users as transit employees does not violate equal protection simply because some methadone users pose no threat to passenger safety, *see New York City Transit Authority v. Beazer*, 440 U.S. 568 (1979), and just as a mandatory retirement age of 50 for police officers does not violate equal protection even though it prematurely ends the careers of many policemen over 50 who still have the capacity to do the job, *see Massachusetts Bd. of Retirement v. Murgia*, 427 U.S. 307 (1976) (*per curiam*), Amendment 2 is not constitutionally invalid simply because it could have been drawn more precisely so as to withdraw special antidiscrimination protections only from those of homosexual "orientation" who actually engage in homosexual conduct. As JUSTICE KENNEDY wrote, when he was on the Court of Appeals, in a case involving discharge of homosexuals from the Navy: "Nearly any statute which classifies people may be irrational as applied in particular cases. Discharge of the particular plaintiffs before us would be rational, under minimal scrutiny, not because their particular cases present the dangers which justify Navy policy, but instead because the general policy of discharging all homosexuals is rational." *Beller v. Middendorf*, 632 F.2d 788, 808–809, n. 20 (9th Cir. 1980) (citation omitted). See also *Ben-Shalom v. Marsh*, 881 F.2d 454, 464 (7th Cir. 1989), cert. denied, 494 U.S. 1004 (1990).

Moreover, even if the provision regarding homosexual "orientation" were invalid, respondents' challenge to Amendment 2—which is a facial challenge—must fail. "A facial challenge to a legislative Act is, of course, the most difficult challenge to mount successfully, since the challenger must establish that no set of circumstances exists under which the Act would be valid." *United States v. Salerno*, 481 U.S. 739, 745 (1987). It would not be enough for respondents to establish (if they could) that Amendment 2 is unconstitutional as applied to those of homosexual "orientation"; since, under *Bowers*, Amendment 2 is unquestionably constitutional as applied to those who engage in homosexual conduct, the facial challenge cannot succeed. Some individuals of homosexual "orientation" who do not engage in homosexual acts might successfully bring an as-applied challenge to Amendment 2, but so far as the record indicates, none of the respondents is such a person. *See* App. 4–5 (complaint describing each of the individual respondents as either "a gay man" or "a lesbian").[2]

---

2   The Supreme Court of Colorado stated: "We hold that the portions of Amendment 2 that would remain if only the provision concerning sexual orientation were stricken are not autonomous and thus, not severable," 882 P.2d at 1349. That statement was premised, however, on the proposition that "[the] four characteristics [described in the Amendment—sexual orientation, conduct, practices, and relationships] are not truly severable from one another because each provides nothing more than a different way of identifying *the same class of persons*." *Id.*, at 1349–1350 (emphasis added). As I have discussed above, if that premise is true—if the entire class affected by the Amendment takes part in homosexual conduct, practices and relationships—*Bowers* alone suffices to answer all constitutional objections. Separate consideration of persons of homosexual "orientation" is necessary only if one believes (as the Supreme Court of Colorado did not) that that is a distinct class.

III

The foregoing suffices to establish what the Court's failure to cite any case remotely in point would lead one to suspect: No principle set forth in the Constitution, nor even any imagined by this Court in the past 200 years, prohibits what Colorado has done here. But the case for Colorado is much stronger than that. What it has done is not only unprohibited, but eminently reasonable, with close, congressionally approved precedent in earlier constitutional practice.

First, as to its eminent reasonableness. The Court's opinion contains grim, disapproving hints that Coloradans have been guilty of "animus" or "animosity" toward homosexuality, as though that has been established as un-American. Of course it is our moral heritage that one should not hate any human being or class of human beings. But I had thought that one could consider certain conduct reprehensible—murder, for example, or polygamy, or cruelty to animals—and could exhibit even "animus" toward such conduct. Surely that is the only sort of "animus" at issue here: moral disapproval of homosexual conduct, the same sort of moral disapproval that produced the centuries-old criminal laws that we held constitutional in *Bowers*. The Colorado amendment does not, to speak entirely precisely, prohibit giving favored status to people who are homosexuals; they can be favored for many reasons—for example, because they are senior citizens or members of racial minorities. But it prohibits giving them favored status *because of their homosexual conduct*—that is, it prohibits favored status *for homosexuality*.

But though Coloradans are, as I say, *entitled* to be hostile toward homosexual conduct, the fact is that the degree of hostility reflected by Amendment 2 is the smallest conceivable. The Court's portrayal of Coloradans as a society fallen victim to pointless, hate-filled "gay-bashing" is so false as to be comical. Colorado not only is one of the 25 States that have repealed their antisodomy laws, but was among the first to do so. See 1971 Colo. Sess. Laws, ch. 121, § 1. But the society that eliminates criminal punishment for homosexual acts does not necessarily abandon the view that homosexuality is morally wrong and socially harmful; often, abolition simply reflects the view that enforcement of such criminal laws involves unseemly intrusion into the intimate lives of citizens. *Cf.* Brief for Lambda Legal Defense and Education Fund, Inc., et al. as *Amici Curiae* in *Bowers v. Hardwick*, O.T.1985, No. 85–140, p. 25, n. 21 (antisodomy statutes are "unenforceable by any but the most offensive snooping and wasteful allocation of law enforcement resources"); Kadish, *The Crisis of Overcriminalization*, 374 The Annals of the American Academy of Political and Social Science 157, 161 (1967) ("To obtain evidence [in sodomy cases], police are obliged to resort to behavior which tends to degrade and demean both themselves personally and law enforcement as an institution").

There is a problem, however, which arises when criminal sanction of homosexuality is eliminated but moral and social disapprobation of homosexuality is meant to be retained. The Court cannot be unaware of that problem; it is evident in many cities of the country, and occasionally bubbles to the surface of the news, in heated political disputes over such matters as the introduction into local schools of books teaching that homosexuality is an optional and fully acceptable "alternate life style." The problem (a problem, that is, for those who wish to retain social disapprobation of homosexuality) is that, because those who engage in homosexual conduct tend to reside in disproportionate numbers in certain communities, have high disposable income, and of course care about homosexual-rights issues much more ardently than the public at large, they possess political power much greater than their numbers, both locally and statewide. Quite understandably, they devote this political power to achieving not merely a grudging social toleration, but full social acceptance, of homosexuality. *See, e.g.*, Jacobs, *The Rhetorical Construction of Rights: The Case of the Gay Rights Movement, 1969–1991*, 72 Neb. L. Rev. 723, 724 (1993) ("The task of gay rights proponents is to move the center of public discourse along a continuum from the rhetoric of disapprobation, to rhetoric of tolerance, and finally to affirmation").

By the time Coloradans were asked to vote on Amendment 2, their exposure to homosexuals' quest for social endorsement was not limited to newspaper accounts of happenings in places such as New York, Los Angeles, San Francisco, and Key West. Three Colorado cities—Aspen, Boulder, and Denver—had enacted ordinances that listed "sexual orientation" as an impermissible ground for discrimination, equating the moral disapproval of homosexual conduct with racial and religious bigotry. *See* Aspen Municipal Code § 13–98 (1977); Boulder Rev. Municipal Code §§ 12–1–1 to 12–1–11 (1987); Denver Rev. Municipal Code, Art. IV §§ 28–91 to 28–116 (1991). The phenomenon had even appeared statewide: the Governor of Colorado had signed an executive order pronouncing that "in the State of Colorado we recognize the diversity in our pluralistic society and strive to bring an end to discrimination in any form," and directing state agencyheads to "ensure non-discrimination" in hiring and promotion based on, among other things, "sexual orientation." Executive Order No. D0035 (Dec. 10, 1990). I do not mean to be critical of these legislative successes; homosexuals are as entitled to use the legal system for reinforcement of their moral sentiments as are the rest of society. But they are subject to being countered by lawful, democratic countermeasures as well.

That is where Amendment 2 came in. It sought to counter both the geographic concentration and the disproportionate political power of homosexuals by (1) resolving the controversy at the statewide level, and (2) making the election a single-issue contest for both sides. It put directly, to all the citizens of the State, the question: Should homosexuality be given special protection? They answered no. The Court today asserts that this most democratic of procedures is unconstitutional. Lacking any cases to establish that facially absurd proposition, it simply asserts that it must be unconstitutional, because it has never happened before.

> "[Amendment 2] identifies persons by a single trait and then denies them protection across the board. The resulting disqualification of a class of persons from the right to seek specific protection from the law is unprecedented in our jurisprudence. The absence of precedent for Amendment 2 is itself instructive. . . .
>
> It is not within our constitutional tradition to enact laws of this sort. Central both to the idea of the rule of law and to our own Constitution's guarantee of equal protection is the principle that government and each of its parts remain open on impartial terms to all who seek its assistance."

As I have noted above, this is proved false every time a state law prohibiting or disfavoring certain conduct is passed, because such a law prevents the adversely affected group—whether drug addicts, or smokers, or gun owners, or motorcyclists—from changing the policy thus established in "each of [the] parts" of the State. What the Court says is even demonstrably false at the constitutional level. The Eighteenth Amendment to the Federal Constitution, for example, deprived those who drank alcohol not only of the power to alter the policy of prohibition locally or through state legislation, but even of the power to alter it through state constitutional amendment or federal legislation. The Establishment Clause of the First Amendment prevents theocrats from having their way by converting their fellow citizens at the local, state, or federal statutory level; as does the Republican Form of Government Clause prevent monarchists.

But there is a much closer analogy, one that involves precisely the effort by the majority of citizens to preserve its view of sexual morality statewide, against the efforts of a geographically concentrated and politically powerful minority to undermine it. The constitutions of the States of Arizona, Idaho, New Mexico, Oklahoma, and Utah to this day contain provisions stating that polygamy is "forever prohibited." Polygamists, and those who have a polygamous "orientation," have been "singled out" by these provisions for much more severe treatment than merely denial of favored status; and that treatment can only be changed by achieving amendment of the state constitutions. The Court's disposition today suggests that these provisions are unconstitutional, and that polygamy must be permitted in these States on a state-legislated, or perhaps even local-option, basis—unless, of course, polygamists for some reason have fewer constitutional rights than homosexuals.

The United States Congress, by the way, *required* the inclusion of these antipolygamy provisions in the constitutions of Arizona, New Mexico, Oklahoma, and Utah, as a condition of their admission to statehood. See Arizona Enabling Act, 36 Stat. 569; New Mexico Enabling Act, 36 Stat. 558; Oklahoma Enabling Act, 34 Stat. 269; Utah Enabling Act, 28 Stat. 108. (For Arizona, New Mexico, and Utah, moreover, the Enabling Acts required that the antipolygamy provisions be "irrevocable without the consent of the United States and the people of said State"—so that not only were "each of [the] parts" of these States not "open on impartial terms" to polygamists, but even the States as a whole were not; polygamists would have to persuade the whole country to their way of thinking.) Idaho adopted the constitutional provision on its own, but the 51st Congress, which admitted Idaho into the Union, found its constitution to be "republican in form and . . . in conformity with the Constitution of the United States." Act of Admission of Idaho, 26 Stat. 215 (emphasis added). Thus, this "singling out" of the sexual practices of a single group for statewide, democratic vote—so utterly alien to our constitutional system, the Court would have us believe—has not only happened, but has received the explicit approval of the United States Congress.

I cannot say that this Court has explicitly approved any of these state constitutional provisions; but it has approved a territorial statutory provision that went even further, depriving polygamists of the ability even to achieve a constitutional amendment, by depriving them of the power to vote. In *Davis v. Beason*, 133 U.S. 333 (1890), Justice Field wrote for a unanimous Court:

> "In our judgment, § 501 of the Revised Statutes of Idaho Territory, which provides that 'no person . . . who is a bigamist or polygamist or who teaches, advises, counsels, or encourages any person or persons to become bigamists or polygamists, or to commit any other crime defined by law, or to enter into what is known as plural or celestial marriage, or who is a member of any order, organization or association which teaches, advises, counsels, or encourages its members or devotees or any other persons to commit the crime of bigamy or polygamy, or any other crime defined by law . . . is permitted to vote at any election, or to hold any position or office of honor, trust, or profit within this Territory,' *is not open to any constitutional or legal objection.*" *Id.*, at 346–347 (emphasis added).

To the extent, if any, that this opinion permits the imposition of adverse consequences upon mere abstract advocacy of polygamy, it has of course been overruled by later cases. *See Brandenburg v. Ohio*, 395 U.S. 444 (1969) (per curiam). But the proposition that polygamy can be criminalized, and those engaging in that crime deprived of the vote, remains good law. *See Richardson v. Ramirez*, 418 U.S. 24, 53 (1974). *Beason* rejected the argument that "such discrimination is a denial of the equal protection of the laws." Brief for Appellant in *Davis v. Beason*, O.T. 1889, No. 1261, p. 41. Among the Justices joining in that rejection were the two whose views in other cases the Court today treats as equal-protection lodestars—Justice Harlan, who was to proclaim in *Plessy v. Ferguson*, 163 U.S. 537, 559 (1896) (dissenting opinion), that the Constitution "neither knows nor tolerates classes among citizens," quoted ante, at 1, and Justice Bradley, who had earlier declared that "class legislation ... [is] obnoxious to the prohibitions of the Fourteenth Amendment," *Civil Rights Cases*, 109 U.S. 3, 24 (1883), quoted ante, at 14.[3]

This Court cited *Beason* with approval as recently as 1993, in an opinion authored by the same Justice who writes for the Court today. That opinion said: "Adverse impact will not always lead to a finding of impermissible targeting. For example, a social harm may have been a legitimate concern of government for reasons quite apart from discrimination. ... *See, e.g.,* ... *Davis v. Beason*, 133 U.S. 333 (1890)." *Church of Lukumi Babalu Aye, Inc. v. Hialeah*, 508 U.S. 520, 535 (1993). It remains to be explained how § 501 of the Idaho Revised Statutes was not an "impermissible targeting" of polygamists, but (the much more mild) Amendment 2 is an "impermissible targeting" of homosexuals. Has the Court concluded that the perceived social harm of polygamy is a "legitimate concern of government," and the perceived social harm of homosexuality is not?

---

[3]   The Court labors mightily to get around *Beason*, but cannot escape the central fact that this Court found the statute at issue—which went much further than Amendment 2, denying polygamists not merely special treatment but the right *to vote*—"not open to any constitutional or legal objection," rejecting the appellant's argument (much like the argument of respondents today) that the statute impermissibly "singled him out," Brief for Appellant in *Davis v. Beason*, O.T.1889, No. 1261, p. 41. The Court adopts my conclusions that (a) insofar as *Beason* permits the imposition of adverse consequences based upon mere advocacy, it has been overruled by subsequent cases, and (b) insofar as *Beason* holds that convicted felons may be denied the right to vote, it remains good law. To these conclusions, it adds something new: the claim that "to the extent [*Beason*] held that the groups designated in the statute may be deprived of the right to vote because of their status, its ruling could not stand without surviving strict scrutiny, a most doubtful outcome." But if that is so, it is only because we have declared the right to *vote* to be a "fundamental political right," see, *e.g., Dunn v. Blumstein*, 405 U.S. 330, 336 (1972), deprivation of which triggers strict scrutiny. Amendment 2, of course, does not deny the fundamental right to vote, and the Court rejects the Colorado court's view that there exists a fundamental right to participate in the political process. Strict scrutiny is thus not in play here. Finally, the Court's suggestion that § 501 of the Revised Statutes of Idaho, and Amendment 2, deny rights on account of "status" (rather than conduct) opens up a broader debate involving the significance of *Bowers* to this case, a debate which the Court is otherwise unwilling to join.

IV

I strongly suspect that the answer to the last question is yes, which leads me to the last point I wish to make: The Court today, announcing that Amendment 2 "defies . . . conventional [constitutional] inquiry," and "confounds [the] normal process of judicial review," employs a constitutional theory heretofore unknown to frustrate Colorado's reasonable effort to preserve traditional American moral values. The Court's stern disapproval of "animosity" towards homosexuality might be compared with what an earlier Court (including the revered Justices Harlan and Bradley) said in *Murphy v. Ramsey*, 114 U.S. 15 (1885), rejecting a constitutional challenge to a United States statute that denied the franchise in federal territories to those who engaged in polygamous cohabitation:

> "[C]ertainly no legislation can be supposed more wholesome and necessary in the founding of a free, self-governing commonwealth, fit to take rank as one of the co-ordinate States of the Union, than that which seeks to establish it on the basis of the idea of the family, as consisting in and springing from the union for life of one man and one woman in the holy estate of matrimony; the sure foundation of all that is stable and noble in our civilization; the best guaranty of that reverent morality which is the source of all beneficent progress in social and political improvement." *Id.*, at 45.

I would not myself indulge in such official praise for heterosexual monogamy, because I think it no business of the courts (as opposed to the political branches) to take sides in this culture war.

But the Court today has done so, not only by inventing a novel and extravagant constitutional doctrine to take the victory away from traditional forces, but even by verbally disparaging as bigotry adherence to traditional attitudes. To suggest, for example, that this constitutional amendment springs from nothing more than " 'a bare . . . desire to harm a politically unpopular group,' " is nothing short of insulting. (It is also nothing short of preposterous to call "politically unpopular" a group which enjoys enormous influence in American media and politics, and which, as the trial court here noted, though composing no more than 4% of the population had the support of 46% of the voters on Amendment 2.)

When the Court takes sides in the culture wars, it tends to be with the knights rather than the villeins—and more specifically with the Templars, reflecting the views and values of the lawyer class from which the Court's Members are drawn. How that class feels about homosexuality will be evident to anyone who wishes to interview job applicants at virtually any of the Nation's law schools. The interviewer may refuse to offer a job because the applicant is a Republican; because he is an adulterer; because he went to the wrong prep school or belongs to the wrong country club; because he eats snails; because he is a womanizer; because she wears real-animal fur; or even because he hates the Chicago Cubs. But if the interviewer should wish not to be an associate or partner of an applicant because he disapproves of the applicant's homosexuality, *then* he will have violated the pledge which the Association of American Law Schools requires all its member-schools to exact from job interviewers: "assurance of the employer's willingness" to hire homosexuals. This law-school view of what "prejudices" must be stamped out may be contrasted with the more plebeian attitudes that apparently still prevail in the United States Congress, which has been unresponsive to repeated attempts to extend to homosexuals the protections of federal civil rights laws, *see, e.g.*, Employment Non-Discrimination Act of 1994, S. 2238, 103d Cong., 2d Sess. (1994); Civil Rights Amendments of 1975, H.R. 5452, 94th Cong., 1st Sess. (1975), and which took the pains to exclude them specifically from the Americans With Disabilities Act of 1990, see 42 U.S.C. § 12211(a) (1988 ed., Supp. V). * * *

Today's opinion has no foundation in American constitutional law, and barely pretends to. The people of Colorado have adopted an entirely reasonable provision which does not even disfavor homosexuals in any substantive sense, but merely denies them preferential treatment. Amendment 2 is designed to prevent piecemeal deterioration of the sexual morality favored by a majority of Coloradans, and is not only an appropriate means to that legitimate end, but a means that Americans have employed before. Striking it down is an act, not of judicial judgment, but of political will. I dissent.

NOTES

1.   For a sampling of scholarly commentary on *Romer*, see Akhil Reed Amar, *Attainder and Amendment 2:* Romer's *Rightness*, 95 MICH. L. REV. 203 (1996); Lynn Baker, *The Missing Pages of the Majority Opinion in* Romer v. Evans, 68 U. COLO. L. REV. 387 (1997); Dale Carpenter, *A Conservative Defense of* Romer v. Evans, 76 IND. L.J. 403 (2000); Richard Duncan, *The Narrow and Shallow Bite of* Romer *and the Eminent Rationality of Dual-Gender Marriage: A (Partial) Response to Professor Koppelman*, 6 WM. & MARY BILL RTS. J. 147 (1997); Daniel Farber & Suzanna Sherry, *The Pariah Principle*, 13 CONST. COMMENT. 257 (1996); Roderick M. Hills, Jr., *Is Amendment 2 Really a Bill of Attainder? Some Questions About Professor Amar's Analysis of* Romer, 95 MICH. L. REV. 236 (1996); Nan D. Hunter, *Proportional Equality: Readings of* Romer, 89 KY. L.J. 885 (2000); Louis Michael Seidman, Romer's *Radicalism: The Unexpected Revival of Warren Court Activism*, 1996 SUP. CT. REV. 67; Jane S. Schacter, Romer v. Evans *and Democracy's Domain*, 50 VAND. L. REV. 361 (1997); Cass R. Sunstein, *The*

Supreme Court, 1995 Term—Foreword: Leaving Things Undecided, 110 HARV. L. REV. 6, 53–71 (1996).

    2.   From the time it was decided, *Romer* was greeted with uncertainty about its doctrinal basis. One reason is that the Colorado Supreme Court's decisions in the Amendment 2 case—like most of the legal and academic commentary—had focused on the applicability of the "political participation" theory to this context. In *Romer*, however, the U.S. Supreme Court ultimately declined to follow this path. As suggested by the opinion's reference to a "denial of equal protection of the laws in its most literal sense," the Court was apparently influenced by an amicus brief filed by a number of leading constitutional scholars. The brief, filed on behalf of Professors John Hart Ely, Gerald Gunther, Philip Kurland, Kathleen Sullivan, and Laurence Tribe, argued that Amendment 2 constituted an "inherent" violation of the equal protection clause:

> Colorado's Amendment 2 constitutes a *per se* violation of the Equal Protection Clause of the Fourteenth Amendment, which provides that "[n]o state shall . . . deny to any person within its jurisdiction the equal protection of the laws." That command is violated when a state's constitution renders some persons ineligible for "the . . . protection of the laws" from an entire category of mistreatment— here, the mistreatment of discrimination, however invidious and unwarranted. If Colorado had declared some people within its jurisdiction completely ineligible for the protection of its laws, existing or future, from some other form of mistreatment— unjustified physical assault, for example—no one would doubt that such state action would constitute a *per se* denial of the equal protection of the laws. Selectively decreeing some "person or class of persons," to use Amendment 2's language, ineligible for legal protection from mistreatment in which the wrong charged takes the form of *discrimination as such* is every bit as offensive on its face to the principle of equality before the law.

> States have no affirmative duty to enact or retain special laws for each individual or group who might be victimized by discriminatory treatment—that is, by injurious treatment that reflects prejudice and is neither privileged nor rationally justified by the context in which it occurs—just as they may well have no affirmative duty to enact or retain laws directed at other forms of wrongful treatment. But it is quite another matter for a state's constitution absolutely to preclude, for a selected set of persons, even the possibility of protection under any state or local law from a whole category of harmful conduct, including some that is undeniably wrongful. . . .

> To recognize that Amendment 2 works a *per se* violation of the Equal Protection Clause requires no benign or even neutral view of what Amendment 2 calls "homosexual . . . orientation, conduct, practices or relationships." For literally *any* characteristic—even

one on the basis of which a state may properly deny benefits or impose disabilities in a wide variety of circumstances—can sometimes become the basis for deprivations that are prejudiced rather than justified, and that are not privileged by the special context in which they occur. When Amendment 2 explicitly creates, for selected persons, a unique hole in the state's fabric of existing and potential legal protections against that admitted wrong, it provides a paradigm case of what it means for a state to structure its legal system so as to "deny" to "person[s] within its jurisdiction the equal protection of the laws."

Brief of Laurence H. Tribe et al. as Amici Curiae Supporting Respondents, *Romer v. Evans*, 517 U.S. 620, 116 S.Ct. 1620, 134 L.Ed.2d 855 (1996) (No. 94–1039), 1995 WL 17008432 at 1–2.

3.   Another reason for doctrinal uncertainty about *Romer* is that the rational basis standard applied by the Court is usually very forgiving to the government. Why didn't the government prevail in this case, given the relaxed standard applied? And, if the Court had, indeed, embraced the "per se" equal protection violation asserted in the scholars' amicus brief discussed above, why did the Court also apply rational basis? Wouldn't the very idea of a per se violation of the equal protection clause seem to obviate the need to apply any standard of review?

4.   It is notable that *Romer* simply applied rational basis without discussing the standard of review. You will find in the opinion no analysis of whether heightened scrutiny for sexual orientation-based claims might be warranted. The Court's silence on the question has not, however, prevented some federal circuit courts from citing *Romer* for the proposition that sexual orientation is not a suspect classification. *E.g., Equality Found. of Greater Cincinnati, Inc. v. City of Cincinnati*, 128 F.3d 289, 294 (6th Cir. 1997); *Richenberg v. Perry*, 97 F.3d 256, 260 (8th Cir. 1996); *Holmes v. Cal. Army Nat'l Guard*, 124 F.3d 1126, 1132 (9th Cir. 1997); *Lofton v. Secretary of Dep't of Children & Family Servs.*, 358 F.2d 804, 818 (11th Cir. 2004); *Price-Cornelison v. Brooks*, 524 F.3d 1103, 1113 (10th Cir. 2008). As indicated in the notes in section II.B.1, however, recall that in 2012, the Second Circuit became the first federal court of appeals to apply heightened scrutiny to a sexual orientation-based claim. *Windsor v. United States*, 699 F.3d 169 (2d Cir. 2012). In that case, the court said that it did not understand the decision to apply rational basis in *Romer* to imply a rejection of intermediate scrutiny, and that the plaintiffs in *Romer* had not pressed a claim for intermediate scrutiny in the Supreme Court. 699 F.3d at 179.

5.   A final reason that *Romer* has been regarded as enigmatic is its failure to mention—let alone distinguish—*Bowers v. Hardwick*, a case that was still good law when *Romer* was decided. That puzzling aspect of the opinion has receded in importance since the Court overruled *Hardwick* in *Lawrence*.

6.   To what extent, if any, is the *Romer* ruling traceable to the fact that Amendment 2 was passed through the initiative process? The Court did not focus on that issue in its opinion, but some research in political science suggests that direct democracy is particularly unfavorable terrain for minorities, including sexual minorities. For example, one leading study found that gay and lesbian citizens have faced measures putting their rights to a popular vote at an unusually high rate. Barbara Gamble, *Putting Civil Rights to a Popular Vote*, 41 AM. J. POL. SCI. 245–269 (1997). Gamble noted that nearly 60% of all state and local initiatives relating to civil rights in the period between 1959–1993 concerned the rights of gays and lesbians. Gamble's study also found that 88% of these gay-related initiatives proposed restricting lesbian and gay rights by repealing existing protective laws or banning the enactment of protective laws in the future; and that voters approved some 79% of these restrictive measures. This study also reported a high rate of rights-restrictive measures affecting other minority groups. And, measures affecting minorities in general, and gays and lesbians in particular, both passed at a notably higher rate than the general pool of ballot measures, where voters have traditionally voted "no" in a high percentage of cases. *Id.* What might explain these patterns? What factors might make direct democracy inhospitable to sexual or other minorities?

7.   In a consideration of the political as well as the legal strategies that underlie the debate about statutory protections against sexual orientation discrimination, Professor Jane Schacter analyzed the rhetoric of a number of the ballot initiative fights:

> The discourse of equivalents claims that the legitimacy of gay civil rights laws can be determined only by express comparison with existing antidiscrimination law. The discourse invokes two related themes in rejecting the gay civil rights claim: first, that the experience of gay men and lesbians is insufficiently "like" the experience of other already-protected groups; and second, that sexual orientation is insufficiently "like" other protected aspects of identity, such as race, gender, disability, religion, and national origin.

> These themes sustain two contradictory lines of argument that gay rights opponents frequently offer. The first *denies* that gay men and lesbians are victims of discrimination at all. It depicts homosexuals as privileged and powerful actors who covet new and unwarranted "special rights." The underlying theme is that the *experience* of gay men and lesbians does not reflect the same kinds of disadvantage as that suffered by groups protected by existing civil rights law. The second argument concedes that gay men and lesbians are the objects of discrimination, but *defends* such discrimination as fully appropriate, based on the claim that homosexuality is an objectionable "chosen behavior." Sexual orientation is depicted as different from other protected aspects of identity in ways that

disqualify gay men and lesbians from the protection of civil rights laws.

Jane S. Schacter, *The Gay Civil Rights Debate in the States: Decoding the Discourse of Equivalents*, 29 HARV. C.R.-C.L. L. REV. 283, 291 (1994). *See also* Samuel A. Marcosson, *The Special Rights Canard in the Debate over Lesbian and Gay Civil Rights*, 9 NOTRE DAME J.L. ETHICS & PUB. POL'Y 137 (1995).

4. Sexual Orientation and the Equal Protection Clause After *Romer*: Significant Post-*Romer* Decisions

One of the major questions after *Romer* has been the reach of the landmark decision. Just how robust is the protection that *Romer* affords sexual minorities? As might have been predicted from the many uncertainties about *Romer*'s holding, discussed above, the results have been mixed.

The most important development has been the Supreme Court's landmark 2013 decision in *United States v. Windsor*, striking down a portion of the Defense of Marriage Act. *Windsor* is excerpted and addressed at length in Chapter 6. For present purposes, the important thing to note is that the majority opinion relied on *Romer* and twice mentioned the "unusual character" of DOMA's discrimination, reflected in the federal government's departure from its common practice of deferring to states' definitions of marriage. This echoed *Romer*'s emphasis on the "unprecedented" character of Amendment 2, and the resulting inference drawn by the Court that the Amendment could be explained only by animus. While the *Windsor* Court stopped short of treating federal regulation in the area of marriage as violating federalism doctrines, it explicitly linked the rare federal entry into the field to the sort of "animus or improper purpose" emphasized in *Romer*. *Windsor*, 133 S. Ct. at 2692–93. In linking federalism to *Romer* in this way, the Court seemed to follow a novel First Circuit decision that had struck down DOMA. *Massachusetts v. U.S. Dep't of Health & Human Serv.*, 682 F.3d 1, 13 (1st Cir. 2012) ("Given that DOMA intrudes broadly into an area of traditional state regulation, a closer examination of the justifications that would prevent DOMA from violating equal protection (and thus from exceeding federal authority) is uniquely reinforced by federalism concerns.").

In addition, *Romer* played a pivotal role in Justice O'Connor's concurrence in *Lawrence*. Indeed, some have read the *Romer-Lawrence* combination to signal that the Supreme Court is, in reality, applying some form of heightened scrutiny to sexual orientation claims, even as it deploys the rhetoric of rational basis. *See* Nan D. Hunter, *Sexual Orientation and the Paradox of Heightened Scrutiny*, 102 MICH. L. REV. 1528, 1529, 1552 (2004).

On the other hand, there are signs that *Romer* has been weaker in its application than some might have predicted. Indeed, one early post-*Romer* decision suggested that the case would be read narrowly. Just a year after *Romer* was decided, the Sixth Circuit upheld on remand a Cincinnati city charter amendment that banned—as Colorado's Amendment 2 had—the enactment of gay civil rights protections. The Supreme Court declined to review the Sixth Circuit's disposition. *Equality Found. of Greater Cincinnati, Inc. v. City of Cincinnati*, 128 F.3d 289 (6th Cir. 1997), *cert. denied*, 525 U.S. 943, 119 S.Ct. 365, 142 L.Ed.2d 302 (1998). The circuit court distinguished *Romer* by emphasizing that the Cincinnati measure was a municipal, not a statewide measure, and was not as broadly drafted. *Id.* at 296–97. One might reasonably have thought, however, that—at the very least—*Romer* made unconstitutional measures flatly banning the addition of sexual orientation to anti-discrimination laws. Additional grounds to conclude that *Romer* has not been expansively understood can be found in the domain of family law. For example, in *Lofton v. Secretary of Department of Children & Family Services*, 358 F.3d 804, 827 (11th Cir. 2004), *cert. denied*, 543 U.S. 1081, 125 S.Ct. 869, 160 L.Ed.2d 825 (2005), the Eleventh Circuit upheld Florida's policy banning adoption of children by "practicing homosexuals." The *Lofton* decision is considered below in Chapter 7, Section III.A.1.

Consider now how three courts have applied *Romer*. The first case involves inequality in the criminal penalties meted out for certain versions of statutory rape. The remaining two are federal courts of appeals decisions relating to same-sex marriage. Consider how these understandings of *Romer* differ from one another.

KANSAS V. LIMON
Kansas Supreme Court, 2005
122 P.3d 22, 280 Kan. 275

LUCKERT, JUDGE.

The principal issue presented in this case is whether the Kansas unlawful voluntary sexual relations statute, K.S.A. 2004 Supp. 21–3522, violates the equal protection provision of the Fourteenth Amendment to the United States Constitution. Matthew Limon argues that the United States Supreme Court decision in *Lawrence v. Texas* requires this court to find the statute unconstitutional because it results in a punishment for unlawful voluntary sexual conduct between members of the opposite sex that is less harsh than the punishment for the same conduct between members of the same sex.

The statute subject to this challenge, commonly referred to as the Romeo and Juliet statute, applies to voluntary sexual intercourse, sodomy, or lewd touching when, at the time of the incident, (1) the victim is a child of 14 or 15; (2) the offender is less than 19 years of age and less than 4 years older than the victim; (3) the victim and offender are the only ones involved; and (4) the victim and offender are members of the opposite sex. K.S.A. 2004 Supp. 21–3522. Limon's conduct meets all of the elements of the Romeo and Juliet statute except the one limiting application to acts between members of the opposite sex.

When the Romeo and Juliet statute applies, prison terms are shorter and other consequences, such as postrelease supervision periods and sex offender registration requirements, are less harsh than when general rape, sodomy, and lewd touching statutes apply. Because these disparities are based upon the homosexual nature of Limon's conduct, he argues the Romeo and Juliet statute creates a classification which violates the equal protection principles announced by the United States Supreme Court. Limon suggests we apply a strict level of scrutiny when reviewing his claim, but asserts that even if the rational basis test applies, under the guidance of *Lawrence*, the classification bears no rational relationship to legitimate State interests.

We agree that the United States Supreme Court's decision in *Lawrence* controls our analysis and, when considered in conjunction with several equal protection decisions of the United States Supreme Court, requires us to hold that the State does not have a rational basis for the statutory classification created in the Romeo and Juliet statute. * * *

Limon was convicted of criminal sodomy pursuant to K.S.A. 21–3505(a)(2) after a bench trial on stipulated facts. The stipulation established that on February 16, 2000, Limon had consensual oral contact with the genitalia of M.A.R. Both Limon and M.A.R. are male. Limon turned 18 years of age just 1 week before the incident; his date of birth is February 9, 1982. He was less than 4 years older than M.A.R., who turned 15 years of age the month following the incident. M.A.R.'s date of birth is March 17, 1985. * * *

The contact occurred at a school for developmentally disabled children where Limon and M.A.R. were residents. Although there is a discrepancy between Limon's and M.A.R.'s functioning, the difference is minor. Intellectually, Limon falls between the ranges described as borderline intellectual functioning and mild mental retardation. M.A.R. functions in the upper limits of the range of mild mental retardation. M.A.R. consented to the sexual contact, and when he asked Limon to stop, Limon did so.

The trial court rejected Limon's equal protection argument and denied the motion for downward durational departure. * * *

In this appeal, Limon primarily argues that to punish criminal voluntary sexual conduct between teenagers of the same sex more harshly than criminal voluntary sexual conduct between teenagers of the opposite sex is a violation of the equal protection provision of the United States Constitution. * * *

Limon's arguments are constructed entirely upon the precedent of United States Supreme Court cases, and those precedents command our decision in this case. However, Limon also cites § 1 of the Kansas Constitution Bill of Rights and, thus, preserves a state constitutional claim. * * *

Traditionally, when analyzing an equal protection claim, the United States and Kansas Supreme Courts employ three levels of scrutiny: strict scrutiny, intermediate scrutiny, and the rational basis test. The level of scrutiny applied by the court depends on the nature of the legislative classification and the rights affected by that classification. *Romer v. Evans.* The general rule is that a law will be subject to the rational basis test unless the legislative classification targets a suspect class or burdens a fundamental right. * * *

Classification

In the first step, we must examine the nature of the classification created by the Romeo and Juliet statute. The State argues that the statute applies only to conduct and does not discriminate against any class of individual, in particular against homosexual persons. The State also argues that nothing in the record establishes that either Limon or M.A.R. is homosexual.

Indeed, there is no per se classification of homosexuals, bisexuals, or heterosexuals in the statute, nor do we know which classification applies to Limon or M.A.R. However, that does not mean that Limon's argument fails. As Justice Scalia noted in his dissent in *Romer*, "there can hardly be more palpable discrimination against a class than making the *conduct* that defines the class criminal." (Emphasis added.) The majority in *Lawrence* similarly noted that making homosexual conduct criminal and not legislating against "deviate sexual intercourse" committed by persons of different sexes "in and of itself is an invitation to subject homosexual persons to discrimination both in the public and in the private spheres." Throughout the *Lawrence* opinion, the majority refers to the stigmatizing and demeaning effect of criminalizing conduct commonly engaged in by homosexuals and concludes that a state may not "demean their existence or control their destiny." Additionally, *Lawrence* makes it clear that *Romer* applies to "persons who were homosexuals, lesbians, or bisexual either by 'orientation, conduct, practices or relationships.'"

This case is different from *Lawrence*, where homosexual conduct was criminal and heterosexual conduct was not. The *Lawrence* Court focused upon the "stigma" the criminal statute imposed which it characterized as "not trivial." Here, both types of conduct are criminalized and, thus, stigma attaches to the heterosexual conduct covered by the Romeo and

Juliet statute. However, there is an enormous escalation in the severity of punishment for those punished under the general rape, sodomy, and lewd act statutes. The Kansas Sentencing Guidelines impose a presumptive sentence of prison upon all defendants, including those with no prior criminal history, who are convicted of a severity level 3 felony, the severity level applying to Limon's conviction. In contrast, a presumption of probation applies to all sentences, except those for defendants with criminal histories of "A" or "B," who are sentenced for a severity level 9 crime, which would be the applicable severity level for sodomy if the Romeo and Juliet statute applied.

Additionally, the presumptive terms of imprisonment for a severity level 3 felony, as noted earlier, are approximately 15 times that of a severity level 9 felony. As also discussed earlier, for Limon, whose criminal history score was a B, this classification means the difference between a 13-, 14-, or 15-month prison sentence and a 206-month prison sentence. K.S.A. 2004 Supp. 21–4704. For a defendant with no criminal history, a conviction of criminal sodomy (as charged in this case) entails a sentencing range of 55–59–61 months' presumptive imprisonment while a conviction of unlawful voluntary sexual relations under the Romeo and Juliet statute entails a sentencing range of 5–6–7 months with the presumption of *probation*. K.S.A. 2004 Supp. 21–4704. This represents an extreme disparity in sentencing.

There is also the distinction that Limon faces the stigma of sex offender registration; those convicted under the Romeo and Juliet statute do not. K.S.A. 22–4902.

Furthermore, the demeaning and stigmatizing effect upon which the *Lawrence* Court focused is at least equally applicable to teenagers, both the victim and the offender, as it is to adults and, according to some, the impact is greater upon a teen.

Based upon these considerations we conclude there is a discriminatory classification requiring us to examine the level of scrutiny to be applied in testing the constitutionality of the classification. * * *

The next step of our analysis is to determine the appropriate level of scrutiny to apply. Limon argues that under the holding in *Lawrence* the highest level of scrutiny should apply because the statute creates a classification of homosexuals which the *Lawrence* Court recognized as suspect. Contrary to this argument, the United States Supreme Court has not recognized homosexuals as a suspect classification. In addition, as Justice Scalia notes in his dissenting opinion in *Lawrence*, "Though there is discussion of 'fundamental proposition[s]' and 'fundamental decisions,' nowhere does the Court's opinion declare that homosexual sodomy is a 'fundamental right.'" See *Lofton v. Secretary of Dept. of Children & Family*, 358 F.3d 804, 817 (11th Cir. 2004) (concluding it would be "a strained and ultimately incorrect reading of *Lawrence* to interpret it to announce a new fundamental right"); *Standhardt v. Superior Court ex rel. County of Maricopa*, 206 Ariz. 276, 77 P.3d 451 (2003), *rev. denied*, May 26, 2004 (no fundamental right to same-sex marriage where *Lawrence* did not recognize fundamental right to engage in same-sexual conduct). Thus strict scrutiny does not apply to our analysis of whether the Romeo and Juliet provision unconstitutionally discriminates based upon sexual orientation.

Justice O'Connor, in her concurring opinion in *Lawrence*, suggests "a more searching form of rational basis review" applies when a law exhibits a "desire to harm a politically unpopular group." * * *

Despite not deciding the case on equal protection grounds and never explicitly identifying the standard utilized for its due process analysis, the *Lawrence* majority, by approvingly citing and discussing the equal protection analysis in *Romer*, at least implied that the rational basis test is the appropriate standard when a statute is attacked because of its classification of homosexual conduct. * * *

The *Lawrence* opinion contains another oblique indication that the rational basis test would apply, stating: "The Texas statute furthers no *legitimate* state interest which can justify its intrusion into the personal and private life of the individual." 539 U.S. at 578. (Emphasis added.) Typically, a search for a legitimate interest signifies a rational basis analysis.

Hence, we apply the rational basis test to determine whether the Romeo and Juliet statute is unconstitutional because of its exclusion of homosexual conduct.

Rational Basis Test

The Court of Appeals applied the rational basis test and upheld the statute upon finding minimal congruence between the classifying means and the one legislative end upon which the two judges who comprised the majority could agree: public health.

As the Court of Appeals noted, the basic contours of the rational basis test are well-defined: "For a statute to pass constitutional muster under the rational basis standard, it therefore must meet a two-part test: (1) It must implicate legitimate goals, and (2) the means chosen by the legislature must bear a rational relationship to those goals."

In explaining the test, the United States Supreme Court has said that, although the rational basis test is "the most deferential of standards, we insist on knowing the relation between the classification adopted and the object obtained." *Romer.* * * *

Romer and other United States Supreme Court decisions instruct that we must examine the scope of the classification. Over-inclusiveness, where the legislation burdens a wider range of individuals than necessary given the State's interest, may be particularly invidious and unconstitutional. *Romer*. Likewise, a failure to create a classification which is sufficiently broad to effectively accommodate the State's interest, *i.e.*, the creation of an under-inclusive class, may evidence an animus toward those burdened. *Cleburne*. Paradoxically, a class may be both under-and over-inclusive; Limon argues the Romeo and Juliet statute creates such a class.

> [The Court goes on to quote Justice O'Connor's concurring opinion in *Lawrence* and its reckoning of *Moreno, Eisenstadt, Cleburne* and *Romer* (*see supra* Chapter 2, Section III.D)].

Of the four cases Justice O'Connor discusses, two are particularly analogous to this case. As Justice O'Connor indicated, in *Eisenstadt v. Baird*, the Court invalidated on rational basis grounds a Massachusetts statute banning the distribution of contraceptives to unmarried persons. The state's highest court had found the legislative purpose to be "the State's interest in protecting the health of its citizens" by "preventing the distribution of articles designed to prevent conception which may have undesirable, if not dangerous, physical consequences" and "to protect morals" by discouraging premarital sexual intercourse. Addressing the purpose of preventing premarital sex, the Supreme Court concluded: " 'The rationality of this justification is dubious, particularly in light of the admitted widespread availability to all persons . . . , unmarried as well as married, of birth-control devices for the prevention of disease, as distinguished from the prevention of contraception. [*sic*]' " The Court concluded that "the Massachusetts statute is thus so riddled with exceptions that deterrence of premarital sex cannot reasonably be regarded as its aim."

The *Eisenstadt* Court also explained, if the State genuinely considered contraceptives to pose a health risk, it would have banned their use by both married and unmarried persons. Protecting only single persons from the alleged dangers of contraceptives, and even then only when used to prevent pregnancy rather than the spread of disease, was "both discriminatory and overbroad" and "illogical to the point of irrationality." *Eisenstadt*.

In the other case cited by Justice O'Connor which is particularly analogous, *Romer*, the Court was reviewing the Colorado constitutional amendment which the State argued protected the associational rights of landlords and employers with moral objections to homosexuality and furthered the State's interest in "conserving resources to fight discrimination against other groups." *Romer*. The Court found it "impossible to credit" these proffered purposes. * * *

The Court faulted the Colorado constitutional amendment for imposing a "broad and undifferentiated disability on a single named group." The Court further condemned the statute because "its sheer breadth is so discontinuous with the reasons offered for it that the amendment seems inexplicable by anything but animus toward the class it affects." Additionally, the amendment was "a status-based enactment divorced from any factual context from which we could discern a relationship to legitimate state interests." Because of these faults, the Court reached "the inevitable inference that the disadvantage imposed is born of animosity toward the class of persons affected." * * *

With these holdings to direct us, we begin our search for a rational basis for the harshly disparate sentencing treatment of those 18 years old and younger who engage in voluntary sex with an underage teenager of the same sex. * * *

Legislative History

Although the legislature need not have articulated the basis for the classification the State relies upon when the classification is challenged, we begin with an examination of the legislative record to determine if a purpose for the classification is suggested therein.

The Kansas unlawful voluntary sexual relations (Romeo and Juliet) statute was originally drafted as an amendment to K.S.A. 21–3520, rather than as a free-standing statute. See L.1999, ch. 164, sec. 38; 1999 S.B. 131. As it appeared in S.B. 131, the provision contained no requirement that the prohibited activity occur between members of the opposite sex. In other words, it would not have differentiated between a Romeo and Juliet relationship, a Romeo and Romeo relationship, or a Juliet and Juliet relationship. * * *

There was significant opposition to the provision, although none of the recorded criticism faulted the statute for not containing language limiting the provision to heterosexual teen relations. * * *

[T]here is nothing in the legislative record regarding the legislative purpose for adding the opposite sex requirement. The only legislative purposes recorded relate to the general goal of less harsh punishment for those 18 years old and younger who had voluntary sex with another teen who was at least 14 and the goal of adjusting sentence disparities. It was opponents to the legislation who raised public health and moral concerns and none of them related to the difference between heterosexual and homosexual conduct.

Although the legislative history does not suggest the State's interest in including the phrase "and are members of the opposite sex," the State argues several possibilities. In addition, we must consider the rationales utilized by the Court of Appeals majority. These various possible State interests can be categorized as: (1) the protection and preservation of the traditional sexual mores of society; (2) preservation of the historical notions of appropriate sexual development of children; (3) protection of teenagers against coercive relationships; (4) protection of teenagers from the increased health risks that accompany sexual activity; (5) promotion of parental responsibility and procreation; and (6) protection of those in group homes.

Traditional Sexual Mores and Development

Limon counters this theoretical justification by arguing that the State's moral disapproval of homosexuality is an illegitimate justification for discrimination.

The *Lawrence decision* rejected a morality-based rationale as a legitimate State interest. The Court recognized that many people condemn homosexuality as immoral. * * *

However, the Court continued by stating: "These considerations do not answer the question before us." 539 U.S. at 571, 123 S.Ct. 2472. The Court framed the issue as "whether the majority may use the power of the State to enforce these views on the whole society through operation of the criminal law. 'Our obligation is to define the liberty of all, not to mandate our own moral code.' *Planned Parenthood of Southeastern Pa. v. Casey*, 505 U.S. 833, 850 [112 S.Ct. 2791, 120 L.Ed.2d 674] (1992)." 539 U.S. at 571, 123 S.Ct. 2472. * * *

The Court of Appeals majority would dismiss this analysis in *Lawrence* because of the due process context in which the discussion was made. The *Lawrence* majority, however, signaled application of the principles to equal protection analysis: "Equality of treatment and the due process right to demand respect for conduct protected by the substantive guarantee of liberty are linked in important respects, and a decision on the latter point advances both interests." 539 U.S. at 575, 123 S.Ct. 2472. In essence, the *Lawrence* decision recognized that the substantive due process analysis at issue in that case and the equal protection analysis necessary in this case are inevitably linked.

This court has described this link as follows:

"The difference between the constitutional concepts of due process and equal protection is that due process emphasizes fairness between the State and the individual dealing with the State, regardless of how other individuals in the same situation are treated, while equal protection emphasizes disparity in treatment by a State between classes of individuals whose situations are arguably indistinguishable. The test in determining the constitutionality of a statute under due process or equal protection concepts weighs almost identical factors." (Emphasis added.) *Chiles v. State*, 254 Kan. 888, Syl. ¶ 10, 869 P.2d 707 (1994).

Thus, we are directed in our equal protection analysis by the United States Supreme Court's holding in *Lawrence* that moral disapproval of a group cannot be a legitimate governmental interest.

Historical Notions of Appropriate Sexual Development of Children

The Court of Appeals also determined the *Lawrence* holding did not apply to this case because *Lawrence* involved adults and this case involved an adult in a relationship with a minor. Likewise, the State focuses its argument on the State's interest in the moral and sexual development of children.

Undoubtedly, the State has broad powers to protect minors. This point was noted by the United States Supreme Court in *Carey v. Population Services International*, 431 U.S. 678, 97 S.Ct. 2010, 52 L.Ed.2d 675 (1977). *Carey* involved a constitutional challenge to a prohibition on distribution of contraceptives to persons under 16 years of age. The appellants argued that the free availability of contraceptives might encourage sexual activity among minors and the State had a legitimate interest in discouraging such behavior. In response, the appellees argued that minors as well as adults had a privacy right to engage in consensual sexual behavior. * * *

Neither the Court of Appeals nor the State cites any scientific research or other evidence justifying the position that homosexual sexual activity is more harmful to minors than adults. * * *

We conclude, as the United States Supreme Court stated in *Romer*, the "status-based enactment [is so] divorced from any factual context" we cannot "discern a relationship" to the espoused State interest (*Romer*, 517 U.S. at 635, 116 S.Ct. 1620) that the law preserves the sexual development of children consistent with traditional sexual mores. Additionally, we again recognize the *Lawrence* Court's conclusion that moral disapproval of a group cannot be a legitimate governmental interest.

Coercive Effect Upon Minors

The State at various times refers to the coercive effect often existing in a relationship between an adult and a child. Certainly, the State has a significant interest in prohibiting sex between adults and minors, not only because of the potentially coercive effect of an adult's influence but also because of concern regarding the minor's ability to arrive at an informed consent. These concerns are addressed by and form the fundamental policy rationale of statutory rape provisions. Limon's argument accepts and supports this State interest; he agrees he deserves punishment. He simply disputes that he should be punished more severely for having sex with a member of the same sex.

Additionally, the policy decision made by the legislature in enacting the Romeo and Juliet statute undercuts this argument. The legislature determined, at least as to those in a heterosexual relationship, that a mutual relationship between teenagers is less likely to involve the same coercion that a relationship between an older adult and a child might and is more likely to be one where the minor's participation is voluntary, although not legally consensual.

This, however, begs the question of whether there is a rational basis to distinguish between a class of those 18 years old and younger who engage in voluntary sex with minors aged 14 or 15 who are of the same sex and a class of those 18 years old and younger who engage in voluntary sex with such minors of the opposite sex. We see no basis to determine that as a class one group or the other would have a higher tendency to be coercive. A distinction on this basis has no factual support.

The State makes the same argument in a narrower fashion as applied to the facts of this case, stating the activity between Limon and M.A.R. was "less than consensual and more likely coercive." Where the State stipulated below that the sexual activity between Limon and M.A.R. was consensual, it cannot be heard to argue on appeal that Limon's actions were "coercive and predatory." We agree the wording in the stipulation that the oral sex between Limon and M.A.R. was "consensual" was a legal misnomer and a better term would have been "voluntary," but that distinction does not permit the State to back away from its stipulation at this stage of the case.

Public Health

As to the public health justification, Limon argues that excluding gay teenagers from the lesser penalties of the Romeo and Juliet law has no connection with the State's interest in reducing the spread of sexually transmitted diseases. Specifically, the State focuses upon the risks of HIV and in support of its argument cites briefs filed before the United States Supreme Court in the *Lawrence* case. * * *

At a minimum, we cannot distinguish between the health risks for the adults involved in *Lawrence* and the minor involved in this case. Additionally, we find persuasive Limon's argument that for this justification to be rational, the prohibited sexual activities would have to be more likely to transmit disease when engaged in by homosexuals than by heterosexuals; however, this proposition is not grounded in fact. * * *

Using statistics from the United States Centers for Disease Control and Prevention (CDC) and other studies, the amici support the argument that the Court of Appeals majority and the State focus on the wrong population in citing the statistics regarding the incidence of HIV infection in adult homosexual males. Significantly, they point to the CDC's Basic Statistics which reflect that among the population of HIV-positive young people ages 13–19, which includes the age range covered by the Romeo and Juliet statute, 61 percent are female. Yet, the risk of transmission of the HIV infection through female to female contact is negligible. Recognizing that HIV is transmitted through intravenous drug use of shared needles and other mechanisms besides sexual transmission, the gravest risk of sexual transmission for females is through heterosexual intercourse. * * *

In essence, the Romeo and Juliet statute is over-inclusive because it increases penalties for sexual relations which are unlikely to transmit HIV and other sexually transmitted diseases. Thus, the statute burdens a wider range of individuals than necessary for public health purposes. Simultaneously, the provision is under-inclusive because it lowers the penalty for heterosexuals engaging in high-risk activities. In other words, the statute proscribes conduct unrelated to a public health purpose and does not proscribe conduct which is detrimental to public health. * * *

Promoting Parental Responsibility and Procreation

Limon also contends that there is no rational connection between the classification and the Court of Appeals's parental responsibility and procreation justifications. The Court of Appeals stated that the legislature might have determined that lengthy incarceration of a young adult offender who has become a parent as a result of a heterosexual relationship with a minor would be counterproductive to that young adult's duty to support his or her child. But, because same-sex relationships do not lead to unplanned pregnancies, the need to release a same-sex offender from incarceration is absent.

Limon argues this justification and Judge Green's findings regarding the State's interest in relationships which lead to procreation make no sense since the State's interest is to discourage teen pregnancies, not encourage them. Further, the statute does not reduce penalties solely for conduct that results in pregnancy, but also for heterosexual intercourse which does not result in pregnancy, i.e., sodomy and lewd contact. Again, the relationship between the objective and the classification is so strained that we cannot conclude it is rational.

Protection of Those in Group Homes

The State also makes an argument that the State has an interest in gender segregation in group homes. The Romeo and Juliet statute has no limitation related to living arrangements or disability. If the statute punished similar behavior in segregated group homes for juveniles, the State's argument could conceivably justify a harsher penalty. However, the statute is not limited in this manner. If the legislative purpose is to protect those in group homes, the statute's overbreadth in covering situations both inside and outside residential living environments suggests animus toward teenagers who engage in homosexual sex. See *Romer*, 517 U.S. at 632, 116 S.Ct. 1620

No Rational Basis

We conclude that K.S.A. 2004 Supp. 21–3522, the Kansas unlawful voluntary sexual relations statute, does not pass rational basis scrutiny under the United States Constitution Equal Protection Clause or, because we traditionally apply the same analysis to our state constitution, under the Kansas Constitution Equal Protection Clause. The Romeo and Juliet statute suffers the same faults as found by the United States Supreme Court in *Romer* and *Eisenstadt*; adding the phrase "and are members of the opposite sex" created a broad, overreaching, and undifferentiated status-based classification which bears no rational relationship to legitimate State interests. Paraphrasing the United States Supreme Court's decision in *Romer*, the statute inflicts immediate, continuing, and real injuries that outrun and belie any legitimate justification that may be claimed for it. Furthermore, the State's interests fail under the holding in *Lawrence* that moral disapproval of a group cannot be a legitimate governmental interest. As Justice Scalia stated: "If, as the [United States Supreme] Court asserts, the promotion of majoritarian sexual morality is not even a *legitimate* state interest," the statute cannot "survive rational-basis review."

Because we determine the statute violates constitutional equal protection guarantees based upon a rational basis analysis, we need not reach Limon's other arguments that strict scrutiny should be applied, including his argument that the statute discriminates based on sex.

———————

Contrast the role of *Romer* (and *Lawrence*) in *Limon* with the view taken by the Court of Appeals for the Eighth Circuit in the next case, which focuses on a broadly-worded state ballot initiative denying legal protections to same-sex couples. The last several years have seen a rapid proliferation of ballot measures around the country that address not only same-sex marriage, but other forms of legal protection for same-sex couples. As it was in *Romer* itself, the initiative process has been a losing venue for LGBT citizens. We defer until Chapter 6 full consideration of the relevance of *Romer* to laws allowing only opposite-sex couples to wed. But consider here whether, under *Romer*, a state may deny same-sex couples the right to other forms of legal protection for their relationships.

Did the Eighth Circuit give *Romer* its due in this case? Note, as well, how little *Lawrence* figures in the court's analysis. Why might that be so?

CITIZENS FOR EQUAL PROTECTION V. BRUNING

United States Court of Appeals, Eighth Circuit, 2006
455 F.3d 859

LOKEN, CHIEF JUDGE.

In November 2000, Nebraska voters passed by a large majority a constitutional amendment, codified as Article I, § 29 of the Nebraska Constitution, providing:

> Only marriage between a man and a woman shall be valid or recognized in Nebraska. The uniting of two persons of the same sex in a civil union, domestic partnership, or other similar same-sex relationship shall not be valid or recognized in Nebraska.

Three public interest groups whose members include gay and lesbian citizens of Nebraska commenced this action against the Governor and the Attorney General in their official capacities seeking an order declaring that § 29 violates the Equal Protection Clause and is an unconstitutional bill of attainder, and permanently enjoining its enforcement. * * *

After the parties submitted the case on a Joint Stipulation of Facts, the district court held that § 29 violates the Equal Protection Clause, is an unconstitutional bill of attainder, and deprives gays and lesbians of their First Amendment rights. *Citizens for Equal Protection, Inc. v. Bruning*, 368 F. Supp. 2d 980 (D. Neb. 2005). The State appeals. We reverse. * * *

Relying primarily on *Romer*, Appellees argue that § 29 violates the Equal Protection Clause because it raises an insurmountable political barrier to same-sex couples obtaining the many governmental and private sector benefits that are based upon a legally valid marriage relationship. Appellees do not assert a right to marriage or same-sex unions. Rather, they seek "a level playing field, an equal opportunity to convince the people's elected representatives that same-sex relationships deserve legal protection." *Citizens for Equal Protection*, 368 F. Supp. 2d at 985 n.1. The argument turns on the fact that § 29 is an amendment to the Nebraska Constitution. Unlike state-wide legislation restricting marriage to a man and a woman, a constitutional amendment deprives gays and lesbians of "equal footing in the political arena" because state and local government officials now lack the power to address issues of importance to this minority.

The district court agreed, concluding "that Section 29 is indistinguishable from the Colorado constitutional amendment at issue in *Romer*." 368 F. Supp. 2d at 1002. In this part of its opinion, the district court purported to apply conventional, "rational-basis" equal protection analysis—"If a legislative classification or distinction neither burdens a fundamental right nor targets a suspect class, we will uphold it so long as it bears a rational relation to some legitimate [government] end." *Vacco v. Quill*, 521 U.S. 793, 799, 117 S. Ct. 2293, 138 L. Ed. 2d 834 (1997), quoting *Romer*, 517 U.S. at 631. But the court in its discussion, 368 F. Supp. 2d at 997–1005, applied the same strict scrutiny analysis applied by the Colorado Supreme Court, but not by the United States Supreme Court, in *Romer*. Like the Colorado Court, the district court based its heightened scrutiny on Appellees' "fundamental right of access to the political process." *Id.* at 1003.

As Supreme Court decisions attest, the level of judicial scrutiny to be applied in determining the validity of state legislative and constitutional enactments under the Fourteenth Amendment is a subject of continuing debate and disagreement among the Justices. Though the most relevant precedents are murky, we conclude for a number of reasons that § 29 should receive rational-basis review under the Equal Protection Clause, rather than a heightened level of judicial scrutiny.

While voting rights and apportionment cases establish the fundamental right to access the political process, it is not an absolute right. In a multi-tiered democracy, it is inevitable that interest groups will strive to make it more difficult for competing interest groups to achieve contrary legislative objectives. This can be done, for example, by having the state legislature repeal a local ordinance, or by having the electorate adopt a constitutional amendment barring future legislation. As the Supreme Court said in upholding a state constitutional amendment in *James v. Valtierra*, 402 U.S. 137, 141–43, 91 S. Ct. 1331, 28 L. Ed. 2d 678 (1971):

> Provisions for referendums demonstrate devotion to democracy, not to bias, discrimination, or prejudice. Nonetheless, appellees contend that Article XXXIV denies them equal protection because . . . it hampers persons desiring public housing from achieving their objective when no such roadblock faces other groups seeking to influence other public decisions to their advantage. . . . Under any such holding, presumably a State would not be able to require referendums on any subject unless referendums were required on all, because they would always disadvantage some group. And this Court would be required to analyze governmental structures to determine whether a gubernatorial veto provision or a filibuster rule is likely to "disadvantage" any of the diverse and shifting groups that make up the American people.

Similarly, Justice Scalia's discussion of the anti-polygamy provisions in many state constitutions illustrates the chaos that would result if all enactments that allegedly deprive a group of "equal" political access must survive the rigors of strict judicial scrutiny. *Romer*, 517 U.S. at 648–51 (Scalia, J., dissenting). * * *

If sexual orientation, like race, were a "suspect classification" for purposes of the Equal Protection Clause, then Appellees' focus on the political burden erected by a constitutional amendment would find support in cases like *Reitman v. Mulkey*, 387 U.S. 369, 87 S. Ct. 1627, 18 L. Ed. 2d 830 (1967), *Hunter v. Erickson*, 393 U.S. 385, 89 S. Ct. 557, 21 L. Ed. 2d 616 (1969), and *Washington v. Seattle School District No. 1*, 458 U.S. 457, 102 S. Ct. 3187, 73 L. Ed. 2d 896 (1982). But the Supreme Court has never ruled that sexual orientation is a suspect classification for equal protection purposes. The Court's general standard is that rational-basis review applies "where individuals in the group affected by a law have distinguishing characteristics relevant to interests the State has the authority to implement." *City of Cleburne v. Cleburne Living Center*, 473 U.S. 432, 441, 105 S. Ct. 3249, 87 L. Ed. 2d 313 (1985). As we will explain, that is the case here, and therefore Appellees are not entitled to strict scrutiny review on this ground.

Rational-basis review is highly deferential to the legislature or, in this case, to the electorate that directly adopted § 29 by the initiative process. "In areas of social and economic policy, a statutory classification that neither proceeds along suspect lines nor infringes fundamental constitutional rights must be upheld against equal protection challenge if there is any reasonably conceivable state of facts that could provide a rational-basis for the classification." *F.C.C. v. Beach Communications, Inc.*, 508 U.S. 307, 313, 113 S. Ct. 2096, 124 L. Ed. 2d 211 (1993). Thus, the classification created by § 29 and other laws defining marriage as the union between one man and one woman is afforded a "strong presumption of validity." *Heller v. Doe*, 509 U.S. 312, 319, 113 S. Ct. 2637, 125 L. Ed. 2d 257 (1993). * * *

Our rational-basis review begins with an historical fact—the institution of marriage has always been, in our federal system, the predominant concern of state government. * * *

This necessarily includes the power to classify those persons who may validly marry. "Surely, for example, a State may legitimately say that no one can marry his or her sibling, that no one can marry who is not at least 14 years old, that no one can marry without first passing an examination for venereal disease, or that no one can marry who has a living husband or wife." *Zablocki v. Redhail*, 434 U.S. 374, 392, 98 S. Ct. 673, 54 L. Ed. 2d 618 (1978) (Stewart, J., concurring). In this constitutional environment, rational-basis review must be particularly deferential.

The State argues that the many laws defining marriage as the union of one man and one woman and extending a variety of benefits to married couples are rationally related to the government interest in "steering procreation into marriage." By affording legal recognition and a basket of rights and benefits to married heterosexual couples, such laws "encourage procreation to take place within the socially recognized unit that is best situated for raising children." The State and its supporting amici cite a host of judicial decisions and secondary authorities recognizing and upholding this rationale. The argument is based in part on the traditional notion that two committed heterosexuals are the optimal partnership for raising children, which modern-day homosexual parents understandably decry. But it is also based on a "responsible procreation" theory that justifies conferring the inducements of marital recognition and benefits on opposite-sex couples, who can otherwise produce children by accident, but not on same-sex couples, who cannot. *See Hernandez v. Robles*, 7 N.Y.3d 338, 855 N.E.2d 1, 821 N.Y.S.2d 770 (2006); *Morrison v. Sadler*, 821 N.E.2d 15, 24–26 (Ind. Ct. App. 2005). Whatever our personal views regarding this political and sociological debate, we cannot conclude that the State's justification "lacks a rational relationship to legitimate state interests." *Romer*, 517 U.S. at 632.[3]

The district court rejected the State's justification as being "at once too broad and too narrow." *Citizens for Equal Protection*, 368 F. Supp. 2d at 1002. But under rational-basis review, "Even if the classification . . . is to some extent both underinclusive and overinclusive, and hence the line drawn . . . imperfect, it is nevertheless the rule that . . . perfection is by no means required." *Vance v. Bradley*, 440 U.S. 93, 108, 99 S. Ct. 939, 59 L. Ed. 2d 171 (1979). Legislatures are permitted to use generalizations so long as "the question is at least debatable." *Heller*, 509 U.S. at 326 (quotation omitted). The package of government benefits and restrictions that accompany the institution of formal marriage serve a variety of other purposes. The legislature—or the people through the initiative process— may rationally choose not to expand in wholesale fashion the groups entitled to those benefits. * * *

---

[3]   When the Supreme Court invalidated a state law criminalizing sodomy in *Lawrence v. Texas*, 539 U.S. 558, 123 S. Ct. 2472, 156 L. Ed. 2d 508 (2003), only Justice O'Connor relied on the Equal Protection Clause, rather than the substantive component of the Due Process Clause. Of particular relevance to this case, Justice O'Connor concluded that moral disapproval of private, consensual homosexual conduct "is an interest that is insufficient to satisfy rational basis review under the Equal Protection Clause," but she expressly noted that "other reasons exist [for the State] to promote the institution of marriage beyond mere moral disapproval of an excluded group." 539 U.S. at 582, 585 (O'Connor, J., concurring). The *Lawrence* majority, too, was careful to note that the Texas statute at issue "does not involve whether the government must give formal recognition to any relationship that homosexual persons seek to enter." *Id.* at 578.

We likewise reject the district court's conclusion that the Colorado enactment at issue in *Romer* is indistinguishable from § 29. The Colorado enactment repealed all existing and barred all future preferential policies based on "orientation, conduct, practices, or relationships." The Supreme Court struck it down based upon this "unprecedented" scope. See *Romer*, 517 U.S. at 626, 633. Here, § 29 limits the class of people who may validly enter into marriage and the legal equivalents to marriage emerging in other States—civil unions and domestic partnerships. This focus is not so broad as to render Nebraska's reasons for its enactment "inexplicable by anything but animus" towards same-sex couples. *Id.* at 632.

Appellees argue that § 29 does not rationally advance this purported state interest because "prohibiting protection for gay people's relationships" does not steer procreation into marriage. This demonstrates, Appellees argue, that § 29's only purpose is to disadvantage gay people. But the argument disregards the expressed intent of traditional marriage laws—to encourage heterosexual couples to bear and raise children in committed marriage relationships. Appellees attempt to isolate § 29 from other state laws limiting marriage to heterosexual couples. But as we have explained, there is no fundamental right to be free of the political barrier a validly enacted constitutional amendment erects. If the many state laws limiting the persons who may marry are rationally related to a legitimate government interest, so is the reinforcing effect of § 29. * * *

In the nearly one hundred and fifty years since the Fourteenth Amendment was adopted, to our knowledge no Justice of the Supreme Court has suggested that a state statute or constitutional provision codifying the traditional definition of marriage violates the Equal Protection Clause or any other provision of the United States Constitution. * * *

We hold that § 29 and other laws limiting the state-recognized institution of marriage to heterosexual couples are rationally related to legitimate state interests and therefore do not violate the Constitution of the United States.

Compare *Bruning*'s treatment of *Romer* with how the court understood the case in the next opinion, *Perry v. Brown*, in which the Ninth Circuit struck down California's Proposition 8. As you will see in Chapter 6, the Supreme Court's later decision in *Perry* held that Proposition 8's ballot proponents lacked standing to pursue an appeal from the district court decision invalidating the measure. The effect of that holding was to wipe out the Ninth Circuit's opinion and reinstate the earlier decision of the district court. While the next opinion is no longer good law, it is worth studying because it contrasts so sharply with the Eighth Circuit's approach in *Bruning*.

PERRY V. BROWN

United States Court of Appeals, Ninth Circuit, 2011
671 F.3d 1052, *vacated* 133 S. Ct. 2652 (2013)

REINHARDT, CIRCUIT JUDGE.

[Proposition 8, passed by California's voters in 2008, amended the state constitution to override a state supreme court ruling that had accorded same-sex couples the constitutional right to marry. Even as Proposition 8 eliminated the right to marry, however, California's domestic partnership law remained in effect and continued to grant same-sex couples substantially all the rights of married couples.]

This is not the first time the voters of a state have enacted an initiative constitutional amendment that reduces the rights of gays and lesbians under state law. In 1992, Colorado adopted Amendment 2 to its state constitution, which prohibited the state and its political subdivisions from providing any protection against discrimination on the basis of sexual orientation. * * *

Proposition 8 is remarkably similar to Amendment 2. Like Amendment 2, Proposition 8 "single[s] out a certain class of citizens for disfavored legal status. . . ." Like Amendment 2, Proposition 8 has the "peculiar property," of "withdraw[ing] from homosexuals, but no others," an existing legal right—here, access to the official designation of 'marriage'—that had been broadly available, notwithstanding the fact that the Constitution did not compel the state to confer it in the first place. Like Amendment 2, Proposition 8 denies "equal protection of the laws in the most literal sense," because it "carves out" an "exception" to California's equal protection clause, by removing equal access to marriage, which gays and lesbians had previously enjoyed, from the scope of that constitutional guarantee. Like Amendment 2, Proposition 8 "by state decree . . . put[s] [homosexuals] in a solitary class with respect to" an important aspect of human relations, and accordingly "imposes a special disability upon [homosexuals] alone." And like Amendment 2, Proposition 8 constitutionalizes that disability, meaning that gays and lesbians may overcome it "only by enlisting the citizenry of [the state] to amend the State Constitution" for a second time. * * *

To be sure, there are some differences between Amendment 2 and Proposition 8. Amendment 2 "impos[ed] a broad and undifferentiated disability on a single named group" by "identif[ying] persons by a single trait and then den[ying] them protection across the board." Proposition 8, by contrast, excises with surgical precision one specific right: the right to use the designation of 'marriage' to describe a couple's officially recognized relationship. Proponents argue that Proposition 8 thus merely "restor[es] the traditional definition of marriage while otherwise leaving undisturbed the manifold rights and protections California law provides gays and lesbians," making it unlike Amendment 2, which eliminated various substantive rights.

These differences, however, do not render *Romer* less applicable. It is no doubt true that the "special disability" that Proposition 8 "imposes upon" gays and lesbians has a less sweeping effect on their public and private transactions than did Amendment 2. Nevertheless, Proposition 8 works a meaningful harm to gays and lesbians, by denying to their committed lifelong relationships the societal status conveyed by the designation of 'marriage,' and this harm must be justified by some legitimate state interest. Proposition 8 is no less problematic than Amendment 2 merely because its effect is narrower; to the contrary, the surgical precision with which it excises a right belonging to gay and lesbian couples makes it even more suspect. A law that has no practical effect except to strip one group of the right to use a state-authorized and socially meaningful designation is all the more "unprecedented" and "unusual" than a law that imposes broader changes, and raises an even stronger "inference that the disadvantage imposed is born of animosity toward the class of persons affected." In short, *Romer* governs our analysis notwithstanding the differences between Amendment 2 and Proposition 8. * * *

To the extent that it has been argued that withdrawing from same-sex couples access to the designation of 'marriage'—without in any way altering the substantive laws concerning their rights regarding childrearing or family formation—will encourage heterosexual couples to enter into matrimony, or will strengthen their matrimonial bonds, we believe that the People of California "could not reasonably" have "conceived" such an argument "to be true." It is implausible to think that denying two men or two women the right to call themselves married could somehow bolster the stability of families headed by one man and one woman. While deferential, the rational-basis standard "is not a toothless one." * * *

Proponents offer an alternative justification for Proposition 8: that it advances California's interest in "proceed[ing] with caution" when considering changes to the definition of marriage. But this rationale, too, bears no connection to the reality of Proposition 8. The amendment was enacted *after* the State had provided same-sex couples the right to marry and *after* more than 18,000 couples had married (and remain married even after Proposition 8).

Perhaps what Proponents mean is that California had an interest in pausing at 18,000 married same-sex couples to evaluate whether same-sex couples should continue to be allowed to marry, or whether the same-sex marriages that had already occurred were having any adverse impact on society. Even if that were so, there could be no rational connection between the asserted purpose of *"proceeding* with caution" and the enactment of an absolute ban, unlimited in time, on same-sex marriage in the state constitution. * * *

Had Proposition 8 imposed not a total ban but a time-specific moratorium on same-sex marriages, during which the Legislature would have been authorized to consider the question in detail or at the end of which the People would have had to vote again to renew the ban, the amendment might plausibly have been designed to "proceed with caution." * * *

When directly enacted legislation "singl[es] out a certain class of citizens for disfavored legal status," we must "insist on knowing the relation between the classification adopted and the object to be attained," so that we may ensure that the law exists "to further a proper legislative end" rather than "to make the[ ] [class] unequal to everyone else." Proposition 8 fails this test. Its sole purpose and effect is "to eliminate the right of same-sex couples to marry in California"—to dishonor a disfavored group by taking away the official designation of approval of their committed relationships and the accompanying societal status, and nothing more. * * *

NOTES

1.   Does the *Bruning* or *Perry* opinion offer a better understanding of *Romer*? Does the *Perry* approach have any application in a state, like Nebraska, that bans domestic partnership protections as well as marriage?

2.   Another recent opinion in the Ninth Circuit—one also written by Judge Stephen Reinhardt—may have significant implications for equality claims. In *SmithKline Beecham Corp. v. Abbott Labs.*, 740 F.3d 471 (9th Cir. 2014), the court held that prospective jurors cannot be subject to a peremptory strike based on sexual orientation. *Abbott* was the first federal appellate ruling to apply to sexual orientation discrimination the line of cases that began when *Batson v. Kentucky*, 476 U.S. 79, 106 S.Ct. 1712, 90 L.Ed.2d 69 (1986) outlawed race-based peremptory challenges. The Supreme Court has applied the *Batson* approach to gender. *J.E.B. v. Alabama, ex rel. T.B.*, 511 U.S. 127, 114 S. Ct. 1419, 128 L. Ed. 2d 89 (1994). Beyond the issue of juror discrimination, *Abbott* contained an extended analysis that read the Supreme Court's 2013 decision in *Windsor* to require the application of heightened scrutiny to equal protection claims involving sexual orientation discrimination. Although *Windsor* itself did not say it was applying heightened scrutiny, the Ninth Circuit's opinion identified numerous aspects of the *Windsor* analysis that were inconsistent with traditional rational basis review. The court concluded:

> At a minimum . . . *Windsor* scrutiny "requires something more than traditional rational basis review." *Windsor* requires that

when state action discriminates on the basis of sexual orientation, we must examine its actual purposes and carefully consider the resulting inequality to ensure that our most fundamental institutions neither send nor reinforce messages of stigma or second-class status. In short, *Windsor* requires heightened scrutiny. *** Thus, there can no longer be any question that gays and lesbians are no longer a "group or class of individuals normally subject to 'rational basis' review."

740 F. 3d. at 483–84.

III.   SEXUAL ORIENTATION DISCRIMINATION AS A FORM OF SEX DISCRIMINATION

The standard of review applied to claims of sexual orientation discrimination would be less consequential if sexual orientation discrimination were itself to be seen as a form of sex discrimination. In that case, heightened scrutiny would apply. This argument has featured prominently in recent litigation and scholarship.

A. VARIATIONS ON A THEME

1.   The Formal Argument

Baehr v. Lewin is an early and influential case concerning the rights of same-sex couples to marry. Indeed, it may fairly be said to have inaugurated the current debate about marriage by putting the possibility of same-sex marriage on the national screen for the first time. The case is addressed further in Chapter 6, Section II.A.2.b, but for present purposes, focus on the argument made by the court that denial of marriage rights to same-sex partners can be seen as a form of sex discrimination. Then, look at the more recent debate over that argument between the majority and dissenting opinions in the *Hernandez v. Robles* marriage decision by New York's highest court.

BAEHR V. LEWIN

Supreme Court of Hawaii, 1993
852 P.2d 44, 74 Haw. 645

LEVINSON, JUDGE, in which MOON, CHIEF JUDGE, joins.

The equal protection clauses of the United States and Hawaii Constitutions are not mirror images of one another. The fourteenth amendment to the United States Constitution somewhat concisely provides, in relevant part, that a state may not "deny to any person within its jurisdiction the equal protection of the laws." Hawaii's counterpart is more elaborate. Article I, section 5 of the Hawaii Constitution provides in relevant part that "[n]o person shall . . . be denied the equal protection of the laws, *nor be denied the enjoyment of the person's civil rights or be discriminated against in the exercise thereof because of race, religion, sex, or ancestry.*" (Emphasis added.) Thus, by its plain language, the Hawaii Constitution prohibits state-sanctioned discrimination against any person in the exercise of his or her civil rights on the basis of sex.

"The freedom to marry has long been recognized as one of the vital personal rights essential to the orderly pursuit of happiness by free [people]." *Loving*, 388 U.S. at 12. So "fundamental" does the United States Supreme Court consider the institution of marriage that it has deemed marriage to be "one of the 'basic civil rights of [men and women].'" *Id.* (quoting *Skinner*, 316 U.S. at 541).

* * * This court has held, in another context, that such "privilege[s] of citizenship . . . cannot be taken away [on] any of the prohibited bases of race, religion, sex or ancestry" enumerated in article I, section 5 of the Hawaii Constitution and that to do so violates the right to equal protection of the laws as guaranteed by that constitutional provision. * * *

Rudimentary principles of statutory construction render manifest the fact that, by its plain language, HRS § 572–1 restricts the marital relation to a male and a female. . . . Accordingly, on its face and (as Lewin admits) as applied, HRS § 572–1 denies same-sex couples access to the marital status and its concomitant rights and benefits. It is the state's regulation of access to the status of married persons, on the basis of the applicants' sex, that gives rise to the question whether the applicant couples have been denied the equal protection of the laws in violation of article I, section 5 of the Hawaii Constitution. * * *

As we have indicated, HRS § 572–1, on its face and as applied, regulates access to the marital status and its concomitant rights and benefits on the basis of the applicants' sex. As such, HRS § 572–1 establishes a sex-based classification. * * *

Our decision in *Holdman* [*v. Olim*, an earlier case brought under the Hawaii constitution] is key to the present case in several respects. First, we clearly and unequivocally established, for purposes of equal protection analysis under the Hawaii Constitution, that sex-based classifications are subject, as a per se matter, to some form of "heightened" scrutiny, be it "strict" or "intermediate," rather than mere "rational basis" analysis. Second, we assumed, arguendo, that such sex-based classifications were subject to "strict scrutiny." Third, we reaffirmed the longstanding principle that this court is free to accord greater protections to Hawaii's citizens under the state constitution than are recognized under the United States Constitution. And fourth, we looked to the then current case law of the United States Supreme Court for guidance.

Of the decisions of the United States Supreme Court cited in *Holdman, Frontiero v. Richardson* was by far the most significant. * * *

Particularly noteworthy in *Frontiero*, however, was the concurring opinion of Justice Powell, joined by the Chief Justice and Justice Blackmun (the Powell group). The Powell group agreed that "the challenged statutes constitute[d] an unconstitutional discrimination against servicewomen," but deemed it "unnecessary for the Court in this case to characterize sex as a suspect classification, with all of the far-reaching implications of such a holding." Central to the Powell group's thinking was the following explanation:

> There is another . . . reason for deferring a general categorizing of sex classifications as invoking the strictest test of judicial scrutiny. The Equal Rights Amendment, which if adopted will resolve the substance of this precise question, has been approved by Congress and submitted for ratification by the States. If this Amendment is duly adopted, it will represent the will of the people accomplished in the manner prescribed by the Constitution. By acting prematurely and unnecessarily, . . . the Court has assumed a decisional responsibility at the very time when state legislatures, functioning within the traditional democratic process, are debating the proposed Amendment. It seems . . . that this reaching out to preempt by judicial action a major political decision which is currently in process of resolution does not reflect appropriate respect for duly prescribed legislative processes.

411 U.S. at 727 (emphasis added).

The Powell group's concurring opinion therefore permits but one inference: had the Equal Rights Amendment been incorporated into the United States Constitution, at least seven members (and probably eight) of the *Frontiero* Court would have subjected statutory sex-based classifications to "strict" judicial scrutiny.

In light of the interrelationship between the reasoning of the Brennan plurality and the Powell group in *Frontiero*, on the one hand, and the presence of article I, section 3—the Equal Rights Amendment—in the Hawaii Constitution, on the other, it is time to resolve once and for all the question left dangling in *Holdman*. Accordingly, we hold that sex is a "suspect category" for purposes of equal protection analysis under article I, section 5 of the Hawaii Constitution[33] and that HRS § 572–1 is subject to the "strict scrutiny" test. It therefore follows, and we so hold, that (1) HRS § 572–1 is presumed to be unconstitutional (2) unless Lewin, as an agent of the State of Hawaii, can show that (a) the statute's sex-based

---

[33] Our holding in this regard is *not*, as the dissent suggests, "[t]hat Appellants are a 'suspect class.'"

classification is justified by compelling state interests and (b) the statute is narrowly drawn to avoid unnecessary abridgements of the applicant couples' constitutional rights. * * *

Because, for the reasons stated in this opinion, the circuit court erroneously granted Lewin's motion for judgment on the pleadings and dismissed the plaintiffs' complaint, we vacate the circuit court's order and judgment and remand this matter for further proceedings consistent with this opinion. On remand, in accordance with the "strict scrutiny" standard, the burden will rest on Lewin to overcome the presumption that HRS § 572–1 is unconstitutional by demonstrating that it furthers compelling state interests and is narrowly drawn to avoid unnecessary abridgements of constitutional rights.

HERNANDEZ V. ROBLES

Court of Appeals of New York, 2006
855 N.E.2d 1, 7 N.Y.3d 338, 821 N.Y.S.2d 770

SMITH, JUDGE.

Plaintiffs claim that the distinction made by the Domestic Relations Law between opposite-sex and same-sex couples deprives them of the equal protection of the laws. [The Court notes that plaintiffs argued that the denial of marriage rights to same-sex couples constituted sex discrimination, and rejects this claim.] * * *

By limiting marriage to opposite-sex couples, New York is not engaging in sex discrimination. The limitation does not put men and women in different classes, and give one class a benefit not given to the other. Women and men are treated alike—they are permitted to marry people of the opposite sex, but not people of their own sex. This is not the kind of sham equality that the Supreme Court confronted in *Loving*; the statute there, prohibiting black and white people from marrying each other, was in substance anti-black legislation. Plaintiffs do not argue here that the legislation they challenge is designed to subordinate either men to women or women to men as a class.

KAYE, CHIEF JUDGE, dissenting.

The exclusion of same-sex couples from civil marriage also discriminates on the basis of sex, which provides a further basis for requiring heightened scrutiny. * * *

Under the Domestic Relations Law, a woman who seeks to marry another woman is prevented from doing so on account of her sex—that is, because she is not a man. If she were, she would be given a marriage license to marry that woman. That the statutory scheme applies equally to both sexes does not alter the conclusion that the classification here is based on sex. The "equal application" approach to equal protection analysis was expressly rejected by the Supreme Court in *Loving*: "We reject the notion that the mere 'equal application' of a statute containing [discriminatory] classifications is enough to remove the classifications from the [constitutional] proscription of all invidious . . . discriminations" (388 U.S. at 8). Instead, the *Loving* Court held that "there can be no question but that Virginia's miscegenation statutes rest solely upon distinctions drawn according to race [where the] statutes proscribe generally accepted conduct if engaged in by members of different races."

2.   The Argument from Gender Roles

A different approach to conceptualizing sexual orientation discrimination as sex discrimination has been advanced by various scholars. Consider the argument set out in an influential early article by Professor Sylvia Law, and think about how it is different from the argument presented above.

HOMOSEXUALITY AND THE SOCIAL MEANING OF GENDER*
Sylvia A. Law

[H]omosexuality is censured because it violates the prescriptions of gender role expectations. A panoply of legal rules and cultural institutions reinforce the assumption that heterosexual intimacy is the only natural and legitimate form of sexual expression. The presumption and prescription that erotic interests are exclusively directed to the opposite sex define an important aspect of masculinity and femininity. Real men are and should be sexually attracted to women, and real women invite and enjoy that attraction. Though complex rules govern the ways in which heterosexual attraction may appropriately be expressed, the allure of the opposite sex is pervasively assumed. Conversely, the culture and law presume and prescribe an absence of sexual attraction between people of the same sex.

But sexual intimacies are only one piece of the presumption and prescription of heterosexuality. In our culture, the adult heterosexual couple forms the nucleus of networks of social and kinship relations, which are socially supported and privileged. The pleasure most people feel when a single friend forms a close relationship with a congenial person of the opposite sex is not based simply, or even primarily, on an appreciation of erotic or procreative possibilities. Rather, it reflects a broad understanding that life as half of a heterosexual couple is generally easier, and more pleasant and satisfying, in part because dominant prevailing structures of social and family life make it so.

---

* Sylvia A. Law, *Homosexuality and the Social Meaning of Gender*, 1988 WIS. L. REV. 187, 196–202 (1998).

Homosexual relationships challenge dichotomous concepts of gender. These relationships challenge the notion that social traits, such as dominance and nurturance, are naturally linked to one sex or the other. Moreover, those involved in homosexual relations implicitly reject the social institutions of family, economic and political life that are premised on gender inequality and differentiation. * * *

In the nineteenth century, industrialization and urbanization profoundly altered American family circumstances and values. Economically, families were no longer integrated units of production. Rather, men sold their labor in exchange for a wage, and women were assigned and assumed responsibility for maintaining the home as locus of consumption, reproduction and refuge. In many ways, women's situation improved: birth rates declined, women acquired wider educational opportunities and minimal legal rights, and a feminist movement gave voice to their interests. Urban families were less integrated with the community. Individuals, particularly men and people of means, could exercise greater choice over their family arrangements; some chose to avoid the expectations of patriarchal family life.

These profound changes in the economic and social function of the family and its relation to a larger community generated great anxiety and produced strong reaction from many sources. For the first time, the American family developed a self-conscious "image." Central to this new image was a perception of a sharp separation between public and private, male and female. The sense of individual identity, of oneness with others, and of purpose to life that were once associated with patriarchal family and religion were now more closely tied to gender.

Many social forces worked to reinforce this new gender-dichotomous concept of family. Conventional morality praised the purity of women and of the home. Late nineteenth century social purity movements promoted temperance and suppression ˉof sexually explicit materials, including contraceptive information. In England, the historic concept of "sodomy" was broadened to encompass all forms of non-procreative sex, including advocacy of birth control. Feminists promoted "voluntary motherhood," a concept which glorified the maternal role, urged male self-restraint, and sought to empower women within the family. With the development of opportunities for independent living in the nineteenth century, homosexual identity first became possible.

Only when individuals began to make their living through wage labor instead of as parts of an interdependent family unit, was it possible for homosexual desire to coalesce into a personal identity—an identity based on the ability to remain outside the heterosexual family and to construct a personal life based on attraction to one's own sex.

Simultaneous with the emergence of the possibility of homosexual identity, nineteenth century social condemnation of homosexuality intensified and sought to reinforce sharp differences in the meaning of gender. As the material and social functions of the family became less clear, and family size decreased, the attractiveness of the ideological and emotional ideal of the family intensified. Many trends made homosexual liaisons more threatening: as the economic basis of family cohesion attenuated, emotional expectations increased; with smaller families, each child bore greater responsibility for carrying on the family line; women's claims for emancipation and participation in wage labor challenged traditional division of functions.

Nineteenth century grounds for ostracism of homosexuals differed for men and women. Lesbians were censured by silence; sexual acts between two women were unimaginable. Men, by contrast, were judged guilty of effeminacy. For both men and women, homosexual behavior came to be seen as a manifestation of "inversion." Effeminate men or masculine women violated the prescriptions of gender. The men particularly served as popular symbols of perversion and moral contagion.

NOTES

1.   Professor Law emphasizes the role that prescriptive gender roles play in the regulation of sexual orientation. Her approach has affinities with ideas about sex stereotyping and employment embraced by the U.S. Supreme Court in *Price Waterhouse v. Hopkins*, 490 U.S. 228, 109 S.Ct. 1775, 104 L.Ed.2d 268 (1989), a leading case on statutory sex discrimination claims under Title VII (*see infra* Chapter 5, Section II.B).

2.   In 2010, Judge Vaughn Walker ruled that California's Proposition 8 lacked a rational basis and was therefore unconstitutional under the federal equal protection clause. One of Judge Walker's rationales for the ruling seemed to embrace strongly the link between excluding same-sex couples from marriage and maintaining traditional gender roles:

> Proponents first argue that Proposition 8 is rational because it preserves: (1) "the traditional institution of marriage as the union of a man and a woman"; (2) "the traditional social and legal purposes, functions, and structure of marriage"; and (3) "the traditional meaning of marriage as it has always been defined in the English language. . . ." These interests relate to maintaining the definition of marriage as the union of a man and a woman for its own sake.

> Tradition alone, however, cannot form a rational basis for a law. The "ancient lineage" of a classification does not make it rational. Rather, the state must have an interest apart from the fact of the tradition itself.

> The evidence shows that the tradition of restricting an individual's choice of spouse based on gender does not rationally further a state

interest despite its "ancient lineage." Instead, the evidence shows that the tradition of gender restrictions arose when spouses were legally required to adhere to specific gender roles. California has eliminated all legally mandated gender roles except the requirement that a marriage consist of one man and one woman. Proposition 8 thus enshrines in the California Constitution a gender restriction that the evidence shows to be nothing more than an artifact of a foregone notion that men and women fulfill different roles in civic life.

> The tradition of restricting marriage to opposite-sex couples does not further any state interest. Rather, the evidence shows that Proposition 8 harms the state's interest in equality, because it mandates that men and women be treated differently based only on antiquated and discredited notions of gender.

Perry v. Schwarzenegger, 704 F. Supp. 2d 921, 999 (N.D. Cal. 2010). For further discussion of _Perry_, see Chapter 6.

3. Transgender Rights as Gender Discrimination

In a major ruling, the Eleventh Circuit became the first court of appeals in a constitutional case to hold that discrimination based on gender identity is a form of sex discrimination that triggers intermediate scrutiny. As you will see in Chapter 5, most of the law regarding employment discrimination against transgender people has developed under statutory frameworks. The next case is important because it utilizes the equal protection clause and thus might offer a blueprint for constitutional claims against state actors in realms beyond employment.

GLENN V. BRUMBY
United States Court of Appeals, Eleventh Circuit, 2011
663 F.3d 1312

BARKETT, CIRCUIT JUDGE.

* * * Vandiver Elizabeth Glenn was born a biological male. Since puberty, Glenn has felt that she is a woman, and in 2005, she was diagnosed with GID, a diagnosis listed in the American Psychiatric Association's Diagnostic and Statistical Manual of Mental Disorders.

Starting in 2005, Glenn began to take steps to transition from male to female under the supervision of health care providers. This process included living as a woman outside of the workplace, which is a prerequisite to sex reassignment surgery. In October 2005, then known as Glenn Morrison and presenting as a man, Glenn was hired as an editor by the Georgia General Assembly's OLC. Sewell Brumby is the head of the OLC and is responsible for OLC personnel decisions, including the decision to fire Glenn.

In 2006, Glenn informed her direct supervisor, Beth Yinger, that she was a transsexual and was in the process of becoming a woman. On Halloween in 2006, when OLC employees were permitted to come to work wearing costumes, Glenn came to work presenting as a woman. When Brumby saw her, he told her that her appearance was not appropriate and asked her to leave the office. Brumby deemed her appearance inappropriate "[b]ecause he was a man dressed as a woman and made up as a woman." Brumby stated that "it's unsettling to think of someone dressed in women's clothing with male sexual organs inside that clothing," and that a male in women's clothing is "unnatural." Following this incident, Brumby met with Yinger to discuss Glenn's appearance on Halloween of 2006 and was informed by Yinger that Glenn intended to undergo a gender transition.

In the fall of 2007, Glenn informed Yinger that she was ready to proceed with gender transition and would begin coming to work as a woman and was also changing her legal name. Yinger notified Brumby, who subsequently terminated Glenn because "Glenn's intended gender transition was inappropriate, that it would be disruptive, that some people would view it as a moral issue, and that it would make Glenn's coworkers uncomfortable."

Glenn sued, alleging two claims of discrimination under the Equal Protection Clause. First, Glenn alleged that Brumby "discriminat[ed] against her because of her sex, including her female gender identity and her failure to conform to the sex stereotypes associated with the sex Defendant[ ] perceived her to be." [Glenn also alleged that Brumby discriminated against her because of a medical condition]. * * *

The Equal Protection Clause requires the State to treat all persons similarly situated alike or, conversely, to avoid all classifications that are "arbitrary or irrational" and those that reflect "a bare . . . desire to harm a politically unpopular group." States are presumed to act lawfully, and therefore state action is generally upheld if it is rationally related to a legitimate governmental purpose. However, more than a rational basis is required in certain circumstances. * * * In *United States v. Virginia*, the Supreme Court reaffirmed its prior holdings that sex-based discrimination is subject to intermediate scrutiny under the Equal Protection Clause. This standard requires the government to show that its "gender classification . . . is substantially related to a sufficiently important government interest." Moreover, this test requires a "genuine" justification, not one that is "hypothesized or invented *post hoc* in response to litigation." In *Virginia*, the state's policy of excluding women from the Virginia Military Institute failed this test because the state could not rely on generalizations about different aptitudes of males and females to support the exclusion of women. * * *

The question here is whether discriminating against someone on the basis of his or her gender non-conformity constitutes sex-based discrimination under the Equal Protection Clause. For the reasons discussed below, we hold that it does.

In *Price Waterhouse v. Hopkins*, the Supreme Court held that discrimination on the basis of gender stereotype is sex-based discrimination. In that case, the Court considered allegations that a senior manager at Price Waterhouse was denied partnership in the firm because she was considered "macho," and "overcompensated for being a woman." * * *

A person is defined as transgender precisely because of the perception that his or her behavior transgresses gender stereotypes. "[T]he very acts that define transgender people as transgender are those that contradict stereotypes of gender-appropriate appearance and behavior." Ilona M. Turner, *Sex Stereotyping Per Se: Transgender Employees and Title VII*, 95 Cal. L. Rev. 561, 563 (2007); *see also* Taylor Flynn, *Transforming the Debate: Why We Need to Include Transgender Rights in the Struggles for Sex and Sexual Orientation Equality*, 101 Colum. L. Rev. 392, 392 (2001) (defining transgender persons as those whose "appearance, behavior, or other personal characteristics differ from traditional gender norms"). There is thus a congruence between discriminating against transgender and transsexual individuals and discrimination on the basis of gender-based behavioral norms. Accordingly, discrimination against a transgender individual because of her gender-nonconformity is sex discrimination, whether it's described as being on the basis of sex or gender. * * *

All persons, whether transgender or not, are protected from discrimination on the basis of gender stereotype. For example, courts have held that plaintiffs cannot be discriminated against for wearing jewelry that was considered too effeminate, carrying a serving tray too gracefully, or taking too active a role in child-rearing. An individual cannot be punished because of his or her perceived gender-nonconformity. Because these protections are afforded to everyone, they cannot be denied to a transgender individual. The nature of the discrimination is the same; it may differ in degree but not in kind, and discrimination on this basis is a form of sex-based discrimination that is subject to heightened scrutiny under the Equal Protection Clause. Ever since the Supreme Court began to apply heightened scrutiny to sex-based classifications, its consistent purpose has been to eliminate discrimination on the basis of gender stereotypes.

* * * Accordingly, governmental acts based upon gender stereotypes—which presume that men and women's appearance and behavior will be determined by their sex—must be subjected to

heightened scrutiny because they embody "the very stereotype the law condemns." *J.E.B. v. Alabama* (declaring unconstitutional a government attorney's use of peremptory juror strikes based on the presumption that potential jurors' views would correspond to their sexes). * * *

* * * In this case, Brumby testified at his deposition that he fired Glenn because he considered it "inappropriate" for her to appear at work dressed as a woman and that he found it "unsettling" and "unnatural" that Glenn would appear wearing women's clothing. Brumby testified that his decision to dismiss Glenn was based on his perception of Glenn as "a man dressed as a woman and made up as a woman," and Brumby admitted that his decision to fire Glenn was based on "the sheer fact of the transition." Brumby's testimony provides ample direct evidence to support the district court's conclusion that Brumby acted on the basis of Glenn's gender non-conformity.

[The remainder of the opinion is excerpted in Chapter 5, sec. III. A].

NOTES

1.   For more on transgender rights and sex discrimination, see Taylor Flynn, *Transforming the Debate: Why We Need to Include Transgender Rights in the Struggles for Sex and Sexual Orientation Equality*, 101 COLUM. L. REV. 392 (2001); Franklin H. Romeo, *Beyond a Medical Model: Advocating for a New Conception of Gender Identity in the Law*, 36 COLUM. HUM. RTS. L. REV. 713 (2005); Stevie V. Tran & Elizabeth M. Glazer, *Transgenderless*, 35 HARV. J.L. & GENDER 399 (2012); Dylan Vade, *Expanding Gender and Expanding the Law: Toward a Social and Legal Conceptualization of Gender That Is More Inclusive of Transgender People*, 11 MICH. J. GENDER & L. 253 (2005). While many transgender rights cases are litigated under a theory of sex discrimination, advocates have used a variety of other legal strategies, including disability law and the First Amendment. For articles advocating transgender rights through other means, see Jeffrey Kosbie, *(No) State Interests in Regulating Gender: How Suppression of Gender Nonconformity Violates Freedom of Speech*, 19 WM. & MARY J. WOMEN & L. 187 (2013); S. Elizabeth Malloy, *What Best to Protect Transsexuals from Discrimination: Using Current Legislation or Adopting a New Judicial Framework*, 32 WOMEN'S RTS. L. REP. 283 (2011); Daniella A. Schmidt, *Bathroom Bias: Making the Case for Trans Rights Under Disability Law*, 20 MICH. J. GENDER & L. 155 (2013).

2.   Some of the sex-based medical discrimination faced by transgender persons is starkly portrayed in Kate Davis's 2001 documentary film, *Southern Comfort*. The film depicts the last year in the life of Robert Eads, a transgender man. Eads was diagnosed with ovarian cancer after his transition, but doctors refused to treat him because of his gender presentation. For information about the film, see http://www.imdb.com/title/tt0276515/.

B. DEBATING THE SEX DISCRIMINATION ARGUMENT

EVALUATING THE SEX DISCRIMINATION ARGUMENT FOR LESBIAN AND GAY RIGHTS*

Edward Stein

In order to elucidate the problems with the sex discrimination argument, consider a hypothetical argument that could be made against antimiscegenation laws. Various scholars have noted that there were sex hierarchies implicit in antimiscegenation statutes—a significant purpose of such laws was to protect white women from black men. Sex classifications clearly played a role in the development and articulation of antimiscegenation laws. In light of this fact, one could make a sex discrimination argument against antimiscegenation laws, pointing out that women were disadvantaged by antimiscegenation laws and that such laws were justified by sexism. * * * *removed a woman's right to decide for herself*

Overturning antimiscegenation laws because they discriminate on the basis of sex would mischaracterize the core of the problem with such laws.

To put a finer point on my claim, there are three related problems with the sex discrimination argument against antimiscegenation laws in particular and against racially discriminatory laws in general. First, this argument misidentifies the class disadvantaged by antimiscegenation laws. Nonwhites, more than women, are disadvantaged by such a law. Call this the _sociological_ mistake of the sex discrimination argument against antimiscegenation laws. The sex discrimination argument against antimiscegenation laws overemphasizes the ways these laws disadvantage women as compared to the ways they disadvantage people of color. * * *

Second, the sex discrimination argument against antimiscegenation laws misidentifies the belief system that justifies antimiscegenation laws. Even granting that racism and sexism complement each other in providing the justification for antimiscegenation laws, racism, not sexism, is the belief system that primarily underlies these laws. Call this the _theoretical_ mistake of the sex discrimination argument against antimiscegenation laws. * * *

Third, a court that overturned an antimiscegenation law on the grounds that the law discriminated on the basis of sex would, in so doing, fail to take a stand on the central moral issue underlying the legal questions about antimiscegenation laws, namely that racial discrimination is morally wrong. If the _Loving_ Court, in overturning

---

* Edward Stein, _Evaluating the Sex Discrimination Argument for Lesbian and Gay Rights_, 49 UCLA L. REV. 471, 496–504, 509–15 (2001).

Virginia's antimiscegenation law, had focused on the sexist rather than the racist assumptions that justified the law, it would have made a moral mistake, not just a theoretical one. Call this the *moral* mistake of the sex discrimination argument against antimiscegenation laws. The three mistakes of the sex discrimination argument against antimiscegenation laws—the sociological, the theoretical, and the moral—are interconnected. The theoretical mistake builds on the sociological mistake: If women are in fact greatly disadvantaged by antimiscegenation laws, then it would make sense to say that sexism plays a role in the justification of such laws. The moral mistake builds on the other two: It is tempting to see the moral issue of antimiscegenation laws in terms of mistaken and unjust views of women because of the sociological and theoretical claims linking racism and sexism.

The three problems with the sex discrimination argument against antimiscegenation laws parallel problems with the sex discrimination argument as applied to laws that discriminate against lesbians, gay men, and bisexuals. I turn now to these parallel problems with the sex discrimination argument for lesbian and gay rights. * * *

Various scholars have argued for the need to analyze sexual orientation and sex separately. For example, Cheshire Calhoun, in her article *Separating Lesbian Theory from Feminist Theory*, says that:

> patriarchy and heterosexual dominance are two, in principle, separable systems. Even where they work together, it is possible conceptually to pull the patriarchal aspect of male-female relationships apart from their heterosexual dimensions. . . . Even if empirically and historically heterosexual dominance and patriarchy are completely intertwined, it does not follow from this fact that the collapse [or weakening] of patriarchy will bring about the collapse [or weakening] of heterosexual dominance.

While an advocate of the sex discrimination argument might admit that sexual-orientation inequality and homophobia could continue to exist even if there were sex equality and no sexism, I want to make a stronger claim. Building on the work of Calhoun and of others, I claim that there are actual and significant differences between sexism and homophobia in contemporary American and other western societies. Simply put, sexism and homophobia are coming apart. Consider, for example, the dramatic changes in family law in the past century. Whereas women were once viewed as the property of their husbands and had few rights as wives, today the legal status of women and men in the context of the family are basically equal. In contrast, with the notable exception of the creation of civil unions in Vermont, the legal recognition for lesbian and gay relationships and families lags dramatically behind those of heterosexuals. This one example illustrates how homophobia, though it has gradually become disentangled from sexism, remains entrenched in our society. * * *

It mischaracterizes the nature of laws that discriminate against lesbians and gay men to see them as primarily harming women (or even as harming women as much as they harm gay men, lesbians, and bisexuals). Further, it mischaracterizes laws that discriminate on the basis of sexual orientation to see them as primarily justified by sexism rather than by homophobia. * * * *homophobia is seen as much worse —*

[T]o simply deploy the sex discrimination argument against sodomy laws would, for example, ignore the central role that conceptions of sexual desire play in such laws. Making the sex discrimination argument also overlooks the distinctive role that "the closet," and the associated invisibility of lesbians, gay men, and bisexuals, play in the justification and maintenance of sodomy laws and of sexual orientation discrimination generally. Various theorists have shown how the element of secrecy, sometimes in the form of an "open secret," is a central aspect of the experience of lesbians, gay men, and bisexuals. The centrality of the closet can be seen in such legal policies as the military's "don't ask, don't tell" policy and the varied policies of public school districts towards teachers who are open about their homosexuality or bisexuality. * * *

I agree that some laws that disadvantage one group may also disadvantage another and that more than one belief system may undergird some laws. Sometimes, however, one group may be more disadvantaged than another and one belief system may play a much more central role than another. * * *

A parallel point can be made concerning the sex discrimination argument for lesbian and gay rights: Women, compared to men, may be more disadvantaged by laws that discriminate on the basis of sexual orientation, but lesbians, gay men, and bisexuals are more significantly disadvantaged by such laws than are women in general. Similarly, while sexism plays a role in maintaining laws relating to sexual orientation, homophobia plays a much more central role. * * *

In an essay written before *Loving* but after *Brown v. Board of Education*, Herbert Wechsler argued that the questions posed by state-enforced segregation (in both education and marriage) do not primarily concern discrimination or equal protection but rather primarily concern freedom of association. He argued that the prohibition of miscegenation affected both whites and nonwhites; the prohibition, properly understood, did not discriminate against blacks and did not violate the Equal Protection Clause but rather restricted the freedom of association of everyone, regardless of race.

Charles Black, in response, said that as a member of this society, he has no doubt why segregation laws exist. He argued that Wechsler ignored the obvious ways in which segregation (in marriage, education, and other contexts) clearly offends equality. It was ridiculous to claim that such laws were unconstitutional because they restrict the right to free association:

> [I]f a whole race of people finds itself confined within a system which is set up and continued for the very purpose of keeping it in an inferior station, and if the question is then solemnly propounded whether such a race is being treated "equally," I think we ought to exercise one of the sovereign prerogatives of philosophers—that of laughter.

Black convincingly—and presciently (in light of the Court's decision in *Loving*)—argued that segregation was designed to keep African Americans "in their place" and to sustain white supremacy.

The moral objection to the sex discrimination argument is similar to Black's objection to Wechsler's argument against segregation: Laws that discriminate against lesbians, gay men, and bisexuals should be overturned on the grounds that they make invidious distinctions on the basis of sexual orientation, not on other grounds. Overturning laws that discriminate on the basis of sexual orientation because they discriminate on the basis of sex (or gender) mischaracterizes the core wrong of these laws. . . . By failing to address arguments about the morality of same-sex sexual acts and the moral character of lesbians, gay men, and bisexuals, the sex discrimination argument "closets," rather than confronts, homophobia. * * *

In virtue of the fact that sex and sexual orientation are conceptually and culturally distinct, not all laws that discriminate on the basis of sexual orientation in fact make use of sex classifications. In his book, *Gaylaw*, William Eskridge distinguishes among three different types of laws that discriminate on the basis of sexual orientation: (1) laws that explicitly discriminate on the basis of sexual orientation (*type-1 laws*; an example would be the military's policy concerning homosexuality); (2) laws that discriminate on the basis of sex but that have their primary effect on gay people (*type-2 laws*; an example would be marriage laws that prohibit same-sex couples from marrying); and (3) other laws that do not facially discriminate against either sex or sexual orientation but that have discriminatory effects on lesbians and gay men (*type-3 laws*).

As an example of a type-1 law, consider the military's policy concerning homosexuality. This law and the regulations that implement it, often referred to collectively as the "don't ask, don't tell" policy, do not facially discriminate on the basis of sex or even mention sex classifications. Under this policy, one of the several ways that lesbians, gay men, and bisexuals can be discharged is if they engage in sexual activities with people of the same-sex. This policy does not, however, discharge *heterosexuals* who engage in same-sex sexual acts (as some heterosexuals do). Specifically, the law provides for an exemption from discharge of a member of the armed forces who "engages in a homosexual act . . . [if] such conduct is a departure from the member's usual and customary behavior; such conduct . . . is unlikely to recur; . . . and the member does not have a propensity or intent to engage in homosexual acts." In other words, heterosexuals who occasionally engage in same-sex sexual acts might not be discharged for engaging in such acts, even if such acts are discovered. Only lesbians, gay men, and bisexuals will be discharged for engaging in same-sex sexual acts, because, by virtue of their sexual orientations, only they have the propensity to engage in such acts. In light of this exemption, the military policy is a type-1 law: It does not discriminate on the basis of sex, but it discriminates on the basis of sexual orientation—it discharges lesbians, gay men, and bisexuals for engaging in a behavior for which heterosexuals are not discharged.

Although the sex discrimination argument could be applied to type-1 laws as well as to type-3 laws, the sex discrimination argument has its greatest potential applied to type-2 laws, that is, laws that discriminate on the basis of sex. The sex discrimination argument will be much harder for judges to accept when it is applied to type-1 laws or to type-3 laws, that is, laws that discriminate on the basis of sexual orientation that do *not* make use of sex classifications. This is a significant practical limitation of the sex discrimination argument. * * *

Legislatures that wish to restrict lesbian and gay rights will try to immunize themselves against the sex discrimination argument by not using sex classifications in laws relating to sexual orientation and by explicitly stating that such laws do not discriminate against sex. * * *

[Another] practical problem for the sex discrimination argument for lesbian and gay rights is that any practical successes for the sex discrimination argument could lead to a weakening of protections against sex discrimination. This is because a strong backlash typically occurs when lesbians, gay men, and bisexuals make legal and political advances. In fact, some have argued that the link to lesbian and gay rights, especially to same-sex marriage, had a deleterious effect on the Equal Rights Amendment. A backlash to any success of the sex discrimination argument could undermine both women's rights and lesbian and gay rights. In effect, this is what happened in Hawaii. The 1999 decision of the state's supreme court construed the 1998 constitutional amendment as taking Hawaii's marriage law "out of the ambit of the equal protection clause of the Hawaii constitution," thereby weakening sex discrimination jurisprudence in Hawaii. * * *

[M]y view is that the sex discrimination argument, given its practical and theoretical pitfalls, if presented at all, should be used with caution.

Making this argument in conjunction with other sorts of arguments for lesbian and gay rights might mitigate some of the practical problems with the sex discrimination argument, but some serious worries would remain. A law that discriminates on the basis of sexual orientation that is overturned in the face of the sex discrimination argument could reappear in a slightly different form, recast so that it does not make use of sex classifications. Further, when a law that discriminates on the basis of sexual orientation is overturned in the face of the sex discrimination argument, the central moral debates about homosexuality are bracketed. Perhaps Herbert Wechsler's argument that appealed to the freedom of association could have worked to persuade judges who would have otherwise upheld racial segregation, but such an argument would have lacked the moral force of the Supreme Court's opinion in *Loving*. When the basic human rights of a despised minority are at issue, the judiciary needs to speak in a strong moral voice.

DEFENDING THE SEX DISCRIMINATION ARGUMENT FOR LESBIAN AND GAY RIGHTS: A REPLY TO EDWARD STEIN*

Andrew Koppelman

So many things are wrong with laws that discriminate against gay people that it is hard to know where to begin. They intrude on citizens' privacy. They enforce indefensible beliefs about sexual morality. They give the state's imprimatur to a theology, and a dubious one at that. They interfere with matters in which the law has no competence and that are none of the state's business. They oppress a long-suffering minority. Their enforcement typically involves cruelty and hypocrisy.

They also discriminate on the basis of sex, and they depend on and reinforce the subordination of women.

Each of the preceding seven sentences is an inadequate portrait of antigay oppression to the extent that it fails to mention the wrongs cited by the others. This is one of the limitations of language. Edward Stein's critique of the sex discrimination argument for gay rights is concerned about what the argument leaves out. I do not want to leave them out, either. But that is not a reason to neglect the wrongs specifically revealed by the sex discrimination argument. * * *

The formal argument that discrimination against gays is a kind of sex discrimination is stated briefly and accurately by Stein:

> If a person's sexual orientation is a dispositional property that concerns the sex of people to whom he or she is attracted, then, to determine a person's sexual orientation, one needs to know

---

* Andrew Koppelman, *Defending the Sex Discrimination Argument for Lesbian and Gay Rights: A Reply to Edward Stein*, 49 UCLA L. REV. 519, 519–34 (2001).

the person's sex and the sex of the people to whom he or she is primarily sexually attracted. For example, if A is sexually attracted exclusively to men, then A is a heterosexual only if A is a woman, and A is a homosexual only if A is a man.

This argument is formally incomplete, Stein thinks, because a law that discriminates against gays may just as easily be understood as treating both sexes equally by forbidding both to engage in sexual conduct with persons of the same sex. "Deciding whether a statute that discriminates on the basis of sexual orientation discriminates on the basis of sex seems, in light of this problem, like deciding whether a glass is half empty or half full."

Stein acknowledges that the miscegenation cases presented a similar problem, and that the U.S. Supreme Court ultimately rejected the idea that both races were treated identically by laws against interracial marriage. But, he claims, in those cases there was "a fit between the class disadvantaged by the law and the suspect classification the law employs." And he proceeds to raise questions about the sociological connection between antigay animus and sexism.

This, however, leaves legal doctrine behind, because it misstates what the Court did in the miscegenation cases. Stein is correct that *Loving v. Virginia* noted a connection between the miscegenation prohibition and racism. But *Loving* was preceded by *McLaughlin v. Florida*, in which the Court unanimously invalidated a criminal statute prohibiting an unmarried interracial couple from habitually living in and occupying the same room at night. "It is readily apparent," the Court held, that the statute "treats the interracial couple made up of a white person and a Negro differently than it does any other couple." Racial classifications, it concluded, can only be sustained by a compelling state interest. Because the State had failed to establish that the statute served "some overriding statutory purpose requiring the proscription of the specified conduct when engaged in by a white person and a Negro, but not otherwise," the statute necessarily fell as "an invidious discrimination forbidden by the Equal Protection Clause."

McLaughlin, not *Loving*, was the groundbreaking case that laid the equal application argument to rest, and *McLaughlin*, not *Loving*, is the crucial precedent on which the sex discrimination argument relies. It should not even be necessary to cite it as a precedent, because it stated the obvious. If prohibited conduct is defined by reference to the actor's own race or sex, the prohibition is not neutral with reference to that characteristic. Indeed, in the states that specifically prohibit homosexual sex, the defendant's own sex would appear to be one of the essential elements of the crime that the prosecution must prove.

McLaughlin did not rely on any claims whatsoever about the motive for the law or about the class that was harmed by the law. It simply noted that there was a racial classification and applied heightened scrutiny. The sex discrimination argument for protecting gays from discrimination requires nothing more. * * *

Stein correctly observes that sex discrimination doctrine permits discrimination in cases in which the discrimination reflects real differences between men and women. Courts have relied on that doctrine to reject the sex discrimination argument. But does current doctrine permit this result? There are a few cases, which Stein notes, that do permit reliance on those differences. The laws upheld in those decisions, however, reflected accurate empirical rather than normative generalizations. More importantly, the generalizations they reflected were exceptionless. If it were otherwise—if a sex-based classification could be justified by what is usually the case, or what is true about most members of either sex—then the constitutional doctrine would be eviscerated, because even the most invidiously sexist laws have been justifiable in terms of some argument of this sort.

What "real differences" could courts cite? Stein notes that some states have tried to defend some kinds of discrimination by arguing:

> that marriage is related to childrearing (and that . . . lesbians and gay men are bad parents compared to heterosexuals), that lesbians and gay men are less able to sustain the sort of long-term commitments the state wants to encourage in its citizens, and that the incidence of sodomy can be reduced by preventing homosexuals from marrying.

All of these claims involve the kind of stereotyping that the Court has consistently rejected in the sex discrimination cases. Some, such as the claim about parenting, are not even statistically accurate. More importantly, none of them are true of all gay couples. Such generalizations have been relied on by courts denying gays' sex discrimination claims. But such generalizations have also been relied on to justify *all* forms of sex discrimination. * * *

Drawing on a taxonomy developed by William Eskridge, Jr., Stein observes that the sex discrimination argument does not reach all antigay laws. Specifically, he claims that sex classifications are found neither in laws that explicitly discriminate on the basis of sexual orientation (what he calls "type-1 laws"), nor in laws that do not facially discriminate but have discriminatory effects on gays ("type-3 laws").

With respect to type-3 laws, Stein is undoubtedly correct. This objection is not confined to the sex discrimination argument, however. It also deflates the argument that homosexuality is a suspect classification like race and the argument that sexual orientation discrimination is like religious discrimination. Disparate impact based on race or religion is not now recognized as a basis for a constitutional claim. In this regard, the sex discrimination argument fares no worse than its rivals.

The sex discrimination argument does, however, reach type-1 laws. Any law that discriminates against gays as such must be predicated on some procedure for determining who is gay. Stein acknowledges that "to determine a person's sexual orientation, one needs to know the person's sex and the sex of the people to whom he or she is primarily sexually attracted." He thinks that the sex discrimination argument would not reach a law that prohibited gay people from marrying anyone of either sex. In order to enforce this law, though, the registrar of marriages would need to know what A's sex is in order to decide whether A's attraction to B marks A as a gay person. Imagine a law that discriminated against "miscegenosexuals" and denied them the right to marry or other benefits. Does Stein really think that such a law is not racially discriminatory, or that it would not be immediately recognized as such? * * *

The big problem with his sociological objection is that it implies that *Loving* was wrong to talk about white supremacy. The same objection could have been raised in that case: Miscegenation laws primarily harmed, not blacks as such, but interracial heterosexual couples (a group that, by definition, included equal numbers of blacks and whites). While the harm to blacks was recognized even by the most obtuse judges as a "stigma, of the deepest degradation . . . fixed upon the whole [black] race," it would be callous not to notice that the persons who were *most* severely harmed by those laws were the ones whose marriages were voided and who were, in many cases, sent to prison. If the harm to blacks counts against the miscegenation laws, then for the same reasons, the harm to women should count against antigay laws. * * *

What Stein calls the "theoretical" objection (it appears just as sociological as its predecessor) is that "while sexism plays a role in the justification of laws that discriminate against lesbians, gay men, and bisexuals, homophobia plays a more central role." I do not know how to evaluate that comparative claim, which pertains to complex social and psychological processes that are largely mysterious (and that take very different forms in the psyches of different people). * * *

At one point Stein makes the stronger claim that in contemporary America, "sexism and homophobia are coming apart." I would have to see better evidence than that which Stein cites before I believed this. The most thorough documentation of the linkage is the work of Francisco Valdes, which illustrates the ways in which literature, the discourse of scholarly psychologists, politics, public opinion, popular culture, and judicial decisionmaking have conflated sex, gender, and sexual orientation throughout the last century. Valdes concludes that "sex, gender, and sexual orientation *never* have been constructed independently of each other in our society." If someone wanted to refute him, they could begin by citing instances of discourse in which sexual orientation is constructed without reference to gender norms. However, this would not be an easy task. I cannot imagine where they would begin. The mere fact that women's status has improved, which is all that Stein cites, hardly suffices. The status of gays has improved at the same time, and those who have struggled against heterosexism and sexism are acutely conscious of the link. * * *

Finally, Stein objects that the sex discrimination argument "mischaracterizes the core wrong" of antigay laws. "By failing to address arguments about the morality of same-sex sexual acts and the moral character of lesbians, gay men, and bisexuals, the sex discrimination argument 'closets,' rather than confronts, homophobia."

This is a powerful claim. Stein is only the latest of many writers who have worried that the sex discrimination argument marginalizes gays' moral claims. Jack Balkin writes that the sex discrimination argument implies "that discrimination against homosexuals is merely a 'side effect' of discrimination against women, and therefore somehow less important." John Gardner thinks that "those committed to the moral wrongfulness of sexuality discrimination should not be at all happy to find this wrongfulness appended to the moral margins of somebody else's grievance, namely the grievance of those who are victims of sex discrimination." William Eskridge writes that the sex discrimination argument has "a transvestite quality," because "it dresses a gay rights issue up in gender rights garb." Danielle Kie Hart argues that the sex discrimination argument "makes the lives of homosexuals invisible; it sends a clear message to society that it is not acceptable to discuss homosexuality in a public forum; and it reflects and may perpetuate negative attitudes about lesbians and gay men."

All these concerns are valid. One can make the same point about the interracial couple prosecuted in *Loving*: the racist system primarily harmed blacks, but the white husband's interests were hardly unimportant. Balkin's rephrasing of the point is helpful: "gender categories are general forms of social subordination that subordinate the feminine and all things associated with the feminine. Thus, this system subordinates not only women, but homosexuals, bisexuals, and effeminate men."

The problem here is the problem with any legal claim. Law always picks and chooses among facts in the world, deeming some relevant and ignoring others. It thus flattens the richness of human life. Law is not literature. Its capacity "to speak in a strong moral voice" is inevitably limited. When we evaluate a human life, we do not just ask whether the person followed the rules. Othello and Iago both killed their wives; the law would make no distinction between them, even though any reader of Shakespeare's play knows that the two men lived in different moral universes. Facts are messy. Legal categories make them clean, usually by stripping off the living flesh. There is a danger, which should always be resisted, that stories deemed irrelevant for legal purposes will be deemed irrelevant *simpliciter*.

The sex discrimination argument relies on settled law that was established for the benefit of women, not of gays. It can be relied on because it is settled, but it is settled only because it was devised without thinking about (to some extent, by deliberately ignoring) the claims of gays. Accepting and relying on the sex discrimination argument thus means accepting and relying on a view of the world in which gays are at best marginal.

On the other hand, the marginalization of gays is precisely why the argument has the comparative advantages that it does. Each of the other principal arguments for gay equality—the privacy and suspect classification arguments—depend on an innovative extension of existing law to cover gays. The sex discrimination argument does not. On the contrary, it is its opponents who must ask for legal innovation, by carving out an exception to a settled rule.

NOTES

1.   Who do you think has the better of this exchange? What light is shed on the questions debated by Professors Stein and Koppelman by the argument offered by Professor Law earlier in this Chapter?

2.   As you reflect on the cogency of conceptualizing sexual orientation discrimination as a form of sex discrimination, recall the *Brumby* court's framing of discrimination based on gender identity as sex discrimination. Does that analysis bear on the issue debated by Stein and Koppelman? For analysis of whether discrimination based on gender identity is a form of sex discrimination covered by Title VII of the Civil Rights Act of 1964, see Chapter 5, sec. II. B. 2.

CHAPTER 4

SEXUALITY, GENDER, & FREE SPEECH

■ ■ ■

I.   INTRODUCTION

Sexual orientation and gender identity have vital expressive dimensions. Key milestones of an open life—coming out, meeting other LGBT people, finding a partner, participating in social and political activity—depend to some extent on self-identification. This is especially so given that LGBT people, unlike many other minority groups, are typically not visually identifiable. As society presumes heterosexuality, gay and bisexual people simply do not "exist" to the public until choosing to self-identify by "coming out."

Free expression enables LGBT persons to create their own groups, communities, and cultures. Absent self-identification, gay people would never be able to meet with one another to form meaningful friendships; intimate relationships; support, lobbying, or educational groups; or, for example, legal-aid organizations.

This Chapter explores the role of First Amendment freedoms in the lives of LGBT individuals and in the LGBT community. Section II of this Chapter focuses on the lives of high school and college students and on issues associated with asserting sexual and gender identity at school. (We defer until Chapter 5 issues about LGBT persons being open about their identities at work). Section II also includes some historical material on the regulation of lesbian/gay/bisexual meeting places and participation in public life. Section III considers legal issues that have come to the fore over the last few decades, as private, non-governmental organizations (like the Boy Scouts and religiously-affiliated entities) have sought to deny equal access to LGBT people. The organizing legal principle of this Chapter is the First Amendment. We will see expressive liberties asserted as both a "sword" in favor of LGBT presence and inclusion and as a "shield" against it—that is, as a source of constitutional protection claimed by those seeking to exclude LGBT persons from areas of social life. The historical trajectory of First Amendment claims in the realm of LGBT issues has been toward "shield" claims that pit values of equality against values of liberty. Increasingly, these liberty claims involve not only free speech, but also religious freedom. Conflicts of this type have become especially salient with the rise of same-sex marriage and will be revisited in Chapter 6, but as we will see, the issues are by no means limited to that context.

II.　ASSERTING LGBT IDENTITY

A.　HIGH SCHOOL AND COLLEGE

FRICKE V. LYNCH

United States District Court, District of Rhode Island, 1980
491 F. Supp. 381

PETTINE, CHIEF JUDGE.

Most of the time, a young man's choice of a date for the senior prom is of no great interest to anyone other than the student, his companion, and, perhaps, a few of their classmates. But in Aaron Fricke's case, the school authorities actively disapprove of his choice, the other students are upset, the community is abuzz, and out-of-state newspapers consider the matter newsworthy. All this fuss arises because Aaron Fricke's intended escort is another young man. Claiming that the school's refusal to allow him to bring a male escort violates his First and Fourteenth Amendment rights, Fricke seeks a preliminary injunction ordering the school officials to allow him to attend with a male escort.

Two days of testimony have revealed the following facts. The senior reception at Cumberland High School is a formal dinner-dance sponsored and run by the senior class. It is held shortly before graduation but is not a part of the graduation ceremonies. This year the students have decided to hold the dance at the Pleasant Valley Country Club in Sutton, Massachusetts on Friday, May 30. All seniors except those on suspension are eligible to attend the dance; no one is required to go. All students who attend must bring an escort, although their dates need not be seniors or even Cumberland High School students. Each student is asked the name of his date at the time he buys the tickets.

The principal testified that school dances are chaperoned by him, two assistant principals, and one or two class advisers. They are sometimes joined by other teachers who volunteer to help chaperone; such teachers are not paid. Often these teachers will drop in for part of the dance. Additionally, police officers are on duty at the dance. Usually two officers attend; last year three plainclothes officers were at the junior prom.

The seeds of the present conflict were planted a year ago when Paul Guilbert, then a junior at Cumberland High School, sought permission to bring a male escort to the junior prom. The principal, Richard Lynch (the defendant here), denied the request, fearing that student reaction could lead to a disruption at the dance and possibly to physical harm to Guilbert. The request and its denial were widely publicized and led to widespread community and student reaction adverse to Paul. Some students taunted and spit at him, and once someone slapped him; in response, principal Lynch arranged an escort system, in which Lynch or an assistant principal accompanied Paul as he went from one class to the next. No other incidents or violence occurred. Paul did not attend the prom. At that time Aaron Fricke (plaintiff here) was a friend of Paul's and supported his position regarding the dance.

This year, during or after an assembly in April in which senior class events were discussed, Aaron Fricke, a senior at Cumberland High School, decided that he wanted to attend the senior reception with a male companion. Aaron considers himself a homosexual, and has never dated girls, although he does socialize with female friends. He has never taken a girl to a school dance. Until this April, he had not "come out of the closet" by publicly acknowledging his sexual orientation.

Aaron asked principal Lynch for permission to bring a male escort, which Lynch denied. A week later (during vacation), Aaron asked Paul Guilbert—who now lives in New York—to be his escort (if allowed), and Paul accepted. Aaron met again with Lynch, at which time they discussed Aaron's commitment to homosexuality; Aaron indicated that although it was possible he might someday be bisexual, at the present he is exclusively homosexual and could not conscientiously date girls. Lynch gave Aaron written reasons for his action;[2] his prime concern was the fear that a disruption would occur and Aaron or, especially, Paul would be hurt. He indicated in court that he would allow Aaron to bring a male escort if there were no threat of violence.

After Aaron filed suit in this Court, an event reported by the Rhode Island and Boston papers, a student shoved and, the next day, punched Aaron. The unprovoked, surprise assault necessitated five stitches under Aaron's right eye. The assailant was suspended for nine days. After this, Aaron was given a special parking space closer to the school doors and

---

[2] Principal Lynch sent the following letter to Aaron's home and handed it to him in person: I am denying your request for the following reasons:

1. The real and present threat of physical harm to you, your male escort and to others;

2. The adverse effect among your classmates, other students, the school and the town of Cumberland, which is certain to follow approval of such a request for overt homosexual interaction (male or female) at a class function;

3. Since the dance is being held out of state and this is a function of the students of Cumberland High School, the school department is powerless to insure protection in Sutton, Massachusetts. That protection would be required of property as well as persons and would expose all concerned to liability for harm which might occur;

4. It is long-standing school policy that no unescorted student, male or female, is permitted to attend. To enforce this rule, a student must identify his or her escort before the committee will sell the ticket. I suspect that other objections will be raised by your fellow students, the Cumberland School Department, parents and other citizens, which will heighten the potential for harm.

has been provided with an escort (principal or assistant principal) between classes. No further incidents have occurred. * * *

Aaron contends that the school's action violates his First Amendment right of association, his First Amendment right to free speech, and his Fourteenth Amendment right to equal protection of the laws. (The equal protection claim is a "hybrid" one—that he has been treated differently than others because of the content of his communication.)[3]

The starting point in my analysis of Aaron's First Amendment free speech claim must be, of course, to determine whether the action he proposes to take has a "communicative content sufficient to bring it within the ambit of the First Amendment." *Gay Students Organization v. Bonner*, 509 F.2d 652 (1st Cir. 1974) (hereinafter *Bonner*).... [T]he "speech pure" / "speech plus" demarcation is problematic, both in logic and in practice. This normally difficult task is made somewhat easier here, however, by the precedent set in *Bonner*, *supra*. In that case, the University of New Hampshire prohibited the Gay Students' Organization (GSO) from holding dances and other social events. The First Circuit explicitly rejected the idea that traditional First Amendment rights of expression were not involved. The Court found that not only did discussion and exchange of ideas take place at informal social functions, but also that:

> beyond the specific communications at such events is the basic "message" GSO seeks to convey—that homosexuals exist, that they feel repressed by existing laws and attitudes, that they wish to emerge from their isolation, and that public understanding of their attitudes and problems is desirable for society.

Here too the proposed activity has significant expressive content. Aaron testified that he wants to go because he feels he has a right to attend and participate just like all the other students and that it would be dishonest to his own sexual identity to take a girl to the dance. He went on to acknowledge that he feels his attendance would have a certain political element and would be a statement for equal rights and human rights. Admittedly, his explanation of his "message" was hesitant and not nearly as articulate as Judge Coffin's restatement of the GSO's message, cited above. Nevertheless, I believe Aaron's testimony that he is sincerely— although perhaps not irrevocably—committed to a homosexual orientation and that attending the dance with another young man would be a political statement. While mere communicative intent may not

---

[3] The plaintiff has not advanced the plausible arguments that homosexuals constitute a suspect class, *see* L. Tribe, *American Constitutional Law* (1978) at 944–45 n. 17, or that one has a constitutional right to be a homosexual, *see, e.g.*, *Acanfora v. Board of Education*, 359 F. Supp. 843 (D. Md. 1973), *aff'd on other grounds*, 491 F.2d 498 (4th Cir. 1974). The first amendment aspect of the case makes it unnecessary for me to reach these issues, although they may very well be applicable to this kind of case.

always transform conduct into speech, *United States v. O'Brien*, 391 U.S. 367, 376 (1968), *Bonner* makes clear that this exact type of conduct as a vehicle for transmitting this very message can be considered protected speech.

Accordingly, the school's action must be judged by the standards articulated in *United States v. O'Brien*, 391 U.S. 367 (1968), and applied in *Bonner*: (1) was the regulation within the constitutional power of the government; (2) did it further an important or substantial governmental interest; (3) was the governmental interest unrelated to the suppression of free expression; and (4) was the incidental restriction on alleged first amendment freedoms no greater than essential to the furtherance of that interest?

I need not dwell on the first two *O'Brien* requirements: the school unquestionably has an important interest in student safety and has the power to regulate students' conduct to ensure safety. As to the suppression of free expression, Lynch's testimony indicated that his personal views on homosexuality did not affect his decision, and that but for the threat of violence he would let the two young men go together. Thus the government's interest here is not in squelching a particular message because it objects to its content as such. On the other hand, the school's interest is in suppressing certain speech activity because of the reaction its message may engender. Surely this is still suppression of free expression.

It is also clear that the school's action fails to meet the last criterion set out in *O'Brien*, the requirement that the government employ the "least restrictive alternative" before curtailing speech. The plaintiff argues, and I agree, that the school can take appropriate security measures to control the risk of harm. Lynch testified that he did not know if adequate security could be provided, and that he would still need to sit down and make the necessary arrangements. In fact he has not made any effort to determine the need for and logistics of additional security. Although Lynch did not say that any additional security measures would be adequate, from the testimony I find that significant measures could be taken and would—in all probability—critically reduce the likelihood of any disturbance. As Lynch's own testimony indicates, police officers and teachers will be present at the dance, and have been quite successful in the past in controlling whatever problems arise, including unauthorized drinking. Despite the ever-present possibility of violence at sports events, adequate discipline has been maintained. From Lynch's testimony, I have every reason to believe that additional school or law enforcement personnel could be used to "shore up security" and would be effective. It should also be noted that Lynch testified that if he considered it impossible to provide adequate security he would move to cancel the dance. The Court appreciates that controlling high school students is no easy task. It is, of course, impossible to guarantee that no harm will occur, no matter what measures are taken. But only one student so far has attempted to harm Aaron, and no evidence was introduced of other threats. The measures taken already, especially the escort system, have been highly effective in preventing any further problems at school. Appropriate security measures coupled with a firm, clearly communicated attitude by the administration that any disturbance will not be tolerated appear to be a realistic, and less restrictive, alternative to prohibiting Aaron from attending the dance with the date of his choice.

The analysis so far has been along traditional First Amendment lines, making no real allowance for the fact that this case arises in a high school setting. The most difficult problem this controversy presents is how this setting should affect the result. *Tinker v. Des Moines Independent Community School District*, 393 U.S. 503 (1969), makes clear that high school students do not "shed their constitutional rights to freedom of speech or expression at the schoolhouse gate." * * *

Tinker did, however, indicate that there are limits on first amendment rights within the school:

> A student's rights, therefore, do not embrace merely the classroom hours. When he is in the cafeteria, or on the playing field, or on the campus during the authorized hours, he may express his opinions, even on controversial subjects like the conflict in Vietnam, if he does so without "materially and substantially interfer[ing] with the requirements of appropriate discipline in the operation of the school" and without colliding with the rights of others. *But conduct by the student, in class or out of it, which for any reason—whether it stems from time, place or type of behavior—materially disrupts classwork or involves substantial disorder or invasion of the rights of others is, of course, not immunized by the constitutional guarantee of freedom of speech.*

It seems to me that here, not unlike in *Tinker*, the school administrators were acting on "an undifferentiated fear or apprehension of disturbance." True, Aaron was punched and then security measures were taken, but since that incident he has not been threatened with violence nor has he been attacked. There has been no disruption at the school; classes have not been cancelled, suspended, or interrupted. In short, while the defendants have perhaps shown more of a basis for fear of harm than in *Tinker*, they have failed to make a "showing" that Aaron's conduct would "materially and substantially interfere" with school discipline. However, even if the Court assumes that there is justifiable fear and that Aaron's peaceful speech leads, or may lead, to a violent reaction from others, the question remains: may the school prohibit the speech, or must it protect the speaker?

It is certainly clear that outside of the classroom the fear—however justified—of a violent reaction is not sufficient reason to restrain such speech in advance, and an actual hostile reaction is rarely an adequate basis for curtailing free speech. Thus, the question here is whether the interest in school discipline and order, recognized in *Tinker*, requires a different approach.

After considerable thought and research, I have concluded that even a legitimate interest in school discipline does not outweigh a student's right to peacefully express his views in an appropriate time, place, and manner.[5] To rule otherwise would completely subvert free speech in the schools by granting other students a "heckler's veto," allowing them to decide—through prohibited and violent methods—what speech will be heard. The First Amendment does not tolerate mob rule by unruly school children. This conclusion is bolstered by the fact that any disturbance here, however great, would not interfere with the main business of school—education. No classes or school work would be affected; at the very worst an optional social event, conducted by the students for their own enjoyment, would be marred. In such a context, the school does have an obligation to take reasonable measures to protect and foster free speech, not to stand helpless before unauthorized student violence. * * *

The present case is so difficult because the court is keenly sensitive to the testimony regarding the concerns of a possible disturbance, and of physical harm to Aaron or Paul. However, I am convinced that meaningful security measures are possible, and the First Amendment

---

[5] The second reason relied upon by the *Bonner* court in finding the GSO social events to be speech-related was the interpretation placed upon those events by the community. There the university prohibited the gay social events because the community considered them "shocking and offensive," "a spectacle, an abomination," an "affront" to townspeople, "grandstanding," inflammatory, "undermin[ing] the university within the state," and distasteful. The first circuit concluded that "[we] do not see how these statements can be interpreted to avoid the conclusion that the regulation imposed was based in large measure, if not exclusively, on the content of the GSO's expression." *Bonner* at 661. I quite agree that these statements of community outrage indicate that the *content*, i.e. the homosexual-ness, of the GSO's activities led to the strong reaction and the prohibition, not the fact that they were dances. With all due respect, however, I am puzzled by how this reaction proves the *expressive* nature of these activities. Community outrage per se does not transform conduct into speech, or even indicate that it is speech; communities have reacted with outrage similar to that of the citizens of New Hampshire to such non-expressive activities as Hester Prynne's adultery, the dumping of chemicals into Love Canal, and the Son of Sam murders. It is hard in *Bonner* to separate the community's opposition to the GSO's acts from its opposition to its message (if the acts had a message); surely they opposed both. Same-sex dancing may have an expressive element, but it is also action, and potentially objectionable as such.

Insofar as *Bonner* directs me to consider community reaction in assessing expressive content, I conclude that the community disapproves of the content of Aaron's message and that the vehemence of their opposition to his intended escort is based in part on this disapproval of what he is trying to communicate. The school here professes to be unconcerned with the content of the plaintiff's message, but their concern with townspeople's reaction is, indirectly, content-related.

requires that such steps be taken to protect—rather than to stifle—free expression. Some may feel that Aaron's attendance at the reception and the message he will thereby convey is trivial compared to other social debates, but to engage in this kind of a weighing in process is to make the content-based evaluation forbidden by the First Amendment.

As to the other concern raised by *Tinker*, some people might say that Aaron Fricke's conduct would infringe the rights of the other students, and is thus unprotected by *Tinker*. This view is misguided, however. Aaron's conduct is quiet and peaceful; it demands no response from others and—in a crowd of some five hundred people—can be easily ignored. Any disturbance that might interfere with the rights of others would be caused by those students who resort to violence, not by Aaron and his companion, who do not want a fight.

Because the free speech claim is dispositive, I find it unnecessary to reach the plaintiff's right of association argument or to deal at length with his equal protection claim.[6] I find that the plaintiff has established a probability of success on the merits and has shown irreparable harm; accordingly his request for a preliminary injunction is hereby granted.

As a final note, I would add that the social problems presented by homosexuality are emotionally charged; community norms are in flux, and the psychiatric profession itself is divided in its attitude toward homosexuality. This Court's role, of course, is not to mandate social norms or impose its own view of acceptable behavior. It is instead, to interpret and apply the Constitution as best it can. The Constitution is not self-explanatory, and answers to knotty problems are inevitably inexact. All that an individual judge can do is to apply the legal precedents as accurately and as honestly as he can, uninfluenced by personal predilections or the fear of community reaction, hoping each time to disprove the legal maxim that "hard cases make bad law."

---

[6] This case can also be profitably analyzed under the Equal Protection Clause of the fourteenth amendment. In preventing Aaron Fricke from attending the senior reception, the school has afforded disparate treatment to a certain class of students—those wishing to attend the reception with companions of the same sex. Ordinarily, a government classification need only bear a rational relationship to a legitimate public purpose; . . . [however] [w]here, as here, government classification impinges on a first amendment right, the government is held to a higher level of scrutiny. *Chicago Police Department v. Mosley*, 408 U.S. 92 (1972). I find that principal Lynch's reason for prohibiting Aaron's attendance at the reception—the potential for disruption—is not sufficiently compelling to justify a classification that would abridge first amendment rights.

McMillen v. Itawamba County School District

United States District Court, Northern District of Mississippi, 2010
702 F. Supp. 2d 699

DAVIDSON, DISTRICT JUDGE.

Plaintiff, Constance McMillen ("Constance"), is a senior at Itawamba Agricultural High School ("IAHS") in Fulton, Mississippi. Constance has been openly identified as a lesbian at school since the eighth grade. Last semester, Constance asked her girlfriend, who is a fellow student at IAHS, to be her date to the IAHS Junior and Senior prom ("prom") and her girlfriend accepted her invitation.

According to a Memorandum to IAHS Juniors and Seniors issued on February 5, 2010, the prom was scheduled to be held in the IAHS Commons on April 2, 2010 . . . Constance approached the assistant principal, Rick Mitchell, to ask permission to bring her girlfriend as her date to the prom. Constance was informed that they could attend with two guys as their dates but could not attend together as a couple.

Constance then met with Principal Trae Wiygul ("Wiygul") and Superintendent Teresa McNeese ("McNeese") to ask for permission to bring her girlfriend as her date to the prom and was told the two could attend separately but not together as a couple. In addition, Constance was informed that she and her girlfriend would not be allowed to slow dance together because it could "push people's buttons." Constance testified that Superintendent McNeese also informed her that if she and her girlfriend made anyone uncomfortable while at the prom, they would be "kicked out." Constance also inquired as to whether she would be allowed to wear a tuxedo to the prom. Both Wiygul and McNeese informed Constance that only boys were allowed to wear tuxedos. Further, after checking with the Itawamba County Board of Education, Superintendent McNeese informed Constance that girls were not allowed to even wear slacks and a nice top but must wear a dress. Disappointed by Defendants' answers, Constance contacted the ACLU. The ACLU then sent Defendants a letter demanding it change its policies which prevent Constance from attending the prom with a same-sex date and from wearing a tuxedo. * * *

On March 10, 2010, after [a] special meeting was held, the Itawamba County Board of Education, issued a statement to the press, announcing its intent to cancel the prom. The School Board stated in its announcement, in part:

> Due to the distractions to the educational process caused by recent events, the Itawamba School District has decided to not host a prom at Itawamba Agricultural High School this year. It is our hope that private citizens will organize an event for the juniors and seniors. However, at this time, we feel that it is in

the best interest of the Itawamba County School District, after taking into consideration the education, safety, and well being of our students, that the Itawamba County School District not host a junior/senior prom at [IAHS].

* * * Constance testified that she considered it important to attend prom because it is a "part of high school that everyone remembers" and that she wanted to share that with her girlfriend who is special to her. Constance wants to attend the prom with her girlfriend because she does not want to hide her sexual orientation. Constance further testified that she feels that the school is attempting to force her to pretend that she is someone she is not by going with a male date. Constance testified that she believes gay students have the same right as straight students to not only attend the prom with the person they are dating but also to dance with that person. According to Constance, "if [she] cannot share the prom experience with [her] girlfriend then there is not any point in going." Constance also believes that students should not be forced to wear clothes that conform to traditional gender norms and testified that she wants to wear a tuxedo to the prom so that she can express to her school community that "it's perfectly okay for a woman to wear a tuxedo, and that the school shouldn't be allowed to make girls wear a dress if that's not what they are comfortable in." Constance does not want to attend the prom if IAHS does not allow female students to wear tuxedos. * * *

In order for the court to grant a preliminary injunction, Constance must establish the following elements:

(1) a substantial likelihood of success on the merits;

(2) a substantial threat that the plaintiff will suffer irreparable injury if the injunction is denied;

(3) that the threatened injury to the plaintiff outweighs any damage that an injunction might cause the defendant; and

(4) that granting the injunction will not disserve the public interest.

a.   Substantial Likelihood of Success on the Merits

The First Amendment of the Constitution states that "Congress shall make no law . . . abridging the freedom of speech." U.S. Const. amend. I. "[I]f the constitutional conception of 'equal protection of the laws' means anything, it must at the very least mean that a bare desire to harm a politically unpopular group cannot constitute a legitimate governmental interest." *Romer v. Evans*, 517 U.S. 620, 634–35, 116 S. Ct. 1620, 1628 134 L. Ed. 2d 855 (1996). The United States Supreme Court has "recognized that the 'vigilant protection of constitutional freedoms is nowhere more vital than in the community of American schools.'" The Fifth Circuit has established that the "expression of one's identity and affiliation to unique social groups" may constitute "speech" as envisioned by the First Amendment. *See Canady v. Bossier Parish Sch. Bd.*, 240 F.3d 437, 441 (5th Cir. 2001). The United States Supreme Court has also held that "states and their agencies, such as the Defendant, cannot set-out homosexuals for special treatment, neither inclusive or [sic] exclusive." *Collins v. Scottsboro City Bd. of Educ.*, CV–2008–90 (38th Judicial District March 28, 2008) (*citing Romer v. Evans*, 517 U.S. 620, 116 S. Ct. 1620, 134 L. Ed. 2d 855 (1996)). * * *

In *Fricke v. Lynch*, 491 F. Supp. 381, 385 (D.R.I. 1980), a factually similar case, the United States District Court of Rhode Island held that a male high school student's desire to take a same-sex date to his prom had significant expressive content which brought it within the ambit of the First Amendment. *See Fricke v. Lynch*, 491 F. Supp. at 385. The Rhode Island district court found that Fricke's belief that he had "a right to attend and participate just like all other students and that it would be dishonest to his own sexual identity to take a girl to the dance" coupled with the fact he felt "his attendance would have a certain political element and would be a statement for equal rights and human rights" is "the exact type of conduct" that "can be considered protected speech." *Id.* at 385.

In *Gay Students Organization of New Hampshire v. Bonner*, 509 F.2d 652, 659 (1st Cir. 1974), the First Circuit opined that "GSO social functions do not constitute 'pure speech', but conduct may have a communicative content sufficient to bring it within the ambit of the First Amendment." * * * The First Circuit held that the University's policy banning the GSO from holding social functions was content related and "the curtailing of expression which [the University] find[s] abhorrent or offensive cannot provide the important governmental interest upon which impairment of First Amendment freedoms must be predicated." *Gay Students Org.*, 509 F.2d at 662 (citations omitted).

According to the clearly established case law, Defendants have violated her First Amendment rights by denying Constance's request to bring her girlfriend as her date to the prom.

Constance further believes that females should be allowed to dress in non-gender-conforming attire, and that, in particular, she should be permitted to wear a tuxedo to the prom. In *Canady,* the Fifth Circuit recognized that "[c]lothing may also symbolize ethnic heritage religious beliefs, and political and social views." *Canady,* 240 F.3d at 440. The Fifth Circuit stated that "the choice to wear clothing as a symbol of an opinion or cause is undoubtedly protected under the First Amendment if the message is likely to be understood by those intended to view it." *Id.* at 441 (*citing Texas v. Johnson*, 491 U.S. 397, 404, 109 S. Ct. 2533, 105 L. Ed. 2d 342 (1989)).

The United States Supreme Court has held that "[i]n deciding whether particular conduct possesses sufficient communicative elements to bring the First Amendment into play, we have asked whether '[a]n intent to convey a particularized message was present, and [whether] the likelihood was great that the message would be understood by those who viewed it.'" * * *

In *Tinker*, students were suspended from school for wearing black armbands in protest of the Vietnam War. *See Tinker*, 393 U.S. at 508–14, 89 S. Ct. 733. The United States Supreme Court held that students may wear color patterns or styles with the intent to express a particular matter unless school officials can demonstrate the expression would "substantially interfere with the work of the school or impinge upon the rights of the other students." *Id.* at 509, 89 S. Ct. 733 (citations omitted).

In *ACT-UP v. Walp*, 755 F. Supp. 1281 (M.D. Pa. 1991), the District Court of the Middle District of Pennsylvania found that the Pennsylvania House of Representatives violated the Plaintiffs' First Amendment rights when it closed the gallery during the governor's speech to prevent members of ACT-UP from expressing their views in an attempt to raise public awareness of acquired immune deficiency syndrome (AIDS). * * *

In the case *sub judice*, Constance requested permission to wear a tuxedo, or even pants and a nice shirt, to her prom with the intent of communicating to the school community her social and political views that women should not be constrained to wear clothing that has traditionally been deemed "female" attire. * * *

The record shows Constance has been openly gay since eighth grade and she intended to communicate a message by wearing a tuxedo and to express her identity through attending prom with a same-sex date. The Court finds this expression and communication of her viewpoint is the type of speech that falls squarely within the purview of the First Amendment. * * * The Court finds that Constance's First Amendment rights have been violated and therefore, she has established * * * a substantial likelihood of success on the merits with respect to her First Amendment claim.

[The court went on to find that Constance had demonstrated both a substantial threat of imminent injury and that the threat of injury to her outweighed any injury that granting an injunction might cause.] * * *

d. Public Interest

"[I]t is in the public's interest to protect rights guaranteed under the Constitution of the United States." The United States Supreme Court has stated, "[t]he right to speak freely and to promote diversity of ideas and programs is therefore one of the chief distinctions that sets us apart from totalitarian regimes." * * *

However, the Court is of the opinion that its failure to grant an injunction in this instance does not disserve the public interest. Defendants testified that a parent sponsored prom which is open to *all* IAHS students has been planned and is scheduled for April 2, 2010. Though the details of the "private" prom are unknown to the Court, Defendants have made representations, upon which this Court relies, that *all* IAHS students, including the Plaintiff, are welcome and encouraged to attend. The Court finds that requiring Defendants to step-back into a sponsorship role at this late date would only confuse and confound the community on the issue. Parents have taken the initiative to plan and pay for a "private" prom for the Juniors and Seniors of IAHS and to now require Defendants to host one as it had originally planned would defeat the purpose and efforts of those individuals.

In addition, the power and interests of an Article III Court has its limits and under the circumstances, the Court cannot go into the business of planning and overseeing a prom hosted by Defendants, especially in light of the fact that the parents of IAHS students have already undertaken such tasks. Therefore, the Court finds that issuing an injunction would be disruptive to the efforts of the community and would not be in the public's interest. * * *

[T]he Court finds that Plaintiff's motion for preliminary injunction should be denied. This case remains active and Plaintiff, is she so desires, will be permitted to amend her Complaint to seek compensatory damages and any other appropriate relief.

DOE V. YUNITS

Superior Court of Massachusetts, 2000
2000 WL 33162199

GILES, JUDGE.

Plaintiff Pat Doe ("plaintiff"), a fifteen-year-old student, has brought this action by her next friend, Jane Doe, requesting that this court prohibit defendants from excluding the plaintiff from South Junior High School ("South Junior High"), Brockton, Massachusetts, on the basis of the plaintiff's sex, disability, or gender identity and expression. Plaintiff has been diagnosed with gender identity disorder, which means that, although plaintiff was born biologically male, she has a female gender identity. Plaintiff seeks to attend school wearing clothes and fashion accouterments that are consistent with her gender identity. Defendants have informed plaintiff that she could not enroll in school this academic year if she wore girls' clothes or accessories. . . .

Plaintiff began attending South Junior High, a Brockton public school, in September 1998, as a 7th grader. In early 1999, plaintiff first began to express her female gender identity by wearing girls' make-up, shirts, and fashion accessories to school. South Junior High has a dress code which prohibits, among other things, "clothing which could be disruptive or distractive to the educational process or which could affect the safety of students." In early 1999, the principal, Kenneth Cardone ("Cardone"), would often send the plaintiff home to change if she arrived at school wearing girls' apparel. On some occasions, plaintiff would change and return to school; other times, she would remain home, too upset to return. In June 1999, after being referred to a therapist by the South Junior High, plaintiff was diagnosed with gender identity disorder. Plaintiff's treating therapist, Judith Havens ("Havens"), determined that it was medically and clinically necessary for plaintiff to wear clothing consistent with the female gender and that failure to do so could cause harm to plaintiff's mental health.

Plaintiff returned to school in September 1999, as an 8th grader, and was instructed by Cardone to come to his office every day so that he could approve the plaintiff's appearance. Some days the plaintiff would be sent home to change, sometimes returning to school dressed differently and sometimes remaining home. During the 1999–2000 school year, plaintiff stopped attending school, citing the hostile environment created by Cardone. Because of plaintiff's many absences during the 1999–2000 school year, plaintiff was required to repeat the 8th grade this year.

Over the course of the 1998–1999 and 1999–2000 school years, plaintiff sometimes arrived at school wearing such items as skirts and dresses, wigs, high-heeled shoes, and padded bras with tight shirts. The school faculty and administration became concerned because the plaintiff was experiencing trouble with some of her classmates. Defendants cite one occasion when the school adjustment counselor had to restrain a male student because he was threatening to punch the plaintiff for allegedly spreading rumors that the two had engaged in oral sex. Defendants also point to an instance when a school official had to break up a confrontation between the plaintiff and a male student to whom plaintiff persistently blew kisses. At another time, plaintiff grabbed the buttock of a male student in the school cafeteria. Plaintiff also has been known to primp, pose, apply make-up, and flirt with other students in class. Defendants also advance that the plaintiff sometimes called attention to herself by yelling and dancing in the halls. Plaintiff has been suspended at least three times for using the ladies' restroom after being warned not to.

On Friday, September 1, 2000, Cardone and Dr. Kenneth Sennett ("Sennett"), Senior Director for Pupil Personnel Services, met with the plaintiff relative to repeating the 8th grade. At that meeting, Cardone and Sennett informed the plaintiff that she would not be allowed to attend South Junior High if she were to wear any outfits disruptive to the educational process, specifically padded bras, skirts or dresses, or wigs. On September 21, 2000, plaintiff's grandmother tried to enroll plaintiff in school and was told by Cardone and Sennett that plaintiff would not be permitted to enroll if she wore any girls' clothing or accessories. Defendants allege that they have not barred the plaintiff from school but have merely provided limits on the type of dress the plaintiff may wear. Defendants claim it is the plaintiff's own choice not to attend school because of the guidelines they have placed on her attire. Plaintiff is not currently attending school, but the school has provided a home tutor for her to allow her to keep pace with her classmates. * * *

The Massachusetts Declaration of Rights, Article XVI (as amended by Article 77) provides, "the right of free speech shall not be abridged" . . . . The analysis of this article is guided by federal free speech analysis. According to federal analysis, this court must first determine whether the plaintiff's symbolic acts constitute expressive speech which is protected, in this case, by Article VXI of the Massachusetts Declaration of Rights. See *Texas v. Johnson, supra,* [491 U.S. 397, 109 S. Ct. 2533, 105 L. Ed. 2d 342 (1989)] citing *Spence v. Washington, supra,* [418 U.S. 405, 94 S. Ct. 2727, 41 L. Ed. 2d 842 (1974)]. If the speech is expressive, the court must next determine if the defendants' conduct was impermissible because it was meant to suppress that speech. See *Texas v. Johnson,* 491 U.S. 397, 403, 105 L. Ed. 2d 342, 109 S. Ct. 2533 (1989), citing *United States v. O'Brien,* 391 U.S. 367, 377, 20 L. Ed. 2d 672, 88 S. Ct. 1673 (1968); see also *Spence v. Washington,* 418 U.S. 405, 414 n. 8, 41 L. Ed. 2d 842, 94 S. Ct. 2727 (1974). If the defendants' conduct is not related to the suppression of speech, furthers an important or substantial governmental interest, and is within the constitutional powers of the government, and if the incidental restriction on speech is no greater than necessary, the government's conduct is permissible. See *United States v. O'Brien, supra.* In addition, because this case involves public school students, suppression of speech that "materially and substantially interferes with the work of the school" is permissible. See *Tinker v. Des Moines Community School District,* 393 U.S. 503, 21 L. Ed. 2d 731, 738, 89 S. Ct. 733 (1969). * * *

Symbolic acts constitute expression if the actor's intent to convey a particularized message is likely to be understood by those perceiving the message. . . .

Plaintiff in this case is likely to establish that, by dressing in clothing and accessories traditionally associated with the female gender, she is expressing her identification with that gender. In addition, plaintiff's ability to express herself and her gender identity through dress is important to her health and well-being, as attested to by her treating therapist. Therefore, plaintiff's expression is not merely a personal preference but a necessary symbol of her very identity. . . .

This court must next determine if the plaintiff's message was understood by those perceiving it, i.e., the school faculty and plaintiff's fellow students. . . . In the case at bar, defendants contend that junior high school students are too young to understand plaintiff's expression of her female gender identity through dress and that "not every defiant act by a high school student is constitutionally protected speech." *Id.* at 558. However . . . here there is strong evidence that plaintiff's message is well understood by faculty and students. The school's vehement response and some students' hostile reactions are proof of the fact that the plaintiff's message clearly has been received. Moreover, plaintiff is likely to establish, through testimony, that her fellow students are well aware of the fact that she is a biological male more comfortable wearing traditionally "female"-type clothing because of her identification with that gender. * * *

Plaintiff also will probably prevail on the merits of the second prong of the *Texas v. Johnson* test, that is, the defendants' conduct was meant to suppress plaintiff's speech. Defendants in this case have prohibited the plaintiff from wearing items of clothing that are traditionally labeled girls' clothing, such as dresses and skirts, padded bras, and wigs. This constitutes direct suppression of speech because biological females who wear items such as tight skirts to school are unlikely to be disciplined by school officials, as admitted by defendants' counsel at oral argument. . . . Therefore, the test set out in *United States v. O'Brien*, which permits restrictions on speech where the government motivation is not directly related to the content of the speech, cannot apply here. Further, defendants' argument that the school's policy is a content-neutral regulation of speech is without merit because, as has been discussed, the school is prohibiting the plaintiff from wearing clothes a biological female would be allowed to wear. Therefore, the plaintiff has a likelihood of fulfilling the *Texas v. Johnson* test that her speech conveyed a particularized message understood by others and that the defendants' conduct was meant to suppress that speech. * * *

This court also must consider if the plaintiff's speech "materially and substantially interferes with the work of the school." . . . Defendants argue that they are merely preventing disruptive conduct on the part of the plaintiff by restricting her attire at school. Their argument is unpersuasive. Given the state of the record thus far, the plaintiff has demonstrated a likelihood of proving that defendants, rather than attempting to restrict plaintiff's wearing of distracting items of clothing, are seeking to ban her from donning apparel that can be labeled "girls' clothes" and to encourage more conventional, male-oriented attire. Defendants argue that any other student who came to school dressed in distracting clothing would be disciplined as the plaintiff was. However, defendants overlook the fact that, if a female student came to school in a frilly dress or blouse, make-up, or padded bra, she would go, and presumably has gone, unnoticed by school officials. Defendants do not find plaintiff's clothing distracting *per se*, but, essentially, distracting simply because plaintiff is a biological male.

In addition to the expression of her female gender identity through dress, however, plaintiff has engaged in behavior in class and towards other students that can be seen as detrimental to the learning process. This deportment, however, is separate from plaintiff's dress. Defendants vaguely cite instances when the principal became aware of threats by students to beat up the "boy who dressed like a girl" to support the notion that plaintiff's dress alone is disruptive. To rule in defendants' favor in this regard, however, would grant those contentious students a "heckler's veto." See *Fricke v. Lynch*, 491 F. Supp. 381, 387 (D.R.I. 1980). The majority of defendants' evidence of plaintiff's disruption is based on plaintiff's actions as distinct from her mode of dress. Some of these acts may be a further expression of gender identity, such as applying make-up in class; but many are instances of misconduct for which any student would be punished. Regardless of plaintiff's gender identity, any student should be punished for engaging in harassing behavior towards classmates. Plaintiff is not immune from such punishment but, by the same token, should not be punished on the basis of dress alone.

Plaintiff has framed this issue narrowly as a question of whether or not it is appropriate for defendants to restrict the manner in which she can dress. Defendants, on the other hand, appear unable to distinguish between instances of conduct connected to plaintiff's expression of her female gender identity, such as the wearing of a wig or padded bra, and separate from it, such as grabbing a male student's buttocks or blowing kisses to a male student. The line between expression and flagrant behavior can blur, thereby rendering this case difficult for the court. It seems, however, that expression of gender identity through dress can be divorced from conduct in school that warrants punishment, regardless of the gender or gender identity of the offender. Therefore, a school should not be allowed to bar or discipline a student because of gender-identified dress but should be permitted to ban clothing that would be inappropriate if worn by any student, such as a theatrical costume, and to punish conduct that would be deemed offensive if committed by any student, such as harassing, threatening, or obscene behavior. See *Bethel v. Fraser*, 478 U.S. 675, 92 L. Ed. 2d 549, 106 S. Ct. 3159 (1986).

NOTES

1.   *Proms.* Aaron Fricke told his story of going to the prom in detail in Aaron Fricke, *One Life, One Prom, in* THE CHRISTOPHER STREET READER 21 (Michael Denneny et al. eds., 1983). There are reasons to believe that things

may have changed since Fricke's struggle, at least in some parts of the country. Commentator Andrew Sullivan observes:

> I grew up in a world where I literally never heard the word "homosexual" until I went to college. It is not uncommon to meet gay men in their early 20s who took a boy as their date to the high school prom. . . . [T]he psychological impact [of this cultural shift] on the younger generation cannot be overstated.

Andrew Sullivan, *The End of Gay Culture and the Future of Gay Life*, CHI. SUN-TIMES, Nov. 27, 2005, at B1. *See also* Julie Hubbard, *Bleckley School Officials Allowing Gay Prom Date*, MACON TELEGRAPH, Mar. 23, 2010 (story of gay teen receiving permission to bring his male prom date). In some schools, openly gay and lesbian students have been elected as homecoming king or queen. *Lesbian Becomes College Homecoming King*, ASSOCIATED PRESS, Mar. 2, 2006; Sarah Kershaw et al., *Gay Students Force New Look at Homecoming Traditions*, N.Y. TIMES, Nov. 27, 2004, at A12. In others, gay students have staged their own prom. *See, e.g.*, Cheryl Winkelman, *Tracy's Inaugural Gay Prom Goes Smoothly Despite Threats*, ALAMEDA TIMES-STAR, Apr. 14, 2006.

Transgender students have also made their presence more visible at school dances. In 2013, Cassidy Lynn Campbell of Huntington Beach, California became the first transgender student to be elected homecoming queen at a public high school. Treye Green, *Who Is Cassidy Lynn Campbell? Meet Transgender Teen Crowned High School's Homecoming Queen*, INT'L BUS. TIMES (Sept. 21, 2013, 5:52 PM), http://www.ibtimes.com/who-cassidy-lynn-campbell-meet-transgender-teen-crowned-high-schools-homecoming-queen-1409254. Several transgender high school students have also been elected prom queen or king. *See, e.g.*, Ross Forman, *Lesbian Wins Prom King at Lane Tech*, WINDY CITY TIMES (June 23, 2013), http://www.windycitymediagroup.com/lgbt/Lesbian-wins-prom-king-at-Lane-Tech/43366.html; *Transgender Teen Elected Prom Queen*, THE ADVOCATE (May 31, 2011, 5:40 PM), http://www.advocate.com/news/daily-news/2011/05/31/transgender-teen-elected-prom-queen.

However, as the events surrounding Constance McMillen's 2010 lawsuit reflect, problems still arise. Eventually, two private proms were held in Constance's community, both organized by parents. One, which a majority of the students attended, was not mentioned to McMillen. The second, which McMillen attended, had only five other student attendees and was deemed by media accounts to be a "fake prom." Subsequently, McMillen became a poster-child for the LGBT movement, including appearances on numerous TV shows and serving as a Grand Marshall of the 2010 New York City Pride Parade. *School Wrong, but Prom Won't Go On*, THE ADVOCATE, March 23, 2010, *available* at http://www.advocate.com/News/Daily_News/2010/03/23/McMillens_School_Wrong_But_Prom_Wont_Have_to_Go_On/. In addition, she won a $35,000 settlement from the school district for the violation of her rights, found by the district judge who had previously denied injunctive relief.

See Chris Joyner, *Mississippi School District Pays Lesbian Teen Over Prom*, USA Today, July 21, 2010, at 3A.

    2.   *Gender Identity and Dress.* Compare the *Fricke, McMillen* and *Doe* cases. How are they similar and how are they different? The two issues intersect in a concrete way when a transgender student seeks to attend a prom in gender-variant clothing. *See* Meg Kissinger & Meg Jones, *Crossing the Line?; Lake Geneva Student Who Wore Dress to Prom Is Suspended, Fined $249*, Milwaukee J. Sentinel, May 11, 2005, at B1; Shamus Toomey, *No Prom but Lots of Support for Man Who Wore Gown: School Officials Say He Violated Dress Code*, Chi. Sun-Times, May 26, 2006, at 4.

Straights & Gays for Equality v. Osseo Area Schools

United States Court of Appeals, Eighth Circuit, 2006
471 F.3d 908

Before Sprecher, Circuit Judge, Durfee, Senior Judge, and Eschbach, District Judge.

    The Osseo Area School District ("School District"), Maple Grove Senior High School ("MGSH"), and various school board members and school staff (collectively referred to as "appellants") appeal from an order of the district court granting the Straights and Gays for Equality ("SAGE"), N.R., and H.W.'s (collectively referred to as "appellees") motion for a preliminary injunction. The district court granted appellees' motion for a preliminary injunction on their Equal Access Act (EAA) claim and ordered appellants to grant SAGE the same access for meetings, avenues of communication, and other miscellaneous rights afforded to groups referred to as "curricular." We affirm.

    SAGE, an unincorporated association of students enrolled at MGSH, was formed to "promote tolerance and respect for [MGSH] students and faculty through education and activities relevant to gay, lesbian, bisexual, and transgender ('GLBT') individuals and their allies." N.R. and H.W. are students at MGSH and members of SAGE.

    MGSH, a high school within the School District, recognizes approximately 60 student groups, including SAGE. MGSH classifies student groups as either "curricular" or "noncurricular" under the Student Group Framework ("Framework"). The Framework defines "curricular" groups as those "[r]elated to the school's curriculum" and sponsored by the school. Curricular groups are allowed to "communicate via PA [public address system], Yearbook, scrolling screen" and "use other avenues of communication." They may also participate in "fundraising or field trips at principal [sic] discretion." Groups classified as "curricular" include, inter alia, cheerleading and synchronized swimming.

The Framework defines "noncurricular groups" as those "[n]ot related to the school's curriculum" and not sponsored by the school. The school limits noncurricular groups's [*sic*] communication avenues. They may only announce meetings by placing posters on a community bulletin board and outside their meeting places. They are prohibited from making announcements on the PA, in the yearbook, on the scrolling screen, or by other avenues of communication. They also may not fundraise or take field trips. The Framework classifies nine groups as "noncurricular," including SAGE.

Appellees contended that appellants were violating the EAA by affording certain noncurricular groups designated as curricular student groups, such as cheerleading and synchronized swimming, with greater access to school facilities and communication options than noncurricular groups such as SAGE. * * *

The EAA prohibits public secondary schools with a "limited open forum" from discriminating against students desiring to hold meetings on the basis of political, religious, philosophical, or other content of the speech. *Bd. of Educ. of the Westside Cmty. Sch. v. Mergens*, 496 U.S. 226, 235, 110 S. Ct. 2356, 110 L. Ed. 2d 191 (1990) (citing 20 U.S.C. §§ 4071(a), (b)). A public secondary school creates a "limited open forum" whenever it " 'grants an offering to or opportunity for one or more noncurriculum related student groups to meet on school premises during noninstructional time.' " *Id.* (quoting 20 U.S.C. § 4071(b)). Thus, a school's obligations under the EAA are "triggered" even if the school only permits one noncurriculum group to meet. Once triggered the EAA forbids a school from prohibiting other groups, based on the content of their speech, from having "equal access" to meet on school premises.

> [Under *Mergens*, a] "curriculum related student group" is one that:

> directly relates to a school's curriculum if the subject matter of the group is actually taught, or will soon be taught, in a regularly offered course; if the subject matter of the group concerns the body of courses as a whole; if participation in the group is required for a particular course; or if participation in the group results in academic credit.

The circle of groups considered "curriculum related" has a relatively small circumference and does not include "anything remotely related to abstract educational goals"; instead, the Court limited the definition of "curriculum related student group" to support "Congress's intent to provide a low threshold for triggering the Act's requirements."

For example, a French club is directly related to the school's curriculum if the school teaches French in a regularly offered course or plans to teach French in the foreseeable future. Likewise, a student government organization is directly related to the curriculum if it addresses matters relating to the body of courses offered by the school. *Id.* Also, both band and choir directly relate to the school's curriculum if they are offered as part of the school's regular curriculum.

In contrast, although the EAA does not define "noncurriculum related student group," the Supreme Court has interpreted the phrase broadly to mean "any student group that does not *directly* relate to the body of courses offered by the school." (emphasis in original) "Whether a specific student group is a 'noncurriculum related student group' will [ ] depend on a particular school's curriculum, but such determinations [are] subject to factual findings well within the competence of trial courts to make." Additionally, courts must look to the school's "actual practice rather than its stated policy" in determining whether a student group is noncurriculum related. * * *

Here, MGSH does not prohibit SAGE from meeting at the school or utilizing some avenues of communication; however, the issue is not whether SAGE has access to some avenues of communication but whether it has equal access to the same avenues of communication as other noncurriculum related groups. We hold that it does not.[4]

First, no regularly offered course at MGSH teaches or will teach the subject matter of cheerleading or synchronized swimming. With regard to cheerleading, the "subject matter" of cheerleading is dance, gymnastics, jumps, and stunts, which are performed for the purpose of creating team spirit at athletic contests. While the MGSH Registration Handbook does list "Body Control" as a "theme" for its physical education classes—which includes dance, gymnastics, and tumbling—none of the offered courses listed in the Handbook, as in *Pope*, actually teach all of the subject matter performed in cheerleading. Likewise, although synchronized swimming involves both swimming and gymnastics, which are listed under the "Body Control" theme and "Fitness" theme in the Handbook, it is not taught in a regularly offered course at MGSH.

Second, cheerleading and synchronized swimming do not concern the body of courses as a whole. Unlike a student government organization, neither the cheerleading squad nor the synchronized swimming team address concerns or formulate proposals relating to the body of courses as a whole at MGSH.

Finally, participation in cheerleading or synchronized swimming does not result in academic credit and is not required for a particular course.

---

[4] Appellants have not alleged that SAGE's meetings could "materially and substantially interfere with the orderly conduct of educational activities within the school" or interfere with MGSH's ability to maintain order and discipline at the school. *Mergens*, 496 U.S. at 241 (internal quotations and citation omitted). Therefore, our analysis is restricted to the issue of whether SAGE has equal access to the same avenues of communication as other noncurriculum related groups.

Because cheerleading and synchronized swimming, like SAGE, are noncurriculum related groups, SAGE is entitled to the same avenues of communication as those groups. Our conclusion that SAGE is likely to prevail on the merits of its EAA claim, however, does not mean that MGSH "can never close a limited open forum once such a forum has been created." *Pope*, 12 F.3d at 1254. MGSH is "free to wipe out all of its noncurriculum related student groups and totally close its forum." *Id.* Furthermore, our holding does not prevent MGSH from legitimately categorizing cheerleading, synchronized swimming, and any other athletic groups as "curriculum related" by granting physical education academic credit to students who participate in such groups. * * *

Here, although MGSH has afforded students the opportunity to hold SAGE meetings in school classrooms and place posters on a community bulletin board and outside the meeting place, they have not, like student members of cheerleading and synchronized swimming, been allowed to communicate via the PA, yearbook, and scrolling screen. Additionally, the students have been prohibited from holding fundraising events or having field trips. Therefore, the student members of SAGE are entitled to a presumption of irreparable harm, as they will not be able to exercise their rights absent a preliminary injunction.

NOTES

1.   As gay-straight alliances have proliferated in high schools across the country, the Equal Access Act, enacted in 1984, has increasingly become part of the litigation landscape. In an example of a recent successful case, the American Civil Liberties Union pressured a public high school in Corpus Christi, Texas into recognizing a gay-straight alliance by threatening to sue under the EAA. *Flour Bluff High School Acknowledges Gay-Straight Alliance Club Has the Right to Meet*, AMERICAN CIVIL LIBERTIES UNION (Mar. 9, 2011), https://www.aclu.org/lgbt-rights/flour-bluff-high-school-acknowledges-gay-straight-alliance-club-has-right-meet. For a general overview, see Todd A. DeMitchell & Richard Fossey, *Student Speech: School Boards, Gay/Straight Alliances, and the Equal Access Act*, 2008 B.Y.U. EDUC. & L.J. 89 (2008); Eric W. Schulze, *Gay-Related Student Groups and the Equal Access Act*, 196 ED. L. REP. 369 (2005). In 2011, the U.S. Department of Education issued guidelines about the Act intended "to provide schools with the information and resources they need to help ensure that all students, including LGBT and gender non-conforming students, have a safe place to learn, meet, share experiences, and discuss matters that are important to them." *Key Policy Letters from the Education Secretary and Deputy Secretary*, U.S. DEP'T OF EDUC. (June 14, 2011), http://www2.ed.gov/policy/elsec/guid/secletter/110607.html.

2.   High school students are increasingly using the Fourteenth Amendment's equal protection clause to insist that public schools protect them from anti-gay harassment and discrimination. A landmark Seventh

Circuit ruling in 1996 authorized such a suit to go forward. *See Nabozny v. Podlesny*, 92 F.3d 446 (7th Cir. 1996). Following the Seventh Circuit's decision in *Nabozny*, a jury found that school officials had "failed to protect" Nabozny. Before the jury could award damages, the parties reached a settlement of nearly $1 million, covering damages and medical costs. *See* Terry Wilson, *Gay-Bashing Victim Awarded $1 Million for School Incident*, CHI. TRIB., Nov. 21, 1996, at 12.

Following *Nabozny*, the Ninth Circuit held that students may establish an equal protection violation by demonstrating that school officials either intentionally discriminated or acted with deliberate indifference. *Flores v. Morgan Hill Unified Sch. Dist.*, 324 F.3d 1130 (9th Cir. 2003).

3.   The social and psychological obstacles for LGBT students can be intense. Rates of harassment directed against LGBT teenagers are high. *See* Rebecca Bethard, *Chalk Talk: New York's Harvey Milk School: A Viable Alternative*, 33 J.L. & EDUC. 417, 417–18 (2004) (reporting a 1999 study indicating that 41.7% of LGBT students did not feel safe in school and that 69% had experienced harassment). A 1989 report on youth suicide issued by the U.S. Department of Health and Human Services (HHS) reported that gay and lesbian youth were more likely to suffer chronic depression and alcoholism and were "2 to 3 times more likely to attempt suicide than other young people." Paul Gibson, *Gay Male and Lesbian Youth Suicide, in* U.S. DEP'T OF HEALTH & HUMAN SERVS., 3 REPORT OF THE SECRETARY'S TASK FORCE ON YOUTH SUICIDE 110 (Marcia R. Feinleib ed., 1989). The report also found that such youth were more often forced to leave their homes as "push-aways" or "throw-aways" rather than running away on their own. *Id.* at 112. Gibson's stated assumptions that homosexuality was natural and that homosexuals should not be subject to discrimination proved quite controversial and drew a public disapproval of the report from then-HHS Secretary Louis W. Sullivan.

In 2011, the U.S. Centers for Disease Control and Prevention (CDC) released the results of a new study on lesbian, gay, and bisexual youth. Dana Rudolph, *Gay, Lesbian, Bisexual Youth More at Risk, Federal Study Finds*, KEEN NEWS SERV. (June 8, 2011), http://www.keennewsservice.com/2011/06/08/gay-lesbian-bisexual-youth-more-at-risk-federal-study-finds/. The CDC found that gay and lesbian students had higher risks than heterosexual students in seven of ten major health risk categories: behaviors related to violence, attempted suicide, tobacco use, alcohol use, other drug use, sexual behaviors, and weight management. *Id.* Bisexual students were at even higher risk. *Id.*

Recent state-level reports also suggest that LGBT youths continue to have higher incidence of suicide attempts. *See, e.g.*, CAL. SAFE SCH. COAL. & 4-H CTR. FOR YOUTH DEV., UNIV. CAL., DAVIS, SAFE PLACE TO LEARN: CONSEQUENCE OF HARASSMENT BASED ON ACTUAL OR PERCEIVED SEXUAL ORIENTATION AND GENDER NON-CONFORMITY AND STEPS FOR MAKING SCHOOLS SAFER 8 (2004), *available at* http://casafeschools.org/Safe

PlacetoLearnLow.pdf (finding that 45% of "students harassed based on actual or perceived sexual orientation . . . seriously consider[ed] suicide" and 35% "made a plan for suicide," compared to 14% and 9% for other students); MASS. DEP'T OF EDUC., 2003 YOUTH RISK BEHAVIOR SURVEY RESULTS 49 (2004) (finding that 32% of "sexual minority youth" attempt suicide, as compared to 7% of other students). Such suicides received increased news coverage in 2010, when a spate of a half-dozen teenagers killed themselves after anti-gay bullying. *See* Jeremy Hubbard, *Fifth Gay Teen Suicide in Three Weeks Sparks Debate*, ABC NEWS (Oct. 3, 2010), http://abcnews.go.com/US/gay-teen-suicide-sparks-debate/story?id=11788128. The suicides led to the "It Gets Better" campaign, organized by columnist Dan Savage, in which individuals posted videos to YouTube indicating support for gay youth, including such visible supporters as President Obama. *See* Brian Stelter, *Campaign Offers Help to Gay Youths*, N.Y. TIMES, Oct. 19, 2010, at A16.

4. Nineteen states and the District of Columbia have passed laws providing protection to gay students against discrimination or bullying based on their sexual orientation and/or gender identity. ARK. CODE ANN. § 6–18–514 (2011); CAL. EDUC. CODE § 220 (2006); CAL. PENAL CODE § 422.55 (2006); COLO. REV. STAT. § 22–32–109.1(1)(b) (2009); COLO. REV. STAT. § 24–34–301(7) (2008); CONN. GEN. STAT. § 10–15c (2006); D.C. CODE § 2–1402.41 (2006); 105 ILL. COMP. STAT. 5/27–23.7 (2010); IOWA CODE § 216.9; ME. REV. STAT. ANN. tit. 5, §§ 4601–02 (2006); MD. CODE ANN. EDUC. § 7–421 (2005); MASS. GEN. LAWS ch. 76, § 5 (2006); MINN. STAT. § 363A.13 (2005); N.C. GEN. STAT. § 115C-407.15; N.H. REV. STAT. § 193–F:1 (2010); N.J. STAT. ANN. §§ 18A:37–13 (2010); N.Y. EDUC. LAW § 313 (2006); OR. REV. STAT. § 659A.403 (2007); R.I. GEN. LAWS § 16–21–33 (2012); VT. STAT. ANN. tit. 16, § 11 (2001); WASH. REV. CODE §§ 28A.300.285(2), 9A.36.080(1) (2007); WIS. STAT. § 118.13 (2006).

In 2013, California became the first state to enact a broad law protecting the rights of transgender students, including the right to play on sex-segregated sports teams and access sex-segregated restrooms. Tom Verdin, *California's Transgender-Student Law: Kids Can Choose Bathrooms, Sports Teams*, CHRISTIAN SCI. MONITOR (Aug. 12, 2013), http://www.csmonitor.com/USA/Latest-News-Wires/2013/0812/California-s-transgender-student-law-Kids-can-choose-bathrooms-sports-teams. Also in 2013, Colorado parents won a lawsuit under the Colorado Anti-Discrimination Act against their transgender daughter's school. Ed Payne, *Transgender First-Grader Wins the Right to Use Girls' Restroom*, CNN (June 24, 2013, 3:15 PM), http://www.cnn.com/2013/06/24/us/colorado-transgender-girl-school/index. html. As a result of the lawsuit, their daughter will be allowed to use the girl's restroom at school. *Id.*

But laws against bullying and harassment have resulted in some pushback. State legislators in Arizona and Tennessee, for example, have introduced legislation to prevent anti-discrimination laws from taking effect. Hannah Ridge, *On LGBT Rights, Some States Are Actually Banning Bans on Discrimination*, POLICYMIC (Mar. 21, 2013), http://www.policymic.com/

articles/30641/on-lgbt-rights-some-states-are-actually-banning-bans-on-discrimination.

5. *Federal Legislation*. In 2010, members of Congress introduced the Student Non-Discrimination Act (SNDA), legislation to protect LGBT students from discrimination modeled after Title IX's gender discrimination protections. As of 2013, however, the legislation had not yet made it out of committee. Joy Resmovits, *Student Non-Discrimination Act: Jared Polis, Ileana Ros-Lehtinen Reintroduce Anti-Bullying Bill*, HUFFINGTON POST (Apr. 18, 2013, 1:57 PM), http://www.huffingtonpost.com/2013/04/18/student-non-discrimination-act_n_3110436.html.

6. In addition to the guidelines on the Equal Access Act described in Note 1, the U.S. Department of Education issued interpretive guidance to schools in 2010 indicating various mechanisms that can be used to enforce anti-bullying policies, including against LGBT youth. *See* October 26, 2010 Dear Colleague Letter, United States Department of Education Office for Civil Rights, http://www2.ed.gov/about/offices/list/ocr/letters/colleague-201010.pdf. The guidance arose out of a coordinated effort between the Departments of Education, Defense, Justice, Health and Human Services, Interior, and Agriculture. It indicated that the Department of Education considered anti-gay bullying a potential violation of Title IX's bar on gender harassment and thus would hold schools accountable for ensuring the safety of gay students. For an academic call for inclusive anti-bullying laws, such as those indicated by the Department of Education as being appropriate, see Julie Sacks and Robert S. Salem, *Victims Without Legal Remedies: Why Kids Need Schools to Develop Comprehensive Anti-Bullying Policies*, 72 ALB. L. REV. 147 (2009).

HARPER V. POWAY UNIFIED SCHOOL DISTRICT

United States Court of Appeals, Ninth Circuit, 2006
445 F.3d 1166, *vacated* 127 S. Ct. 1484 (2007) (mem.)

REINHARDT, CIRCUIT JUDGE.

May a public high school prohibit students from wearing T-shirts with messages that condemn and denigrate other students on the basis of their sexual orientation? Appellant in this action is a sophomore at Poway High School who was ordered not to wear a T-shirt to school that read, "BE ASHAMED, OUR SCHOOL EMBRACED WHAT GOD HAS CONDEMNED" handwritten on the front, and "HOMOSEXUALITY IS SHAMEFUL" handwritten on the back. He appeals the district court's order denying his motion for a preliminary injunction. Because he is not likely to succeed on the merits, we affirm the district court's order. Poway High School ("the School") has had a history of conflict among its students over issues of sexual orientation. In 2003, the School permitted a student group called the Gay-Straight Alliance to hold a "Day of Silence" at the School which, in the words of an Assistant Principal, is intended to "teach tolerance of others, particularly those of a different sexual orientation." During the days surrounding the 2003 "Day of Silence," a series of incidents and altercations occurred on the school campus as a result of anti-homosexual comments that were made by students. One such confrontation required the Principal to separate students physically. According to David LeMaster, a teacher at Poway, several students were suspended as a result of these conflicts. Moreover, a week or so after the "Day of Silence," a group of heterosexual students informally organized a "Straight-Pride Day," during which they wore T-shirts which displayed derogatory remarks about homosexuals. According to Assistant Principal Lynell Antrim, some students were asked to remove the shirts and did so, while others "had an altercation and were suspended for their actions."

Because of these conflicts in 2003, when the Gay-Straight Alliance sought to hold another "Day of Silence" in 2004, the School required the organization to consult with the Principal to "problem solve" and find ways to reduce tensions and potential altercations. On April 21, 2004, the date of the 2004 "Day of Silence," appellant Tyler Chase Harper wore a T-shirt to school on which "I WILL NOT ACCEPT WHAT GOD HAS CONDEMNED," was handwritten on the front and "HOMOSEXUALITY IS SHAMEFUL 'Romans 1:27' " was handwritten on the back. There is no evidence in the record that any school staff saw Harper's T-shirt on that day. The next day, April 22, 2004, Harper wore the same T-shirt to school, except that the front of the shirt read "BE ASHAMED, OUR SCHOOL EMBRACED WHAT GOD HAS CONDEMNED," while the back retained the same message as before, "HOMOSEXUALITY IS SHAMEFUL 'Romans 1:27.' " LeMaster, Harper's second period teacher, noticed Harper's shirt and observed "several students off-task talking about" the shirt. LeMaster, recalling the altercations that erupted as a result of "anti-homosexual speech" during the previous year's "Day of Silence," explained to Harper that he believed that the shirt was "inflammatory," that it violated the School's dress code, and that it "created a negative and hostile working environment for others." When Harper refused to remove his shirt and asked to speak to an administrator, LeMaster gave him a dress code violation card to take to the front office.

When Harper arrived at the front office, he met Assistant Principal Antrim. She told Harper that the "Day of Silence" was "not about the school promoting homosexuality but rather it was a student activity trying to raise other students' awareness regarding tolerance in their judgement [sic] of others." Antrim believed that Harper's shirt "was inflammatory under the circumstances and could cause disruption in the educational setting." Like LeMaster, she also recalled the altercations that had arisen as a result of anti-homosexual speech one year prior. According to her affidavit, she "discussed [with Harper] ways that he and students of his faith could bring a positive light onto this issue without the condemnation that he displayed on his shirt." Harper was informed that if he removed the shirt he could return to class. When Harper again refused to remove his shirt, the Principal, Scott Fisher, spoke with him, explaining his concern that the shirt was "inflammatory" and that it was the School's "intent to avoid physical conflict on campus." Fisher also explained to Harper that it was not healthy for students to be addressed in such a derogatory manner. According to Fisher, Harper informed him that he had already been "confronted by a group of students on campus" and was "involved in a tense verbal conversation" earlier that morning. The Principal eventually decided that Harper could not wear his shirt on campus, a decision that, he asserts, was influenced by "the fact that during the previous year, there was tension on campus surrounding the Day of Silence between certain gay and straight students." Fisher proposed some alternatives to wearing the shirt, all of which Harper turned down. Harper asked two times to be suspended. Fisher "told him that [he] did not want him suspended from school, nor did [he] want him to have something in his disciplinary record because of a stance he felt strongly about." Instead, Fisher told Harper that he would be required to remain in the front office for the remainder of the school day. * * *

Harper remained in the office for the last period of the day, after which he was instructed to proceed directly off campus. Harper was not suspended, no disciplinary record was placed in his file, and he received full attendance credit for the day.

[Harper filed a lawsuit raising several constitutional claims, including one based on his right to free speech. The district c-ourt denied Harper's motion for a preliminary injunction. Harper then filed an interlocutory appeal.]

The district court concluded that Harper failed to demonstrate a likelihood of success on the merits of his claim that the School violated his First Amendment right to free speech because, under *Tinker v. Des Moines Independent Community School District*, the evidence in the record was sufficient to permit the school officials to "reasonably . . . forecast substantial disruption of or material interference with school activities." 393 U.S. 503, 514 (1969). . . . We affirm the district court's denial of the requested preliminary injunction. Although we, like the district court, rely on *Tinker*, we rely on a different provision—that schools may prohibit speech that "intrudes upon . . . the rights of other students." *Tinker*, 393 U.S. at 508.

Public schools are places where impressionable young persons spend much of their time while growing up. They do so in order to receive what society hopes will be a fair and full education—an education without which they will almost certainly fail in later life, likely sooner rather than later. See *Brown v. Bd. of Educ.*, 347 U.S. 483, 493 (1954) ("[I]t is doubtful that any child may reasonably be expected to succeed in life if he is denied the opportunity of an education."). The public school, with its free education, is the key to our democracy. Almost all young Americans attend public schools. During the time they do—from first grade through twelfth—students are discovering what and who they are. Often, they are insecure. Generally, they are vulnerable to cruel, inhuman, and prejudiced treatment by others.

The courts have construed the First Amendment as applied to public schools in a manner that attempts to strike a balance between the free speech rights of students and the special need to maintain a safe, secure and effective learning environment. . . . In *Tinker*, the Supreme Court confirmed a student's right to free speech in public schools. In balancing that right against the state interest in maintaining an ordered and effective public education system, however, the Court declared that a student's speech rights could be curtailed under two circumstances. First, a school may regulate student speech that would "impinge upon the rights of other students." Second, a school may prohibit student speech that would result in "substantial disruption of or material interference with school activities." Because, as we explain below, the School's prohibition of the wearing of the demeaning T-shirt is constitutionally permissible under the first of the *Tinker* prongs, we conclude that the district court did not abuse its discretion in finding that Harper failed to demonstrate a likelihood of success on the merits of his free speech claim.

* * * Harper argues that *Tinker*'s reference to the "rights of other students" should be construed narrowly to involve only circumstances in which a student's right to be free from direct physical confrontation is infringed. * * *

We conclude that Harper's wearing of his T-shirt "colli[des] with the rights of other students" in the most fundamental way. Public school students who may be injured by verbal assaults on the basis of a core identifying characteristic such as race, religion, or sexual orientation, have a right to be free from such attacks while on school campuses. As *Tinker* clearly states, students have the right to "be secure and to be let alone." *Id.* Being secure involves not only freedom from physical assaults but from psychological attacks that cause young people to question their self-worth and their rightful place in society. The "right to be let alone" has been recognized by the Supreme Court, of course, as " 'the most comprehensive of rights and the right most valued by civilized men.' " Indeed, the "recognizable privacy interest in avoiding unwanted communication" is perhaps most important "when persons are 'powerless to avoid' it." Because minors are subject to mandatory attendance requirements, the Court has emphasized "the obvious concern on the part of parents, and school authorities acting in loco parentis, to protect children—especially in a captive audience. . . ." Although name-calling is ordinarily protected outside the school context, "[s]tudents cannot hide behind the First Amendment to protect their 'right' to abuse and intimidate other students at school."

Speech that attacks high school students who are members of minority groups that have historically been oppressed, subjected to verbal and physical abuse, and made to feel inferior, serves to injure and intimidate them, as well as to damage their sense of security and interfere with their opportunity to learn. The demeaning of young gay and lesbian students in a school environment is detrimental not only to their psychological health and well-being, but also to their educational development. Indeed, studies demonstrate that "academic underachievement, truancy, and dropout are prevalent among homosexual youth and are the probable consequences of violence and verbal and physical abuse at school." Susanne M. Stronski Huwiler and Gary Remafedi, *Adolescent Homosexuality*, 33 REV. JUR. U.I.P.R. REV. JUR. U.I.P.R. 151, 164 (1999); see also Thomas A. Mayes, *Confronting Same-Sex, Student-to-Student Sexual Harassment: Recommendations for Educators and Policy Makers*, 29 FORDHAM URB. L.J. 641, 655 (2001) (describing how gay students are at a greater risk of school failure and dropping out, most likely as a result of "social pressure and isolation"); Amy Lovell, *"Other Students Always Used to Say, 'Look At The Dykes' ": Protecting Students From Peer Sexual Orientation Harassment*, 86 CAL. L. REV. 617, 625–28 (1998) (summarizing the negative effects on gay students of peer sexual orientation harassment). One study has found that among teenage victims of anti-gay discrimination, 75% experienced a decline in academic performance, 39% had truancy problems and 28% dropped out of school. See Courtney Weiner, Note, *Sex Education: Recognizing Anti-Gay Harassment as Sex Discrimination Under Title VII and Title IX*, 37 COLUM. HUM. RTS. L. REV. 189, 225 (2005). Another study confirmed that gay students had difficulty concentrating in school and feared for their safety as a result of peer harassment, and that verbal abuse led some gay students to skip school and others to drop out altogether. HUMAN RIGHTS WATCH, HATRED IN THE HALLWAYS (1999), http://hrw.org/reports/2001/uslgbt/Final-05.htm#P609_91364. Indeed, gay teens suffer a school dropout rate over three times the national average. NAT'L MENTAL HEALTH ASS'N, BULLYING IN SCHOOLS: HARASSMENT PUTS GAY YOUTH AT RISK, http://www.nmha.org/pbedu/backtoschool/bullying GayYouth.pdf; see also Maurice R. Dyson, *Safe Rules or Gays' Schools? The Dilemma of Sexual Orientation Segregation in Public Education*, 7 U. PA. J. CONST. L. 183, 187 (2004) (gay teens face greater risks of "dropping out [and] performing poorly in school"); Kelli Armstrong, *The Silent Minority Within a Minority: Focusing on the Needs of Gay Youth in Our Public Schools*, 24 GOLDEN GATE U. L. REV. 67, 76–77 (1994) (describing how abuse by peers causes gay youth to experience social isolation and drop out of school). In short, it is well established that attacks on students on the basis of their sexual orientation are harmful not only to the students' health and welfare, but also to their educational performance and their ultimate potential for success in life.

Those who administer our public educational institutions need not tolerate verbal assaults that may destroy the self-esteem of our most vulnerable teenagers and interfere with their educational development. * * *

The dissent claims that we should not take notice of the fact that gay students are harmed by derogatory messages such as Harper's because there is no "evidence" that they are in fact injured by being shamed or humiliated by their peers. It is simply not a novel concept, however, that such attacks on young minority students can be harmful to their self-esteem and to their ability to learn. As long ago as in *Brown v. Board of Education*, the Supreme Court recognized that "[a] sense of inferiority affects the motivation of a child to learn." 347 U.S. at 494, 74 S.Ct. 686 (internal quotation marks omitted). If a school permitted its students to wear shirts reading, "Negroes: Go Back To Africa," no one would doubt that the message would be harmful to young black students. So, too, in the case of gay students, with regard to messages such as those written on Harper's T-shirt. As our dissenting colleague recently concluded, "[y]ou don't need an expert witness to figure out" the self-evident effect of certain policies or messages. *Jespersen v. Harrah's Operating Co., Inc.*, 444 F.3d 1104, 1117, at *13 (9th Cir. 2006) (Kozinski, Circuit Judge, dissenting). * * *

The dissent takes comfort in the fact that there is a political disagreement regarding homosexuality in this country. We do not deny that there is, just as there was a longstanding political disagreement about racial equality that reached its peak in the 1950's and about whether religious minorities should hold high office that lasted at least until after the 1960 presidential election, or whether blacks or Jews should be permitted to attend private universities and prep schools, work in various industries such as banks, brokerage houses, and Wall Street law firms, or stay at prominent resorts or hotels. Such disagreements may justify social or political debate, but they do not justify students in high schools or elementary schools assaulting their fellow students with demeaning statements: by calling gay students shameful, by labeling black students inferior or by wearing T-shirts saying that Jews are doomed to Hell. Perhaps our dissenting colleague believes that one can condemn homosexuality without condemning homosexuals. If so, he is wrong. To say that homosexuality is shameful is to say, necessarily, that gays and lesbians are shameful. There are numerous locations and opportunities available to those who wish to advance such an argument. It is not necessary to do so by directly condemning, to their faces, young

students trying to obtain a fair and full education in our public schools.
* * *

In his declaration in the district court, the school principal justified his actions on the basis that "any shirt which is worn on campus which speaks in a derogatory manner towards an individual or group of individuals is not healthy for young people. . . ." If, by this, the principal meant that all such shirts may be banned under *Tinker*, we do not agree. T-shirts proclaiming, "Young Republicans Suck," or "Young Democrats Suck," for example, may not be very civil but they would certainly not be sufficiently damaging to the individual or the educational process to warrant a limitation on the wearer's First Amendment rights. Similarly, T-shirts that denigrate the President, his administration, or his policies, or otherwise invite political disagreement or debate, including debates over the war in Iraq, would not fall within the "rights of others" *Tinker* prong.

Although we hold that the School's restriction of Harper's right to carry messages on his T-shirt was permissible under *Tinker*, we reaffirm the importance of preserving student speech about controversial issues generally and protecting the bedrock principle that students "may not be confined to the expression of those sentiments that are officially approved." *Tinker*. It is essential that students have the opportunity to engage in full and open political expression, both in and out of the school environment. Engaging in controversial political speech, even when it is offensive to others, is an important right of all Americans and learning the value of such freedoms is an essential part of a public school education. Indeed, the inculcation of "the fundamental values necessary to the maintenance of a democratic political system" is "truly the 'work of the schools.' " Limitations on student speech must be narrow, and applied with sensitivity and for reasons that are consistent with the fundamental First Amendment mandate. Accordingly, we limit our holding to instances of derogatory and injurious remarks directed at students' minority status such as race, religion, and sexual orientation. Moreover, our decision is based not only on the type and degree of injury the speech involved causes to impressionable young people, but on the locale in which it takes place. See *Tinker* (student rights must be construed "in light of the special characteristics of the school environment"). Thus, it is limited to conduct that occurs in public high schools (and in elementary schools). As young students acquire more strength and maturity, and specifically as they reach college age, they become adequately equipped emotionally and intellectually to deal with the type of verbal assaults that may be prohibited during their earlier years. Accordingly, we do not condone the use in public colleges or other public institutions of higher learning of restrictions similar to those permitted here.

Finally, we emphasize that the School's actions here were no more than necessary to prevent the intrusion on the rights of other students. Aside from prohibiting the wearing of the shirt, the School did not take the additional step of punishing the speaker: Harper was not suspended from school nor was the incident made a part of his disciplinary record. * * *

The dissent claims that although the School may have been justified in banning discussion of the subject of sexual orientation altogether, it cannot "gag[] only those who oppose the Day of Silence." As we have explained, however, although *Tinker* does not allow schools to restrict the non-invasive, non-disruptive expression of political viewpoints, it does permit school authorities to restrict "one particular opinion" if the expression would "impinge upon the rights of other students" or substantially disrupt school activities. *Tinker.* Accordingly, a school may permit students to discuss a particular subject without being required to allow them to launch injurious verbal assaults that intrude upon the rights of other students.

"A school need not tolerate student speech that is inconsistent with its basic educational mission, [] even though the government could not censor similar speech outside the school." Part of a school's "basic educational mission" is the inculcation of "fundamental values of habits and manners of civility essential to a democratic society." For this reason, public schools may permit, and even encourage, discussions of tolerance, equality, and democracy without being required to provide equal time for student or other speech espousing intolerance, bigotry, or hatred. As we have explained, because a school sponsors a "Day of Religious Tolerance," it need not permit its students to wear T-shirts reading, "Jews Are Christ-Killers" or "All Muslims Are Evil Doers." Such expressions would be "wholly inconsistent with the 'fundamental values' of public school education." Similarly, a school that permits a "Day of Racial Tolerance," may restrict a student from displaying a swastika or a Confederate Flag. * * *

We again emphasize that we do not suggest that all debate as to issues relating to tolerance or equality may be prohibited. As we have stated repeatedly, we consider here only the question of T-shirts, banners, and other similar items bearing slogans that injure students with respect to their core characteristics. Other issues must await another day. * * *

KOZINSKI, CIRCUIT JUDGE, dissenting:

While I find this a difficult and troubling case, I can agree with neither the majority's rationale nor its conclusion. On the record to date, the school authorities have offered no lawful justification for banning Harper's t-shirt and the district court should therefore have enjoined them from doing so pending the outcome of this case. * * *

School authorities may ban student speech based on the existence of "any facts which might reasonably [lead] school authorities to forecast substantial disruption." *Tinker*. The school authorities here have shown precious little to support an inference that Harper's t-shirt would "materially disrupt[ ] classwork." [Although the majority opinion ruled only on the "rights of others" prong of *Tinker*, the dissent offered a lengthy challenge to the factual basis for a finding of "substantial disruption" under the other *Tinker* prong. Much of this part of the dissent is omitted].

But there is a more fundamental issue here. The record reveals quite clearly that Harper's t-shirt was not an out-of-the-blue affront to fellow students who were minding their own business. Rather, Harper wore his t-shirt in response to the Day of Silence, a political activity that was sponsored or at the very least tolerated by school authorities. The Day of Silence is a protest sponsored by the Gay, Lesbian and Straight Education Network (GLSEN). According to a GLSEN press release, the Day of Silence is "an annual, national student-led effort in which participants take a vow of silence to peacefully protest the discrimination and harassment faced by lesbian, gay, bisexual and transgender (LGBT) youth in schools." Press Release, GLSEN, A New Record for the Day of Silence (Apr. 14, 2004), available at http://www.glsen.org/cgi-bin/iowa/all/news/record/1655.html. The point of this protest, as I understand it, is to promote tolerance toward all students, regardless of their sexual orientation.

Tolerance is a civic virtue, but not one practiced by all members of our society toward all others. This may be unfortunate, but it is a reality we must accept in a pluralistic society. Specifically, tolerance toward homosexuality and homosexual conduct is anathema to those who believe that intimate relations among people of the same sex are immoral or sinful. So long as the subject is kept out of the school environment, these differences of opinion need not clash. But a visible and highly publicized political action by those on one side of the issue will provoke those on the other side to express a different point of view, if only to avoid the implication that they agree. See Robert Bolt, A Man for All Seasons act 2, at 88 (1962) ("The maxim of the law is 'Silence gives consent.'").

Given the history of violent confrontation between those who support the Day of Silence and those who oppose it, the school authorities may have been justified in banning the subject altogether by denying both sides permission to express their views during the school day. I find it far more problematic—and more than a little ironic—to try to solve the problem of violent confrontations by gagging only those who oppose the Day of Silence and the point of view it represents. * * *

I cannot imagine that my colleagues would approve this in other situations. Say, for example, one school group—perhaps the Young Republicans—were to organize a day of support for the war in Iraq by encouraging students to wear a yellow armband. And suppose that other students responded by wearing t-shirts with messages such as "Marines are Murderers" and "U.S. Bombs Kill Babies." If a student whose brother was killed in Iraq assaulted a student wearing one of the anti-war t-shirts, would we approve a school's response that banned the t-shirts but continued to permit the yellow armbands? Not to worry, says the majority, because students can still sport t-shirts that criticize "the President, his administration, or his policies, or otherwise invite political disagreement or debate." But acceptance of homosexuality is a political disagreement and debate. It's not at all clear to me how one can criticize public officers and their policies without also addressing the controversial policies they adopt. For example, in 2004, San Francisco mayor Gavin Newsom issued marriage licenses to nearly 4,000 gay and lesbian couples. While some people view this as a courageous and principled action, others consider it an abomination. It's not at all clear to me how those in the latter camp could go about expressing their vehement disagreement with Mayor Newsom's policy without also expressing disdain for those who turned out at City Hall to take advantage of the policy.

[The dissent then moved on to the "rights of others" analysis]. Tinker does contain an additional ground for banning student speech, namely where it is an "invasion of the rights of others." The school authorities suggest that Harper's t-shirt violates California Education Code § 201(a), which provides that "[a]ll pupils have the right to participate fully in the educational process, free from discrimination and harassment." Defendants cite no California case holding that the passive display by one student of a message another student finds offensive violates this provision, and I am reluctant to so conclude on my own. The interaction between harassment law and the First Amendment is a difficult and unsettled one because much of what harassment law seeks to prohibit, the First Amendment seems to protect. Certainly, state law cannot trump the First Amendment by defining "harassment" as any conduct that another person finds offensive; far too much core First Amendment speech could thus be squelched.

* * * The "rights of others" language in *Tinker* can only refer to traditional rights, such as those against assault, defamation, invasion of privacy, extortion and blackmail, whose interplay with the First Amendment is well established. Surely, this language is not meant to give state legislatures the power to define the First Amendment rights of students out of existence by giving others the right not to hear that speech. Otherwise, a state legislature could effectively overrule *Tinker* by granting students an affirmative right not to be offended. To the extent

that state law purports to prohibit such language in the school context, it is patently unconstitutional. * * *

Nor can I join my colleagues in concluding that Harper's t-shirt violated the rights of other students by disparaging their homosexual status. As I understand the opinion, my colleagues are saying that messages such as Harper's are so offensive and demeaning that they interfere with the ability of homosexual students to partake of the educational environment. * * *

[This argument] raises many problems, the first of which is that it finds no support in the record. What my colleagues say could be true, but the only support they provide are a few law review articles, a couple of press releases by advocacy groups and some pop psychology. Aside from the fact that published articles are hardly an adequate substitute for record evidence, the cited materials are just not specific enough to be particularly helpful. None would seem to meet the standard of *Daubert v. Merrell Dow Pharmaceuticals, Inc.*, 509 U.S. 579, 592–94 (1993).

The first article, written by physicians but apparently not peer-reviewed, makes a general statement to the effect that academic under-achievement and other problems of homosexual youths "are the probable consequence of violence and verbal and physical abuse at school." Susanne M. Stronski Huwiler & Gary Remafedi, *Adolescent Homosexuality*, 33 REV. JUR. U.I.P.R. 151, 164 (1999). The article does not explain what the authors mean by "verbal . . . abuse," so it's not clear that Harper's t-shirt is even covered by the article's findings. Nor does the article explain the degree to which statements, as opposed to physical abuse, are responsible for the ill effects it discusses. The second article, written by a lawyer, not a health-care professional, merely points to general problems suffered by gay and lesbian youths during their school years—problems that are reinforced by a variety of school practices and policies. See Thomas A. Mayes, *Confronting Same-Sex, Student-to-Student Sexual Harassment: Recommendations for Educators and Policy Makers*, 29 FORDHAM URB. L.J. 641, 655–58 (2001). The other articles the majority cites also focus on physical abuse or threats, which the school can and should stamp out in a viewpoint neutral way. The majority finally resorts to press releases from advocacy groups—hardly a source "whose accuracy cannot reasonably be questioned." Fed.R.Evid. 201(b). What the materials the majority cites do establish is that the success of gay and lesbian teens in school is a complicated phenomenon, influenced by many factors. Even taking the sources on their own terms, none provides support for the notion that disparaging statements by other students, in the context of a political debate, materially interfere with the ability of homosexual students to profit from the school environment.

Nor do I find the proposition at the heart of the majority's opinion—that homosexual students are severely harmed by any and all statements casting aspersions on their sexual orientation—so self-evident as to require no evidentiary support. We take judicial notice of facts that aren't reasonably subject to dispute—gravity, the temperature at which ice melts, that commercial goods cost money, that time flows forward but not backward. But the fact that we can take judicial notice of certain indisputable facts does not mean that all facts are indisputable. Predicting the effect of certain kinds of statements on the learning ability of high school students is simply not the kind of "fact" that is judicially noticeable under any fair reading of Federal Rule of Evidence 201. Even the articles that the majority cites admit that the research on these effects is not unanimous. We have no business assuming without proof that the educational progress of homosexual students would be stunted by Harper's statement.

I find it significant, moreover, that Harper did not thrust his view of homosexuality into the school environment as part of a campaign to demean or embarrass other students. Rather, he was responding to public statements made by others with whom he disagreed. Whatever one might think are the psychological effects of unprovoked demeaning statements by one student against another, the effects may be quite different when they are part of a political give-and-take. By participating in the Day of Silence activities, homosexual students perforce acknowledge that their status is not universally admired or accepted; the whole point of the Day of Silence, as I understand it, is to dispute views like those characterized by Harper's t-shirt. Supporters of the Day of Silence may prefer to see views such as Harper's channeled into public discourse rather than officially suppressed but whispered behind backs or scribbled on bathroom walls. Confronting—and refuting—such views in a public forum may well empower homosexual students, contributing to their sense of self-esteem.

Beyond the question of evidentiary support, I have considerable difficulty understanding the source and sweep of the novel doctrine the majority announces today. Not all statements that demean other students can be banned by schools; the majority is very clear about this. The new doctrine applies only to statements that demean students based on their "minority status such as race, religion, and sexual orientation." Is this a right created by state law? By federal law? By common law? And if interference with the learning process is the keystone to the new right, how come it's limited to those characteristics that are associated with minority status? Students may well have their self-esteem bruised by being demeaned for being white or Christian, or having bad acne or weight problems, or being poor or stupid or any one of the infinite number of characteristics that will not qualify them for minority status. Under the rule the majority announces today, schools would be able to ban t-shirts with pictures of Mohammed wearing a bomb turban but not those with pictures of a Crucifix dipped in urine—yet Muslim and Christian children, respectively, may have their learning equally disrupted.

Even the concept of minority status is not free from doubt. In defining what is a minority—and hence protected—do we look to the national community, the state, the locality or the school? In a school that has 60 percent black students and 40 percent white students, will the school be able to ban t-shirts with anti-black racist messages but not those with anti-white racist messages, or vice versa? Must a Salt Lake City high school prohibit or permit Big Love t-shirts?

And at what level of generality do we define a minority group? If the Pope speaks out against gay marriage, can gay students wear to school t-shirts saying "Catholics Are Bigots," or will they be demeaning the core characteristic of a religious minority? And, are Catholics part of a monolithic Christian majority, or a minority sect that has endured centuries of discrimination in America? * * *

The fundamental problem with the majority's approach is that it has no anchor anywhere in the record or in the law. It is entirely a judicial creation, hatched to deal with the situation before us, but likely to cause innumerable problems in the future. Respectfully, I cannot go along. * * *

I also have sympathy for defendants' position that students in school are a captive audience and should not be forced to endure speech that they find offensive and demeaning. There is surely something to the notion that a Jewish student might not be able to devote his full attention to school activities if the fellow in the seat next to him is wearing a t-shirt with the message "Hitler Had the Right Idea" in front and "Let's Finish the Job!" on the back. This t-shirt may well interfere with the educational experience even if the two students never come to blows or even have words about it.

Perhaps school authorities should have greater latitude to control student speech than allowed them by [Tinker]. Perhaps the narrow exceptions of Tinker should be broadened and multiplied. Perhaps Tinker should be overruled. But that is a job for the Supreme Court, not for us. While I sympathize with my colleagues' effort to tinker with the law in this area, I am not convinced we have the authority to do so, which is why I must respectfully dissent.

Exhibit A

NOTES

1. After the Ninth Circuit's decision, the Supreme Court granted certiorari, vacated the judgment, and remanded the case with instructions to the Ninth Circuit to dismiss it as moot. *Harper ex rel. Harper v. Poway Unified Sch. Dist.*, 127 S. Ct. 1484 (2007) (mem.). By the time the Court acted, Tyler Harper had graduated. In its decision, the Court also denied the motion to intervene filed on behalf of Tyler Harper's younger sister, who had sought to continue the case.

2. The *Harper* case is hardly an isolated incident. There have been a number of recent flashpoints of controversy involving LGBT students and schools. For other cases involving students wearing t-shirts expressing a view on LGBT issues, see *Nuxoll v. Indian Prairie School District #204*, 523 F.3d 668 (7th Cir. 2008); *Okwedy v. Molinari*, 333 F.3d 339 (2d Cir. 2003). For scholarly perspectives, see Michael Kent Curtis, *Be Careful What You Wish for: Dueling High School T-Shirts, and the Perils of Suppression*, 44 WAKE FOREST L. REV. 431 (2009); Shannon Gilreath, *"Tell Your Faggot Friend He Owes Me $500 for My Broken Hand": Thoughts on a Substantive Equality Theory of Free Speech*, 44 WAKE FOREST L. REV. 557 (2009); John E. Taylor, Tinker *and Viewpoint Discrimination*, 77 U.M.K.C. L. REV. 569 (2009). There have also been curricular controversies. One high profile case involved parental protests in Massachusetts about grade school children reading books

featuring gay families. *See* Parker v. Hurley, 514 F.3d 87 (1st Cir. 2008), *cert. denied,* 129 S.Ct. 56, 172 L.Ed.2d 24 (2008). That controversy made its way to the Proposition 8 campaign in 2008, and provided the basis for claims about how schoolchildren would be affected by legalizing marriage in California. For more on the Proposition 8 campaign, see Chapter 6, Section II.B.1 *infra.*

3. In light of the obstacles confronted by openly gay students in some high schools, consider the idea that school districts ought to offer students the option of attending a separate LGBT school, like the Harvey Milk High School in New York. That school aims to protect LGBT youth from physical violence and emotional harm. For more about Harvey Milk High, see *The Harvey Milk High School*, HETRICK-MARTIN INST., http://www.hmi.org/page.aspx?pid=230 (last visited Oct. 17, 2013).

4. The difficulties encountered by some gay and transgender students in K-12 schools do not necessarily evaporate at the college level, but they can change. In the 1970s and 1980s, the major litigation battles involved securing recognition, funding, and equal facility access for LGBT student groups on campus. Many state universities fought student groups on this score, and the groups compiled an impressive record of litigation victories. *See, e.g., Gay & Lesbian Students Ass'n v. Gohn,* 850 F.2d 361 (8th Cir. 1988); *Gay Student Servs. v. Tex. A & M Univ.,* 737 F.2d 1317 (5th Cir. 1984), *cert. denied,* 471 U.S. 1001, 105 S.Ct. 1860, 85 L.Ed.2d 155 (1985); *Gay Lib v. Univ. of Mo.,* 558 F.2d 848 (8th Cir. 1977), *cert. denied sub nom. Ratchford v. Gay Lib,* 434 U.S. 1080, 98 S. Ct. 1276, 55 L. ed. 2d 789 (1978); *Gay Alliance of Students v. Matthews,* 544 F.2d 162 (4th Cir. 1976); *Gay Students Org. of Univ. of N.H. v. Bonner,* 509 F.2d 652 (1st Cir. 1974); *Student Coalition for Gay Rights v. Austin Peay State Univ.,* 477 F. Supp. 1267 (M.D. Tenn. 1979); *Wood v. Davison,* 351 F. Supp. 543 (N.D. Ga. 1972). *See also* Jane S. Schacter, *Sexual Orientation, Social Change, and the Courts,* 54 DRAKE L. REV. 861, 873 (2006) ("By interpreting the First Amendment to require that universities recognize and provide space to gay student groups, courts helped to establish a visible gay presence on college campuses. Student activism was the driving force in establishing this presence, but the substantial string of litigation victories was necessary to counter the recalcitrance of several universities. This was no small accomplishment. Coerced gay invisibility has historically been a central part of gay inequality. And, these cases facilitated not only visibility, but subsequent student and university activism in support of a broader range of non-discrimination policies.").

5. Compared to students at public universities, gay and bisexual students wishing to organize on private college campuses do not have the same legal recourse if denied resources or administrative recognition. In the District of Columbia, gay students at a private Catholic school, Georgetown University, filed suit under the local human rights act, which prohibits discrimination in public and private educational institutions on the basis of sexual orientation. Georgetown interposed a First Amendment defense, arguing that forced recognition of the gay student group would violate its rights of free exercise of religion. The District of Columbia's highest court, the

D.C. Court of Appeals, reached a compromise that neither party contemplated in their pleadings. It chose not to interpret the local human rights law as requiring Georgetown to "endorse" the student group, agreeing that this would violate the school's First Amendment rights. It did interpret the law, however, to require Georgetown to grant equal benefits to the group. "Although a compelling state interest may justify regulation of religiously motivated conduct," the court reasoned, "nothing can penetrate the constitutional shield protecting against official coercion to renounce a religious belief or to endorse a principle opposed to that belief." *Gay Rights Coalition of Georgetown Univ. Law Ctr. v. Georgetown Univ.*, 536 A.2d 1, 25 (D.C. 1987). With regard to the use of University resources, the court held that the District's compelling interest in eradicating discrimination on the basis of sexual orientation outweighed the University's First Amendment religious rights:

The [District of Columbia] Council determined that a person's sexual orientation, like a person's race and sex, for example, tells nothing of value about his or her attitudes, characteristics, abilities or limitations. It is a false measure of individual worth, one unfair and oppressive to the person concerned, one harmful to others because discrimination inflicts a grave and recurring injury upon society as a whole. . . . Only by eradicating discrimination based on sexual orientation, along with all other forms of discrimination unrelated to individual merit, could the District eliminate recurrent personal injustice and build a society which encourages and expects the full contribution of *every* member of the community in all their diversity and potential. * * *

> The compelling interests, therefore, that any state has in eradicating discrimination against the homosexually or bisexually oriented include the fostering of individual dignity, the creation of a climate and environment in which each individual can utilize his or her potential to contribute to and benefit from society, and equal protection of the life, liberty and property that the Founding Fathers guaranteed us all.

Id. at 32, 37.

Following the *Georgetown* decision, Congress initially attempted to force the District of Columbia City Council to amend its human rights law to exempt religiously-affiliated educational institutions from having to comply with the gay rights provisions of the law. Nation's Capital Religious Liberty and Academic Freedom Act, Pub. L. No. 100–462, § 145, 102 Stat. 2269 (1988) (adopting the Armstrong Amendment). The federal appellate court in the District of Columbia, however, ruled that forcing the Council to adopt such an amendment violated the First Amendment speech rights of the city councilors. *Clarke v. United States*, 886 F.2d 404 (D.C. Cir. 1989), *reh'g denied*, 898 F.2d 161, *vacated on other grounds*, 915 F.2d 699 (D.C. Cir. 1990). In response, Congress went ahead the next year and, with its plenary authority over the District of Columbia, amended the human rights law directly to exempt Georgetown and other religiously-affiliated institutions from the gay rights law. District of Columbia Appropriations Act of 1990, Pub. L. No. 101–168, § 141, 103 Stat. 1267, 1284 (1989).

In the meantime, Georgetown University announced its intention to abide by the initial court result, regardless of the later Congressional intervention, and signed a consent decree to that effect. *See* Lawrence Feinberg, *GU to Treat Homosexuals Equally*, WASH. POST, Nov. 1, 1988, at D5. Georgetown has become more hospitable to LGBT students since 2008, when the school opened an LGBTQ resource center in response to student protests about the school's response to anti-gay incidents. Kyle Spencer, *A Rainbow over Catholic Colleges*, N.Y. TIMES, July 30, 2013, at ED22. In 2013, Georgetown elected its first openly gay student body president. *Id.*

6.   LGBT students face particular challenges at religiously affiliated colleges and universities. Some Christian schools prohibit "homosexual behavior," raising questions for gay and lesbian students about whether they could lose scholarships or be expelled for holding hands with a partner or posting a picture on a gay website. Erik Eckholm, *Even on Religious Campuses, Students Fight for Gay Identity*, N.Y. TIMES, Apr. 19, 2011, at A1.

7.   Transgender students face additional challenges when they attend, or wish to attend, single-sex colleges and universities. Smith College rejected a transgender woman's application in 2013 because government documents listed the applicant as male. Zach Howard, *Elite Women's College Rejects Transgender Student, Prompts Outcry*, REUTERS (Mar. 28, 2013, 4:51 PM), http://www.reuters.com/article/2013/03/28/us-usa-college-transgender-idUS BRE92R0YT20130328. In response, activists pressured Smith to form a committee to address transgender applications. Glennisha Morgan, *Smith College Plans Committee to Address Transgender Student Applicants*, HUFFINGTON POST (May 5, 2013, 8:38 PM), http://www.huffingtonpost.com/ 2013/05/03/smith-college-transgender-committee-_n_3209606.html.   A transgender student was accepted during that same application cycle at Simmons College, a women's college in Massachusetts. *Simmons Primacy*, TRANSWOMEN @ SMITH (Mar. 21, 2013, 6:25 PM), http://calliowong.tumblr. com/post/45942592041/simmons-primacy.

8.   Anti-gay bullying and harassment cases are not restricted to incidents at K-12 schools. One particularly controversial case involved college roommates at Rutgers University. In 2010, Dharun Ravi and another classmate, Molly Wei, used a webcam to spy on Ravi's roommate, Tyler Clementi, having sex with a man. Lisa W. Foderaro, *Private Moment Made Public, Then a Fatal Jump*, N.Y. TIMES, Sept. 30, 2010, at A1. Ravi and Wei streamed Clementi's sexual encounter on the Internet and encouraged their friends to watch. *Id.* Only three days later, Clementi committed suicide. In 2012, Wei made a deal with the prosecution, but Ravi was convicted on fifteen charges and sentenced to thirty days in jail. Kate Zernike, *Judge Defends Penalty in Rutgers Spying Case, Saying It Fits Crime*, N.Y. TIMES, May 31, 2012, at A22. Ravi's trial raised questions as to whether his actions

should be considered a hate crime. *See, e.g.,* Lila Shapiro, *Dharun Ravi Appeals Highlight the Continued Hate-Crime Law Debate*, HUFFINGTON POST (June 13, 2012, 4:51 PM), http://www.huffingtonpost.com/2012/06/13/dharun-ravi-appeals-hate-crime_n_1594320.html. The case brought tremendous attention to the anti-LGBT bullying issue. For a review of the case that urges a nuanced understanding of students like Tyler Clementi, see Andrew Gilden, *Cyberbullying and the Innocence Narrative*, 48 HARV. C.R.-C.L. L. REV. 357 (2013) (arguing that the media oversimplified Clementi's narrative by painting him as only a victim).

B. HISTORICAL REGULATION OF ASSOCIATIONS AND MEETING PLACES

Historically, bars have been an important meeting place for LGBT people. According to historian Allan Bérubé, "bars were the first institution in the United States that contradicted . . . stigmas and gave gay Americans a sense of pride in themselves and their sexuality. . . . In a nation which has for generations mobilized its institutions toward making gay people invisible, illegal, isolated, ignorant and silent, the creation of gay . . . bars were daring, political acts, the first stages in creating the roots of America's national movement for civil rights for gay people."[1] In fact, the beginning of the modern era of the movement for lesbian/gay rights is marked from the 1969 riot at the Stonewall Bar in Greenwich Village, New York, when the patrons fought back during a police raid of the bar. *See supra* Chapter 1, Section II. The next reading captures the atmosphere before Stonewall, in the 1950s in a big city.

AN UNDERGROUND BAR[*]

Judy Grahn

In the closeted world of the late 1950s, when you brought me out, Von, we worried a great deal that you might lose your teaching credentials if we were seen as Lesbians. We made up stories for people about phony boyfriends and husbands. We told some people we were sisters-in-law. And we were frightened all the time. Yet still we found our world exciting and wouldn't have stopped being Gay for anything. We loved being able to love each other and to explore areas of human behavior that didn't seem to be open to other young women we knew. We were part of a secret network of Lesbians who knew each other, who were busy learning the stances and attitudes of Gayness, and who met for

---

[1]   Declaration of Allan Bérubé in Support of Memorandum of Points and Authorities in Support of Ex Parte Application for Leave to Intervene, *State ex rel. Agnost v. Owen*, No. 830–321, at 4 (Cal. Super. Ct. 1984).

[*]   Judy Grahn, *An Underground Bar, in* ANOTHER MOTHER TONGUE: GAY WORDS, GAY WORLDS 28–33 (1984).

parties or to play cards. There was yet another part of the Gay underground culture that I would get to know in the next couple of years: the Gay bar. This was to be the only public expression of Gay culture that I would find in a closeted world.

During the late fifties and early sixties, my Von, when virtually everyone was in the closet, including you as you finished college after tearfully sending me on my way out into the world to become a "real writer," the only place I found to locate a gathering of Gay people was a downtown big-city bar. . . .

I can see now it was a necessary part of my initiation; going to my first Gay bar certainly felt as terrifying, mystifying, and life-altering as any ritual procedure could have felt.

The bar was on a sleazy street of pawnshops, clubs featuring women dancers pushing watered-down drinks on a quota system between dances, tattoo parlors, rundown hotels, and hamburger counters staying open till just past bar-closing time to serve coffee and sobering-up food to customers too drunk to walk to a bus stop. A nearby bus stand for service personnel dropped off loads of sailors and soldiers with weekend passes and just enough money to get drunk and do a little carousing. MPs patrolled the block as often as did the city police.

The street had a permanently dislocated look, unwashed and untended, a look of transience and worn-out baggage. Our fresh young faces, not yet wary, cynical, or bitter, were a startling contrast to the environment. Dim, multicolored neon lights added to the dinginess and aura of danger. Brassy whores in tight, bright mini-skirts were trailed down the street by knots of self-conscious sailors and singular, decrepit winos.

Nothing distinguished the Rendezvous Bar from any of the others except that its reputation among queers was that it was "ours." Why we should have wanted it is anybody's guess. Perhaps we took what dregs were available. All the world at that time was divided very severely into male and female, with no one crossing the line easily; there was no androgyny. Women did not wear pants on the street; men did not make graceful gestures, let alone carry purses or wear make-up. In those days homosexuality was so closely guarded and so heavily punished that it might as well have been illegal just to gather in a bar together. Only heavy payoffs, I have heard, kept any of the bars open for business to a Gay clientele. Quite a contrast to the snazzy, clean, well-lit, beautiful, and often Gay-owned bars of today. . . . But the sleazy Rendezvous was where we bottom-of-the-world overt Gay people could go and be "ourselves."

I went there one night with another Lesbian I had met in the service; I remember the fear I felt on the bus ride downtown. The bus passed through a dark tunnel and the driver had a black curtain wrapped around his seat. I felt I was on a journey to hell and had to laugh at my young self for undertaking such a perilous journey. There would be no turning back for me once I had entered such a place; I knew very distinctly that I had "crossed over."

From the minute I entered the doors of the Rendezvous, past the Gay bouncer (who looked exactly like Li'l Abner in the comics), and gaped in thrilled shock at the self-assured, proud Lesbians in pants and the men in make-up and sculptured, displayed, eerily beautiful faces, I saw myself as part of a group that included some very peculiar characters and characteristics. I ceased then to be a nice white Protestant girl with a tomboy nature who had once had a secret and very loving Lesbian relationship with another nice girl who was attending college to become a teacher. That definition no longer applied, as I stepped into my first Gay bar to become a full-fledged dike, a more-than-a-Lesbian.

Imitating the women I found at the Rendezvous, I dressed for the dike part each evening before riding the bus to my new world. I combed my hair back from my face, having cut it as short as I could and still hold my job. Using men's hairdressing I slicked it into a duck tail; with peroxide I streaked a blond swath into the front and arranged a curl to fall down the center of my forehead. Next came boys' trousers and either a black turtleneck sweater or a boys' white shirt with a T-shirt underneath. Black clothing was the color of choice. Cigarettes tucked in the front pocket, boys' black loafers, and a comb completed the outfit. No makeup of any kind, certainly no purse. A jacket, if it were pouring rain or freezing cold. The boys' heavy black loafers that I had invaded a men's shoe store to buy were a special point of pride; they had taken real courage to get.

No one in the bar used a last name in front of the others, and I suspect that all first names were assumed: We had names we took for ourselves as dikes or fairies in that particular setting, just as we had a special slang language. I took the name Sonny.

For all our boyish clothes and mannerisms (known as being "butch") we women did not pass as men or boys. We dikes did not want to be taken for men and were insulted and ashamed (I certainly was, anyhow) when someone said we were "trying to be men" or when a clerk called me "Sir." In fact, on those rare occasions when a woman came in who was passing in society as a man, word about this went around the tables and we studied her secretly and gossiped about her. For our point was not to be men; our point was to be butch and get away with it. We always kept something back: a highpitched voice, a slant of the head, or a limpness of hand gestures, something that was clearly labeled female. I believe our statement was "Here is another way of being a woman," not "Here is a woman trying to be taken for a man."

The fairies also held something back that prevented them from passing over into the female gender; no matter how many sequins or feathers she wore, a drag queen was a Gay queen, not a man-passing-as-a-woman. Proper bar etiquette required that the drag queens be called "she." They referred to each other as "sister" (by which they meant friends with whom one did not have sex). "Mary" was another term for male homosexuals, and so was "Nellie" (used as an adjective). We dikes were sometimes spoken of as "he," but this was relatively rare compared to the use of female pronouns to indicate the queens.

A hawk-eyed, bent-over old crone with a heavy European accent and not a trace of warmth or goodwill owned the bar, cheating us nightly on the beer and refusing to supply toilet paper or other niceties. She glared at all of us equally with apparent rank contempt when we stood at the bar to order our beers. Her standard method of letting us know it was closing time was to shine a blazing searchlight into our beer-sodden faces until we got the message, stumbling out into the starkly unwelcoming streets.

The bar had considerable dangers. Sailors lurked in the alleys outside, waiting to prove their "manhood" on our bodies; more than once they beat someone I knew—dike or faggot—on her or his way home. A brick crashed through the front window one night, scattering glass splinters over the dance floor where, fortunately, none of us were clenched together swaying to early sixties "Moon River" melodies, thrilled to death (in my case at least) to be holding a member of the same sex in her arms, to be two women publicly dancing.

One night a furious femme wearing a tight dress and carrying a purse attacked one of the dikes at another table—a woman dressed like myself in sedate dark colors and men's clothing, slicked-back hair. The femme stormed up behind the dike, who was probably her girlfriend, beating her on the head with the sharp peg of her high-heeled shoe. It was my first understanding that women fight each other.

Another night two policemen came up to the table where I sat with my friend from the service. They shined a flashlight into our eyes and commanded us to stand up or else be arrested. Then they demanded that we say our real names, first and last, several times, as loud as we could. Sweat poured down my ribs as I obeyed. After they left, my friend and I sat with our heads lowered, too ashamed of our weakness to look around or even to look each other in the face. We had no internal defense from the self-loathing our helplessness inspired and no analysis that would help us perceive oppression as oppression and not as a personal taint of character. Only the queens with their raucous sly tongues helped us get over these kinds of incidents. They called the policemen "Alice Blue Gowns," insulting them behind their backs. "Alice Blue Gown tried to sit on *my* nightstick but I said No! You dirty boy! I know you're menthtrating!" one plump faggot in a cashmere sweater would begin and soon we would be laughing and feeling strong again.

The dikes had a special way of talking, with a minimum of inflection, a flat matter-of-fact, everything-is-under-control effect. It was considered more dikish to be planted solidly in one place than to flit, to use tightly controlled gestures rather than anything grandiose.

The dikes and femmes of the bar provided a kind of low-key, solid background of being; the queens (often with a sailor or two in tow) took the foreground, talking in loud voices, using flamboyant costumes and body language to create a starry effect. Sometimes they came in full drag, with wigs and makeup, and at other times just with a big fluffy sweater for a costume but always with the particular broad gestures, lilting voice, and special queen talk. Or shrieking. The special language of a queen, or even an ordinary garden-variety faggot, is so distinct I find I can distinguish it even in a crowd of men in a restaurant or on the street, far from any Gay scene. It's a full or modified lisp coupled with dramatic inflection and, as used in full-drag queen-style, it accompanies a running monologue of commentary, jokes, puns and "Gay talk," most of it sexual but with a great deal of social and political content. Bruce Rodgers's dictionary of Gay slang, *Gay Talk* (originally called *The Queen's Vernacular*), has more than 12,000 entries. This slang talk is used most particularly by Gay men, especially the fairy queens, and less so by the bar dikes.

I noticed some differences between my experience as a single woman in that Gay bar and my experiences in other kinds of bars, where, of course, I did not dress in an extreme dyke fashion. In the Gay bar I could sit and drink and not be surrounded by men demanding my attention. I could ask someone to dance. I could lead when we danced, or I could find someone who liked to lead and let her do it. I could dance with either men or women. I could sing along with the lyrics and not be embarrassed to be using the "wrong" gender. I could sit with a serious face and not have smiles and pleasantries demanded of me. I noticed also great differences in Gay coupling; for the most part, lovers who were going together for any length of time were of similar size; one did not tower over the other. In the playing they did together in company, there was not the same stress on conquering-male, conquered-female that I saw in straight bars, where the pairing was different, with different purposes and a different social structure to support it.

NOTES

1. *Gay Bars.* State officials often attempted to close down gay bars, generating a series of cases concerning the right of liquor licensees to sell

alcohol to gay people. *E.g., One Eleven Wines & Liquors, Inc. v. Div. of Alcoholic Beverage Control*, 235 A.2d 12, 50 N.J. 329 (1967); *Stoumen v. Reilly*, 234 P.2d 969, 37 Cal.2d 713 (1951). These are important early "gay rights" cases because they prohibited state actors from closing important meeting places for lesbians and gay men. Other cases upheld such closings. *E.g., Kotteman v. Grevemberg*, 96 So.2d 601, 603, 233 La. 328, 335 (1957) (upholding the revocation of a beer permit of a "notorious . . . place in which perverts and sex deviates congregated"); *Kifisia Foods, Inc. v. N.Y. State Liquor Auth.*, 281 N.Y.S.2d 611, 28 A.D.2d 841 (1967) (per curiam) (upholding the Authority's revocation of a license when policemen testified about homosexual solicitation); *In re Freedman Liquor License Case*, 235 A.2d 624, 625, 211 Pa.Super. 132, 134 (1967) (upholding the suspension of a license on the basis of unspecified "revolting" testimony about homosexuals).

The *Stoumen* case was the first decision in a line of cases prohibiting the closure of bars simply because they served homosexuals. Professor Arthur Leonard's analysis of the *Stoumen* decision is generally applicable to this line of cases:

> In some respects the court's decision [in *Stoumen*] was a major breakthrough. The highest court of a major state had ruled that it could not be assumed that an assembly of homosexuals was unlawful *per se*, and indeed that homosexuals had a right to assemble for lawful purposes of socializing. Unfortunately, the court's opinion was long on factual assertion and short on careful legal analysis. No particular constitutional provision or statute was cited in support of the asserted right of assembly, and the decision was quite narrowly drawn. Its protection for social meeting places for gay people seemed illusory in the years that followed for two reasons. First, by basing its decision explicitly on the construction of the Alcoholic Beverage Control law and a particular reading of the constitutional authorization for the Board of Equalization, the court was apparently leaving the matter open for simple legislative overruling. Second, and more important, within a legal framework that criminalized same-sex sexual activity and solicitation for same, it would be an easy matter for plainclothes policemen to document the sort of illegal activity that the court had stated could be used to justify a license revocation. * * *

> [Thus,] these decisions did not make the gay bars a safe place in which people could connect with others for romantic purposes, and it was not until the increasingly militant gay rights movement of the 1970s had organized to gain political power (and the state had moved to decriminalize consensual sodomy) that police actions predicated primarily on sexual conduct became a thing of the past. Police continued to carry out plainclothes operations to combat drug trafficking and bar raids are still a frequent occurrence in some parts of the country, but they focus primarily on allegations (albeit

sometimes pretextual) of serving liquor to minors, prostitution, and drug dealing.

ARTHUR S. LEONARD, *The Gay Bar and The Right To Hang Out Together*, *in* SEXUALITY AND THE LAW: AN ENCYCLOPEDIA OF MAJOR LEGAL CASES 190, 192, 195 (1993).

Some state liquor boards also tried to prevent lesbians and gay men from congregating by forcing organizations to disclose their membership lists before granting a liquor license. At least one court has upheld the right of a liquor board to require such disclosure. *Freeman v. Hittle*, 747 F.2d 1299 (9th Cir. 1984). For a general discussion of this topic, see M.J. Greene, Annotation, *Sale of Liquor to Homosexuals or Permitting Their Congregation at Licensed Premises as Ground for Suspension or Revocation of Liquor License*, 27 A.L.R.3d 1254 (2007).

2.   *Gay Meetings.* In *Cyr v. Walls*, 439 F. Supp. 697 (N.D. Tex. 1977), it was alleged that the police department of Fort Worth, Texas, harassed attendees at the 1974 Texas Gay Conference. Challenging the police practices as violations of their constitutional rights, the gay plaintiffs claimed that the police "circled the church repeatedly, recorded the license plate numbers of numerous parked automobiles, and stopped some of the participants leaving the meeting for questioning and driver's license checks. . . . The license numbers and names recorded were later released for publication to Forth Worth newspaper reporters." *Id.* The court refused to grant defendants' motion to dismiss this case, affirming that plaintiffs had stated a claim upon which relief could be granted for the violation of their constitutional rights.

3.   *Bathhouses.* In the early 1980s, in response to the AIDS crisis, public authorities in New York City closed that city's bathhouses, another popular meeting spot for gay men. The courts rejected claims similar to those raised in *One Eleven* and *Cyr*, and concluded that the state interest in health and safety outweighed the right of association. *See City of New York v. New St. Mark's Baths*, 497 N.Y.S.2d 979, 130 Misc. 2d 911 (1986), *aff'd*, 505 N.Y.S.2d 1015, 122 A.D.2d 747 (1986), *appeal dismissed*, 512 N.E.2d 555, 70 N.Y.2d 693, 518 N.Y.S.2d 1029 (1987).

4.   *Gay Groups.* Some states refused to permit the incorporation of gay rights organizations. *See, e.g., State ex rel. Grant v. Brown*, 313 N.E.2d 847, 39 Ohio St. 2d 112 (1974), *cert. denied sub nom. Duggan v. Brown*, 420 U.S. 916, 95 S. Ct. 1110, 43 L. Ed. 2d 388 (1975). For a critique of the type of discretion granted to the state in cases similar to *State ex rel. Grant v. Brown*, see Henry B. Hansmann, *Reforming Nonprofit Corporation Law*, 129 U. PA. L. REV. 497, 526 & n. 70 (1981).

In 1972 the highest court in New York ordered a lower court to allow the incorporation of a lesbian and gay legal organization, Lambda Legal Defense and Education Fund. *In re Thom*, 301 N.E.2d 542, 33 N.Y.2d 609, 347 N.Y.S.2d 571 (1973). The lower court had denied Lambda's application to become a recognized public interest organization. *In re Thom*, 337 N.Y.S.2d

588, 40 A.D.2d 787 (1972). The same year it decided *In re Thom*, the New York Court of Appeals ordered the New York Secretary of State to incorporate the Gay Activists Alliance, a nonprofit organization. *Gay Activists Alliance v. Lomenzo*, 293 N.E.2d 255, 31 N.Y.2d 965, 341 N.Y.S.2d 108 (1973). The court held that the Secretary of State's denial of incorporation on "public policy" grounds was arbitrary and that incorporation could not be denied if the formal filing requirements were met and if the organization's purposes were lawful. It also affirmed the lower court's ruling that the word "gay" was permissible and that there was no criterion of appropriateness for corporate names.

5.   The difficulty that some nonprofit gay organizations experienced when seeking tax-exempt status under state and federal law parallels the obstacles faced historically by groups simply seeking incorporation. In *Big Mama Rag, Inc. v. United States*, 631 F.2d 1030, 1034–35 (D.C. Cir. 1980), the Court of Appeals for the District of Columbia Circuit struck down as unconstitutionally vague a Treasury Department regulation that was relied on to deny federal tax-exempt status to a feminist magazine that addressed lesbian issues. *See also* Rev. Rul. 78–305, 1978–2 C.B. 172 (1978) (providing that nonprofit organizations that educate about homosexuality qualify for tax-exempt status).

C. OUTING

Much of the preceding material has concerned LGBT persons who seek to reveal their sexual identities. But there has been a vigorous debate over the years about the ethics and legality of revealing that someone is gay, lesbian, bisexual or transgender *without* that person's consent. "Outing" has occupied the uneasy space "between those who live openly lesbian and gay lives and those who remain closeted."[1]

When, if ever, do you think it is ethical to reveal that someone is LGBT against that person's wishes? Does it matter if that person has come out in some, but not all, settings? Is a public figure? Has taken anti-gay positions? The notes that follow consider both the ethical and legal implications of this controversial practice.

NOTES

1.   Proponents of outing often defend it as ethical based on several arguments. The core claim is frankly consequentialist: outing is proffered as necessary to realize equality for the LGBT community. Publicly identifying famous gay people may demonstrate that gay people are worthy of admiration and capable of success, or it may shame closeted individuals who have opposed pro-gay policies. Sometimes outing is defended based on its

---

[1]   Michael Bronski, *Outing: The Power of the Closet*, GAY COMMUNITY NEWS, June 3–9, 1990, *reprinted in* LARRY GROSS, CONTESTED CLOSETS: THE POLITICS AND ETHICS OF OUTING 262, 264 (1993).

ability to secure a different, perhaps more ironic brand of equality—the equal treatment of gay and straight public figures with respect to the revelation of their personal lives in the media. In other accounts, outing is justified based on its asserted capacity to "help" someone closeted toward self-realization as gay.

Opponents of outing respond that it is an unjustified imposition on personal privacy that can have harmful effects on a closeted individual, including emotional and psychological problems and the loss of one's family and job. Moreover, opponents contend, it is the process of *voluntarily* coming out that is beneficial for gays and lesbians, not the fact of being out, irrespective of the circumstances. Opponents place personal autonomy at the center of the gay rights movement and view outing as antithetical to that core value.

For extended analysis of the ethics of outing, see LARRY GROSS, CONTESTED CLOSETS: THE POLITICS AND ETHICS OF OUTING (1993); GAY ETHICS: CONTROVERSIES IN OUTING, CIVIL RIGHTS, AND SEXUAL SCIENCE (Timothy F. Murphy ed., 1994); WARREN JOHANSSON & WILLIAM A. PERCY, OUTING: SHATTERING THE CONSPIRACY OF SILENCE (1994); RICHARD D. MOHR, GAY IDEAS: OUTING AND OTHER CONTROVERSIES (1992); MICHELANGELO SIGNORILE, QUEER IN AMERICA: SEX, THE MEDIA, AND THE CLOSETS OF POWER (1993).

2. In addition to ethical considerations, outing also raises legal issues. One principal issue relates to defamation and arises because of the traditional tort rule that referring publicly to a person as a "homosexual" was libel per se. This "per se" rule was based on the idea that characterization of someone as gay implied (1) commission of the crime of sodomy, *e.g., Plumley v. Landmark Chevrolet, Inc.,* 122 F.3d 308 (5th Cir. 1997); *Buck v. Savage,* 323 S.W.2d 363 (Tex. Civ. App. 1959); (2) professional incompetence, *see, e.g., Manale v. City of New Orleans, Dep't of Police,* 673 F.2d 122, 125 (5th Cir. 1982); (3) unchastity, *e.g., Schomer v. Smidt,* 170 Cal. Rptr. 662, 666, 113 Cal. App. 3d 828, 835 (1980); or (4) contracting a loathsome disease, *see Sleem v. Yale University,* 843 F. Supp. 57, 63 n. 4 (M.D.N.C. 1993). Some courts have found homosexuality to constitute an independent fifth category of libel per se. *E.g. Privitera v. Town of Phelps,* 435 N.Y.S.2d 402, 79 A.D.2d 1 (1981). A majority of courts, however, have moved away from the libel per se rule, with many expressing skepticism about the legal distinction between per se and per quod defamation in libel and slander generally. *See, e.g., Hayes v. Smith,* 832 P.2d 1022 (Colo. Ct. App. 1991), *cert. denied,* (Colo. July 20, 1992); *Boehm v. American Bankers Ins. Group,* 557 So. 2d 91, 94 (Fla. Dist. Ct. App. 1990); *Moricoli v. Schwartz,* 46 Ill. App. 3d 481, 5 Ill. Dec. 74, 361 N.E.2d 74 (1977); *Nazeri v. Mo. Valley Coll.,* 860 S.W. 2d 303 (Mo. 1993); *Wilson v. Harvey,* 842 N.E.2d 83, 164 Ohio App. 3d 278 (2005). The issues are addressed in Patrice S. Arend, *Defamation in an Age of Political Correctness: Should a False Public Statement That a Person Is Gay Be Defamatory?,* 18 N. ILL. U. L. REV. 99 (1997); Randy M. Fogle, *Is Calling Someone "Gay" Defamatory?: The Meaning of Reputation, Community Mores, Gay Rights and Free Speech,* 3 L.

& Sexuality 165 (1993); Patricia C. Kussman, Annotation, Imputation of Homosexuality as Defamation, 7 A.L.R. 6th 135 (2005).

3.   Another set of legal issues raised by outing relates to the tort of invasion of privacy. *See generally Ozer v. Borquez*, 940 P.2d 371, 377 (Colo. 1997) ("[A] majority of jurisdictions have recognized that the right of privacy encompasses a tort claim based on unreasonable publicity given to one's private life."). To succeed, a claim for invasion of privacy generally must establish three elements: (1) the disclosure of the private facts was public; (2) the facts disclosed were private; and (3) the facts disclosed "would be offensive and objectionable to a reasonable person of ordinary sensibilities." *Sipple v. Chronicle Publ'g Co.*, 201 Cal. Rptr. 665, 667–68, 154 Cal. App. 3d 1040, 1045 (1984) (citations omitted). Under the Restatement (Second) of Torts, sexual relations are presumptively private, as are "unpleasant or disgraceful or humiliating illnesses." Restatement (Second) of Torts § 652D cmt. b (1977). Nonetheless, lawsuits of gay claimants may fail if they are out in some settings but not others. *E.g., Sipple*, 201 Cal. Rptr. at 671, 154 Cal. App. 3d at 1050 (denying judgment for a gay man who prevented the assassination of President Ford after national publications reported on his homosexuality because he had been out in the gay community and because his homosexuality was newsworthy); *Crumrine v. Harte-Hanks Television, Inc.*, 37 S.W.3d 124 (Tex. Ct. App. 2001) (denying the claim of a gay, HIV positive father against broadcast accounts of his identity and status because they had been discussed in court during a child custody dispute and because his status was newsworthy where child safety was an issue). For a general discussion of outing and invasion of privacy, see Barbara Moretti, *Outing: Justifiable or Unwarranted Invasion of Privacy? The Private Facts Tort as a Remedy for Disclosures of Sexual Orientation*, 11 Cardozo Arts & Ent. L.J. 857 (1993).

4.   A proposed bill in Tennessee, known colloquially as the "Don't Say Gay" bill, would require that teachers inform parents when they suspect that a student is gay or might be gay:

> The general assembly recognizes that certain subjects are particularly sensitive and are, therefore, best explained and discussed within the home. Because of its complex societal, scientific, psychological, and historical implications, human sexuality is one such subject. Human sexuality is best understood by children with sufficient maturity to grasp its complexity and implications . . .
>
> [School policies shall not prohibit a] school counselor, nurse, principal or assistant principal from counseling a student who is engaging in, or who may be at risk of engaging in, behavior injurious to the physical or mental health and well-being of the student or another person; provided, that wherever possible such counseling shall be done in consultation with the student's parents or legal guardians. Parents or legal guardians of students who

receive such counseling shall be notified as soon as practicable that such counseling has occurred.

Katie McDonough, *Tennessee "Don't Say Gay" Bill Could Require Schools to Out Their Students*, SALON (Jan. 30, 2013, 11:16 AM), http://www.salon.com/2013/01/30/tennessee_dont_say_gay_bill_now_requires_teachers_to_out_their_students/ (citing S.B. 234, 108th S., Reg. Sess. (Tenn. 2013)).

What do you believe a teacher should do in this situation? Should she be required to tell a student's family about her student's sexuality? Forbidden from discussing this information with the student's family? What if the teacher has concerns about the student's mental or physical well-being?

III.   FREE (ANTI-GAY) SPEECH

This Section looks at the assertion of LGBT identity from the other end of the telescope. The legal issues we examine here arise when *private, non-governmental* organizations deny equal access and opportunities to LGBT people. In such cases, those who are excluded or whose identities are suppressed cannot rely on constitutional protections applicable to state actors, but must seek legal recourse—if any—in the application of non-discrimination statutes and principles to the private actors. Conversely, the private actors often raise the First Amendment as a defense, alleging that the application of a law prohibiting them from discriminating against LGBT people violates their First Amendment rights. The structures of some of these cases recall disputes about the entry of racial minorities and women into the nation's public life. The unit accordingly begins with the *Roberts* case, in which the U.S. Supreme Court considered the constitutionality of the Jaycees' ban on women members. The cases and notes that follow consider the exclusion of openly gay persons from parades, from groups like the Boy Scouts, from officially recognized student groups on campus, and most recently, from businesses who do not wish to serve them. The Chapter closes with consideration of the Solomon Amendment, a measure that had required law schools to host military recruiters who excluded openly gay students during the time that Don't Ask, Don't Tell was still the law. As you review these materials, consider the overarching question of how courts should resolve conflicts between equality and expressive or religious liberty.

ROBERTS V. UNITED STATES JAYCEES
Supreme Court of the United States, 1984
468 U.S. 609, 104 S.Ct. 3244, 82 L.Ed.2d 462

JUSTICE BRENNAN delivered the opinion of the Court.

This case requires us to address a conflict between a State's efforts to eliminate gender-based discrimination against its citizens and the constitutional freedom of association asserted by members of a private organization. In the decision under review, the Court of Appeals for the Eighth Circuit concluded that, by requiring the United States Jaycees to admit women as full voting members, the Minnesota Human Rights Act violates the First and Fourteenth Amendment rights [of association] of the organization's members. We . . . reverse. * * *

Our decisions have referred to constitutionally protected "freedom of association" in two distinct senses. In one line of decisions, the Court has concluded that choices to enter into and maintain certain intimate human relationships must be secured against undue intrusion by the State because of the role of such relationships in safeguarding the individual freedom that is central to our constitutional scheme. In this respect, freedom of association receives protection as a fundamental element of personal liberty. In another set of decisions, the Court has recognized a right to associate for the purpose of engaging in those activities protected by the First Amendment—speech, assembly, petition for the redress of grievances, and the exercise of religion. The Constitution guarantees freedom of association of this kind as an indispensable means of preserving other individual liberties.

The intrinsic and instrumental features of constitutionally protected association may, of course, coincide. In particular, when the State interferes with individuals' selection of those with whom they wish to join in a common endeavor, freedom of association in both of its forms may be implicated. The Jaycees contend that this is such a case. Still, the nature and degree of constitutional protection afforded freedom of association may vary depending on the extent to which one or the other aspect of the constitutionally protected liberty is at stake in a given case. We therefore find it useful to consider separately the effect of applying the Minnesota statute to the Jaycees on what could be called its members' freedom of intimate association and their freedom of expressive association.

A

The Court has long recognized that, because the Bill of Rights is designed to secure individual liberty, it must afford the formation and preservation of certain kinds of highly personal relationships a substantial measure of sanctuary from unjustified interference by the State. *E.g., Pierce v. Society of Sisters*, 268 U.S. 510, 534–535 (1925); *Meyer v. Nebraska*, 262 U.S. 390, 399 (1923). Without precisely identifying every consideration that may underlie this type of constitutional protection, we have noted that certain kinds of personal bonds have played a critical role in the culture and traditions of the Nation by cultivating and transmitting shared ideals and beliefs; they thereby foster diversity and act as critical buffers between the individual and the power of the State. *See, e.g., Zablocki v. Redhail*, 434 U.S. 374, 383–386 (1978); *Moore v. East Cleveland*, 431 U.S. 494, 503–504 (1977) (plurality opinion); *Wisconsin v. Yoder*, 406 U.S. 205, 232 (1972); *Griswold v. Connecticut*, 381 U.S. 479, 482–485 (1965). Moreover, the constitutional shelter afforded such relationships reflects the realization that individuals draw much of their emotional enrichment from close ties with others. Protecting these relationships from unwarranted state interference therefore safeguards the ability independently to define one's identity that is central to any concept of liberty. *See, e.g., Quilloin v. Walcott*, 434 U.S. 246, 255 (1978); *Smith v. Organization of Foster Families*, 431 U.S. 816, 844 (1977); *Cleveland Board of Education v. LaFleur*, 414 U.S. 632, 639–640 (1974); *Stanley v. Illinois*, 405 U.S. 645, 651–652 (1972); *Stanley v. Georgia*, 394 U.S. 557, 564 (1969); *Olmstead v. United States*, 277 U.S. 438, 478 (1928) (Brandeis, J., dissenting).

The personal affiliations that exemplify these considerations, and that therefore suggest some relevant limitations on the relationships that might be entitled to this sort of constitutional protection, are those that attend the creation and sustenance of a family—marriage, *e.g., Zablocki v. Redhail*; childbirth, *e.g., Carey v. Population Services International*; the raising and education of children, *e.g., Smith v. Organization of Foster Families*; and cohabitation with one's relatives, *e.g., Moore v. East Cleveland*. Family relationships, by their nature, involve deep attachments and commitments to the necessarily few other individuals with whom one shares not only a special community of thoughts, experiences, and beliefs but also distinctively personal aspects of one's life. Among other things, therefore, they are distinguished by such attributes as relative smallness, a high degree of selectivity in decisions to begin and maintain the affiliation, and seclusion from others in critical aspects of the relationship. As a general matter, only relationships with these sorts of qualities are likely to reflect the considerations that have led to an understanding of freedom of association as an intrinsic element of personal liberty. Conversely, an association lacking these qualities— such as a large business enterprise—seems remote from the concerns giving rise to this constitutional protection. Accordingly, the Constitution undoubtedly imposes constraints on the State's power to control the selection of one's spouse that would not apply to regulations affecting the choice of one's fellow employees. *Compare Loving v. Virginia*, 388 U.S. 1, 12 (1967), *with Railway Mail Assn. v. Corsi*, 326 U.S. 88, 93–94 (1945).

Between these poles, of course, lies a broad range of human relationships that may make greater or lesser claims to constitutional protection from particular incursions by the State. Determining the limits of state authority over an individual's freedom to enter into a particular association therefore unavoidably entails a careful assessment of where that relationship's objective characteristics locate it on a spectrum from the most intimate to the most attenuated of personal attachments. We need not mark the potentially significant points on this terrain with any precision. We note only that factors that may be relevant include size, purpose, policies, selectivity, congeniality, and other characteristics that in a particular case may be pertinent. In this case, however, several features of the Jaycees clearly place the organization outside of the category of relationships worthy of this kind of constitutional protection.

The undisputed facts reveal that the local chapters of the Jaycees are large and basically unselective groups. At the time of the state administrative hearing, the Minneapolis chapter had approximately 430 members, while the St. Paul chapter had about 400. Apart from age and sex, neither the national organization nor the local chapters employ any criteria for judging applicants for membership, and new members are routinely recruited and admitted with no inquiry into their backgrounds. In fact, a local officer testified that he could recall no instance in which an applicant had been denied membership on any basis other than age or sex. Furthermore, despite their inability to vote, hold office, or receive certain awards, women affiliated with the Jaycees attend various meetings, participate in selected projects, and engage in many of the organization's social functions. Indeed, numerous non-members of both genders regularly participate in a substantial portion of activities central to the decision of many members to associate with one another, including many of the organization's various community programs, awards ceremonies, and recruitment meetings.

In short, the local chapters of the Jaycees are neither small nor selective. Moreover, much of the activity central to the formation and maintenance of the association involves the participation of strangers to that relationship. Accordingly, we conclude that the Jaycees chapters lack the distinctive characteristics that might afford constitutional protection to the decision of its members to exclude women. We turn therefore to consider the extent to which application of the Minnesota statute to compel the Jaycees to accept women infringes the group's freedom of expressive association.

B

An individual's freedom to speak, to worship, and to petition the government for the redress of grievances could not be vigorously protected from interference by the State unless a correlative freedom to engage in group effort toward those ends were not also guaranteed. *See, e.g., Citizens Against Rent Control/Coalition for Fair Housing v. Berkeley*, 454 U.S. 290, 294 (1981). According protection to collective effort on behalf of shared goals is especially important in preserving political and cultural diversity and in shielding dissident expression from suppression by the majority. *See, e.g., Gilmore v. City of Montgomery*, 417 U.S., at 575; *Griswold v. Connecticut*, 381 U.S., at 482–485; *NAACP v. Button*, 371 U.S. 415, 431 (1963); *NAACP v. Alabama ex rel. Patterson*, 357 U.S., at

462. Consequently, we have long understood as implicit in the right to engage in activities protected by the First Amendment a corresponding right to associate with others in pursuit of a wide variety of political, social, economic, educational, religious, and cultural ends. *See, e.g., NAACP v. Claiborne Hardware Co.*, 458 U.S. 886, 907–909, 932–933; *Larson v. Valente*, 456 U.S. 228, 244–246 (1982); *In re Primus*, 436 U.S. 412, 426 (1978); *Abood v. Detroit Board of Education*, 431 U.S. 209, 231 (1977). In view of the various protected activities in which the Jaycees engage (*see infra*) that right is plainly implicated in this case.

Government actions that may unconstitutionally infringe upon this freedom can take a number of forms. Among other things, government may seek to impose penalties or withhold benefits from individuals because of their membership in a disfavored group, *e.g., Healy v. James*, 408 U.S. 169, 180–184 (1972); it may attempt to require disclosure of the fact of membership in a group seeking anonymity, *e.g., Brown v. Socialist Workers '74 Campaign Committee*, 459 U.S. 87, 91–92 (1982); and it may try to interfere with the internal organization or affairs of the group, *e.g., Cousins v. Wigoda*, 419 U.S. 477, 487–488 (1975). By requiring the Jaycees to admit women as full voting members, the Minnesota Act works an infringement of the last type. There can be no clearer example of an intrusion into the internal structure or affairs of an association than a regulation that forces the group to accept members it does not desire. Such a regulation may impair the ability of the original members to express only those views that brought them together. Freedom of association therefore plainly presupposes a freedom not to associate. *See Abood v. Detroit Board of Education*, 431 U.S., at 234–235.

The right to associate for expressive purposes is not, however, absolute. Infringements on that right may be justified by regulations adopted to serve compelling state interests, unrelated to the suppression of ideas, that cannot be achieved through means significantly less restrictive of associational freedoms. We are persuaded that Minnesota's compelling interest in eradicating discrimination against its female citizens justifies the impact that application of the statute to the Jaycees may have on the male members' associational freedoms.

On its face, the Minnesota Act does not aim at the suppression of speech, does not distinguish between prohibited and permitted activity on the basis of viewpoint, and does not license enforcement authorities to administer the statute on the basis of such constitutionally impermissible criteria. Nor does the Jaycees contend that the Act has been applied in this case for the purpose of hampering the organization's ability to express its views. Instead, as the Minnesota Supreme Court explained, the Act reflects the State's strong historical commitment to eliminating discrimination and assuring its citizens equal access to publicly available goods and services. That goal, which is unrelated to the suppression of

expression, plainly serves compelling state interests of the highest order.
* * *

By prohibiting gender discrimination in places of public accommodation, the Minnesota Act protects the State's citizenry from a number of serious social and personal harms. In the context of reviewing state actions under the Equal Protection Clause, this Court has frequently noted that discrimination based on archaic and overbroad assumptions about the relative needs and capacities of the sexes forces individuals to labor under stereotypical notions that often bear no relationship to their actual abilities. It thereby both deprives persons of their individual dignity and denies society the benefits of wide participation in political, economic, and cultural life. These concerns are strongly implicated with respect to gender discrimination in the allocation of publicly available goods and services. Thus, in upholding Title II of the Civil Rights Act of 1964, which forbids race discrimination in public accommodations, we emphasized that its "fundamental object . . . was to vindicate 'the deprivation of personal dignity that surely accompanies denials of equal access to public establishments.'" *Heart of Atlanta Motel, Inc. v. United States*, 379 U.S. 241, 250 (1964). That stigmatizing injury, and the denial of equal opportunities that accompanies it, is surely felt as strongly by persons suffering discrimination on the basis of their sex as by those treated differently because of their race.

Nor is the state interest in assuring equal access limited to the provision of purely tangible goods and services. A State enjoys broad authority to create rights of public access on behalf of its citizens. *PruneYard Shopping Center v. Robins*, 447 U.S. 74, 81–88 (1980). Like many States and municipalities, Minnesota has adopted a functional definition of public accommodations that reaches various forms of public, quasi-commercial conduct. This expansive definition reflects a recognition of the changing nature of the American economy and of the importance, both to the individual and to society, of removing the barriers to economic advancement and political and social integration that have historically plagued certain disadvantaged groups, including women. Thus, in explaining its conclusion that the Jaycees local chapters are "place[s] of public accommodations" within the meaning of the Act, the Minnesota court noted the various commercial programs and benefits offered to members and stated that "[l]eadership skills are 'goods,' [and] business contacts and employment promotions are 'privileges' and 'advantages'. . . ." Assuring women equal access to such goods, privileges, and advantages clearly furthers compelling state interests.

In applying the Act to the Jaycees, the State has advanced those interests through the least restrictive means of achieving its ends. Indeed, the Jaycees has failed to demonstrate that the Act imposes any serious burdens on the male members' freedom of expressive association. To be sure, as the Court of Appeals noted, a "not insubstantial part" of the Jaycees' activities constitutes protected expression on political, economic, cultural, and social affairs. Over the years, the national and local levels of the organization have taken public positions on a number of diverse issues, and members of the Jaycees regularly engage in a variety of civic, charitable, lobbying, fundraising, and other activities worthy of constitutional protection under the First Amendment. There is, however, no basis in the record for concluding that admission of women as full voting members will impede the organization's ability to engage in these protected activities or to disseminate its preferred views. The Act requires no change in the Jaycees' creed of promoting the interests of young men, and it imposes no restrictions on the organization's ability to exclude individuals with ideologies or philosophies different from those of its existing members. Moreover, the Jaycees already invites women to share the group's views and philosophy and to participate in much of its training and community activities. Accordingly, any claim that admission of women as full voting members will impair a symbolic message conveyed by the very fact that women are not permitted to vote is attenuated at best.

While acknowledging that "the specific content of most of the resolutions adopted over the years by the Jaycees has nothing to do with sex," the Court of Appeals nonetheless entertained the hypothesis that women members might have a different view or agenda with respect to these matters so that, if they are allowed to vote, "some change in the Jaycees' philosophical cast can reasonably be expected." It is similarly arguable that, insofar as the Jaycees is organized to promote the views of young men whatever those views happen to be, admission of women as voting members will change the message communicated by the group's speech because of the gender-based assumptions of the audience. Neither supposition, however, is supported by the record. In claiming that women might have a different attitude about such issues as the federal budget, school prayer, voting rights, and foreign relations, or that the organization's public positions would have a different effect if the group were not "a purely young men's association," the Jaycees relies solely on unsupported generalizations about the relative interests and perspectives of men and women. Although such generalizations may or may not have a statistical basis in fact with respect to particular positions adopted by the Jaycees, we have repeatedly condemned legal decisionmaking that relies uncritically on such assumptions. *See, e.g., Palmore v. Sidoti*, 466 U.S. 429, 433–434 (1984). In the absence of a showing far more substantial than that attempted by the Jaycees, we decline to indulge in the sexual stereotyping that underlies appellee's contention that, by allowing women to vote, application of the Minnesota Act will change the content or impact of the organization's speech.

In any event, even if enforcement of the Act causes some incidental abridgment of the Jaycees' protected speech, that effect is no greater than is necessary to accomplish the State's legitimate purposes. As we have explained, acts of invidious discrimination in the distribution of publicly available goods, services, and other advantages cause unique evils that government has a compelling interest to prevent—wholly apart from the point of view such conduct may transmit. Accordingly, like violence or other types of potentially expressive activities that produce special harms distinct from their communicative impact, such practices are entitled to no constitutional protection. In prohibiting such practices, the Minnesota Act therefore "responds precisely to the substantive problem which legitimately concerns" the State and abridges no more speech or associational freedom than is necessary to accomplish that purpose.

HURLEY V. IRISH-AMERICAN GAY, LESBIAN & BISEXUAL GROUP OF BOSTON

Supreme Court of the United States, 1995
515 U.S. 557, 115 S.Ct. 2338, 132 L.Ed.2d 487

JUSTICE SOUTER delivered the opinion of the Court.

The issue in this case is whether Massachusetts may require private citizens who organize a parade to include among the marchers a group imparting a message the organizers do not wish to convey. We hold that such a mandate violates the First Amendment.

I

March 17 is set aside for two celebrations in South Boston. As early as 1737, some people in Boston observed the feast of the apostle to Ireland, and since 1776 the day has marked the evacuation of royal troops and Loyalists from the city, prompted by the guns captured at Ticonderoga and set up on Dorchester Heights under General Washington's command. Washington himself reportedly drew on the earlier tradition in choosing "St. Patrick" as the response to "Boston," the password used in the colonial lines on evacuation day. Although the General Court of Massachusetts did not officially designate March 17 as Evacuation Day until 1938, the City Council of Boston had previously sponsored public celebrations of Evacuation Day, including notable commemorations on the centennial in 1876, and on the 125th anniversary in 1901, with its parade, salute, concert, and fireworks display.

The tradition of formal sponsorship by the city came to an end in 1947, however, when Mayor James Michael Curley himself granted authority to organize and conduct the St. Patrick's Day-Evacuation Day Parade to the petitioner South Boston Allied War Veterans Council, an unincorporated association of individuals elected from various South Boston veterans groups. Every year since that time, the Council has applied for and received a permit for the parade, which at times has included as many as 20,000 marchers and drawn up to 1 million watchers. No other applicant has ever applied for that permit. Through 1992, the city allowed the Council to use the city's official seal, and provided printing services as well as direct funding.

1992 was the year that a number of gay, lesbian, and bisexual descendants of the Irish immigrants joined together with other supporters to form the respondent organization, GLIB, to march in the parade as a way to express pride in their Irish heritage as openly gay, lesbian, and bisexual individuals, to demonstrate that there are such men and women among those so descended, and to express their solidarity with like individuals who sought to march in New York's St. Patrick's Day Parade. Although the Council denied GLIB's application to take part in the 1992 parade, GLIB obtained a state-court order to include its contingent, which marched "uneventfully" among that year's 10,000 participants and 750,000 spectators.

In 1993, after the Council had again refused to admit GLIB to the upcoming parade, the organization and some of its members filed this suit against the Council, the individual petitioner John J. "Wacko" Hurley, and the City of Boston, alleging violations of the State and Federal Constitutions and of the state public accommodations law, which prohibits "any distinction, discrimination or restriction on account of . . . sexual orientation . . . relative to the admission of any person to, or treatment in any place of public accommodation, resort or amusement." After finding that "[f]or at least the past 47 years, the Parade has traveled the same basic route along the public streets of South Boston, providing entertainment, amusement, and recreation to participants and spectators alike," the state trial court ruled that the parade fell within the statutory definition of a public accommodation. The court found that the Council had no written criteria and employed no particular procedures for admission, voted on new applications in batches, had occasionally admitted groups who simply showed up at the parade without having submitted an application, and did "not generally inquire into the specific messages or views of each applicant." The court consequently rejected the Council's contention that the parade was "private" (in the sense of being exclusive), holding instead that "the lack of genuine selectivity in choosing participants and sponsors demonstrates that the Parade is a public event." It found the parade to be "eclectic," containing a wide variety of "patriotic, commercial, political, moral, artistic, religious, athletic, public service, trade union, and eleemosynary themes," as well as conflicting messages. While noting that the Council had indeed excluded the Ku Klux Klan and ROAR (an antibusing group), it attributed little significance to these facts, concluding ultimately that "[t]he only common theme among the participants and sponsors is their public involvement in the Parade."

The court rejected the Council's assertion that the exclusion of "groups with sexual themes merely formalized [the fact] that the Parade expresses traditional religious and social values," and found the Council's "final position [to be] that GLIB would be excluded because of its values and its message, *i.e.*, its members' sexual orientation." This position, in the court's view, was not only violative of the public accommodations law but "paradoxical" as well, since "a proper celebration of St. Patrick's and Evacuation Day requires diversity and inclusiveness." The court rejected the notion that GLIB's admission would trample on the Council's First Amendment rights since the court understood that constitutional protection of any interest in expressive association would "requir[e] focus on a specific message, theme, or group" absent from the parade. "Given the [Council's] lack of selectivity in choosing participants and failure to circumscribe the marchers' message," the court found it "impossible to discern any specific expressive purpose entitling the Parade to protection under the First Amendment." It concluded that the parade is "not an exercise of [the Council's] constitutionally protected right of expressive association," but instead "an open recreational event that is subject to the public accommodations law."

The court held that because the statute did not mandate inclusion of GLIB but only prohibited discrimination based on sexual orientation, any infringement on the Council's right to expressive association was only "incidental" and "no greater than necessary to accomplish the statute's legitimate purpose" of eradicating discrimination (citing *Roberts v. United States Jaycees*, 468 U.S. 609, 628–629 (1984)). Accordingly, it ruled that "GLIB is entitled to participate in the Parade on the same terms and conditions as other participants."

The Supreme Judicial Court of Massachusetts affirmed, seeing nothing clearly erroneous in the trial judge's findings that GLIB was excluded from the parade based on the sexual orientation of its members, that it was impossible to detect an expressive purpose in the parade, that there was no state action, and that the parade was a public accommodation within the meaning of [the Massachusetts statute]. * * *

We granted certiorari to determine whether the requirement to admit a parade contingent expressing a message not of the private organizers' own choosing violates the First Amendment. We hold that it does and reverse.

II

Given the scope of the issues as originally joined in this case, it is worth noting some that have fallen aside in the course of the litigation, before reaching us. Although the Council presents us with a First

Amendment claim, respondents do not. Neither do they press a claim that the Council's action has denied them equal protection of the laws in violation of the Fourteenth Amendment. While the guarantees of free speech and equal protection guard only against encroachment by the government and "erec[t] no shield against merely private conduct," *Shelley v. Kraemer*, 334 U.S. 1 (1948), respondents originally argued that the Council's conduct was not purely private, but had the character of state action. The trial court's review of the city's involvement led it to find otherwise, however, and although the Supreme Judicial Court did not squarely address the issue, it appears to have affirmed the trial court's decision on that point as well as the others. In any event, respondents have not brought that question up either in a cross-petition for certiorari or in their briefs filed in this Court. When asked at oral argument whether they challenged the conclusion by the Massachusetts' courts that no state action is involved in the parade, respondents' counsel answered that they "do not press that issue here." In this Court, then, their claim for inclusion in the parade rests solely on the Massachusetts public accommodations law.

There is no corresponding concession from the other side, however, and certainly not to the state courts' characterization of the parade as lacking the element of expression for purposes of the First Amendment. Accordingly, our review of petitioners' claim that their activity is indeed in the nature of protected speech carries with it a constitutional duty to conduct an independent examination of the record as a whole, without deference to the trial court. *See Bose Corp. v. Consumers Union of United States, Inc.*, 466 U.S. 485, 499 (1984). The "requirement of independent appellate review . . . is a rule of federal constitutional law," *id.*, at 510, which does not limit our deference to a trial court on matters of witness credibility, *Harte-Hanks Communications, Inc. v. Connaughton*, 491 U.S. 657, 688 (1989), but which generally requires us to "review the finding of facts by a State court . . . where a conclusion of law as to a Federal right and a finding of fact are so intermingled as to make it necessary, in order to pass upon the Federal question, to analyze the facts," *Fiske v. Kansas,* 274 U.S. 380, 385–386 (1927). This obligation rests upon us simply because the reaches of the First Amendment are ultimately defined by the facts it is held to embrace, and we must thus decide for ourselves whether a given course of conduct falls on the near or far side of the line of constitutional protection. Even where a speech case has originally been tried in a federal court, subject to the provision of Federal Rule of Civil Procedure 52(a) that "[f]indings of fact . . . shall not be set aside unless clearly erroneous," we are obliged to make a fresh examination of crucial facts. Hence, in this case, though we are confronted with the state courts' conclusion that the factual characteristics of petitioners' activity place it within the vast realm of non-expressive conduct, our obligation is to " 'make an independent examination of the whole record,' . . . so as to assure ourselves that th[is] judgment does not constitute a forbidden intrusion on the field of free expression." *New York Times Co. v. Sullivan*, 376 U.S. 254, 285 (1964) (footnote omitted), quoting *Edwards v. South Carolina*, 372 U.S. 229, 235 (1963).

III

A

If there were no reason for a group of people to march from here to there except to reach a destination, they could make the trip without expressing any message beyond the fact of the march itself. Some people might call such a procession a parade, but it would not be much of one. Real "[p]arades are public dramas of social relations, and in them performers define who can be a social actor and what subjects and ideas are available for communication and consideration." S. Davis, Parades and Power: Street Theatre in Nineteenth-Century Philadelphia 6 (1986). Hence, we use the word "parade" to indicate marchers who are making some sort of collective point, not just to each other but to bystanders along the way. Indeed a parade's dependence on watchers is so extreme that nowadays, as with Bishop Berkeley's celebrated tree, "if a parade or demonstration receives no media coverage, it may as well not have happened." *Id.*, at 171. Parades are thus a form of expression, not just motion, and the inherent expressiveness of marching to make a point explains our cases involving protest marches. . . .

The protected expression that inheres in a parade is not limited to its banners and songs, however, for the Constitution looks beyond written or spoken words as mediums of expression. Noting that "[s]ymbolism is a primitive but effective way of communicating ideas," *West Virginia Bd. of Ed. v. Barnette*, 319 U.S. 624, 632 (1943), our cases have recognized that the First Amendment shields such acts as saluting a flag (and refusing to do so), *id.*, at 632, 642, wearing an arm band to protest a war, *Tinker v. Des Moines Independent Community School Dist.*, 393 U.S. 503, 505–506 (1969), displaying a red flag, *Stromberg v. California*, 283 U.S. 359, 369 (1931), and even "[m]arching, walking or parading" in uniforms displaying the swastika, *National Socialist Party of America v. Skokie*, 432 U.S. 43 (1977). As some of these examples show, a narrow, succinctly articulable message is not a condition of constitutional protection, which if confined to expressions conveying a "particularized message," *cf. Spence v. Washington*, 418 U.S. 405, 411 (1974) (*per curiam*), would never reach the unquestionably shielded painting of Jackson Pollock, music of Arnold Schonberg, or Jabberwocky verse of Lewis Carroll.

Not many marches, then, are beyond the realm of expressive parades, and the South Boston celebration is not one of them. Spectators line the streets; people march in costumes and uniforms, carrying flags and banners with all sorts of messages (*e.g.*, "England get out of Ireland,"

"Say no to drugs"); marching bands and pipers play, floats are pulled along, and the whole show is broadcast over Boston television. To be sure, we agree with the state courts that in spite of excluding some applicants, the Council is rather lenient in admitting participants. But a private speaker does not forfeit constitutional protection simply by combining multifarious voices, or by failing to edit their themes to isolate an exact message as the exclusive subject matter of the speech. Nor, under our precedent, does First Amendment protection require a speaker to generate, as an original matter, each item featured in the communication. Cable operators, for example, are engaged in protected speech activities even when they only select programming originally produced by others. *Turner Broadcasting System, Inc. v. FCC*, 512 U.S. 622, 636, 114 S.Ct. 2445, 129 L.Ed.2d 497 (1994). For that matter, the presentation of an edited compilation of speech generated by other persons is a staple of most newspapers' opinion pages, which, of course, fall squarely within the core of First Amendment security, *Miami Herald Publishing Co. v. Tornillo*, 418 U.S. 241 (1974), as does even the simple selection of a paid noncommercial advertisement for inclusion in a daily paper, see *New York Times*, 376 U.S., at 265–266. The selection of contingents to make a parade is entitled to similar protection.

Respondents' participation as a unit in the parade was equally expressive. GLIB was formed for the very purpose of marching in it, as the trial court found, in order to celebrate its members' identity as openly gay, lesbian, and bisexual descendants of the Irish immigrants, to show that there are such individuals in the community, and to support the like men and women who sought to march in the New York parade. The organization distributed a fact sheet describing the members' intentions, and the record otherwise corroborates the expressive nature of GLIB's participation. In 1993, members of GLIB marched behind a shamrock-strewn banner with the simple inscription "Irish American Gay, Lesbian and Bisexual Group of Boston." GLIB understandably seeks to communicate its ideas as part of the existing parade, rather than staging one of its own.

B

The Massachusetts public accommodations law under which respondents brought suit has a venerable history. . . .

As with many public accommodations statutes across the Nation, the legislature continued to broaden the scope of legislation, to the point that the law today prohibits discrimination on the basis of "race, color, religious creed, national origin, sex, sexual orientation . . . deafness, blindness or any physical or mental disability or ancestry" in "the admission of any person to, or treatment in any place of public accommodation, resort or amusement." Provisions like these are well within the State's usual power to enact when a legislature has reason to believe that a given group is the target of discrimination, and they do not, as a general matter, violate the First or Fourteenth Amendments. Nor is this statute unusual in any obvious way, since it does not, on its face, target speech or discriminate on the basis of its content, the focal point of its prohibition being rather on the act of discriminating against individuals in the provision of publicly available goods, privileges, and services on the proscribed grounds.

C

In the case before us, however, the Massachusetts law has been applied in a peculiar way. Its enforcement does not address any dispute about the participation of openly gay, lesbian, or bisexual individuals in various units admitted to the parade. The petitioners disclaim any intent to exclude homosexuals as such, and no individual member of GLIB claims to have been excluded from parading as a member of any group that the Council has approved to march. Instead, the disagreement goes to the admission of GLIB as its own parade unit carrying its own banner. Since every participating unit affects the message conveyed by the private organizers, the state courts' application of the statute produced an order essentially requiring petitioners to alter the expressive content of their parade. Although the state courts spoke of the parade as a place of public accommodation, once the expressive character of both the parade and the marching GLIB contingent is understood, it becomes apparent that the state courts' application of the statute had the effect of declaring the sponsors' speech itself to be the public accommodation. Under this approach any contingent of protected individuals with a message would have the right to participate in petitioners' speech, so that the communication produced by the private organizers would be shaped by all those protected by the law who wished to join in with some expressive demonstration of their own. But this use of the State's power violates the fundamental rule of protection under the First Amendment, that a speaker has the autonomy to choose the content of his own message.

"Since *all* speech inherently involves choices of what to say and what to leave unsaid," *Pacific Gas & Electric Co. v. Public Utilities Comm'n of Cal.*, 475 U.S. 1, 11 (1986) (plurality opinion) (emphasis in original), one important manifestation of the principle of free speech is that one who chooses to speak may also decide "what not to say," *id.*, at 16. Although the State may at times "prescribe what shall be orthodox in commercial advertising" by requiring the dissemination of "purely factual and uncontroversial information," *Zauderer v. Office of Disciplinary Counsel of Supreme Court of Ohio*, 471 U.S. 626, 651 (1985), outside that context it may not compel affirmance of a belief with which the speaker disagrees, see *Barnette*, 319 U.S., at 642. Indeed this general rule, that the speaker has the right to tailor the speech, applies not only to expressions of value, opinion, or endorsement, but equally to statements of fact the speaker would rather avoid, subject, perhaps, to the permissive law of defamation. Nor is the rule's benefit restricted to the press, being enjoyed by business corporations generally and by ordinary people engaged in unsophisticated expression as well as by professional publishers. Its point is simply the point of all speech protection, which is to shield just those choices of content that in someone's eyes are misguided, or even hurtful.

Petitioners' claim to the benefit of this principle of autonomy to control one's own speech is as sound as the South Boston parade is expressive. Rather like a composer, the Council selects the expressive units of the parade from potential participants, and though the score may not produce a particularized message, each contingent's expression in the Council's eyes comports with what merits celebration on that day. Even if this view gives the Council credit for a more considered judgment than it actively made, the Council clearly decided to exclude a message it did not like from the communication it chose to make, and that is enough to invoke its right as a private speaker to shape its expression by speaking on one subject while remaining silent on another. The message it disfavored is not difficult to identify. Although GLIB's point (like the Council's) is not wholly articulate, a contingent marching behind the organization's banner would at least bear witness to the fact that some Irish are gay, lesbian, or bisexual, and the presence of the organized marchers would suggest their view that people of their sexual orientations have as much claim to unqualified social acceptance as heterosexuals and indeed as members of parade units organized around other identifying characteristics. The parade's organizers may not believe these facts about Irish sexuality to be so, or they may object to unqualified social acceptance of gays and lesbians or have some other reason for wishing to keep GLIB's message out of the parade. But whatever the reason, it boils down to the choice of a speaker not to propound a particular point of view, and that choice is presumed to lie beyond the government's power to control.

Respondents argue that any tension between this rule and the Massachusetts law falls short of unconstitutionality, citing the most recent of our cases on the general subject of compelled access for expressive purposes, *Turner Broadcasting System Inc. v. FCC,*, 512 U.S. 622, 114 S.Ct. 2445, 129 L.Ed.2d 497 (1994). There we reviewed regulations requiring cable operators to set aside channels for designated broadcast signals, and applied only intermediate scrutiny. Respondents contend on this authority that admission of GLIB to the parade would not threaten the core principle of speaker's autonomy because the Council, like a cable operator, is merely "a conduit" for the speech of participants in the parade "rather than itself a speaker." But this metaphor is not apt here, because GLIB's participation would likely be perceived as having resulted from the Council's customary determination about a unit admitted to the parade, that its message was worthy of presentation and quite possibly of support as well. A newspaper, similarly, "is more than a passive receptacle or conduit for news, comment, and advertising," and we have held that "[t]he choice of material . . . and the decisions made as to limitations on the size and content . . . and treatment of public issues . . .—whether fair or unfair—constitute the exercise of editorial control and judgment" upon which the State can not intrude. *Tornillo*, 418 U.S., at 258. Indeed, in *Pacific Gas & Electric*, we invalidated coerced access to the envelope of a private utility's bill and newsletter because the utility "may be forced either to appear to agree with [the intruding leaflet] or to respond." 475 U.S., at 15 (plurality) (citation omitted). The plurality made the further point that if "the government [were] freely able to compel . . . speakers to propound political messages with which they disagree, . . . protection [of a speaker's freedom] would be empty, for the government could require speakers to affirm in one breath that which they deny in the next." *Id.*, at 16. Thus, when dissemination of a view contrary to one's own is forced upon a speaker intimately connected with the communication advanced, the speaker's right to autonomy over the message is compromised.

In *Turner Broadcasting*, we found this problem absent in the cable context, because "[g]iven cable's long history of serving as a conduit for broadcast signals, there appears little risk that cable viewers would assume that the broadcast stations carried on a cable system convey ideas or messages endorsed by the cable operator." We stressed that the viewer is frequently apprised of the identity of the broadcaster whose signal is being received via cable and that it is "common practice for broadcasters to disclaim any identity of viewpoint between the management and the speakers who use the broadcast facility."

Parades and demonstrations, in contrast, are not understood to be so neutrally presented or selectively viewed. Unlike the programming offered on various channels by a cable network, the parade does not consist of individual, unrelated segments that happen to be transmitted together for individual selection by members of the audience. Although each parade unit generally identifies itself, each is understood to contribute something to a common theme, and accordingly there is no customary practice whereby private sponsors disavow "any identity of viewpoint" between themselves and the selected participants. Practice follows practicability here, for such disclaimers would be quite curious in a moving parade. Without deciding on the precise significance of the likelihood of misattribution, it nonetheless becomes clear that in the context of an expressive parade, as with a protest march, the parade's overall message is distilled from the individual presentations along the way, and each unit's expression is perceived by spectators as part of the whole.

An additional distinction between *Turner Broadcasting* and this case points to the fundamental weakness of any attempt to justify the state court order's limitation on the Council's autonomy as a speaker. A cable is not only a conduit for speech produced by others and selected by cable operators for transmission, but a franchised channel giving monopolistic opportunity to shut out some speakers. This power gives rise to the government's interest in limiting monopolistic autonomy in order to allow for the survival of broadcasters who might otherwise be silenced and consequently destroyed. The government's interest in *Turner Broadcasting* was not the alteration of speech, but the survival of speakers. In thus identifying an interest going beyond abridgment of speech itself, the defenders of the law at issue in *Turner Broadcasting* addressed the threshold requirement of any review under the Speech Clause, whatever the ultimate level of scrutiny, that a challenged restriction on speech serve a compelling, or at least important, governmental object.

In this case, of course, there is no assertion comparable to the *Turner Broadcasting* claim that some speakers will be destroyed in the absence of the challenged law. True, the size and success of petitioners' parade makes it an enviable vehicle for the dissemination of GLIB's views, but that fact, without more, would fall far short of supporting a claim that petitioners enjoy an abiding monopoly of access to spectators. Considering that GLIB presumably would have had a fair shot (under neutral criteria developed by the city) at obtaining a parade permit of its own, respondents have not shown that petitioners enjoy the capacity to "silence the voice of competing speakers," as cable operators do with respect to program providers who wish to reach subscribers. Nor has any other legitimate interest been identified in support of applying the Massachusetts statute in this way to expressive activity like the parade.

The statute is a piece of protective legislation that announces no purpose beyond the object both expressed and apparent in its provisions, which is to prevent any denial of access to (or discriminatory treatment in) public accommodations on proscribed grounds, including sexual orientation. On its face, the object of the law is to ensure by statute for gays and lesbians desiring to make use of public accommodations what the old common law promised to any member of the public wanting a meal at the inn, that accepting the usual terms of service, they will not be turned away merely on the proprietor's exercise of personal preference. When the law is applied to expressive activity in the way it was done here, its apparent object is simply to require speakers to modify the content of their expression to whatever extent beneficiaries of the law choose to alter it with messages of their own. But in the absence of some further, legitimate end, this object is merely to allow exactly what the general rule of speaker's autonomy forbids.

It might, of course, have been argued that a broader objective is apparent: that the ultimate point of forbidding acts of discrimination toward certain classes is to produce a society free of the corresponding biases. Requiring access to a speaker's message would thus be not an end in itself, but a means to produce speakers free of the biases, whose expressive conduct would be at least neutral toward the particular classes, obviating any future need for correction. But if this indeed is the point of applying the state law to expressive conduct, it is a decidedly fatal objective. Having availed itself of the public thoroughfares "for purposes of assembly [and] communicating thoughts between citizens," the Council is engaged in a use of the streets that has "from ancient times, been a part of the privileges, immunities, rights, and liberties of citizens." *Hague v. Committee for Industrial Organization*, 307 U.S. 496, 515 (1939) (opinion of Roberts, J.). Our tradition of free speech commands that a speaker who takes to the street corner to express his views in this way should be free from interference by the State based on the content of what he says. The very idea that a noncommercial speech restriction be used to produce thoughts and statements acceptable to some groups or, indeed, all people, grates on the First Amendment, for it amounts to nothing less than a proposal to limit speech in the service of orthodox expression. The Speech Clause has no more certain antithesis. While the law is free to promote all sorts of conduct in place of harmful behavior, it is not free to interfere with speech for no better reason than promoting an approved message or discouraging a disfavored one, however enlightened either purpose may strike the government. * * *

New York State Club Association is also instructive by the contrast it provides. There, we turned back a facial challenge to a state antidiscrimination statute on the assumption that the expressive associational character of a dining club with over 400 members could be sufficiently attenuated to permit application of the law even to such a private organization, but we also recognized that the State did not prohibit exclusion of those whose views were at odds with positions espoused by the general club memberships. *See also Roberts*, 468 U.S., at 627. In other words, although the association provided public benefits to which a State could ensure equal access, it was also engaged in expressive activity; compelled access to the benefit, which was upheld, did not trespass on the organization's message itself. If we were to analyze this case strictly along those lines, GLIB would lose. Assuming the parade to be large enough and a source of benefits (apart from its expression) that would generally justify a mandated access provision, GLIB could nonetheless be refused admission as an expressive contingent with its own message just as readily as a private club could exclude an applicant whose manifest views were at odds with a position taken by the club's existing members.

IV

Our holding today rests not on any particular view about the Council's message but on the Nation's commitment to protect freedom of speech. Disapproval of a private speaker's statement does not legitimize use of the Commonwealth's power to compel the speaker to alter the message by including one more acceptable to others. Accordingly, the judgment of the Supreme Judicial Court is reversed and the case remanded for proceedings not inconsistent with this opinion. *It is so ordered.*

NOTES

1.   *Roberts.* Chief Justice Burger and Justice Blackmun, both former members of Twin Cities chapters of the Jaycees, recused themselves from *Roberts.* Justice O'Connor filed a concurrence in which she criticized the majority's opinion for overlooking the commercial nature of the opportunities afforded to men by membership in the Jaycees. "An association must choose its market. Once it enters the marketplace of commerce in any substantial degree it loses the complete control over its membership that it would otherwise enjoy if it confined its affairs to the marketplace of ideas." *Roberts,* 468 U.S. at 636, 104 S. Ct. at 3259 (O'Connor, J., concurring in part and in judgment).

2.   *Hurley.* Under state court order, the GLIB organization marched in the 1992 and 1993 Boston parades. The Allied War Veterans Council cancelled the parade in 1994 rather than allow GLIB to march. Shortly after the U.S. Supreme Court granted a writ of certiorari in *Hurley,* but prior to the case's resolution, the parade organizers brought a declaratory judgment action to prevent GLIB from marching in the 1995 parade. In an attempt to distinguish the event from the 1993 parade at issue in the Supreme Court case, the organizers styled the 1995 parade as a protest against the court order of the Massachusetts high court that forced inclusion of GLIB in previous parades. "[T]he 1995 Parade will begin with a motorcade of vehicles exhibiting black flags, Parade officials will wear black armbands, rather than the traditional green attire, and each of the several divisions of the Parade will be led by a black flag." *S. Bos. Allied War Veterans Council v. City of Boston,* 875 F. Supp. 891, 911 (D. Mass. 1995). Applying the balancing test from *Roberts,* a federal judge ruled that the event was a "sincere and significant protest" which would be compromised by the forced inclusion of GLIB. *S. Bos. Allied War Veterans Council,* 875 F. Supp. at 895. Many prominent public officials refused to march in the Veterans Council parade, including the Mayor of Boston, who barred all city employees from participating in their official capacity. *See Black Flags in Boston Protest Gay Group,* N.Y. TIMES, Mar. 20, 1995, at A10.

3. *Public Violence.* Increasing violence against gay and transgender people on public streets has threatened the expressive rights of the LGBT community. Transgender members of racial minorities have been particularly vulnerable. Jamilah King, *Hate Violence Against LGBT Community on Dangerous Rise*, COLORLINES (June 4, 2013, 1:19 PM), http://colorlines.com/ archives/2013/06/hate_violence_against_lgbt_is_one_a_dangerous_rise.html. From 2010–2011, the New York Anti-Violence Project reported a 13% increase in anti-gay violence in New York City, and the Federal Bureau of Investigation also noted an increase in violence from 1996–2011. *Anti-Gay Crimes Set to Double in New York City in 2013*, RT (Aug. 19, 2013, 8:37 PM), http://rt.com/usa/anti-gay-crimes-double-691/. Attacks in 2013 ranged from verbal slurs to physical attacks and in one case, murder. *Id.* In Washington, D.C., six separate attacks were reported over a span of thirteen days in June and July of 2013. Jase Peeples, *Violence Against LGBT People Continues to Rise in Washington, D.C.*, THE ADVOCATE (July 2, 2013, 7:08 PM), http://www. advocate.com/crime/2013/07/02/violence-against-lgbt-people-continues-rise-washington-dc. Four of the six attacks were against transgender persons. *Id.*

4. *The Olympics.* Russia stirred controversy in June 2013 when President Vladimir Putin signed a law that prohibited the promotion of "nontraditional sexual relationships" to minors. Kathy Lally, *Russia Anti-Gay Law Casts a Shadow over Sochi's 2014 Olympics*, WASH. POST (Sept. 29, 2013), http://articles.washingtonpost.com/2013-09-29/world/42510859_1_sochi -russia-anti-gay-law-olympic-boycott. Enacted shortly before the 2014 Winter Olympics, the law was interpreted to prohibit gay pride parades and any discussion of sexuality among teenagers. *Id.* Russia has also seen an increase in anti-gay violence, with commentators blaming the rise on the new law. Alec Luhn, *Russian Anti-Gay Law Prompts Rise in Homophobic Violence*, THE GUARDIAN (Sept. 1, 2013, 10:01 AM), http://www.theguardian. com/world/2013/sep/01/russia-rise-homophobic-violence.

BOY SCOUTS OF AMERICA V. DALE

Supreme Court of the United States, 2000
530 U.S. 640, 120 S.Ct. 2446, 147 L.Ed.2d 554

CHIEF JUSTICE REHNQUIST delivered the opinion of the Court.

James Dale entered scouting in 1978 at the age of eight by joining Monmouth Council's Cub Scout Pack 142. Dale became a Boy Scout in 1981 and remained a Scout until he turned 18. By all accounts, Dale was an exemplary Scout. In 1988, he achieved the rank of Eagle Scout, one of Scouting's highest honors. Dale applied for adult membership in the Boy Scouts in 1989. The Boy Scouts approved his application for the position of assistant scoutmaster of Troop 73. Around the same time, Dale left home to attend Rutgers University. After arriving at Rutgers, Dale first acknowledged to himself and others that he is gay. He quickly became involved with, and eventually became the copresident of, the Rutgers University Lesbian/Gay Alliance. In 1990, Dale attended a seminar addressing the psychological and health needs of lesbian and gay teenagers. A newspaper covering the event interviewed Dale about his advocacy of homosexual teenagers' need for gay role models. In early July 1990, the newspaper published the interview and Dale's photograph over a caption identifying him as the copresident of the Lesbian/Gay Alliance.

Later that month, Dale received a letter from Monmouth Council Executive James Kay revoking his adult membership. Dale wrote to Kay requesting the reason for Monmouth Council's decision. Kay responded by letter that the Boy Scouts "specifically forbid membership to homosexuals." In 1992, Dale filed a complaint against the Boy Scouts in the New Jersey Superior Court [alleging violations of a New Jersey statute that prohibits discrimination on the basis of sexual orientation by places of public accommodation. The New Jersey Supreme Court ruled in Dale's favor.]

In *Roberts v. United States Jaycees*, 468 U.S. 609 (1984), we observed that "implicit in the right to engage in activities protected by the First Amendment" is "a corresponding right to associate with others in pursuit of a wide variety of political, social, economic, educational, religious, and cultural ends." This right is crucial in preventing the majority from imposing its views on groups that would rather express other, perhaps unpopular, ideas. Government actions that may unconstitutionally burden this freedom may take many forms, one of which is "intrusion into the internal structure or affairs of an association" like a "regulation that forces the group to accept members it does not desire." *Id.* at 623. Forcing a group to accept certain members may impair the ability of the group to express those views, and only those views, that it intends to express. Thus, "[f]reedom of association . . . plainly presupposes a freedom not to associate." *Id.*

The forced inclusion of an unwanted person in a group infringes the group's freedom of expressive association if the presence of that person affects in a significant way the group's ability to advocate public or private viewpoints. But the freedom of expressive association, like many freedoms, is not absolute. [It can] be overridden "by regulations adopted to serve compelling state interests, unrelated to the suppression of ideas, that cannot be achieved through means significantly less restrictive of associational freedoms." *Id.* at 623.

To determine whether a group is protected by the First Amendment's expressive associational right, we must determine whether the group engages in "expressive association." The First Amendment's protection of expressive association is not reserved for advocacy groups. But to come within its ambit, a group must engage in some form of expression, whether it be public or private. * * *

The Boy Scouts is a private, nonprofit organization. According to its mission statement:

It is the mission of the Boy Scouts of America to serve others by helping to instill values in young people and, in other ways, to prepare them to make ethical choices over their lifetime in achieving their full potential. The values we strive to instill are based on those found in the Scout Oath and Law:

<u>Scout Oath</u> On my honor I will do my best:
To do my duty to God and my country and to obey the Scout Law;
To help other people at all times;
To keep myself physically strong, mentally awake, and morally straight.

<u>Scout Law</u> A Scout is:

Trustworthy	Obedient
Loyal	Cheerful
Helpful	Thrifty
Friendly	Brave
Courteous	Clean
Kind	Reverent.

Thus, the general mission of the Boy Scouts is clear: "[T]o instill values in young people." The Boy Scouts seeks to instill these values by having its adult leaders spend time with the youth members, instructing and engaging them in activities like camping, archery, and fishing. During the time spent with the youth members, the scoutmasters and assistant scoutmasters inculcate them with the Boy Scouts' values—both expressly and by example. It seems indisputable that an association that seeks to transmit such a system of values engages in expressive activity.

Given that the Boy Scouts engages in expressive activity, we must determine whether the forced inclusion of Dale as an assistant scoutmaster would significantly affect the Boy Scouts' ability to advocate public or private viewpoints. This inquiry necessarily requires us first to explore, to a limited extent, the nature of the Boy Scouts' view of homosexuality.

The values the Boy Scouts seeks to instill are "based on" those listed in the Scout Oath and Law. The Boy Scouts explains that the Scout Oath and Law provide "a positive moral code for living; they are a list of 'do's' rather than 'don'ts.'" The Boy Scouts asserts that homosexual conduct is inconsistent with the values embodied in the Scout Oath and Law, particularly with the values represented by the terms "morally straight" and "clean."

Obviously, the Scout Oath and Law do not expressly mention sexuality or sexual orientation. And the terms "morally straight" and "clean" are by no means self-defining. Different people would attribute to those terms very different meanings. For example, some people may believe that engaging in homosexual conduct is not at odds with being "morally straight" and "clean." And others may believe that engaging in homosexual conduct is contrary to being "morally straight" and "clean." The Boy Scouts says it falls within the latter category. * * *

The Boy Scouts asserts that it "teach[es] that homosexual conduct is not morally straight," and that it does "not want to promote homosexual conduct as a legitimate form of behavior." We accept the Boy Scouts' assertion. We need not inquire further to determine the nature of the Boy Scouts' expression with respect to homosexuality. . . . We cannot doubt that the Boy Scouts sincerely holds this view.

We must then determine whether Dale's presence as an assistant scoutmaster would significantly burden the Boy Scouts' desire to not "promote homosexual conduct as a legitimate form of behavior." As we give deference to an association's assertions regarding the nature of its expression, we must also give deference to an association's view of what would impair its expression. That is not to say that an expressive association can erect a shield against antidiscrimination laws simply by asserting that mere acceptance of a member from a particular group would impair its message. But here Dale, by his own admission, is one of a group of gay Scouts who have "become leaders in their community and are open and honest about their sexual orientation." Dale was the copresident of a gay and lesbian organization at college and remains a gay rights activist. Dale's presence in the Boy Scouts would, at the very least, force the organization to send a message, both to the youth members and the world, that the Boy Scouts accepts homosexual conduct as a legitimate form of behavior.

Hurley [v. *Irish-American Gay, Lesbian and Bisexual Group of Boston, Inc.*, 515 U.S. 557 (1995)], is illustrative on this point. . . . As the presence of GLIB in Boston's St. Patrick's Day parade would have interfered with the parade organizers' choice not to propound a particular point of view, the presence of Dale as an assistant scoutmaster would just as surely interfere with the Boy Scout's choice not to propound a point of view contrary to its beliefs.

The New Jersey Supreme Court determined that the Boy Scouts' ability to disseminate its message was not significantly affected by the forced inclusion of Dale as an assistant scoutmaster because of the following findings:

Boy Scout members do not associate for the purpose of disseminating the belief that homosexuality is immoral; Boy

Scouts discourages its leaders from disseminating any views on sexual issues; and Boy Scouts includes sponsors and members who subscribe to different views in respect of homosexuality.

Boy Scouts of America v. Dale, 734 A.2d 1196, 1223 (N.J. 1999). We disagree with the New Jersey Supreme Court's conclusion drawn from these findings.

First, associations do not have to associate for the "purpose" of disseminating a certain message in order to be entitled to the protections of the First Amendment. An association must merely engage in expressive activity that could be impaired in order to be entitled to protection. For example, the purpose of the St. Patrick's Day parade in *Hurley* was not to espouse any views about sexual orientation, but we held that the parade organizers had a right to exclude certain participants nonetheless.

Second, even if the Boy Scouts discourages Scout leaders from disseminating views on sexual issues—a fact that the Boy Scouts disputes with contrary evidence—the First Amendment protects the Boy Scouts' method of expression. If the Boy Scouts wishes Scout leaders to avoid questions of sexuality and teach only by example, this fact does not negate the sincerity of its belief discussed above.

Third, the First Amendment simply does not require that every member of a group agree on every issue in order for the group's policy to be "expressive association." The Boy Scouts takes an official position with respect to homosexual conduct, and that is sufficient for First Amendment purposes. In this same vein, Dale makes much of the claim that the Boy Scouts does not revoke the membership of heterosexual Scout leaders that openly disagree with the Boy Scouts' policy on sexual orientation. But if this is true, it is irrelevant.[1] The presence of an avowed homosexual and gay rights activist in an assistant scoutmaster's uniform sends a distinctly different message from the presence of a heterosexual assistant scoutmaster who is on record as disagreeing with Boy Scouts policy. The Boy Scouts has a First Amendment right to choose to send one message but not the other. The fact that the organization does not trumpet its views from the housetops, or that it tolerates dissent within its ranks, does not mean that its views receive no First Amendment protection.

Having determined that the Boy Scouts is an expressive association and that the forced inclusion of Dale would significantly affect its expression, we inquire whether the application of New Jersey's public

---

[1] The record evidence sheds doubt on Dale's assertion. For example, the National Director of the Boy Scouts certified that "any persons who advocate to Scouting youth that homosexual conduct is" consistent with Scouting values will not be registered as adult leaders. And the Monmouth Council Scout Executive testified that the advocacy of the morality of homosexuality to youth members by any adult member is grounds for revocation of the adult's membership.

accommodations law to require that the Boy Scouts accept Dale as an assistant scoutmaster runs afoul of the Scouts' freedom of expressive association. We conclude that it does. * * *

[A] state requirement that the Boy Scouts retain Dale as an assistant scoutmaster would significantly burden the organization's right to oppose or disfavor homosexual conduct. The state interests embodied in New Jersey's public accommodations law do not justify such a severe intrusion on the Boy Scouts' rights to freedom of expressive association. That being the case, we hold that the First Amendment prohibits the State from imposing such a requirement through the application of its public accommodations law.

JUSTICE STEVENS' dissent makes much of its observation that the public perception of homosexuality in this country has changed. Indeed, it appears that homosexuality has gained greater societal acceptance. But this is scarcely an argument for denying First Amendment protection to those who refuse to accept these views. The First Amendment protects expression, be it of the popular variety or not. And the fact that an idea may be embraced and advocated by increasing numbers of people is all the more reason to protect the First Amendment rights of those who wish to voice a different view.

JUSTICE STEVENS, with whom JUSTICE SOUTER, JUSTICE GINSBURG and JUSTICE BREYER join, dissenting.

> [Justice Stevens's dissent begins with a lengthy review of the factual record, aimed at demonstrating that the Boy Scouts, as an organization, did not maintain an explicit anti-gay policy or propound a consistent or coherent anti-gay message.]

[O]ther than [in] a single sentence, BSA fails to show that it ever taught Scouts that homosexuality is not "morally straight" or "clean," [phrases used in the Scout oath] or that such a view was part of the group's collective efforts to foster a belief. Furthermore, BSA's policy statements fail to establish any clear, consistent, and unequivocal position on homosexuality. * * *

[BSA] was clearly on notice by 1990 that it might well be subjected to state public accommodation antidiscrimination laws, and that a court might one day reject its claimed right to associate. Yet it took no steps prior to Dale's expulsion to clarify how its exclusivity was connected to its expression. It speaks volumes about the credibility of BSA's claim to a shared goal that homosexuality is incompatible with Scouting that since at least 1984 it had been aware of this issue . . . yet it did nothing in the intervening six years (or even in the years after Dale's expulsion) to explain clearly and openly why the presence of homosexuals would affect its expressive activities, or to make the view of "morally straight" and "clean" taken in its 1991 and 1992 policies a part of the values actually instilled in Scouts through the Handbook, lessons, or otherwise.

* * * The relevant question is whether the mere inclusion of the person at issue would "impose any serious burden," "affect in any significant way," or be "a substantial restraint upon" the organization's "shared goals," "basic goals," or "collective effort to foster beliefs." Accordingly, it is necessary to examine what, exactly, are BSA's shared goals and the degree to which its expressive activities would be burdened, affected, or restrained by including homosexuals.

The evidence before this Court makes it exceptionally clear that BSA has, at most, simply adopted an exclusionary membership policy and has no shared goal of disapproving of homosexuality. BSA's mission statement and federal charter say nothing on the matter; its official membership policy is silent; its Scout Oath and Law—and accompanying definitions—are devoid of any view on the topic; its guidance for Scouts and Scoutmasters on sexuality declare that such matters are "not construed to be Scouting's proper area," but are the province of a Scout's parents and pastor; and BSA's posture respecting religion tolerates a wide variety of views on the issue of homosexuality. Moreover, there is simply no evidence that BSA otherwise teaches anything in this area, or that it instructs Scouts on matters involving homosexuality in ways not conveyed in the Boy Scout or Scoutmaster Handbooks. In short, Boy Scouts of America is simply silent on homosexuality. There is no shared goal or collective effort to foster a belief about homosexuality at all—let alone one that is significantly burdened by admitting homosexuals.

* * * The majority pretermits this entire analysis. It finds that BSA in fact " 'teach[es] that homosexual conduct is not morally straight.' " This conclusion, remarkably, rests entirely on statements in BSA's briefs. Moreover, the majority insists that we must "give deference to an association's assertions regarding the nature of its expression" and "we must also give deference to an association's view of what would impair its expression." So long as the record "contains written evidence" to support a group's bare assertion, "[w]e need not inquire further." Once the organization "asserts" that it engages in particular expression, "[w]e cannot doubt" the truth of that assertion.

This is an astounding view of the law. I am unaware of any previous instance in which our analysis of the scope of a constitutional right was determined by looking at what a litigant asserts in his or her brief and inquiring no further. It is even more astonishing in the First Amendment area, because, as the majority itself acknowledges, "we are obligated to independently review the factual record." It is an odd form of independent review that consists of deferring entirely to whatever a litigant claims. But the majority insists that our inquiry must be "limited," because "it is not the role of the courts to reject a group's expressed values because they disagree with those values or find them internally inconsistent."

But nothing in our cases calls for this Court to do any such thing. An organization can adopt the message of its choice, and it is not this Court's place to disagree with it. But we must inquire whether the group is, in fact, expressing a message (whatever it may be) and whether that message (if one is expressed) is significantly affected by a State's antidiscrimination law. More critically, that inquiry requires our independent analysis, rather than deference to a group's litigating posture. Reflection on the subject dictates that such an inquiry is required.

Surely there are instances in which an organization that truly aims to foster a belief at odds with the purposes of a State's antidiscrimination laws will have a First Amendment right to association that precludes forced compliance with those laws. But that right is not a freedom to discriminate at will, nor is it a right to maintain an exclusionary membership policy simply out of fear of what the public reaction would be if the group's membership were opened up. It is an implicit right designed to protect the enumerated rights of the First Amendment, not a license to act on any discriminatory impulse. To prevail in asserting a right of expressive association as a defense to a charge of violating an antidiscrimination law, the organization must at least show it has adopted and advocated an unequivocal position inconsistent with a position advocated or epitomized by the person whom the organization seeks to exclude. If this Court were to defer to whatever position an organization is prepared to assert in its briefs, there would be no way to mark the proper boundary between genuine exercises of the right to associate, on the one hand, and sham claims that are simply attempts to insulate nonexpressive private discrimination, on the other hand. Shielding a litigant's claim from judicial scrutiny would, in turn, render civil rights legislation a nullity, and turn this important constitutional right into a farce. Accordingly, the Court's prescription of total deference will not do. . . .

Even if BSA's right to associate argument fails, it nonetheless might have a First Amendment right to refrain from including debate and dialogue about homosexuality as part of its mission to instill values in Scouts. . . . Dale's right to advocate certain beliefs in a public forum or in a private debate does not include a right to advocate these ideas when he is working as a Scoutmaster. And BSA cannot be compelled to include a message about homosexuality among the values it actually chooses to teach its Scouts, if it would prefer to remain silent on that subject. * * *

In its briefs, BSA implies, even if it does not directly argue, that Dale would use his Scoutmaster position as a "bully pulpit" to convey immoral messages to his troop, and therefore his inclusion in the group would compel BSA to include a message it does not want to impart. Even though the majority does not endorse that argument, I think it is important to explain why it lacks merit, before considering the argument the majority does accept. BSA has not contended, nor does the record support, that Dale had ever advocated a view on homosexuality to his troop before his membership was revoked. Accordingly, BSA's revocation could only have been based on an assumption that he would do so in the future. But the only information BSA had at the time it revoked Dale's membership was a newspaper article describing a seminar at Rutgers University on the topic of homosexual teenagers that Dale attended. The relevant passage reads:

> James Dale, 19, co-president of the Rutgers University Lesbian Gay Alliance with Sharice Richardson, also 19, said he lived a double life while in high school, pretending to be straight while attending a military academy. He remembers dating girls and even laughing at homophobic jokes while at school, only admitting his homosexuality during his second year at Rutgers. " 'I was looking for a role model, someone who was gay and accepting of me,' Dale said, adding he wasn't just seeking sexual experiences, but a community that would take him in and provide him with a support network and friends."

Nothing in that article, however, even remotely suggests that Dale would advocate any views on homosexuality to his troop. . . . [T]here is no basis for BSA to presume that a homosexual will be unable to comply with BSA's policy not to discuss sexual matters any more than it would presume that politically or religiously active members could not resist the urge to proselytize or politicize during troop meetings.[19] As BSA itself puts it, its rights are "not implicated *unless* a prospective leader *presents himself* as a role model inconsistent with Boy Scouting's understanding of the Scout Oath and Law."

The majority, though, does not rest its conclusion on the claim that Dale will use his position as a bully pulpit. Rather, it contends that Dale's mere presence among the Boy Scouts will itself force the group to convey a message about homosexuality—even if Dale has no intention of doing so. The majority holds that "[t]he presence of an avowed homosexual and gay rights activist in an assistant scoutmaster's uniform sends a distinc[t] . . . message," and, accordingly, BSA is entitled to exclude that message.

---

[19] Consider, in this regard, that a heterosexual, as well as a homosexual, could advocate to the Scouts the view that homosexuality is not immoral. BSA acknowledges as much by stating that a heterosexual who advocates that view to Scouts would be expelled as well. But BSA does not expel heterosexual members who take that view outside of their participation in Scouting, as long as they do not advocate that position to the Scouts. And if there is no reason to presume that such a heterosexual will openly violate BSA's desire to express no view on the subject, what reason—other than blatant stereotyping—could justify a contrary presumption for homosexuals?

In particular, "Dale's presence in the Boy Scouts would, at the very least, force the organization to send a message, both to the youth members and the world, that the Boy Scouts accepts homosexual conduct as a legitimate form of behavior."

The majority's argument relies exclusively on *Hurley*. Dale's inclusion in the Boy Scouts is nothing like the case in *Hurley*. . . . His participation sends no cognizable message to the Scouts or to the world. Unlike GLIB, Dale did not carry a banner or a sign; he did not distribute any fact sheet; and he expressed no intent to send any message. If there is any kind of message being sent, then, it is by the mere act of joining the Boy Scouts. Such an act does not constitute an instance of symbolic speech under the First Amendment. * * *

The only apparent explanation for the majority's holding, then, is that homosexuals are simply so different from the rest of society that their presence alone—unlike any other individual's—should be singled out for special First Amendment treatment. Under the majority's reasoning, an openly gay male is irreversibly affixed with the label "homosexual." That label, even though unseen, communicates a message that permits his exclusion wherever he goes. His openness is the sole and sufficient justification for his ostracism. Though unintended, reliance on such a justification is tantamount to a constitutionally prescribed symbol of inferiority. As counsel for the Boy Scouts remarked, Dale "put a banner around his neck when he . . . got himself into the newspaper. . . . He created a reputation. . . . He can't take that banner off. He put it on himself and, indeed, he has continued to put it on himself." * * *

Furthermore, it is not likely that BSA would be understood to send any message, either to Scouts or to the world, simply by admitting someone as a member. Over the years, BSA has generously welcomed over 87 million young Americans into its ranks. In 1992 over one million adults were active BSA members. The notion that an organization of that size and enormous prestige implicitly endorses the views that each of those adults may express in a non-Scouting context is simply mind boggling. Indeed, in this case there is no evidence that the young Scouts in Dale's troop, or members of their families, were even aware of his sexual orientation, either before or after his public statements at Rutgers University. It is equally farfetched to assert that Dale's open declaration of his homosexuality, reported in a local newspaper, will effectively force BSA to send a message to anyone simply because it allows Dale to be an Assistant Scoutmaster. For an Olympic gold medal winner or a Wimbledon tennis champion, being "openly gay" perhaps communicates a message—for example, that openness about one's sexual orientation is more virtuous than concealment; that a homosexual person can be a capable and virtuous person who should be judged like anyone else; and that homosexuality is not immoral—but it certainly does not follow that they necessarily send a message on behalf of the organizations that sponsor the activities in which they excel. The fact that such persons participate in these organizations is not usually construed to convey a message on behalf of those organizations any more than does the inclusion of women, African-Americans, religious minorities, or any other discrete group. Surely the organizations are not forced by antidiscrimination laws to take any position on the legitimacy of any individual's private beliefs or private conduct.

The State of New Jersey has decided that people who are open and frank about their sexual orientation are entitled to equal access to employment as school teachers, police officers, librarians, athletic coaches, and a host of other jobs filled by citizens who serve as role models for children and adults alike. Dozens of Scout units throughout the State are sponsored by public agencies, such as schools and fire departments, that employ such role models. BSA's affiliation with numerous public agencies that comply with New Jersey's law against discrimination cannot be understood to convey any particular message endorsing or condoning the activities of all these people.

ACCOMMODATING THE PUBLIC SPHERE: BEYOND THE MARKET MODEL*
Nan D. Hunter

II.   An Expressive Identity Critique of *Dale*

The clash between an openly gay scoutmaster and the Boy Scouts presents a particularly rich illustration of what I have called an expressive identity claim. An expressive identity claim is one in which an equality claim incorporates a message in which the assertion of self-worth is inseparable from the equal treatment demand. Because lesbian and gay rights cases center on an identity that is not visible, the separation of expression and identity is easiest in those cases. It is my contention, however, that virtually all equality cases consist of an expressive identity claim, either implicitly or explicitly.

In most race cases, for example, the factor of visibility itself functions to communicate both difference and, implicitly, self-worth. The expressive content of visible racial difference is powerfully demonstrated by the impulse to exclude. "I don't want blacks in this group" reveals two political stances: explicitly that of the speaker and implicitly that of the African-American person whose claim to a right of presence and inclusion inherently rejects the attempted imposition of a badge of inferiority. The impulse to exclude is always the signifier of a viewpoint entitled to protection under the First Amendment.

*   Nan D. Hunter, *Accommodating the Public Sphere: Beyond the Market Model*, 85 MINN. L. REV. 1591, 1605–36 (2001).

In most lesbian and gay cases, coming out speech serves the function of communicating both self-worth and self-identification. The fact that the self-worth message materializes in speech, rather than in physical presence, should not lead to a different constitutional standard for whether those who object to that belief in equality should be exempt from anti-discrimination laws. A belief in superiority in any form—racial, sexual, or other—cannot be completely silenced by the state.

The Boy Scouts' position is not entirely clear. Their first briefs refer to the condemnation or immorality of homosexual conduct. In their reply brief, they assert the desire to remain silent about homosexuality, although apparently they do not intend their silence to indicate neutrality. The Court's holding is phrased in terms of the BSA's right "to 'not promote homosexual conduct,' " quoting the reply brief. In whatever form, the essence of their position is disapproval. Requiring that they state it more clearly, if only internally, does not seem an unfair prerequisite for a group seeking an expression-based exemption from a generally applicable law.

In *Dale*, however, the Court was unable to escape a cultural distortion chamber in its assessment of these competing interests. As a result, it over-read the expressive component of both Dale's identity as a gay man and the BSA's statements on homosexuality. I shall discuss each of these points in turn, and close this Part with some thoughts on the category of cases where group beliefs and exclusion of persons overlap.

A.   The Demonization of Dale

Compared to the unabashedly homophobic language of the Court in *Bowers v. Hardwick*, or of the dissent in *Romer v. Evans*, the tone of the majority opinion in *Dale* is almost bland. There is a careful evenhandedness whenever the text trenches on the morality question itself. The Court rejects the Boy Scouts' argument that the terms "morally straight" and "clean" in the Boy Scout Oath and Law are on their face synonymous with condemnation of homosexuality: "Some people may believe that engaging in homosexual conduct is not at odds with being 'morally straight' and 'clean.' And others may believe that engaging in homosexual conduct is contrary to being 'morally straight' and 'clean.' " The Court itself professes to give no weight to meanings of morality: "We are not, as we must not be, guided by our views of whether the Boy Scouts' teachings with respect to homosexual conduct are right or wrong; public or judicial disapproval of a tenet of an organization's expression does not justify [its abridgement]."

Without making a direct statement, however, the Court's language invokes another canard: the intrinsic uncontrollability of gay male sexuality. In the text of *Dale*, that specter has been modernized. Sexuality has been merged into identity, but not tamed. Dale's coming out replaces sexual acts per se as the socially explosive moment. Once he had come out in any respect, his identity as "homosexual," like his sexuality, became impossible to control.

In the critical portion of the opinion in which the Court found that Dale's mere presence would force the Boy Scouts to send a message, the Court described him as "by his own admission, . . . one of a group of gay Scouts who have become leaders in their community and are open and honest about their sexual orientation." In the next sentence, the Court introduces a key word: "Dale was the copresident of a gay and lesbian organization at college and remains a gay rights activist." The Court goes on to join these elements: "The presence of an avowed homosexual and gay rights activist in an assistant scoutmaster's uniform sends a distinct . . . message."

As the dissent argues, these passages insinuate that Dale would attempt to use an assistant scoutmaster position for purposes of proclaiming the value of homosexuality. In fact, Dale stated that he would agree to be bound by the organization's rules against that in his capacity as scoutmaster. The initial newspaper article contained Dale's statements to a reporter covering a conference that he attended in which the Boy Scouts were not mentioned. Nor, as the dissent notes, did anyone contend that Dale was a person so publicly identified with gay rights that he could be said to epitomize the issue, thus justifying his particular exclusion (rather than as a member of the class).

Instead, the Court impliedly finds that almost any openly gay or lesbian person is radioactive. Nothing in the record marks Dale as an "activist" other than his copresidency of a college student group, yet "activist" carries the unmistakable whiff of extremism and zeal. It is difficult to imagine that the copresident of a student Spanish club or drama club or Catholic Youth Organization would be labeled, ten years later, an activist. Despite the rhetorical focus on his insinuated proclivity to proselytize, it is also difficult to imagine that the Court would have ruled differently if Dale had been a member rather than copresident; or indeed, if he had never joined any organization in his life except the Boy Scouts. Since there is no indication that Dale sought out the reporter or initiated the interview, the conclusion must be that nothing more than his willingness to self-identify as gay justifies his exclusion. As the dissent concludes, the result is that socially visible homosexuality creates a basis for exclusion to an extent that no other minority characteristic does.

Anthropologist Gayle S. Rubin would characterize this as an example of "the fallacy of misplaced scale":

> Throughout much of European and American history, a single act of consensual anal penetration was grounds for execution. . . .

Although people can be intolerant, silly, or pushy about what constitutes proper diet, differences in menu rarely provoke the kinds of rage, anxiety, and sheer terror that routinely accompany differences in erotic taste. Sexual acts are burdened with an excess of significance.

The Court attaches an excess of significance to Dale's homosexuality and then declares that as the self-evident import of his presence. * * *

Most importantly, the case illustrates that the rhetoric of egalitarian masculinity that is the hallmark of the Boy Scouts is no longer a satisfactory substitute for a fully inclusive concept of citizenship. The Boy Scouts' image as a paragon of good citizenship begins to fade when their strongest argument to the Court is the right to believe in inequality. Dale tells us that the assumption that conforming to gender norms is the price of admission to a shared civic culture is under severe challenge.

C.   The Expression-Exclusion Continuum

The concept of expressive identity is an attempt to normalize equality claims in which expression is somehow required in order to make the identity characteristic socially visible. It is an argument that they should be treated the same as other equality claims, those based on immediately visible characteristics, because ultimately all equality claims are expressive. This, however, does not answer the question of when, if ever, identity is acceptable as a basis for exclusion.

The tension in the expressive association cases involving membership organizations arises from the prohibition of discrimination based on certain identity characteristics combined with the constitutional right to associate. In order to protect the group's right, we allow them to exclude persons "whose manifest views are at odds" with a group policy, whose presence would impede their ability to communicate their message "nearly as effectively."

Under this principle, the Boy Scouts unquestionably has a right to exclude persons with views contrary to its own. Granting them the deference shown by the majority and accepting as bona fide that the Boy Scouts command to be "morally straight" communicates disapproval of homosexuality, they have the right to exclude all who would communicate approval. In *Dale*, however, that dog did not bark: the Boy Scouts have not genuinely sought to exclude everyone communicating approval of homosexuality.

Dale is an example of a case that sits at the border between expression and discriminatory exclusion. The Court has not developed an adequate methodology for assessing when an organization has crossed that line. Although organizations can lawfully exclude persons for a number of reasons, cases such as *Dale* arise when an organization seeks an exemption from a statute that protects persons with certain characteristics from discrimination based on a legislative judgment that prejudice is frequently directed against members of this group.

I suggest thinking of this situation as a continuum. Seeking group unity based on shared beliefs/goals lies at one end of a continuum. Excluding persons solely because their identity renders them somehow undesirable is at the other end. In my view, a group's right to exclude should generally extend from that first starting point as far as reasonably necessary to achieve the goal of shared beliefs.

In some situations, applying that principle will allow a group to exclude for the full length of the continuum. For some groups, especially social clubs, celebration of the shared identity is itself the entire or primary purpose of the group. For other groups, the core organizing purpose is a belief in some form of superiority, such as the inevitable example of the Ku Klux Klan. The Klan meets this test: only believers in white supremacy may join. Given the overwhelming importance to the Klan of its beliefs in supremacy and segregation, I would argue that they should be permitted to extend their exclusions to include the far point on the continuum, in other words, to exclude all non-whites. The Klan is nothing if not consistent.

What a group drawn together by shared beliefs or goals should not be permitted to do is to start at the other end of the continuum, to use a protected characteristic as its only basis for seeking unity. In other words, although I recognize that an identity characteristic might function reasonably well as a proxy for certain beliefs, it can only be a partial proxy. I would require the organization to, in essence, have the courage of its convictions and accept only members or leaders who shared those beliefs, whatever they were. If a belief is important enough to serve as a basis for excluding a group of people specifically protected by law, then it should be important enough to define eligibility for membership. If it does define eligibility for everyone seeking to join, then the organization has a much more genuine claim to reach the identity end of the continuum in its exclusions.

I acknowledge that this approach would lead to some intrusion in internal organization affairs, a disadvantage that must be acknowledged. That limited intrusions can be justified by a compelling interest in securing full civil rights for historically disadvantaged groups is, however, well established by the *United States Jaycees-Rotary Club-New York State Club Ass'n* line of cases. This proposal for intrusion has the advantage that its effect will be to produce more, not less, expression of the organization's contrary beliefs.

The *Dale* Court rejected this approach, saying that the Boy Scouts were entitled to choose to send one message but not the other—to reject sending the message that Dale represented but to accept sending the message conveyed by heterosexual scoutmasters who believed there to be nothing wrong with homosexuality. This statement invites an organization engaged primarily in expressive activity on any topic to simply adopt a resolution barring gay members. It eliminates any basis upon which a court could assess whether the exclusion is necessary to the preservation of the group's shared beliefs. On this logic, there is dangerously little left of the anti-discrimination protection. * * *

NOTES

1. Not all supporters of gay equality necessarily regard the *Dale* decision as wrongly decided. Professor Dale Carpenter, for example, has argued that:

> The First Amendment created gay America. For advocates of gay legal and social equality there has been no more reliable and important constitutional text. The freedoms it guarantees have protected gay cultural and political institutions from state regulation designed to impose a contrary vision of the good life. Gay organizations, clubs, bars, politicians, journals, newspapers, radio programs, television shows—all these would be swept away in the absence of a strong First Amendment.
>
> The First Amendment, evenhanded and detached from passions to an unusual degree for a jurisprudence, sheltered gays even when most of the country thought they were not just immoral, but also sick and dangerous. . . .
>
> By contrast, the Due Process Clause (in its substantive dimension) has been faithless. The Equal Protection Clause has been impotent. The Ninth Amendment has been missing in action. . . . And the Fourteenth Amendment's Privileges and Immunities Clause has not been seen since it was banished at the age of five.

Dale Carpenter, *Expressive Association and Anti-Discrimination Law After Dale*, 85 MINN. L. REV. 1515, 1525–27 (2001).

2. For scholarly commentary on *Dale* from different perspectives, see Yaacov Ben-Shemesh, *Multiculturalism and the Anti-Discrimination Principle: Law and Intercultural Conflicts*, 1 LAW & ETHICS HUM. RTS. 271 (2007); Erwin Chemerinsky & Catherine Fisk, *The Expressive Interest of Associations*, 9 WM. & MARY BILL RTS. J. 595 (2001); Richard A. Epstein, *The Constitutional Perils of Moderation: The Case of the Boy Scouts*, 74 S. CAL. L. REV. 119 (2000); Nancy J. Knauer, *"Simply So Different": The Uniquely Expressive Character of the Openly Gay Individual After* Boy Scouts of America v. Dale, 89 KY. L.J. 997 (2001); Andrew Koppelman, *Sign of the Times:* Dale v. Boy Scouts of America *and the Changing Meaning of Nondiscrimination*, 23 CARDOZO L. REV. 1819 (2002); Jed Rubenfeld, *The First Amendment's Purpose*, 53 STAN. L. REV. 767 (2001); Seana Valentine

Shiffrin, *What Is Really Wrong with Compelled Association*, 99 NW. U. L. REV. 839 (2005); Laurence H. Tribe, *Disentangling Symmetries: Speech, Association, Parenthood*, 28 PEPP. L. REV. 641 (2001); Neal Troum, *Expressive Association and the Right to Exclude: Reading Between the Lines in* Boy Scouts of America v. Dale, 35 CREIGHTON L. REV. 641 (2002).

3.   As early as 1991, the San Francisco Board of Education voted to eject the Boy Scouts from operating on public school property during school hours. Nanette Asimov, *S.F. Schools Break Ties with Boy Scouts; Board Cites Discriminatory Membership Policy*, S.F. CHRON., Sept. 14, 1991 at A14. In the wake of the *Dale* decision, several public schools across the country followed suit by eliminating sponsorship of Boy Scout troops and ending special privileges allowing the Scouts to distribute literature in schools. *Group: Supreme Court Ruling Yields Unexpected Lesson for Boy Scouts; One Year Later, Discrimination Still Outrages Americans*, U.S. NEWSWIRE, June 21, 2001. In response to policies like these, Congress enacted the Boy Scouts of America Equal Access Act as part of the No Child Left Behind Act of 2001. The measure prevented public schools that let youth or community groups use its facilities from discriminating against the Boy Scouts. *Boy Scouts of America Equal Access Act*, U.S. Department of Education, http://www2.ed.gov/about/offices/list/ocr/boyscouts.html (last visited Oct. 16, 2013).

4.   In May 2013, the leadership of the Boy Scouts of America voted to allow openly gay youths to participate in the organization. Erik Eckholm, *Boy Scouts End Longtime Ban on Openly Gay Youths*, N.Y. TIMES, May 23, 2013, at A1. But the group still forbids openly gay adults and leaders from participating. The policy change followed a vocal campaign by members of the scouting community, including a campaign in which many Eagle Scouts renounced their status or returned their badges in protest of the Boy Scouts' exclusionary policies. Gabriel Rodriguez, *This Brave Eagle Scout Won't Tolerate the Boy Scouts' Anti-Gay Policy*, POLICYMIC (April 7, 2013), http://www.policymic.com/articles/33409/this-brave-eagle-scout-won-t-tolerate-the-boy-scouts-anti-gay-policy.

5.   Note that not all youth organizations similar to the Boy Scouts have pursued policies of exclusion. The Girl Scouts of the United States of America explicitly address homosexuality in its membership policy:

> As a private organization, Girl Scouts of the U.S.A. respects the values and beliefs of its members and does not intrude into personal matters. Therefore, there are no membership policies on sexual preference. However, Girl Scouts of the U.S.A. has firm standards relating to the appropriate conduct of adult volunteers and staff. The Girl Scout organization does not condone or permit sexual displays of any sort by its members during Girl Scout activities, nor does it permit the advocacy or promotion of a personal lifestyle or sexual preference. These are private matters for girls and their families to address.

Girl Scouts of the United States of America, Statements on GSUSA Membership Policies (Oct. 1991). Indeed, in October 2011, a Girl Scout troop in Colorado admitted a transgender member, Bobby Montoya. Katia Hetter, *Girl Scouts Accepts Transgender Kid, Provokes Cookie Boycott*, CNN (Jan. 13, 2012, 7:23 PM), http://www.cnn.com/2012/01/13/living/girl-scout-boycott/. The Girl Scouts of Colorado said, "If a child identifies as a girl and the child's family presents her as a girl, Girl Scouts of Colorado welcomes her as a Girl Scout." *Id.*

Big Brothers/Big Sisters of America's policy, adopted first in 1977, now reads:

> It is the historical practice of BB/BS to consider and communicate . . . before a match is made, any past or present pertinent factors in the health, personality and behavior of the other, which in the professional judgment of the agency staff may have a significant effect upon the prospective relationship (between volunteer and child). . . . This practice covers such issues as religious and cultural background, marital status, affectional preference, physical and mental health, drug or alcohol use, criminal convictions and other such matters.

Big Brothers/Big Sisters of America, Policy Statement: Volunteer Selection and Assignment (July 1988 Executive Newsletter) (on file with national headquarters). In 2002, Big Brothers/Big Sisters updated its policy to require chapters to allow gay and lesbian individuals to volunteer as mentors. Ray Delgado, *Big Brothers, Sisters Hit by Religious Right / Group Attacked for Welcoming Gay and Lesbian Mentors*, S.F. CHRON. (Aug. 15, 2002, 4:00 AM), http://www.sfgate.com/news/article/Big-Brothers-Sisters-hit-by-religious-right -2809844.php. The YMCA of the USA, which does not enunciate policies for autonomous local branches, includes "lifestyle" as one of several categories which do not diminish individual value. YMCA of the USA, Managing Cultural Diversity (May 1995) (on file with national headquarters). The Boys and Girls Club has no official policy regarding homosexuality.

The next two cases bring squarely into focus the tension between some religious beliefs and anti-discrimination laws. This tension has become increasingly prominent over the last several years, especially in the context of the debate over marriage equality. (*See* Chapter 6, Sec. II.) As you consider these cases, think about if and how the religious nature of the claims changes the issue from what we have seen thus far. Notice, as well, that the second case involves a *commercial* actor who resists application of a non-discrimination norm. How should that fact weigh in the analysis?

CHRISTIAN LEGAL SOCIETY V. MARTINEZ

Supreme Court of the United States, 2010
561 U.S. ___, 130 S.Ct. 2971, 177 L.Ed.2d 838

JUSTICE GINSBURG delivered the opinion of the Court.

In a series of decisions, this Court has emphasized that the First Amendment generally precludes public universities from denying student organizations access to school-sponsored forums because of the groups' viewpoints. See *Rosenberger* v. *Rector and Visitors of Univ. of Va.*, 515 U.S. 819 (1995); *Widmar* v. *Vincent*, 454 U.S. 263 (1981); *Healy* v. *James*, 408 U.S. 169 (1972). This case concerns a novel question regarding student activities at public universities: May a public law school condition its official recognition of a student group—and the attendant use of school funds and facilities—on the organization's agreement to open eligibility for membership and leadership to all students?

In the view of petitioner Christian Legal Society (CLS), an accept-all-comers policy impairs its First Amendment rights to free speech, expressive association, and free exercise of religion by prompting it, on pain of relinquishing the advantages of recognition, to accept members who do not share the organization's core beliefs about religion and sexual orientation. From the perspective of respondent Hastings College of the Law (Hastings or the Law School), CLS seeks special dispensation from an across-the-board open-access requirement designed to further the reasonable educational purposes underpinning the school's student-organization program. * * *

Founded in 1878, Hastings was the first law school in the University of California public-school system. Like many institutions of higher education, Hastings encourages students to form extracurricular associations that "contribute to the Hastings community and experience." These groups offer students "opportunities to pursue academic and social interests outside of the classroom [to] further their education" and to help them "develo[p] leadership skills."

Through its "Registered Student Organization" (RSO) program, Hastings extends official recognition to student groups. Several benefits attend this school-approved status. RSOs are eligible to seek financial assistance from the Law School, which subsidizes their events using funds from a mandatory student-activity fee imposed on all students. RSOs may also use Law-School channels to communicate with students: They may place announcements in a weekly Office-of-Student-Services newsletter, advertise events on designated bulletin boards, send e-mails using a Hastings-organization address, and participate in an annual Student Organizations Fair designed to advance recruitment efforts. In addition, RSOs may apply for permission to use the Law School's facilities for meetings and office space. Finally, Hastings allows officially recognized groups to use its name and logo.

In exchange for these benefits, RSOs must abide by certain conditions. Only a "non-commercial organization whose membership is limited to Hastings students may become [an RSO]." A prospective RSO must submit its bylaws to Hastings for approval, and if it intends to use the Law School's name or logo, it must sign a license agreement. Critical here, all RSOs must undertake to comply with Hastings' "Policies and Regulations Applying to College Activities, Organizations and Students."

The Law School's Policy on Nondiscrimination (Nondiscrimination Policy), which binds RSOs, states:

> "[Hastings] is committed to a policy against legally impermissible, arbitrary or unreasonable discriminatory practices. All groups, including administration, faculty, student governments, [Hastings]-owned student residence facilities and programs sponsored by [Hastings], are governed by this policy of nondiscrimination. [Hasting's] policy on nondiscrimination is to comply fully with applicable law.

> "[Hastings] shall not discriminate unlawfully on the basis of race, color, religion, national origin, ancestry, disability, age, sex or sexual orientation. This nondiscrimination policy covers admission, access and treatment in Hastings-sponsored programs and activities."

Hastings interprets the Nondiscrimination Policy, as it relates to the RSO program, to mandate acceptance of all comers: School-approved groups must "allow any student to participate, become a member, or seek leadership positions in the organization, regardless of [her] status or beliefs." Other law schools have adopted similar all-comers policies. See, e.g., Georgetown University Law Center, Office of Student Life: Student Organizations, available at http://www.law.georgetown.edu/StudentLife/ StudentOrgs/NewGroup.htm (All Internet materials as visited June 24, 2010, and included in Clerk of Court's case file) (Membership in registered groups must be "open to all students."); Hofstra Law School Student Handbook 2009–2010, p.49, available at http://law.hofstra.edu/ pdf/StudentLife/StudentAffairs/Handbook/stuhb_handbook.pdf ("[Student] organizations are open to all students."). From Hastings' adoption of its Nondiscrimination Policy in 1990 until the events stirring this litigation, "no student organization at Hastings . . . ever sought an exemption from the Policy."

In 2004, CLS became the first student group to do so. At the beginning of the academic year, the leaders of a predecessor Christian organization—which had been an RSO at Hastings for a decade—formed CLS by affiliating with the national Christian Legal Society (CLS-

National). CLS-National, an association of Christian lawyers and law students, charters student chapters at law schools throughout the country. CLS chapters must adopt bylaws that, *inter alia*, require members and officers to sign a "Statement of Faith" and to conduct their lives in accord with prescribed principles.[1] Among those tenets is the belief that sexual activity should not occur outside of marriage between a man and a woman; CLS thus interprets its bylaws to exclude from affiliation anyone who engages in "unrepentant homosexual conduct." CLS also excludes students who hold religious convictions different from those in the Statement of Faith.

On September 17, 2004, CLS submitted to Hastings an application for RSO status, accompanied by all required documents, including the set of bylaws mandated by CLS-National. Several days later, the Law School rejected the application; CLS's bylaws, Hastings explained, did not comply with the Nondiscrimination Policy because CLS barred students based on religion and sexual orientation.

CLS formally requested an exemption from the Nondiscrimination Policy, but Hastings declined to grant one. "[T]o be one of our student-recognized organizations," Hastings reiterated, "CLS must open its membership to all students irrespective of their religious beliefs or sexual orientation." If CLS instead chose to operate outside the RSO program, Hastings stated, the school "would be pleased to provide [CLS] the use of Hastings facilities for its meetings and activities." CLS would also have access to chalkboards and generally available campus bulletin boards to announce its events. In other words, Hastings would do nothing to suppress CLS's endeavors, but neither would it lend RSO-level support for them.

Refusing to alter its bylaws, CLS did not obtain RSO status. It did, however, operate independently during the 2004–2005 academic year. . . .

On October 22, 2004, CLS filed suit against various Hastings officers and administrators . . . alleg[ing] that Hastings' refusal to grant the organization RSO status violated CLS's First and Fourteenth Amendment rights to free speech, expressive association, and free exercise of religion.

On cross-motions for summary judgment, the U. S. District Court for the Northern District of California ruled in favor of Hastings. The Law

---

[1]   The Statement of Faith provides: "Trusting in Jesus Christ as my Savior, I believe in:

• One God, eternally existent in three persons, Father, Son and Holy Spirit.

• God the Father Almighty, Maker of heaven and earth.

• The Deity of our Lord, Jesus Christ, God's only Son conceived of the Holy Spirit, born of the Virgin Mary; His vicarious death for our sins through which we receive eternal life; His bodily resurrection and personal return.

• The presence and power of the Holy Spirit in the work of regeneration.

• The Bible as the inspired Word of God." App. 226.

School's all-comers condition on access to a limited public forum, the court held, was both reasonable and viewpoint neutral, and therefore did not violate CLS's right to free speech.

Nor, in the District Court's view, did the Law School impermissibly impair CLS's right to expressive association. * * *

The court also rejected CLS's Free Exercise Clause argument. "[T]he Nondiscrimination Policy does not target or single out religious beliefs," the court noted; rather, the policy "is neutral and of general applicability." * * *

On appeal, the Ninth Circuit affirmed in an opinion that stated, in full:

> "The parties stipulate that Hastings imposes an open membership rule on all student groups—all groups must accept all comers as voting members even if those individuals disagree with the mission of the group. The conditions on recognition are therefore viewpoint neutral and reasonable. *Truth v. Kent Sch. Dist.*, 542 F. 3d 634, 649–50 (9th Cir. 2008)." *Christian Legal Soc. Chapter of Univ. of Cal.* v. *Kane*, 319 Fed. Appx. 645, 645–646 (CA9 2009).

[We] now affirm the Ninth Circuit's judgment.

Before considering the merits of CLS's constitutional arguments, we must resolve a preliminary issue: CLS urges us to review the Nondiscrimination Policy as written—prohibiting discrimination on several enumerated bases, including religion and sexual orientation—and not as a requirement that all RSOs accept all comers. The written terms of the Nondiscrimination Policy, CLS contends, "targe[t] solely those groups whose beliefs are based on religion or that disapprove of a particular kind of sexual behavior," and leave other associations free to limit membership and leadership to individuals committed to the group's ideology. Brief for Petitioner 19 (internal quotation marks omitted). For example, "[a] political . . . group can insist that its leaders support its purposes and beliefs," CLS alleges, but "a religious group cannot."

CLS's assertion runs headlong into the stipulation of facts it jointly submitted with Hastings at the summary-judgment stage. In that filing, the parties specified:

> "Hastings requires that registered student organizations allow *any* student to participate, become a member, or seek leadership positions in the organization, regardless of [her] status or beliefs. Thus, for example, the Hastings Democratic Caucus cannot bar students holding Republican political beliefs from becoming members or seeking leadership positions in the organization." * * *

In support of the argument that Hastings' all-comers policy treads on its First Amendment rights to free speech and expressive association, CLS draws on two lines of decisions. First, in a progression of cases, this Court has employed forum analysis to determine when a governmental entity, in regulating property in its charge, may place limitations on speech. Recognizing a State's right "to preserve the property under its control for the use to which it is lawfully dedicated," *Cornelius* v. *NAACP Legal Defense & Ed. Fund, Inc.*, 473 U. S. 788, 800 (1985) (internal quotation marks omitted), the Court has permitted restrictions on access to a limited public forum, like the RSO program here, with this key caveat: Any access barrier must be reasonable and viewpoint neutral. * * *

Second, as evidenced by another set of decisions, this Court has rigorously reviewed laws and regulations that constrain associational freedom. In the context of public accommodations, we have subjected restrictions on that freedom to close scrutiny; such restrictions are permitted only if they serve "compelling state interests" that are "unrelated to the suppression of ideas"—interests that cannot be advanced "through . . . significantly less restrictive [means]." *Roberts* v. *United States Jaycees*, 468 U.S. 609, 623 (1984). See also, *e.g., Boy Scouts of America* v. *Dale*, 530 U.S. 640, 648 (2000). "Freedom of association," we have recognized, "plainly presupposes a freedom not to associate." *Roberts*, 468 U.S., at 623. Insisting that an organization embrace unwelcome members, we have therefore concluded, "directly and immediately affects associational rights." *Dale*, 530 U.S., at 659.

CLS would have us engage each line of cases independently, but its expressive-association and free-speech arguments merge: *Who* speaks on its behalf, CLS reasons, colors *what* concept is conveyed. It therefore makes little sense to treat CLS's speech and association claims as discrete. Instead, three observations lead us to conclude that our limited-public-forum precedents supply the appropriate framework for assessing both CLS's speech and association rights.

First, the same considerations that have led us to apply a less restrictive level of scrutiny to speech in limited public forums as compared to other environments apply with equal force to expressive association occurring in limited public forums. . . .

Second, and closely related, the strict scrutiny we have applied in some settings to laws that burden expressive association would, in practical effect, invalidate a defining characteristic of limited public forums—the State may "reserv[e] [them] for certain groups." *Rosenberger*, 515 U.S., at 829. . . .

Third, this case fits comfortably within the limited-public-forum category, for CLS, in seeking what is effectively a state subsidy, faces only indirect pressure to modify its membership policies; CLS may exclude any person for any reason if it forgoes the benefits of official recognition. The expressive-association precedents on which CLS relies, in contrast, involved regulations that *compelled* a group to include unwanted members, with no choice to opt out. See, *e.g., Dale*, 530 U.S., at 648 (regulation "forc[ed] [the Boy Scouts] to accept members it [did] not desire" (internal quotation marks omitted)); *Roberts*, 468 U. S., at 623 ("There can be no clearer example of an intrusion into the internal structure or affairs of an association than" forced inclusion of unwelcome participants.).

In diverse contexts, our decisions have distinguished between policies that require action and those that withhold benefits. Application of the less-restrictive limited-public-forum analysis better accounts for the fact that Hastings, through its RSO program, is dangling the carrot of subsidy, not wielding the stick of prohibition.

In sum, we are persuaded that our limited-public-forum precedents adequately respect both CLS's speech and expressive-association rights, and fairly balance those rights against Hastings' interests as property owner and educational institution. We turn to the merits of the instant dispute, therefore, with the limited-public-forum decisions as our guide. * * *

"Once it has opened a limited [public] forum," we emphasized, "the State must respect the lawful boundaries it has itself set." The constitutional constraints on the boundaries the State may set bear repetition here: "The State may not exclude speech where its distinction is not reasonable in light of the purpose served by the forum, . . . nor may it discriminate against speech on the basis of . . . viewpoint." *Rosenberger*, 515 U.S., at 829.

Our inquiry is shaped by the educational context in which it arises: "First Amendment rights," we have observed, "must be analyzed in light of the special characteristics of the school environment." *Widmar*, 454 U.S., at 268, n. 5 (internal quotation marks omitted). * * *

A college's commission—and its concomitant license to choose among pedagogical approaches—is not confined to the classroom, for extracurricular programs are, today, essential parts of the educational process. Schools, we have emphasized, enjoy "a significant measure of authority over the type of officially recognized activities in which their students participate."

With appropriate regard for school administrators' judgment, we review the justifications Hastings offers in defense of its all-comers requirement. First, the open-access policy "ensures that the leadership, educational, and social opportunities afforded by [RSOs] are available to all students." Just as "Hastings does not allow its professors to host classes open only to those students with a certain status or belief," so the Law School may decide, reasonably in our view, "that the . . . educational experience is best promoted when all participants in the forum must provide equal access to all students." RSOs, we count it significant, are eligible for financial assistance drawn from mandatory student-activity fees; the all-comers policy ensures that no Hastings student is forced to fund a group that would reject her as a member.

Second, the all-comers requirement helps Hastings police the written terms of its Nondiscrimination Policy without inquiring into an RSO's motivation for membership restrictions. To bring the RSO program within CLS's view of the Constitution's limits, CLS proposes that Hastings permit exclusion because of *belief* but forbid discrimination due to *status*. But that proposal would impose on Hastings a daunting labor. How should the Law School go about determining whether a student organization cloaked prohibited status exclusion in belief-based garb? If a hypothetical Male-Superiority Club barred a female student from running for its presidency, for example, how could the Law School tell whether the group rejected her bid because of her sex or because, by seeking to lead the club, she manifested a lack of belief in its fundamental philosophy?

This case itself is instructive in this regard. CLS contends that it does not exclude individuals because of sexual orientation, but rather "on the basis of a conjunction of conduct and the belief that the conduct is not wrong." Our decisions have declined to distinguish between status and conduct in this context. See *Lawrence* v. *Texas*, 539 U.S. 558, 575 (2003) ("When homosexual *conduct* is made criminal by the law of the State, that declaration in and of itself is an invitation to subject homosexual *persons* to discrimination." (emphasis added)); *id.,* at 583 (O'Connor, J., concurring in judgment) ("While it is true that the law applies only to conduct, the conduct targeted by this law is conduct that is closely correlated with being homosexual. Under such circumstances, [the] law is targeted at more than conduct. It is instead directed toward gay persons as a class.").

Third, the Law School reasonably adheres to the view that an all-comers policy, to the extent it brings together individuals with diverse backgrounds and beliefs, "encourages tolerance, cooperation, and learning among students." And if the policy sometimes produces discord, Hastings can rationally rank among RSO-program goals development of conflict-resolution skills, toleration, and readiness to find common ground.

Fourth, Hastings' policy, which incorporates—in fact, subsumes—state-law proscriptions on discrimination, conveys the Law School's decision "to decline to subsidize with public monies and benefits conduct of which the people of California disapprove." State law, of course, may not *command* that public universities take action impermissible under the First Amendment.

In sum, the several justifications Hastings asserts in support of its all-comers requirement are surely reasonable in light of the RSO forum's purposes.

The Law School's policy is all the more creditworthy in view of the "substantial alternative channels that remain open for [CLS-student] communication to take place." If restrictions on access to a limited public forum are viewpoint discriminatory, the ability of a group to exist outside the forum would not cure the constitutional shortcoming. But when access barriers are viewpoint neutral, our decisions have counted it significant that other available avenues for the group to exercise its First Amendment rights lessen the burden created by those barriers.

In this case, Hastings offered CLS access to school facilities to conduct meetings and the use of chalkboards and generally available bulletin boards to advertise events. Although CLS could not take advantage of RSO-specific methods of communication, the advent of electronic media and social-networking sites reduces the importance of those channels.

Private groups, from fraternities and sororities to social clubs and secret societies, commonly maintain a presence at universities without official school affiliation. Based on the record before us, CLS was similarly situated: It hosted a variety of activities the year after Hastings denied it recognition, and the number of students attending those meetings and events doubled.

CLS nevertheless deems Hastings' all-comers policy "frankly absurd." "There can be no diversity of viewpoints in a forum," it asserts, "if groups are not permitted to form around viewpoints." *Id.*, at 50; accord *post*, at 25 (Alito, J., dissenting). This catchphrase confuses CLS's preferred policy with constitutional limitation—the *advisability* of Hastings' policy does not control its *permissibility*.

CLS also assails the reasonableness of the all-comers policy in light of the RSO forum's function by forecasting that the policy will facilitate hostile takeovers; if organizations must open their arms to all, CLS contends, saboteurs will infiltrate groups to subvert their mission and message. This supposition strikes us as more hypothetical than real. CLS points to no history or prospect of RSO-hijackings at Hastings. Students tend to self-sort and presumably will not endeavor en masse to join—let alone seek leadership positions in—groups pursuing missions wholly at odds with their personal beliefs. And if a rogue student intent on sabotaging an organization's objectives nevertheless attempted a takeover, the members of that group would not likely elect her as an officer.

RSOs, moreover, in harmony with the all-comers policy, may condition eligibility for membership and leadership on attendance, the payment of dues, or other neutral requirements designed to ensure that students join because of their commitment to a group's vitality, not its demise. Several RSOs at Hastings limit their membership rolls and officer slates in just this way.

Hastings, furthermore, could reasonably expect more from its law students than the disruptive behavior CLS hypothesizes—and to build this expectation into its educational approach. A reasonable policy need not anticipate and preemptively close off every opportunity for avoidance or manipulation. If students begin to exploit an all-comers policy by hijacking organizations to distort or destroy their missions, Hastings presumably would revisit and revise its policy. See Tr. of Oral Arg. 41 (counsel for Hastings); Brief for Hastings 38.

Finally, CLS asserts (and the dissent repeats, *post*, at 29) that the Law School lacks any legitimate interest—let alone one reasonably related to the RSO forum's purposes—in urging "religious groups not to favor co-religionists for purposes of their religious activities." CLS's analytical error lies in focusing on the benefits it must forgo while ignoring the interests of those it seeks to fence out: Exclusion, after all, has two sides. Hastings, caught in the crossfire between a group's desire to exclude and students' demand for equal access, may reasonably draw a line in the sand permitting *all* organizations to express what they wish but *no* group to discriminate in membership.

D.

We next consider whether Hastings' all-comers policy is viewpoint neutral.

Although this aspect of limited-public-forum analysis has been the constitutional sticking point in our prior decisions . . . we need not dwell on it here. It is, after all, hard to imagine a more viewpoint-neutral policy than one requiring *all* student groups to accept *all* comers. In contrast to *Healy*, *Widmar*, and *Rosenberger*, in which universities singled out organizations for disfavored treatment because of their points of view, Hastings' all-comers requirement draws no distinction between groups based on their message or perspective. An all-comers condition on access to RSO status, in short, is textbook viewpoint neutral. . . .

Hastings' requirement that student groups accept all comers, we are satisfied, "is justified without reference to the content [or viewpoint] of the regulated speech." The Law School's policy aims at the *act* of rejecting would-be group members without reference to the reasons motivating that behavior: Hastings' "desire to redress th[e] perceived harms" of exclusionary membership policies "provides an adequate explanation for its [all-comers condition] over and above mere disagreement with [any student group's] beliefs or biases." CLS's conduct—not its Christian perspective—is, from Hastings' vantage point, what stands between the group and RSO status. "In the end," as Hastings observes, "CLS is simply confusing its *own* viewpoint-based objections to . . . nondiscrimination laws (which it is entitled to have and [to] voice) with viewpoint *discrimination.*" * * *

JUSTICE ALITO, with whom THE CHIEF JUSTICE, JUSTICE SCALIA, and JUSTICE THOMAS join, dissenting.

The proudest boast of our free speech jurisprudence is that we protect the freedom to express "the thought that we hate." Today's decision rests on a very different principle: no freedom for expression that offends prevailing standards of political correctness in our country's institutions of higher learning. * * *

The Court's treatment of this case is deeply disappointing. The Court does not address the constitutionality of the very different policy that Hastings invoked when it denied CLS's application for registration. Nor does the Court address the constitutionality of the policy that Hastings now purports to follow. And the Court ignores strong evidence that the accept-all-comers policy is not viewpoint neutral because it was announced as a pretext to justify viewpoint discrimination. Brushing aside inconvenient precedent, the Court arms public educational institutions with a handy weapon for suppressing the speech of unpopular groups—groups to which, as Hastings candidly puts it, these institutions "do not wish to . . . lend their name[s]." * * *

The Court bases all of its analysis on the proposition that the relevant Hastings' policy is the so-called accept-all-comers policy. This frees the Court from the difficult task of defending the constitutionality of either the policy that Hastings actually—and repeatedly—invoked when it denied registration, *i.e.*, the school's written Nondiscrimination Policy, or the policy that Hastings belatedly unveiled when it filed its brief in this Court. Overwhelming evidence, however, shows that Hastings denied CLS's application pursuant to the Nondiscrimination Policy and that the accept-all-comers policy was nowhere to be found until it was mentioned by a former dean in a deposition taken well after this case began. [The dissent then supplies its view of the facts and its reading of the joint stipulation]. * * *

I must comment on the majority's emphasis on funding. According to the majority, CLS is "seeking what is effectively a state subsidy," and the question presented in this case centers on the "use of school funds." In fact, funding plays a very small role in this case. Most of what CLS sought and was denied—such as permission to set up a table on the law school patio—would have been virtually cost free. If every such activity is regarded as a matter of funding, the First Amendment rights of students at public universities will be at the mercy of the administration. As CLS notes, "[t]o university students, the campus is their world. The right to meet on campus and use campus channels of communication is at least as important to university students as the right to gather on the town square and use local communication forums is to the citizen." * * *

The Court pays little attention to *Healy* and instead focuses solely on the question whether Hastings' registration policy represents a permissible regulation in a limited public forum. While I think that *Healy* is largely controlling, I am content to address the constitutionality of Hastings' actions under our limited public forum cases, which lead to exactly the same conclusion.

In this case, the forum consists of the RSO program. Once a public university opens a limited public forum, it "must respect the lawful boundaries it has itself set." The university "may not exclude speech where its distinction is not 'reasonable in light of the purpose served by the forum.'" And the university must maintain strict viewpoint neutrality.

This requirement of viewpoint neutrality extends to the expression of religious viewpoints. In an unbroken line of decisions analyzing private religious speech in limited public forums, we have made it perfectly clear that "[r]eligion is [a] viewpoint from which ideas are conveyed." * * *

Analyzed under this framework, Hastings' refusal to register CLS pursuant to its Nondiscrimination Policy plainly fails. As previously noted, when Hastings refused to register CLS, it claimed that the CLS bylaws impermissibly discriminated on the basis of religion and sexual orientation. As interpreted by Hastings and applied to CLS, both of these grounds constituted viewpoint discrimination. * * *

Here, the Nondiscrimination Policy permitted membership requirements that expressed a secular viewpoint. See App. 93. (For example, the Hastings Democratic Caucus and the Hastings Republicans were allowed to exclude members who disagreed with their parties' platforms.) But religious groups were not permitted to express a religious viewpoint by limiting membership to students who shared their religious viewpoints. Under established precedent, this was viewpoint discrimination.

It bears emphasis that permitting religious groups to limit membership to those who share the groups' beliefs would not have the effect of allowing other groups to discriminate on the basis of religion. It would not mean, for example, that fraternities or sororities could exclude students on that basis. As our cases have recognized, the right of expressive association permits a group to exclude an applicant for membership only if the admission of that person would "affec[t] in a significant way the group's ability to advocate public or private viewpoints." *Dale*, 530 U.S., at 648. Groups that do not engage in expressive association have no such right. Similarly, groups that are dedicated to expressing a viewpoint on a secular topic (for example, a political or ideological viewpoint) would have no basis for limiting membership based on religion because the presence of members with diverse religious beliefs would have no effect on the group's ability to express its views. But for religious groups, the situation is very different. This point was put well by a coalition of Muslim, Christian, Jewish, and Sikh groups: "Of course there is a strong interest in prohibiting religious discrimination where religion is irrelevant. But it is fundamentally confused to apply a rule against religious discrimination to a religious association."

The Hastings Nondiscrimination Policy, as interpreted by the law school, also discriminated on the basis of viewpoint regarding sexual morality. CLS has a particular viewpoint on this subject, namely, that sexual conduct outside marriage between a man and a woman is wrongful. Hastings would not allow CLS to express this viewpoint by limiting membership to persons willing to express a sincere agreement with CLS's views. By contrast, nothing in the Nondiscrimination Policy prohibited a group from expressing a contrary viewpoint by limiting membership to persons willing to endorse that group's beliefs. A Free Love Club could require members to affirm that they reject the traditional view of sexual morality to which CLS adheres. It is hard to see how this can be viewed as anything other than viewpoint discrimination. * * *

I come now to the version of Hastings' policy that the Court has chosen to address. This is not the policy that Hastings invoked when CLS was denied registration. Nor is it the policy that Hastings now proclaims—and presumably implements. It is a policy that, as far as the record establishes, was in force only from the time when it was first disclosed by the former dean in July 2005 until Hastings filed its brief in this Court in March 2010. Why we should train our attention on this particular policy and not the other two is a puzzle. But in any event, it is clear that the accept-all-comers policy is not reasonable in light of the purpose of the RSO forum, and it is impossible to say on the present record that it is viewpoint neutral.

Once a state university opens a limited forum, it "must respect the lawful boundaries it has itself set." *Rosenberger*, 515 U.S., at 829. Hastings' regulations on the registration of student groups impose only two substantive limitations: A group seeking registration must have student members and must be non-commercial. Access to the forum is not limited to groups devoted to particular purposes. The regulations provide that a group applying for registration must submit an official document including "a statement of *its purpose*," *id.* but the regulations make no attempt to define the limits of acceptable purposes. The regulations do not require a group seeking registration to show that it has a certain number of members or that its program is of interest to any particular number of Hastings students. Nor do the regulations require that a group serve a need not met by existing groups. * * *

Taken as a whole, the regulations plainly contemplate the creation of a forum within which Hastings students are free to form and obtain registration of essentially the same broad range of private groups that nonstudents may form off campus. That is precisely what the parties in this case stipulated: The RSO forum "seeks to promote a diversity of viewpoints *among* registered student organizations, including viewpoints on religion and human sexuality."

The way in which the RSO forum actually developed corroborates this design. As noted, Hastings had more than 60 RSOs in 2004–2005, each with its own independently devised purpose. Some addressed serious social issues; others—for example, the wine appreciation and ultimate Frisbee clubs—were simply recreational. Some organizations focused on a subject but did not claim to promote a particular viewpoint on that subject (for example, the Association of Communications, Sports & Entertainment Law); others were defined, not by subject, but by viewpoint. The forum did not have a single Party Politics Club; rather, it featured both the Hastings Democratic Caucus and the Hastings Republicans. There was no Reproductive Issues Club; the forum included separate pro-choice and pro-life organizations. Students did not see fit to create a Monotheistic Religions Club, but they have formed the Hastings Jewish Law Students Association and the Hastings Association of Muslim Law Students. In short, the RSO forum, true to its design, has allowed Hastings students to replicate on campus a broad array of private, independent, noncommercial organizations that is very similar to those that nonstudents have formed in the outside world.

The accept-all-comers policy is antithetical to the design of the RSO forum for the same reason that a state-imposed accept-all-comers policy would violate the First Amendment rights of private groups if applied off campus. As explained above, a group's First Amendment right of expressive association is burdened by the "forced inclusion" of members whose presence would "affec[t] in a significant way the group's ability to advocate public or private viewpoints." *Dale*, 530 U.S., at 648. The Court has therefore held that the government may not compel a group that engages in "expressive association" to admit such a member unless the government has a compelling interest, " 'unrelated to the suppression of ideas, that cannot be achieved through means significantly less restrictive of associational freedoms.' " * * *

In sum, Hastings' accept-all-comers policy is not reasonable in light of the stipulated purpose of the RSO forum: to promote a diversity of viewpoints *"among"*—not within—"registered student organizations." * * *

One final aspect of the Court's decision warrants comment. In response to the argument that the accept-all-comers-policy would permit a small and unpopular group to be taken over by students who wish to silence its message, the Court states that the policy would permit a registered group to impose membership requirements "designed to ensure that students join because of their commitment to a group's vitality, not its demise." *Ante*, at 27. With this concession, the Court tacitly recognizes that Hastings does not really have an accept-all-comers policy—it has an accept-some-dissident-comers policy—and the line between members who merely seek to change a group's message (who apparently must be admitted) and those who seek a group's "demise" (who may be kept out) is hopelessly vague.

Here is an example. Not all Christian denominations agree with CLS's views on sexual morality and other matters. During a recent year, CLS had seven members. Suppose that 10 students who are members of denominations that disagree with CLS decided that CLS was misrepresenting true Christian doctrine. Suppose that these students joined CLS, elected officers who shared their views, ended the group's affiliation with the national organization, and changed the group's message. The new leadership would likely proclaim that the group was "vital" but rectified, while CLS, I assume, would take the view that the old group had suffered its "demise." Whether a change represents reform or transformation may depend very much on the eye of the beholder.

Justice Kennedy takes a similarly mistaken tack. He contends that CLS "would have a substantial case on the merits if it were shown that the all-comers policy was . . . used to infiltrate the group or challenge its leadership in order to stifle its views," *ante*, at 4 (concurring opinion), but he does not explain on what ground such a claim could succeed. The Court holds that the accept-all-comers policy is viewpoint neutral and reasonable in light of the purposes of the RSO forum. How could those characteristics be altered by a change in the membership of one of the forum's registered groups? No explanation is apparent.

In the end, the Court refuses to acknowledge the consequences of its holding. A true accept-all-comers policy permits small unpopular groups to be taken over by students who wish to change the views that the group expresses. Rules requiring that members attend meetings, pay dues, and behave politely, see *ante*, at 27, would not eliminate this threat.

The possibility of such takeovers, however, is by no means the most important effect of the Court's holding. There are religious groups that cannot in good conscience agree in their bylaws that they will admit persons who do not share their faith, and for these groups, the consequence of an accept-all-comers policy is marginalization. See Brief for Evangelical Scholars (Officers and 24 Former Presidents of the Evangelical Theological Society) et al. as *Amici Curiae* 19 (affirmance in this case "will allow every public college and university in the United States to exclude all evangelical Christian organizations"); Brief for Agudath Israel of America as *Amicus Curiae* 3, 8 (affirmance would "point a judicial dagger at the heart of the Orthodox Jewish community in the United States" and permit that community to be relegated to the status of "a second-class group"); Brief for Union of Orthodox Jewish Congregations of America as *Amicus Curiae* 3 (affirmance "could significantly affect the ability of [affiliated] student clubs and youth movements . . . to prescribe requirements for their membership and leaders based on religious beliefs and commitments"). This is where the Court's decision leads.

I do not think it is an exaggeration to say that today's decision is a serious setback for freedom of expression in this country. Our First Amendment reflects a "profound national commitment to the principle that debate on public issues should be uninhibited, robust, and wide-open." *New York Times Co.* v. *Sullivan*, 376 U.S. 254, 270 (1964). Even if the United States is the only Nation that shares this commitment to the same extent, I would not change our law to conform to the international norm. I fear that the Court's decision marks a turn in that direction. Even those who find CLS's views objectionable should be concerned about the way the group has been treated—by Hastings, the Court of Appeals, and now this Court. I can only hope that this decision will turn out to be an aberration.

ELANE PHOTOGRAPHY, LLC V. WILLOCK

Supreme Court of New Mexico, 2013
309 P. 3d 53

CHAVEZ, JUDGE.

[Vanessa Willock and Misti Collingsworth were planning a commitment ceremony. Willock e-mailed a local business, Elane Photography, to inquire about its services. The lead photographer and co-owner of the business, Elaine Huguenin, replied that she would not photograph a same-sex ceremony because she considered it to violate her religious beliefs, and that she photographed only "traditional weddings." The couple filed a complaint alleging discrimination in violation of the New Mexico Human Rights Act's provisions prohibiting discrimination based on sexual orientation by businesses that meet the definition of a public accommodation. On appeal from a judgment against it, Elane Photography did not contest that it was a public accommodation, but argued that applying the statute to it violated its rights under the Free Speech and Free Exercise Clause of the First Amendment. The New Mexico Supreme Court first rejected Elane's argument that the refusal to serve the same-sex couple was not based on their sexual orientation. On this point, the court invoked the analysis of status and conduct in *CLS v. Martinez*, among other things. The court then turned to the First Amendment issues].

* * * Elane Photography observes that photography is an expressive art form and that photographs can fall within the constitutional protections of free speech. *See Hurley v. Irish-Am. Gay, Lesbian & Bisexual Grp. of Boston*, 515 U.S. 557, 569, 115 S. Ct. 2338, 132 L. Ed. 2d 487 (1995) (observing that abstract art and instrumental music are "unquestionably shielded" by the First Amendment). Elane Photography also states that in the course of its business, it creates and edits photographs for its clients so as to tell a positive story about each wedding it photographs, and the company and its owners would prefer not to send a positive message about same-sex weddings or same-sex marriage. Elane Photography concludes that by requiring it to photograph same-sex weddings on the same basis that it photographs opposite-sex weddings, the NMHRA unconstitutionally compels it to "create and engage in expression" that sends a positive message about same-sex marriage not shared by its owner.

The compelled-speech doctrine on which Elane Photography relies is comprised of two lines of cases. The first line of cases establishes the proposition that the government may not require an individual to "speak the government's message." *Rumsfeld v. Forum for Academic & Institutional Rights, Inc.*, 547 U.S. 47, 63, 126 S. Ct. 1297, 164 L. Ed. 2d 156 (2006). The second line of cases prohibits the government from requiring a private actor "to host or accommodate another speaker's message." *Id.*

The right to refrain from speaking was established in *West Virginia State Board of Education v. Barnette*, in which the United States Supreme Court held that the State of West Virginia could not constitutionally require students to salute the American flag and recite the Pledge of Allegiance. The Court held that a state could not require "affirmation of a belief and an attitude of mind," and that the state had impermissibly "invade[d] the sphere of intellect and spirit which it is the purpose of the First Amendment to our Constitution to reserve from all official control."

Similarly, in *Wooley v. Maynard,* the United States Supreme Court held that the State of New Hampshire could not constitutionally punish a man for covering the state motto on the license plate of his car. The *Wooley* plaintiffs considered "Live Free or Die," the state motto, "repugnant to their moral, religious, and political beliefs," and they raised a First Amendment challenge to the state's law forbidding residents to hide or alter the motto. * * *

However, [*Barnette* and *Wooley*] . . . involve situations in which the speakers were compelled to publicly "speak the government's message." *Rumsfeld.* * * * Both cases stand for the proposition that the First Amendment does not permit the government to "prescribe what shall be orthodox in politics, nationalism, religion, or other matters of opinion or force citizens to confess by word or act their faith therein." However, unlike the laws at issue in *Wooley* and *Barnette,* the NMHRA does not require Elane Photography to recite or display any message. It does not even require Elane Photography to take photographs. The NMHRA only mandates that if Elane Photography operates a business as a public accommodation, it cannot discriminate against potential clients based on their sexual orientation.

Furthermore, the laws at issue in *Wooley* and *Barnette* had little purpose other than to promote the government-sanctioned message. * * * Antidiscrimination laws have important purposes that go beyond expressing government values: they ensure that services are freely available in the market, and they protect individuals from humiliation and dignitary harm. * * *

Elane Photography's argument here is more analogous to the claims raised by the law schools in *Rumsfeld.* In that case, a federal law made universities' federal funding contingent on the universities allowing military recruiters access to university facilities and services on the same basis as other, non-military recruiters. A group of law schools that objected to the ban on gays in the military challenged the law on a number of constitutional grounds, including that the law in question compelled them to speak the government's message. In order to assist the military recruiters, schools had to provide services that involved speech, "such as sending e-mails and distributing flyers."

The United States Supreme Court held that this requirement did not constitute compelled speech. The Court observed that the federal law "neither limits what law schools may say nor requires them to say anything." Schools were compelled only to provide the type of speech-related services to military recruiters that they provided to non-military recruiters. "There [was] nothing . . . approaching a Government-mandated pledge or motto that the school [had to] endorse."

The same situation is true in the instant case. Like the law in *Rumsfeld,* the NMHRA does not require any affirmation of belief by regulated public accommodations; instead, it requires businesses that offer services to the public at large to provide those services without regard for race, sex, sexual orientation, or other protected classifications.

The fact that these services may involve speech or other expressive services does not render the NMHRA unconstitutional. *See Rumsfeld* ("The compelled speech to which the law schools point is plainly incidental to the [law's] regulation of conduct, and it has never been deemed an abridgment of freedom of speech or press to make a course of conduct illegal merely because the conduct was in part initiated, evidenced, or carried out by means of language, either spoken, written, or printed." (internal quotation marks and citation omitted)). Elane Photography is compelled to take photographs of same-sex weddings only to the extent that it would provide the same services to a heterosexual couple. *See id.* (speech assisting military recruiters was "only 'compelled' if, and to the extent, the school provide[d] such speech for other recruiters").

The second line of compelled-speech cases deals with situations in which a government entity has required a speaker to "host or accommodate another speaker's message." *Id.* at 63, 126 S.Ct. 1297. Elane Photography argues that a same-sex wedding or commitment ceremony is an expressive event, and that by requiring it to accept a client who is having a same-sex wedding, the NMHRA compels it to facilitate the messages inherent in that event. Elane Photography argues that there are two messages conveyed by a same-sex wedding or commitment ceremony: first, that such ceremonies exist, and second, that these occasions deserve celebration and approval. Elane Photography does not wish to convey either of these messages.

The United States Supreme Court has never found a compelled-speech violation arising from the application of antidiscrimination laws to a for-profit public accommodation.... [The Court] has found constitutional problems with some applications of state public accommodation laws, but those problems have arisen when states have applied their public accommodation laws to free-speech events such as privately organized parades, and private membership organizations. Elane Photography, however, is an ordinary public accommodation, a "clearly commercial entit[y]," that sells goods and services to the public.

* * * If Elane Photography took photographs on its own time and sold them at a gallery, or if it was hired by certain clients but did not offer its services to the general public, the [public accommodations] law would not apply to Elane Photography's choice of whom to photograph or not. The difference in the present case is that the photographs that are allegedly compelled by the NMHRA are photographs that Elane Photography produces for hire in the ordinary course of its business as a public accommodation. This determination has no relation to the artistic merit of photographs produced by Elane Photography. If Annie Leibovitz or Peter Lindbergh worked as public accommodations in New Mexico, they would be subject to the provisions of the NMHRA. Unlike the defendants

in *Hurley* or the other cases in which the United States Supreme Court has found compelled-speech violations, Elane Photography sells its expressive services to the public. It may be that Elane Photography expresses its clients' messages in its photographs, but only because it is hired to do so.

* * * *Hurley* is different from the instant case in two significant ways. First, the Massachusetts courts appear to have erroneously classified the privately organized parade as a public accommodation. *See id.* ("[T]he state courts' application of the statute had the effect of declaring the sponsors' speech itself to be the public accommodation."). Second, parades by their nature express a message to the public. By requiring the parade organizers to include GLIB, the Massachusetts courts directly altered the expressive content of the parade. The presence of a group in a parade carries expressive weight, and Hurley implicated associational rights as well as free-speech rights. Elane Photography argues that photographs are also inherently expressive, so *Hurley* must apply to this case as well. However, the NMHRA applies not to Elane Photography's photographs but to its business operation, and in particular, its business decision not to offer its services to protected classes of people. While photography may be expressive, the operation of a photography business is not. By way of analogy, the NMHRA could not dictate which groups a parade organizer had to include. However, if a business sold parade-planning services, and that business operated as a public accommodation, the NMHRA would prohibit that business from refusing to offer parade-planning services to persons because of their sexual orientation. Thus, Elane Photography's reliance on *Hurley* is misplaced.

* * * Elane Photography also argues that if it is compelled to photograph same-sex weddings, observers will believe that it and its owners approve of same-sex marriage. * * * The *Hurley* Court observed that admitting GLIB or any other organization into a parade would likely be perceived as a message from the parade organizers "that [GLIB's] message was worthy of presentation and quite possibly of support as well."

* * * The *Rumsfeld* Court held that students "can appreciate the difference between speech a school sponsors and speech the school permits because legally required to do so," and that the law schools were free to express their disagreement with the military's policy.

* * * Elane Photography makes an argument very similar to one rejected by the *Rumsfeld* Court: by treating customers alike, regardless of whether they are having same-sex or opposite-sex weddings, Elane Photography is concerned that it will send the message that it sees nothing wrong with same-sex marriage. Reasonable observers are unlikely to interpret Elane Photography's photographs as an

endorsement of the photographed events. It is well known to the public that wedding photographers are hired by paying customers and that a photographer may not share the happy couple's views on issues ranging from the minor (the color scheme, the hors d'oeuvres) to the decidedly major (the religious service, the choice of bride or groom). As in *Rumsfeld* . . . Elane Photography is free to disavow, implicitly or explicitly, any messages that it believes the photographs convey. We note that after *Rumsfeld,* many law schools published open letters expressing their continued opposition to military policies and military recruitment on campus.

* * * [The Court then turned to the First Amendment free exercise claim]. It is an open question whether Elane Photography, which is a limited liability company rather than a natural person, has First Amendment free exercise rights. Several federal courts have recently addressed this question with differing outcomes. However, it is not necessary for this Court to address whether Elane Photography has a constitutionally protected right to exercise its religion. Assuming that Elane Photography has such rights, they are not offended by enforcement of the NMHRA.

Under established law, "the right of free exercise does not relieve an individual of the obligation to comply with a valid and neutral law of general applicability on the ground that the law proscribes (or prescribes) conduct that his religion prescribes (or proscribes)." *Emp't Div., Dep't of Human Res. of Or. v. Smith,* 494 U.S. 872, 879 (1990). In order to state a valid First Amendment free exercise claim, a party must show [among others] that the law in question is not a "neutral law of general applicability," *id.* * * *

The United States Supreme Court elaborated on the rule concerning "law that is neutral and of general applicability" in *Church of the Lukumi Babalu Aye, Inc. v. City of Hialeah,* 508 U.S. 520, 531, 546 (1993). A law is not neutral "if [its] object . . . is to infringe upon or restrict practices because of their religious motivation." It is not generally applicable if it "impose[s] burdens only on conduct motivated by religious belief" while permitting exceptions for secular conduct or for favored religions. *Id.* These inquiries are related; the Court observed that improper intent could be inferred if the law was a " 'religious gerrymander' " that burdened religion but exempted similar secular activity. If a law is neither neutral nor generally applicable, it "must be justified by a compelling governmental interest and must be narrowly tailored to advance that interest."

* * * In *Lukumi Babalu Aye,* the city of Hialeah had passed several ordinances that prohibited religious sacrifice of animals but exempted secular slaughterhouses, kosher slaughterhouses, hunting, fishing, euthanasia of unwanted animals, and extermination of pests. The Court held that this was a "religious gerrymander," the result of which was "that few if any killings of animals [were] prohibited other than Santeria sacrifice." The Court concluded that "[t]he ordinances had as their object the suppression of religion" and were therefore nonneutral. The Court then examined whether the ordinances were generally applicable and whether the government was selectively burdening only religiously motivated conduct. The Court did not precisely define the standard for assessing general applicability, but it did observe that the Hialeah ordinances were grossly under-inclusive with respect to the laws' stated goals, and it concluded that the laws burdened "only . . . conduct motivated by religious belief." The Court applied strict scrutiny to the ordinances and found them unconstitutional.

* * * Elane Photography argues that the NMHRA is not generally applicable and that this Court therefore should apply strict scrutiny to the application of the NMHRA to Elane Photography. Elane Photography identifies several exemptions from the antidiscrimination provisions of the NMHRA and argues that these exemptions make it not generally applicable. Specifically, Elane Photography points to Section 28–1–9(A)(1), which exempts sales or rentals of single-family homes if the owner does not own more than three houses, and Section 28–1–9(D), which exempts owners who live in small multi-family dwellings and rent out the other units. Elane Photography argues that these exemptions . . . "impermissibly prefer the secular to the religious."

This is a misreading of Section 28–1–9. Unlike the exemptions in *Lukumi Babalu Aye,* the exemptions in Section 28–1–9(A) and (D) apply equally to religious and secular conduct. Neither subsection discusses motivation; homeowners who meet the criteria of Section 28–1–9(A) and (D) are permitted to discriminate regardless of whether they do so on religious or nonreligious grounds. Therefore, the NMHRA does not target only religiously motivated discrimination, and these exemptions do not prevent the NMHRA from being generally applicable. These exemptions also do not indicate any animus toward religion by the Legislature that might render the law nonneutral; similar exemptions commonly appear in housing discrimination laws, including the federal Fair Housing Act. . . .

Elane Photography also argues that the exemptions to the NMHRA for religious organizations undercut the purpose of the statute. In particular, Elane Photography highlights Section 28–1–9(B) and (C), which in its reading permits religious organizations to "decline same-sex couples as customers."

Once again, Elane Photography's interpretation rests on a distorted reading of the statute. Section 28–1–9(B) allows religious organizations to "limit[ ] admission to or giv[e] preference to persons of the same religion or denomination or [to make] selections of buyers, lessees or tenants" that promote the organization's religious principles. In the context of "buyers, lessees or tenants," "buyers" clearly refers to purchasers of real estate rather than retail customers. *Id.* Subsection (C) exempts religious organizations from provisions of the NMHRA governing sexual orientation and gender identity, but only regarding "employment or renting." If a religious organization sold goods or services to the general public, neither subsection would allow the organization to turn away same-sex couples while catering to opposite-sex couples of all faiths. Subsection (B) permits religious organizations to serve only or primarily people of their own faith, as well as to discriminate in certain limited real estate transactions; Subsection (C) applies only to employment and, again, to real estate.

In other words, neither of the religious exemptions in Section 28–1–9 would permit a religious organization to take the actions that Elane Photography did in this case. Furthermore, these exemptions do not prevent the NMHRA from being generally applicable. Exemptions for religious organizations are common in a wide variety of laws, and they reflect the attempts of the Legislature to respect free exercise rights by reducing legal burdens on religion. Such exemptions are generally permissible, and in some situations they may be constitutionally mandated, *see Hosanna-Tabor Evangelical Lutheran Church & Sch. v. EEOC,* ___ U.S. ___, ___, 132 S. Ct. 694, 705–06 (2012) (holding that the First Amendment precludes the application of employment discrimination laws to disputes between religious organizations and their ministers).

The exemptions in the NMHRA are ordinary exemptions for religious organizations and for certain limited employment and real-estate transactions. The exemptions do not prefer secular conduct over religious conduct or evince any hostility toward religion. We hold that the NMHRA is a neutral law of general applicability, and as such it does not offend the Free Exercise Clause of the First Amendment. * * *

NOTES

1. For academic analysis of the CLS case, see Richard A. Epstein, *Church and State at the Crossroads*: Christian Legal Society v. Martinez, 2010 CATO SUP. CT. REV. 105 (2010); William N. Eskridge, Jr., *Noah's Curse: How Religion Often Conflates Status, Belief, and Conduct to Distort Antidiscrimination Norms*, 45 GA. L. REV. 657 (2011); John D. Inazu, *The Unsettling "Well-Settled" Law of Freedom of Association*, 43 CONN. L. REV. 149 (2010) (positing that Freedom of Association has been misunderstood since *Roberts v. Jaycees* and that *CLS* continues in this tradition of incorrectly decided Supreme Court cases); Kathleen M. Sullivan, *Two Concepts of the Freedom of Speech*, 124 HARV. L. REV. 143 (2010); *Symposium, Christian Legal Society v. Martinez*, 38 Hastings Con. L. Qrtrly (2011).

2. There is a burgeoning academic literature on the kinds of issues posed in *Elane Photography* and the larger conflict implicated by the case. For a variety of perspectives, see Thomas C. Berg, *What Same-Sex Marriage and Religious-Liberty Claims Have in Common*, 5 NW. J.L. & SOC. POL'Y 206 (2010); Jennifer Gerarda Brown, *Peacemaking in the Culture War Between Gay Rights and Religious Liberty*, 95 IOWA L. REV. 747 (2010); Chai R. Feldblum, *Moral Conflict and Liberty: Gay Rights and Religion*, 72 BROOK. L. REV. 61 (2006); James Gottry, Note, *Just Shoot Me: Antidiscrimination Laws Take Aim at First Amendment Freedoms*, 64 VAND. L. REV. 961 (2011); Laura K. Klein, *Rights Clash: How Conflicts Between Gay Rights and Religious Freedom Challenge the Legal System*, 98 GEO. L.J. 505 (2010); Douglas Laycock, *Religious Liberty and the Culture Wars*, U. ILL. L. REV. (forthcoming 2014); Douglas Laycock & Thomas C. Berg, *Protecting Same-Sex Marriage and Religious Liberty*, 99 VA.. L. REV. IN BRIEF 1 (2013); Douglas NeJaime, *Inclusion, Accommodation and Recognition: Accounting for Differences Based on Religion and Sexual Orientation*, 32 HARV. J. L. & GENDER 303 (2009); Douglas NeJaime, *Marriage Inequality: Same-Sex Relationships, Religious Exemptions, and the Production of Sexual Orientation Discrimination*, 100 CAL. L. REV. 1169 (2012); *Symposium, Religious Liberty and Non-Discrimination Law,* 5 NW. J. L. & SOC. POL. 206 (2010); Laura S. Underkuffler, *Odious Discrimination and the Religious Exemption Question*, 32 CARDOZO L. REV. 2069 (2011); Robin Fretwell Wilson, *The Calculus of Accommodation: Contraception, Abortion, Same-Sex Marriage, and Other Clashes Between Religion and the State*, 53 B.C. L. REV. 1417 (2012).

3. Notice that the New Mexico Supreme Court declined to decide the "open question" whether a company like *Elane Photography* could assert religious rights under the First Amendment. As this edition of the Casebook goes to press, the United States Supreme Court has before it a case presenting that question for decision in the context of a religious challenge to parts of the Affordable Care Act. *Hobby Lobby Stores, Inc. v. Sebelius,* 723 F.3d 1114 (10th Cir. 2013) (*en banc*), *cert. granted Sebelius v. Hobby Lobby Stores, Inc.*, 2013 WL 5297798 (2013).

4. *Elane Photography* is by no means the only dispute that has placed a commercial actor in conflict with a law banning discrimination based on sexual orientation. Several high-profile recent disputes have involved small business owners who refused to serve LGBT individuals, including a bakery in Oregon that did not want to bake a wedding cake for a lesbian couple, a florist in Washington who did not want to provide flowers for a gay wedding, and a Kentucky printer who declined to print t-shirts for a gay pride parade. *See* Sarah Pulliam Bailey, *Religious Liberty Pitted Against Gay Rights in Discrimination Lawsuits*, HUFFINGTON POST (Sept. 8, 2013, 9:03 AM), http://www.huffingtonpost.com/2013/09/08/discrimination-lawsuits-gay-rights_n_3882450.html; Alex Roarty, *Are Gay Rights Trampling on Freedom of Religion?*, THE ATLANTIC (Sept. 23, 2013, 2:45 PM), http://www.theatlantic.com/politics/archive/2013/09/are-gay-rights-laws-trampling-on-freedom-of-religion/279908/.

5.   The conflict between LGBT equality and religious liberty seemed to reach a new level of public salience in early 2014, when the Arizona legislature passed a controversial bill that would expand religious liberties. The bill was ultimately vetoed by the state's governor, in the face of opposition from business, many conservative public officials (including Senators John McCain and Jeff Flake), and several groups who threatened to cancel major events in the state—including the National Football League, which had scheduled the 2015 Super Bowl for Glendale, Arizona. Fernanda Santos, *Arizona Governor Vetoes Bill on Refusal of Service to Gays*, N.Y. Times, Feb. 27, 2014, at A1. Notably, at the time the bill was passed, Arizona neither banned discrimination in public accommodations based on sexual orientation, nor permitted same-sex marriage. Notwithstanding that state law already permitted discrimination, the bill served as a flashpoint for a larger national debate. In the wake of the controversy, some scholars of law and religion argued that the bill had been grossly misrepresented. Rick Garnett, *The Veto, Coverage, and Misrepresentation of AZ 1062*, MIRROR OF JUSTICE, Feb. 27, 2014 (http://mirrorofjustice.blogs.com/mirrorofjustice/2014/02/the-veto-coverage-and-misrepresentation-of-az-1062.html)   Columnist   Ross Douthat wrote that same-sex marriage in all 50 states was now a foregone conclusion, and that what remained to be seen was whether it would be possible to carve out any legal protections for religious objectors. He lamented that "now, apparently, the official line is that *you bigots don't get to negotiate anymore*." Ross Douthat, *The Terms of Our Surrender*, N.Y. Times, March 2, 2014, at SR 12 (italics in original).

6.   Related to legal disputes like *Elane Photography* are the cultural and political faceoffs epitomized by the 2012 controversy involving the fast-food chain, Chick-Fil-A. That business made headlines when its founder, Dan Cathy, publicly spoke against marriage equality and said his company supported the "biblical definition of the family unit." His statements triggered a "kiss-in" protest, which then triggered a counter-action that organizers called "Chick-Fil-A Appreciation Day." *See* Kim Severson, *Chick-Fil-A Thrust Back into Spotlight on Gay Rights*, N. Y. TIMES, July 25, 2012, at A13. Unlike Elane Photography, however, the Chik-Fil-A chain did not seek to turn away gay customers.

7.   For a variation on the conflict between a commercial actor and a non-discrimination norm, consider the controversy about "conversion therapy" designed to change a person's sexual orientation to heterosexual. In 2013, the Ninth Circuit upheld the state of California's ban on gay conversion therapy for minors. *Pickup v. Brown*, 728 F.3d 1042 (9th Cir. 2013). The court concluded that the ban did not violate the First Amendment rights of therapists and that it was within the state's prerogative to regulate a treatment that it considered harmful. The court viewed the ban as a regulation of conduct, not speech. The opinion emphasized that practitioners remained free to express their views about homosexuality to parents, patients and others, but were not free to employ this therapy. The state of New Jersey has also banned gay conversion therapy. Its ban has, thus far,

survived legal challenge. See King v. Christie, ___ F. Supp. 2d ___, 2013 WL 5970343 (D.N.J.).

IV.   FREE (ANTI-ANTI-GAY) SPEECH

RUMSFELD V. FAIR

Supreme Court of the United States, 2006
547 U.S. 47, 126 S.Ct. 1297, 164 L.Ed.2d 156

CHIEF JUSTICE ROBERTS delivered the opinion of the Court.

When law schools began restricting the access of military recruiters to their students because of disagreement with the Government's policy on homosexuals in the military, Congress responded by enacting the Solomon Amendment. That provision specifies that if any part of an institution of higher education denies military recruiters access equal to that provided other recruiters, the entire institution would lose certain federal funds. The law schools responded by suing, alleging that the Solomon Amendment infringed their First Amendment freedoms of speech and association. The District Court disagreed but was reversed by a divided panel of the Court of Appeals for the Third Circuit, which ordered the District Court to enter a preliminary injunction against enforcement of the Solomon Amendment. We granted certiorari.

Respondent Forum for Academic and Institutional Rights, Inc. (FAIR), is an association of law schools and law faculties. Its declared mission is "to promote academic freedom, support educational institutions in opposing discrimination and vindicate the rights of institutions of higher education." FAIR members have adopted policies expressing their opposition to discrimination based on, among other factors, sexual orientation. They would like to restrict military recruiting on their campuses because they object to the policy Congress has adopted with respect to homosexuals in the military. [Under this policy, a person generally may not serve in the Armed Forces if he has engaged in homosexual acts, stated that he is a homosexual, or married a person of the same sex. Respondents do not challenge that policy in this litigation.] The Solomon Amendment, however, forces institutions to choose between enforcing their nondiscrimination policy against military recruiters in this way and continuing to receive specified federal funding. * * *

The Solomon Amendment denies federal funding to an institution of higher education that "has a policy or practice . . . that either prohibits, or in effect prevents" the military "from gaining access to campuses, or access to students . . . on campuses, for purposes of military recruiting in a manner that is at least equal in quality and scope to the access to campuses and to students that is provided to any other employer." 10 U.S.C.A. § 983(b). The statute provides an exception for an institution with "a longstanding policy of pacifism based on historical religious affiliation." The Government and FAIR agree on what this statute requires: In order for a law school and its university to receive federal funding, the law school must offer military recruiters the same access to its campus and students that it provides to the nonmilitary recruiter receiving the most favorable access.

Certain law professors participating as *amici*, however, argue that the . . . Solomon Amendment's equal-access requirement is satisfied when an institution applies to military recruiters the same policy it applies to all other recruiters. On this reading, a school excluding military recruiters would comply with the Solomon Amendment so long as it also excluded any other employer that violates its nondiscrimination policy. . . . We . . . consider whether institutions can comply with the Solomon Amendment by applying a general nondiscrimination policy to exclude military recruiters.

We conclude that they cannot and that the Government and FAIR correctly interpret the Solomon Amendment. The statute requires the Secretary of Defense to compare the military's "access to campuses" and "access to students" to "the access to campuses and to students that is provided to *any other employer*." The statute does not call for an inquiry into why or how the "other employer" secured its access. Under *amici's* reading, a military recruiter has the same "access" to campuses and students as, say, a law firm when the law firm is permitted on campus to interview students and the military is not. We do not think that the military recruiter has received equal "access" in this situation— regardless of whether the disparate treatment is attributable to the military's failure to comply with the school's nondiscrimination policy.

The Solomon Amendment does not focus on the *content* of a school's recruiting policy, as the *amici* would have it. Instead, it looks to the *result* achieved by the policy and compares the "access . . . provided" military recruiters to that provided other recruiters. Applying the same policy to all recruiters is therefore insufficient to comply with the statute if it results in a greater level of access for other recruiters than for the military. Law schools must ensure that their recruiting policy operates in such a way that military recruiters are given access to students at least equal to that "*provided* to any other employer."

Not only does the text support this view, but this interpretation is necessary to give effect to the Solomon Amendment's recent revision. Under the prior version, the statute required "entry" without specifying how military recruiters should be treated once on campus. The District Court thought that the DOD policy, which required equal access to students once recruiters were on campus, was unwarranted based on the text of the statute. Congress responded directly to this decision by codifying the DOD policy. Under *amici*'s interpretation, this legislative change had no effect—law schools could still restrict military access, so long as they do so under a generally applicable nondiscrimination policy. Worse yet, the legislative change made it *easier* for schools to keep military recruiters out altogether: under the prior version, simple access could not be denied, but under the amended version, access could be denied altogether, so long as a nonmilitary recruiter would also be denied access. That is rather clearly *not* what Congress had in mind in codifying the DOD policy. We refuse to interpret the Solomon Amendment in a way that negates its recent revision, and indeed would render it a largely meaningless exercise.

We therefore read the Solomon Amendment the way both the Government and FAIR interpret it. It is insufficient for a law school to treat the military as it treats all other employers who violate its nondiscrimination policy. Under the statute, military recruiters must be given the same access as recruiters who comply with the policy.

The Constitution grants Congress the power to "provide for the common Defence," "[t]o raise and support Armies," and "[t]o provide and maintain a Navy." Art. I, § 8, cls. 1, 12–13. Congress' power in this area is broad and sweeping, and there is no dispute in this case that it includes the authority to require campus access for military recruiters. That is, of course, unless Congress exceeds constitutional limitations on its power in enacting such legislation. But the fact that legislation that raises armies is subject to First Amendment constraints does not mean that we ignore the purpose of this legislation when determining its constitutionality; . . . "judicial deference . . . is at its apogee" when Congress legislates under its authority to raise and support armies.

Although Congress has broad authority to legislate on matters of military recruiting, it nonetheless chose to secure campus access for military recruiters indirectly, through its Spending Clause power. The Solomon Amendment gives universities a choice: Either allow military recruiters the same access to students afforded any other recruiter or forgo certain federal funds. Congress' decision to proceed indirectly does not reduce the deference given to Congress in the area of military affairs. Congress' choice to promote its goal by creating a funding condition deserves at least as deferential treatment as if Congress had imposed a mandate on universities.

Congress' power to regulate military recruiting under the Solomon Amendment is arguably greater because universities are free to decline the federal funds. In *Grove City College v. Bell*, 465 U.S. 555, 575–576 (1984), we rejected a private college's claim that conditioning federal funds on its compliance with Title IX of the Education Amendments of 1972 violated the First Amendment. We thought this argument "warrant[ed] only brief consideration" because "Congress is free to attach reasonable and unambiguous conditions to federal financial assistance that educational institutions are not obligated to accept." We concluded that no First Amendment violation had occurred—without reviewing the substance of the First Amendment claims—because Grove City could decline the Government's funds.

Other decisions, however, recognize a limit on Congress' ability to place conditions on the receipt of funds. We recently held that " 'the government may not deny a benefit to a person on a basis that infringes his constitutionally protected . . . freedom of speech even if he has no entitlement to that benefit.' " *United States v. American Library Assn., Inc.*, 539 U.S. 194, 210 (2003). Under this principle, known as the unconstitutional conditions doctrine, the Solomon Amendment would be unconstitutional if Congress could not directly require universities to provide military recruiters equal access to their students.

This case does not require us to determine when a condition placed on university funding goes beyond the "reasonable" choice offered in *Grove City* and becomes an unconstitutional condition. It is clear that a funding condition cannot be unconstitutional if it could be constitutionally imposed directly. See *Speiser v. Randall*, 357 U.S. 513, 526 (1958). Because the First Amendment would not prevent Congress from directly imposing the Solomon Amendment's access requirement, the statute does not place an unconstitutional condition on the receipt of federal funds.

A

The Solomon Amendment neither limits what law schools may say nor requires them to say anything. Law schools remain free under the statute to express whatever views they may have on the military's congressionally mandated employment policy, all the while retaining eligibility for federal funds. See Tr. of Oral Arg. 25 (Solicitor General acknowledging that law schools "could put signs on the bulletin board next to the door, they could engage in speech, they could help organize student protests"). As a general matter, the Solomon Amendment regulates conduct, not speech. It affects what law schools must *do*—afford equal access to military recruiters—not what they may or may not *say*.

Nevertheless, the Third Circuit concluded that the Solomon Amendment violates law schools' freedom of speech in a number of ways. First, in assisting military recruiters, law schools provide some services, such as sending e-mails and distributing flyers, that clearly involve speech. The Court of Appeals held that in supplying these services law schools are unconstitutionally compelled to speak the Government's message. Second, military recruiters are, to some extent, speaking while they are on campus. The Court of Appeals held that, by forcing law schools to permit the military on campus to express its message, the

Solomon Amendment unconstitutionally requires law schools to host or accommodate the military's speech. Third, although the Court of Appeals thought that the Solomon Amendment regulated speech, it held in the alternative that, if the statute regulates conduct, this conduct is expressive and regulating it unconstitutionally infringes law schools' right to engage in expressive conduct. We consider each issue in turn.

1

Some of this Court's leading First Amendment precedents have established the principle that freedom of speech prohibits the government from telling people what they must say. In *West Virginia Bd. of Ed. v. Barnette*, 319 U.S. 624, 642 (1943), we held unconstitutional a state law requiring schoolchildren to recite the Pledge of Allegiance and to salute the flag. And in *Wooley v. Maynard*, 430 U.S. 705, 717 (1977), we held unconstitutional another that required New Hampshire motorists to display the state motto—"Live Free or Die"—on their license plates.

The Solomon Amendment does not require any similar expression by law schools. Nonetheless, recruiting assistance provided by the schools often includes elements of speech. For example, schools may send e-mails or post notices on bulletin boards on an employer's behalf. Law schools offering such services to other recruiters must also send e-mails and post notices on behalf of the military to comply with the Solomon Amendment. As FAIR points out, these compelled statements of fact ("The U.S. Army recruiter will meet interested students in Room 123 at 11 a.m."), like compelled statements of opinion, are subject to First Amendment scrutiny.

This sort of recruiting assistance, however, is a far cry from the compelled speech in *Barnette* and *Wooley*. The Solomon Amendment, unlike the laws at issue in those cases, does not dictate the content of the speech at all, which is only "compelled" if, and to the extent, the school provides such speech for other recruiters. There is nothing in this case approaching a Government-mandated pledge or motto that the school must endorse.

The compelled speech to which the law schools point is plainly incidental to the Solomon Amendment's regulation of conduct, and "it has never been deemed an abridgment of freedom of speech or press to make a course of conduct illegal merely because the conduct was in part initiated, evidenced, or carried out by means of language, either spoken, written, or printed." *Giboney v. Empire Storage & Ice Co.*, 336 U.S. 490, 502 (1949). Congress, for example, can prohibit employers from discriminating in hiring on the basis of race. The fact that this will require an employer to take down a sign reading "White Applicants Only" hardly means that the law should be analyzed as one regulating the employer's speech rather than conduct. See *R.A.V. v. St. Paul*, 505 U.S.

377, 389 (1992) ("[W]ords can in some circumstances violate laws directed not against speech but against conduct"). Compelling a law school that sends scheduling e-mails for other recruiters to send one for a military recruiter is simply not the same as forcing a student to pledge allegiance, or forcing a Jehovah's Witness to display the motto "Live Free or Die," and it trivializes the freedom protected in *Barnette* and *Wooley* to suggest that it is.

2

Our compelled-speech cases are not limited to the situation in which an individual must personally speak the government's message. We have also in a number of instances limited the government's ability to force one speaker to host or accommodate another speaker's message. See *Hurley v. Irish-American Gay, Lesbian and Bisexual Group of Boston, Inc.*, 515 U.S. 557, 566 (1995) (state law cannot require a parade to include a group whose message the parade's organizer does not wish to send). *Pacific Gas & Elec. Co. v. Public Util. Comm'n of Cal.*, 475 U.S. 1, 20–21 (1986) (plurality opinion); accord, *id.*, at 25 (Marshall, J., concurring in judgment) (state agency cannot require a utility company to include a third-party newsletter in its billing envelope); *Miami Herald Publishing Co. v. Tornillo*, 418 U.S. 241, 258 (1974) (right-of-reply statute violates editors' right to determine the content of their newspapers). Relying on these precedents, the Third Circuit concluded that the Solomon Amendment unconstitutionally compels law schools to accommodate the military's message "[b]y requiring schools to include military recruiters in the interviews and recruiting receptions the schools arrange."

The compelled-speech violation in each of our prior cases, however, resulted from the fact that the complaining speaker's own message was affected by the speech it was forced to accommodate. The expressive nature of a parade was central to our holding in *Hurley* ("Parades are . . . a form of expression, not just motion, and the inherent expressiveness of marching to make a point explains our cases involving protest marches"). We concluded that because "every participating unit affects the message conveyed by the [parade's] private organizers," a law dictating that a particular group must be included in the parade "alter[s] the expressive content of th[e] parade." As a result, we held that the State's public accommodation law, as applied to a private parade, "violates the fundamental rule of protection under the First Amendment, that a speaker has the autonomy to choose the content of his own message."

The compelled-speech violations in *Tornillo* and *Pacific Gas* also resulted from interference with a speaker's desired message. In *Tornillo*, we recognized that "the compelled printing of a reply . . . tak[es] up space that could be devoted to other material the newspaper may have preferred to print," and therefore concluded that this right-of-reply statute infringed the newspaper editors' freedom of speech by altering the message the paper wished to express. The same is true in *Pacific Gas.* There, the utility company regularly included its newsletter, which we concluded was protected speech, in its billing envelope. Thus, when the state agency ordered the utility to send a third-party newsletter four times a year, it interfered with the utility's ability to communicate its own message in its newsletter. A plurality of the Court likened this to the situation in *Tornillo* and held that the forced inclusion of the other newsletter interfered with the utility's own message.

In this case, accommodating the military's message does not affect the law schools' speech, because the schools are not speaking when they host interviews and recruiting receptions. Unlike a parade organizer's choice of parade contingents, a law school's decision to allow recruiters on campus is not inherently expressive. Law schools facilitate recruiting to assist their students in obtaining jobs. A law school's recruiting services lack the expressive quality of a parade, a newsletter, or the editorial page of a newspaper; its accommodation of a military recruiter's message is not compelled speech because the accommodation does not sufficiently interfere with any message of the school.

The schools respond that if they treat military and nonmilitary recruiters alike in order to comply with the Solomon Amendment, they could be viewed as sending the message that they see nothing wrong with the military's policies, when they do. We rejected a similar argument in *PruneYard Shopping Center v. Robins*, 447 U.S. 74 (1980). In that case, we upheld a state law requiring a shopping center owner to allow certain expressive activities by others on its property. We explained that there was little likelihood that the views of those engaging in the expressive activities would be identified with the owner, who remained free to disassociate himself from those views and who was "not . . . being compelled to affirm [a] belief in any governmentally prescribed position or view."

The same is true here. Nothing about recruiting suggests that law schools agree with any speech by recruiters, and nothing in the Solomon Amendment restricts what the law schools may say about the military's policies. We have held that high school students can appreciate the difference between speech a school sponsors and speech the school permits because legally required to do so, pursuant to an equal access policy. *Board of Ed. of Westside Community Schools (Dist.66) v. Mergens*, 496 U.S. 226, 250 (1990) (plurality opinion); see also *Rosenberger v. Rector and Visitors of Univ. of Va.*, 515 U.S. 819, 841 (1995) (attribution concern "not a plausible fear"). Surely students have not lost that ability by the time they get to law school.

3

Having rejected the view that the Solomon Amendment impermissibly regulates *speech*, we must still consider whether the expressive nature of the *conduct* regulated by the statute brings that conduct within the First Amendment's protection. In *O'Brien*, we recognized that some forms of " 'symbolic speech' " were deserving of First Amendment protection. But we rejected the view that "conduct can be labeled 'speech' whenever the person engaging in the conduct intends thereby to express an idea." Instead, we have extended First Amendment protection only to conduct that is inherently expressive. In *Texas v. Johnson*, 491 U.S. 397, 406 (1989), for example, we applied *O'Brien* and held that burning the American flag was sufficiently expressive to warrant First Amendment protection.

Unlike flag burning, the conduct regulated by the Solomon Amendment is not inherently expressive. Prior to the adoption of the Solomon Amendment's equal-access requirement, law schools "expressed" their disagreement with the military by treating military recruiters differently from other recruiters. But these actions were expressive only because the law schools accompanied their conduct with speech explaining it. For example, the point of requiring military interviews to be conducted on the undergraduate campus is not overwhelmingly apparent. An observer who sees military recruiters interviewing away from the law school has no way of knowing whether the law school is expressing its disapproval of the military, all the law school's interview rooms are full, or the military recruiters decided for reasons of their own that they would rather interview someplace else.

The expressive component of a law school's actions is not created by the conduct itself but by the speech that accompanies it. The fact that such explanatory speech is necessary is strong evidence that the conduct at issue here is not so inherently expressive that it warrants protection under *O'Brien*. If combining speech and conduct were enough to create expressive conduct, a regulated party could always transform conduct into "speech" simply by talking about it. For instance, if an individual announces that he intends to express his disapproval of the Internal Revenue Service by refusing to pay his income taxes, we would have to apply *O'Brien* to determine whether the Tax Code violates the First Amendment. Neither *O'Brien* nor its progeny supports such a result.

Although the Third Circuit also concluded that *O'Brien* does not apply, it held in the alternative that the Solomon Amendment does not pass muster under *O'Brien* because the Government failed to produce evidence establishing that the Solomon Amendment was necessary and effective. The Court of Appeals surmised that "the military has ample resources to recruit through alternative means," suggesting "loan repayment programs" and "television and radio advertisements." As a result, the Government—according to the Third Circuit—failed to establish that the statute's burden on speech is no greater than essential to furthering its interest in military recruiting.

We disagree with the Court of Appeals' reasoning and result. We have held that "an incidental burden on speech is no greater than is essential, and therefore is permissible under *O'Brien*, so long as the neutral regulation promotes a substantial government interest that would be achieved less effectively absent the regulation." The Solomon Amendment clearly satisfies this requirement. Military recruiting promotes the substantial Government interest in raising and supporting the Armed Forces—an objective that would be achieved less effectively if the military were forced to recruit on less favorable terms than other employers. The Court of Appeals' proposed alternative methods of recruiting are beside the point. The issue is not whether other means of raising an army and providing for a navy might be adequate. That is a judgment for Congress, not the courts. It suffices that the means chosen by Congress add to the effectiveness of military recruitment. Accordingly, even if the Solomon Amendment were regarded as regulating expressive conduct, it would not violate the First Amendment under *O'Brien*.

B

The Solomon Amendment does not violate law schools' freedom of speech, but the First Amendment's protection extends beyond the right to speak. We have recognized a First Amendment right to associate for the purpose of speaking, which we have termed a "right of expressive association." See, e.g., *Boy Scouts of America v. Dale*, 530 U.S. 640, 644 (2000). The reason we have extended First Amendment protection in this way is clear: The right to speak is often exercised most effectively by combining one's voice with the voices of others. See *Roberts v. United States Jaycees*, 468 U.S. 609, 622 (1984). If the government were free to restrict individuals' ability to join together and speak, it could essentially silence views that the First Amendment is intended to protect.

FAIR argues that the Solomon Amendment violates law schools' freedom of expressive association. According to FAIR, law schools' ability to express their message that discrimination on the basis of sexual orientation is wrong is significantly affected by the presence of military recruiters on campus and the schools' obligation to assist them. Relying heavily on our decision in *Dale*, the Court of Appeals agreed.

In *Dale*, we held that the Boy Scouts' freedom of expressive association was violated by New Jersey's public accommodations law, which required the organization to accept a homosexual as a scoutmaster. After determining that the Boy Scouts was an expressive association, that "the forced inclusion of Dale would significantly affect its expression," and that the State's interests did not justify this intrusion, we concluded that the Boy Scout's First Amendment rights were violated.

The Solomon Amendment, however, does not similarly affect a law school's associational rights. To comply with the statute, law schools must allow military recruiters on campus and assist them in whatever way the school chooses to assist other employers. Law schools therefore "associate" with military recruiters in the sense that they interact with them. But recruiters are not part of the law school. Recruiters are, by definition, outsiders who come onto campus for the limited purpose of trying to hire students—not to become members of the school's expressive association. This distinction is critical. Unlike the public accommodations law in *Dale*, the Solomon Amendment does not force a law school " 'to accept members it does not desire.' " The law schools *say* that allowing military recruiters equal access impairs their own expression by requiring them to associate with the recruiters, but just as saying conduct is undertaken for expressive purposes cannot make it symbolic speech, so too a speaker cannot "erect a shield" against laws requiring access "simply by asserting" that mere association "would impair its message."

FAIR correctly notes that the freedom of expressive association protects more than just a group's membership decisions. For example, we have held laws unconstitutional that require disclosure of membership lists for groups seeking anonymity, *Brown v. Socialist Workers '74 Campaign Comm.*, 459 U.S. 87, 101–102 (1982), or impose penalties or withhold benefits based on membership in a disfavored group, *Healy v. James*, 408 U.S. 169, 180–184 (1972). Although these laws did not directly interfere with an organization's composition, they made group membership less attractive, raising the same First Amendment concerns about affecting the group's ability to express its message.

The Solomon Amendment has no similar effect on a law school's associational rights. Students and faculty are free to associate to voice their disapproval of the military's message; nothing about the statute affects the composition of the group by making group membership less desirable. The Solomon Amendment therefore does not violate a law school's First Amendment rights. A military recruiter's mere presence on campus does not violate a law school's right to associate, regardless of how repugnant the law school considers the recruiter's message. * * *

In this case, FAIR has attempted to stretch a number of First Amendment doctrines well beyond the sort of activities these doctrines protect. The law schools object to having to treat military recruiters like other recruiters, but that regulation of conduct does not violate the First Amendment. To the extent that the Solomon Amendment incidentally affects expression, the law schools' effort to cast themselves as just like the schoolchildren in *Barnette*, the parade organizers in *Hurley*, and the

Boy Scouts in *Dale* plainly overstates the expressive nature of their activity and the impact of the Solomon Amendment on it, while exaggerating the reach of our First Amendment precedents.

Because Congress could require law schools to provide equal access to military recruiters without violating the schools' freedoms of speech or association, the Court of Appeals erred in holding that the Solomon Amendment likely violates the First Amendment. We therefore reverse the judgment of the Third Circuit and remand the case for further proceedings consistent with this opinion. *It is so ordered.*

JUSTICE ALITO took no part in the consideration or decision of this case.

NOTES

1.   In the wake of the *FAIR* decision, opponents of the Solomon Amendment have focused on "amelioration" strategies available to law schools who wish to express their continuing opposition to discrimination by military recruiters. This effort has been enhanced by the statement of the Solicitor General in oral argument at the U.S. Supreme Court affirming that law schools could, consistent with the Solomon Amendment, "put signs on the bulletin board next to the door, they could engage in speech, they could help organize student protests," and by Chief Justice Roberts's quotation of this language in the Court's opinion.

2.   One amelioration strategy that was used by many law schools was the strict enforcement of non-discrimination policies in other contexts. As the CLS case above reflects, however, this policy itself can lead to First Amendment challenges.

3.   In late 2010, Congress passed the Don't Ask, Don't Tell Repeal Act of 2010 (H.R. 2965, S. 4023) as one of its last acts of the Congressional session. (For more information on the repeal itself, see Chapter 5). Following the repeal of the policy, several colleges and universities indicated a willingness to explore whether they would invite the ROTC back onto campus, including Harvard, Yale, and Columbia. *See* Tamar Lewin, *Colleges Rethink R.O.T.C. After "Don't Ask" Repeal*, N.Y. TIMES, December 21, 2010, at A18. President Lee Bollinger of Columbia was particularly outspoken about how important the repeal was to his university's assessment of their relationship with the United States military. What role, if any, do you think the repeal of Don't Ask, Don't Tell should play in allowing the programs back onto campus? Prior to reconsideration of these university's policies, many students who wished to enroll in the R.O.T.C. program had to travel to other colleges, often very early in the morning, to attend mandatory physical training and leadership courses. Does your opinion change if the other colleges are located nearby? Given that many of the students receive scholarships to participate in R.O.T.C., does this financial incentive, potentially allowing individuals that could otherwise not afford to attend college to do so, make a difference to your opinion?

CHAPTER 5

WORKING

■ ■ ■

I. INTRODUCTION

A. BACKGROUND READINGS

Lesbians, gay men, bisexual, and transgender individuals confront significant discrimination, both explicit and subtle, in the workplace. Some employers fire or refuse to hire individuals solely on the basis of their articulated or perceived sexual orientation or gender identity. Those LGBT individuals who do have jobs often must hide their identity. Richard Mohr has argued that gay people (and the same is true of transgender individuals) begin to "underidentify with their jobs ... [feeling] no security ... [and consequently are prevented from] giving it a proper degree of commitment, a proper link to self ..." Or LGBT employees become workaholics to "show themselves [they are] productive enough, worthy enough, good enough, [to] overcome the invisible stigma that lurks within them waiting to suppurate."[1] On-the-job discrimination also has a concrete component: persons in same-sex couples usually do not receive the employment benefits for their life partners that married persons receive for their spouses. As a result, LGBT employees do not get "equal pay for equal work." The following readings provide background information about the challenges facing LGBT individuals in the workplace.

PRIVATE EXPERIENCES IN THE PUBLIC DOMAIN: LESBIANS IN ORGANIZATIONS*

Marny Hall

THE LESBIAN CORPORATE EXPERIENCE

The danger of disclosure

Constantly occurring in the work setting were experiences that triggered the women's awareness of their lesbianism. Anti-gay jokes, or comments presuming heterosexuality, such as "Why don't you get married? ... you're almost twenty-eight", stimulated an awareness of

---

[1] RICHARD D. MOHR, GAYS/JUSTICE: A STUDY OF ETHICS, SOCIETY, AND LAW 149 (1988).

* Marny Hall, *Private Experiences in the Public Domain: Lesbians in Organizations*, *in* WOMEN'S STUDIES: ESSENTIAL READINGS 167–73 (Stevi Jackson et al. eds., 1993).

being different. Because the revelation of one's lesbianism could have serious consequences, these women were constantly preoccupied with concealing that aspect of their lives. Sometimes concealment occurred as automatically as retinal adjustment to light change. At other times, it was deliberate and felt more stressful. Whether automatic or deliberate, the process of concealment called for constant attention to every nuance of social interaction. The background buzz of assumptions became centrally important for the lesbian because it signalled where vigilance was necessary or where she could relax and "be herself." The workplace reality for the lesbian, therefore, was one of heightened awareness and sensitivity toward the usually hidden matrices of behaviour, values and attitudes in self and others. * * *

Dangers of non-disclosure

Accompanying the need for protective secrecy was a "state-of-siege" mentality, a feeling of "us and them". Often the feeling associated with these states was anxiety or anger, or both, sometimes in the form of intellectual distance: "I don't fit in, and I don't necessarily want to"; "They're so ignorant"; "You just have to see where they're coming from."

Even if a subject's lesbianism continued to be a well-kept secret, it was perceived as a disadvantage that caused lesbians to receive "unfair treatment". No matter how long they had lived with their partners, lesbians couldn't tap corporate benefits, such as "family" health insurance or travel bonuses which included spouses. One woman, who had lived with her lover for seven years, had earned enough sales points for a company-sponsored trip to Hawaii; however, she had to go alone. There were no family allowances for lesbians who were relocated and whose partners chose to accompany them. Nor could lesbians play the management game, because they would never have the requisite opposite-sexed spouse and a country club membership in the suburbs.

Being secretive created inner conflicts: "I wanted to come out, but I just couldn't," as well as constant anxiety about discovery: "If my bosses knew, they'd find a way to get rid of me"; "In the case of my supervisees, sometimes it gets emotional, and they might hug me. What would go through their minds if they knew I was a lesbian?" Several women felt that their lesbianism, because it was invisible, was less of a hindrance than their gender, which they could not disguise. Being a woman was seen as a major disadvantage in the corporate world: "As a woman, I'm generally assumed to be incompetent whereas the men are assumed to be competent unless proven otherwise."

Their lesbianism reinforced separation between work and leisure. Some respondents contended that this was congruent with their needs: "I am a private person anyway. Even if I weren't gay, I wouldn't want to mix work with my life outside work." For the others the discontinuity was a source of frustration and anger: "These guys go home and their friends are the same people they see all day. For me, coming to work is bowing out of my world completely and going into theirs." * * *

Even though the non-disclosure of their homosexuality was crucial, several respondents felt the secret was not always within their control. For example, one woman was showing a friend from work the plans of the new house she and her lover had bought. Pointing-out the main bedroom, she accidentally said, "This is where we sleep." She was appalled to have revealed the intimate nature of her relationship. Other respondents felt they revealed their lesbianism through their physical appearance. A lesbian who wore jeans to a clerical job said, "The way I dress I was in a way forcing it down their throats." Another woman said, "At the time they started suspecting, I made a mistake and cut my hair short. That was the tip-off."

Many of the interviewees said their homosexuality had been revealed inadvertently. In one instance, a woman was featured in the business section of her home-town newspaper when she became the 300th member to join a local gay business organization. She had been assured, falsely, by the photographer who covered the event that the story would appear only in gay publications. Another woman said her co-workers found out about her when her lover, wearing jeans and short hair, stopped by her office one day to drop something off. These accidental disclosures generated embarrassment and fear and were perceived by respondents as an "Oh no!" experience. Even when these near-calamities did not trigger the expected dire consequences, the incidents themselves were remembered vividly. * * *

The neuterized/neutralized strategy

Femaleness is the discredited and visible side of one's lesbianism. Consequently if gender can be minimized, lesbianism is less likely to come into focus. Computer-related jobs were particularly popular. One can speculate that, because they combine the masculine aspects of technology with the female tradition of keyboard work, computers effectively de-gender their programmers. Consequently sexuality and sexual preference questions are neutralized. In a related strategy, women who are perceived as masculine can tap positive qualities attributed to males. In a corporation, the advantages occasioned by such perceptions may outweigh, or at least balance, the disadvantages of being seen as "unfeminine". * * *

Strategies that balance non-disclosure

All forms of non-disclosure, whether the occasional substitute of "he" for "she" when describing a weekend outing with a lover or the complete fabrication of a heterosexual life, leave a lesbian in a difficult moral position. Not only is she denying what she knows to be true, but she is also ignoring the strong exhortations of the lesbian community to come out. * * *

Denial and dissociation. Frequently respondents would insist they were not in the closet, and in response to further questioning would contradict themselves, for example, "No, I haven't actually told anyone I'm gay." They continued to deny, however, that they were being secretive. Others claimed they felt comfortable in the face of homophobic remarks. Though no respondent said it, I speculate that these respondents were using a dissociative strategy; it was not *they* who were being discussed contemptuously. One respondent distinguished between "dykey women", and gays who "handled their gayness discreetly". The dichotomization between good and bad gays is another dissociative strategy.

Avoidance. Several respondents simply avoided personal situations at work. Some regretted the absence of social interactions with co-workers. Others said they did not want to get close to co-workers because they had nothing in common with them.

Distraction. Respondents purposefully cultivated images that conveyed differentness—a feminist, a liberal—in order to distract from the more discreditable identification of lesbian. Unfavourable self-assessments about being duplicitous could thus be balanced by principled stand-taking.

Token disclosure. While concealing the true nature of their relationships, some respondents let it be known that they had done something with "a room-mate". This was a partial disclosure since their room-mates were also their lovers. Similarly, after Harvey Milk's assassination, one woman asked a homophobic job supervisor for time off to go to the funeral of a friend. She did not mention that the "friend" was Milk. In response to an anti-gay joke, one lesbian said, "You'd better get yourself some new material", revealing her irritation, but not her gay identity.

The most common partial-disclosure strategy was simply to disclose their homosexuality only to certain people they felt they could trust. Because this information could leak, such a partial disclosure often set off a new round of strategies to find out if one's secret had been more widely revealed.

All of these balancing strategies seemed to restore to some degree respondents' threatened sense of integrity.

Implications and conclusions

Rather like a horse that finds itself simultaneously reined in and spurred on, corporate lesbians are caught in a crossfire of conflicting cultural and subcultural imperatives. The strategies lesbians used to manoeuver their ways through this thicket of contradictions reveal that the old reductionist notion of "coming out" is not an act, but rather a never-ending and labyrinthine process of decision and indecision, of nuance and calculated presentations as well as impulsive and inadvertent revelations—a process, in short, as shifting as the contexts in which it occurs.

Is there, one might ask, a position beyond strategy, of simply acting naturally as one respondent claimed she did? Upon examination the "natural" stance is simply another ploy, an "as-if" strategy in which the respondent acted as if she were entitled to the same social prerogatives, could count on the same good will assumed by her heterosexual co-workers. According to Goffman, this sort of "open" strategy thrusts a new career upon the stigmatized person, "that of representing [her] category. [She] finds [herself] too eminent to avoid being presented by [her] own as an instance of them".[8] And, one might add, or tokenized by heterosexual co-workers.

And so the final irony for those who are thoroughly, consistently and extensively open at work is that they are effectively shorn of the authenticity and individuality they sought by this "naturalness". As Laing writes, "lonely and painful . . . to be misunderstood, but to be correctly understood is also to be in danger of being engulfed, when the 'understanding' occurs within a framework that one had hoped to break out of".[9] And Goffman notes, "There may be no 'authentic' solution at all".[10]

The rare lesbian who reveals her orientation, and who survives the consequences of violating the gendered expectations which structure the organization succumbs, then, to the organization in another way. Stylized out of existence, she forfeits her private mutinies, cannot mobilize the resistance necessary to shield her individuality from engulfment by the collective purpose of the organization. Homogenized, the token corporate lesbian becomes the consummate "organization (wo)man".

OUT AT WORK: A TRANS PERSPECTIVE*
Bay Windows

Andrea Dawn Verville is seated in the facility where she earns her living teaching adult education classes for unemployed and underemployed veterans. Clad in a woman's suit but without make-up, Verville says that until a legal name change comes through, she still identifies at her workplace by her male birth name.

---

[8] E. Goffman, *Stigma*, Englewood Cliffs, NJ: Prentice Hall, 1964, p. 26.

[9] R.D. Laing, *The Divided Self*, New York: Pantheon, 1970, p. 76.

[10] Goffman, *Stigma*, p. 124.

* Allen Richards, *Out at Work: A Trans Perspective*, BAY WINDOWS, June 27, 2003.

"Once the legal name change goes through, I will go full-time," Verville explains. Of her co-workers, she observes, "It's hard enough for people to take in a new person, but [it is particularly hard] to take in a new person and attach old names to her. . . . [My supervisor and I have agreed to] let things slide for now, until everything becomes legal in the courts of Massachusetts. Then it will be OK [for us] to say 'OK, these are the new rules we play by.' "

Verville identifies as a male-to-female (MTF) pre-operative transsexual. Still in the early stages of transition—she began undergoing hormone replacement therapy several months ago—Verville is nonetheless taking a bold step: Transitioning on a job she has held for the past several years. She admits to having had a high level of anxiety, she says, "because there is always the real threat of violence. Even here in Boston, there have been transgender people who have been killed in the past."

Ironically, Verville is confident that she could defend herself physically. Her self-described "hyper-masculine" past included stints in the Marines as a marksmanship instructor and aircraft mechanic, as well as receiving certification as a firefighter and working security jobs that on one occasion had her guarding former Vice President Al Gore.

But she is well aware of the disadvantages transgender individuals face in court and oftentimes in employment. In her case, however, Verville says, "I have the back-up of the administration." Verville's supervisor was supportive as she advised colleagues of her upcoming change. "It was the entire staff of the school, which was comprised of about twenty people," Verville recalls. "[At the end of a regular meeting], my boss said that I had an announcement to make. I basically laid everything out on the table and tried to allay some of their unspoken fears right off the bat. It was met with quiet acceptance and a 'Good for you' kind of thing."

"Afterward, that's when you start hearing people talking about you. Now, there's a slight level of humor, trying to break the ice and let them know that it's OK to come to me and talk about these things. It's not anything that most people have any sort of background with so part of who I am is an educator." * * *

. . . [W]hile transgender issues have moved farther into the mainstream in recent years, many trans people still have difficulty gaining acceptance in the mainstream workforce. According to Jennifer Levi, a staff attorney at Gay and Lesbian Advocates and Defenders (GLAD), transgendered individuals can face a host of workplace issues because of their gender identities. "It can be a difficult situation for trans people to transition during the course of employment, or it can be difficult if people have taken a job and then other co-workers learn that they are transgender," says Levi. "The ultimate goal is for people to retain their jobs and to be able to work both in safety and just to be comfortable in the workplace."

Certainly, transgendered people have made gains toward better treatment in the workplace as well: Like Verville, others who spoke to Bay Windows for this story spoke positively of coming out or transitioning on the job.

Take Cole Thaler, a recent graduate of Northeastern University School of Law, who is now employed as a law clerk. Thaler, a female-to-male transgendered person (FTM) and co-founder of the Massachusetts transgender Political Coalition, said that his school records list him as female, which causes discrepancies when employers are checking references. "Generally I have had good experiences," he says. "I have been really lucky in that at all the jobs I have had since I identified as trans, all of my co-workers have been very willing to educate themselves and have been very respectful toward me."

Because he is not taking hormones and described himself as small of stature, Thaler explains, "I'm in a place where sometimes I pass and sometimes I don't, which has created any number of interesting situations in the workplace." For instance, Thaler once interviewed for a position for which one of his references referred to Thaler with male pronouns. Thaler explained to the interviewer that he identified as transgender; the interviewer then asked if that meant he would be using the men's restroom. Thaler said it was appropriate for him to do so if there was no single occupancy restroom. To this, the interviewer responded that he would send a memo out to other staff offering his support. "It set the pace so that when I came in people were expecting to see a guy and responded to me professionally," says Thaler.

"There is this sort of ethic of professionalism [in some high-level occupations] that has definitely worked to my advantage," Thaler admits. But there are still instances of highly paid white-collar workers being fired as well as the familiar stories of blue-collar individuals facing termination, he maintains. "I think it's just maybe less overt [in the white-collar world]."

Trans activist Holly Ryan credits the acceptance of her co-workers to her self-acceptance. Ryan, a purchasing director for a human service agency who also trains staff on dealing with trans individuals in rehabs, detoxes and educational facilities, transitioned on the job five years ago. She has been promoted three times since then. Ryan describes herself as expecting fair treatment and getting it. "I don't look at the ground. I don't whimper. I don't blame the world for anything. I just feel that, you know, it's going to be harder for me," she says. "But if I carry myself right, then it's not a problem. Not to say that there is not discrimination, but I think it's all in how you carry yourself."

The change did not require a huge leap of imagination for her co-workers, Ryan says. "I was pretty androgynous for years before that. I have long hair and I had electrolysis done even before I transitioned. I wore small hoop earrings. A lot of people thought that I was going to come out as gay," she explains. "I guess trans is the last thing on their minds. But when they thought about it for a day or two, they just said 'Oh, yeah, we get it now.'" Of her role in the company, Ryan says, "I'm not kept in the closet at my job. I'm out front."

Despite her own good fortune transitioning at work, Ryan personally knows of at least one person who hasn't fared as well: "I have a friend, who transitioned six months ago. Had a $75,000 a year job in manufacturing, came back, and three months later was fired for some other trumped up reason." * * *

While it appears that employers are becoming more open to gender diversity, climbing the ladder of success is still a challenge for many. Writer/activist Nancy Nangeroni, host of WMBR's Gender Talk, a radio program devoted to transgender issues, observes that many people start their own businesses rather than deal with the difficulties involved in attempting to be accepted as a trans person by potential employers.

Nangeroni, an MTF, is an MIT graduate who works as a design engineer. She transitioned on the job several years ago but within six months she knew staying at the company wasn't going to work for her. Nangeroni describes a feeling of undefined discomfort with her former co-workers, which she now acknowledges was at least partly on her end as well. A self-described former jock, Nangeroni had a falling out with a colleague with whom she had previously bonded over sports talk. "When I transitioned, he and I had a big blowout two or three months after I transitioned," Nangeroni recalls. "After that, he treated me with respect, I treated him with respect and it was much better. We agreed that we needed to be more professional and we were. So I respect him a lot for that."

After leaving that job, Nangeroni went on job interviews where she disclosed her trans status. "I think six or eight times I disclosed, and no offer. The first job that I didn't disclose, I got an offer," she notes. "So that pretty much was a lesson. Then later on, when the guy hired me, I asked him if he would have hired me if I had told him [I was trans]. He said no, because he would have wondered why I was telling him. He thought there would have been a problem."

"There's no point in my going for an interview if I'm going to tell them I'm trans," Nangeroni concludes. "It's just a waste of time.

"When I went to work at Lucent, they had previously had a person who transitioned there ten years before and it went badly. When I first arrived there, everyone loved me," Nangeroni recalled. "I started getting invited to all kinds of high level management meetings, including meetings in managers' homes. Until they found out I was a transsexual. Overnight everything changed. I never got another invitation."

But for Mike West, there are more pros than cons to coming out as trans. "I do plan on discussing my trans identity with potential employers and co-workers [when I return to work]," says West, a transitional male who is currently on long-term disability. "I have found that when I have been 100 percent honest with people that I get a very good response from them. I have actually had people approach me [to say] how impressed they are with my honesty and how much credit they give me for the whole thing. I think being honest also makes me relax more; there are no secrets. I'd be a liar if I said that someday I didn't hope that I have transitioned so well into my male role that I don't have to disclose the fact that I am transsexual. But at this moment in my life, I am still in the early stages of transition, so I feel it's best to just be up front and honest with everyone."

BIAS IN THE WORKPLACE: CONSISTENT EVIDENCE OF SEXUAL ORIENTATION AND GENDER IDENTITY DISCRIMINATION 1998–2008*

M.V. Lee Badgett et al.

Over the last ten years, many researchers have conducted studies to find out whether LGBT people face sexual orientation discrimination in the workplace. These studies include surveys of LGBT individuals' workplace experiences, wage comparisons between lesbian, gay, and bisexual (LGB) and heterosexual persons, analyses of discrimination complaints filed with administrative agencies, and testing studies and controlled experiments.

Studies conducted from the mid-1980s to mid-1990s revealed that 16% to 68% of LGB respondents reported experiencing employment discrimination at some point in their lives. Since the mid-1990s, an additional fifteen studies found that 15% to 43% of LGB respondents experienced discrimination in the workplace.

When asked more specific questions about the type of discrimination experienced, LGB respondents reported the following experiences that were related to their sexual orientation: 8% to 17% were fired or denied employment, 10% to 28% were denied a promotion or given negative

* M.V. Lee Badgett, Brad Sears, Holning Lau, Deborah Ho, *Bias in the Workplace: Consistent Evidence of Sexual Orientation and Gender Identity Discrimination 1998–2008*, 84 CHI.-KENT L. REV. 559 (2009).

performance evaluations, 7% to 41% were verbally/physically abused or had their workplace vandalized, and 10% to 19% reported receiving unequal pay or benefits.

Although data on the transgender population are scarce, several studies have brought to light the presence of discrimination against this community. When transgender individuals were surveyed separately, they reported similar or higher levels of employment discrimination. In six studies conducted between 1996 and 2006, 20% to 57% of transgender respondents reported having experienced employment discrimination at some point in their life. More specifically, 13% to 56% were fired, 13% to 47% were denied employment, 22% to 31% were harassed, and 19% were denied a promotion based on their gender identity.

Beyond survey responses, collection and analysis of state-level discrimination complaint data allow another lens through which to measure sexual orientation discrimination. Individual complaints of discrimination filed with government agencies provide another measure of perceived discrimination. In 1997 the General Accounting Office (or GAO, now known as the Government Accountability Office) collected the number of complaints filed in states that outlaw sexual orientation discrimination and found that 1% of all discrimination complaints related to sexual orientation. However, comparisons of data from sixteen states and the District of Columbia show that the rate of sexual orientation discrimination complaints per LGB person is 5 per 10,000, which is roughly equivalent to gender-based discrimination complaints.

A wage or income gap between LGB people and heterosexual people with the same job and personal characteristics provides another indicator of sexual orientation discrimination. A growing number of studies using data from the National Health and Social Life Survey, the General Social Survey, the United States Census, and the National Health and Nutrition Examination Survey show that gay men earn 10% to 32% less than otherwise similar heterosexual men. The findings for lesbians, however, are less clear. In some studies they earn more than heterosexual women but less than heterosexual or gay men. [The fact that lesbians consistently earn less than men suggests that gender discrimination has a greater impact on lesbians' wages than sexual orientation discrimination.]

Controlled experiments reveal sexual orientation discrimination in workplace settings. In controlled experiments, researchers manufacture scenarios that allow comparisons of the treatment of LGB people with treatment of heterosexuals. Seven out of eight studies using controlled experiments related to employment and public accommodation find evidence of sexual orientation discrimination.

Despite the variations in methodology, context, and time period in the studies reviewed in this report, our review of the evidence demonstrates one disturbing and consistent pattern: sexual orientation-based and gender identity discrimination is a common occurrence in many workplaces across the country.

B. AMERICAN EMPLOYMENT LAW

In focusing on the working lives of LGBT individuals, this Chapter explores the landscape of employment discrimination law in the United States. Such an examination is an immense and complex task. Employment discrimination protections can be established by all three branches of the government—legislative (through statutes), executive (through rules, regulations, and executive orders), and judicial (through court decisions)—and by all levels of government—federal, state, and local. Moreover, employers, and therefore jobs themselves, are highly differentiated: military, civil service, public and private education, quasi-public utilities, government contractors, large and small corporations, partnerships, and other private employers. Employment discrimination law is also inconsistent, not only between jurisdictions and job types, but also on its own terms. The terrain is constantly shifting—particularly with the changing nature of the American judiciary and with the changing nature of American industry—and is thus difficult to capture in a study such as this.

This Chapter attempts to organize the vast subject of employment discrimination by dividing it into two parts—one explores the "private" workplace (corporate America and other non-governmental jobs), the other the "public" workplace (government employment). Employees in both are generally protected by antidiscrimination statutes such as Title VII. In addition, government employees are protected from discrimination by constitutional provisions, civil service rules, and executive orders.

II.   PRIVATE EMPLOYMENT

The traditional concept governing relations between workers and employers in America has historically been "employment at will." "Employment at will" means that employment is solely within the discretion of, or "at the will of," the employer. An employee can be hired or fired for good reason, bad reason, or no reason at all.[2]

Throughout the last fifty years, the employment-at-will concept has been altered by expanding notions of rights for employees and restrictions on the unfettered discretion of employers. Some of these restrictions are statutory protections, created by Congress and state legislatures. The

---

[2] *See generally* MICHAEL J. ZIMMER, CHARLES A. SULLIVAN & REBECCA HANNER WHITE, CASES AND MATERIALS ON EMPLOYMENT DISCRIMINATION 4–5 (6th ed. 2003).

most important of these laws is Title VII of the Civil Rights Act of 1964.[3] Title VII makes it unlawful for an employer "to fail or refuse to hire or to discharge any individual, or otherwise to discriminate against any individual with respect to his compensation, terms, conditions, or privileges of employment, because of such individual's race, color, religion, sex, or national origin."[4] Congress has further extended employment protections to bar discrimination on the basis of age, *see* Age Discrimination in Employment Act,[5] disability, *see* Americans with Disabilities Act,[6] and genetic information. *See* Genetic Information Non-Discrimination Act.[7]

A. EMPLOYMENT NON-DISCRIMINATION ACT (ENDA)

There have been several bills introduced in Congress during the last four decades seeking to prohibit employment discrimination on the basis of sexual orientation. Early efforts focused on simply amending Title VII to include "sexual orientation" as a protected class. A more recent proposal, known as the Employment Non-Discrimination Act (ENDA), calls for the enactment of a separate statute explicitly addressing the issue of sexual orientation discrimination.

ENDA would prohibit employers with more than fifteen employees from discriminating on the basis of sexual orientation. It would cover instances of disparate treatment (i.e. intentional discrimination) but not of disparate impact. (Disparate impact claims are those that challenge facially neutral policies that have a negative and disproportionate effect on a protected class.) It would also exclude religious organizations and the armed forces from its coverage and would not require employers to provide domestic partnership benefits.

---

[3]   Pub. L. No. 88–352, § 701, 78 Stat. 241 (1964) (codified at 42 U.S.C.A.§§ 2000e to 2000e–17 (West 2007)).

[4]   42 U.S.C.A. § 2000e–2(a)(1).

[5]   Pub. L. No. 90–202, § 2, 81 Stat. 602 (1967) (codified at 29 U.S.C.A. §§ 621–634 (West 2007)).

[6]   Pub. L. No. 101–336, § 2, 104 Stat. 328 (1990) (codified at 42 U.S.C.A. §§ 12101–12213 (West 2007)). In enacting the Americans with Disabilities Act in 1990, Congress specifically exempted these types of claims from the law's coverage:

(a) Homosexuality and Bisexuality. For purposes of the definition of "disability" in section 3(2) [42 U.S.C. § 12102(2)], homosexuality and bisexuality are not impairments and as such are not disabilities under this Act.

(b) Certain conditions. Under this Act, the term "disability" shall not include—

(1) transvestism, transsexualism, pedophilia, exhibitionism, voyeurism, gender identity disorders not resulting from physical impairments, or other sexual behavior disorders; * * *

Id. at § 12211. The Supreme Court has held, however, that individuals who are HIV-positive, even when they are asymptomatic, can be disabled within the meaning of the ADA. *See Bragdon v. Abbott*, 524 U.S. 624, 118 S.Ct. 2196, 141 L.Ed.2d 540 (1998).

[7]   Pub. L. No. 110–233, 122 Stat. 881 (2008) (codified as amended in scattered sections of 2, 29, 42 U.S.C.).

When ENDA was first proposed in the mid-1990's, it did not include a prohibition on discrimination on the basis of gender identity. Some of the bill's supporters were opposed to including such a provision, reasoning that the chances that Congress would enact the law would be considerably diminished if gender identity was included as a protected category. Not surprisingly, the transgender community was not pleased with this decision and soon began working to add gender identity to the bill. In 2004, the Human Rights Campaign, one of the leading gay rights organizations that lobby at the federal level, modified its position and came out in support of expanding ENDA to include gender identity.[8]

In 2007, a new ENDA bill, which included gender identity as a protected class for the first time, was introduced in the House of Representatives. But later that year, the bill was substituted with two different ones, one addressing sexual orientation and the other gender identity discrimination. The former was approved by the House of Representatives by a vote of 235 to 184. The Senate, however, did not take up the measure, and neither body voted on the gender identity version of ENDA.

In 2013, the Senate voted to pass an ENDA bill that included gender identity protection by a margin of 64 to 32. As this casebook was going to press, however, the legislation's prospects in the House of Representatives remained uncertain.

B. TITLE VII

The absence of a federal law explicitly prohibiting discrimination on the basis of either sexual orientation or gender identity means that the most important issue for LGBT rights under federal antidiscrimination law relates to Title VII's prohibition of discrimination on the basis of sex. Subsection 1, therefore, provides a brief primer on Title VII law as it applies to sex discrimination, with an emphasis on claims of sexual harassment and gender stereotyping. Although courts have almost uniformly rejected the notion that either sexual orientation or gender identity as such fall within the meaning of "sex" under Title VII, some LGBT plaintiffs have succeeded in bringing sex employment discrimination cases under sexual harassment and/or gender stereotyping theories. These issues are explored in Subsections 2 (sexual orientation) and 3 (gender identity).

1. Sex

The original version of the bill that eventually became Title VII did not include sex as a protected category. In fact, the amendment to prohibit sex discrimination was proposed by an *opponent* of Title VII on

---

[8] *See* Bob Roehr, *HRC Moves to Add Trans to ENDA*, WINDY CITY TIMES, Aug. 11, 2004.

the floor of the House of Representatives. It was the legislator's hope that the amendment would prove to be so divisive that it would lead to the eventual defeat of the entire legislation. The amendment, however, was approved and so was, of course, Title VII.

The statute does not define "sex." Furthermore, because of the unusual way in which sex was added to the statute as a protected category, there is little legislative history to provide guidance on the meaning of the term. As a result, it has been largely up to the courts to define the term.

One of the earliest Supreme Court cases that addressed the meaning of "sex" under Title VII was *Phillips v. Martin Marrietta Corp.*[9] The employer in that case had a policy that excluded from its workplace women, but not men, with young children. The employer argued that it was not discriminating on the basis of sex because it was not refusing to hire all women, but only certain women, that is, women with young children. The Court rejected the notion that a "sex-plus" policy, namely, one that takes into account sex plus another factor (such as having children), is exempt from the scope of Title VII.

Perhaps surprisingly, given the reasoning of *Martin Marietta*, the Court several years later concluded that the exclusion of pregnancy from a disability insurance plan did not violate Title VII. The Court explained in *General Electric Co. v. Gilbert* that the insurance plan distinguished between pregnant women and nonpregnant persons (both men and women), and as such did not constitute sex discrimination.[10] Congress did not agree, and quickly amended Title VII by enacting the Pregnancy Discrimination Act of 1978, which explicitly prohibited discrimination on the basis of pregnancy.

The Court was more open to the idea that sexual harassment could constitute a form of sex discrimination under Title VII, concluding in *Meritor Savings Bank v. Vinson* that the statute is violated when the harassment is "sufficiently severe or pervasive 'to alter the conditions of [the victim's] employment and create an abusive working environment.' "[11] The Court distinguished between two different categories of sexual harassment claims: "quid pro quo" cases and "hostile work environment" cases.[12] The former cases involve demands on employees to engage in sexual relationships in order to avoid being demoted or fired, or as a condition for promotion. The latter cases, which are more common, involve the creation of a workplace environment that

---

[9] 400 U.S. 542, 91 S.Ct. 496, 27 L.Ed.2d 613 (1971).

[10] 429 U.S. 125, 97 S.Ct. 401, 50 L.Ed.2d 343 (1976).

[11] 477 U.S. 57, 67, 106 S.Ct. 2399, 2405, 91 L.Ed.2d 49, 60 (1986).

[12] *Id.* at 65–66, 106 S. Ct. at 2404–05, L. Ed. 2d at 58–9.

is sufficiently hostile to the members of one sex so as to make it difficult for the subjects of the harassment to do their jobs.[13]

In "quid pro quo" cases, it is alleged that an employer or supervisor has taken a "tangible employment action" as a result of the employee's refusal to submit (or continue to submit) to sexual relations, which, if proven, by itself "constitutes a change in the terms and conditions of employment . . . actionable under Title VII."[14] On the other hand, in "hostile work environment" cases, the harassment usually takes place *before* a tangible employment decision is made regarding the employee. As a result, in order to establish that the harassment affects the terms and conditions of employment, the plaintiff must show that it is "severe or pervasive."[15] The Court has added that "in order to be actionable under the statute, a sexually objectionable environment must be both objectively and subjectively offensive, one that a reasonable person would find hostile or abusive, and one that the victim in fact did perceive to be so."[16]

In addition to recognizing sexual harassment, in its different manifestations, as a form of sex discrimination, the Court, in the following opinion, concluded that making employment decisions based on gender stereotypes also constitutes impermissible discrimination under Title VII.

PRICE WATERHOUSE V. HOPKINS

Supreme Court of the United States, 1989
490 U.S. 228, 109 S.Ct. 1775, 104 L.Ed.2d 268

JUSTICE BRENNAN.

Ann Hopkins was a senior manager in an office of Price Waterhouse when she was proposed for partnership in 1982. She was neither offered nor denied admission to the partnership; instead, her candidacy was held for reconsideration the following year. When the partners in her office later refused to repropose her for partnership, she sued Price Waterhouse under Title VII of the Civil Rights Act of 1964, charging that the firm had discriminated against her on the basis of sex in its decisions regarding partnership. * * *

Ann Hopkins had worked at Price Waterhouse's Office of Government Services in Washington, D.C., for five years when the partners in that office proposed her as a candidate for partnership. Of the

---

[13] For a further exploration of the two categories of sexual harassment cases, see HAROLD S. LEWIS, JR. & ELIZABETH J. NORMAN, EMPLOYMENT DISCRIMINATION LAW AND PRACTICE 98–120 (2nd ed. 2004).

[14] *Burlington Indus., Inc. v. Ellerth*, 524 U.S. 742, 754, 118 S.Ct. 2257, 2265, 141 L.Ed.2d 633, 648 (1998).

[15] *Id.* at 754, 118 S. Ct. at 2265, 141 L. Ed. 2d at 648.

[16] *Faragher v. City of Boca Raton*, 524 U.S. 775, 787, 118 S.Ct. 2275, 2283, 141 L.Ed.2d 662, 676 (1998).

662 partners at the firm at that time, 7 were women. Of the 88 persons proposed for partnership that year, only 1—Hopkins—was a woman. Forty-seven of these candidates were admitted to the partnership, 21 were rejected, and 20—including Hopkins—were "held" for reconsideration the following year. Thirteen of the 32 partners who had submitted comments on Hopkins supported her bid for partnership. Three partners recommended that her candidacy be placed on hold, eight stated that they did not have an informed opinion about her, and eight recommended that she be denied partnership.

In a jointly prepared statement supporting her candidacy, the partners in Hopkins' office showcased her successful 2-year effort to secure a $25 million contract with the Department of State, labeling it "an outstanding performance" and one that Hopkins carried out "virtually at the partner level." . . .

The partners in Hopkins' office praised her character as well as her accomplishments, describing her in their joint statement as "an outstanding professional" who had a "deft touch," a "strong character, independence and integrity." Clients appear to have agreed with these assessments. At trial, one official from the State Department described her as "extremely competent, intelligent," "strong and forthright, very productive, energetic and creative." Another high-ranking official praised Hopkins' decisiveness, broadmindedness, and "intellectual clarity"; she was, in his words, "a stimulating conversationalist." Evaluations such as these led [the district court] Judge Gesell to conclude that Hopkins "had no difficulty dealing with clients and her clients appear to have been very pleased with her work" and that she "was generally viewed as a highly competent project leader who worked long hours, pushed vigorously to meet deadlines and demanded much from the multidisciplinary staffs with which she worked."

On too many occasions, however, Hopkins' aggressiveness apparently spilled over into abrasiveness. Staff members seem to have borne the brunt of Hopkins' brusqueness. Long before her bid for partnership, partners evaluating her work had counseled her to improve her relations with staff members. Although later evaluations indicate an improvement, Hopkins' perceived shortcomings in this important area eventually doomed her bid for partnership. Virtually all of the partners' negative remarks about Hopkins—even those of partners supporting her—had to do with her "interpersonal skills." Both "[s]upporters and opponents of her candidacy," stressed Judge Gesell, "indicated that she was sometimes overly aggressive, unduly harsh, difficult to work with and impatient with staff."

There were clear signs, though, that some of the partners reacted negatively to Hopkins' personality because she was a woman. One partner described her as "macho"; another suggested that she "overcompensated for being a woman"; a third advised her to take "a course at charm school". Several partners criticized her use of profanity; in response, one partner suggested that those partners objected to her swearing only "because it's a lady using foul language." Another supporter explained that Hopkins "ha[d] matured from a tough-talking somewhat masculine hard-nosed mgr to an authoritative, formidable, but much more appealing lady ptr candidate." But it was the man who, as Judge Gesell found, bore responsibility for explaining to Hopkins the reasons for the Policy Board's decision to place her candidacy on hold who delivered the *coup de grace*: in order to improve her chances for partnership, Thomas Beyer advised, Hopkins should "walk more femininely, talk more femininely, dress more femininely, wear make-up, have her hair styled, and wear jewelry."

Dr. Susan Fiske, a social psychologist and Associate Professor of Psychology at Carnegie-Mellon University, testified at trial that the partnership selection process at Price Waterhouse was likely influenced by sex stereotyping. Her testimony focused not only on the overtly sex-based comments of partners but also on gender-neutral remarks, made by partners who knew Hopkins only slightly, that were intensely critical of her. One partner, for example, baldly stated that Hopkins was "universally disliked" by staff, and another described her as "consistently annoying and irritating"; yet these were people who had had very little contact with Hopkins. According to Fiske, Hopkins' uniqueness (as the only woman in the pool of candidates) and the subjectivity of the evaluations made it likely that sharply critical remarks such as these were the product of sex stereotyping—although Fiske admitted that she could not say with certainty whether any particular comment was the result of stereotyping. Fiske based her opinion on a review of the submitted comments, explaining that it was commonly accepted practice for social psychologists to reach this kind of conclusion without having met any of the people involved in the decisionmaking process.

In previous years, other female candidates for partnership also had been evaluated in sex-based terms. As a general matter, Judge Gesell concluded, "[c]andidates were viewed favorably if partners believed they maintained their femin[in]ity while becoming effective professional managers"; in this environment, "[t]o be identified as a 'women's lib[b]er' was regarded as [a] negative comment." In fact, the judge found that in previous years "[o]ne partner repeatedly commented that he could not consider any woman seriously as a partnership candidate and believed that women were not even capable of functioning as senior managers—yet the firm took no action to discourage his comments and recorded his vote in the overall summary of the evaluations."

Judge Gesell found that Price Waterhouse legitimately emphasized interpersonal skills in its partnership decisions, and also found that the firm had not fabricated its complaints about Hopkins' interpersonal skills as a pretext for discrimination. Moreover, he concluded, the firm did not give decisive emphasis to such traits only because Hopkins was a woman; although there were male candidates who lacked these skills but who were admitted to partnership, the judge found that these candidates possessed other, positive traits that Hopkins lacked.

The judge went on to decide, however, that some of the partners' remarks about Hopkins stemmed from an impermissibly cabined view of the proper behavior of women, and that Price Waterhouse had done nothing to disavow reliance on such comments. He held that Price Waterhouse had unlawfully discriminated against Hopkins on the basis of sex by consciously giving credence and effect to partners' comments that resulted from sex stereotyping. * * *

In saying that gender played a motivating part in an employment decision, we mean that, if we asked the employer at the moment of the decision what its reasons were and if we received a truthful response, one of those reasons would be that the applicant or employee was a woman. In the specific context of sex stereotyping, an employer who acts on the basis of a belief that a woman cannot be aggressive, or that she must not be, has acted on the basis of gender.

Although the parties do not overtly dispute this last proposition, the placement by Price Waterhouse of "sex stereotyping" in quotation marks throughout its brief seems to us an insinuation either that such stereotyping was not present in this case or that it lacks legal relevance. We reject both possibilities. As to the existence of sex stereotyping in this case, we are not inclined to quarrel with the District Court's conclusion that a number of the partners' comments showed sex stereotyping at work. As for the legal relevance of sex stereotyping, we are beyond the day when an employer could evaluate employees by assuming or insisting that they matched the stereotype associated with their group, for " '[i]n forbidding employers to discriminate against individuals because of their sex, Congress intended to strike at the entire spectrum of disparate treatment of men and women resulting from sex stereotypes.' " *Los Angeles Dept. of Water and Power v. Manhart*, 435 U.S. 702, 707, n. 13, 98 S.Ct. 1370, 55 L.Ed.2d 657 (1978), quoting *Sprogis v. United Air Lines, Inc.*, 444 F.2d 1194, 1198 (7th Cir. 1971). An employer who objects to aggressiveness in women but whose positions require this trait places women in an intolerable and impermissible catch 22: out of a job if they behave aggressively and out of a job if they do not. Title VII lifts women out of this bind.

Remarks at work that are based on sex stereotypes do not inevitably prove that gender played a part in a particular employment decision. The plaintiff must show that the employer actually relied on her gender in making its decision. In making this showing, stereotyped remarks can certainly be *evidence* that gender played a part. In any event, the stereotyping in this case did not simply consist of stray remarks. On the contrary, Hopkins proved that Price Waterhouse invited partners to submit comments; that some of the comments stemmed from sex stereotypes; that an important part of the Policy Board's decision on Hopkins was an assessment of the submitted comments; and that Price Waterhouse in no way disclaimed reliance on the sex-linked evaluations. This is not, as Price Waterhouse suggests, "discrimination in the air"; rather, it is, as Hopkins puts it, "discrimination brought to ground and visited upon" an employee. By focusing on Hopkins' specific proof, however, we do not suggest a limitation on the possible ways of proving that stereotyping played a motivating role in an employment decision, and we refrain from deciding here which specific facts, "standing alone," would or would not establish a plaintiff's case, since such a decision is unnecessary in this case. * * *

In finding that some of the partners' comments reflected sex stereotyping, the District Court relied in part on Dr. Fiske's expert testimony. Without directly impugning Dr. Fiske's credentials or qualifications, Price Waterhouse insinuates that a social psychologist is unable to identify sex stereotyping in evaluations without investigating whether those evaluations have a basis in reality. This argument comes too late. At trial, counsel for Price Waterhouse twice assured the court that he did not question Dr. Fiske's expertise and failed to challenge the legitimacy of her discipline. Without contradiction from Price Waterhouse, Fiske testified that she discerned sex stereotyping in the partners' evaluations of Hopkins and she further explained that it was part of her business to identify stereotyping in written documents. We are not inclined to accept petitioner's belated and unsubstantiated characterization of Dr. Fiske's testimony as "gossamer evidence" based only on "intuitive hunches" and of her detection of sex stereotyping as "intuitively divined". Nor are we disposed to adopt the dissent's dismissive attitude toward Dr. Fiske's field of study and toward her own professional integrity.

Indeed, we are tempted to say that Dr. Fiske's expert testimony was merely icing on Hopkins' cake. It takes no special training to discern sex stereotyping in a description of an aggressive female employee as requiring "a course at charm school." Nor, turning to Thomas Beyer's memorable advice to Hopkins, does it require expertise in psychology to know that, if an employee's flawed "interpersonal skills" can be corrected by a soft-hued suit or a new shade of lipstick, perhaps it is the employee's sex and not her interpersonal skills that has drawn the criticism.

Price Waterhouse also charges that Hopkins produced no evidence that sex stereotyping played a role in the decision to place her candidacy on hold. As we have stressed, however, Hopkins showed that the partnership solicited evaluations from all of the firm's partners; that it generally relied very heavily on such evaluations in making its decision; that some of the partners' comments were the product of stereotyping; and that the firm in no way disclaimed reliance on those particular comments, either in Hopkins' case or in the past. Certainly a plausible— and, one might say, inevitable—conclusion to draw from this set of circumstances is that the Policy Board in making its decision did in fact take into account all of the partners' comments, including the comments that were motivated by stereotypical notions about women's proper deportment.

[Concurring opinions by JUSTICE WHITE and JUSTICE O'CONNOR, as well as a dissenting opinion by JUSTICE KENNEDY, are omitted.]

JESPERSEN V. HARRAH'S OPERATING COMPANY, INC.
United States Court of Appeals, Ninth Circuit, 2006 (en banc)
444 F.3d 1104

SCHROEDER, CHIEF JUDGE.

We took this sex discrimination case en banc in order to reaffirm our circuit law concerning appearance and grooming standards, and to clarify our evolving law of sex stereotyping claims. * * *

Plaintiff Darlene Jespersen worked successfully as a bartender at Harrah's for twenty years and compiled what by all accounts was an exemplary record. During Jespersen's entire tenure with Harrah's, the company maintained a policy encouraging female beverage servers to wear makeup. The parties agree, however, that the policy was not enforced until 2000. In February 2000, Harrah's implemented a "Beverage Department Image Transformation" program at twenty Harrah's locations, including its casino in Reno. Part of the program consisted of new grooming and appearance standards, called the "Personal Best" program. The program contained certain appearance standards that applied equally to both sexes, including a standard uniform of black pants, white shirt, black vest, and black bow tie. Jespersen has never objected to any of these policies. The program also contained some sex-differentiated appearance requirements as to hair, nails, and makeup.

In April 2000, Harrah's amended that policy to require that women wear makeup. Jespersen's only objection here is to the makeup requirement. The amended policy provided in relevant part:

> All Beverage Service Personnel, in addition to being friendly, polite, courteous and responsive to our customer's needs, must possess the ability to physically perform the essential factors of the job as set forth in the standard job descriptions. They must be well groomed, appealing to the eye, be firm and body toned, and be comfortable with maintaining this look while wearing the specified uniform. Additional factors to be considered include, but are not limited to, hair styles, overall body contour, and degree of comfort the employee projects while wearing the uniform.

* * *

Beverage Bartenders and Barbacks will adhere to these additional guidelines:

- Overall Guidelines (applied equally to male/ female):
    - Appearance: Must maintain Personal Best image portrayed at time of hire.
    - Jewelry, if issued, must be worn. Otherwise, tasteful and simple jewelry is permitted; no large chokers, chains or bracelets.
    - No faddish hairstyles or unnatural colors are permitted.
- Males:
    - Hair must not extend below top of shirt collar. Ponytails are prohibited.
    - Hands and fingernails must be clean and nails neatly trimmed at all times. No colored polish is permitted.
    - Eye and facial makeup is not permitted.
    - Shoes will be solid black leather or leather type with rubber (non skid) soles.
- Females:
    - Hair must be teased, curled, or styled every day you work. Hair must be worn down at all times, no exceptions.
    - Stockings are to be of nude or natural color consistent with employee's skin tone. No runs.
    - Nail polish can be clear, white, pink or red color only. No exotic nail art or length.

- Shoes will be solid black leather or leather type with rubber (non skid) soles.
- *Make up (face powder, blush and mascara) must be worn and applied neatly in complimentary colors. Lip color must be worn at all times.* (emphasis added).

Jespersen did not wear makeup on or off the job, and in her deposition stated that wearing it would conflict with her self-image. It is not disputed that she found the makeup requirement offensive, and felt so uncomfortable wearing makeup that she found it interfered with her ability to perform as a bartender. Unwilling to wear the makeup, and not qualifying for any open positions at the casino with a similar compensation scale, Jespersen left her employment with Harrah's.

After exhausting her administrative remedies with the Equal Employment Opportunity Commission and obtaining a right to sue notification, Jespersen filed this action in July 2001. In her complaint, Jespersen sought damages as well as declaratory and injunctive relief for discrimination and retaliation for opposition to discrimination, alleging that the "Personal Best" policy discriminated against women by "(1) subjecting them to terms and conditions of employment to which men are not similarly subjected, and (2) requiring that women conform to sex-based stereotypes as a term and condition of employment."

Harrah's moved for summary judgment, supporting its motion with documents giving the history and purpose of the appearance and grooming policies. Harrah's argued that the policy created similar standards for both men and women, and that where the standards differentiated on the basis of sex, as with the face and hair standards, any burdens imposed fell equally on both male and female bartenders.

In her deposition testimony, attached as a response to the motion for summary judgment, Jespersen described the personal indignity she felt as a result of attempting to comply with the makeup policy. Jespersen testified that when she wore the makeup she "felt very degraded and very demeaned." In addition, Jespersen testified that "it prohibited [her] from doing [her] job" because "[i]t affected [her] self-dignity . . . [and] took away [her] credibility as an individual and as a person." Jespersen made no cross-motion for summary judgment, taking the position that the case should go to the jury. Her response to Harrah's motion for summary judgment relied solely on her own deposition testimony regarding her subjective reaction to the makeup policy, and on favorable customer feedback and employer evaluation forms regarding her work.

The record therefore does not contain any affidavit or other evidence to establish that complying with the "Personal Best" standards caused burdens to fall unequally on men or women, and there is no evidence to suggest Harrah's motivation was to stereotype the women bartenders.

Jespersen relied solely on evidence that she had been a good bartender, and that she had personal objections to complying with the policy, in order to support her argument that Harrah's "'sells' and exploits its women employees." Jespersen contended that as a matter of law she had made a prima facie showing of gender discrimination, sufficient to survive summary judgment on both of her claims.

The district court granted Harrah's motion for summary judgment on all of Jespersen's claims. In this appeal, Jespersen maintains that the record before the district court was sufficient to create triable issues of material fact as to her unlawful discrimination claims of unequal burdens and sex stereotyping. We deal with each in turn.

UNEQUAL BURDENS

In order to assert a valid Title VII claim for sex discrimination, a plaintiff must make out a prima facie case establishing that the challenged employment action was either intentionally discriminatory or that it had a discriminatory effect on the basis of gender. *McDonnell Douglas Corp. v. Green,* 411 U.S. 792, 802, 93 S.Ct. 1817, 36 L.Ed.2d 668 (1973). Once a plaintiff establishes such a prima facie case, "[t]he burden then must shift to the employer to articulate some legitimate, nondiscriminatory reason for the employee's rejection." *McDonnell,* 411 U.S. at 802.

In this case, Jespersen argues that the makeup requirement itself establishes a prima facie case of discriminatory intent and must be justified by Harrah's as a bona fide occupational qualification. Our settled law in this circuit, however, does not support Jespersen's position that a sex-based difference in appearance standards alone, without any further showing of disparate effects, creates a prima facie case.

In *Gerdom v. Cont'l Airlines, Inc.,* 692 F.2d 602 (9th Cir.1982), we considered the Continental Airlines policy that imposed strict weight restrictions on female flight attendants, and held it constituted a violation of Title VII. We did so because the airline imposed no weight restriction whatsoever on a class of male employees who performed the same or similar functions as the flight attendants. Indeed, the policy was touted by the airline as intended to "create the public image of an airline which offered passengers service by thin, attractive women, whom executives referred to as Continental's 'girls.'" *Id.* at 604. In fact, Continental specifically argued that its policy was justified by its "desire to compete [with other airlines] by featuring attractive female cabin attendants[,]" a justification which this court recognized as "discriminatory on its face." *Id.* at 609. The weight restriction was part of an overall program to create a sexual image for the airline.

In contrast, this case involves an appearance policy that applied to both male and female bartenders, and was aimed at creating a professional and very similar look for all of them. All bartenders wore the same uniform. The policy only differentiated as to grooming standards. * * *

... [H]ere we deal with requirements that, on their face, are not more onerous for one gender than the other. Rather, Harrah's "Personal Best" policy contains sex-differentiated requirements regarding each employee's hair, hands, and face. While those individual requirements differ according to gender, none on its face places a greater burden on one gender than the other. Grooming standards that appropriately differentiate between the genders are not facially discriminatory.

We have long recognized that companies may differentiate between men and women in appearance and grooming policies, and so have other circuits. The material issue under our settled law is not whether the policies are different, but whether the policy imposed on the plaintiff creates an "unequal burden" for the plaintiff's gender ... Under established equal burdens analysis, when an employer's grooming and appearance policy does not unreasonably burden one gender more than the other, that policy will not violate Title VII.

Jespersen asks us to take judicial notice of the fact that it costs more money and takes more time for a woman to comply with the makeup requirement than it takes for a man to comply with the requirement that he keep his hair short, but these are not matters appropriate for judicial notice. Judicial notice is reserved for matters "generally known within the territorial jurisdiction of the trial court" or "capable of accurate and ready determination by resort to sources whose accuracy cannot reasonably be questioned." Fed.R.Evid. 201. The time and cost of makeup and haircuts is in neither category. The facts that Jespersen would have this court judicially notice are not subject to the requisite "high degree of indisputability" generally required for such judicial notice. Fed.R.Evid. 201 advisory committee's note. * * *

SEX STEREOTYPING

... The stereotyping in *Price Waterhouse* interfered with Hopkins' ability to perform her work; the advice that she should take "a course at charm school" was intended to discourage her use of the forceful and aggressive techniques that made her successful in the first place. Impermissible sex stereotyping was clear because the very traits that she was asked to hide were the same traits considered praiseworthy in men.

Harrah's "Personal Best" policy is very different. The policy does not single out Jespersen. It applies to all of the bartenders, male and female. It requires all of the bartenders to wear exactly the same uniforms while interacting with the public in the context of the entertainment industry. It is for the most part unisex, from the black tie to the non-skid shoes. There is no evidence in this record to indicate that the policy was adopted to make women bartenders conform to a commonly-accepted stereotypical image of what women should wear. The record contains nothing to suggest the grooming standards would objectively inhibit a woman's ability to do the job. The only evidence in the record to support the stereotyping claim is Jespersen's own subjective reaction to the makeup requirement. * * *

We respect Jespersen's resolve to be true to herself and to the image that she wishes to project to the world. We cannot agree, however, that her objection to the makeup requirement, without more, can give rise to a claim of sex stereotyping under Title VII. If we were to do so, we would come perilously close to holding that every grooming, apparel, or appearance requirement that an individual finds personally offensive, or in conflict with his or her own self-image, can create a triable issue of sex discrimination.

This is not a case where the dress or appearance requirement is intended to be sexually provocative, and tending to stereotype women as sex objects . . . The "Personal Best" policy does not, on its face, indicate any discriminatory or sexually stereotypical intent on the part of Harrah's. * * *

Nor is there evidence in this record that Harrah's treated Jespersen any differently than it treated any other bartender, male or female, who did not comply with the written grooming standards applicable to all bartenders. Jespersen's claim here materially differs from Hopkins' claim in *Price Waterhouse* because Harrah's grooming standards do not require Jespersen to conform to a stereotypical image that would objectively impede her ability to perform her job requirements as a bartender. * * * AFFIRMED.

PREGERSON, CIRCUIT JUDGE, with whom JUDGES KOZINSKI, GRABER, and W. FLETCHER join, dissenting:

* * * The majority contends that it is bound to reject Jespersen's sex stereotyping claim because she presented too little evidence—only her "own subjective reaction to the makeup requirement." I disagree. Jespersen's evidence showed that Harrah's fired her because she did not comply with a grooming policy that imposed a facial uniform (full makeup) on only female bartenders. Harrah's stringent "Personal Best" policy required female beverage servers to wear foundation, blush, mascara, and lip color, and to ensure that lip color was on at all times. Jespersen and her female colleagues were required to meet with professional image consultants who in turn created a facial template for each woman. Jespersen was required not simply to wear makeup; in addition, the consultants dictated where and how the makeup had to be applied.

Quite simply, her termination for failing to comply with a grooming policy that imposed a facial uniform on only female bartenders is discrimination "because of" sex. Such discrimination is clearly and unambiguously impermissible under Title VII, which requires that "gender must be *irrelevant* to employment decisions." *Price Waterhouse v. Hopkins,* 490 U.S. 228, 240, 109 S.Ct. 1775, 104 L.Ed.2d 268 (1989) (plurality opinion) (emphasis added).[2]

Notwithstanding Jespersen's failure to present additional evidence, little is required to make out a sex-stereotyping—as distinct from an undue burden—claim in this situation . . . *Price Waterhouse* recognizes that gender discrimination may manifest itself in stereotypical notions as to how women should dress and present themselves, not only as to how they should behave. * * *

. . . The fact that Harrah's required female bartenders to conform to a sex stereotype by wearing full makeup while working is not in dispute, and the policy is described at length in the majority opinion. This policy did not, as the majority suggests, impose a "grooming, apparel, or appearance requirement that an individual finds personally offensive," but rather one that treated Jespersen differently from male bartenders "because of" her sex. I believe that the fact that Harrah's designed and promoted a policy that required women to conform to a sex stereotype by wearing full makeup is sufficient "direct evidence" of discrimination.

The majority contends that Harrah's "Personal Best" appearance policy is very different from the policy at issue in *Price Waterhouse* in that it applies to both men and women. I disagree. As the majority concedes, "Harrah's 'Personal Best' policy contains sex-differentiated requirements regarding each employee's hair, hands, and face." The fact that a policy contains sex-differentiated requirements that affect people of both genders cannot excuse a particular requirement from scrutiny. By refusing to consider the makeup requirement separately, and instead stressing that the policy contained some gender-neutral requirements, such as color of clothing, as well as a variety of gender-differentiated requirements for "hair, hands, and face," the majority's approach would permit otherwise impermissible gender stereotypes to be neutralized by the presence of a stereotype or burden that affects people of the opposite gender, or by some separate non-discriminatory requirement that applies to both men and women . . .

---

[2]   Title VII identifies only one circumstance in which employers may take gender into account in making an employment decision-namely, "when gender is a 'bona fide occupational qualification [(BFOQ)] reasonably necessary to the normal operation of th[e] particular business or enterprise.'" *Price Waterhouse,* 490 U.S. at 242 (quoting 42 U.S.C. § 2000e–2(e)). Harrah's has not attempted to defend the "Personal Best" makeup requirement as a BFOQ. In fact, there is little doubt that the "Personal Best" policy is not a business necessity, as Harrah's quietly disposed of this policy after Jespersen filed this suit . . .

Because I believe that we should be careful not to insulate appearance requirements by viewing them in broad categories, such as "hair, hands, and face," I would consider the makeup requirement on its own terms. Viewed in isolation—or, at the very least, as part of a narrower category of requirements affecting employees' faces—the makeup or facial uniform requirement becomes closely analogous to the uniform policy held to constitute impermissible sex stereotyping in *Carroll v. Talman Federal Savings & Loan Ass'n of Chicago,* 604 F.2d 1028, 1029 (7th Cir.1979). In *Carroll,* the defendant bank required women to wear employer-issued uniforms, but permitted men to wear business attire of their own choosing. The Seventh Circuit found this rule discriminatory because it suggested to the public that the uniformed women held a "lesser professional status" and that women could not be trusted to choose appropriate business attire.

Just as the bank in *Carroll* deemed female employees incapable of achieving a professional appearance without assigned uniforms, Harrah's regarded women as unable to achieve a neat, attractive, and professional appearance without the facial uniform designed by a consultant and required by Harrah's. The inescapable message is that women's undoctored faces compare unfavorably to men's, not because of a physical difference between men's and women's faces, but because of a cultural assumption—and gender-based stereotype—that women's faces are incomplete, unattractive, or unprofessional without full makeup. We need not denounce all makeup as inherently offensive, just as there was no need to denounce all uniforms as inherently offensive in *Carroll,* to conclude that *requiring* female bartenders to wear full makeup is an impermissible sex stereotype and is evidence of discrimination because of sex. * * *

KOZINSKI, CIRCUIT JUDGE, with whom JUDGES GRABER and W. FLETCHER join, dissenting:

I agree with Judge Pregerson and join his dissent-subject to one caveat: I believe that Jespersen also presented a triable issue of fact on the question of disparate burden . . . I find it perfectly clear that Harrah's overall grooming policy is substantially more burdensome for women than for men. Every requirement that forces men to spend time or money on their appearance has a corresponding requirement that is as, or more, burdensome for women: short hair v. "teased, curled, or styled" hair; clean trimmed nails v. nail length and color requirements; black leather shoes v. black leather shoes. The requirement that women spend time and money applying full facial makeup has no corresponding requirement for men, making the "overall policy" more burdensome for the former than for the latter. The only question is how much.

It is true that Jespersen failed to present evidence about what it costs to buy makeup and how long it takes to apply it. But is there any doubt that putting on makeup costs money and takes time? Harrah's policy requires women to apply face powder, blush, mascara and lipstick. You don't need an expert witness to figure out that such items don't grow on trees.

Nor is there any rational doubt that application of makeup is an intricate and painstaking process that requires considerable time and care. Even those of us who don't wear makeup know how long it can take from the hundreds of hours we've spent over the years frantically tapping our toes and pointing to our wrists. It's hard to imagine that a woman could "put on her face," as they say, in the time it would take a man to shave—certainly not if she were to do the careful and thorough job Harrah's expects. Makeup, moreover, must be applied and removed every day; the policy burdens men with no such daily ritual. While a man could jog to the casino, slip into his uniform, and get right to work, a woman must travel to work so as to avoid smearing her makeup, or arrive early to put on her makeup there.

It might have been tidier if Jespersen had introduced evidence as to the time and cost associated with complying with the makeup requirement, but I can understand her failure to do so, as these hardly seem like questions reasonably subject to dispute. We could—and should—take judicial notice of these incontrovertible facts.

Alternatively, Jespersen did introduce evidence that she finds it burdensome to *wear* makeup because doing so is inconsistent with her self-image and interferes with her job performance. My colleagues dismiss this evidence, apparently on the ground that wearing makeup does not, as a matter of law, constitute a substantial burden. This presupposes that Jespersen is unreasonable or idiosyncratic in her discomfort. Why so? Whether to wear cosmetics—literally, the face one presents to the world— is an intensely personal choice. Makeup, moreover, touches delicate parts of the anatomy—the lips, the eyes, the cheeks—and can cause serious discomfort, sometimes even allergic reactions, for someone unaccustomed to wearing it. If you are used to wearing makeup—as most American women are—this may seem like no big deal. But those of us not used to wearing makeup would find a requirement that we do so highly intrusive. Imagine, for example, a rule that all judges wear face powder, blush, mascara and lipstick while on the bench. Like Jespersen, I would find such a regime burdensome and demeaning; it would interfere with my job performance. I suspect many of my colleagues would feel the same way.

Everyone accepts this as a reasonable reaction from a man, but why should it be different for a woman? It is not because of anatomical differences, such as a requirement that women wear bathing suits that cover their breasts. Women's faces, just like those of men, can be perfectly presentable without makeup; it is a cultural artifact that most women raised in the United States learn to put on—and presumably enjoy wearing—cosmetics. But cultural norms change; not so long ago a man wearing an earring was a gypsy, a pirate or an oddity. Today, a man wearing body piercing jewelry is hardly noticed. So, too, a large (and perhaps growing) number of women choose to present themselves to the world without makeup. I see no justification for forcing them to conform to Harrah's quaint notion of what a "real woman" looks like.

NOTES

1.   As explored below in Subsections 2.A and 3, many of the gender stereotyping claims that have followed *Price Waterhouse* have been brought by LGBT employees. Such claims, of course, have also been raised in cases where neither issues of sexual orientation nor gender identity were present. In *Back v. Hastings on Hudson Union Free School District*, 365 F.3d 107 (2d Cir. 2004), for example, a female teacher who alleged she was denied tenure because the defendant did not believe she could be both a good worker and a good mother at the same time was allowed by the court to proceed with her gender-stereotyping lawsuit.

2.   The *Jespersen* court has not been alone in upholding dress and grooming policies that are different for men and women. *See e.g., Harper v. Blockbuster Entm't Corp.*, 139 F.3d 1385 (11th Cir. 1998) (upholding employer's grooming policy, which prohibited men, but not women, from having long hair); *Tavora v. New York Mercantile Exch.*, 101 F.3d 907 (2d Cir. 1996) (same). *But see, e.g., Frank v. United Airlines, Inc.*, 216 F.3d 845 (9th Cir. 2000) (holding that airline's weight policy for flight attendants that based women's weight maximums on medium frame category, and men's maximums on large frame category, was discriminatory).

2.   Sexual Orientation

In an important early case, the U.S. Court of Appeals for the Ninth Circuit held in 1979 that discrimination on the basis of sexual orientation is not "sex" discrimination within the meaning of Title VII.[17] In doing so, it quoted from an earlier ruling rejecting the view that Title VII protected transgender individuals from discrimination:

> The cases interpreting Title VII sex discrimination provisions agree that they were intended to place women on an equal footing with men. . . . Giving the statute its plain meaning, this court concludes that Congress had only the traditional notions of "sex" in mind. Later legislative activity makes this narrow definition even more evident. Several bills have been introduced to amend the Civil Rights Act to prohibit discrimination against

---

[17]   *DeSantis v. Pacific Telephone & Telegraph*, 608 F.2d 327 (9th Cir. 1979).

"sexual preference." None have [sic] been enacted into law. . . . Congress has not shown any intent other than to restrict the term "sex" to its traditional meaning. Therefore, this court will not expand Title VII's application in the absence of Congressional mandate.[18]

Many other courts have since agreed.[19] But there has been considerable less agreement among courts, as we will explore in this Subsection, on the extent to which the sexual orientation of plaintiffs impacts their ability to make out gender stereotyping and/or sexual harassment claims under Title VII.

a. Gender Stereotyping

DAWSON V. BUMBLE & BUMBLE

United States Court of Appeals, Second Circuit, 2005
398 F.3d 211

POOLER, CIRCUIT JUDGE:

This is an employment discrimination case. Plaintiff-Appellant Dawn Dawson, a self-described "lesbian female, who does not conform to gender norms in that she does not meet stereotyped expectations of femininity and may be perceived as more masculine than a stereotypical woman," claims that she suffered discrimination on the basis of sex, sex stereotyping, and/or sexual orientation in violation of federal, state, and municipal law. *See* Title VII of the Civil Rights Act of 1964 ("Title VII"), 42 U.S.C. § 2000e *et seq.;* New York State Human Rights Law, N.Y. Exec. Law § 290 *et seq.;* New York City Human Rights Law, N.Y.C. Admin. Code, Title 8. Dawson's former employer, Defendant-Appellee Bumble & Bumble, describes itself as "a prestigious, high-end hair salon in Manhattan, known for its innovative hair cutting techniques."

Dawson was hired by Bumble & Bumble in early 1999 as a "hair assistant." Dawson describes the duties of this position as including "assisting [hair] stylists in all aspects of their jobs, keeping their work areas in the salon clean, escorting clients to different areas of the salon, shampooing clients' hair, and blow-drying clients' hair."

---

[18] *Id.* at 329 (quoting *Holloway v. Arthur Andersen & Co.,* 566 F.2d 659, 662–63 (9th Cir. 1977)).

[19] *See, e.g., Schroeder v. Hamilton Sch. Dist.,* 282 F.3d 946, 951 (7th Cir. 2002); *Bibby v. Philadelphia Coca–Cola Bottling Co.,* 260 F.3d 257, 265 (3d Cir. 2001); *Higgins v. New Balance Athletic Shoe, Inc.,* 194 F.3d 252, 259 (1st Cir. 1999); *Hopkins v. Baltimore Gas & Elec. Co.,* 77 F.3d 745, 751–52 & n. 3 (4th Cir. 1996); *Simonton v. Runyon,* 232 F.3d 33, 35–36 (2d Cir. 2000); *Williamson v. A.G. Edwards & Sons,* 876 F.2d 69, 70 (8th Cir. 1989). *See also Medina v. Income Support Div.,* 413 F.3d 1131, 1135 (10th Cir. 2005) (concluding that plaintiff, in effect, "alleg[ed] that she was discriminated against because she is a heterosexual" and holding that the "protections [of the statute] do not extend . . . to a person's sexuality.").

In addition to her duties as a hair assistant, Dawson was simultaneously enrolled in Bumble & Bumble's training program for hair stylists . . . Dawson alleges in her complaint that she "was confident that she would be able to graduate from the hair assistant training program to a stylist in an expedited fashion." We do not see, however, that Dawson disputes Bumble & Bumble's contention that "[o]nly about 10–15% of the total number of assistants at the Salon at any given time typically complete the educational program" and that it generally takes these successful candidates at least two and sometimes three years to complete the program.

The district court observed that the Bumble & Bumble salon is an unconventional workplace, a "heterogenous environment that strives for the avant garde and extols the unconventional." *Dawson v. Bumble & Bumble,* 246 F.Supp.2d 301, 311 (S.D.N.Y.2003). The district court also found that the salon's employees "embody many lifestyles and sexual preferences and reflect varying physical appearances, overall looks, and different manners of hair [,] dress and clothing." *Id.* at 310. Bumble & Bumble itself contends that "[i]f there is a 'norm' for Bumble employees, it is the norm of non-conformance." Thus, Bumble & Bumble asserts that the salon regularly employs "sexually 'non-stereotypical' individuals, including a female-to-male transsexual, [an] openly bisexual Education Coordinator, numerous other openly gay employees, and both male and female gay employees, including . . . lesbian employees with very androgynous looks." The district court found it to be particularly significant that Connie Voines, the manager of the salon and the individual who ultimately decided to terminate Dawson, is "a pre-surgery male-to-female transsexual who . . . at the time of the events in question, was transitioning from appearing male to appearing female." *Dawson,* 246 F.Supp.2d at 309.

Dawson does not seriously contest the depiction of the Bumble & Bumble salon as an environment in which conformance to gender norms was something less than a prerequisite for continued employment. When asked at her deposition if the salon employed "nonconformists" other than herself, Dawson replied: "It's like, you know, I don't think hairdressers are conformists anyway, so I would say the whole lot of them." Further, Dawson testified that she was not at all reticent about her lesbianism while working at the salon, but rather "discussed my life like anybody else would discuss their life and you know and I wasn't hidden about who I was." Dawson also stated that she was a willing participant in the sexually-charged banter that took place among the salon's employees, and that she would sometimes refer to herself as a "dyke." More generally, she stated that "lesbian jokes were brought up" and "you know, I like myself, I'm happy, so if this is light and funny, I'm with that."

The issue on which the parties disagree sharply is the quality of Dawson's performance as a hair assistant and as a participant in Bumble & Bumble's training program. Dawson alleges in her complaint that "her work was consistently praised by Connie Voines, . . . by other stylists, and clients" and that "several individuals who evaluated her work progress in the training program gave [her] positive feedback."

Dawson was terminated on July 15, 2000. According to Bumble & Bumble, Dawson's firing was the result of poor performance on the job and in the training program:

> Dawson's performance at the Salon was erratic: sometimes she performed well and with an enthusiastic attitude; other times, she did not. Over time, her performance on the Salon floor and in the educational program declined until it was unacceptable. For example, Dawson's performance in the basic cutting class was inadequate to advance to basic razor.

> Dawson also demonstrated significant performance deficiencies on the Salon floor. Several clients complained that she had been rude or abrupt with them or rough with their hair—more than with any other assistant. Similarly, several stylists complained that she was hostile or disrespectful. * * *

Appellee's Br. at 4–6 (internal citations omitted).

Dawson contends, however, that her failure to advance in Bumble & Bumble's training program and her termination are the result of discriminatory animus. As to the training program, Dawson alleges that it was repeatedly made clear to her that females rarely attained the position of hair stylist. Specifically, Dawson asserts that on one occasion when she asked Voines to place her in an editorial styling class, Voines stated, "How many women do you see doing editorial . . . They only want men with accents." Dawson also points to an affidavit from Amy Strober, another hair assistant, in which Strober states that when she asked to be assigned to a styling class, Voines said, "Do you know how many famous female editorial stylists there are? There is one."

With respect to her work on the salon floor as a hair assistant, Dawson alleges that she was subjected to a hostile work environment in that "[s]he was constantly harassed about her appearance, that she did not conform to the image of women, and that she should act in a manner less like a man and more like a woman." Dawson alleges that a range of invective was directed at her by fellow Bumble & Bumble employees: (1) two stylists, Howard McLaren and Raymond McLaren, repeatedly referred to her "in front of colleagues and clients, by the name 'Donald' "; (2) a stylist named Ralph Formisano once stated that she was " 'wearing her sexuality like a costume,' implying that she did not conform to gender norms and appeared to be a lesbian"; and (3) a fellow hair assistant named Deniz Uzunoglu once "loudly proclaimed to [her], in extremely vulgar and threatening terms, that he thought she 'needed to have sex with a man.' "

In addition, Dawson asserts that the McLarens stated to educators in Bumble's education department that they wanted to fire her because of her " 'dyke' attitude." Finally, Dawson alleges that her termination took place as follows:

> On or about July 15, 2000, Voines informed Dawson that she was terminated because she "seemed unhappy" and because of the way she dressed and wore her hair. When Dawson asked for clarification, Voines stated that she could not send her to New Jersey or any place outside New York City. She added, "People won't understand you . . . you'll frighten them."

The United States District Court for the Southern District of New York granted Bumble & Bumble's motion for summary judgment with respect to all of Dawson's Title VII, NYSHRL, and NYCHRL claims. * * *

As already noted, Dawson defines herself in her complaint as "a lesbian female, who does not conform to gender norms in that she does not meet stereotyped expectations of femininity and may be perceived as more masculine than a stereotypical woman." In her brief on this appeal, Dawson further explains that she "is in three distinct, but somewhat interrelated protected classes . . . because (1) she is a woman [,] . . . (2) she does not conform to gender norms in that she appears more like a man than a woman, . . . [and] she is (3) gay." The district court, however, observed that "because the borders [between these classes] are so imprecise, it is not eviden[t] exactly what conduct by Bumble Dawson claims as the gravamen of the claims she asserts on sex or gender grounds, as opposed to what actions she bases on sexual orientation or sexual stereotyping." *Dawson,* 246 F.Supp.2d at 311. The district court further opined that

> Dawson's claims of sexual discrimination, as she articulates them in the Complaint and elaborates in her deposition, [possess a] somewhat protean quality, [such that it is] hard to grasp or pinpoint precisely what conduct she accuses of offending whatever behavioral norms she asserts govern the circumstances. At various times in her pleadings and testimony, she asserts that she was disparately treated because of the way she looked, because she was a woman, because she was not a man, because she was a lesbian, because she was a lesbian who did not conform to gender norms.

We find ourselves in full agreement with these assertions. Both in her complaint and in her briefing on this appeal, Dawson has significantly conflated her claims. As a result, it is often difficult to discern when Dawson is alleging that the various adverse employment actions allegedly visited upon her by Bumble & Bumble were motivated by animus toward her gender, her appearance, her sexual orientation, or some combination of these. The following excerpt from her deposition testimony, in which Dawson states the reasons why she believed she had been terminated, is indicative of the problem:

> A. Because of the way I look . . . [M]y visual presence was not acceptable. And the constant remarks about me being a lesbian . . . made it clear that they were none too happy with that.

> Q. . . . [I]s it fair to say that one of the things you're saying . . . is that you believe you were discriminated against because of your sexual orientation?

> A. Yes.

> Q. . . . Is it fair to state that another thing that you're complaining about in this action is that you were discriminated against because you're a lesbian who looks a certain way?

> A. Yes.

Such confusion as to the sources of the discriminatory animus allegedly visited upon Dawson complicates her claims under Title VII because "[t]he law is well-settled in this circuit and in all others to have reached the question that. . . . Title VII does not prohibit harassment or discrimination because of sexual orientation." *Simonton v. Runyon*, 232 F.3d 33, 35 (2d Cir.2000). Thus, to the extent that she is alleging discrimination based upon her lesbianism, Dawson cannot satisfy the first element of a prima facie case under Title VII because the statute does not recognize homosexuals as a protected class.

Realizing that discrimination based upon sexual orientation is not actionable under Title VII, Dawson avails herself of the "gender stereotyping" theory of Title VII liability according to which individuals who fail or refuse to comply with socially accepted gender roles are members of a protected class. * * *

When utilized by an avowedly homosexual plaintiff, however, gender stereotyping claims can easily present problems for an adjudicator. This is for the simple reason that "[s]tereotypical notions about how men and women should behave will often necessarily blur into ideas about heterosexuality and homosexuality." *Howell v. North Cent. Coll.,* 320 F.Supp.2d 717, 723 (N.D.Ill.2004). Like other courts, we have therefore recognized that a gender stereotyping claim should not be used to "bootstrap protection for sexual orientation into Title VII." *Simonton*, 232 F.3d at 38. * * *

Generally speaking, one can fail to conform to gender stereotypes in two ways: (1) through behavior or (2) through appearance. Dawson makes no assertion with respect to behavioral non-conformance. That is, unlike the plaintiff in *Price Waterhouse,* she was not told by anyone at Bumble & Bumble that her continued employment depended upon her acting and speaking in a more "feminine" manner. There is also no allegation that Dawson's work assignments were restricted in any way to those considered "appropriate" for a woman to perform.

Dawson's claim with respect to gender stereotyping thus rests upon the contention that her appearance was unacceptable in the eyes of Bumble & Bumble. Dawson states her position in this regard most comprehensively in an affidavit filed after she was deposed:

> My outward appearance does not conform to the traditional expectations of the way a woman would look. I do not conform to our society's gender norms because of the way I present myself, including my manner of dress, hair style, my lack of feminine jewelry, lack of feminine perfume, and lack of makeup. I also do not have a noticeable chest or wide hips, and my body type is more like a male than a female. In sum, my overall appearance is more like a male than a female. In fact, many people think that I look less like a female and more like a male.

Whatever the accuracy of this statement, the record in this case is simply devoid of any substantial evidence that Dawson was subjected to any adverse employment consequences as a result of her appearance. With respect to her "manner of dress," there is no evidence that the Bumble & Bumble salon even employed a formal dress code for its employees, let alone a dress code that reinforced gender stereotypes. On the contrary, Dawson has not contradicted the assertion of Connie Voines, the salon manager, to the effect that Dawson "generally wore leather pants and a jean jacket when working, none of which was objectionable from the Salon's point of view."

The only evidence presented by Dawson which tends to show that her style of dress was not acceptable comes in the form of alleged statements by co-workers. First, in her complaint Dawson alleges that she was "harassed by Ralph [Formisano], a stylist. He accused Dawson of 'wearing her sexuality like a costume,' implying that she did not conform to gender norms and appeared to be a lesbian." Only in her post-deposition affidavit does Dawson clearly state that this comment had anything to do with her "overall appearance" and was not simply concerned with her sexual orientation. Dawson's complaint also contains the allegation that "Howard and Raymond McLaren repeatedly referred to Dawson, in front of colleagues and clients, by the name 'Donald.'" Realizing that these comments also provide ambiguous support for a gender stereotyping claim, Dawson asserts in her brief on this appeal that she "believed the comments were related to her masculine appearance and/or her sexual orientation."

Bumble & Bumble *does* have a policy regarding hairstyles: employees must have their hair cut by Bumble & Bumble stylists as a means of advertising the salon's techniques. Dawson does not argue that this rule is discriminatory in itself, and any claim that it improperly enforces employees to conform to gender stereotypes is decisively belied by Connie Voines' uncontested assertion that for part of the time during which she was employed at the salon, Dawson was allowed to wear her hair "in a 'mohawk' style (in her case, extremely short in the back and on the sides, with a strip of longer hair down the center of her head)." Because this haircut was performed by a Bumble & Bumble stylist, the salon had no objection to it. Indeed, Voines states without contradiction that "many women [besides Dawson] who have worked at the Salon have had very short hair" and that one female employee had *all* of the hair on her head shaved down to only fuzz." * * *

In sum, in contrast to the plaintiff in *Price Waterhouse,* who proffered evidence that her promotion to partnership depended upon her changing her behavior to better conform to gender stereotypes, . . . Dawson has produced no substantial evidence from which we may plausibly infer that her alleged failure to conform her appearance to feminine stereotypes resulted in her suffering any adverse employment action at the hands of Bumble & Bumble. Thus, her Title VII claim based upon a gender stereotyping theory must fail. * * * AFFIRMED.

PROWEL V. WISE BUSINESS FORMS, INC.

United States Court of Appeals, Third Circuit, 2009
579 F.3d 285

HARDIMAN, CIRCUIT JUDGE.

Brian Prowel appeals the District Court's summary judgment in favor of his former employer, Wise Business Forms, Inc. Prowel sued under Title VII of the Civil Rights Act of 1964 and the Pennsylvania Human Relations Act, alleging that Wise harassed and retaliated against him because of sex . . . The principal issue on appeal is whether Prowel has marshaled sufficient facts for his claim of "gender stereotyping" discrimination to be submitted to a jury. * * *

Prowel began working for Wise in July 1991. A producer and distributor of business forms, Wise employed approximately 145 workers at its facility in Butler, Pennsylvania. From 1997 until his termination, Prowel operated a machine called a nale encoder, which encodes numbers and organizes business forms. On December 13, 2004, after 13 years with the company, Wise informed Prowel that it was laying him off for lack of work. * * *

Prowel identifies himself as an effeminate man and believes that his mannerisms caused him not to "fit in" with the other men at Wise. Prowel described the "genuine stereotypical male" at the plant as follows:

> [B]lue jeans, t-shirt, blue collar worker, very rough around the edges. Most of the guys there hunted. Most of the guys there fished. If they drank, they drank beer, they didn't drink gin and tonic. Just you know, all into football, sports, all that kind of stuff, everything I wasn't.

In stark contrast to the other men at Wise, Prowel testified that he had a high voice and did not curse; was very well-groomed; wore what others would consider dressy clothes; was neat; filed his nails instead of ripping them off with a utility knife; crossed his legs and had a tendency to shake his foot "the way a woman would sit"; walked and carried himself in an effeminate manner; drove a clean car; had a rainbow decal on the trunk of his car; talked about things like art, music, interior design, and decor; and pushed the buttons on the nale encoder with "pizzazz."

Some of Prowel's co-workers reacted negatively to his demeanor and appearance. During the last two years of his employment at Wise, a female co-worker frequently called Prowel "Princess." In a similar vein, co-workers made comments such as: "Did you see what Rosebud was wearing?"; "Did you see Rosebud sitting there with his legs crossed, filing his nails?"; and "Look at the way he walks."

Prowel also testified that he is homosexual. At some point prior to November 1997, Prowel was "outed" at work when a newspaper clipping of a "man-seeking-man" ad was left at his workstation with a note that read: "Why don't you give him a call, big boy." Prowel reported the incident to two management-level personnel and asked that something be done. The culprit was never identified, however.

After Prowel was outed, some of his co-workers began causing problems for him, subjecting him to verbal and written attacks during the last seven years of his tenure at Wise. In addition to the nicknames "Princess" and "Rosebud," a female co-worker called him "fag" and said: "Listen, faggot, I don't have to put up with this from you." Prowel reported this to his shift supervisor but received no response.

At some point during the last two years of Prowel's employment, a pink, light-up, feather tiara with a package of lubricant jelly was left on his nale encoder. The items were removed after Prowel complained to Henry Nolan, the shift supervisor at that time. On March 24, 2004, as Prowel entered the plant, he overheard a co-worker state: "I hate him.

They should shoot all the fags." Prowel reported this remark to Nolan, who said he would look into it. Prowel also overheard conversations between co-workers, one of whom was a supervisor, who disapproved of how he lived his life. Finally, messages began to appear on the wall of the men's bathroom, claiming Prowel had AIDS and engaged in sexual relations with male co-workers. After Prowel complained, the company repainted the restroom. * * *

On December 13, 2004, Prowel was summoned to meet with his supervisors, who informed him that he was terminated effective immediately for lack of work. * * *

In evaluating Wise's motion for summary judgment, the District Court properly focused on our decision in *Bibby v. Philadelphia Coca Cola Bottling Co.,* 260 F.3d 257 (3d Cir.2001), wherein we stated: "Title VII does not prohibit discrimination based on sexual orientation. Congress has repeatedly rejected legislation that would have extended Title VII to cover sexual orientation." *Id.* at 261 (citations omitted). This does not mean, however, that a homosexual individual is barred from bringing a *sex discrimination* claim under Title VII, which plainly prohibits discrimination "because of sex."

Both Prowel and Wise rely heavily upon *Bibby.* Wise claims this appeal is indistinguishable from *Bibby* and therefore we should affirm its summary judgment for the same reason we affirmed summary judgment in *Bibby.* Prowel counters that reversal is required here because gender stereotyping was not at issue in *Bibby.* As we shall explain, *Bibby* does not dictate the result in this appeal. Because it guides our analysis, however, we shall review it in some detail.

John Bibby, a homosexual man, was a long-time employee of the Philadelphia Coca Cola Bottling Company. The company terminated Bibby after he sought sick leave, but ultimately reinstated him. After Bibby's reinstatement, he alleged that he was assaulted and harmed by co-workers and supervisors when he was subjected to crude remarks and derogatory sexual graffiti in the bathrooms.

Bibby filed a complaint with the Philadelphia Commission on Human Relations (PCHR), alleging sexual orientation discrimination. After the PCHR issued a right-to-sue letter, Bibby sued in federal court alleging, *inter alia,* sexual harassment in violation of Title VII. The district court granted summary judgment for the company because Bibby was harassed not "because of sex," but rather because of his sexual orientation, which is not cognizable under Title VII.

On appeal, this Court affirmed, holding that Bibby presented insufficient evidence to support a claim of same-sex harassment under Title VII. Despite acknowledging that harassment based on sexual orientation has no place in a just society, we explained that Congress chose not to include sexual orientation harassment in Title VII. Nevertheless, we stated that employees may—consistent with the Supreme Court's decision in *Price Waterhouse*—raise a Title VII *gender stereotyping* claim, provided they can demonstrate that "the[ir] harasser was acting to punish [their] noncompliance with gender stereotypes." *Id.* at 264. Because Bibby did not claim gender stereotyping, however, he could not prevail on that theory. We also concluded, in dicta, that even had we construed Bibby's claim to involve gender stereotyping, he did not marshal sufficient evidence to withstand summary judgment on that claim.

In light of the foregoing discussion, we disagree with both parties' arguments that *Bibby* dictates the outcome of this case. *Bibby* does not carry the day for Wise because in that case, the plaintiff failed to raise a gender stereotyping claim as Prowel has done here. Contrary to Prowel's argument, however, *Bibby* does not require that we reverse the District Court's summary judgment merely because we stated that a gender stereotyping claim is cognizable under Title VII; such has been the case since the Supreme Court's decision in *Price Waterhouse*. Instead, we must consider whether the record, when viewed in the light most favorable to Prowel, contains sufficient facts from which a reasonable jury could conclude that he was harassed and/or retaliated against "because of sex." * * *

As this appeal demonstrates, the line between sexual orientation discrimination and discrimination "because of sex" can be difficult to draw. In granting summary judgment for Wise, the District Court found that Prowel's claim fell clearly on one side of the line, holding that Prowel's sex discrimination claim was an artfully-pleaded claim of sexual orientation discrimination. However, our analysis—viewing the facts and inferences in favor of Prowel—leads us to conclude that the record is ambiguous on this dispositive question. Accordingly, Prowel's gender stereotyping claim must be submitted to a jury.

Wise claims it laid off Prowel because the company decided to reduce the number of nale encoder operators from three to two. This claim is not without support in the record. After Prowel was laid off, no one was hired to operate the nale encoder during his shift. Moreover, market conditions caused Wise to lay off 44 employees at its Pennsylvania facility between 2001 and September 2006, and the company's workforce shrank from 212 in 2001 to 145 in 2008. General Manager Straub testified that in determining which nale encoder operator to lay off, he considered various factors, including customer service, productivity, cooperativeness, willingness to perform other tasks (the frequency with which employees complained about working on other machines), future advancement opportunities, and cost. According to Wise, Prowel was laid off because: comments on his daily production reports reflected an uncooperative and insubordinate attitude; he was the highest paid operator; he complained when asked to work on different machines; and he did not work to the best of his ability when operating the other machines.

Prowel asserts that these reasons were pretextual and he was terminated because of his complaints to management about harassment and his discussions with co-workers regarding a potential lawsuit against the company. In this respect, the record indicates that Prowel's work compared favorably to the other two nale encoder operators. Specifically, Prowel worked on other equipment fifty-four times during the last half of 2004 while a co-worker did so just once; Prowel also ran more jobs and impressions per hour than that same co-worker; and Prowel's attendance was significantly better than the third nale encoder operator. Finally, although Wise laid off forty-four workers between 2001 and 2006, it laid off no one in 2003, only Prowel in 2004, and just two in 2005. Although Prowel is unaware what role his sexual orientation played in his termination, he alleges that he was harassed and retaliated against not because of the quality of his work, but rather because he failed to conform to gender stereotypes.

The record demonstrates that Prowel has adduced evidence of harassment based on gender stereotypes. He acknowledged that he has a high voice and walks in an effeminate manner. In contrast with the typical male at Wise, Prowel testified that he: did not curse and was very well-groomed; filed his nails instead of ripping them off with a utility knife; crossed his legs and had a tendency to shake his foot "the way a woman would sit." Prowel also discussed things like art, music, interior design, and decor, and pushed the buttons on his nale encoder with "pizzazz." Prowel's effeminate traits did not go unnoticed by his co-workers, who commented: "Did you see what Rosebud was wearing?"; "Did you see Rosebud sitting there with his legs crossed, filing his nails?"; and "Look at the way he walks." Finally, a co-worker deposited a feathered, pink tiara at Prowel's workstation. When the aforementioned facts are considered in the light most favorable to Prowel, they constitute sufficient evidence of gender stereotyping harassment—namely, Prowel was harassed because he did not conform to Wise's vision of how a man should look, speak, and act-rather than harassment based solely on his sexual orientation.

To be sure, the District Court correctly noted that the record is replete with evidence of harassment motivated by Prowel's sexual orientation. Thus, it is possible that the harassment Prowel alleges was because of his sexual orientation, not his effeminacy. Nevertheless, this does not vitiate the possibility that Prowel was also harassed for his failure to conform to gender stereotypes. *See* 42 U.S.C. § 2000e–2(m) ("[A]n unlawful employment practice is established when the complaining party demonstrates that . . . sex . . . was a motivating factor for any employment practice, even though other factors also motivated the practice."). Because both scenarios are plausible, the case presents a question of fact for the jury and is not appropriate for summary judgment.

In support of the District Court's summary judgment, Wise argues persuasively that every case of sexual orientation discrimination cannot translate into a triable case of gender stereotyping discrimination, which would contradict Congress's decision not to make sexual orientation discrimination cognizable under Title VII. Nevertheless, Wise cannot persuasively argue that *because* Prowel is homosexual, he is precluded from bringing a gender stereotyping claim. There is no basis in the statutory or case law to support the notion that an effeminate *heterosexual* man can bring a gender stereotyping claim while an effeminate *homosexual* man may not. As long as the employee— regardless of his or her sexual orientation—marshals sufficient evidence such that a reasonable jury could conclude that harassment or discrimination occurred "because of sex," the case is not appropriate for summary judgment. For the reasons we have articulated, Prowel has adduced sufficient evidence to submit this claim to a jury.

NOTES

1.   Why the different outcomes in *Dawson* and *Prowel*? Were the plaintiff's facts in the latter case stronger than in the former? Did the nature of the workplace (a high-end hair salon vs. a printing plant) matter? Why did the *Dawson* court view the plaintiff's case as an improper effort to "bootstrap" a sexual orientation claim onto a gender stereotyping claim? Why was the *Prowel* court apparently not concerned about "bootstrapping"?

2.   Consider the following critique by Professor Zachary Kramer of judicial rulings (like *Dawson*) that have rejected, on "bootstrapping" grounds, Title VII sex discrimination claims brought by lesbian and gay plaintiffs:

> [T]here is a double standard at work in employment discrimination cases. For lesbian and gay employees, sexual orientation is a burden because courts are primed to reject otherwise actionable discrimination claims on the theory that such claims are an attempt to bootstrap protection for sexual orientation into Title VII. However, rather than being burdened by their sexual orientation in employment discrimination cases, heterosexual employees are not affected by theirs. Because heterosexuality is invisible in our culture, courts simply fail to recognize when an employee's discrimination claim implicates her heterosexuality. As a result, no court will ever conclude that a heterosexual employee is raising a sex discrimination claim as a means to bootstrap protection for sexual orientation into Title VII. Put simply, heterosexuals and homosexuals are not similarly situated under Title VII.

Zachary A. Kramer, *Heterosexuality and Title VII*, 103 NW. U. L. REV. 205, 207–08 (2009). Kramer elaborates on the invisibility of heterosexuality by explaining that "in our culture, heterosexuals are typically thought of as not having a sexual orientation. Instead, heterosexuality is merely the normative baseline against which all other sexual orientations are tested. As such, heterosexuality tends to be missing altogether from discussions about sex and sexuality." *Id*. at 209. He adds that "the invisibility of heterosexuality has seeped into employment discrimination jurisprudence, creating a doctrinal privilege for heterosexual employees in the sense that they do not risk losing their discrimination claims because of their sexual orientation." *Id*. at 230.

3.   Did Dawson lose in part because the employer seemed willing to hire and promote other LGBT individuals? Notice that Dawson claimed that she was discriminated against "because she was a lesbian who looks a certain way." Dawson's claim, therefore, might have been based on the idea that even an employer who is willing to promote gay men who are perceived to be effeminate, as well transgender employees who are gender nonconforming, might nonetheless be unwilling to promote lesbians who are perceived to be "too masculine." Is this claim analogous to one based on an employer's willingness to promote some racial minority groups and not others? An employer who refuses to promote African Americans while promoting Asians would clearly violate Title VII. Would not the same be true of an employer who refuses to promote "masculine" lesbians while promoting "feminine" gay men? Or is the problem that neither lesbians nor gay men, as such, are protected by the statute, while African Americans are protected?

b.   Sexual Harassment

ONCALE V. SUNDOWNER OFFSHORE SERVICES, INC.
Supreme Court of the United States, 1998
523 U.S. 75, 118 S.Ct. 998, 140 L.Ed.2d 201

JUSTICE SCALIA.

This case presents the question whether workplace harassment can violate Title VII's prohibition against "discriminat[ion] . . . because of . . . sex," 42 U.S.C. § 2000e–2(a)(1), when the harasser and the harassed employee are of the same sex.

The District Court having granted summary judgment for respondent, we must assume the facts to be as alleged by petitioner Joseph Oncale. The precise details are irrelevant to the legal point we must decide, and in the interest of both brevity and dignity we shall describe them only generally. In late October 1991, Oncale was working for respondent Sundowner Offshore Services on a Chevron U.S.A., Inc., oil platform in the Gulf of Mexico. He was employed as a roustabout on an eight-man crew which included respondents John Lyons, Danny Pippen, and Brandon Johnson. Lyons, the crane operator, and Pippen, the driller, had supervisory authority. On several occasions, Oncale was forcibly subjected to sex-related, humiliating actions against him by Lyons, Pippen and Johnson in the presence of the rest of the crew. Pippen and Lyons also physically assaulted Oncale in a sexual manner, and Lyons threatened him with rape.

Oncale's complaints to supervisory personnel produced no remedial action; in fact, the company's Safety Compliance Clerk, Valent Hohen, told Oncale that Lyons and Pippen "picked [on] him all the time too," and called him a name suggesting homosexuality. Oncale eventually quit— asking that his pink slip reflect that he "voluntarily left due to sexual harassment and verbal abuse." When asked at his deposition why he left Sundowner, Oncale stated "I felt that if I didn't leave my job, that I would be raped or forced to have sex."

Oncale filed a complaint against Sundowner in the United States District Court for the Eastern District of Louisiana, alleging that he was discriminated against in his employment because of his sex. Relying on the Fifth Circuit's decision in *Garcia v. Elf Atochem North America*, 28 F.3d 446, 451–452 (5th Cir. 1994), the district court held that "Mr. Oncale, a male, has no cause of action under Title VII for harassment by male co-workers." On appeal, a panel of the Fifth Circuit concluded that *Garcia* was binding Circuit precedent, and affirmed. 83 F.3d 118 (5th Cir. 1996). . . .

Title VII of the Civil Rights Act of 1964 provides, in relevant part, that "[i]t shall be an unlawful employment practice for an employer . . . to discriminate against any individual with respect to his compensation, terms, conditions, or privileges of employment, because of such individual's race, color, religion, sex, or national origin." 42 U.S.C. § 2000e–2(a)(1). We have held that this not only covers "terms" and "conditions" in the narrow contractual sense, but "evinces a congressional intent to strike at the entire spectrum of disparate treatment of men and women in employment." *Meritor Savings Bank, FSB v. Vinson*, 477 U.S. 57, 64, 106 S.Ct. 2399, 91 L.Ed.2d 49 (1986). "When the workplace is permeated with discriminatory intimidation, ridicule, and insult that is sufficiently severe or pervasive to alter the conditions of the victim's employment and create an abusive working environment, Title VII is violated." *Harris v. Forklift Systems, Inc.*, 510 U.S. 17, 21, 114 S.Ct. 367, 126 L.Ed.2d 295 (1993).

Title VII's prohibition of discrimination "because of . . . sex" protects men as well as women, *Newport News Shipbuilding & Dry Dock Co. v. EEOC*, 462 U.S. 669, 682, 103 S.Ct. 2622, 77 L.Ed.2d 89 (1983), and in the related context of racial discrimination in the workplace we have rejected any conclusive presumption that an employer will not discriminate against members of his own race. "Because of the many facets of human motivation, it would be unwise to presume as a matter of law that human beings of one definable group will not discriminate against other members of that group." *Castaneda v. Partida*, 430 U.S. 482, 499, 97 S.Ct. 1272, 51 L.Ed.2d 498 (1977). In *Johnson v. Transportation Agency, Santa Clara Cty.*, 480 U.S. 616, 107 S.Ct. 1442, 94 L.Ed.2d 615 (1987), a male employee claimed that his employer discriminated against him because of his sex when it preferred a female employee for promotion. Although we ultimately rejected the claim on other grounds, we did not consider it significant that the supervisor who made that decision was also a man. If our precedents leave any doubt on the question, we hold today that nothing in Title VII necessarily bars a claim of discrimination "because of . . . sex" merely because the plaintiff and the defendant (or the person charged with acting on behalf of the defendant) are of the same sex.

Courts have had little trouble with that principle in cases like *Johnson*, where an employee claims to have been passed over for a job or promotion. But when the issue arises in the context of a "hostile environment" sexual harassment claim, the state and federal courts have taken a bewildering variety of stances. Some, like the Fifth Circuit in this case, have held that same-sex sexual harassment claims are never cognizable under Title VII. Other decisions say that such claims are actionable only if the plaintiff can prove that the harasser is homosexual (and thus presumably motivated by sexual desire). *Compare McWilliams v. Fairfax County Board of Supervisors*, 72 F.3d 1191 (4th Cir. 1996), *with Wrightson v. Pizza Hut of America*, 99 F.3d 138 (4th Cir. 1996). Still others suggest that workplace harassment that is sexual in content is always actionable, regardless of the harasser's sex, sexual orientation, or motivations. *See Doe v. Belleville*, 119 F.3d 563 (7th Cir. 1997).

We see no justification in the statutory language or our precedents for a categorical rule excluding same-sex harassment claims from the coverage of Title VII. As some courts have observed, male-on-male sexual harassment in the workplace was assuredly not the principal evil Congress was concerned with when it enacted Title VII. But statutory prohibitions often go beyond the principal evil to cover reasonably comparable evils, and it is ultimately the provisions of our laws rather than the principal concerns of our legislators by which we are governed. Title VII prohibits "discriminat[ion] . . . because of . . . sex" in the "terms" or "conditions" of employment. Our holding that this includes sexual harassment must extend to sexual harassment of any kind that meets the statutory requirements.

Respondents and their amici contend that recognizing liability for same-sex harassment will transform Title VII into a general civility code for the American workplace. But that risk is no greater for same-sex than for opposite-sex harassment, and is adequately met by careful attention to the requirements of the statute. Title VII does not prohibit all verbal or physical harassment in the workplace; it is directed only at "discriminat[ion] ... because of ... sex." We have never held that workplace harassment, even harassment between men and women, is automatically discrimination because of sex merely because the words used have sexual content or connotations. "The critical issue, Title VII's text indicates, is whether members of one sex are exposed to disadvantageous terms or conditions of employment to which members of the other sex are not exposed." *Harris*, supra, at 25 (GINSBURG, J., concurring).

Courts and juries have found the inference of discrimination easy to draw in most male-female sexual harassment situations, because the challenged conduct typically involves explicit or implicit proposals of sexual activity; it is reasonable to assume those proposals would not have been made to someone of the same sex. The same chain of inference would be available to a plaintiff alleging same-sex harassment, if there were credible evidence that the harasser was homosexual. But harassing conduct need not be motivated by sexual desire to support an inference of discrimination on the basis of sex. A trier of fact might reasonably find such discrimination, for example, if a female victim is harassed in such sex-specific and derogatory terms by another woman as to make it clear that the harasser is motivated by general hostility to the presence of women in the workplace. A same-sex harassment plaintiff may also, of course, offer direct comparative evidence about how the alleged harasser treated members of both sexes in a mixed-sex workplace. Whatever evidentiary route the plaintiff chooses to follow, he or she must always prove that the conduct at issue was not merely tinged with offensive sexual connotations, but actually constituted "discrimina[tion] ... because of ... sex."

And there is another requirement that prevents Title VII from expanding into a general civility code: As we emphasized in *Meritor* and *Harris*, the statute does not reach genuine but innocuous differences in the ways men and women routinely interact with members of the same sex and of the opposite sex. The prohibition of harassment on the basis of sex requires neither asexuality nor androgyny in the workplace; it forbids only behavior so objectively offensive as to alter the "conditions" of the victim's employment. "Conduct that is not severe or pervasive enough to create an objectively hostile or abusive work environment—an environment that a reasonable person would find hostile or abusive—is beyond Title VII's purview." *Harris*, 510 U.S., at 21. We have always regarded that requirement as crucial, and as sufficient to ensure that courts and juries do not mistake ordinary socializing in the workplace—

such as male-on-male horseplay or intersexual flirtation—for discriminatory "conditions of employment."

We have emphasized, moreover, that the objective severity of harassment should be judged from the perspective of a reasonable person in the plaintiff's position, considering "all the circumstances." *Harris*, 510 U.S., at 23. In same-sex (as in all) harassment cases, that inquiry requires careful consideration of the social context in which particular behavior occurs and is experienced by its target. A professional football player's working environment is not severely or pervasively abusive, for example, if the coach smacks him on the buttocks as he heads onto the field—even if the same behavior would reasonably be experienced as abusive by the coach's secretary (male or female) back at the office. The real social impact of workplace behavior often depends on a constellation of surrounding circumstances, expectations, and relationships which are not fully captured by a simple recitation of the words used or the physical acts performed. Common sense, and an appropriate sensitivity to social context, will enable courts and juries to distinguish between simple teasing or roughhousing among members of the same sex, and conduct which a reasonable person in the plaintiff's position would find severely hostile or abusive.

Because we conclude that sex discrimination consisting of same-sex sexual harassment is actionable under Title VII, the judgment of the Court of Appeals for the Fifth Circuit is reversed, and the case is remanded for further proceedings consistent with this opinion.

Justice THOMAS, concurring.

I concur because the Court stresses that in every sexual harassment case, the plaintiff must plead and ultimately prove Title VII's statutory requirement that there be discrimination "because of . . . sex."

EQUAL EMPLOYMENT OPPORTUNITY COMMISSION v. BOH BROTHERS CONSTRUCTION COMPANY

United States Court of Appeals, Fifth Circuit, 2013 (en banc)
731 F.3d 444

JENNIFER WALKER ELROD, CIRCUIT JUDGE.

This Title VII case arises out of alleged sexual harassment by Chuck Wolfe, the superintendent of an all-male crew on a construction site operated by Boh Bros. Construction Company ("Boh Brothers"). During a three-day jury trial, the Equal Employment Opportunity Commission ("EEOC") presented evidence that Wolfe subjected Kerry Woods, an iron worker on Wolfe's crew, to almost-daily verbal and physical harassment because Woods did not conform to Wolfe's view of how a man should act. The jury found in favor of the EEOC on its hostile-environment claim, awarding compensatory and punitive damages. Boh Brothers appeals the district court's denial of its motion for judgment as a matter of law and motion for new trial. * * *

Woods is an iron worker and structural welder. Boh Brothers hired Woods on November 3, 2005, to work on crews repairing the Twin Spans bridges between New Orleans and Slidell after Hurricane Katrina. In January 2006, the company transferred Woods to a bridge-maintenance crew. Wolfe was the crew superintendent, with about five employees under his supervision.

The worksite was an undeniably vulgar place. Wolfe and the crew regularly used "very foul language" and "locker room talk." According to other crew members, Wolfe was a primary offender: he was "rough" and "mouthy" with his co-workers and often teased and "ribbed on" them.

By April 2006, Woods had become a specific and frequent target of Wolfe's abuse. Wolfe referred to Woods as "pu—y," "princess," and "fa—ot," often "two to three times a day." About two to three times per week—while Woods was bent over to perform a task—Wolfe approached him from behind and simulated anal intercourse with him. Woods felt "embarrassed and humiliated" by the name-calling and began to look over his shoulder before bending down. In addition, Wolfe exposed his penis to Woods about ten times while urinating, sometimes waving at Woods and smiling.

One time, Wolfe approached Woods while Woods was napping in his locked car during a break. According to Woods, Wolfe "looked like he was zipping his pants" and said, "[i]f your door wouldn't have been locked, my d-ck probably would have been in your mouth."

According to Wolfe, some of his teasing originated from Woods's use of Wet Ones instead of toilet paper, which Wolfe viewed as "kind of gay" and "feminine." In an interview with the EEOC, Wolfe explained:

> Mr. Woods sat at a table with a bunch of iron workers and told us that he brought, you know, feminine wipes—not feminine wipes—but Wet Ones or whatever to work with him because he didn't like it, didn't like to use toilet paper. It's [not] the kind of thing you'd want to say in front of a bunch [of] rough iron workers that they had there. They all picked on him about it. They said that's kind of feminine to bring these, that's for girls. To bring Wet Ones to work to wipe your ass, you damn sure don't sit in front of a bunch of iron workers and tell them about it. You keep that to yourself if in fact that's what you do.

Woods complained about Wolfe's treatment to his foreman, Tim Carpenter, "two or three times." Specifically, Woods said that he "didn't like how [Wolfe] spoke to" him and asked Carpenter to reprimand Wolfe for urinating on the bridge. According to Woods, he elected not to complain about all of Wolfe's behavior because he was afraid "to cause more of a conflict." * * *

. . . Woods [also met] with [Wayne] Duckworth, [the general superintendent for Boh Brothers' Heavy Highway Department]. . . . At the end of the conversation, Duckworth indicated that he would "look into" the alleged harassment. He sent Woods home without pay because, according to Duckworth, he feared "further problems" between Woods and Wolfe. Woods, believing that he had been fired, called Carpenter and asked him to intervene and "see if he could put [Woods] to work." Two days later, Carpenter called Woods and told him to report to work at the Almonaster yard.

Duckworth subsequently investigated Woods's complaint, although he did not document any aspect of his investigation. He spoke with both Wolfe and a crew foreman for about ten minutes each and determined that Wolfe's behavior, though unprofessional, did not constitute sexual harassment. Duckworth did not notify the company's general counsel about Woods's harassment allegations. . . .

Woods initially filed an EEOC charge questionnaire in November 2006, shortly after his removal from the Twin Spans maintenance crew, alleging he had been "fired" from that job and, three days later, hired to work at a different Boh Brothers location. In February 2007, Boh Brothers laid Woods off for lack of work. That March, Woods filed an EEOC charge of discrimination, alleging sexual harassment and, on the basis of his November 2006 removal from the maintenance crew, retaliation.

The EEOC brought this enforcement action on Woods's behalf in September 2009, claiming sexual harassment and retaliation under Title VII. Following a three-day trial, the jury returned a verdict in favor of Woods on the harassment claim and in favor of Boh Brothers on the retaliation claim. The jury awarded Woods $201,000 in compensatory damages and $250,000 in punitive damages. The district court reduced the compensatory damages award to $50,000 to comply with the $300,000 statutory damages cap. 42 U.S.C. § 1981a(b)(3)(D). Boh Brothers filed a renewed motion for judgment as a matter of law following entry of judgment and a motion for new trial, both of which the court denied. Boh Brothers timely appealed.

A panel of this court overturned the jury verdict. According to the panel, the evidence was insufficient as a matter of law to sustain the jury's finding that Wolfe discriminated against Woods "because of . . . sex" in violation of Title VII. *EEOC v. Boh Bros. Constr. Co., L.L.C.,* 689 F.3d 458, 459 (5th Cir.2012). The EEOC subsequently sought and obtained *en banc* review. * * *

[W]e must draw all reasonable inferences in the light most favorable to the verdict and cannot substitute other inferences that we might regard as more reasonable. * * *

[T]he most critical issues on appeal are whether the EEOC presented sufficient evidence that (1) Wolfe harassed Woods "because of . . . sex" as required by Title VII, and (2) Wolfe's harassment was severe or pervasive. We turn to the because-of-sex issue first.

At trial, the EEOC relied on gender-stereotyping evidence to prove that Woods suffered discrimination on the basis of sex. Specifically, the EEOC asserted that Wolfe harassed Woods because Woods was not a manly-enough man in Wolfe's eyes. On appeal, Boh Brothers argues that (1) the EEOC cannot, as a matter of law, rely on gender-stereotyping evidence to establish a same-sex harassment claim, and (2) even if it could, the evidence here was insufficient to sustain the jury verdict. As explained below, both of these arguments fail.

[Boh Brothers argued that the three evidentiary paths mentioned in *Oncale* "are the *exclusive* paths to success on a Title VII same-sex harassment claim." The court disagreed, noting that the *Oncale* Court "used 'for example' and '[w]hatever evidentiary route the plaintiff chooses to follow' in its discussion of those categories."] Boh Brothers further argues that, even if the EEOC's sex-stereotyping theory is cognizable in this context, the evidence is insufficient to support the jury's finding that Wolfe harassed Woods "because of . . . sex." We disagree.

In conducting this intent-based inquiry, we focus on the alleged harasser's subjective perception of the victim. Thus, even an employer's wrong or ill-informed assumptions about its employee may form the basis of a discrimination claim. *See, e.g., Black v. Pan Am. Labs., L.L.C.,* 646 F.3d 254, 260 (5th Cir.2011) (affirming a jury verdict in favor of a female sexual-harassment plaintiff who introduced evidence that decision-makers made sex-based comments—that "women [are] a detriment to the company," women "get hired on, get married, and/or get pregnant and they leave," and that the plaintiff did not need to worry about her sales quota because "it shouldn't matter to you, you're not the breadwinner anyway"—without requiring the plaintiff to show that her harasser's obviously sexist perceptions were true); *EEOC v. WC&M Enters., Inc.,* 496 F.3d 393, 401–02 (5th Cir.2007) (holding that a Muslim man's national-origin discrimination claim survived summary judgment even though his harassers did not know his country of origin). We do not require a plaintiff to prop up his employer's subjective discriminatory animus by proving that it was rooted in some objective truth; here, for example, that Woods was not, in fact, "manly." Rather, in considering the *motivation* behind a harasser's behavior, we look to evidence of the harasser's subjective view of the victim.

Applying these principles here, and drawing all reasonable inferences in the light most favorable to the verdict, there is enough evidence to support the jury's conclusion that Wolfe harassed Woods because of sex. Specifically, the EEOC offered evidence that Wolfe, the crew superintendent, thought that Woods was not a manly-enough man and taunted him tirelessly. Wolfe called Woods sex-based epithets like "fa—ot," "pu—y," and "princess," often "two to three times" per day. Wolfe himself admitted that these epithets were directed at Woods's masculinity:

Q. Now, when you said that Mr. Woods was kind of gay for using Wet Ones, you were saying that he was feminine; is that correct?

A. I didn't say he was gay. Said it . . . seemed kind of gay. . . .

Q. So you wouldn't say that he was gay, but you say his conduct was kind of gay?

A. Yes, sir[.]

Q. By saying that, you were saying he was feminine; correct?

A. Yes.

Q. You meant he was not being manly; is that correct?

A. Yes, sir.

Q. When you said that Mr. Woods'[s] conduct sounded like a homo, that again refers to Mr. Woods being feminine for using Wet Ones; is that correct?

A. Yes, sir. . . .

Q. And . . . when you were talking with the EEOC investigator about the wet wipes or the Wet Ones, you initially called them feminine wipes; correct?

A. Yes, sir. I believe I did.

Q. And that's because you believed that Wet Ones [are] something that girls should use but men should not?

A. Or babies, yeah, that's correct.

Q. So you had stereotypes of how a man should act, and Mr. Woods didn't fit in to those stereotypes because he used Wet Ones and then talked about it in front of a bunch of hairy iron workers; correct?

A. I don't agree with that, no, no. He was an iron worker just like the rest of [t]hem. He performed and did his job just like everyone else. We was just playing. . . . * * *

In addition to this name-calling, Wolfe mocked Woods with several other sexualized acts. For example, Woods testified that Wolfe would approach him from behind and "hump" him two to three times per week (which equates to more than 60 instances of simulated anal sex), that Wolfe exposed his genitals to Woods (sometimes while smiling and waving) about ten times, and that Wolfe suggested that he would put his penis in Woods's mouth.

Viewing the record as a whole, a jury could view Wolfe's behavior as an attempt to denigrate Woods because—at least in Wolfe's view—Woods fell outside of Wolfe's manly-man stereotype. Thus, we cannot say that no reasonable juror could have found that Woods suffered harassment because of his sex. Having reached this conclusion, we turn to the second critical question on appeal: whether the alleged abuse was sufficiently severe or pervasive to support Title VII liability.

Boh Brothers asserts that, even if Wolfe harassed Woods because of sex, the district court should have granted its Rule 50(b) motion because Wolfe's harassment was not severe or pervasive as a matter of law. * * * Woods specifically testified that he was a unique and constant target of Wolfe's abuse. For example, Woods testified on direct examination:

Q. In your experience, is it common on a construction site for this type of behavior you've described to take place?

A. No.

Q. Has any supervisor ever treated you like this at any other job you've held?

A. No.

Q. Has anybody ever treated you like this on any job you've held?

A. No.

Q. In your opinion, did Mr. Wolfe treat the other members of the maintenance crew the same way he treated you?

A. No.

Q. What was the difference?

A. He treated them—he treated them more like you're supposed to treat a grown man. He didn't pick—he didn't harass them like he harassed me all the time.

Q. Did you ever see Mr. Wolfe show somebody else his penis?

A. No.

Q. Did you ever hear Mr. Wolfe say anything about putting his penis in somebody's mouth to somebody else?

A. No.

Wolfe himself conceded that he called *only* Woods "queer"; he did not recall whether he called anyone else "fa—ot," a name he used regarding Woods on a consistent basis. This, alongside all of the evidence discussed above . . .—the repeated humping, the reference to oral sex, etc.—is sufficient for a reasonable juror to conclude that Wolfe's harassment was sufficiently severe or pervasive to alter the conditions of Woods's employment. Wolfe hurled raw sex-based epithets uniquely at Woods two-to-three times a day, almost every day, for months on end. We have upheld a jury verdict on analogous facts. Accordingly, we conclude that there was sufficient evidence for a reasonable juror to conclude that Wolfe's harassment of Woods was severe or pervasive.

E. GRADY JOLLY, CIRCUIT JUDGE, dissenting,

Let me first acknowledge that the facts and language in this case, which occurred in an all-male workforce on an ironworker construction site, are not for tender ears. The vulgarities can cast turmoil in a strong stomach, but that does not mean that the laws of the United States have been violated, and it does not require Title VII and the EEOC to serve as federal enforcer of clean talk in a single sex workforce.

The majority notes that the EEOC "may rely on evidence that Wolfe viewed Woods as insufficiently masculine to prove its Title VII claim." That may be true, but the fatal vacuum in the majority's reasoning is that the EEOC, in fact, produced no evidence that Wolfe believed Woods was not a "manly man." This lack of regard for the very foundational requirement that some *reason* for alleged sexual discrimination be presented allows this alleged same-sex stereotyping case to untether Title VII from its current mooring in sexual discrimination. Its application now veers from the realm of valid action against actual *sexual* harassment to a new world, in which Title VII prevents not only sexual harassment, but also myriad other undesirable conduct—regardless of whether that conduct, in fact, even resembles *sexual discrimination*. Accordingly, I respectfully dissent.

While the Supreme Court has made clear that same-sex sexual harassment claims are cognizable under Title VII, it has further acknowledged that proving such claims is more demanding and cumbersome than proving traditional opposite-sex sexual harassment claims. *See Oncale v. Sundowner Offshore Servs., Inc.*, 523 U.S. 75, 80–81, 118 S.Ct. 998, 140 L.Ed.2d 201 (1998). Thus, in *Oncale* the Court recognized that there must be some identifiable basis for inferring that an alleged harasser is intending to discriminate against a victim on the basis of his or her sex in same-sex discrimination cases. For instance, the Court observed that same-sex harassment claims could be viable when there is credible evidence a harasser is homosexual, or when it has been made clear "the harasser is motivated by general hostility to the presence of [members of his or her same sex] in the workplace," or when there is "direct comparative evidence about how the alleged harasser treated members of both sexes in a mixed-sex workplace." *Id.* at 80. Each of these examples is a mechanism for ascertaining an intent to discriminate based upon sex. It is compelling, in the first instance, that none of these factors are present in this case.

But regardless of whether there are other methods for making this determination, the EEOC proffered no basis for inferring discriminatory intent based upon Woods's sex—subjective or objective. Rather, it moves quickly from asserting that other evidentiary paths are available to a conclusion that, because Wolfe targeted certain words and acts at Woods, Wolfe's mal intent to sexually discriminate against Woods was proved. This line of reasoning completely abdicates the burden prescribed to plaintiffs in same-sex sexual discrimination cases by the Supreme Court in *Oncale*—which is not simply to assert the basis for the inference of harassment based upon sex, but to further prove the truth of that assertion. The *Oncale* Court specifically held "[t]he same chain of inference" present in male-female sexual harassment claims—i.e., the assumption that certain "proposals would not have been made to someone of the same sex"—is available in same-sex sexual harassment cases only if an additional step is taken to illuminate the basis of the inference. *Id.* at 80, 118 S.Ct. 998. Unlike opposite sex Title VII claims, therefore, in same-sex suits a plaintiff must elucidate and prove the premise of his assertion that the harassment is *because of* sex—it is not assumed automatically.

In this case, the EEOC's proffered premise is that Wolfe subjectively believed Woods was somehow not "manly." But the only evidence the EEOC provided supporting this premise related to Woods's use of Wet Ones; Wolfe himself testified that, aside from this, he emphatically did not believe or consider Woods feminine, but, instead, Woods was "an iron worker just like the rest of [t]hem." And Woods himself offered no other explanation as to why he believed Wolfe was sexually harassing him, as opposed to simply taunting him as Wolfe did every other iron worker on the all-male job site. Indeed, Woods never stated that he felt Wolfe called him names and behaved crudely with him because Wolfe believed Woods did not conform to gender norms. Thus, even the plaintiff did not contend his alleged harasser harassed him because he did not act "manly."

Moreover, there is simply no evidence, garnered from Woods, Wolfe, or any of the other men who testified, that Woods failed objectively to conform to traditional "male gender norms." The majority notes that "[w]e do not require a plaintiff to prop up his employer's subjective discriminatory animus by proving that it was rooted in some objective truth." In other cases this assertion may be true. When, however, the subjective discriminatory animus of the employer is itself in question, objective evidence may be necessary to demonstrate the presence or absence of such an intent. *See, e.g., Medina v. Income Support Div., New Mexico,* 413 F.3d 1131, 1135 (10th Cir.2005) (finding no sexual harassment based upon gender stereotyping when "there [wa]s no evidence ... that [the plaintiff] did not dress or behave like a stereotypical woman"). If a victim possesses no characteristics, exhibited or unexhibited, of nonconformance with gender stereotypes, then there would appear to be no basis for an alleged harasser to possess a subjective intent to discriminate against that victim because of nonconformance. And in cases such as this, where the alleged harasser does not consider the victim to be unmanly—and even the victim does not testify otherwise—and the alleged harasser further treats the victim with the same or similar disrespect with which he treats his other coworkers, we are left without anything tethering a claim of discrimination because of sex to the realities of the workplace. To reach any other conclusion is to say that when a supervisor persists in referring to an unquestionably manly man as a sissy, the laws of the United States have been broken, requiring the full force of the United States executive and judiciary to descend upon some small business and extract hundreds of thousands of dollars in fees and damages from its till. Such a result is simply at odds with Title VII, which is only violated in cases of discrimination based upon the victim's sex.

The majority ... relies on the harassment, in and of itself, as a substitute for actual evidence reflecting a subjective intent of Wolfe to engage in *sex* discrimination against Woods—completely ignoring the all male iron worker environment where it occurred. The majority thus engages in a distraction from the proper legal analysis by treating this case as if it were sexual harassment between male and female when the inference of sex discrimination may be presumed by words and conduct. In same-sex sexual harassment cases, particularly in an all-male workforce where rowdy language is commonplace, the reason for harassment (i.e. whether it is because of *sex*) must be distilled and proved by the plaintiff, a showing which the majority has utterly failed in making. The majority should call it for what it is: immature and gutter behavior between and among male coworkers. And then drop it.

It is especially inappropriate in this case to assume that Wolfe's use of words like "pu—y" and "fa—ot" necessarily connoted a desire to sexually discriminate, because all of the evidence indicates Wolfe used these and similar words towards the other men on site on a daily basis. In fact, the record is replete with testimony that Wolfe was vulgar with everyone on site, aiming derogatory terms with sexual innuendoes at each of them, exposing himself to them, and pretending to "hump" several men on site. And while Wolfe was unquestionably the crudest ironworker on the site, the evidence indicates all the men were generally more vulgar here than they would have been in a mixed-sex society, and that such sexually-charged words were bandied about regularly. The EEOC has identified no basis for presuming that Wolfe directed these words and actions at Woods, particularly, or at any of the other ironworkers for that matter, out of a subjective intent to sexually discriminate against him or them. This failure should end the discussion and the case. * * *

Finally, the majority opinion takes no account of the overall social context in which this case occurred. It is important to the case, and to any conclusion of sexual harassment, that these actions occurred in an all-male environment and on the construction site. This setting is customarily vulgar and crude. And the Supreme Court has clearly and repeatedly held that "an appropriate sensitivity to social context," and a recognition that the same actions taken on "the field" versus in the office are importantly different, are considerations preventing Title VII from mutating into an all-encompassing code of civility. *Oncale,* 523 U.S. at 81. In fact, the Court explicitly found that "[t]he real social impact of workplace behavior depends on a constellation of surrounding circumstances, expectations, and relationships which are not fully captured by a simple recitation of the words used or the physical acts performed." *Id.* at 81–82. Despite this clear admonition, the majority quotes extensively from the record and recounts various actions in which Wolfe engaged without ever taking account of the environment surrounding these events, or explaining how behavior occurring on and characteristic of the construction site can constitute *sexual* harassment. * * *

EDITH H. JONES, CIRCUIT JUDGE, dissenting,

Bad facts often inspire bad law. And sex talk doesn't always mean that sex is involved. Supervisor Wolfe's conduct was, indeed, bad, boorish and juvenile. What elevated grossness in an all-male environment to a Title VII claim of employment discrimination "because of" Woods's "sex"? The EEOC had to offer an expert witness to explain its case. That should tell us something. In Title VII opposite-sex cases, we need no expert to explain the employment implications of sexual come-ons, put-downs, pat-downs, and stereotyping. Here, an all-male, heterosexual crew was performing a "macho" job. We know that men behave differently when women aren't around (as do women surrounded by women). No physical touching, threats, sexual *quid pro quo,* or employment retaliation was imposed on the plaintiff. Yet without such hard proof of sexually-motivated harassment, the majority affirms a substantial sexual harassment verdict for Kerry Woods. . . . [B]ased on this decision, every one of Woods's co-workers could have filed suit against Boh Brothers.

This decision, however, goes further than its application to single-sex workplaces. EEOC claimed to advocate that there is "no coarse workplace exclusion" from Title VII, especially for classically male locales like the oil patch. What it has persuaded the majority to adopt is the disturbing proposition that, to avoid exposure to Title VII liability, employers must purge every workplace of speech and gestures that might be viewed in any way as tokens of sex discrimination. Consider the attached memorandum, "Etiquette for Ironworkers," which suggests how prudent employers may respond to the majority decision. . . .

ETIQUETTE FOR IRONWORKERS

MEMO TO: Management

FROM: Legal Department of Apex Co.

DATE: September 2013

In keeping up with the newest developments in employment law, we have carefully reviewed and hired specialist outside counsel to give us a legal opinion concerning the implications of a recent Fifth Circuit en banc decision. *EEOC v. Boh Bros.* . . . Like us, the employer in that case engaged in heavy construction and often operated in all-male crews. Like us, it had an unblemished record, years without a Title VII case. But the court ruled that common sexual epithets and vulgar gestures, when used too frequently by a male, heterosexual supervisor, can support a verdict against the company on behalf of another male, heterosexual plaintiff. Instead of looking on these actions as horseplay or, at worst, bullying, the court approved a jury verdict for "gender-stereotyping harassment." The EEOC intends to make this case an example for similar workplaces.

We need not advise you of the costs a company can incur in these cases. In addition to hundreds of thousands in outside legal fees, a judgment for damages may run into six figures. The EEOC requested, and got, a sweeping and intrusive injunction that will require significant expenditures in paperwork compliance costs and regular workplace sensitivity training for over one thousand employees.

To avert these consequences, we recommend that the company immediately issue the following rules for proper, non-gender-stereotyping workplace behavior. Employees should be informed that the rules apply across the board, to all-male, all-female, and mixed-sex offices and positions. The workplace must be cleansed of speech and actions that may be misperceived or twisted as reflecting gender stereotyping harassment.

NOTICE CONCERNING TITLE VII

To our Associates:

You are all aware of this company's unwavering policy to prevent discrimination of any kind based on sex, race, religion or national origin. Because of a new court decision, we must now focus on eliminating same-sex "gender stereotyping" of any kind as well. This means that men may expose this company to liability for their speech and behavior in the presence of other men, and women in the presence of other women. Although these rules will apply throughout the company, you IRONWORKERS have to take special notice. The rules apply throughout the workday, during breaks and lunch hours, and whenever two or more workers are gathered together.

1. At the most general level, all employees must refrain from any communication—spoken, written, or gesticulated—that may create any suggestion of "sexual stereotyping" or "gender-based bullying." Please consider the broad implications of this prohibition, some of which follow. All employee interactions must be fully gender inclusive (or at least gender ambiguous). Careless phrases and jokes will not be tolerated if they may be interpreted to carry a stereotyping overtone.

2. No more banter about bodily functions, sexual or otherwise, or human physical appearance. Those who do not enjoy references to sweat, toilet humor, tattoos, tight jeans, muscles, or large beards may feel singled out as not "man enough" for such speech.

3. Do not discuss the appearance of women or any intimate sexual encounters, and do not refer to or use words that refer to sex in any way. This includes CUSS WORDS.

4. Do not swivel your hips, make obscene gestures or mimic "twerking."

5. Avoid discussing topics that may be viewed as "non-inclusive": bodybuilding, Boy Scouts, hunting, fishing, and riflery. Football and other "macho" sports may be an unwelcome subject to those who consider them boorishly aggressive.

6. Do not engage in any competitive activity, like lifting heavy objects, on the worksite. This can create a sense of unmanly inferiority for non-participants.

7. Do not use gender-stereotyped nicknames or name-calling. Supervisors may not encourage you to work harder by saying "put your backs into it," or "man up," and terms like "ladies" or "sissies" will be grounds for immediate discipline.

8. Schoolyard humor, which is common at our jobsites to fill down-times and relieve boredom, raises sensitive issues. Some workers may be put off by jokes about personal grooming, scented deodorant, chest hair, or clothing as a form of gender hostility. Poking fun at a worker for drinking a diet soda, not being able to eat a raw jalapeno, using "Wet Ones" or "Purell" to clean himself, or calling someone a "wimp" or "wuss" or "geek" may get us sued and you in serious trouble.

9. Asinine locker room behavior is forbidden. Examples of this would be comments about anatomy, crude gestures, actions like towel-swatting, simulated sexual acts, and any behavior that would make someone ill at ease with his personal expression of his gender. Relieving yourself in the presence of others is forbidden; the company is reconfiguring all restrooms to prevent any worker from observing another worker's bodily functions.

10. Avoid touching any coworker in any manner, except if asked to rescue the person from physical danger, and even then, avoid touching private areas.

PENALTIES: A first violation of these rules will result in a warning, a second violation in suspension without pay, and successive violations will result in termination. We will not call this a "three-strikes" policy, as that term might be interpreted to refer to the principally male sport of baseball. We need hardly explain that any worker terminated for same-sex gender stereotyping will have a hard time finding future employment.

The Company will conduct quarterly sensitivity sessions, where you can learn more about offensive gender stereotyping against fellow males and what you can do to prevent or correct it. As questions arise at any time, call our newly hired Sex Stereotype Counselor in the HR Department.

[Dissenting opinions by SMITH, J., and DEMOSS, J., are omitted].

NOTES

1. The Court in *Oncale* concluded that it was appropriate to infer that different-sex sexual harassment constitutes sex discrimination "because the challenged conduct typically involves explicit or implicit proposals of sexual activity; it is reasonable to assume those proposals would not have been made to someone of the same sex." *Oncale v. Sundowner Offshore Services, Inc.*, 523 U.S. 75, 80, 118 S.Ct. 998, 140 L.Ed.2d 201 (1998). Why is it reasonable to so assume? Is it because most people are heterosexual?

2. Plaintiffs in some post-*Oncale* same-sex sexual harassment cases have had a difficult time establishing that the harassment was "because of sex." Part of the problem seems to be that several courts have not been persuaded that the harassment was motivated by the plaintiffs' sex, as opposed to by their sexual orientation. In *Simonton v. Runyon*, 232 F.3d 33, 35 (2d Cir. 2000), for example, the plaintiff (Simonton) alleged that

> his co-workers repeatedly assaulted him with such comments as "go fuck yourself, fag," "suck my dick," and "so you like it up the ass?" Notes were placed on the wall in the employees' bathroom with Simonton's name and the name of celebrities who had died of AIDS. Pornographic photographs were taped to his work area, male dolls were placed in his vehicle, and copies of Playgirl magazine were

sent to his home. Pictures of an erect penis were posted in his work place, as were posters stating that Simonton suffered from mental illness as a result of "bung hole disorder." There were repeated statements that Simonton was a "fucking faggot."

Although the court noted that the alleged behavior was "morally reprehensible," it dismissed the Title VII claim, deeming it to be based on an allegation of sexual orientation, rather than sex, discrimination. Other courts have reached the same conclusion in similar cases. *See, e.g., Higgins v. New Balance Athletic Shoe, Inc.*, 194 F.3d 252 (1st Cir. 1999); *Bibby v. Philadelphia Coca-Cola Bottling Co.*, 260 F.3d 257 (3rd Cir. 2001).

3.   Christopher Vickers worked as a private police officer at an Ohio hospital. After some of his co-workers began suspecting that he might be gay, they started to harass him. They frequently called him a "fag," subjected him to vulgar gestures, and made lewd remarks suggesting that Vickers provide them with sexual favors. During a training on how to use handcuffs, one of the co-workers handcuffed Vickers and then simulated sex with him while another co-worker photographed the incident. "On other occasions, Vickers' co-workers repeatedly touched his crotch with a tape measure, grabbed Vickers' chest while making derogatory comments, tried to shove a sanitary napkin in Vickers' face, and simulated sex with a stuffed animal and then tried to push the stuffed animal into Vickers' crotch." *Vickers v. Fairfield Med. Ctr.*, 453 F.3d 757, 760 (6th Cir. 2006).

The Sixth Circuit Court of Appeals upheld the dismissal of Vickers's gender stereotyping claim by reasoning that "a gender stereotyping claim should not be used to bootstrap protection for sexual orientation into Title VII." *Id.* at 764. The court added that if Vickers succeeded with his claim, "any discrimination based on sexual orientation would be actionable under a sex stereotyping theory . . . , as all homosexuals, by definition, fail to conform to traditional gender norms in their sexual practices." *Id.* The court also rejected the sex harassment claim: "Nothing in Vickers' complaint indicates that his harassers acted out of sexual desire. Similarly, the complaint does not support an inference that there was general hostility toward men in the workplace. Finally, Vickers included no information regarding how women were treated in comparison to men at [the hospital]. In fact, defendants-appellees maintain that Vickers worked in an all-male workforce, an assertion that Vickers has apparently not disputed." *Id.* at 7654.

4.   It is important that lawyers representing plaintiffs in same-sex sexual harassment cases under Title VII think carefully about how to handle evidence relating to harassment on the basis of sexual orientation. Focusing on such evidence, without linking it to discrimination "because of sex," might imperil the lawsuit. For example, the court in *Simonton, supra* Note 2, concluded that it was not possible "to infer from the [plaintiff's] complaint that the harassment [he] suffered was because of his sex and not, *as he urges throughout his complaint*, because of his sexual orientation." *Simonton*, 232 F.3d at 37 (emphasis added).

The fact, however, that there might have been discrimination on the basis of sexual orientation, alongside discrimination "because of sex," should not be held against plaintiffs in Title VII cases because "they do[ ] not need to allege that [they] suffered discrimination on the basis of [their] sex *alone* or that sexual orientation played no part in their treatment." *Centola v. Potter*, 183 F. Supp. 2d 403, 409 (D. Mass. 2002) (emphasis added). Part of the problem, of course, is that "the line between discrimination because of sexual orientation and discrimination because of sex is hardly clear." *Id.* at 408. While some judges may believe that they can neatly distinguish between both types of discrimination, it is not clear that the individuals who engage in the harassing conduct make such distinctions. Male supervisors and co-employees, for example, may dislike a male employee who is perceived to be gay and effeminate both because of his sexual orientation and because he does not "act like a man."

5.   In *Rene v. MGM Grand Hotel*, 305 F.3d 1061 (9th Cir. 2002) (en banc), *cert. denied*, 538 U.S. 922, 123 S.Ct. 1573, 155 L.Ed.2d 313 (2003), the full U.S. Court of Appeals for the Ninth Circuit reversed the granting of a summary judgment motion filed by the employer in a same-sex sexual harassment case. The plaintiff in *Rene*, who worked as a butler for a Las Vegas hotel,

> provided extensive evidence that, over the course of a two-year period, his supervisor and several of his fellow butlers subjected him to a hostile work environment on almost a daily basis. The harassers' conduct included whistling and blowing kisses at Rene, calling him "sweetheart" and "muñeca" (Spanish for "doll"), telling crude jokes and giving sexually oriented "joke" gifts, and forcing Rene to look at pictures of naked men having sex. On "more times than [Rene said he] could possibly count," the harassment involved offensive physical conduct of a sexual nature. Rene gave deposition testimony that he was caressed and hugged and that his coworkers would "touch [his] body like they would to a woman." On numerous occasions, he said, they grabbed him in the crotch and poked their fingers in his anus through his clothing. When asked what he believed was the motivation behind this harassing behavior, Rene responded that the behavior occurred because he is gay.

Id. at 1064. The court, in a plurality opinion, concluded that the conduct in question was "of a sexual nature" and that it was therefore enough to establish a cause of action of sexual harassment under Title VII. *Id.* at 1068. The plurality noted that

> [i]n granting MGM Grand's motion for summary judgment, the district court did not deny that the sexual assaults alleged by Rene were so objectively offensive that they created a hostile working environment. Rather, it appears to have held that Rene's otherwise viable cause of action was defeated because he believed he was targeted because he is gay. This is not the law. We have surveyed

the many cases finding a violation of Title VII based on the offensive touching of the genitalia, buttocks, or breasts of women. In none of those cases has a court denied relief because the victim was, or might have been, a lesbian. The sexual orientation of the victim was simply irrelevant. If sexual orientation is irrelevant for a female victim, we see no reason why it is not also irrelevant for a male victim.

Id. at 1066. A concurring opinion also sided with the plaintiff, but under the theory that he had made out a case of gender stereotyping harassment. *See id.* at 1064 (Pregerson, J., concurring). For its part, the dissent took issue with the notion that harassment of a "sexual nature" was enough to satisfy the statute's causation requirement in a same-sex sexual harassment case: "The alleged harassment in this case was not on account of the plaintiff's sex, i.e., this plaintiff was not treated differently from all the other male butlers because he was male. Rene contended [instead] that he was treated differently because he was homosexual." *Id.* at 1074 (Hug, J., dissenting). The dissenting opinion also concluded that the plaintiff did not claim "before the district court that the harassment [he] experienced was because he acted effeminately on the job, or for any reason other than his sexual orientation. The first line of the legal argument presented to the district court in opposition to the motion for summary judgment crystalizes this point in stating: 'The question raised by the motion is whether the conduct as alleged by Rene is prohibited by Title VII even though it was directed at Rene because of his sexual orientation.'" *Id.* at 1077.

6.   Courts have split on the question of whether Title VII polices the so-called "bisexual harasser" who sexually harasses subordinates regardless of their gender. Since an "equal opportunity" harasser arguably treats men and women in the same way, some courts have concluded that that harassment is not "because of sex." *See, e.g., EEOC v. Harbert-Yeargin, Inc.,* 266 F.3d 498, 520 (6th Cir. 2001) (noting that if the harasser "had been an equal opportunity gooser, there would be no cause of action here."); *Holman v. State of Indiana,* 211 F.3d 399, 403 (7th Cir. 2000) ("Title VII does not cover the 'equal opportunity' or 'bisexual' harasser . . . because such a person is not *discriminating* on the basis of sex."); *Barnes v. Costle,* 561 F.2d 983, 990 n. 55 (D.C. Cir. 1977) ("In case of the bisexual superior, the insistence upon sexual favors would not constitute gender discrimination because it would apply to male and female employees alike."). Other courts have rejected this view. *See, e.g., Brown v. Henderson,* 257 F.3d 246, 254 (2d Cir. 2001) ("the inquiry into whether ill treatment was actually sex-based discrimination cannot be short-circuited by the mere fact that both men and women are involved"). *See also McDonnell v. Cisneros,* 84 F.3d 256, 260 (7th Cir. 1996) ("It would be exceedingly perverse if a male worker could buy his supervisors and his company immunity from Title VII liability by taking care to harass sexually an occasional male worker, though his preferred targets were female.").

7.   While the bisexuality of the harasser might undermine a sexual harassment claim, the homosexuality of the harasser might bolster it. Recall that in *Oncale*, the Supreme Court stated that

> [c]ourts and juries have found the inference of discrimination easy to draw in most male-female sexual harassment situations, because the challenged conduct typically involves explicit or implicit proposals of sexual activity; it is reasonable to assume those proposals would not have been made to someone of the same sex. *The same chain of inference would be available to a plaintiff alleging same-sex harassment, if there were credible evidence that the harasser was homosexual.*

Oncale, 523 U.S. at 80 (emphasis added). The emphasized sentence has given rise to cases in which plaintiffs have attempted to make out their harassment claims by trying to establish the same-sex sexual orientation of their harassers. *See, e.g., Love v. Motiva Enterprises*, 2009 WL 3334610, at *2–3 (Ct. App. 5th Cir. 2009); La Day v. Catalyst Technology, Inc., 302 F.3d 474, 480–81 (5th Cir. 2002); *Cooke v. Stefani Mgmt. Servs., Inc.*, 250 F.3d 564, 565–66 (7th Cir. 2001); *Shepherd v. Slater Steels Corp.*, 168 F.3d 998, 1009–1010 (7th Cir. 1999); *Merritt v. Delaware River Port Auth.*, 1999 WL 285900, at *3–4 (E.D. Pa. 1999). Although most of these courts spent time discussing the harassers' sexual orientation, it is not clear that *Oncale* requires that type of inquiry in cases where plaintiffs seek to use the existence of sexual desire to establish that the discrimination was "because of sex." As one federal Court of Appeals has put it,

> a plaintiff need not, in every first-evidentiary-route [i.e. sexual desire] case, establish that her harasser is homosexual in order to demonstrate that the harassing conduct was motivated by sexual desire. . . . [It is possible] that an alleged harasser may consider herself "heterosexual" but nonetheless propose or desire sexual activity with another woman in a harassing manner. In that scenario, evidence of homosexuality beyond that of her conduct itself may not be forthcoming, although the harasser still acted out of sexual desire. Indeed, aside from testimonial evidence or the fact of the harassing conduct, we find it would often be extremely difficult to obtain evidence tending to show a person's sexual orientation. Therefore, while the fact that the harasser is homosexual may support a finding that her conduct was motivated by sexual desire, we do not read *Oncale* to require a plaintiff to demonstrate, in every first-evidentiary-route case, such a fact. We emphasize that *Oncale's* first evidentiary route turns on whether the harasser acted out of sexual desire. A plaintiff who makes this showing establishes that the harassment took place because of her sex, regardless whether she has also demonstrated that her harasser is homosexual.

Dick v. Phone Directories Company, Inc., 397 F.3d 1256, 1265 (10th Cir. 2005).

8. In addition to pursuing sexual harassment and/or gender stereotyping claims under Title VII, lesbians, gay men, and bisexuals in twenty-one states (CA, CO, CT, DE, HW, IA, IL, MA, MD, ME, MN, NH, NJ, NV, NM, NY, OR, RI, VT, WI, WA) and the District of Columbia can sue under state statutes prohibiting employment discrimination on the basis of sexual orientation. For examples of such lawsuits, see *Wiedemeier v. AWS Convergence Technologies*, Inc. 2009 WL 3165746 (Cal.App. 2 Dist. 2009); *Dominguez v. Washington Mutual* Bank, 168 Cal.App.4th 714, 85 Cal.Rptr.3d 705 (2008); *Cookson v. Brewer Sch. Dep't*, 2009 ME 57, 974 A.2d 276 (2009); *Kwiatkowski v. Merrill Lynch*, 2008 WL 3875417 (N.J.Super.A.D. 2008); *Taylor v. N.Y.U Med. Ctr.*, 21 Misc.3d 23, 871 N.Y.S.2d 568 (App.Term 2008). There are also currently over 250 municipalities that have local ordinances prohibiting employment discrimination on the basis of sexual orientation.

9. State laws prohibiting employment discrimination on the basis of sexual orientation usually have some exemption for religious organizations. Minnesota's statute, for example, contains a provision stating that the discrimination prohibition does not apply to "a religious . . . association with respect to qualifications based on religion or sexual orientation, when religion or sexual orientation shall be a bona fide occupational qualification for employment." MINN. STAT. § 363A.20, subd. 2 (2006). The application of this provision has led to the dismissal of, for example, discrimination claims brought by a gay pastor and secular teacher in a religious high school, *Doe v. Lutheran High Sch. of Greater Minneapolis*, 702 N.W.2d 322 (Minn. Ct. App. 2005), and the gay music director of a church, *Egan v. Hamline United Methodist Church*, 679 N.W.2d 350 (Minn. Ct. App. 2004).

Minnesota's statute simultaneously makes it illegal for a religious association to discriminate on the basis of sexual orientation in "secular business activities . . . unrelated to the religious and educational purposes for which it is organized." MINN. STAT. § 363A.26(2) (2006). In *Thorson v. Billy Graham Evangelistic Assoc.*, 687 N.W.2d 652 (Minn.Ct.App.2004), the female plaintiff, who worked in the mailroom of the defendant evangelical association, was fired when two co-employees observed her kissing a woman in the parking lot at work. The plaintiff argued that "because she was engaged in a secular business activity as a mailroom employee, [the defendant was] not exempt from the operation of the [statute]." *Id.*, 687 N.W.2d at 655. The court disagreed, concluding that the statute was inapplicable to *all* of the activities of organizations, such as the defendant, whose "activities are exclusively evangelical and are entirely related to the religious purpose for which it is organized." *Id.* at 657.

3. Gender Identity

ULANE V. EASTERN AIRLINES, INC.

United States Court of Appeals, Seventh Circuit, 1984
742 F.2d 1081, *cert. denied*, 471 U.S. 1017, 105 S.Ct. 2023, 85 L.Ed.2d 304 (1985)

HARLINGTON WOOD, JR., CIRCUIT JUDGE.

Plaintiff, as Kenneth Ulane, was hired in 1968 as a pilot for defendant, Eastern Air Lines, Inc., but was fired as Karen Frances Ulane in 1981. Ulane filed a timely charge of sex discrimination with the Equal Employment Opportunity Commission, which subsequently issued a right to sue letter. This suit followed. Counts I and II allege that Ulane's discharge violated Title VII of the Civil Rights Act of 1964: Count I alleges that Ulane was discriminated against as a female; Count II alleges that Ulane was discriminated against as a transsexual. The judge ruled in favor of Ulane on both counts after a bench trial. The court awarded her[2] reinstatement as a flying officer with full seniority and back pay, and attorneys' fees. This certified appeal followed pursuant to Federal Rule of Civil Procedure 54(b).

Counsel for Ulane opens their brief by explaining: "This is a Title VII case brought by a pilot who was fired by Eastern Airlines for no reason other than the fact that she ceased being a male and became a female." That explanation may give some cause to pause, but this briefly is the story.

Ulane became a licensed pilot in 1964, serving in the United States Army from that time until 1968 with a record of combat missions in Vietnam for which Ulane received the Air Medal with eight clusters. Upon discharge in 1968, Ulane began flying for Eastern. With Eastern, Ulane progressed from Second to First Officer, and also served as a flight instructor, logging over 8,000 flight hours.

Ulane was diagnosed a transsexual[3] in 1979. She explains that although embodied as a male, from early childhood she felt like a female. Ulane first sought psychiatric and medical assistance in 1968 while in the military. Later, Ulane began taking female hormones as part of her

---

[2] Since Ulane considers herself to be female, and appears in public as female, we will use feminine pronouns in referring to her.

[3] Transsexualism is a condition that exists when a physiologically normal person (*i.e.*, not a hermaphrodite—a person whose sex is not clearly defined due to a congenital condition) experiences discomfort or discontent about nature's choice of his or her particular sex and prefers to be the other sex. This discomfort is generally accompanied by a desire to utilize hormonal, surgical, and civil procedures to allow the individual to live in his or her preferred sex role. The diagnosis is appropriate only if the discomfort has been continuous for at least two years, and is not due to another mental disorder, such as schizophrenia. To be distinguished are homosexuals, who are sexually attracted to persons of the same sex, and transvestites, who are generally male heterosexuals who cross-dress, *i.e.*, dress as females, for sexual arousal rather than social comfort; both homosexuals and transvestites are content with the sex into which they were born.

treatment, and eventually developed breasts from the hormones. In 1980, she underwent "sex reassignment surgery."[4] After the surgery, Illinois issued a revised birth certificate indicating Ulane was female, and the FAA certified her for flight status as a female. Ulane's own physician explained, however, that the operation would not create a biological female in the sense that Ulane would "have a uterus and ovaries and be able to bear babies." Ulane's chromosomes,[5] all concede, are unaffected by the hormones and surgery. Ulane, however, claims that the lack of change in her chromosomes is irrelevant.[6] Eastern was not aware of Ulane's transsexuality, her hormone treatments, or her psychiatric counseling until she attempted to return to work after her reassignment surgery. Eastern knew Ulane only as one of its male pilots.

A. TITLE VII AND ULANE AS A TRANSSEXUAL.

The district judge first found under Count II that Eastern discharged Ulane because she was a transsexual, and that Title VII prohibits discrimination on this basis.[7] While we do not condone discrimination in any form, we are constrained to hold that Title VII does not protect transsexuals, and that the district court's order on this count therefore must be reversed for lack of jurisdiction.

[Title VII] provides in part that: "It shall be an unlawful employment practice for an employer to . . . discharge any individual . . . because of such individual's . . . sex. . . ." Other courts have held that the term "sex" as used in the statute is not synonymous with "sexual preference." *See, e.g., De Santis v. Pacific Telephone & Telegraph Co.*, 608 F.2d 327, 329–30 (9th Cir. 1979). The district court recognized this, and agreed that homosexuals and transvestites do not enjoy Title VII protection, but distinguished transsexuals as persons who, unlike homosexuals and transvestites, have sexual *identity* problems; the judge agreed that the

---

[4]   Sex reassignment surgery for male-to-female transsexuals "involves the removal of the external male sexual organs and the construction of an artificial vagina by plastic surgery. It is supplemented by hormone treatments that facilitate the change in secondary sex characteristics," such as breast development.

[5]   The normal individual has 46 chromosomes, two of which designate sex. An XX configuration denotes female; XY denotes male. These chromosome patterns cannot be surgically altered.

[6]   Biologically, sex is defined by chromosomes, internal and external genitalia, hormones, and gonads. Chromosomal sex cannot be changed, and a uterus and ovaries cannot be constructed. This leads some in the medical profession to conclude that hormone treatments and sex reassignment surgery can alter the evident makeup of an individual, but cannot change the individual's innate sex. Others disagree, arguing that one must look beyond chromosomes when determining an individual's sex and consider factors such as psychological sex or assumed sex role. These individuals conclude that post-operative male-to-female transsexuals do in fact qualify as females and are not merely "facsimiles."

[7]   Not all of the experts who testified agreed that Ulane is a transsexual. (Although doctors attempt to perform sex reassignment surgery only on transsexuals—as opposed, for example, on transvestites or schizophrenics, that an individual has undergone such surgery is not determinative of whether he or she is a true transsexual.) If Ulane is not a transsexual, then she is a transvestite. Even in the trial judge's view, transvestites are not covered by Title VII.

term "sex" does not comprehend "sexual preference," but held that it does comprehend "sexual identity." The district judge based this holding on his finding that "sex is not a cut-and-dried matter of chromosomes," but is in part a psychological question—a question of self-perception; and in part a social matter—a question of how society perceives the individual. The district judge further supported his broad view of Title VII's coverage by recognizing Title VII as a remedial statute to be liberally construed. He concluded that it is reasonable to hold that the statutory word "sex" literally and scientifically applies to transsexuals even if it does not apply to homosexuals or transvestites.[10] We must disagree.

Even though Title VII is a remedial statute, and even though some may define "sex" in such a way as to mean an individual's "sexual identity," our responsibility is to interpret this congressional legislation and determine what Congress intended when it decided to outlaw discrimination based on sex. The district judge did recognize that Congress manifested an intention to exclude homosexuals from Title VII coverage. Nonetheless, the judge defended his conclusion that Ulane's broad interpretation of the term "sex" was reasonable and could therefore be applied to the statute by noting that transsexuals are different than homosexuals, and that Congress never considered whether it should include or exclude transsexuals. While we recognize distinctions among homosexuals, transvestites, and transsexuals, we believe that the same reasons for holding that the first two groups do not enjoy Title VII coverage apply with equal force to deny protection for transsexuals.

It is a maxim of statutory construction that, unless otherwise defined, words should be given their ordinary, common meaning. The phrase in Title VII prohibiting discrimination based on sex, in its plain meaning, implies that it is unlawful to discriminate against women because they are women and against men because they are men. The words of Title VII do not outlaw discrimination against a person who has a sexual identity disorder, *i.e.*, a person born with a male body who believes himself to be female, or a person born with a female body who believes herself to be male; a prohibition against discrimination based on an individual's sex is not synonymous with a prohibition against discrimination based on an individual's sexual identity disorder or discontent with the sex into which they were born. The dearth of legislative history on section 2000e–2(a)(1) strongly reinforces the view that that section means nothing more than its plain language implies.

---

[10] Judge Grady explained:

I have no problem with the idea that the statute was not intended and cannot reasonably be argued to have been intended to cover the matter of sexual preference, the preference of a sexual partner, or the matter of sexual gratification from wearing the clothes of the opposite sex. It seems to me an altogether different question as to whether the matter of sexual identity is comprehended by the word, "sex."

When Congress enacted the Civil Rights Act of 1964 it was primarily concerned with race discrimination. "Sex as a basis of discrimination was added as a floor amendment one day before the House approved Title VII, without prior hearing or debate." *Holloway v. Arthur Andersen & Co.*, 566 F.2d 659, 662 (9th Cir. 1977). This sex amendment was the gambit of a congressman seeking to scuttle adoption of the Civil Rights Act. The ploy failed and sex discrimination was abruptly added to the statute's prohibition against race discrimination.

The total lack of legislative history supporting the sex amendment coupled with the circumstances of the amendment's adoption clearly indicates that Congress never considered nor intended that this 1964 legislation apply to anything other than the traditional concept of sex. Had Congress intended more, surely the legislative history would have at least mentioned its intended broad coverage of homosexuals, transvestites, or transsexuals, and would no doubt have sparked an interesting debate. There is not the slightest suggestion in the legislative record to support an all-encompassing interpretation.

Members of Congress have, moreover, on a number of occasions, attempted to amend Title VII to prohibit discrimination based upon "affectational or sexual orientation." Each of these attempts has failed. While the proposed amendments were directed toward homosexuals, their rejection strongly indicates that the phrase in the Civil Rights Act prohibiting discrimination on the basis of sex should be given a narrow, traditional interpretation, which would also exclude transsexuals. Furthermore, Congress has continued to reject these amendments even after courts have specifically held that Title VII does not protect transsexuals from discrimination.

Although the maxim that remedial statutes should be liberally construed is well recognized, that concept has reasonable bounds beyond which a court cannot go without transgressing the prerogatives of Congress. In our view, to include transsexuals within the reach of Title VII far exceeds mere statutory interpretation. Congress had a narrow view of sex in mind when it passed the Civil Rights Act, and it has rejected subsequent attempts to broaden the scope of its original interpretation. For us to now hold that Title VII protects transsexuals would take us out of the realm of interpreting and reviewing and into the realm of legislating. This we must not and will not do.

Congress has a right to deliberate on whether it wants such a broad sweeping of the untraditional and unusual within the term "sex" as used in Title VII. Only Congress can consider all the ramifications to society of such a broad view. We do not believe that the interpretation of the word "sex" as used in the statute is a mere matter of expert medical testimony or the credibility of witnesses produced in court. Congress may, at some future time, have some interest in testimony of that type, but it does not control our interpretation of Title VII based on the legislative history or lack thereof. If Congress believes that transsexuals should enjoy the protection of Title VII, it may so provide. Until that time, however, we decline in behalf of the Congress to judicially expand the definition of sex as used in Title VII beyond its common and traditional interpretation.

Our view of the application of Title VII to this type of case is not an original one. *Sommers v. Budget Marketing, Inc.*, 667 F.2d 748, 750 (8th Cir. 1982) (per curiam), and *Holloway v. Arthur Andersen & Co.*, 566 F.2d 659, 662–63 (9th Cir. 1977), the only two circuit court cases we found that have specifically addressed the issue, both held that discrimination against transsexuals does not fall within the ambit of Title VII. In *Sommers*, Budget Marketing fired an anatomical male who claimed to be female once Budget Marketing discovered that he had misrepresented himself as female when he applied for the job. In *Holloway*, Arthur Andersen, an accounting firm, dismissed the plaintiff after he informed his superior that he was undergoing treatment in preparation for sex change surgery. We agree with the Eighth and Ninth Circuits that if the term "sex" as it is used in Title VII is to mean more than biological male or biological female, the new definition must come from Congress.

B. TITLE VII AND ULANE AS A FEMALE.

The trial judge originally found only that Eastern had discriminated against Ulane under Count II as a transsexual. The judge subsequently amended his findings to hold that Ulane is also female and has been discriminated against on this basis. Even if we accept the district judge's holding that Ulane is female, he made no factual findings necessary to support his conclusion that Eastern discriminated against her on this basis. All the district judge said was that his previous "findings and conclusions concerning sexual discrimination against the plaintiff by Eastern Airlines, Inc. apply with equal force whether plaintiff be regarded as a transsexual or a female." This is insufficient to support a finding that Ulane was discriminated against because she is *female* since the district judge's previous findings all centered around his conclusion that Eastern did not want "[a] *transsexual* in the cockpit" (emphasis added).

Ulane is entitled to any personal belief about her sexual identity she desires. After the surgery, hormones, appearance changes, and a new Illinois birth certificate and FAA pilot's certificate, it may be that society, as the trial judge found, considers Ulane to be female. But even if one believes that a woman can be so easily created from what remains of a man, that does not decide this case. If Eastern had considered Ulane to be female and had discriminated against her because she was female (*i.e.*, Eastern treated females less favorably than males), then the argument might be made that Title VII applied, but that is not this case. It is clear from the evidence that if Eastern did discriminate against Ulane, it was not because she is female, but because Ulane is a transsexual—a biological male who takes female hormones, cross-dresses, and has surgically altered parts of her body to make it appear to be female.

Since Ulane was not discriminated against as a female, and since Title VII is not so expansive in scope as to prohibit discrimination against transsexuals, we reverse the order of the trial court and remand for entry of judgment in favor of Eastern on Count I and dismissal of Count II. Reversed.

SMITH V. CITY OF SALEM

United States Court of Appeals, Sixth Circuit, 2004
378 F.3d 566

COLE, CIRCUIT JUDGE.

Plaintiff-Appellant Jimmie L. Smith appeals from a judgment of the United States District Court for the Northern District of Ohio dismissing his claims against his employer, Defendant-Appellant City of Salem, Ohio, and various City officials, and granting judgment on the pleadings to Defendants, pursuant to Federal Rule of Civil Procedure 12(c). Smith, who considers himself a transsexual and has been diagnosed with Gender Identity Disorder, alleged that Defendants discriminated against him in his employment on the basis of sex. He asserted claims pursuant to Title VII of the Civil Rights Act of 1964, 42 U.S.C. § 2000e *et seq.*, and 42 U.S.C. § 1983. The district court dismissed those claims pursuant to Rule 12(c). . . . For the following reasons, we reverse the judgment of the district court and remand the case for further proceedings consistent with this opinion. * * *

Smith is—and has been, at all times relevant to this action—employed by the city of Salem, Ohio, as a lieutenant in the Salem Fire Department (the "Fire Department"). Prior to the events surrounding this action, Smith worked for the Fire Department for seven years without any negative incidents. Smith—biologically and by birth a male—is a transsexual and has been diagnosed with Gender Identity Disorder ("GID"), which the American Psychiatric Association characterizes as a disjunction between an individual's sexual organs and sexual identity. American Psychiatric Association, Diagnostic and Statistical Manual of Mental Disorders 576–582 (4th ed. 2000). After being diagnosed with GID, Smith began "expressing a more feminine appearance on a full-time basis"—including at work—in accordance with international medical protocols for treating GID. Soon thereafter, Smith's co-workers began questioning him about his appearance and commenting that his appearance and mannerisms were not "masculine enough." As a result,

Smith notified his immediate supervisor, Defendant Thomas Eastek, about his GID diagnosis and treatment. He also informed Eastek of the likelihood that his treatment would eventually include complete physical transformation from male to female. Smith had approached Eastek in order to answer any questions Eastek might have concerning his appearance and manner and so that Eastek could address Smith's co-workers' comments and inquiries. Smith specifically asked Eastek, and Eastek promised, not to divulge the substance of their conversation to any of his superiors, particularly to Defendant Walter Greenamyer, Chief of the Fire Department. In short order, however, Eastek told Greenamyer about Smith's behavior and his GID.

Greenamyer then met with Defendant C. Brooke Zellers, the Law Director for the City of Salem, with the intention of using Smith's transsexualism and its manifestations as a basis for terminating his employment. On April 18, 2001, Greenamyer and Zellers arranged a meeting of the City's executive body to discuss Smith and devise a plan for terminating his employment. The executive body included Defendants Larry D. DeJane, Salem's mayor; James A. Armeni, Salem's auditor; and Joseph S. Julian, Salem's service director. Also present was Salem Safety Director Henry L. Willard, now deceased, who was never a named defendant in this action. * * *

During the meeting, Greenamyer, DeJane, and Zellers agreed to arrange for the Salem Civil Service Commission to require Smith to undergo three separate psychological evaluations with physicians of the City's choosing. They hoped that Smith would either resign or refuse to comply. If he refused to comply, Defendants reasoned, they could terminate Smith's employment on the ground of insubordination. Willard, who remained silent during the meeting, telephoned Smith afterwards to inform him of the plan, calling Defendants' scheme a "witch hunt."

Two days after the meeting, on April 20, 2001, Smith's counsel telephoned DeJane to advise him of Smith's legal representation and the potential legal ramifications for the City if it followed through on the plan devised by Defendants during the April 18 meeting. On April 22, 2001, Smith received his "right to sue" letter from the U.S. Equal Employment Opportunity Commission ("EEOC"). Four days after that, on April 26, 2001, Greenamyer suspended Smith for one twenty-four hour shift, based on his alleged infraction of a City and/or Fire Department policy. * * *

Defendants do not challenge Smith's complaint with respect to any of the other elements necessary to establish discrimination and retaliation claims pursuant to Title VII. In any event, we affirmatively find that Smith has made out a *prima facie* case for both claims. To establish a *prima facie* case of employment discrimination pursuant to Title VII, Smith must show that: (1) he is a member of a protected class; (2) he suffered an adverse employment action; (3) he was qualified for the position in question; and (4) he was treated differently from similarly situated individuals outside of his protected class. His complaint asserts that he is a male with Gender Identity Disorder, and Title VII's prohibition of discrimination "because of . . . sex" protects men as well as women. The complaint also alleges both that Smith was qualified for the position in question—he had been a lieutenant in the Fire Department for seven years without any negative incidents—and that he would not have been treated differently, on account of his non-masculine behavior and GID, had he been a woman instead of a man. * * *

In his complaint, Smith asserts Title VII claims of retaliation and employment discrimination "because of . . . sex." The district court dismissed Smith's Title VII claims on the ground that he failed to state a claim for sex stereotyping pursuant to *Price Waterhouse v. Hopkins*, 490 U.S. 228, 109 S.Ct. 1775, 104 L.Ed.2d 268 (1989). The district court implied that Smith's claim was disingenuous, stating that he merely "invokes the term-of-art created by *Price Waterhouse*, that is, 'sex-stereotyping,'" as an end run around his "real" claim, which, the district court stated, was "based upon his transsexuality." The district court then held that "Title VII does not prohibit discrimination based on an individual's transsexualism."

Relying on *Price Waterhouse*—which held that Title VII's prohibition of discrimination "because of . . . sex" bars gender discrimination, including discrimination based on sex stereotypes—Smith contends on appeal that he was a victim of discrimination "because of . . . sex" both because of his gender non-conforming conduct and, more generally, because of his identification as a transsexual.

. . . As Judge Posner has pointed out, the term "gender" is one "borrowed from grammar to designate the sexes as viewed as social rather than biological classes." Richard A. Posner, Sex and Reason, 24–25 (1992). The Supreme Court made clear that in the context of Title VII, discrimination because of "sex" includes gender discrimination: "In the context of sex stereotyping, an employer who acts on the basis of a belief that a woman cannot be aggressive, or that she must not be, has acted on the basis of gender." *Price Waterhouse*, 490 U.S. at 250. The Court emphasized that "we are beyond the day when an employer could evaluate employees by assuming or insisting that they matched the stereotype associated with their group." *Id.* at 251.

Smith contends that the same theory of sex stereotyping applies here. His complaint sets forth the conduct and mannerisms which, he alleges, did not conform with his employers' and co-workers' sex stereotypes of how a man should look and behave. Smith's complaint states that, after being diagnosed with GID, he began to express a more feminine appearance and manner on a regular basis, including at work. The complaint states that his co-workers began commenting on his appearance and mannerisms as not being masculine enough; and that his supervisors at the Fire Department and other municipal agents knew about this allegedly unmasculine conduct and appearance. The complaint then describes a high-level meeting among Smith's supervisors and other municipal officials regarding his employment. Defendants allegedly schemed to compel Smith's resignation by forcing him to undergo multiple psychological evaluations of his gender non-conforming behavior. The complaint makes clear that these meetings took place soon after Smith assumed a more feminine appearance and manner and after his conversation about this with Eastek. In addition, the complaint alleges that Smith was suspended for twenty-four hours for allegedly violating an unenacted municipal policy, and that the suspension was ordered in retaliation for his pursuing legal remedies after he had been informed about Defendants' plan to intimidate him into resigning. In short, Smith claims that the discrimination he experienced was based on his failure to conform to sex stereotypes by expressing less masculine, and more feminine mannerisms and appearance.

Having alleged that his failure to conform to sex stereotypes concerning how a man should look and behave was the driving force behind Defendants' actions, Smith has sufficiently pleaded claims of sex stereotyping and gender discrimination.

In so holding, we find that the district court erred in relying on a series of pre-*Price Waterhouse* cases from other federal appellate courts holding that transsexuals, as a class, are not entitled to Title VII protection because "Congress had a narrow view of sex in mind" and "never considered nor intended that [Title VII] apply to anything other than the traditional concept of sex." *Ulane v. Eastern Airlines, Inc.*, 742 F.2d 1081, 1085, 1086 (7th Cir. 1984); *see also Holloway v. Arthur Andersen & Co.*, 566 F.2d 659, 661–63 (9th Cir. 1977) (refusing to extend protection of Title VII to transsexuals because discrimination against transsexuals is based on "gender" rather than "sex"). It is true that, in the past, federal appellate courts regarded Title VII as barring discrimination based only on "sex" (referring to an individual's anatomical and biological characteristics), but not on "gender" (referring to socially-constructed norms associated with a person's sex). In this earlier jurisprudence, male-to-female transsexuals . . .—as biological males whose outward behavior and emotional identity did not conform to socially-prescribed expectations of masculinity—were denied Title VII protection by courts because they were considered victims of "gender" rather than "sex" discrimination.

However, th[is] approach . . . has been eviscerated by *Price Waterhouse*. By holding that Title VII protected a woman who failed to conform to social expectations concerning how a woman should look and behave, the Supreme Court established that Title VII's reference to "sex" encompasses both the biological differences between men and women, and gender discrimination, that is, discrimination based on a failure to conform to stereotypical gender norms.

After *Price Waterhouse*, an employer who discriminates against women because, for instance, they do not wear dresses or makeup, is engaging in sex discrimination because the discrimination would not occur but for the victim's sex. It follows that employers who discriminate against men because they *do* wear dresses and makeup, or otherwise act femininely, are also engaging in sex discrimination, because the discrimination would not occur but for the victim's sex.

Yet some courts have held that this latter form of discrimination is of a different and somehow more permissible kind. For instance, the man who acts in ways typically associated with women is not described as engaging in the same activity as a woman who acts in ways typically associated with women, but is instead described as engaging in the different activity of being a transsexual (or in some instances, a homosexual or transvestite). Discrimination against the transsexual is then found not to be discrimination "because of . . . sex," but rather, discrimination against the plaintiff's unprotected status or mode of self-identification. In other words, these courts superimpose classifications such as "transsexual" on a plaintiff, and then legitimize discrimination based on the plaintiff's gender non-conformity by formalizing the non-conformity into an ostensibly unprotected classification. *See, e.g., Dillon v. Frank*, 952 F.2d 403, 1992 WL 5436 (6th Cir. 1992).

Such was the case here: despite the fact that Smith alleges that Defendants' discrimination was motivated by his appearance and mannerisms, which Defendants felt were inappropriate for his perceived sex, the district court expressly declined to discuss the applicability of *Price Waterhouse*. The district court therefore gave insufficient consideration to Smith's well-pleaded claims concerning his contra-gender behavior, but rather accounted for that behavior only insofar as it confirmed for the court Smith's status as a transsexual, which the district court held precluded Smith from Title VII protection.

Such analyses cannot be reconciled with *Price Waterhouse*, which does not make Title VII protection against sex stereotyping conditional or provide any reason to exclude Title VII coverage for non sex-stereotypical behavior simply because the person is a transsexual. As such, discrimination against a plaintiff who is a transsexual—and therefore fails to act and/or identify with his or her gender—is no different from the discrimination directed against Ann Hopkins in *Price Waterhouse*, who, in sex-stereotypical terms, did not act like a woman. Sex stereotyping based on a person's gender non-conforming behavior is impermissible discrimination, irrespective of the cause of that behavior; a label, such as "transsexual," is not fatal to a sex discrimination claim where the victim has suffered discrimination because of his or her gender non-conformity. Accordingly, we hold that Smith has stated a claim for relief pursuant to Title VII's prohibition of sex discrimination.

Finally, we note that, in its opinion, the district court repeatedly places the term "sex stereotyping" in quotation marks and refers to it as a "term of art" used by Smith to disingenuously plead discrimination because of transsexualism. Similarly, Defendants refer to sex stereotyping as "the *Price Waterhouse* loophole." These characterizations are almost identical to the treatment that Price Waterhouse itself gave sex stereotyping in its briefs to the U.S. Supreme Court. As we do now, the Supreme Court noted the practice with disfavor, stating:

> In the specific context of sex stereotyping, an employer who acts on the basis of a belief that a woman cannot be aggressive, or that she must not be, has acted on the basis of gender. Although the parties do not overtly dispute this last proposition, the placement by Price Waterhouse of "sex stereotyping" in quotation marks throughout its brief seems to us an insinuation either that such stereotyping was not present in this case or that it lacks legal relevance. We reject both possibilities.

Price Waterhouse, 490 U.S. at 250.

SCHROER V. BILLINGTON

U.S. District Court, District of Columbia, 2008
577 F. Supp. 2d 293

ROBERTSON, DISTRICT JUDGE.

Diane Schroer claims that she was denied employment by the Librarian of Congress because of sex, in violation of Title VII of the Civil Rights Act of 1964, 42 U.S.C. § 2000e–2(a)(1). Evidence was taken in a bench trial on August 19–22, 2008.

Diane Schroer is a male-to-female transsexual. Although born male, Schroer has a female gender identity—an internal, psychological sense of herself as a woman. In August 2004, before she changed her legal name or began presenting as a woman, Schroer applied for the position of Specialist in Terrorism and International Crime with the Congressional Research Service (CRS) at the Library of Congress. The terrorism specialist provides expert policy analysis to congressional committees, members of Congress and their staffs. The position requires a security clearance.

Schroer was well qualified for the job. She is a graduate of both the National War College and the Army Command and General Staff College, and she holds masters degrees in history and international relations. During Schroer's twenty-five years of service in the U.S. Armed Forces, she held important command and staff positions in the Armored Calvary, Airborne, Special Forces and Special Operations Units, and in combat operations in Haiti and Rwanda. Before her retirement from the military in January 2004, Schroer was a Colonel assigned to the U.S. Special Operations Command, serving as the director of a 120-person classified organization that tracked and targeted high-threat international terrorist organizations. In this position, Colonel Schroer analyzed sensitive intelligence reports, planned a range of classified and conventional operations, and regularly briefed senior military and government officials, including the Vice President, the Secretary of Defense, and the Chairman of the Joint Chiefs of Staff. At the time of her military retirement, Schroer held a Top Secret, Sensitive Compartmented Information security clearance, and had done so on a continuous basis since 1987. After her retirement, Schroer joined a private consulting firm, Benchmark International, where, when she applied for the CRS position, she was working as a program manager on an infrastructure security project for the National Guard.

When Schroer applied for the terrorism specialist position, she had been diagnosed with gender identity disorder and was working with a licensed clinical social worker . . . to develop a medically appropriate plan for transitioning from male to female. The transitioning process was guided by a set of treatment protocols formulated by the leading organization for the study and treatment of gender identity disorders, the Harry Benjamin International Gender Dysphoria Association. Because she had not yet begun presenting herself as a woman on a full-time basis, however, she applied for the position as "David J. Schroer," her legal name at the time. In October 2004, two months after submitting her application, Schroer was invited to interview with three members of the CRS staff . . . Charlotte Preece, the Assistant Director for Foreign Affairs, Defense and Trade, was the selecting official for the position. Schroer attended the interview dressed in traditionally masculine attire—a sport coat and slacks with a shirt and tie.

Schroer received the highest interview score of all eighteen candidates. In early December, Preece called Schroer, told her that she was on the shortlist of applicants still in the running, and asked for several writing samples and an updated list of references. After receiving these updated materials, the members of the selection committee unanimously recommended that Schroer be offered the job. In mid-December, Preece called Schroer [and] offered her the job . . . The next day, after Preece confirmed that the Library would be able to offer comparable pay, Schroer accepted the offer, and Preece began to fill out the paperwork necessary to finalize the hire.

Before Preece had completed and submitted these documents, Schroer asked her to lunch on December 20, 2004. Schroer's intention was to tell Preece about her transsexuality. She was about to begin the phase of her gender transition during which she would be dressing in traditionally feminine clothing and presenting as a woman on a full-time basis. She believed that starting work at CRS as a woman would be less disruptive than if she started as a man and later began presenting as a woman. * * * As they were sitting down to lunch, Preece stated that they were excited to have Schroer join CRS because she was "significantly better than the other candidates." Schroer asked why that was so, and Preece explained that her skills, her operational experience, her ability creatively to answer questions, and her contacts in the military and in defense industries made her application superior.

About a half hour into their lunch, Schroer told Preece that she needed to discuss a "personal matter." She began by asking Preece if she knew what "transgender" meant. Preece responded that she did, and Schroer went on to explain that she was transgender, that she would be transitioning from male to female, and that she would be starting work as "Diane." Preece's first reaction was to ask, "Why in the world would you want to do that?" Schroer explained that she did not see being transgender as a choice and that it was something she had lived with her entire life. Preece then asked her a series of questions, starting with whether she needed to change Schroer's name on the hiring documentation. Schroer responded that she did not because her legal name, at that point, was still David. Schroer went on to explain the Harry Benjamin Standards of Care and her own medical process for transitioning. She told Preece that she planned to have facial feminization surgery in early January and assured her that recovery from this surgery was quick and would pose no problem for a mid-January start date. In the context of explaining the Benjamin Standards of Care, Schroer explained that she would be living full-time as a woman for at least a year before having sex reassignment surgery. Such surgery, Schroer explained, could normally be accomplished during a two-week vacation period and would not interfere with the requirements of the job.

Preece then raised the issue of Schroer's security clearance, asking what name ought to appear on hiring documents. Schroer responded that she had several transgender friends who had retained their clearances while transitioning and said that she did not think it would be an issue in her case. Schroer also mentioned that her therapist would be available to answer any questions or provide additional background as needed. Because Schroer expected that there might be some concern about her appearance when presenting as a woman, she showed Preece three photographs of herself, wearing traditionally feminine professional attire. Although Preece did not say it to Schroer, her reaction on seeing these photos was that Schroer looked like "a man dressed in women's clothing." * * * Although Schroer initially thought that her conversation with Preece had gone well, she thought it "ominous" that Preece ended it by stating "Well, you've given me a lot to think about. I'll be in touch."

Preece did not finish Schroer's hiring memorandum when she returned to the Library after lunch . . . Preece testified that at this point . . . she was leaning against hiring Schroer. She said that Schroer's transition raised five concerns for her. First, she was concerned about Schroer's ability to maintain her contacts within the military . . . Second, Preece was concerned with Schroer's credibility when testifying before Congress . . . Third, Preece testified that she was concerned with Schroer's trustworthiness because she had not been up front about her transition from the beginning of the interview process . . . Fourth, Preece thought that Schroer's transition might distract her from her job . . . Finally, Preece was concerned with Schroer's ability to maintain her security clearance. In Preece's mind, "David Schroer" had a security clearance, but "Diane Schroer" did not . . . She had this concern, but she did not ask Schroer for any information on the people she knew who had undergone gender transitions while retaining their clearances. * * *

. . . [The next day, after meeting with other Library officials, Preece decided that] she no longer wanted to recommend Schroer for the terrorism specialist position. Preece testified that the security clearance was the critical, deciding factor because of "how long it would take." She also testified, however, that she would have leaned against hiring Schroer even if she had no concerns regarding the security clearance, because her second candidate, John Rollins, presented "fewer complications"— because, unlike Schroer, he was not transitioning from male to female. * * *

Later that same afternoon, Preece called Schroer to rescind the job offer. She said, "Well, after a long and sleepless night, based on our conversation yesterday, I've determined that you are not a good fit, not what we want." Schroer replied that she was very disappointed. Preece ended the conversation by thanking Schroer for her honesty. Preece then called John Rollins, who had a lower total interview score than Schroer, and offered him the position. He accepted.

Since January 2005, Schroer has lived full-time as a woman. She has changed her legal name to Diane Schroer and obtained a Virginia driver's license and a United States Uniformed Services card reflecting her name change and gender transition.

. . . The Library argues that it had a number of non-discriminatory reasons for refusing to hire Schroer, including concerns about her ability to maintain or timely receive a security clearance, her trustworthiness, and the potential that her transition would distract her from her job. The

Library also argues that a hiring decision based on transsexuality is not unlawful discrimination under Title VII.

[The court concluded that the three reasons for not hiring Schroer were pretextual. It then proceeded to address the legal issue of transsexuality and Title VII.]

Schroer contends that the Library's decision not to hire her is sex discrimination banned by Title VII, advancing two legal theories. The first is unlawful discrimination based on her failure to conform with sex stereotypes. The second is that discrimination on the basis of gender identity is literally discrimination "because of . . . sex."

A.   *Sex Stereotyping*

Plaintiff's sex stereotyping theory is grounded in the Supreme Court's decision in *Price Waterhouse v. Hopkins,* 490 U.S. 228 (1989). * * * Schroer's case . . . rests on direct evidence, and compelling evidence, that the Library's hiring decision was infected by sex stereotypes. Charlotte Preece, the decisionmaker, admitted that when she viewed the photographs of Schroer in traditionally feminine attire, with a feminine hairstyle and makeup, she saw a man in women's clothing. In conversations Preece had with colleagues at the Library after her lunch with Schroer, she repeatedly mentioned these photographs. Preece testified that her difficulty comprehending Schroer's decision to undergo a gender transition was heightened because she viewed David Schroer not just as a man, but, in light of her Special Forces background, as a particularly masculine kind of man. Preece's perception of David Schroer as especially masculine made it all the more difficult for her to visualize Diane Schroer as anyone other than a man in a dress. Preece admitted that she believed that others at CRS, as well as Members of Congress and their staffs, would not take Diane Schroer seriously because they, too, would view her as a man in women's clothing.

What makes Schroer's sex stereotyping theory difficult is that, when the plaintiff is transsexual, direct evidence of discrimination based on sex stereotypes may look a great deal like discrimination based on transsexuality itself, a characteristic that, in and of itself, nearly all federal courts have said is unprotected by Title VII. *See Ulane v. Eastern Airlines,* 742 F.2d 1081, 1085 (7th Cir.1984). Take Preece's testimony regarding Schroer's credibility before Congress. As characterized by Schroer, the Library's credibility concern was that she "would not be deemed credible by Members of Congress and their staff because people would perceive her to be a woman, and would refuse to believe that she could possibly have the credentials that she had." Plaintiff argues that this is "quintessential sex stereotyping" because Diane Schroer is a woman and does have such a background. But Preece did not testify that she was concerned that Members of Congress would perceive Schroer simply to be a woman. Instead, she testified that "everyone would know that [Schroer] had transitioned from male to female because only a man could have her military experiences."

Ultimately, I do not think that it matters for purposes of Title VII liability whether the Library withdrew its offer of employment because it perceived Schroer to be an insufficiently masculine man, an insufficiently feminine woman, or an inherently gender-nonconforming transsexual. One or more of Preece's comments could be parsed in each of these three ways. While I would therefore conclude that Schroer is entitled to judgment based on a *Price Waterhouse*-type claim for sex stereotyping, I also conclude that she is entitled to judgment based on the language of the statute itself.

B. *Discrimination Because of Sex*

Schroer's second legal theory is that, because gender identity is a component of sex, discrimination on the basis of gender identity is sex discrimination. In support of this contention, Schroer adduced the testimony of Dr. Walter Bockting, a tenured associate professor at the University of Minnesota Medical School who specializes in gender identity disorders. Dr. Bockting testified that it has long been accepted in the relevant scientific community that there are nine factors that constitute a person's sex. One of these factors is gender identity, which Dr. Bockting defined as one's personal sense of being male or female.[7]

The Library adduced the testimony of Dr. Chester Schmidt, a professor of psychiatry at the Johns Hopkins University School of Medicine and also an expert in gender identity disorders. Dr. Schmidt disagreed with Dr. Bockting's view of the prevailing scientific consensus and testified that he and his colleagues regard gender identity as a component of "sexuality" rather than "sex." According to Dr. Schmidt, "sex" is made up of a number of facets, each of which has a determined biologic etiology. Dr. Schmidt does not believe that gender identity has a single, fixed etiology.

The testimony of both experts—on the science of gender identity and the relationship between intersex conditions and transsexuality—was impressive. Resolving the dispute between Dr. Schmidt and Dr. Bockting as to the proper scientific definition of sex, however, is not within this Court's competence. More importantly (because courts render opinions about scientific controversies with some regularity), deciding whether Dr. Bockting or Dr. Schmidt is right turns out to be unnecessary.

The evidence establishes that the Library was enthusiastic about hiring David Schroer—until she disclosed her transsexuality. The Library

---

[7] The other eight factors, according to Dr. Bockting, are chromosomal sex, hypothalamic sex, fetal hormonal sex, pubertal hormonal sex, sex of assignment and rearing, internal morphological sex, external morphological sex, and gonads.

revoked the offer when it learned that a man named David intended to become, legally, culturally, and physically, a woman named Diane. This was discrimination "because of . . . sex." * * *

Imagine that an employee is fired because she converts from Christianity to Judaism. Imagine too that her employer testifies that he harbors no bias toward either Christians or Jews but only "converts." That would be a clear case of discrimination "because of religion." No court would take seriously the notion that "converts" are not covered by the statute. Discrimination "because of religion" easily encompasses discrimination because of a *change* of religion. But in cases where the plaintiff has changed her sex, and faces discrimination because of the decision to stop presenting as a man and to start appearing as a woman, courts have traditionally carved such persons out of the statute by concluding that "transsexuality" is unprotected by Title VII. In other words, courts have allowed their focus on the label "transsexual" to blind them to the statutory language itself.

In *Ulane v. Eastern Airlines,* the Seventh Circuit held that discrimination based on sex means only that "it is unlawful to discriminate against women because they are women and against men because they are men." The Court reasoned that the statute's legislative history "clearly indicates that Congress never considered nor intended that [Title VII] apply to anything other than the traditional concept of sex." 742 F.2d 1081, 1085 (7th Cir.1984). The Ninth Circuit took a similar approach, holding that Title VII did not extend protection to transsexuals because Congress's "manifest purpose" in enacting the statute was only "to ensure that men and women are treated equally." *Holloway v. Arthur Andersen & Co.,* 566 F.2d 659, 663 (9th Cir.1977). More recently, the Tenth Circuit has also held that because "sex" under Title VII means nothing more than "male and female," the statute only extends protection to transsexual employees "if they are discriminated against because they are male or because they are female." *Etsitty v. Utah Transit Authority,* 502 F.3d 1215, 1222 (10th Cir.2007).

The decisions holding that Title VII only prohibits discrimination against men because they are men, and discrimination against women because they are women, represent an elevation of "judge-supposed legislative intent over clear statutory text." *Zuni Pub. Sch. Dist. No. 89 v. Dep't of Educ.,* 550 U.S. 81, 127 S.Ct. 1534, 1551, 167 L.Ed.2d 449 (2007) (Scalia, J., dissenting).

For Diane Schroer to prevail on the facts of her case, however, it is not necessary to draw sweeping conclusions about the reach of Title VII. Even if the decisions that define the word "sex" in Title VII as referring only to anatomical or chromosomal sex are still good law—after that approach "has been eviscerated by *Price Waterhouse,*" *Smith* [*v. City of*

Salem], 378 F.3d at 573—the Library's refusal to hire Schroer after being advised that she planned to change her anatomical sex by undergoing sex reassignment surgery was *literally* discrimination "because of . . . sex."

In 2007, a bill that would have banned employment discrimination on the basis of sexual orientation and gender identity was introduced in the House of Representatives. *See* H.R.2015, 110 Cong., 1st Sess. (2007). Two alternate bills were later introduced: one that banned discrimination only on the basis of sexual orientation, H.R. 3685, 110 Cong., 1st Sess. (2007), and another that banned only gender identity discrimination, H.R. 3686, 110 Cong., 1st Sess. (2007). None of those bills was enacted.

The Library asserts that the introduction and non-passage of H.R.2015 and H.R. 3686 shows that transsexuals are not currently covered by Title VII and also that Congress is content with the status quo. However, as Schroer points out, another reasonable interpretation of that legislative non-history is that some Members of Congress believe that the *Ulane* court and others have interpreted "sex" in an unduly narrow manner, that Title VII means what it says, and that the statute requires, not amendment, but only correct interpretation.

In refusing to hire Diane Schroer because her appearance and background did not comport with the decisionmaker's sex stereotypes about how men and women should act and appear, and in response to Schroer's decision to transition, legally, culturally, and physically, from male to female, the Library of Congress violated Title VII's prohibition on sex discrimination.

NOTES

1.   The *Schroer* court's second holding, that discrimination on the basis of gender identity "was *literally* discrimination 'because of . . . sex,'" is noteworthy because most courts that have recognized Title VII claims in gender identity cases have instead adopted the gender stereotyping theory embraced by the U.S. Court of Appeals for the Sixth Circuit in *Smith. See, e.g., Barnes v. Cincinnati*, 401 F.3d 729 (6th Cir. 2005), *cert. denied*, 546 U.S. 1003, 126 S.Ct. 624, 163 L.Ed.2d 506 (2005); *Kastl v. Maricopa Co. Cmty. Coll. Dist.*, 325 Fed. Appx. 492, 493 (9th Cir. 2009); *Lopez v. River Oaks Imaging & Diagnostic Group, Inc.*, 542 F.Supp.2d 653, 667–68 (S.D.Tex. 2008). On the other hand, some courts continue to follow *Ulane* in holding that Title VII does not prohibit discrimination on the basis of gender identity. *See, e.g., Etsitty v. Utah Transit Authority*, 502 F.3d 1215, 1222 (10th Cir. 2007); *Oiler v. Winn-Dixie Louisiana, Inc.*, 2002 WL 31098541 (E.D. La. 2002).

2.   In 2012, the Equal Opportunity Employment Commission (EEOC), the agency charged with enforcing federal employment antidiscrimination law, reversed its earlier position by issuing a ruling explaining that a "complaint of discrimination based on gender identity, change of sex, and/or

transgender status is cognizable under Title VII." *Macy v. Holder*, Appeal No. 0120120821(EEOC, April 20, 2012). In doing so, the Commission explained that gender stereotyping was not a required element of the claim:

> Although most courts have found protection for transgender people under Title VII under a theory of gender stereotyping, evidence of gender stereotyping is simply one means of proving sex discrimination. Title VII prohibits discrimination based on sex whether motivated by hostility, by a desire to protect people of a certain gender, by assumptions that disadvantage men [or women], by gender stereotypes, or by the desire to accommodate other people's prejudices or discomfort. While evidence that an employer has acted based on stereotypes about how men or women should act is certainly one means of demonstrating disparate treatment based on sex, "sex stereotyping" is not itself an independent cause of action. As the *Price Waterhouse* Court noted, while "stereotyped remarks can certainly be *evidence* that gender played a part" in an adverse employment action, the central question is always whether the "employer actually relied on [the employee's] gender in making its decision." [*Price Waterhouse v. Hopkins,* 490 U.S. 228, 251 (1989)].

> Thus, a transgender person who has experienced discrimination based on his or her gender identity may establish a prima facie case of sex discrimination through any number of different formulations. * * * For example, Complainant could establish a case of sex discrimination under a theory of gender stereotyping by showing that she did not get the job . . . because the employer believed that biological men should consistently present as men and wear male clothing. Alternatively, if Complainant can prove that the reason that she did not get the job . . . is that the Director was willing to hire her when he thought she was a man, but was not willing to hire her once he found out that she was now a woman—she will have proven that the Director discriminated on the basis of sex. Under this theory, there would actually be no need, for purposes of establishing coverage under Title VII, for Complainant to compile any evidence that the Director was engaging in gender stereotyping.

> In this respect, gender is no different from religion. Assume that an employee considers herself Christian and identifies as such. But assume that an employer finds out that the employee's parents are Muslim, believes that the employee should therefore be Muslim, and terminates the employee on that basis. No one would doubt that such an employer discriminated on the basis of religion. There would be no need for the employee who experienced the adverse employment action to demonstrate that the employer acted on the basis of some religious stereotype—although, clearly, discomfort with the choice made by the employee with regard to religion would presumably be at the root of the employer's actions. But for

purposes of establishing a prima facie case that Title VII has been violated, the employee simply must demonstrate that the employer impermissibly used religion in making its employment decision.

3. *Restrooms.* Because most employers designate restrooms "men" or "women," bathroom use is a recurring issue in gender identity employment litigation. In *Goins v. West Group*, 635 N.W.2d 717 (Minn. 2001), the plaintiff, a male-to-female transgender individual, brought suit under Minnesota's state sexual orientation discrimination law. That law bans sexual orientation discrimination and includes within the definition of "sexual orientation" the "having or being perceived as having a self-image or identity not traditionally associated with one's biological maleness or femaleness." Goins challenged her employer's refusal to permit her to use the women's room. The Minnesota Supreme Court ruled against her, noting that

> Goins does not argue that an employer engages in impermissible discrimination by designating the use of restrooms according to gender. Rather, her claim is that the MHRA prohibits West's policy of designating restroom use according to biological gender, and requires instead that such designation be based on self-image of gender. Goins alleges that West engaged in impermissible discrimination by denying her access to a restroom consistent with her self-image of gender. We do not believe the MHRA can be read so broadly. As the district court observed, where financially feasible, the traditional and accepted practice in the employment setting is to provide restroom facilities that reflect the cultural preference for restroom designation based on biological gender. To conclude that the MHRA contemplates restrictions on an employer's ability to designate restroom facilities based on biological gender would likely restrain employer discretion in the gender designation of workplace shower and locker room facilities, a result not likely intended by the legislature. We believe, as does the Department of Human Rights, that the MHRA neither requires nor prohibits restroom designation according to self-image of gender or according to biological gender. While an employer may elect to offer education and training as proposed by Goins, it is not for us to condone or condemn the manner in which West enforced the disputed employment policy. Bearing in mind that the obligation of the judiciary in construing legislation is to give meaning to words accorded by common experience and understanding, to go beyond the parameters of a legislative enactment would amount to an intrusion upon the policy-making function of the legislature. Accordingly, absent more express guidance from the legislature, we conclude that an employer's designation of employee restroom use based on biological gender is not sexual orientation discrimination in violation of the MHRA.

Id. at 723.

For its part, the court in *Etsitty v. Utah Transit Authority*, 502 F.3d 1215 (10th Cir. 2007), held that an employer's concern about liability constituted a valid ground under Title VII to deny a male-to-female transgender employee the opportunity to use female public bathrooms while wearing a work uniform. The court noted that "because an employer's requirement that employees use restrooms matching their biological sex does not expose biological males to disadvantageous terms and does not discriminate against employees who fail to conform to gender stereotypes, [the defendant's] proffered reason of concern over restroom usage is not discriminatory on the basis of sex." *Id*. at 1225.

Employers sometimes do not allow transgender employees to use the bathrooms of their choice on the ground that to do so would lead to objections from other employees. *Cf. Cruzan v. Special School District #1*, 294 F.3d 981, 984 (8th Cir. 2002) (holding that the use of a female bathroom by a male-to-female transgender employee did not constitute sexual harassment of co-employee plaintiff given that the latter had easy access to other restrooms not used by the former and that the plaintiff did not assert that the transgender employee "engaged in any inappropriate conduct other than merely being present in the . . . restroom").

4.   In addition to pursuing Title VII claims, transgender individuals in seventeen states (CA, CO, CT, DE, HW, IA, IL, MA, ME, MN, NJ, NM, NV, OR, RI, VT, and WA) and the District of Columbia can sue under state statutes that prohibit employment discrimination on the basis of gender identity. Furthermore, over one hundred municipalities have ordinances prohibiting that type of discrimination.

III.   PUBLIC EMPLOYMENT

The statutes that protect employees in the private sector from discrimination (like Title VII) usually also apply to public sector employees. What distinguishes public employment is that government employees, unlike their private sector counterparts, are protected not only by statutes, but also by constitutional law (as well as by civil service rules and executive orders).

The first Subsection that follows explores issues of gender identity and sexual orientation as they relate to general civilian jobs. The second Subsection addresses the military's "Don't Ask, Don't Tell" policy, which until it was repealed by Congress in 2010, was the last federal employment policy that made explicit distinctions on the basis of sexual orientation. The third Subsection discusses LGBT teachers, while the fourth explores the provision by state and local governments of employment benefits in ways that exclude unmarried partners.

A. CIVILIAN JOBS

Glenn v. Brumby

United States Court of Appeals, Eleventh Circuit, 2011
663 F.3d 1312

Barkett, Circuit Judge.

[For an excerpt setting forth the facts of the case, as well as the court's holding that "discriminating against someone on the basis of his or her gender non-conformity constitutes sex-based discrimination under the Equal Protection Clause," see Chapter 3, Section III.A.3]

We now turn to whether Glenn was fired on the basis of gender stereotyping. The first inquiry is whether Brumby acted on the basis of Glenn's gender-nonconformity. *See Vill. of Arlington Heights v. Metro. Hous. Dev. Corp.*, 429 U.S. 252, 266, 97 S.Ct. 555 (1977) (requiring proof of discriminatory intent). If so, we must then apply heightened scrutiny to decide whether that action was substantially related to a sufficiently important governmental interest.

A plaintiff can show discriminatory intent through direct or circumstantial evidence. In this case, Brumby testified at his deposition that he fired Glenn because he considered it "inappropriate" for her to appear at work dressed as a woman and that he found it "unsettling" and "unnatural" that Glenn would appear wearing women's clothing. Brumby testified that his decision to dismiss Glenn was based on his perception of Glenn as "a man dressed as a woman and made up as a woman," and Brumby admitted that his decision to fire Glenn was based on "the sheer fact of the transition." Brumby's testimony provides ample direct evidence to support the district court's conclusion that Brumby acted on the basis of Glenn's gender non-conformity.

If this were a Title VII case, the analysis would end here. *See Lewis v. Smith*, 731 F.2d 1535, 1537–38 (11th Cir.1984) ("If the evidence consists of direct testimony that the defendant acted with a discriminatory motive, and the trier of fact accepts this testimony, the ultimate issue of discrimination is proved."). However, because Glenn's claim is based on the Equal Protection Clause, we must, under heightened scrutiny, consider whether Brumby succeeded in showing an "exceedingly persuasive justification," *Virginia*, 518 U.S. at 546, 116 S.Ct. 2264, that is, that there was a "sufficiently important governmental interest" for his discriminatory conduct, *Cleburne*, 473 U.S. at 441, 105 S.Ct. 3249. This burden "is demanding and it rests entirely on the State." *Virginia*, 518 U.S. at 533, 116 S.Ct. 2264. The defendant's burden cannot be met by relying on a justification that is "hypothesized or invented post hoc in response to litigation." *Id.*

On appeal, Brumby advances only one putative justification for Glenn's firing: his purported concern that other women might object to Glenn's restroom use. However, Brumby presented insufficient evidence to show that he was actually motivated by concern over litigation regarding Glenn's restroom use. To support the justification that he now argues, Brumby points to a single statement in his deposition where he referred to a speculative concern about lawsuits arising if Glenn used the women's restroom. The district court recognized that this single reference, based on speculation, was overwhelmingly contradicted by specific evidence of Brumby's intent, and we agree. Indeed, Brumby testified that he viewed the possibility of a lawsuit by a co-worker if Glenn were retained as unlikely and the record indicates that the OLC, where Glenn worked, had only single-occupancy restrooms. Brumby advanced this argument before the district court only as a *conceivable* explanation for his decision to fire Glenn under rational basis review. *See Glenn*, 724 F.Supp.2d at 1302 ("Defendant based his entire defense on the argument that Plaintiff was not a member of a protected class and therefore his actions must only survive the rational relationship test."). The fact that such a hypothetical justification may have been sufficient to withstand rational-basis scrutiny, however, is wholly irrelevant to the heightened scrutiny analysis that is required here.

Brumby has advanced no other reason that could qualify as a governmental purpose, much less an "important" governmental purpose, and even less than that, a "sufficiently important governmental purpose" that was achieved by firing Glenn because of her gender non-conformity. *Cleburne*, 473 U.S. at 441, 105 S.Ct. 3249.

We therefore AFFIRM the judgment of the district court granting summary judgment in favor of Glenn on her sex-discrimination claim.

NOTES

1. Since most federal circuits have held that sexual orientation does not constitute a suspect classification, most lesbian, gay, and bisexual plaintiffs in equal protection employment discrimination cases have failed to persuade courts to apply heightened scrutiny. Some plaintiffs, however, have succeeded in their claims by arguing that the discrimination in question did not pass muster under the type of rational-basis review called for by *Romer v. Evans*. Examples include the following cases:

    * In *Quinn v. Nassau County Police Department*, 53 F. Supp. 2d 347 (E.D.N.Y. 1999), the plaintiff, who was a gay officer, endured years of harassment by his supervisors and fellow officers. "During a three-week jury trial, the plaintiff testified that approximately a year after he joined the police force in 1986, other officers learned he was gay and over a nine-year period, tormented him with pornographic cartoons and photographs, anti-gay remarks, and barbaric pranks." *Id.* at 350. After a trial on a Section 1983 claim, the jury awarded the plaintiff $380,000 in compensatory and punitive damages. In upholding the verdict, the court relied on *Romer* to hold "that a hostile work environment directed against homosexuals based on their sexual orientation constitute[s] an Equal Protection violation."

* In *Weaver v. Nebo School District*, 29 F. Supp. 2d 1279 (D. Utah 1998), a high school teacher was removed as the school's volleyball coach after she, in direct response to a student's question, stated that she was gay. The court concluded that the defendant, by its actions, violated both the First Amendment and the Equal Protection Clause. On the latter claim, the court noted that the only reason the plaintiff was removed was because of the "negative reaction" by the community to the plaintiff's sexual orientation, which amounted to an irrational justification for the decision under *Romer*. For other cases involving lesbian, gay, or bisexual teachers, see Section III.C, below.

* In *Miguel v. Guess*, 51 P.3d 89, 112 Wash.App. 536 (2002), a lesbian, who worked at a public hospital, alleged that she was dismissed because of her sexual orientation. The court relied on *Romer* to support its holding that "a state actor violates a homosexual employee's right of equal protection when it treats that person differently than it treats heterosexual employees, based solely upon the employee's sexual orientation."

2. In the 1990s, most agencies and departments of the federal government adopted explicit policies stating that they would not discriminate on the basis of sexual orientation. And in 1998, President Bill Clinton issued an executive order adding sexual orientation to the list of prohibited bases for discrimination. Exec. Order No. 13,087, 63 Fed. Reg. 30,097 (May 29, 1998).

3. Security risk was often cited as a rationale for denying employment to gay people in intelligence and military fields—lesbians, gay men, and bisexuals are closeted and frightened about others discovering their sexual orientation, it was argued, and thus foreign operatives could readily prey on such fear, manipulating closeted individuals to reveal government secrets. *See* JONATHAN KATZ, 1950–55: WITCH-HUNT; THE UNITED STATES GOVERNMENT VERSUS HOMOSEXUALS, *in* GAY AMERICAN HISTORY: LESBIANS AND GAY MEN IN THE U.S.A. 139–155 (1976).

The same concerns were used to deny security clearances to employees of military contractors. The Defense Department's Industrial Security Clearance Office (or DISCO) is the branch of the government responsible for issuing such clearances. Until 1995, DISCO utilized regulations that subjected lesbian, gay, and bisexual employees to heightened security clearance checks. While many gay employees were able to obtain clearances, the extra steps they had to take delayed their applications and often cost them their jobs. In 1984, a group of gay employees working in the Silicon

Valley in California called "High Tech Gays" filed suit against DISCO challenging this system. In an important 1987 decision, the federal district court declared the agency's process of using special checks on gay employees unconstitutional. *High Tech Gays v. Defense Indus. Sec. Clearance Office*, 668 F.Supp. 1361 (D. Cal. 1987). In so doing, the court employed heightened judicial scrutiny, finding that classifications based on sexual orientation were constitutionally suspect. The Ninth Circuit reversed, holding that sexual orientation classifications were only entitled to rational-basis review because sexual orientation is not immutable and "homosexuals are not without political power." 895 F.2d 563, 574 (9th Cir. 1990). The court concluded that the regulations were rationally related to the goal of preventing counterintelligence agencies from targeting gay employees.

In 1995, President Clinton signed an executive order removing sexual orientation as a factor in security clearance decisions. Exec. Order 12,968, 60 Fed. Reg. 40,245 (Aug. 7, 1995).

SHAHAR V. BOWERS

United States Court of Appeals, Eleventh Circuit, 1997
114 F.3d 1097 (en banc), *cert. denied*, 522 U.S. 1049, 118 S.Ct. 693, 139 L.Ed.2d 638 (1998)

EDMONDSON, CIRCUIT JUDGE.

In this government-employment case, Plaintiff-Appellant contends that the Attorney General of the State of Georgia violated her federal constitutional rights by revoking an employment offer because of her purported "marriage"[1] to another woman. The district court concluded that Plaintiff's rights had not been violated. We affirm.

Given the culture and traditions of the Nation, considerable doubt exists that Plaintiff has a constitutionally protected federal right to be "married" to another woman: the question about the right of intimate association. Given especially that Plaintiff's religion requires a woman neither to "marry" another female—even in the case of lesbian couples— nor to marry at all, considerable doubt also exists that she has a constitutionally protected federal right to be "married" to another woman to engage in her religion: the question about the right of expressive association. . . .

Because even a favorable decision on these constitutional questions would entitle Plaintiff to no relief in this case, powerful considerations of judicial restraint call upon us not to decide these constitutional issues. . . . So, today we do stop short of making a final decision about such claimed rights. Instead, we assume (for the sake of argument only) that Plaintiff

---

[1] For clarity's sake, we use the words "marriage" and "wedding" (in quotation marks) to refer to Shahar's relationship with her partner; we use the word marriage (absent quotation marks) to indicate legally recognized heterosexual marriage.

has these rights; but we conclude that the Attorney General's act—as an employer—was still lawful.

The facts are not much in dispute; but we accept Plaintiff's view when there is uncertainty. Plaintiff Robin Joy Shahar is a woman who has "married" another woman in a ceremony performed by a rabbi within the Reconstructionist Movement of Judaism. According to Shahar, though the State of Georgia does not recognize her "marriage" and she does not claim that the "marriage" has legal effect, she and her partner consider themselves to be "married."

Since August 1981, Defendant-Appellee Michael J. Bowers has been the Attorney General of the State of Georgia, a statewide elective office. He has been elected to the office four times. As the Attorney General, Bowers is the chief legal officer of the State of Georgia and head of the Georgia Department of Law (the "Department"). His responsibilities include enforcing the laws of the State by acting as a prosecutor in certain criminal actions; conducting investigations; representing Georgia, its agencies and officials in all civil litigation (including habeas corpus matters); and providing legal advice (including advice on the proper interpretation of Georgia law) to Georgia's executive branch.

While a law student, Shahar spent the summer of 1990 as a law clerk with the Department. In September 1990, the Attorney General offered Shahar the position of Staff Attorney when she graduated from law school. Shahar accepted the offer and was scheduled to begin work in September 1991.

In the summer of 1990, Shahar began making plans for her "wedding." Her rabbi announced the expected "wedding" to the congregation at Shahar's synagogue in Atlanta. Shahar and her partner invited approximately 250 people, including two Department employees, to the "wedding." The written invitations characterized the ceremony as a "Jewish, lesbian-feminist, out-door wedding." The ceremony took place in a public park in South Carolina in June 1991.

In November 1990, Shahar filled out the required application for a Staff Attorney position. In response to the question on "marital status," Shahar indicated that she was "engaged." She altered "spouse's name" to read "future spouse's name" and filled in her partner's name: "Francine M. Greenfield." In response to the question "Do any of your relatives work for the State of Georgia?" she filled in the name of her partner as follows: "Francine Greenfield, future spouse."

Sometime in the spring of 1991, Shahar and her partner were working on their "wedding" invitations at an Atlanta restaurant. While there, they ran into Elizabeth Rowe and Susan Rutherford. Rowe was employed by the Department as a paralegal, Rutherford as an attorney. Rowe was invited to, and did attend, Shahar's ceremony. The four women had a brief conversation, which included some discussion of the "wedding" preparations.

In June 1991, Shahar told Deputy Attorney General Robert Coleman that she was getting married at the end of July, changing her last name, taking a trip to Greece and, accordingly, would not be starting work with the Department until mid-to-late September. At this point, Shahar did not say that she was "marrying" another woman. Senior Assistant Attorney General Jeffrey Milsteen, who had been co-chair of the summer clerk committee, was in Coleman's office at the time and heard Coleman congratulate Shahar. Milsteen later mentioned to Rutherford that Shahar was getting married. Rutherford then told Milsteen that Shahar was planning on "marrying" another woman. This revelation caused a stir.

Senior aides to the Attorney General became concerned about what they viewed as potential problems in the office resulting from the Department's employment of a Staff Attorney who purported to be part of a same-sex "marriage." As the Attorney General was out of the office that week, the five aides held several meetings among themselves to discuss the situation.

Upon the Attorney General's return to the office, he was informed of the situation. He held discussions with the senior aides, as well as a few other lawyers within the Department. After much discussion, the Attorney General decided, with the advice of his senior lawyers, to withdraw Shahar's job offer. In July 1991, he did so in writing. The pertinent letter stated that the withdrawal of Shahar's offer:

> has become necessary in light of information which has only recently come to my attention relating to a purported marriage between you and another woman. As chief legal officer of this state, inaction on my part would constitute tacit approval of this purported marriage and jeopardize the proper functioning of this office. * * *

Shahar brought the present action against the Attorney General, individually and in his official capacity, seeking both damages and injunctive relief (including "reinstatement"). She said revoking her offer violated her free exercise and free association rights and her rights to equal protection. * * *

Bowers moved for summary judgment on all causes of action. On that same day, Shahar moved for partial summary judgment. The district court granted the Attorney General's motion for summary judgment and denied Shahar's.

Even when we assume, for argument's sake, that either the right to intimate association or the right to expressive association or both are present, we know they are not absolute. . . . Georgia and its elected

Attorney General also have rights and duties which must be taken into account, especially where (as here) the State is acting as employer. . . . We also know that because the government's role as employer is different from its role as sovereign, we review its acts differently in the different contexts. . . . In reviewing Shahar's claim, we stress that this case is about the government acting as employer. * * *

We conclude that the appropriate test for evaluating the constitutional implications of the State of Georgia's decision—as an employer—to withdraw Shahar's job offer based on her "marriage" is the same test as the test for evaluating the constitutional implications of a government employer's decision based on an employee's exercise of her right to free speech, that is, the *Pickering* balancing test. [*Pickering v. Board of Education*, 391 U.S. 563, 88 S.Ct. 1731, 20 L.Ed.2d 811 (1968).] * * *

We have previously pointed out that government employees who have access to their employer's confidences or who act as spokespersons for their employers, as well as those employees with some policy-making role, are in a special class of employees and might seldom prevail under the First Amendment in keeping their jobs when they conflict with their employers.

Put differently, the government employer's interest in staffing its offices with persons the employer fully trusts is given great weight when the pertinent employee helps make policy, handles confidential information or must speak or act—for others to see—on the employer's behalf. Staff Attorneys inherently do (or must be ready to do) important things, which require the capacity to exercise good sense and discretion (as the Attorney General, using his considered judgment, defines those qualities): advise about policy; have access to confidential information (for example, litigation strategies); speak, write and act on behalf of the Attorney General and for the State.

In a case such as this one, the employee faces a difficult situation. In fact, we know of no federal appellate decision in which a subordinate prosecutor, state's attorney or like lawyer has prevailed in keeping his job over the chief lawyer's objection. . . . We conclude that the Attorney General—who is an elected official with great duties and with no job security except that which might come from his office's performing well— may properly limit the lawyers on his professional staff to persons in whom he has trust.

As both parties acknowledge, this case arises against the backdrop of an ongoing controversy in Georgia about homosexual sodomy, homosexual marriages, and other related issues, including a sodomy prosecution—in which the Attorney General's staff was engaged—resulting in the well-known Supreme Court decision in *Bowers v. Hardwick*, 478 U.S. 186,

190–92, 106 S.Ct. 2841, 92 L.Ed.2d 140 (1986) (criminal prosecution of homosexual sodomy does not violate substantive due process). When the Attorney General viewed Shahar's decision to "wed" openly—complete with changing her name—another woman (in a large "wedding") against this background of ongoing controversy, he saw her acts as having a realistic likelihood to affect her (and, therefore, the Department's) credibility, to interfere with the Department's ability to handle certain kinds of controversial matters (such as claims to same-sex marriage licenses, homosexual parental rights, employee benefits, insurance coverage of "domestic partners"), to interfere with the Department's efforts to enforce Georgia's laws against homosexual sodomy, and to create other difficulties within the Department which would be likely to harm the public perception of the Department.

In addition, because of Shahar's decision to participate in such a controversial same-sex "wedding" and "marriage" and the fact that she seemingly did not appreciate the importance of appearances and the need to avoid bringing "controversy" to the Department, the Attorney General lost confidence in her ability to make good judgments for the Department. Whatever our individual, personal estimates might be, we—as we observe throughout this opinion—cannot say that the Attorney General's worries and view of the circumstances that led him to take the adverse personnel action against Shahar are beyond the broad range of reasonable assessments of the facts.

We must decide whether Shahar's interests outweigh the disruption and other harm the Attorney General believes her employment could cause. *Pickering* balancing is never a precise mathematical process: it is a method of analysis by which a court compares the *relative* values of the things before it. A person often knows that "x" outweighs "y" even without first determining exactly what either "x" or "y" weighs. And it is this common experience that illustrates the workings of a *Pickering* balance.

To decide this case, we are willing to accord Shahar's claimed associational rights (which we have assumed to exist) substantial weight. But, we know that the weight due intimate associational rights, such as, those involved in even a state-authorized marriage, can be overcome by a government employer's interest in maintaining the effective functioning of his office.

In weighing her interest in her associational rights, Shahar asks us also to consider the "non-employment related context" of her "wedding" and "marriage" and that "[s]he took no action to transform her intimate association into a public or political statement." In addition, Shahar says that we should take into account that she has affirmatively disavowed a right to benefits from the Department based on her "marriage." To the extent that Shahar disclaims benefits bestowed by the State based on marriage, she is merely acknowledging what is undisputed, that Georgia law does not and has not recognized homosexual marriage. We fail to see how that technical acknowledgment counts for much in the balance.

If Shahar is arguing that she does not hold herself out as "married," the undisputed facts are to the contrary. Department employees, among many others, were invited to a "Jewish, lesbian-feminist, out-door wedding" which included exchanging wedding rings: the wearing of a wedding ring is an outward sign of having entered into marriage. Shahar listed her "marital status" on her employment application as "engaged" and indicated that her future spouse was a woman. She and her partner have both legally changed their family name to Shahar by filing a name change petition with the Fulton County Superior Court. They sought and received the married rate on their insurance. And, they, together, own the house in which they cohabit. These things were not done secretly, but openly.

Even if Shahar is not married to another woman, she, for appearance purposes, might as well be. We suppose that Shahar could have done more to "transform" her intimate relationship into a public statement. But after (as she says) "sanctifying" the relationship with a large "wedding" ceremony by which she became—and remains for all to see—"married," she has done enough to warrant the Attorney General's concern. He could conclude that her acts would give rise to a likelihood of confusion in the minds of members of the public: confusion about her marital status and about his attitude on same-sex marriage and related issues. * * *

As we have already written, the Attorney General's worry about his office being involved in litigation in which Shahar's special personal interest might appear to be in conflict with the State's position has been borne out in fact. This worry is not unreasonable. In addition, the Department, when the job offer was withdrawn, had already engaged in and won a recent battle about homosexual sodomy—highly visible litigation in which its lawyers worked to uphold the lawful prohibition of homosexual sodomy. This history makes it particularly reasonable for the Attorney General to worry about the internal consequences for his professional staff (for example, loss of morale, loss of cohesiveness and so forth) of allowing a lawyer, who openly—for instance, on her employment application and in statements to coworkers—represents herself to be "married" to a person of the same sex, to become part of his staff. Doubt and uncertainty of purpose can undo an office; he is not unreasonable to guard against that potentiality.

Shahar also argues that, at the Department, she would have handled mostly death penalty appeals and that the *Pickering* test requires evidence of potential interference with these particular duties. Even assuming Shahar is correct about her likely assignment within the Department, a particularized showing of interference with the provision of public services is not required. In addition, the Attorney General must be able to reassign his limited legal staff as the needs of his office require. * * *

In a similar way, it is not for this court to tie the Department's hands by telling it which Staff Attorneys may be assigned to which cases or duties or to force upon the Attorney General a Staff Attorney of limited utility. Such an interference by the federal judiciary into the internal organization of the executive branch of a state government is almost always unwarranted.

As we have already touched upon, the Attorney General, for balancing purposes, has pointed out, among other things, his concern about the public's reaction—the public that elected him and that he serves—to his having a Staff Attorney who is part of a same-sex "marriage." Shahar argues that he may not justify his decision by reference to perceived public hostility to her "marriage." We have held otherwise about the significance of public perception when law enforcement is involved. In *McMullen v. Carson*, 754 F.2d 936 (11th Cir. 1985), we held that a sheriff's clerical employee's First Amendment interest in an off-duty statement that he was employed by the sheriff's office and also was a recruiter for the Ku Klux Klan was outweighed by the sheriff's interest in esprit de corps and credibility in the community the sheriff policed. More important, we relied, in large part, on public perceptions of the employee's constitutionally protected act. *Id.* at 938–940.

In *McMullen*, both public perception and the anticipated effect that the employee's constitutionally protected activity would have on cohesion within the office were crucial in tipping the scales in the sheriff's favor. Nothing indicates that the employee had engaged in a criminal act or that he had joined an organization (he had joined the Invisible Empire) that had engaged in any criminal act. Given that it was additionally undisputed that neither the employee's statements nor his protected expressive association hindered his ability to perform his clerical duties and that the specific clerk "performed his duties in exemplary fashion," *id.* at 937, the two factors—public perception and anticipated effect— seemed to be the only ones weighing on the sheriff's side of the scale. But that was enough. * * *

Shahar says that by taking into account these concerns about public reaction, the Attorney General impermissibly discriminated against homosexuals; and she refers us to the Supreme Court's recent decision in *Romer v. Evans*, 517 U.S. 620, 116 S.Ct. 1620, 134 L.Ed.2d 855 (1996). * * *

Romer is about people's condition; this case is about a person's conduct. And, *Romer* is no employment case. Considering (in deciding to revoke a job offer) public reaction to a future Staff Attorney's conduct in taking part in a same-sex "wedding" and subsequent "marriage" is not the same kind of decision as an across-the-board denial of legal protection to a group because of their condition, that is, sexual orientation or preference. * * *

We do not decide today that the Attorney General did or did not do the right thing when he withdrew the pertinent employment offer. That decision is properly not ours to make. What we decide is much different and less: For the Law Department's professional staff, Georgia's Attorney General has made a personnel decision which none of the asserted federal constitutional provisions prohibited him from making. AFFIRMED

[JUDGE TJOFLAT'S concurring opinion is omitted.]

GODBOLD, SENIOR CIRCUIT JUDGE, dissenting.

The Attorney General did not act reasonably. One must focus on what he knew and what he did. Post-event rationalizations of what he might have done, thought up afterwards in ivory towers, will not do. Two statements are central, the termination letter and the Attorney General's statement of position made to the panel of this court. The termination letter said in part:

> This action has become necessary in light of information which has only recently come to my attention relating to a purported marriage between you and another woman. As the chief legal officer of this state inaction on my part would constitute tacit approval of this purported marriage and jeopardize the proper function of this office.

The Attorney General's position before the panel was expressed in a significant three-prong statement:

> The Attorney General did not withdraw Shahar's offer of employment because of her association, religious or otherwise, with other homosexuals or her female partner, but rather because she invoked the civil and legal significance of being "married" to another woman. Shahar is still free to associate with her female partner, as well as other homosexuals, for religious and other purposes.

Examine the three prongs. They are: (1) Shahar's employment was not withdrawn for her association with her partner; (2) It was withdrawn because she invoked the civil and legal status of being married to another woman; (3) She is free to associate with her partner for religious reasons.

As to (1), the undisputed evidence is that in fact the Attorney General *did* terminate Shahar because of her religious-based association with her partner. As I explain below, he feared that he *might be* infringing on Shahar's religious beliefs, but he failed to make reasonable inquiry to determine if he was. As to (3), plainly Shahar was not free to associate with her partner for religious purposes. That is exactly what she had done, and it cost her employment agreement.

The prong that requires discussion is (2). The termination letter is plainly based on the Attorney General's conclusion that Shahar was falsely holding herself out as becoming married in the civil and legal sense, i.e., proposing to engage in a "purported marriage." In search of evidence of holding out by Shahar this court relies upon her use of the words "marriage" and "wedding." This implicates differing perceptions of what words mean. In a common law/statutory/traditional sense "marriage" describes a ceremony as a relationship or status between two persons as defined by common law or statute, involving two heterosexual persons, one male and one female. But, as this case tells us, that is not the only and ineluctable meaning. To a person of Shahar's faith as a Reconstructionist Jew "marriage" refers to the formal Jewish wedding ceremony recommended and carried out pursuant to the participants' Jewish faith by two persons (including two homosexuals) who have made a lifelong commitment to each other and are bound to each other by the ceremony in a relationship that can be terminated only within their faith and who, by engaging in the ceremony, made a commitment to the Jewish people as well. "Marriage" also refers to the status thereby conveyed upon them. In the eyes of Shahar and her partner they engaged in a Jewish marriage and they are accepted by their faith as married and accordingly they may use the term "marriage" to refer to the ceremonial event and to the status created by it.

This court, in its footnote 1, recognizes the duality of meaning that I have described for "wedding" and "marriage" [and "spouse"]. Throughout its opinion the court attempts to indicate (not always successfully) by quotation marks and limiting words which meaning it is referring to. But the decision of the en banc court is based upon, and approves, the Attorney General's attribution to these words of only a single meaning, the statutory/common-law/traditional meaning, and his perception that any other meaning is either false or non-existent, i.e., Shahar proposed to engage in a "purported marriage." The court simply adopts one perception and excludes the other as though it did not exist for Shahar and for others of her faith.

What the Attorney General knew was that Shahar had used the terms "marriage" and "spouse" and "marriage ceremony" in referring to the ceremony she planned and to the status to be created by it. She had used the terms "honeymoon" or "wedding trip" in describing her plans.

Within the office there was information that she planned to send, or had sent, invitations to the ceremony and that some staff members were on the invitation list, and other information that, as the Attorney General described it, the planned ceremony would be "a big or church wedding, I don't remember which." Possessed of some, or all, of this knowledge, the Attorney General neither saw Shahar nor talked to her but built a Chinese wall around himself and concluded that she had falsely invoked the civil/statutory/common-law meaning that he attributed to the terms. We know that it occurred to him that assigning a single meaning to "marriage" and "wedding ceremony" might not be correct, for he talked with a female Jewish member of his staff, who told him that the wedding was to be performed by a rabbi from New York who performed homosexual marriages but that "she was not aware of homosexual marriages or gay and lesbian marriages being recognized in Judaism." At best the response was ambiguous—on the one hand the wedding was to be done by a rabbi, but on the other hand the staff member was not aware that it would be recognized in Judaism. As it turned out, she was correct about the rabbi but incorrect or uninformed about recognition of the marriage. * * *

The Attorney General and his staff acted in ignorance of the religious roots of the association that Shahar planned, the centrality of it to her faith, and the recognition of it by the religion to which she was committed. Staff members could recall no discussion of or inquiry into the religious aspects of the matter. The actions by the Attorney General do not meet the constitutional requirements of reasonableness.

BIRCH, CIRCUIT JUDGE, dissenting.

I might have found the majority's application of the *Pickering* balancing test more convincing were it not for the Supreme Court's recent decision in *Romer v. Evans*, 517 U.S. 620, 116 S.Ct. 1620, 134 L.Ed.2d 855 (1996). In my opinion, the Court's recognition in *Romer* that homosexuals, as a class, are entitled to some protection under the Equal Protection Clause bears on the validity—and therefore the weight in applying the *Pickering* balancing test—of Bowers' justifications for his action. With *Romer* in the balance, the scales tip decidedly in favor of Shahar because Bowers' asserted interests are not a legitimate basis for infringing Shahar's constitutionally-protected right of intimate association. For this reason, I dissent from the en banc court's affirmance of the district court's order granting summary judgment to Bowers. * * *

The *Pickering* balance in this case requires us to measure Shahar's right of intimate association against Bowers' asserted interests in infringing that right in the context of an employment relationship. The weight we accord to Bowers' asserted interests, however, hinges entirely on the reasonableness of his predictions as to how Shahar's homosexual relationship might affect or disrupt the Attorney General's office, significantly, it is undisputed that Bowers has made no showing of actual disruption to the office. When we closely examine these predictions, we discover that each one is based on a series of assumptions and unsupported inferences about Shahar *because of her status as a homosexual*. I cannot agree with the majority that these inferences and assumptions constitute a legitimate state interest to discriminate against Shahar in light of the Supreme Court's teaching just last term that mere "animosity toward the class" of homosexuals is not a rational basis for state action.

The first inference that Bowers drew from Shahar's status as a lesbian who married another woman is that the public might be hostile to her participation in a same-sex marriage and might view Shahar's employment by his Department as inconsistent with Georgia law. Bowers argued in his brief that "the public perception is that 'the natural consequence of a marriage is some sort of sexual conduct, . . . and if it's homosexual, it would have to be sodomy.' " As the Supreme Court made clear in *Palmore v. Sidoti*, 466 U.S. 429, 104 S.Ct. 1879, 80 L.Ed.2d 421 (1984), the government may not transform private biases into legitimate state interests by relying on the prejudices of the public. . . .

In applying the principle of *Palmore* to this case, the key question is not whether the government official reasonably could assume that the public might have a negative reaction to the employee's presence; it is whether the public's perception upon which the official relies is itself a legitimate basis for government action. If the public's perception is borne of no more than unsupported assumptions and stereotypes, it is irrational and cannot serve as the basis of legitimate government action. In this instance, the public's (alleged) blanket assumption that "if it's homosexual, it would have to be sodomy" is based not on anything set forth in the record but rather on public stereotyping and animosity toward homosexuals. Under the principles articulated in *Romer*, this does not provide the state with a legitimate, rational basis to discriminate against Shahar. Bowers' "concern" for the public's perception of homosexuals, therefore, is entitled to no weight in balancing Shahar's right of intimate association. * * *

Bowers' argument with respect to the alleged deleterious effect of Shahar's status and conduct on "morale" within the office is another attempt to legitimize his adverse action against Shahar on the basis of inferences that others—here, his employees—might derive from her status as a lesbian. The inferences from Shahar's acknowledged homosexuality that she is likely to violate Georgia's sodomy law, or would be unable or unwilling to enforce Georgia's sodomy or marriage laws, is no more justified on behalf of Bowers or his employees than it is on behalf of the public. Moreover, it is important to note that Bowers' speculation regarding Shahar's ability to handle certain types of cases is just that: speculation. Bowers has emphatically refused to meet with Shahar to discuss any of his concerns. Compounding this deficiency in Bowers' assertion that his prediction is "reasonable" is the fact that Bowers does not make the same assumption with respect to any of his other employees: He does not assume, for instance, that an unmarried employee who is openly dating an individual of the opposite sex has likely committed fornication, a criminal offense in Georgia, and thus may have a potential conflict in enforcing the fornication law. Nor, for that matter, does he apparently assume that married employees could well have committed sodomy—i.e., oral or anal sex, and could themselves have a potential conflict in enforcing Georgia's sodomy law.

In short, Bowers' asserted interests in taking adverse action against Shahar are based on inferences from her status as a homosexual which Bowers claims that he, the public, and department staff are entitled to make. In light of the Supreme Court's decision in *Romer*, these status-based inferences, unsupported by any facts in the record and explained only by animosity toward and stereotyping of homosexuals, do not constitute a legitimate interest that outweighs Shahar's First Amendment right of intimate association. Accordingly, I would reverse the district court's order granting summary judgment to Bowers.

[The dissenting opinions of JUDGES BARKETT and KRAVITCH are omitted.]

COVERING[*]
Kenji Yoshino

Assimilation is the magic in the American Dream. Just as in our actual dreams, magic permits us to transform into better, more beautiful creatures, so too in the American Dream, assimilation permits us to become not only Americans, but the kind of Americans we seek to be. Justice Scalia recently expressed this pro-assimilation sentiment when he joined a Supreme Court majority to strike down an affirmative action program. Calling for the end of race-consciousness by public actors, Scalia said: In the eyes of government, we are just one race here. It is American.[1] Packed into this statement is the idea that we should set aside the racial identifications that divide us—black, white, Asian, Latino—and embrace the Americanness that unites us all.

This vision of assimilation is profoundly seductive and is, at some level, not just American but human. Surrendering our individuality is what permits us to enter communities larger than the narrow stations of

---

[*]   Kenji Yoshino, *Covering*, 111 YALE L.J. 769 (2002).

[1]   Adarand Constructors v. Pena, 515 U.S. 200, 239 (1995) (Scalia, J., concurring).

our individual lives. Especially when the traits that divide us are, like race, morally arbitrary, this surrender seems like something to be prized. Indeed, assimilation is not only often beneficial, but sometimes necessary. To speak a language, to wear clothes, to have manners—all are acts of assimilation.

This assimilationist dream has its grip on the law. The American legal antidiscrimination paradigm has been dominated by the cases of race, and, to a lesser extent, sex. The solicitude directed toward racial minorities and women has been justified in part by the fact that they are marked by immutable and visible characteristics—that is, that such groups cannot assimilate into mainstream society because they are marked as different. The law must step in because these groups are physiologically incapable of blending into the mainstream. In contrast, major strands of American antidiscrimination law direct much less concern toward groups that can assimilate. Such groups, after all, can engage in self-help by assimilating into mainstream society. In law, as in broader culture, assimilation is celebrated as the cure to many social ills. One would have to be antisocial to argue against it.

So it is with great trepidation but greater conviction that I come to do so. For the past few years, I have been working on issues relating to sexual minorities. That work has persuaded me that gays (by which I mean both lesbians and gay men) can proffer a new perspective on the relationship between assimilation and discrimination. I believe that the gay context demonstrates in a particularly trenchant manner that assimilation can be an effect of discrimination as well as an evasion of it. My goal here is to develop this idea in the context of orientation, and then to demonstrate the applicability of this insight to the race-and-sex-based contexts.

I believe gays may have theorized some dimensions of the relationship between assimilation and discrimination differently from either racial minorities or women. This is because gays are generally able to assimilate in more ways than either racial minorities or women. In fact or in the imagination of others, gays can assimilate in three ways: conversion, passing, and covering. Conversion means the underlying identity is altered. Conversion occurs when a lesbian changes her orientation to become straight. Passing means the underlying identity is not altered, but hidden. Passing occurs when a lesbian presents herself to the world as straight. Covering means the underlying identity is neither altered nor hidden, but is downplayed. Covering occurs when a lesbian both is, and says she is, a lesbian, but otherwise makes it easy for others to disattend her orientation.

Of these three forms of assimilation, covering will probably be least familiar. The term and concept come from sociologist Erving Goffman's groundbreaking work on stigma. Goffman observed that even persons who are ready to admit possession of a stigma . . . may nonetheless make a great effort to keep the stigma from looming large. Thus a lesbian might be comfortable being gay and saying she is gay, but might nonetheless modulate her identity to permit others to ignore her orientation. She might, for example, (1) not engage in public displays of same-sex affection; (2) not engage in gender-atypical activity that could code as gay; or (3) not engage in gay activism. * * *

[A]s the gay rights movement has become stronger, the assimilationist demands made on gays have become weaker, shifting in emphasis from conversion, to passing, to covering. A quick way of demonstrating that shift is to consider the gay-related issues that have figured in the mainstream press over the last decades. In the early 1970s, the press widely discussed the American Psychiatric Association's deletion of homosexuality from its taxonomy of mental disorders. The controversy over this deletion was a debate about conversion, that is, about whether gays were mentally diseased individuals who needed to change their orientations. In the early 1990s, the press debated the practice of outing—the revelation of an individual's homosexuality against her will—and the military's don't ask, don't tell policy. These topics pertained not to conversion, but to passing, that is, to whether a gay individual could or should self-identify as straight. Finally, at the turn of the millennium, the press has been devoting much of its gay-related coverage to same-sex marriage. The right of gays to marry is a question of covering, as it pertains not to the ability of gays to be gay or to self-identify as gay, but to their ability to signal that identity beyond the simple act of self-identification.

Again, the demand to cover may be the least intuitive. A recent example may clarify how gays are increasingly encountering covering demands. In 1990, a lesbian lawyer named Robin Shahar was fired from her job at the Georgia Attorney General's Office. Her employer emphasized that he had not fired Shahar for being a homosexual or for saying she was a homosexual, but for flaunting her homosexuality by engaging in a same-sex commitment ceremony. Thus Shahar was terminated not for failing to convert or to pass, but for failing to cover. As time progresses, I posit that more and more discrimination against gays will take the form of covering demands, rather than taking the historical forms of categorical exclusion or don't ask, don't tell. * * *

No historical moment has existed in which one demand has categorically supplanted another, as suggested by the coexistence of all three demands today. I thus am not arguing that we have definitively moved into a covering phase of anti-gay discrimination in which conversion and passing are no longer at issue. To the contrary, I believe that one of the challenging aspects of being gay today lies in the very multiplicity of the assimilationist demands that gays encounter. Moreover, the attenuation of assimilationist demands made on gays in the past few decades does not mean this shift is inexorable. The ascendance of the demand to convert in medical circles in the years after Freud's death is but one of many examples of how fragile progress in this area has been. . . .

Any real engagement with gay history . . . shows that in some instances, the shift from conversion to passing or covering can be experienced by gays as no shift at all. One such shift is the military's movement from its 1981 policy, which excluded gays on the basis of their homosexual status, to its 1993 don't ask, don't tell policy . . . which excludes gays on the basis of homosexual self-identification or homosexual conduct. The 1981 policy was a conversion policy, as it required gays to convert to heterosexuality to serve. The don't ask, don't tell policy is popularly understood as a passing policy (as its moniker would suggest) and is defended by the military as a covering policy. This shift thus appears to represent progress for gays—no longer will they be excluded for their status, but only for their self-identification or conduct. Yet this shift has not improved the material or dignitary conditions of gays in the military, as homosexual self-identification and homosexual conduct are sufficiently central to gay identity that burdening such acts is tantamount to burdening gay status. Indeed, exclusions under the new policy have skyrocketed, suggesting that the shift is the reverse of a progress narrative for gays. * * *

[It is generally thought] that gays can convert and pass, while racial minorities and women cannot. To a significant extent, the antidiscrimination jurisprudence arising under the equal protection guarantees of the Federal Constitution and Title VII of the Civil Rights Act of 1964 has accepted these distinctions, maintaining that racial minorities and women are more deserving of legal protection in part because they cannot convert or pass. Such jurisprudence embodies an assimilationist bias. It maintains that groups that can assimilate are less worthy of protection than groups that cannot. It further suggests that the only acceptable defense to a demand for assimilation is the inability to accede to it. In doing so, the jurisprudence reflects and reinforces a schism between gays on the one hand and racial minorities and women on the other.

. . . [E]ven if we accept these distinctions for the sake of argument, gays can still find common cause with racial minorities and women. Conversion and passing do not exhaust the forms of assimilation. There is also covering. And while racial minorities and women may be differently situated from gays along the axes of conversion and passing, all three groups are similarly situated along the axis of covering.

Like gays, racial minorities and women cover, and are asked to cover, all the time. The African-American woman who stops wearing cornrows to succeed at work may be covering. The native Hawaiian broadcaster who mutes his accent to retain his broadcasting job may be covering. The Latino venireperson who denies knowledge of Spanish to remain on a jury may be covering. Women also cover. The woman who seeks to downplay her status as a mother or her pregnancy for fear of being penalized as an inauthentic worker may be covering. The female scholar who eschews feminist topics may be covering. The woman who strives to be as aggressive or tearless as the stereotypical man may be covering. In all these instances, the individual is not attempting to change or hide her identity. Nonetheless, she is assimilating by making a disfavored trait easy for others to disattend.

Framing analogies among the covering strategies of these different groups merits some qualification. As an initial matter, these groups are obviously not distinct. When I state that women cover, I am focusing on how they cover as women—I do not foreclose the possibility that they will also cover along other dimensions. Understanding the intersectionality of identity is crucial to comprehending the difficulty of declaring that an individual is covering. For example, if a lesbian wears her hair long and down, is she covering her status as a gay person, refusing to cover as a woman, or exercising a grooming preference that has nothing to do with either axis of identity? If this question seems unanswerable, it is because—like most intersectional analysis—it honors the complexity of the underlying practice. * * *

. . . [T]he contemporary forms of discrimination to which racial minorities and women are most vulnerable often take the guise of enforced covering. A member of a racial minority cannot be sanctioned for failing to convert or to pass without having a Title VII employment discrimination claim. But he can be sanctioned for failing to cover—for wearing cornrows,[26] or lapsing into Spanish,[27] or for speaking with an accent.[28] Similarly, a woman generally cannot be burdened for failing to convert or to pass. Yet it is still true that for constitutional purposes, state actors can burden pregnancy without triggering a sex discrimination analysis.[29]

This commonality suggests that racial minorities and women have much to gain from a theory of discrimination that focuses on the harms of coerced assimilation. Members of these groups are not as impervious to the assimilationist bias in the current antidiscrimination paradigm as

---

[26] Rogers v. Am. Airlines, Inc., 527 F. Supp. 229 (S.D.N.Y. 1981).

[27] Garcia v. Gloor, 618 F.2d 264 (5th Cir. 1980).

[28] Kahakua v. Friday, No. 88–1668, 1989 WL 61762 (9th Cir. June 2, 1989).

[29] Geduldig v. Aiello, 417 U.S. 484 (1974); see also Bray v. Alexandria Women's Health Clinic, 506 U.S. 263, 272 n.3 (1993) (noting the continuing vitality of *Geduldig*).

their inability to convert or to pass might suggest. If the only defense against an assimilationist demand is that one cannot accede to it, racial minorities and women are left completely unprotected against covering demands, as anyone is assumed to be able to cover. My model thus shows a ground on which racial minorities, women, and gays can make common cause. That common ground will become more evident as anti-gay claims shift in emphasis away from conversion and passing and toward covering.

As the number of employers that welcome lesbian, gay, and bisexual employees grow, they may face resistance from other employees. The following case deals with some of the same legal issues as *Shahar*, except that it does so in the context of a heterosexual public employee who expressed anti-gay rights views that her employer claimed were inconsistent with its policies.

DIXON V. UNIVERSITY OF TOLEDO

United States Court of Appeals, Sixth Circuit, 2012
702 F.3d 269, *cert. denied*, 134 S.Ct. 119 (2013)

KAREN NELSON MOORE, CIRCUIT JUDGE.

In 2008, Plaintiff-Appellant Crystal Dixon, an African-American woman and then-interim Associate Vice President for Human Resources at the University of Toledo (the "University"), wrote an op-ed column in the *Toledo Free Press* rebuking comparisons drawn between the civil-rights and gay-rights movements. Shortly thereafter, Dixon was fired. Claiming violations of her First and Fourteenth Amendment rights, Dixon subsequently filed a § 1983 suit against the University and Defendants-Appellees University President Lloyd Jacobs and University Vice President for Human Resources and Campus Safety William Logie (collectively, "the defendants"). The district court granted summary judgment to the defendants on all claims, and Dixon appeals.

The issues raised in this appeal turn primarily on the resolution of a narrow inquiry: whether the speech of a high-level Human Resources official who writes publicly against the very policies that her government employer charges her with creating, promoting, and enforcing is protected. We conclude that, given the nature of her position, Dixon did not engage in protected speech. We therefore affirm the judgment of the district court.

Dixon began her career at the University in January 2002. At this time, she was recruited by Logie to become the Administrative Director of Employee Relations at the Medical College of Ohio (the "College"). On July 1, 2006, the College merged with the University, and Dixon was promoted to Associate Vice President for Human Resources for the Health

Sciences Campus. In July 2007, Dixon was promoted to interim Associate Vice President for Human Resources for both campuses, the position she held until she was terminated on May 8, 2008.

On April 4, 2008, Michael Miller, Editor-in-Chief of the *Toledo Free Press,* wrote an editorial titled "Gay rights and wrongs." In this piece, Miller implicitly compared the civil-rights movement with the gay-rights movement: "As a middle-aged, overweight white guy with graying facial hair, I am America's ruling demographic, so the gay rights struggle is something I experience secondhand, like my black friends' struggles and my wheelchair-bound friend's struggles." Miller then focused on a purported denial of healthcare benefits to same-sex couples at the University, explaining that "[w]hen [the College and the University] merged, [University] employees retained the domestic-partner benefits, but [College] employees were not offered them. So, people working for the same employer do not have access to the same benefits."

On April 18, 2008, Dixon responded to Miller with her op-ed column "Gay rights and wrongs: another perspective." Dixon addressed both points highlighted above, but did not identify her official position at the University. Dixon first rejected the comparison made by Miller between the gay-rights and civil-rights movements:

> As a Black woman who happens to be an alumnus of the University of Toledo's Graduate School, an employee and business owner, I take great umbrage at the notion that those choosing the homosexual lifestyle are "civil rights victims." Here's why. I cannot wake up tomorrow and not be a Black woman. I am genetically and biologically a Black woman and very pleased to be so as my Creator intended. Daily, thousands of homosexuals make a life decision to leave the gay lifestyle evidenced by the growing population of PFOX (Parents and Friends of Ex Gays) and Exodus International just to name a few. . . .

Additionally, Dixon addressed Miller's discussion of the healthcare benefits system at the University:

> The reference to the alleged benefits disparity at the University of Toledo was rather misleading. When the University of Toledo and former Medical University of Ohio merged, both entities had multiple contracts for different benefit plans at substantially different employee cost sharing levels. To suggest that homosexual employees on one campus are being denied benefits avoids the fact that ALL employees across the two campuses regardless of their sexual orientation, have different benefit plans. The university is working diligently to address this issue

in a reasonable and cost-efficient manner, for all employees, not just one segment.

On April 21, 2008, as a result of her op-ed column, Dixon received a letter placing her on paid administrative leave. On May 4, 2008, Jacobs wrote a guest column in the *Toledo Free Press* responding to Dixon's op-ed column. Jacobs stated that "[a]lthough I recognize it is common knowledge that Crystal Dixon is associate vice president for Human Resources at the University of Toledo, her comments do not accord with the values of the University of Toledo." Jacobs then explained the various programs instituted at the University aimed at expanding and supporting diversity on campus.

A hearing was held on May 5, 2008, at which Dixon read a prepared statement reiterating the beliefs stated in her op-ed column, expressing her view that she had been speaking as a private citizen, and accusing the University of treating her differently than other employees. Dixon also asserted that her personal views did not affect her performance as Associate Vice President of Human Resources:

> If the University is taking the Herculean leap to assume that my convictions affect my service to or decisions about those practicing homosexuality, please consider this: it is commonly believed/perceived that there are one, possibly two practicing homosexuals in the Human Resources Department. I hired both of them (one last year and one earlier this year)! I hired both of them with the perception that while they may be homosexual, more importantly they were competent, motivated and simply the best candidates for the jobs. One individual, I actually hired this year *after* observing a questionable exchange between he and his male roommate in the parking lot one day. . . .

On May 8, 2008, Dixon received a letter from Jacobs terminating her from the position of Associate Vice President for Human Resources for the following reasons:

> The public position you have taken in the Toledo Free Press is in direct contradiction to University policies and procedures as well as the Core Values of the Strategic Plan which is mission critical. Your position also calls into question your continued ability to lead a critical function within the Administration as personnel actions or decisions taken in your capacity as Associate Vice President for Human Resources could be challenged or placed at risk. The result is a loss of confidence in you as an administrator.

On December 1, 2008, Dixon filed suit in the U.S. District Court for the Northern District of Ohio against the University, Jacobs, and Logie. . . . On April 29, 2011, Dixon filed a motion for summary judgment, and the remaining defendants cross-moved for summary judgment in response. The district court granted the defendants' motion, and Dixon appealed. *Dixon v. University of Toledo,* 842 F.Supp.2d 1044 (N.D.Ohio 2012).

Dixon appeals the district court order granting summary judgment to the defendants on her First Amendment retaliation claim and her equal-protection claim. . . . Dixon argues that the district court erred in its First Amendment retaliation analysis, contending that the defendants "violated [her] right to freedom of speech by terminating her employment because she authored an opinion piece in a local newspaper in which she expressed her *personal* opinion and viewpoint on the issue of homosexuality and civil rights from the perspective of a Christian, African-American woman." Dixon further asserts that the district court misapprehended the equal-protection standard, arguing that "when government officials engage in discriminatory treatment based on the exercise of the fundamental right to freedom of speech they violate not only the First Amendment, but they also violate the equal protection guarantee of the Fourteenth Amendment."

First Amendment Retaliation

First Amendment retaliation claims are analyzed under a burden-shifting framework. A plaintiff must first make a prima facie case of retaliation, which comprises the following elements: "(1) he engaged in constitutionally protected speech or conduct; (2) an adverse action was taken against him that would deter a person of ordinary firmness from continuing to engage in that conduct; (3) there is a causal connection between elements one and two—that is, the adverse action was motivated at least in part by his protected conduct." *Scarbrough v. Morgan Cnty. Bd. of Educ.,* 470 F.3d 250, 255 (6th Cir.2006). If the employee establishes a prima facie case, the burden then shifts to the employer to demonstrate "by a preponderance of the evidence that the employment decision would have been the same absent the protected conduct." *Eckerman v. Tenn. Dep't of Safety,* 636 F.3d 202, 208 (6th Cir.2010).

Only the first element, whether the speech was protected, is at issue on appeal[1]. . . . In order to establish that her speech was protected, Dixon must first show that the speech touched on a matter of public concern. Dixon must then show that under the *Pickering* balancing test, her "free speech interests outweigh the efficiency interests of the government as employer." Finally, Dixon must demonstrate that the speech was not made pursuant to her official duties as Associate Vice President of Human Resources. . . .

---

[1]   Termination is an adverse employment action, and it is clear that Dixon was terminated because of her speech.

Because the parties do not dispute that Dixon spoke on a matter of public concern, we turn to whether Dixon satisfies the *Pickering* requirement. The defendants argue that Dixon's speech falls into the presumption set forth in *Rose v. Stephens,* 291 F.3d 917 (6th Cir.2002). If this presumption applies, then Dixon's speech is not protected as a matter of law. Alternatively, the defendants argue that under the traditional *Pickering* balancing test, the balance of interests weighs in favor of the defendants rather than Dixon. The district court addressed both issues, concluding that the presumption applied to Dixon and that "the balance of [Dixon's] interest in making a comment of public concern is clearly outweighed by the University's interest as her employer in carrying out its own objectives." *Dixon,* 842 F.Supp.2d at 1051, 1053.

The *Rose* presumption dictates that "where a confidential or policymaking public employee is discharged on the basis of speech related to his political or policy views, the *Pickering* balance favors the government as a matter of law." *Rose,* 291 F.3d at 921. Therefore, in order for the presumption to apply, Dixon must (1) hold a confidential or policymaking position, and (2) have spoken on a matter related to political or policy views. An application of this presumption "renders the fact-intensive inquiry normally required by *Pickering* unnecessary because under these circumstances it is appropriate to presume that the government's interest in efficiency will predominate." *Rose,* 291 F.3d at 923.

Although there is no clear line drawn between policymaking and non-policymaking positions, we have previously outlined the following four categories of individuals to whom the *Rose* presumption will always apply:

> **Category One:** positions specifically named in relevant federal, state, county, or municipal law to which discretionary authority with respect to the enforcement of that law or the carrying out of some other policy of political concern is granted;

> **Category Two:** positions to which a significant portion of the total discretionary authority available to category one position-holders has been delegated; or positions not named in law, possessing by virtue of the jurisdiction's pattern or practice the same quantum or type of discretionary authority commonly held by category one positions in other jurisdictions;

> **Category Three:** confidential advisors who spend a significant portion of their time on the job advising category one or category two position-holders on how to exercise their statutory or delegated policymaking authority or other confidential employees who control the lines of communications to category

one positions, category two positions or confidential advisors; and

Category Four: positions that are part of a group of positions filled by balancing out political party representation, or that are filled by balancing out selections made by different governmental agents or bodies.

Latham v. Office of Attorney Gen. of Ohio, 395 F.3d 261, 267 (6th Cir.2005). "In determining whether an employee falls into one of these categories, we must examine the inherent duties of the position, rather than the actual tasks undertaken by the employee." *Id.* "While the inherent duties of the position are not necessarily those that appear in the written job description and authorizing statute, such descriptions can be instructive." *Id.*

The district court determined that as Associate Vice President for Human Resources, Dixon "was vested with a significant portion of the statutory authority available, placing her within category two." *Dixon,* 842 F.Supp.2d at 1051. The district court reasoned that her delegated appointing authority, including the authority to hire and fire, was significant and discretionary. Dixon contends on appeal that the district court erred in reaching this conclusion because "[a]lthough [Dixon] had authority to make some hiring decisions . . . she had *no* discretion to make policy regarding hiring practices nor was she delegated *any* such authority, let alone a 'significant portion' of it. Moreover, she had *no* authority, delegated or otherwise, to make any other policy of political concern." Appellant Br. at 26 (emphasis in original).

In Resolution No. 07–10–10, effective October 1, 2007, the Board of Trustees of the University delegated appointing authority to the Associate Vice President for Human Resources. Further, the official job description for Associate Vice President for Human Resources, which Dixon verified as accurate in her deposition, listed the most important job duty as "Policy Development and Application." Specifically, this duty requires that the Associate Vice President "[p]rovide leadership in recommending, implementing and overseeing human resource policies and procedures that support the university's strategic direction; reflect fair and equitable practices; and that are a model for innovative regulatory compliant and contemporary practice." The job description further notes that the Associate Vice President directs employee relations and "represent[s] the University in relevant employee relations actions brought before the . . . Ohio Civil Rights Commission, Equal Employment Opportunity Commission, . . . and other federal and state regulatory agencies."

Additionally, Dixon's own testimony regarding her job responsibilities reflects significant discretionary authority. Dixon testified that she was responsible for answering grievances, issuing disciplinary and corrective action, serving on various task forces, supervising approximately forty employees, overseeing benefits administration, setting compensation, and making presentations at town-hall meetings.

This evidence establishes that Dixon was delegated appointing authority and was responsible for recommending, implementing, and overseeing policy. The district court was thus correct in determining that these responsibilities constituted a policymaking position, i.e., that Dixon, as Associate Vice President for Human Resources, was a category-two policymaker.

In addition to holding a policymaking position, Dixon must have spoken on a political or policy issue in order to be subject to the *Rose* presumption. In *Rose,* we reasoned that "[t]he additional restriction that this presumption applies only to cases where the employee speaks on political or policy issues ensures that the content of the employee's speech directly implicates the loyalty requirements of the position and thus will adversely affect a central aspect of the working relationship in all cases." 291 F.3d at 923. Dixon argues that her op-ed column expressed a matter of personal concern and "was not speech that relates to either [her] political affiliation or substantive policy." Appellant Br. at 26–27.

Dixon's argument, however, ignores critical policies developed in and promoted by the Human Resources Department at the University. Dixon's public statement implying that LGBT individuals should not be compared with and afforded the same protections as African-Americans directly contradicts several such substantive policies instituted by the University. For example, the University's Strategic Plan included pursuing a strategy that will "[r]ealize the strength and distinction to be derived from diversity in all its dimensions [and] recruit, retain, and celebrate a diverse university community." Additionally, the University enacted a Plan for Diversity that explicitly included sexual orientation. The University also included sexual orientation and gender identity and expression in its Equal Opportunity Policy and in its anti-harassment policy. Finally, as explained by Jacobs in his op-ed column, the University enacted the Spectrum Safe Places Program, which encourages "faculty, staff and graduate assistants and resident advisers to open their space as a Safe Place for Lesbian, Gay, Bisexual, Transgender, Queer, and Questioning . . . individuals."

Although Dixon correctly contends that she never explicitly stated that the University diversity policies should not extend to LGBT students and employees, by voicing her belief that members of the LGBT community do not possess an immutable characteristic in the way that she as an African-American woman does, the implication is clear: Dixon does not think LGBT students and employees of the University are entitled to civil-rights protections, even though the University, in part through the Human Resources Department, expressly provides them. In writing her op-ed column, Dixon not only spoke on policy issues, but also spoke on policy issues related directly to her position at the University.

In sum, the *Rose* presumption applies to Dixon because there is evidence establishing that she was a policymaker who engaged in speech on a policy issue related to her position. The government's interests thus outweigh Dixon's interests as a matter of law, and we affirm the district court's grant of summary judgment to the defendants on this basis. Because the *Rose* presumption is dispositive, it is unnecessary for us to consider the district court's *Pickering* [analysis]. * * *

Equal-Protection Claim

Dixon also alleges an equal-protection claim against the defendants, arguing on appeal that the defendants "punished Plaintiff because she expressed a 'less favored' viewpoint—one grounded in her strong Christian faith no less—in this very same forum in violation of the First Amendment (freedom of speech) *and* the Fourteenth Amendment (equal protection)." Appellant Br. at 34. The district court granted summary judgment to the defendants on this claim because Dixon "has not presented anyone who was 'similarly-situated' and engaged in similar conduct." *Dixon,* 842 F.Supp.2d at 1055.

"The Equal Protection Clause prohibits a state from denying to any person within its jurisdiction the equal protection of the laws." *Scarbrough,* 470 F.3d at 260. "The threshold element of an equal protection claim is disparate treatment; once disparate treatment is shown, the equal protection analysis to be applied is determined by the classification used by government decision-makers." *Id.* "Fundamentally, the Clause protects against invidious discrimination among similarly-situated individuals or implicating fundamental rights." *Id.* Although Dixon recites this standard in her argument, she has failed to produce sufficient evidence in support of her equal-protection claim. To begin, as discussed above, she has not shown that the defendants violated a fundamental right, as her speech was not protected. Moreover, Dixon has not shown that the individuals she argues were allowed to engage in public speech on the issue of LGBT rights and protections without penalty—Jacobs and Vice Provost Carol Bresnahan—are similarly situated.

Dixon's comparison with Jacobs is easily distinguishable. Jacobs, as President of the University, wrote an op-ed column detailing the University's stance on diversity, specifically as it relates to sexual orientation. Jacobs was speaking in his official capacity as the President of the University in order to explain the University's position on a policy matter. Dixon, on the other hand, wrote an op-ed column that was not commissioned by the University and that contradicted the very policies that she was charged with creating, promoting, and enforcing.

The comparison with Bresnahan, although intuitively more germane, fails because it is unsupported by sufficient evidence in the record. The evidence proffered by Dixon establishes that in December 2007, Bresnahan and her partner "became the first same-sex couple to file under the city's new domestic-partner registry." After she and her partner filed under the registry, Bresnahan was interviewed by the *Toledo Blade* and made the following statement regarding opposition of others to the registry: "It's their religious beliefs, and bigotry in the name of religion is still bigotry." Bresnahan was identified as Vice Provost of the University in the article, yet she was not terminated or disciplined as a result of this statement.

Importantly, however, the record is silent as to the responsibilities and authority of the vice-provost position at the University. "Inevitably, the degree to which others are viewed as similarly situated depends substantially on the facts and context of the case." *Loesel v. City of Frankenmuth,* 692 F.3d 452, 463 (6th Cir.2012). In this case, the critical inquiry centers on Dixon's role at the University. Therefore, in order to determine whether Bresnahan and Dixon are similarly situated, we must at the very least have before us a description of the duties inherent in Bresnahan's role at the University. Without such evidence, we cannot engage in an accurate comparison of the two individuals for the purposes of summary judgment in this case. Although Dixon has identified another administrator at the University who also spoke publicly on the issue of LGBT rights, Dixon has not shown that Bresnahan is similarly situated. We thus affirm the district court's grant of summary judgment in favor of the defendants on the equal-protection claim.

NOTES

1.   Notice that the government employers prevailed in both *Shahar* and *Dixon*. Does this suggest that public employees in positions of responsibility would do well to make sure that their public actions and statements as they relate to LGBT rights issues are consistent with their employers' views? If it was constitutionally permissible for the University of Toledo to terminate Dixon for publicly expressing her views on LGBT rights issues, does that mean that the Georgia Attorney General could constitutionally terminate Shahar for publicizing and speaking about her commitment ceremony?

2.   Should it have mattered in *Dixon* that the plaintiff was apparently speaking as a private citizen and did not claim to be representing the views of the University? Should it have mattered that she did not directly criticize her employer or any of its policies?

B. THE MILITARY

Few gay issues have received more attention in the past few years than that of lesbians, gay men, and bisexuals in the military. Following President Clinton's election in November of 1992, a national debate on the subject erupted. Clinton had promised during his campaign that he would eliminate the ban on military service by gay people. At the outset of his term, in January of 1993, Clinton ordered his Administration to study the issue and propose a plan of action by July. Throughout the spring and early summer of 1993, Congress held hearings on the subject. In mid-July, the Department of Defense issued new military regulations, which are commonly referred to as the "Don't Ask, Don't Tell" (DADT) policy. The policy was codified by Congress in a law enacted in late 1993 and put into effect with new implementing Defense Department regulations in early 1994. The statute remained in place for seventeen years until Congress repealed it in 2010.

The first Subsection below provides a history of the military's approach to homosexuality, as well as excerpts from the DADT Act of 1993. The second Subsection traces the constitutional challenges to the military's personnel policies on sexual orientation from the 1950s until 2010. Finally, the third Subsection covers the end of DADT.

1. Background Documents

U.S. MILITARY POLICY ON HOMOSEXUALITY AND SODOMY—1916–1993[*]

RAND Corporation Report to the Secretary of Defense

U.S. MILITARY POLICY ON HOMOSEXUALITY AND SODOMY

Since World War I, homosexuals have been restricted from serving in the Armed Forces of the United States through either personnel regulations or the application of the sodomy provisions of military law. Sodomy was defined as anal or oral sex between men or between a man and a woman. At the end of World War II, the legal definition was changed to include sexual relations between women as well.

Homosexuality and the Military, 1916 to 1940

Early attempts to regulate homosexual behaviors within the Armed Forces were sporadic and inchoate. The Articles of War of 1916 went into effect on 1 March 1917. As the first complete revision of military law in over 100 years, this new codification was the first legal document to address the incidence of sodomy within the military population. The first mention of sodomy in military law was in Article 93, which prohibited

---

[*] SEXUAL ORIENTATION AND U.S. MILITARY PERSONNEL POLICY: OPTIONS AND ASSESSMENT 3–10 (RAND Corporation, National Defense Research Institute ed., 1993).

assault with the intent to commit sodomy.[2] In their 1920 revision, the Articles of War included sodomy as a separate offense. This statute did not change until 1951.

Between the two World Wars, the military attempted to screen and exclude homosexuals from service by utilizing contemporary biological theories about the causes and manifestations of homosexuality. In 1921, for example, the Army's "stigmata of degeneration" included men who appeared overly feminine, with sloping shoulders, broad hips, and an absence of secondary sex characteristics, including facial and body hair. Also among the exclusion criteria was the degenerative characteristic of "sexual psychopathy," which included sexual relations between men.

During the interwar period the military discharged homosexuals administratively more frequently than they formally court-martialed them, despite the official stance that sodomists had to be court-martialed under the Articles of War. Individuals suspected of homosexual acts were released under a "Section VIII" discharge for unsuitability. While in theory these could be honorable discharges, in cases of psychopathic behavior, the discharge was normally less-than-honorable, or "blue."

World War II: 1941 to 1946

In an attempt to rationalize policy concerning homosexuals in the months preceding America's entry into World War II, the Army Judge Advocate General tried to assess how existing policy was being applied in the field. In the absence of aggravating factors, the Army removed most sodomists from service through administrative proceedings. Court-martial was indicated, however, in those cases where force was employed, when minors were involved, or when the sexual partner was incapable of consent due to intoxication or other impairing condition.

During World War II, a lively debate took place among military authorities concerning the policies and practices regulating homosexual activity and the exclusion of homosexuals in the Armed Forces. Within the Army alone, for example, there were twenty-four separate revisions of regulations concerning homosexuality between 1941 and 1945, compared with eleven revisions before the war and seventeen between the end of the war and the passage of the Uniform Code of Military Justice in 1950. This debate had several causes. First, there was widespread variance in the treatment of individual cases within the military. Second, military authorities seemed increasingly willing to consult with and accept the

---

[2]   The Manuals for Court–Martial, 1917, defined sodomy as anal penetration of a man or woman by a man; both parties involved were equally guilty of the offense. In these regulations, penetration of the mouth did not constitute sodomy. In the regulations that accompanied the revision of the Articles of War in 1920, however, The Manuals for Courts–Martial redefined sodomy as anal or oral copulation between men or between a man and a woman (Jeffrey S. Davis, "Military Policy Toward Homosexuals: Scientific, Historical, and Legal Perspectives." *Military Law Review* 131, 1991, p. 73).

recommendations of medical and psychiatric personnel with regard to homosexuals. The American Psychiatric Association's Military Mobilization Committee helped develop the procedures that would be used to evaluate the more than 18 million men who would be examined for induction during the course of the war. By the beginning of the war, Army and Navy Departments, along with Selective Service, had determined that overt homosexual behavior could be used to deny entry into the military.[5]

During World War II, the prewar practice of separating homosexuals from service through the use of the administrative discharge was continued and articulated as part of Army regulations. By the end of the war, military policy concerning homosexuality had undergone several important changes. First and most important, the "homosexual" had replaced the "sodomist" as the focal point of legal concern, although the criminal aspects of same-sex behaviors had been neither eliminated nor elucidated in any clear manner. People who engaged in same-sex behaviors could be separated from the service through their resignation or by administrative discharge. Even if no sexual activity had occurred, a growing body of policy supported the view that a homosexual personality could readily be identified, and that such persons were to be barred from military service at induction or separated from the service upon discovery.

The Cold War Era: 1946 to 1956

Immediately after the war, in 1946, the Army liberalized policies toward homosexual personnel by increasing the likelihood of their receiving an honorable discharge. Attitudes shifted soon afterward, however, and, in 1948, the provision for honorable discharge was deleted.[6] On October 11, 1949, the Department of Defense issued a memorandum that unified military policy toward homosexual behavior:

> Homosexual personnel, irrespective of sex, should not be permitted to serve in any branch of the Armed Services in any capacity, and prompt separation of known homosexuals from the Armed Forces be made mandatory.

The Eisenhower Administration, with the signing of Executive Order 10450 in 1953, codified "sexual perversion" as grounds for dismissal from federal jobs. By some estimates, dismissals from federal employment increased tenfold. In the military, the number of discharges for homosexuality remained about the same as it had been during World War II—roughly 2000 per year—but from the much smaller post-war force of

---

[5] Alan Bérubé, *Coming Out Under Fire: The History of Gay Men and Women in World War Two*, New York: The Free Press, 1990, pp. 10–18.

[6] Those men and women with good service records, however, were to be separated from the service with a general, rather than a dishonorable, discharge.

1.4 million. The rate of discharge in the military, therefore, was also approximately ten times greater than it had been during the war.

The Military and Homosexuality in the 1960s and 1970s

Within the military, the separation of homosexuals proceeded unchallenged throughout the late 1950s and early 1960s. DoD policy was revised in 1959, with the issuance of the first version of DoD Directive 1332.14 on the subject of Administrative Discharges. Section VII.I of that directive indicated that among the reasons for discharge for "unfitness" was "sexual perversion," including homosexual acts and sodomy. This remained the policy of the Department throughout the 1960s. . . .

The 1965 DoD directive revised the regulations surrounding the separation of homosexual personnel. Members facing a less-than-honorable discharge were allowed the chance to present their cases before administrative discharge boards and to be represented by counsel. By liberalizing the rights of service members, the 1965 separation directives marked a turning point in the legal history of homosexuals in the services. Before the 1965 directive, most service members accused of homosexuality cooperated without protest in order to protect others or to avoid more severe punishment.[8] Inconsistency in the standards, in the documentation required, and in administrative procedures, however, led to a review during the Carter Administration of the policy and procedures for discharge.[9]

The results of the review were reflected in the new edition of DoD Directive 1332.14, issued on January 16, 1981. In a memorandum accompanying the new directive, outgoing Deputy Secretary of Defense Graham Claytor, noting that his revision "contains no change in policy," explained that the enclosure on homosexuality had been completely revised. The purpose of the new enclosure was to make it clear that, based on an investigative finding that a person "engaged in, has attempted to engage in, or has solicited another to engage in a homosexual act," discharge was mandatory.

The revised enclosure in 1981 also for the first time stated that "Homosexuality is incompatible with military service" and provided the following explanation for the exclusion of homosexuals:

> The presence of such members [homosexuals] adversely affects the ability of the armed forces to maintain discipline, good order, and morale; to foster mutual trust and confidence among

---

[8] Colin J. Williams and Martin S. Weinberg, *Homosexuals in the Military: A Study of Less Than Honorable Discharge*, New York: Harper and Row, 1971, p. 102. The procedures of interrogation are outlined on pp. 100–114.

[9] The directive was issued in response to numerous court challenges, such as *Matlovich v. Secretary of the Air Force*, 591 F.2d 852, D.C. Cir. 1978, questioning why some open homosexuals were discharged while others were retained. The 1981 directive removed the military's discretion in deciding whether to retain an open homosexual, making such discharge mandatory.

servicemembers; to insure the integrity of the system of rank and command; to facilitate assignment and worldwide deployment of servicemembers who frequently must live and work under close conditions affording minimal privacy; to recruit and retain members of the armed forces; to maintain the public acceptability of military service; and to prevent breaches of security.

The revision also affected policy on discharges by making it clear that homosexuality alone did not require a *misconduct* discharge. In the absence of other actions (such as violence), the discharge could be under honorable conditions. As promulgated by Deputy Secretary Claytor, DoD Directive 1332.14 and its provisions concerning homosexuality remained the policy governing enlisted separations until January 1993.

1993 CONGRESSIONAL LAW
10 U.S.C.A. § 654 (2007)

§ 654. Policy concerning homosexuality in the armed forces

(a) Findings. Congress makes the following findings: * * *

(12) The worldwide deployment of United States military forces, the international responsibilities of the United States, and the potential for involvement of the armed forces in actual combat routinely make it necessary for members of the armed forces involuntarily to accept living conditions and working conditions that are often spartan, primitive, and characterized by forced intimacy with little or no privacy.

(13) The prohibition against homosexual conduct is a long-standing element of military law that continues to be necessary in the unique circumstances of military service.

(14) The armed forces must maintain personnel policies that exclude persons whose presence in the armed forces would create an unacceptable risk to the armed forces' high standards of morale, good order and discipline, and unit cohesion that are the essence of military capability.

(15) The presence in the armed forces of persons who demonstrate a propensity or intent to engage in homosexual acts would create an unacceptable risk to the high standards of morale, good order and discipline, and unit cohesion that are the essence of military capability.

(b) Policy. A member of the armed forces shall be separated from the armed forces under regulations prescribed by the Secretary of Defense if one or more of the following findings is made and approved in accordance with procedures set forth in such regulations:

(1) That the member has engaged in, attempted to engage in, or solicited another to engage in a homosexual act or acts unless there are further findings, made and approved in accordance with procedures set forth in such regulations, that the member has demonstrated that—

(A) such conduct is a departure from the member's usual and customary behavior;

(B) such conduct, under all the circumstances, is unlikely to recur;

(C) such conduct was not accomplished by use of force, coercion, or intimidation;

(D) under the particular circumstances of the case, the member's continued presence in the armed forces is consistent with the interests of the armed forces in proper discipline, good order, and morale; and

(E) the member does not have a propensity or intent to engage in homosexual acts.

(2) That the member has stated that he or she is a homosexual or bisexual, or words to that effect, unless there is a further finding, made and approved in accordance with procedures set forth in the regulations, that the member has demonstrated that he or she is not a person who engages in, attempts to engage in, has a propensity to engage in, or intends to engage in homosexual acts.

(3) That the member has married or attempted to marry a person known to be of the same biological sex. * * *

(f) Definitions. In this section:

(1) The term "homosexual" means a person, regardless of sex, who engages in, attempts to engage in, has a propensity to engage in, or intends to engage in homosexual acts, and includes the terms "gay" and "lesbian".

(2) The term "bisexual" means a person who engages in, attempts to engage in, has a propensity to engage in, or intends to engage in homosexual and heterosexual acts.

(3) The term "homosexual act" means:

(A) any bodily contact, actively undertaken or passively permitted, between members of the same sex for the purpose of satisfying sexual desires; and

(B) any bodily contact which a reasonable person would understand to demonstrate a propensity or intent to engage in an act described in subparagraph (A).

2.　Legal Challenges

Legal challenges to the military's sexual orientation personnel policy can be traced back to the 1950s and fall into several distinct historical periods. Early challenges were aimed at ensuring that discharges comported with basic notions of due process of law—such as notice and an opportunity to be heard—and generally did not question the constitutionality of the military's underlying approach.[20] In one of the earliest challenges to the constitutionality of the policy itself, the U.S. Court of Appeals for the Ninth Circuit held in 1980 that it did not violate substantive due process principles.[21]

That ruling was followed by the election of Ronald Reagan and the adoption of regulations in 1981 that clarified and tightened the exclusionary policy. Several decisions in the early 1980s rejected the argument that those regulations impinged on a right to privacy,[22] thus foreshadowing the Supreme Court's decision in *Bowers v. Hardwick*.[23]

Hardwick made it considerably more difficult for plaintiffs to argue that the right to privacy prohibited the government from making employment decisions based on sexual conduct. Accordingly, subsequent litigation challenging the military's policy focused on cases in which lesbians and gay men were discharged not for specific same-sex sexual conduct but solely on the basis of their sexual orientation. Such discharges were challenged under both the First Amendment and the Equal Protection Clause.

One of those cases was *Watkins v. United States Army*, in which a panel of the U.S. Court of Appeals for the Ninth Circuit first found the military regulations unconstitutional under the Equal Protection Clause, only to be vacated by the full circuit sitting en banc in a ruling that sided with Mr. Watkins, but only on estoppel grounds.[24] Several other post-

---

[20] *See, e.g., Clackum v. United States*, 148 Ct.Cl. 404, 296 F.2d 226 (Ct. Cl. 1960); *Matlovich v. Secretary of the Air Force*, 591 F.2d 852 (D.C. Cir. 1978).

[21] *Beller v. Middendorf*, 632 F.2d 788 (9th Cir. 1980), *cert. denied*, 452 U.S. 905, 101 S.Ct. 3030, 69 L.Ed.2d 405 (1981).

[22] *See, e.g., Rich v. Secretary of the Army*, 735 F.2d 1220 (10th Cir. 1984); *Dronenburg v. Zech*, 741 F.2d 1388 (D.C. Cir. 1984).

[23] 478 U.S. 186, 218–19 (1986).

[24] Watkins v. United States Army, 837 F.2d. 1428, amended by 847 F.2d 1329 (9th Cir. 1988), different results reached on rehearing, 875 F.2d 699 (9th Cir. 1989) (en banc), cert. denied, 498 U.S. 957, 111 S.Ct. 384, 112 L.Ed.2d 395 (1990).

Hardwick federal appellate court rejected the argument that the military's 1981 policy violated the Constitution.[25]

Like the 1981 regulations, the 1993 DADT policy was repeatedly challenged in court. Most of those efforts were unsuccessful. The following case is representative of federal appellate court opinions rejecting constitutional challenges brought against the DADT policy.

THOMASSON V. PERRY

United States Court of Appeals, Fourth Circuit, 1996
80 F.3d 915 (en banc), *cert. denied*, 519 U.S. 948, 117 S.Ct. 358, 136 L.Ed.2d 250 (1996)

WILKINSON, CHIEF JUDGE.

Paul G. Thomasson, the plaintiff in this case, rose to the rank of Lieutenant in his ten year Naval career. Thomasson's service record has been a commendable one. Thomasson consistently received the highest possible performance ratings, he was one of a few junior officers selected for a Joint Chiefs of Staff Internship, and his supervisors, including senior Naval officers, praised his work. Rear Admiral Lee F. Gunn, for example, stated in an evaluation that Thomasson was "a true 'front runner' who should be groomed for the most senior leadership in tomorrow's Navy."

In early March, 1994, soon after reading the Navy message implementing the DoD Directives, Thomasson wrote and presented a letter to four Admirals for whom he served. Noting in the letter that "the time has come when I can remain silent no longer," Thomasson stated "I am gay" and expressed strong disagreement with the military's policy. In accordance with that policy, the Navy initiated separation proceedings against him. In May, 1994, a three-member Board of Inquiry convened and conducted a two day hearing. At the hearing, the Navy conceded that Thomasson had an "enviable" service record ... [but], it argued, Thomasson's letter gave rise to a presumption that he had a propensity or intent to engage in homosexual acts which, if unrebutted, warranted separation.

For his part, Thomasson presented a copy of his service record, live and written testimony from co-workers who expressed admiration for his capabilities and professionalism, a statement recounting his career and his decision to write the letter announcing that he was gay, and expert testimony on both homosexuality and the meaning of the military's policy. But Thomasson did not, as the district court observed, tender evidence to rebut the presumption that arose from his declaration of homosexuality;

---

[25] See, e.g., *Ben–Shalom v. Marsh*, 881 F.2d 454 (7th Cir. 1989), cert. denied, 494 U.S. 1004, 110 S.Ct. 1296, 108 L.Ed.2d 473 (1990); *Woodward v. United States*, 871 F.2d 1068 (Fed. Cir. 1989), cert. denied, 494 U.S. 1003, 110 S.Ct. 1295, 108 L.Ed.2d 473 (1990); *Steffan v. Perry*, 41 F.3d 677 (D.C. Cir. 1994) (en banc).

that is, he presented no specific evidence on whether he engaged in or had a propensity or intent to engage in homosexual acts. In fact, Thomasson's statement averred that he would "not go further in degrading myself by disproving a charge about sexual conduct that no one has made." The Navy argued that this defense fell short of rebutting the presumption that arose from Thomasson's declaration of his homosexuality, and therefore that he should be honorably discharged.

The Board unanimously found that Thomasson's announcement of his homosexuality gave rise to a presumption of a propensity or intent to engage in homosexual acts and that this presumption had not been rebutted. Because he thus violated Navy policy, Thomasson "failed to demonstrate acceptable qualities of leadership required of an officer in his grade" and the Board recommended that Thomasson be honorably discharged. A three-member Board of Review unanimously upheld this finding, and the Chief of Navy Personnel signed Thomasson's discharge orders. He was scheduled to be separated in February, 1995.

Thomasson brought this action in February, 1995, seeking declaratory and injunctive relief to prevent his discharge. The district court preliminarily enjoined Thomasson's discharge pending resolution of his claims. Ultimately, however, the court granted summary judgment for the government. . . . A panel of this court heard argument in September, 1995, and the full court subsequently voted to hear the case en banc.

II.

[The court begins with a lengthy review of the history of President Clinton's and Congress's action in enacting the military law at issue.]

Thomasson requests that we simply set aside these lengthy labors of the legislative process and supplant with our own judicial judgment the product of a serious and prolonged debate on a subject of paramount national importance. This would, however, be a step of substantial gravity. The courts were not created to award by judicial decree what was not achievable by political consensus. Our power to resolve particular controversies carries with it an obligation to respect general solutions. To overturn those solutions in the absence of a clear constitutional mandate would transform the judiciary into an instrument of disenfranchisement for all who use the political process to register the democratic will. * * *

III.

* * * None of this means, of course, that the statute before us may escape constitutional scrutiny. Rather, it is part of the process of constitutional scrutiny to recognize when the Constitution itself requires special deference. In the area of military affairs, the constitutional chartering of popular control is powerfully clear and purposefully

redundant. Ultimately, "[t]he special status of the military has required, the Constitution has contemplated, Congress has created, and [the Supreme] Court has long recognized" that constitutional challenges to military personnel policies and decisions face heavy burdens. *Chappell v. Wallace*, 462 U.S. 296, 303–04, 103 S.Ct. 2362, 76 L.Ed.2d 586 (1983). It is with those burdens in mind that we address appellant's particular arguments.

IV.

We turn first to Thomasson's contention that the statute, on its face and as applied, contravenes the Fifth Amendment's guarantee of equal protection of the laws. . . .

A.

. . . The statutory classification here is not suspect, nor does it burden any fundamental right. Section 654(b) is aimed at service members who engage in or have a propensity to engage in homosexual acts. A class comprised of service members who engage in or have a propensity or intent to engage in such acts is not inherently suspect. *Steffan v. Perry*, 41 F.3d 677, 684 n. 3 (D.C. Cir. 1994) (en banc) (classification comprised of persons who engage in acts that the military can legitimately proscribe is not suspect). Similarly, there is no fundamental constitutional right on the part of a service member to engage in homosexual acts and there is a legitimate military interest in preventing the same. Heightened scrutiny of this statute would involve the judiciary in an inventive constitutional enterprise, and it would frustrate the elected branches of government in their efforts to deal with this question. Rational basis is accordingly the suitable standard of review.

B.

It is settled law that rational basis review "is not a license for courts to judge the wisdom, fairness, or logic of legislative choices." *F.C.C. v. Beach Communications, Inc.*, 508 U.S. 307, 313, 113 S.Ct. 2096, 124 L.Ed.2d 211 (1993). The question is simply whether the legislative classification is rationally related to a legitimate governmental interest. * * *

1.

Under these standards, the Act does not violate the equal protection guarantee. Instead, it reflects a legitimate legislative choice. Whether members of the judicial branch agree or disagree with that choice is irrelevant, for the Constitution envisions the rule of law, not the reign of judges. Congress, after months of discussion, concluded that those who engage in or have a propensity to engage in homosexual acts impair military readiness. The Act accordingly observes that the "long-standing" prohibition on homosexual conduct "continues to be necessary in the unique circumstances of military service," 10 U.S.C. § 654(a)(13), and that "[t]he presence in the armed forces of persons who demonstrate a propensity or intent to engage in homosexual acts would create an unacceptable risk to the high standards of morale, good order and discipline, and unit cohesion that are the essence of military capability," 10 U.S.C. § 654(a)(15).

These judgments reflect in turn Congress' view of military life, which can be, on a round-the-clock basis, "spartan, primitive, and characterized by forced intimacy with little or no privacy." 10 U.S.C. § 654(a)(12). Out of this forced intimacy are forged the bonds that create unit cohesion, which Congress found to be a "critical element[ ]" of combat readiness. 10 U.S.C. § 654(a)(7). In short, "to win wars, we create cohesive teams of warriors who will bond so tightly that they are prepared to go into battle and give their lives if necessary for the accomplishment of the mission and for the cohesion of the group. . . . We cannot allow anything to happen which would disrupt that feeling of cohesion within the force." Senate Hearings, at 708 (Statement of Chairman of the Joint Chiefs of Staff, General Colin L. Powell). Military leaders testified time and again how unit cohesion would be undermined: "[I]n my years of military service, I have experienced the fact that the introduction of an open homosexual into a small unit immediately polarizes that unit and destroys the very bonding that is so important for the unit's survival in time of war." S.Rep. No. 112, at 280 (Statement of General H. Norman Schwarzkopf).

It was legitimate, therefore, for Congress to conclude that sexual tensions and attractions could play havoc with a military unit's discipline and solidarity. It was appropriate for Congress to believe that a military force should be as free as possible of sexual attachments and pressures as it prepared to do battle. Any argument that Congress was misguided in this view is one of legislative policy, not constitutional law. Courts have held that military authorities may discharge those who engage in homosexual acts. Given that it is legitimate for Congress to proscribe homosexual acts, it is also legitimate for the government to seek to forestall these same dangers by trying to prevent the commission of such acts. The statements provision, by discharging those with a propensity or intent to engage in homosexual acts, operates in this preventive way. As the Senate Committee described the provision: "[i]t is appropriate for the armed forces to separate the individual from military service without waiting until the individual's propensity or intent . . . ripens into specific conduct prejudicial to good order and discipline." This goal is itself a valid one. No constitutional constraint prohibits the military from preventing acts that would threaten combat capability.

The conditions of military life, whether in barracks or aboard ship or in situations of collective peril, may throw service members into situations where sexual tensions are especially unwelcome. "Many soldiers experience a forced association 24 hours a day. They work together; they eat together; they share living space together; they train together; they shop for groceries together; they worship together. Same-gender sexual attraction in such a 'forced association' environment is something that civilians rarely experience and cannot fully understand." Senate Hearings, at 762 (Statement of General Gordon Sullivan). Section 654(b) thus accommodates the reasonable privacy concerns of heterosexual service members and reduces the sexual problems that may arise when some members of the unit have a propensity or intent to engage in homosexual acts and others do not. These same concerns for privacy and sexual tension explain the military's policy of providing service men and women with separate living quarters.

2.

. . . [T]he means chosen by Congress in the Act are rationally related to legitimate legislative ends. The presumption that declared homosexuals have a propensity or intent to engage in homosexual acts certainly has a rational factual basis. In fact, the presumption, which Thomasson was explicitly advised of, represents perhaps the most sensible inference raised by a declaration of one's sexual orientation. As the Senate Committee noted: "It would be irrational . . . to develop military personnel policies on the basis that all gays and lesbians will remain celibate. . . ."

Although Thomasson argues that some declared homosexuals have not engaged in or do not have a propensity or intent to engage in homosexual acts, "courts are compelled . . . to accept a legislature's generalizations even when there is an imperfect fit between means and ends." *Heller*, 113 S. Ct. at 2643. As a general matter, the legislature was certainly entitled to presume that a service member who declares that he is gay has a propensity to engage in homosexual acts. While some service members have rebutted that presumption before military boards of review, *see Richenberg v. Perry*, 909 F.Supp. 1303, 1313 (D. Neb. 1995); *Able v. United States*, 880 F.Supp. 968, 976 (D.N.Y. 1995), Thomasson did not demonstrate that he lacked a propensity to engage in homosexual acts. The general evidence offered at his discharge hearing had no bearing on this particular question.

Not only is the presumption rational, it is also permissible. Thomasson argues that it is illegitimate to separate him for a mere "propensity" to engage in acts. But in the civil context, the government can fashion general employment policies to prevent unsatisfactory conduct. In fact, the statements presumption is a reasonable means of allocating the burden of proof: It places the burden on the party with the most knowledge of the facts (here the military officer), and it frees the military from engaging in detective work. . . .

Finally, the statute is not, as Thomasson maintains, irrational due to any purported distinction between declared and undeclared homosexuals. The policy instead rationally initiates discharge proceedings when service members, by declaring their homosexuality, thereby provide affirmative evidence to military officials of their propensity or intent to engage in homosexual acts. Thomasson apparently argues that the failure of military authorities to inquire into all service members' propensity to engage in homosexual acts somehow renders the policy unconstitutionally imprecise. But the decision to stop questioning new recruits about their sexual orientation reflects an allocation of military resources and a balance of competing interests, one that does not undermine the basic constitutionality of the Act. Under rational basis review, a classification does not fail because it "is not made with mathematical nicety or because in practice it results in some inequality." *Dandridge v. Williams,* 397 U.S. 471, 485, 90 S.Ct. 1153, 25 L.Ed.2d 491 (1970). * * *

V.

Thomasson also argues that the statute, both on its face and as applied, violates the First Amendment. He was, he contends, separated from the service for doing nothing more than declaring he was gay. According to Thomasson, the statements provision of 10 U.S.C. § 654 thus operates to suppress speech on the basis of its content and viewpoint. It does so, he asserts, by making a specific category of speech—a statement declaring a service member's homosexuality—itself a basis for discharge. . . .

Thomasson, however, misinterprets the basic purpose of the policy. The statute does not target speech declaring homosexuality; rather, it targets homosexual acts and the propensity or intent to engage in homosexual acts, and permissibly uses the speech as evidence. The use of speech as evidence in this manner does not raise a constitutional issue— "the First Amendment does not prohibit the evidentiary use of speech to establish the elements of a crime," or, as is the case here, "to prove motive or intent." *Wisconsin v. Mitchell,* 508 U.S. 476, 489, 113 S.Ct. 2194, 124 L.Ed.2d 436 (1993). Discriminatory words often provide the basis for challenges to discriminatory acts under Title VII, for instance, *see Price Waterhouse v. Hopkins,* 490 U.S. 228, 251–52, 109 S.Ct. 1775, 104 L.Ed.2d 268 (1989) (plurality opinion), yet employers enjoy no First Amendment right to keep those words out of court. *See R.A.V. v. City of St. Paul,* 505 U.S. 377, 389, 112 S.Ct. 2538, 120 L.Ed.2d 305 (1992) (observing that "sexually derogatory 'fighting words,' among other words, may produce a violation of Title VII's general prohibition against sexual discrimination in employment practices").

There is no constitutional impediment, therefore, to the use of speech as relevant evidence of facts that may furnish a permissible basis for separation from military service. No First Amendment concern would arise, for instance, from the discharge of service members for declaring that they would refuse to follow orders, or that they were addicted to controlled substances. Such remarks provide evidence of activity that the military may validly proscribe. And, as we discussed above, the military may take measures to prevent the commission of sexual activity that it deems detrimental to its mission. . . .

Thomasson asserts, however, that this reasoning is not applicable to the new policy. He points to language in the DoD Directive stating that "sexual orientation is considered a personal and private matter" and "is not a bar to continued service." He infers from this language that speech disclosing one's homosexuality admits to nothing unlawful, and hence lacks any evidentiary value. According to Thomasson, the policy thus at bottom distinguishes declared homosexuals from undeclared homosexuals, penalizing only the former on the basis of their speech.

While imaginative, Thomasson's argument fails to alter our conclusion that the new policy is in fact directed at the propensity or intent of service members to engage in homosexual acts, and uses speech declaring homosexuality as evidence thereof. First, Thomasson's charge that such a declaration lacks any evidentiary value is patently erroneous. As we explained in rejecting Thomasson's equal protection challenge, a service member's statement that he is a homosexual has substantial evidentiary value regarding whether he has a propensity to engage in homosexual acts—"the military may reasonably assume that when a member states that he is a homosexual, that member means that he either engages or is likely to engage in homosexual conduct." *Steffan*, 41 F.3d at 686.

Second, the statutory provision does not at its core distinguish between declared and undeclared homosexuals, the central premise of Thomasson's First Amendment argument. Instead, it distinguishes service members who have a propensity or intent to engage in homosexual acts from other members, and uses a declaration of homosexuality as evidence. The statute's operation confirms as much. Service members who state that they are homosexual can avoid separation by rebutting the presumption that they have a propensity or intent to engage in homosexual acts. Although Thomasson chose not to come forward with evidence in this regard, other members subject to discharge under the statements provision have successfully demonstrated that they lack a propensity or intent to engage in homosexual acts. *See Richenberg*, 909 F.Supp. at 1313; *Able*, 880 F.Supp. at 976. Moreover, service members who have never spoken about their sexual orientation are still subject to separation if they are found to have engaged or attempted to engage in homosexual acts. In a similar vein, service members who have not publicly declared their homosexuality are nevertheless subject to discharge if they have made private statements to that effect, when those statements are brought to the attention of commanding officers and the evidence regarding any such private statement is credible. Again, the statute's essential concern is not with speech declaring homosexuality, as Thomasson alleges, but is instead with the propensity or intent to engage in acts which Congress has deemed detrimental to the military's mission.

Because the statute aims at this propensity, not at speech, it is not a viewpoint-based or content-based regulation. With respect to the former, the statute's treatment of a declaration of homosexuality is not based on a desire to suppress any viewpoint that the statement might convey. The declaration asserts a fact, one that the military uses as evidence of a propensity or intent to engage in homosexual acts. The military, however, allows service members to express views on issues that affect homosexuals. As the district court found, members are "free to affiliate with a group that opposes the policy, to make statements criticizing the policy, to attend demonstrations in favor of homosexual rights, to read homosexual newspapers, or engage in other such expressive activities."

The statute likewise does not discriminate on the basis of the content of speech. Whenever a provision prohibits certain acts, it necessarily chills speech that constitutes evidence of the acts. A regulation directed at acts thus inevitably restricts a certain type of speech; this policy is no exception. But effects of this variety do not establish a content-based restriction of speech. . . .

The military policy here is justified on a content-neutral, nonspeech basis: preventing the disruptions that homosexual activity among service members might have on military readiness. That the policy may hinge the commencement of administrative proceedings on a particular type of statement does not convert it into a content-based enactment. * * *

HALL, CIRCUIT JUDGE, dissenting (JUDGES ERVIN, MICHAEL and MOTZ join in this dissent):

I.

It is critical in this case to resist falling into discussion of generalities, as if each homosexual were a clone of some preening archetype. This case is about Lieutenant Paul Thomasson, and only him. The behavior of others is beside the point. Even without the challenged policy, some homosexuals would be unfit for military service, and some among them whose sexual misconduct were the root of their unfitness. The same, of course, can be said for heterosexuals. One need only to read the newspaper to know that the libidos of heterosexual American servicemen are not always restrained by military codes of conduct. But most are.

So, why was Lt. Paul Thomasson discharged?

It was not because of "conduct" in any ordinary sense of the word. To say his service record is "spotless" risks understatement; "sparkling" is a better choice. In his decade in the Navy, Lt. Thomasson rose through the ranks from ensign to full lieutenant. He has excelled in every task assigned him. In April 1991, he was chosen over numerous peers to be an intern to the Joint Chiefs of Staff at the Pentagon. He spent a year there, preparing briefs for Joint Chiefs Chairman Gen. Colin Powell and Secretary of Defense Richard Cheney, and he accompanied them to Congressional hearings on the military budget and force reductions. He was awarded the Joint Service Commendation Medal for "superlative performance" of that role, and, at the end of his internship, Gen. Powell thanked him in a personal letter for "contribut[ing] immeasurably" to the Joint Chiefs' success. Thomasson closed his career in the service of Rear Admiral Albert Konetzni, who, ironically, was in charge of implementing the policy on homosexuality at issue here; nevertheless, Admiral Konetzni recommended him for immediate promotion to Lieutenant Commander on the very day of his discharge.

The performance coin has no other side: the Navy does not complain that Thomasson ever rendered middling, let alone deficient, service. Moreover, the Navy has no proof that Thomasson has engaged in sodomy or broken any other conduct rule, high or petty. Conduct cannot be the cause of his discharge. Likewise, the discharge cannot be explained by Thomasson's homosexual status per se. Under the policy, homosexuals are expressly permitted to serve.

It is only because he has said that he is homosexual.

There is no difference between being and saying except that saying produces a reaction in others. The issue, then, is whether saying, and producing a reaction, is a ground for discharge that may constitutionally be applied to Lt. Thomasson. I believe that it is not.

II.

* * * There is a great deal of evidence that the statute was motivated by a desire to accommodate prejudice against homosexuals. In announcing the policy, the President stated that "those who oppose lifting the ban are clearly focused not on the conduct of individual gay service members, but on how nongay service members feel about gays in general and, in particular, those in the military service." Assistant Secretary of Defense Edwin Dorn testified that "much of the resistance to gays is grounded in fear and prejudice." Retired Admiral Thomas Moorer, former Chairman of the Joint Chiefs of Staff, served on an advisory committee during development of the new policy. He was quite blunt about his views: homosexuals engage in "a filthy, disease-ridden practice," are "inherently promiscuous," and have no place in the military. He stated that many other "military people" share his views. Finally, Lt. General John Otjen, who chaired the Military Working Group, stated that "there's a collective sense in the military . . . that homosexuality is wrong." Gen. Otjen believed that all members of the Military Working Group shared this "collective sense." Moreover, he conceded that, but for fear of and prejudice against homosexuals, the policy would be unnecessary. The evidence that prejudice against homosexuals is a purpose of "don't ask, don't tell" is therefore quite strong.

III.

A.

We are told, though, that tolerating this intolerance is essential to "unit cohesion." Even if accommodating the supposedly widespread disdain for gays were a permissible governmental purpose—and it is not—there is no evidence that the discharge of Lt. Thomasson will rationally further that purpose. Indeed, there is only speculation that the discharge of any homosexual would do so.

Dr. Lawrence J. Korb, Assistant Secretary of Defense under President Reagan, offered this critique of the "unit cohesion" rationale:

> There are at least three . . . major problems with the "unit cohesion" argument. First, it represents a severe and somewhat defeatist underestimation of the ability of today's servicemembers to keep their focus on professional military concerns; it also represents a uniquely curious (and, I believe, incorrect) admission that our soldiers and sailors could not effectively follow orders and do their jobs if we lifted the ban. Second, kowtowing to the prejudices of some by excluding others has never been an acceptable policy rationale, either in the military or in our society at large. And third, in the several units where acknowledged homosexuals are serving today (usually, by court order), there are no signs of unit disintegration or bad morale.

General Otjen, while a strong supporter of the "unit cohesion" hypothesis, admitted that it was based on the personal views of members of the Military Working Group rather than hard facts. The lack of real evidence is not for lack of investigating. In 1992, the General Accounting Office investigated similar organizations that permit open homosexuality in their ranks, and, the next year, the Secretary of Defense commissioned a study of analogous organizations and foreign militaries by the Defense Research Institute of the RAND Corporation. Both studies reported no serious problems resulting from the presence of open homosexuals.

In any event, we have in the record before us a real homosexual, a real unit, and hence a real test of the "unit cohesion" hypothesis.

Lieutenant Thomasson served for over fifteen months after admitting his homosexuality. His stellar job performance continued. There were in fact persons in his unit who disapproved of homosexuality, but they continued to do their duty and had no difficulty working with Lt. Thomasson. In fact, some were forced to question their preconceptions in light of Lt. Thomasson's example. Not a single sailor testified that he had suffered even mildly diminished morale.

B.

The actual experience in Thomasson's unit should not surprise us. The ability of the American soldier to put duty before prejudice has been tested before. "Unit cohesion" is a facile way for the ins to put a patina of rationality on their efforts to exclude the outs. The concept has therefore been a favorite of those who, through the years, have resisted the irresistible erosion of white male domination of the armed forces. Though the prejudices underlying such resistance have doubtless outlived the erosion, they have not manifested themselves in a loss of "unit cohesion."

Race is the obvious example. "Don't ask, don't tell" was formulated when the chairman of the joint chiefs of staff was a black man, a black man whose presence in the otherwise all-white inner circle of our military caused no apparent friction or decay in its morale, performance, or cohesion. Likewise, I am enough of a realist to know that there are racists serving in our armed forces, racists to whom Gen. Powell's high rank must have been distasteful. They did their duty anyway. * * *

C.

Another incongruity of the "unit cohesion" hypothesis behind "don't tell" is that it encourages lying in the interest of building and maintaining "bonds of trust" among the troops. A relationship built on deception is anything but a "bond of trust."

* * * The sad corollary of this "policy of pretense" is that moral courage like that displayed by Lt. Thomasson is punished.

IV.

The policy also operates in an unconstitutional manner. Its bedrock is a presumption that everyone will fail to comply with rules of conduct— a declared homosexual is bound to misbehave, and the members of his unit will doubtless allow private prejudice to override discipline. A presumption of misconduct from a person's status, or even from his private prejudices, does not comport with due process.

An analogy offered by Lt. Thomasson at oral argument makes the point well. The Supreme Court has upheld the constitutionality of the military's uniform regulations, notwithstanding that they bar the wearing of yarmulkes. *Goldman v. Weinberger*, 475 U.S. 503, 106 S.Ct.

1310, 89 L.Ed.2d 478 (1986). Now suppose a serviceman writes a letter to his superior stating, "I am an Orthodox Jew." Has he broken the uniform regulations? Of course not. Should he be disciplined or discharged on account of his presumed "propensity" to wear a yarmulke? Of course not. Should he be discharged because his status and accompanying presumed propensity are presumed to stir up anti-Semitism among the majority gentiles? Of course not. In America, we presume that individuals obey the rules until they prove otherwise. If persons do not obey rules with which they disagree, or are presumed to act upon every urge or desire whatever the legal consequences, then rules are a vain exercise indeed. . . .

V.

The intolerability of a presumption of misconduct from a status renders irrelevant the majority's unremarkable holding that the First Amendment does not bar the evidentiary use of an "admission." Of course it does not. But Thomasson did not "admit" anything that could justify his discharge. He said, "I am gay." Let us take that as admitted. . . . Thomasson has not "admitted" any homosexual conduct.

The rejoinder, of course, is that the statute and policy define speech as "conduct." This definition fails to withstand constitutional scrutiny, for two reasons. First, as I have already discussed, it impermissibly presumes that homosexuals are unable to obey rules of conduct. Second, it creates a classification among homosexuals based solely on speech. Because there is no reason even to "rationally speculate" that declared homosexuals are more likely to break the rules than undeclared—the opposite speculation seems far more accurate—this rule must be targeted at suppressing the speech itself.

Here we meet up with the First Amendment, but on much different ground than the majority tackles it. Suppressing speech is "grave[ ] and most delicate" stuff. The military has a broader power to control speech than a civilian government, *Brown v. Glines*, 444 U.S. 348 (1980), but even there the power is exceedingly narrow: speech may be suppressed only if it is likely to interfere with vital prerequisites to military effectiveness. The "vital prerequisite" here is, I suppose, the accommodation of the prejudices of heterosexual servicemen. I very much doubt that such accommodation—never a legitimate legislative end—can ever be a "vital prerequisite" to the military's mission. In any event, Lt. Thomasson has proved beyond any doubt that his speech had no deleterious impact at all, let alone to some "vital prerequisite" to military effectiveness. If anything, the expulsion of a fine officer in retaliation for his speech will ultimately prove worse for the Navy * * *

In the final analysis, the expression of Lt. Thomasson's thoughts, without more, is the cause of his "honorable" banishment from the Navy. "I think we must let his mind alone." *American Communications Ass'n v.*

Douds, 339 U.S. 382, 444, 70 S.Ct. 674, 94 L.Ed. 925 (1950) (Jackson, J., concurring and dissenting).

NOTES

1.   Several other federal appellate courts upheld the DADT policy in the years following *Thomasson. See, e.g., Cook v. Gates*, 528 F.3d 42 (1st Cir. 2008); *Able v. United States*, 155 F.3d 628 (2d Cir. 1998); *Richenberg v. Perry*, 97 F.3d 256 (8th Cir. 1996), *cert. denied*, 522 U.S. 807, 118 S.Ct. 45, 139 L.Ed.2d 12 (1997).

2.   The number of annual discharges under the DADT policy were as follows:

1994	617
1995	772
1996	870
1997	1007
1998	1163
1999	1046
2000	1241
2001	1273
2002	906
2003	787
2004	668
2005	742
2006	612
2007	627
2008	619
2009	275

Log Cabin Republicans v. United States, 2010 WL 3526272 (C.D. Cal. 2010) at *28.

3.   The *Log Cabin* court was one of two federal district courts that struck down the DADT Act in the fall of 2010. (The other was *Witt v. Department of the Air Force*, 739 F.Supp.2d 1308 (W.D.Wash. 2010), which is discussed in *supra* Chapter 2, Section F.2). In striking down the statute, the *Log Cabin* court explained that the military's insistence that the ban promoted military effectiveness was significantly undermined by the fact that discharges under the policy had fallen by more than half since the start of the Afghanistan and Iraq wars. As the court put it, "if the presence of a homosexual soldier in the Armed Forces were a threat to military readiness or unit cohesion, it surely follows that in times of war it would be more urgent, not less, to discharge him or her, and to do so with dispatch." *Log Cabin Republicans*, 2010 WL 3526272 at *35.

The court also concluded that the plaintiff showed the following at trial:

- by impeding the efforts to recruit and retain an all-volunteer military force, the Act contributes to critical troop shortages and thus harms rather than furthers the Government's interest in military readiness;

- by causing the discharge of otherwise qualified servicemembers with critical skills such as Arabic, Chinese, Farsi, and Korean language fluency; military intelligence; counterterrorism; weapons development; and medical training, the Act harms rather than furthers the Government's interest in military readiness;

- by contributing to the necessity for the Armed Forces to permit enlistment through increased use of the "moral waiver" policy and lower educational and physical fitness standards, the Act harms rather than furthers the Government's interest in military readiness;

- Defendants' actions in delaying investigations regarding and enforcement of the Act until after a servicemember returns from combat deployment show that the Policy is not necessary to further the Government's interest in military readiness or unit cohesion;

- by causing the discharge of well-trained and competent servicemembers who are well-respected by their superiors and subordinates, the Act has harmed rather than furthered unit cohesion and morale;

- the Act is not necessary to protect the privacy of servicemembers because military housing quarters already provide sufficient protection for this interest.

Id. at 36. The court then held that

[t]he Don't Ask, Don't Tell Act infringes the fundamental rights of United States servicemembers in many ways . . . [It] denies homosexuals serving in the Armed Forces the right to enjoy "intimate conduct" in their personal relationships. The Act denies them the right to speak about their loved ones while serving their country in uniform; . . . it discharges them for including information in a personal communication from which an unauthorized reader might discern their homosexuality. In order to justify the encroachment on these rights, Defendants [under *Witt v. Department of Air Force*, 527 F.3d 806 (9th Cir. 2008)] faced the burden at trial of showing the Don't Ask, Don't Tell Act was necessary to significantly further the Government's important interests in military readiness and unit cohesion. Defendants failed to meet that burden.

Id.

3. The End of "Don't Ask, Don't Tell"

The efforts to end the DADT policy were not limited to lawsuits. Many groups and individuals also tried for years to persuade Congress to repeal the DADT Act. Those efforts intensified after the 2008 elections, which not only resulted in the election of President Barack Obama (a strong critic of the military's exclusionary policy), but also handed both chambers of Congress to large Democratic majorities.

In the spring of 2010, the House of Representatives approved a Defense Authorization Act bill that included a repeal of DADT. Although the repeal's supporters believed that including the measure as part of the military's annual funding bill would make it more difficult for opponents to vote against it, Republican Senators during the fall of that year twice voted unanimously to block debate on the bill.

These defeats let repeal supporters in the House to change tactics by introducing a stand-alone bill calling for the end of DADT. That measure passed the House on December 15, 2010, by a vote of 250 to 175. Three days later, the Senate approved the bill by a vote of 65 to 31.

As Congress considered the ban's fate, senior military officials also expressed their views. Admiral Mike Mullen, the Chairman of the Joint Chiefs of Staff, told the Senate Armed Services Committee that "[n]o matter how I look at the issue, I cannot escape being troubled by the fact that we have in place a policy which forces young men and women to lie about who they are in order to defend their fellow citizens."[26] But General James Amos, commandant of the Marines Corps, expressed reservations about ending the policy, apparently reflecting the greater support for the ban in his branch of the Armed Services. Amos explained that "[t]here is nothing more intimate than young men and young women—and when you talk of infantry, we're talking [about] our young men—laying out, sleeping alongside of one another and sharing death, fear and loss of brothers. I don't know what the effect of [lifting the policy] will be on cohesion [and] combat effectiveness."[27]

Three weeks before Congress repealed the law, the Department of Defense issued a report on the findings of a working group named by the Secretary of Defense that spent nine months studying the implications of repealing the DADT policy. The working group solicited the views of hundreds of thousands of armed service members and conducted almost one hundred "information exchange meetings" with military personnel at dozens of military bases and installations around the world. The working group also received input from former and current lesbian and gay service

---

[26] Elisabeth Bumiller, *Top Defense Officials Seek to End "Don't Ask, Don't Tell,"* N.Y. TIMES, Feb. 2, 2010, at A1.

[27] *Marines Commandant Says Ending Ban on Gays is Risky,* N.Y. TIMES, Nov. 7, 2010, at A15.

members. The following is an excerpt from the report's executive summary.

REPORT OF THE COMPREHENSIVE REVIEW OF THE ISSUES ASSOCIATED WITH A REPEAL OF "DON'T ASK, DON'T TELL"*
Department of Defense

The results of the Service member survey reveal a widespread attitude among a solid majority of Service members that repeal of Don't Ask, Don't Tell will not have a negative impact on their ability to conduct their military mission . . . The survey was one of the largest in the history of the military. We heard from over 115,000 Service members, or 28% of those solicited.

The results of the survey are best represented by the answers to three questions:

- When asked about how having a Service member in their immediate unit who said he or she is gay would affect the unit's ability to "work together to get the job done," 70% of Service members predicted it would have a positive, mixed, or no effect.

- When asked "in your career, have you ever worked in a unit with a co-worker that you believed to be homosexual," 69% of Service members reported that they had.

- When asked about the actual experience of serving in a unit with a co-worker who they believed was gay or lesbian, 92% stated that the unit's "ability to work together" was "very good," "good," or "neither good nor poor."

Consistently, the survey results revealed a large group of around 50–55% of Service members who thought that repeal of Don't Ask, Don't Tell would have mixed or no effect; another 15–20% who said repeal would have a positive effect; and about 30% who said it would have a negative effect . . .

To be sure, these survey results reveal a significant minority—around 30% overall (and 40–60% in the Marine Corps and in various combat arms specialties)—who predicted in some form and to some degree negative views or concerns about the impact of a repeal of Don't Ask, Don't Tell. Any personnel policy change for which a group that size predicts negative consequences must be approached with caution.

---

* U.S. Department of Defense, *Report of the Comprehensive Review of the Issues Associated with a Repeal of "Don't Ask, Don't Tell"* (2010).

However, there are a number of other factors that still lead us to conclude that the risk of repeal to overall military effectiveness is low.

The reality is that there are gay men and lesbians already serving in today's U.S. military, and most Service members recognize this . . . [Sixty-nine percent] of the force recognizes that they have at some point served in a unit with a co-worker they believed to be gay or lesbian. Of those who have actually had this experience in their career, 92% stated that the unit's "ability to work together" was "very good," "good," or "neither good nor poor," while only 8% stated it was "poor" or "very poor." Anecdotally, we also heard a number of Service members tell us about a leader, co-worker, or fellow Service member they greatly liked, trusted, or admired, who they later learned was gay; and how once that person's sexual orientation was revealed to them, it made little or no difference to the relationship. Both the survey results and our own engagement of the force convinced us that when Service members had the actual experience of serving with someone they believe to be gay, in general unit performance was not affected negatively by this added dimension.

Yet, a frequent response among Service members at information exchange forums, when asked about the widespread recognition that gay men and lesbians are already in the military, were words to the effect of: "yes, but I don't know they are gay." Put another way, the concern with repeal among many is with "open" service.

In the course of our assessment, it became apparent to us that, aside from the moral and religious objections to homosexuality, much of the concern about "open" service is driven by misperceptions and stereotypes about what it would mean if gay Service members were allowed to be "open" about their sexual orientation. Repeatedly, we heard Service members express the view that "open" homosexuality would lead to widespread and overt displays of effeminacy among men, homosexual promiscuity, harassment and unwelcome advances within units, invasions of personal privacy, and an overall erosion of standards of conduct, unit cohesion, and morality. Based on our review, however, we conclude that these concerns about gay and lesbian Service members who are permitted to be "open" about their sexual orientation are exaggerated, and not consistent with the reported experiences of many Service members.

In today's civilian society, where there is no law that requires gay men and lesbians to conceal their sexual orientation in order to keep their job, most gay men and lesbians still tend to be discrete about their personal lives, and guarded about the people with whom they share information about their sexual orientation. We believe that, in the military environment, this would be true even more so. According to a survey conducted by RAND of a limited number of individuals who anonymously self-identified as gay and lesbian Service members, even if Don't Ask, Don't Tell were repealed, only 15% of gay and lesbian Service members would like to have their sexual orientation known to everyone in their unit. This conclusion is also consistent with what we heard from gay Service members in the course of this review . . .

If gay and lesbian Service members in today's U.S. military were permitted to make reference to their sexual orientation, while subject to the same standards of conduct as all other Service members, we assess that most would continue to be private and discreet about their personal lives. This discretion would occur for reasons having nothing to do with law, but everything to do with a desire to fit in, co-exist, and succeed in the military environment . . .

In communications with gay and lesbian current and former Service members, we repeatedly heard a patriotic desire to serve and defend the Nation, subject to the same rules as everyone else. In the words of one gay Service member, repeal would simply "take a knife out of my back. . . . You have no idea what it is like to have to serve in silence." Most said they did not desire special treatment, to use the military for social experimentation, or to advance a social agenda. Some of those separated under Don't Ask, Don't Tell would welcome the opportunity to rejoin the military if permitted. From them, we heard expressed many of the same values that we heard over and over again from Service members at large—love of country, honor, respect, integrity, and service over self. We simply cannot square the reality of these people with the perceptions about "open" service.

Given that we are in a time of war, the combat arms communities across all Services required special focus and analysis. Though the survey results demonstrate a solid majority of the overall U.S. military who predict mixed, positive or no effect in the event of repeal, these percentages are lower, and the percentage of those who predict negative effects are higher, in combat arms units. For example, . . . while the percentage of the overall U.S. military that predicts negative or very negative effects on their unit's ability to "work together to get the job done" is 30%, the percentage is 43% for the Marine Corps, 48% within Army combat arms units, and 58% within Marine combat arms units.

However, while a higher percentage of Service members in warfighting units predict negative effects of repeal, the percentage distinctions between warfighting units and the entire military are almost non-existent when asked about the actual experience of serving in a unit with someone believed to be gay. For example, when those in the overall military were asked about the experience of working with someone they believed to be gay or lesbian, 92% stated that their unit's "ability to work together," was "very good," "good" or "neither good nor poor." Meanwhile, in response to the same question, the percentage is 89% for those in Army combat arms units and 84% for those in Marine combat arms units—all very high percentages . . .

Our assessment here is also informed by the lessons of history in this country. Though there are fundamental differences between matters of race, gender, and sexual orientation, we believe the U.S. military's prior experiences with racial and gender integration are relevant. In the late 1940s and early 1950s, our military took on the racial integration of its ranks, before the country at large had done so. Our military then was many times larger than it is today, had just returned from World War II, and was in the midst of Cold War tensions and the Korean War. By our assessment, the resistance to change at that time was far more intense: surveys of the military revealed opposition to racial integration of the Services at levels as high as 80–90%. Some of our best-known and most-revered military leaders from the World War II-era voiced opposition to the integration of blacks into the military, making strikingly similar predictions of the negative impact on unit cohesion. But by 1953, 95% of all African-American soldiers were serving in racially integrated units, while public buses in Montgomery, Alabama and other cities were still racially segregated.

Today, the U.S. military is probably the most racially diverse and integrated institution in the country—one in which an African American rose through the ranks to become the senior-most military officer in the country 20 years before Barack Obama was elected President.

The story is similar when it came to the integration of women into the military. In 1948, women were limited to 2% of active duty personnel in each Service, with significant limitations on the roles they could perform. Currently, women make up 14% of the force, and are permitted to serve in 92% of the occupational specialties. Along the way to gender integration, many of our Nation's military leaders predicted dire consequences for unit cohesion and military effectiveness if women were allowed to serve in large numbers. As with racial integration, this experience has not always been smooth. But, the consensus is the same: the introduction and integration of women into the force has made our military stronger.

The general lesson we take from these transformational experiences in history is that in matters of personnel change within the military, predictions and surveys tend to overestimate negative consequences, and underestimate the U.S. military's ability to adapt and incorporate within its ranks the diversity that is reflective of American society at large.

Our conclusions are also informed by the experiences of our foreign allies. To be sure, there is no perfect comparator to the U.S. military, and the cultures and attitudes toward homosexuality vary greatly among nations of the world. However, in recent times a number of other countries have transitioned to policies that permit open military service by gay men and lesbians. These include the United Kingdom, Canada, Australia, Germany, Italy, and Israel.

Significantly, prior to change, surveys of the militaries in Canada and the U.K. indicated much higher levels of resistance than our own survey results—as high as 65% for some areas—but the actual implementation of change in those countries went much more smoothly than expected, with little or no disruption. * * *

Our most significant recommendations are as follows:

Leadership, Training, and Education. Successful implementation of repeal of Don't Ask, Don't Tell will depend upon strong leadership, a clear message, and proactive education . . .

Standards of Conduct. Throughout our engagement with the force, we heard many concerns expressed by Service members about possible inappropriate conduct that might take place in the event of repeal, including unprofessional relationships between Service members; public displays of affection; inappropriate dress and appearance; and acts of violence, harassment, and disrespect. Many of these concerns were about conduct that is already regulated in the military environment, regardless of the sexual orientation of the persons involved, or whether it involves persons of the same sex or the opposite sex. For instance, military standards of conduct—as reflected in the Uniform Code for Military Justice, Service regulations and policies, and unwritten Service customs and traditions—already prohibit fraternization and unprofessional relationships. They also address various forms of harassment and unprofessional behavior, prescribe appropriate dress and appearance, and provide guidelines on public displays of affection.

We believe that it is not necessary to establish an extensive set of new or revised standards of conduct in the event of repeal. Concerns for standards in the event of repeal can be adequately addressed through training and education about how already existing standards of conduct continue to apply to all Service members, regardless of sexual orientation, in a post-repeal environment. We do recommend, however, that the Department of Defense issue guidance that all standards of conduct apply uniformly, without regard to sexual orientation. We also recommend that the Department of Defense direct the Services to review their current standards to ensure that they are sexual-orientation neutral and that they provide adequate guidance to the extent each Service considers appropriate on unprofessional relationships, harassment, public displays of affection, and dress and appearance. Part of the education process should include a reminder to commanders about the tools they already have in hand to punish and remedy inappropriate conduct that may arise in a post-repeal environment . . .

Moral and Religious Concerns. In the course of our review, we heard a large number of Service members raise religious and moral objections to homosexuality or to serving alongside someone who is gay. Some feared repeal of Don't Ask, Don't Tell might limit their individual freedom of expression and free exercise of religion, or require them to change their personal beliefs about the morality of homosexuality. The views expressed to us in these terms cannot be downplayed or dismissed. Special attention should also be given to address the concerns of our community of 3,000 military chaplains. Some of the most intense and sharpest divergence of views about Don't Ask, Don't Tell exists among the chaplain corps. A large number of military chaplains (and their followers) believe that homosexuality is a sin and an abomination, and that they are required by God to condemn it as such.

However, the reality is that in today's U.S. military, people of sharply different moral values and religious convictions—including those who believe that abortion is murder and those who do not, and those who believe Jesus Christ is the Son of God and those who do not—and those who have no religious convictions at all, already co-exist, work, live, and fight together on a daily basis. The other reality is that policies regarding Service members' individual expression and free exercise of religion already exist, and we believe they are adequate. Service members will not be required to change their personal views and religious beliefs; they must, however, continue to respect and serve with others who hold different views and beliefs . . .

Privacy and Cohabitation. In the course of our review we heard from a very large number of Service members about their discomfort with sharing bathroom facilities or living quarters with those they know to be gay or lesbian. Some went so far to suggest that a repeal of Don't Ask, Don't Tell may even require separate bathroom and shower facilities for gay men and lesbians. We disagree, and recommend against separate facilities. Though many regard the very discussion of this topic as offensive, given the number of Service members who raised it, we are obliged to address it. The creation of a third and possibly fourth category of bathroom facilities and living quarters, whether at bases or forward deployed areas, would be a logistical nightmare, expensive, and impossible to administer. And, even if it could be achieved and administered, separate facilities would, in our view, stigmatize gay and lesbian Service members in a manner reminiscent of "separate but equal" facilities for blacks prior to the 1960s. Accordingly, we recommend that the Department of Defense expressly prohibit berthing or billeting assignments or the designation of bathroom facilities based on sexual orientation. At the same time, commanders would retain the authority they currently have to alter berthing or billeting assignments or accommodate privacy concerns on an individualized, case-by-case basis, in the interests of morale, good order and discipline, and consistent with performance of mission. It should also be recognized that commanders already have the tools—from counseling, to non-judicial punishment, to UCMJ prosecution—to deal with misbehavior in either living quarters or showers, whether the person who engages in the misconduct is gay or straight.

Most concerns we heard about showers and bathrooms were based on stereotype—that gay men and lesbians will behave as predators in these situations, or that permitting homosexual and heterosexual people of the same sex to shower together is tantamount to allowing men and women to shower together. However, common sense tells us that a situation in which people of different anatomy shower together is different from a situation in which people of the same anatomy but different sexual orientations shower together. The former is uncommon and unacceptable to almost everyone in this country; the latter is a situation most in the military have already experienced. Indeed, the survey results indicate 50% of Service members recognize they have already had the experience of sharing bathroom facilities with someone they believed to be gay. This is also a situation resembling what now exists in hundreds of thousands of college dorms, college and high school gyms, professional sports locker rooms, police and fire stations, and athletic clubs around the nation. And, as one gay former Service member told us, to fit in, co-exist, and conform to social norms, gay men have learned to avoid making heterosexuals feel uncomfortable or threatened in these situations . . .

Benefits. As part of this review, we considered appropriate changes, in the event of repeal, to benefits to be accorded to same-sex partners and families of gay Service members. This issue is itself large and complex, and implicates the ongoing national political and legal debate regarding same-sex relationships. Members of the U.S. military are eligible for and receive a wide array of benefits and support resources, both for themselves and their families. A reality is that, given current law, particularly the Defense of Marriage Act, there are a number of those benefits that cannot legally be extended to gay and lesbian Service members and their same-sex partners, even if they are lawfully married in a state that permits same-sex marriage. An example of this is the Basic Allowance for Housing at the "with-dependent rate." The "with-dependent" rate is limited by statute to Service members with "dependents." The word "dependent" is also defined by statute and is limited to the Service member's "spouse" or dependent parents, unmarried children, or certain others under the age of 23 who are placed in the legal custody of the Service member. And, the Defense of Marriage

Act limits the definition of the word "spouse" to mean "only a person of the opposite sex who is a husband or wife."

However, there are some benefits that are now, under current law and regulations, fully available to anyone of a Service member's choosing, including a same-sex partner, because they are "member-designated" benefits. Examples here are beneficiaries for Servicemembers' Group Life Insurance and Thrift Savings Plan, missing member notification, and hospital visitation access. If Don't Ask, Don't Tell is repealed, Service members may designate a same-sex partner for these benefits without then having to conceal the nature of the relationship from the military . . .

Re-accession. In the event of repeal, we recommend that Service members who have been previously separated under Don't Ask, Don't Tell be permitted to apply for reentry into the military, pursuant to the same criteria as others who seek reentry. The fact that their separation was for homosexual conduct would not be considered as part of the Service member's application for re-accession.

UCMJ. We support the pre-existing proposals to repeal Article 125 of the Uniform Code of Military Justice and remove private consensual sodomy between adults as a criminal offense. This change in law is warranted irrespective of whether Don't Ask, Don't Tell is repealed, to resolve any constitutional concerns about the provision in light of *Lawrence v. Texas* and *United States v. Marcum*. We also support revising offenses involving sexual conduct or inappropriate relationships to ensure sexual orientation neutral application, consistent with the recommendations of this report. For example, the offense of adultery defined in the Manual for Courts-Martial should be revised to apply equally to heterosexual and homosexual sex that is engaged in by or with a married person.

NOTES

1. In 2012, the Palm Center, a research institute that focuses on issues of gender, sexuality, and the military, issued a report on the effects of the repeal of DADT on military effectiveness. Aaron Belkin et al., *One Year Out: An Assessment of DADT Reapeal's Impact on Military Readiness* (Palm Center, 2012), available at http://www.palmcenter.org/files/One%20Year%20 Out_0.pdf. The report found that the repeal had no impact on the cohesion of units that included openly gay, lesbian, or bisexual members. It also had no impact on recruiting, which remained robust. As for retention, the authors, after noting that some critics had predicted that the repeal would lead to mass resignations, found only two resignations (both involving chaplains) that were linked to the change in policy. Finally, the report found no evidence of an increase in the harassment of gay, lesbian, and bisexual members and no decline in morale among the troops.

2.   After the Supreme Court struck down DOMA in *Windsor v. United States*, ___ U.S. ___, 133 S.Ct. 2675 (2013), the Department of Defense announced that it would make spousal and family benefits, including health care, housing, and survival benefits, available to all of its uniformed service members and civilian employees regardless of sexual orientation as long as the employees presented a marriage license that was "valid in the place of celebration." Emmarie Huetteman, *Gay Spouses of Members of Military Get Benefits*, N.Y. TIMES, Aug. 15, 2013, A15. The Department also announced that it would grant service members in same-sex relationships, who were stationed in jurisdictions that did not recognize same-sex marriages, leaves of absence to travel to states where they could marry. *Id.*

3.   In 1993, the same year that President Clinton announced the adoption of the DADT policy, the military "formally restricted women from artillery, armor, infantry, and other such ground-combat roles." Tanya L. Domi, *Women in Combat: Policy Catches up with Reality*, N. Y. TIMES, Feb. 8, 2013, A30. Two decades later, and only a year after the repeal of DADT, the military lifted its ban on women in combat. Elisabeth Bumiller and Thom Shanker, *Military Chiefs' Personal Encounters Influenced Lifting Women's Combat Ban*, N.Y. TIMES, Jan. 24, 2013, A16.

4.   The DADT policy addressed issues of sexual orientation and not of gender identity. As a result, the repeal of DADT left in place medical regulations that prohibit transgender individuals from serving in the military. Under these regulations, the armed services can discharge, or refuse to admit, individuals on the basis of a "[h]istory of major abnormalities or defects of the genitalia such as change of sex [or] hermaphroditism." Instruction 6130.03, §15(r), "Medical Standards for Appointment, Enlistment, or Induction in the Military Services," U.S. Department of Defense (2011). In addition, "[c]urrent or history of psychosexual conditions, including but not limited to transsexualism, exhibitionism, transvestism, voyeurism, and other paraphilias" constitute grounds for exclusion. *Id.* at § 29(r). *See also* "Standards of Medical Fitness," § 3–35, Army Regulation 40–501, U.S. Department of Defense (2011) ("A history of, or current manifestations of, personality disorders, disorders of impulse control not elsewhere classified, transvestism, voyeurism, other paraphilias, or factitious disorders, psychosexual conditions, transsexual, gender identity disorder to include major abnormalities or defects of the genitalia such as change of sex or a current attempt to change sex, hermaphroditism, pseudohermaphroditism, or pure gonadal dysgenesis or dysfunctional residuals from surgical correction of these conditions render an individual administratively unfit."). In contrast, the armed services of some nations, including Canada, the Czech Republic, Israel, Spain, and Thailand, permit transgender individuals to serve. *See* Tarynn M. Witten, "Gender Identity and the Military: Transgender, Transsexual, and Intersex-Identified Individuals in the U.S. Armed Forces" 5 (Palm Center, 2007), available at http://www.palmcenter.org/files/active/0/ TransMilitary2007.pdf.

5.   Legal challenges to the U.S. military's gender identity exclusionary regulations have not succeeded. *See, e.g., Leyland v. Orr*, 828 F.2d 584, 586 (9th Cir. 1987); *DeGroat v. Townsend*, 495 F.Supp.2d 845, 850 (S.D. Ohio 2007); *Davis v. Alexander*, 510 F.Supp. 900, 904 (D. Minn. 1981). The military has also successfully prosecuted biologically male service members for wearing female clothing under Article 134 of the Uniform Code of Military Justice, which prohibits "disorders and neglects to the prejudice of good order and discipline," as well as conduct that "bring[s] discredit upon the armed forces." 10 U.S.C. § 934 (2012). *See, e.g., United States v. Guerrero*, 33 M.J. 295 (Ct.Mil.App. 1991); *United States v. Davis*, 26 M.J. 445 (Ct.Mil.App. 1988).

6.   In 2013, army private Chelsea (formerly Bradley) Manning was sentenced under the Espionage Act to thirty-five years in a military prison for providing the WikiLeaks organization with classified materials. A few days later, Manning released a statement announcing that "as I transition into this next phase of my life, I want everyone to know the real me. I am Chelsea Manning. I am female." *Manning's Case Broadens Awareness of Transgender People*, WASH. POST, Sept. 1, 2013. Shortly thereafter, the military announced that it would not provide Manning with any medical treatment, including the hormone therapy she requested, while incarcerated at the military prison in Fort Leavenworth, Kansas. *Id.* The military's position on this issue is inconsistent with that of other federal agencies. For example, the federal Bureau of Prisons in 2011, as a result of a settlement following a lawsuit, agreed to provide transgender inmates with hormone therapy. *Private Manning's Transition*, N.Y. TIMES, Aug. 28, 2013, A26. In addition, the Department of Veterans Affairs in 2013 issued a policy directive announcing that it would provide "medically necessary care . . . to enrolled or otherwise eligible intersex and transgender Veterans, including hormonal therapy, mental health care, preoperative evaluation, and medically necessary post-operative and long-term care following sex reassignment surgery." *Providing Health Care for Transgender and Intersex Veterans*, Directive 2013–03, Department of Veterans Affairs (Feb. 8, 2013), p. 2. At the same time, the directive explained that the Department would not perform or fund sex reassignment surgeries. *Id.*

C. TEACHERS

The issue of lesbian, gay, and bisexual school teachers has given rise to a terrific amount of public concern, legislation, and litigation. These cases add an extra dimension to a standard government employee case— namely, the relationship of gay people to children. Two related issues arise in this context: first, the baseless concern that there is some connection between sexual orientation and child molestation; and second, a concern about whether gay people are good "role models" for children.

In 1977, the Washington Supreme Court upheld the firing of a gay school teacher. The court concluded that "the plaintiff's performance as a teacher was sufficiently impaired by his known homosexuality."[28] In particular, the court pointed to the fact that

> at least one student expressly objected to Gaylord teaching at the high school because of his homosexuality. Three fellow teachers testified against Gaylord remaining on the teaching staff, testifying it was objectionable to them both as teachers and parents. The vice-principal and the principal, as well as the retired superintendent of instruction, testified his presence on the faculty would create problems. . . . The testimony of the school teachers and administrative personnel constituted substantial evidence sufficient to support the findings as to the impairment of the teacher's efficiency.

> It is important to remember that Gaylord's homosexual conduct must be considered in the context of his position of teaching high school students. Such students could treat the retention of the high school teacher by the school board as indicating adult approval of his homosexuality. It would be unreasonable to assume as a matter of law a teacher's ability to perform as a teacher required to teach principles of morality is not impaired and creates no danger of encouraging expression of approval and of imitation. Likewise to say that school directors must wait for prior specific overt expression of homosexual conduct before they act to prevent harm from one who chooses to remain "erotically attracted to a notable degree towards persons of his own sex and is psychologically, if not actually disposed to engage in sexual activity prompted by this attraction" is to ask the school directors to take an unacceptable risk in discharging their fiduciary responsibility of managing the affairs of the school district.[29]

A year later, California State Senator John Briggs proposed a statewide initiative calling for the firing of any school employee who engaged in "advocating, soliciting, imposing, encouraging or promoting of private or public homosexual activity directed at, or likely to come to the attention of schoolchildren and/or other employees."[30] The Briggs Initiative was defeated at the polls by California voters.

A law very similar to the Briggs Initiative was proposed in several states around the country and enacted in Oklahoma. The statute, provided as follows:

---

[28] *Gaylord v. Tacoma Sch. Dist. No. 10*, 559 P.2d 1340, 1346, 88 Wash.2d 286, 297 (1977).

[29] *Id.* at 1346–47, 88 Wash.2d at 298.

[30] Karen M. Harbeck, *Gay and Lesbian Educators: Past History/Future Prospects, in* COMING OUT OF THE CLASSROOM CLOSET: GAY AND LESBIAN STUDENTS, TEACHERS, AND CURRICULA 121, 129 & n.25 (Karen M. Harbeck ed. 1992).

A. As used in this section:

1. "Public homosexual activity" means the commission of an act defined in Section 886 of Title 21 of the Oklahoma Statutes, if such act is:

a. committed with a person of the same sex, and

b. indiscreet and not practiced in private;

2. "Public homosexual conduct" means advocating, soliciting, imposing, encouraging or promoting public or private homosexual activity in a manner that creates a substantial risk that such conduct will come to the attention of school children or school employees; * * *

B. . . . [A] teacher, student teacher or a teachers' aide may be refused employment, or reemployment, dismissed, or suspended after a finding that the teacher or teachers' aide has:

1. Engaged in public homosexual conduct or activity; and

2. Has been rendered unfit, because of such conduct or activity, to hold a position as a teacher, student teacher or teachers' aide.

C. The following factors shall be considered in making the determination whether the teacher, student teacher or teachers' aide has been rendered unfit for his position:

1. The likelihood that the activity or conduct may adversely affect students or school employees;

2. The proximity in time or place the activity or conduct to the teacher's, student teacher's or teachers' aide's official duties;

3. Any extenuating or aggravating circumstances; and

4. Whether the conduct or activity is of a repeated or continuing nature which tends to encourage or dispose school children toward similar conduct or activity.[31]

The National Gay Task Force challenged the law in federal court. The U.S. Court of Appeals for the Tenth Circuit Court rejected the due process/privacy challenge to the statute because it "does not punish acts performed in private between adults."[32] It also rejected the equal protection challenge because "[s]urely a school may fire a teacher for engaging in an indiscreet public act of oral or anal intercourse."[33] The

---

[31] OKLA.STAT. tit. 70, § 6–103.15 (1981).

[32] *National Gay Task Force v. Board of Educ. of Oklahoma City*, 729 F.2d 1270, 1273 (10th Cir. 1984).

[33] *Id.*

court, however, upheld the free speech challenge to the statute by noting that

> [t]he First Amendment protects "advocacy" even of illegal conduct except when "advocacy" is "directed to inciting or producing imminent lawless action and is likely to incite or produce such action." *Brandenburg v. Ohio*, 395 U.S. 444, 447, 89 S.Ct. 1827, 23 L.Ed.2d 430 (1969). The First Amendment does not permit someone to be punished for advocating illegal conduct at some indefinite future time.

> "Encouraging" and "promoting," like "advocating," do not necessarily imply incitement to imminent action. A teacher who went before the Oklahoma legislature or appeared on television to urge the repeal of the Oklahoma anti-sodomy statute would be "advocating," "promoting," and "encouraging" homosexual sodomy and creating a substantial risk that his or her speech would come to the attention of school children or school employees if he or she said, "I think it is psychologically damaging for people with homosexual desires to suppress those desires. They should act on those desires and should be legally free to do so." Such statements, which are aimed at legal and social change, are at the core of First Amendment protections. . . . Finally, the deterrent effect of § 6–103.15 is both real and substantial. It applies to all teachers, substitute teachers, and teachers aides in Oklahoma. To protect their jobs they must restrict their expression. Thus, the § 6–103.15 proscription of advocating, encouraging, or promoting homosexual activity is unconstitutionally overbroad.

> We recognize that a state has interests in regulating the speech of teachers that differ from its interests in regulating the speech of the general citizenry. *Pickering v. Board of Education*, 391 U.S. 563, 568, 88 S.Ct. 1731, 20 L.Ed.2d 811 (1968). But a state's interests outweigh a teacher's interests only when the expression results in a material or substantial interference or disruption in the normal activities of the school. *See Tinker v. Des Moines Independent Community School District*, 393 U.S. 503, 89 S.Ct. 733, 21 L.Ed.2d 731 (1969). * * *

> . . . An adverse effect on students or other employees is the only factor among those listed in § 6–103.15 that is even related to a material and substantial disruption. And although a material and substantial disruption is an adverse effect, many adverse effects are not material and substantial disruptions. The statute does not require that the teacher's public utterance occur in the classroom. Any public statement that would come to the

attention of school children, their parents, or school employees that might lead someone to object to the teacher's social and political views would seem to justify a finding that the statement "may adversely affect" students or school employees.[34]

The U.S. Supreme Court granted certiorari and heard oral argument in the Oklahoma teachers case. However, Justice Powell fell ill, and the Court split 4–4 and thus, being evenly split, simply affirmed the Tenth Circuit's decision without an opinion of its own.[35]

SCHROEDER V. HAMILTON SCHOOL DISTRICT

United States Court of Appeals, Seventh Circuit, 2002
282 F.3d 946, *cert. denied*, 537 U.S. 974, 123 S.Ct. 435, 154 L.Ed.2d 330 (2002)

MANION, CIRCUIT JUDGE.

Tommy Schroeder, a school teacher, filed suit against his former employer, the Hamilton [Wisconsin] School District, the school district administrator, and several staff administrators (including school principals and human resource directors), pursuant to 42 U.S.C. § 1983, alleging that they violated his right to equal protection by failing to take reasonable measures to prevent students and parents, and occasionally fellow staff members, from harassing him about his homosexuality. The district court granted summary judgment for the defendants. Schroeder appeals, and we affirm.

In 1990, after teaching for approximately 15 years in the Hamilton School District, Tommy Schroeder began teaching sixth grade at Templeton Middle School in Hamilton, Wisconsin. Shortly after arriving at Templeton, Schroeder disclosed his homosexuality to a few of his fellow staff members and, during his second or third year at the school, made the same disclosure at a public meeting. This information eventually spread throughout the Templeton community, and, beginning with the 1993–94 school year, Schroeder began receiving unpleasant inquiries and crude, occasionally cruel, taunts from students regarding his homosexuality.

While there were isolated incidents involving parents, as well as some of Schroeder's colleagues, the bulk of the harassment he endured at Templeton came from students. Some of the incidents were rather mild. For example, a fifth-grade girl asked Schroeder to verify a rumor that he was gay. Another student authored a note complaining that she had been disciplined by "the gay man." Finally, other students were found discussing Schroeder's homosexuality during homeroom. Many of the reported student comments and actions, however, were far worse-

---

[34] *Id.* at 1274–75.

[35] *Board of Educ. of Oklahoma City v. National Gay Task Force*, 470 U.S. 903, 105 S.Ct. 1858, 84 L.Ed.2d 776 (1984).

accusations that he had AIDS; a student calling him a faggot and remarking "How sad there are any gays in the world"; another student physically confronted Schroeder after shouting obscenities at him; catcalls in the hallways that he was a "queer" or a "faggot"; obscenities shouted at him during bus duty; harassing phone calls with students chanting "faggot, faggot, faggot" and other calls where he was asked whether he was a "faggot"; and bathroom graffiti identifying Schroeder as a "faggot," and describing, in the most explicit and vulgar terms, the type of sexual acts they presumed he engaged in with other men. He reported this harassment on several occasions, and the defendants "consequenced" (i.e., a term of art in education circles for student discipline) the students identified with the offensive behavior. Much of the harassment, however, was anonymous, and therefore went unpunished. As Patty Polczynski, the associate principal at Templeton, told Schroeder, "[i]t makes it difficult to consequence if you don't know who it is to consequence."

Because of the widespread, anonymous nature of the harassment, Schroeder demanded that the defendants conduct "sensitivity training" to condemn discrimination against homosexuals (presumably for the students at Templeton—the chief perpetrators of the harassment). Instead, Polczynski, after several meetings with Schroeder, circulated a memorandum to teachers and other staff noting that students were continuing to use "inappropriate and offensive racial and/or gender-related words or phrases," and that "[i]f you observe or overhear students using inappropriate language or gestures, please consequence them as you feel appropriate. . . ." Schroeder considered this memorandum to be a milquetoast response to the harassment he was receiving, especially in comparison to a previous Polczynski memorandum warning staff that "derogatory racial comments and symbols" were "totally unacceptable" and "contrary to [the school's] efforts to create a positive academic environment for all students." When the harassment continued, Schroeder expressed his frustration to Polczynski, and she responded by telling him that "you can't stop middle school kids from saying things. Guess you'll just have to ignore it."

Finally, after several requests for a transfer, Schroeder was moved to Lannon Elementary School in the fall of 1996, where he taught first-and second-grade classes. After a year's respite, the taunts resumed. This time, however, they came primarily from adults, presumably the parents of students at Lannon. At the beginning of his second year at Lannon, an anonymous memo was circulated by a parent proclaiming, "Mr. Schroeder openly admitted at a district meeting that he was homosexual. Is that a good role model for our 5-, 6- and 7-year-old children?" Schroeder also claims that he began hearing that certain staff members and parents were calling him a pedophile and accusing him of sexually abusing small boys. One parent removed his child from Schroeder's class because of

Schroeder's homosexuality. Another parent's fear that Schroeder was a pedophile led defendant Richard Ladd, Lannon's principal, to raise the possibility of "proximity supervision" (i.e., meaning that Schroeder could not be alone with male students). The tires on Schroeder's car were slashed, and he began receiving anonymous, harassing phone calls at home (e.g. "Faggot, stay away from our kids" and "We just want you to know you . . . queer that when we pull out all our kids, you will have no job").

In February 1998, Schroeder, who has a protracted history of psychiatric problems, experienced a "mental breakdown." On February 11, 1998, Schroeder's last day at Lannon, Ladd approached him about complaints that he had received from some of his students' parents. Schroeder told Ladd that he did not want to talk about it, and that he was resigning. Later that day, Schroeder handed Ladd a letter of resignation. At this point, Ladd offered to arrange for a substitute teacher to take over Schroeder's class and requested that he take some time to think about whether he really wanted to resign. Schroeder declined the request, and never reported to work at Lannon again. Schroeder did, however, apply for medical leave and long-term disability insurance. Pursuant to terms of the collective bargaining agreement between the teacher's union and the Hamilton School District, the district terminated Schroeder's employment at the end of the 1998–99 school year.

Schroeder contends that the harassment he received from students, parents, and fellow teachers/staff members at Templeton and Lannon, coupled with the defendants' failure to properly address the problem, caused him to have a nervous breakdown that ultimately resulted in his termination. He therefore filed suit against the defendants, pursuant to 42 U.S.C. § 1983, alleging that they denied him equal protection of the law by failing to take effective steps to prevent him from being harassed on account of his sexual orientation. The parties filed cross motions for summary judgment, and the district court granted summary judgment in favor of the defendants. Schroeder appeals the decision. * * *

In order to establish an equal protection violation, Schroeder must show that the defendants: (1) treated him differently from others who were similarly situated, (2) intentionally treated him differently because of his membership in the class to which he belonged (i.e., homosexuals), and (3) because homosexuals do not enjoy any heightened protection under the Constitution, *see, e.g., Romer v. Evans*, 517 U.S. 620, 634–35, 116 S.Ct. 1620, 134 L.Ed.2d 855 (1996); *Bowers v. Hardwick*, 478 U.S. 186, 196, 106 S.Ct. 2841, 92 L.Ed.2d 140 (1986), that the discriminatory intent was not rationally related to a legitimate state interest. As we noted in *Nabozny v. Podlesny*,

The gravamen of equal protection lies not in the fact of deprivation of a right but in the invidious classification of persons aggrieved by the state's action. A plaintiff must demonstrate intentional or purposeful discrimination to show an equal protection violation. Discriminatory purpose, however, implies more than intent as volition or intent as awareness of consequences. It implies that a decisionmaker singled out a particular group for disparate treatment and selected his course of action at least in part for the purpose of causing its adverse effects on the identifiable group.

[92 F.3d 446, 453–54 (7th Cir. 1996)].

* * * The district court's decision to grant the defendants' motion for summary judgment of this claim must be sustained if the defendants demonstrate that they did not deny Schroeder equal protection on account of his sexual orientation, or that they had a "rational basis" for doing so. * * *

Schroeder would have us *infer* differential treatment because: (1) a memorandum circulated by the associate principal at Templeton, Patty Polczynski, failed to address and condemn the widespread use by students of "heterosexist" and "anti-gay" comments in the same manner that a previous memorandum had done with respect to racist comments and symbols, and (2) while the Hamilton School District held several district-wide staff/teacher training sessions and conducted annual student orientation programs to implement its policies prohibiting race and sex discrimination, the district never held similar training sessions or student programs to address sexual orientation discrimination.

These events do not, however, demonstrate that Schroeder was treated differently from his non-homosexual colleagues, or that he was discriminated against on the basis of his homosexuality. First, as Schroeder acknowledges, the initial memorandum circulated by Polczynski was generated in response to the pervasive use of racist comments and symbols by students in the Hamilton School District. Polczynski explained her motivation for circulating the memorandum in the memorandum itself, noting that the derogatory racial comments being made by students were "contrary to [the school's] efforts to create a positive academic environment for all students." Additionally, the district-wide staff/teacher training sessions on race discrimination, referred to in Schroeder's appellate briefs, were conducted in the early 1990's when the Hamilton School District began busing black students into its schools from the Milwaukee County Schools. The training sessions and student orientation programs were conducted to ensure that incoming minority students were not subjected to racial discrimination, and to increase sensitivity to racial issues among school district personnel and students. By citing these examples, Schroeder attempts to set up a false dichotomy—i.e., disparity of treatment/protection given to blacks/women as compared with homosexuals. In reality, these examples merely demonstrate the school district's priorities for use of time and resources in favor of its students. And this is certainly understandable given the limited resources of today's public schools.

Furthermore, in a school setting, the well-being of students, not teachers, must be the primary concern of school administrators. Not only are schools primarily for the benefit of students, but it is also clear that children between the ages 6 to 14 are much more vulnerable to intimidation and mockery than teachers with advanced degrees and 20 years of experience. Likewise, with this vulnerability in mind, school administrators must be particularly steadfast in addressing and preventing any form of verbal or physical harassment/abuse directed at their students. They must also be cautious about using police tactics to deal with nonviolent harassment of a teacher by students, even if that harassment is offensive and cruel. * * *

. . . Schroeder [also] contends that the defendants discriminated against him because the Hamilton School District had policies against race and sex discrimination, but did not have one against sexual orientation discrimination. While this is most certainly true, the lack of such a policy is not evidence that the defendants were deliberately indifferent to his complaints of harassment. As previously noted, unlike blacks and women, homosexuals are not entitled to any heightened protection under the Constitution. Therefore, discrimination against homosexuals, or for that matter the elderly, overweight, undersized, or disfigured, will only constitute a violation of equal protection if it lacks a rational basis. Here, there is no evidence that the defendants' decision not to implement a separate policy against sexual orientation discrimination was based on any animus toward Schroeder or homosexuals in general. Schroeder appears to suggest, however, that the only way the defendants could have prevented the harassment was by requiring all Hamilton School District personnel and students to attend mandatory training sessions on sexual orientation discrimination. There are several problems with this argument.

First of all, it is hardly reasonable to expect a school district to devote a substantial amount of resources to curb the harassment of one teacher, regardless of the basis for the harassment. In this case, other than Schroeder's situation, there is no evidence of any discrimination against homosexual teachers or students in the Hamilton School District. Instead, the evidence shows that one teacher, who happened to be a homosexual, was harassed because of his homosexuality. As emphasized in *Equal. Found. of Greater Cincinnati, Inc. v. City of Cincinnati*, 128 F.3d 289, 300–01 (6th Cir. 1997), another decision involving a claim of denial of equal protection on grounds of sexual orientation discrimination, it is not irrational to prioritize protective activities. It is in fact unavoidable, because of limitations of time and other resources. * * *

Schroeder's exhortation to adopt a specific policy requiring students to be sensitive to, or accepting of, homosexuals is especially problematic in an elementary or early middle school (i.e., sixth grade) setting. What would such a policy say? It is relatively simple to explain to a child that he or she should not criticize or offend someone because of the color of their skin, or because they are a boy or a girl. This is why blacks and women are described as "discrete and insular" groups. Unfortunately, there is no simple way of explaining to young students why it is wrong to mock homosexuals without discussing the underlying lifestyle or sexual behavior associated with such a designation.

Schools can, however, teach their students that it is wrong to mock anyone, for any reason. School administrators can, and should, insist that students behave in a courteous and respectful manner toward their teachers and other students. Such a policy would not require any discussion of homosexuality, or any other characteristic or behavior associated with it. If a student calls a teacher or another student a "faggot," he should be disciplined for violating the school's general civility code. If a student assaults a faculty member or another student because he is a homosexual, or because he is overweight, disfigured, undersized, or aged, he should be suspended or expelled for the assault. Students who are inconsiderate, disrespectful, mean, or even vicious, to others should be "consequenced" for what they do, not for the underlying motivation. Students must be taught—at school if not at home—that it is reprehensible to cruelly mock and malign staff members and other students—for any reason. In this case, the record is clear: When school administrators determined that a student harassed Schroeder by using derogatory terms like "faggot," the student was punished. By punishing these students, the defendants made it abundantly clear to the student population that such terms were totally unacceptable in polite society. This is all that was required of them.

That being said about disrespectful students, a short word about difficult parents. Schroeder asserts that he was also harassed by parents, and that the defendants did nothing about it because of his homosexuality. In support of his claim, Schroeder points to a memorandum, apparently circulated by a parent, which questions his qualifications to teach and criticizes the school's decision to blend first- and second-grade classes. The first paragraph alerted parents to the fact that Schroeder was an admitted homosexual, and presented the rhetorical question, "Is this a good role model for five-, six- and seven-year-old children?" Schroeder, like any well-qualified teacher, should be a good role model for his students, not because he is homosexual, but because he is an effective and enthusiastic teacher who wants them to learn. Regardless of the parental attitude displayed in the memorandum, however, school administrators have little or no power to "consequence" the parents of students. Obviously, if a child picks up foul language and prejudicial views from his parents at home, and then displays them at school, he should be disciplined. A student cannot, however, be disciplined for expressing a home-taught religious belief that homosexual acts are immoral. Administrators have to tiptoe on a narrow path when dealing with a child's unwarranted prejudices as opposed to his sincerely held religious beliefs. Beyond that, the Equal Protection Clause does not require a school district to do anything about parental unpleasantries unless they take place on school grounds. Schroeder could have reported the anonymous harassing phone calls he received, presumably from parents, to the telephone company, and any threats of physical violence to the police. School administrators have little authority to control parental activity. * * *

The question in this case is not whether the defendants did enough to engender a more positive attitude among its students and staff toward homosexuality. Rather, the only issue is whether the manner in which the defendants handled Schroeder's complaints of harassment denied him equal protection under the law. School administrators disciplined the identified students who misbehaved and degraded him, and made an effort to discover those not identified. There is no evidence that the defendants were deliberately indifferent to his situation, or that they did not make a sincere effort to deal with his complaints. On the contrary, the record shows that the school district was genuinely concerned about the treatment Schroeder experienced, and that it did what reasonably could be expected under the circumstances. The record is replete with memos, correspondence, and testimony indicating that various administrators and staff positively responded to his requests. In the absence of deliberate indifference, federal judges should not use rational basis review as a mechanism to impose their own social values on public school administrators who already have innumerable challenges to face.

Schroeder's breakdown and his current psychological condition are unfortunate. To the extent that student and parental harassment of him exacerbated his long history of personal and psychological problems, that is also unfortunate. There is, however, no evidence that the defendants denied him the equal protection of the law. * * * Affirmed.

[Concurring opinion by JUDGE POSNER is omitted.]

DIANE P. WOOD, CIRCUIT JUDGE, dissenting.

In this case, the majority holds that Tommy Schroeder, an openly homosexual teacher who was subjected to severe harassment on the job, cannot survive summary judgment on his claim under 42 U.S.C. § 1983 that defendant Hamilton School District and some of its administrators violated his rights under the Equal Protection Clause of the United States Constitution. In my view, this holding and the rationale both the majority and concurrence have used to reach it are inconsistent with the Supreme Court's recognition in *Romer v. Evans*, 517 U.S. 620, 116 S.Ct. 1620, 134 L.Ed.2d 855 (1996), that the Equal Protection Clause does protect homosexuals as a class and that this protection may not be denied simply because they may be an unpopular class in a given state or local community. I therefore respectfully dissent.

Because the majority has already furnished many of the relevant facts, I will simply highlight those that appear especially important to me. First, there is no dispute that Schroeder was a very good teacher; he taught successfully for the District for 22 years. Whatever psychiatric problems he may have had, it is clear that he had them under control until the unrelenting harassment to which he was subjected on the job caused him to have a full mental breakdown on February 11, 1998. He left the school that day a ruined man; when it became apparent that he could not return, the District terminated him. His vulnerability in no way excuses the District for the well-known reason that tortfeasors take their victims as they find them.

In addition, Schroeder complained repeatedly to the school officials about the vicious harassment the students and occasionally others directed toward him. His efforts to alert the District to the problem and to seek redress eliminate any possibility of the District's defeating this claim of intentional discrimination through a claim of lack of knowledge.

Despite the majority's efforts to find remedial efforts in the District's generalized responses, it is plain that the District never in any way took action specifically designed to inform the students that certain words or phrases that reflect negative views about homosexuals were out-of-bounds, nor in any other way did it tell them that harassment or discrimination based upon Schroeder's sexual orientation was impermissible. It would have been easy enough, as part of the philosophy of "courtesy to all" that the majority advocates, to prohibit certain words or actions without a detailed discussion of the sexual behavior of adults.

Finally, the District treated the class of homosexuals differently from the way it treated other classes, such as racial minorities or gender, as illustrated by the memorandum it circulated cautioning the community to avoid "offensive racial and/or gender related words or phrases." Even the majority concedes this when it admits that the District had no policy against discrimination based on sexual orientation and did have such policies against other forms of discrimination. Since even this court believes that discrimination based on sexual orientation is not "gender-related," *see, e.g., Spearman v. Ford Motor Co.*, 231 F.3d 1080, 1084 (7th

Cir. 2000), there is every reason to think that the students of the Hamilton School District might have thought the same thing and concluded that the District's policy did not require them to avoid what is often referred to as gay-bashing.

The majority acknowledges that the core violation of the Equal Protection Clause is "precisely the selective withdrawal of police protection from a disfavored group. . . ." It also appears to admit that homosexuals might constitute one such group. Indeed so, as the Supreme Court's *Romer* decision makes clear. And, it is worth noting that *Romer* is the only decision from the Supreme Court in recent years to address an equal protection argument where the class of homosexuals were singled out for uniquely disfavored treatment. *Bowers v. Hardwick*, 478 U.S. 186, 106 S.Ct. 2841, 92 L.Ed.2d 140 (1986), looked only at the question whether the enforcement of the Georgia sodomy statute violated the fundamental rights (meaning substantive due process rights) of homosexuals in that state. The Court was careful to note that it was not addressing any equal protection argument. . . . The later case of *Boy Scouts of America v. Dale*, 530 U.S. 640, 120 S.Ct. 2446, 147 L.Ed.2d 554 (2000), dealt with the question whether the First Amendment associational rights of the Boy Scouts organization would be infringed if it was compelled to accept a scout leader it did not want. In that case, the reason the Boy Scouts did not want respondent Dale in its organization was Dale's sexual orientation. But the Equal Protection Clause naturally enough did not figure in the Court's opinion because the Boy Scouts is a private organization and thus not a "state actor" for purposes of the Fourteenth Amendment. That leaves us with *Romer* as the governing Supreme Court decision on the applicability of the Equal Protection Clause to the class of homosexuals.

Nothing in *Romer* justifies a system under which a state or state actors like the District and its officials deliberately either omit altogether or give a diminished form of legal protection from verbal or physical assaults to individuals in certain disfavored classes. Yet both the majority opinion and the concurrence see no problem in the fact that the defendants intentionally responded less vigorously to the abuse that finally broke Schroeder than they themselves would have done for others. In fact, the majority seriously understates the case. *Never*, in the course of these events, did the administration ever attempt to dissuade either students, parents, or anyone else in the broader community of the school district, to refrain from discrimination or harassment based upon sexual orientation. Indeed, as I have already noted, school officials never even told the students that the words being used to describe Schroeder transgressed the general code of civility the majority is recommending to schools. Schroeder was just told to tough it out. The majority also makes the unwarranted factual finding that there was no evidence of hostility to

Schroeder. Even a glance at the facts the majority itself has set out shows that this is, at a minimum, a disputed point of fact.

Last, the majority seems to believe that a lack of resources might have prevented the District from responding to Schroeder's complaints. This cannot be a serious point. Adding two words, "sexual orientation," to the memorandum that was circulated could hardly have added a second to the secretarial time involved, nor could it have added appreciably to the amount of toner consumed by the photocopying machine. This case is nothing like *Equality Foundation of Greater Cincinnati, Inc. v. City of Cincinnati*, 128 F.3d 289 (6th Cir. 1997). . . . *Equality Foundation* was a case in which the court upheld the city's refusal to include homosexuals in a specially protected class, whereas here the only thing Schroeder wants is the *same* treatment that everyone else is receiving—that is, the kind of treatment to which the Constitution entitles him, according to *Romer v. Evans.* The glaring absence of the words "sexual orientation" in the memorandum, coming on the heels of the offensive incidents and Schroeder's complaint about exactly that kind of harassment, implies official tolerance, if not endorsement, of the behavior in which the students and others had been engaging. As I believe the majority acknowledges, the mere fact that members of some religious groups think that homosexuality is immoral also in no way excuses a public school's tolerance of harassing *conduct* based on sexual preference. Some religions profess beliefs that are incompatible with the individual guarantees found in the Bill of Rights, as we have seen to our sorrow in the recent history of the Taliban group in Afghanistan, whose views about the role of women in society could never be adopted by a public body here. In this country, nondiscriminatory secular norms of conduct ordinarily prevail even if they conflict with particular religious beliefs or practices.

I do not disagree that each case of harassment or discrimination must be evaluated on its own facts. Nor do I quarrel with the proposition that proper allocation of investigative resources may require devoting less time and effort to some complaints than to others. That decision, however, must be made on a case-by-case basis. Systematically to put cases involving harassment based on homosexuality (or any other recognized classification) below the threshold for any action at all amounts to the kind of differential unfavorable treatment that the Equal Protection Clause reaches. I had thought that *Nabozny v. Podlesny*, 92 F.3d 446 (7th Cir. 1996), . . . settled the point that sexual orientation discrimination could not be treated in such a cavalier fashion.

Schroeder has shown that he suffered harassment so severe that he experienced a total mental breakdown; he has shown that a reasonable trier of fact could find that the school district officials acted intentionally when they failed to respond to his complaints; and he has shown that the trier of fact could also infer that his unfavorable treatment occurred because of his homosexuality. This is more than enough, in my view, to allow him to proceed to trial in his case against the District. I would Reverse the district court's judgment and Remand for that trial.

NOTES

1.   In *Rowland v. Mad River Local School District*, the school district did not renew plaintiff's contract to continue her work as a high school guidance counselor after she informed co-workers that she was bisexual. The plaintiff sued and a jury awarded her damages, finding a violation of her constitutional rights under the First Amendment and the Fourteenth Amendment's Equal Protection Clause. The U.S. Court of Appeals for the Sixth Circuit reversed, 730 F.2d 444 (6th Cir. 1984), rewriting the facts of the case to find that the plaintiff was actually dismissed for violating the confidentiality of her students. The court asserted that the breach of confidence rationale in no way related to plaintiff's sexual orientation and, thus, the equal protection and free speech issues were not addressed. Although certiorari was denied by the U.S. Supreme Court, Justice Brennan wrote a powerful dissenting opinion. 470 U.S. 1009–18, 105 S.Ct. 1373–79, 84 L.Ed.2d 392–98 (1985) (Brennan, J., dissenting from the denial of certiorari). His dissent is the first explication by a Supreme Court Justice of why classifications based on sexual orientation are suspect and should be carefully scrutinized by the courts.

2.   In *Collins v. Faith School District #46–2*, 574 N.W.2d 889, 1998 S.D. 17 (1998), a school board fired a teacher for discussing male homosexual sexual activities with his fourth grade class in the context of a sexual education program. The South Dakota Supreme Court overturned the board's decision. The court held that the board's decision that the teacher was "incompetent" on the basis of this one class was irrational in light of his otherwise meritorious 29-year teaching record. *See also Glover v. Williamsburg Local Sch. Dist. Bd. of Educ.*, 20 F. Supp. 2d 1160 (S.D. Ohio 1998) (holding that non-renewal of teaching contract because of sexual orientation violates Equal Protection Clause).

3.   In *Lovell v. Comsewogue School District*, 214 F. Supp. 2d 319 (E.D.N.Y. 2002), a lesbian teacher alleged a violation of her constitutional rights to equal protection when the school refused to discipline students who were harassing her because of her sexual orientation. As in *Schroeder*, the teacher argued that the school took harassment on the basis of sexual orientation less seriously than harassment on other grounds, such as race. She alleged, for example "that when a black teacher had the word 'nigger' written on her blackboard, the school called in the Police Bias Unit and the School District held numerous faculty meetings concerning the incident. Similarly, when a student used the same racial epithet against another student, the offending student was suspended. On the other hand, when students harassed [her] due to her sexual orientation, including calling her a 'dyke,' no action was taken." *Id.* at 322. The court denied the defendant's

motion to dismiss by concluding that "the use of disparaging remarks based on sexual orientation is sufficiently similar to the use of racial epithets [and] that [the plaintiff] was treated differently than other similarly situated teachers, which is sufficient to support a [*sic*] equal protection claim at this stage of the litigation." *Id.* at 322–23.

D. EMPLOYMENT BENEFITS

GLOSSIP V. MISSOURI DEPARTMENT OF TRANSPORTATION
Missouri Supreme Court, 2013
411 S.W.3d 796

PER CURIAM

* * * On December 25, 2009, Corporal Dennis Engelhard, a nine-year veteran of the Missouri State Highway Patrol, was killed in the line of duty. At the time of his death, Glossip was Engelhard's same-sex domestic partner. Engelhard had no children.

Following Engelhard's death, Glossip applied to the Missouri Department of Transportation and Highway Patrol Employees' Retirement System ("MPERS") for survivor benefits under section 104.140.3, RSMo Supp. 2002, which provides survivor benefits to the surviving spouse of a highway patrol employee who is killed in the line of duty. The application for survivor benefits asked Glossip to submit a copy of a valid driver's license, a death certificate, and a marriage license. Glossip submitted his driver's license, Engelhard's death certificate, and an affidavit describing his relationship with Engelhard. Glossip's affidavit acknowledged that he and Engelhard were never married, but stated that they had cohabitated in a same-sex relationship since 1995. He further stated that they "held [themselves] out to [their] families and [their] community as a couple in a committed, marital relationship" and "would have entered into a civil marriage if it were legal to do so in Missouri."

MPERS denied Glossip's application for survivor benefits. The denial letter stated that the denial was "based upon the lack of a valid marriage certificate and based upon Sections 104.012 and 451.022." Section 104.012, RSMo Supp. 2001, provides that "for the purposes of public retirement systems administered pursuant to this chapter, any reference to the term 'spouse' only recognizes marriage between a man and a woman." Section 451.022, RSMo Supp. 2001, provides in relevant part that "[i]t is the public policy of this state to recognize marriage only between a man and a woman." Glossip appealed the denial to MPERS's Board of Trustees, but the appeal was also denied.

Glossip subsequently filed a petition requesting declaratory and injunctive relief in the circuit court. He argued that the survivor benefits statute and section 104.012 violate the Missouri Constitution's equal protection clause, MO. CONST. art. I, sec. 2, by excluding him from survivor benefits because of his sexual orientation. . . . Glossip does not challenge the Missouri Constitution's ban on same-sex marriage, MO. CONST. art. I, sec. 33, or its statutory counterpart, section 451.022.

MPERS moved to dismiss Glossip's amended petition on the ground that it failed to state a claim for which relief could be granted, and Glossip moved for summary judgment. The trial court granted MPERS's motion to dismiss, dismissed Glossip's motion for summary judgment as moot, and dismissed his amended petition with prejudice. Glossip timely appealed. . . .

Glossip contends that section 104.140.3, the survivor benefits statute, and section 104.012 violate the Missouri Constitution's equal protection clause in that they discriminate on the basis of sexual orientation and are not sufficiently related to an adequate government purpose to survive the appropriate level of equal protection scrutiny. Significantly, he does not challenge Missouri's constitutional and statutory provisions banning same-sex marriage. Instead, Glossip argues that the survivor benefits statute and section 104.012 unconstitutionally exclude him from eligibility for benefits.

Statutes are presumed constitutional. This Court will construe a statute in favor of its constitutional validity, and a statute will not be invalidated on constitutional grounds unless it clearly and undoubtedly violates a constitutional provision. The party challenging a statute's validity bears the burden of proving the statute clearly and undoubtedly violates the constitution.

The equal protection clause of the Missouri Constitution provides "that all persons are created equal and are entitled to equal rights and opportunity under the law." MO. CONST. art. I, sec. 2. Determining whether a statute violates equal protection involves a two-part analysis. First, the Court determines whether the statute contains a classification that "operates to the disadvantage of some suspect class or impinges upon a fundamental right explicitly or implicitly protected by the Constitution." *In re Marriage of Kohring,* 999 S.W.2d 228, 231–32 (Mo. banc 1999). If so, the Court will apply strict scrutiny, and the statute will be invalid unless it serves compelling state interests and is narrowly tailored to meet those interests. If the statute does not disadvantage a suspect class or impair a fundamental right, in most cases the Court will apply rational basis scrutiny, and the statute will be valid as long as it bears a reasonable relationship to a legitimate state purpose. In some circumstances, such as in cases involving gender discrimination, the United States Supreme Court has also recognized and applied an intermediate level of scrutiny. *See United States v. Virginia,* 518 U.S. 515, 533 (1996). In such cases, the state has the burden of demonstrating that the statute serves important government interests and is substantially related to achieving those interests.

The Survivor Benefits Statute Does Not Discriminate on the Basis of Sexual Orientation

Glossip argues that the survivor benefits statute violates the Missouri Constitution's equal protection clause because it discriminates against him on the basis of sexual orientation. Glossip's claim, however, fails at the threshold inquiry because the survivor benefits statute does not discriminate on the basis of sexual orientation. Instead, it draws a distinction on the basis of marital status.

The survivor benefits statute creates a death benefit on behalf of a highway patrol employee who dies in the line of duty in favor of the employee's surviving spouse to whom the employee was married at the time of death. The word "spouse" is defined as "joined in wedlock" or "married." WEBSTER'S THIRD NEW INTERNATIONAL DICTIONARY 2208 (1993). As such, the statute imposes a threshold requirement for a prospective beneficiary: the person must have been married to the deceased employee at the time of the latter's death. If a prospective beneficiary fails to satisfy this condition, no benefit is available.

Glossip is not eligible for survivor benefits because he failed to satisfy the threshold spousal requirement. Under the plain language of the survivor benefits statute, to be entitled to the survivor benefit, a person must have been married to the deceased employee and survived him. Because Glossip was not married to Engelhard at the time of his death, he is not eligible for survivor benefits. . . . The question, then, is whether the state may constitutionally condition the receipt of benefits on marital status.

The dissent is incorrect in suggesting that this Court must decide whether the state may condition the receipt of benefits on marital status so long as that classification remains burdened by the ban on same-sex marriage. The dissent's concern with the survivor benefits statute is not the spousal requirement as such but rather the legal context, namely the burdens imposed on the spousal requirement by the same-sex marriage ban. It would have the Court reach the issue whether conditioning the receipt of benefits on marital status is in fact sexual orientation discrimination and must be stricken on that basis. But this ignores the fact that Glossip specifically disclaimed any challenge to the ban on same-sex marriage, a fact that sets this case apart from the landmark civil rights cases cited by the dissent. Glossip was certainly free to make this choice, but it is fatal to his claim. This Court rejects the notion that the unchallenged constitutional and statutory provisions banning same-sex marriage nevertheless transform the survivor benefits statute's spousal requirement into sexual orientation discrimination.

The Survivor Benefits Statute Is Subject to Rational Basis Scrutiny

In an equal protection case, this Court's first step is to determine whether the challenged statute disadvantages a suspect class or impinges on a fundamental right. If so, it is subject to strict scrutiny. If not, then it is subject to rational basis review unless intermediate scrutiny applies.

In this case, the survivor benefits statute excludes Glossip from eligibility for survivor benefits because he and Engelhard were not married. The United States Supreme Court has never held that marital status is a classification triggering heightened equal protection scrutiny. *See Eisenstadt v. Baird*, 405 U.S. 438, 446–47 (1972) (invalidating a Massachusetts law denying unmarried persons access to contraceptives for want of a rational basis). Neither has this Court. *Cf. In re Marriage of Kohring*, 999 S.W.2d at 232 (holding there is no suspect class of "unmarried, divorced, or legally separated persons"). Glossip does not contend the survivor benefits statute violates a fundamental right. Glossip has cited no case holding that laws conditioning the receipt of benefits on marital status are subject to heightened scrutiny. Rational basis review applies in this case.

The dissent argues that this Court should apply heightened "intermediate" scrutiny in this case in light of the long history of discrimination against gays and lesbians. But, as just explained, Glossip is not eligible for survivor benefits because he is not a surviving spouse, not because he is gay. The cited cases just do not apply here, where the issue is discrimination based on marital status, not sexual orientation.

Had this case required this Court to determine the constitutionality of discrimination based on sexual orientation, it would be guided by federal law, for the Missouri Constitution's equal protection clause is coextensive with the Fourteenth Amendment, and this Court has been reluctant to extend the scope of the Missouri Constitution's equal protection clause beyond that of its federal cognate.

The United States Supreme Court left open the question of what level of scrutiny should apply to sexual orientation discrimination in *Windsor*. *See* 133 S. Ct. at 2696. There, as in *Lawrence v. Texas*, 539 U.S. 558 (2003), it took a tangential approach to the constitutionality of the challenged statute and held that the statute failed even the most deferential level of scrutiny. *Windsor*, 133 S. Ct. at 2696. Neither of these cases identified what level of scrutiny applies to cases alleging discrimination based on sexual orientation. This Court also need not reach that issue here because the survivor benefits statute does not discriminate on the basis of sexual orientation, and Glossip has elected not to challenge Missouri's statutory and constitutional proscription against same-sex marriage.

The Survivor Benefits Statute's Spousal Requirement Bears a Reasonable Relation to Legitimate State Interests

* * * Here, the General Assembly could have reasonably concluded that limiting survivor benefits to spouses would serve the death benefit's intended purpose as well as the interests of administrative efficiency and controlling costs. Providing survivor benefits to persons who are economically dependent on a deceased state employee is a legitimate state interest, and the General Assembly could have reasonably concluded that the spousal requirement would serve that purpose. The General Assembly could reasonably conceive that there might be a greater incidence of economic interdependence among married couples than among unmarried couples. Furthermore, under Missouri law, spouses owe each other a duty of financial support, but no such duty exists for unmarried couples. Consequently, the General Assembly could have concluded that a spousal requirement would serve as a reasonable proxy for a person likely to depend on the deceased employee for support.

Glossip argues that the spousal requirement does not bear a reasonable relation to the purpose of assisting dependent persons because the category is both over-inclusive and under-inclusive. It may be true that there are spouses of highway patrol employees who are not economically dependent on the employee and that there are non-spouses who are economically dependent on the employee. Rational basis review, however, does not require that the fit between the classification and government interest be exact, but merely "reasonable," and "this Court will not substitute its judgment for that of the legislature as to the wisdom, social desirability or economic policy underlying a statute." *Pemiscot Cnty.*, 256 S.W.3d at 102. It is reasonably conceivable that many spouses of highway patrol employees depend on their spouse's economic contributions. In light of the strong presumption in favor of a statute's validity, particularly a statute creating an economic interest, this Court cannot conclude that the spousal requirement is not reasonably related to the legitimate state interest of assisting dependent persons.

The spousal requirement also serves the interest of controlling costs. The General Assembly was free to provide survivor benefits to a larger class of beneficiaries, such as all people who could demonstrate any measure of financial dependence on the deceased employee. But it was not required to do so. Here, the General Assembly apparently believed that limiting survivor benefit beneficiaries to a smaller class of people would preserve MPERS's limited resources. Given that choice, the General Assembly was free to limit survivor benefits to a sub-class of those people who depend financially on deceased employees—as long as that classification does not require heightened scrutiny and bears a reasonable relationship to legitimate state interests. As discussed above, the spousal requirement is subject to rational basis review and is reasonably related to the purpose of assisting dependent persons. The cost savings realized by limiting survivor benefits to a smaller group of people, here surviving spouses and minor children, provides additional support for the statute's rationality.

Finally, the spousal requirement serves the interest of administrative efficiency. The General Assembly could have reasonably anticipated that expanding survivor benefits beyond surviving spouses and surviving children could create a risk of competing claims and subjective eligibility determinations and that such claims would increase the time and cost necessary to resolve benefits claims. Accordingly, the General Assembly could have reasonably concluded that limiting the death benefit to spouses, rather than, for example, all committed or financially interdependent couples, would provide an objective criterion for the efficient resolution of claims. Where, for the reasons already noted, the statute is subject only to rational basis review rather than to heightened scrutiny, such administrative considerations are reasonable.

Glossip argues that the spousal requirement must fail even rational basis scrutiny because the statute was motivated by a desire to harm gays and lesbians. Glossip cites the United States Supreme Court's recent decision in *Windsor* for the proposition that "'a bare . . . desire to harm a politically unpopular group cannot' justify disparate treatment of that group." *Windsor*, 133 S. Ct. at 2693 (quoting *Dep't of Agric. v. Moreno*, 413 U.S. 528, 534 (1973)). As already discussed at length, Glossip's argument fails because the survivor benefits statute restricts benefits based on marital status, not sexual orientation. Further, the history of section 104.140 demonstrates that the spousal requirement was not enacted to harm gays and lesbians. Section 104.140 has limited survivor benefits to a deceased employee's surviving spouse since the first death benefit was enacted in 1969, predating Missouri's first statute limiting marriage to opposite-sex couples by over 25 years. Instead, the spousal requirement is reasonably related to several government interests distinct from the public policy limiting marriage to opposite-sex couples. * * *

TEITELMAN, J., dissenting.

For decades, indeed centuries, gay men and lesbians have been subjected to persistent, unyielding discrimination, both socially and legally. That shameful history continues to this day. The statutes at issue in this case, sections 104.140.3, RSMo 2002, and 104.012, RSMo Supp. 2001, bear witness to that history and help ensure that this unfortunate past remains a prologue to the continued state-sanctioned marginalization of our fellow citizens. The plain meaning and intended application of sections 104.140.3 and 104.012 is to discriminate specifically against gay men and lesbians by categorically denying them crucial state benefits when their partner dies in the line of duty. This type of intentional, invidious and specifically targeted discrimination is fundamentally inconsistent with the constitutional guarantee of equal protection under the law.

Against this backdrop, the principal opinion holds that section 104.140.3 does not discriminate on the basis of sexual orientation because it draws a distinction only on the basis of marital status. This holding overlooks the fact that section 104.140.3 employs a definition of "spouse" that operates to the unique disadvantage of gay men and lesbians, even when, like Corporal Engelhard, they devote their lives to the defense of the same rule of law that relegates them to the status of second-class citizens. For these reasons, I respectfully dissent.

I. Equal Protection

* * * For nearly a hundred years following the Civil War, "separate but equal" and the attendant legally sanctioned racial segregation was held to satisfy the guarantee of equal protection. *See Brown v. Board of Education*, 347 U.S. 483 (1954). Bans on interracial marriage were held to be consistent with equal protection during the lifetime of every member of this Court. See Loving v. Virginia, 388 U.S. 1 (1967). The guarantee of equal protection was not made conclusively applicable to women until 1971. See Reed v. Reed, 404 U.S. 71 (1971). With the benefit of hindsight, the various decisions extending the guarantee of equal protection to racial minorities and women, though intensely controversial at the time, now seem obvious to a vast majority of Americans. * * *

Kelly Glossip's case raises the contemporary corollary to this old issue. By overlooking the actual impact of sections 104.140.3 and 104.012, the principal opinion leaves Glossip and others similarly situated left to wonder when courts finally will square the textual guarantee of equal protection with the continued and blatant discrimination against gays and lesbians.

The question posed by Glossip's case is simply whether the equal protection clause prevents the state from extending survivor benefits only to married opposite-sex couples when state law makes any same sex-marriage a legal impossibility. To answer this question, this Court employs the following two-step analysis. In the first step, the challenged law is analyzed to determine the classification created by the law. Once the relevant classification is identified, the court must apply the appropriate level of scrutiny to determine whether there is a sufficient justification for the classification at issue.

II. The Classification

. . . Despite the fact that the state has elected to provide survivor benefits on terms that make it legally impossible for any same sex-couple ever to receive survivor benefits, the principal opinion concludes that these statutes draw a distinction solely on the basis of marital status and in no way discriminate on the basis of sexual orientation. In one sense, the principal opinion is correct. The statutes do draw a distinction on the basis of marital status. This distinction, however, is drawn in a context in which same-sex couples are barred from marriage by the state constitution, a state statute provides that any same-sex marriage is a legal nullity, and section 104.012 defines a "spouse" as including only a marriage between a man and a woman. By tying the payment of survivor benefits to a definition of "spouse" that renders access to those benefits legally impossible to obtain only for gays and lesbians, the purported marital distinction is also necessarily a distinction based on sexual orientation. *See Alaska Civil Liberties Union v. State*, 122 P.3d 781 (AK. Sup. Ct. 2005); *Diaz v. Brewer*, 656 F.3d 1008 (9th Cir. 2011), and *Dragovich v. U.S. Dept. of the Treasury*, 848 F.Supp. 2d 1091, 1100 (N.D. Cal. 2012). Under these circumstances, there is no plausible way to conclude that sections 140.104.3 and 104.012 draw a distinction only on the basis of marital status and are somehow neutral on the issue of sexual orientation. Instead, it is clear that the statutes necessarily operate to the unique disadvantage of gays and lesbians precisely because of their sexual orientation. To conclude otherwise is akin to arguing that a statute that eliminates health benefits only for those who may have a child with sickle cell anemia is not discriminatory because it draws a distinction solely on the basis of a medical condition rather than on the basis of race.[1] At some point, equal protection analysis requires an assessment of the practical reality of the case. In this case, the reality is that Glossip's sexual orientation made it legally impossible for him to obtain survivor benefits. Sections 104.140.3 and 104.012 thereby turn the legal status of marriage into a proxy for discrimination on the basis of sexual orientation.

The principal opinion asserts that the fact that Glossip disclaimed any challenge to the ban on same-sex marriage is fatal to his claim. That is incorrect. The fact that sections 104.140.3 and 104.012 draw a distinction on the basis of marriage and, by necessity, sexual orientation, does not mean that Glossip's case hinges on a challenge to the legal bar on same sex marriages. The crux of Glossip's argument is not based on any assertion that he should have had the legal right to marry Engelhard. As a matter of state constitutional law, that argument is foreclosed by article I, section 33 of the Missouri Constitution, which provides that "marriage shall exist only between a man and a woman." The plain

---

[1] Sickle cell anemia is a disease that almost exclusively affects African-Americans. While the analogy is imperfect, it illustrates the key shortcoming with the principal opinion's analysis, which is that it does not account for the fact that the marital status distinction drawn by sections 104.140.3 and 104.012 necessarily operates to the unique disadvantage of gays and lesbians. This analogy is intended only to illustrate this point and is in no way intended to equate the distinct histories of African-Americans and gays and lesbians.

language of article I, section 33 does nothing more than limit the state's recognition of marriage to opposite-sex couples. The fact that the state does not recognize same-sex marriages does not mean that gays and lesbians are deprived of their other fundamental individual constitutional rights. Nothing in the short, simple text of article I, section 33 in any way overrides the separate constitutional guarantee of equal protection by justifying other forms of discrimination on the basis of sexual orientation.

Glossip's sole claim is that the benefits statutes violate equal protection because those statutes employ a definition of "spouse" that allows opposite-sex couples the opportunity to receive benefits while making it legally impossible for same-sex couples ever to receive benefits should one partner die in the line of duty. The state can dispense benefits equally to gay and lesbian survivors without providing a legal status such as marriage. By choosing to dispense benefits only to those who are married, however, the state has elected to make the receipt of such benefits a legal impossibility for one and only one group of people. It is that group of people, gay and lesbian couples, who are specifically disadvantaged by sections 104.140.3 and 104.012 and who define the class subject to discriminatory treatment. The state constitutional ban on same-sex marriages is essentially irrelevant to Glossip's claim.

III. Level of Scrutiny

Having determined that the statutes at issue necessarily discriminate on the basis of sexual orientation, the next analytical step requires an assessment of the state's justification for its discrimination. * * * The principal opinion correctly recites the standards for strict scrutiny and rational basis review but omits mention of the well-established equal protection jurisprudence holding that courts must apply heightened or "intermediate" scrutiny to a classification that disadvantages a group that has been subjected to historic patterns of disadvantage. Under intermediate or heightened scrutiny, the classification is permissible only if it is substantially related to the achievement of important governmental objectives. *See Craig v. Boren*, 429 U.S. 190, 197 (1976) (applying intermediate scrutiny to a gender classification); *Clark v. Jeter*, 486 U.S. 456, 461(1988) (applying intermediate scrutiny to a classification based on "illegitimacy").

More than a quarter century ago, this Court recognized that "[i]t cannot be doubted that historically homosexuals have been subjected to 'antipathy [and] prejudice.'" *State v. Walsh*, 713 S.W.2d 508, 511 (Mo. banc 1986). Although *Walsh* held that classifications based on sexual orientation were not subject to heightened equal protection scrutiny, that conclusion was based on the fact that homosexual behavior was, at that time, a crime. The rationale of *Walsh* is no longer viable in light of *Lawrence v. Texas*, 539 U.S. 558 (2003), which held that homosexual behavior is no longer subject to criminalization. What remains of *Walsh*, however, is this Court's accurate recognition of a historical pattern of state-sanctioned discrimination directed at gays and lesbians. The only defensible, reality-based conclusion to be drawn is that gay men and lesbians have been and, as this case illustrates, continue to be singled out for disparate treatment even though the immutable fact of whom one loves neither interferes with the rights of others nor has any relevance to one's ability to contribute to society. The legal import of this fact is that classifications aimed at disadvantaging people on the basis of their sexual orientation should be subjected to heightened scrutiny. *See Varnum v. Brien*, 763 N.W.2d 862 (Iowa 2009); *Kerrigan v. Comm'r of Pub. Health*, 957 A.2d 407 (Conn. 2008); *In re Marriage Cases*, 183 P.3d 384 (Cal. 2008).

IV. Sections 104.140.3 and 104.012 are not substantially related to the achievement of important governmental objectives

Sections 104.140.3 and 104.012 do not withstand heightened scrutiny. The state argues that the benefits statutes are justified by the state's interest in dispensing survivor benefits to those most likely to be economically dependent on the deceased trooper; ensuring that objective criteria dictate benefit eligibility; and that costs are controlled. None of these justifications are plausible.

The state's assertion that limiting survivor benefits to "spouses" will ensure that benefits are payable only to those who are most financially dependent on the deceased trooper is implausible. There is also no dispute that, at all times, Missouri law absolutely barred Glossip and Engelhard from becoming legally married. There is also no dispute in this case that Glossip and Engelhard were in a long-term, committed and financially interdependent relationship. Yet, under the guise of ensuring that benefits are paid only to those couples who are truly financially interdependent, the state denied Glossip any survivor benefit following Engelhard's death. As this case demonstrates, the relationship between marriage and financial interdependence fails to provide a rational basis, let alone a substantial justification, for categorically excluding same-sex couples from crucial benefits, particularly when, as in this case, the state effectively concedes that Glossip and Engelhard were, in fact, financially interdependent. Marriage simply cannot be a proxy for financial interdependence when only gays and lesbians—a relatively small, readily identifiable and historically marginalized group—are excluded categorically from being married legally.

The state also argues that it has an interest in ensuring that objective criteria dictate benefit eligibility. That is true. However, the state is not free to choose whatever "objective" criteria it wants. Objectivity is not synonymous with constitutional validity. National origin and sex are objective criteria, yet no one would contend seriously that the objectivity of either classification conclusively would establish the constitutional validity of statutes based on those classifications. Yet the state asserts that the "objective" criterion of same-sex marriage is a valid proxy for commitment and financial interdependence. As noted above, for purposes of this case and others like it, same-sex marriage is not a valid proxy for financial interdependence. When the state's asserted interest is in ensuring that benefits are paid to a survivor who was in a committed, financially interdependent relationship with a deceased trooper, then the criteria that bear the most substantial relationship to the goal of objectivity would be none other than evidence of long-term commitment and financial interdependence.

Finally, the state asserts that excluding all same sex couples from benefits is justified on cost-control grounds. If "cost control" constitutes a substantial justification for the denial of benefits in cases subject to heightened scrutiny, discrimination always would be justified on purely economic grounds. In other words, discrimination is cheaper than equal protection. The state's interest in efficiency cannot justify the discriminatory treatment of one group of citizens in favor of another. *See Varnum v. Brien*, 763 N.W.2d at 896–897; *In re Balas*, 449 B.R. 567, 579 (Bankr. N.D. Cal. 2011).

The statutes at issue discriminate on the basis of sexual orientation. The discrimination is not substantially related to a legitimate state purpose. Consequently, I would reverse the judgment dismissing Glossip's claim for survivor benefits.

IRIZARRY V. BOARD OF EDUCATION OF CHICAGO

United States Court of Appeals, Seventh Circuit, 2001
251 F.3d 604

POSNER, CIRCUIT JUDGE.

Although Milagros Irizarry has lived with the same man for more than two decades and they have two (now adult) children, they have never married. As an employee of the Chicago public school system, she receives health benefits but he does not, even though he is her "domestic partner" (the term for persons who are cohabiting with each other in a relationship similar to marriage), though he would if he were her husband. In July 1999, the Chicago Board of Education extended spousal health benefits to domestic partners—but only if the domestic partner was of the same sex as the employee, which excluded Irizarry's domestic partner, an exclusion that she contends is unconstitutional.

Besides being of the same sex, applicants for domestic-partner status must be unmarried, unrelated, at least 18 years old, and "each other's sole domestic partner, responsible for each other's common welfare." They must satisfy two of the following four additional conditions as well: that they have been living together for a year; that they jointly own their home; that they jointly own other property of specified kinds; that the domestic partner is the primary beneficiary named in the employee's will. Although the board's purpose in entitling domestic partners so defined to spousal benefits was to extend such benefits to homosexual employees, homosexual marriage not being recognized by Illinois, 750 ILCS 5/212, 5/213.1, entitlement to the benefits does not require proof of sexual orientation.

Irizarry's domestic partner satisfies all the conditions for domestic-partner benefits except being of the same sex. She argues that the board's policy denies equal protection and, secondarily, due process. The district court dismissed her suit for failure to state a claim.

The board of education makes two arguments for treating homosexual couples differently from unmarried heterosexual couples. First, since homosexual marriage is not possible in Illinois (or anywhere else in the United States, though it is now possible in the Netherlands), and heterosexual marriage of course is, the recognition of a domestic-partnership surrogate is more important for homosexual than for heterosexual couples, who can obtain the benefits simply by marrying. Second, the board wants to attract homosexual teachers in order to provide support for homosexual students. According to its brief, the board "believes that lesbian and gay male school personnel who have a healthy acceptance of their own sexuality can act as role models and provide emotional support for lesbian and gay students. . . . They can support students who are questioning their sexual identities or who are feeling alienated due to their minority sexual orientation. They can also encourage all students to be tolerant and accepting of lesbians and gay males, and discourage violence directed at these groups."

This line of argument will shock many people even today; it was not that long ago when homosexual teachers were almost universally considered a public menace likely to seduce or recruit their students into homosexuality, then regarded with unmitigated horror. The plaintiff does not argue, however, that the Chicago Board of Education is irrational in having turned the traditional attitude toward homosexual teachers upside down. It is not for a federal court to decide whether a local government agency's policy of tolerating or even endorsing homosexuality is sound. Even if the judges consider such a policy morally repugnant— even dangerous—they may not interfere with it unless convinced that it lacks even minimum rationality, which is a permissive standard. It is a fact that some school children are homosexual, and the responsibility for dealing with that fact is lodged in the school authorities, and (if they are public schools) ultimately in the taxpaying public, rather than in the federal courts.

The efficacy of the policy may be doubted. Although it had been in effect for a year and a half when the appeal was argued, only nine employees out of some 45,000 had signed up for domestic-partner benefits and none of the nine indicated whether he or she was homosexual; they may not all have been, as we shall see—perhaps none were. Nor is there any indication that any of the nine are new employees attracted to teach in the Chicago public schools by the availability of health benefits for same-sex domestic partners. Maybe it's too early, though, to assess the efficacy of the policy. No matter; limited efficacy does not make the policy irrational—not even if we think limited efficacy evidence that the policy is more in the nature of a political gesture than a serious effort to improve the lot of homosexual students—if only because with limited efficacy comes limited cost. Because homosexuals are a small fraction of the population, because the continuing stigma of homosexuality discourages many of them from revealing their sexual orientation, and because nowadays a significant number of heterosexuals substitute cohabitation for marriage in response to the diminishing stigma of cohabitation, extending domestic-partner benefits to mixed-sex couples would greatly increase the expense of the program.

Irizarry argues that the child of an unmarried couple ought equally to be entitled to the mentoring and role-model benefits of having teachers who live in the same way the student's parents do. Cost considerations to one side, the argument collides with a nationwide policy in favor of marriage. True, it is no longer widely popular to try to pressure homosexuals to marry persons of the opposite sex. But so far as heterosexuals are concerned, the evidence that on average married couples live longer, are healthier, earn more, have lower rates of substance abuse and mental illness, are less likely to commit suicide, and report higher levels of happiness—that marriage civilizes young males, confers economies of scale and of joint consumption, minimizes sexually transmitted disease, and provides a stable and nourishing framework for child rearing—*see, e.g.*, Linda J. Waite & Maggie Gallagher, *The Case for Marriage: Why Married People Are Happier, Healthier, and Better Off Financially* (2000); David Popenoe, *Life without Father: Compelling New Evidence That Fatherhood and Marriage Are Indispensable for the Good of Children and Society* (1996); George W. Dent, Jr., "The Defense of Traditional Marriage," 15 *J.L. & Pol.* 581 (1999), refutes any claim that policies designed to promote marriage are irrational. The Chicago Board of Education cannot be faulted, therefore, for not wishing to encourage heterosexual cohabitation; and, though we need not decide the point, the refusal to extend domestic-partner benefits to heterosexual cohabitators could be justified on the basis of the policy favoring marriage for heterosexuals quite apart from the reasons for wanting to extend the spousal fringe benefits to homosexual couples.

Of course, self-selection is important; people are more likely to marry who believe they have characteristics favorable to a long-term relationship. But the Chicago Board of Education would not be irrational (though it might be incorrect) in assigning some causal role to the relationship itself. Linda J. Waite, "Does Marriage Matter?" 32 *Demography* 483, 498–99 (1995), finds that

> cohabitants are much less likely than married couples to pool financial resources, more likely to assume that each partner is responsible for supporting himself or herself financially, more likely to spend free time separately, and less likely to agree on the future of the relationship. This makes both investment in the relationship and specialization with this partner much riskier than in marriage, and so reduces them. Whereas marriage connects individuals to other important social institutions, such as organized religion, cohabitation seems to distance them from these institutions.

Irizarry and her domestic partner may, given the unusual duration of their relationship, be an exception to generalizations about the benefits of marriage. We are not aware of an extensive scholarly literature comparing marriage to long-term cohabitation. This may be due to the fact that long-term cohabitation is rare—only ten percent of such relationships last for five years or more, Pamela J. Smock, "Cohabitation in the United States: An Appraisal of Research Themes, Findings, and Implications," 26 *Ann. Rev. Sociology* 1 (2000). But there is evidence that the widespread substitution of cohabitation for marriage in Sweden has given that country the highest rate of family dissolution and single parenting in the developed world. David Popenoe, *Disturbing the Nest: Family Change and Decline in Modern Societies* 173–74 (1988). It is well known that divorce is harmful to children, and presumably the same is true for the dissolution of a cohabitation—and a cohabitation is more likely to dissolve than a marriage. True, Irizarry's cohabitation has not dissolved; but law and policy are based on the general rather than the idiosyncratic, as the Supreme Court noted with reference to other benefits tied to marital status in *Califano v. Jobst*, 434 U.S. 47, 53–54, 98 S.Ct. 95, 54 L.Ed.2d 228 (1977). Nor is it entirely clear that this couple ought to be considered an exception to the general concern with heterosexuals who choose to have a family outside of marriage. For when asked at argument why the couple had never married, Irizarry's counsel replied that he had asked his client that question and she had told him that "it just never came up." There may be good reasons why a particular couple would not marry even after producing children, but that the thought of marriage would not even occur to them is disquieting.

The Lambda Legal Defense and Education Fund has filed an amicus curiae brief surprisingly urging reversal—surprisingly because Lambda is an organization for the promotion of homosexual rights, and if it is the law that domestic-partnership benefits must be extended to heterosexual couples, the benefits are quite likely to be terminated for everyone lest the extension to heterosexual cohabitors impose excessive costs and invite criticism as encouraging heterosexual cohabitation and illegitimate births and discouraging marriage and legitimacy. But Lambda is concerned with the fact that state and national policy encourages (heterosexual) marriage in all sorts of ways that domestic-partner health benefits cannot begin to equalize. Lambda wants to knock marriage off its perch by requiring the board of education to treat unmarried heterosexual couples as well as it treats married ones, so that marriage will lose some of its luster.

This is further evidence of the essentially symbolic or political rather than practical significance of the board's policy. Lambda is not jeopardizing a substantial benefit for homosexuals because very few of them want or will seek the benefit. In any event, it would not be proper for judges to use the vague concept of "equal protection" to undermine marriage just because it is a heterosexual institution. The desire of the board of education to increase the employment of homosexual teachers is admittedly a striking manifestation of the sexual revolution that has characterized, some would say convulsed, the United States in the last forty years. The courts did not try to stop the revolution. On the contrary, they spurred it on, most pertinently to this case by their decisions removing legal disabilities of birth out of wedlock, disabilities that if they still existed might have induced Ms. Irizarry and the father of her children to marry in order to remove those disabilities from their children. Likewise relevant are cases such as *Stanley v. Illinois*, 405 U.S. 645, 92 S.Ct. 1208, 31 L.Ed.2d 551 (1972), that confer constitutional rights on unwed fathers. But no court has gone so far as to deem marriage a suspect classification because government provides benefits to married persons that it withholds from cohabiting couples. That would be a bizarre extension of case law already criticized as having carried the courts well beyond the point at which the Constitution might be thought to provide guidance to social policy.

To the board's argument that it has extended spousal benefits to the domestic partners of homosexual employees because homosexual marriage is not a status available to its employees, Irizarry replies that the argument depends on the board's groundless decision to provide benefits to spouses, rather than domestic partners, of its employees. She says that all the board has to do to purge the constitutional violation is to condition all nonemployee fringe benefits on satisfaction of its domestic-partnership conditions other than that the domestic partner be of the same sex as the employee; and then the "discrimination" in favor of heterosexuals that the extension of spousal benefits to homosexual domestic partners was intended to erase will be eliminated without discrimination against heterosexual domestic partners. She points to Chicago's Human Rights Ordinance, which forbids discrimination on the basis of marital status. But the purpose, at least the primary purpose, of such a prohibition is surely not to dethrone marriage; it is to prevent discrimination against married women, who employers might think have divided loyalties. Such laws are pro-marriage, not anti- as the plaintiff suggests.

All other considerations to one side, the board reaps cost savings by basing dependent benefits on marital status—savings distinct from those discussed earlier that depend simply on the much smaller number of homosexuals than heterosexuals likely to seek or qualify for domestic-partner benefits. It is easier to determine whether the claimant is married to an employee than to determine whether the claimant satisfies the multiple criteria for domestic partnership. . . . And we do not understand the plaintiff to be arguing that the board of education must have anything more than a rational basis for its action in order to defeat the plaintiff's equal protection claim. Only when the plaintiff in an equal protection case is complaining of a form of discrimination that is suspect because historically it was irrational or invidious is there a heavier burden of justifying a difference in treatment than merely showing that it is rational. Heterosexuals cohabiting outside of marriage are not such a class. There is a history of disapproval of (nonmarital) cohabitation, and some states still criminalize it. *See, e.g.*, Ariz. Rev. Stat. Ann. § 13–1409; Mich. Comp. Laws Ann. § 750.355; N.D. Cent. Code § 12.1–20–10—as indeed Illinois did until 1990. *United States v. Nichols*, 937 F.2d 1257, 1263 (7th Cir. 1991). But the disapproval is not necessarily irrational or invidious, given the benefits of marriage discussed earlier. It was rational for the board to refuse to extend domestic-partnership benefits to persons who can if they wish marry and by doing so spare the board from having to make a factual inquiry into the nature of their relationship.

The least rational feature of the board's policy, though not emphasized by the plaintiff, is that although-domestic-partner benefits are confined to persons of the same sex, the partners need not be homosexual. They could be roommates who have lived together for a year and own some property jointly and for want of relatives are each other's "sole domestic-partner," and if so they would be entitled to domestic-partner benefits under the board of education's policy. To distinguish between roommates of the same and of different sexes, as the policy implicitly does, cannot be justified on the ground that the latter but not the former could marry each other!

So the policy does not make a very close fit between end and means. But it doesn't have to, provided there is a rational basis for the loose fit. This follows from our earlier point that cost is a rational basis for treating people differently. Economy is one of the principal reasons for using rules rather than standards to govern conduct. Rules single out one or a few facts from the welter of possibly relevant considerations and make that one or those few facts legally determinative, thus dispensing with inquiry into the other considerations. A standard that takes account of all relevant considerations will produce fewer arbitrary differences in outcome, but at a cost in uncertainty, administrative burden, and sometimes even—as here—in invading people's privacy. It is easy to see why the board of education does not want to put applicants to the proof of their sexual preference. That would be resented. The price of avoiding an inquiry that would be costly because it would be obnoxious is that a few roommates may end up with windfall benefits. We cannot say that the board is being irrational in deciding to pay that price rather than snoop into people's sex lives.

If the result is, as it may be, that none of the nine employees who have opted for domestic-partner benefits is homosexual (or at least that none is willing to acknowledge his homosexuality publicly, for that is not required by the board's policy though it would seem implicit in the board's desire to attract homosexuals who have "a healthy acceptance of their own sexuality"), this would lend a note of irony to the board's policy and would reinforce our earlier conjecture that the purpose is to make a statement rather than to confer actual monetary benefits. But "making a statement" is a common purpose of legislation and does not condemn it as irrational.

NOTES

1.   The first appellate court to hold that a failure by a state employer to provide domestic partnership benefits to lesbian and gay employees violated the state constitution was the Oregon Court of Appeals in *Tanner v. Oregon Health Sciences University*, 971 P.2d 435, 157 Or.App. 502 (1998). In its analysis, the court concluded that lesbians and gay men are a suspect class under the Oregon constitution, a determination that required the state to show that the failure to provide health and life insurance benefits to the same-sex partners of its employees was "justified by genuine differences between the class and those to whom the privileges and immunities are made available." *Id.* at 447, 971 Or. App. at 524. (For a further discussion of the standard of review applied to sexual orientation discrimination cases brought under state constitutions, see *supra* Chapter 3, Section II.B.) Instead of providing such a justification, the state, as in *Glossip*, argued that its benefits policy made distinctions on the basis of marital status rather than on sexual orientation. While the Missouri court in *Glossip* accepted that argument, the Oregon court rejected it after noting that "[h]omosexual couples may not marry [and as a result] the benefits are not made available on equal terms. They are [instead] made available on terms that, for gay and lesbian couples, are a legal impossibility." *Id.* at 448, 971 Or. App. at 525. *See also Alaska Civil Liberties Union v. Alaska,* 122 P.3d 781, 788 (Alaska 2005) (holding that

policy denying health insurance and other benefits to the same-sex partners of government employees constituted a sexual orientation classification rather than a marital classification and that the policy violated the state constitution's equal protection guarantee); *Snetsinger v. Montana Univ. System*, 104 P.3d 445, 452, 325 Mont. 148, 157 (2004) (same).

2.   According to the National Conference of State Legislatures, eighteen states (AK, AZ, CA, CT, HA, IL, IA, ME, MD, MT, NJ, NM, NY, OR, RI, VT, WA, and WY) and the District of Columbia provide domestic partnership benefits to their employees. *See* http://www.ncsl.org/research/ human-services/states-offering-benefits-for-same-sex-partners-of.aspx.
Arizona in 2008 adopted a regulation making health benefits available to the domestic partners of state employees. The legislature responded a year later by enacting a statute limiting those benefits to the legal spouses (and children) of those employees. In 2010, a federal district court issued a preliminary injunction prohibiting enforcement of the statute after concluding that lesbian and gay employees were likely to prevail in an equal protection challenge to the statute, see *Collins v. Brewer*, 727 F.Supp.2d 797 (D.Ariz. 2010), a ruling that was affirmed by the Court of Appeals. *See Diaz v. Brewer*, 656 F.3d 1008 (9th Cir. 2011), *cert. denied*, ___ U.S. ___, 133 S.Ct. 2884 (2013).

3.   More than 100 municipalities have enacted ordinances offering domestic partnership benefits to their employees. Some of these ordinances have been challenged by taxpayer plaintiffs who claim that the local governments lack the authority, under their respective state laws, to enact them. The outcomes of the cases vary. The ordinances were upheld in *Schaefer v. City & County of Denver*, 973 P.2d 717 (Colo. Ct. App. 1998); *Crawford v. City of Chicago*, 304 Ill.App.3d 818, 237 Ill.Dec. 668, 710 N.E.2d 91 (1999); and *City of Atlanta v. Morgan*, 492 S.E.2d 193, 268 Ga. 586 (1997). The ordinances were struck down in *Connors v. City of Boston*, 714 N.E.2d 335, 430 Mass. 31 (1999); *Lilly v. City of Minneapolis*, 527 N.W.2d 107 (Minn. Ct. App. 1995); *Arlington County v. White*, 528 S.E.2d 706, 259 Va. 708 (2000). Some municipalities, such as San Francisco and New York City, have also enacted ordinances requiring entities that contract with them to provide domestic partnership benefits. San Francisco's ordinance was upheld in *S.D. Myers, Inc. v. City & County of San Francisco*, 253 F.3d 461 (9th Cir. 2001) (holding that ordinance did not violate commerce or due process clause). New York City's ordinance was struck down in *Council of New York v. Bloomberg*, 846 N.E.2d 433, 6 N.Y.3d 380, 813 N.Y.S.2d 3 (2006) (holding inter alia that law was preempted by the Employee Retirement Income Security Act (ERISA)).

4.   The Michigan Supreme Court has held that the state's anti-gay marriage constitutional amendment, which states that "the union of one man and one woman in marriage shall be the only agreement recognized as a marriage or similar union for any purpose," prohibits public employers from providing benefits to the same-sex partners of their employees. *See National*

Pride at Work, Inc. v. Governor of Michigan, 748 N.W.2d 524, 481 Mich. 56 (2008).

In 2011, the Michigan Civil Service Commission extended health care benefits to one adult co-resident (who was designated as an "Other Eligible Adult Individual" (OEAI)) of state employees. The co-resident could not be a member of the employee's immediate family, which was defined as "spouse, children, parents, grandparents or foster parents, grandchildren, parents-in-law, brothers, sisters, aunts, uncles, or cousins." The state Attorney General filed an action against the Commission claiming *inter alia* that its new policy violated the Marriage Amendment. The Michigan Court of Appeals rejected that claim, noting that the extension of benefits was gender neutral and that it did "not depend on the employee being in a close relationship of any particular kind with the OEAI beyond a common residence." Attorney General v. Civil Service Commission, 2013 WL 85805 (Mich.App.), *2.

For its part, the Michigan legislature enacted a statute prohibiting public employers from providing health benefits and other fringe benefits to anyone other than their employees' spouses and children. 2011 Mich. Pub. Acts 297; Mich. Comp. Laws §§ 15.583–.584. The governor signed the bill, but included a signing statement declaring that the law did not apply to university or state employees, which, if accurate, limited the statute's application to other public entities, such as local governments and school districts. Shortly thereafter, five same-sex couples, all of which included one partner who worked for a local government or school district, filed a lawsuit in federal court claiming that the statute violated their rights to Equal Protection and Due Process. A district court issued a preliminary injunction prohibiting the enforcement of the statute after it concluded that the plaintiffs were likely to prevail with their equal protection challenge. Bassett v. Snyder, 951 F.Supp.2d 939 (E.D.Mich. 2013)). In doing so, the court noted that "[t]he historical background and legislative history of the Act demonstrate that it was motivated by animus against gay men and lesbians." *Id.* at 24.

CHAPTER 6

COUPLING

■ ■ ■

I.   INTRODUCTION

Until relatively recently, no jurisdiction in the United States legally recognized same-sex relationships and, in the years leading up to *Lawrence*, some still criminalized same-sex sexual acts. The landscape has shifted dramatically, however, in the last several years. A decade after the Hawaii Supreme Court issued a decision indicating that it was poised to allow same-sex couples to marry,[1] the Massachusetts Supreme Judicial Court became the first state supreme court to affirm the constitutional right of same-sex couples to marry.[2] As this Chapter will explore, several other states have since followed Massachusetts' lead. And when the Supreme Court eventually weighed in, it struck down the federal law banning recognition of same-sex marriage.

This Chapter maps out the search for legal recognition of same-sex relationships. After this introductory Section, the second Section explores marriage: it considers the special constitutional status of marriage; chronicles the variety of efforts to achieve legal recognition of same-sex marriage in the United States; considers alternatives to marriage that have emerged during this time; probes the unfolding backlash; explores the question of federal and interstate recognition, including the Supreme Court's treatment of the Defense of Marriage Act (DOMA); and considers the relationship between same-sex marriage and religious liberty. The Section includes a case study of California's Proposition 8 ("Prop 8"). The developments in California before and after Prop 8, and the ballot campaign itself, capture many of the important legal and social dynamics that have shaped the contemporary debate about same-sex marriage. The Chapter concludes by looking at a debate within the LGBT community concerning the propriety and priority of efforts to legalize same-sex marriage, in light of the shortcomings of the marriage model.

* * *

Beginning in 2004, advocates for same-sex marriage filed a series of lawsuits in California. Phyllis Lyon and Del Martin were the first couple

---

[1]   *Baehr v. Lewin*, 852 P.2d 44, 74 Haw. 530 (1993).

[2]   *Goodridge v. Dep't of Pub. Health*, 798 N.E.2d 941, 440 Mass. 309 (2003).

to be married in that state. As chronicled in a declaration filed in one of the lawsuits, Lyon and Martin played a prominent role in the LGBT movement over many decades.

DECLARATION OF PHYLLIS LYON*

I, PHYLLIS LYON, declare as follows:

1.   I make this declaration of my own personal and first-hand knowledge. If called as a witness, I would be competent to testify to the contents hereof. My beloved intended spouse, Del Martin ("Del")[,] and I have joined the other Petitioner couples in this lawsuit because we wish to be married and treated as fully equal, respected citizens under the law of our home state of California.

2.   Del and I have been in a loving, committed relationship of mutual support for more than 51 years. We are registered as domestic partners with the City of San Francisco and with the State of California. On February 12, 2004 we received a marriage license and were married in a ceremony performed for us by the Assessor for the City and County of San Francisco, Mabel Teng. As far as we know, it was the first civil marriage conducted knowingly for a lesbian or gay couple by a government official and with a government-issued license to take place in the United States.

3.   Our marriage ceremony was very moving and emotional for Del and me. It meant a great deal to have legal recognition for our relationship after over five decades of devotion to each other. . . . While Del and I had pledged our love and dedication to each other for life 51 years before, it was immensely meaningful and important for us to do so before witnesses in an official, public ceremony, with the intention of being legally bound as spouses.

4.   Del and I vowed on February 12 to "love and comfort, honor and keep in sickness and in health, for richer [or] for poorer, for better or for worse and be faithful as long as we both shall live." We have lived these vows for all our time together and we believe it is long past time for the State of California to acknowledge and respect who we are to each other. We had not anticipated that we would have the chance to be married in our lifetimes. But when the opportunity presented itself back in February— just as we were celebrating our 51st anniversary—we realized how gratifying it would be finally to take that simple, public, legal step.

5.   After our marriage, we received an extraordinary amount of support from friends and from people around the City and around the world. Some sent us flowers; a great many sent cards or letters. On Sunday, February 22, 2004, over two thousand people attended a wedding reception for us. We even received calls from as far away as Melbourne,

---

*   Appendix for Respondent, Woo v. Lockyer, (No. A110451), 143 Cal. App. 4th 873, 49 Cal. Rptr. 3d 675 (Cal. Ct. App. 2006) (Nov. 9, 2005).

Australia and Bogota, Colombia, from people who wanted to speak with us, to congratulate us and to thank us for helping others understand that lesbian and gay couples love each other just like heterosexual couples do.

6. Although the amount of warmth and support was almost overwhelming, we appreciated and shared the upwelling of joy at seeing such a positive change taking place. We have seen incredible, amazing changes in public awareness and attitudes towards lesbians and gay men over the years we have been together. We hadn't really expected to be as visible as we were on our wedding day and in the weeks that followed. But, it has given us deep satisfaction to know that our happiness has helped move human understanding forward in such an affirmative way. In truth, this has been a goal Del and I have shared during all our time together.

7. Del and I met in 1950, when we were working for the same company in Seattle. After having moved to San Francisco, we purchased a home together in 1955. We have been living together in San Francisco since that time. I will turn 80 in a couple of months, and Del is 83. She was previously married and has a daughter who is in her sixties.

8. We are both retired now. I previously worked as a journalist and a sexologist. Del worked as a bookkeeper. In addition to our paid jobs, we both have spent decades doing political and community work as community leaders, authors, and activists—striving to increase visibility and understanding, and always working toward full equality for lesbian, gay, bisexual, and transgender ("LGBT") people and their families.

9. We have seen attitudes change enormously over these years. In the mid-fifties, lesbian and gay couples certainly didn't talk about getting married. People were far too preoccupied with fear of losing their jobs. Today it seems that most heterosexual people realize they know at least a few lesbians or gay men, and many know they have lesbian or gay people within their extended families. Back when Del and I started doing educational work about sexual orientation, most lesbians and gay men didn't even identify themselves to other lesbian and gay people, let alone to their heterosexual coworkers, neighbors and relatives. We have seen that society as a whole has become healthier and safer for everyone as lesbian and gay people have become more visible and familiar, and much of the rest of society has relaxed a bit about the fact that we exist. It has been reassuring to see medical and sociological policies, as well as legal policies, becoming much more reasonable about sexual orientation and LGBT people.

10. Del and I had not thought much about marriage in the early years. Back then, it seemed as if marriage was wholly unobtainable in our lifetime. It wasn't until the early 1970s that same-sex marriage was advocated for publicly. In fact, it was heterosexual people, including

friends of ours, who first raised the issue publicly in the early 1970s. The San Francisco Chronicle published an editorial in 1970, probably in July, calling for equal marriage rights for lesbians and gay men. We remember fondly some years later when John Burton (then a new member of the state Assembly) introduced a bill to remove the different-sex restriction in California's marriage law. Then, in the late 1970s or early 1980s, a friend of ours—a married woman lawyer—sponsored a successful marriage equality resolution within the San Francisco Bar Association and then within the California State Bar. And today, we see Mrs. Cheney and Vice President Cheney supporting their daughter and acknowledging that it would hurt their family if she were denied equal freedom to have a happy family life. We are encouraged that, both now and in the past, many heterosexual people have appreciated how much same-sex couples are denied—and how much our families and friends are denied—by our exclusion from marriage.

11. We registered as domestic partners when the City and County of San Francisco set up a local registry years ago. There were a few limited rights that came with registration, as well as a nice feeling that our local government was respecting and caring about us. At one point, the City started holding an annual celebration of same-sex couples. The second or third time it was held, Del and I participated and spoke during the ceremony. It was a sweet validation to have Mayor Brown and other officials honor our commitment in a way that was both formal and festive. But none of us could confuse those domestic partnerships with marriage. They did not have the same social meaning as a marriage, nor the comprehensive legal protections of marriage.

12. The legal protections are of great concern to us. Because I am nearly 80 and Del already is in her 80s, we both are rather anxious about what will happen to the other when one of us dies or becomes seriously ill. In particular, although we have executed documents giving each other the right to make medical decisions for the other, and giving each other the right to hospital visitation, we worry that we may misplace these forms and be unable to find them when we need them, and that, as a result, we will be prevented from making decisions for each other or from seeing each other in the hospital, despite having been life partners for over 50 years. Because this issue is of such concern for us, and because we are so worried about making sure the documents are accurate and properly filled out, we have filled out these documents several times. But we still experience stress about what may happen in an emergency.

13. Our fears are exacerbated by the fact that we often travel and we worry that hospital officials may not respect our relationship even if we have our documents with us. What if we are in a state that does not honor this type of document? Or, what if the hospital staff says they are not familiar with domestic partnerships and do not consider same-sex couples

to be next-of-kin even if they do have proper legal documentation? We have seen friends deal with similar problems over the years and it has been tragic to hear about a person's wishes being ignored just when they are struggling with physical pain, incapacity and fear. These concerns make us feel quite vulnerable.

14. We also worry about losing our home should one of us have to go into a nursing home and have expensive bills, while the other may not be able to claim the kinds of exemptions for the home that protect spouses from financial ruin in such circumstances. We are fearful as well about whether we will be allowed to live together and whether we will be treated respectfully if we both have to go to a nursing home or assisted living facility.

* * *

On February 12, 2004, Martin and Lyon were the first couple to be married when San Francisco began issuing marriage licenses to same-sex couples. San Francisco Mayor Gavin Newsom decided to allow same-sex marriage on a unilateral basis, without waiting for judicial or legislative action. The idea was not universally popular with LGBT rights activists, with some feeling that the move might spur a backlash. Newsom and his team decided to proceed, however, and Martin and Lyon were invited to be the first couple to participate. Rachel Gordon, *The Battle Over Same-Sex Marriage*, S.F. CHRONICLE, Feb. 15, 2004, at A1. Their marriage and all the other same-sex marriages that occurred in San Francisco were later voided by the court after a legal challenge by the State of California. *Lockyer v. City & County of San Francisco*, 95 P.3d 459, 495, 33 Cal. 4th 1055, 1113, 17 Cal. Rptr. 225, 268 (2004). In 2008, the California Supreme Court held that same-sex couples had a right to marry under the state's constitution. *In re Marriage Cases*, 43 Cal. 4th 757, 76 Cal. Rptr. 3d 683, 183 P.3d 384 (2008). Martin and Lyon were legally married in June 2008, after the California Supreme Court's ruling. Martin died in August of that year, but Lyon later noted that "[s]he died a married woman" because Proposition 8 had not yet been enacted at the polls. *See* Phyllis Lyon, *On Gay Marriage,* L.A. Times, May 26, 2009, at A21.

II.   THE MARRIAGE EQUALITY DEBATE

A. THE CONSTITUTIONAL FOUNDATION

Marriage is fundamentally a matter for the states, but has long held a special place in federal constitutional law. As long ago as 1923, the U.S. Supreme Court stated that the liberty guaranteed by the due process clause includes the right to marry. *Meyer v. Nebraska*, 262 U.S. 390, 43 S.Ct. 625, 67 L.Ed. 1042 (1923). The Court went on to elaborate the contours of that right, most famously in the next case.

LOVING V. VIRGINIA

Supreme Court of the United States, 1967
388 U.S. 1, 87 S.Ct. 1817, 18 L.Ed.2d 1010

MR. CHIEF JUSTICE WARREN.

This case presents a Constitutional question never addressed by this Court: whether a statutory scheme adopted by the State of Virginia to prevent marriages between persons solely on the basis of racial classifications violates the equal protection and due process clauses of the Fourteenth Amendment. For reasons which seem to us to reflect the central meaning of those Constitutional commands, we conclude that these statutes cannot stand consistently with the Fourteenth Amendment.

In June 1958, two residents of Virginia, Mildred Jeter, a Negro woman, and Richard Loving, a white man, were married in the District of Columbia pursuant to its laws. Shortly after their marriage, the Lovings returned to Virginia and established their marital abode in Caroline County. At the October Term, 1958, of the Circuit Court of Caroline County, a grand jury issued an indictment charging the Lovings with violating Virginia's ban on interracial marriages. On January 6, 1959, the Lovings pleaded guilty to the charge and were sentenced to one year in jail; however, the trial judge suspended the sentence for a period of 25 years on the condition that the Lovings leave the State and not return to Virginia together for 25 years. He stated in an opinion that:

> "Almighty God created the races white, black, yellow, malay and red, and He placed them on separate continents. And but for the interference with His arrangement there would be no cause for such marriages. The fact that He separated the races shows that He did not intend for the races to mix."

After their convictions, the Lovings took up residence in the District of Columbia. On November 6, 1963, they filed a motion in the state trial court to vacate the judgment and set aside the sentence on the ground that the statutes which they had violated were repugnant to the Fourteenth Amendment ... On January 22, 1965, the state trial judge denied the motion to vacate the sentences, and the Lovings perfected an appeal to the Supreme Court of Appeals of Virginia. . . .

The Supreme Court of Appeals upheld the constitutionality of the antimiscegenation statutes and, after modifying the sentence, affirmed the convictions.

The two statutes under which appellants were convicted and sentenced are part of a comprehensive statutory scheme aimed at prohibiting and punishing interracial marriages. The Lovings were convicted of violating § 20–58 of the Virginia Code:

"*Leaving State to evade law.* If any white person and colored person shall go out of this State, for the purpose of being married, and with the intention of returning, and be married out of it, and afterwards return to and reside in it, cohabiting as man and wife, they shall be punished as provided in § 20–59, and the marriage shall be governed by the same law as if it had been solemnized in this State. The fact of their cohabitation here as man and wife shall be evidence of their marriage."

Section 20–59, which defines the penalty for miscegenation, provides:

"*Punishment for marriage.* If any white person intermarry with a colored person, or any colored person intermarry with a white person, he shall be guilty of a felony and shall be punished by confinement in the penitentiary for not less than one nor more than five years."

Other central provisions in the Virginia statutory scheme are § 20–57, which automatically voids all marriages between "a white person and a colored person" without any judicial proceeding,[2] and §§ 20–54 and 1–14 which, respectively, define "white persons" and "colored persons and Indians" for purposes of the statutory prohibitions.[3] The Lovings have never disputed in the course of this litigation that Mrs. Loving is a "colored person" or that Mr. Loving is a "white person" within the meanings given those terms by the Virginia statutes.

---

[2]   Section 20–57 of the Virginia Code provides:

"*Marriages void without decree.* All marriages between a white person and a colored person shall be absolutely void without any decree of divorce or other legal process." *Va. Code Ann.*, § 20–57 (1960 Repl. Vol.).

[3]   Section 20–54 of the Virginia Code provides:

"*Intermarriage prohibited; meaning of term 'white persons.'* It shall hereafter be unlawful for any white person in this State to marry any save a white person, or a person with no other admixture of blood than white and American Indian. For the purpose of this chapter, the term 'white person' shall apply only to such person as has no trace whatever of any blood other than Caucasian; but persons who have one-sixteenth or less of the blood of the American Indian and have no other non-Caucasic blood shall be deemed to be white persons. All laws heretofore passed and now in effect regarding the intermarriage of white and colored persons shall apply to marriages prohibited by this chapter." *Va. Code Ann.*, § 20–54 (1960 Repl. Vol.).

The exception for persons with less than one-sixteenth "of the blood of the American Indian" is apparently accounted for, in the words of a tract issued by the Registrar of the State Bureau of Vital Statistics, by "the desire of all to recognize as an integral and honored part of the white race the descendants of John Rolfe and Pocahontas. . . ." Plecker, The New Family and Race Improvement, 17 Va.Health Bull., Extra No. 12, at 25–26 (New Family Series No. 5, 1925), cited in Wadlington, *The* Loving *Case: Virginia's Anti–Miscegenation Statute in Historical Perspective,* 52 VA. L. REV. 1189, 1202, n. 93 (1966).

Section 1–14 of the Virginia Code provides:

"*Colored persons and Indians defined.* Every person in whom there is ascertainable any Negro blood shall be deemed and taken to be a colored person, and every person not a colored person having one fourth or more of American Indian blood shall be deemed an American Indian; except that members of Indian tribes existing in this Commonwealth having one fourth or more of Indian blood and less than one sixteenth of Negro blood shall be deemed tribal Indians." *Va. Code Ann.* § 1–14 (1960 Repl. Vol.).

Virginia is now one of 16 States which prohibit and punish marriages on the basis of racial classifications.[4] Penalties for miscegenation arose as an incident to slavery and have been common in Virginia since the colonial period. The present statutory scheme dates from the adoption of the Racial Integrity Act of 1924, passed during the period of extreme nativism which followed the end of the First World War. The central features of this Act, and current Virginia law, are the absolute prohibition of a "white person" marrying other than another "white person," a prohibition against issuing marriage licenses until the issuing official is satisfied that the applicants' statements as to their race are correct, certificates of "racial composition" to be kept by both local and state registrars, and the carrying forward of earlier prohibitions against racial intermarriage.

I

In upholding the constitutionality of these provisions in the decision below, the Supreme Court of Appeals of Virginia referred to its 1955 decision in *Naim v. Naim*, 87 S.E.2d 749 (Va.1955), as stating the reasons supporting the validity of these laws. In *Naim*, the state court concluded that the State's legitimate purposes were "to preserve the racial integrity of its citizens," and to prevent "the corruption of blood," "a mongrel breed of citizens," and "the obliteration of racial pride," obviously an endorsement of the doctrine of White Supremacy. The court also reasoned that marriage has traditionally been subject to state regulation without federal intervention, and, consequently, the regulation of marriage should be left to exclusive state control by the Tenth Amendment.

While the state court is no doubt correct in asserting that marriage is a social relation subject to the State's police power, *Maynard v. Hill*, 125 U.S. 190 (1888), the State does not contend in its argument before this Court that its powers to regulate marriage are unlimited notwithstanding the commands of the Fourteenth Amendment. Nor could it do so in light of *Meyer v. Nebraska*, 262 U.S. 390 (1923), and *Skinner v. Oklahoma*, 316 U.S. 535 (1942). Instead, the State argues that the meaning of the Equal Protection Clause, as illuminated by the statements of the Framers, is only that state penal laws containing an interracial element as part of the definition of the offense must apply equally to whites and Negroes in the sense that members of each race are punished to the same degree. Thus,

---

[4] After the initiation of this litigation, Maryland repealed its prohibitions against interracial marriage, *Md. Laws* 1967, c. 6, leaving Virginia and 15 other States [Alabama; Arkansas; Delaware; Florida; Georgia; Kentucky; Louisiana; Mississippi; Missouri; North Carolina; Oklahoma; South Carolina; Tennessee; Texas; West Virginia] with statutes outlawing interracial marriage. * * *

Over the past 15 years, 14 states have repealed laws outlawing interracial marriages: Arizona, California, Colorado, Idaho, Indiana, Maryland, Montana, Nebraska, Nevada, North Dakota, Oregon, South Dakota, Utah, and Wyoming. The first state court to recognize that miscegenation statutes violate the Equal Protection Clause was the Supreme Court of California. *Perez v. Sharp*, 198 P.2d 17 (Cal. 1948).

the State contends that, because its miscegenation statutes punish equally both the white and the Negro participants in an interracial marriage, these statutes, despite their reliance on racial classifications, do not constitute an invidious discrimination based upon race. The second argument advanced by the State assumes the validity of its equal application theory. The argument is that, if the Equal Protection Clause does not outlaw miscegenation statutes because of their reliance on racial classifications, the question of constitutionality would thus become whether there was any rational basis for a State to treat interracial marriages differently from other marriages. On this question, the State argues, the scientific evidence is substantially in doubt and, consequently, this Court should defer to the wisdom of the state legislature in adopting its policy of discouraging interracial marriages.

Because we reject the notion that the mere "equal application" of a statute containing racial classifications is enough to remove the classifications from the Fourteenth Amendment's proscription of all invidious racial discriminations, we do not accept the State's contention that these statutes should be upheld if there is any possible basis for concluding that they serve a rational purpose. The mere fact of equal application does not mean that our analysis of these statutes should follow the approach we have taken in cases involving no racial discrimination where the Equal Protection Clause has been arrayed against a statute discriminating between the kinds of advertising which may be displayed on trucks in New York City, *Railway Express Agency, Inc. v. New York*, 336 U.S. 106 (1949), or an exemption in Ohio's ad valorem tax for merchandise owned by a nonresident in a storage warehouse, *Allied Stores of Ohio, Inc. v. Bowers*, 358 U.S. 522 (1959). In these cases, involving distinctions not drawn according to race, the Court has merely asked whether there is any rational foundation for the discriminations, and has deferred to the wisdom of the state legislatures. In the case at bar, however, we deal with statutes containing racial classifications, and the fact of equal application does not immunize the statute from the very heavy burden of justification which the Fourteenth Amendment has traditionally required of state statutes drawn according to race.

The State argues that statements in the Thirty-ninth Congress about the time of the passage of the Fourteenth Amendment indicate that the Framers did not intend the Amendment to make unconstitutional state miscegenation laws. Many of the statements alluded to by the State concern the debates over the Freedmen's Bureau Bill, which President Johnson vetoed, and the Civil Rights Act of 1866, enacted over his veto. While these statements have some relevance to the intention of Congress in submitting the Fourteenth Amendment, it must be understood that they pertained to the passage of specific statutes and not to the broader, organic purpose of a constitutional amendment. As for the various statements directly concerning the Fourteenth Amendment, we have said in connection with a related problem, that although these historical sources "cast some light" they are not sufficient to resolve the problem; "[a]t best, they are inconclusive. The most avid proponents of the post-War Amendments undoubtedly intended them to remove all legal distinctions among 'all persons born or naturalized in the United States.' Their opponents, just as certainly, were antagonistic to both the letter and the spirit of the Amendments and wished them to have the most limited effect." *Brown v. Board of Education*, 347 U.S. 483, 489 (1954). *See also Strauder v. West Virginia*, 100 U.S. 303, 310 (1880). We have rejected the proposition that the debates in the Thirty-ninth Congress or in the state legislatures which ratified the Fourteenth Amendment supported the theory advanced by the State, that the requirement of equal protection of the laws is satisfied by penal laws defining offenses based on racial classifications so long as white and Negro participants in the offense were similarly punished. *McLaughlin v. Florida*, 379 U.S. 184 (1964).

The State finds support for its "equal application" theory in the decision of the Court in *Pace v. Alabama*, 106 U.S. 583 (1883). In that case, the Court upheld a conviction under an Alabama statute forbidding adultery or fornication between a white person and a Negro which imposed a greater penalty than that of a statute proscribing similar conduct by members of the same race. The Court reasoned that the statute could not be said to discriminate against Negroes because the punishment for each participant in the offense was the same. However, as recently as the 1964 Term, in rejecting the reasoning of that case, we stated "*Pace* represents a limited view of the Equal Protection Clause which has not withstood analysis in the subsequent decisions of this Court." *McLaughlin v. Florida*, 379 U.S. at 188. As we there demonstrated, the Equal Protection Clause requires the consideration of whether the classifications drawn by any statute constitute an arbitrary and invidious discrimination. The clear and central purpose of the Fourteenth Amendment was to eliminate all official state sources of invidious racial discrimination in the States. *Slaughter-House Cases*, 16 Wall. 36, 71 (1873); *Strauder v. West Virginia*, 100 U.S. 303, 307–308 (1880); *Ex parte Virginia*, 100 U.S. 339, 344–345 (1880); *Shelley v. Kraemer*, 334 U.S. 1 (1948); *Burton v. Wilmington Parking Authority*, 365 U.S. 715 (1961).

There can be no question but that Virginia's miscegenation statutes rest solely upon distinctions drawn according to race. The statutes proscribe generally accepted conduct if engaged in by members of different races. Over the years, this Court has consistently repudiated "[d]istinctions between citizens solely because of their ancestry" as being "odious to a free people whose institutions are founded upon the doctrine of equality." *Hirabayashi v. United States*, 320 U.S. 81, 100 (1943). At the very least, the Equal Protection Clause demands that racial classifications, especially suspect in criminal statutes, be subjected to the "most rigid scrutiny," *Korematsu v. United States*, 323 U.S. 214, 216 (1944), and, if they are ever to be upheld, they must be shown to be necessary to the accomplishment of some permissible state objective, independent of the racial discrimination which it was the object of the Fourteenth Amendment to eliminate. Indeed, two members of this Court have already stated that they "cannot conceive of a valid legislative purpose . . . which makes the color of a person's skin the test of whether his conduct is a criminal offense." *McLaughlin v. Florida*, 379 U.S. at 198 (Stewart, J., joined by Douglas, J., concurring).

There is patently no legitimate overriding purpose independent of invidious racial discrimination which justifies this classification. The fact that Virginia prohibits only interracial marriages involving white persons demonstrates that the racial classifications must stand on their own justification, as measures designed to maintain White Supremacy.[5] We have consistently denied the constitutionality of measures which restrict the rights of citizens on account of race. There can be no doubt that restricting the freedom to marry solely because of racial classifications violates the central meaning of the Equal Protection Clause.

II

These statutes also deprive the Lovings of liberty without due process of law in violation of the Due Process Clause of the Fourteenth Amendment. The freedom to marry has long been recognized as one of the vital personal rights essential to the orderly pursuit of happiness by free men.

Marriage is one of the "basic civil rights of man," fundamental to our very existence and survival. *Skinner v. Oklahoma*, 316 U.S. 535, 541 (1942). *See also Maynard v. Hill*, 125 U.S. 190 (1888). To deny this fundamental freedom on so unsupportable a basis as the racial classifications embodied in these statutes, classifications so directly subversive of the principle of equality at the heart of the Fourteenth Amendment, is surely to deprive all the State's citizens of liberty without due process of law. The Fourteenth Amendment requires that the

---

[5]   Appellants point out that the State's concern in these statutes, as expressed in the words of the 1924 Act's title, "An Act to Preserve Racial Integrity," extends only to the integrity of the white race. While Virginia prohibits whites from marrying any nonwhite (subject to the exception for the descendants of Pocahontas), Negroes, Orientals, and any other racial class may intermarry without statutory interference. Appellants contend that this distinction renders Virginia's miscegenation statutes arbitrary and unreasonable even assuming the constitutional validity of an official purpose to preserve "racial integrity." We need not reach this contention because we find the racial classifications in these statutes repugnant to the Fourteenth Amendment, even assuming an even-handed state purpose to protect the "integrity" of all races.

freedom of choice to marry not be restricted by invidious racial discriminations. Under our Constitution, the freedom to marry, or not marry, a person of another race resides with the individual and cannot be infringed by the State.

These convictions must be reversed. *It is so ordered.*

MR. JUSTICE STEWART, concurring.

I have previously expressed the belief that "it is simply not possible for a state law to be valid under our Constitution which makes the criminality of an act depend upon the race of the actor." *McLaughlin v. Florida*, 379 U.S. 184, 198 (concurring opinion). Because I adhere to that belief, I concur in the judgment of the Court.

NOTES

1.   After *Loving*, the Supreme Court struck down a state statute that burdened the marriage rights of those who have outstanding child support obligations, *Zablocki v. Redhail*, 434 U.S. 374, 390–91, 98 S.Ct. 673, 683, 54 L.Ed.2d 618, 633 (1978), as well as a state regulation that burdened the marriage rights of prisoners, *Turner v. Safley*, 482 U.S. 78, 100, 107 S.Ct. 2254, 2267, 96 L.Ed.2d 64, 86 (1987). In *Turner,* the Court identified what it regarded as the central elements of marriage:

> It is settled that a prison inmate "retains those [constitutional] rights that are not inconsistent with his status as a prisoner or with the legitimate penological objectives of the corrections system." The right to marry, like many other rights, is subject to substantial restrictions as a result of incarceration. Many important attributes of marriage remain, however, after taking into account the limitations imposed by prison life. First, inmate marriages, like others, are expressions of emotional support and public commitment. These elements are an important and significant aspect of the marital relationship. In addition, many religions recognize marriage as having spiritual significance; for some inmates and their spouses, therefore, the commitment of marriage may be an exercise of religious faith as well as an expression of personal dedication. Third, most inmates eventually will be released by parole or commutation, and therefore most inmate marriages are formed in the expectation that they ultimately will be fully consummated. Finally, marital status often is a precondition to the receipt of government benefits (e.g., Social Security benefits), property rights (e.g., tenancy by the entirety, inheritance rights), and other, less tangible benefits (e.g., legitimation of children born out of wedlock). These incidents of marriage, like the religious and personal aspects of the marriage commitment, are unaffected by the fact of confinement or the pursuit of legitimate corrections goals. . . . Taken together, we conclude that these remaining elements are

sufficient to form a constitutionally protected marital relationship in the prison context.

482 U.S. at 95–96, 107 S.Ct. at 2265, 96 L.Ed. at 83.

2.   The right to marry established in *Loving* is closely related to the right of (marital) privacy established in *Griswold v. Connecticut*, 381 U.S. 479, 485–86, 85 S.Ct. 1678, 1682, 14 L.Ed.2d 510, 515–16 (1965) (striking down ban on contraceptive use by married couples), where the Court observed that marriage "is an association that promotes a way of life, not causes; a harmony in living, not political faiths; a bilateral loyalty, not commercial or social projects" and "for as noble a purpose as any involved in our prior decisions." 381 U.S. at 486.

3.   Although this Chapter is concerned primarily with same-sex relationships, it should be noted that lesbians and gay men sometimes find themselves in different-sex marriages. Moreover, different-sex marriages also include many bisexual men and women. *See generally* BRENDA MADDOX, MARRIED AND GAY: AN INTIMATE LOOK AT A DIFFERENT RELATIONSHIP (1982).

MARRIAGE AND THE STRUGGLE FOR GAY, LESBIAN, AND BLACK LIBERATION*
Randall Kennedy

The central claim of those who invoke *Loving* on behalf of the right to same-sex marriage is that prohibiting same-sex couples from marrying is as illegitimate as prohibiting different-race couples from marrying. It is this use of *Loving* that I refer to as the *Loving* analogy. This analogy, however, is conceptualized in a variety of ways.

One conception emphasizes marriage as a fundamental right. It contends that the right to marry is so essential that only the weightiest and most narrowly tailored policy can justify an abridgement of this right. Under this view, due process is violated if the state bars eligibility for marriage pursuant to a rationale that is insufficiently substantial and narrow. Just as the rationales supporting antimiscegenation laws were deemed in *Loving* to be insufficiently compelling to justify barring different-race couples from marriage, so too should the rationales supporting the heterosexual monopoly be deemed insufficiently compelling to justify banning same-sex couples from marriage.

A second conception notes that, as a formal matter, bars to same-sex marriage are gender discrimination. Such barriers do not expressly prohibit gays or lesbians from marrying; rather, they expressly prevent a man from marrying a person that a woman would be allowed to marry, and prevent a woman from marrying a person that a man would be

---

    *   Randall Kennedy, *Marriage and the Struggle for Gay, Lesbian, and Black Liberation*, 2005 UTAH L. REV. 781, 786–94.

allowed to marry. Proponents of this argument contend that the aim of these gender restrictions is to perpetuate traditional, patriarchal gender conventions, particularly those that keep women in a dependent relationship to men. According to one proponent of this theory, the prohibition on same-sex marriage preserves the polarities of gender on which the subordination of women rests in a similar fashion as the prohibition of interracial marriage preserved the polarization of race "on which white supremacy rested." As the *Loving* decision invalidated the use of antimiscegenation laws as weapons of continued racial oppression, so too should a latter-day *Loving*-like ruling invalidate the use of gender restrictions as weapons of continued gender oppression.

A third conception is the most common, the most influential, the one I prefer, and the one I will use for the balance of this Article. It focuses upon the same-sex prohibition as a means by which the heterosexual—"straight"—majority oppresses gays and lesbians. Under this view, the bar to same-sex marriage stigmatizes gays and lesbians on behalf of heterosexualist caste assumptions in a fashion comparable to the way in which antimiscegenation laws wrongfully stigmatized blacks on behalf of white supremacist caste assumptions. Many adherents to this sexual orientation equal protection conception of the *Loving* analogy argue that governmental distinctions based on sexual orientation should be subjected to strict judicial scrutiny as are governmental distinctions based on racial classifications.

Those who deploy the *Loving* analogy do not—and should not—claim that prohibitions against interracial marriage and prohibitions against same-sex marriage are the same. Obviously they are not. As Professor George Chauncey observes, "[c]laiming the two experiences have been the same does no justice to history and no service to the gay cause." For one thing, antimiscegenation policies, though prevalent, were never as pervasive as bars to same-sex marriage. From early in the history of the United States, there were at least some locales where people of different races could lawfully marry. Eight states never enacted antimiscegenation laws, and at the time the United States Supreme Court invalidated such statutes, thirty-four states permitted interracial marriage. By contrast, until recently, same-sex marriage was either unimagined or prohibited in every state. . . . On the other hand, while criminal punishments played a substantial part in the enforcement of antimiscegenation statutes, criminal law has played a negligible part in the enforcement of prohibitions of same-sex marriage (though it was not until 2003 that the Court barred states from punishing people engaged in sexual intimacy solely because the parties involved were of the same gender).

Another difference between prohibitions on interracial marriage and prohibitions on same-sex marriage has to do with the salience of the marriage issue in the campaign for gay and lesbian liberation. Marriage has emerged as a prominent—indeed a central—issue for many activists who champion the interests of gays and lesbians. By contrast, few activists championing the interests of African Americans openly campaigned to eradicate antimiscegenation laws. When pressed, they condemned these laws, rightly perceiving them as government-sponsored, antiblack stigmata. But they refrained from making the destruction of antimiscegenation statutes a priority. They feared that aggressive action on this front would provoke a dangerous backlash and divert resources from more popular concerns such as voting and schooling.

Clearly then, differences distinguish conflicts over interracial and same-sex marriage. They are not the same—a point that one might almost assume given its obviousness. After all, by definition, an analogy involves a comparison of distinct, albeit arguably related, phenomena. It bears noting, moreover, given the criticism aimed at the *Loving* analogy, that there are few instances in which proponents have made the total equivalency claims that Professor Chauncey rightly abjures. Partisans of the *Loving* analogy typically go out of their way to acknowledge distinctions between hierarchies grounded on race and hierarchies grounded on sexual orientation. Indeed, if anything, they have often been unduly diffident in defending their use of *Loving*.

The *Loving* analogy is a heuristic device that acknowledges the distinctions but underscores the similarities between prohibitions on interracial marriage and prohibitions on same-sex marriage. Partisans of the *Loving* analogy rightly maintain that the similarities place a heavy pall over bars to same-sex marriage given the now widely recognized illegitimacy of antimiscegenation laws. They contend that in both cases popular prejudices, nourished by deeply entrenched mythologies, were translated into laws or policies that have wrongly prevented or impeded couples from marrying.

Many defenders of prohibitions to same-sex marriage indignantly reject comparisons that place them on a moral or political par with racial segregationists. Some deny being homophobic. Some even suggest that their defense of the heterosexual monopoly on marriage is actually a boon to gays and lesbians. Declaring that "[t]he stigmatization of homosexuals is wrong and makes no contribution to the moral health of our society," Shelby Steele, nonetheless, defends prohibitions against same-sex marriage and maintains that marriage is bad for gays and lesbians. "The true problem with gay marriage," Steele writes, "is that it consigns gays to a life of mimicry and pathos. It shoehorns them into an institution that does not reflect the best possibilities of their own sexual orientation."

Such claims recall yet another useful lesson highlighted by the *Loving* analogy—the reminder that many racial segregationists believed that apartheid American style was good for blacks and for whites and that, viewed properly, the race line was reasonable and not invidious. Remember that in its infamous decision in *Plessy v. Ferguson*, upholding the constitutionality of racial segregation in intrastate transportation, the United States Supreme Court rejected the claim that state-enforced racial separation in railroad cars stigmatized blacks. "Negroes," the Court insinuated, were simply being unduly sensitive. According to the Court, the enforced separation of the races did not stamp blacks with a badge of inferiority. "If this be so," the Court averred, "it is not by anything found in the act, but solely because the colored race chooses to put that construction upon it."

Today, Americans look back upon segregationist apologetics with disbelief, amazed that millions of apparently decent and sensible people could have accepted those rationalizations and misperceived (or ignored) the cruel reality of segregation. That they did, however, should caution us to the possibility that familiarity with traditional and widely accepted arrangements can blind people to forms of oppression that are inconsistent with fundamental legal and moral requirements.

It is a mistake to think that cruel policies can only be established or maintained by those who are conspicuously evil. Typically, horrible social injustices sanctioned by law are perpetrated not by individuals who are self-consciously criminal, but instead by individuals who are soberingly normal and sincerely believe that what they are doing is right. Many slaveholders sincerely believed that for Negroes, bondage was a positive good. Similarly, many segregationists believed, honestly, that keeping blacks in their "place" would redound to their benefit as well as to the interests of white society. That is why many segregationists were surprised—and hurt—when blacks began to protest openly and aggressively against the Jim Crow system. They actually, though mistakenly, believed that blacks were satisfied with their lot absent outside agitation, and that segregation was a prudent and fair social arrangement. A great achievement of the civil rights movement was to remove layers of obfuscation that had blinded or confused people about the realities of segregation. The litigation that produced *Brown* and *Loving* assisted in enabling people, including some former segregationists, to see that laws requiring racial separation did not represent mere innocent racial distinctions, but represented instead manifestations of racial subordination.

Advocates for gays and lesbians are embarked on a similar endeavor. They, too, are attempting to show that a familiar policy—heterosexual monopoly of marriage—that millions of ordinary, decent people accept as a given is instead a choice that wrongs same-sex couples. As champions for the advancement of African Americans mobilized historians, sociologists, anthropologists, theologians, political theorists, journalists, medical theorists, and other interpreters of the social and scientific world to challenge mythologies that stigmatized blacks, so too are champions for the advancement of gays and lesbians engaged in a wide-ranging attack upon the numerous, taken-for-granted ways in which oppressive assumptions of heterosexual superiority are inscribed in virtually every nook and cranny of our culture. The *Loving* analogy, with its explicit plea for empathy, is part of that campaign.

Efforts to elevate the status of gays and lesbians have often imitated the tactics, imagery, and rhetoric of the various campaigns to advance the status of African Americans. Seeking to dramatize the deplorable but neglected oppression of sexual minorities, Bayard Rustin, a key advisor to Martin Luther King, Jr. in the 1950s and 1960s, declared in the 1970s that "the new niggers are gays." Champions of gay liberation seek to end what they call "the apartheid of the closet." "Black is beautiful" is echoed by "gay is good." "Black pride" is echoed by "gay pride." The Lambda Legal Defense and Education Fund models itself on the legendary National Association for the Advancement of Colored People (NAACP) Legal Defense and Education Fund. The killing of Matthew Shepherd is analogized to the killing of Emmet Till.

Clearly useful in attracting support in certain quarters, this effort to appropriate by analogy some of the goodwill, inspiration, and sympathy generated by the black civil rights movement has also prompted negative reactions. Recognizing the potency of the *Loving* analogy, detractors have sought to delegitimize it. A telling example is David Orgon Coolidge's article, *Playing the Loving Card: Same-Sex Marriage and the Politics of Analogy.* "Of all the legal arguments offered in favor of legalizing same-sex marriage," he writes, "the one with the greatest rhetorical punch is the *Loving* analogy. . . . In one fell swoop one can invoke race, civil rights, and the freedom to marry while simultaneously painting one's opponents [as latter-day] Bull Connors." According to Coolidge, the *Loving* analogy is mere demagoguery—"the race card" of the marriage debate.

Although Coolidge was a white cultural conservative, those who oppose the *Loving* analogy may be found on a broad demographic and ideological spectrum that includes black liberals as well as black conservatives. "A lot of blacks are upset that the feminist movement pimped off the black movement," declared Alveda Celeste King, the niece of Martin Luther King, Jr. "Now here comes the gay movement. Blacks resent it very much, because they do not see a parallel, nor do I." King's remark encapsulates succinctly what I shall refer to as the racial critique of the *Loving* analogy. The racial critique asserts that, in the United States, discrimination based on race has been so fundamentally different from and worse than discrimination based on sexual orientation that analogizing the two is wrong and misleading.

Many who voice the racial critique emphasize that race is an unchangeable characteristic that is visible, while sexual orientation is a matter of chosen behavior which, in any event, can be hidden. Hence, in the course of deriding the *Loving* analogy, journalist Gwen Daye Richardson emphasized the visibility of race: "Skin color is an immediately obvious and permanent characteristic present at birth," she averred, "[h]omosexuality is not. Unless gay people tell someone they are gay, no one knows. Blacks have no such option." Emphasizing the supposed immutability of race, Reverend Walter E. Fauntroy maintained that "[t]he essential difference between the Black civil rights struggle and the gay rights struggle is that Black people are discriminated against on the basis of something we cannot change, our race; gays are discriminated against on the basis of their behavior, something that can be changed." Fauntroy inferred that it is not fair to deny rights on the basis of something a person cannot change.

In its characteristic articulation, the racial critique of the *Loving* analogy is beset by a number of weaknesses. Leaving to one side the intensely debated issue of the mutability of sexual orientation, the racial critique overlooks the extent to which racial identity can be chosen and is thus changeable. Some people elect to be black insofar as they present themselves publicly as black even though they have physical characteristics that would otherwise prompt many onlookers to perceive them as "white." It is also true that some people who are, by certain definitions, "black" (perhaps they have black parents or grandparents) choose to think of themselves and present themselves as "white." To an appreciable extent, then, race is or can be a chosen category. * * *

More importantly, positing immutability—"we are not responsible for our condition and cannot change it"—as a basis for legal solicitude and social exoneration implicitly concedes that the trait in question is regrettable, like a disease one has caught through no fault of his own. Portraying blackness or homosexuality as a tragic pathology is itself demeaning.

Still more importantly, visibility and immutability render blacks more eligible for solicitude than gays and lesbians because African Americans are a discrete and insular minority distinguishable from the white majority by differences (especially skin color) that are visible and unchangeable. But if these features make blacks more eligible for solicitude than gays and lesbians, the logic of the detractors would seem to dictate that blacks should lose their eligibility for heightened solicitude if their blackness was not unchangeably visible. The unspoken corollary to claiming that it is objectionable to withhold rights on the basis of something a person cannot change is claiming that it is less objectionable to deny rights on the basis of something a person can change. This logic is hardly appealing. Racial oppression would not be one whit less dreadful and needful of judicial (and other forms of) intervention if blacks were somehow afforded the option of changing their color. As noted above, an appreciable number of blacks have complexions that allow them to be perceived as "white." But blacks who can "pass" should receive no less protection from racial oppression than "visible" blacks even though the former could, if they wished, blend in with the white majority. Walter White should have been protected against Jim Crow legislation as much as any black person (or any person of whatever complexion) even though Walter White looked like a white man. The ability of people to "pass," convert, retreat into a closet, or go underground should provide no basis for lessened attention to invidious discriminations.

B. LITIGATING FOR SAME-SEX MARRIAGE

1. First Generation Cases

SINGER V. HARA
Court of Appeals of Washington, 1974
522 P.2d 1187, 11 Wash. App. 247, *review denied*, 84 Wash. 2d 1008 (1974)

SWANSON, CHIEF JUDGE.

... [A]ppellants applied for a marriage license on September 20, 1971, and after respondent Hara refused to grant such a license, the motion to show cause was filed on April 27, 1972. . . .

[Appellants argue] that the state prohibition of same-sex marriages violates the ERA which recently became part of our state constitution. The question thus presented is a matter of first impression in this state and, to our knowledge, no court in the nation has ruled upon the legality of same-sex marriage in light of an equal rights amendment. The ERA provides, in relevant part:

> Equality of rights and responsibility under the law shall not be denied or abridged on account of sex. * * *

Although appellants suggest an analogy between the racial classification involved in *Loving* and *Perez* and the alleged sexual classification involved in the case at bar, we do not find such an analogy. The operative distinction lies in the relationship which is described by the term "marriage" itself, and that relationship is the legal union of one man and one woman. Washington statutes, specifically those relating to marriage (RCW 26.04) and marital (community) property (RCW 26.16), are clearly founded upon the presumption that marriage, as a legal relationship, may exist only between one man and one woman who are otherwise qualified to enter that relationship. Similarly although it appears that the appellate courts of this state until now have not been required to define specifically what constitutes a marriage, it is apparent from a review of cases dealing with legal questions arising out of the marital relationship that the definition of marriage as the legal union of one man and one woman who are otherwise qualified to enter into the relationship not only is clearly implied from such cases, but also was deemed by the court in each case to be so obvious as not to require recitation. Finally, the courts known by us to have considered the question have all concluded that same-sex relationships are outside of the proper definition of marriage. * * *

* * * We do not believe that approval of the ERA by the people of this state reflects any intention upon their part to offer couples involved in same-sex relationships the protection of our marriage laws. A consideration of the basic purpose of the ERA makes it apparent why that amendment does not support appellants' claim of discrimination. The primary purpose of the ERA is to overcome discriminatory legal treatment as between men and women "on account of sex." The popular slogan, "Equal pay for equal work," particularly expresses the rejection of the notion that merely because a person is a woman, rather than a man, she is to be treated differently than a man with qualifications equal to her own.

Prior to adoption of the ERA, the proposition that women were to be accorded a position in the law inferior to that of men had a long history. Thus, in that context, the purpose of the ERA is to provide the legal protection, as between men and women, that apparently is missing from the state and federal Bills of Rights, and it is in light of that purpose that the language of the ERA must be construed. To accept the appellants' contention that the ERA must be interpreted to prohibit statutes which refuse to permit same-sex marriages would be to subvert the purpose for which the ERA was enacted by expanding its scope beyond that which was undoubtedly intended by the majority of the citizens of this state who voted for the amendment. * * *

In the instant case, it is apparent that the state's refusal to grant a license allowing the appellants to marry one another is not based upon appellants' status as males, but rather it is based upon the state's recognition that our society as a whole views marriage as the appropriate and desirable forum for procreation and the rearing of children. This is true even though married couples are not required to become parents and even though some couples are incapable of becoming parents and even though not all couples who produce children are married. These, however, are exceptional situations. The fact remains that marriage exists as a protected legal institution primarily because of societal values associated with the propagation of the human race. Further, it is apparent that no same-sex couple offers the possibility of the birth of children by their union. Thus the refusal of the state to authorize same-sex marriages results from such impossibility of reproduction rather than from an invidious discrimination "on account of sex." Therefore, the definition of marriage as the legal union of one man and one woman is permissible as applied to appellants, notwithstanding the prohibition contained in the ERA, because it is founded upon the unique physical characteristics of the sexes and appellants are not being discriminated against because of their status as males per se. In short, we hold the ERA does not require the state to authorize same-sex marriage.

Appellants' final assignment of error is based primarily upon the proposition that the state's failure to grant them a marriage license violates the Equal Protection Clause of the Fourteenth Amendment to the United States Constitution. The threshold question presented involves the standard by which to measure appellants' constitutional argument.
* * *

Although appellants present argument to the contrary, we agree with the state's contention that to define marriage to exclude homosexual or any other same-sex relationships is not to create an inherently suspect legislative classification requiring strict judicial scrutiny to determine a compelling state interest. *Baker v. Nelson*, 191 N.W.2d 185 (Minn.1971); *see Jones v. Hallahan, supra*. . . . The state contends that the exclusion of same-sex relationships from our marriage statutes may be upheld under the traditional "reasonable basis" or "rational relationship" test to which we have previously made reference. We agree.

There can be no doubt that there exists a rational basis for the state to limit the definition of marriage to exclude same-sex relationships. . . .

As the court observed in *Baker v. Nelson, supra* at 186:

The institution of marriage as a union of man and woman, uniquely involving the procreation and rearing of children within a family, is as old as the book of Genesis. . . . This historic institution manifestly is more deeply founded than the asserted contemporary concept of marriage and societal interests for which petitioners contend. The due process clause of the Fourteenth Amendment is not a charter for restructuring it by judicial legislation. . . .

The equal protection clause of the Fourteenth Amendment, like the due process clause, is not offended by the state's classification of persons authorized to marry.

Thus, for the reasons stated in this opinion, we hold that the trial court correctly concluded that the state's denial of a marriage license to appellants is required by our state statutes and permitted by both the state and federal constitutions. The judgment is affirmed.

NOTES

1. In addition to the *Singer* case, two other cases in the early 1970s, cited in *Singer*, upheld state marriage laws against constitutional challenges by same-sex couples—*Jones v. Hallahan*, 501 S.W.2d 588, 590 (Ky. Ct. App. 1973), and *Baker v. Nelson*, 191 N.W.2d 185, 187, 291 Minn. 310, 315 (1971). The U.S. Supreme Court dismissed the appeal in *Baker* for "want of a substantial federal question." 409 U.S. 810, 93 S.Ct. 37, 34 L.Ed.2d 65 (1972). Two later challenges also failed: one in the 1980s, *DeSanto v. Barnsley*, 476 A.2d 952, 328 Pa. Super. 181 (1984), and another in the 1990s, *Dean v. District of Columbia*, 653 A.2d 307 (D.C. 1995). In more recent federal litigation, opponents of same-sex marriage have used *Baker* to argue that the "Supreme Court has already decided the question[.]" Defendant-Intervenors-Appellants' Opening Brief at 16, *Perry v. Brown*, 671 F.3d 1052 (9th Cir. 2012).

2. Other courts ruled against same-sex marriage in different contexts. An intermediate appellate court in New York, faced with a case in which a man had married another man whom he thought was a woman, relied on dictionary definitions of marriage in ruling that "[t]he marriage ceremony itself was a nullity." *Anonymous v. Anonymous*, 325 N.Y.S.2d 499, 501, 67 Misc.2d 982, 982 (1971). In 1988, a circuit judge in Indiana denied two gay prisoners a license to marry and fined them $2,800 because "[t]heir claims about Indiana law and constitutional rights are wacky and sanctionably so." *See* Arthur Leonard, *Judge Denies Marriage License to Gay Male Prisoners*, 1988 LESBIAN/GAY L. NOTES 63. And in October 1991 an Ohio probate judge denied a marriage license to a gay couple, asserting that state law prohibits same-sex marriage. *See* Arthur Leonard, *Gay Washingtonians Sue for Marriage License*, 1991 LESBIAN/GAY L. NOTES 3.

2. Second Generation Cases

In 1993, Hawaii's Supreme Court reinstated a same-sex marriage challenge that had been dismissed by a trial court. *Baehr v. Lewin*, 852 P.2d 44, 68, 74 Haw. 530, 582 (1993). The court held that the denial of marriage licenses to same-sex couples articulated a claim of sex discrimination under the Hawaii state constitution, and it remanded the case for trial on the question of whether the state could satisfy strict scrutiny in defending its policy. The Hawaii Supreme Court's opinion on the sex discrimination claim is reprinted above, in Chapter 3, Section III.A.1. That opinion is widely seen to have opened the contemporary public debate over same-sex marriage. On remand, after a full trial on the merits, the trial court ruled that the state's ban on same-sex marriage was unconstitutional. *Baehr v. Miike*, 1996 WL 694235, at *22 (Haw. Cir. Ct. 1996). The trial court decision was stayed pending the state's appeal to the Hawaii Supreme Court. Meanwhile, in November 1998, the voters amended the state's constitution to permit the legislature to reserve marriage to opposite-sex couples—a reservation that the legislature, in fact, made. Legislative action associated with the ballot initiative on same-sex marriage also resulted in the enactment of the first statewide law providing rights and benefits to same-sex couples through a nonmarital designation. The "reciprocal beneficiaries" law included not only same-sex couples but also other pairings, such as blood relatives, excluded from marriage. The law included survivorship rights, health benefits, property rights, and legal standing regarding wrongful death and victims' rights. It went into effect on July 1, 1997. *See* HAW. REV. STAT. §§ 572C–1 to 572C–7 (2006).

Shortly after the Hawaii law went into effect, the Alaska electorate amended its state constitution to block same-sex marriage. As in Hawaii, the amendment was a response to a court decision. In *Brause v. Bureau of Vital Statistics*, 1998 WL 88743, at *6 (Alaska Super. Ct. 1998), a trial court had affirmed the right to marry asserted by two gay men. In November 1998, the Alaska electorate amended the state constitution to read:

> To be valid or recognized in this State, a marriage may exist only between one man and one woman.

ALASKA CONST. art. I, § 25 (amended 1998). The Alaska voters thereby ended the marriage litigation just as the Hawaii voters had ended the marriage challenge in their state.

Six years after the Hawaii decision, the Vermont Supreme Court, in a landmark decision, ruled that same-sex couples must be provided the same benefits and protections as married couples. The court did not, however, require the state's legislature to open marriage to same-sex couples. In *Baker v. Vermont*, 744 A.2d 864, 170 Vt. 194 (1999), the court said:

> May the State of Vermont exclude same-sex couples from the benefits and protections that its laws provide to opposite-sex married couples? That is the fundamental question we address in this appeal, a question that the Court well knows arouses deeply-felt religious, moral, and political beliefs. Our constitutional responsibility to consider the legal merits of issues properly before us provides no exception for the controversial case. The issue before the Court, moreover, does not turn on the religious or moral debate over intimate same-sex relationships, but rather on the statutory and constitutional basis for the exclusion of same-sex couples from the secular benefits and protections offered married couples. We conclude that under the Common Benefits Clause of the Vermont Constitution, which, in pertinent part, reads, "That government is, or ought to be, instituted for the common benefit, protection, and security of the people, nation, or community, and not for the particular

emolument or advantage of any single person, family, or set of persons, who are a part only of that community," Vt. Const., ch. I, art 7., plaintiffs may not be deprived of the statutory benefits and protections afforded persons of the opposite sex who choose to marry. We hold that the State is constitutionally required to extend to same-sex couples the common benefits and protections that flow from marriage under Vermont law. Whether this ultimately takes the form of inclusion within the marriage laws themselves or a parallel "domestic partnership" system or some equivalent statutory alternative, rests with the Legislature. Whatever system is chosen, however, must conform with the constitutional imperative to afford all Vermonters the common benefit, protection, and security of the law. * * *

While the laws relating to marriage have undergone many changes during the last century, largely toward the goal of equalizing the status of husbands and wives, the benefits of marriage have not diminished in value. On the contrary, the benefits and protections incident to a marriage license under Vermont law have never been greater. They include, for example, the right to receive a portion of the estate of a spouse who dies intestate and protection against disinheritance through elective share provisions; preference in being appointed as the personal representative of a spouse who dies intestate; the right to bring a lawsuit for the wrongful death of a spouse; the right to bring an action for loss of consortium; the right to workers' compensation survivor benefits; the right to spousal benefits statutorily guaranteed to public employees, including health, life, disability, and accident insurance; the opportunity to be covered as a spouse under group life insurance policies issued to an employee; the opportunity to be covered as the insured's spouse under an individual health insurance policy; the right to claim an evidentiary privilege for marital communications; homestead rights and protections; the presumption of joint ownership of property and the concomitant right of survivorship; hospital visitation and other rights incident to the medical treatment of a family member; and the right to receive, and the obligation to provide, spousal support, maintenance, and property division in the event of separation or divorce. [statutory citations have been omitted] * * *

It is important to state clearly the parameters of today's ruling. Although plaintiffs sought injunctive and declaratory relief designed to secure a marriage license, their claims and arguments here have focused primarily upon the consequences of official exclusion from the statutory benefits, protections, and security incident to marriage under Vermont law. While some future case may attempt to establish that—notwithstanding equal benefits and protections under Vermont law—the denial of a marriage license operates per se to deny constitutionally-protected rights, that is not the claim we address today. We hold only that plaintiffs are entitled under Chapter I, Article 7, of the Vermont Constitution to obtain the same benefits and protections afforded by Vermont law to married opposite-sex couples. We do not purport to infringe upon the prerogatives of the Legislature to craft an appropriate means of addressing this constitutional mandate, other than to note that the record here refers to a number of potentially constitutional statutory schemes from other jurisdictions. These include what are typically referred to as "domestic partnership" or "registered partnership" acts, which generally establish an alternative legal status to marriage for same-sex couples, impose similar formal requirements and limitations, create a parallel licensing or registration scheme, and extend all or most of the same rights and obligations provided by the law to married partners.

744 A.2d at 867, 883–86, 170 Vt. at 197–98, 221–25. In the wake of the state supreme court decision, the Vermont legislature complied with the court's mandate in 2000 by enacting a law recognizing "civil unions" for same-sex couples. VT. STAT. ANN. tit. 15, §§ 1201–1207 (2007).

After *Baker*, the U.S. Supreme Court decided *Lawrence* (2003). That case did not speak directly to marriage, but had powerful implications for the issue. Professor Carlos Ball has explained *Lawrence*'s implications for the constitutional case for same-sex marriage:

The Court in *Lawrence* understood that the Texas sodomy statute implicated liberty interests associated with personal relationships as much as liberty interests associated with sexual conduct. For the Court, in fact, it made no sense to discuss the freedom to engage in sexual conduct without bringing into the liberty analysis the ability of individuals to form and maintain the kinds of personal relationships that often accompany that conduct. The impact of the Texas sodomy statute on the freedom of individuals to form and maintain personal relationships, in other words, was for the Court as important as the statute's impact on the freedom of individuals to make decisions about their sexual conduct without fear of criminal repercussions. . . .

The *Lawrence* Court recognized that the criminalization of particular kinds of sexual intimacy not only limits the autonomy of individuals to decide which kinds of sexual acts they want to engage in and with whom; it also, directly and necessarily, has an impact on the autonomy of individuals to build relationships that are based, in part, upon that sexual intimacy. Thus the Court, in one of the most important sentences in the opinion, noted that "[w]hen sexuality finds overt expression in intimate conduct with another person, the conduct can be but one element in a personal bond that is more enduring."

The Court in *Lawrence* understood that relationships are central to the dignity and autonomy of all individuals, including those who are lesbian or gay. As the Court saw it, what was ultimately at issue in the case was the ability of individuals to "retain their dignity as free persons" in the face of regulations such as Texas's sodomy statute that "seek to control . . . personal relationship[s]." The crucial point is this: The *Lawrence* Court understood that there is more to lesbian and gay individuals than their interest in having sex and that there is more to gay rights positions than simply the right to have sex.

Carlos A. Ball, *The Positive in the Fundamental Right to Marry: Same-Sex Marriage in the Aftermath of* Lawrence v. Texas, 88 MINN. L. REV. 1184, 1212–13 (2004).

Within six months of the *Lawrence* decision, the Massachusetts Supreme Judicial Court held that the denial of marriage licenses to same-sex couples violated its state's constitution. These developments—and reactions to them—are captured in the readings that follow.

3. The Recognition of Same-Sex Marriage

a. *The Door Opens: Goodridge*

GOODRIDGE V. DEPARTMENT OF PUBLIC HEALTH

Supreme Judicial Court of Massachusetts, 2003
798 N.E.2d 941, 440 Mass. 309

MARSHALL, C.J.

The plaintiffs are fourteen individuals from five Massachusetts counties. * * *

In March and April, 2001, each of the plaintiff couples attempted to obtain a marriage license from a city or town clerk's office. * * *

In each case, the clerk either refused to accept the notice of intention to marry or denied a marriage license to the couple on the ground that Massachusetts does not recognize same-sex marriage. Because obtaining a marriage license is a necessary prerequisite to civil marriage in Massachusetts, denying marriage licenses to the plaintiffs was tantamount to denying them access to civil marriage itself, with its appurtenant social and legal protections, benefits, and obligations.[6]

On April 11, 2001, the plaintiffs filed suit in the Superior Court against the department and the commissioner seeking a judgment that "the exclusion of the [p]laintiff couples and other qualified same-sex couples from access to marriage licenses, and the legal and social status of civil marriage, as well as the protections, benefits and obligations of marriage, violates Massachusetts law." * * *

A Superior Court judge ruled for the department. * * *

III

A

The larger question is whether, as the department claims, government action that bars same-sex couples from civil marriage constitutes a legitimate exercise of the State's authority to regulate conduct, or whether, as the plaintiffs claim, this categorical marriage exclusion violates the Massachusetts Constitution. * * *

For the reasons we explain below, we conclude that the marriage ban does not meet the rational basis test for either due process or equal protection. * * *

The department posits three legislative rationales for prohibiting same-sex couples from marrying: (1) providing a "favorable setting for procreation"; (2) ensuring the optimal setting for child rearing, which the department defines as "a two-parent family with one parent of each sex"; and (3) preserving scarce State and private financial resources. We consider each in turn.

The judge in the Superior Court endorsed the first rationale, holding that "the state's interest in regulating marriage is based on the traditional concept that marriage's primary purpose is procreation." This is incorrect. Fertility is not a condition of marriage, nor is it grounds for divorce. People who have never consummated their marriage, and never plan to, may be and stay married. People who cannot stir from their deathbed may marry. While it is certainly true that many, perhaps most,

---

[6] The complaint alleged various circumstances in which the absence of the full legal protections of civil marriage has harmed them and their children. For example, Hillary and Julie Goodridge alleged that, when Julie gave birth to their daughter (whom Hillary subsequently coadopted) during a delivery that required the infant's transfer to neonatal intensive care, Hillary "had difficulty gaining access to Julie and their newborn daughter at the hospital"; Gary Chalmers and Richard Linnell alleged that "Gary pays for a family health insurance policy at work which covers only him and their daughter because Massachusetts law does not consider Rich to be a 'dependent.' This means that their household must purchase a separate individual policy of health insurance for Rich at considerable expense. . . . Gary has a pension plan at work, but under state law, because he is a municipal employee, that plan does not allow him the same range of options in providing for his beneficiary that a married spouse has and thus he cannot provide the same security to his family that a married person could if he should predecease Rich."

married couples have children together (assisted or unassisted), it is the exclusive and permanent commitment of the marriage partners to one another, not the begetting of children, that is the sine qua non of civil marriage.[23]

* * * The "marriage is procreation" argument singles out the one unbridgeable difference between same-sex and opposite-sex couples, and transforms that difference into the essence of legal marriage. Like Amendment 2 to the Constitution of Colorado, which effectively denied homosexual persons equality under the law and full access to the political process, the marriage restriction impermissibly "identifies persons by a single trait and then denies them protection across the board." *Romer v. Evans*, 517 U.S. 620, 633 (1996). In so doing, the State's action confers an official stamp of approval on the destructive stereotype that same-sex relationships are inherently unstable and inferior to opposite-sex relationships and are not worthy of respect.

The department's first stated rationale, equating marriage with unassisted heterosexual procreation, shades imperceptibly into its second: that confining marriage to opposite-sex couples ensures that children are raised in the "optimal" setting. Protecting the welfare of children is a paramount State policy. Restricting marriage to opposite-sex couples, however, cannot plausibly further this policy. "The demographic changes of the past century make it difficult to speak of an average American family. The composition of families varies greatly from household to household." *Troxel v. Granville*, 530 U.S. 57, 63 (2000). Massachusetts has responded supportively to the changing realities of the American family and has moved vigorously to strengthen the modern family in its many variations. Moreover, we have repudiated the common-law power of the State to provide varying levels of protection to children based on the circumstances of birth. The "best interests of the child" standard does not turn on a parent's sexual orientation or marital status.

The department has offered no evidence that forbidding marriage to people of the same sex will increase the number of couples choosing to enter into opposite-sex marriages in order to have and raise children. There is thus no rational relationship between the marriage statute and the Commonwealth's proffered goal of protecting the "optimal" child rearing unit. Moreover, the department readily concedes that people in

---

[23] It is hardly surprising that civil marriage developed historically as a means to regulate heterosexual conduct and to promote child rearing, because until very recently unassisted heterosexual relations were the only means short of adoption by which children could come into the world, and the absence of widely available and effective contraceptives made the link between heterosexual sex and procreation very strong indeed. Punitive notions of illegitimacy, and of homosexual identity, further cemented the common and legal understanding of marriage as an unquestionably heterosexual institution. But it is circular reasoning, not analysis, to maintain that marriage must remain a heterosexual institution because that is what it historically has been.

same-sex couples may be "excellent" parents. These couples (including four of the plaintiff couples) have children for the reasons others do—to love them, to care for them, to nurture them. But the task of child rearing for same-sex couples is made infinitely harder by their status as outliers to the marriage laws. Given the wide range of public benefits reserved only for married couples, we do not credit the department's contention that the absence of access to civil marriage amounts to little more than an inconvenience to same-sex couples and their children. Excluding same-sex couples from civil marriage will not make children of opposite-sex marriages more secure, but it does prevent children of same-sex couples from enjoying the immeasurable advantages that flow from the assurance of a stable family structure in which children will be reared, educated, and socialized.[26]

. . . The third rationale advanced by the department is that limiting marriage to opposite-sex couples furthers the Legislature's interest in conserving scarce State and private financial resources. The marriage restriction is rational, it argues, because the General Court logically could assume that same-sex couples are more financially independent than married couples and thus less needy of public marital benefits, such as tax advantages, or private marital benefits, such as employer-financed health plans that include spouses in their coverage.

An absolute statutory ban on same-sex marriage bears no rational relationship to the goal of economy. First, the department's conclusory generalization—that same-sex couples are less financially dependent on each other than opposite-sex couples—ignores that many same-sex couples, such as many of the plaintiffs in this case, have children and other dependents (here, aged parents) in their care. The department does not contend, nor could it, that these dependents are less needy or deserving than the dependents of married couples. Second, Massachusetts marriage laws do not condition receipt of public and private financial benefits to married individuals on a demonstration of financial dependence on each other; the benefits are available to married couples regardless of whether they mingle their finances or actually depend on each other for support. * * *

The department has had more than ample opportunity to articulate a constitutionally adequate justification for limiting civil marriage to opposite-sex unions. It has failed to do so.

The marriage ban works a deep and scarring hardship on a very real segment of the community for no rational reason. The absence of any

---

[26] The [dissent's] claim that the constitutional rights to bear and raise a child are "not implicated or infringed" by the marriage ban does not stand up to scrutiny. The absolute foreclosure of the marriage option for the class of parents and would-be parents at issue here imposes a heavy burden on their decision to have and raise children that is not suffered by any other class of parent.

reasonable relationship between, on the one hand, an absolute disqualification of same-sex couples who wish to enter into civil marriage and, on the other, protection of public health, safety, or general welfare, suggests that the marriage restriction is rooted in persistent prejudices against persons who are (or who are believed to be) homosexual. "The Constitution cannot control such prejudices but neither can it tolerate them. Private biases may be outside the reach of the law, but the law cannot, directly or indirectly, give them effect." *Palmore v. Sidoti*, 466 U.S. 429, 433 (1984). Limiting the protections, benefits, and obligations of civil marriage to opposite-sex couples violates the basic premises of individual liberty and equality under law protected by the Massachusetts Constitution.

IV

We consider next the plaintiffs' request for relief. * * *

In their complaint the plaintiffs request only a declaration that their exclusion and the exclusion of other qualified same-sex couples from access to civil marriage violates Massachusetts law. We declare that barring an individual from the protections, benefits, and obligations of civil marriage solely because that person would marry a person of the same sex violates the Massachusetts Constitution. We vacate the summary judgment for the department. We remand this case to the Superior Court for entry of judgment consistent with this opinion. Entry of judgment shall be stayed for 180 days to permit the Legislature to take such action as it may deem appropriate in light of this opinion.

GREANEY, J. (concurring).

I agree with the result reached by the court, the remedy ordered, and much of the reasoning in the court's opinion. In my view, however, the case is more directly resolved using traditional equal protection analysis. Analysis begins with the indisputable premise that the deprivation suffered by the plaintiffs is no mere legal inconvenience. The right to marry is not a privilege conferred by the State, but a fundamental right that is protected against unwarranted State interference. * * *

Because our marriage statutes intend, and state, the ordinary understanding that marriage under our law consists only of a union between a man and a woman, they create a statutory classification based on the sex of the two people who wish to marry. * * *

With these two propositions established (the infringement on a fundamental right and a sex-based classification), the enforcement of the marriage statutes as they are currently understood is forbidden by our Constitution unless the State can present a compelling purpose furthered by the statutes that can be accomplished in no other reasonable manner. This the State has not done. The justifications put forth by the State to sustain the statute's exclusion of the plaintiffs are insufficient for the reasons explained by the court. * * *

I do not doubt the sincerity of deeply held moral or religious beliefs that make inconceivable to some the notion that any change in the common-law definition of what constitutes a legal civil marriage is now, or ever would be, warranted. But, as matter of constitutional law, neither the mantra of tradition, nor individual conviction, can justify the perpetuation of a hierarchy in which couples of the same sex and their families are deemed less worthy of social and legal recognition than couples of the opposite sex and their families. See *Lawrence v. Texas.* * * *

SPINA, J. (dissenting, with whom SOSMAN and CORDY, JJ., join).

What is at stake in this case is not the unequal treatment of individuals or whether individual rights have been impermissibly burdened, but the power of the Legislature to effectuate social change without interference from the courts, pursuant to art. 30 of the Massachusetts Declaration of Rights. The power to regulate marriage lies with the Legislature, not with the judiciary. Today, the court has transformed its role as protector of individual rights into the role of creator of rights, and I respectfully dissent.

1. *Equal protection.* [The marriage law] creates no distinction between the sexes, but applies to men and women in precisely the same way. It does not create any disadvantage identified with gender, as both men and women are similarly limited to marrying a person of the opposite sex. Similarly, the marriage statutes do not discriminate on the basis of sexual orientation. The marriage statutes do not disqualify individuals on the basis of sexual orientation from entering into marriage. All individuals, with certain exceptions not relevant here, are free to marry. Whether an individual chooses not to marry because of sexual orientation or any other reason should be of no concern to the court. * * *

2. *Due process.* The marriage statutes do not impermissibly burden a right protected by our constitutional guarantee of due process implicit in art. 10 of our Declaration of Rights. There is no restriction on the right of any plaintiff to enter into marriage. Each is free to marry a willing person of the opposite sex. * * *

... Same-sex marriage, or the "right to marry the person of one's choice" as the court today defines that right, does not fall within the fundamental right to marry. Same-sex marriage is not "deeply rooted in this Nation's history," and the court does not suggest that it is. * * *

[JUSTICE SOSMAN's dissent, which JUSTICES SPINA and CORDY joined, is omitted.]

CORDY, J. (dissenting, with whom SPINA and SOSMAN, JJ., join).

The Massachusetts marriage statute does not impair the exercise of a recognized fundamental right, or discriminate on the basis of sex in violation of the equal rights amendment to the Massachusetts Constitution. Consequently, it is subject to review only to determine whether it satisfies the rational basis test. Because a conceivable rational basis exists upon which the Legislature could conclude that the marriage statute furthers the legitimate State purpose of ensuring, promoting, and supporting an optimal social structure for the bearing and raising of children, it is a valid exercise of the State's police power. * * *

* * * *State purpose.* The court's opinion concedes that the civil marriage statute serves legitimate State purposes, but further investigation and elaboration of those purposes is both helpful and necessary. Civil marriage is the institutional mechanism by which societies have sanctioned and recognized particular family structures, and the institution of marriage has existed as one of the fundamental organizing principles of human society. Marriage has not been merely a contractual arrangement for legally defining the private relationship between two individuals (although that is certainly part of any marriage). Rather, on an institutional level, marriage is the "very basis of the whole fabric of civilized society," and it serves many important political, economic, social, educational, procreational, and personal functions.

Paramount among its many important functions, the institution of marriage has systematically provided for the regulation of heterosexual behavior, brought order to the resulting procreation, and ensured a stable family structure in which children will be reared, educated, and socialized. Admittedly, heterosexual intercourse, procreation, and child care are not necessarily conjoined (particularly in the modern age of widespread effective contraception and supportive social welfare programs), but an orderly society requires some mechanism for coping with the fact that sexual intercourse commonly results in pregnancy and childbirth. The institution of marriage is that mechanism.

The institution of marriage provides the important legal and normative link between heterosexual intercourse and procreation on the one hand and family responsibilities on the other. The partners in a marriage are expected to engage in exclusive sexual relations, with children the probable result and paternity presumed. Whereas the relationship between mother and child is demonstratively and predictably created and recognizable through the biological process of pregnancy and childbirth, there is no corresponding process for creating a relationship between father and child.... The alternative, a society without the institution of marriage, in which heterosexual intercourse, procreation, and child care are largely disconnected processes, would be chaotic.

The marital family is also the foremost setting for the education and socialization of children. Children learn about the world and their place in it primarily from those who raise them, and those children eventually grow up to exert some influence, great or small, positive or negative, on society. The institution of marriage encourages parents to remain committed to each other and to their children as they grow, thereby encouraging a stable venue for the education and socialization of children. * * *

It is undeniably true that dramatic historical shifts in our cultural, political, and economic landscape have altered some of our traditional notions about marriage, including the interpersonal dynamics within it, the range of responsibilities required of it as an institution, and the legal environment in which it exists. Nevertheless, the institution of marriage remains the principal weave of our social fabric. A family defined by heterosexual marriage continues to be the most prevalent social structure into which the vast majority of children are born, nurtured, and prepared for productive participation in civil society. It is difficult to imagine a State purpose more important and legitimate than ensuring, promoting, and supporting an optimal social structure within which to bear and raise children. At the very least, the marriage statute continues to serve this important State purpose. * * *

In considering whether such a rational basis exists, we defer to the decision-making process of the Legislature, and must make deferential assumptions about the information that it might consider and on which it may rely. We must assume that the Legislature (1) might conclude that the institution of civil marriage has successfully and continually provided this structure over several centuries; (2) might consider and credit studies that document negative consequences that too often follow children either born outside of marriage or raised in households lacking either a father or a mother figure, and scholarly commentary contending that children and families develop best when mothers and fathers are partners in their parenting; and (3) would be familiar with many recent studies that variously support the proposition that children raised in intact families headed by same-sex couples fare as well on many measures as children raised in similar families headed by opposite-sex couples; support the proposition that children of same-sex couples fare worse on some measures; or reveal notable differences between the two groups of children that warrant further study.

We must also assume that the Legislature would be aware of the critiques of the methodologies used in virtually all of the comparative studies of children raised in these different environments, cautioning that the sampling populations are not representative, that the observation periods are too limited in time, that the empirical data are unreliable, and that the hypotheses are too infused with political or agenda driven bias.

Taking all of this available information into account, the Legislature could rationally conclude that a family environment with married opposite-sex parents remains the optimal social structure in which to bear children, and that the raising of children by same-sex couples, who by definition cannot be the two sole biological parents of a child and cannot provide children with a parental authority figure of each gender,[29] presents an alternative structure for child rearing that has not yet proved itself beyond reasonable scientific dispute to be as optimal as the biologically based marriage norm. Working from the assumption that a recognition of same-sex marriages will increase the number of children experiencing this alternative, the Legislature could conceivably conclude that declining to recognize same-sex marriages remains prudent until empirical questions about its impact on the upbringing of children are resolved.

* * * In addition, the Legislature could conclude that redefining the institution of marriage to permit same-sex couples to marry would impair the State's interest in promoting and supporting heterosexual marriage as the social institution that it has determined best normalizes, stabilizes, and links the acts of procreation and child rearing. While the plaintiffs argue that they only want to take part in the same stabilizing institution, the Legislature conceivably could conclude that permitting their participation would have the unintended effect of undermining to some degree marriage's ability to serve its social purpose.

* * * Given the critical importance of civil marriage as an organizing and stabilizing institution of society, it is eminently rational for the Legislature to postpone making fundamental changes to it until such time as there is unanimous scientific evidence, or popular consensus, or both, that such changes can safely be made.

There is no reason to believe that legislative processes are inadequate to effectuate legal changes in response to evolving evidence, social values, and views of fairness on the subject of same-sex

---

[29] This family structure raises the prospect of children lacking any parent of their own gender. For example, a boy raised by two lesbians as his parents has no male parent. Contrary to the suggestion that concerns about such a family arrangement is [sic] based on "stereotypical" views about the differences between sexes, concern about such an arrangement remains rational. It is, for example, rational to posit that the child himself might invoke gender as a justification for the view that neither of his parents "understands" him, or that they "don't know what he is going through," particularly if his disagreement or dissatisfaction involves some issue pertaining to sex. Given that same-sex couples raising children are a very recent phenomenon, the ramifications of an adolescent child's having two parents but not one of his or her own gender have yet to be fully realized and cannot yet even be tested in significant numbers.

relationships. Deliberate consideration of, and incremental responses to rapidly evolving scientific and social understanding is the norm of the political process—that it may seem painfully slow to those who are already persuaded by the arguments in favor of change is not a sufficient basis to conclude that the processes are constitutionally infirm. The Legislature is the appropriate branch, both constitutionally and practically, to consider and respond to it. It is not enough that we as Justices might be personally of the view that we have learned enough to decide what is best. So long as the question is at all debatable, it must be the Legislature that decides.

NOTES

1.   With echoes of the Vermont Supreme Court's resolution of the *Baker* case, the Massachusetts state legislature, after *Goodridge* was decided, asked the Supreme Judicial Court whether an equal benefits law short of full marriage recognition would satisfy the court's mandate. The Court replied that it would not. *Opinion of the Justices to the Senate*, 802 N.E.2d 565, 572, 440 Mass. 1201, 1210 (2004). On May 17, 2004, at the expiration of the Court's original 180-day mandate, same-sex couples began to marry in Massachusetts. *See* Yvonne Abraham & Rick Klein, *Free to Marry: Historic Date Arrives for Same-Sex Couples in Massachusetts*, BOSTON GLOBE, May 17, 2004, at A1.

2.   As had the Hawaii decision before it, the *Goodridge* decision provoked a wave of backlash against same-sex marriage. The backlash is discussed below, in Section II.C.

3.   Justice Cordy's dissent articulates the "responsible procreation" argument against same-sex marriage. This argument has been particularly influential in litigation. You should consider its various iterations and responses by lawyers and courts in the remainder of this chapter.

b.   Marriage Litigation in the State Courts after Goodridge

After *Goodridge* made same-sex marriage a reality in the United States, several important questions came to the fore. One was whether other state supreme courts would follow *Goodridge's* lead. Another was whether courts would use the doctrinal apparatus of fundamental rights, grounded in substantive due process, or would instead employ equality analysis. Note that *Goodridge* blended the two frameworks. A third question was whether courts would apply rational basis review (as the court did in *Goodridge*) or would deem heightened scrutiny appropriate. Since *Goodridge,* state supreme courts have varied on each of these points. The cases below reveal some of the fault lines in the debates about the merits, the appropriate doctrinal approach, and the correct standard of review.

Hernandez v. Robles

Court of Appeals of New York, 2006
855 N.E.2d 1, 7 N.Y.3d 338, 821 N.Y.S.2d 770

Smith, J.

It is undisputed that the benefits of marriage are many. The diligence of counsel has identified 316 such benefits in New York law, of which it is enough to summarize some of the most important: Married people receive significant tax advantages, rights in probate and intestacy proceedings, rights to support from their spouses both during the marriage and after it is dissolved, and rights to be treated as family members in obtaining insurance coverage and making health care decisions. Beyond this, they receive the symbolic benefit, or moral satisfaction, of seeing their relationships recognized by the State.

The critical question is whether a rational legislature could decide that these benefits should be given to members of opposite-sex couples, but not same-sex couples. The question is not, we emphasize, whether the Legislature must or should continue to limit marriage in this way; of course the Legislature may (subject to the effect of the Federal Defense of Marriage Act, Pub. L. 104 110 Stat. 2419) extend marriage or some or all of its benefits to same-sex couples. We conclude, however, that there are at least two grounds that rationally support the limitation on marriage that the Legislature has enacted. Others have been advanced, but we will discuss only these two, both of which are derived from the undisputed assumption that marriage is important to the welfare of children.

First, the Legislature could rationally decide that, for the welfare of children, it is more important to promote stability, and to avoid instability, in opposite-sex than in same-sex relationships. Heterosexual intercourse has a natural tendency to lead to the birth of children; homosexual intercourse does not. Despite the advances of science, it remains true that the vast majority of children are born as a result of a sexual relationship between a man and a woman, and the Legislature could find that this will continue to be true. The Legislature could also find that such relationships are all too often casual or temporary. It could find that an important function of marriage is to create more stability and permanence in the relationships that cause children to be born. It thus could choose to offer an inducement—in the form of marriage and its attendant benefits—to opposite-sex couples who make a solemn, long-term commitment to each other.

The Legislature could find that this rationale for marriage does not apply with comparable force to same-sex couples. These couples can become parents by adoption, or by artificial insemination or other technological marvels, but they do not become parents as a result of accident or impulse. The Legislature could find that unstable relationships between people of the opposite sex present a greater danger that children will be born into or grow up in unstable homes than is the case with same-sex couples, and thus that promoting stability in opposite-sex relationships will help children more. This is one reason why the Legislature could rationally offer the benefits of marriage to opposite-sex couples only.

There is a second reason: The Legislature could rationally believe that it is better, other things being equal, for children to grow up with both a mother and a father. Intuition and experience suggest that a child benefits from having before his or her eyes, every day, living models of what both a man and a woman are like. It is obvious that there are exceptions to this general rule—some children who never know their fathers, or their mothers, do far better than some who grow up with parents of both sexes—but the Legislature could find that the general rule will usually hold. * * *

Plaintiffs seem to assume that they have demonstrated the irrationality of the view that opposite-sex marriages offer advantages to children by showing there is no scientific evidence to support it. Even assuming no such evidence exists, this reasoning is flawed. In the absence of conclusive scientific evidence, the Legislature could rationally proceed on the common-sense premise that children will do best with a mother and father in the home. And a legislature proceeding on that premise could rationally decide to offer a special inducement, the legal recognition of marriage, to encourage the formation of opposite-sex households.

In sum, there are rational grounds on which the Legislature could choose to restrict marriage to couples of opposite sex. Plaintiffs have not persuaded us that this long-accepted restriction is a wholly irrational one, based solely on ignorance and prejudice against homosexuals. This is the question on which these cases turn. If we were convinced that the restriction plaintiffs attack were founded on nothing but prejudice—if we agreed with the plaintiffs that it is comparable to the restriction in *Loving v. Virginia*, a prohibition on interracial marriage that was plainly "designed to maintain White Supremacy"—we would hold it invalid, no matter how long its history. As the dissent points out, a long and shameful history of racism lay behind the kind of statute invalidated in *Loving*.

But the historical background of *Loving* is different from the history underlying this case. Racism has been recognized for centuries—at first by a few people, and later by many more—as a revolting moral evil. This country fought a civil war to eliminate racism's worst manifestation, slavery, and passed three constitutional amendments to eliminate that curse and its vestiges. *Loving* was part of the civil rights revolution of the

1950's and 1960's, the triumph of a cause for which many heroes and many ordinary people had struggled since our nation began.

It is true that there has been serious injustice in the treatment of homosexuals also, a wrong that has been widely recognized only in the relatively recent past, and one our Legislature tried to address when it enacted the Sexual Orientation Non-Discrimination Act four years ago. But the traditional definition of marriage is not merely a by-product of historical injustice. Its history is of a different kind.

The idea that same-sex marriage is even possible is a relatively new one. Until a few decades ago, it was an accepted truth for almost everyone who ever lived, in any society in which marriage existed, that there could be marriages only between participants of different sex. A court should not lightly conclude that everyone who held this belief was irrational, ignorant or bigoted. We do not so conclude. * * *

We resolve this question in this case on the basis of the Supreme Court's observation that no more than rational basis scrutiny is generally appropriate "where individuals in the group affected by a law have distinguishing characteristics relevant to interests the State has the authority to implement" (*City of Cleburne*). * * *

Where rational basis scrutiny applies, "[t]he general rule is that legislation is presumed to be valid and will be sustained if the classification drawn by the statute is rationally related to a legitimate state interest." Plaintiffs argue that a classification distinguishing between opposite-sex couples and same-sex couples cannot pass rational basis scrutiny, because if the relevant State interest is the protection of children, the category of those permitted to marry—opposite-sex couples—is both underinclusive and overinclusive. We disagree.

Plaintiffs argue that the category is underinclusive because, as we recognized above, same-sex couples, as well as opposite-sex couples, may have children. That is indeed a reason why the Legislature might rationally choose to extend marriage or its benefits to same-sex couples; but it could also, for the reasons we have explained, rationally make another choice, based on the different characteristics of opposite-sex and same-sex relationships. Our earlier discussion demonstrates that the definition of marriage to include only opposite-sex couples is not irrationally underinclusive.

In arguing that the definition is overinclusive, plaintiffs point out that many opposite-sex couples cannot have or do not want to have children. How can it be rational, they ask, to permit these couples, but not same-sex couples, to marry? The question is not a difficult one to answer. While same-sex couples and opposite-sex couples are easily distinguished, limiting marriage to opposite-sex couples likely to have children would require grossly intrusive inquiries, and arbitrary and unreliable line-drawing. A legislature that regarded marriage primarily or solely as an institution for the benefit of children could rationally find that an attempt to exclude childless opposite-sex couples from the institution would be a very bad idea.

Rational basis scrutiny is highly indulgent towards the State's classifications. Indeed, it is a paradigm of judicial restraint. We conclude that permitting marriage by all opposite-sex couples does not create an irrationally over-narrow or overbroad classification.

IN RE MARRIAGE CASES

California Supreme Court, 2008
43 Cal. 4th 757, 76 Cal. Rptr. 3d 683, 183 P.3d 384

GEORGE, C.J.

* * * Although our state Constitution does not contain any explicit reference to a "right to marry," past California cases establish beyond question that the right to marry is a fundamental right whose protection is guaranteed to all persons by the California Constitution. * * *

Plaintiffs challenge the Court of Appeal's characterization of the constitutional right they seek to invoke as the right to same-sex marriage, and on this point we agree with plaintiffs' position. In *Perez v. Sharp*, *supra*, 32 Cal.2d 711—this court's 1948 decision holding that the California statutory provisions prohibiting interracial marriage were unconstitutional—the court did not characterize the constitutional right that the plaintiffs in that case sought to obtain as "a right to interracial marriage" and did not dismiss the plaintiffs' constitutional challenge on the ground that such marriages never had been permitted in California. * * *

The flaw in characterizing the constitutional right at issue as the right to same-sex marriage rather than the right to marry goes beyond mere semantics. It is important both analytically and from the standpoint of fairness to plaintiffs' argument that we recognize they are not seeking to create a new constitutional right—the right to "same-sex marriage"—or to change, modify, or (as some have suggested) "deinstitutionalize" the existing institution of marriage. Instead, plaintiffs contend that, properly interpreted, the state constitutional right to marry affords same-sex couples the same rights and benefits—accompanied by the same mutual responsibilities and obligations—as this constitutional right affords to opposite-sex couples. * * *

The opportunity of a couple to establish an officially recognized family of their own not only grants access to an extended family but also permits the couple to join the broader family social structure that is a significant feature of community life. * * *

It is true, of course, that as an historical matter in this state marriage always has been limited to a union between a man and a woman. Tradition alone, however, generally has not been viewed as a sufficient justification for perpetuating, without examination, the restriction or denial of a fundamental *constitutional* right. * * *

There can be no question but that, in recent decades, there has been a fundamental and dramatic transformation in this state's understanding and legal treatment of gay individuals and gay couples. California has repudiated past practices and policies that were based on a once common viewpoint that denigrated the general character and morals of gay individuals, and at one time even characterized homosexuality as a mental illness rather than as simply one of the numerous variables of our common and diverse humanity. This state's current policies and conduct regarding homosexuality recognize that gay individuals are entitled to the same legal rights and the same respect and dignity afforded all other individuals and are protected from discrimination on the basis of their sexual orientation, and, more specifically, recognize that gay individuals are fully capable of entering into the kind of loving and enduring committed relationships that may serve as the foundation of a family and of responsibly caring for and raising children. * * *

Pointing out that past cases often have linked marriage and procreation, [intervenors, opponents of same-sex marriage] argue that because only a man and a woman can produce children biologically with one another, the constitutional right to marry necessarily is limited to opposite-sex couples.

This contention is fundamentally flawed for a number of reasons. . . . Men and women who desire to raise children with a loved one in a recognized family but who are physically unable to conceive a child with their loved one never have been excluded from the right to marry. * * *

A variant of the contention that the right to marry is limited to couples who are capable of procreation is that the purpose of marriage is to promote "responsible procreation" and that a restriction limiting this right exclusively to opposite-sex couples follows from this purpose. A number of recent state court decisions, applying the rational basis equal protection standard, have relied upon this purpose as a reasonably conceivable justification for a statutory limitation of marriage to opposite-sex couples. These decisions have explained that although same-sex couples can have or obtain children through assisted reproduction or adoption, resort to such methods demonstrates, in the case of a same-sex couple, that parenthood necessarily is an *intended* consequence because each of these two methods requires considerable planning and expense, whereas in the case of an opposite-sex couple a child often is the *unintended* consequence of the couple's sexual intercourse. These courts reason that a state plausibly could conclude that although affording the benefits of marriage to opposite-sex couples is an incentive needed to ensure that *accidental* procreation is channeled into a stable family relationship, a similar incentive is not required for same-sex couples because they cannot produce children accidentally.

Whether or not the state's interest in encouraging responsible procreation properly can be viewed as a reasonably conceivable justification for the statutory limitation of marriage to a man and a woman for purposes of the rational basis equal protection standard, this interest clearly does not provide an appropriate basis for defining or limiting the scope of the constitutional right to marry. None of the past cases discussing the right to marry—and identifying this right as one of the fundamental elements of personal autonomy and liberty protected by our Constitution—contains any suggestion that the constitutional right to marry is possessed only by individuals who are at risk of producing children accidentally, or implies that this constitutional right is not equally important for and guaranteed to responsible individuals who can be counted upon to take appropriate precautions in planning for parenthood. Thus, although the state undeniably has a legitimate interest in promoting "responsible procreation," that interest cannot be viewed as a valid basis for defining or limiting the class of persons who may claim the protection of the fundamental constitutional right to marry. * * *

[Intervenors] also rely upon several academic commentators who maintain that the constitutional right to marry should be viewed as inapplicable to same-sex couples because a contrary interpretation assertedly would sever the link that marriage provides between procreation and child rearing and would "send a message" to the public that it is immaterial to the state whether children are raised by their biological mother and father. Although we appreciate the genuine concern for the well-being of children underlying that position, we conclude this claim lacks merit. Our recognition that the core substantive rights encompassed by the constitutional right to marry apply to same-sex as well as opposite-sex couples does not imply in any way that it is unimportant or immaterial to the state whether a child is raised by his or her biological mother and father . . . Instead, such an interpretation of the constitutional right to marry simply confirms that a stable two-parent family relationship, supported by the state's official recognition and protection, is equally as important for the numerous children in California who are being raised by same-sex couples as for those children being raised by opposite-sex couples (whether they are biological parents or adoptive parents). This interpretation also guarantees individuals who are in a same-sex relationship, and who are raising children, the opportunity to obtain from the state the official recognition and support accorded a family by agreeing to take on the substantial and long-term mutual obligations and responsibilities that are an essential and inseparable part of a family relationship.

[Portions of the opinion rejecting the claim that California's domestic partnership option for same-sex couples satisfies the state constitution are reprinted in section II.B.4(a), below].

VARNUM V. BRIEN

Supreme Court of Iowa, 2009
763 N.W.2d 862

CADY, J.

* * * This requirement of equal protection—that the law must treat all similarly situated people the same—has generated a narrow threshold test. Under this threshold test, if plaintiffs cannot show as a preliminary matter that they are similarly situated, courts do not further consider whether their different treatment under a statute is permitted under the equal protection clause. * * *

In considering whether two classes are similarly situated, a court cannot simply look at the trait used by the legislature to define a classification under a statute and conclude a person without that trait is not similarly situated to persons with the trait. . . . The equal protection clause does not merely ensure the challenged statute applies equally to all people in the legislative classification. "'[S]imilarly situated' cannot mean simply 'similar in the possession of the classifying trait.' All members of any class are similarly situated in this respect and consequently, any classification whatsoever would be reasonable by this test." Tussman & tenBroek, 37 Cal. L. Rev. at 345. In the same way, the similarly situated requirement cannot possibly be interpreted to require plaintiffs to be identical in every way to people treated more favorably by the law. No two people or groups of people are the same in every way, and nearly every equal protection claim could be run aground onto the shoals of a threshold analysis if the two groups needed to be a mirror image of one another. Such a threshold analysis would hollow out the constitution's promise of equal protection.

Thus, equal protection before the law demands more than the equal application of the classifications made by the law. The law itself must be equal. . . . In other words, to truly ensure equality before the law, the equal protection guarantee requires that laws treat all those who are similarly situated with respect to the purposes of the law alike. This requirement makes it "impossible to pass judgment on the reasonableness of a [legislative] classification without taking into consideration, or identifying, the purpose of the law." Tussman & tenBroek, 37 Cal. L. Rev. at 347. The purposes of the law must be referenced in order to meaningfully evaluate whether the law equally protects all people similarly situated with respect to those purposes. For these reasons, the trait asserted by the County is insufficient to support its threshold argument. * * *

Therefore, with respect to the subject and purposes of Iowa's marriage laws, we find that the plaintiffs are similarly situated compared to heterosexual persons. Plaintiffs are in committed and loving relationships, many raising families, just like heterosexual couples. Moreover, official recognition of their status provides an institutional basis for defining their fundamental relational rights and responsibilities, just as it does for heterosexual couples. Society benefits, for example, from providing same-sex couples a stable framework within which to raise their children and the power to make health care and end-of-life decisions for loved ones, just as it does when that framework is provided for opposite-sex couples.

In short, for purposes of Iowa's marriage laws, which are designed to bring a sense of order to the legal relationships of committed couples and their families in myriad ways, plaintiffs are similarly situated in every important respect, but for their sexual orientation. As indicated above, this distinction cannot defeat the application of equal protection analysis through the application of the similarly situated concept because, under this circular approach, all distinctions would evade equal protection review. Therefore, with respect to the government's purpose of "providing an institutional basis for defining the fundamental relational rights and responsibilities of persons," same-sex couples are similarly situated to opposite-sex couples. . . .

It is true the marriage statute does not expressly prohibit gay and lesbian persons from marrying; it does, however, require that if they marry, it must be to someone of the opposite sex. Viewed in the complete context of marriage, including intimacy, civil marriage with a person of the opposite sex is as unappealing to a gay or lesbian person as civil marriage with a person of the same sex is to a heterosexual. Thus, the right of a gay or lesbian person under the marriage statute to enter into a civil marriage only with a person of the opposite sex is no right at all. Under such a law, gay or lesbian individuals cannot simultaneously fulfill their deeply felt need for a committed personal relationship, as influenced by their sexual orientation, and gain the civil status and attendant benefits granted by the statute. Instead, a gay or lesbian person can only gain the same rights under the statute as a heterosexual person by negating the very trait that defines gay and lesbian people as a class— their sexual orientation.

* * * Plaintiffs argue sexual-orientation based statutes should be subject to the most searching scrutiny. The County asserts Iowa's marriage statute, section 595.2, may be reviewed, at most, according to an

intermediate level of scrutiny. Because we conclude Iowa's same-sex marriage statute cannot withstand intermediate scrutiny, we need not decide whether classifications based on sexual orientation are subject to a higher level of scrutiny. Thus, we turn to a discussion of the intermediate scrutiny standard.

* * * Even assuming there may be a rational basis at this time to believe the legislative classification advances a legitimate government interest, this assumed fact would not be sufficient to survive the equal protection analysis applicable in this case. In order to ensure this classification based on sexual orientation is not borne of prejudice and stereotype, intermediate scrutiny demands a closer relationship between the legislative classification and the purpose of the classification than mere rationality. Under intermediate scrutiny, the relationship between the government's goal and the classification employed to further that goal must be "substantial."

* * * As applied to this case, it could be argued the same-sex marriage ban is just one legislative step toward ensuring the optimal environment for raising children. Under this argument, the governmental objective is slightly more modest. It seeks to reduce the number of same-sex parent households, nudging our state a step closer to providing the asserted optimal milieu for children. Even evaluated in light of this narrower objective, however, the ban on same-sex marriage is flawed.

The ban on same-sex marriage is substantially over-inclusive because not all same-sex couples choose to raise children. Yet, the marriage statute denies civil marriage to all gay and lesbian people in order to discourage the limited number of same-sex couples who desire to raise children. In doing so, the legislature includes a consequential number of "individuals within the statute's purview who are not afflicted with the evil the statute seeks to remedy."

At the same time, the exclusion of gay and lesbian people from marriage is underinclusive, even in relation to the narrower goal of improving child rearing by limiting same-sex parenting. Quite obviously, the statute does not prohibit same-sex couples from raising children. Same-sex couples currently raise children in Iowa, even while being excluded from civil marriage, and such couples will undoubtedly continue to do so. Recognition of this under-inclusion puts in perspective just how minimally the same-sex marriage ban actually advances the purported legislative goal. A law so simultaneously over-inclusive and under-inclusive is not substantially related to the government's objective. In the end, a careful analysis of the over and underinclusiveness of the statute reveals it is less about using marriage to achieve an optimal environment for children and more about merely precluding gay and lesbian people from civil marriage.

* * * Having examined each proffered governmental objective through the appropriate lens of intermediate scrutiny, we conclude the sexual-orientation-based classification under the marriage statute does not substantially further any of the objectives. While the objectives asserted may be important (and many undoubtedly are important), none are furthered in a substantial way by the exclusion of same-sex couples from civil marriage. Our equal protection clause requires more than has been offered to justify the continued existence of the same-sex marriage ban under the statute."

NOTES

1.   The history of the institution of marriage features centrally in the same-sex marriage debate, with opponents routinely arguing that marriage has always been restricted to one man and one woman. Several scholars, however, have contested that idea and suggested that same-sex marriage has its own historical lineage, one that includes some religious acceptance of the practice. The late John Boswell, a prominent historian, argued that there was strong evidence that the Catholic Church consecrated same-sex marriages from the fifth through at least the thirteenth century. *See* John Boswell, *Homosexuality and Religious Life: A Historical Approach*, *in* HOMOSEXUALITY IN THE PRIESTHOOD AND RELIGIOUS LIFE 3, 11 (Jeanne Gramick ed., 1989). *See generally* JOHN BOSWELL, SAME-SEX UNIONS IN PREMODERN EUROPE 283–344 (1994) (including an appendix of translations of ancient religious texts for such ceremonies); JOHN BOSWELL, CHRISTIANITY, SOCIAL TOLERANCE, AND HOMOSEXUALITY (1980). Same-sex marriages have also been recognized by many cultures outside the Judeo-Christian tradition. *See* William N. Eskridge, Jr., *A History of Same-Sex Marriage*, 79 VA. L. REV. 1419, 1437–69 (1993) (arguing that same-sex marriages existed in ancient Greece, Crete, Native American, African and Asian cultures, and may have existed in Egypt and Mesopotamia).

2.   As of early 2014, seventeen states (California, Connecticut, Delaware, Hawaii, Illinois, Iowa, Maine, Maryland, Massachusetts, Minnesota, New Hampshire, New Jersey, New Mexico, New York, Rhode Island, Vermont, and Washington) plus the District of Columbia have opened marriage to same-sex couples. *See* http://www.hrc.org/files/assets/resources/marriage_equality_082013.pdf. After a federal district court declared Utah's ban on same-sex marriage unconstitutional in December 2013, same-sex couples in that state obtained marriage licenses. *See Kitchen v. Herbert*, ___ F. Supp. 2d ___, 2013 WL 6697874 (D. Utah Dec. 20, 2013). But the U.S. Supreme Court eventually stayed the injunction issued by the district court pending appeal. *See Herbert v. Kitchen*, 571 U.S. ___ (Jan. 6, 2014). As explained more fully below, some states maintain civil union or domestic partnership laws that provide the state-law rights and benefits of marriage to same-sex couples.

3.   While the earliest victories for the marriage equality movement came through litigation, eventually legislatures began to pass marriage equality bills. More recently, in November 2012, voters in Maine, Maryland, and Washington passed marriage equality at the ballot box; in addition, voters in Minnesota rejected a constitutional amendment banning same-sex marriage, and lawmakers in the state subsequently passed marriage equality legislation.

4.   As of early 2014, sixteen countries allow same-sex couples to marry nationwide. The Netherlands first opened marriage to same-sex couples in 2001. These countries eventually did the same: Belgium (2003), Spain (2005), Canada (2005), South Africa (2006), Norway (2009), Sweden (2009), Portugal (2010), Iceland (2010), Argentina (2010), Denmark (2012), Brazil (2013), France (2013), Uruguay (2013), New Zealand (2013), and Great Britain (England and Wales, 2013; Scotland, 2014). Same-sex couples can marry in parts of Mexico.

Denmark first provided nonmarital recognition to same-sex couples in 1989. Now, other countries have nationwide same-sex civil union or partnership laws: Andorra (2005), Austria (2010), Colombia (2009), Czech Republic (2006), Ecuador (2009), Finland (2002), Germany (2001), Greenland (1996), Hungary (2009), Ireland (2011), Luxembourg (2004), Slovenia (2006), and Switzerland (2007). *See* http://www.freedomtomarry.org/landscape/entry/c/international.

5.   Regardless of their legal rights, many same-sex couples choose to "marry" in a social or religious sense. As early as 1988—well before the contemporary same-sex marriage debate was seriously engaged—the Partners National Survey of Lesbian and Gay Couples showed that same-sex couples observed the following relationship rituals: 57 percent of women and 36 percent of men wore rings; 19 percent of women and 11 percent of men held a ceremony; and 12 percent of women and 9 percent of men participated in some other ritual. *See* Elizabeth Rhodes, *New Ties That Bind*, SEATTLE TIMES, July 21, 1991, at K1.

4. Alternatives to Marriage: Civil Unions, Domestic Partnerships, and Other Forms of Recognition

a. Can Marriage Alternatives Satisfy the Demands of Constitutional Equality?

Consistent with the constitutional demands of a state constitution, may a state decide to offer same-sex couples civil unions or more limited forms of domestic partnership in lieu of marriage? Recall that the Vermont Supreme Court approved that choice in the *Baker* decision (sec. II.B.2 above). As the following cases reflect, courts have disagreed on this question.

LEWIS V. HARRIS

Supreme Court of New Jersey, 2006
908 A.2d 196, 188 N.J. 415

ALBIN, J.

[Plaintiffs, several committed same-sex couples,] contend that the right to marry a person of the same sex is a fundamental right secured by the liberty guarantee of Article I, Paragraph 1 of the New Jersey Constitution . . . which provides:

> All persons are by nature free and independent, and have certain natural and unalienable rights, among which are those of enjoying and defending life and liberty, of acquiring, possessing, and protecting property, and of pursuing and obtaining safety and happiness.

* * * In searching for the meaning of "liberty" under Article I, Paragraph 1, we must resist the temptation of seeing in the majesty of that word only a mirror image of our own strongly felt opinions and beliefs. Under the guise of newly found rights, we must be careful not to impose our personal value system on eight-and-one-half million people, thus bypassing the democratic process as the primary means of effecting social change in this State. That being said, this Court will never abandon its responsibility to protect the fundamental rights of all of our citizens, even the most alienated and disfavored, no matter how strong the winds of popular opinion may blow.

Despite the rich diversity of this State, the tolerance and goodness of its people, and the many recent advances made by gays and lesbians toward achieving social acceptance and equality under the law, we cannot find that a right to same-sex marriage is so deeply rooted in the traditions, history, and conscience of the people of this State that it ranks as a fundamental right. . . . We now must examine whether those laws that deny to committed same-sex couples both the right to and the rights of marriage afforded to heterosexual couples offend the equal protection principles of our State Constitution. * * *

In 2004, the Legislature passed the Domestic Partnership Act, making available to committed same-sex couples "certain rights and benefits that are accorded to married couples under the laws of New Jersey." * * *

In passing the Act, the Legislature expressed its clear understanding of the human dimension that propelled it to provide relief to same-sex couples. It emphasized that the need for committed same-sex partners "to have access to these rights and benefits is paramount in view of their essential relationship to any reasonable conception of basic human dignity and autonomy, and the extent to which they will play an integral role in enabling these persons to enjoy their familial relationships as domestic partners." * * *

We next examine the extent to which New Jersey's laws continue to restrict committed same-sex couples from enjoying the full benefits and privileges available through marriage. Although under the Domestic Partnership Act same-sex couples are provided with a number of important rights, they still are denied many benefits and privileges accorded to their similarly situated heterosexual counterparts. Thus, the Act has failed to bridge the inequality gap between committed same-sex couples and married opposite-sex couples. . . . [The court details the rights afforded to married couples but denied to committed same-sex couples.]

We now must assess the public need for denying the full benefits and privileges that flow from marriage to committed same-sex partners. At this point, we do not consider whether committed same-sex couples should be allowed to marry, but only whether those couples are entitled to the same rights and benefits afforded to married heterosexual couples. * * *

The Legislature has recognized that the "rights and benefits" provided in the Domestic Partnership Act are directly related "to any reasonable conception of basic human dignity and autonomy." It is difficult to understand how withholding the remaining "rights and benefits" from committed same-sex couples is compatible with a "reasonable conception of basic human dignity and autonomy." There is no rational basis for, on the one hand, giving gays and lesbians full civil rights in their status as individuals, and, on the other, giving them an incomplete set of rights when they follow the inclination of their sexual orientation and enter into committed same-sex relationships.

Disparate treatment of committed same-sex couples, moreover, directly disadvantages their children . . .

The equal protection requirement of Article I, Paragraph 1 leaves the Legislature with two apparent options. The Legislature could simply amend the marriage statutes to include same-sex couples, or it could create a separate statutory structure, such as a civil union, as Connecticut and Vermont have done. Plaintiffs argue that even equal social and financial benefits would not make them whole unless they are allowed to call their committed relationships by the name of marriage. They maintain that a parallel legal structure, called by a name other than marriage, which provides the social and financial benefits they have sought, would be a separate-but-equal classification that offends Article I, Paragraph 1. From plaintiffs' standpoint, the title of marriage is an intangible right, without which they are consigned to second-class citizenship. * * *

Raised here is the perplexing question—"what's in a name?"—and is a name itself of constitutional magnitude after the State is required to provide full statutory rights and benefits to same-sex couples? We are mindful that in the cultural clash over same-sex marriage, the word marriage itself—independent of the rights and benefits of marriage—has an evocative and important meaning to both parties. Under our equal protection jurisprudence, however, plaintiffs' claimed right to the name of marriage is surely not the same now that equal rights and benefits must be conferred on committed same-sex couples. * * *

[I]t is not our role to suggest whether the Legislature should either amend the marriage statutes to include same-sex couples or enact a civil union scheme. Our role here is limited to constitutional adjudication, and therefore we must steer clear of the swift and treacherous currents of social policy when we have no constitutional compass with which to navigate. * * *

We cannot escape the reality that the shared societal meaning of marriage—passed down through the common law into our statutory law—has always been the union of a man and a woman. To alter that meaning would render a profound change in the public consciousness of a social institution of ancient origin. When such change is not compelled by a constitutional imperative, it must come about through civil dialogue and reasoned discourse, and the considered judgment of the people in whom we place ultimate trust in our republican form of government. Whether an issue with such far-reaching social implications as how to define marriage falls within the judicial or the democratic realm, to many, is debatable. Some may think that this Court should settle the matter, insulating it from public discussion and the political process. Nevertheless, a court must discern not only the limits of its own authority, but also when to exercise forbearance, recognizing that the legitimacy of its decisions rests on reason, not power. We will not short-circuit the democratic process from running its course.

New language is developing to describe new social and familial relationships, and in time will find its place in our common vocabulary. Through a better understanding of those new relationships and acceptance forged in the democratic process, rather than by judicial fiat, the proper labels will take hold. However the Legislature may act, same-sex couples will be free to call their relationships by the name they choose and to sanctify their relationships in religious ceremonies in houses of worship. * * *

Our decision today significantly advances the civil rights of gays and lesbians. We have decided that our State Constitution guarantees that every statutory right and benefit conferred to heterosexual couples through civil marriage must be made available to committed same-sex couples. Now the Legislature must determine whether to alter the long accepted definition of marriage. The great engine for social change in this country has always been the democratic process. Although courts can ensure equal treatment, they cannot guarantee social acceptance, which must come through the evolving ethos of a maturing society. Plaintiffs' quest does not end here. Their next appeal must be to their fellow citizens whose voices are heard through their popularly elected representatives. * * *

The constitutional relief that we give to plaintiffs cannot be effectuated immediately or by this Court alone. The implementation of this constitutional mandate will require the cooperation of the Legislature. To bring the State into compliance with Article I, Paragraph 1 so that plaintiffs can exercise their full constitutional rights, the Legislature must either amend the marriage statutes or enact an appropriate statutory structure within 180 days of the date of this decision.

NOTE

After *Lewis*, the New Jersey legislature voted to allow civil unions for same-sex couples. The bill took effect in February 2007. *See* N.J. STAT. ANN. §§ 37:1–1 to 37:1–36 (2007). Couples in civil unions had the same legal rights and responsibilities as married couples under New Jersey law. LGBT rights advocates continued to push for marriage legislatively while also challenging civil unions in state court as constitutionally inadequate. After the U.S. Supreme Court struck down Section 3 of the Defense of Marriage Act (DOMA) and federal agencies began providing federal rights and benefits to married same-sex couples, the New Jersey courts determined that civil unions failed to satisfy the equality mandate announced in *Lewis*. *See Garden State Equality v. Dow*, 79 A.3d 1036, 216 N.J. 314 (N.J. 2013). Accordingly, same-sex couples obtained the right to marry in New Jersey. These developments are discussed more fully below in Section II.D.4.

In the two cases that follow, states offered same-sex couples comprehensive protections through civil unions or domestic partnerships but withheld access to marriage. Same-sex couples challenged the constitutional adequacy of these separate nonmarital regimes.

KERRIGAN V. COMMISSIONER OF PUBLIC HEALTH
Supreme Court of Connecticut, 2008
957 A.2d 407, 289 Conn. 135

PALMER, J.

In view of the exalted status of marriage in our society, it is hardly surprising that civil unions are perceived to be inferior to marriage. We therefore agree with the plaintiffs that "[m]aintaining a second-class citizen status for same-sex couples by excluding them from the institution of civil marriage is the constitutional infirmity at issue."

Accordingly, we reject the trial court's conclusion that marriage and civil unions are "separate" but "equal" legal entities; and that it therefore "would be the elevation of form over substance" to conclude that the constitutional rights of same sex couples are implicated by a statutory scheme that restricts them to civil unions. Although marriage and civil unions do embody the same legal rights under our law, they are by no means "equal." As we have explained, the former is an institution of transcendent historical, cultural and social significance, whereas the latter most surely is not. Even though the classifications created under our statutory scheme result in a type of differential treatment that generally may be characterized as symbolic or intangible, this court correctly has stated that such treatment nevertheless "is every bit as restrictive as naked exclusions"; because it is no less real than more tangible forms of discrimination, at least when, as in the present case, the statute singles out a group that historically has been the object of scorn, intolerance, ridicule or worse.

We do not doubt that the civil union law was designed to benefit same sex couples by providing them with legal rights that they previously did not have. If, however, the intended effect of a law is to treat politically unpopular or historically disfavored minorities differently from persons in the majority or favored class, that law cannot evade constitutional review under the separate but equal doctrine. *See, e.g., Brown v. Board of Education*, 347 U.S. 483, 495, In such circumstances, the very existence of the classification gives credence to the perception that separate treatment is warranted for the same illegitimate reasons that gave rise to the past discrimination in the first place. Despite the truly laudable effort of the legislature in equalizing the legal rights afforded same sex and opposite sex couples, there is no doubt that civil unions enjoy a lesser status in our society than marriage. We therefore conclude that the plaintiffs have alleged a constitutionally cognizable injury, that is, the denial of the right to marry a same sex partner. We next must determine whether the state's differential treatment of same sex and opposite sex couples nevertheless satisfies state constitutional requirements. [The court concluded that the state did not satisfy constitutional requirements by offering same-sex couples civil unions.]

In re Marriage Cases

Supreme Court of California, 2008
43 Cal. 4th 757, 76 Cal. Rptr. 3d 683, 183 P.3d 384

George, C.J.

We have no occasion in this case to determine whether the state constitutional right to marry necessarily affords all couples the constitutional right to require the state to designate their official family relationship a "marriage," or whether, as the Attorney General suggests, the Legislature would not violate a couple's constitutional right to marry if—perhaps in order to emphasize and clarify that this civil institution is distinct from the religious institution of marriage—it were to assign a name other than marriage as the official designation of the family relationship for *all* couples. The current California statutes, of course, do not assign a name other than marriage for *all* couples, but instead reserve exclusively to opposite-sex couples the traditional designation of marriage, and assign a different designation—domestic partnership—to the only official family relationship available to same-sex couples.

Whether or not the name "marriage," in the abstract, is considered a core element of the state constitutional right to marry, one of the core elements of this fundamental right is the right of same-sex couples to have their official family relationship accorded the same dignity, respect, and stature as that accorded to all other officially recognized family relationships. The current statutes—by drawing a distinction between the name assigned to the family relationship available to opposite-sex couples and the name assigned to the family relationship available to same-sex couples, and by reserving the historic and highly respected designation of marriage exclusively to opposite-sex couples while offering same-sex couples only the new and unfamiliar designation of domestic partnership—pose a serious risk of denying the official family relationship of same-sex couples the equal dignity and respect that is a core element of the constitutional right to marry. As observed by the City at oral argument, this court's conclusion in *Perez*, *supra*, 32 Cal.2d 711, that the statutory provision barring interracial marriage was unconstitutional, undoubtedly would have been the same even if alternative nomenclature, such as "transracial union," had been made available to interracial couples.

Accordingly, although we agree with the Attorney General that the provisions of the Domestic Partner Act afford same-sex couples most of the substantive attributes to which they are constitutionally entitled under the state constitutional right to marry, we conclude that the current statutory assignment of different designations to the official family relationship of opposite-sex couples and of same-sex couples properly must be viewed as potentially impinging upon the state constitutional right of same-sex couples to marry.

b. A Closer Look at Alternative Sources of Legal Recognition

Domestic partnerships provide some external recognition, as well as packages of rights, benefits, and responsibilities that some same-sex couples find attractive. The term "civil union" is now commonly used to describe the most comprehensive form of domestic partnership—a form that grants to same-sex couples all the rights of marriage that a state can itself bestow. Some laws denominated "domestic partnership" laws are equally broad. For instance, California's law, which in the excerpt above the California Supreme Court rejected as a substitute for marriage, provided domestic partners with the state-law rights and benefits of marriage. Other domestic partnership regimes, such as Wisconsin's, grant only limited benefits. Aside from civil unions and domestic partnerships, some states have offered statuses such as "designated beneficiary" or "reciprocal beneficiary." These regimes provide fewer rights and often include relationships other than intimate couples, such as blood relatives and close friends.[3] Compare the following "domestic partnership" provisions from California and Wisconsin with the "designated beneficiary" provisions from Colorado:

CALIFORNIA DOMESTIC PARTNERSHIP STATUTE

§ 297. Domestic partners defined; Requirements for establishing domestic partnership

(a) Domestic partners are two adults who have chosen to share one another's lives in an intimate and committed relationship of mutual caring.

(b) A domestic partnership shall be established in California when both persons file a Declaration of Domestic Partnership with the Secretary of State pursuant to this division, and, at the time of filing, all of the following requirements are met:

   (1) Both persons have a common residence.

   (2) Neither person is married to someone else or is a member of another domestic partnership with someone else that has not been terminated, dissolved, or adjudged a nullity.

   (3) The two persons are not related by blood in a way that would prevent them from being married to each other in this state.

---

[3] Vermont's reciprocal beneficiary law includes only blood relatives excluded from marriage. 15 VT. STAT. ANN. § 1301.

(4) Both persons are at least 18 years of age.

(5) Either of the following:

    (A) Both persons are members of the same sex.

    (B) One or both of the persons meet the eligibility criteria under Title II of the Social Security Act as defined in 42 U.S.C. Section 402(a) for old-age insurance benefits or Title XVI of the Social Security Act as defined in 42 U.S.C. Section 1381 for aged individuals. Notwithstanding any other provision of this section, persons of opposite sexes may not constitute a domestic partnership unless one or both of the persons are over the age of 62.

(6) Both persons are capable of consenting to the domestic partnership.

§ 297.5. Rights, protections, benefits and responsibilities of present, former, and surviving registered domestic partners; Federal provisions; Long-term care plans; Constitutional provisions and provisions adopted by initiative

(a) Registered domestic partners shall have the same rights, protections, and benefits, and shall be subject to the same responsibilities, obligations, and duties under law, whether they derive from statutes, administrative regulations, court rules, government policies, common law, or any other provisions or sources of law, as are granted to and imposed upon spouses.

(b) Former registered domestic partners shall have the same rights, protections, and benefits, and shall be subject to the same responsibilities, obligations, and duties under law, whether they derive from statutes, administrative regulations, court rules, government policies, common law, or any other provisions or sources of law, as are granted to and imposed upon former spouses.

(c) A surviving registered domestic partner, following the death of the other partner, shall have the same rights, protections, and benefits, and shall be subject to the same responsibilities, obligations, and duties under law, whether they derive from statutes, administrative regulations, court rules, government policies, common law, or any other provisions or sources of law, as are granted to and imposed upon a widow or a widower.

(d) The rights and obligations of registered domestic partners with respect to a child of either of them shall be the same as those of spouses. The rights and obligations of former or surviving registered domestic partners with respect to a child of either of them shall be the same as those of former or surviving spouses.

CAL. FAM. CODE §§ 297, 297.5 (2005).

Wisconsin Domestic Partnership Statute

770.001 Declaration of policy.

The legislature finds that it is in the interests of the citizens of this state to establish and provide the parameters for a legal status of domestic partnership. The legislature further finds that the legal status of domestic partnership as established in this chapter is not substantially similar to that of marriage. Nothing in this chapter shall be construed as inconsistent with or a violation of article XIII, section 13, of the Wisconsin Constitution ["Only a marriage between one man and one woman shall be valid or recognized as a marriage in this state. A legal status identical or substantially similar to that of marriage for unmarried individuals shall not be valid or recognized in this state."]

770.05   Criteria for forming a domestic partnership.

Two individuals may form a domestic partnership if they satisfy all of the following criteria:

    (1) Each individual is at least 18 years old and capable of consenting to the domestic partnership.

    (2) Neither individual is married to, or in a domestic partnership with, another individual.

    (3) The 2 individuals share a common residence. . . .

    (4) The 2 individuals are not nearer of kin to each other than 2nd cousins, whether of the whole or half blood or by adoption.

    (5) The individuals are members of the same sex.

770.10   Completion and filing of declaration.

In order to form the legal status of domestic partners, the individuals shall complete the declaration of domestic partnership, sign the declaration, having their signatures acknowledged before a notary, and submit the declaration to the register of deeds of the county in which they reside.

WIS. STAT. ANN. § 770.001–10 (2009).

[Unlike the more robust statutory rights and responsibilities afforded by California's domestic partnership law, the Wisconsin law grants domestic partners a more limited set of protections. The principal provisions grant domestic partners hospital visitation rights (WIS. STAT. ANN. § 50.36), family and medical leave rights (WIS. STAT. ANN. § 103.10), inheritance rights under intestacy law (WIS. STAT. ANN. § 852.01), the right to sue for wrongful death (WIS. STAT. ANN. § 895.04), worker's compensation death benefits (WIS. STAT. ANN. § 40.65), and property ownership with rights of survivorship (WIS. STAT. ANN. § 852.09).]

Colorado Designated Beneficiary Statute

15–22–104. Requirements for a valid designated beneficiary agreement.

(1) A designated beneficiary agreement shall be legally recognized if:

    (a) The parties to the designated beneficiary agreement satisfy all of the following criteria:

        (I) Both are at least eighteen years of age;

        (II) Both are competent to enter into a contract;

        (III) Neither party is married to another person;

        (IV) Neither party is a party to another designated beneficiary agreement; and

        (V) Both parties enter into the designated beneficiary agreement without force, fraud, or duress[.]

COLO. REV. STAT. § 15–22–106

[Unlike the domestic partnership laws above, which assign a set of rights and responsibilities to the partners, the Colorado law allows the beneficiaries to choose rights and responsibilities from a menu. The menu offers only a limited set of rights. These include the right to act as a proxy decision-maker or surrogate decision-maker for medical care; the right to inherit real or personal property through intestate succession; the right to sue for wrongful death; and the right to direct the disposition of the beneficiary's remains. COLO. REV. STAT. § 15–22–105.]

NOTES

1. As of early 2014, of the states that have not provided same-sex couples access to marriage, four offer some form of nonmarital recognition for same-sex relationships, with one offering limited benefits (Wisconsin) and the others comprehensive substitutes for marriage (Colorado, Nevada, and Oregon). For a listing and taxonomy of statewide nonmarital measures, see the Human Rights Campaign's "relationship recognition" map, available at http://www.hrc.org/files/assets/resources/marriage_equality_082013.pdf. Note that many individual municipalities provide some recognition to same-sex couples in those areas under their jurisdiction.

2. States offering civil unions or domestic partnerships must decide whether to limit these forms of recognition to same-sex couples only, or to extend them to different-sex couples who do not wish to marry. As a matter of policy, how would you approach that question? How about as a matter of constitutional equality? Should these nonmarital relationship statuses be extended, like Colorado's "designated beneficiary" law, beyond intimate couples to include other relationships? If so, which relationships should be covered?

3. As states with nonmarital recognition regimes begin to allow same-sex couples to marry, will they maintain these nonmarital statuses? *Should* they maintain these statuses? Does it matter whether the nonmarital statuses include only same-sex couples? Whether the status grants fewer rights than marriage?

Once Connecticut offered marriage to same-sex couples, it converted civil unions, which had been available only to same-sex couples, into marriages by statute: "Two persons who are parties to a civil union . . . that has not been dissolved or annulled by the parties or merged into a marriage . . . as of October 1, 2010, shall be deemed to be married . . . and such civil union shall be merged into such marriage by operation of law on said date." CT. STAT. ANN. § 46b-38rr (2009). In contrast, Washington, D.C., which offered domestic partnerships to same-sex and different-sex couples, maintained its nonmarital status after it opened marriage to same-sex couples. *See* D.C. Code § 32–701 (2012). Which course do you prefer—the one taken in Connecticut or Washington, D.C.? Why?

Some employers have also ceased offering domestic partner benefits once same-sex couples have access to marriage. See Nancy D. Polikoff, *What Marriage Equality Arguments Portend for Domestic Partner Employee Benefits*, 37 N.Y.U. REV. L. & SOC. CHANGE 49 (2012). As an employer, would you continue to offer domestic partner benefits even after same-sex couples can marry? If so, which relationships would be eligible for benefits?

4. Domestic partnerships raise a number of novel tax issues. *See, e.g.,* Patricia A. Cain, *Dependency, Taxes, and Alternative Families*, 5 IOWA J. GENDER, RACE & JUST. 267 (2002); Nancy J. Knauer, *Heteronormativity and Federal Tax Policy*, 101 W. VA. L. REV. 129 (1998); Adam Chase, *Tax Planning for Same-Sex Couples*, 72 DENV. U. L. REV. 359 (1995).

c. *Other Sources of Protection*

In the absence of marriage or statutory schemes offering nonmarital rights, same-sex couples have sought to create or receive some of the rights and benefits that are automatically enjoyed by married couples. These include: rights to spousal shares of marital property upon death of one partner; tax benefits (including joint income tax returns, dependency deductions, gift tax exemptions, and exemptions for alimony and property settlements); rights in tort law (including emotional distress, wrongful death actions, and loss of consortium); rights in criminal law (including immunity from compelled testimony and the marital communication privilege); non-exclusion under zoning laws; visitation privileges in hospitals and other institutions; authority to make decisions for an ill spouse; employee benefits for spouses (including health insurance, medical leave, and bereavement leave); government benefits (including Social Security and veterans payments to spouses, workers compensation for those whose spouses move for job-related reasons); lower fees for married couples (including automobile and life insurance, family travel rates, and family memberships); immigration benefits; and draft exemptions.

Same-sex couples have used a variety of legal instruments as a means of asserting their rights. These include the simple (wills, powers of attorney) to the complicated (adoption). *See, e.g., Marvin v. Marvin*, 18 Cal. 3d 660, 134 Cal. Rptr. 815, 557 P.2d 106 (1976); *Whorton v. Dillingham*, 248 Cal. Rptr. 405, 202 Cal. App. 3d 447 (1988); and *Jones v. Daly*, 176 Cal. Rptr. 130, 122 Cal. App. 3d 500 (1981). But contractual arrangements can only go so far.

Another strategy has been to seek recognition for purposes of specific benefits and programs. In 1989, LGBT rights lawyers achieved a landmark victory in *Braschi v. Stahl Associates Co.*, 543 N.E.2d 49, 74 N.Y.2d 201, 544 N.Y.S.2d 784 (1989). Braschi, a gay man, sought to remain in his rent-controlled New York City apartment after the death of his partner, Blanchard. The rent-control law allowed a "surviving spouse of the deceased tenant or some other member of the deceased tenant's *family* who has been living with the tenant" to remain in the apartment. In the following passage, the court adopted a functional, rather than formal, definition of family:

> [W]e conclude that the term family, as used in 9 NYCRR 2204.6(d), should not be rigidly restricted to those people who have formalized their relationship by obtaining, for instance, a marriage certificate or an adoption order. The intended protection against sudden eviction should not rest on fictitious legal distinctions or genetic history, but instead should find its foundation in the reality of family life. In the context of eviction, a more realistic, and certainly equally valid, view of a family includes two adult lifetime partners whose relationship is long term and characterized by an emotional and financial commitment and interdependence. This view comports both with our society's traditional concept of "family" and with the expectations of individuals who live in such nuclear units. In fact, Webster's Dictionary defines "family" *first* as "a group of people united by certain convictions or common affiliation" (WEBSTER'S NINTH NEW COLLEGIATE DICTIONARY 448 (1984). . . . Hence, it is reasonable to conclude that, in using the term

"family," the Legislature intended to extend protection to those who reside in households having all of the normal familial characteristics. Appellant Braschi should therefore be afforded the opportunity to prove that he and Blanchard had such a household.

This definition of "family" is consistent with both of the competing purposes of the rent-control laws: the protection of individuals from sudden dislocation and the gradual transition to a free market system. Family members, whether or not related by blood, or law who have always treated the apartment as their family home will be protected against the hardship of eviction following the death of the named tenant, thereby furthering the Legislature's goals of preventing dislocation and preserving family units which might otherwise be broken apart upon eviction. * * *

Appellant and Blanchard lived together as permanent life partners for more than 10 years. They regarded one another, and were regarded by friends and family, as spouses. * * * In addition to their interwoven social lives, appellant clearly considered the apartment his home. He lists the apartment as his address on his driver's license and passport, and receives all his mail at the apartment address. * * * Financially, the two men shared all obligations including a household budget. . . . Additionally, Blanchard executed a power of attorney in appellant's favor so that appellant could make necessary decisions—financial, medical and personal—for him during his illness. Finally, appellant was the named beneficiary of Blanchard's life insurance policy, as well as the primary legatee and coexecutor of Blanchard's estate. Hence, a court examining these facts could reasonably conclude that these men were much more than mere roommates.

NOTES

1.   Even as the *Braschi* court adopted a functional definition of family, it seems to have hewed to a model of family shaped by marriage. The court may have treated the couple as a family because they functioned like a married couple, despite the fact that they were in a same-sex relationship. *See, e.g.,* Ariela R. Dubler, *Wifely Behavior: A Legal History of Acting Married*, 100 COLUM. L. REV. 957, 1020 (2000).

2.   The issue of legal recognition of same-sex couples has arisen in domestic violence cases. In *State v. Hadinger*, 573 N.E.2d 1191, 61 Ohio App. 3d 820 (1991), the Ohio Court of Appeals overturned a trial court ruling that Hadinger could not be convicted of domestic violence because she could not be a "person living as a spouse" with the woman she abused, as required under

the statute. The Court of Appeals held that, because the statute defines "person living as a spouse" as "a person . . . who otherwise is cohabiting with the offender," 573 N.E.2d at 1192, the definition was broad enough to encompass two people of the same sex, *id.* at 1193.

3. The question of guardianship rights for a same-sex partner was litigated in an early Minnesota case that became a powerful symbol of the need for the law to recognize same-sex couples. In *In re Guardianship of Kowalski*, 478 N.W.2d 790, 797 (Minn. Ct. App. 1991), the Court of Appeals of Minnesota granted the petition for guardianship of Sharon Kowalski that had been filed by Sharon's partner, Karen Thompson. Sharon had suffered severe brain damage in a car accident. The guardianship petition was challenged by Sharon's family. The family had not been aware of Sharon's sexual orientation before the accident, and they disapproved of the lesbian relationship. They sought guardianship in a third-party, a family friend. Karen remained active in Sharon's care, visiting her at least three times a week, re-outfitting their home to be handicap-accessible, and taking Sharon for weekend visits, despite a previous four-year period in which she was refused visitation rights by the family. The trial court awarded guardianship to the family friend "despite the uncontradicted medical testimony" that Sharon expressed a preference to be cared for by Thompson, that Thompson had a strong interest in Sharon's care and an "exceptional" understanding of Sharon's needs, and was "strongly equipped" to provide care for Sharon outside of an institutional setting. *Id.* at 793–94. The Court of Appeals reversed and held that, in light of the overwhelming evidence, Karen's petition for guardianship should be granted. *See id.* at 797.

C. THE MARRIAGE EQUALITY MOVEMENT AND BACKLASH

Over the last several years, as the LGBT movement has sought protection for same-sex couples, it has concentrated on winning access to marriage. This mobilization in favor of marriage equality has long since been met with countermobilization. Virtually as soon as the Hawaii Supreme Court signaled its apparent intention to announce a state constitutional right to marry, efforts to oppose that change in marriage law began. The passage of the Defense of Marriage Act (DOMA), further discussed in Parts II.D and II.E, and many mini-DOMA's in the ensuing years, evidenced substantial popular resistance to the legalization of same-sex marriage. After *Goodridge* was decided, that resistance reached a new level, when a federal constitutional amendment to ban same-sex marriage was endorsed by President George W. Bush. A leading version of the amendment proposed:

> Marriage in the United States shall consist only of the union of a man and a woman. Neither this Constitution, nor the constitution of any State, shall be construed to require that

marriage or the legal incidents thereof be conferred upon any union other than the union of a man and a woman.

H.R.J. Res. 88, 109th Cong. (2006).

In addition to promoting a federal constitutional amendment, opponents of same-sex marriage sought additional restrictions in the states. The early mini-DOMA's enacted after the *Baehr* decision in Hawaii generally focused on banning same-sex marriage on the state level and/or denying recognition to same-sex marriages performed elsewhere. Some were codified by statute, others by state constitutional amendment. After *Goodridge*, the trend was for states to pass constitutional amendments, not statutes. Indeed, some states that already had DOMA statutes on the books added new constitutional amendments. And many of the measures passed after *Goodridge* were so-called "super-DOMA's"—laws that reach beyond same-sex marriage to restrict civil unions and domestic partnerships, as well.[4] Recall the Nebraska initiative at issue in the *Bruning* case, *supra* Chapter 3, Section II.B.4. The state constitutional amendment upheld by the Eighth Circuit in that case provided that:

> Only marriage between a man and a woman shall be valid or recognized in Nebraska. The uniting of two persons of the same sex in a civil union, domestic partnership, or other similar same-sex relationship shall not be valid or recognized in Nebraska.

NEB. CONST., art. I, § 29. The Nebraska measure is among the most explicitly far-reaching in the nation. Other post-*Goodridge* amendments move in a similar direction, but many are not as precise about their scope. For example, the Ohio amendment provides that:

> Only a union between one man and one woman may be a marriage valid in or recognized by this state and its political subdivisions. This state and its political subdivisions shall not create or recognize a legal status for relationships of unmarried individuals that intends to approximate the design, qualities, significance or effect of marriage.

OHIO CONST., art. XV, § 11. The Michigan amendment reflects a similar approach:

> To secure and protect the benefits of marriage for our society and for future generations of children, the union of one man and one woman in marriage shall be the only agreement recognized as a marriage or similar union for any purpose.

---

[4] For an updated taxonomy of state laws restricting same-sex marriage, see the map frequently updated by the Human Rights Campaign at http://www.hrc.org/files/assets/resources/marriage_prohibitions_072013.pdf.

MICH. CONST., art. I, § 25. Measures like Ohio's and Michigan's require judicial interpretation to determine their reach.[5]

1. Perspectives on Marriage Backlash

Details about form and scope aside, there is no question that the backlash against same-sex marriage advocacy has been widespread.[6] This Section explores various dimensions of the backlash. Consider the following perspectives.

BROWN AND *LAWRENCE* (AND *GOODRIDGE*)[*]
Michael Klarman

Court rulings such as *Brown* and *Goodridge* produce political backlashes for three principal reasons: They raise the salience of an issue, they incite anger over "outside interference" or "judicial activism," and they alter the order in which social change would otherwise have occurred.

Brown was harder to ignore than earlier changes in southern racial practices. Most white southerners did not see black jurors or black police officers, who policed black neighborhoods only, and they would have been largely unaware of the dramatic increases in black voter registration that had occurred since World War II. Even some instances of integration— such as on city buses or golf courses—would have gone unnoticed by many white southerners. But they could not miss *Brown*, which received front-page coverage in virtually every newspaper in the country and was a constant topic of southern conversations. A northern white visitor found after *Brown* that segregation "is the foremost preoccupation of the Southern mind. . . . [It] intrudes into almost every conversation. It nags, it bothers and it will not be ignored." One white-supremacist leader credited the Court with "awakening us from a slumber of about 30 years," and an Alabama public official noted that white southerners owed the Justices "a debt of gratitude" for "causing us to become organized and unified."

Lawrence and, to an even greater extent, *Goodridge*, have dramatically raised the salience of gay-rights issues. Many other reforms on issues of sexual orientation—such as repeal of criminal prohibitions on

---

[5]   The Michigan Supreme Court ruled that the amendment prevents public employers from offering domestic partnership benefits to employees. *National Pride At Work v. Governor of Michigan*, 481 Mich. 56, 748 N.W.2d 524 (2008).

[6]   In 2010, the backlash took a new form when three Iowa supreme court justices who had ruled in favor of marriage equality in the *Varnum* case excerpted earlier lost their seats in a retention election. See John Gramlich, *Judges' Battles Signal a New Era for Retention Elections*, Wash. Post, Dec. 5, 2010, at A8. Normally, such elections return incumbent justices to the bench at a high rate. In the Iowa case, large sums were spent to defeat the justices.

[*]   Michael Klarman, Brown *and* Lawrence *(and* Goodridge*)*, 104 MICH. L. REV. 431, 473–85 (2005).

sodomy, expansion of partnership benefits, and enactment of statutory protections against discrimination in employment and public accommodations—have occurred without riveting public attention. Since *Goodridge*, though, same-sex marriage has constantly captured front-page newspaper headlines, and the issue received enormous attention during the 2004 presidential election campaign. Court rulings such as *Lawrence* and *Goodridge* forced people who previously had not paid much attention to gay-rights issues to notice what has been happening and to form an opinion on it. As one social conservative observed not long after the Massachusetts decision, "the more people focus on [gay marriage], the less they support it." Another critic of same-sex marriage noted that *Goodridge* "slapped American Christians in their face and woke them up." In the spring of 2004 in Oregon, the Christian Coalition sent out 75,000 voter guides opposing the reelection of Justice Rives Kistler of the state supreme court, denouncing him as "the only open homosexual supreme court judge in the nation"; it was the same-sex marriage issue that had given salience to the jurist's sexual orientation.

The second reason that rulings such as *Brown* and *Goodridge* produce political backlashes is that judicially mandated social reform may mobilize greater resistance than change accomplished through legislatures or with the acquiescence of other democratically operated institutions. *Brown* represented federal interference in southern race relations—something that white southerners, harboring deep historical resentments over military rule and "carpetbag" government during Reconstruction—could not easily tolerate. . . .

Goodridge, decided by the Massachusetts Supreme Court, cannot be seen as outside interference—at least with regard to ramifications for Massachusetts—in the same way that white southerners tended to regard the U.S. Supreme Court ruling in *Brown*. However, because it was a court decision, rather than a reform adopted by voters or popularly elected legislators, critics were able to deride it as the handiwork of arrogant "activist judges" defying the will of the people. . . . Karl Rove declared that President Bush believed that "5,000 years of human history should not be overthrown by the acts of a few liberal judges." The president himself stated during one of the presidential debates, "I'm deeply concerned that judges are making those decisions, and not the citizenry of the United States." Even a prominent gay-rights activist such as Andrew Sullivan, former editor of the New Republic, conceded that "court-imposed mandates rub people the wrong way, even those who support including gay couples within the family structure." The *Goodridge* ruling on same-sex marriage contrasts with other gay-rights reforms such as decriminalization of same-sex sodomy or the expansion of antidiscrimination laws to cover sexual orientation, where legislatures have been the driving force.

Moreover, because the Full Faith & Credit Clause of the federal constitution conceivably—though doubtfully—would place other states under some obligation to respect Massachusetts marriages, critics of *Goodridge* were able to rally support for a federal constitutional amendment, which was said to be necessary to protect the rest of the nation from the "activist judges" of Massachusetts. . . .

Third and perhaps most important, court decisions produce backlashes by commanding that social reform take place in a different order than might otherwise have occurred. On subjects such as race and sexual orientation, public attitudes often vary across a range of issues. Under Jim Crow, whites were generally more opposed to interracial marriage and the integration of grade schools than they were to desegregating transportation or permitting blacks to vote. Similarly, heterosexuals today tend to be far more committed to preventing same-sex marriage than to barring same-sex "civil unions" or to permitting employers to discriminate based on sexual orientation. Heterosexuals are least determined to retain criminal prohibitions on private, consensual, adult same-sex sodomy. * * *

By contrast, *Lawrence* dealt with an issue on which heterosexuals are most tolerant of change. Whatever most Americans today think of same-sex marriage or gays openly serving in the military, few favor punishing the private sexual conduct of gays and lesbians. As one leading social conservative put it after *Lawrence*, "even most Christians believe that what is done in the privacy of one's home is not the government's business." In 1961 all fifty states punished same-sex sodomy; in 1986 only twenty-five did so; and only thirteen states did so at the time of *Lawrence* (and only four of these had statutes that were explicitly addressed to same-sex sodomy). Even in those holdout states, virtually no prosecutions actually occurred. Thus, *Lawrence* was about as (politically) easy a constitutional case as the Court ever confronts: The Justices were asked to translate into constitutional law a social norm that commanded overwhelming popular support. Thus, they probably anticipated a relatively placid response to their ruling, unlike in *Brown*, where some of the Justices expected white southerners to respond with violence and school closures.

Goodridge produced a political backlash for the same reason that *Brown* did. By the early twenty-first century, most Americans were willing to accept decriminalization of same-sex sodomy, statutory bans on employment discrimination based on sexual orientation, and perhaps even civil unions for same-sex couples. Before *Lawrence* and, even more so, *Goodridge* gave same-sex marriage special prominence, many Democratic politicians—including most of those competing for the party's presidential nomination in 2004—supported civil unions, but not formal marriage, for gays and lesbians. This compromise position was an effort to appeal to homosexual voters, who disproportionately support the Democratic party, without alienating those heterosexuals who are willing to countenance progressive change on issues involving sexual orientation but not same-sex marriage.

After *Goodridge*, that compromise position became untenable. With gay and lesbian couples demanding marriage licenses across the country, it became harder to divert public attention from same-sex marriage to civil unions. * * *

. . . Inspired by the ruling of the Massachusetts court, thousands of same-sex couples applied for and received marriage licenses in San Francisco and in Multnomah County, Oregon, and smaller numbers did so in several other cities across the nation. Office-holders in local communities where public opinion supported same-sex marriage had obvious incentives to grant such licenses; their defiance of higher authority converted them into local heroes (much as southern governors such as Orval Faubus and George Wallace became virtually unbeatable politically by defying federal-court integration orders after *Brown*). For example, Mayor Newsom, who had won a narrow victory in the San Francisco mayoral election in December 2003, saw his approval ratings rise to a staggering eighty-five percent after he ordered local officials to begin issuing marriage licenses in February 2004. As the threat that same-sex marriage would expand beyond the boundaries of Massachusetts became real, opponents mobilized behind state and federal constitutional amendments to limit marriage to unions between men and women.

After the 2004 election, many prominent Democrats blamed Mayor Newsom of San Francisco for providing conservatives with an issue to rally around. Senator Dianne Feinstein of California observed that the thousands of same-sex weddings in San Francisco "energized a very conservative vote" and that the "whole issue has been too much, too fast, too soon. And people aren't ready for it." Representative Barney Frank of Massachusetts, one of the few openly gay representatives in the U.S. Congress, said that Newsom had "helped to galvanize Mr. Bush's conservative supporters in those states by playing into people's fears of same-sex weddings." . . .

Thus, the most significant short-term consequence of *Goodridge*, as with *Brown*, may have been the political backlash that it inspired. By outpacing public opinion on issues of social reform, such rulings mobilize opponents, undercut moderates, and retard the cause they purport to advance. And while the violent southern backlash produced by *Brown* generated a counterbacklash in northern opinion, in the wake of *Goodridge* gays and lesbians have not faced the sort of pervasive public violence that outrages moderates and turns the tide of public opinion once and for all. * * *

The future may be even easier to predict with regard to gay rights. Although the election results in 2004 confirm that most Americans are not yet ready for same-sex marriage, on other gay-rights issues the trend is plainly in the direction of expanded rights. In 2004, voters in Cincinnati overturned a city ordinance adopted ten years earlier that had barred the city council from passing any laws giving "minority or protected status" to gays and lesbians. In both North Carolina and Idaho, states not normally considered strong bastions of gay rights, voters elected their first openly gay state legislators, and voters in Dallas County, Texas elected as sheriff an openly lesbian Democrat—the first woman ever to hold the post and the first Democrat to do so in nearly three decades. On January 1, 2005, the nation's most far-reaching domestic partnership law went into effect in California, granting nearly all the rights of married couples to thousands of same-sex partners. Moreover, despite election results revealing powerful public opposition to same-sex marriage, lower courts—even in socially conservative states—have continued to expand gay rights in other contexts. In December 2004, a state court in Arkansas invalidated a regulation banning gays and lesbians from serving as foster parents, and the Montana Supreme Court ruled that public universities in the state were constitutionally obliged to provide gay employees with insurance coverage for domestic partners. * * *

The demographics of public opinion on issues of sexual orientation virtually ensure that one day in the not-too-distant future a substantial majority of Americans will support same-sex marriage: young people are much more likely to support gay rights than are their elders. Indeed, a poll taken in June 2003 showed that sixty-one percent of respondents aged eighteen to twenty-nine already supported the legalization of same-sex marriage, while among those aged 65 and over just twenty-two percent did so. There is little reason to believe that as people get older, their attitudes on such issues become more conservative (unlike attitudes toward wealth redistribution, which do become more conservative as people age and acquire more property). As an older generation holding more traditional views about sexual orientation fades from the scene and today's youth become tomorrow's policymakers, same-sex marriage will become increasingly accepted.

GOODRIDGE IN CONTEXT[*]

Mary L. Bonauto

At GLAD [Gay & Lesbian Advocates & Defenders], we had assumed that some day we would have to litigate the denial of marriage. My own experience with GLAD's intake calls demonstrated over and over again that many of the people who called us with legal problems could trace their problems to nonrecognition of their relationships. I had turned down requests for representation in such cases several times. The real question was when would LGBT people denied marriage rights get a fair hearing in court, in the legislature, and in public opinion in Massachusetts. . . . [W]ith each passing year, the increase in support for ending discrimination against LGBT people by non-LGBT people became phenomenal. This increase was essential because, as Rev. Dr. Martin Luther King, Jr. explained, no minority can succeed without the assistance of the majority. For this and other reasons, some of which are discussed below, we thought the answer was, "In 2001." * * *

GLAD did not litigate the marriage issue in Massachusetts precipitously. Short of constitutional litigation, we had made concerted efforts to secure rights and protections for LGBT families through other means, but knew those tools could not address the enormous architecture of protections provided by marriage. For example . . . GLAD used statutory construction principles to include LGBT families within the meanings of words like "person" in the adoption context. We worked within the equitable powers of the courts to address the needs of LGBT families when the legislature had not spoken, as in the de facto parenting case. We tried to secure a rule of even-handedness—that LGBT people should be able to contract regarding their affairs under ordinary rules of contract. We were unable to persuade the court that the term "dependent" could include same-sex domestic partners, a failure that effectively nullified governmental domestic partner programs for health insurance. . . .

. . . [F]rom our perspective on the ground, we thought the conventional wisdom that a civil union "compromise" would be more palatable than marriage was overstated. Much of the public debate in Vermont in the early months of 2000 had to do with the fundamental humanity and equal citizenship of LGBT people, i.e., the same issues involved in seeking marriage. Thus, any alleged advantage of civil unions seemed de minimis and certainly outweighed by the enormous legal disadvantages of civil unions vis-a-vis marriage for couples. Although this is too crude a formulation, we expected that those who opposed any rights for LGBT people would reject both marriage and civil unions and that

---

[*] Mary L. Bonauto, Goodridge *in Context*, 40 HARV. C.R.–C.L. L. REV. 1, 21–69 (2005). Bonauto was the lead lawyer in the *Goodridge* litigation.

those who accepted civil unions could come to see marriage as the fairer and simpler alternative over time. Those who protested most vociferously opposed marriage, civil unions, and any legal protections whatsoever. In short, we considered and rejected the idea of litigating for civil unions as opposed to marriage.

Second, we believed that the public education accompanying the case as well as the Vermont court ruling enormously advanced the standing of LGBT families and people in Vermont. We hoped that a case in Massachusetts, along with public education and legislative involvement, would make relationship recognition and access to legal protections an increasingly urgent priority in all branches of government.

Third, we anticipated political fallout in both states and expected (with enormous work) we could weather it. We saw that significant numbers of non-LGBT people came to the fore when the courts finally rejected discrimination in Vermont and anticipated that would be true in Massachusetts as well. Despite some legislators being turned out of office for their civil union votes, there was no undoing of the court decision in Vermont: the legislature refused to advance for electoral consideration any amendment to the state constitution that would have either reversed the *Baker* [*v. Vermont*] decision or amended the constitution to add a restriction on marriage. * * *

. . . Another factor sped the timing of the decision to litigate: we knew we would soon be on the defense in a constitutional amendment campaign. The Massachusetts Citizens Alliance, later known as Massachusetts Citizens for Marriage, was planning to come straight at the marriage issue with a citizen initiative to place an anti-LGBT marriage amendment on the ballot by November 2004. In order for the measure to advance, it needed the support of 50 of 200 legislators in a joint session. At GLAD, we knew no ballot campaign on marriage had yet been won and we assumed the issues would be framed in a way favorable to our opponents, putting LGBT people and families on the defense. In short, we calculated that the signature gathering process would succeed, that 50 or more legislators would support it, and that we would likely be facing a ballot measure in 2004.

Knowing that the legislature and public would be embroiled in the marriage and amendment discussions in any event, and aware of the generally favorable momentum toward relationship recognition, we viewed an affirmative marriage case as an opportunity to frame the issues positively and in the voices of LGBT people. We also thought the best defense was the same thing that had moved us forward so far: shining a light (this time through a lawsuit) on the lives of the real people affected and the bedrock American principles of fairness and equality. We knew we had a window of opportunity: a constitutional amendment must be approved by two legislatures before it can be put out to the voters for ratification at a general election.

If the case were resolved successfully, then Massachusetts voters would have the chance to see for themselves that relationship recognition and marriage rights for LGBT people were fair before they voted on the question of taking away those rights. If we lost the case, there would be less impetus to vote in favor of an amendment. Even more importantly, many more people in the electorate would understand the harms to our communities from being denied relationship recognition and marriage rights, thus increasing pressure on the Massachusetts legislature to take steps to ameliorate the discrimination. * * *

[Bonauto then discusses anti-marriage initiatives around the country after *Goodridge*.]

. . . Is all of this legislative activity a "backlash" to *Goodridge*, or to San Francisco Mayor Gavin Newsom's move to issue marriage licenses starting in February? On balance, it is more "lash" than "backlash." Without a doubt, these developments have agitated some and spurred others to take more drastic steps to preempt the otherwise natural course of events. Thirty-seven states enacted laws or constitutional amendments denying marriage to LGBT people before *Goodridge* was even decided. The proposed federal amendment was drafted in 2000–2001, and Congress passed the Defense of Marriage Act in 1996, both long before any state ended the exclusion of same-sex couples from marriage. The new marriage restrictions and amendments are not spontaneous developments, but the result of a premeditated campaign. George Chauncey's overview shows how marriage has been an obsession of the radical right, and Evan Wolfson notes, on the eve of the 1996 Presidential Caucuses in Iowa, leading "family values" groups—the same ones active in Massachusetts and around the country today—forced the candidates to take a position on a so-called Marriage Protection Pledge, the sole purpose of which was to deny marriage rights to LGBT people without "protecting" marriage in any other way. . . .

Beyond accelerating the conversation about fairness, staying the course means allowing legal systems and private entities to take measure of these new legal developments. In Massachusetts, some employers and trusts initially withheld employment benefits but then changed course to explicitly include same-sex married couples within their benefit plans.

. . . The public policy discussions are advancing as well and will continue. Already, some states have begun ameliorating the harsh consequences of the total exclusion of LGBT people from marriage. While the steps taken toward statewide domestic partnership registries in Maine and New Jersey are modest, they are particularly notable because Maine's follows a legislative enactment of a state anti-LGBT marriage law, and New Jersey's accompanies pending marriage litigation. California's newest law, effective January 1, 2005, provides registered domestic partners with almost every state-conferred right and responsibility of married persons and may soon be superceded by marriage. . . .

Many in the LGBT community feel lifted up by the *Goodridge* decision, just as the *Brown* decision had a "powerfully inspirational effect" on politically minded African Americans. We need this spirit, just as we need urgency because the harms to families and their children demand it. We must not be self-abnegating, but we also need the tempering influence of a longer term perspective: the nearly sixty years it took to dismantle the "separate but equal" doctrine, and the even longer fight for women to win the right to vote—plus the fact that it took a constitutional amendment to do so. While the path of LGBT people will be different from those in other justice movements, I draw solace from California's *Perez* case where that state's high court, in a four-to-three decision with a bitter dissent, ended race discrimination in marriage in that state. It was the first state supreme court to do so, and the existing legal precedents around the country were contrary, and the cultural landscape was inauspicious. Yet, many of us are now grateful that the court saw the issue as one of human equality and dignity and broke what had been a logjam of discrimination. A large number of states repealed their bans on interracial marriage by the time the U.S. Supreme Court decided *Loving v. Virginia* nineteen years later. While Dr. King was correct that progress is anything but inevitable, it is certainly a better bet that with determined time and effort, LGBT people will be part of constitutional history in this country, a story of the "extension of constitutional rights and protections to people once formerly ignored or excluded."

NOTES

1. The reality of same-sex marriage, achieved first through litigation, likely affects public perception. As Professor Carlos Ball explains, "Although implacable opponents of same-sex marriage are unlikely to allow facts such as these to weaken their resolve, more open-minded citizens are likely to be persuaded of the moral legitimacy behind claims for gay equality by simply observing and getting to know lesbian and gay couples as married couples." Carlos A. Ball, *The Backlash Thesis and Same-Sex Marriage: Learning from* Brown v. Board of Education *and its Aftermath*, 14 WM. & MARY BILL RTS. J. 1493, 1527 (2006).

2. The ferocity and scope of the backlash against same-sex marriage rulings raise the question why the earliest state court constitutional ruling in favor of interracial marriage—by the California Supreme Court in 1948—did not trigger comparable backlash. Opinion polls suggest that interracial marriage was subject to very high rates of disapproval when the California

Supreme Court struck down that state's ban on interracial unions in *Perez v. Sharp,* 32 Cal. 2d 711, 198 P.2d 17 (1948). Under Professor Klarman's analysis, above, one might have expected a backlash. The disparity in the aftermaths is likely traceable to a range of legal, political and cultural differences between the historical episodes that suggest that broad generalizations about backlash against court decisions should be avoided in favor of a fact-intensive, contextualized inquiry. *See* Jane S. Schacter, *Courts and the Politics of Backlash: Marriage Equality Litigation, Then and Now*, 82 S. Cal. L. Rev. 1153 (2009).

2. Proposition 8 in California: A Case Study of Backlash and Its Complex Aftermath

The same-sex marriage debate was highly visible and sharply contested in California. In March 2000, the voters passed a statute, Proposition 22, that defined marriage as limited to a man and a woman. In 2004, San Francisco Mayor Gavin Newsom made national headlines by directing that marriage licenses be issued to same-sex couples in the city, Prop 22 notwithstanding. (Recall from Section I of this Chapter that Del Martin and Phyllis Lyon were the first couple to wed when the mayor made this decision.) Mayor Newsom's argument was that he was authorized to act because Prop 22 violated the California Constitution.

Unlike in Massachusetts, LGBT rights advocates in California deliberately avoided litigation challenging the state's marriage law. They were not merely concerned about the uncertainty of litigation but were also worried that a favorable decision could easily be reversed through the state initiative system. Yet Mayor Newsom's actions pushed the issue in California and invited litigation by opponents of same-sex marriage seeking to halt the marriages.

The marriages permitted by Newsom's action were eventually voided by the California Supreme Court in *Lockyer v. City & County of San Francisco*, 33 Cal. 4th 1055, 17 Cal. Rptr. 3d 225, 95 P.3d 459 (2004). The opinion in *Lockyer,* however, expressly turned on the finding that, in the absence of a judicial determination that Prop 22 was unconstitutional, city officials lacked authority to act based on their own views of the measure's constitutional defects. The court's opinion reserved for another day the question whether Prop 22 violated the state constitution.

Soon after the *Lockyer* decision, several lawsuits were brought to challenge the constitutionality of Prop 22. With the issue now in the courts, LGBT rights advocates affirmatively litigated for marriage equality in the state. In California, events outside the control of LGBT rights lawyers forced them into litigation involving the constitutionality of the state's marriage ban. This feature is noteworthy, given that backlash critics often blame advocates for the choice to litigate prematurely. *See* Scott L. Cummings & Douglas NeJaime, *Lawyering for*

Marriage Equality, 57 UCLA L. REV. 1235, 1240–41 (2010) (explaining how the situation in California calls into question a central assumption of the backlash thesis).

In May 2008, the California Supreme Court overturned Prop 22 under the California Constitution. (Excerpts of the decision, *In re Marriage Cases*, 43 Cal. 4th 757, 76 Cal. Rptr. 3d 683, 183 P.3d 384 (2008)), appear in Section II.B. of this Chapter.) With its ruling, the California Supreme Court became the first state supreme court in the country to follow *Goodridge*. Same-sex couples began to marry in June 2008, but did not enjoy that freedom for long. Even before the *Marriage Cases* decision, efforts were underway to replace Prop 22—a statute— with a state constitutional amendment limiting marriage to a man and a woman. Opponents of same-sex marriage completed their efforts in time to qualify Prop 8 for the November 2008 ballot. Prop 8 went on to pass at the polls with 52% of the vote. This was down substantially from the 61% approval Prop 22 had secured in 2000, but was enough to bring same-sex marriage to a halt in the nation's most populous state. After its passage, Prop 8 came to represent the face of the same-sex marriage debate in the United States. In this section, we explore the campaign that led to passage of the measure, the litigation it spawned, and its ultimate demise after it made its way all the way to the U.S. Supreme Court.

a. Proposition 8

Full Text of Proposition 8

This initiative measure is submitted to the people in accordance with the provisions of Article II, Section 8, of the California Constitution.

This initiative measure expressly amends the California Constitution by adding a section thereto; therefore, new provisions proposed to be added are printed in italic type to indicate that they are new.

SECTION 1. Title This measure shall be known and may be cited as the "California Marriage Protection Act."

SECTION 2. Section 7.5 is added to Article I of the California Constitution, to read:

SEC. 7.5. Only marriage between a man and a woman is valid or recognized in California.

The Official Ballot Pamphlet from Proposition

Arguments for Proposition 8

Proposition 8 is simple and straightforward. It contains the same 14 words that were previously approved in 2000 by over 61% of

California voters: "Only marriage between a man and a woman is valid or recognized in California."

Because four activist judges in San Francisco wrongly overturned the people's vote, we need to pass this measure as a constitutional amendment to RESTORE THE DEFINITION OF MARRIAGE as a man and a woman.

Proposition 8 is about preserving marriage; *it's not an attack on the gay lifestyle.* Proposition 8 doesn't take away any rights or benefits of gay or lesbian domestic partnerships. Under California law, "domestic partners shall have the same rights, protections, and benefits" as married spouses. (Family Code § 297.5.) There are NO exceptions. Proposition 8 WILL NOT change this.

YES on Proposition 8 does three simple things:

- *It restores the definition of marriage* to what the vast majority of California voters already approved and human history has understood marriage to be.

- *It overturns the outrageous decision of four activist Supreme Court judges who ignored the will of the people.*

- *It protects our children from being taught in public schools that "same-sex marriage" is the same as traditional marriage.*

Proposition 8 protects marriage as an essential institution of society. While death, divorce, or other circumstances may prevent the ideal, the best situation for a child is to be raised by a married mother and father.

The narrow decision of the California Supreme Court isn't just about "live and let live." State law may require teachers to instruct children as young as kindergarteners about marriage. (Education Code § 51890.) If the gay marriage ruling is not overturned, TEACHERS COULD BE REQUIRED to teach young children there is *no difference* between gay marriage and traditional marriage.

We should not accept a court decision that may result in public schools teaching our kids that gay marriage is okay. That is an issue for parents to discuss with their children according to their own values and beliefs. *It shouldn't be forced on us against our will.*

Some will try to tell you that Proposition 8 takes away legal rights of gay domestic partnerships. That is false. Proposition 8 DOES NOT take away any of those rights and does not interfere with gays living the lifestyle they choose.

However, while gays have the right to their private lives, *they do not have the right to redefine marriage for everyone else.*

CALIFORNIANS HAVE NEVER VOTED FOR SAME-SEX MARRIAGE. If gay activists want to legalize gay marriage, they should put it on the ballot. Instead, they have gone behind the backs of voters and convinced four activist judges in San Francisco to redefine marriage for the rest of society. That is the wrong approach.

Voting YES on Proposition 8 RESTORES the definition of marriage that was approved by over 61% of voters. Voting YES overturns the decision of four activist judges. Voting YES *protects our children.*

Please vote YES on Proposition 8 to RESTORE the meaning of marriage.

RON PRENTICE, President

California Family Council

ROSEMARIE "ROSIE" AVILA, Governing Board Member

Santa Ana Unified School District

BISHOP GEORGE McKINNEY, Director

Coalition of African American Pastors

Arguments Against Proposition 8

————

OUR CALIFORNIA CONSTITUTION—the law of our land— SHOULD GUARANTEE THE SAME FREEDOMS AND RIGHTS TO EVERYONE—NO ONE group SHOULD be singled out to BE TREATED DIFFERENTLY.

In fact, our nation was founded on the principle that all people should be treated equally. EQUAL PROTECTION UNDER THE LAW IS THE FOUNDATION OF AMERICAN SOCIETY.

That's what this election is about—equality, freedom, and fairness, for all.

Marriage is the institution that conveys dignity and respect to the lifetime commitment of any couple. PROPOSITION 8 WOULD DENY LESBIAN AND GAY COUPLES that same DIGNITY AND RESPECT.

That's why Proposition 8 is wrong for California.

Regardless of how you feel about this issue, the freedom to marry is fundamental to our society, just like the freedoms of religion and speech.

PROPOSITION 8 MANDATES ONE SET OF RULES FOR GAY AND LESBIAN COUPLES AND ANOTHER SET FOR EVERYONE ELSE. That's just not fair. OUR LAWS SHOULD TREAT EVERYONE EQUALLY.

In fact, the government has no business telling people who can and cannot get married. Just like government has no business telling us what to read, watch on TV, or do in our private lives. We don't need Prop. 8; WE DON'T NEED MORE GOVERNMENT IN OUR LIVES.

REGARDLESS OF HOW ANYONE FEELS ABOUT MARRIAGE FOR GAY AND LESBIAN COUPLES, PEOPLE SHOULD NOT BE SINGLED OUT FOR UNFAIR TREATMENT UNDER THE LAWS OF OUR STATE. Those committed and loving couples who want to accept the responsibility that comes with marriage should be treated like everyone else.

DOMESTIC PARTNERSHIPS ARE NOT MARRIAGE.

When you're married and your spouse is sick or hurt, there is no confusion: you get into the ambulance or hospital room with no questions asked. IN EVERYDAY LIFE, AND ESPECIALLY IN EMERGENCY SITUATIONS, DOMESTIC PARTNERSHIPS ARE SIMPLY NOT ENOUGH. Only marriage provides the certainty and the security that people know they can count on in their times of greatest need.

EQUALITY UNDER THE LAW IS A FUNDAMENTAL CONSTITUTIONAL GUARANTEE. Prop. 8 separates one group of Californians from another and excludes them from enjoying the same rights as other loving couples.

Forty-six years ago I married my college sweetheart, Julia. We raised three children—two boys and one girl. The boys are married, with children of their own. Our daughter, Liz, a lesbian, can now also be married—if she so chooses.

All we have ever wanted for our daughter is that she be treated with the same dignity and respect as her brothers—with the same freedoms and responsibilities as every other Californian.

My wife and I never treated our children differently, we never loved them any differently, and now the law doesn't treat them differently, either.

Each of our children now has the same rights as the others, to choose the person to love, commit to, and to marry.

Don't take away the equality, freedom, and fairness that everyone in California—straight, gay, or lesbian—deserves.

Please join us in voting NO on Prop. 8.

SAMUEL THORON, Former President

Parents, Families and Friends of Lesbians and Gays

JULIA MILLER THORON, Parent

NOTES

1. How would you assess the competing arguments in the ballot pamphlet? Are each side's arguments the most effective available for its position?

2. More money was spent by both sides in the Prop 8 campaign than had ever been spent on any initiative involving a social issue. Expenses exceeded $80 million, with donations coming from individuals in all fifty states and from around the world. The vast sums of funding in the campaigns largely went to the television ads, some of which echoed the themes in the ballot arguments. For an in-depth analysis of several of the major ads used in the campaign, see Melissa Murray, *Marriage Rights and Parental Rights: Parents, the State, and Proposition 8*, 5 STAN. J. C.R. & C.L. 357 (2009).

3. One of the more controversial aspects of the funding of Prop 8 was the substantial role played by the Mormon Church. *See* Jesse McKinley & Kirk Johnson, *Mormons Tipped Scale in Ban on Gay Marriage*, N.Y. Times, Nov. 15, 2008, at A1. Proceedings before the California Fair Political Practices Commission resulted in the Church's agreement to pay a $5,500 fine for failing to report $37,000 worth of assistance to the pro-Prop 8 campaign shortly before the 2008 election. Bob Egelko, *Judge Poses Tough Questions for Each Side of Prop 8 Debate*, S.F. CHRONICLE, June 9, 2010, at C5.

b. State Court Challenge

Shortly following its passage, Prop 8 was challenged in state court. The central claim was that Prop 8 was procedurally invalid because it constituted a "revision" to—and not a mere "amendment" of—the state constitution, and therefore could not, under the terms of the state constitution, be enacted through a ballot initiative alone. Then-Attorney General Jerry Brown contested the claim that Prop 8 was a "revision," but nevertheless asserted that it violated the state constitution because it denied same-sex couples a fundamental right made inalienable under that document. Because of Brown's stance, ProtectMarriage.com was permitted to intervene.

In *Strauss v. Horton*, 46 Cal. 4th 364, 93 Cal. Rptr. 3d 591, 207 P.3d 48 (2009), the state supreme court rejected the challenge to Prop 8. Chief Justice George, who authored the opinion in the *Marriage Cases*, wrote for the majority:

> [A]s originally adopted, the constitutional amendment/revision dichotomy in California-which mirrored the framework set forth in many other state constitutions of the same vintage—indicates that the category of *constitutional revision* referred to the kind of wholesale or fundamental alteration of the constitutional structure that appropriately could be undertaken only by a constitutional convention, in contrast to the category of *constitutional amendment,* which included any and all of the more discrete changes to the Constitution that thereafter might be proposed. . . .

> [A]mong the various constitutional protections recognized in the *Marriage Cases* as available to same-sex couples, it is only the designation of marriage—albeit significant—that has been removed by this initiative measure.

> Taking into consideration the actual limited effect of Proposition 8 upon the preexisting state constitutional right of privacy and due process and upon the guarantee of equal protection of the laws, and after comparing this initiative measure to the many other constitutional changes that have been reviewed and evaluated in numerous prior decisions of this court, we conclude Proposition 8 constitutes a constitutional amendment rather than a constitutional revision. As a quantitative matter, petitioners concede that Proposition 8—which adds but a single, simple section to the Constitution—does not constitute a revision. As a qualitative matter, the act of limiting access to the designation of marriage to opposite-sex couples does not have a substantial or, indeed, even a minimal effect on *the governmental plan or framework of California* that existed prior to the amendment. Contrary to petitioners' claim in this regard, the measure does not transform or undermine the judicial function; this court will continue to exercise its traditional responsibility to faithfully enforce *all* of the provisions of the California Constitution, which now include the new section added through the voters' approval of Proposition 8. Furthermore, the judiciary's authority in applying the state Constitution always has been limited by the content of the provisions set forth in our Constitution, and that limitation remains unchanged.

The court also upheld the validity of the approximately 18,000 same-sex marriages that had occurred between the *Marriage Cases* decision and Prop 8's passage.

c. Moving to the Federal Courts

Strauss was immediately followed by the announcement of a federal lawsuit challenging the constitutionality of Prop 8. As the next reading explains, the decision to go to federal court marked a new—and controversial—chapter in same-sex marriage advocacy.

GAY ON TRIAL: WHY MORE THAN MARRIAGE IS AT STAKE IN THE FEDERAL LEGAL CHALLENGE TO PROP 8[*]

Gabriel Arana

On Nov. 4, 2008, when the polls closed on the West Coast and media outlets reported that California voters had passed Proposition 8, gay-rights supporters across the country were stunned. How could the purported gay haven of *California*—home to Hollywood, Harvey Milk, and the Castro—have rejected same-sex marriage?

After months of scapegoating, soul-searching, and regrouping, gay-rights leaders settled on a two-part strategy: Fight the measure in state court and work on overturning it at the ballot box in 2010 or 2012. The state Supreme Court challenge to Prop 8, which argued that the measure was not an "amendment" to the California Constitution but a "revision" requiring legislative approval, was widely considered a long shot. Few were surprised when the court upheld Prop 8.

What did come as a surprise was the news, that same day, that two relative strangers to civil-rights litigation, David Boies and Ted Olson, had filed a suit against the amendment in federal court. It was a decision so rash that it could only have come from outsiders. Olson, a prominent figure in the conservative legal movement, had represented George W. Bush in *Bush v. Gore*, a case in which he faced off against Boies, a high-profile lawyer who made his name defending Wall Street, not civil rights. They intend to take their challenge to Prop 8 all the way. . . .

For decades, groups like the ACLU and Lambda have taken an incremental approach to fighting for gay rights in court, concentrating on establishing legal precedents and popular support in states before going federal. In California, Connecticut, New York, and Iowa, gay-rights attorneys have pursued many big-ticket cases, with mixed results. But in federal courts, their aims have been more modest; it was only in 2003 that Lambda succeeded in decriminalizing sodomy nationwide.

---

[*] Gabriel Arana, *Gay on Trial: Why More than Marriage is at Stake in the Federal Legal Challenge to Prop. 8*, THE AMERICAN PROSPECT, November 23, 2009

To some, both within the movement and outside it, this tentative approach has been frustrating. As Olson said, "People should not have to beg to be treated equally or wait for decades for popular approval to be treated equally." But even among those of us who believe LGBT Americans deserve equal rights *now*, the fear is that jumping the gun will lead to harmful court precedents and social backlash [as followed the Hawaii Supreme Court's 1993 ruling]. * * *

"The debate is never about whether equality means equality for gay people, too. There have been debates about timing as long as there have been queer people to have a conversation," says Jennifer Pizer, the Lambda attorney who argued the state-level challenge to Prop 8. "The question always is a matter of how much development of the doctrine and how much social and political change should be achieved before asking the ultimate question." * * *

The fact that two straight, white-shoe lawyers have taken on the case shows the broad support gay rights have gained. But there is also the sense that Boies and Olson stand to lose nothing. The possible reward, on the other hand, is clear: For two attorneys who have pursued high-profile cases throughout their careers, this could be the defining win that puts them in history books. *Perry v. Schwarzenegger* is one of the rare cases that redraws battle lines and upsets traditional alliances. Like *Brown v. Board of Education* or *Roe v. Wade*, it has the potential to change American life. * * *

The stakes are high. If *Perry v. Schwarzenegger* reaches the Supreme Court and Boies and Olson are successful, gays and lesbians nationwide would not only have the right to marry, they stand to gain many of the legal rights they have sought for decades. In the eyes of the law, gay people would be equal to straight people, and any legislation that discriminated against them could be challenged and easily struck down against this precedent. However, defeat could legitimize such discrimination against LGBT Americans, making it far more difficult to sue for parental or housing rights. The door to any federal litigation on marriage equality would be shut for decades.

This is risky because Boies and Olson are entering a legal no-man's land. The coalition of lawyers who fought to overturn Prop 8 at the state level decided not to mount a federal challenge "because federal litigation puts in play the federal doctrines that as yet are underdeveloped," Pizer says. Marriage and family law tend to be state law, she explains, and the federal framework is sketchy.

Legal experts say getting judges to recognize gays as a suspect class will be a tough sell; the Supreme Court has long refused to make age or disability a protected category. And even those who think the legal arguments are compelling say that swaying a conservative Supreme

Court is the real challenge. "If you just look at the criteria, they'll be able to make a very powerful case," says William Eskridge, a professor at Yale Law School who was involved in gay-marriage litigation in the early 1990s. "[But] if the case comes to the Supreme Court in the next three years, given its membership, the conventional wisdom is that they don't have five votes." * * *

The quandary for the court in January is, in effect, how to name a reality that we do not all share. The real fight is not over marriage itself. *Perry v. Schwarzenegger* is only about gay marriage in the sense that *Roe v. Wade* was about privacy, or *Brown v. Board of Education* was about school choice. The case is really about the place of gay people in society. * * *

As Eskridge points out, the best turn the Prop 8 case could take is that it would be rendered moot by California voters . . . But even if Boies and Olson lose the case, it would not be the disaster that some gay-rights supporters fear. A Supreme Court loss could galvanize a movement that, at least in California, was dumbstruck that gay rights didn't just come as a matter of course. Indeed . . . the promise of equality seems to lie increasingly in local, grass-roots efforts. Decades of fervent activism are what made the legislative victories in Vermont and New Hampshire possible, and they are an indication of public support that no court can grant. It is better not to be the victim of discrimination in the first place than to have the law on your side when you are.

NOTES

1. The decision by Olson and Boies to file in federal court starkly raises the question of who should decide matters of crucial strategy in law reform litigation. For a scholarly perspective, see William B. Rubenstein, *Divided We Litigate*: *Addressing Disputes Among Group Members and Lawyers in Civil Rights Campaigns*, 106 YALE L.J. 1623 (1997). Do you think it was wise to file in federal court? Why or why not? What role do you think the consensus of major LGBT rights organizations should play in determining the path forged in such cases?

2. How does the involvement of Ted Olson—most famous for representing George W. Bush in *Bush v. Gore*—affect the cause? Is there a "conservative" case for same-sex marriage that is different from a "progressive" case? If so, how?

3. As you assess the wisdom of the federal litigation, consider the character of the marriage backlash. As we have seen, after 1993, same-sex marriage produced a sweeping *policy* backlash around the country, reflected in a rash of anti-marriage measures at both the state and federal levels. Prop 22 and Prop 8 were parts of this response. Yet, over the same time period, there was no *public opinion* backlash. Quite the contrary, polls show that public attitudes toward same-sex marriage have warmed considerably in the

last several years, with Gallup now showing majority support. *See, e.g.,* Lydia Saad, *In U.S., 52% Back Law to Legalize Gay Marriage in 50 States*, GALLUP, INC., July 29, 2013, *available at* http://www.gallup.com/poll/163730/back-law-legalize-gay-marriage-states.aspx (last accessed Dec. 11, 2013) ("Gallup used two separate approaches to measure public support for gay marriage this month, and they produced similar results: 52% would vote for a federal law legalizing same-sex marriages in all 50 states, and 54% think gay marriages should be recognized as valid, with the same rights as marriages between men and women."). When Gallup first asked about the legality of same-sex marriage in 1996, it found that 68% of Americans were opposed while only 27% were in favor. Jeffrey M. Jones, *American's Opposition to Gay Marriage Eases Slightly*, GALLUP, INC., May 4, 2010, *available at* http://www.gallup.com/poll/128291/americans-opposition-gay-marriage-eases-slightly.aspx (last accessed Dec. 11, 2013).

Does rising public support of this kind suggest that court decisions in favor of marriage equality may have speeded public acceptance, even as they have also helped to generate measures like Prop 8?

Judge Vaughn Walker of the Northern District of California was assigned the *Perry* case. Contrary to prior practice in the state court litigation on marriage equality, he decided to hold a full trial on the merits. He took steps to allow cameras in the courtroom during the trial, but, after an expedited appeal of his order, the Supreme Court barred cameras. *Hollingsworth v. Perry*, 558 U.S. 183 (2010). The trial ultimately lasted thirteen days and produced a transcript of 3115 pages.[7] Both sides offered expert testimony on questions relevant to Prop 8's constitutionality. In August 2010, Judge Walker issued the following opinion.

PERRY V. SCHWARZENEGGER

District Court of Northern California, 2010
704 F.Supp.2d 921

WALKER, J.

[Plaintiffs, same-sex couples wishing to marry in California, claimed that Prop 8 deprived them of due process and equal protection of the laws contrary to the Fourteenth Amendment. The Governor and Attorney General appeared in court, but declined to defend the measure. The initiative's sponsors, known as ProtectMarriage.com-Yes on 8, a Project of California Renewal ("Protect Marriage"), were permitted to intervene in the district court proceedings.]

* * * A state's interest in an enactment must of course be secular in nature. The state does not have an interest in enforcing private moral or religious beliefs without an accompanying secular purpose. See *Lawrence v. Texas,* 539 U.S. 558, 571 (2003).

---

[7]   The trial transcripts are available at http://www.afer.org/our-work/hearing-transcripts/.

Perhaps recognizing that Proposition 8 must advance a secular purpose to be constitutional, proponents abandoned previous arguments from the campaign that had asserted the moral superiority of opposite-sex couples. Instead, in this litigation, proponents asserted that Proposition 8:

1. Maintains California's definition of marriage as excluding same-sex couples;

2. Affirms the will of California citizens to exclude same-sex couples from marriage;

3. Promotes stability in relationships between a man and a woman because they naturally (and at times unintentionally) produce children; and

4. Promotes "statistically optimal" child-rearing households; that is, households in which children are raised by a man and a woman married to each other.

While proponents vigorously defended the constitutionality of Proposition 8, they did so based on legal conclusions and cross-examinations of some of plaintiffs' witnesses, eschewing all but a rather limited factual presentation. * * *

At oral argument on proponents' motion for summary judgment, the court posed to proponents' counsel the assumption that "the state's interest in marriage is procreative" and inquired how permitting same-sex marriage impairs or adversely affects that interest. Counsel replied that the inquiry was "not the legally relevant question," but when pressed for an answer, counsel replied: "Your honor, my answer is: I don't know. I don't know."

Despite this response, proponents in their trial brief promised to "demonstrate that redefining marriage to encompass same-sex relationships" would effect some twenty-three specific harmful consequences. At trial, however, proponents presented only one witness, David Blankenhorn, to address the government interest in marriage. Blankenhorn's testimony is addressed at length hereafter; suffice it to say that he provided no credible evidence to support any of the claimed adverse effects proponents promised to demonstrate. During closing arguments, proponents again focused on the contention that "responsible procreation is really at the heart of society's interest in regulating marriage." When asked to identify the evidence at trial that supported this contention, proponents' counsel replied, "you don't have to have evidence of this point."

Proponents' procreation argument, distilled to its essence, is as follows: the state has an interest in encouraging sexual activity between people of the opposite sex to occur in stable marriages because such sexual activity may lead to pregnancy and children, and the state has an interest in encouraging parents to raise children in stable households. The state therefore, the argument goes, has an interest in encouraging all opposite-sex sexual activity, whether responsible or irresponsible, procreative or otherwise, to occur within a stable marriage, as this encourages the development of a social norm that opposite-sex sexual activity should occur within marriage. Entrenchment of this norm increases the probability that procreation will occur within a marital union. Because same-sex couples' sexual activity does not lead to procreation, according to proponents the state has no interest in encouraging their sexual activity to occur within a stable marriage. Thus, according to proponents, the state's only interest is in opposite-sex sexual activity. * * *

[Judge Walker then discusses the evidence presented at trial by the various expert witnesses and then presents an extensive set of findings of fact].

CONCLUSIONS OF LAW

* * * The freedom to marry is recognized as a fundamental right protected by the Due Process Clause.

* * * The parties do not dispute that the right to marry is fundamental. The question presented here is whether plaintiffs seek to exercise the fundamental right to marry; or, because they are couples of the same sex, whether they seek recognition of a new right.

To determine whether a right is fundamental under the Due Process Clause, the court inquires into whether the right is rooted "in our Nation's history, legal traditions, and practices." *Glucksberg,* 521 U.S. at 710. Here, because the right to marry is fundamental, the court looks to the evidence presented at trial to determine: (1) the history, tradition and practice of marriage in the United States; and (2) whether plaintiffs seek to exercise their right to marry or seek to exercise some other right. * * *

The marital bargain in California (along with other states) traditionally required that a woman's legal and economic identity be subsumed by her husband's upon marriage under the doctrine of coverture; this once-unquestioned aspect of marriage now is regarded as antithetical to the notion of marriage as a union of equals. As states moved to recognize the equality of the sexes, they eliminated laws and practices like coverture that had made gender a proxy for a spouse's role within a marriage. Marriage was thus transformed from a male-dominated institution into an institution recognizing men and women as equals. Yet, individuals retained the right to marry; that right did not become different simply because the institution of marriage became compatible with gender equality.

The evidence at trial shows that marriage in the United States traditionally has not been open to same-sex couples. The evidence suggests many reasons for this tradition of exclusion, including gender roles mandated through coverture, social disapproval of same-sex relationships, and the reality that the vast majority of people are heterosexual and have had no reason to challenge the restriction. The evidence shows that the movement of marriage away from a gendered institution and toward an institution free from state-mandated gender roles reflects an evolution in the understanding of gender rather than a change in marriage. The evidence did not show any historical purpose for excluding same-sex couples from marriage, as states have never required spouses to have an ability or willingness to procreate in order to marry. Rather, the exclusion exists as an artifact of a time when the genders were seen as having distinct roles in society and in marriage. That time has passed.

The right to marry has been historically and remains the right to choose a spouse and, with mutual consent, join together and form a household. Race and gender restrictions shaped marriage during eras of race and gender inequality, but such restrictions were never part of the historical core of the institution of marriage. Today, gender is not relevant to the state in determining spouses' obligations to each other and to their dependents. Relative gender composition aside, same-sex couples are situated identically to opposite-sex couples in terms of their ability to perform the rights and obligations of marriage under California law. Gender no longer forms an essential part of marriage; marriage under law is a union of equals. * * *

Plaintiffs do not seek recognition of a new right. To characterize plaintiffs' objective as "the right to same-sex marriage" would suggest that plaintiffs seek something different from what opposite-sex couples across the state enjoy—namely, marriage. Rather, plaintiffs ask California to recognize their relationships for what they are: marriages. * * *

Because plaintiffs seek to exercise their fundamental right to marry, their claim is subject to strict scrutiny. *Zablocki,* 434 U.S. at 388. That the majority of California voters supported Proposition 8 is irrelevant, as "fundamental rights may not be submitted to [a] vote; they depend on the outcome of no elections." Under strict scrutiny, the state bears the burden of producing evidence to show that Proposition 8 is narrowly tailored to a compelling government interest. Because the government defendants declined to advance such arguments, proponents seized the role of asserting the existence of a compelling California interest in Proposition 8.

As explained in detail in the equal protection analysis, Proposition 8 cannot withstand rational basis review. Still less can Proposition 8 survive the strict scrutiny required by plaintiffs' due process claim. The minimal evidentiary presentation made by proponents does not meet the heavy burden of production necessary to show that Proposition 8 is narrowly tailored to a compelling government interest. Proposition 8 cannot, therefore, withstand strict scrutiny. Moreover, proponents do not assert that the availability of domestic partnerships satisfies plaintiffs' fundamental right to marry; proponents stipulated that "[t]here is a significant symbolic disparity between domestic partnership and marriage." Accordingly, Proposition 8 violates the Due Process Clause of the Fourteenth Amendment.

EQUAL PROTECTION

* * * The guarantee of equal protection coexists, of course, with the reality that most legislation must classify for some purpose or another. See *Romer v. Evans,* 517 U.S. 620, 631 (1996). When a law creates a classification but neither targets a suspect class nor burdens a fundamental right, the court presumes the law is valid and will uphold it as long as it is rationally related to some legitimate government interest . . .

The court defers to legislative (or in this case, popular) judgment if there is at least a debatable question whether the underlying basis for the classification is rational. Even under the most deferential standard of review, however, the court must "insist on knowing the relation between the classification adopted and the object to be attained." *Romer,* 517 U.S. at 632; *Heller,* 509 U.S. at 321 (basis for a classification must "find some footing in the realities of the subject addressed by the legislation"). The court may look to evidence to determine whether the basis for the underlying debate is rational. *Plyler v. Doe,* 457 U.S. 202, 228 (1982) (finding an asserted interest in preserving state resources by prohibiting undocumented children from attending public school to be irrational because "the available evidence suggests that illegal aliens underutilize public services, while contributing their labor to the local economy and tax money to the state fisc"). . . .

Yet, to survive rational basis review, a law must do more than disadvantage or otherwise harm a particular group. *United States Department of Agriculture v. Moreno,* 413 U.S. 528 (1973).

SEXUAL ORIENTATION OR SEX DISCRIMINATION

Plaintiffs challenge Proposition 8 as violating the Equal Protection Clause because Proposition 8 discriminates both on the basis of sex and on the basis of sexual orientation. Sexual orientation discrimination can take the form of sex discrimination. Thus, Proposition 8 operates to restrict Perry's choice of marital partner because of her sex. But

Proposition 8 also operates to restrict Perry's choice of marital partner because of her sexual orientation; her desire to marry another woman arises only because she is a lesbian. * * *

STANDARD OF REVIEW

* * * The trial record shows that strict scrutiny is the appropriate standard of review to apply to legislative classifications based on sexual orientation. All classifications based on sexual orientation appear suspect, as the evidence shows that California would rarely, if ever, have a reason to categorize individuals based on their sexual orientation. Here, however, strict scrutiny is unnecessary. Proposition 8 fails to survive even rational basis review.

PROPOSITION 8 DOES NOT SURVIVE RATIONAL BASIS

Proposition 8 cannot withstand any level of scrutiny under the Equal Protection Clause, as excluding same-sex couples from marriage is simply not rationally related to a legitimate state interest. One example of a legitimate state interest in not issuing marriage licenses to a particular group might be a scarcity of marriage licenses or county officials to issue them. But marriage licenses in California are not a limited commodity, and the existence of 18,000 same-sex married couples in California shows that the state has the resources to allow both same-sex and opposite-sex couples to wed. * * *

PURPORTED INTEREST #1: RESERVING MARRIAGE AS A UNION BETWEEN A MAN AND A WOMAN AND EXCLUDING ANY OTHER RELATIONSHIP

Proponents first argue that Proposition 8 is rational because it preserves: (1) "the traditional institution of marriage as the union of a man and a woman"; (2) "the traditional social and legal purposes, functions, and structure of marriage"; and (3) "the traditional meaning of marriage as it has always been defined in the English language." . . .

Tradition alone, however, cannot form a rational basis for a law.

. . . [T]he evidence shows that the tradition of gender restrictions arose when spouses were legally required to adhere to specific gender roles. California has eliminated all legally mandated gender roles except the requirement that a marriage consist of one man and one woman. Proposition 8 thus enshrines in the California Constitution a gender restriction that the evidence shows to be nothing more than an artifact of a foregone notion that men and women fulfill different roles in civic life.

The tradition of restricting marriage to opposite-sex couples does not further any state interest. Rather, the evidence shows that Proposition 8 harms the state's interest in equality, because it mandates that men and women be treated differently based only on antiquated and discredited notions of gender. * * *

PURPORTED INTEREST #2: PROCEEDING WITH CAUTION WHEN IMPLEMENTING SOCIAL CHANGES

Proponents next argue that Proposition 8 is related to state interests in: (1) "[a]cting incrementally and with caution when considering a radical transformation to the fundamental nature of a bedrock social institution"; (2) "[d]ecreasing the probability of weakening the institution of marriage"; (3) "[d]ecreasing the probability of adverse consequences that could result from weakening the institution of marriage"; and (4) "[d]ecreasing the probability of the potential adverse consequences of same-sex marriage." * * *

[P]roponents presented no reliable evidence that allowing same-sex couples to marry will have any negative effects on society or on the institution of marriage. The process of allowing same-sex couples to marry is straightforward, and no evidence suggests that the state needs any significant lead time to integrate same-sex couples into marriage. The evidence shows that allowing same-sex couples to marry will be simple for California to implement because it has already done so; no change need be phased in. California need not restructure any institution to allow same-sex couples to marry. * * *

PURPORTED INTEREST #3: PROMOTING OPPOSITE-SEX PARENTING OVER SAME-SEX PARENTING

... Proponents argue Proposition 8: (1) promotes "stability and responsibility in naturally procreative relationships"; (2) promotes "enduring and stable family structures for the responsible raising and care of children by their biological parents"; (3) increases "the probability that natural procreation will occur within stable, enduring, and supporting family structures"; (4) promotes "the natural and mutually beneficial bond between parents and their biological children"; (5) increases "the probability that each child will be raised by both of his or her biological parents"; (6) increases "the probability that each child will be raised by both a father and a mother"; and (7) increases "the probability that each child will have a legally recognized father and mother."

The evidence supports two points which together show Proposition 8 does not advance any of the identified interests: (1) same-sex parents and opposite-sex parents are of equal quality, and (2) Proposition 8 does not make it more likely that opposite-sex couples will marry and raise offspring biologically related to both parents. * * *

Proponents argue Proposition 8 advances a state interest in encouraging the formation of stable households. Instead, the evidence

shows that Proposition 8 undermines that state interest, because same-sex households have become less stable by the passage of Proposition 8.
* * *

PURPORTED INTEREST #4: PROTECTING THE FREEDOM OF THOSE WHO OPPOSE MARRIAGE FOR SAME-SEX COUPLES

Proponents next argue that Proposition 8 protects the First Amendment freedom of those who disagree with allowing marriage for couples of the same sex. Proponents argue that Proposition 8: (1) preserves "the prerogative and responsibility of parents to provide for the ethical and moral development and education of their own children"; and (2) accommodates "the First Amendment rights of individuals and institutions that oppose same-sex marriage on religious or moral grounds."

These purported interests fail as a matter of law. Proposition 8 does not affect any First Amendment right or responsibility of parents to educate their children. Californians are prevented from distinguishing between same-sex partners and opposite-sex spouses in public accommodations, as California antidiscrimination law requires identical treatment for same-sex unions and opposite-sex marriages. . . .

To the extent proponents argue that one of the rights of those morally opposed to same-sex unions is the right to prevent same-sex couples from marrying, as explained presently those individuals' moral views are an insufficient basis upon which to enact a legislative classification.

PURPORTED INTEREST #5: TREATING SAME-SEX COUPLES DIFFERENTLY FROM OPPOSITE-SEX COUPLES

Proponents argue that Proposition 8 advances a state interest in treating same-sex couples differently from opposite-sex couples by: (1) "[u]sing different names for different things"; (2) "[m]aintaining the flexibility to separately address the needs of different types of relationships"; (3) "[e]nsuring that California marriages are recognized in other jurisdictions"; and (4) "[c]onforming California's definition of marriage to federal law."

Here, proponents assume a premise that the evidence thoroughly rebutted: rather than being different, same-sex and opposite-sex unions are, for all purposes relevant to California law, exactly the same. The evidence shows conclusively that moral and religious views form the only basis for a belief that same-sex couples are different from opposite-sex couples. The evidence fatally undermines any purported state interest in treating couples differently; thus, these interests do not provide a rational basis supporting Proposition 8.

In addition, proponents appear to claim that Proposition 8 advances a state interest in easing administrative burdens associated with issuing and recognizing marriage licenses. . . . Even assuming the state were to have an interest in administrative convenience, Proposition 8 actually creates an administrative burden on California because California must maintain a parallel institution for same-sex couples to provide the equivalent rights and benefits afforded to married couples. * * *

PURPORTED INTEREST #6: THE CATCHALL INTEREST

Finally, proponents assert that Proposition 8 advances "[a]ny other conceivable legitimate interests identified by the parties, amici, or the court at any stage of the proceedings." * * *

Many of the purported interests identified by proponents are nothing more than a fear or unarticulated dislike of same-sex couples. . . . The evidence shows that, by every available metric, opposite-sex couples are not better than their same-sex counterparts; instead, as partners, parents and citizens, opposite-sex couples and same-sex couples are equal. Proposition 8 violates the Equal Protection Clause because it does not treat them equally.

A PRIVATE MORAL VIEW THAT SAME-SEX COUPLES ARE INFERIOR TO OPPOSITE-SEX COUPLES IS NOT A PROPER BASIS FOR LEGISLATION

In the absence of a rational basis, what remains of proponents' case is an inference, amply supported by evidence in the record, that Proposition 8 was premised on the belief that same-sex couples simply are not as good as opposite-sex couples. Whether that belief is based on moral disapproval of homosexuality, animus towards gays and lesbians or simply a belief that a relationship between a man and a woman is inherently better than a relationship between two men or two women, this belief is not a proper basis on which to legislate. * * *

The arguments surrounding Proposition 8 raise a question similar to that addressed in *Lawrence*, when the Court asked whether a majority of citizens could use the power of the state to enforce "profound and deep convictions accepted as ethical and moral principles" through the criminal code. 539 U.S. at 571. The question here is whether California voters can enforce those same principles through regulation of marriage licenses. They cannot. California's obligation is to treat its citizens equally, not to "mandate [its] own moral code." *Id.* (citing *Planned Parenthood of Southeastern Pa. v. Casey,* 505 U.S. 833 (1992)). "[M]oral disapproval, without any other asserted state interest," has never been a rational basis for legislation. *Lawrence,* 539 U.S. at 582 (O'Connor, J, concurring). Tradition alone cannot support legislation. See *Williams,* 399 U.S. at 239; *Romer,* 517 U.S. at 635; *Lawrence,* 539 U.S. at 579. * * *

The evidence at trial regarding the campaign to pass Proposition 8 uncloaks the most likely explanation for its passage: a desire to advance the belief that opposite-sex couples are morally superior to same-sex couples. The campaign relied heavily on negative stereotypes about gays and lesbians and focused on protecting children from inchoate threats vaguely associated with gays and lesbians. * * *

Because Proposition 8 disadvantages gays and lesbians without any rational justification, Proposition 8 violates the Equal Protection Clause of the Fourteenth Amendment.

NOTES

1. Contrast the opinion in *Perry* with the Eighth Circuit's rejection of an equal protection-based challenge to Nebraska's anti-same-sex marriage amendment in *Bruning* (see Chapter 3, Section II.A.4). Nebraska's measure goes further than Prop 8 by denying not only access to marriage, but any legal protections to same-sex couples. Is the federal constitutional challenge to the Nebraska measure the stronger of the two challenges because of the Nebraska measure's breadth? Or is Prop 8, ironically, more legally vulnerable because California already offered same-sex couples comprehensive marriage-like protections through its domestic partnership law?

2. The proponents of Prop 8, who had intervened at the district court, appealed Judge Walker's ruling to the Ninth Circuit Court of Appeals. None of the state defendants appealed the judgment, and the question was raised whether intervenors had Article III standing to appeal a judgment when state officials chose not to appeal. The Ninth Circuit asked the California Supreme Court for its opinion on whether state law authorized ballot sponsors to appeal in the unusual circumstances presented in *Perry*, and the state court answered affirmatively. *See Perry v. Brown*, 52 Cal. 4th 1116, 134 Cal. Rptr. 3d 499, 265 P.3d 1002 (2011). Thereafter, the Ninth Circuit found that the initiative proponents had Article III standing and ruled that Prop 8 was unconstitutional. In doing so, the court adopted a narrower line of reasoning than the district court and limited its ruling to the unique situation in California, where voters had eliminated same-sex couples' existing right to marry while maintaining a comprehensive domestic partnership scheme. The Ninth Circuit explained:

> All that Proposition 8 accomplished was to take away from same-sex couples the right to be granted marriage licenses and thus legally to use the designation of 'marriage,' which symbolizes state legitimization and societal recognition of their committed relationships. Proposition 8 serves no purpose, and has no effect, other than to lessen the status and human dignity of gays and lesbians in California, and to officially reclassify their relationships and families as inferior to those of opposite-sex couples. The Constitution simply does not allow for "laws of this sort."

Perry v. Brown, 671 F.3d 1052, 1063–64 (9th Cir. 2012). The court relied extensively on *Romer v. Evans*, 517 U.S. 620 (1996).

d.   Prop 8 at the U.S. Supreme Court

After the Ninth Circuit's ruling, the proponents of Prop 8 sought certiorari from the U.S. Supreme Court. In addition to accepting a case challenging Section 3 of the federal Defense of Marriage Act (discussed below in Section II.D), the Court accepted the Prop 8 case, now captioned *Hollingsworth v. Perry*. In addition to briefing the merits, the Court specifically asked the parties to address whether the Prop 8 proponents had standing to appeal the district court's adverse ruling.

Ultimately, the Court did not address the merits of Prop 8 and instead, in a 5–4 decision, held that the proponents lacked standing to appeal. Writing for the Court, Chief Justice Roberts explained:

> Federal courts have authority under the Constitution to answer such questions only if necessary to do so in the course of deciding an actual "case" or "controversy." As used in the Constitution, those words do not include every sort of dispute, but only those "historically viewed as capable of resolution through the judicial process." This is an essential limit on our power: It ensures that we act *as judges,* and do not engage in policymaking properly left to elected representatives. For there to be such a case or controversy, it is not enough that the party invoking the power of the court have a keen interest in the issue. That party must also have "standing," which requires, among other things, that it have suffered a concrete and particularized injury. Because we find that petitioners do not have standing, we have no authority to decide this case on the merits, and neither did the Ninth Circuit.

Hollingsworth v. Perry, 570 U.S. ___ (2013) (citations omitted). Accordingly, the Court vacated the Ninth Circuit's ruling, thus leaving Judge Walker's district court decision as the decisive ruling in the case.

The Justices themselves may have been concerned about the political reaction to a broad substantive ruling and therefore may have wished to avoid the merits for institutional reasons. Indeed, Justice Kennedy, writing for the dissenting Justices, raised the tension that confronted the Court:

> Of course, the Court must be cautious before entering a realm of controversy where the legal community and society at large are still formulating ideas and approaches to a most difficult subject. But it is shortsighted to misconstrue principles of justiciability to avoid that subject.

570 U.S. ___ (2013) (Kennedy, J., dissenting). Ultimately, Justice Kennedy would have reached the merits in order to preserve the integrity of the state initiative system.

After some wrangling in the California Supreme Court over the breadth of Judge Walker's order, same-sex couples have access to marriage in California. The federal litigation challenging Prop 8 ultimately produced its demise but in unexpected ways—without a U.S. Supreme Court decision on the merits and without a direct impact on marriage bans in other states.

D. FEDERAL RECOGNITION OF SAME-SEX COUPLES' MARRIAGES

1. The Federal Defense of Marriage Act

Soon after the Hawaii Supreme Court issued its 1993 decision in *Baehr*, opponents of same-sex marriage argued that, absent legislation, Hawaii would set off a national chain reaction in which the federal government and other states would be compelled to recognize same-sex marriage. Accordingly, in 1996, Congress passed, and President Bill Clinton signed, the Defense of Marriage Act ("DOMA"):

DEFENSE OF MARRIAGE ACT
Pub. L. No. 104–199, 110 Stat. 2419 (1996)

An Act to define and protect the institution of marriage.

SECTION 2. POWERS RESERVED TO THE STATES.

(a) IN GENERAL. Chapter 115 of title 28, United States Code, is amended by adding after section 1738B the following:

§ 1738C. Certain acts, records, and proceedings and the effect thereof

> No State, territory, or possession of the United States, or Indian tribe, shall be required to give effect to any public act, record, or judicial proceeding of any other State, territory, possession, or tribe respecting a relationship between persons of the same sex that is treated as a marriage under the laws of such other State, territory, possession, or tribe, or a right or claim arising from such relationship. [28 U.S.C.A. § 1738C (2007).]

SECTION 3. DEFINITION OF MARRIAGE.

(a) IN GENERAL. Chapter 1 of title 1, United States Code, is amended by adding at the end the following:

Sec. 7.   Definition of "marriage" and "spouse"

In determining the meaning of any Act of Congress, or of any ruling, regulation, or interpretation of the various administrative bureaus and agencies of the United States, the word "marriage" means only a legal union between one man and one woman as husband and wife, and the word "spouse" refers only to a person of the opposite sex who is a husband or a wife. [1 U.S.C.A. § 7 (2007).]

Note that DOMA has two different sections. One, which we address in Section E below, states that federal law does not require any state to recognize a same-sex marriage duly entered into in another state. The other, which is the focus of this Section, provides that, for purposes of any federal law, the definition of marriage is limited to one man and one woman.

2. DOMA Litigation and the Executive Branch's Position

DOMA's definition of marriage applied to an enormous array of federal programs and, in one fell swoop, severely limited the benefits and protections available to same-sex couples across many areas of law. For many years, the organized LGBT rights bar steered clear of challenging DOMA in federal court, for many of the same reasons that federal lawsuits against state mini-DOMA's were avoided before the *Perry* litigation was brought to challenge Prop 8. A lawsuit filed in Massachusetts in 2009 changed that. Lawyers at Gay & Lesbian Advocates & Defenders (GLAD) brought suit on behalf of married same-sex couples disadvantaged in relation to particular federal programs. In a parallel suit, lawyers for the Commonwealth of Massachusetts challenged DOMA as applied to the state, which authorized marriage for same-sex couples. These lawsuits challenged only Section 3 of DOMA, regarding the federal definition of marriage, and did not raise claims against Section 2, regarding interstate recognition. In June 2010, just a few weeks before Judge Walker issued his *Perry* decision, a federal district judge in Massachusetts struck down Section 3 of DOMA as unconstitutional.

After this favorable result, LGBT rights lawyers filed additional challenges to Section 3 of DOMA in other federal district courts. Two such cases, *Windsor v. United States*, 833 F. Supp. 2d 394 (S.D.N.Y. 2012), and *Pedersen v. Office of Personnel Management*, 881 F. Supp. 2d 294 (D. Conn. 2012), were filed in federal district courts in the Second Circuit. Unlike the First Circuit, where the Massachusetts district court sat, the Second Circuit lacked precedent on the question of whether sexual orientation-based classifications merit heightened scrutiny for federal equal protection purposes.

In response, Attorney General Eric Holder, who had been defending Section 3 of DOMA on behalf of the United States, announced that the

President's position on DOMA had shifted in light of resolution of this new issue. On February 23, 2011, the Attorney General sent the letter excerpted below to the Speaker of the House. As you review the letter, consider whether you think it is appropriate for the President unilaterally to decline to defend a statute in circumstances presented here. Does it pose any systemic risks?

The Honorable John A. Boehner

Speaker

U.S. House of Representatives

Washington, DC 20515

Re: Defense of Marriage Act

Dear Mr. Speaker:

After careful consideration, including review of a recommendation from me, the President of the United States has made the determination that Section 3 of the Defense of Marriage Act ("DOMA"), 1 U.S.C. § 7, as applied to same-sex couples who are legally married under state law, violates the equal protection component of the Fifth Amendment. Pursuant to 28 U.S.C. § 530D, I am writing to advise you of the Executive Branch's determination and to inform you of the steps the Department will take in two pending DOMA cases to implement that determination.

While the Department has previously defended DOMA against legal challenges involving legally married same-sex couples, recent lawsuits that challenge the constitutionality of DOMA Section 3 have caused the President and the Department to conduct a new examination of the defense of this provision. In particular, in November 2011, plaintiffs filed two new lawsuits challenging the constitutionality of Section 3 of DOMA in jurisdictions without precedent on whether sexual-orientation classifications are subject to rational basis review or whether they must satisfy some form of heightened scrutiny.... Previously, the Administration has defended Section 3 in jurisdictions where circuit courts have already held that classifications based on sexual orientation are subject to rational basis review, and it has advanced arguments to defend DOMA Section 3 under the binding standard that has applied in those cases.

These new lawsuits, by contrast, will require the Department to take an affirmative position on the level of scrutiny that should be applied to DOMA Section 3 in a circuit without binding precedent on the issue. As described more fully below, the President and I have concluded that classifications based on sexual orientation warrant heightened scrutiny and that, as applied to same-sex couples legally married under state law, Section 3 of DOMA is unconstitutional.

Standard of Review

The Supreme Court has yet to rule on the appropriate level of scrutiny for classifications based on sexual orientation. It has, however, rendered a number of decisions that set forth the criteria that should inform this and any other judgment as to whether heightened scrutiny applies. [The criteria cited here are discussed in Chapter 3, Section 2, above.] * * *

Each of these factors counsels in favor of being suspicious of classifications based on sexual orientation. First and most importantly, there is, regrettably, a significant history of purposeful discrimination against gay and lesbian people, by governmental as well as private entities, based on prejudice and stereotypes that continue to have ramifications today. Indeed, until very recently, states have "demean[ed] the[ ] existence" of gays and lesbians "by making their private sexual conduct a crime." *Lawrence v. Texas*, 539 U.S. 558, 578 (2003).

Second, while sexual orientation carries no visible badge, a growing scientific consensus accepts that sexual orientation is a characteristic that is immutable, *see* Richard A. Posner, Sex and Reason 101 (1992); it is undoubtedly unfair to require sexual orientation to be hidden from view to avoid discrimination, *see* Don't Ask, Don't Tell Repeal Act of 2010. . . .

Third, the adoption of laws like those at issue in *Romer v. Evans,* 517 U.S. 620 (1996), and *Lawrence*, the longstanding ban on gays and lesbians in the military, and the absence of federal protection for employment discrimination on the basis of sexual orientation show the group to have limited political power and "ability to attract the [favorable] attention of the lawmakers." *Cleburne*, 473 U.S. at 445. And while the enactment of the Matthew Shepard Act and pending repeal of Don't Ask, Don't Tell indicate that the political process is not closed *entirely* to gay and lesbian people, that is not the standard by which the Court has judged "political powerlessness." Indeed, when the Court ruled that gender-based classifications were subject to heightened scrutiny, women already had won major political victories such as the Nineteenth Amendment (right to vote) and protection under Title VII (employment discrimination).

Finally, there is a growing acknowledgment that sexual orientation "bears no relation to ability to perform or contribute to society. . . ." *Frontiero v. Richardson*, 411 U.S. 677, 686 (1973) (plurality). Recent evolutions in legislation (including the pending repeal of Don't Ask, Don't Tell), in community practices and attitudes, in case law (including the Supreme Court's holdings in *Lawrence* and *Romer*), and in social science regarding sexual orientation all make clear that sexual orientation is not a characteristic that generally bears on legitimate policy objectives. *See, e.g.,* Statement by the President on the Don't Ask, Don't Tell Repeal Act of 2010 ("It is time to recognize that sacrifice, valor and integrity are no more defined by sexual orientation than they are by race or gender, religion or creed.")

To be sure, there is substantial circuit court authority applying rational basis review to sexual-orientation classifications. We have carefully examined each of those decisions. Many of them reason only that if consensual same-sex sodomy may be criminalized under *Bowers v. Hardwick*, then it follows that no heightened review is appropriate—a line of reasoning that does not survive the overruling of *Bowers* in *Lawrence v. Texas*, 539 U.S. 558 (2003). Others rely on claims regarding "procreational responsibility" that the Department has disavowed already in litigation as unreasonable, or claims regarding the immutability of sexual orientation that we do not believe can be reconciled with more recent social science understandings. And none engages in an examination of all the factors that the Supreme Court has identified as relevant to a decision about the appropriate level of scrutiny. Finally, many of the more recent decisions have relied on the fact that the Supreme Court has not recognized that gays and lesbians constitute a suspect class or the fact that the Court has applied rational basis review in its most recent decisions addressing classifications based on sexual orientation, *Lawrence* and *Romer*. But neither of those decisions reached, let alone resolved, the level of scrutiny issue because in both the Court concluded that the laws could not even survive the more deferential rational basis standard.

Application to Section 3 of DOMA

* * * [U]nder heightened scrutiny, the United States cannot defend Section 3 by advancing hypothetical rationales, independent of the legislative record, as it has done in circuits where precedent mandates application of rational basis review. Instead, the United States can defend Section 3 only by invoking Congress' actual justifications for the law.

Moreover, the legislative record underlying DOMA's passage contains discussion and debate that undermines any defense under heightened scrutiny. The record contains numerous expressions reflecting moral disapproval of gays and lesbians and their intimate and family relationships—precisely the kind of stereotype-based thinking and animus the Equal Protection Clause is designed to guard against. * * *

Application to Second Circuit Cases

After careful consideration, including a review of my recommendation, the President has concluded that given a number of factors, including a documented history of discrimination, classifications based on sexual orientation should be subject to a heightened standard of scrutiny. The President has also concluded that Section 3 of DOMA, as applied to legally married same-sex couples, fails to meet that standard and is therefore unconstitutional. . . .

Notwithstanding this determination, the President has informed me that Section 3 will continue to be enforced by the Executive Branch. To that end, the President has instructed Executive agencies to continue to comply with Section 3 of DOMA, consistent with the Executive's obligation to take care that the laws be faithfully executed, unless and until Congress repeals Section 3 or the judicial branch renders a definitive verdict against the law's constitutionality. This course of action respects the actions of the prior Congress that enacted DOMA, and it recognizes the judiciary as the final arbiter of the constitutional claims raised.

As you know, the Department has a longstanding practice of defending the constitutionality of duly-enacted statutes if reasonable arguments can be made in their defense, a practice that accords the respect appropriately due to a coequal branch of government. However, the Department in the past has declined to defend statutes despite the availability of professionally responsible arguments, in part because the Department does not consider every plausible argument to be a "reasonable" one. "[D]ifferent cases can raise very different issues with respect to statutes of doubtful constitutional validity," and thus there are "a variety of factors that bear on whether the Department will defend the constitutionality of a statute." Letter to Hon. Orrin G. Hatch from Assistant Attorney General Andrew Fois at 7 (Mar. 22, 1996). This is the rare case where the proper course is to forgo the defense of this statute. Moreover, the Department has declined to defend a statute "in cases in which it is manifest that the President has concluded that the statute is unconstitutional," as is the case here. Seth P. Waxman, *Defending Congress*, 79 N.C. L. Rev. 1073, 1083 (2001).

In light of the foregoing, I will instruct the Department's lawyers to immediately inform the district courts in *Windsor* and *Pedersen* of the Executive Branch's view that heightened scrutiny is the appropriate standard of review and that, consistent with that standard, Section 3 of DOMA may not be constitutionally applied to same-sex couples whose marriages are legally recognized under state law. If asked by the district courts in the Second Circuit for the position of the United States in the event those courts determine that the applicable standard is rational basis, the Department will state that, consistent with the position it has taken in prior cases, a reasonable argument for Section 3's constitutionality may be proffered under that permissive standard. Our attorneys will also notify the courts of our interest in providing Congress a full and fair opportunity to participate in the litigation in those cases. We will remain parties to the case and continue to represent the interests of the United States throughout the litigation. * * *

Sincerely yours,

Eric H. Holder, Jr.

Attorney General

Ultimately, the Second Circuit Court of Appeals in *Windsor* held that intermediate scrutiny should apply to sexual-orientation-based classifications:

Analysis of these four factors supports our conclusion that homosexuals compose a class that is subject to heightened scrutiny. We further conclude that the class is quasi-suspect (rather than suspect) based on the weight of the factors and on analogy to the classifications recognized as suspect and quasi-suspect. While homosexuals have been the target of significant and long-standing discrimination in public and private spheres, this mistreatment "is not sufficient to require 'our most exacting scrutiny.'"

Windsor v. United States, 699 F.3d 169, 185 (2d Cir. 2012). Applying intermediate scrutiny, the court found Section 3 of DOMA unconstitutional. *See id.* at 185–88. Meanwhile, the First Circuit also found Section 3 unconstitutional but did so without applying intermediate scrutiny. *See Gill v. Office of Pers. Mgmt.*, 682 F.3d 1 (1st Cir. 2012).

3. DOMA at the U.S. Supreme Court

As the number of federal court decisions invalidating Section 3 of DOMA grew, the U.S. Supreme Court granted certiorari in *Windsor*. As in *Hollingsworth v. Perry*, the Court confronted significant questions of justiciability. Given that the federal executive branch refused to defend DOMA, the Bipartisan Legal Advisory Group (BLAG), composed of five Congressional leaders, intervened to defend the law. BLAG's decision divided along party lines, with the three Republican members voting to defend DOMA. In *Windsor*, the Court considered whether, given the President's agreement with the plaintiff and the Second Circuit, a case or controversy existed and whether BLAG had standing. While some Justices would have found these issues dispositive such that they would not have reached the merits, a majority reached the merits and ultimately struck down Section 3 of DOMA.

UNITED STATES V. WINDSOR

Supreme Court of the United States, 2013
570 U.S. ___, 133 S.Ct. 2675, 186 L.Ed.2d 808

JUSTICE KENNEDY delivered the opinion of the Court.

Two women then resident in New York were married in a lawful ceremony in Ontario, Canada, in 2007. Edith Windsor and Thea Spyer returned to their home in New York City. When Spyer died in 2009, she left her entire estate to Windsor. Windsor sought to claim the estate tax exemption for surviving spouses. She was barred from doing so, however, by a federal law, the Defense of Marriage Act, which excludes a same-sex partner from the definition of "spouse" as that term is used in federal statutes. Windsor paid the taxes but filed suit to challenge the constitutionality of this provision. The United States District Court and the Court of Appeals ruled that this portion of the statute is unconstitutional and ordered the United States to pay Windsor a refund. This Court granted certiorari and now affirms the judgment in Windsor's favor.

I

In 1996, as some States were beginning to consider the concept of same-sex marriage, see, *e.g.*, *Baehr v. Lewin*, 74 Haw. 530, 852 P. 2d 44 (1993), and before any State had acted to permit it, Congress enacted the Defense of Marriage Act (DOMA), 110 Stat. 2419. DOMA contains two operative sections: Section 2, which has not been challenged here, allows States to refuse to recognize same-sex marriages performed under the laws of other States. See 28 U. S. C. §1738C.

Section 3 is at issue here. It amends the Dictionary Act in Title 1, §7, of the United States Code to provide a federal definition of "marriage" and "spouse." Section 3 of DOMA provides as follows:

> "In determining the meaning of any Act of Congress, or of any ruling, regulation, or interpretation of the various administrative bureaus and agencies of the United States, the word 'marriage' means only a legal union between one man and one woman as husband and wife, and the word 'spouse' refers only to a person of the opposite sex who is a husband or a wife." 1 U. S. C. §7.

The definitional provision does not by its terms forbid States from enacting laws permitting same-sex marriages or civil unions or providing state benefits to residents in that status. The enactment's comprehensive definition of marriage for purposes of all federal statutes and other regulations or directives covered by its terms, however, does control over 1,000 federal laws in which marital or spousal status is addressed as a matter of federal law.

Edith Windsor and Thea Spyer met in New York City in 1963 and began a long-term relationship. Windsor and Spyer registered as domestic partners when New York City gave that right to same-sex couples in 1993. Concerned about Spyer's health, the couple made the 2007 trip to Canada for their marriage, but they continued to reside in New York City. The State of New York deems their Ontario marriage to be a valid one.

Spyer died in February 2009, and left her entire estate to Windsor. Because DOMA denies federal recognition to same-sex spouses, Windsor did not qualify for the marital exemption from the federal estate tax, which excludes from taxation "any interest in property which passes or has passed from the decedent to his surviving spouse." Windsor paid $363,053 in estate taxes and sought a refund. The Internal Revenue Service denied the refund, concluding that, under DOMA, Windsor was not a "surviving spouse." Windsor commenced this refund suit in the United States District Court for the Southern District of New York. She contended that DOMA violates the guarantee of equal protection, as applied to the Federal Government through the Fifth Amendment.

While the tax refund suit was pending, the Attorney General of the United States notified the Speaker of the House of Representatives, pursuant to 28 U. S. C. §530D, that the Department of Justice would no longer defend the constitutionality of DOMA's §3. . . .

Although "the President . . . instructed the Department not to defend the statute in *Windsor*," he also decided "that Section 3 will continue to be enforced by the Executive Branch" and that the United States had an "interest in providing Congress a full and fair opportunity to participate in the litigation of those cases." The stated rationale for this dual-track procedure (determination of unconstitutionality coupled with ongoing enforcement) was to "recogniz[e] the judiciary as the final arbiter of the constitutional claims raised."

In response to the notice from the Attorney General, the Bipartisan Legal Advisory Group (BLAG) of the House of Representatives voted to intervene in the litigation to defend the constitutionality of §3 of DOMA. . . .

On the merits of the tax refund suit, the District Court ruled against the United States. It held that §3 of DOMA is unconstitutional and ordered the Treasury to refund the tax with interest. . . . [T]he Court of Appeals for the Second Circuit affirmed the District Court's judgment. It applied heightened scrutiny to classifications based on sexual orientation, as both the Department and Windsor had urged. The United States has not complied with the judgment. Windsor has not received her refund, and the Executive Branch continues to enforce §3 of DOMA. * * *

[In Part II, the Court found that "prudential and Article III requirements are met" such that it did not need to determine BLAG's standing and could proceed directly to the merits.]

III

. . . It seems fair to conclude that, until recent years, many citizens had not even considered the possibility that two persons of the same sex might aspire to occupy the same status and dignity as that of a man and woman in lawful marriage. For marriage between a man and a woman no doubt had been thought of by most people as essential to the very definition of that term and to its role and function throughout the history of civilization. That belief, for many who long have held it, became even more urgent, more cherished when challenged. For others, however, came the beginnings of a new perspective, a new insight. Accordingly some States concluded that same-sex marriage ought to be given recognition and validity in the law for those same-sex couples who wish to define themselves by their commitment to each other. The limitation of lawful marriage to heterosexual couples, which for centuries had been deemed both necessary and fundamental, came to be seen in New York and certain other States as an unjust exclusion.

Slowly at first and then in rapid course, the laws of New York came to acknowledge the urgency of this issue for same-sex couples who wanted to affirm their commitment to one another before their children, their family, their friends, and their community. And so New York recognized same-sex marriages performed elsewhere; and then it later amended its own marriage laws to permit same-sex marriage. New York, in common with, as of this writing, 11 other States and the District of Columbia, decided that same-sex couples should have the right to marry and so live with pride in themselves and their union and in a status of equality with all other married persons. After a statewide deliberative process that enabled its citizens to discuss and weigh arguments for and against same-sex marriage, New York acted to enlarge the definition of marriage to correct what its citizens and elected representatives perceived to be an injustice that they had not earlier known or understood.

Against this background of lawful same-sex marriage in some States, the design, purpose, and effect of DOMA should be considered as the beginning point in deciding whether it is valid under the Constitution. By history and tradition the definition and regulation of marriage, as will be discussed in more detail, has been treated as being within the authority and realm of the separate States. Yet it is further established that Congress, in enacting discrete statutes, can make determinations that bear on marital rights and privileges. . . . Congress has the power both to ensure efficiency in the administration of its programs and to choose what larger goals and policies to pursue. . . .

Though . . . discrete examples establish the constitutionality of limited federal laws that regulate the meaning of marriage in order to further federal policy, DOMA has a far greater reach; for it enacts a directive applicable to over 1,000 federal statutes and the whole realm of federal regulations. And its operation is directed to a class of persons that the laws of New York, and of 11 other States, have sought to protect.

In order to assess the validity of that intervention it is necessary to discuss the extent of the state power and authority over marriage as a matter of history and tradition. State laws defining and regulating marriage, of course, must respect the constitutional rights of persons, see, e.g., *Loving v. Virginia*, 388 U. S. 1 (1967); but, subject to those guarantees, "regulation of domestic relations" is "an area that has long been regarded as a virtually exclusive province of the States." [citation omitted]

The recognition of civil marriages is central to state domestic relations law applicable to its residents and citizens. The definition of marriage is the foundation of the State's broader authority to regulate the subject of domestic relations with respect to the "[p]rotection of offspring, property interests, and the enforcement of marital responsibilities." "[T]he states, at the time of the adoption of the Constitution, possessed full power over the subject of marriage and divorce . . . [and] the Constitution delegated no authority to the Government of the United States on the subject of marriage and divorce." [citations omitted]

* * * The significance of state responsibilities for the definition and regulation of marriage dates to the Nation's beginning; for "when the Constitution was adopted the common understanding was that the domestic relations of husband and wife and parent and child were

matters reserved to the States." [citation omitted] Marriage laws vary in some respects from State to State. For example, the required minimum age is 16 in Vermont, but only 13 in New Hampshire. Likewise the permissible degree of consanguinity can vary (most States permit first cousins to marry, but a handful—such as Iowa and Washington, prohibit the practice). But these rules are in every event consistent within each State.

Against this background DOMA rejects the long-established precept that the incidents, benefits, and obligations of marriage are uniform for all married couples within each State, though they may vary, subject to constitutional guarantees, from one State to the next. Despite these considerations, it is unnecessary to decide whether this federal intrusion on state power is a violation of the Constitution because it disrupts the federal balance. The State's power in defining the marital relation is of central relevance in this case quite apart from principles of federalism. Here the State's decision to give this class of persons the right to marry conferred upon them a dignity and status of immense import. When the State used its historic and essential authority to define the marital relation in this way, its role and its power in making the decision enhanced the recognition, dignity, and protection of the class in their own community. DOMA, because of its reach and extent, departs from this history and tradition of reliance on state law to define marriage. "'[D]iscriminations of an unusual character especially suggest careful consideration to determine whether they are obnoxious to the constitutional provision.'" *Romer v. Evans*, 517 U. S. 620, 633 (1996).

The Federal Government uses this state-defined class for the opposite purpose—to impose restrictions and disabilities. That result requires this Court now to address whether the resulting injury and indignity is a deprivation of an essential part of the liberty protected by the Fifth Amendment. What the State of New York treats as alike the federal law deems unlike by a law designed to injure the same class the State seeks to protect.

In acting first to recognize and then to allow same-sex marriages, New York was responding "to the initiative of those who [sought] a voice in shaping the destiny of their own times." These actions were without doubt a proper exercise of its sovereign authority within our federal system, all in the way that the Framers of the Constitution intended. The dynamics of state government in the federal system are to allow the formation of consensus respecting the way the members of a discrete community treat each other in their daily contact and constant interaction with each other.

The States' interest in defining and regulating the marital relation, subject to constitutional guarantees, stems from the understanding that marriage is more than a routine classification for purposes of certain statutory benefits. Private, consensual sexual intimacy between two adult persons of the same sex may not be punished by the State, and it can form "but one element in a personal bond that is more enduring." *Lawrence v. Texas*, 539 U. S. 558, 567 (2003). By its recognition of the validity of same-sex marriages performed in other jurisdictions and then by authorizing same-sex unions and same-sex marriages, New York sought to give further protection and dignity to that bond. For same-sex couples who wished to be married, the State acted to give their lawful conduct a lawful status. This status is a far-reaching legal acknowledgment of the intimate relationship between two people, a relationship deemed by the State worthy of dignity in the community equal with all other marriages. It reflects both the community's considered perspective on the historical roots of the institution of marriage and its evolving understanding of the meaning of equality.

IV

DOMA seeks to injure the very class New York seeks to protect. By doing so it violates basic due process and equal protection principles applicable to the Federal Government. See U. S. Const., Amdt. 5; *Bolling v. Sharpe*, 347 U. S. 497 (1954). The Constitution's guarantee of equality "must at the very least mean that a bare congressional desire to harm a politically unpopular group cannot" justify disparate treatment of that group. *Department of Agriculture v. Moreno*, 413 U. S. 528, 534–535 (1973). In determining whether a law is motived by an improper animus or purpose, "'[d]iscriminations of an unusual character'" especially require careful consideration. *Supra*, at 19 (quoting *Romer, supra*, at 633). DOMA cannot survive under these principles. The responsibility of the States for the regulation of domestic relations is an important indicator of the substantial societal impact the State's classifications have in the daily lives and customs of its people. DOMA's unusual deviation from the usual tradition of recognizing and accepting state definitions of marriage here operates to deprive same-sex couples of the benefits and responsibilities that come with the federal recognition of their marriages. This is strong evidence of a law having the purpose and effect of disapproval of that class. The avowed purpose and practical effect of the law here in question are to impose a disadvantage, a separate status, and so a stigma upon all who enter into same-sex marriages made lawful by the unquestioned authority of the States.

The history of DOMA's enactment and its own text demonstrate that interference with the equal dignity of same-sex marriages, a dignity conferred by the States in the exercise of their sovereign power, was more than an incidental effect of the federal statute. It was its essence. The House Report announced its conclusion that "it is both appropriate and necessary for Congress to do what it can to defend the institution of traditional heterosexual marriage. . . . H. R. 3396 is appropriately entitled the 'Defense of Marriage Act.' The effort to redefine 'marriage' to extend to homosexual couples is a truly radical proposal that would fundamentally alter the institution of marriage." The House concluded that DOMA expresses "both moral disapproval of homosexuality, and a moral conviction that heterosexuality better comports with traditional (especially Judeo- Christian) morality." The stated purpose of the law was to promote an "interest in protecting the traditional moral teachings reflected in heterosexual-only marriage laws." Were there any doubt of this far-reaching purpose, the title of the Act confirms it: The Defense of Marriage.

* * * When New York adopted a law to permit same-sex marriage, it sought to eliminate inequality; but DOMA frustrates that objective through a system-wide enactment with no identified connection to any particular area of federal law. DOMA writes inequality into the entire United States Code. The particular case at hand concerns the estate tax, but DOMA is more than a simple determination of what should or should not be allowed as an estate tax refund. Among the over 1,000 statutes and numerous federal regulations that DOMA controls are laws pertaining to Social Security, housing, taxes, criminal sanctions, copyright, and veterans' benefits.

DOMA's principal effect is to identify a subset of state-sanctioned marriages and make them unequal. The principal purpose is to impose inequality, not for other reasons like governmental efficiency. Responsibilities, as well as rights, enhance the dignity and integrity of the person. And DOMA contrives to deprive some couples married under the laws of their State, but not other couples, of both rights and responsibilities. By creating two contradictory marriage regimes within the same State, DOMA forces same-sex couples to live as married for the purpose of state law but unmarried for the purpose of federal law, thus diminishing the stability and predictability of basic personal relations the State has found it proper to acknowledge and protect. By this dynamic DOMA undermines both the public and private significance of state-sanctioned same-sex marriages; for it tells those couples, and all the world, that their otherwise valid marriages are unworthy of federal recognition. This places same-sex couples in an unstable position of being in a second-tier marriage. The differentiation demeans the couple, whose moral and sexual choices the Constitution protects, see *Lawrence*, 539 U.S. 558, and whose relationship the State has sought to dignify. And it humiliates tens of thousands of children now being raised by same-sex couples. The law in question makes it even more difficult for the children to understand the integrity and closeness of their own family and its concord with other families in their community and in their daily lives.

Under DOMA, same-sex married couples have their lives burdened, by reason of government decree, in visible and public ways. By its great reach, DOMA touches many aspects of married and family life, from the mundane to the profound. It prevents same-sex married couples from obtaining government healthcare benefits they would otherwise receive. It deprives them of the Bankruptcy Code's special protections for domestic-support obligations. It forces them to follow a complicated procedure to file their state and federal taxes jointly. It prohibits them from being buried together in veterans' cemeteries.

* * * DOMA also brings financial harm to children of same-sex couples. It raises the cost of health care for families by taxing health benefits provided by employers to their workers' same-sex spouses. And it denies or reduces benefits allowed to families upon the loss of a spouse and parent, benefits that are an integral part of family security.

DOMA divests married same-sex couples of the duties and responsibilities that are an essential part of married life and that they in most cases would be honored to accept were DOMA not in force. * * *

* * *

The power the Constitution grants it also restrains. And though Congress has great authority to design laws to fit its own conception of sound national policy, it cannot deny the liberty protected by the Due Process Clause of the Fifth Amendment.

What has been explained to this point should more than suffice to establish that the principal purpose and the necessary effect of this law are to demean those persons who are in a lawful same-sex marriage. This requires the Court to hold, as it now does, that DOMA is unconstitutional as a deprivation of the liberty of the person protected by the Fifth Amendment of the Constitution.

The liberty protected by the Fifth Amendment's Due Process Clause contains within it the prohibition against denying to any person the equal protection of the laws. See *Bolling*, 347 U. S., at 499–500; *Adarand Constructors, Inc. v. Peña*, 515 U. S. 200, 217–218 (1995). While the Fifth Amendment itself withdraws from Government the power to degrade or demean in the way this law does, the equal protection guarantee of the Fourteenth Amendment makes that Fifth Amendment right all the more specific and all the better understood and preserved.

The class to which DOMA directs its restrictions and restraints are those persons who are joined in same-sex marriages made lawful by the State. DOMA singles out a class of persons deemed by a State entitled to recognition and protection to enhance their own liberty. It imposes a disability on the class by refusing to acknowledge a status the State finds to be dignified and proper. DOMA instructs all federal officials, and indeed all persons with whom same-sex couples interact, including their own children, that their marriage is less worthy than the marriages of others. The federal statute is invalid, for no legitimate purpose overcomes the purpose and effect to disparage and to injure those whom the State, by its marriage laws, sought to protect in personhood and dignity. By seeking to displace this protection and treating those persons as living in marriages less respected than others, the federal statute is in violation of the Fifth Amendment. This opinion and its holding are confined to those lawful marriages.

The judgment of the Court of Appeals for the Second Circuit is affirmed.

It is so ordered.

CHIEF JUSTICE ROBERTS, dissenting.

* * * [W]hile I disagree with the result to which the majority's analysis leads it in this case, I think it more important to point out that its analysis leads no further. The Court does not have before it, and the logic of its opinion does not decide, the distinct question whether the States, in the exercise of their "historic and essential authority to define the marital relation," may continue to utilize the traditional definition of marriage.

The majority goes out of its way to make this explicit in the penultimate sentence of its opinion. It states that "[t]his opinion and its holding are confined to those lawful marriages,"—referring to same-sex marriages that a State has already recognized as a result of the local "community's considered perspective on the historical roots of the institution of marriage and its evolving understanding of the meaning of equality." Justice SCALIA believes this is a "'bald, unreasoned disclaime[r].'" In my view, though, the disclaimer is a logical and necessary consequence of the argument the majority has chosen to adopt. The dominant theme of the majority opinion is that the Federal Government's intrusion into an area "central to state domestic relations law applicable to its residents and citizens" is sufficiently "unusual" to set off alarm bells. I think the majority goes off course, as I have said, but it is undeniable that its judgment is based on federalism.

* * * We may in the future have to resolve challenges to state marriage definitions affecting same-sex couples. That issue, however, is not before us in this case. . . . I write only to highlight the limits of the majority's holding and reasoning today, lest its opinion be taken to resolve not only a question that I believe is not properly before us— DOMA's constitutionality—but also a question that all agree, and the Court explicitly acknowledges, is not at issue.

JUSTICE SCALIA, with whom JUSTICE THOMAS joins, and with whom THE CHIEF JUSTICE joins as to Part I, dissenting.[8]

This case is about power in several respects. It is about the power of our people to govern themselves, and the power of this Court to pronounce the law. Today's opinion aggrandizes the latter, with the predictable consequence of diminishing the former. We have no power to decide this case. And even if we did, we have no power under the Constitution to invalidate this democratically adopted legislation. The Court's errors on both points spring forth from the same diseased root: an exalted conception of the role of this institution in America. * * *

II.

* * * I think that this Court has, and the Court of Appeals had, no power to decide this suit. We should vacate the decision below and remand to the Court of Appeals for the Second Circuit, with instructions to dismiss the appeal. Given that the majority has volunteered its view of the merits, however, I proceed to discuss that as well.

A

There are many remarkable things about the majority's merits holding. The first is how rootless and shifting its justifications are. For example, the opinion starts with seven full pages about the traditional power of States to define domestic relations—initially fooling many readers, I am sure, into thinking that this is a federalism opinion. But we are eventually told that "it is unnecessary to decide whether this federal intrusion on state power is a violation of the Constitution," and that "[t]he State's power in defining the marital relation is of central relevance in this case quite apart from principles of federalism" because "the State's decision to give this class of persons the right to marry conferred upon them a dignity and status of immense import." *Ante*, at 18. But no one questions the power of the States to define marriage (with the concomitant conferral of dignity and status), so what is the point of devoting seven pages to describing how long and well established that power is? Even after the opinion has formally disclaimed reliance upon principles of federalism, mentions of "the usual tradition of recognizing and accepting state definitions of marriage" continue. See, *e.g.*, *ante*, at 20. What to make of this? The opinion never explains. My guess is that the majority, while reluctant to suggest that defining the meaning of "marriage" in federal statutes is unsupported by any of the Federal Government's enumerated powers, nonetheless needs some rhetorical basis to support its pretense that today's prohibition of laws excluding same-sex marriage is confined to the Federal Government (leaving the

---

8   *Editor's Note*: Part I, which Chief Justice Roberts joined, explained why the Court should not have reached the merits.

second, state-law shoe to be dropped later, maybe next Term). But I am only guessing.

Equally perplexing are the opinion's references to "the Constitution's guarantee of equality." *Ibid*. Near the end of the opinion, we are told that although the "equal protection guarantee of the Fourteenth Amendment makes [the] Fifth Amendment [due process] right all the more specific and all the better understood and preserved"—what can that mean?— "the Fifth Amendment itself withdraws from Government the power to degrade or demean in the way this law does." *Ante*, at 25. The only possible interpretation of this statement is that the Equal Protection Clause, even the Equal Protection Clause as incorporated in the Due Process Clause, is not the basis for today's holding. But the portion of the majority opinion that explains why DOMA is unconstitutional (Part IV) begins by citing *Bolling v. Sharpe*, 347 U. S. 497 (1954), *Department of Agriculture v. Moreno*, 413 U. S. 528 (1973), and *Romer v. Evans*, 517 U.S. 620 (1996)—all of which are equal-protection cases. And those three cases are the only authorities that the Court cites in Part IV about the Constitution's meaning, except for its citation of *Lawrence v. Texas*, 539 U. S. 558 (2003) (not an equal-protection case) to support its passing assertion that the Constitution protects the "moral and sexual choices" of same-sex couples.

Moreover, if this is meant to be an equal-protection opinion, it is a confusing one. The opinion does not resolve and indeed does not even mention what had been the central question in this litigation: whether, under the Equal Protection Clause, laws restricting marriage to a man and a woman are reviewed for more than mere rationality. That is the issue that divided the parties and the court below. In accord with my previously expressed skepticism about the Court's "tiers of scrutiny" approach, I would review this classification only for its rationality. See *United States v. Virginia*, 518 U. S. 515, 567–570 (1996) (SCALIA, J., dissenting). As nearly as I can tell, the Court agrees with that; its opinion does not apply strict scrutiny, and its central propositions are taken from rational-basis cases like *Moreno*. But the Court certainly does not apply anything that resembles that deferential framework.

The majority opinion need not get into the strict-vs.-rational-basis scrutiny question, and need not justify its holding under either, because it says that DOMA is unconstitutional as "a deprivation of the liberty of the person protected by the Fifth Amendment of the Constitution"; that it violates "basic due process" principles; and that it inflicts an "injury and indignity" of a kind that denies "an essential part of the liberty protected by the Fifth Amendment". The majority never utters the dread words "substantive due process," perhaps sensing the disrepute into which that doctrine has fallen, but that is what those statements mean. Yet the opinion does not argue that same-sex marriage is "deeply rooted in this

Nation's history and tradition," a claim that would of course be quite absurd. So would the further suggestion (also necessary, under our substantive-due-process precedents) that a world in which DOMA exists is one bereft of "'ordered liberty.'" [citations omitted]

Some might conclude that this loaf could have used a while longer in the oven. But that would be wrong; it is already overcooked. The most expert care in preparation cannot redeem a bad recipe. The sum of all the Court's nonspecific hand-waving is that this law is invalid (maybe on equal-protection grounds, maybe on substantive-due-process grounds, and perhaps with some amorphous federalism component playing a role) because it is motivated by a "'bare . . . desire to harm'" couples in same-sex marriages. It is this proposition with which I will therefore engage.

B

As I have observed before, the Constitution does not forbid the government to enforce traditional moral and sexual norms. See *Lawrence v. Texas*, 539 U. S. 558, 599 (2003) (SCALIA, J., dissenting). I will not swell the U. S. Reports with restatements of that point. It is enough to say that the Constitution neither requires nor forbids our society to approve of same-sex marriage, much as it neither requires nor forbids us to approve of no-fault divorce, polygamy, or the consumption of alcohol.

However, even setting aside traditional moral disapproval of same-sex marriage (or indeed same-sex sex), there are many perfectly valid—indeed, downright boring—justifying rationales for this legislation. Their existence ought to be the end of this case. For they give the lie to the Court's conclusion that only those with hateful hearts could have voted "aye" on this Act. And more importantly, they serve to make the contents of the legislators' hearts quite irrelevant: "It is a familiar principle of constitutional law that this Court will not strike down an otherwise constitutional statute on the basis of an alleged illicit legislative motive." *United States v. O'Brien*, 391 U. S. 367, 383 (1968). Or at least it was a familiar principle. By holding to the contrary, the majority has declared open season on any law that (in the opinion of the law's opponents and any panel of like-minded federal judges) can be characterized as mean-spirited.

The majority concludes that the only motive for this Act was the "bare . . . desire to harm a politically unpopular group." Bear in mind that the object of this condemnation is not the legislature of some once-Confederate Southern state (familiar objects of the Court's scorn, see, *e.g.*, *Edwards v. Aguillard*, 482 U.S. 578 (1987)), but our respected coordinate branches, the Congress and Presidency of the United States. Laying such a charge against them should require the most extraordinary evidence, and I would have thought that every attempt would be made to indulge a more anodyne explanation for the statute. The majority does the opposite—affirmatively concealing from the reader the arguments that exist in justification. It makes only a passing mention of the "arguments put forward" by the Act's defenders, and does not even trouble to paraphrase or describe them. See *ante*, at 21. I imagine that this is because it is harder to maintain the illusion of the Act's supporters as unhinged members of a wild-eyed lynch mob when one first describes their views as they see them.

To choose just one of these defenders' arguments, DOMA avoids difficult choice-of-law issues that will now arise absent a uniform federal definition of marriage. See, *e.g.*, Baude, Beyond DOMA: Choice of State Law in Federal Statutes, 64 Stan. L. Rev. 1371 (2012). Imagine a pair of women who marry in Albany and then move to Alabama, which does not "recognize as valid any marriage of parties of the same sex." When the couple files their next federal tax return, may it be a joint one? Which State's law controls, for federal-law purposes: their State of celebration (which recognizes the marriage) or their State of domicile (which does not)? (Does the answer depend on whether they were just visiting in Albany?) Are these questions to be answered as a matter of federal common law, or perhaps by borrowing a State's choice-of-law rules? If so, *which* State's? And what about States where the status of an out-of-state same-sex marriage is an unsettled question under local law? DOMA avoided all of this uncertainty by specifying which marriages would be recognized for federal purposes. That is a classic purpose for a definitional provision. [citations omitted]

Further, DOMA preserves the intended effects of prior legislation against then-unforeseen changes in circumstance. When Congress provided (for example) that a special estate-tax exemption would exist for spouses, this exemption reached only *opposite-sex* spouses—those being the only sort that were recognized in any State at the time of DOMA's passage. When it became clear that changes in state law might one day alter that balance, DOMA's definitional section was enacted to ensure that state-level experimentation did not automatically alter the basic operation of federal law, unless and until Congress made the further judgment to do so on its own. That is not animus—just stabilizing prudence. Congress has hardly demonstrated itself unwilling to make such further, revising judgments upon due deliberation. [citations omitted]

The Court mentions none of this. Instead, it accuses the Congress that enacted this law and the President who signed it of something much worse than, for example, having acted in excess of enumerated federal powers—or even having drawn distinctions that prove to be irrational. Those legal errors may be made in good faith, errors though they are. But the majority says that the supporters of this Act acted with malice—with the "purpose" "to disparage and to injure" same-sex couples. It says that the motivation for DOMA was to "demean," to "impose inequality," to "impose . . . a stigma," to deny people "equal dignity," to brand gay people as "unworthy," and to "humiliat[e]" their children.

I am sure these accusations are quite untrue. To be sure (as the majority points out), the legislation is called the Defense of Marriage Act. But to defend traditional marriage is not to condemn, demean, or humiliate those who would prefer other arrangements, any more than to defend the Constitution of the United States is to condemn, demean, or humiliate other constitutions. To hurl such accusations so casually demeans *this institution*. In the majority's judgment, any resistance to its holding is beyond the pale of reasoned disagreement. To question its high-handed invalidation of a presumptively valid statute is to act (the majority is sure) with *the purpose* to "disparage," "injure," "degrade," "demean," and "humiliate" our fellow human beings, our fellow citizens, who are homosexual. All that, simply for supporting an Act that did no more than codify an aspect of marriage that had been unquestioned in our society for most of its existence—indeed, had been unquestioned in virtually all societies for virtually all of human history. It is one thing for a society to elect change; it is another for a court of law to impose change by adjudging those who oppose it hostes humani generis, enemies of the human race.

* * *

The penultimate sentence of the majority's opinion is a naked declaration that "[t]his opinion and its holding are confined" to those couples "joined in same-sex marriages made lawful by the State." I have heard such "bald, unreasoned disclaimer[s]" before. *Lawrence*, 539 U. S., at 604. When the Court declared a constitutional right to homosexual sodomy, we were assured that the case had nothing, nothing at all to do with "whether the government must give formal recognition to any relationship that homosexual persons seek to enter." *Id.*, at 578. Now we are told that DOMA is invalid because it "demeans the couple, whose moral and sexual choices the Constitution protects," *ante*, at 23—with an accompanying citation of *Lawrence*. It takes real cheek for today's majority to assure us, as it is going out the door, that a constitutional requirement to give formal recognition to same-sex marriage is not at issue here—when what has preceded that assurance is a lecture on how superior the majority's moral judgment in favor of same-sex marriage is to the Congress's hateful moral judgment against it. I promise you this: The only thing that will "confine" the Court's holding is its sense of what it can get away with.

I do not mean to suggest disagreement with THE CHIEF JUSTICE's view that lower federal courts and state courts can distinguish today's case when the issue before them is state denial of marital status to same-sex couples—or even that this Court could theoretically do so. Lord, an opinion with such scatter-shot rationales as this one (federalism noises among them) can be distinguished in many ways. And deserves to be. State and lower federal courts should take the Court at its word and distinguish away.

In my opinion, however, the view that this Court will take of state prohibition of same-sex marriage is indicated beyond mistaking by today's opinion. As I have said, the real rationale of today's opinion, whatever disappearing trail of its legalistic argle-bargle one chooses to follow, is that DOMA is motivated by "'bare . . . desire to harm'" couples in same-sex marriages. How easy it is, indeed how inevitable, to reach the same conclusion with regard to state laws denying same-sex couples marital status. Consider how easy (inevitable) it is to make the following substitutions in a passage from today's opinion:

> "~~DOMA's~~ *This state law's* principal effect is to identify a subset of ~~state-sanctioned marriages~~ *constitutionally protected sexual relationships*, see *Lawrence*, and make them unequal. The principal purpose is to impose inequality, not for other reasons like governmental efficiency. Responsibilities, as well as rights, enhance the dignity and integrity of the person. And ~~DOMA~~ *this state law* contrives to deprive some couples ~~married under the laws of their State~~ *enjoying constitutionally protected sexual relationships,* but not other couples, of both rights and responsibilities."

Or try this passage:

> "~~[DOMA]~~ *This state law* tells those couples, and all the world, that their otherwise valid ~~marriages~~ *relationships* are unworthy of ~~federal~~ *state* recognition. This places same-sex couples in an unstable position of being in a second-tier ~~marriage~~ *relationship*. The differentiation demeans the couple, whose moral and sexual choices the Constitution protects, see *Lawrence*. . . ."

Or this—which does not even require alteration, except as to the invented number:

> "And it humiliates ~~tens of~~ thousands of children now being raised by same-sex couples. The law in question makes it even more difficult for the children to understand the integrity and closeness of their own family and its concord with other families in their community and in their daily lives."

Similarly transposable passages—deliberately transposable, I think—abound. In sum, that Court which finds it so horrific that Congress irrationally and hatefully robbed same-sex couples of the "personhood and dignity" which state legislatures conferred upon them, will of a certitude be similarly appalled by state legislatures' irrational and hateful failure to acknowledge that "personhood and dignity" in the first place. As far as this Court is concerned, no one should be fooled; it is just a matter of listening and waiting for the other shoe.

By formally declaring anyone opposed to same-sex marriage an enemy of human decency, the majority arms well every challenger to a state law restricting marriage to its traditional definition. Henceforth those challengers will lead with this Court's declaration that there is "no legitimate purpose" served by such a law, and will claim that the traditional definition has "the purpose and effect to disparage and to injure" the "personhood and dignity" of same-sex couples. The majority's limiting assurance will be meaningless in the face of language like that, as the majority well knows. That is why the language is there. The result will be a judicial distortion of our society's debate over marriage—a debate that can seem in need of our clumsy "help" only to a member of this institution.

As to that debate: Few public controversies touch an institution so central to the lives of so many, and few inspire such attendant passion by good people on all sides. Few public controversies will ever demonstrate so vividly the beauty of what our Framers gave us, a gift the Court pawns today to buy its stolen moment in the spotlight: a system of government that permits us to rule ourselves. Since DOMA's passage, citizens on all sides of the question have seen victories and they have seen defeats. There have been plebiscites, legislation, persuasion, and loud voices—in other words, democracy. Victories in one place for some are offset by victories in other places for others. [citations omitted] Even in a single State, the question has come out differently on different occasions. Compare Maine Question 1 (permitting "the State of Maine to issue marriage licenses to same-sex couples") (approved by a popular vote, 53% to 47%, on November 6, 2012) with Maine Question 1 (rejecting "the new law that lets same-sex couples marry") (approved by a popular vote, 53% to 47%, on November 3, 2009).

In the majority's telling, this story is black-and-white: Hate your neighbor or come along with us. The truth is more complicated. It is hard to admit that one's political opponents are not monsters, especially in a struggle like this one, and the challenge in the end proves more than today's Court can handle. Too bad. A reminder that disagreement over something so fundamental as marriage can still be politically legitimate would have been a fit task for what in earlier times was called the judicial temperament. We might have covered ourselves with honor today, by promising all sides of this debate that it was theirs to settle and that we would respect their resolution. We might have let the People decide.

But that the majority will not do. Some will rejoice in today's decision, and some will despair at it; that is the nature of a controversy that matters so much to so many. But the Court has cheated both sides, robbing the winners of an honest victory, and the losers of the peace that comes from a fair defeat. We owed both of them better. I dissent.

JUSTICE ALITO, with whom JUSTICE THOMAS joins as to Parts II and III, dissenting.[9]

Our Nation is engaged in a heated debate about same-sex marriage. That debate is, at bottom, about the nature of the institution of marriage. Respondent Edith Windsor, supported by the United States, asks this Court to intervene in that debate, and although she couches her argument in different terms, what she seeks is a holding that enshrines in the Constitution a particular understanding of marriage under which the sex of the partners makes no difference. The Constitution, however, does not dictate that choice. It leaves the choice to the people, acting through their elected representatives at both the federal and state levels. I would therefore hold that Congress did not violate Windsor's constitutional rights by enacting §3 of [DOMA]. . . .

II

* * * Same-sex marriage presents a highly emotional and important question of public policy—but not a difficult question of constitutional law. The Constitution does not guarantee the right to enter into a same-sex marriage. Indeed, no provision of the Constitution speaks to the issue.

The Court has sometimes found the Due Process Clauses to have a substantive component that guarantees liberties beyond the absence of physical restraint. And the Court's holding that "DOMA is unconstitutional as a deprivation of the liberty of the person protected by the Fifth Amendment of the Constitution," suggests that substantive due process may partially underlie the Court's decision today. But it is well established that any "substantive" component to the Due Process Clause protects only "those fundamental rights and liberties which are, objectively, 'deeply rooted in this Nation's history and tradition,'" as well as "'implicit in the concept of ordered liberty,' such that 'neither liberty nor justice would exist if they were sacrificed.'" [citations omitted]

It is beyond dispute that the right to same-sex marriage is not deeply rooted in this Nation's history and tradition. In this country, no State permitted same-sex marriage until the Massachusetts Supreme Judicial Court held in 2003 that limiting marriage to opposite-sex couples violated the State Constitution. . . .

---

9   *Editor's Note*: In Part I, Justice Alito explained his view that BLAG had Article III standing in the case such that the Court should reach the merits.

What Windsor and the United States seek, therefore, is not the protection of a deeply rooted right but the recognition of a very new right, and they seek this innovation not from a legislative body elected by the people, but from unelected judges. Faced with such a request, judges have cause for both caution and humility.

The family is an ancient and universal human institution. Family structure reflects the characteristics of a civilization, and changes in family structure and in the popular understanding of marriage and the family can have profound effects. Past changes in the understanding of marriage—for example, the gradual ascendance of the idea that romantic love is a prerequisite to marriage—have had far-reaching consequences. But the process by which such consequences come about is complex, involving the interaction of numerous factors, and tends to occur over an extended period of time.

We can expect something similar to take place if same-sex marriage becomes widely accepted. The long-term consequences of this change are not now known and are unlikely to be ascertainable for some time to come. There are those who think that allowing same-sex marriage will seriously undermine the institution of marriage. Others think that recognition of same-sex marriage will fortify a now-shaky institution.

At present, no one—including social scientists, philosophers, and historians—can predict with any certainty what the long-term ramifications of widespread acceptance of same-sex marriage will be. And judges are certainly not equipped to make such an assessment. The Members of this Court have the authority and the responsibility to interpret and apply the Constitution. Thus, if the Constitution contained a provision guaranteeing the right to marry a person of the same sex, it would be our duty to enforce that right. But the Constitution simply does not speak to the issue of same-sex marriage. In our system of government, ultimate sovereignty rests with the people, and the people have the right to control their own destiny. Any change on a question so fundamental should be made by the people through their elected officials.

III

Perhaps because they cannot show that same-sex marriage is a fundamental right under our Constitution, Windsor and the United States couch their arguments in equal protection terms. They argue that § 3 of DOMA discriminates on the basis of sexual orientation, that classifications based on sexual orientation should trigger a form of "heightened" scrutiny, and that § 3 cannot survive such scrutiny. They further maintain that the governmental interests that § 3 purports to serve are not sufficiently important and that it has not been adequately shown that § 3 serves those interests very well. The Court's holding, too, seems to rest on "the equal protection guarantee of the Fourteenth

Amendment"—although the Court is careful not to adopt most of Windsor's and the United States' argument.

In my view, the approach that Windsor and the United States advocate is misguided. Our equal protection framework, upon which Windsor and the United States rely, is a judicial construct that provides a useful mechanism for analyzing a certain universe of equal protection cases. But that framework is ill suited for use in evaluating the constitutionality of laws based on the traditional understanding of marriage, which fundamentally turn on what marriage is. * * *

By asking the Court to strike down DOMA as not satisfying some form of heightened scrutiny, Windsor and the United States are really seeking to have the Court resolve a debate between two competing views of marriage.

The first and older view, which I will call the "traditional" or "conjugal" view, sees marriage as an intrinsically opposite-sex institution. BLAG notes that virtually every culture, including many not influenced by the Abrahamic religions, has limited marriage to people of the opposite sex. And BLAG attempts to explain this phenomenon by arguing that the institution of marriage was created for the purpose of channeling heterosexual intercourse into a structure that supports child rearing. . . . While modern cultural changes have weakened the link between marriage and procreation in the popular mind, there is no doubt that, throughout human history and across many cultures, marriage has been viewed as an exclusively opposite-sex institution and as one inextricably linked to procreation and biological kinship.

The other, newer view is what I will call the "consent-based" vision of marriage, a vision that primarily defines marriage as the solemnization of mutual commitment—marked by strong emotional attachment and sexual attraction—between two persons. At least as it applies to heterosexual couples, this view of marriage now plays a very prominent role in the popular understanding of the institution. Indeed, our popular culture is infused with this understanding of marriage. Proponents of same-sex marriage argue that because gender differentiation is not relevant to this vision, the exclusion of same-sex couples from the institution of marriage is rank discrimination.

The Constitution does not codify either of these views of marriage (although I suspect it would have been hard at the time of the adoption of the Constitution or the Fifth Amendment to find Americans who did not take the traditional view for granted). The silence of the Constitution on this question should be enough to end the matter as far as the judiciary is concerned. Yet, Windsor and the United States implicitly ask us to endorse the consent-based view of marriage and to reject the traditional view, thereby arrogating to ourselves the power to decide a question that philosophers, historians, social scientists, and theologians are better qualified to explore.[7] Because our constitutional order assigns the resolution of questions of this nature to the people, I would not presume to enshrine either vision of marriage in our constitutional jurisprudence.

Legislatures, however, have little choice but to decide between the two views. We have long made clear that neither the political branches of the Federal Government nor state governments are required to be neutral between competing visions of the good, provided that the vision of the good that they adopt is not countermanded by the Constitution. Accordingly, both Congress and the States are entitled to enact laws recognizing either of the two understandings of marriage. * * *

* * *

For these reasons, I would hold that §3 of DOMA does not violate the Fifth Amendment. I respectfully dissent.

NOTES

1. Justice Kennedy's majority opinion includes elements of equality, liberty, and federalism. What role did each doctrinal area play? On what doctrinal principle does the decision ultimately rest? What role does dignity play in Justice Kennedy's reasoning?

2. What level of scrutiny does Justice Kennedy apply? Why did he not explicitly engage the issue of heightened scrutiny addressed by the Second Circuit?

In a significant decision involving peremptory challenges based on sexual orientation, the Ninth Circuit Court of Appeals recently held that *Windsor* requires the application of heightened scrutiny to sexual orientation classifications. *SmithKline Beecham Corp. v. Abbott Labs.*, 740 F.3d 471 (9th Cir. 2014). The court reasoned that while *Windsor* "did not expressly announce the level of scrutiny it applied to the equal protection claim . . . an express declaration is not necessary." *Id.* at 480. The court then explained: "Unlike in rational basis review, hypothetical reasons for DOMA's enactment were not a basis of the Court's inquiry." *Id.* at 481. It continued:

---

[7] The degree to which this question is intractable to typical judicial processes of decisionmaking was highlighted by the trial in *Hollingsworth v. Perry*. In that case, the trial judge, after receiving testimony from some expert witnesses, purported to make "findings of fact" on such questions as why marriage came to be, what marriage is, and the effect legalizing same-sex marriage would have on opposite-sex marriage.

At times, the trial reached the heights of parody, as when the trial judge questioned his ability to take into account the views of great thinkers of the past because they were unavailable to testify in person in his courtroom.

And, if this spectacle were not enough, some professors of constitutional law have argued that we are bound to accept the trial judge's findings—including those on major philosophical questions and predictions about the future—unless they are "clearly erroneous." Only an arrogant legal culture that has lost all appreciation of its own limitations could take such a suggestion seriously.

Rational basis is ordinarily unconcerned with the inequality that results from the challenged state action. Due to this distinctive feature of rational basis review, words like *harm* or *injury* rarely appear in the Court's decisions applying rational basis review. *Windsor*, however, uses these words repeatedly.

Id. at 482 (citation omitted). Finally, the court noted that "[a]bsent from *Windsor*'s review of DOMA are the 'strong presumption' in favor of constitutionality of laws and the 'extremely deferential' posture toward government action that are the marks of rational basis review." *Id.* at 483. What do you think of the Ninth Circuit's reasoning? Do you agree?

3.   How does Justice Kennedy analyze the governmental interests put forward to support DOMA? Why are those interests not valid justifications for the law?

4.   In his dissent, Chief Justice Roberts emphasizes the federalism dimensions of the majority opinion to distinguish the constitutional question regarding state marriage prohibitions. For his part, Justice Scalia suggests a closer relationship between the Court's decision and the constitutionality of state marriage bans. To what extent did principles of federalism guide the Court's decision? What does the equal protection reasoning in *Windsor* reveal about the constitutionality of state laws excluding same-sex couples from marriage?

5.   Even though *Windsor* did not involve a claim to the fundamental right to marry, Justices Scalia and Alito both engage this issue. Does excluding same-sex couples from marriage infringe on the fundamental right to marry? Is there anything in Justice Kennedy's opinion that reveals his outlook on this question? For analysis of *Windsor*'s right-to-marry dimensions, see Douglas NeJaime, Windsor*'s Right to Marry*, 123 YALE L.J. ONLINE 219 (2013).

6.   In his dissent, Justice Alito explains how the debate over same-sex marriage implicates a broader debate over the meaning and purpose of marriage. What is the distinction between the "conjugal" and "consent-based" understandings of marriage? How do same-sex couples relate to each? What does Justice Kennedy's opinion suggest are the central features of marriage? How do these features relate to the view of marriage espoused by the Court in *Loving* and *Turner*, excerpted above in Section II.A?

7.   Justice Kennedy concludes that DOMA "humiliates tens of thousands of children now being raised by same-sex couples." How does this argument relate to the claims of same-sex marriage opponents regarding procreation and childrearing? What is the relationship between marriage and parenting? What should it be?

4. Challenges to State Marriage Laws after *Windsor*

a. *Lawsuits in State Court*

Soon after the Court issued its decision in *Windsor*, lawyers filed new motions in pending state-court cases challenging the constitutionality of civil union regimes in New Jersey and Illinois. (Before the Illinois litigation was resolved, the legislature in that state passed a marriage equality law.) The lawyers in the New Jersey suit, which included both state and federal constitutional claims, relied on Justice Kennedy's language about stigma to frame civil unions as a dignitary harm: "As with DOMA, having 'two contradictory . . . regimes within the same state . . . tells those couples and all the world that their [civil unions] are unworthy of federal protection.'" "Just like with DOMA," the lawyers argued, "'[t]he differentiation' effected by the New Jersey scheme 'demeans the couple.'"[10]

Windsor, however, did more than simply lend support to arguments based on dignitary harm. Instead, by striking down Section 3 of DOMA, *Windsor* dramatically increased the material harm that same-sex couples in nonmarital recognition regimes experienced; without marriage, these couples could not access significant federal rights and benefits available to married same-sex couples after *Windsor*. The lawyers in the New Jersey litigation pointed to this development to support the equal protection claim. The trial court accepted this argument and resolved the case based on state equal protection principles:

> Because plaintiffs, and all same-sex couples in New Jersey, cannot access many federal marital benefits as partners in civil unions, this court holds that New Jersey's denial of marriage to same-sex couples now violates Article 1, Paragraph 1 of the New Jersey Constitution as interpreted by the New Jersey Supreme Court in *Lewis v. Harris*. The equality demanded by *Lewis v. Harris* now requires that same-sex couples in New Jersey be allowed to marry.

Garden State Equality v. Dow, 82 A.3d 336, 367, 434 N.J. Super. 163, 217 (N.J. Super. Ct. 2013). The trial court refused to stay its order, thereby opening marriage to same-sex couples. The New Jersey Supreme Court upheld the trial court's denial of the state's motion to stay. In doing so, the state supreme court explained that because *Windsor* "paved the way to extending federal benefits to married same-sex couples" and "because a number of federal agencies responded and now provide various benefits to married same-sex couples," "same-sex couples in New Jersey [were] being deprived of the full rights and benefits the State Constitution

---

[10] Plaintiffs' Brief in Support of Motion for Summary Judgment at 44, *Garden State Equality v. Dow*, No. MER L–1729–11 (N.J. Super. filed July 3, 2013).

guarantees." *Garden State Equality v. Dow*, 79 A.3d 1036, 1042, 216 N.J. 314, 325 (N.J. 2013). The state subsequently dropped its appeal. Same-sex couples in New Jersey now have access to marriage.

Meanwhile, in New Mexico, after county clerks began to issue marriage licenses to same-sex couples, the state supreme court resolved the issue. The state had been providing some recognition to same-sex couples' marriages from other states, but was not itself offering any relationship recognition to same-sex couples. In *Griego v. Oliver*, the court held that sexual orientation merited intermediate scrutiny for state equal protection purposes. 316 P.3d 865, 880–89 (N.M. 2013). Applying that standard, the court invalidated same-sex couples' exclusion from marriage:

> Excluding same-gender couples from civil marriage prevents children of same-gender couples from enjoying the security that flows from the rights, protections, and responsibilities that accompany civil marriage. There is no substantial relationship between New Mexico's marriage laws and the purported governmental interest of responsible child-rearing.

Id. at 888.

b. *Lawsuits in Federal Court*

In *Windsor*'s wake, same-sex couples around the country filed a number of lawsuits in federal court challenging state marriage bans. In addition to federal constitutional claims based on the fundamental right to marry, the plaintiffs in these suits asserted federal equal protection claims that relied on the Court's reasoning in *Windsor*. At the same time, federal lawsuits filed before the Court's decision moved forward with new energy.

In two of those cases, both of which involved states that offered no relationship recognition to same-sex couples, the federal district courts struck down state marriage laws. In *Kitchen v. Herbert*, the court found Utah's constitutional ban, which voters had passed in 2004, unconstitutional. The court held that "Plaintiffs have a fundamental right to marry that protects their choice of a same-sex partner." ___ F. Supp. 2d ___, 2013 WL 6697874, at *18 (D. Utah Dec. 20, 2013). The court then found that the law failed to survive strict scrutiny. *Id.* Separately, the court subjected the plaintiffs' equal protection claim to rational basis review and concluded that the state marriage ban failed even this more deferential standard:

> The State's position appears to be based on an assumption that the availability of same-sex marriage will somehow cause opposite-sex couples to forego marriage. But the State has not presented any evidence that heterosexual individuals will be any

less inclined to enter into an opposite-sex marriage simply because their gay and lesbian fellow citizens are able to enter into a same-sex union. Similarly, the State has not shown any effect of the availability of same-sex marriage on the number of children raised by either opposite-sex or same-sex partners.

In contrast to the State's speculative concerns, the harm experienced by same-sex couples in Utah as a result of their inability to marry is undisputed. To apply the Supreme Court's reasoning in *Windsor*, [the Utah law] "tells those couples and all the world that their otherwise valid [relationships] are unworthy of [state] recognition. This places same-sex couples in an unstable position of being in a second-tier [relationship]. The differentiation demeans the couple, whose moral and sexual choices the Constitution protects." *Windsor*, 133 S.Ct. at 2694; *see also id.* at 2710 (Sclia, J., dissenting) (suggesting that the majority's reasoning could be applied to the state-law context in precisely this way). And while [the Utah law] does not offer any additional protection to children being raised by opposite-sex couples, it demeans the children of same-sex couples who are told that their families are less worthy of protection than other families.

Id. at *28. Interestingly, the court forecefully relied on Justice Scalia's dissent in *Windsor*:

The Constitution's protection of the individual rights of gay and lesbian citizens is equally dispositve whether this protection requires a court to respect state law, as in *Windsor*, or strike down a state law, as the Plaintiffs ask the court to do here. In his dissenting opinion, the Honorable Antonin Scalia recognized that this result was the logical outcome of the Court's ruling in *Windsor*[.]

Id. at *7.

The district court issued an injunction and refused to stay its order, thus allowing same-sex couples in Utah to obtain marriage licenses. Eventually, the U.S. Supreme Court stayed the injunction pending appeal. *See Herbert v. Kitchen*, 571 U.S. ___ (Jan. 6, 2014). The federal government declared that it would recognize the marriages performed in Utah up to that point. Dep't of Justice, Statement by Attorney General Eric Holder on Federal Recognition of Same-Sex Marriages in Utah (Jan. 10, 2014). But for state-law purposes, the Utah Attorney General announced that the state would "neither recognize nor confer new marital benefits" on married same-sex couples. Utah Att'y General, Official Statement (Jan. 8, 2014). The Tenth Circuit Court of Appeals decided to review the case on an expedited basis.

The Tenth Circuit also has a second marriage case before it. A few weeks after the *Kitchen* decision, a federal district court struck down Oklahoma's constitutional ban on same-sex marriage. In *Bishop v. United States*, the court applied rational basis review to the law's sexual orientation classification and concluded that the law constituted "an arbitrary, irrational exclusion of just one class of Oklahoma citizens from a governmental benefit." ___ F. Supp. 2d ___, 2014 WL 116013, at *33 (D. Okla. Jan. 14, 2014). The court noted the influence of the Supreme Court's decisions:

> The Supreme Court has not expressly reached the issue of whether state laws prohibiting same-sex marriage violate the U.S. Constitution. However, Supreme Court law now prohibits states from passing laws that are born of animosity against homosexuals, extends constitutional protection to the moral and sexual choices of homosexuals, and prohibits the federal government from treating opposite-sex marriages and same-sex marriages differently. There is no precise legal label for what has occurred in Supreme Court jurisprudence beginning with *Romer* in 1996 and culminating in *Windsor* in 2013, but this Court knows a rhetorical shift when it sees one.

Id. at *33. The court stayed its ruling pending appeal, and the Tenth Circuit also expedited its review of the case.[11]

Meanwhile, the Ninth Circuit Court of Appeals is considering a case challenging same-sex couples' exclusion from marriage in Nevada, a state that provides domestic partnership. *See Sevcik v. Sandoval*, 911 F. Supp. 2d 996 (D. Nev. 2012). The Ninth Circuit's decision in *SmithKline* (noted above), which interpreted *Windsor* to require heightened scrutiny for sexual orientation classifications, may have significant implications for the marriage case.

5. Federal Recognition after *Windsor*

As the Court's opinion in *Windsor* makes clear, the federal government traditionally deferred to state-law determinations regarding a couple's marital status, rather than include an independent federal definition of marriage. Therefore, in the wake of *Windsor*, the federal government confronted the issue of how to recognize same-sex couples' marriages at a time when only some states allow same-sex couples to marry. Indeed, Justice Scalia's dissent points to avoidance of this choice-of-law issue as a potential justification for DOMA. To understand the

---

[11] Other federal district courts have found state marriage bans unconstitutional. *See DeBoer v. Snyder*, ___ F. Supp. 2d ___, 2014 WL 1100794 (E.D. Mich. Mar. 21, 2014); *De Leon v. Perry*, ___ F. Supp. 2d ___, 2014 WL 715741 (W.D. Tex. Feb. 26, 2014); *Bostic v. Rainey*, ___ F. Supp. 2d ___, 2014 WL 561978 (E.D. Va. Feb. 13, 2014).

choice-of-law implications after *Windsor*, consider the following excerpt from an article that Justice Scalia cites in his *Windsor* dissent:

BEYOND DOMA: CHOICE OF STATE LAW IN FEDERAL STATUTES*
William Baude

How should the federal government decide what state's law applies when a federal statute incorporates state law? * * * For purposes of federal choice of law, state status is what counts. To the extent they borrow from state law, the federal statutes ask who is married, not whether the couple happens to get one or another benefit under state law. * * *

The Constitution provides that "Full Faith and Credit shall be given in each State to the public Acts, Records, and judicial Proceedings of every other State. And the Congress may by general Laws prescribe the Manner in which such Acts, Records, and Proceedings shall be proved, and the Effect thereof." The Full Faith and Credit Clause has sometimes been cited by those who urge that states have a duty to recognize marriages from other states. But that clause has generally not been interpreted to extend as broadly to legislative rulings (like those concerning which marriages are valid) as it does to judicial judgments (like specific custody orders that might be premised on those marriages). Moreover, even if one thinks that marriages are entitled to full faith and credit as "public Acts, Records, and judicial Proceedings," the Full Faith and Credit Clause empowers Congress to decide what "effect" those acts, records, and proceedings shall have, and Congress has explicitly provided (in a separate section—section 2—of DOMA) that states are not required to recognize same-sex marriages from other states.

On top of that, states have traditionally invoked a "public policy" exception to resist implementing foreign laws that their legislatures find particularly objectionable. The many state statutes that deny recognition to foreign same-sex marriages are intended in part as a legislative expression of such policy. Section 2 of DOMA is expressly intended to ratify such policies (if any ratification were needed). * * *

CHOICE OF LAW IN FEDERAL LEGISLATION

Choice of Law as Statutory Interpretation

. . . Recall that DOMA operate[d] by effectively amending a thousand different legal provisions that invoke marital status. The federal

---

* William Baude, *Beyond DOMA: Choice of State Law in Federal Statutes*, 64 STAN. L. REV. 1371, 1374, 1390–92, 1399–1402, 1404–08, 1410, 1412, 1414, 1417, 1421 (2012). By permission of the Board of Trustees of the Leland Stanford Junior University, from the Stanford Law Review at Vol. 64 Stan. L. Rev. 1371 (2012). For more information, visit http://www.stanfordlaw review.org.

government has no cause to "recognize" marital status—under state law or otherwise—in the abstract. It ascertains who is married only to the extent it is required to under another statutory or regulatory rule. Thus, . . . interpreters must decide: who does this statute refer to when it refers to married couples?

Federal courts "choose" state law as part of an answer to that statutory interpretation question. . . .

Thus, what courts have been calling a choice-of-law problem when federal law incorporates state law categories is really just a two-part statutory-interpretation problem: Federal law contains an undefined term whose meaning is ordinarily a legal category. To figure out the meaning of that category, one must first decide whether state law is relevant, and if it is, which state's law. . . .

[P]erhaps the most important implication is that Congress has total authority to solve the so-called choice-of-law problem. It is generally accepted that "definition of legislative terms must, as an original matter, be an incident of the legislative power," because Congress's power to decide what the statute says entails the power to do so through the use of definitions. It follows that Congress can decide which states' laws are incorporated by its statutes, because those rules are simply a form of definition—of defining more precisely what Congress meant in referring to the state law term.

A Congressional Choice-of-Law Rule

. . . Congress should decide what law governs marriage for federal purposes. Such a provision could cut across all of the regulatory and statutory definitions and provide a uniform and predictable approach. For example, Congress might replace DOMA's definition of marriage with one saying that in determining the meaning of any law or regulation, the word "marriage" means a marriage that is recognized as valid in the state where the marriage was celebrated, or one that is recognized as valid in a state where one of the parties is domiciled.

Congress has made such determinations on occasion. Veterans' benefits based on marriage, for example, are awarded "according to the law of the place where the parties resided at the time of the marriage or the law of the place where the parties resided when the right to benefits accrued." Similarly, the Social Security Act provides that marital status determinations will be made by reference to the law of the parties' domicile. Both of these statutes predate (and are partly eclipsed by) DOMA, but might apply again if it is repealed. Congress should go further, providing a single, clear rule to regulate marriage wherever it interacts with the federal code.

To Congress's credit, some of the more recent proposals to repeal DOMA would have provided a choice-of-law rule in its stead. The bills would have provided federal recognition for any marriage that was valid in the state where it was celebrated. . . .

Of course, those measures have not passed, but whatever one thinks of the substance of the proposed choice-of-law rules, Congress is the best institution to provide them. Congressional action provides a clear, stable, ex ante rule for determining a couple's marital status—whether on a statute-by-statute basis or across all statutes at once. It can solve the marital choice-of-law problem for all areas of federal law.

* * * [W]hile congressional action is possible, it is not certain, and . . . even if it does come, it may not come for a while. So it is worthwhile to examine the alternatives to legislation.

Regulatory Choice of Law

In the face of congressional inaction, administrative agencies might fill the gap instead. Congress frequently fails to legislate the pesky implementing details of the statutes it passes, and agencies fill the gap by issuing regulations to which the courts might defer. . . . Agencies can also create law through administrative adjudications rather than regulation. * * *

While agency resolution has some of the virtues of congressional resolution, it also may be inadequate to solve the post-DOMA choice-of-law problem. There is no single federal agency in charge of marriage. As discussed above, DOMA cuts a swath through thousands of different statutes and regulations within the jurisdiction of many different administrative bodies—the Social Security Administration, the Internal Revenue Service, the Board of Immigration Appeals, and more. Each body would presumably have to separately provide its own marital choice-of-law rules, and those rules might differ, just as the Bureau of Immigration Affairs and the Veterans Administration provided different choice-of-law rules in their respective fields. That could mean that a couple is married for purposes of some federal statutes but not others, potentially leading to odd conflicts. . . .

Regulatory uniformity would have to be accomplished through executive branch coordination. * * *

FEDERAL CHOICE OF LAW IN THE FEDERAL COURTS

It seems at least somewhat likely that neither Congress nor administrative agencies will codify conflicts rules for federal statutes that rely on state marital status. In that event, the task of interpreting that universe of statutes will fall to the courts. In every case in which federal marital status is at issue, they must decide what law controls marital status.

. . . [F]ederal courts should turn to what they have called the "federal common law" of conflicts if there is no statutory or regulatory choice-of-law provision.

* * * Federal courts should follow the whole law of the parties' domicile. . . . [T]he parties' current domicile will sometimes choose to recognize a marriage that would not be valid there, and sometimes it will decide that its preference is so strong that it invalidates the marriage entirely. By relying on the choice-of-law rules of the marital domicile, the federal government comes as close as possible to taking itself out of the equation. Federal courts should therefore treat parties as married if their home state—their domicile—treats them that way.

NOTES

1.   Should Congress adopt a choice-of-law rule that governs all federal statutes keyed to marital status? If so, which rule is best: place-of-celebration or place-of-residence? If Congress does not adopt a choice-of-law rule, what is the alternative?

2.   At this point, Congress has not adopted a uniform choice-of-law rule. Instead, consistent with what Professor Baude terms "regulatory choice of law," many federal agencies individually have provided guidance on how marital status will be determined for purposes of the statutory schemes they are charged with administering. Agencies consider both the extent to which the relevant statutory schemes provide guidance and the policy considerations at stake.

A place-of-residence or domicile rule is explicitly embedded in some federal statutes. For instance, the Social Security Act invokes a place-of-residence rule. While the Social Security Administration continues to assess the impact of *Windsor*, at least one agency has provided guidance applying a place-of-residence rule. In the context of the Family and Medical Leave Act (FMLA), the Department of Labor issued an updated fact sheet explaining that while same-sex spouses are included after *Windsor*, the spouses must reside in a state that recognizes their marriage. According to the fact sheet: "Spouse means a husband or wife as defined or recognized under state law for purposes of marriage in the state where the employee resides, including 'common law' marriage and same-sex marriage." U.S. Dep't of Labor, Wage and Hour Div., *Fact Sheet #28F: Qualifying Reasons for Leave under the Family and Medical Leave Act* (Aug. 2013).

In contrast, many agencies have adopted a place-of-celebration rule. One of the most significant announcements came from the Internal Revenue Service:

[I]ndividuals of the same sex will be considered to be lawfully married under the [Internal Revenue] Code as long as they were married in a state whose laws authorize the marriage of two individuals of the same sex, even if they are domiciled in a state that does not recognize the validity of same-sex marriages. For over half a century, for Federal income tax purposes, the Service has recognized marriages based on the laws of the state in which they were entered into, without regard to subsequent changes in domicile, to achieve uniformity, stability, and efficiency in the application and administration of the Code. Given our increasingly mobile society, it is important to have a uniform rule of recognition that can be applied with certainty by the Service and taxpayers alike for all Federal tax purposes. Those overriding tax administration policy goals generally apply with equal force in the context of same-sex marriages.

In most Federal tax contexts, a state-of-domicile rule would present serious administrative concerns. For example, spouses are generally treated as related parties for Federal tax purposes, and one spouse's ownership interest in property may be attributed to the other spouse for purposes of numerous Code provisions. If the Service did not adopt a uniform rule of recognition, the attribution of property interests could change when a same-sex couple moves from one state to another with different marriage recognition rules. The potential adverse consequences could impact not only the married couple but also others involved in a transaction, entity, or arrangement. This would lead to uncertainty for both taxpayers and the Service.

A rule of recognition based on the state of a taxpayer's current domicile would also raise significant challenges for employers that operate in more than one state, or that have employees (or former employees) who live in more than one state, or move between states with different marriage recognition rules. Substantial financial and administrative burdens would be placed on those employers, as well as the administrators of employee benefit plans.

Rev. Rul. 2013–17, 2013–38 I.R.B. 201, at § 3. Federal agencies have also announced a place-of-celebration rule in other crucial areas, including immigration and military spousal benefits. With regard to programs it administers, the Department of Justice has made federal rights and benefits, including joint filing in bankruptcy proceedings, recognition of federal inmates' marriages, and benefits for surviving spouses of public safety officers, available to married same-sex couples based on a place-of-celebration rule. For guidance on federal agency rules after *Windsor*, see http://www.lambdalegal.org/publications/after-doma.

    3.   As the discussion regarding the adequacy of civil unions after *Windsor* suggests, the federal government has not extended federal rights and benefits to nonmarital relationships, such as civil unions or domestic partnerships. As the IRS explained in its post-*Windsor* ruling, "For Federal tax purposes, the term 'marriage' does not include registered domestic partnerships, civil unions, or other similar formal relationships recognized

under state law that are not denominated as a marriage under that state's law[.]" Rev. Rul. 2013–17, 2013–38 I.R.B. 201, at § 4. This development has provided additional support to same-sex couples' claim that state-level nonmarital recognition fails to satisfy equal protection requirements.

E. INTERSTATE RECOGNITION OF SAME-SEX COUPLES' MARRIAGES

As the Court's opinion made clear, *Windsor* did not involve a challenge to Section 2 of DOMA, which relates to interstate recognition of same-sex marriage. When DOMA was passed in 1996, supporters of the law pointed to the Full Faith and Credit Clause in Article IV of the federal Constitution to argue that states would have to recognize same-sex marriages from other states. That Clause provides that:

> Full faith and credit shall be given in each State to the public Acts, Records, and judicial Proceedings of every other State. And the Congress may by general Laws prescribe the manner in which such Acts, Records, and Proceedings shall be proved, and the effect thereof.

U.S. CONST. art. IV, § 1. However, as Professor Baude's article suggests, the idea that the Full Faith and Credit Clause would, in fact, compel interstate recognition of same-sex marriage is hardly the inevitability that opponents claimed. Nevertheless, the claim proved politically potent. As discussed above, in Section II.B, many states passed their own "mini-DOMA" laws defining marriage as an exclusively different-sex union and expressly declining to recognize same-sex marriages performed in other states. This Section considers the significance of DOMA and these "mini-DOMA's" within the established framework for interstate recognition of marriages. It does so by using developments from Maryland and Texas to show the different positions that states have taken. It then provides a more recent example from a federal district court in Ohio. Together these decisions illustrate the importance of principles of comity in the specific context of interstate recognition. Yet they also show how the issue may ultimately rest on some of the same constitutional questions raised by same-sex marriage bans more generally.

Maryland voters approved marriage equality in November 2012. Before that, the Maryland Court of Appeals, which is the state's highest court, rejected same-sex couples' marriage claims under the state constitution. *See Conaway v. Deane*, 932 A.2d 571, 401 Md. 219 (2007). Yet that decision did not resolve the question of whether Maryland would recognize same-sex couples' marriages from other states. In the excerpts that follow, the state's Attorney General and the Maryland Court of Appeals answer that question affirmatively. As you read the following excerpts, consider why the state would recognize same-sex couples' marriages even as the state refused to allow same-sex couples to marry. Consider also whether recognition should depend on either the couple's relationship to Maryland or the marital rights or obligations at issue.

OFFICE OF THE ATTORNEY GENERAL, STATE OF MARYLAND

95 Md. Op. Att. Gen. 3 (Md. A.G. 2010)

THE HONORABLE RICHARD S. MADALENO, JR.

Maryland Senate

You asked whether the State may recognize same-sex marriages legally performed in other jurisdictions. . . .

Same-Sex Marriages from Other Jurisdictions in Maryland

This opinion does not concern whether individuals of the same sex may wed in Maryland. The General Assembly has clearly answered that question "no"[12]—an answer that the Court of Appeals has found to be constitutional.

Rather, your inquiry raises the question whether the State may recognize a same-sex marriage *that is valid in the jurisdiction in which it was contracted.* . . .

Although two individuals are married in another jurisdiction, their marital status in Maryland can become significant in a variety of ways. A same-sex couple validly married in another state or country may move to Maryland for employment. A same-sex couple validly married in another state or country may vacation in the State—or may stop temporarily in the State while traveling to another destination. A same-sex couple in Maryland may go to another state for the specific purpose of marrying under that state's law, and then return to Maryland. A same-sex couple married in another state may never set foot in Maryland, yet their marital status may have legal significance for others in Maryland.

You have asked whether those marriages *may* be recognized under State law. The answer to that question is clearly "yes." * * *

Choice-of-law, or conflict-of-laws, is the body of common law that the courts apply when the laws of more than one jurisdiction potentially govern a particular situation. In regard to out-of-state marriages the courts apply the principle of comity, a term that describes the respect that one state has for the laws of another in light of its own public policy.

---

12 *Editor's Note*: In 1973, the Maryland legislature passed FL § 2–201, which provided: "Only a marriage between a man and a woman is valid in this State."

Out-of-State Marriages and the Principle of Comity

The Court of Appeals would start from the general principle that a marriage that is valid in the place of celebration remains valid in Maryland. There is an exception to that rule if the particular marriage is contrary to a strong State public policy. A statute that limits marriage in Maryland to opposite-sex couples could be said to embody a policy against same-sex marriage. However, there are many restrictions in the State's marriage statutes and the Court of Appeals has not construed the public policy exception to encompass all those restrictions. For example, it has recognized common law marriages from other states, although there is no common law marriage in Maryland, and has recognized a Rhode Island marriage between an uncle and a niece, although a statute prohibits marriage between an uncle and a niece in Maryland. Indeed, the public policy exception is a very limited one that the Court has seldom invoked.

While the matter is not free from all doubt, in our view, the Court is likely to respect the law of other states and recognize a same-sex marriage contracted validly in another jurisdiction. In light of Maryland's developing public policy concerning intimate same-sex relationships, the Court would not readily invoke the public policy exception to the usual rule of recognition. * * *

Relationship of Out-of-State Marriage to Maryland

[A]n out-of-state marriage may come within Maryland's jurisdiction in a variety of ways. . . . [T]he particular category to which a marriage belongs may affect a court's application of the public policy exception. While it is not clear whether Maryland Court of Appeals will draw such distinctions among these categories, the categories provide a useful rubric for describing the circumstances in which the question of recognition of a marriage may arise.

"Migratory" or *"mobile"* marriages. A couple marries in the jurisdiction where they happen to reside at the time of their marriage. They move to Maryland for reasons that have nothing to do with the marriage laws of the respective jurisdictions. This is the classic scenario in which the Maryland courts apply the standard rule that a marriage that is valid in the place of celebration is also generally valid in the couple's new residence, subject to the public policy exception.

"Transient" or *"visitor"* marriages. The couple marries in another jurisdiction in which they reside. They later travel to or through Maryland temporarily without any intention of residing in the State, but their marital status becomes legally significant for some reason. For example, a same-sex couple validly married in Massachusetts may travel to Maryland for vacation or pass through en route to Washington, D.C. An event may occur while the couple is in Maryland in which their marital status plays a role. In such a situation, the State is called upon to

recognize the married status of a couple that had never resided in Maryland, and indeed never intended to do so, for a very specific purpose. A court may be particularly reluctant to invoke the public policy exception in such circumstances.

"Extraterritorial" marriages. The couple marries in the jurisdiction in which they reside outside Maryland. However, unlike the previous two categories, in this scenario, the married couple never sets foot in Maryland. The validity of their marriage is significant in Maryland only because it affects a legal determination being made in Maryland, such as the probate of an estate. Again, a court may be reluctant to invoke the public policy exception, particularly if there are adverse effects on third parties.

"Evasive" marriages. Residents of a state that bars same-sex marriage travel to a jurisdiction that allows same-sex marriages for the specific purpose of avoiding the prohibition in their own state. They contract a valid marriage in the other jurisdiction—the place of celebration—and return to their own state. This may be the category in which a court would be least sympathetic to recognition of the marriage. Unlike some other states, however, Maryland has never had a statute directing the courts to withhold recognition of evasive marriages. . . . Moreover, the factual inquiry required to distinguish "evasive" marriages from others might make such a distinction impractical in many contexts. * * *

Summary

[The state statute limiting marriage to opposite-sex unions] embodies a policy against same-sex marriage, but likely was not originally intended to govern recognition of out-of-state marriages. The development of Maryland's public policy as to committed same-sex relationships over the past decade makes it increasingly unlikely that the Court would rely on the statute to invoke the public policy exception to the general rule of recognition of out-of-state marriages. Thus, in our view, the Court is likely to abide by the general rule of recognition, especially if the particular circumstances fit within the migratory, transient, or extraterritorial categories described above. While the Court may be least sympathetic in the context of an evasive marriage, there may be little basis under Maryland law for distinguishing that category from the others. Whether the Court will in fact recognize such an out-of-state marriage may also be affected by the facts and circumstances of the particular case before it, the particular incident of marriage at stake, and whether the particular issue is governed by or linked to federal law.

Douglas F. Gansler   Robert N. McDonald

Attorney General   Chief Counsel, Opinions and Advice

[Eventually, the Maryland Court of Appeals settled the question that the Attorney General addressed in 2010.]

PORT V. COWAN

Court of Appeals of Maryland, 2012
44 A.3d 970, 426 Md. 435

HARRELL, J.

Port and Cowan were wed in a civil ceremony in California on 10 October 2008. At that time, California recognized domestic same-sex marriage. That the parties' marriage was formed validly in California is neither contested nor at issue on this record.

Approximately eight months after marrying, the parties agreed to separate on or about 24 June 2009. After the requisite period of separation, Port filed in the Circuit Court for Prince George's County on 12 July 2010 a complaint for an absolute divorce. Cowan filed timely a "no contest" answer to Port's divorce complaint.

Port and Cowan present in their respective appeals the same, single question for our consideration: "Must the Circuit Court grant a divorce to two people of the same sex who were validly married in another jurisdiction and who otherwise meet the criteria for divorce under Maryland law?"

Because we resolve this appeal on the non-constitutional ground of comity, we shall not reach the parties' equal protection and due process arguments. * * *

A. The Doctrine of Comity

Under the doctrine of comity, long applied in our State, Maryland courts "will give effect to laws and judicial decisions of another state or jurisdiction, not as a matter of obligation but out of deference and respect." When considering a foreign marriage specifically, Maryland courts follow the choice-of-law rule of *lex loci celebrationis,* applying the substantive law of the place where the contract of marriage was formed.

Generally, Maryland courts will honor foreign marriages as long as the marriage was valid in the state where performed. There are two exceptions to this rule: the foreign marriage may not be "repugnant" to Maryland public policy and may not be prohibited expressly by the General Assembly.

Maryland recognizes liberally foreign marriages, even those marriages that may be prohibited from being formed if conducted in this State. * * *

B. *Applying* Lex Loci Celebrationis *to the Parties' Valid Foreign Same-Sex Marriage*

* * * The parties' California same-sex marriage is valid. Therefore, in order for their marriage to be valid for purposes of whether Maryland will adjudicate its dissolution, it must not run afoul of either exception to *lex loci celebrationis*: that is, it cannot be prohibited by statute or "repugnant" to the public policies of Maryland. For the following reasons, Port's and Cowan's entitlement, on this record, to a Maryland divorce from their California same-sex marriage is not prohibited, as a matter of law and on this record, by these exceptions.

Regarding the statutory prohibition exception, Family Law Article § 2–201 does not forbid expressly valid-where-formed foreign same-sex marriages. The plain wording of § 2–201 provides that "[o]nly a marriage between a man and a woman is valid in this State." It does not preclude from recognition same-sex marriages solemnized validly in another jurisdiction, only those sought-to-be, or actually, performed in Maryland. To preclude the former from being valid, the statute in question must express a clear mandate voiding such marriages and abrogating the common law.

Other states intending to prevent recognition of valid foreign same-sex marriages have done so expressly and clearly, rather than by implication, subtlety, or indirection.

On at least eight occasions, the Maryland General Assembly failed to amend § 2–201 to preclude valid out-of-state same-sex marriages from being recognized in Maryland.

This pattern permits an inference, which we take, that the General Assembly intended the doctrine of comity regarding foreign same-sex marriages to remain the proper analysis to employ here.

We conclude also that the parties' same-sex marriage is not "repugnant" to Maryland "public policy," as that term is understood properly in applying the doctrine of comity in modern times.

With regard to the second exception to *lex loci celebrationis*, recognizing valid foreign same-sex marriages is consistent actually with Maryland public policy. Prior to the Attorney General's opinion surmising that this Court would recognize foreign same-sex marriages (valid where entered), the General Assembly enacted several laws that protect and support same-sex couples, as alluded to earlier in this opinion. An array of statutes prohibit public or private discrimination based on sexual orientation in the areas of employment, public accommodations, leasing commercial property, and housing. Maryland's domestic partner statute extends to same-sex couples, who qualify as domestic partners, certain medical and decision-making rights as regards one another.

* * * A valid out-of-state same-sex marriage should be treated by Maryland courts as worthy of divorce, according to the applicable statutes, reported cases, and court rules of this State.

[Months after the *Port* decision, Maryland voters approved marriage equality at the ballot box. Now, same-sex couples can marry in Maryland.]

The *Port* court applied principles of comity to recognize the same-sex couple's marriage such that the couple could divorce. Now consider the contrasting approach of the Texas Court of Appeals, which refused to recognize a same-sex couple's marriage for purposes of administering the couple's divorce.

IN RE MARRIAGE OF J.B. AND H.B.
Court of Appeals of Texas, 2010
326 S.W.3d 654

FITZGERALD, J.

Does a Texas district court have subject-matter jurisdiction over a divorce case arising from a same-sex marriage that occurred in Massachusetts? . . . We hold that Texas district courts do not have subject-matter jurisdiction to hear a same-sex divorce case. Texas's laws compelling this result do not violate the Equal Protection Clause of the Fourteenth Amendment.

BACKGROUND

Appellee filed a petition for divorce in Dallas County in which he sought a divorce from H.B., whom appellee alleged to be his husband. Appellee alleged that he and H.B. were lawfully married in Massachusetts in September 2006 and moved to Texas in 2008. Appellee further alleged that he and H.B. "ceased to live together as husband and husband" in November 2008. . . .

A few days after appellee filed suit, the State intervened in the action "as a party respondent to oppose the Petition for Divorce and defend the constitutionality of Texas and federal law." The Texas laws in question are article I, section 32(a) of the Texas Constitution and section 6.204 of the Texas Family Code. The federal law in question is the Defense of Marriage Act (DOMA), 28 U.S.C. § 1738C. The State alleged that appellee is not a party to a "marriage" under Texas law, that he is therefore not eligible for the remedy of divorce, and that the trial court cannot grant a divorce without violating Texas law. At the end of its petition in intervention, the State prayed for dismissal of the petition for divorce. * * *

Texas Courts Lack Subject-Matter Jurisdiction Over Same-Sex Divorce Cases

The Texas Constitution and Texas Family Code

The Texas Constitution was amended in 2005 to provide as follows:

(a) Marriage in this state shall consist only of the union of one man and one woman.

(b) This state or a political subdivision of this state may not create or recognize any legal status identical or similar to marriage.

TEX. CONST. art. I, § 32.

. . . In 2003, the legislature declared that same-sex marriages are void by adopting section 6.204, which provides in pertinent part as follows:

(b) A marriage between persons of the same sex or a civil union is contrary to the public policy of this state and is void in this state.

(c) The state or an agency or political subdivision of the state may not give effect to a:

(1) public act, record, or judicial proceeding that creates, recognizes, or validates a marriage between persons of the same sex or a civil union in this state or in any other jurisdiction; or

(2) right or claim to any legal protection, benefit, or responsibility asserted as a result of a marriage between persons of the same sex or a civil union in this state or in any other jurisdiction.

Id. § 6.204(b)–(c) (Vernon 2006). * * *

Application of Texas Law

Section 6.204(b) declares same-sex marriages void and against Texas public policy. Thus, section 6.204(b) means that same-sex marriages have no legal effect in Texas.

Next, section 6.204(c)(1) provides that Texas and its agencies and subdivisions may not give any effect to any public act, record, or judicial proceeding that creates, recognizes, or validates a same-sex marriage "in this state or in any other jurisdiction." Thus, section 6.204(c)(1) amplifies section 6.204(b) by providing explicitly that the rule of voidness applies even to same-sex marriages that have been recognized by another jurisdiction. Further, section 6.204(c)(1) mandates that Texas courts may not give any legal effect whatsoever to a public act, record, or judicial proceeding that validates a same-sex marriage. . . .

Section 6.204(c)(2) forbids the state and its subdivisions from giving any effect to a "right or claim to any legal protection, benefit, or responsibility asserted as a result of a" same-sex marriage. Thus, the State may not give any legal effect even to a claim to a protection or benefit predicated on a same-sex marriage. A petition for divorce is a claim—that is, "a demand of a right or supposed right,"—to legal protections, benefits, or responsibilities "asserted as a result of a marriage," TEX. FAM.CODE ANN. § 6.204(c)(2), one example of such a benefit being community-property rights. Under section 6.204(c)(2), the State cannot give any effect to such a petition when it is predicated on a same-sex marriage. If a trial court were to exercise subject-matter jurisdiction over a same-sex divorce petition, even if only to deny the petition, it would give that petition some legal effect in violation of section 6.204(c)(2). In order to comply with this statutory provision and accord appellee's same-sex divorce petition no legal effect at all, the trial court must not address the merits. In other words, the court must dismiss for lack of subject-matter jurisdiction.

Thus, in the instant case, section 6.204(c) precludes a trial court from giving any legal effect to appellee's petition for divorce and all supporting documentation, and it deprives the trial court of subject-matter jurisdiction. * * *

Comity

Appellee argues that the trial court possesses subject-matter jurisdiction based on principles of comity because he was legally married in Massachusetts. Appellee further contends that Texas courts have long employed the comity-based "place-of-celebration rule" to determine whether a foreign marriage is valid for purposes of hearing a divorce, and that we should continue to apply that rule. * * *

Texas has repudiated the place-of-celebration rule with respect to same-sex unions on public-policy grounds. . . . Any common-law principle recognizing same-sex marriages performed in other jurisdictions must yield to the constitution. Moreover, the legislature has declared that same-sex marriages are contrary to Texas public policy. . . . Accordingly, we conclude that neither comity nor the place-of-celebration rule overcome the jurisdictional bar of section 6.204(c)(2). . . .

Conclusion

We hold that Texas courts lack subject-matter jurisdiction to entertain a suit for divorce that is brought by a party to a same-sex marriage, even if the marriage was entered in another state that recognizes the validity of same-sex marriages. We must therefore proceed to consider whether the Texas laws compelling this result offend the Constitution.

TEXAS LAW DOES NOT VIOLATE THE EQUAL PROTECTION CLAUSE OF THE FOURTEENTH AMENDMENT

The question presented is whether Texas law proscribing the adjudication of a petition for divorce by a party to a same-sex marriage violates the Equal Protection Clause of the Fourteenth Amendment.

* * * Because Texas's laws stripping the courts of jurisdiction to adjudicate claims for same-sex divorce do not discriminate against a suspect class or burden a fundamental right, we evaluate the law under the rational-basis test.

* * * The state has a legitimate interest in promoting the raising of children in the optimal familial setting. It is reasonable for the state to conclude that the optimal familial setting for the raising of children is the household headed by an opposite-sex couple. . . . Because only relationships between opposite-sex couples can naturally produce children, it is reasonable for the state to afford unique legal recognition to that particular social unit in the form of opposite-sex marriage. * * *

Conclusion

. . . Texas's laws providing that its courts have no subject-matter jurisdiction to adjudicate a petition for divorce by a party to a same-sex marriage do not violate the Equal Protection Clause of the Fourteenth Amendment, a provision never before construed as a charter for restructuring the traditional institution of marriage by judicial legislation.

While the Maryland court in *Port* had found that it need not decide the constitutional issues, the Texas court reached those issues. Now consider the contrasting constitutional view of the federal district court in Ohio. Unlike the Maryland and Texas cases, the following case was decided after *Windsor*.

OBERGEFELL v. KASICH

United States District Court, Southern District of Ohio, 2013
2013 WL 3814262

This is not a complicated case. The issue is whether the State of Ohio can discriminate against same sex marriages lawfully solemnized out of state, when Ohio law has historically and unambiguously provided that the validity of a marriage is determined by whether it complies with the law of the jurisdiction where it was celebrated.

Throughout Ohio's history, Ohio law has been clear: a marriage solemnized outside of Ohio is valid in Ohio if it is valid where solemnized.

Thus, for example, under Ohio law, out-of-state marriages between first cousins are recognized by Ohio, even though Ohio law does not authorize marriages between first cousins. Likewise, under Ohio law, out of state marriages of minors are recognized by Ohio, even though Ohio law does not authorize marriages of minors.

How then can Ohio, especially given the historical status of Ohio law, single out same sex marriages as ones it will not recognize? The short answer is that Ohio cannot . . . at least not under the circumstances here.

By treating lawful same sex marriages differently than it treats lawful opposite sex marriages (*e.g.,* marriages of first cousins and marriages of minors), Ohio law, as applied to these Plaintiffs, likely violates the United States Constitution which guarantees that "No State shall make or enforce any law which shall . . . deny to any person within its jurisdiction equal protection of the laws."

The end result here and now is that the local Ohio Registrar of death certificates is hereby **ORDERED** not to accept for recording a death certificate for John Arthur that does not record Mr. Arthur's status at death as "married" and James Obergefell as his "surviving spouse."

AGREED FACTS AND CIRCUMSTANCES

Less than a month ago, on June 26, 2013, the United States Supreme Court issued its historic decision in [*Windsor*]. The Supreme Court held that the federal Defense of Marriage Act ("DOMA"), which denied recognition to same-sex marriages for purposes of federal law, was unconstitutional, as it denied fundamental fairness and equal protection of the law to gay citizens. While the holding in *Windsor* is ostensibly limited to a finding that the federal government cannot refuse to recognize state laws authorizing same sex marriage, the issue whether States can refuse to recognize out-of-state same sex marriages is now surely headed to the fore. Indeed, just as Justice Scalia predicted in his animated dissent, by virtue of the present lawsuit, "the state-law shoe" has now dropped in Ohio.

Plaintiffs James Obergefell and John Arthur are male Cincinnati residents who have been living together in a committed and intimate relationship for more than twenty years, and they were very recently legally married in the state of Maryland pursuant to the laws of Maryland recognizing same sex marriage.

Mr. Arthur is currently a hospice patient. He is dying of amyotrophic lateral sclerosis ("ALS"). ALS is a progressive disease that has caused Mr. Arthur severe and worsening muscle deterioration, has no known cure, and is fatal.

On July 11, 2013, Plaintiffs traveled to Maryland in a special jet equipped with medical equipment and a medical staff necessary to serve

Mr. Arthur's needs, whereupon Plaintiffs were married in the jet as it sat on the tarmac in Anne Arundel County, Maryland. They returned to Cincinnati that same day.

Plaintiffs' marriage is legally recognized in Maryland and by the federal government by virtue of the very recent and historic decision of the United States Supreme Court in [*Windsor*]. Plaintiffs' marriage is not recognized in Ohio, as legal recognition of same-sex marriages is prohibited by Ohio law enacted in 2004.

Mr. Arthur is certain to die soon. Consistent with Ohio law, his death record will list his "marital status at time of death" as "unmarried" and will not record Mr. Obergefell as the "surviving spouse." * * *

ANALYSIS

* * * Plaintiffs, a same-sex couple, are legally married in Maryland. They reside in Ohio where their marriage is not recognized as valid. They are treated differently than they would be if they were in a comparable opposite-sex marriage. By treating lawful same sex marriages differently than it treats lawful opposite sex marriages (*e.g.,* marriages of first cousins and marriages of minors), Plaintiffs assert that the Ohio laws barring recognition of out-of-state same sex marriages, enacted in 2004, violate equal protection.

Although the law has long recognized that marriage and domestic relations are matters generally left to the states, the restrictions imposed on marriage by states, however, must nonetheless comply with the Constitution. *Loving v. Virginia*, 388 U.S. 1, 12 (1967); *Zablocki v. Redhail*, 434 U.S. 374, 383 (1978).

In *Windsor,* the Supreme Court again applied the principle of equal protection to a statute restricting marriage when it reviewed the constitutionality of the federal Defense of Marriage Act ("DOMA"), which denied recognition to same-sex marriages for purposes of federal law. This included marriages from the twelve states and District of Columbia in which same-sex couples could legally marry. The Supreme Court held that the federal law was unconstitutional because it violated equal protection and due process principles guaranteed by the Fifth Amendment.

In reality, the decision of the United States Supreme Court in *Windsor* was not unprecedented as the Supreme Court relied upon its equal protection analysis from an earlier case, where, in 1996, the Court held that an amendment to a state constitution, ostensibly just prohibiting any special protections for gay people, in truth violated the Equal Protection Clause, under even a rational basis analysis. *Romer v. Evans*, 517 U.S. 620 (1996).

* * * Under Supreme Court jurisprudence, states are free to determine conditions for valid marriages, but these restrictions must be supported by legitimate state purposes because they infringe on important liberty interests around marriage and intimate relations.

In derogation of law, the Ohio scheme has unjustifiably created two tiers of couples: (1) opposite-sex married couples legally married in other states; and (2) same-sex married couples legally married in other states. This lack of equal protection of law is fatal.

As a threshold matter, it is absolutely clear that under Ohio law, from the founding of the State through at least 2004, the validity of an opposite-sex marriage is to be determined by whether it complies with the law of the jurisdiction where it was celebrated. That is, a marriage solemnized outside of Ohio is valid in Ohio if it is valid where solemnized. * * *

Quintessentially, Plaintiffs have established a substantial likelihood that they will prevail at trial on their claim that by treating lawful same sex marriages differently than it treats lawful opposite sex marriages (*e.g.,* marriages of first cousins and marriages of minors), Ohio law, as applied here, violates the United States Constitution which guarantees that "No State shall make or enforce any law which shall . . . deny to any person within its jurisdiction equal protection of the laws."

Moreover, as the United States Supreme Court found in *Windsor,* there is no legitimate state purpose served by refusing to recognize same-sex marriages celebrated in states where they are legal. Instead, as in *Windsor,* and at least on this early record here, the very purpose of the Ohio provisions, enacted in 2004, is to "impose a disadvantage, a separate status, and so a stigma upon all who enter into same-sex marriages made lawful by the unquestioned authority of the States." The purpose served by treating same-sex married couples differently than opposite-sex married couples is the same improper purpose that failed in *Windsor* and in *Romer:* "to impose inequality" and to make gay citizens unequal under the law. It is beyond cavil that it is constitutionally prohibited to single out and disadvantage an unpopular group.

* * * Even if the classification of same-sex couples legally married in other states is reviewed under the least demanding rational basis test, this Court on this record cannot find a rational basis for the Ohio provisions discriminating against lawful, out-of-state same sex marriages that is not related to the impermissible expression of disapproval of same-sex married couples.

Consequently, Plaintiffs have demonstrated a strong likelihood of success on the merits.

NOTES

1.   John Arthur died on October 22, 2013. On December 23, 2013, the *Obergefell* court issued a permanent injunction and quoted at length from its earlier opinion. *See Obergefell v. Wymyslo*, ___ F. Supp. 2d ___, 2013 WL 7869139 (S.D. Ohio Dec. 23, 2013). In a significant move, the court also held that while Ohio's lack of recognition could not survive mere rational basis review, sexual orientation classifications merited heightened scrutiny for federal equal protection purposes. *See id.* at *18.

2.   What are the differences between the comity and equal protection approaches? Why does the *Port* court take the first approach while the *Obergefell* court takes the second? How do the background state-law regimes governing same-sex marriage influence the choice between the comity and equal protection approaches?

3.   How does the Supreme Court's intervention in *Windsor* explain the outcome in *Obergefell*? Do you think the Texas Court of Appeals that decided *Marriage of J.B. and H.B.* would reach a different result now that *Windsor* has been decided? After *Windsor*, what is the difference between a challenge to a state's refusal to recognize a same-sex marriage from another state and a challenge to a state's refusal to allow same-sex couples to marry in the state?[13]

4.   Were the marriages in *Port, Marriage of J.B. and H.B.*, and *Obergefell* migratory? evasive? Can you tell? How does that matter? How should it matter?

5.   When a same-sex couple moves to a state that refuses to recognize their marriage, what problems might they face? How should they dissolve their relationship if they choose to do so? Can they plan for the possibility for a state's refusal to recognize their marriage? If so, how?

6.   There is a large body of scholarly work on the recognition question. *See, e.g.*, Barbara J. Cox, *Same-Sex Marriage and Choice-of-Law: If We Marry in Hawaii, Are We Still Married When We Return Home?*, 1994 WIS. L. REV. 1033; Herma Hill Kay, *Same-Sex Marriage in the Conflict of Laws: A Critique of the Proposed "Defense of Marriage Act,"* in THE CIVIL LAW IN THE 21ST CENTURY 902 (1997); Andrew Koppelman, *Interstate Recognition of Same-Sex Marriages and Civil Unions: A Handbook for Judges*, 153 U. PA. L. REV. 2143 (2005); Gillian E. Metzger, *Congress, Article IV, and Interstate Relations*, 120 HARV. L. REV. 1468 (2007); Andrew Koppelman, *Same-Sex Marriage, Choice of Law, and Public Policy*, 76 TEX. L. REV. 921 (1998); Larry Kramer, *Same-Sex Marriage, Conflict of Laws, and the Unconstitutional Public Policy Exception*, 106 YALE L.J. 1965 (1997); Gary J. Simson, *Beyond Interstate Recognition in the Same-Sex Marriage Debate*, 40 U.C. DAVIS L. REV. 313

---

[13] *See Bourke v. Beshear*, ___ F. Supp. 2d ___, 2014 WL 556729, at *10 (W.D. Ky. Feb. 12, 2014) (after holding unconstitutional Kentucky's lack of recognition of same-sex couples' valid marriages, the court explained that while it "was not presented with the particular question whether Kentucky's ban on same-sex marriage is constitutional . . . , there is no doubt that *Windsor* and this Court's analysis suggest a possible result to that question").

(2006); Mark Strasser, *For Whom the Bell Tolls: On Subsequent Domiciles' Refusing to Recognize Same-Sex Marriages*, 66 U. CINN. L. REV. 339 (1998); Tobias Barrington Wolff, *Interest Analysis in Interjurisdictional Marriage Disputes*, 153 U. PA. L. REV. 2215 (2005); John Yarwood, *Breaking Up is Hard to Do: Mini-DOMA States, Migratory Same-Sex Marriage, Divorce, and a Practical Solution to Property* Division, 89 B.U.L. REV. 1355 (2009); Symposium, *The Interstate Effects of Legalizing Same-Sex Marriage*, 16 QUINNIPIAC L. REV. 1 (1996); Note, *In Sickness and in Health, in Hawaii and Where Else?: Conflict of Laws and Recognition of Same-Sex Marriages*, 109 HARV. L. REV. 2038 (1996). Professor Kramer's article is particularly important because, as a leading scholar in the field, he challenges the constitutionality of the existing approach to Full Faith and Credit Clause jurisprudence, which permits the courts of one state to reject the policies of another state that violate their own forum's public policy. Kramer also contends that the Defense of Marriage Act exceeds Congress's Article IV authority.

F. RELIGIOUS OBJECTIONS AND SAME-SEX MARRIAGE

In the past few years, many states have passed marriage equality legislatively. Often this legislative process features debate over whether and to what extent the marriage law should include religious exemptions. This debate raises questions about who should be covered—religious and religiously-affiliated organizations? secular businesses? individuals? government employees?—and what activity should be exempted—goods and services related to the wedding? goods and services sought by the couple after the wedding? spousal benefits in employment? housing for the couple? More broadly, this debate raises the question of whether the marriage law is the proper vehicle through which to accommodate religious objectors. Instead, might the appropriate target be the state's antidiscrimination law?

In thinking about these issues, consider the following letter that a group of religious liberty scholars sent to the Illinois Governor upon that state's consideration of a marriage equality bill.[*] They proposed a series of religious exemptions as part of a "marriage conscience protection" to be included in the marriage law. This group also proposed the "marriage conscience protection" to lawmakers in other states.

The Honorable Pat Quinn, Governor of Illinois
207 State Capitol Bldg.

---

[*] Letter from Robin Fretwell Wilson, Chair of 1958 Law Alumni Professor of Law, Washington & Lee University School of Law, Thomas C. Berg, James Oberstar Professor of Law & Public Policy, University of St. Thomas School of Law (Minnesota), Carl H. Esbeck, Professor of Law, University of Missouri, Richard W. Garnett, Professor of Law, University of Notre Dame Law School, & Edward McGlynn Gaffney, Jr., Professor of Law, Valparaiso University School of Law, to Gov. Pat Quinn, Illinois (Dec. 18, 2012).

Springfield, IL 62706

Re: Religious Liberty Implications of Legalizing Same-Sex Marriage

Dear Governor Quinn:

We write to urge the Illinois General Assembly to ensure that any bill legalizing same-sex marriage does not infringe the religious liberty of organizations and individuals who, for religious reasons, conscientiously object to facilitating same-sex marriages. . . .

This letter analyzes the potential effects of same-sex marriage on religious conscience in Illinois and proposes a solution to address the conflicts: a specific religious liberty protection that should be an integral part of any proposed legislation. This proposal clarifies that individuals and organizations may refuse to provide services for a wedding if doing so would violate deeply held beliefs, while ensuring that the refusal creates no substantial hardship for the couple seeking the service. We write not to support or oppose same-sex marriage in Illinois. Rather, our aim is to define a "middle way" to address the needs of same-sex couples while honoring and respecting religious liberty.

As this letter details, the conflicts between same-sex marriage and religious conscience will be both certain and considerable if adequate protections are not provided. Without adequate safeguards, many religious individuals will be forced to engage in conduct that violates their deepest religious beliefs, and religious organizations will be constrained in crucial aspects of their religious exercise. * * *

Proposed Religious Conscience Protection

The many potential conflicts between same-sex marriage and religious liberty are avoidable. But they are avoidable only if the Illinois General Assembly takes the time and effort to craft the "robust religious-conscience exceptions" to same-sex marriage that leading voices on both sides of the public debate over same-sex marriage call for. The juncture for balancing religious liberty and legal recognition of same-sex unions is now.

Any proposed marriage bill can provide reasonable, carefully tailored protections for religious conscience by including a simple "marriage conscience protection" modeled, in part, on existing conscience protections in Illinois' nondiscrimination laws, which provide religious protections in the strongest of terms. The "marriage conscience protection" would provide as follows:

Section ___

(a) Religious organizations protected.

No religious or denominational organization, no organization operated for charitable or educational purposes which is supervised or controlled by or in connection with a religious organization, and no individual employed by any of the foregoing organizations, while acting in the scope of that employment, shall be required to

(1) provide services, accommodations, advantages, facilities, goods, or privileges for a purpose related to the solemnization or celebration of any marriage; or

(2) solemnize any marriage; or

(3) treat as valid any marriage

if such providing, solemnizing, or treating as valid would cause such organizations or individuals to violate their sincerely held religious beliefs.

(b) Individuals and small businesses protected.

(1) Except as provided in paragraph (b)(2), no individual, sole proprietor, or small business shall be required to

(A) provide goods or services that assist or promote the solemnization or celebration of any marriage, or provide counseling or other services that directly facilitate the perpetuation of any marriage; or

(B) provide benefits to any spouse of an employee; or

(C) provide housing to any married couple

if providing such goods, services, benefits, or housing would cause such individuals or sole proprietors, or owners of such small businesses, to violate their sincerely held religious beliefs.

(2) Paragraph (b)(1) shall not apply if

(A) a party to the marriage is unable to obtain any similar good[s] or services, employment benefits, or housing elsewhere without substantial hardship; or

(B) in the case of an individual who is a government employee or official, if another government employee or official is not promptly available and willing to provide the requested government service without inconvenience or delay; provided that no judicial officer authorized to solemnize marriages shall be required to solemnize any marriage if to do so would violate the judicial officer's sincerely held religious beliefs.

(3) A "small business" within the meaning of paragraph (b)(1) is a legal entity other than a natural person

(A) that provides services which are primarily performed by an owner of the business; or

(B) that has five or fewer employees; or

(C) in the case of a legal entity that offers housing for rent, that owns five or fewer units of housing.

(c) No civil cause of action or other penalties.

No refusal to provide services, accommodations, advantages, facilities, goods, or privileges protected by this section shall

(1) result in a civil claim or cause of action challenging such refusal; or

(2) result in any action by the State or any of its subdivisions to penalize or withhold benefits from any protected entity or individual, under any laws of this State or its subdivisions, including but not limited to laws regarding employment discrimination, housing, public accommodations, educational institutions, licensing, government contracts or grants, or tax-exempt status.

* * *

CONFLICTS BETWEEN SAME-SEX MARRIAGE AND RELIGIOUS LIBERTY

The conflicts between religious conscience and same-sex marriage generally take one of two forms. First, if same-sex marriage is legalized without appropriate statutory accommodations, religious organizations and individuals that object to same-sex marriage will face new lawsuits under the state nondiscrimination act and other similar laws. So will many small businesses, which are owned by individual conscientious objectors. Likely lawsuits include claims where:

- Individuals of conscience, who run a small business, such as wedding photographers, florists, banquet halls, or making wedding cakes in one's home, can be sued under public accommodations laws for refusing to offer their services in connection with a same-sex marriage ceremony.

- Religious summer camps, day care centers, retreat centers, counseling centers, meeting halls, or adoption agencies can be sued under public accommodations laws for refusing to offer their facilities or services to members of a same-sex marriage.

- A church or other religious nonprofit that dismisses an employee, such as an organist or secretary, for entering into a same-sex marriage can be sued under employment discrimination laws that prohibit discrimination on the basis of marital status.

The second form of conflict involving religious organizations and individuals (or the small businesses that they own) that conscientiously object to same-sex marriage is that they will be labeled unlawful "discriminators" under state or municipal laws and thus face a range of penalties at the hand of state agencies and local governments, such as the withdrawal of government contracts or exclusion from government facilities. * * *

All of these conflicts either did not exist before, or will significantly intensify after, the legalization of same-sex marriage. Thus, legalizing same-sex marriage without adequate protections for religious liberty will have at least two unintended consequences: It will harm religious organizations and individuals of conscience, and it will spawn costly, unnecessary conflicts, many of which will lead to litigation. * * *

Respectfully yours,

Robin Fretwell Wilson
Class of 1958 Law Alumni
Professor of Law
Washington and Lee University
School of Law

Thomas C. Berg
James Oberstar Professor of Law
& Public Policy
University of St. Thomas School of
Law (Minnesota)

Carl H. Esbeck
Professor of Law
University of Missouri School of
Law

Richard W. Garnett
Professor of Law
University of Notre Dame Law
School

Edward McGlynn Gaffney, Jr.
Professor of Law
Valparaiso University School of
Law

The scholars writing to Governor Quinn urged lawmakers to include religious exemptions in the marriage legislation, and their proposed exemptions covered a broad range of both actors and activity. Consider the following response, which raises objections to the breadth of the "marriage conscience protection" and explores its relationship to existing antidiscrimination law.

MARRIAGE INEQUALITY: SAME-SEX RELATIONSHIPS, RELIGIOUS EXEMPTIONS, AND THE PRODUCTION OF SEXUAL ORIENTATION DISCRIMINATION*

Douglas NeJaime

The focus on religious exemptions in the marriage context fails to reflect where issues actually arise—and will continue to arise—on the ground. Clashes between sexual orientation equality and religious freedom prominently feature same-sex *relationships*, rather than same-sex *marriages*. Religious objections are based largely on the public, relational component of sexual orientation—the fact that lesbians and gay men enact their sexual orientation through same-sex relationships. * * *

While the focus on marriage obscures the centrality of same-sex relationships, the "marriage conscience protection," which purports to accommodate religious objections to same-sex marriage specifically, would in practice burden lesbians and gay men based on their relationships more generally. Through provisions authorizing religious objectors to refuse to "treat as valid" any same-sex marriage and extending religious exemptions to secular, commercial actors, the "protection" would reach far outside the marriage context and permit discrimination against same-sex couples throughout the life of their (marital) relationships. * * *

SAME-SEX RELATIONSHIPS AND LESBIAN AND GAY IDENTITY

Uncovering Same-Sex Relationships

* * * To make their case for religious exemptions in marriage equality legislation, scholars typically deploy two high-profile lawsuits that pit gay rights against religious freedom. Neither case, however, implicates marriage for same-sex couples. Instead, both highlight the public, relationship-based feature of sexual orientation discrimination and the importance of existing antidiscrimination law, thereby demonstrating commentators' misplaced emphasis on marriage. The first comes from New Mexico, a state with a sexual orientation nondiscrimination law but no relationship recognition regime for same-sex couples. The second emerges from New Jersey, a state with a civil union regime (but no marriage recognition) and an antidiscrimination law that includes both sexual orientation and civil union status.[14]

In *Willock v. Elane Photography*, a photographer, based on her religious beliefs, refused to photograph a same-sex couple's commitment

---

* Douglas NeJaime, *Marriage Inequality: Same-Sex Relationships, Religious Exemptions, and the Production of Sexual Orientation Discrimination*, 100 CALIF. L. REV. 1169, 1175–77, 1195–96, 1200–04, 1225–26, 1230–33, 1236 (2012). © 2012 by the California Law Review, Inc. Reprinted by permission of the California Law Review.

14 *Editor's Note*: Since publication of this article, both New Mexico and New Jersey opened marriage to same-sex couples.

ceremony. The couple sued under New Mexico's public accommodations antidiscrimination law. The state Human Rights Commission found in their favor, and the state courts affirmed that ruling.[15] Religious liberty scholars frequently appeal to this case in arguing for religious exemptions in legislation recognizing marriage for same-sex couples. . . . [But] [i]t makes little sense, as a matter of law, to think that the New Mexico case illustrates a problem that [a state] would newly confront if it allowed same-sex couples to marry; New Mexico [did] not offer any relationship recognition to same-sex couples, let alone marriage. It was the existence of the antidiscrimination law—not the nature of the commitment ceremony—that allowed the case to go forward in New Mexico.

In *Bernstein v. Ocean Grove Camp Meeting Association*, the New Jersey Department of Law and Public Safety Division on Civil Rights found probable cause to credit the allegations of a complaint that a nonprofit ministry organization unlawfully refused to permit a civil union ceremony on a beachfront boardwalk pavilion open to all others for various events and ceremonies. The Ocean Grove Camp Meeting Association is a Methodist organization whose mission is "to provide opportunities for spiritual birth, growth and renewal through worship, education, cultural and recreational programs for persons of all ages in a Christian seaside setting." The Association consistently rented its facility for Christian, non-Christian, and secular weddings, as well as for a host of other secular events, including fundraisers, musical performances, and meetings. Since the pavilion was open for public use, based on both actual practice and the earlier representations of the Association itself, the Division on Civil Rights found that the facility was a public accommodation, and that under the state's antidiscrimination regime, the Association could not therefore discriminate between different-sex wedding ceremonies and same-sex civil union ceremonies. An Administrative Law Judge ultimately agreed with the Division on Civil Rights.[16] Again, scholars and advocates consistently point to this case in calling for religious accommodations in marriage equality legislation.

These on-the-ground examples, however, do not demonstrate the unique threat of marriage equality. Instead, they undermine the exceptional treatment of marriage and point to the public, relational enactment of sexual orientation identity actually at stake—and to the importance of handling conflicts between same-sex couples and religious objectors in the domain of antidiscrimination law. Both *Willock* and *Bernstein* involved nonmarital same- sex relationships. In both cases, objections arose in response to the same-sex relationship, regardless of

---

[15] *See Elane Photography, LLC v. Willock*, 309 P.3d 53 (N.M. 2013).

[16] *See Bernstein v. Ocean Grove Camp Meeting Ass'n*, No. CRT 6145–09 (Off. of Admin. Law decision issued January 12, 2012), available at http://www.adfmedia.org/files/OGCMA-Bernstein Ruling.pdf.

marriage. And, in both cases, the courts applied existing antidiscrimination protections. * * *

THE PERVERSE EFFECTS OF MARRIAGE LAWS ON ANTIDISCRIMINATION

The Refusal to "Treat as Valid" and Extension to Secular Actors

. . . As its title suggests, the "marriage conscience protection" purports to be marriage specific. Yet the proposed provision would permit discrimination against same-sex relationships in situations far removed from marriage, sweeping within its reach (marital) same-sex relationships throughout the entire course of those relationships. By covering the relationships of lesbians and gay men so comprehensively, the "marriage conscience protection" would target the enactment of sexual orientation identity in ways that sexual orientation antidiscrimination law otherwise would not tolerate.

While there are several problems with the "marriage conscience" proposal, one particularly problematic component—legal shielding of "refusing to treat as valid any marriage"—illustrates its troubling breadth. With this language, the provision reaches into key areas addressed by antidiscrimination law and leaves same-sex couples vulnerable to discrimination based on their sexual orientation identity. The proposed religious accommodations threaten to subject same-sex couples to discrimination in employment, public accommodations, and housing for the duration of the marriage and in situations far removed from the marriage celebration.

A religious employer allowed to refuse to "treat as valid" a same-sex couple's marriage could refuse to provide healthcare benefits to the spouses of lesbian and gay employees, regardless of whether the employees' positions directly relate to the employer's religious mission, while providing such benefits to the spouses of heterosexual employees. Under the "marriage conscience protection," the married same-sex couple would be deprived of [spousal] healthcare benefits throughout the course of their relationship without legal recourse. This sexual orientation discrimination, which might otherwise be prohibited under state antidiscrimination law, would be justified as merely a religious distinction.

While the broad accommodations for religious organizations are troubling, the application of the religious exemption to secular actors in the stream of commerce threatens to cut back existing antidiscrimination protections in a much more sweeping fashion. Allowing such individuals and businesses to avail themselves of the "marriage conscience protection" is alarming even as it relates to marriage celebrations. It would, for instance, allow the florist, the baker, and the photographer to refuse service. But the application of this exemption across the life of the same-sex couple's marriage cuts a broad swath out of many states' antidiscrimination laws. That is, the interaction of the "treat as valid" language with the inclusion of "individuals" and "small businesses" among those entitled to accommodation renders the exemptions even more potent and pushes far beyond existing antidiscrimination exemptions.

To be clear, the scholars advancing the "marriage conscience protection" have refined their proposal over time. The more recent iteration of the "marriage conscience protection" uses "treat as valid" terminology for religious organizations, but is more specific for secular actors, allowing them to refuse to "provide goods or services . . . that directly facilitate the perpetuation of any marriage," refuse to "provide benefits to any spouse of an employee," and refuse to "provide housing to any married couple." In practice, this language would likely have the same impact as the "treat as valid" language. It simply suggests with greater specificity what the refusal to "treat as valid" may mean. Furthermore, the more recent proposal also limits exemptions in the commercial context to individuals, sole proprietors, and small businesses.

Even with these modifications and limitations, the religious exemption would allow the relationship counselor to refuse to counsel the (married) same-sex couple, the landlord to refuse to rent an apartment to the (married) same-sex couple, the bed-and-breakfast proprietor to refuse to lodge the (married) same-sex couple, and the caterer to refuse to cater the (married) same-sex couple's anniversary party. Similarly, small secular employers, who claim religious convictions authorizing opposition to same-sex marriage, could provide benefits for the spouses of heterosexual employees but refuse to provide such benefits to the legal spouses of lesbian and gay employees.

Therefore, an actor otherwise covered by antidiscrimination law could treat a same-sex couple's marital relationship differently than it treats other marital relationships. The actor could do this in the first year of the couple's marriage, and in the twenty-first year. And the actor could do so even if existing antidiscrimination laws protect on the basis of sexual orientation and thereby prohibit the discrimination at issue. In other words, the exemption would allow a covered actor to provide unequal treatment to same-sex relationships by channeling that unequal treatment through religiously grounded marriage objections and thereby avoiding existing antidiscrimination obligations. * * *

Shrouding Discrimination

* * * Worse yet, the proposal categorizes discrimination against same-sex couples as "marriage conscience protection" and thereby obscures the actual occurrence of sexual orientation discrimination. The law would condone discrimination against marital same-sex relationships

without ever labeling it sexual orientation discrimination. Businesses, for instance, could turn away married or soon-to-be-married same-sex couples by invoking religious objections to same-sex marriage. Their decisions, which would constitute sexual orientation discrimination under existing antidiscrimination law, would be framed instead as permissible, religiously motivated conduct relating to marriage. "Marriage conscience" would provide a new language with which to describe—and allow—sexual orientation discrimination against married same-sex couples.

NOTES

1.　A group of legal scholars responded to the "marriage conscience protection" proposal in Illinois by pointing to some of the objections raised in Professor NeJaime's article. *See* Letter of Dale Carpenter *et al.* (Oct. 23, 2013), *available at* http://blogs.chicagotribune.com/files/five-law-professors-against-changing-sb-10.pdf. Ultimately, legislators in Illinois provided a narrow exemption protecting religious entities in the context of the marriage celebration: "No church, mosque, synagogue, temple, nondenominational ministry [etc.] . . . is required to provide religious facilities for the solemnization ceremony or celebration associated with the solemnization ceremony of a marriage if the solemnization ceremony or celebration associated with the solemnization is in violation of its religious beliefs." ILL. H.B. 5170 (2013). The marriage law also provides that "[n]othing in this Act is intended to abrogate, limit, or expand" the state's antidiscrimination law, which includes sexual orientation. *Id.*

2.　No state has adopted the broad "marriage conscience protection" that some religious liberty scholars have proposed. Instead, most states that have codified marriage equality have included exemptions for religious and religiously-affiliated organizations, rather than secular businesses and individuals in the commercial marketplace or government employees. *See, e.g.,* N.Y. DOM. REL. LAW A8520–2011, § 10B (Consol. 2011). And these exemptions have generally focused on celebration and solemnization of the marriage, rather than more broadly on recognition. *See, e.g.,* CT. STAT. ANN. § 46b-35a (2009). In addition, lawmakers in some states have explicitly acknowledged that antidiscrimination law continues to govern conflicts between sexual orientation equality and religious objections. *See, e.g.,* MINN. STAT. § 517.201 (2013).

3.　Debates over religious exemptions have also emerged in the wake of *Windsor* as some lawmakers have pressed federal legislation, such as the Marriage and Religious Freedom Act, to allow federal employees, contractors, and grantees to refuse to serve same-sex couples.

G.　THE COMMUNITY'S DEBATE OVER MARRIAGE

There has been a different kind of debate about same-sex marriage, one less polarized and noisy than the public debate explored throughout this Chapter. The LGBT community has had its own internal debate about whether marriage is a wise or desirable priority for the movement. The debate began years before the Hawaii Supreme Court's decision in *Baehr*. The following important exchange between Thomas Stoddard and Paula Ettelbrick, two gay and lesbian rights advocates, inaugurated the debate and appeared under the heading *Gay Marriage: A Must or a Bust?* in OUT/LOOK magazine in 1989.

WHY GAY PEOPLE SHOULD SEEK THE RIGHT TO MARRY*
Thomas Stoddard

Even though, these days, few lesbians and gay men enter into marriages recognized by law, absolutely every gay person has an opinion on marriage as an "institution." (The word "institution" brings to mind, perhaps appropriately, museums.) After all, we all know quite a bit about the subject. Most of us grew up in marital households. Virtually all of us, regardless of race, creed, gender, and culture, have received lectures on the propriety, if not the sanctity, of marriage—which usually suggests that those who choose not to marry are both unhappy and unhealthy. We all have been witnesses, willing or not, to a lifelong parade of other people's marriages, from Uncle Harry and Aunt Bernice to the Prince and Princess of Wales. And at one point or another, some nosy relative has inevitably inquired of every gay person when he or she will finally "tie the knot" (an intriguing and probably apt cliché).

I must confess at the outset that I am no fan of the "institution" of marriage as currently constructed and practiced. I may simply be unlucky, but I have seen preciously few marriages over the course of my forty years that invite admiration and emulation. All too often, marriage appears to petrify rather than satisfy and enrich, even for couples in their twenties and thirties who have had a chance to learn the lessons of feminism. Almost inevitably, the partners seem to fall into a "husband" role and a "wife" role, with such latter-day modifications as the wife who works in addition to raising the children and managing the household.

Let me be blunt: in its traditional form, marriage has been oppressive, especially (although not entirely) to women. Indeed, until the middle of the last century, marriage was, at its legal and social essence, an extension of the husband and his paternal family. Under the English common law, wives were among the husband's "chattel"—personal property—and could not, among other things, hold property in their own names. The common law crime of adultery demonstrates the unequal treatment accorded to husbands and wives: while a woman who slept with a man who wasn't her husband committed adultery, a man who slept with a woman not his wife committed fornication. A man was legally

---

* Thomas Stoddard, *Why Gay People Should Seek The Right To Marry*, OUT/LOOK, Fall 1989, at 9, 9–13.

incapable of committing adultery, except as an accomplice to an errant wife. The underlying offense of adultery was not the sexual betrayal of one partner by the other, but the wife's engaging in conduct capable of tainting the husband's bloodlines. (I swear on my *Black's Law Dictionary* that I have not made this up!)

Nevertheless, despite the oppressive nature of marriage historically, and in spite of the general absence of edifying examples of modern heterosexual marriage, I believe very strongly that every lesbian and gay man should have the right to marry the same-sex partner of his or her choice, and that the gay rights movement should aggressively seek full legal recognition for same-sex marriages. To those who might not agree, I respectfully offer three explanations, one practical, one political and one philosophical.

THE PRACTICAL EXPLANATION

The legal status of marriage rewards the two individuals who travel to the altar (or its secular equivalent) with substantial economic and practical advantages. Married couples may reduce their tax liability by filing a joint return. They are entitled to special government benefits, such as those given surviving spouses and dependents through the Social Security program. They can inherit from one another even when there is no will. They are immune from subpoenas requiring testimony against the other spouse. And marriage to an American citizen gives a foreigner a right to residency in the United States.

Other advantages have arisen not by law but by custom. Most employers offer health insurance to their employees, and many will include an employee's spouse in the benefits package, usually at the employer's expense. Virtually no employer will include a partner who is not married to an employee, whether of the same sex or not. Indeed, very few insurance companies even offer the possibility of a group health plan covering "domestic partners" who are not married to one another. Two years ago, I tried to find such a policy for Lambda, and discovered that not one insurance company authorized to do business in New York—the second-largest state in the country with more than 17 million residents— would accommodate us. (Lambda has tried to make do by paying for individual insurance policies for the same-sex partners of its employees who otherwise would go uninsured but these individual policies are usually narrower in scope than group policies, often require applicants to furnish individual medical information not required under most group plans, and are typically much more expensive per person.)

In short, the law generally presumes in favor of every marital relationship, and acts to preserve and foster it, and to enhance the rights of the individuals who enter into it. It is usually possible, with enough money and the right advice, to replicate some of the benefits conferred by the legal status of marriage through the use of documents like wills and power of attorney forms, but that protection will inevitably, under current circumstances, be incomplete.

The law (as I suspect will come as no surprise to the readers of this journal) still looks upon lesbians and gay men with suspicion, and this suspicion casts a shadow over the documents they execute in recognition of a same-sex relationship. If a lesbian leaves property to her lover, her will may be invalidated on the grounds that it was executed under the "undue influence" of the would-be beneficiary. A property agreement may be denied validity because the underlying relationship is "meretricious"— akin to prostitution. (Astonishingly, until the mid-seventies, the law throughout the United States deemed "meretricious" virtually *any* formal economic arrangement between two people not married to one another, on the theory that an exchange of property between them was presumably payment for sexual services; the Supreme Court of California helped unravel this quaint legal fantasy in its 1976 ruling in the first famous "alimony" case, *Marvin v. Marvin.*) The law has progressed considerably beyond the uniformly oppressive state of affairs before 1969, but it is still far from enthusiastic about gay people and their relationships—to put it mildly.

Moreover, there are some barriers one simply cannot transcend outside of a formal marriage. When the Internal Revenue Code or the Immigration and Naturalization Act say "married," they mean "married" by definition of state statute. When the employer's group health plan says "spouse," it means "spouse" in the eyes of the law, not the eyes of the loving couple.

But there is another drawback. Couples seeking to protect their relationship through wills and other documents need knowledge, determination and—most importantly—money. No money, no lawyer. And no lawyer, no protection. Those who lack the sophistication or the wherewithal to retain a lawyer are simply stuck in most circumstances. Extending the right to marry to gay couples would assure that those at the bottom of the economic ladder have a chance to secure their relationship rights, too.

THE POLITICAL EXPLANATION

The claim that gay couples ought to be able to marry is not a new one. In the seventies, same-sex couples in three states—Minnesota, Kentucky and Washington—brought constitutional challenges to the marriage statutes, and in all three instances they failed. In each of the three, the court offered two basic justifications for limiting marriage to male-female couples: history and procreation. Witness this passage from the Supreme Court of Minnesota's 1971 opinion in *Baker v. Nelson*: "The institution of marriage as a union of man and woman, uniquely involving the procreating and rearing of children within a family, is as old as the book of Genesis. . . . This historic institution manifestly is more deeply founded than the asserted contemporary concept of marriage and societal interests for which petitioners contend."

Today no American jurisdiction recognizes the right of two women or two men to marry one another, although several nations in Northern Europe do. Even more telling, until earlier this year, there was little discussion within the gay rights movement about whether such a right should exist. As far as I can tell, no gay organization of any size, local or national, has yet declared the right to marry as one of its goals.

With all due respect to my colleagues and friends who take a different view, I believe it is time to renew the effort to overturn the existing marriage laws, and to do so in earnest, with a commitment of money and energy, through both the courts and the state legislatures. I am not naive about the likelihood of imminent victory. There is none. Nonetheless—and here I will not mince words—I would like to see the issue rise to the top of the agenda of every gay organization, including my own (although the judgment is hardly mine alone).

Why give it such prominence? Why devote resources to such a distant goal? Because marriage is, I believe, the political issue that most fully tests the dedication of people who are *not* gay to full equality for gay people, and also the issue most likely to lead ultimately to a world free from discrimination against lesbians and gay men.

Marriage is much more than a relationship sanctioned by law. It is the centerpiece of our entire social structure, the core of the traditional notion of "family." Even in its present tarnished state, the marital relationship inspires sentiments suggesting that it is something almost suprahuman. The Supreme Court, in striking down an anti-contraception statute in 1965, called marriage "noble" and "intimate to the degree of being sacred." The Roman Catholic Church and the Moral Majority would go—and have gone—considerably further.

Lesbians and gay men are now denied entry to this "noble" and "sacred" institution. The implicit message is this: two men or two women are incapable of achieving such an exalted domestic state. Gay relationships are somehow less significant, less valuable. Such relationships may, from time to time and from couple to couple, give the appearance of a marriage, but they can never be of the same quality or importance.

I resent—indeed, I loathe—that conception of same-sex relationships. And I am convinced that ultimately the only way to overturn it is to remove the barrier to marriage that now limits the freedom of every gay man and lesbian.

That is not to deny the value of "domestic partnership" ordinances, statutes that prohibit discrimination based on "marital status," and other legal advances that can enhance the rights (as well as the dignity) of gay couples. Without question, such advances move us further along the path to equality. But their value can only be partial. (The recently enacted San Francisco "domestic partnership" ordinance, for example, will have practical value only for gay people who happen to be employed by the City of San Francisco and want to include their non-marital spouses in part of the city's fringe benefit package; the vast majority of gay San Franciscans—those employed by someone other than the city—have only a symbolic victory to savor.) Measures of this kind can never assure full equality. Gay relationships will continue to be accorded a subsidiary status until the day that gay couples have *exactly* the same rights as their heterosexual counterparts. To my mind, that means either that the right to marry be extended to us, or that marriage be abolished in its present form for all gay couples, presumably to be replaced by some new legal entity—an unlikely alternative.

THE PHILOSOPHICAL EXPLANATION

I confessed at the outset that I personally found marriage in its present avatar rather, well, unattractive. Nonetheless, even from a philosophical perspective, I believe the right to marry should become a stated goal of the gay rights movement.

First, and most basically, the issue is not the desirability of marriage, but rather the desirability of the *right* to marry. That I think two lesbians or two gay men should be entitled to a marriage license does not mean that I think all gay people should find appropriate partners and exercise the right, should it eventually exist. I actually rather doubt that I, myself, would want to marry, even though I share a household with another man who is exceedingly dear to me. There are others who feel differently, for economic, symbolic, or romantic reasons. They should, to my mind, unquestionably have the opportunity to marry if they wish and otherwise meet the requirements of the state (like being old enough).

Furthermore, marriage may be unattractive and even oppressive as it is currently structured and practiced, but enlarging the concept to embrace same-sex couples would necessarily transform it into something new. If two women can marry, or two men, marriage—even for heterosexuals—need not be a union of a "husband" and a "wife." Extending the right to marry to gay people—that is, abolishing the traditional gender requirements of marriage—can be one of the means, perhaps the principal one, through which the institution divests itself of the sexist trappings of the past.

Some of my colleagues disagree with me. I welcome their thoughts and the debates and discussions our different perspectives will trigger.

The movement for equality for lesbians and gay men can only be enriched through this collective exploration of the question of marriage. But I do believe many thousands of gay people want the right to marry. And I think, too, they will earn that right for themselves sooner than most of us imagine.

SINCE WHEN IS MARRIAGE A PATH TO LIBERATION?*

Paula Ettelbrick

"Marriage is a great institution, if you like living in institutions," according to a bit of T-shirt philosophy I saw recently. Certainly, marriage is an institution. It is one of the most venerable, impenetrable institutions in modern society. Marriage provides the ultimate form of acceptance for personal intimate relationships in our society, and gives those who marry an insider status of the most powerful kind.

Steeped in a patriarchal system that looks to ownership, property, and dominance of men over women as its basis, the institution of marriage long has been the focus of radical feminist revulsion. Marriage defines certain relationships as more valid than all others. Lesbian and gay relationships, being neither legally sanctioned or commingled by blood, are always at the bottom of the heap of social acceptance and importance.

Given the imprimatur of social and personal approval which marriage provides, it is not surprising that some lesbians and gay men among us would look to legal marriage for self-affirmation. After all, those who marry can be instantaneously transformed from "outsiders" to "insiders," and we have a desperate need to become insiders.

It could make us feel OK about ourselves, perhaps even relieve some of the internalized homophobia that we all know so well. Society will then celebrate the birth of our children and mourn the death of our spouses. It would be easier to get health insurance for our spouses, family memberships to the local museum, and a right to inherit our spouse's cherished collection of lesbian mystery novels even if she failed to draft a will. Never again would she have to go to a family reunion and debate about the correct term for introducing our lover/partner/significant other to Aunt Flora. Everything would be quite easy and very nice.

So why does this unlikely event so deeply disturb me? For two major reasons. First, marriage will not liberate us as lesbians and gay men. In fact, it will constrain us, make us more invisible, force our assimilation into the mainstream, and undermine the goals of gay liberation. Second, attaining the right to marry will not transform our society from one that

---

* Paula Ettelbrick, *Since When Is Marriage a Path To Liberation?*, OUT/LOOK, Fall 1989, at 9, 14–17.

makes narrow, but dramatic, distinctions between those who are married and those who are not married to one that respects and encourages choice of relationships and family diversity. Marriage runs counter to two of the primary goals of the lesbian and gay movement: the affirmation of gay identity and culture; and the validation of many forms of relationships.

When analyzed from the standpoint of civil rights, certainly lesbians and gay men should have a right to marry. But obtaining a right does not always result in justice. White male firefighters in Birmingham, Alabama have been fighting for their "rights" to retain their jobs by overturning the city's affirmative action guidelines. If their "rights" prevail, the courts will have failed in rendering justice. The "right" fought for by the white male firefighters, as well as those who advocate strongly for the "rights" to legal marriage for gay people, will result, at best, in limited or narrowed "justice" for those closest to power at the expense of those who have been historically marginalized.

The fight for justice has as its goal the realignment of power imbalances among individuals and classes of people in society. A pure "rights" analysis often fails to incorporate a broader understanding of the underlying inequities that operate to deny justice to a fuller range of people and groups. In setting our priorities as a community, we must combine the concept of both rights and justice. At this point in time, making legal marriage for lesbian and gay couples a priority would set an agenda of gaining rights for a few, but would do nothing to correct the power imbalances between those who are married (whether gay or straight) and those who are not. Thus, justice would not be gained. Justice for gay men and lesbians will be achieved only when we are accepted and supported in this society *despite* our differences from the dominant culture and the choices we make regarding our relationships. Being queer is more than setting up house, sleeping with a person of the same gender, and seeking state approval for doing so. It is an identity, a culture with many variations. It is a way of dealing with the world by diminishing the constraints of gender roles which have for so long kept women and gay people oppressed and invisible. Being queer means pushing the parameters of sex, sexuality, and family, and in the process transforming the very fabric of society. Gay liberation is inexorably linked to women's liberation. Each is essential to the other.

The moment we argue, as some among us insist on doing, that we should be treated as equals because we are really just like married couples and hold the same values to be true, we undermine the very purpose of our movement and begin the dangerous process of silencing our different voices. As a lesbian, I am fundamentally different from non-lesbian women. That's the point. Marriage, as it exists today, is antithetical to my liberation as a lesbian and as a woman because it mainstreams my life and voice. I do not want to be known as "Mrs.

Attached-To-Somebody-Else." Nor do I want to give the state the power to regulate my primary relationship.

Yet, the concept of equality in our legal system does not support differences, it only supports sameness. The very standard for equal protection is that people who are similarly situated must be treated equally. To make an argument for equal protection, we will be required to claim that gay and lesbian relationships are the same as straight relationships. To gain the right, we must compare ourselves to married couples. The law looks to the insiders as the norm, regardless of how flawed or unjust their institutions, and requires that those seeking the law's equal protection situate themselves in a similar posture to those who are already protected. In arguing for the right to legal marriage, lesbians and gay men would be forced to claim that we are just like heterosexual couples, have the same goals and purposes, and vow to structure our lives similarly. The law provides no room to argue that we are different, but are nonetheless entitled to equal protection.

The thought of emphasizing our sameness to married heterosexuals in order to obtain this "right" terrifies me. It rips away the very heart and soul of what I believe it is to be a lesbian in this world. It robs me of the opportunity to make a difference. We end up mimicking all that is bad about the institution of marriage in our effort to appear to be the same as straight couples.

By looking to our sameness and de-emphasizing our differences, we don't even place ourselves in a position of power that would allow us to transform marriage from an institution that emphasizes property and state regulation of relationships to an institution which recognizes one of many types of valid and respected relationships. Until the constitution is interpreted to respect and encourage differences, pursuing the legalization of same-sex marriage would be leading our movement into a trap; we would be demanding access to the very institution which, in its current form, would undermine *our* movement to recognize many different kinds of relationships. We would be perpetuating the elevation of married relationships and of "couples" in general, and further eclipsing other relationships of choice.

Ironically, gay marriage, instead of liberating gay sex and sexuality, would further outlaw all gay and lesbian sex which is not performed in a marital context. Just as sexually active non-married women face stigma and double standards around sex and sexual activity, so too would non-married gay people. The only legitimate gay sex would be that which is cloaked in and regulated by marriage. Its legitimacy would stem not from an acceptance of gay sexuality, but because the Supreme Court and society in general fiercely protect the privacy of marital relationships.

Lesbians and gay men who did not seek the state's stamp of approval would clearly face increased sexual oppression.

Undoubtedly, whether we admit it or not, we all need to be accepted by the broader society. That motivation fuels our work to eliminate discrimination in the workplace and elsewhere, fight for custody of our children, create our own families, and so on. The growing discussion about the right to marry may be explained in part by this need for acceptance. Those closer to the norm or to power in this country are more likely to see marriage as a principle of freedom and equality. Those who are more acceptable to the mainstream because of race, gender, and economic status are more likely to want the right to marry. It is the final acceptance, the ultimate affirmation of identity.

On the other hand, more marginal members of the lesbian and gay community (women, people of color, working class and poor) are less likely to see marriage as having relevance to our struggles for survival. After all, what good is the affirmation of our relationships (that is, marital relationships) if we are rejected as women, black, or working class?

The path to acceptance is much more complicated for many of us. For instance, if we choose legal marriage, we may enjoy the right to add our spouse to our health insurance policy at work, since most employment policies are defined by one's marital status, not family relationship. However, that choice assumes that we have a job *and* that our employer provides us with health benefits. For women, particularly women of color who tend to occupy the low-paying jobs that do not provide healthcare benefits at all, it will not matter one bit if they are able to marry their women partners. The opportunity to marry will neither get them the health benefits nor transform them from outsider to insider.

Of course, a white man who marries another white man who has a full-time job with benefits will certainly be able to share in those benefits and overcome the only obstacle left to full societal assimilation—the goal of many in his class. In other words, gay marriage will not topple the system that allows only the privileged few to obtain decent health care. Nor will it close the privilege gap between those who are married and those who are not.

Marriage creates a two-tier system that allows the state to regulate relationships. It has become a facile mechanism for employers to dole out benefits, for businesses to provide special deals and incentives, and for the law to make distinctions in distributing meager public funds. None of these entities bothers to consider the relationship among people; the love, respect, and need to protect that exists among all kinds of family members. Rather, a simple certificate of the state, regardless of whether the spouses love, respect, or even see each other on a regular basis, dominates and is supported. None of this dynamic will change if gay men and lesbians are given the option of marriage.

Gay marriage will not help us address the systemic abuses inherent in a society that does not provide decent health care to all of its citizens, a right that should not depend on whether the individual (1) has sufficient resources to afford health care or health insurance, (2) is working and receives health insurance as part of compensation, or (3) is married to a partner who is working and has health coverage which is extended to spouses. It will not address the underlying unfairness that allows businesses to provide discounted services or goods to families and couples—who are defined to include straight, married people and their children, but not domestic partners.

Nor will it address the pain and anguish of an unmarried lesbian who receives word of her partner's accident, rushes to the hospital and is prohibited from entering the intensive ward or obtaining information about her condition solely because she is not a spouse or family member. Likewise, marriage will not help the gay victim of domestic violence who, because he chose not to marry, finds no protection under the law to keep his violent lover away.

If the laws change tomorrow and lesbians and gay men were allowed to marry, where would we find the incentive to continue the progressive movement we have started that is pushing for societal and legal recognition of all kinds of family relationships? To create other options and alternatives? To find a place in the law for the elderly couple who, for companionship and economic reasons, live together but do not marry? To recognize the right of a long-time, but unmarried, gay partner to stay in his rent-controlled apartment after the death of his lover, the only named tenant on the lease? To recognize the family relationship of the lesbian couple and the two gay men who are jointly sharing child-raising responsibilities? To get the law to acknowledge that we may have more than one relationship worthy of legal protection?

Marriage for lesbians and gay men still will not provide a real choice unless we continue the work our community has begun to spread the privilege around to other relationships. We must first break the tradition of piling benefits and privileges on to those who are married, while ignoring the real life needs of those who are not. Only when we de-institutionalize marriage and bridge the economic and privilege gap between the married and the unmarried will each of us have a true choice. Otherwise, our choice not to marry will continue to lack legal protection and societal respect.

The lesbian and gay community has laid the groundwork for revolutionizing society's views of family. The domestic partnership movement has been an important part of this progress insofar as it validates non-marital relationships. Because it is not limited to sexual or romantic relationships, domestic partnership provides an important opportunity for many who are not related by blood or marriage to claim certain minimal protections.

It is crucial, though, that we avoid the pitfall of framing the push for legal recognition of domestic partners (those who share a primary residence and financial responsibilities for each other) as a stepping stone to marriage. We must keep our eyes on the goals of providing true alternatives to marriage and of radically reordering society's views of family.

The goals of lesbian and gay liberation must simply be broader than the right to marry. Gay and lesbian marriages may minimally transform the institution of marriage by diluting its traditional patriarchal dynamic, but they will not transform society. They will not demolish the two-tier system of the "haves" and the "have-nots." We must not fool ourselves into believing that marriage will make it acceptable to be gay or lesbian. We will be liberated only when we are respected and accepted for our differences and the diversity we provide to this society. Marriage is not a path to that liberation.

In 2006, a coalition of LGBT activists and authors, along with allies, issued the following statement.

BEYOND SAME-SEX MARRIAGE: A NEW STRATEGIC VISION FOR ALL OUR FAMILIES AND RELATIONSHIPS*
Various Signatories

The time has come to reframe the narrow terms of the marriage debate in the United States. Conservatives are seeking to enshrine discrimination in the U.S. Constitution through the Federal Marriage Amendment. But their opposition to same-sex marriage is only one part of a broader pro-marriage, "family values" agenda that includes abstinence-only sex education, stringent divorce laws, coercive marriage promotion policies directed toward women on welfare, and attacks on reproductive freedom. Moreover, a thirty-year political assault on the social safety net has left households with more burdens and constraints and fewer resources.

Meanwhile, the LGBT movement has recently focused on marriage equality as a stand-alone issue. While this strategy may secure rights and benefits for some LGBT families, it has left us isolated and vulnerable to

----

* This is the executive summary of a document entitled *Beyond Same–Sex Marriage: A New Strategic Vision For All Our Families and Relationships*, which is available at http://www.beyondmarriage.org.

a virulent backlash. We must respond to the full scope of the conservative marriage agenda by building alliances across issues and constituencies. Our strategies must be visionary, creative, and practical to counter the right's powerful and effective use of marriage as a "wedge" issue that pits one group against another. The struggle for marriage rights should be part of a larger effort to strengthen the stability and security of diverse households and families. To that end, we advocate:

- Legal recognition for a wide range of relationships, households and families—regardless of kinship or conjugal status.

- Access for all, regardless of marital or citizenship status, to vital government support programs including but not limited to health care, housing, Social Security and pension plans, disaster recovery assistance, unemployment insurance and welfare assistance.

- Separation of church and state in all matters, including regulation and recognition of relationships, households and families.

- Freedom from state regulation of our sexual lives and gender choices, identities and expression.

Marriage is not the only worthy form of family or relationship, and it should not be legally and economically privileged above all others. A majority of people—whatever their sexual and gender identities—do not live in traditional nuclear families. They stand to gain from alternative forms of household recognition beyond one-size-fits-all marriage. For example:

- Single parent households

- Senior citizens living together and serving as each other's caregivers (think *Golden Girls*)

- Blended and extended families

- Children being raised in multiple households or by unmarried parents

- Adult children living with and caring for their parents

- Senior citizens who are the primary caregivers to their grandchildren or other relatives

- Close friends or siblings living in non-conjugal relationships and serving as each other's primary support and caregivers

- Households in which there is more than one conjugal partner

- Care-giving relationships that provide support to those living with extended illness such as HIV/AIDS.

The current debate over marriage, same-sex and otherwise, ignores the needs and desires of so many in a nation where household diversity is the demographic norm. We seek to reframe this debate. Our call speaks to the widespread hunger for authentic and just community in ways that are both pragmatic and visionary. It follows in the best tradition of the progressive LGBT movement, which invented alternative legal statuses such as domestic partnership and reciprocal beneficiary. We seek to build on these historic accomplishments by continuing to diversify and democratize partnership and household recognition. We advocate the expansion of existing legal statuses, social services and benefits to support the needs of all our households.

We call on colleagues working in various social justice movements and campaigns to read the full-text of our statement . . . and to join us in our call for government support of *all* our households.

NOTES

1.   Professor Nan Hunter has suggested that, in arguing that lesbians and gay men should not want to enter the institution of marriage, Ettelbrick "essentialized" marriage and failed to appreciate the ways in which "[m]arriage between men or between women could . . . destabilize the cultural meaning of marriage," with positive implications for the institution. Nan D. Hunter, *Marriage, Law, and Gender: A Feminist Inquiry*, 1 L. & SEXUALITY 9, 17 (1991).

2.   Others, like Ettelbrick, have lamented that the focus on marriage equality eclipses other important goals. Professor Angela Harris, for example, argues that the LGBT community has historically worked:

> to queer "the family," to bring its contradictions and its inadequacies to the surface, to make it visible as a set of economic and political entitlements, a tentacular institution with roots in the state and the market and not simply a private relation of intimacy.

Angela Harris, *From Stonewall to the Suburbs?: Toward a Political Economy of Sexuality*, 14 WM. & MARY BILL RTS. J. 1539, 1568 (2006). Harris argues that, with the focus now turned almost exclusively on marriage equality, the work of expanding the meaning of family will cease and recognition of families that fit the traditional mold will take precedence.

3.   The Stoddard-Ettelbrick debate was revisited, modernized, and reconfigured to some extent in *Updating the LGBT Intra-Community Debate on Same-Sex Marriage*, 61 RUTGERS L. REV. 493 (2009).

Professor Nancy Polikoff, in her piece "Equality and Justice for Lesbian and Gay Families and Relationships," updated and defended Ettelbrick's view:

I advocate law reform that values all families and relationships. This does not mean that the law should treat all relationships in the same way. It means that we should identify the purpose of any law and include within that law the relationships that will further its purpose. Marriage should never be the dividing line between who is in and who is out.

I do not start with marriage, or with the package of rights that marriage gives different-sex couples, and work down from there, strategizing about how many of those rights politicians are willing to grant same-sex couples who sign up with the state in a status called civil union or domestic partnership. Instead, I start by identifying the needs of all LGBT people and work up from there to craft legislative proposals to meet those needs.

Laws that value all families are not primarily about legitimating gay relationships that mirror marriage. They are about ensuring that every relationship and every family has the legal framework for economic and emotional security. Laws that value all families value same-sex couples but not only same-sex couples. Lesbian, gay, bisexual, and transgender people live in varied households and families. A valuing-all-families approach strives to meet the needs of all of them, making real the vision in the Beyond Same-Sex Marriage statement that "marriage is not the only worthy form of family or relationship, and it should not be legally and economically privileged above all others."

61 RUTGERS L. REV. 529, 558–60. In 2008, Polikoff published BEYOND (STRAIGHT AND GAY) MARRIAGE, a book that examined in depth the ways that marriage as an institution leaves unmet the important material needs of many individuals—LGBT and straight.

In his symposium essay, *A Little Older, a Little Wiser, and Still Committed*, Professor Mark Strasser defended Stoddard's view:

Two issues should not be conflated: (1) whether married individuals are more willing to sacrifice for the sake of the family, thereby making all members of the family better off in the long run, and (2) whether women in different-sex marriages are often asked to bear disproportionate burdens. Both (1) and (2) may be true. The point here is merely that the recognition of same-sex marriage would likely result in LGBT couples investing more in their families, redounding to the benefit of all. It is simply unclear whether the recognition of same-sex marriage would promote egalitarian sharing of burdens in different-sex relationships.

61 RUTGERS L. REV. 507, 519.

In the same issue, Professor Edward Stein charted a middle path between the two views:

My look backward from today to 1989 indicates that both Stoddard and Ettelbrick were right. The aggressive push for marriage equality has made a surprising amount of progress: not only has it produced substantial legal reform in a few states, but it has also contributed to a significant change in attitudes toward LGBT people and their families. The pluralist, reformed-minded approach has also borne fruit. Various alternatives to marriage have been developed, functional accounts of family have been embraced, and the institution of marriage and its legal significance have changed. The different strategies that Stoddard and Ettelbrick proposed have both worked and, rather than being in opposition to each other, have worked well together. When, for example, attempts to achieve marriage equality have failed, alternative forms of relationship recognition have been created instead of same-sex marriage. This has happened, for example, in Maryland, where domestic partnership laws were passed after the state's supreme court rejected a legal challenge to prohibitions on same-sex marriages. Sometimes, the relationship-recognition form that results is effectively a consolation prize from the perspective of the marriage-equality approach, but these alternative forms, under the influence of Ettelbrick's approach, may blossom into relationship pluralism, especially if the new form of relationship recognition develops in a sedimentary fashion. The two approaches also work synergistically in that, as functional and alternative family forms are implemented and people get used to them, resistance to same-sex marriage often weakens. By giving domestic partner benefits to employees in same-sex relationships, employers and some municipalities helped people get used to same-sex relationships and gave them recognition. This process helped facilitate support for and acceptance of same-sex marriages, civil unions, and more robust domestic partnerships. Similarly, people living in states that have had civil union or domestic partner laws for some years tend to be more supportive of same-sex relationships. The Vermont legislature, which in 1999 struggled to respond to their state supreme court's order to give same-sex relationships the same rights and benefits that different-sex couples received through marriage, just recently, and by an overwhelming majority, enacted legislation giving full marriage equality to same-sex couples. This demonstrates how recognition of nonmarital same-sex relationships can pave the way to full marriage equality for same-sex couples.

Marriage or Liberation?: Reflections on Two Strategies in the Struggle for Lesbian and Gay Rights and Relationship Recognition, 61 RUTGERS L. REV. 567, 591.

4. The materials in the preceding notes show that the issues joined by Stoddard and Ettelbrick remain in contention in some quarters, but the internal LGBT community debate about marriage has become quite muted in

recent years. Why might that be so? One likely explanation is the widespread backlash against same-sex marriage advocacy by opponents of LGBT rights. Consider this view:

> For all the fiery rhetoric and deep disagreements dividing opponents and proponents of same-sex marriage, however, there are some surprising points of confluence between the two sides in how they frame the debate. First, both supporters and opponents of same-sex marriage characterize the institution of marriage as a centrally important and positive force in communal life. Such a characterization is, of course, utterly predictable for those opposing same-sex marriage . . . Yet it is hardly obvious that prominent supporters of LGBT rights would also have such high praise for marriage . . . A second point of confluence is that both sides frame the marriage debate as something of an epochal showdown on LGBT equality. Both, in other words, seem to see the stakes as high, the outcome as a proxy statement about LGBT equality, and the struggle as a cultural moment of truth . . . The fact that the public debate about same-sex marriage has been framed as the true test of LGBT equality undoubtedly has been a prime force in quieting any internal resistance to same-sex marriage. The internal critics have always had political commitments that place them in deep and passionate opposition to the "external" critics of same-sex marriage—the cultural and religious traditionalists who oppose LGBT equality in all its forms. Indeed, the internal and external resistance to same-sex marriage are strikingly converse to one another. The internal resistance to marriage advocacy came from those strongly committed to gay equality, but doubtful about the institution of marriage. The external resistance comes from those strongly opposed to gay equality, but reverent about the traditional institution of marriage.

Jane S. Schacter, *The Other Same-Sex Marriage Debate,* 84 CHICAGO-KENT L. REV. 379, 381–83 (2009). In this article, Professor Schacter asks, in counterfactual fashion, whether it is possible to imagine the history unfolding differently. Might LGBT advocates have affirmatively sought an institution separate from marriage—one that might have allowed more flexibility than marriage, and thus met a wider range of needs of the kind that Polikoff identified? Might LGBT advocates, alternatively, have sought to eliminate civil marriage, leaving marriage to religious institutions, while the state offered a secular partnership to all couples? Would either of these courses, or another one you might imagine, have been preferable to concentrating heavily on securing access to marriage per se? Why or why not?

Professor Doug NeJaime analyzes the viability of these alternative paths by revisiting the earlier era of nonmarital advocacy, before the movement made explicit claims to marriage. Through a case study of domestic partnership work in California in the 1980s and 1990s, he shows how marriage anchored nonmarital recognition. In this excerpt, NeJaime summarizes some of the case study's implications:

> Even for activists resisting marriage, marriage functioned like a riptide. Advocates were swimming with *and* against marriage, often at the same time. That is, they challenged marriage's role even as they submitted to its pull. LGBT advocates' claims [to nonmarital recognition] did not simply succeed or fail on their own, but were met with reactions from a range of relevant actors who shaped the content and influenced the viability of those claims. Government actors, including judges and lawmakers, privileged marriage in law and policy. Countermovement activists, who influenced officials and mobilized voters, sought to both restore the centrality of marriage and cut back on LGBT rights. And private institutions, including employers and insurers sympathetic to sexual orientation equality, acted on financial incentives to limit the types of nonmarital relationships that would qualify for benefits. Overall, then, marriage constituted a deeply entrenched legal norm, a powerful but controversial cultural priority, and a well-understood limiting principle. Both supportive and hostile responses filtered LGBT claims through the lens of marriage, and such responses often redirected advocates' energy and constrained potentially more transformative visions.
>
> . . . Marriage rendered intimate couples the appropriate targets of reform. Those who mapped onto a particular notion of the marital family gained support by distinguishing themselves from other relationships that failed to fit the marital mold. Furthermore, marriage distinguished same-sex couples from their different-sex, unmarried counterparts. This produced an emphasis on marriage access over marriage choice in ways that gradually propped up marriage as an LGBT movement goal. Indeed, supportive allies frequently cast domestic partnership as a compromise solution that avoided the more radical possibility of same-sex marriage.
>
> Accordingly, the power of marriage as a legal and cultural norm structured claims, debates, and outcomes regarding family reform such that advocates did not—and could not—simply reject marriage. Even if advocates hoped otherwise, domestic partnership in many ways solidified, rather than resisted, the power of marriage.

Douglas NeJaime, *Before Marriage: The Unexplored History of Nonmarital Recognition and Its Relationship to Marriage*, 102 CALIF. L. REV. 87, 161 (2014).

CHAPTER 7

PARENTING

■ ■ ■

It is estimated that "as many as 6 million American children and adults have an LGBT parent."[1] It is also estimated that "nearly half of LGBT women (48%)" and "a fifth of LGBT men (20%)" are raising a child under 18.[2]

The law first encountered LGBT parents in the context of the dissolution of heterosexual marriages. Those cases continue to arise today. Lesbians, gay men, and bisexuals also often become parents through adoption or foster care. In addition, many same-sex couples and LGBT individuals use reproductive technologies to become parents.

This Chapter's first section explores the role that sexual orientation and gender identity play in child custody and visitation disputes between LGBT persons and heterosexuals. The second section then considers the legal issues that are raised when families are formed by LGBT individuals through adoption, alternative insemination, ova donation/sharing, and surrogacy. It also explores the family law issues that arise when the relationships of LGBT parents dissolve.

I. PARENTING DISPUTES BETWEEN LGBT PERSONS AND HETEROSEXUALS

A. BACKGROUND AND SOCIAL SCIENCE

Many cases involving parenting by lesbians, gay men, and bisexuals concern the dissolution of mixed-gender marriages. Sexual orientation is often put at issue in these cases when it turns out that one of the divorcing parents is lesbian, gay, or bisexual. Courts then struggle with

---

[1] Gary J. Gates, *LGBT Parenting in the United States* (The Willimans Institute, 2013), p.1, available at http://williamsinstitute.law.ucla.edu/wp-content/uploads/LGBT-Parenting.pdf.

[2] *Id.* "An estimated 39% of individuals in same-sex couples who have children under age 18 in the home are people of color, compared to 36% of different-sex couples who are non-White." *Id.* In addition, "[a]mong children under age 18 living with same-sex couples, half (50%) are non-White compared to 41% of children living with different-sex couples." *Id.* There is also evidence that same-sex couples raising children face economic disadvantages. The median annual household income of same-sex couples with children under 18 is lower ($63,000) than that of different-sex couples with children ($74,000). In addition, single LGBT adults raising children are three times as likely to report income near the poverty threshold than single non-LGBT parents. *Id.* As for married or partnered LGBT couples with children, they are two times as likely as non-LGBT couples with children to report household income near the poverty line. *Id.*

the extent to which that parent's sexuality ought to influence the decision about placement of any children. These family law decisions are based on state law, and thus there are essentially 51 different sets of rules in the United States. Some general principles, however, do apply. In considering the extent to which a parent's sexuality is an issue in such a case, courts are governed by general rules that vary according to at least three different concerns—the relationships among the parties; the right at issue; and the time at which the dispute arises.

Parties. Courts apply different legal standards depending upon whether the dispute at issue is between a child's biological parents; between a parent and a non-parent third party; or between a parent and the government.

- In the two-parent dispute—the most common form in which these cases arise—the standard used throughout the country is the "best interests of the child"; i.e., the court assigns custody according to what it perceives as the child's best interests.[3]

- At the other end of the spectrum, state statutes authorize the government to terminate permanently parental rights in "neglect" proceedings; the state must demonstrate by clear and convincing evidence that the parent is unfit.[4] While governed by neglect statutes, these state actions are simultaneously bounded by constitutional norms.[5] "There are no reported dependency or neglect cases in which sexual orientation alone was found sufficient to terminate a natural parent's rights. However, courts do sometimes mention the parent's sexual orientation as one of several factors leading to the termination of parental rights."[6]

- Disputes pitting parents against non-parents occupy a poorly-defined middle ground in most jurisdictions. Most states appear to follow the traditional " 'parent's rights doctrine' and award custody to a nonparent only if the parent is shown to be unfit. In other jurisdictions, however, the nonparent need not prove unfitness but rather must make a strong showing that awarding custody to the natural parent will not be in the child's best interest."[7]

---

[3] HOMER H. CLARK, JR., THE LAW OF DOMESTIC RELATIONS IN THE UNITED STATES 797–98 (2d ed. 1988).

[4] *Id.* at 357.

[5] *Id.* at 350–5.

[6] EDITORS OF THE HARVARD LAW REVIEW, SEXUAL ORIENTATION AND THE LAW 125 (1990).

[7] *Id.* at 124.

Timing. Unlike most judicial decrees, custody and visitation decisions are never final. Courts are available to entertain claims by parents that "changed circumstances" warrant a change in custody or revision to a visitation allotment. In such cases, courts are forced to balance the child's interest in stability against the claimed change in circumstance. Typically, the change must be significant before a court will amend an earlier order.[8] As is evident in the cases below, "[n]oncustodial parents often seek to change the custody order on the grounds that the sexual orientation of the custodial parent has changed, or, more often, that the court's awareness of the custodial parent's sexual orientation has changed. . . . [M]ost courts have found that a change in a parent's sexual orientation or in the courts' knowledge of it is material."[9]

Lesbian/Gay/Bisexual Cases. Courts articulate and/or employ one of two different tests in considering the relevance of a parent's sexual orientation: a "per se" test or a "nexus" test. There is a thread in caselaw that supports the concept that homosexuality alone is a per se reason for denying custody or visitation rights.[10] These cases are rare, and most courts eschew such language in favor of some nexus test—a parent's sexuality may only be taken into account when it has some relationship to her parenting abilities.[11] While an improvement on a per se test, the

---

[8]   *See, e.g.,* UNIF. MARRIAGE & DIVORCE ACT § 409(b), 9A U.L.A. 628 (2007) ("the court shall not modify a prior custody decree unless it finds ... that a change has occurred in the circumstances of the child or his custodian, and that the modification is necessary to serve the best interest of the child").

[9]   EDITORS OF THE HARVARD LAW REVIEW, SEXUAL ORIENTATION AND THE LAW 123–24 (1990).

[10]   *E.g., S v. S,* 608 S.W.2d 64, 65, 66 (Ky. Ct. App. 1980) (while "wife denies any overt lesbian relationship in the presence of the child and there is no proof to the contrary," court denies her custody based both on testimony that " 'there is social stigma attached to homosexuality' " and speculation from data on parental modeling on children); *S.E.G. v. R.A.G.,* 735 S.W.2d 164, 166 (Mo. Ct. App. 1987) ("Such conduct [i.e., lesbian mother showing affection toward and sleeping with her partner] can never be kept private enough to be a neutral factor in the development of a child's values and character."); *M.J.P. v. J.G.P.,* 640 P.2d 966, 967, 1982 OK 13 (1982) ("The question before us is whether this acknowledged, open homosexual relationship involving the custodial parent was shown by the facts to be sufficient change of condition to warrant modification of a child custody order? We answer in the affirmative."); *Dailey v. Dailey,* 635 S.W.2d 391, 396 (Tenn. Ct. App. 1981) ("To permit this small child to be subjected to the type of sexually related behavior that has been carried on in his presence in the past under the proof in this record could provide nothing but harmful effects on his life in the future."); *Roe v. Roe,* 324 S.E.2d 691, 694, 228 Va. 722, 728 (1985) ("[W]e have no hesitancy in saying that the conditions under which this child must live daily are not only unlawful but also impose an intolerable burden upon her by reason of the social condemnation attached to them.").

[11]   *E.g., S.N.E. v. R.L.B.,* 699 P.2d 875 (Alaska 1985) (finding that social stigma, real or imagined, associated with parent's homosexuality does not affect child's best interests); *Jacoby v. Jacoby,* 763 So.2d 410, 413 (Fla. Dist. Ct. App. 2000) (holding that "[f]or a court to properly consider conduct such as [the mother's] sexual orientation on the issue of custody, the conduct must have a direct effect or impact upon the children"); *Hassenstab v. Hassenstab,* 570 N.W.2d 368, 372–73, 6 Neb.App. 13, 18–19 (Ct. App. 1997) (affirming refusal to modify custody based on mother's lesbian relationship in absence of evidence child was directly exposed to sexual activity or harmed by mother's relationship); *Inscoe v. Inscoe,* 700 N.E.2d 70, 82, 121 Ohio App.3d 396, 415 (Ct. App. 1997) (ruling that trial court "may consider a parent's sexual orientation only if the sexual orientation has a direct adverse impact" on the child); *Fox v. Fox,* 904 P.2d 66, 69, 1995 OK 87 (1995) (holding that lesbian mother's "sexual proclivities" are not grounds for changing

nexus test by no means produces determinant results in favor of lesbian, gay, or bisexual parents; not surprisingly, courts have articulated a nexus test in cases that both protect and discriminate against these parents.[12] Accordingly, in reviewing the cases in this Section, you should consider in what circumstances courts find that the relevant nexus does exist and consider upon whom the burden of proof, vis-à-vis this nexus, is placed.

Transgender Cases. Custody cases involving transgender parents are fewer in number than those involving gay, lesbian, or bisexual parents. Nonetheless, there are some similarities between the two groups of cases as courts struggle to determine what role, if any, gender identity should play in the assignation of parental rights and responsibilities. *See* Helen Y. Chang, *My Father is a Woman, Oh No!: The Failure of the Courts to Uphold Individual Substantive Due Process Rights for Transgender Parents Under the Guise of the Best Interest of the Child*, 43 SANTA CLARA L. REV. 649, 685–98 (2003) (arguing that courts in cases involving transgender parents should apply the same nexus test that many courts apply in cases involving gay, lesbian, or bisexual parents).

Social Science Data. As will be evident in the following caselaw, a recurring issue in cases between LGBT parents and their former heterosexual spouses is whether sexuality affects parenting ability. Social scientists have studied this question for decades, generally concluding that there are no meaningful differences in the children of lesbians and gay men when compared to children of heterosexual parents—in other words, that a parent's homosexuality has no discernable impact on the child's well-being or upbringing.

In an influential 1997 law review article, BYU Law Professor Lynn Wardle argued that this social science research was methodologically flawed because it relied inter alia on small, non-random samples that seldom used married heterosexual families as the control groups. *See* Lynn D. Wardle, *The Potential Impact of Homosexual Parenting on Children*, 1997 U. ILL. L. REV. 833. Despite the flaws, Wardle used the

---

custody absent evidence of "significant change of circumstances which directly and adversely affects the children"); *Van Driel v. Van Driel*, 525 N.W.2d 37, 39 (S.D. 1994) (explicitly rejecting *per se* test and holding that lesbian mother's "conduct must be shown to have had some harmful effect on the children"). *See also In re Marriage of Birdsall*, 243 Cal.Rptr. 287, 291, 197 Cal.App.3d 1024, 1031 (1988) (holding that a parent is not unfit, as a matter of law, merely because he or she is homosexual); *McGriff v. McGriff*, 99 P.3d 111, 117, 140 Idaho 642, 648 (2004) (holding that "[s]exual orientation, in and of itself cannot be the basis for awarding or removing custody"); *Teegarden v. Teegarden*, 642 N.E.2d 1007, 1010 (Ind. Ct. App. 1994) (holding that lesbian mother's custody could not be conditioned on her behavior absent evidence that such behavior would adversely affect children); *Paul C. v. Tracy C.*, 622 N.Y.S.2d 159, 160, 209 A.D.2d 955, 956 (App. Div. 1994) (holding that mother's alleged lesbian relationship did not preclude her from custody absent evidence that such relationship had negative affect on children).

[12] *Compare, e.g., In re Marriage of Martins*, 269 Ill.App.3d 380, 390, 206 Ill.Dec. 562, 645 N.E.2d 567, 574 (Ct. App. 1995) (granting custody to father after finding lesbian mother's "lifestyle had adversely affected the children") *with Large v. Large*, 1993 WL 498127, at *5 (Ohio Ct. App. 1993) (affirming grant of custody to lesbian mother after finding no evidence indicating that her sexual orientation negatively effected children).

data to argue that the studies suggest that children raised by lesbians and gay men are at risk of the following potential harms: a greater incidence of same-sex sexual activity, which then leads to a greater incidence of HIV, drug abuse, and suicide; negative effects on gender roles, gender identity, and self-esteem; and a greater likelihood of being sexually molested. Wardle's article touched off a lively debate in the scholarly literature; for a response, see, e.g., Carlos A. Ball & Janice Farrell Pea, *Warring with Wardle: Morality, Social Science, and Gay and Lesbian Parents*, 1998 U. ILL. L. REV. 253.

Most of the responses to Wardle continued to insist that children raised by gay parents were no different than those raised by heterosexuals. Consider, by contrast, the argument in the following reading.

(HOW) DOES THE SEXUAL ORIENTATION OF PARENTS MATTER?*

Judith Stacey & Timothy J. Biblarz

... [W]e examined the findings of 21 psychological studies ... published between 1981 and 1998 that we considered best equipped to address sociological questions about how parental sexual orientation matters to children. One meta-analysis of 18 such studies (11 of which are included among our 21) characteristically concludes that "the results demonstrate no differences on any measures between the heterosexual and homosexual parents regarding parenting styles, emotional adjustment, and sexual orientation of the child(ren)." ... Echoing th[is] conclusion of meta-analysts Allen and Burrell (1996), the authors of all 21 studies almost uniformly claim to find no differences in measures of parenting or child outcomes. In contrast, our careful scrutiny of the findings they report suggests that on some dimensions—particularly those related to gender and sexuality—the sexual orientations of these parents matter somewhat more for their children than the researchers claimed. * * *

CHILDREN'S GENDER PREFERENCES AND BEHAVIOR

The findings demonstrate that, as we would expect, on some measures meaningful differences have been observed in predictable directions. For example, lesbian mothers in R. Green et al. [*Lesbian Mothers and their Children: A Comparison with Solo Parent Heterosexual Mothers and Their Children*, 15 ARCHIVES SEXUAL BEHAV. 167] (1986) reported that Their children, especially daughters, more frequently dress, play, and behave in ways that do not conform to sex-typed cultural norms. Likewise, daughters of lesbian mothers reported greater interest in

---

* Judith Stacey & Timothy J. Biblarz, *(How) Does the Sexual Orientation of Parents Matter?*, 66 AM. SOC. REV. 159, 167–71, 176–79 (2001).

activities associated with both "masculine" and "feminine" qualities and that involve the participation of both sexes, whereas daughters of heterosexual mothers report significantly greater interest in traditionally feminine, same-sex activities. Similarly, daughters with lesbian mothers reported higher aspirations to nontraditional gender occupations. For example, in R. Green et al. (1986), 53 percent (16 out of 30) of the daughters of lesbians aspired to careers such as doctor, lawyer, engineer, and astronaut, compared with only 21 percent (6 of 28) of the daughters of heterosexual mothers.

Sons appear to respond in more complex ways to parental sexual orientations. On some measures, like aggressiveness and play preferences, the sons of lesbian mothers behave in less traditionally masculine ways than those raised by heterosexual single mothers. However, on other measures, such as occupational goals and sartorial styles, they also exhibit greater gender conformity than do daughters with lesbian mothers (but they are not more conforming than sons with heterosexual mothers). Such evidence, albeit limited, implies that lesbian parenting may free daughters and sons from a broad but uneven range of traditional gender prescriptions. It also suggests that the sexual orientation of mothers interacts with the gender of children in complex ways to influence gender preferences and behavior. Such findings raise provocative questions about how children assimilate gender culture and interests—questions that the propensity to downplay differences deters scholars from exploring. * * *

Children's Sexual Preferences And Behavior

. . . [We pay] particular attention to thought-provoking findings from the Tasker and Golombok [Growing Up In a Lesbian Family] (1997) study, the only comparative study we know of that follows children raised in lesbian-headed families into young adulthood and hence that can explore the children's sexuality in meaningful ways. A significantly greater proportion of young adult children raised by lesbian mothers than those raised by heterosexual mothers in the Tasker and Golombok sample reported having had a homoerotic relationship (6 of the 25 young adults raised by lesbian mothers—24 percent—compared with 0 of the 20 raised by heterosexual mothers). The young adults reared by lesbian mothers were also significantly more likely to report having thought they might experience homoerotic attraction or relationships. The difference in their openness to this possibility is striking: 64 percent (14 of 22) of the young adults raised by lesbian mothers report having considered same-sex relationships (in the past, now, or in the future), compared with only 17 percent (3 of 18) of those raised by heterosexual mothers. Of course, the fact that 17 percent of those raised by heterosexual mothers also report some openness to same-sex relationships, while 36 percent of those raised by lesbians do not, underscores the important reality that parental influence on children's sexual desires is neither direct nor easily predictable.

If these young adults raised by lesbian mothers were more open to a broad range of sexual possibilities, they were not statistically more likely to self-identify as bisexual, lesbian, or gay. To be coded as such, the respondent not only had to currently self-identify as bisexual/lesbian/gay, but also to express a commitment to that identity in the future. Tasker and Golombok employ a measure of sexual identity with no "in-between" categories for those whose identity may not yet be fully fixed or embraced. Thus, although a more nuanced measure or a longer period of observation could yield different results, Golombok and Tasker choose to situate their findings within the "overall no difference" interpretation:

> The commonly held assumption that children brought up by lesbian mothers will themselves grow up to be lesbian or gay is not supported by the findings of the study: the majority of children who grew up in lesbian families identified as heterosexual in adulthood, and there was no statistically significant difference between young adults from lesbian and heterosexual family backgrounds with respect to sexual orientation.

This reading, while technically accurate, deflects analytic attention from the rather sizable differences in sexual attitudes and behaviors that the study actually reports. . . .

Tasker and Golombok also report some fascinating findings on the number of sexual partners children report having had between puberty and young adulthood. Relative to their counterparts with heterosexual parents, the adolescent and young adult girls raised by lesbian mothers appear to have been more sexually adventurous and less chaste, whereas the sons of lesbians evince the opposite pattern—somewhat less sexually adventurous and more chaste (the finding was statistically significant for the 25-girl sample but not for the 18-boy sample). In other words, once again, children (especially girls) raised by lesbians appear to depart from traditional gender-based norms, while children raised by heterosexual mothers appear to conform to them. Yet this provocative finding of differences in sexual behavior and agency has not been analyzed or investigated further. * * *

CHILDREN'S MENTAL HEALTH

. . . [The] studies find no significant differences between children of lesbian mothers and children of heterosexual mothers in anxiety, depression, self-esteem, and numerous other measures of social and psychological adjustment. The roughly equivalent level of psychological well-being between the two groups holds true in studies that test children directly, rely on parents' reports, and solicit evaluations from teachers.

The few significant differences found actually tend to favor children with lesbian mothers. Given some credible evidence that children with gay and lesbian parents, especially adolescent children, face homophobic teasing and ridicule that many find difficult to manage, the children in these studies seem to exhibit impressive psychological strength. * * *

NO DIFFERENCES OF SOCIAL CONCERN

Lesbigay parents and their children in these studies display no differences from heterosexual counterparts in psychological well-being or cognitive functioning. Scores for lesbigay parenting styles and levels of investment in children are at least as "high" as those for heterosexual parents. Levels of closeness and quality of parent/child relationships do not seem to differentiate directly by parental sexual orientation, but indirectly, by way of parental gender. Because every relevant study to date shows that parental sexual orientation per se has no measurable effect on the quality of parent-child relationships or on children's mental health or social adjustment, there is no evidentiary basis for considering parental sexual orientation in decisions about children's "best interest." In fact, given that children with lesbigay parents probably contend with a degree of social stigma, these similarities in child outcomes suggest the presence of compensatory processes in lesbigay-parent families. * * *

HOW THE SEXUAL ORIENTATION OF PARENTS MATTERS

* * * First, our analysis of the psychological research indicates that the effects of parental gender trump those of sexual orientation. A diverse array of gender theories (social learning theory, psychoanalytic theory, materialist, symbolic inter-actionist) would predict that children with two same-gender parents, and particularly with co-mother parents, should develop in less gender-stereotypical ways than would children with two heterosexual parents. There is reason to credit the perception of lesbian co-mothers in a qualitative study that they "were redefining the meaning and content of motherhood, extending its boundaries to incorporate the activities that are usually dichotomized as mother and father." Children who derive their principal source of love, discipline, protection, and identification from women living independent of male domestic authority or influence should develop less stereotypical symbolic, emotional, practical, and behavioral gender repertoires. Indeed, it is the claim that the gender mix of parents has no effect on their children's gender behavior, interests, or development that cries out for sociological explanation. Only a crude theory of cultural indoctrination that posited the absolute impotence of parents might predict such an outcome, and the remarkable variability of gender configurations documented in the anthropological record readily undermines such a theory. The burden of proof in the domain of gender and sexuality should rest with those who embrace the null hypothesis.

Second, because homosexuality is stigmatized, selection effects may yield correlations between parental sexual orientation and child development that do not derive from sexual orientation itself. For example, social constraints on access to marriage and parenting make lesbian parents likely to be older, urban, educated, and self-aware—factors that foster several positive developmental consequences for their children. On the other hand, denied access to marriage, lesbian co-parent relationships are likely to experience dissolution rates somewhat higher than those among heterosexual co-parents. Not only do same-sex couples lack the institutional pressures and support for commitment that marriage provides, but qualitative studies suggest that they tend to embrace comparatively high standards of emotional intimacy and satisfaction. The decision to pursue a socially ostracized domain of intimacy implies an investment in the emotional regime that Giddens terms "the pure relationship" and "confluent love." Such relationships confront the inherent instabilities of modern or postmodern intimacy, what Beck and . . . Gersheim term "the normal chaos of love." Thus, a higher dissolution rate would be correlated with but not causally related to sexual orientation, a difference that should erode were homophobia to disappear and legal marriage be made available to lesbians and gay men.

Most of the differences in the findings discussed above cannot be considered deficits from any legitimate public policy perspective. They either favor the children with lesbigay parents, are secondary effects of social prejudice, or represent "just a difference" of the sort democratic societies should respect and protect. Apart from differences associated with parental gender, most of the presently observable differences in child "outcomes" should wither away under conditions of full equality and respect for sexual diversity. * * *

Even in a utopian society, however, one difference seems less likely to disappear: The sexual orientation of parents appears to have a unique (although not large) effect on children in the politically sensitive domain of sexuality. The evidence, while scanty and underanalyzed, hints that parental sexual orientation is positively associated with the possibility that children will be more likely to attain a similar orientation—and theory and common sense also support such a view. Children raised by lesbian co-parents should and do seem to grow up more open to homoerotic relationships. This may be partly due to genetic and family socialization processes, but what sociologists refer to as "contextual effects" not yet investigated by psychologists may also be important. Because lesbigay parents are disproportionately more likely to inhabit diverse, cosmopolitan cities—Los Angeles, New York and San Francisco—and progressive university communities-such as Santa Cruz, Santa Rosa, Madison, and Ann Arbor—their children grow up in comparatively tolerant school, neighborhood, and social contexts, which foster less hostility to homoeroticism. * * *

We recognize the political dangers of pointing out that recent studies indicate that a higher proportion of children with lesbigay parents are themselves apt to engage in homosexual activity. In a homophobic world, anti-gay forces deploy such results to deny parents custody of their own children and to fuel backlash movements opposed to gay rights. Nonetheless, we believe that denying this probability capitulates to heterosexist ideology and is apt to prove counterproductive in the long run. It is neither intellectually honest nor politically wise to base a claim for justice on grounds that may prove falsifiable empirically. Moreover, the case for granting equal rights to nonheterosexual parents should not require finding their children to be identical to those reared by heterosexuals. Nor should it require finding that such children do not encounter distinctive challenges or risks, especially when these derive from social prejudice. * * *

Thus, while we disagree with those who claim that there are no differences between the children of heterosexual parents and children of lesbigay parents, we unequivocally endorse their conclusion that social science research provides no grounds for taking sexual orientation into account in the political distribution of family rights and responsibilities.

NOTES

1.   The Stacey and Biblarz essay has been cited in appellate opinions, both by judges who argue that the social science literature shows that the sexual orientation of gay and lesbian parents does not negatively affect their children, see *Snetsinger v. Montana Univ. Sys.*, 104 P.3d 445, 455, 325 Mont. 148, 162 (2004) (Nelson, J., concurring); *Hernandez v. Robles*, 805 N.Y.S.2d 354, 387, 26 A.D.3d 98, 141 (App. Div. 2005) (Saxe, J., dissenting), and by judges who claim that the empirical evidence on whether the sexual orientation of lesbian and gay parents harms children is at best inconclusive, see *Lofton v. Secretary of Dep't of Children & Family Servs.*, 358 F.3d 804, 825 nn. 24 & 25 (11th Cir. 2004); *Ex parte H.H.*, 830 So.2d 21, 36 n. 11 (Ala. 2002) (Moore, C.J., concurring).

2.   In an article reviewing the social science studies on the children of lesbians and gay men, including several conducted after the publication of the Stacey and Biblarz essay, Professor Carlos Ball divides the literature into three distinct subject areas of investigation. *See* Carlos A. Ball, *Social Science Studies and the Children of Lesbians and Gay Men: The Rational Basis Perspective*, 21 WILL. & MARY BILL RIGHTS JR. 691 (2013). The first area addresses the children's psychological adjustment and social functioning, "including matters such as behavioral adjustment, emotional well-being, self-esteem, school performance, and peer relations. The second area consists of the gender attitudes and interests of the children of lesbians and gay men.

Finally, the third area relates to the sexual orientation of those children." *Id.* at 697. In terms of the first area of study, Ball concludes that "the social science evidence showing a lack of an association between parental sexual orientation and the psychological and social functioning of children is so conclusive and so uniform, that efforts to impose marriage and parenting restrictions on lesbians and gay men based on concerns about such functioning are irrational (and therefore unconstitutional) because they lack a defensible factual foundation." *Id.* at 698.

But Ball found that the social science literature is somewhat less consistent on the questions of gender role development and sexual orientation, with a minority of studies suggesting possible associations with parental sexual orientation. "Specifically, . . . a minority of studies suggest that the daughters of lesbian mothers evince attitudes and engage in play and school activities that are less consistent with traditional gender expectations when compared to the daughters of heterosexual parents. Similarly, . . . a minority of studies suggest that the daughters of lesbian mothers express a greater interest in participating in same-sex relationships than do the daughters of heterosexual parents." *Id.* at 699. Ball then proceeds to argue that even if these indicia of possible differences can be shown to exist conclusively, they cannot constitutionally be used to justify the differential treatment of lesbians and gay men in matters associated with parenting because the state does not have a legitimate interest "in encouraging individuals to behave in certain ways (or to pursue certain preferences) based on their gender" or "in attempting to influence the sexual orientation of individuals, or in discouraging individuals (including adolescents) from engaging in same-sex as opposed to different-sex sexual conduct." *Id.* at 701. Do you agree? If so, does that mean that much of the social science literature on the children of lesbians and gay men is constitutionally *irrelevant*?

B. CUSTODY CASES

EX PARTE J.M.F.
Supreme Court of Alabama, 1998
730 So.2d 1190

LYONS, JUSTICE.

I.

The parties were divorced in January 1993, after a six-year marriage, and the trial court awarded custody of the parties' minor daughter to the mother. Shortly thereafter, the mother began a homosexual relationship with G.S., and in April 1992 she and her daughter moved into an apartment with G.S. Although the apartment had three bedrooms, the mother began sharing a bedroom with G.S. The father was aware of the relationship but, according to him, his conversations with the mother led him to believe that the mother and G.S. would maintain a discreet relationship, that they would not share a bedroom, and that they would represent themselves to the child and others as being merely roommates.

The father subsequently remarried, and the child regularly visited him and his new wife in their home. During the course of these visits, the father learned that his former wife and G.S. were sharing a bedroom, that the child occasionally slept with them in their bed, and that they kissed in the presence of the child. The father also noticed one instance where the child, while playing a game with her stepmother, grabbed the stepmother's breast in a way that appeared to him to be inappropriate. During visitation, the child remarked to the father that "girls could marry girls and boys could marry boys."

After the father learned that the mother and G.S. were not conducting a discreet relationship but were, in fact, openly displaying their affair to the child, and after observing the effect that this was having upon the child, he moved to modify the divorce judgment in order to obtain custody of the daughter. The child underwent expert psychological evaluation and was represented in the modification proceedings by a guardian ad litem.

The evidence presented during the ... proceeding shows that since the divorce, the mother and G.S. have not conducted their relationship with discretion and have not concealed the nature of their union from the child. The mother and G.S. have exchanged rings and have a committed relationship as "life partners" that includes ongoing sexual activity. The mother and G.S. share a bed and the child has at times slept in the bed with them. They kiss and show romantic affection for each other in the child's presence.[1]

The mother has explained to the daughter that she and G.S. love each other the way that the child's father and stepmother love each other. The mother and G.S. testified that G.S. shares in the child's upbringing in the way of a devoted stepmother and that the child accepts and loves her as a parental figure. G.S. regularly attends school functions and meetings with the mother, accompanies the child on school field trips, and eats lunch with the child at school twice a month.

The record contains evidence indicating that the child has remarked several times that girls may marry girls and that boys may marry boys. The mother and G.S. have homosexual couples as guests in their home, and they have taken the daughter with them on an overnight trip to visit a male homosexual couple; during this visit, the child slept with the mother and G.S. in one room, while their hosts shared a bedroom.

---

[1] The record contains no evidence indicating that the mother and G.S. have displayed any sexual activity in the presence of the child, other than hand-holding and kissing that is not prolonged.

During her testimony, the mother repeatedly denied that her lifestyle had resulted in, or would result in, problems for the child. She denied that other children would shun the child based upon the obvious relationship between her mother and G.S., which they regularly display to those at the child's school. The mother stated in deposition testimony that if others showed "prejudice" against the child it would be "up to the child" to decide how to deal with it because "kids have to deal with peer pressure in their own ways anyway." The mother pointed out that children reject other children for a variety of reasons and that her daughter was "going to have to learn about prejudice in her daily life anyway." The mother was confident that the child could decide for herself what to tell her friends and that whatever the child was comfortable with would be fine.

The other evidence adduced during the trial showed, without dispute, that the child has a loving relationship with her father and her stepmother and that she accepts the stepmother as a parental figure. It is undisputed that she enjoys visiting them in their home and that the father and stepmother share in the care of the child when she is with them. The stepmother testified as to her love for the child and her commitment to sharing the responsibility of her upbringing. The father and the stepmother are both employed and can make satisfactory arrangements for the care of the child while they are working; the father, in particular, has a flexible work schedule in his job as an electrician that allows him to be available to care for the child.

There was also expert testimony at trial from the psychologists who examined the child. Dr. Sharon Gotlieb, who was the child's primary therapist, opined that the child's relationship with her mother is excellent, that the two are well bonded, and that the child exhibited no pathology or mental illness. She also stated that the child had a good relationship with G.S. and that the relationship is beneficial to the child. Dr. Gotlieb expressed concern that a change in custody would have a substantial detrimental effect on the child, perhaps causing her to have immediate and/or long-term behavior problems, school problems, or depression. Dr. Gotlieb did testify that a child is best served by having both a male and a female role model in the house, rather than two male, or two female, role models; however, she qualified this statement by opining that the gender of a new adult introduced into the home of a custodial parent after the biological parents divorced would make no difference to the child because the principal role models in her life would remain her parents.

Dr. Daniel McKeever, a pastoral counselor, testified that the father brought the child to him to be evaluated after observing her touching herself "excessively" in the genital area. He testified that, utilizing play therapy, he detected that the child might have issues of anger and sexuality, based upon his perceptions of the child's play with anatomically correct dolls. He also expressed a suspicion that the child might have experienced sexual abuse; however, he also stated that he had only two appointments with the child and that the father's suspicion of sexual abuse stemmed from the fact of the mother's lesbianism. Dr. McKeever did not interview the mother, G.S., or the child's stepmother.

Dr. Karen Turnbow, the court-appointed psychologist, stated in her report to the court that her evaluation of the child revealed no indication of sexual abuse or exposure to sexual acts. She reported that she spent time with both parents, with G.S., and with the child's stepmother, and concluded that the child has a good relationship with each of them and is resilient. Dr. Turnbow stated that, based upon her review of available literature on the subject of a child being reared by an openly homosexual parent, she did not think the homosexuality of a parent should be the sole consideration in a custody situation; rather, she said, the literature suggested that custody should be determined on the basis of individual character and parenting skills.

Dr. James B. Collier testified on behalf of the mother concerning scientific studies as to the effect growing up in a homosexual household had on children. He testified that he had reviewed at least 50 articles, all from journals that are subject to peer review, and that these studies consistently found no adverse consequences for children growing up in such a household.

In addition to the foregoing evidence, the trial court also had before it the report of Terry M. Cromer, the child's appointed guardian ad litem; the report summarized the evidence and scientific studies submitted to the court and presented Cromer's own observations. Cromer confirmed the unanimous opinion of all the psychologists that the child was pretty, well-groomed, intelligent, energetic, healthy, and generally happy. He also confirmed that the child is bonded with both parents and enjoys a loving relationship with both. He recognized that, as Dr. Collier and Dr. Gotlieb had stated, there were studies that had determined that there is generally no significant difference in various factors between a child who has been reared by a heterosexual couple and one who has been reared by a homosexual couple. He also pointed out that there are studies that come to the opposite conclusion and that the child's therapist, Dr. Gotlieb, appeared reluctant to consider studies which suggest that a child reared by homosexual parents could suffer exclusion, isolation, a drop in school grades, and other problems. After summarizing the evidence, Cromer recommended to the trial court that it grant the father's motion to change custody.

After considering all the evidence, the trial court entered an order changing custody to the father, finding that the change would materially promote the child's best interests and setting forth the mother's visitation rights. The trial court initially restricted the mother's visits by ordering that she not "exercise her right of visitation with the minor child of the parties in the presence of a person to whom she is not related by blood or marriage." However, upon motion of the mother, the trial court modified the order to provide that the restriction "shall not apply and be considered as being applicable to the general public, casual, professional, platonic or business relationships."

In reviewing the trial court's judgment, the Court of Civil Appeals pointed out that, in Alabama, evidence of a parent's heterosexual misconduct cannot, in itself, support a change of custody unless the trial court finds that the misconduct has a detrimental effect upon the child. The Court of Civil Appeals emphasized that this standard has been applied in other jurisdictions to cases involving homosexual conduct on the part of a custodial parent, and it adopted this standard for use in such cases in Alabama. In applying this standard, the Court of Civil Appeals determined that the record contained no evidence indicating that the mother's relationship with G.S. has a detrimental effect upon the child, and it thus concluded that the trial court had improperly changed custody based solely upon the mother's homosexuality.

II.

It is, of course, well established that a noncustodial parent seeking a change of custody must show not only that he or she is fit to have custody, but that the change would materially promote the child's best interests. This requires a showing that the positive good brought about by the modification would more than offset the inherently disruptive effect caused by uprooting the child. Where a parent seeks a change of custody based solely upon the heterosexual misconduct of the custodial parent, our law requires that there be an additional showing that the misconduct has a detrimental effect upon the child.

In this case, however, the father has not sought to change the custody of the child based upon the fact that the mother is engaged in a homosexual affair; indeed, the father was aware of the mother's feelings for G.S. at the time of the divorce and was aware that they cohabitated thereafter, but he did not immediately seek a change of custody. The father sought custody of the child only after he had remarried and had discovered that the mother and G.S. were not conducting a discreet affair in the guise of "roommates" but were, instead, presenting themselves openly to the child as affectionate "life partners" with a relationship similar to that of the father and the stepmother. This is, therefore, not a custody case based solely upon the mother's sexual conduct, where the "substantial detrimental effect" element might be applicable. Rather, it is a custody case based upon two distinct changes in the circumstances of the parties: (1) the change in the father's life, from single parenthood to marriage and the creation of a two-parent, heterosexual home environment, and (2) the change in the mother's homosexual relationship, from a discreet affair to the creation of an openly homosexual home environment. The father was not, as the Court of Civil Appeals erroneously held, required to show that the mother's relationship with the child was having a "substantial detrimental effect" upon the child. Rather, he was required to establish that, based upon the changes in the circumstances of the parties, a change in custody would materially promote the child's best interests and that the positive good brought by this change would more than offset the inherently disruptive effect of uprooting the child.

III.

* * * The trial court was presented with evidence of two important changes in the circumstances of the parties that had occurred since their divorce; we will address both of those changes. There is evidence that the mother had expressed feelings for G.S. just before the divorce and that the father was aware of this. There is evidence that, when the mother subsequently moved into a three-bedroom apartment with G.S. and the child, she represented to the father that she and G.S. would not share a room and would represent themselves to be roommates. However, the mother and G.S. subsequently established an open lesbian relationship, which they explained to the child and which they demonstrate with affection in the presence of the child on a regular basis.

The mother has testified that she has not had any significant concern about the adverse effect her transformation from a married heterosexual to a committed homosexual could have on the child. The mother has repeatedly denied that the child will suffer any ill effects from the mother's choice of lifestyle; however, the mother has also testified that it will be up to the child to cope with any ridicule or prejudice that the child might suffer as she gets older, because, she said, "all children have to cope with prejudice anyway."

The mother and G.S. have homosexual couples as guests in their home, and the evidence suggests that the child believes that "girls can marry girls." Both the mother and G.S. have testified that they would not discourage the child from adopting a homosexual lifestyle. In short, the mother and G.S. have established a two-parent home environment where their homosexual relationship is openly practiced and presented to the child as the social and moral equivalent of a heterosexual marriage.[3]

---

[3]   Act 98–500, Ala. Acts 1998, approved by the Governor on May 1, 1998, forbids the issuance of a marriage license "in the State of Alabama to parties of the same sex" and provides that the State of Alabama "shall not recognize as valid any marriage of parties of the same sex that occurred or was alleged to have occurred" anywhere else.

The trial court also heard evidence indicating that the father is no longer a single parent, but has now established a happy marriage with a woman who loves the child, assists in her care, and has demonstrated a commitment to sharing the responsibility of rearing the child should the father gain custody of her. The child has consistently expressed love for the stepmother and acceptance of her as a parental figure. The father and the stepmother have a house with ample room for the child, and they are able to provide for her material needs, as well as her emotional and physical needs. In short, the father and the stepmother have established a two-parent home environment where heterosexual marriage is presented as the moral and societal norm.

The trial court had before it a number of scientific studies as to the effect of child-rearing by homosexual couples, and much of the information presented by those studies suggests that a homosexual couple with good parenting skills is just as likely to successfully rear a child as is a heterosexual couple. The trial court was also presented with studies indicating that a child reared by a homosexual couple is more likely to experience isolation, behavioral problems, and depression and that the optimum environment for rearing a child is one where both a male and a female role model are present, living together in a marriage relationship. There was evidence that the child displayed conduct that gave her father cause for concern.

After carefully considering all of the evidence, we simply cannot hold that the trial court abused its discretion in determining that the positive good brought about by placing the child in the custody of her father would more than offset the inherent disruption brought about by uprooting the child from her mother's custody. While the evidence shows that the mother loves the child and has provided her with good care, it also shows that she has chosen to expose the child continuously to a lifestyle that is "neither legal in this state, nor moral in the eyes of most of its citizens." *Ex parte D.W.W.*, 717 So.2d 793, 796 (Ala.1998).[4] The record contains evidence from which the trial court could have concluded that "[a] child raised by two women or two men is deprived of extremely valuable developmental experience and the opportunity for optimal individual growth and interpersonal development" and that "the degree of harm to children from the homosexual conduct of a parent is uncertain . . . and the range of potential harm is enormous." Lynn D. Wardle, *The Potential*

---

[4] Under Ala. Code 1975, § 13A–6–65, it is a Class A misdemeanor to engage in consensual "deviate sexual intercourse with another person"; this statute was specifically altered by the legislature from the original draft of the "Alabama Criminal Code" proposed to the legislature, so as "to make all homosexual conduct criminal." See Commentary to § 13A–6–65 and § 13A–1–1.

In addition, Alabama has established that "[c]ourse materials and instruction" in the public schools "that relate to [sex] education" shall emphasize, "in a factual manner and from a public health perspective, that homosexuality is not a lifestyle acceptable to the general public and that homosexual conduct is a criminal offense under the laws of the state." Ala. Code 1975, § 16–40A–2(c)(8).

Impact of Homosexual Parenting on Children, 1997 U. Ill. L. Rev. 833, 895 (1997).

While much study, and even more controversy, continue to center upon the effects of homosexual parenting, the inestimable developmental benefit of a loving home environment that is anchored by a successful marriage is undisputed. The father's circumstances have changed, and he is now able to provide this benefit to the child. The mother's circumstances have also changed, in that she is unable, while choosing to conduct an open cohabitation with her lesbian life partner, to provide this benefit. The trial court's change of custody based upon the changed circumstances of the parties was not an abuse of discretion; thus, the Court of Civil Appeals erred in reversing the trial court's judgment. * * *

The judgment of the Court of Civil Appeals is reversed and the cause is remanded for that court to enter a judgment affirming the trial court's order insofar as it changes custody and to consider the issue regarding the restrictions placed upon the mother's visitation rights.

JACOBY V. JACOBY
Florida Court of Appeals, 2000
763 So.2d 410

NORTHCUTT, JUDGE.

The circuit court dissolved the marriage of Julie and David Jacoby in November 1998. Mrs. Jacoby challenges several aspects of the final judgment, including the court's designation of Mr. Jacoby as primary residential parent of the parties' children. We agree with Mrs. Jacoby on the custody issue, and reverse on that point. * * *

Two daughters were born during the marriage, one in August 1989 and the other in October 1992. In November 1996, Mrs. Jacoby informed her husband that she had fallen in love with a longstanding family friend who is a lesbian. The parties separated. Mrs. Jacoby and the children moved into the home of her lesbian partner; Mr. Jacoby stayed in the marital home. After the separation, the children began to visit Mr. Jacoby every other weekend. Then, in September or November 1997, the parties agreed to rotating custody, and the children alternated between the two homes on a weekly basis. This arrangement continued until November 1998, when the circuit court entered its final judgment. During the period of separation and rotating custody, the children continued attending a private school affiliated with a Baptist church, where they had been enrolled before the break-up of the marriage.

Both parties sought primary residential custody of the two girls. Mrs. Jacoby proposed that they live with her and her partner in the home they had shared since the separation. The father became engaged while the divorce was pending. He intended to marry and move into a home owned by his new wife when the dissolution was final. If he were awarded custody, the girls would live with him, his new wife and her teenaged children. They would attend public school in the neighborhood of his new home, which was in the same county as the marital home, but not nearby.

Numerous witnesses testified at trial, including the mother, her partner, the father, his fiancée and a court appointed psychologist. The mother had been the children's primary caretaker during the marriage and the initial period of separation, and the father admitted she was a great parent. But the father, too, had become a better and more involved parent during the rotating custody. The psychologist confirmed that both parties were good parents, but he concluded that Mrs. Jacoby had an edge in parenting skills. She was more adept at demonstrating affection, he said. In addition, the children had stronger emotional ties to her, and she could provide a fine home environment. The psychologist also believed that Mrs. Jacoby would be the custodial parent more likely to encourage contact with the noncustodial parent. He recommended that she be assigned primary residential responsibility for the children.

As often happens in child custody cases, each parent attempted to prove examples of the other's lapses in parental judgment. The court wisely refused to consider a number of these minor conflicts in deciding which parent should have primary residential responsibility for the girls. At the same time, however, the court's remarks during the final hearing and in the final judgment demonstrate that it succumbed to the father's attacks on the mother's sexual orientation, which were the primary feature of this case.

For a court to properly consider conduct such as Mrs. Jacoby's sexual orientation on the issue of custody, the conduct must have a direct effect or impact upon the children. See *Maradie v. Maradie*, 680 So.2d 538 (Fla. 1st DCA 1996). "[T]he mere possibility of negative impact on the child is not enough." *Id.* at 543. The connection between the conduct and the harm to the children must have an evidentiary basis; it cannot be assumed. We have reviewed the court's comments concerning the negative impact of the mother's sexual orientation on the children, and have found them to be conclusory or unsupported by the evidence.

For example, the final judgment stated that "[t]here is no doubt that the husband feels the current living arrangement of the wife is immoral and an inappropriate place in which to rear their children. . . . Obviously, this opinion is shared by others in the community." But the latter is not obvious to us from this record. In fact, there was no evidence addressing "the community's" beliefs about the morality of homosexuals or their child rearing abilities.

The order then addressed the community's reaction to homosexuals, by paraphrasing the psychologist's testimony: "Dr. Merin testified that a *strong stigma* attaches to homosexuality and that while being reared in a homosexual environment does not appear to alter sexual preference, it *does affect* social interaction and that it is likely that the children's peers or their parents will have negative words or thoughts about this." (emphasis supplied). The court mischaracterized Dr. Merin's testimony. In response to the question "and it's your understanding that you say times are changing . . . , but there is still a stigma socially attached with homosexual lifestyles in our society?" Dr. Merin responded "yes." He did not quantify the degree. He did remark that "[i]n our society it is now the likelihood that there would be words spoken or thoughts, negative thoughts or concerns by children's peers or the parent of their peers. . . ." Dr. Merin's actual testimony about social interaction was: "research *would indicate that the considerations would be given more to their social interaction* than to the great degree of probability that they would themselves, you know, develop homosexual characteristics." (emphasis supplied).

But even if the court's comments about the community's beliefs and possible reactions were correct and supported by the evidence in this record, the law cannot give effect to private biases. *See Palmore v. Sidoti*, 466 U.S. 429, 433 (1984). Moreover, even if the law were to permit consideration of the biases of others, and even if we were to accept the assumption that such would necessarily harm the children, the bias and ensuing harm would flow not from the fact that the children were *living* with a homosexual mother, but from the fact that she *is* a homosexual. The circuit court's reliance on perceived biases was an improper basis for a residential custody determination.

The final judgment also contained unsupported findings concerning the effect on the children of religious teachings about homosexuality. The judgment stated: "Dr. Merin testified that once the children learn about homosexuality and religious teachings, real confusion and conflict *will arise* for them." (emphases supplied.) Again, the order does not accurately reflect Dr. Merin's views. Concerning a possible conflict between religious teachings and homosexuality, Dr. Merin opined that as the children get older, they *may* become confused, but that their level of comfort would be affected by how the situation was handled. This was the only testimony about the possible effects of religious teaching on the children, and it did not support a finding that the mother's sexual orientation will harm the children.

Moreover, the record contains no competent evidence about what, if any, religious teaching the children were exposed to. Yet the judge criticized Mrs. Jacoby's decision to keep the children in the church-affiliated school they had been attending, stating he "[could not] determine if [the mother] is naive or simply blase, but she has made absolutely no effort to determine how her current lifestyle might adversely impact the children in their current school environment." These words are disquieting for several reasons. First, ironically, they betray the influence of religious stereotyping. Several witnesses testified about the Baptists' beliefs without ever explaining the sources of their knowledge. When Mr. Jacoby's attorney asked Dr. Merin if he knew the Baptists' position on homosexuality, the doctor responded that they were strongly opposed to it. Mr. Jacoby also testified he had learned that the Baptist religion was against homosexuality. At one point, the trial court itself questioned Mrs. Jacoby directly, asking whether she was aware that "the Baptists" had boycotted Disney World. None of this was competent evidence; nothing in the record suggested that the psychologist, Mr. Jacoby, or the trial court was qualified to expound on Baptist doctrine.

Second, no evidence was presented to show to what degree, how, or even whether this supposed Baptist doctrine of anti-homosexuality was espoused at the children's school or, for that matter, at the church with which it was affiliated. Indeed, the only evidence with any bearing on these questions suggested an atmosphere of tolerance; Mr. and Mrs. Jacoby both testified that the school employed a teacher who was widely known to be homosexual. The court's question about "Disney World" presumably referred to the 1996 and 1997 votes by attendees at the Southern Baptist Convention to boycott the Walt Disney Company in part because it extended health benefits to employees in same-sex relationships. But there was no evidence in this record about that boycott. The court's implication either that Baptists were unanimous in that position or that the Southern Baptist Convention wields some sort of hierarchal authority over Baptist churches and schools had no evidentiary support.

Third, while criticizing Mrs. Jacoby for failing to investigate Baptist teachings on homosexuality, the court chose to ignore Mr. Jacoby's own similar failings. Mr. Jacoby testified that he intended to convert to Catholicism after his remarriage, and he had been taking the girls to a Catholic church. But he conceded that he did not know the Catholic tenets on homosexuality.

In short, there was no evidence to show that the children were being harmed or would be harmed by their continued enrollment in the school they had attended during the parties' marriage. Nor does the record disclose that Mrs. Jacoby's decision to keep the children in that school was any less informed than Mr. Jacoby's desire to take them out of it.

Mrs. Jacoby's sexual orientation found its way into the final judgment in other ways. The judgment referred to the father's fiancée's house as "a very appropriate home" and a "very nice home." It went on to state that "[t]he preference of this home to the one proposed by the wife is obvious. . . ." Again, although we are confident that the court accurately assessed Mr. Jacoby's new home, the obviousness of its preference is not apparent from the evidence. Nothing in the record suggested that Mrs. Jacoby's house was physically inappropriate for raising children; that is, that it was too small or in an unsavory neighborhood, or some such. In fact, the evidence showed it was a three bedroom home, that the girls shared their own bedroom, and that they had a computer complete with children's games.

If the court's "obvious" preference was based on the father's heterosexual relationship, it was akin to the custody award to the father in *Packard v. Packard*, 697 So.2d 1292, 1293 (Fla. 1st DCA 1997), based solely on the fact that he lived in a "more traditional family environment." As did the First District in *Packard*, we reject such a determination when no evidence showed harm to the children resulting from the "nontraditional" environment.

The court also found that when the Jacoby children have spent time with the father in the company of his fiancée and her children "there has been absolutely nothing inappropriate in the presence of the children or during the time they may have spent the night in the home." We have no quarrel with this finding, which is amply supported by the evidence. But Mr. Jacoby's counsel has endeavored to contrast this fact with a charge that Mrs. Jacoby and her partner were not so circumspect in their behavior. In his written closing argument to the circuit court, in his brief on appeal, and at oral argument the father's counsel repeatedly intoned that the evidence proved the two women allowed the children in their bed when the adults were topless. After carefully reviewing the record, we dismiss this accusation as specious innuendo, intended to imply that the women engaged in sexual conduct in the children's presence. The record citation tendered for this assertion was the father's testimony that one of the girls, upon seeing him working in the yard shirtless, commented "that [he] was topless and [he] slept topless like mommy does." While the mother acknowledged that she and her companion slept together, and that sometimes the children were allowed into their mother's bed to snuggle, these facts simply do not support the inference the father promotes. For its part, the trial court made no finding that Mrs. Jacoby had ever engaged in sexual conduct in the children's presence. We are satisfied that it was no more taken in by this canard than we are.

In summary, when making this custody determination the circuit court penalized the mother for her sexual orientation without evidence that it harmed the children. Accordingly, we reverse the court's appointment of the father as primary residential parent, and remand with directions to enter a new custody order.

THREADGILL, ACTING CHIEF JUDGE, Dissenting.

I respectfully dissent from that portion of the majority opinion that reverses the award of primary residential responsibility for the children to Mr. Jacoby.

In reviewing a true discretionary act, such as an award of child custody, an appellate court must fully recognize the superior vantage point of the trial court and apply a test of reasonableness to determine whether the trial court abused its discretion. If reasonable men could differ as to the propriety of the trial court's action, then it cannot be said the trial court abused its discretion.

In this case, I believe the trial court gave thorough consideration to the criteria set forth in section 61.13(3), Florida Statutes (1997). I am convinced that the trial court limited its consideration of Mrs. Jacoby's sexual orientation to the effect it would have on the best interests of the children. Unlike the majority, I believe there is competent, substantial evidence in the record to support the relevant findings of the trial court. Under such circumstances, I conclude that the trial court did not abuse its discretion in awarding primary residential responsibility to Mr. Jacoby. I would affirm on that issue. Otherwise, I concur in the majority opinion.

MAGNUSON V. MAGNUSON

Court of Appeals of Washington, 2007
170 P.3d 65, 141 Wash.App. 347

BROWN, J.

In this parenting plan dispute, Robert S. Magnuson contends the trial court erred by improperly considering transgender status when it granted primary residential placement of the parties' children to Dr. Tracy A. Magnuson. But the court properly focused on the children's needs in making the residential placement decision, not transgender status, conforming to principles established in sexual preference cases. We agree with this extension of principle. Accordingly, we affirm.

In 1985, "Robbie"[1] Magnuson and Tracy A. Magnuson (now Berg) were married. They had two children, Brian (born October 4, 1991) and Meridith (born December 29, 1998). Tracy is a surgeon and Robbie is an attorney. Robbie eventually "announced that [s]he needed to, and would be transitioning from male to female." She took a leave of absence from work and ultimately resigned. Robbie and Tracy separated in October 2004, and Tracy filed to dissolve their marriage.

---

[1] Each party is referred to by first name to avoid confusion without disrespect to individual or professional status. Similarly, Robbie is referred to by pronoun in the female gender consistent with the preference shown in Robbie's briefing and to conform to and avoid confusion with the trial court's quoted findings of fact.

After an eight-day trial, the court entered numerous findings, including: "Both parents are good and loving parents . . . The children's relationship with each parent is approximately equal. Each has performed equal but very different roles with the children. . . . Historically, the parties were a dual professional family, relying on the assistance of nannies[,] and [i]t is somewhat disingenuous for either parent to claim the historical role of primary parent in this case."

The court found both parents acted in ways adversely affecting the children's stability. For example, Tracy denigrated Robbie in front of the children; Robbie's conduct had an "unimaginable impact on Meridith" when she showed up at Meridith's school, pushed Meridith's maternal grandmother out of the way, and "grabbed Meridith, such that observers actually thought a kidnapping was going on." Further, "[Robbie] has indicated she will be undergoing sexual reassignment surgery sometime in the very near future . . . [Robbie's] surgery may be everything [she] has hoped for, or it may be disastrous. No one knows what is ahead[,] and [t]he impact of gender reassignment surgery on the children is unknown."

The court found while Robbie left her job, Tracy "maintained her professional career, has provided for the children in the 'former' family home, and provides an oasis of stability in all of this ongoing change." A previous shared co-equal residential placement did not work, and "[t]hese children, in particular, need environmental and parental stability." Finally, "[w]hile the margin is somewhat slim in this particular case, [Tracy] is in a more stable and predictable place in her life right now to act as the children's primary care giver." Robbie appealed.

The issue is whether the trial court abused its discretion by impermissibly considering Robbie's transgender status in granting residential placement of the parties' two minor children to Tracy. Robbie contends the court erred in rejecting the guardian ad litem's (GAL) recommendation, in finding "[t]he impact of gender reassignment surgery on the children is unknown" [Factual Finding 2.21 X], in failing to properly address the factors in RCW 26.09.187(3)(a), and in restricting Robbie's parental rights.

We review a trial court's child placement decision for abuse of discretion. Trial courts have broad discretion and are not bound by GAL recommendations. * * * Certain factors must be considered when establishing the residential provisions in a permanent parenting plan. RCW 26.09.187(3)(a). These include: the parent/child relationship, the parents' responsibilities in performing parenting functions, parent agreements, "[e]ach parent's past and potential for future performance of parenting functions," the child's "emotional needs and developmental level," the child's relationships and activities, including schooling, the parent's wishes, the wishes of a mature child, and the parents' employment schedules. RCW 26.09.187(3)(a)(iii)(iv).

First, the trial court carefully considered each child's relationship with each parent before [ruling]. The court did not interview the children, but relied upon specific evidence given by the parties and the GAL when finding the impact of Robbie's surgery on the children was unknown. The court acted within its fact-finding discretion when drawing inferences from the given evidence of the children's present uncomfortable and nervous behavior to make the future impact finding. While Robbie points to evidence of the children's adjustment, we are in no position to find facts, reweigh the evidence, or decide witness credibility.

Second, the court was not bound by the GAL's recommendation. The court's oral ruling and its extensive findings of fact show the factors in RCW 26.09.187(3)(a) that were considered; the court is not required to enter written findings on each factor. The record does not support Robbie's assertion that by rejecting the GAL's recommendation, the court impermissibly based its placement decision on transgender status.

Indeed, the court found Robbie was "undergoing an authentic gender transformation," and "has a right to be happy in her chosen life ahead." And, Robbie received substantial residential time with the children without limitation or restriction. *See In re Marriage of Cabalquinto,* 100 Wash.2d 325, 329, 669 P.2d 886 (1983) ("Visitation rights must be determined with reference to the needs of the child rather than the sexual preferences of the parent."). The *Cabalquinto* court's reasoning in a sexual preference visitation context is equally applicable in this transgender residential placement context.

In sum, the need of each child, not Robbie's transgender status, was the court's focus in determining residential placement. The court focused on the children's need for "environmental and parental stability" in granting the majority of residential time to Tracy, a permissible statutory factor addressing the children's emotional needs. RCW 26.09.187(3)(a) . . . Affirmed.

KULIK, J. (dissenting).

I agree with the majority's conclusion that the Supreme Court's reasoning in *In re Marriage of Cabalquinto,* 100 Wash.2d 325, 669 P.2d 886 (1983) is equally applicable to transgender persons. *Cabalquinto* held that a trial court cannot restrict a parent's rights based on sexual orientation, and the majority here extends that holding to transgender persons. However, the trial court erred by doing exactly what the majority here prohibits—the court awarded primary residential placement to Tracy based on Robbie's transgender status. This is a manifest abuse of discretion and, therefore, I respectfully dissent . . .

The trial court's Findings of Fact (FF) 2.21 X provides: "The impact of gender reassignment surgery on the children is unknown." But the trial court's other findings refute the assertion that substantial evidence supports FF 2.21 X. Contrary to the unrebutted expert opinion of Dr. Walter Bockting, the court found that the impact of the gender reassignment surgery on the children was unknown. Dr. Bockting is a national expert in transgender parenting. He presented uncontradicted testimony that transgender status does not ultimately have an impact on the parent's ability to parent.

The court found that the children had approximately equal relationships with each parent. Significantly, the court made no finding that Robbie's transgender status endangered the physical, mental, or emotional health of the children. And, the trial court found that Robbie was the more nurturing parent.

The guardian ad litem (GAL) conducted an exhaustive investigation. He interviewed 23 lay witnesses and 15 professional and expert witnesses, and prepared a 214-page report. The court found that the GAL had done a thorough job and had performed his role in an exemplary way.

The GAL testified that Robbie was the primary parent based on sabbaticals and involvement with the children on a day-to-day basis. The GAL concluded that Robbie was the more nurturing and engaged parent, and he recommended that the court designate Robbie as the primary residential parent. The GAL also concluded that Tracy had always been the secondary parent. Another expert, Dr. Paul Wert, the court-appointed psychologist, stated that psychologically and emotionally, Robbie was capable of continuing to extensively parent.

The trial court also erroneously based its decision to place the children with Tracy on a misreading of RCW 26.09.187(3)(a)(I). Under this statute, the greatest weight shall be given to the "relative strength, nature, and stability of the child's relationship with each parent." RCW 26.09.187(3)(a)(I). Here, the trial court found a lack of stability based on Robbie's transgender status. "The respondent has indicated she will be undergoing sexual reassignment surgery sometime in the very near future. Said surgery may be everything respondent has hoped for, or it may be disastrous. No one knows what is ahead."

However, the statute requires a review of the stability of the child's relationship with the parent—not a review of whether the parent may have a surgery that impacts the parent. The trial court's conclusion that Robbie's life was not stable because of her planned surgery was directly and impermissibly related to Robbie's transgender status. And again, there was no evidence and no finding that Robbie's transgender status would cause any harm or detriment to the children.

Moreover, the proper test of parental fitness is the present condition of the parent. The court's speculation about the future is not an appropriate basis for awarding custody.

Finally, the trial court itself recognized that Robbie's transgender status caused no harm to the children when it placed no restrictions on Robbie's visitation with the children. The court agreed that the children's relationships with each parent were approximately equal. Apparently, the only difference between the parents was that Robbie, the primary parent, planned to have gender reassignment surgery.

"A trial court abuses its discretion when its decision is manifestly unreasonable or based on untenable grounds." *In re Parentage of J.H.,* 112 Wash.App. 486, 492, 49 P.3d 154 (2002). One parent's transgender status is not a tenable ground upon which to decide residential placement. Accordingly, I respectfully dissent.

NOTES

1. *Openness of Relationship.* It appears that the lesbian mother lost in *Ex parte J.M.F.* because she was not sufficiently "discreet" in her relationship with her partner to satisfy the Alabama Supreme Court. Notice how the court did not require the petitioning father to establish that the mother's relationship with another woman adversely affected the child. Instead, the openness of the relationship, both inside and outside of the home, seems to have been enough to justify taking custody away from the lesbian mother and awarding it to the remarried father.

The North Carolina Supreme Court reached a similar conclusion in *Pulliam v. Smith,* 348 N.C. 616, 501 S.E.2d 898 (1998). After Carol and Frederick were divorced in 1991, they entered into a consent decree by which they would have joint legal custody and Frederick would have physical custody of their two children, ages three and six. The mother remarried and subsequently brought a motion to modify the custody judgment based on the fact that Frederick's gay partner had moved in with him and the children. The trial court granted the custody modification petition, but the intermediate appellate court, as in *Ex parte J.M.F.,* reversed concluding that there was insufficient evidence that the father's living arrangement adversely affected the children. The North Carolina Supreme Court reversed, noting that

> uncontroverted evidence was presented that defendant-father and Mr. Tipton engaged in oral sex approximately once a week in the home with the children present [in the home]. Defendant-father and Mr. Tipton intended to continue such homosexual activity in the home. Defendant-father saw nothing wrong with such conduct and would not counsel the two minor children that such conduct was improper.

Evidence was also presented tending to show that the children had seen the two men demonstrate physical affection, including kissing each other on the lips. This activity took place in the home in front of the children as the "provider" of this couple prepared to leave for work. The minor child Joey had observed his father and Mr. Tipton in bed together.

The evidence further tended to show that the door of the bedroom occupied by defendant-father and Mr. Tipton was directly across the hall and approximately three feet from the door to the children's bedroom. Defendant-father and Mr. Tipton testified that both their bedroom door and the children's bedroom door were open at all times, except when the two men engaged in sexual activity. Further, testimony tended to show that the children went in and out of the two men's bedroom at will, often during the night when the two men were in bed together.

Defendant testified that he had told the children that society was not accepting of such a homosexual relationship. There was also evidence that Mr. Tipton kept photographs of "drag queens" in the home, despite his admission that the children should not be exposed to such material. Further, evidence was presented that Mr. Tipton had, on at least one occasion, taken the children away from the home without defendant's knowledge of their whereabouts.

. . . We conclude that activities such as the regular commission of sexual acts in the home by unmarried people, failing and refusing to counsel the children against such conduct while acknowledging this conduct to them, allowing the children to see unmarried persons known by the children to be sexual partners in bed together, keeping admittedly improper sexual material in the home, and Mr. Tipton's taking the children out of the home without their father's knowledge of their whereabouts support the trial court's findings of "improper influences" which are "detrimental to the best interest and welfare of the two minor children."

We do not agree with the conclusion of Justice Webb's dissent that the only basis upon which the trial court changed custody was that the defendant is a "practicing homosexual." Instead, we conclude that the trial court could and did order a change in custody *based in part* on proper findings of fact to the effect that defendant-father was regularly engaging in sexual acts with Mr. Tipton in the home while the children were present and upon other improper conduct by these two men. The trial court did not rely on the mere fact that defendant is a homosexual or a "practicing homosexual." Nor does this Court hold that the mere homosexual status of a parent is sufficient, taken alone, to support denying such parent custody of his or her child or children. That question is not presented by the facts of this case. . . .

... [E]vidence was [also] presented that when Joey was told that defendant-father was involved in a homosexual relationship, Joey was emotionally distraught, covering his face with his hands and running into the bathroom. Later, Joey cried, grasped onto his mother, and asked his mother to get him out of defendant's home. Evidence was also presented that sometime thereafter, Joey told his stepfather, William Pulliam, that he wanted his mother to come and get him and take him to Wichita where she lived. Further, evidence was presented that Joey expressed confusion over defendant's homosexual relationship with Mr. Tipton by asking Mr. Tipton if he was Joey's stepfather.

The trial court could reasonably find from this substantial evidence, as well as the other evidence discussed above, that "[t]he activity of the Defendant will likely create emotional difficulties for the two minor children."

Id. at 900–04.

2.   *Peer/Social Harassment.* In *Jacoby*, the Florida court rejected the argument that custody or visitation should be adjusted because a child may face peer or community ridicule by virtue of being placed with a gay or lesbian parent. Note that the court did not discount the logic of the argument so much as it concluded that it should not be given weight. In reaching that conclusion, the Florida court relied on the U.S. Supreme Court's decision in *Palmore v. Sidoti*, 466 U.S. 429, 433, 104 S.Ct. 1879, 80 L.Ed.2d 421 (1984). In *Palmore*, a white couple divorced with the mother gaining custody of the couple's 3 year-old daughter. Subsequently, the mother began living with— and married—a black man. The Florida trial court granted the father's motion for a change of custody, stating:

The father's evident resentment of the mother's choice of a black partner is not sufficient to wrest custody from the mother. It is of some significance, however, that the mother did see fit to bring a man into her home and carry on a sexual relationship with him without being married to him. Such action tended to place gratification of her own desires ahead of her concern for the child's future welfare. This Court feels that despite the strides that have been made in bettering relations between the races in this country, it is inevitable that Melanie will, if allowed to remain in her present situation and attains school age and thus more vulnerable to peer pressures, suffer from the social stigmatization that is sure to come.

466 U.S. at 431, 104 S.Ct. at 1881, 80 L.Ed.2d at 424.

The U.S. Supreme Court reversed, stating:

It would ignore reality to suggest that racial and ethnic prejudices do not exist or that all manifestations of those prejudices have been eliminated. There is a risk that a child living with a stepparent of a different race may be subject to a variety of pressures and stresses not present if the child were living with parents of the same racial or ethnic origin.

The question, however, is whether the reality of private biases and the possible injury they might inflict are permissible considerations for removal of an infant child from the custody of its natural mother. We have little difficulty concluding that they are not. The Constitution cannot control such prejudices but neither can it tolerate them. Private biases may be outside the reach of the law, but the law cannot, directly or indirectly, give them effect. * * *

The effects of racial prejudice, however real, cannot justify a racial classification removing an infant child from the custody of its natural mother found to be an appropriate person to have such custody.

466 U.S. at 433–34, 104 S.Ct. at 1882–3, 80 L.Ed.2d at 426.

Prior to *Palmore*, courts occasionally used the harassment theory to curtail lesbian/gay custody or visitation rights. Thus, in *Jacobson v. Jacobson*, 314 N.W.2d 78, 82 (N.D. 1981), the North Dakota Supreme Court held that in light of society's mores toward homosexuality and the mother's involvement in a lesbian relationship, it was not in the best interests of the children to be placed in the custody of their mother. The court reasoned:

> [W]e cannot lightly dismiss the fact that living in the same house with their mother and her lover may well cause the children to "suffer from the slings and arrows of a disapproving society" to a much greater extent than would an arrangement wherein the children were placed in the custody of their father with visitation rights in the mother. Although we agree with the trial court that the children will be required to deal with the problem regardless of which parent has custody, it is apparent to us that requiring the children to live, day-to-day, in the same residence with the mother and her lover means that the children will have to confront the problem to a significantly greater degree than they would if living with their father.

Id. at 81.

The North Dakota Supreme Court eventually overruled *Jacobson*. *See Damron v. Damron*, 670 N.W.2d 871, 875 (N.D. 2003). The trial court, relying on *Jacobson*, had granted the father's motion to modify custody because the fact that the children were living with the mother and her female partner created a presumption that they were being harmed. The North Dakota Supreme Court reversed, holding that "a custodial parent's homosexual household is not grounds for modifying custody within two years of a prior custody in the absence of evidence that environment endangers or potentially endangers the children's physical or emotional health or impairs their emotional development." *Id*. at 876. In overruling *Jacobson*, the North

Dakota Supreme Court implicitly rejected the social stigma argument as grounds for awarding parental rights and responsibilities.

Other courts, in addition to the Florida court in *Jacoby*, have explicitly rejected the argument. *See Inscoe v. Inscoe*, 700 N.E.2d 70, 82, 121 Ohio App.3d 396, 415 (Ct. App. 1997) (holding that "[w]hen determining an allocation of parental rights and responsibilities, a trial court must disregard adverse impact on the child that flow from society's disapproval of a parent's sexual orientation") (citing *Palmore v. Sidoti*); *accord S.N.E. v. R.L.B.*, 699 P.2d 875, 879 (Alaska 1985). *See also In re Marriage of R.S.*, 286 Ill.App.3d 1046, 1053, 222 Ill.Dec. 498, 677 N.E.2d 1297, 1301 (Ct. App. 1996) (holding that the possibility that "the children might suffer some future social condemnation" because "of the mother's sexual orientation or conjugal relationship" is not enough to justify modification of custody in the absence of a finding that the children were adversely affected).

3.   *Custody Disputes with Third Parties*. Lesbian and gay parents have not only lost custody of their children to their former spouses, as in *Ex parte J.M.F.*, but they have also lost custody to nonparents. In *Bottoms v. Bottoms*, 457 S.E.2d 102, 249 Va. 410 (1995), the Virginia Supreme Court upheld the change in custody from the child's lesbian mother to the maternal grandmother noting inter alia that "[c]onduct inherent in lesbianism is punishable as a Class 6 felony in the Commonwealth" and "that living daily under conditions stemming from active lesbianism practiced in the home may impose a burden upon a child by reason of the 'social condemnation' attached to such an arrangement, which will inevitably afflict the child's relationships with its 'peers and with the community at large.'" 457 S.E.2d at 108, 249 Va. at 420 (quoting *Roe v. Roe*, 324 S.E.2d 691, 694, 228 Va. 722, 728 (1985)). *See also White v. Thompson*, 569 So.2d 1181, 1184 (Miss. 1990) (upholding the transfer of custody from lesbian mother to paternal grandparents).

In contrast, the court in *In re Strome*, 120 P.3d 499, 505–06, 201 Or.App. 625, 638 (2005), concluded that the mother of a gay father who sought custody of her grandchildren failed to overcome the statutory presumption favoring legal parents in custody disputes. And the court in *Clifford K. v. Paul S.*, 619 S.E.2d 138, 161, 217 W.Va. 625, 648 (2005), ruled that, after the mother of the child died, it was in his best interests to be cared for by the mother's female partner rather than by the deceased mother's father. *See also In re Guardianship of Sophia S.*, 2005 WL 3471671, at *4 (Cal. Ct. App. 2005) (upholding the naming of mother's former lesbian partner as guardian of child rather than the child's maternal grandmother).

4.   Four years after it decided *Ex parte J.M.F.*, the Alabama Supreme Court affirmed a trial court's denial of a motion to modify custody brought by a lesbian mother. *See In re D.H.*, 830 So.2d 21, 26 (Ala. 2002). Although the majority, unlike the trial court, did not dwell on the mother's sexual orientation, Chief Justice Roy Moore stated in a concurring opinion that "the homosexual conduct of a parent—conduct involving a sexual relationship between two persons of the same gender—creates a strong presumption of

unfitness that alone is sufficient justification for denying that parent custody of his or her own children or prohibiting the adoption of the children of others." *Id.* at 26 (Moore, C.J. concurring). For examples of courts that have refused to hold the sexual orientation of lesbian and gay parents against them in custody cases, see *Maxwell v. Maxwell*, 382 S.W.3d 892 (Ky. 2012); *Damron v. Damron*, 670 N.W.2d 871 (N.D. 2003). *But see Brimberry v. Gordon*, 2013 WL 4748028 at *4 (Ark.Ct.App. Sept. 4, 2013) (affirming trial court's decision to deny custody to lesbian mother because of her "lifestyle choices" and noting that the evidence showed "that the mother had her [female] romantic partner spend the night in the home, often when the child was present [and] that the child would climb into bed with them in the morning.").

5. *Transgender Parents.* The Nevada Supreme Court in *Daly v. Daly*, 102 Nev. 66, 715 P.2d 56 (1986), *overruled on other grounds by In re Termination of Parental Rights as to N.J.*, 116 Nev. 790, 8 P.3d 126 (2000), upheld the termination of the parental rights of a male-to-female transgender parent. The child in the case was born more than a dozen years before her father underwent sex-reassignment surgery. When the mother learned of the impending surgery, she petitioned to have the father's parental rights terminated. The court found the termination to be in the child's best interest because of "the substantial risk of emotional or mental injury were she forced to visit with her father." *Id.* at 59. Similarly, the court in *M.B. v. D.W.*, 236 S.W.3d 31 (Ky.Ct.App. 2007), terminated the parental rights of a male-to-female transsexual parent so that her former wife's new husband could adopt the child.

In contrast, the court in *Christian v. Randall*, 516 P.2d 132, 33 Colo.App. 129 (Ct. App. 1973), refused to transfer custody from a female-to-male transgender parent who had custody of the children for many years after the divorce and before he underwent sex-change surgery. The court noted that the sex change did not "adversely affect respondent's relationship with the children nor impair their emotional development." 516 P.2d at 134, 33 Colo.App. at 133. *Cf. In re Marriage of D.F.D & D.G.D.*, 862 P.2d 368, 376, 261 Mont. 186, 200 (1993) (concluding that trial court erred in denying joint custody to father who had in the past dressed in women's clothes in private).

C. VISITATION RESTRICTIONS

MOIX V. MOIX

Supreme Court of Arkansas
___ S.W.3d ___, 2013 Ark. 478, 2013 WL 6118520 (Ark.)

CLIFF HOOFMAN, JUSTICE.

Appellant John Moix appeals from the circuit court's visitation order, which contained a provision prohibiting his long-term, domestic partner from being present during any overnight visitation with appellant's minor child. On appeal, appellant argues that the circuit court's order violated his state and federal constitutional rights to privacy and equal protection, and that the circuit court erred by finding that such a non-cohabitation restriction was required in the absence of any finding of harm to the child. . . . We reverse and remand.

John and Libby Moix were divorced in 2004. The divorce decree incorporated the parties' settlement agreement, which provided that the parties would share joint custody of their three sons, with appellee serving as the primary custodian and appellant receiving reasonable visitation. The settlement agreement also stated that neither party was to have overnight guests of the opposite sex.

In May 2005, appellee filed a petition to modify visitation, alleging that since the entry of the divorce decree, appellant had been having a romantic relationship with a live-in male companion and that the children had been exposed to that relationship on multiple occasions. Appellee asserted that appellant and his partner had recently separated after they were involved in a physical altercation in which appellant was seriously injured, although they had since resumed their relationship and were again residing together. Appellee requested that, due to this change in circumstances, the circuit court grant her sole custody of the children and limit appellant's visitation in such a way as to limit the children's exposure to the illicit relationship and to the danger caused by the volatility of his companion. Appellant agreed to the entry of an order of modification, filed on July 18, 2005, which provided that the existing custody arrangement would continue with the two older twin boys, but that appellee would receive full custody of R.M., who was five years old at the time. The order also restricted appellant to visitation with R.M. on every other weekend and every Wednesday, with no overnight visitation.

Despite the agreed order modifying visitation, it is undisputed by the parties that the order was not followed and that appellant had liberal overnight visitation with R.M. until late 2009 or early 2010, when he became addicted to prescription drugs and sought inpatient treatment after being involved in a hit-and-run accident. After he completed his treatment, appellant was limited to daytime visitation at the discretion of appellee. In May 2012, appellant filed a motion for modification of visitation and child support, in which he alleged that appellee had remarried in 2010 and that she had informed him that R.M. had a new father and no longer needed him. Appellant asserted that the severe reduction in his visitation coincided with appellee's remarriage and that his son had expressed the desire to spend more time with him. Because there had been a material change in circumstances based on appellee's remarriage, her new husband usurping his role as father of R.M., and the fact that R.M. was now twelve years old and wished to spend more time with his father, appellant requested that the circuit court modify visitation to allow overnight visits, as well as holiday and extended summer visitation.

In her response, appellee denied that there had been a material change in circumstances or that it was in R.M.'s best interest to have increased visitation. She asserted that any change in appellant's circumstances had been detrimental, pointing to his arrest for driving while under the influence of prescription drugs and the fact that he had lost his pharmacist license. She further alleged that appellant's relationship with his boyfriend had been volatile and that it was not in R.M.'s best interest to have overnight visitation in such an environment.

At the hearing held on October 9, 2012, appellant testified that he had been a pharmacist for twenty-three years and that he had had previous problems with a prescription-drug addiction in 1993, although he had completed treatment and remained sober until his recent relapse subsequent to his divorce. He testified that he gradually relapsed from 2004 until February 2010, when he was arrested for a DWI after being involved in a hit-and-run accident. Appellant completed several months of inpatient treatment and testified that he had completely abstained from alcohol and prescription drugs since February 2010. He further testified that he was now under a ten-year contract with the pharmacy board, pursuant to which he had been able to regain his pharmacist license, and that he has to call every morning to see if he must undergo a drug screen. So far, appellant stated that he had undergone fifty-nine random drug screens, all of which had been negative. He testified that he has also been regularly attending AA and NA meetings as required under the contract.

With regard to his relationship with his partner, Chad Cornelius, appellant testified that they had been in a committed, monogamous relationship for at least seven years and that they had applied for a marriage license in Iowa. Appellant stated that he had enjoyed overnight visitation with R.M. for five years before appellee forbade it and that even though Chad had been present, R.M. had never been exposed to any type of romantic behavior between them. Appellant testified that he and Chad had never slept in the same bed during any of R.M.'s previous visits and that if overnight visitation were again allowed, he would continue to abstain from bed sharing or other romantic behavior in the presence of his son. Appellant stated that Chad has a son from his previous marriage who often stays overnight at their home and that R.M. and Chad's son have a close relationship that would be greatly hindered if Chad were not allowed to be present during any overnight visits. According to appellant, he and Chad had not had any altercations since the one in 2005, which did not occur in the presence of R.M., and he stated that Chad is a positive role model for his son. Appellant also noted that his two older sons had lived with him during their senior year in high school, that they continued to spend weekends at his home during college, and that one of his sons is moving back home. He testified that all of his children are happy and emotionally, mentally, and physically stable.

Chad also testified and stated that he was a registered nurse at a hospital focusing on children and adolescents with behavioral-health issues. Chad testified that he has had to pass multiple state and federal background checks as a condition of his employment. He agreed that he and appellant had been in a committed relationship since 2005 and that they would like to get married. Chad also confirmed that he always slept in another room when R.M. visited. He testified that his sixteen-year-old son has a great relationship with R.M. Chad confirmed that appellant had been completely abstinent from drugs and alcohol since February 2010, and Chad stated that he personally does not drink alcohol in their home.

[Three other witnesses testified on behalf of the appellant, telling the court that both he and Chad were good and responsible parents.] The final witness to testify was appellee. She testified that she had obtained the 2005 modification order after she became concerned about appellant's and Chad's relationship and how it would affect R.M. She stated that appellant's relationship was not the sole reason why she was contesting his attempt to increase visitation. According to appellee, appellant had complained to her about Chad acting in a threatening and controlling manner, and she indicated that their relationship was unstable and unhealthy. She also indicated that she had found needles and vials of steroids in a guest bedroom of appellant's home while cleaning it in 2009 and that appellant had told her that Chad had a past history of steroid use. She testified that she would like to see appellant exhibit a longer period of being drug and alcohol free before allowing expanded visitation. Appellee further stated that appellant had shared information about the court proceedings with R.M., which she did not feel was appropriate. She admitted that R.M. had a loving relationship with his father and that it was important that they spend time together, but testified that it was not in R.M.'s best interest to have overnight or extended visitation at the present time due to his recent drug issues and his relationship with Chad.

In rebuttal testimony, appellant responded to appellee's allegation about finding needles and steroids in his home. He testified that he was not aware of these items, that he had never used intravenous drugs at any point, and that he was not aware that Chad had ever used them.

The circuit court entered an order on November 14, 2012, granting appellant's motion for modification of visitation. The court found that there had been a material change in circumstances and that it was in R.M.'s best interest to have more time with his father. Appellant was awarded visitation on every other weekend, as well as one evening during the week, in addition to extended summer and holiday visitation. However, the court found that it was required by the public policy of this state to impose a non-cohabitation restriction preventing Chad from being present during any overnight visits. The court noted that appellant and Chad were in a long-term committed relationship, that they had resided together since at least 2007, and that Chad posed "no threat to the health, safety, or welfare" of R.M. Other than the prohibition on unmarried cohabitation with a romantic partner in the presence of a minor child, the circuit court found no other factors present to militate against overnight visitation in this case. The court further found that the non-cohabitation policy, and the mandatory application of that policy, survive both federal and state constitutional scrutiny. Appellant filed a timely notice of appeal from the circuit court's order.

In domestic relations cases, we review the evidence de novo and will not reverse the circuit court's findings unless they are clearly erroneous. We also give special deference to the circuit court's superior position in evaluating the witnesses, their testimony, and the child's best interest. Because a circuit court maintains continuing jurisdiction over visitation, it may modify or vacate a prior visitation order when it becomes aware of a material change in circumstances since the previous order. The party seeking modification has the burden of demonstrating such a material change in circumstances. With regard to visitation, the primary consideration is the best interest of the child. Important factors for the court to consider in determining reasonable visitation are the wishes of the child, the capacity of the party desiring visitation to supervise and care for the child, problems of transportation and prior conduct in abusing visitation, the work schedule or stability of the parties, and relationship with siblings and other relatives. We have held that fixing visitation rights is a matter that lies within the sound discretion of the circuit court.

In his first two points on appeal, appellant argues that the non-cohabitation agreement imposed by the circuit court violates his federal and state constitutional rights to privacy and equal protection. However, because we find merit in appellant's final argument, there is no need to address these constitutional arguments. . . .

In his third and final point on appeal, appellant argues that, contrary to the circuit court's belief, our prior cases do not require the imposition of non-cohabitation provisions in the absence of any finding of evidence of harm to the minor child. . . .

As the circuit court in this case recognized, under the long-standing public policy of the courts in this state, a parent's extramarital cohabitation with a romantic partner in the presence of children, or a parent's promiscuous conduct or lifestyle, has never been condoned. *See, e.g., Alphin v. Alphin,* 364 Ark. 332, 219 S.W.3d 160 (2005); *Taylor v. Taylor,* 353 Ark. 69, 110 S.W.3d 731 (2003); *Campbell v. Campbell,* 336 Ark. 379, 985 S.W.2d 724 (1999). In *Campbell, supra,* this court made it clear that the purpose of non-cohabitation provisions are to promote a stable environment for the children and not merely to monitor a parent's sexual conduct.

We have also repeatedly held, however, that the primary consideration in domestic relations cases is the welfare and best interest of the children and that all other considerations are secondary. Therefore, we have emphasized in more recent cases that the policy against romantic cohabitation in the presence of children must be considered under the circumstances of each particular case and in light of the best interest of the children. For example, in *Taylor, supra,* we reversed the trial court's modification of custody where the finding of a material change in circumstances was based on the trial court's concern about protecting the children from future harm based on public misperception. In that case, the evidence showed that the custodial parent resided with a lesbian woman and that the two sometimes shared a bed, although they denied a romantic or sexual relationship. We cited cases from other states in support of the proposition that there must be concrete proof of likely harm to the children from the parent's living arrangement before a change in custody can be made. We held that "evidence-based factors must govern," rather than stereotypical presumptions of future harm.

We further discussed the issue of non-cohabitation agreements in *Arkansas Department of Human Services v. Cole,* 2011 Ark. 145, 380 S.W.3d 429. In *Cole,* we held that the Arkansas Adoption and Foster Care Act of 2008 (Act 1), which prohibited an individual from adopting or serving as a foster parent if that individual was cohabiting with a sexual partner outside of marriage, was unconstitutional because it violated the fundamental right to privacy implicit in the Arkansas Constitution. In response to the appellants' argument in that case that our holding would render non-cohabitation agreements in custody or dependency-neglect cases unenforceable, we stated the following:

> We strongly disagree with the State and [the Family Council Action Committee's] conclusion that if this court finds that the categorical ban on adoption and fostering for sexual cohabitors put in place by Act 1 violates an individual's fundamental right to sexual privacy in one's home, state courts and DHS will be prohibited henceforth from considering and enforcing non-cohabitation agreements and orders in deciding child-custody and visitation cases as well as dependency-neglect cases. That simply is not the case. The overriding concern in all of these situations is the best interest of the child. *To arrive at what is in the child's best interest, the circuit courts and state agencies look*

*at all the factors, including a non-cohabitation order if one exists,
and make the best-interest determination on a case-by-case basis.*
Act 1's blanket ban provides for no such individualized
consideration or case-by-case analysis in adoption or foster-care
cases and makes the bald assumption that in all cases where
adoption or foster care is the issue it is always against the best
interest of the child to be placed in a home where an individual
is cohabiting with a sexual partner outside of marriage.

But in addition to case-by-case analysis, there is another
difference between cohabitation in the child-custody or
dependency-neglect context and cohabiting sexual partners who
wish to adopt or become foster parents. Third-party strangers
who cohabit with a divorced parent are unknown in many cases
to the circuit court and have not undergone the rigorous
screening associated with foster care or adoption. By everyone's
account, applicants for foster care must comply with a raft of
DHS regulations that include criminal background checks, home
studies, family histories, support systems, and the like.
Adoption, under the auspices of the trial court, requires similar
screening. Unsuitable and undesirable adoptive and foster
parents are thereby weeded out in the screening process. The
same does not pertain to a third-party stranger who cohabits
with a divorced or single parent.

Id. at 16–17, 380 S.W.3d 429, 380 S.W.3d 438 (emphasis added). Thus, we
agree with appellant that the public policy against romantic cohabitation
is not a "blanket ban," as it may not override the primary consideration
for the circuit court in such cases, which is determining what is in the
best interest of the children involved.

In the present case, the circuit court found from the evidence
presented that appellant and his partner are in a long-term, committed
romantic relationship and that "Mr. Cornelius poses no threat to the
health, safety, or welfare of the minor child." The court further found
that, "[o]ther than the prohibition of unmarried cohabitation with a
romantic partner in the presence of the minor child, there are no other
factors that would militate against overnight visitation." However,
because the circuit court also stated that the mandatory application of our
public policy against unmarried cohabitation required it to include a non-
cohabitation provision, it made no finding on whether such a provision
was in the best interest of R.M. Therefore, we reverse and remand for the
circuit court to make this determination.

HUDSON GOODSON, JUSTICE, dissenting.

The majority in this case finds error in the circuit court's conclusion that the restriction on overnight visitation was in the best interest of the child. I must dissent.

Arkansas's appellate courts have steadfastly upheld chancery court orders that prohibit parents from allowing romantic partners to stay or reside in the home when the children are present. This court has gone so far as to say that "a parent's unmarried cohabitation with a romantic partner, or a parent's promiscuous conduct or lifestyle, *in the presence of a child* cannot be abided." *Taylor v. Taylor,* 353 Ark. 69, 80, 110 S.W.3d 731, 737 (2003) (emphasis supplied). This rule has been applied regardless of whether the parent is heterosexual or homosexual. *See Taylor,* 345 Ark. 300, 47 S.W.3d 222 (2001). The laudable purpose of the prohibition is to promote a stable environment for children; it is not imposed merely to monitor a parent's sexual conduct.

In our 2001 decision in *Taylor,* this court affirmed the circuit court's requirement that the mother's female sexual companion move out of the home as a condition of retaining custody of her children. There was no showing of harm occasioned by the companion's presence, as the circuit court expressed the willingness to allow the companion to babysit when the mother was at work. Nonetheless, we held that the circuit court acted within its authority and was not clearly erroneous in determining that it was not in the children's best interests for the mother to continue cohabitating with another adult with whom she was romantically involved. This court said,

> As emphasized by our court's earlier decisions, the trial court's use of the non-cohabitation restriction is a material factor to consider when determining custody issues. Such a restriction or prohibition aids in structuring the home place so as to reduce the possibilities (or opportunities) where children may be present and subjected to a single parent's sexual encounters, whether they be heterosexual or homosexual.

Taylor, 345 Ark. at 304–305, 47 S.W.3d at 225.

We have not completely abandoned the restriction in subsequent caselaw. In *Arkansas Department of Human Services v. Cole,* 2011 Ark. 145, 380 S.W.3d 429, this court determined that Act 1's categorical ban prohibiting sexual cohabitors from adopting or fostering children was unconstitutional as a violation of the fundamental right of privacy found in the Arkansas Constitution. However, we did not disavow the restriction on overnight romantic guests, as we expressly rejected the argument that striking down the categorical ban would prevent our courts from considering and enforcing non-cohabitation orders and agreements in domestic-relations cases.

The primary consideration regarding visitation is the best interest of the child. In its oral ruling from the bench, the circuit court recognized this guiding principle. The court also recognized the settled law permitting the imposition of a restriction on overnight visitation in the presence of sexual partners. Contrary to the majority's assertion, the circuit court did not neglect to make a determination that the restriction was in the best interest of the child. The court quite plainly stated that "the best interest dictates that that be the continued policy of the Court" to not permit overnight visitation in the presence of the child. I would affirm the circuit court's decision in keeping with our time-tested law. The court acted well within in its authority to conclude that the restriction promoted the best interest of this child.

[Dissenting opinion by BAKER, J., is omitted].

NOTES

1. Many lesbian, gay, and bisexual parents, following the dissolution of different-sex relationships, have had to contend with court-imposed visitation restrictions. Some courts have sought to prohibit children from staying overnight with their lesbian, gay, or bisexual parents. *See, e.g., North v. North*, 648 A.2d 1025, 1033, 102 Md.App. 1, 16 (Ct. Spec. App. 1994) (holding that lower court abused its discretion by denying father overnight visitation based on fear that he would display or discuss his "homosexual lifestyle" with children). Other courts have allowed overnight visits as long as particular others are not present. In one case, for example, an appellate court upheld a visitation restriction on a gay dad that prohibited the overnight presence of any non-blood related person. *Marlow v. Marlow*, 702 N.E.2d 733, 738 (Ind. Ct. App. 1998). In another case, a court vacated a visitation restriction prohibiting overnight visitation in the presence of a lesbian mother's female partner. *Eldridge v. Eldridge*, 42 S.W.3d 82, 90 (Tenn. 2001). *See also A.O.V. v. J.R.V.*, 2007 WL 581871, at *6 (Va. Ct. App. 2007) (holding that trial judge did not "abuse his discretion by prohibiting the father from allowing his [male] companion to occupy the home overnight or engaging in displays of affection while the children visit."). Other courts have imposed restrictions on the presence of certain individuals (usually the parent's same-sex partner) regardless of the time of day. *See, e.g., Ex parte D.W.W.*, 717 So.2d 793, 796–97 (Ala. 1998) (upholding visitation restriction that prohibited mother's lesbian partner from being present during visit); *Weigand v. Houghton*, 730 So.2d 581 (Miss. 1999) (same). In addition, some courts have expressed concerns about parents who are actively involved in the LGBT community. One court, for example, upheld an order requiring that a gay father "not include in the children's activities during periods of visitation, any social, religious or educational functions sponsored by or which otherwise promote the homosexual lifestyle." *Marlow, supra*, 702 N.E.2d at 735. Another court, in upholding a restriction prohibiting the presence of a lesbian mother's partner during visitation, noted with concern that "[b]oth women are active

in the homosexual community [and that] [t]hey frequent gay bars and have discussed taking the children to a homosexual church." *See Ex parte D.W.W.*, supra 717 So.2d at 796. Finally, at least one court has upheld similar visitation restrictions imposed on a transgender parent. *See J.L.S. v. D.K.S.*, 943 S.W.2d 766, 772 (Mo. Ct. App. 1997) (upholding visitation restriction imposed on female transgender parent that she not "cohabit with other transsexuals or sleep with another female" during visits).

2.   Other courts, like the Arkansas Supreme Court in *Moix*, have rejected visitation restrictions in cases involving lesbian, gay, and bisexual parents in the absence of a showing that such restrictions are necessary to avoid the risk of harm to children. In *Mongerson v. Mongerson*, 678 S.E.2d 891 (Ga. 2009), for example, the Georgia Supreme Court unanimously overturned a trial judge's ruling that granted visitation to a gay father on the condition that he not "expos[e] the children to his homosexual partners and friends." *Id.* at 894. The court explained that "the prohibition . . . assumes, without evidentiary support, that the children will suffer harm from any such contact. Such an arbitrary classification based on sexual orientation flies in the face of our public policy that encourages divorced parents to participate in the raising of their children." *Id.* at 895. *See also In re Marriage of Dorworth*, 33 P.3d 1260, 1262 (Colo. Ct. App. 2001) (vacating visitation restriction that prohibited presence of any other person at night at home of bisexual father); *Gould v. Dickens*, 143 S.W.3d 639, 644 (Mo. Ct. App. 2004) (vacating visitation restriction prohibiting overnight visitation when lesbian mother shared a bed with her female partner).

II.   LGBT FAMILY FORMATION AND DISSOLUTION

A.   ADOPTION

Many lesbian, gay, and bisexual individuals become parents through adoption. Some adopt children who are part of the foster care system, others pursue private adoptions, while yet others seek to adopt their partners' legal children through second-parent adoptions. This Section begins with a look at legal restrictions on the ability of LGB individuals to adopt. It then explores the implications of placing openly lesbian and gay youth with lesbian and gay adoptive (and foster care) parents. It ends with a consideration of the issue of second-parent adoptions.

1.   Restrictions on Prospective Parents

In 1977, Florida became the first state to enact a law prohibiting lesbians and gay men from adopting. In 2010, an intermediate state appellate court struck down that law as a violation of the state constitution's guarantee of equal protection.[13] The state's subsequent decision not to appeal the ruling to the Florida Supreme Court effectively ended the thirty-three year old ban on gay adoption.

There were several unsuccessful prior challenges to the constitutionality of Florida's adoption ban. Most of those cases were litigated in state court, but one was brought in federal court. This suit eventually led the U.S. Court of Appeals for the Eleventh Circuit, in the case that follows, to hold that a prohibition on gay adoption does not violate the federal Constitution. Despite the fact that the Florida law is no longer enforceable, this ruling remains the leading federal opinion on the authority of the government to prohibit or restrict the ability of lesbians and gay men to serve as adoptive parents.

LOFTON V. SECRETARY OF THE DEPARTMENT OF CHILDREN & FAMILY SERVICES

United States Court of Appeals, Eleventh Circuit, 2004
358 F.3d 804

BIRCH, CIRCUIT JUDGE:

I. BACKGROUND

A. The Challenged Florida Statute

Since 1977, Florida's adoption law has contained a codified prohibition on adoption by any "homosexual" person. 1977 Fla. Laws, ch. 77–140, § 1, Fla. Stat. § 63.042(3) (2002). [The statute provides that "[n]o person eligible to adopt under the statute may adopt if that person is a homosexual." *Id.*] For purposes of this statute, Florida courts have defined the term "homosexual" as being "limited to applicants who are known to engage in current, voluntary homosexual activity," thus drawing "a distinction between homosexual orientation and homosexual activity." *Fla. Dep't of Health & Rehab. Servs. v. Cox*, 627 So.2d 1210, 1215 (Fla. Dist. Ct. App. 1993), *aff'd in relevant part*, 656 So.2d 902, 903 (Fla. 1995). During the past twelve years, several legislative bills have attempted to repeal the statute, and three separate legal challenges to it have been filed in the Florida courts. To date, no attempt to overturn the provision has succeeded. We now consider the most recent challenge to the statute.

B. The Litigants

Six plaintiffs-appellants bring this case. The first, Steven Lofton, is a registered pediatric nurse who has raised from infancy three Florida foster children, each of whom tested positive for HIV at birth. By all accounts, Lofton's efforts in caring for these children have been

---

[13] *Florida Department of Children and Families v. In re Matter of Adoption of X.X.G. and N.R.G.*, 45 So.3d 79 (Fla.Ct.App. 2010).

exemplary, and his story has been chronicled in dozens of news stories and editorials as well as on national television. We confine our discussion of that story to those facts relevant to the legal issues before us and properly before us in the record. John Doe, also named as a plaintiff-appellant in this litigation, was born on 29 April 1991. Testing positive at birth for HIV and cocaine, Doe immediately entered the Florida foster care system. Shortly thereafter, Children's Home Society, a private agency, placed Doe in foster care with Lofton, who has extensive experience treating HIV patients. At eighteen months, Doe sero-reverted and has since tested HIV negative. In September of 1994, Lofton filed an application to adopt Doe but refused to answer the application's inquiry about his sexual preference and also failed to disclose Roger Croteau, his cohabitating partner, as a member of his household. After Lofton refused requests from the Department of Children and Families ("DCF") to supply the missing information, his application was rejected pursuant to the homosexual adoption provision. Shortly thereafter, in early 1995, William E. Adams, Jr., a professor of law who had participated in one of the previous legal challenges to Fla. Stat. § 63.042(3), wrote to the American Civil Liberties Union ("ACLU") and informed it that Lofton and Croteau would make "excellent test plaintiffs." Two years later, in light of the length of Doe's stay in Lofton's household, DCF offered Lofton the compromise of becoming Doe's legal guardian. This arrangement would have allowed Doe to leave the foster care system and DCF supervision. However, because it would have cost Lofton over $300 a month in lost foster care subsidies and would have jeopardized Doe's Medicaid coverage, Lofton declined the guardianship option unless it was an interim stage toward adoption. Under Florida law, DCF could not accommodate this condition, and the present litigation ensued.

Plaintiff-appellant Douglas E. Houghton, Jr., is a clinical nurse specialist and legal guardian of plaintiff-appellant John Roe, who is eleven years old. Houghton has been Roe's caretaker since 1996 when Roe's biological father, suffering from alcohol abuse and frequent unemployment, voluntarily left Roe, then four years old, with Houghton. That same year, Houghton was appointed co-guardian of Roe along with one Robert Obeso (who otherwise has no involvement in this case). After Roe's biological father consented to termination of his parental rights, Houghton attempted to adopt Roe. Because of Houghton's homosexuality, however, he did not receive a favorable preliminary home study evaluation, which precluded him from filing the necessary adoption petition in state circuit court.

Plaintiff-appellants Wayne Larue Smith and Daniel Skahen, an attorney and real estate broker residing together in Key West, became licensed DCF foster parents after completing a requisite ten-week course in January of 2000. Since then, they have cared for three foster children, none of whom has been available for adoption. On 1 May 2000, Smith and Skahen submitted applications with DCF to serve as adoptive parents. On their adoption applications, both Smith and Skahen indicated that they are homosexuals. On 15 May 2000, they received notices from DCF stating that their applications had been denied because of their homosexuality. * * *

II. DISCUSSION

B. Florida's Adoption Scheme

Appellants' challenge cannot be viewed apart from the context in which it arises. Under Florida law, "adoption is not a right; it is a statutory privilege." *Cox*, 627 So.2d at 1216. Unlike biological parentage, which precedes and transcends formal recognition by the state, adoption is wholly a creature of the state.

In formulating its adoption policies and procedures, the State of Florida acts in the protective and provisional role of *in loco parentis* for those children who, because of various circumstances, have become wards of the state. Thus, adoption law is unlike criminal law, for example, where the paramount substantive concern is not intruding on individuals' liberty interests and the paramount procedural imperative is ensuring due process and fairness. Adoption is also distinct from such contexts as government-benefit eligibility schemes or access to a public forum, where equality of treatment is the primary concern. By contrast, in the adoption context, the state's overriding interest is the best interests of the children whom it is seeking to place with adoptive families. Florida, acting *parens patriae* for children who have lost their natural parents, bears the high duty of determining what adoptive home environments will best serve all aspects of the child's growth and development.

Because of the primacy of the welfare of the child, the state can make classifications for adoption purposes that would be constitutionally suspect in many other arenas. For example, Florida law requires that, in order to adopt any child other than a special needs child, an individual's primary residence and place of employment must be located in Florida. In screening adoption applicants, Florida considers such factors as physical and mental health, income and financial status, duration of marriage, housing, and neighborhood, among others. Similarly, Florida gives preference to candidates who demonstrate a commitment to "value, respect, appreciate, and educate the child regarding his or her racial and ethnic heritage." Moreover, prospective adoptive parents are required to sign an affidavit of good moral character. Many of these preferences and requirements, if employed outside the adoption arena, would be unlikely to withstand constitutional scrutiny.

The decision to adopt a child is not a private one, but a public act. At a minimum, would-be adoptive parents are asking the state to confer official recognition—and, consequently, the highest level of constitutional insulation from subsequent state interference—on a relationship where there exists no natural filial bond. In many cases, they also are asking the state to entrust into their permanent care a child for whom the state is currently serving as *in loco parentis*. In doing so, these prospective adoptive parents are electing to open their homes and their private lives to close scrutiny by the state. Florida's adoption application requires information on a variety of private matters, including an applicant's physical and psychiatric medical history, previous marriages, arrest record, financial status, and educational history. In this regard, Florida's adoption scheme is like any "complex social welfare system that necessarily deals with the intimacies of family life." *Bowen v. Gilliard*, 483 U.S. 587 (1987) (citation omitted). Accordingly, such intrusions into private family matters are on a different constitutional plane than those that "seek[ ] to foist orthodoxy on the unwilling by banning or criminally prosecuting" nonconformity. * * *

C.   *Appellants' Due Process Challenges*

1.   *Fundamental Right to "Family Integrity"*

* * * [A]ppellants argue that, by prohibiting homosexual adoption, the state is refusing to recognize and protect constitutionally protected parent-child relationships between Lofton and Doe and between Houghton and Roe. Noting that the Supreme Court has identified "the interest of parents in the care, custody, and control of their children" as "perhaps the oldest of the fundamental liberty interests recognized by this Court," *Troxel v. Granville*, 530 U.S. 57, 65 (2000), appellants argue that they are entitled to a similar constitutional liberty interest because they share deeply loving emotional bonds that are as close as those between a natural parent and child. They further contend that this liberty interest is significantly burdened by the Florida statute, which prevents them from obtaining permanency in their relationships and creates uncertainty about the future integrity of their families. Only by being given the opportunity to adopt, appellants assert, will they be able to protect their alleged right to "family integrity."

Although the text of the Constitution contains no reference to familial or parental rights, Supreme Court precedent has long recognized that "the Due Process Clause of the Fourteenth Amendment protects the fundamental right of parents to make decisions concerning the care, custody, and control of their children." *Id.* at 66. A corollary to this right is the "private realm of family life which the state cannot enter that has been afforded both substantive and procedural protection." *Smith v. Org. of Foster Families for Equal. & Reform*, 431 U.S. 816, 842 (1977). Historically, the Court's family and parental-rights holdings have involved biological families. The Court itself has noted that "the usual understanding of 'family' implies biological relationships, and most decisions treating the relation between parent and child have stressed this element." *Smith*, 431 U.S. at 843. Appellants, however, seize on a few lines of *dicta* from *Smith*, in which the Court acknowledged that "biological relationships are not [the] exclusive determination of the existence of a family," *id.*, and noted that "[a]doption, for instance, is recognized as the legal equivalent of biological parenthood," *id.* at 844 n. 51. Extrapolating from *Smith*, appellants argue that parental and familial rights should be extended to individuals such as foster parents and legal guardians and that the touchstone of this liberty interest is not biological ties or official legal recognition, but the emotional bond that develops between and among individuals as a result of shared daily life.

We do not read *Smith* so broadly. In *Smith*, the Court considered whether the appellee foster families possessed a constitutional liberty interest in "the integrity of their family unit" such that the state could not disrupt the families without procedural due process. Although the Court found it unnecessary to resolve that question, Justice Brennan, writing for the majority, did note that the importance of familial relationships stems not merely from blood relationships, but also from "the emotional attachments that derive from the intimacy of daily association." The *Smith* Court went on, however, to discuss the "important distinctions between the foster family and the natural family," particularly the fact that foster families have their genesis in state law. The Court stressed that the parameters of whatever potential liberty interest such families might possess would be defined by state law and the justifiable expectations it created. The Court found that the expectations created by New York law—which accorded only limited recognition to foster families—supported only "the most limited constitutional 'liberty' in the foster family." Basing its holding on other grounds, the Court concluded that the procedures provided under New York law were "adequate to protect whatever liberty interest appellees may have."

* * * Here, we find that under Florida law neither a foster parent nor a legal guardian could have a justifiable expectation of a permanent relationship with his or her child free from state oversight or intervention. Under Florida law, foster care is designed to be a short-term arrangement while the state attempts to find a permanent adoptive home. For instance, Florida law permits foster care as a "permanency option" only for children at least fourteen years of age, and DCF may remove a foster child anytime that it believes it to be in the child's best interests. Similarly, legal guardians in Florida are subject to ongoing judicial oversight, including the duty to file annual guardianship reports and annual review by the appointing court, and can be removed for a wide variety of reasons ... such ... as incapacity, illness, substance abuse, conviction of a felony, failure to file annual guardianship reports, and

failure to fulfill guardianship education requirements. In both cases, the state is not interfering with natural family units that exist independent of its power, but is regulating ones created by it. Lofton and Houghton entered into relationships to be a foster parent and legal guardian, respectively, with an implicit understanding that these relationships would not be immune from state oversight and would be permitted to continue only upon state approval. The emotional connections between Lofton and his foster child and between Houghton and his ward originate in arrangements that have been subject to state oversight from the outset. We conclude that Lofton, Doe, Houghton, and Roe could have no justifiable expectation of permanency in their relationships. Nor could Lofton and Houghton have developed expectations that they would be allowed to adopt, in light of the adoption provision itself. * * *

2. *Fundamental Right to "Private Sexual Intimacy"*

[The court rejected the plaintiffs' contention that the adoption ban impermissibly burdened their right to private sexual intimacy under *Lawrence v. Texas*, 539 U.S. 558, 123 S.Ct. 2472, 156 L.Ed.2d 508 (2003). This section of the opinion can be found in *supra* Chapter 1, Section F.]

D. *Appellants' Equal Protection Challenge*

1. *Rational-Basis Review*

* * * Unless the challenged classification burdens a fundamental right or targets a suspect class, the Equal Protection Clause requires only that the classification be rationally related to a legitimate state interest. As we have explained, Florida's statute burdens no fundamental rights. Moreover, all of our sister circuits that have considered the question have declined to treat homosexuals as a suspect class. Because the present case involves neither a fundamental right nor a suspect class, we review the Florida statute under the rational-basis standard.

Rational-basis review, a paradigm of judicial restraint, does not provide a license for courts to judge the wisdom, fairness, or logic of legislative choices. The question is simply whether the challenged legislation is rationally related to a legitimate state interest. Under this deferential standard, a legislative classification is accorded a strong presumption of validity and must be upheld against equal protection challenge if there is any reasonably conceivable state of facts that could provide a rational basis for the classification. * * *

2. *Florida's Asserted Rational Bases*

Cognizant of the narrow parameters of our review, we now analyze the challenged Florida law. Florida contends that the statute is only one aspect of its broader adoption policy, which is designed to create adoptive homes that resemble the nuclear family as closely as possible. Florida argues that the statute is rationally related to Florida's interest in furthering the best interests of adopted children by placing them in families with married mothers and fathers. Such homes, Florida asserts, provide the stability that marriage affords and the presence of both male and female authority figures, which it considers critical to optimal childhood development and socialization. In particular, Florida emphasizes a vital role that dual-gender parenting plays in shaping sexual and gender identity and in providing heterosexual role modeling. Florida argues that disallowing adoption into homosexual households, which are necessarily motherless or fatherless and lack the stability that comes with marriage, is a rational means of furthering Florida's interest in promoting adoption by marital families.

Florida clearly has a legitimate interest in encouraging a stable and nurturing environment for the education and socialization of its adopted children. It is chiefly from parental figures that children learn about the world and their place in it, and the formative influence of parents extends well beyond the years spent under their roof, shaping their children's psychology, character, and personality for years to come. In time, children grow up to become full members of society, which they in turn influence, whether for good or ill. The adage that "the hand that rocks the cradle rules the world" hardly overstates the ripple effect that parents have on the public good by virtue of their role in raising their children. It is hard to conceive an interest more legitimate and more paramount for the state than promoting an optimal social structure for educating, socializing, and preparing its future citizens to become productive participants in civil society—particularly when those future citizens are displaced children for whom the state is standing *in loco parentis*.

More importantly for present purposes, the state has a legitimate interest in encouraging this optimal family structure by seeking to place adoptive children in homes that have both a mother and father. Florida argues that its preference for adoptive marital families is based on the premise that the marital family structure is more stable than other household arrangements and that children benefit from the presence of both a father and mother in the home. Given that appellants have offered no competent evidence to the contrary, we find this premise to be one of those "unprovable assumptions" that nevertheless can provide a legitimate basis for legislative action. Although social theorists from Plato to Simone de Beauvoir have proposed alternative child-rearing arrangements, none has proven as enduring as the marital family structure, nor has the accumulated wisdom of several millennia of human experience discovered a superior model. Against this "sum of experience," it is rational for Florida to conclude that it is in the best interests of adoptive children, many of whom come from troubled and unstable backgrounds, to be placed in a home anchored by both a father and a mother.

3. Appellants' Arguments

Appellants offer little to dispute whether Florida's preference for marital adoptive families is a legitimate state interest. Instead, they maintain that the statute is not rationally related to this interest. Arguing that the statute is both overinclusive and underinclusive, appellants contend that the real motivation behind the statute cannot be the best interest of adoptive children. * * *

a. Adoption by Unmarried Heterosexual Persons

Appellants note that Florida law permits adoption by unmarried individuals and that, among children coming out the Florida foster care system, 25% of adoptions are to parents who are currently single. Their argument is that homosexual persons are similarly situated to unmarried persons with regard to Florida's asserted interest in promoting married-couple adoption. According to appellants, this disparate treatment lacks a rational basis and, therefore, disproves any rational connection between the statute and Florida's asserted interest in promoting adoption into married homes. * * *

The Florida legislature could rationally conclude that homosexuals and heterosexual singles are not similarly situated in relevant respects. It is not irrational to think that heterosexual singles have a markedly greater probability of eventually establishing a married household and, thus, providing their adopted children with a stable, dual-gender parenting environment. Moreover, as the state noted, the legislature could rationally act on the theory that heterosexual singles, even if they never marry, are better positioned than homosexual individuals to provide adopted children with education and guidance relative to their sexual development throughout pubescence and adolescence. In a previous challenge to Florida's statute, a Florida appellate court observed:

> [W]hatever causes a person to become a homosexual, it is clear that the state cannot know the sexual preferences that a child will exhibit as an adult. Statistically, the state does know that a very high percentage of children available for adoption will develop heterosexual preferences. As a result, those children will need education and guidance after puberty concerning relationships with the opposite sex. In our society, we expect that parents will provide this education to teenagers in the home. These subjects are often very embarrassing for teenagers and some aspects of the education are accomplished by the parents telling stories about their own adolescence and explaining their own experiences with the opposite sex. It is in the best interests of a child if his or her parents can personally relate to the child's problems and assist the child in the difficult transition to heterosexual adulthood. Given that adopted

children tend to have some developmental problems arising from
adoption or from their experiences prior to adoption, it is
perhaps more important for adopted children than other children
to have a stable heterosexual household during puberty and the
teenage years.

Cox, 627 So.2d at 1220. "It could be that the assumptions underlying
these rationales are erroneous, but the very fact that they are arguable is
sufficient, on rational-basis review, to immunize the legislative choice
from constitutional challenge." *Heller*, 509 U.S. at 333. Although the
influence of environmental factors in forming patterns of sexual behavior
and the importance of heterosexual role models are matters of ongoing
debate, they ultimately involve empirical disputes not readily amenable
to judicial resolution—as well as policy judgments best exercised in the
legislative arena. For our present purposes, it is sufficient that these
considerations provide a reasonably conceivable rationale for Florida to
preclude all homosexuals, but not all heterosexual singles, from adopting.

The possibility, raised by appellants, that some homosexual
households, including those of appellants, would provide a better
environment than would some heterosexual single-parent households
does not alter our analysis. The Supreme Court repeatedly has instructed
that neither the fact that a classification may be overinclusive or
underinclusive nor the fact that a generalization underlying a
classification is subject to exceptions renders the classification irrational.
"[C]ourts are compelled under rational-basis review to accept a
legislature's generalizations even when there is an imperfect fit between
means and ends." *Id.* at 321. We conclude that there are plausible
rational reasons for the disparate treatment of homosexuals and
heterosexual singles under Florida adoption law and that, to the extent
that the classification may be imperfect, that imperfection does not rise to
the level of a constitutional infraction.

b. Current Foster Care Population

Appellants make much of the fact that Florida has over three
thousand children who are currently in foster care and, consequently,
have not been placed with permanent adoptive families. According to
appellants, because excluding homosexuals from the pool of prospective
adoptive parents will not create more eligible married couples to reduce
the backlog, it is impossible for the legislature to believe that the statute
advances the state's interest in placing children with married couples.

We do not agree that the statute does not further the state's interest
in promoting nuclear-family adoption because it may delay the adoption
of some children. Appellants misconstrue Florida's interest, which is not
simply to place children in a permanent home as quickly as possible, but,
when placing them, to do so in an optimal home, i.e., one in which there is

a heterosexual couple or the potential for one. According to appellants' logic, every restriction on adoptive-parent candidates, such as income, in-state residency, and criminal record—none of which creates more available married couples—are likewise constitutionally suspect as long as Florida has a backlog of unadopted foster children. The best interests of children, however, are not automatically served by adoption into *any* available home merely because it is permanent. Moreover, the legislature could rationally act on the theory that not placing adoptees in homosexual households increases the probability that these children eventually will be placed with married-couple families, thus furthering the state's goal of optimal placement. Therefore, we conclude that Florida's current foster care backlog does not render the statute irrational.

c.   Foster Care and Legal Guardianship

Noting that Florida law permits homosexuals to become foster parents and permanent guardians, appellants contend that this fact demonstrates that Florida must not truly believe that placement in a homosexual household is not in a child's best interests. We do not find that the fact that Florida has permitted homosexual foster homes and guardianships defeats the rational relationship between the statute and the state's asserted interest. We have not located and appellants have not cited any precedent indicating that a disparity between a law and its enforcement is a relevant consideration on rational-basis review, which only asks whether the legislature could have reasonably thought that the challenged law would further a legitimate state interest. Thus, to the extent that foster care and guardianship placements with homosexuals are the handiwork of Florida's executive branch, they are irrelevant to the question of the *legislative* rationale for Florida's adoption scheme. To the extent that these placements are the product of an intentional legislative choice to treat foster care and guardianships differently than adoption, the distinction is not an irrational one. Indeed, it bears a rational relationship to Florida's interest in promoting the nuclear-family model of adoption since foster care and guardianship have neither the permanence nor the societal, cultural, and legal significance as does adoptive parenthood, which is the legal equivalent of natural parenthood.

Foster care and legal guardianship are designed to address a different situation than permanent adoption, and "the legislature must be allowed leeway to approach a perceived problem incrementally." *Beach Communications*, 508 U.S. at 316. The fact that "[t]he legislature may select one phase of one field and apply a remedy there, neglecting the others," does not render the legislative solution invalid. *Id.* (citation omitted). We conclude that the rationality of the statute is not defeated by the fact that Florida permits homosexual persons to serve as foster parents and legal guardians.

d. Social Science Research

Appellants cite recent social science research and the opinion of mental health professionals and child welfare organizations as evidence that there is no child welfare basis for excluding homosexuals from adopting. They argue that the cited studies show that the parenting skills of homosexual parents are at least equivalent to those of heterosexual parents and that children raised by homosexual parents suffer no adverse outcomes. Appellants also point to the policies and practices of numerous adoption agencies that permit homosexual persons to adopt.

In considering appellants' argument, we must ask not whether the latest in social science research and professional opinion *support* the decision of the Florida legislature, but whether that evidence is so well established and so far beyond dispute that it would be irrational for the Florida legislature to believe that the interests of its children are best served by not permitting homosexual adoption. Also, we must credit any conceivable rational reason that the legislature might have for choosing not to alter its statutory scheme in response to this recent social science research. We must assume, for example, that the legislature might be aware of the critiques of the studies cited by appellants—critiques that have highlighted significant flaws in the studies' methodologies and conclusions, such as the use of small, self-selected samples; reliance on self-report instruments; politically driven hypotheses; and the use of unrepresentative study populations consisting of disproportionately affluent, educated parents.[24] Alternatively, the legislature might consider and credit other studies that have found that children raised in homosexual households fare differently on a number of measures, doing worse on some of them, than children raised in similarly situated heterosexual households.[25] Or the legislature might consider, and even credit, the research cited by appellants, but find it premature to rely on a very recent and still developing body of research, particularly in light of

---

[24] *See, e.g.,* D. Baumrind, *Commentary on Sexual Orientation: Research and Social Policy Implications,* 31 Developmental Psychol. 130 (No. 1, 1995) (reviewing various studies and questioning them on "theoretical and empirical grounds" because of flaws such as small sample sizes, reliance on self-report instruments, and self-selected, unrepresentative study populations); R. Lerner & A.K. Nagai, *No Basis: What the Studies Don't Tell Us About Same–Sex Parenting,* Marriage Law Project (Jan. 2001) (reviewing forty-nine studies on same-sex parenting and finding recurring methodological flaws, including failure to use testable hypotheses, lack of control methods, unrepresentative study populations, self-selected sample groups, and use of negative hypotheses); J. Stacey & T. Biblarz, *(How) Does the Sexual Orientation of Parents Matter,* 66 Am. Soc. Rev. 159, 166 (2001) (reviewing 21 studies and finding various methodological flaws, leading authors to conclude that "there are no studies of child development based on random, representative samples" of same-sex households).

[25] *See, e.g.,* K. Cameron & P. Cameron, *Homosexual Parents,* 31 Adolescence 757, 770–774 (1996) (reporting study findings that children raised by homosexual parents suffer from disproportionately high incidence of emotional disturbance and sexual victimization); Stacey & Biblarz, *supra,* at 170 (concluding, based on study results, that "parental sexual orientation is positively associated with the possibility that children will attain a similar orientation, and theory and common sense also support such a view").

the absence of longitudinal studies following child subjects into adulthood and of studies of adopted, rather than natural, children of homosexual parents.

We do not find any of these possible legislative responses to be irrational. Openly homosexual households represent a very recent phenomenon, and sufficient time has not yet passed to permit any scientific study of how children raised in those households fare as adults. Scientific attempts to study homosexual parenting in general are still in their nascent stages and so far have yielded inconclusive and conflicting results. Thus, it is hardly surprising that the question of the effects of homosexual parenting on childhood development is one on which even experts of good faith reasonably disagree. Given this state of affairs, it is not irrational for the Florida legislature to credit one side of the debate over the other. Nor is it irrational for the legislature to proceed with deliberate caution before placing adoptive children in an alternative, but unproven, family structure that has not yet been conclusively demonstrated to be equivalent to the marital family structure that has established a proven track record spanning centuries. Accordingly, we conclude that appellants' proffered social science evidence does not disprove the rational basis of the Florida statute.

    e.   *Romer v. Evans*

Finally, we disagree with appellants' contention that *Romer* requires us to strike down the Florida statute. In *Romer*, the Supreme Court invalidated Amendment 2 to the Colorado state constitution, which prohibited all legislative, executive, or judicial action designed to protect homosexual persons from discrimination. The constitutional defect in Amendment 2 was the disjunction between the "[s]weeping and comprehensive" classification it imposed on homosexuals and the state's asserted bases for the classification—respect for freedom of association and conservation of resources to fight race and gender discrimination. The Court concluded that the Amendment's "sheer breadth is so discontinuous with the reasons offered for it that the amendment seems inexplicable by anything but animus toward the class it affects."

Unlike Colorado's Amendment 2, Florida's statute is not so "[s]weeping and comprehensive" as to render Florida's rationales for the statute "inexplicable by anything but animus" toward its homosexual residents. Amendment 2 deprived homosexual persons of "protections against exclusion from an almost limitless number of transactions and endeavors that constitute ordinary civic life in a free society." In contrast to this "broad and undifferentiated disability," the Florida classification is limited to the narrow and discrete context of access to the statutory privilege of adoption and, more importantly, has a plausible connection with the state's asserted interest. Moreover, not only is the effect of

Florida's classification dramatically smaller, but the classification itself is narrower. Whereas Amendment 2's classification encompassed both conduct *and* status, Florida's adoption prohibition is limited to conduct. Thus, we conclude that *Romer*'s unique factual situation and narrow holding are inapposite to this case.

III. CONCLUSION

We exercise great caution when asked to take sides in an ongoing public policy debate, such as the current one over the compatibility of homosexual conduct with the duties of adoptive parenthood. The State of Florida has made the determination that it is not in the best interests of its displaced children to be adopted by individuals who "engage in current, voluntary homosexual activity," *Cox*, 627 So.2d at 1215, and we have found nothing in the Constitution that forbids this policy judgment. Thus, any argument that the Florida legislature was misguided in its decision is one of legislative policy, not constitutional law.

> [The Eleventh Circuit divided evenly six to six on whether to grant a Petition for Rehearing En Banc, and as a result denied the petition. *Lofton v. Secretary of the Dep't of Children & Family Servs.*, 377 F.3d 1275 (11th Cir. 2004). Judge Rosemary Barkett dissented from the denial of rehearing.]

BARKETT, J., dissenting.

Florida is the only state in the union to have such a categorical statutory prohibition targeted solely against homosexuals. This provision finds, as a matter of law, hundreds of thousands of Florida citizens unfit to serve as adoptive parents solely because of constitutionally protected conduct. There is no comparable bar in Florida's adoption statute that applies to any other group. Neither child molesters, drug addicts, nor domestic abusers are categorically barred by the statute from serving as adoptive parents. In a very real sense, Florida's adoption statute treats homosexuals less favorably than even those individuals with characteristics that may pose a threat to the well-being of children.

While Florida claims that it has singled out homosexuals because it wishes to limit adoptions to married couples, the statute in this case says absolutely nothing about married couples. In fact, Florida's adoption statute expressly provides for single persons to adopt. A full twenty-five percent of adoptions out of foster care in Florida are by single people; in the district covering Miami-Dade County, this figure is over forty percent. This is only the first and most glaring of numerous gaps between the state's ban on homosexual adoption and its purported justification. Under Florida law, for example, single persons who are homosexuals but are "not practicing" may adopt. Florida also permits homosexuals (whether sexually active or not) to serve as foster parents on a *permanent* basis, and the state acknowledges that such foster care placements involve a state of "*de facto* permanency." Finally, Florida permits homosexuals to serve as legal guardians. * * *

Florida prohibits homosexuals from being considered as adoptive parents because it wishes to place children with married couples. It wishes to do so for two alleged reasons: (1) to provide "stability" in the home, which the panel apparently believes can only be provided by married couples representing the "nuclear" family model; and (2) to properly shape heterosexual "sexual and gender identity," which the panel asserts should be accomplished by married couples. * * *

[T]he state's proffered rational basis for the statute here (providing adopted children with married couples as parents) cannot be legitimately credited because it fails the equal protection requirement that "all persons similarly situated should be treated alike." . . . [I]t is plainly false that Florida has established a preference for "married mothers and fathers" as adoptive parents. The 1977 statute prohibiting homosexual adoption expresses no preference whatsoever for married couples, expressly permitting an "unmarried adult" to adopt. Moreover, the DCF administrative regulations that are inextricably tied to Florida's adoption statutes do not prefer married over single candidates for adoption. In short, the Florida legislature never did, and the Florida executive no longer does, express a preference for married over unmarried couples or singles in the area of adoption. The fact that Florida places children for adoption with single parents directly and explicitly contradicts Florida's post hoc assertion that the ban is justified by the state's wish to place children for adoption only with "families with married mothers and fathers." This contradiction alone is enough to prove that the state's alleged reasons are "illogical to the point of irrationality." *Eisenstadt v. Baird*, 405 U.S. 438, 451 (1972).

However, instead of acknowledging this glaring gap between the ban on homosexual adoption and the state's purported justification, as did the Supreme Court in invalidating the statutes in *Eisenstadt, Moreno, Cleburne,* and *Romer,* the *Lofton* panel stretches mightily to construct a hypothetical to bridge this gap. "It is not irrational," the panel opines, "to think that heterosexual singles have a markedly greater probability of eventually establishing a married household and, thus, providing their adopted children with a stable, dual-gender parenting environment." The panel's contrived hypothetical offering blatantly ignores not only the absence of any preference in Florida's statute for married couples but also the realities of the adoption process. Evaluations of prospective parents are based on present, not "eventual," status and conditions. Florida does not ask for a commitment of plans to marry someday in the future and permits single adults to adopt without making inquiry into whether they have immediate, or even long-range, marriage plans or prospects. Indeed, that many individuals choose to adopt outside of marriage is an indication that adoption and commitment to a permanent adult relationship are completely separate decisions. Moreover, experience leads one to believe that single heterosexuals who adopt are less likely to marry in the future, not more likely. Finally, this speculative hypothesis also fails to take account of "non-practicing homosexuals" who are not likely to marry but can adopt under Florida law. . . .

In addition to its failure to meaningfully distinguish homosexuals from single heterosexuals, the panel never explains why it is rational to believe that homosexuals, as a class, are unable to provide stable homes and appropriate role models for children. With respect to the first of these arguments, there is absolutely no record evidence to show that homosexuals are incapable of providing the permanent family life sought by Florida. To the contrary, as the facts in this case suggest, many children throughout the country are lovingly and successfully cared for by homosexuals in their capacity as biological parents, foster parents, or legal guardians. Furthermore, it is not marriage that guarantees a stable, caring environment for children but the character of the individual caregiver. Indeed, given the reality of foster care in Florida, the statute actually operates to impede, rather than promote, the placement of a child into a permanent family. . . . Florida's foster care system has a backlog of more than 3,400 children in it, far more than the number of married couples eligible to adopt. Given this backlog, the state's ban on gay adoption does nothing to increase the number of children being adopted, whether by married couples or anyone else. The state is evidently willing to allow children to live with the potential uncertainties of several foster-care placements rather than enjoy the security and certainty of an adoptive home with one or two caring parents who are also homosexual.

Nor does the panel offer a reason for why it is rational to credit the state's second argument: that homosexuals are incapable of providing good role models. The panel claims that "[heterosexual] children will need education and guidance after puberty concerning relationships with the opposite sex. . . . It is in the best interests of a child if his or her parents can personally relate to the child's problems and assist the child in the difficult transition to heterosexual adulthood." Is the panel suggesting that heterosexual parents are necessary in order to tell children about their own dating experiences after puberty? For anyone who has been a parent, this will no doubt seem a very strange, even faintly comical, claim. There is certainly no evidence that the ability to share one's adolescent dating experiences (or lack thereof) is an important, much less essential, facet of parenting. The difficult transition to adulthood is a common human experience, not an experience unique to human beings of a particular race, gender, or sexual orientation. It is downright silly to argue that parents must have experienced everything that a child will experience in order to guide them. Indeed, that will generally not be the case. For example, immigrant parents help their children adjust to a world and culture they have not known. It cannot be suggested that such individuals are unfit to parent any more than it could be suggested that a mother is unfit to parent a son or that a white person is unfit to parent an African-American child. Furthermore, the panel's argument completely neglects to consider the situation of gay children of heterosexual parents. Children simply need parents who will love and support them.

In addition to this contrived argument about teenage dating advice, the panel suggests that placing children with homosexual parents may make it more likely that children will become homosexual, referring cryptically to the "vital role that dual-gender parenting plays in *shaping sexual and gender identity* and in providing heterosexual role modeling." In our democracy, however, it is not the province of the State, even if it were *able* to do so, to dictate or even attempt to influence how its citizens should develop their sexual and gender identities. This approach views homosexuality in and of itself as a social harm that must be discouraged, and so demeans the dignity of homosexuals, something that *Lawrence* specifically proscribes.

> [Judge Barkett also concludes that *Lawrence* reaffirmed a fundamental right in private intimate sexual conduct and that Florida's adoption ban should be subjected to heightened scrutiny because it significantly burdens the right identified in *Lawrence* by making lesbians and gay men choose between engaging in same-sex sexual intimacy and adopting.]

NOTES

1. In state court litigation that followed *Lofton* by several years, Florida continued to insist that "there is a rational basis for the prohibition on homosexual adoption because children will have better role models, and face less discrimination, if they are placed in non-homosexual households, preferably with a husband and wife as the parents." *Florida Department of Children and Families v. In re Matter of Adoption of X.X.G. and N.R.G.*, 45 So.3d 79, 85 (Fla.Ct.App. 2010). Despite the lack of change in the state's position, the *X.X.G.* court accepted many of the arguments against the law that were rejected by the *Lofton* court. After noting that one-third of Florida's adoptions were by single individuals and that the state allowed lesbians and gay men to serve as foster parents and as legal guardians, the state appellate court concluded that there was no rational basis for categorically prohibiting gay people from adopting. *Id.* at 87. The court also reviewed the social science literature on parenting by lesbians and gay men, noting that "[t]hese reports and studies find that there are no differences in the parenting of homosexuals or the adjustment of their children . . . [B]ased on the robust nature of the evidence available in the field, this Court is satisfied that the issue is so far

beyond dispute that it would be irrational to hold otherwise; the best interests of children are not preserved by prohibiting homosexual adoption." *Id.*

2. In 2000, the Mississippi legislature enacted a law prohibiting "adoptions by couples of the same gender." MISS. CODE ANN. § 93–17–3(5) (2006). Unlike Florida's law, however, the Mississippi adoption statute does not deny lesbians and gay men who are single the opportunity to adopt. Also in 2000, Utah enacted a statute prohibiting a child from being adopted "by a person who is cohabiting in a relationship that is not a legally valid and binding marriage under the laws of this state. For purposes of this Subsection[,] 'cohabiting' means residing with another person and being involved in a sexual relationship with that person." UTAH CODE ANN. § 78–30–1–3(b) (2010). Since same-sex couples cannot marry in Utah, this provision makes it impossible for lesbians and gay men who live with their partners to adopt. Note, however, that unlike the Florida ban, the Utah statute is facially neutral as to sexual orientation.

A similar provision was approved by Arkansas voters in 2008. The Arkansas Supreme Court later held that the measure violated the fundamental right to privacy under the state constitution because it penalized individuals for their sexual intimacy choices. See *Arkansas Dep't Human Services v. Cole*, 380 S.W.3d 429 2011 Ark. 145 (2011). An earlier Arkansas regulation prohibiting the placement of foster children with lesbians and gay men was struck down by the Arkansas Supreme Court in 2006. *See Department of Human Services v. Howard*, 367 Ark. 55, 238 S.W.3d 1 (2006). In 2011, the Arizona legislature amended its adoption statute in order to codify a preference in favor of adoption by married couples. *See* ARIZ. REV. STAT. 8–103 (2012). This provision adversely affects same-sex couples because the state constitution prohibits them from marrying. *See* ARIZ. CONST. Art. 30.

3. In 2004, the Oklahoma legislature amended its adoption statute in order to prohibit state agencies and courts from "recogniz[ing] an adoption by more than one individual of the same sex from any other state or foreign jurisdiction." OKLA. STAT. TIT. 10, § 7502–1.4(A) (2006). A federal district court struck down the law for violating the Full Faith and Credit Clause, the Equal Protection Clause, and the Due Process Clause of the U.S. Constitution. *Finstuen v. Edmondson*, 497 F.Supp.2d 1295, 1315 (W.D. Okla. 2006). The U.S. Court of Appeals for the Tenth Circuit affirmed on the first ground without reaching the equal protection and due process claims. *See* 496 F.3d 1139, 1156 (10th Cir. 2007). For a critique of the Oklahoma law, see Carlos A. Ball, *The Immorality of Statutory Restrictions on Adoption by Lesbians and Gay Men*, 38 LOY. U. CHI. L.J. 379 (2007).

4. There is a difference between categorically prohibiting lesbians and gay men to adopt (or to serve as foster care parents) and allowing decision makers to take the sexual orientation of prospective parents into account when making particular placement decisions. Professor Michael Wald, in an

article that forcefully argues against categorical restrictions based on sexual orientation, suggests that in making case-by-case adoption and foster care placement decisions, judges and agencies should be permitted to take sexual orientation into account as long as it is one of several factors that are considered. *See* Michael S. Wald, *Adults' Sexual Orientation and State Determinations Regarding Placement of Children*, 40 FAM. L. Q. 381, 417–422 (2006). Wald explains that "[c]aseworkers or courts could consider the difficulties or advantages a particular child is likely to face in living with a gay family as one of the factors in determining the best placement. Even if the difficulties are related to the fact of stigma, as a general rule, children should not be made to bear the costs of remedying biases that are deemed undesirable by policymakers." *Id*. at 417–18.

Professor Wald adds that the case for allowing decision-makers to take sexual orientation into account is stronger in foster care placements than in adoption ones because "children tend to enter foster care at older ages and face very difficult adjustments. Asking these youth to adjust to a home where the caretakers are of a different sexual orientation may be unwise in some situations. The youth may bring biases that will undermine the chances of a successful placement. Getting foster youth to develop the emotional commitment and sense of trust needed for successful placements is challenging under the best of circumstances. It is likely to be impossible if the youth is resistant." *Id*. at 421. What is your position on this? Do you agree with Professor Wald or do you think that a prospective parent's sexual orientation should *never* be a factor in the placement of children?

2. Matching LGBT Youth with LGBT Parents

Not surprisingly, most of the debate surrounding the adoption (and foster care) placements of children with lesbian, gay, and bisexual parents has focused on the sexual orientation of the adults. But it is important to remember that some of the children, especially the older ones, will have sexual orientations of their own. The following readings address this important, but often ignored, fact.

SEXUAL ORIENTATION AND ADOPTIVE MATCHING[*]
Joseph Evall

A. LOOKING LIKE A BIOLOGICAL FAMILY

. . . [I]n the early days of adoption, when it was a goal to make the adoptive family look to the world as much like a biological family as was possible, physical similarities between child and parent were thought highly desirable. Through careful selection of features such as hair color, eye color, and body type, a family unit could be created in which there was a clear family resemblance. The outside world would not question the

---

[*] Joseph Evall, *Sexual Orientation and Adoptive Matching*, 25 FAM. L.Q. 347, 367–77 (1991).

naturalness of the family, nor be made aware of the likely infertility of one of the parents. * * *

This justification alone would not support the adoptive placement of self-identified gay, lesbian, or bisexual adolescents with gay adults for several obvious reasons. Arriving in the adoptive family as an adolescent, the adoptee already knows that the adoptive parents are not the biological parents. Furthermore, since most gay people are the offspring of heterosexual parents, the mere presence of gay youth and gay parents in the same family would not suggest to onlookers a biological relationship. * * *

B. FURTHERING THE CHILDREN'S UNDERSTANDING OF THEIR LIFECYCLES

Matching children and parents based on similar traits might also be justified on the basis of increasing the children's understanding of how they will develop biologically. For example, a daughter with blond hair might be able to say to herself, if her adoptive mother had blond hair, "This is how my blond hair will look when I'm older." Or, a son prone to obesity might be able to say to himself, "If I keep overeating, that is how I will look," pointing to his overweight father who had been prone to obesity.

This issue is inapplicable to [sexual orientation matching]. Gay and lesbian people do not age in a genetically distinct way that would profit gay and lesbian adolescents to observe. Rather, the benefits accrued from observing older gay and lesbian people are in the nature of the benefits reaped from watching role models, discussed below.

C. TEACHING COPING SKILLS

Teaching the skills needed for survival in society is, of course, one of the functions of a parent. Certain groups of people need special skills relevant to the differences that define those groups of people. For example, modern American society is heterosexist and homophobic. In order to flourish in America today, a member of a sexual minority must learn how to cope successfully in such an environment.

It is important to understand that there is no consensus on what constitutes coping. . . . If an adoption agency wanted to place gay or lesbian youth with gay or lesbian adoptive parents so that they could learn how to cope with homophobia, the agency would be imposing on the children its own view of what constitutes coping. By choosing parents who identify themselves as gay or lesbian as exemplars of people who have coped with homophobia, the agency is telling the world that one component of coping is that self-identification, and that not hiding one's sexual orientation is thereby desirable. Although this might be a desirable symbolic message, one that would send a positive message to *all* children in society, the method might sacrifice the best interests of the child because there is no reason to suspect that particular coping skills can best be learned from parents who also belong to a sexual minority.

The presence in America of well-adjusted gay people who were raised by heterosexual parents suggests that this placement is not necessary. In fact, *most* homosexual children are raised in families led by heterosexual parents. There is no reason to suggest that a loving, nurturing home environment will not teach the self-respect necessary to thrive. Furthermore, gay adopted children can learn particular coping skills from heterosexual parents in the same way that the gay biological children of heterosexual parents learn them—from the gay community at large, through the wisdom and common sense acquired during development, and from gay and lesbian role models. * * *

Matching a child with a like parent so that she can learn coping skills sends two insidious messages to the child. The first message is that the defining difference is so severe that special arrangements must be made to accommodate it. Thus, when the government or even private actors behave in a certain manner because of one's sexual orientation, they are using that person's sexual orientation as a way of both categorizing and defining that person. The greater the emphasis the adoption system places on sexual orientation, the more important sexual orientation seems as a way of defining significant aspects of a person.

When the adoption system matches members of a group on the basis of coping skills, it also tells those children that only someone in that group is capable of understanding and teaching them how to deal with that difference; that for the rest of their lives, an unbridgeable gulf will separate them from others who do not share their "difference."

Perhaps it is true that lesbians and gay men are more likely than others to have learned the particular coping skills that enable them to deal with homophobia and heterosexism in our society. However, that does not mean that simply being lesbian or gay should be used as a proxy for the trait that is desired: the ability to *teach* children to cope.

D. ROLE MODELS

Gay and lesbian adolescents might be matched with gay and lesbian parents to provide the youth with positive role models to whom they may aspire to be. The children would see that they can flourish in society, that they could serve as parents, and that society could one day *choose* them to parent. However, children also have role models other than their parents. Nongay parents could expose them to productive, successful gay people, and thereby show the children that they can succeed in society.

Furthermore, if gay people were limited to parenting gay adolescents, they would be less effective role models. They would only be able to show their children that they have been found capable of parenting gay children, and not other children. Faced with this image, all adopted children would be taught by society that gay people can only parent gay and lesbian adolescents. Moreover, allowing gay and lesbian people to care only for children with HIV disease would be similarly stigmatizing.

E. FOSTERING COMMUNITY

Because of the central role of the family in transmitting community norms, values, and culture, any state participation in the creation of families carries great political implications. First, as discussed above, parents teach children how to cope with the outside world. In selecting adoptive parents from all those in a particular community, the state rewards those parents and their method of coping with a world hostile to their minority status—and thereby encourages others in the community to adhere to act similarly in order to garner the benefit of adopting. In addition, the new generation will be taught those values and mechanisms by their adoptive parents.

Second, by matching children and parents within a community, the adoption system reinforces to society at large, as well as to the particular community, the value and worth of that community and of its members. Thus, matching gay children with gay parents may send a message that each "deserves" the other.

Finally, since much of the culture of a community, as well as its norms and values, is transmitted and preserved through the family, the state's decisions about how to assemble families may affect the strength and viability of the community. Besides helping to inform the richness of American culture, communities pay a crucial role in the American political system. * * *

It is interesting to consider sexual orientation in light of . . . other characteristics, such as race or membership in an Indian tribe, because sexual orientation is an altogether different type of status. First, one typically belongs to the same race, or Indian tribe, or religion, as one's parents. Most gay people, however, are born to heterosexual parents. Thus, the gay community has not developed from within the family unit. One typically does not share membership in this community with one's family. The community is replenished with each generation because gay people arise in each generation out of the general population. In addition, no small part of gay culture arises from challenges to the traditional notions of the family itself.

Second, one is a member of a racial or ethnic community by status; it is determined by birth. The gay community, however, is *not* a community of homosexuals—it is a community of gay people, who have consciously acted on (this means self-identification, not sexual activity) their recognition of their homosexuality.

Third, there is little serious writing that one should alter the features that make one a member of a racial or other ethnic community. Yet, many view homosexuality as a sin or sickness, and argue that one should endeavor to change the behavior—the self-definition or other acts—that makes one a member of the gay community. Thus, it is a community marked by a battle to establish its right to exist. Once these various differences between communities such as the African-American community and the gay community, are understood, it becomes clear that the arguments that may support in-racial adoptive placements do not necessarily apply to other in-community matchings. * * *

Because gay parents *ordinarily* raise nongay children and nongay parents *ordinarily* raise nongay children, it seems no usurpation of autonomy to place children across lines of sexual orientation. Rather, empowerment of the community occurs by recognizing that gay people make fine parents, and placing children with them regardless of sexual orientation. Such a placement will be in the best interests of any child because if gay, the child will recognize that the state has validated his or her right to parent and that he or she is capable of so doing; if nongay, the child will not have to fear that a subsequent recognition of sexual orientation, should it be different than suspected, will result in his or her disempowerment by being plunged into a weakened community.

Finally, there is gay culture as a culture. Control over Native American children or African-American children is important to the survival of these communities; the culture develops, and is transmitted, within the family. Gay culture is not; it is transmitted through a web of institutions and interactions that suffuses society. Access to gay children from within the family is not necessary to transmit gay culture.

RESISTING "DON'T ASK, DON'T TELL" IN THE LICENSING OF LESBIAN AND GAY FOSTER PARENTS: WHY OPENNESS WILL BENEFIT LESBIAN AND GAY YOUTH[*]

Nancy D. Polikoff

The most obvious connection between lesbian and gay youth and foster parents is the importance of the availability of gay and lesbian foster parents to provide homes for gay teenagers who need acceptance and support for their journey into adulthood. But the open, publicly acknowledged and valued existence of gay foster parents serves another function. The state agency that licenses foster parents is the same agency that controls the lives of lesbian and gay youth in its care. Open licensing

---

[*] Nancy D. Polikoff, *Resisting "Don't Ask, Don't Tell" in the Licensing of Lesbian and Gay Foster Parents: Why Openness Will Benefit Lesbian and Gay Youth*, 48 HASTINGS L.J. 1183, 1184–94 (1997).

of gay foster parents sends a powerful message to those youth that it's okay to be gay, and we need the state to send that message in as many ways as possible.

[States should] not only license gay and lesbian foster parents—they [should] do so openly. A "don't ask, don't tell" policy might work for gay adult foster parents. It might be acceptable for a state agency to license foster parents without inquiring into sexual orientation, and to therefore be unable to say whether any of its foster parents were gay, because it is appropriate to believe that a person's sexual orientation is irrelevant to his or her ability to be a good parent. We might say that an agency that doesn't make that kind of inquiry before licensing foster parents is really doing a good job.

This reasoning fails, however, when one considers gay and lesbian teenagers within the foster care system. The child welfare system already ignores the existence of gay, lesbian, bisexual, and transgendered young people who receive their services. Social workers, group home counselors, and foster parents are not trained to understand gay and lesbian adolescent sexual development, to recognize and overcome their own personal discomfort of adolescent sexuality, and to help gay and lesbian teenagers face and respond to social stigma that they experience. "Don't ask, don't tell" is not benign for these adolescents because sexual orientation is always relevant to their development; it must be considered in their case plans and when making placements. Yet an agency that does not openly license gay foster parents cannot be expected to openly address the needs of gay and lesbian teenagers. * * *

[I]t is also critical that the child's welfare system hire social workers and group home counselors who are openly gay and lesbian. This is something, of course, that state and local agencies are not required to do unless there is some legislation or policy in place which prohibits discrimination in employment on the basis of sexual orientation. Many teenagers are never placed in foster homes, but rather wind up in group home settings. There they are vulnerable to peer harassment as well as adult disapproval. These placements chronically fail. For example, consider Rhonda, a sixteen-year old black lesbian. When her grandmother died, there was no one to take her and she moved into a youth shelter. Over the course of sixteen months, she went through every shelter and group home in Los Angeles. Several times between placements she wound up back on the streets. This is how she described her situation:

> Maybe a third of us that hung out on the street together were gay. A lot of them left home because their parents threw them out. You're gay, that's a curse, get out. They treated it like a disease or something. A lot of gay kids would have problems because they wouldn't want to go to a straight foster home, so

they didn't go anywhere. They'd say, "Either I get into a gay home or a shelter where I can be freely gay or I'll stay out here on the streets." But after several months of going from shelter to shelter, you want to say, "Forget it, I'm not ever going to find a home. I'll make it on my own." I finally decided it was time to go to a straight group home, see how it was like there and if I didn't get along, I'd just leave. And I did go and I saw what everybody was afraid of. It was very homophobic. They watched everything I did. They made me sign an agreement not to touch any other girl in the home. They totally blew the subject out of proportion.

A boy tells his story as follows:

I was living at home with my room and she was always on me about acting more like a boy, being more like my brothers and all that mess. I tried but I just couldn't do it. It just wasn't me. Things went from bad to worse and I just couldn't take it anymore. One day my mom and I had this big fight and she said, "Why don't you just take your faggot ass out of my house?" So I left. I went to social services and they put me in this group home. It was horrible. First of all, it was a terrible place and the boys who were there were bad news. Although I didn't say anything about being gay or anything, the staff sensed that something was up with me, that I wasn't like the other boys and they were always watching me. They never said anything to me, but I knew that they were watching me. They sensed I was different, I could just tell by the way they looked at me when I first came in the door. The first night that I was there I got jumped by these guys in the bedroom. When I told the staff they said they could not do anything about it. I complained to my social worker and they moved me to another group home. This one was worse. In that one, I had staff preaching to me and telling me I was going to go to hell. And that I was evil and all of that. I had this psychologist asking me a million questions and asking me if I wanted to be a girl. You know, stupid, ignorant stuff like that. I just didn't fit in. I wasn't comfortable. I complained again and I was sent to another group home. This one was better because they had some gay staff there and they looked out for me so I stayed because the staff was cool with me. So there were other kids that lived there. It's not so bad now.

One study based on interviews with fifty-four gay and lesbian teenagers in foster homes or group home placements in New York, Toronto, and Los Angeles showed that 89% had experienced multiple placements because they didn't fit in where they were originally placed. All but one had experienced verbal harassment due to their sexual orientation, and 52% had experienced physical violence. * * *

On a daily basis, social workers, their supervisors, and their supervisor's supervisors, who are often political appointees, make decisions about homes for children behind closed doors. The news behind these closed doors is not always bad. Social workers often support licensing of gay and lesbian foster parents because they know gay men and lesbians provide good homes for children and because foster homes are always, everywhere, in short supply. Some agencies explicitly place gay and lesbian teenagers in gay foster homes. While programs exist in some places you might expect—New York, Los Angeles, Washington, D.C., and Boston—advocates of gay and lesbian foster parenting have allies in many states. In Iowa, a gay male couple from the town of Eldora was named as the foster parents of the year for 1996 by the Iowa Foster and Adopted Parents Association. They achieved this honor after being nominated by their seventeen-year old foster son. Over the preceding seven years, they had been foster parents to thirteen children, one of whom they adopted. A representative of Iowa's Department of Human Services told the Des Moines Register that the state doesn't ask questions about an applicant's sexual orientation and does not require that applicants be heterosexual. "We have a set of standards," said the Bureau Chief, "and we apply them to all applicants." Iowa places 15–20% of its foster children with parents who are unmarried. We don't know, of course, how many of them are gay.

Perhaps more dramatic was the response of social workers in Nebraska in 1995, when the state social services agency proposed to ban gay men and lesbians from serving as foster parents. The head of the agency suggested the policy without any articulated justification or evidence of problems or bad outcomes for children in gay or lesbian foster homes. The Nebraska chapter of the National Association of Social Workers not only opposed the proposed ban, but publicly announced that implementing the ban would violate the code of ethics of their state licenses, which bans discrimination on the basis of sexual orientation and marital status. They talked about what a difficult position it would put the state social workers in, by forcing them to choose between violating the law and violating their own code of ethics.

The news, of course, is not uniformly good. In Ohio last year, a guardian ad litem challenged a placement of a child by the Department of Human Services with lesbian foster parents. Although the agency announced that it did not discriminate on the basis of sexual orientation, the judge said that he was against gay and lesbian foster homes, and that he was willing to "go to war against the DHS policy." In December 1996, a Kansas City, Missouri newspaper reported that the state's unwritten policy against licensing gay and lesbian parents had been violated. This policy is a verbal one, announced in training sessions. The newspaper knew the policy had been violated because a former employee of the state's division of family services reported that he had been ordered to license a lesbian foster parent. When he refused, citing religious reasons, another employee completed the licensing. * * *

There are two likely reasons [why the placement of gay and lesbian teenagers in gay and lesbian foster homes] is so controversial. One is the notion that such foster parents will make these children become gay or lesbian, especially if they are in a questioning state. And, of course, according to opponents, foster children are by definition in a questioning state of mind, since they couldn't possibly be gay or lesbian. The idea that gay foster parents would somehow force their sexuality on foster children is especially pronounced when you have a teenager who has already identified as gay, lesbian, or questioning. The other likely reason is the continued myth that gay men sexually abuse children, and that therefore any teenager placed with gay foster parents would be at risk for being sexually abused.

In the course of any kind of public campaign against the ban on gay and lesbian foster parenting, if you tout a success story about gay and lesbian teenagers, you will come head on against these controversies. I think that there is no choice but to confront them. We need to do it. We also need to be openly part of a strategy that affirms both the value of gay and lesbian foster parents for gay and lesbian teenagers, and the value of state agencies licensing gay and lesbian foster parents across the board. * * *

. . . [I] am not arguing that gay and lesbian teenagers should only be placed with gay and lesbian foster parents. I certainly think heterosexuals can provide a safe and affirming environment in which to help their gay and lesbian foster children grow into adulthood. But if an agency openly licenses gay and lesbian foster parents, it is more likely to look for positive heterosexual foster placements for gay and lesbian teenagers and therefore will be better able to serve the needs of all the gay and lesbian youth in their care.

3. Second-Parent Adoptions

Distinct from the traditional form of adoption, which extinguishes the parental rights and obligations of the biological or current legal parents, second parent-adoption leaves the parental rights of one legally recognized parent intact and creates another legally recognized parent for the child. All jurisdictions allow individuals to adopt their spouses' children without the latter having to terminate his or her parental rights. The issue then becomes whether the same-sex partners of parents can do the same. This question requires the judicial interpretation of a particular state's adoption statute. By now, several appellate courts across the country have grappled with the issue. The first judicial decision below is representative of opinions that have allowed the same-sex partners of parents to petition for adoption; the second is representative of opinions that have concluded differently.

IN RE ADOPTION OF TAMMY

Supreme Judicial Court of Massachusetts, 1993
619 N.E.2d 315, 416 Mass. 205

GREANEY, JUSTICE.

We summarize the relevant facts as found by the judge. Helen and Susan have lived together in a committed relationship, which they consider to be permanent, for more than ten years. In June, 1983, they jointly purchased a house in Cambridge. Both women are physicians specializing in surgery. At the time the petition was filed, Helen maintained a private practice in general surgery at Mount Auburn Hospital and Susan, a nationally recognized expert in the field of breast cancer, was director of the Faulkner Breast Center and a surgical oncologist at the Dana Farber Cancer Institute. Both women also held positions on the faculty of Harvard Medical School.

For several years prior to the birth of Tammy, Helen and Susan planned to have a child, biologically related to both of them, whom they would jointly parent. Helen first attempted to conceive a child through artificial insemination by Susan's brother. When those efforts failed, Susan successfully conceived a child through artificial insemination by Helen's biological cousin, Francis. The women attended childbirth classes together and Helen was present when Susan gave birth to Tammy on April 30, 1988. Although Tammy's birth certificate reflects Francis as her biological father, she was given a hyphenated surname using Susan and Helen's last names.

Since her birth, Tammy has lived with, and been raised and supported by, Helen and Susan. Tammy views both women as her parents, calling Helen "mama" and Susan "mommy." Tammy has strong emotional and psychological bonds with both Helen and Susan. Together, Helen and Susan have provided Tammy with a comfortable home, and have created a warm and stable environment which is supportive of Tammy's growth and over-all well being. Both women jointly and equally participate in parenting Tammy, and both have a strong financial commitment to her. During the work week, Helen usually has lunch at home with Tammy, and on weekends both women spend time together with Tammy at special events or running errands. When Helen and Susan are working, Tammy is cared for by a nanny. The three vacation together at least ten days every three to four months, frequently spending time with Helen's and Susan's respective extended families in California and Mexico. Francis does not participate in parenting Tammy and does not support her. His intention was to assist Helen and Susan in having a child, and he does not intend to be involved with Tammy, except as a distant relative. Francis signed an adoption surrender and supports the joint adoption by both women.

Helen and Susan, recognizing that the laws of the Commonwealth do not permit them to enter into a legally cognizable marriage, believe that the best interests of Tammy require legal recognition of her identical emotional relationship to both women. Susan expressed her understanding that it may not be in her own long-term interest to permit Helen to adopt Tammy because, in the event that Helen and Susan separate, Helen would have equal rights to primary custody. Susan indicated, however, that she has no reservation about allowing Helen to adopt. Apart from the emotional security and current practical ramifications which legal recognition of the reality of her parental relationships will provide Tammy, Susan indicated that the adoption is important for Tammy in terms of potential inheritance from Helen. Helen and her living issue are the beneficiaries of three irrevocable family trusts. Unless Tammy is adopted, Helen's share of the trusts may pass to others. Although Susan and Helen have established a substantial trust fund for Tammy, it is comparatively small in relation to Tammy's potential inheritance under Helen's family trusts.

Over a dozen witnesses, including mental health professionals, teachers, colleagues, neighbors, blood relatives and a priest and nun, testified to the fact that Helen and Susan participate equally in raising Tammy, that Tammy relates to both women as her parents, and that the three form a healthy, happy, and stable family unit. Educators familiar with Tammy testified that she is an extremely well-adjusted, bright, creative, cheerful child who interacts well with other children and adults. A priest and nun from the parties' church testified that Helen and Susan are active parishioners, that they routinely take Tammy to church and church-related activities, and that they attend to the spiritual and moral development of Tammy in an exemplary fashion. Teachers from Tammy's school testified that Helen and Susan both actively participate as volunteers in the school community and communicate frequently with school officials. Neighbors testified that they would have no hesitation in leaving their own children in the care of Helen or Susan. Susan's father, brother, and maternal aunt, and Helen's cousin testified in favor of the joint adoption. Members of both women's extended families attested to the fact that they consider Helen and Susan to be equal parents of Tammy. Both families unreservedly endorsed the adoption petition.

The Department of Social Services (department) conducted a home study in connection with the adoption petition which recommended the adoption, concluding that "the petitioners and their home are suitable for the proper rearing of this child." Tammy's pediatrician reported to the department that Tammy receives regular pediatric care and that she "could not have more excellent parents than Helen and Susan." A court-appointed guardian ad litem, Dr. Steven Nickman, assistant clinical professor of psychiatry at Harvard Medical School, conducted a clinical assessment of Tammy and her family with a view toward determining whether or not it would be in Tammy's best interests to be adopted by Helen and Susan. Dr. Nickman considered the ramifications of the fact that Tammy will be brought up in a "non-standard" family. As part of his report, he reviewed and referenced literature on child psychiatry and child psychology which supports the conclusion that children raised by lesbian parents develop normally. In sum, he stated that "the fact that this parent-child constellation came into being as a result of thoughtful planning and a strong desire on the part of these women to be parents to a child and to give that child the love, the wisdom and the knowledge that they possess . . . [needs to be taken into account]. . . . The maturity of these women, their status in the community, and their seriousness of purpose stands in contrast to the caretaking environments of a vast number of children who are born to heterosexual parents but who are variously abused, neglected and otherwise deprived of security and happiness." Dr. Nickman concluded that "there is every reason for [Helen] to become a legal parent to Tammy just as [Susan] is," and he recommended that the court so order. An attorney appointed to represent Tammy's interests also strongly recommended that the joint petition be granted.

Despite the overwhelming support for the joint adoption and the judge's conclusion that joint adoption is clearly in Tammy's best interests, the question remains whether there is anything in the law of the Commonwealth that would prevent this adoption. The law of adoption is purely statutory, and the governing statute, is to be strictly followed in all its essential particulars. To the extent that any ambiguity or vagueness exists in the statute, judicial construction should enhance, rather than defeat, its purpose. The primary purpose of the adoption statute, particularly with regard to children under the age of fourteen, is undoubtedly the advancement of the best interests of the subject child. With these considerations in mind, we examine the statute to determine whether adoption in the circumstances of this case is permitted.

1.   The initial question is whether the Probate Court judge had jurisdiction to enter a judgment on a joint petition for adoption brought by two unmarried cohabitants in the petitioners' circumstances. We answer this question in the affirmative.

There is nothing on the face of the statute which precludes the joint adoption of a child by two unmarried cohabitants such as the petitioners. [The law] provides that "[a] person of full age may petition the probate court in the county where he resides for leave to adopt as his child another person younger than himself, unless such other person is his or her wife or husband, or brother, sister, uncle or aunt, of the whole or half blood." Other than requiring that a spouse join in the petition, if the petitioner is married and the spouse is competent to join therein, the statute does not expressly prohibit or require joinder by any person. Although the singular "a person" is used, it is a legislatively mandated rule of statutory construction that "[w]ords importing the singular number may extend and be applied to several persons" unless the resulting construction is "inconsistent with the manifest intent of the law-making body or repugnant to the context of the same statute." In the context of adoption, where the legislative intent to promote the best interests of the child is evidenced throughout the governing statute, and the adoption of a child by two unmarried individuals accomplishes that goal, construing the term "person" as "persons" clearly enhances, rather than defeats, the purpose of the statute. Furthermore, it is apparent from the first sentence of [the law] that the Legislature considered and defined those combinations of persons which would lead to adoptions in violation of public policy. Clearly absent is any prohibition of adoption by two unmarried individuals like the petitioners.

While the Legislature may not have envisioned adoption by same-sex partners, there is no indication that it attempted to define all possible categories of persons leading to adoptions in the best interests of children. Rather than limit the potential categories of persons entitled to adopt . . . the Legislature used general language to define who may adopt and who may be adopted. The Probate Court has thus been granted jurisdiction to consider a variety of adoption petitions. The limitations on adoption that do exist derive from the written consent requirements contained in § 2, from specific conditions set forth in § 2A, which must be satisfied prior to the adoption of a child under the age of fourteen, and from several statutory and judicial directives which essentially restrict adoptions to those which have been found by a judge to be in the best interests of the subject child.

In this case all requirements in §§ 2 and 2A are met, and there is no question that the judge's findings demonstrate that the directives set forth in §§ 5B and 6, and in case law, have been satisfied. Adoption will not result in any tangible change in Tammy's daily life; it will, however, serve to provide her with a significant legal relationship which may be important in her future. At the most practical level, adoption will entitle Tammy to inherit from Helen's family trusts and from Helen and her family under the law of intestate succession to receive support from Helen, who will be legally obligated to provide such support to be eligible for coverage under Helen's health insurance policies, and to be eligible for social security benefits in the event of Helen's disability or death.

Of equal, if not greater significance, adoption will enable Tammy to preserve her unique filial ties to Helen in the event that Helen and Susan separate, or Susan predeceases Helen. As the case law and commentary on the subject illustrate, when the functional parents of children born in circumstances similar to Tammy separate or one dies, the children often remain in legal limbo for years while their future is disputed in the courts. In some cases, children have been denied the affection of a functional parent who has been with them since birth, even when it is apparent that this outcome is contrary to the children's best interests. Adoption serves to establish legal rights and responsibilities so that, in the event that problems arise in the future, issues of custody and visitation may be promptly resolved by reference to the best interests of the child within the recognized framework of the law. There is no jurisdictional bar in the statute to the judge's consideration of this joint petition. The conclusion that the adoption is in the best interests of Tammy is also well warranted.

2. The judge also posed the question whether Susan's legal relationship to Tammy must be terminated if Tammy is adopted. Section 6 provides that, on entry of an adoption decree, "all rights, duties and other legal consequences of the natural relation of child and parent shall . . . terminate between the child so adopted and his natural parents and kindred." Although [the law] clearly permits a child's natural parent to be an adoptive parent, § 6 does not contain any express exceptions to its termination provision. The Legislature obviously did not intend that a natural parent's legal relationship to its child be terminated when the natural parent is a party to the adoption petition.

Section 6 clearly is directed to the more usual circumstances of adoption, where the child is adopted by persons who are not the child's natural parents (either because the natural parents have elected to relinquish the child for adoption or their parental rights have been involuntarily terminated). The purpose of the termination provision is to protect the security of the child's newly-created family unit by eliminating involvement with the child's natural parents. Although it is not uncommon for a natural parent to join in the adoption petition of a spouse who is not the child's natural parent, the statute has never been construed to require the termination of the natural parent's legal relationship to the child in these circumstances. Nor has § 6 been construed to apply when the natural mother petitions alone to adopt her child born out of wedlock. Reading the adoption statute as a whole, we conclude that the termination provision contained in § 6 was intended to apply only when the natural parents (or parent) are not parties to the adoption petition.

3. We conclude that the Probate Court has jurisdiction to enter a decree on a joint adoption petition brought by the two petitioners when the judge has found that joint adoption is in the subject child's best interests. We further conclude that, when a natural parent is a party to a

joint adoption petition, that parent's legal relationship to the child does not terminate on entry of the adoption decree.

[Dissenting opinions by JUSTICE NOLAN and JUSTICE LYNCH are omitted.]

IN RE ADOPTION OF LUKE

Supreme Court of Nebraska, 2002
640 N.W.2d 374, 263 Neb. 365

PER CURIAM.

B.P. is the biological mother of Luke, a minor child born on December 20, 1997. Luke was conceived by artificial insemination using semen from an anonymous donor from the University of Nebraska Medical Center's genetic semen bank. Accordingly, Luke's biological father is unknown and is not a party to this action. For purposes of the Nebraska adoption statutes, Luke was born "out of wedlock."

On October 2, 2000, appellants jointly filed a verified petition in which A.E. sought to adopt Luke. B.P. indicated her "consent" in the petition and in other supporting documents. B.P. did not file a relinquishment of her parental rights to Luke. To the contrary, she indicated on an affidavit attached to the petition that she did not intend to relinquish Luke. The only relief sought in this proceeding was the adoption of Luke by A.E.

A home study of appellants' household was conducted by an adoption specialist. The specialist recommended A.E.'s adoption of Luke be approved by the court.

In an order filed December 1, 2000, the county court denied the petition for adoption. * * *

For an adoption to be valid under Nebraska's adoption statutes, the record must show the following factors: (1) the existence of an adult person or persons entitled to adopt, (2) the existence of a child eligible for adoption, (3) compliance with statutory procedures providing for adoption, and (4) evidence that the proposed adoption is in the child's best interests. Neb. Rev. Stat. § 43–101 et seq. The absence of any one of the necessary factors will preclude the adoption. In this case, Luke was not eligible for adoption, the county court determined that his adoption by A.E. was precluded on this basis, and we affirm on this basis.

The county court stated that "the statu[t]es permit a single adult person to adopt a child after all necessary consents and relinquishments have been filed." On this record, B.P. did not relinquish her parental rights to Luke, and therefore, he was not eligible for adoption by A.E. The county court's denial of the petition due to an absence of a relinquishment was correct. The county court also stated that Nebraska's adoption statutes do not provide for "two non-married persons to adopt a minor child, no matter how qualified they are." Because A.E. alone sought to adopt Luke, the issue of whether two nonmarried persons are entitled to adopt was not presented to the county court in this case. Thus, that issue is not before this court on appeal, and we do not consider it.

Appellants argue that the county court erred in concluding that it could not grant the adoption of Luke by A.E. as an additional parent without a relinquishment of the parental rights of B.P. Appellants contend that "consent is an alternative to a relinquishment," and that where B.P. intended to preserve her parental rights upon the adoption of Luke by A.E., only B.P.'s consent, which was given, was required. . . .

The State responds that the Nebraska adoption statutory scheme does not provide for adoption without relinquishment except in the case of a stepparent where "an adult husband or wife" seeks to "adopt a child of the other spouse." § 43–101(1).[2] The State contends that stepparent adoption is the only explicit adoption scenario outlined in the Nebraska adoption statutes and that it is implicit in this statutorily permitted scenario that the existing parent intends to continue parenting and, therefore, need not relinquish his or her parental rights to the child in question. . . .

With respect to . . . Luke, who is the subject of this case, § 43–101 provides that "any minor child may be adopted." Elsewhere in chapter 43, however, numerous statutory substantive and procedural provisions are set forth which must be read together with § 43–101 and met before "any minor child," § 43–101, is in fact eligible for adoption and a decree of adoption may be properly entered. The statutes which provide for the consequences of adoption also bear on the issue of Luke's eligibility. Reading the various provisions of chapter 43 in pari materia, we conclude that with the exception of the stepparent adoption, the parent or parents possessing existing parental rights must relinquish the child before "any minor child may be adopted by any adult person or persons." Under Nebraska's statutory adoption scheme, the minor child, Luke, was not eligible for adoption by A.E. because B.P. had not relinquished him and the county court's reading of the statute was correct.

In *In re Adoption of Kassandra B. & Nicholas B.*, 540 N.W.2d 554, 558 (Neb. 1995), we observed that as to the biological parent,

---

[2] Section 43–101 is entitled "Children eligible for adoption." Section 43–101(1) provides as follows:

> Except as otherwise provided in the Nebraska Indian Child Welfare Act, any minor child may be adopted by any adult person or persons and any adult child may be adopted by the spouse of such child's parent in the cases and subject to sections 43–101 to 43–115, except that no person having a husband or wife may adopt a minor child unless the husband or wife joins in the petition therefor. If the husband or wife so joins in the petition therefor, the adoption shall be by them jointly, except that an adult husband or wife may adopt a child of the other spouse whether born in or out of wedlock.

"termination of his or her parental rights is the foundation of our adoption statutes." This pronouncement is reflected in the adoption statutes, which require relinquishment or termination prior to adoption, except when a stepparent adopts, and is further reflected in case law interpreting the adoption statutes.

Appellants argue that B.P.'s consent was the equivalent of relinquishment for purposes of the present case. We do not agree. Section § 43–104 provides that "no adoption shall be decreed unless written consents thereto are filed in the court of the county in which the person or persons desiring to adopt reside." . . .

A consent to the proceedings by a parent or parents under § 43–104 is not required when a relinquishment has been executed. § 43–104(3)(a). A relinquishment would preclude the necessity of a consent. B.P. did not sign a relinquishment in this case, and her "consent" is not the equivalent of relinquishment.

We have stated that the consent granted by a court under § 43–104 does nothing more than permit the trial court to entertain the adoption proceedings. *Klein v. Klein*, 230 Neb. 385, 431 N.W.2d 646 (1988). We read "consent" in § 43–104 to mean that the person, persons, or entity authorized to consent to the proceedings has agreed that the proposed adoption should be entertained by the trial court. In the instant case, B.P. "consented" to the proceedings and Luke is not ineligible for adoption due to a lack of such consent; however, B.P.'s consent to the proceedings was not tantamount to a relinquishment of parental rights.

The importance of "relinquishment" in the adoption statutes is apparent in § 43–109, which provides in relevant part:

> If, upon the hearing, the court finds that such adoption is for the best interests of such minor child or such adult child, a decree of adoption shall be entered. No decree of adoption shall be entered unless . . . (c) the court record includes an affidavit or affidavits signed by the *relinquishing biological parent*, or parents if both are available, in which it is affirmed that, pursuant to section 43–106.02, prior to the relinquishment of the child for adoption, the *relinquishing parent* was, or parents if both are available were, (i) presented a copy or copies of the nonconsent form provided for in section 43–146.06 and (ii) given an explanation of the effects of filing or not filing the nonconsent form.

(Emphasis supplied.) The affidavit noted in § 43–109(c) refers to the form completed by the relinquishing parent or parents which indicates whether the parent or parents agree to the release of information about the relinquishing parent or parents to the adopted child. . . .

We have held that in a private adoption case where the prospective adoptive parent was not a spouse of the biological parent, there must be a relinquishment by the biological parent and the relinquishment must be valid in order for the child to become eligible for adoption. See *Gray v. Maxwell*, 293 N.W.2d 90 (Neb. 1993) (stating that where biological mother was paid sum of money in excess of legitimate expenses of confinement and birth in consideration for executing relinquishment, such relinquishment was against public policy and was invalid). In the instant case, B.P. swore in the affidavit required under § 43–109 that "I do not intend to relinquish [Luke] for the ultimate purpose of adoption." Having refused to relinquish Luke, B.P. is not a "relinquishing biological parent." The affidavit B.P. signed did not meet the requirements of § 43–109. Therefore, Luke was not eligible for adoption and "[n]o decree of adoption shall be entered."

The provisions contained in the adoption statutes found at §§ 43–110 and 43–111, pertaining to the consequences of adoption, further buttress our conclusion that "termination" of existing parental rights is the foundation of our adoption statutes. Section 43–110, entitled "Decree; effect as between parties," provides as follows:

> After a decree of adoption is entered, the usual relation of parent and child and all the rights, duties and other legal consequences of the natural relation of child and parent shall thereafter exist between such adopted child and the person or persons adopting such child and his, her or their kindred.

We have stated that the "purpose of § 43–110 is to terminate any relationship which existed between the natural parent and the child and to create a new relationship between the adoptive parent and the child." *In re Estate of Luckey*; *Bailey v. Luckey*, 291 N.W.2d 235, 237–38 (Neb. 1980).

Section 43–111, entitled "Decree; effect as to natural parents," provides:

> Except as provided in section 43–106.01 and the Nebraska Indian Child Welfare Act, after a decree of adoption has been entered, the natural parents of the adopted child shall be relieved of all parental duties toward and all responsibilities for such child and have no rights over such adopted child or to his or her property by descent and distribution.

We have read this section as requiring a relinquishment prior to a private placement adoption. *Gray v. Maxwell, supra.*

Thus, under Nebraska's adoption statutes, the legal consequence of an adoption is that "the natural relation of child and parent shall thereafter exist between such adopted child and the person or persons adopting such child," § 43–110, and the adoption serves to relieve the natural parents of "all parental duties toward and all responsibilities for such child and have no rights over such adopted child," § 43–111. The pleadings in this case indicate that only A.E. sought to adopt Luke. Had the county court permitted the adoption of Luke by A.E., a new relationship between A.E. and Luke would have been created pursuant to § 43–110, and, as an unintended consequence, B.P. would have been relieved of her natural rights to Luke pursuant to § 43–111. In the instant case, B.P. manifestly did not want the consequences ordained by § 43–111 to attach had the county court granted the petition for adoption of Luke by A.E. * * *

Appellants urge this court to ignore the language of § 43–111 and to interpret the adoption statutes as permitting the adoption of Luke by A.E. as a parent in addition to the existing parent, B.P., without consequence to the parental rights of B.P. Appellants acknowledge that the exception providing for a stepparent adoption under § 43–101 permits the addition of a stepparent without relieving the natural parent of rights which would otherwise result under § 43–111. Appellants urge this court to read into the adoption statutes an additional exception for second-parent adoptions and to disregard the fact that the adoption statutes explicitly provide for stepparent adoptions and do not explicitly provide for second-parent adoptions.

The adoption statutes permit only the paradigms which are explicit. With the exception of the statutory stepparent adoption scenario outlined in § 43–101, the adoption statutes neither provide for nor expressly designate who may adopt. When construing a statute, appellate courts are guided by the presumption that the Legislature intended a sensible, rather than an absurd, result in enacting a statute. Because the Nebraska adoption statutes explicitly provide for a stepparent adoption following which the existing parent will inherently continue raising the child, we conclude it would be an absurd result under the statutes as written to require relinquishment by the existing parent in the explicit statutorily permitted case of a stepparent adoption. As compared to a stepparent adoption, however, it is not inherent in § 43–101 that the "person or persons" seeking to adopt will necessarily be in addition to the existing parent who will continue to raise the child. Reading the adoption statutes in their entirety, it is clear that aside from the stepparent adoption scenario, the parents' parental rights must be terminated or the child must be relinquished in order for the child to be eligible for adoption by "any adult person or persons" under § 43–101. * * * AFFIRMED

[Dissenting opinion by JUSTICE WRIGHT is omitted.]

NOTES

1. In addition to Massachusetts, second-parent adoptions have been approved by the highest courts in California, Idaho, New York, Pennsylvania, and Vermont. *See Sharon S. v. Superior Court*, 73 P.3d 554, 574, 31 Cal.4th 417, 446, 2 Cal.Rptr.3d 699, 729 (2003); *Matter of Jacob*, 660 N.E.2d 397, 405, 86 N.Y.2d 651, 669, 636 N.Y.S.2d 716, 724 (1995); *In re Adoption of Doe*, ___ P.3d ___, 2014 WL 527144 (Idaho); *Adoption of R.B.F. & R.C.F.*, 803 A.2d 1195, 1203, 569 Pa. 269, 283 (2002); *In re Adoption of B.L.V.B.*, 628 A.2d 1271, 1276, 160 Vt. 368, 377 (1993).

2. In addition to Nebraska, appellate courts in North Carolina, Ohio and Wisconsin have denied second-parent adoption petitions. *See Boseman v. Jarrell*, 704 S.E.2d 494, 501, 364 N.C. 537, 547 (2010); In *re Adoption of Doe*, 719 N.E.2d 1071, 1073, 130 Ohio App.3d 288, 292 (1998); *In Interest of Angel Lace M.*, 516 N.W.2d 678, 687, 184 Wis.2d 492, 519 (1994). Interestingly, the North Carolina Supreme Court in *Boseman*, after concluding that the state adoption statute did not allow second-parent adoptions, proceeded to affirm the granting of joint custody following the dissolution of a lesbian relationship because the biological mother had invited her partner to form a family unit and to raise the child together. *Boseman*, 704 S.E.2d at 504, 364 N.C. at 552. We explore the rights to custody and visitation of the former partners of legal parents in *infra* Section III.C.

3. Second-parent adoption has been an area of considerable success for LGBT families. Twenty-one states currently allow second-parent adoption in all parts of the state. *See* https://www.hrc.org/files/assets/resources/parenting_second-parent-adoption_012014.pdf. Some states permit such adoptions by statute, but more states have come to allow second-parent adoptions through judicial decisions. This is an area of law where the less glamorous law reform tool of statutory interpretation—and not the higher profile one of constitutional litigation—has produced significant results. *See* Jane S. Schacter, *Constructing Families in a Democracy: Courts, Legislatures and Second-Parent Adoptions*, 75 CHI.-KENT L. REV. 933, 935 (2000). The foundational article on second-parent adoption was Nancy D. Polikoff, *This Child Does Have Two Mothers: Redefining Parenthood To Meet the Needs of Children in Lesbian-Mother and Other Nontraditional Families*, 78 GEO. L.J. 459 (1990).

4. "Second-parent" adoptions should be distinguished from "joint adoptions." The latter term is usually used in instances when neither member of the couple is a legal parent at the time the adoption petition is filed. In joint adoptions, two individuals seek to become legal parents simultaneously (rather than consecutively, as is the case with second-parent adoptions). In 1997, New Jersey instituted an explicit policy, after it settled a lawsuit filed by a gay couple seeking to jointly adopt their foster child, placing same-sex couples on an equal footing with heterosexual married ones for purposes of adoption. *See* Ronald Smothers, *Accord Lets Gay Couples Adopt Jointly*, N.Y. TIMES, Dec. 18, 1997, at B4. Since then, several appellate

courts have held that their state's adoption statutes, which explicitly permit married couples to file joint adoption petitions, do not implicitly prohibit unmarried same-sex couples from doing the same. *See* In re Infant Girl W., 845 N.E.2d 229 (Ind. Ct. App. 2006); *In re Adoption of M.A.*, 930 A.2d 1088, 2007 ME 123 (2007); In re Adoption of Carolyn B., 774 N.Y.S.2d 227, 6 A.D.3d 67 (App.Div. 2004).

B. REPRODUCTION IN LGBT FAMILIES

1. Alternative Insemination

Alternative insemination, which requires virtually no medical expertise, can be performed at home without any involvement by state officials or medical professionals. To perform alternative insemination, a donor's sperm is collected and then injected with an instrument, such as a syringe or turkey baster, into a woman's uterus during her period of ovulation. Because of its simplicity, lesbians have increasingly used alternative insemination as a way of becoming mothers. As the following materials make clear, however, alternative insemination is not without risk. The legal rights and obligations of the sperm donor, the birth mother, and the co-parent are difficult to define in advance of litigation.

THOMAS S. V. ROBIN Y.

Supreme Court of New York, Appellate Division, 1994
618 N.Y.S.2d 356, 209 A.D.2d 298

MEMORANDUM DECISION

This appeal presents the narrow issue of whether a sperm donor who is known to his child as her father and who, despite residing in California, has had considerable contact with her at the instance of her mother, is entitled to an order of filiation, as mandated by Family Court Act § 542. We hold that he is. The broader issue of visitation, while argued extensively in the briefs, has not been adequately explored, and we therefore remand this issue for a hearing.

The child, Ry R.-Y., now 12 years old, lives with her mother, respondent Robin Y., the mother's lifetime companion, Sandra R., and Sandra's child, Cade, now 14, who was also conceived through artificial insemination by a donor known to her mother. Petitioner, who is also gay, was sought out by Robin Y. as a known donor and, after several attempts in both New York and California, Robin Y. successfully inseminated herself with petitioner's semen in February 1981 at the home of a mutual friend.

Ry was born on November 16, 1981 in San Francisco, where the household temporarily relocated in connection with Sandra R.'s employment. Like Cade, Ry was given the last names of R. and Y.

Petitioner is not listed on Ry's birth certificate, and R. and Y. paid all expenses associated with the pregnancy and delivery. Petitioner was, however, informed of the birth and brought congratulatory flowers to R. and Y.'s home. Later that year, the household moved back to New York where they currently occupy an apartment located in a building owned by Sandra R.

For the first three years of her life, petitioner saw Ry only once or twice while in New York on business. In accordance with an oral agreement with R. and Y., he did not call, support or give presents to her during this period. When Cade, at the age of approximately five years, started asking questions about her father, R. and Y., as they had agreed between themselves, made arrangements for Ry and Cade to meet their biological fathers.

Petitioner testified that there were approximately 26 visits with the R. and Y. family over the following six-year period, ranging in duration from a few days to two weeks. Robin Y. estimates that appellant spent a total of sixty days with the R.-Y. family over the course of those six years, and petitioner estimates 148 days. Whatever the figure, it appears that all parties concerned developed a comfortable relationship with one another. Photographs included in the exhibits depict a warm and amicable relationship between petitioner and Ry, and there are numerous cards and letters from Ry to petitioner in which she expressed her love for him.

In July 1990, petitioner asked Robin Y. for permission to take Ry and Cade to see his parents and stay at a beach house with some of his siblings and their children. It seems that petitioner felt awkward about introducing R. and Y. to his parents. R. and Y., however, were not willing to allow petitioner to take the girls unless the mothers accompanied them.

It was apparently during the course of these negotiations that petitioner revealed his desire to establish a paternal relationship with Ry. Y. and R. regarded this as a breach of their oral agreement, insisting that visitation continue on the same terms as over the past six years, *viz.*, with their supervision. They also rejected petitioner's suggestion to consult a family counselor or mediator. Unable to resolve his differences with R. and Y. and unable to see his daughter for a period of several months, petitioner moved, by order to show cause, for an order of filiation and for visitation.

During the course of the proceedings, Family Court ordered blood tests and a psychiatric evaluation of Ry. . . . The tests indicated a 99.9% probability of petitioner's paternity. Psychiatric evaluation revealed a belief on Ry's part that any relationship with petitioner would necessarily disrupt her relationship with Robin Y. and Sandra R. and might therefore undermine the legitimacy of her perception of the family unit. It also revealed that, since these proceedings were instituted, Ry has expressed a desire to end all contact with petitioner.

Family Court found by clear and convincing evidence, based upon the blood tests, that petitioner is the biological father of Ry. Nevertheless, citing the doctrine of equitable estoppel, the court refused to enter an order of filiation and dismissed the proceeding. The court characterized petitioner as an "outsider attacking her [Ry's] family and refusing to give it respect", concluding that "a declaration of paternity would be a statement that her family is other than what she knows it to be and needs it to be" and, therefore, "would not be in her best interests." The court added, "Even were there an adjudication of paternity, I would deny [petitioner's] application for visitation."

It is appropriate to begin with the observation that the effect of Family Court's order is to cut off the parental rights of a man who is conceded by all concerned—the child, her mother and the court—to be the biological father. The legal question that confronts us is not, as Family Court framed it, whether an established family unit is to be broken up. Custody of the child is not now, and is unlikely ever to be, an issue between the parties. Rather the question is whether the rights of a biological parent are to be terminated. Absent strict adherence to statutory provisions, termination of those rights is in violation of well established standards of due process and cannot stand.

The asserted sanctity of the family unit is an uncompelling ground for the drastic step of depriving petitioner of procedural due process. Whatever concerns and misgivings Family Court and the dissenters may entertain about visitation, custody and the child's best interests, it is clear that they are appropriately reserved for a later stage of the proceedings. * * *

The emphasis placed on custody, both by respondent and the dissent, is out of all proportion to its relevance to this proceeding. First, Thomas S. has never asserted a desire to gain custody of Ry. Second, as noted, custody and visitation are matters for subsequent hearings. Finally, the extent of petitioner's involvement in Ry's life is at once characterized by the dissent as both inadequate and overly intrusive. He is vilified for failing to sufficiently undertake his parental responsibility to provide ongoing support for the child and her education, without any consideration for whether support was necessary, solicited or even deemed desirable by her mother and Sandra R. He is criticized for having only a limited experience with the day-to-day events in his child's life, without regard for the three-thousand-mile distance between residences or the degree to which access to the child was limited by respondent and Sandra R. At the same time, petitioner's desire to communicate and visit with his daughter is portrayed as a threat to the stability and legitimacy of the family unit constituted by Ry, respondent and Sandra R. It is distressing that petitioner, who seems to have exhibited sensitivity and respect for the relationship between respondent and her domestic partner, is proposed to be compensated for his understanding by judicial extinguishment of his rights as a father. Such a result is offensive to the Court's sense of equity. Moreover, such an injustice hardly serves to promote tolerance and restraint among persons who may confront similar circumstances. It discourages resolution of disputes involving novel and complex familial relationships without resort to litigation which, ideally, should only be pursued as a last resort. * * *

Family Court's disposition is no more compelled by the equities of this matter than by the law. The notion that a lesbian mother should enjoy a parental relationship with her daughter but a gay father should not is so innately discriminatory as to be unworthy of comment. Merely because petitioner does not have custody of his daughter does not compel the conclusion, embraced by the dissent, that he may not assert any right to maintain a parental relationship with her. While much is made by Family Court of the alleged oral understanding between the parties that petitioner would not assume a parental role towards Ry, any such agreement is unenforceable for failure to comply with explicit statutory requirements for surrender of parental rights as the dissent concedes. * * *

Family Court presumed to apply the doctrine of equitable estoppel to foreclose any attempt by petitioner to obtain judicial consideration of his rights as a parent. However, the doctrine is more appropriately applied against the mother than against petitioner. If respondent now finds petitioner's involvement in his daughter's life to be inconvenient, she cannot deny that her predicament is the result of her own action. Not content with the knowledge of the identity of the biological father that her chosen method of conception afforded, Robin Y. initiated and fostered a relationship between petitioner and Ry. However strenuously this relationship may be gainsaid by respondent, its nature, duration and constancy during the six years prior to the commencement of this proceeding amply demonstrate petitioner's interest and concern for his child so as to preclude summary termination of his parental rights. Nor, given that Ry has known petitioner to be her father since the age of three, is there any credibility to the suggestion that mere acknowledgment of petitioner's legal status will result in a shock to the child's sensibilities. According to the testimony of the court-appointed psychiatrist, Ry's recently expressed desire to sever contact with petitioner, coinciding as it does with the onset of the instant dispute, is based on concerns communicated to her by Robin Y. and Sandra R. These fears are based on the misapprehension that visitation by petitioner necessarily poses an immediate threat to the stability of the household. In any event, Family Court's precipitous pronouncement notwithstanding, visitation is a matter yet to be determined, and the value of therapy in reestablishing the relationship between Ry and her father is an appropriate consideration in that context. Finally, entry of an order of filiation has the advantage of supplying a further source of support, should the necessity arise, together with the potential for substantial inheritance.

We reject the dissent's view that the alleged agreement between the parties constitutes evidence of a lack of commitment to his child on the part of petitioner. As the dissenters concede, legal impediments and public policy considerations bar enforcement of the oral agreement, and it can therefore be accorded no force or effect. It is the longstanding rule of equity, now extended to law, that the facts be viewed in their fullest. The Court cannot simply ignore the significant events that have transpired since Ry's third birthday. In any event, we regard the determination of this matter in any manner that departs from the express procedures delineated in article 5 of the Family Court Act as a violation of petitioner's statutory and Constitutional rights.

Having initiated and encouraged, over a substantial period of time, the relationship between petitioner and his daughter, respondent is estopped to deny his right to legal recognition of that relationship. The provisions of Family Ct. Act § 542(a) are clear and unambiguous and, therefore, there is no room for judicial interpretation. Having found that petitioner is the father of Ry R.-Y., Family Court was commanded by statutory direction to enter an order of filiation.

ELLERIN, JUSTICE (dissenting).

The question before us on this appeal is whether petitioner must be granted an order of filiation, pursuant to Family Court Act § 542, establishing his paternity of the child borne by respondent in November, 1981 as a result of having been artificially inseminated with petitioner's sperm or whether the doctrine of equitable estoppel may be applied to preclude the issuance of such order. . . .

The facts as found by the trial court are as follows. The child Ry was conceived by respondent Robin Y using sperm donated by appellant Thomas S., a gay man, while Robin was living in a stable life partnership relationship with another lesbian mother, Sandra R., and Sandra's then infant child Cade. At the time of appellant's providing his sperm, it was agreed, albeit not in writing, that he would have no parental rights or obligations and that the child would be brought up with Cade in a 2 parent household with 2 mothers. Appellant further agreed that he would make himself known to the child if the child wished to know the identity of her biological progenitor.

Notwithstanding the agreement, it is the manner in which the parties acted during the period from the child's birth up to the time of the commencement of this proceeding that is of critical significance. For the first 3 years of Ry's life there was virtually no contact with appellant. He was neither present at, nor involved with any arrangements for or costs of, her birth. His name was not on her birth certificate, he was not in any way involved in her care or support nor did he indicate the slightest desire to learn of her progress or condition even though for the first 8 months of her life Ry and her family resided in San Francisco where appellant lived.

It was only in 1985 when Cade, then almost 5 years old, began to ask about her biological origins, that contact was made with both Cade's sperm donor and with appellant, both of whom lived in California. At that time Ry was almost 3 and a half years old. In the ensuing 6 years there were periodic contacts between appellant, and both children, usually with both mothers present and always at the complete discretion of the mothers.

The record clearly establishes that for Ry's first 9 and half years of life the appellant at no time sought to establish a true parental relationship with her either by way of seeking to legally establish his paternity and assuming the responsibilities and obligations which that status entailed or by any involvement in her upbringing or schooling or by attempting to provide any support for her. He was not there when she cut her baby teeth, started to walk, was sick or in need of parental comfort or guidance, nor did he seek to involve himself in the every day decisions which are peculiarly the domain of parents—decisions as to what schools she should attend, what camps, what doctors should be consulted, the extent of her after school and social activities, the need for tutors and the like. Perhaps Ry herself best stated it when she said that to her a parent is a person who a child depends on to care for her needs.

The net of petitioner's relationship with Ry during the 6 years that he occasionally saw her until she was almost 10 years old was that of a close family friend or fond surrogate uncle who, while acknowledging that he was her biological sperm donor, fully recognized that her family unit consisted of her two mothers and her sister Cade and that he was not a family member of that unit. Throughout this period he fully acquiesced in the mothers' arrangement for meetings—i.e., to include all 4 members of the Ry family and with Cade to be treated by him in precisely the same way as Ry. While respondent Robin Y. was always agreeable to continuing periodic meetings and contacts with appellant on the same basis, it was appellant who summarily sought to alter this *modus operandi* of the preceding 6 years. He asked that the children visit him by themselves, without the other members of those whom he had always recognized as her family, so that he could introduce Ry to his own biological family, including his parents and siblings. He made clear that he would not feel comfortable introducing the mothers to his family. After respondent refused to accede to this attempt to markedly alter the prior course of the relationship between appellant and Ry's family, fueled by respondent's apprehension of future legal proceedings seeking to undermine that family relationship, appellant filed the instant petition for filiation.

The trial court, sensitive to the issues involved, appointed a law guardian for the child and obtained the agreement of all parties to submit the child to a psychiatric evaluation. Both the law guardian and the psychiatrist strongly recommended against the declaration of paternity and further recommended that there be no court-ordered visitation. . . .

At the outset, it must be emphasized that this proceeding was brought for the purpose of establishing, in the first instance, petitioner's parental status. While, concededly, petitioner provided the sperm for the artificial insemination that resulted in Ry's birth, petitioner at no time, for the almost 10 years prior to the commencement of this proceeding, established any paternal rights either by way of a legal proceeding or by way of fulfilling any of the duties and responsibilities incidental to parenthood. In that setting, the majority's characterization of the denial of the petition as akin to the "termination of [petitioner's] parental rights" is both puzzling and inaccurate. Until it can be established that petitioner has some parental rights, the very relief sought in this proceeding, the question of any "termination" of petitioner's rights never arises and the majority's recourse to Social Services Law § 384–b, governing termination of parental rights, is misplaced.

Nor, it should be made clear, is this case in any way a referendum on the comparative parenting abilities of lesbian mothers versus gay fathers, a gratuitous rhetorical inquiry posed by the majority. That petitioner is a gay man is wholly irrelevant to the question of whether his conduct for a period of almost 10 years during which he acquiesced in, and indeed fostered, Ry's belief that her family unit consisted of her 2 mothers and her sister Cade and that he did not occupy, nor seek to exercise, any parental or family role, should preclude his present attempt to establish parental status. It is the import of appellant's conduct and not his sexual orientation that is controlling. An identical standard would apply if any or all of the parties involved in this case were heterosexual.

The threshold issue that must first be determined is what rights, if any, arise from the fact that petitioner was the sperm donor and paternal biological progenitor of the child Ry. The Court of Appeals has made clear that absent "a full commitment to the responsibilities of parenthood" the mere existence of a biological link does not merit constitutional protection. Thus, an unwed biological father does not automatically have parental rights which must be recognized by the state independent of the child's best interests, since such rights come into existence only if the father has sufficiently grasped the opportunity to "promptly manifest[ed] his willingness to take on parental responsibilities" and it is only when "the opportunity, of limited duration, to manifest a willingness to be a parent" is grasped that an interest arises worthy of protection as a matter of due process.

While providing support for the child, and the child's education, would appear to be a minimal requirement for the manifestation of parenthood, the criteria which are particularly relevant in determining whether an unwed biological father has sufficiently undertaken his parental responsibilities to give him a protected parental interest may be garnered by reference to Domestic Relations Law § 111 which governs adoptions and delineates the various criteria which must be met before an unwed father has any protected right vis-a-vis the child. That statute provides that when the child is more than six months old, the father has a protected parental right to the extent of requiring his consent to the child's adoption, *only if* he has,

> maintained substantial and continuous or repeated contact with the child as manifested by: (i) the payment by the father toward the support of the child of a fair and reasonable sum, according to the father's means, and either (ii) the father's visiting the child at least monthly when physically and financially able to do so and not prevented from doing so by the person or authorized agency having lawful custody of the child, or (iii) the father's regular communication with the child or with the person or agency having the care or custody of the child, when physically and financially unable to visit the child or prevented from doing so by the person or authorized agency having lawful custody of the child.

In this case there is no question that petitioner has never sought to contribute to the ongoing support of the child, or to see to her educational or other needs despite the fact that he is a professional of substantial means. On the contrary, all of the child's economic and educational needs have been provided for through her mothers and she has enjoyed a comfortable standard of living. Nor, after not seeing the child at all for the first 3 years of her life, has petitioner ever sought to visit the child on anything close to a monthly basis. His failure to do so cannot be attributed to respondent since, until very recently, the pattern of occasional visits was one with which he was in full agreement. Whether viewed within the framework of the statutory criteria or the common understanding of what parenthood entails vis-a-vis the multiple daily facets of a child's life, petitioner's conduct until the commencement of this proceeding fell far short of manifesting the willingness to take on the parental responsibilities necessary to invest him with any constitutionally recognized parental "rights" which could be terminated subject to the provisions of Social Services Law § 384–b.

Petitioner argues that, *de hors* any constitutional considerations, Family Court Act § 542 requires that an order of filiation be granted because he is unquestionably the child's biological progenitor. Irrespective of the seemingly mandatory language of Family Court Act § 542, biological fatherhood does not create an absolute right to an order of filiation, and, indeed, the courts of this state have frequently applied the doctrine of equitable estoppel to forestall the entry of such an order regardless of biological relation.

An equitable estoppel will be applied in the interest of fairness where the misleading words or conduct of a party induces justifiable reliance by another to his or her substantial detriment, and may include a situation where the failure of a party to promptly assert a right creates circumstances making it inequitable to permit the right to be exercised after considerable time has elapsed.

Appropriate circumstances for application of an estoppel in a paternity proceeding have been found in a wide variety of situations. For example, in *Matter of Ettore I. v. Angela D.*, 513 N.Y.S.2d 733 (App. Div. 1987), the petitioner was estopped from asserting paternity where he had taken no action for three years and both the child and the mother's husband had regarded the child as the husband's own and had formed a parent-child relationship.

In *Terrence M. v. Gale C.*, 597 N.Y.S.2d 333 (App. Div. 1993), petitioner was estopped from attempting to establish his paternity where he had failed to support or attempt to establish any relationship with the child for almost the entire period of the child's minority. In that case, the person whom the child had previously thought of as her father had never been married to her mother and was, at the time of the proceeding, deceased. * * *

This leads to the issue of whether an estoppel should be applied under the facts of this case. While frequently paternity cases which have involved the application of equitable estoppel have concerned the preservation of the legitimacy of the child in its legal definition, no authority is cited to support the majority's conclusion that the preservation of legitimacy in its legal sense is a *sine qua non* for the imposition of equitable estoppel. On the contrary, the paramount purpose of the equitable estoppel doctrine is to promote fairness and justice, and in considering whether it should be applied in a paternity case the overriding consideration is whether imposition of the estoppel will serve the best interests of the child. * * *

. . . While the child has always known that petitioner is her biological progenitor, it had consistently been demonstrated by petitioner himself that this factor did not confer upon him any authority or power over her life, that it did not mean that Sandra R. was less her mother than Robin Y., and that it did not mean that her sister was not her full sister. To now grant him the standing to claim the very considerable authority and power held by a parent, against her wishes, would change her life in drastic ways. For this reason, I believe that the elements of misrepresentation, reliance and detriment have clearly been established and that the evidence demonstrates that an order of filiation is not in this child's best interests. Under these circumstances, the doctrine should be applied. * * *

Finally, it should be noted that, contrary to respondent's arguments, the fact that the child was conceived by artificial insemination is wholly irrelevant on the question of whether or not petitioner has acquired any parental rights. In this state, the only differentiation drawn between the familial status of a child conceived as a result of artificial insemination, as opposed to intercourse occurs when the child is born to a woman who makes a mutual decision with her husband to conceive a child in this fashion, which is memorialized in a written, signed statement and where the insemination is performed by a licensed physician who certifies that he has performed the procedure. In such a case, Domestic Relations Law § 73 automatically bestows the parental rights of the biological father upon the mother's husband, who is deemed the legal father for all purposes. That statute, of course, has no application to this case and the conclusion that petitioner has no protected parental rights is predicated upon his failure for almost 10 years to manifest his willingness to assume the responsibilities of parenthood or to be a parent irrespective of the manner of the child's conception.

NOTES

1. *Use of an Unknown Sperm Donor.* Using an unknown sperm donor is often considered the best way to guarantee that he will not assert parental rights at a later time. The anonymity of the woman and the donor may be maintained through the use of a sperm bank. Sperm banks often screen donors for health problems. They also keep records on the physical characteristics of donors. Thus, although the mother does not know the donor's identity, she may still screen for certain physical traits and can more safely assume that her own health will not be jeopardized by the insemination.

Some sperm banks have recently adopted policies that allow the child, usually when he or she reaches the age of 18, to learn the identity of the anonymous donor as long as the donor, at the time of donation, consented to have his identity revealed. These sperm banks inform prospective mothers whether donors have agreed to have their identity revealed in the future so that the mothers can take this information into account when choosing a donor.

2. *Use of a Known Sperm Donor*. Some prospective mothers choose known donors because they want to have the option of revealing their identities to their children. Many of these mothers also choose to have the donors play a role in their children's lives. One study of lesbian couples who chose known donors found that they

> struggled with how to maintain themselves as lesbian-headed two-parent families in the face of normative cognitive prescriptions about the two-parent family. Although some solved this problem by simply eliminating the biological father from the picture altogether, replacing him with male role models who had no legal or social claim to father status, others attempted a compromise in which the biological father remained present but was redefined from father to sperm donor and, in some cases, to uncle or close family friend. Men who agreed to play this role often relinquished both their social and legal claim to co-parent status, making it possible for the nonbiological mother to fill that role.

Susan E. Dalton & Denise D. Bielby, *"That's Our Kind of Constellation": Lesbian Mothers Negotiate Institutionalized Understandings of Gender Within the Family*, 14 GENDER & SOCIETY 36, 49 (2000). Dalton and Bielby report that it is difficult for some lesbian coparents to manage a sperm donor's involvement with their family while at the same time making it clear that the donor is not a parent. As one of the lesbian mothers put it, "We were not looking for another parent, we were looking for somebody the kids could know, and that's a hard thing to ask somebody. . . . I think to ask somebody to be an anonymous donor is fairly easy [as is] to ask them to be an involved parent, but [the] . . . in-between, we want you to be a known person but not involved is [not so easy]. . . . [It] takes a fairly special person to be able to have that sort of a role." *Id.* For an extensive study of thirty-four families headed by lesbian mothers whose children were conceived through donor insemination, see MAUREEN SULLIVAN, THE FAMILY OF WOMAN: LESBIAN MOTHERS, THEIR CHILDREN, AND THE UNDOING OF GENDER (2004). *See also* NANCY J. MEZEY, NEW CHOICES, NEW FAMILIES: HOW LESBIANS DECIDE ABOUT MOTHERHOOD (2008).

What advice would you give to prospective mothers when choosing between anonymous and known donors? What are the advantages and disadvantages of each option? If a lesbian couple chooses to use sperm provided by a known donor, what advice would you give them regarding the possible legal implications of that choice? How can they best protect themselves against a possible future parental claim by the known donor?

3. *Use of a Known Sperm Donor and Parentage Statutes*. The Uniform Parentage Act (UPA) of 1973 deemed a known sperm donor not to be the father of a child conceived by a *married* woman as long as the sperm was

provided to a licensed physician. Uniform Parentage Act § (5)(b) (1973). Several states adopted the UPA as written, but others (like California) did not distinguish between married and unmarried women. *See Jhordan C. v. Mary K.*, 224 Cal.Rptr. 530, 534, 179 Cal.App.3d 386, 392 (1986). A more recent version of the UPA also does not differentiate among women based on their marital status (or on the sperm being provided to a licensed physician). *See* Uniform Parentage Act § 703 (2002). Although some state statutes continue to distinguish between married and unmarried women for purposes of terminating the parental rights of known donors, *see, e.g.,* MINN. STAT. ANN. § 257.56(2) (West 2007); MO. ANN. STAT. § 210.824(2) (West 2004); MONT. CODE ANN. § 40–6–106(2) (2007), most statutes do not. The laws that do not take marital status into account can be divided into two groups. Under the first set of statutes, the donor is not a parent and there is "no statutory mechanism for producing a different result even if the parties intend a different outcome." Nancy Polikoff, *A Mother Should Not Have to Adopt Her Own Child: Parentage Laws for Children of Lesbian Couples in the Twenty-First Century*, 5 STAN. J. CIV. RTS. & LIBERTIES 201, 241 (2009) (footnote omitted). In the second group, "the donor is not a parent unless the donor and recipient agree in writing to the contrary." *Id.* at 242 (footnote omitted).

4. *Contract—Use of an Alternative Insemination Donor's Agreement.* In *In re R.C.*, 775 P.2d 27, 35 (Colo. 1989) (en banc), the court held that a statute, which would have otherwise extinguished the rights of a known donor, was inapplicable in a case where there was an agreement between the parties that the donor would have parental rights. In *Matter of Marriage of Leckie & Voorhies*, 875 P.2d 521, 521–22, 128 Or.App. 289, 291–93 (Ct. App. 1994), a donor's agreement that he would not "demand, request, or compel any guardianship or custody," and that he would "have no parental rights whatsoever with said child," was held to control his later claim to filiation, particularly in the absence of "any conduct legally sufficient to vitiate his waiver."

5. *Function—Ongoing Contact with Child.* As *Thomas S.* makes clear, ongoing contact between donor and child may also preclude the extinguishment of the donor's rights. *See* Fred A. Bernstein, *This Child Does Have Two Mothers . . . and a Sperm Donor with Visitation*, 22 N.Y.U. REV. L. & SOC. CHANGE 1, 22–27 (1996); *see also Tripp v. Hinckley*, 736 N.Y.S.2d 506, 508, 290 A.D.2d 767, 768 (App. Div. 2002) (upholding extended visitation rights of donor who was involved in the children's lives after they were born).

6. *Discrimination in the Provision of Reproductive Services.* Although for some women the process of alternative insemination is relatively simple, for others it is not so. Some women require the assistance of reproductive services, such as IVF (or in vitro fertilization), if they are to conceive. Lesbians who need reproductive services are vulnerable to being discriminated against on grounds of sexual orientation and marital status. *See* Andrea D. Gurmakin et al., *Screening Practices and Beliefs of Assisted Reproductive Technology Programs*, 83 FERTILITY & STERILITY 61, 64 (2005) (study found that 17% of providers of reproductive technology services were

very or extremely likely to turn away a lesbian couple). *See also North Coast Women's Care Medical Group, Inc. v. Superior Court*, 44 Cal.4th 1145, 1150, 81 Cal.Rptr.3d 708, 189 P.3d 959, 963 (2008) (lesbian woman alleged that physician refused to perform insemination on her because of her sexual orientation).

2.   Ova Donation/Ova Sharing

D.M.T. v. T.M.H.
Supreme Court of Florida, 2013
129 So.3d 320

PARIENTE, J.

The child at the center of this dispute was born on January 4, 2004. Her birth mother, D.M.T., and her biological mother, T.M.H., were in a long-term committed relationship at the time of the child's birth, and the child began her life by living with both parents. The Fifth District set forth the undisputed facts of this case as follows:

> [T.M.H.] and [D.M.T.] were involved in a committed relationship from 1995 until 2006. They lived together and owned real property as joint tenants, evidenced by a deed in the record. Additionally, both women deposited their income into a joint bank account and used those funds to pay their bills.

> The couple decided to have a baby that they would raise together as equal parental partners. They sought reproductive medical assistance, where they learned [D.M.T.] was infertile. [T.M.H.] and [D.M.T.], using funds from their joint bank account, paid a reproductive doctor to withdraw ova from [T.M.H.], have them fertilized, and implant the fertilized ova into [D.M.T.]. The two women told the reproductive doctor that they intended to raise the child as a couple, and they went for counseling with a mental health professional to prepare themselves for parenthood. The in vitro fertilization procedure that was utilized proved successful, and a child was conceived.

> The child was born in Brevard County on January 4, 2004. The couple gave the child a hyphenation of their last names. Although the birth certificate lists only [D.M.T.] as the mother and does not indicate a father, a maternity test revealed that there is a 99.99% certainty that [T.M.H.] is the biological mother of the child. [T.M.H.] and [D.M.T.] sent out birth announcements with both of their names declaring, "We Proudly Announce the Birth of Our Beautiful Daughter." Both women participated at their child's baptism, and they both took an active role in the child's early education.

> The women separated in May 2006, and the child lived with [D.M.T.]. Initially, [T.M.H.] made regular child support payments, which [D.M.T.] accepted. [T.M.H.] ended the support payments when she and [D.M.T.] agreed to divide the child's time evenly between them. They continued to divide the costs of education.

T.M.H., 79 So.3d at 788–89.

Eventually, the couple's relationship severely deteriorated, and, as is all too commonly seen in child custody proceedings, one parent, D.M.T., unfortunately severed the other parent's, T.M.H.'s, contact with the daughter the couple had jointly planned for, conceived, and raised as a family. Until that time, the child "did not distinguish between one [woman] being the biological or the birth parent." *Id.* at 789. Each party was simply a parent to this child up until and including the point at which D.M.T., the birth mother, absconded to an undisclosed location with the child after the parties' relationship soured.

After finally locating the birth mother in Australia, T.M.H., the biological mother, served the birth mother with a petition to establish parental rights to the couple's child and for declaratory relief, including an adjudication of parentage pursuant to chapter 742, Florida Statutes (2008), and a declaration of statutory invalidity with respect to section 742.14, the assisted reproductive technology statute. In response to the biological mother's action, the birth mother filed a motion for summary judgment, alleging that the biological mother lacked parental rights as a matter of law regardless of the couple's original intent with respect to raising the child. The trial court held a hearing and granted the birth mother's summary judgment motion, explaining that it felt constrained by the current state of the law and expressing hope that an appellate court would reverse its ruling. . . . The biological mother appealed the trial court's ruling to the Fifth District Court of Appeal, [which reversed]. * * *

I. Sections 742.13 and 742.14

* * * Section 742.14, which is Florida's assisted reproductive technology statute, is entitled "Donation of eggs, sperm, or preembryos" and has provided as follows since 1993:

> The donor of any egg, sperm, or preembryo, *other than the commissioning couple* or a father who has executed *a preplanned adoption* agreement under s. 63.212, *shall relinquish all maternal or paternal rights and obligations* with respect to the donation or the resulting children. Only reasonable compensation directly related to the donation of eggs, sperm, and preembryos shall be permitted.

§ 742.14, Fla. Stat. (emphasis added). The term "commissioning couple," as used in section 742.14, is defined in section 742.13(2) as "the *intended mother and father* of a child who will be conceived by means of assisted reproductive technology using the eggs or sperm of at least one of the intended parents." § 742.13(2), Fla. Stat. (emphasis added).

The Fifth District concluded that the assisted reproductive technology statute did not apply to T.M.H. since she always intended to parent the child conceived through her provision of biological material to her partner. Therefore, according to the Fifth District, T.M.H. is not considered a "donor" as that term is used in the statute.

We reject the Fifth District's construction of the assisted reproductive technology statute. The plain language of section 742.14 does not provide for the subjective intentions of someone in T.M.H.'s position to be taken into consideration in determining whether he or she is a "donor" under the terms of the statute. Rather, the statute identifies only two categories of individuals who do not relinquish parental rights as to their provision of biological material during the course of assisted reproductive technology—(1) members of a "commissioning couple"; and (2) fathers who have executed a preplanned adoption agreement. Indeed, the structure of section 742.14 designates these groups as fitting within the term "donor," and then provides that they are specifically exempted from the statutory relinquishment of parental rights. If the statute did not apply to these groups, then they would not need to be exempted from its requirements.

In providing for these two exceptions, the Legislature expressed its intent not to allow the subjective intentions of all other individuals who provide eggs, sperm, or preembryos during the course of assisted reproductive technology to become an issue in need of litigation. Instead, the Legislature articulated a policy of treating all individuals who provide eggs, sperm, or preembryos as part of assisted reproductive technology as "donor[s]" bound by the terms of the statute, and then exempting two specific groups in accordance with the purpose behind the statutory enactment.

To hold that section 742.14 does not apply to T.M.H. in this case because of her subjective intention not to give her egg away would essentially create a third exception in the statute. This Court, however, is "not at liberty to add words to the statute that were not placed there by the Legislature." *Lawnwood Med. Ctr., Inc. v. Seeger,* 990 So.2d 503, 512 (Fla.2008). * * *

II. The Constitutionality of the Statutes

1. Constitutional Right of Parenting

It is a basic tenet of our society and our law that individuals have the fundamental constitutionally protected rights to procreate and to be a parent to their children. * * *

Moreover, "we recognize the sanctity of the biological connection" between parents and children, and thus, "we look carefully at anything that would sever the biological parent-child link." *Baby E.A.W.,* 658 So.2d at 967. With respect to the link between a biological father and his child, we have previously explained that constitutional protection of the individual's right to be a parent applies "when an unwed [biological] father demonstrates a full commitment to the responsibilities of parenthood by coming forward to participate in raising his child." *Id.* at 966–67. The approach this Court has taken regarding the rights of biological but unwed fathers echoes the United States Supreme Court's recognition that a biological father's constitutional rights are inchoate and develop into a fundamental right to be a parent "[w]hen an unwed father demonstrates a full commitment to the responsibilities of parenthood by 'com[ing] forward to participate in the rearing of his child,' . . . [because] his interest in personal contact with his child acquires *substantial protection under the due process clause." Lehr,* 463 U.S. at 261, 103 S.Ct. 2985. * * *

In this case, the biological mother asserts that she has a protected constitutional interest to be a parent to her child, which is a fundamental right unquestionably protected by the Florida and federal Due Process Clauses and specifically by Florida's state constitutional privacy provision. While acknowledging that a mere biological link between parent and child is insufficient to merit substantial constitutional protection, the biological mother argues that we should analogize the nature of her interest to the interest possessed by unwed biological fathers, whose parental rights are inchoate but develop into a fundamental right to be a parent when the biological father demonstrates "a full commitment to the responsibilities of parenthood." *T.M.H.,* 79 So.3d at 797. We agree.

This Court has previously stated that the biological relationship between parent and child provides "the opportunity to assume parental responsibilities." *Doe,* 543 So.2d at 748. In other words, although an unmarried man who impregnates an unmarried woman does not automatically have a fundamental right to be a parent to the child, his right to be a parent develops substantial constitutional protection as a fundamental right if he assumes responsibility for the care and raising of that child. . . .

In this case, the biological connection between mother and daughter is not in dispute. Additionally, T.M.H. and her former partner D.M.T. demonstrated an intent to jointly raise the child through their actions before and after the child's birth, and T.M.H. actively participated as a parent for the first several years of the child's life. Importantly for constitutional purposes, T.M.H. also assumed full parental responsibilities until her contact with her child was suddenly cut off. In this way, this case is wholly unlike cases such as *Lamaritata v. Lucas,* 823 So.2d 316, 319 (Fla. 2d DCA 2002), relied on by the dissent, where the parties seeking the assistance of reproductive technology "joined forces solely for the purpose of artificially inseminating Ms. Lamaritata" and specifically agreed that the individual providing genetic material would not have any rights or obligations with respect to the child.

This case is also completely different from cases involving *nonparents* seeking to establish legal rights to a child, such as *Beagle,* 678 So.2d 1271, which involved grandparents' rights, and *Troxel,* which is relied on by the dissent. *Troxel* concerned a state nonparental visitation statute described as "breathtakingly broad," permitting "*[a]ny person* " to petition the court for visitation rights "*at any time,*" and the court to grant such visitation rights whenever "visitation may serve *the best interest of the child.*" *Troxel,* 530 U.S. at 61, 67, 120 S.Ct. 2054.

Contrary to *Troxel,* which involved a nonparent, there is no doubt that the common law would grant constitutional due process and privacy protection, in the form of a fundamental right to be a parent, to an unwed biological father in this situation who had the proverbial one night stand with a mother but then assumed parental responsibilities for the first several years of the child's life. Of course, the common law was developed before the scientific advancements in reproductive technology that allow individuals to exercise their basic right and desire to have children in ways that were not contemplated by society centuries or even decades ago.

As explained by the Fifth District in this case, it is difficult to understand how rigid legal rules "established during a time so far removed in history when the science of in vitro fertilization was a remote thought in the minds of the scientists of the times [have] much currency today." *T.M.H.,* 79 So.3d at 796. Although the right to procreate has long been described as "one of the basic civil rights" individuals hold, *Skinner,* 316 U.S. at 541, 62 S.Ct. 1110, advances in science and technology now provide innumerable ways for traditional and non-traditional couples alike to conceive a child and, we conclude, in so doing to exercise their "inalienable rights . . . to enjoy and defend life and liberty, [and] to pursue happiness." Art. I, § 2, Fla. Const. * * *

It would indeed be anomalous if, under Florida law, an unwed biological father would have more constitutionally protected rights to parent a child after a one night stand than an unwed biological mother who, with a committed partner and as part of a loving relationship, planned for the birth of a child and remains committed to supporting and raising her own daughter. As the Fifth District stated, "it would pose a substantial equal protection problem to deny an unwed genetic mother the ability to assert parental rights after she established a parental relationship with her child while allowing an unwed genetic father to do so." *T.M.H.*, 79 So.3d at 797 n. 8.

Although the biological mother in this case is seeking vindication of her right to be a parent to her child, this right comes with critical legal and financial responsibilities, including possible child support payments. *See* § 61.29, Fla. Stat. (2012). Unquestionably, these responsibilities are part and parcel of the fundamental right to be a parent. T.M.H., the biological mother, demonstrated her commitment to accepting these responsibilities until her contact with the child was cut off. Because T.M.H. accepted responsibility for raising her child from the beginning and did in fact parent and support the child until D.M.T. prevented her from doing so, we hold that T.M.H.'s inchoate interest has developed into a protected fundamental right to be a parent to her child.

2. Abridgment of Fundamental Right

We subject statutes that interfere with an individual's fundamental rights to strict scrutiny analysis, which requires the State to prove that the legislation furthers a compelling governmental interest through the least intrusive means. * * * Therefore, the burden falls on the birth mother to demonstrate that application of the assisted reproductive technology statute to deprive the biological mother of her fundamental right to be a parent furthers a compelling governmental interest through the least intrusive means. This showing has not been made.

We recognize the important role section 742.14 plays in protecting couples seeking to use assisted reproductive technology to conceive a child from parental rights claims brought by typical third-party providers of the genetic material used in assisted reproductive technology, as well as the State's corresponding interest in furthering that objective. This case, however, does not implicate those concerns. Quite simply, based on the factual situation before us, we do not discern even a legitimate State interest in applying section 742.14 to deny T.M.H. her right to be a parent to her daughter.

This is significant to our as-applied constitutional analysis of the statutory scheme, which is intended to provide statutory protection to a "commissioning couple" from a parental rights claim by a third-party provider of biological material used in assisted reproductive technology.

We therefore reject the dissent's assertion that our analysis has no "logical end point" or "obvious stopping point," as our conclusion is based on the specific facts presented in this case, as set forth in the Fifth District's certified question, which establish that T.M.H. was an intended parent and assumed full parental responsibilities until her contact with the child was cut off. * * *

[3.] Classification Based on Sexual Orientation

We next address the equal protection challenge to the statute, as confronted by the Fifth District, under both the Florida and United States Constitutions. Specifically ... we address whether the statute is unconstitutional as applied under the Florida and federal Equal Protection Clauses by exempting heterosexual couples, but not same-sex couples, from the automatic relinquishment of parental rights when seeking the assistance of reproductive technology to conceive a child with the intent to become the child's parents. Put another way, as Judge Monaco succinctly explained in his concurring opinion below, "[b]ut for the fact that [the biological mother] and [the birth mother] are of the same sex, we would probably consider them to be a 'commissioning couple' under the statute, and the outcome of this case would be easy." *T.M.H.,* 79 So.3d at 804 (Monaco, J., concurring). * * *

Sexual orientation has not been determined to constitute a protected class and therefore sexual orientation does not provide an independent basis for using heightened scrutiny to review State action that results in unequal treatment to homosexuals. *See Romer,* 517 U.S. at 630–32, 116 S.Ct. 1620. Further, even though our state constitution recognizes gender as a specific class, *see* art. I, § 2, Fla. Const., it does not separately recognize sexual orientation as a protected class, and thus we do not rely on our state's Equal Protection Clause to apply a heightened scrutiny examination to statutes discriminating on the basis of sexual orientation. *See Fla. Dep't of Children & Families v. Adoption of X.X.G.,* 45 So.3d 79, 81, 83 (Fla. 3d DCA 2010) (applying rational basis review to a statute prohibiting homosexuals from adopting).

Accordingly, we apply a rational basis analysis to our review of this claim. The specific question we confront is whether the classification between heterosexual and same-sex couples drawn by the assisted reproductive technology statute bears some rational relationship to a legitimate state purpose.

D.M.T. argues that defining the term "commissioning couple" in section 742.13(2), as applied in section 742.14, to include only one male and one female is related to the State's legitimate interest in not extending rights to same-sex couples. Specifically, she cites to Florida law that declines to recognize same-sex marriages and prohibits homosexuals from adopting children. We reject this argument as unavailing for several reasons.

First, section 742.14 does not operate to *grant* parental rights to biological parents, but only to provide for the *relinquishment* of those rights in the case of the typical egg or sperm donor. In other words, section 742.14 allows a member of a "commissioning couple" to preserve his or her interest in the child conceived through assisted reproductive technology; however, that individual becomes a parent only if he or she has some legal basis to be recognized as a parent. This could be due to a biological connection plus the assumption of parental responsibilities, as we have demonstrated applies in this case, or through application of another statute. *See, e.g.,* § 63.032(12), Fla. Stat. (2008) (defining the term "parent" to mean "a woman who gives birth to a child or a man whose consent to the adoption of the child would be required"). That is, sections 742.13 and 742.14 do not create a statutory basis for an individual who would not otherwise have parental rights to claim those rights. Therefore, because section 742.14 does not operate to grant rights, but only to eliminate rights that are already held or that may develop, any State interest that could potentially exist in not extending rights to same-sex couples is not implicated.

Second, there is no indication that the exception provided in section 742.14 for a "commissioning couple" extends only to married couples, so the state constitutional provision against same-sex marriage is also not implicated. By contrast, in the next statutory provisions, sections 742.15–16, Florida Statutes, which relate to gestational surrogacy, the Legislature has specifically provided that the "commissioning couple" must be "legally married" in order to claim protection under the statutes. *See* § 742.15(1), Fla. Stat. (2008). . . .

Third, we reject D.M.T.'s contention that recognizing T.M.H.'s parental rights in this case would undermine the State interest in providing certainty to couples using assisted reproductive technology to become parents because it would increase litigation regarding the intentions of individuals providing genetic material for use in assisted reproductive technology. No one disputes that the State has an interest in ensuring that the parental rights of children conceived through the use of assisted reproductive technology are defined by law, in making sure children have parents to care for them, and in preventing litigation that disrupts families.

In reality, however, the issue of an unmarried mother and father's intent under the statute, including whether they qualify as a "commissioning couple," has been the subject of prior litigation in the courts of this state. Since intent, pursuant to the definition of "commissioning couple" found in section 742.13(2) and used in section

742.14, is the determinative element regarding whether two individuals seeking the assistance of reproductive technology to conceive qualify as a "commissioning couple," it is of course relevant to the inquiry. We conclude, though, that the State does not have a legitimate interest in precluding same-sex couples from being given the same opportunity as heterosexual couples to demonstrate that intent. Consistent with equal protection, a same-sex couple must be afforded the equivalent chance as a heterosexual couple to establish their intentions in using assisted reproductive technology to conceive a child. * * *

III. Waiver of Rights

Lastly, we address the birth mother's contention that, regardless of the application of section 742.14 in this case, the biological mother waived any parental rights to this child by signing a standard informed consent form during the couple's process of seeking medical assistance to conceive. . . .

While it is uncontroverted that the biological mother signed a standard "Informed Consent Oocyte Recipient" form for the Fertility and Reproductive Medicine Center for Women with the birth mother listed as the recipient, the biological mother signed this form as the birth mother's partner and *not* as the individual providing the egg for the couple. Clearly, then, this informed consent does not on its face apply to waive the biological mother's rights to the child, even though this is the document that the birth mother relied on in her initial motion to dismiss and motion for judgment on the pleadings. * * *

[C]ourts that have considered similar standard informed consents used in reproductive technology have held that waiver provisions like the one [in this case] are inapplicable in circumstances like those in this case. This is because it is uncontested that the biological mother was not an anonymous donor, but rather, that the parties were in a committed relationship where reproductive technology was used—with one woman providing her egg and the other partner bearing the child—so that both women became the child's parents.

We reject the dissent's reliance on *Lamaritata* to argue that the biological mother waived her parental rights. *Lamaritata* is completely distinguishable from this case. As the dissent acknowledges, the parties in *Lamaritata* specifically entered into a contract whereby they agreed that the donor would have no parental rights and obligations associated with any child conceived from the use of assisted reproductive technology. . . . As the Second District explained, there were "no facts to show that [the parties] ha[d] any type of relationship that would fall under the rubric of 'couple.' Further, they did not commission or contract to jointly raise the children as mother and father." *Lamaritata,* 823 So.2d at 319. . . .

Despite the dissent's view to the contrary, the facts of this case clearly demonstrate that exactly the opposite of the facts in *Lamaritata* are true here. Not only did the biological mother assume parental obligations, but the couple's actions before and after the child's birth—including their use of funds from their joint bank account, their statements to the reproductive doctor that they intended to raise the child as a couple, the counseling they underwent to prepare themselves for parenthood, the use of a hyphenated last name for the child, and the joint birth announcement—reveal that the couple's agreement in actuality was to both parent the child they intended to conceive. . . .

We also reject the dissent's reliance on *Wakeman v. Dixon,* 921 So.2d 669 (Fla. 1st DCA 2006). Like the Fifth District, we conclude that *Wakeman* "is clearly distinguishable from the instant case because there, one lesbian partner was the birth mother and the partner claiming parental rights was not the biological mother." *T.M.H.,* 79 So.3d at 794 n. 6. As the Fifth District correctly observed, the First District in *Wakeman* held that the individual seeking parental rights was neither a "biological" nor a "natural" parent, whereas in this case, T.M.H. "would fall into both categories under the *Wakeman* rationale." *T.M.H.,* 79 So.3d at 794 n. 6. * * *

POLSTON, C.J., dissenting.

Unlike the majority, I do not believe that sections 742.14 and 742.13(2), Florida Statutes, violate T.M.H.'s constitutional rights to due process, privacy, and equal protection. Instead, contract law, common law, Florida statutory law, and the United States and Florida Constitutions all provide that T.M.H. does not have parental rights with respect to the child born to D.M.T. Therefore, I respectfully dissent.

I refer to the parties in this case using the birth mother's initials, D.M.T., and the egg donor's initials, T.M.H. The majority refers to T.M.H. as the biological mother, but the term might appear to answer the very question addressed by this Court, namely whether T.M.H. is a legal parent. Furthermore, the terms the majority uses to distinguish the parties (birth mother and biological mother) are confusing because "both the genetic and gestational roles in bringing this child into the world are 'biological' processes." *T.M.H. v. D.M.T.,* 79 So.3d 787, 807 (Fla. 5th DCA 2011) (Lawson, J., dissenting). * * *

. . . T.M.H. signed at the time of her egg donation two waivers of all claims and rights she might have regarding any resulting child. Specifically, the informed consent donor form that T.M.H. signed at the time she donated her eggs includes the following language:

> I, the undersigned, [T.M.H.,] forever hereafter relinquish any claims to jurisdiction over the offspring that might result from this donation and waive any and all rights to future consent,

notice, or consultation regarding the donation. I agree that the recipient may regard the donated eggs as her own and any offspring resulted there from as her own children.

In addition to this informed consent donor form, T.M.H. also signed an "Informed Consent Oocyte Recipient" form on the line reserved for the recipient's partner. And, very similar to the donor form, the recipient form provides as follows:

I/We understand that the egg donor has relinquished any claim to, or jurisdiction over the offspring that might result from this donation and waive any and all rights to future consent, notice, or consultation regarding such donation. The donor understands that the recipient may regard the donated eggs as her own and any offspring resulting there from as her own children.

Therefore, T.M.H. signed two contracts that expressly waived any rights she might have with respect to any child resulting from her egg donation.

A person may waive fully vested, fundamental parental rights by completing a form. *See, e.g.,* § 39.806(1)(a), Fla. Stat. (providing that grounds for the termination of parental rights may be established "[w]hen the parent or parents have voluntarily executed a written surrender of the child and consented to the entry of an order giving custody of the child to the department for subsequent adoption"). . . . Further, . . . individuals may waive various constitutional rights, including the right to counsel, the right to remain silent, and the right to a jury.

If one can waive fully vested parental rights and various constitutional rights by signing a written form, an egg donor can certainly waive any potential interest in a possible future child by completing a form. Consequently, I would give effect to the plain language of the two forms that T.M.H. signed and conclude that T.M.H. contractually waived any claim of parental rights.

. . . Notably, the Second District Court of Appeal's decision in *Lamaritata,* 823 So.2d 316, is very persuasively on point. In *Lamaritata,* a donor and recipient "entered into a contract whereby the donor would provide sperm to [the] recipient with the expectation that she would become pregnant through artificial insemination and deliver offspring." 823 So.2d at 318. Further, their "agreement provided that if childbirth resulted, the donor would have no parental rights and obligations." *Id.* The Second District held that "[b]oth the contract between the parties and the Florida statute controlling these arrangements provide that there are no parental rights or responsibilities resulting to the donor of sperm." *Id.* at 319 (citing § 742.14, Fla. Stat.). As a result, "the sperm donor is a nonparent, a statutory stranger to the children." *Id.* The donor's status as a nonparent continued to be true, even though the donor and recipient "entered into subsequent stipulations, purportedly to give visitation rights to this [donor.]" *Id.* The Second District explained that the subsequent visitation rights agreement between the parties was not enforceable because "[t]here are numerous Florida cases holding that nonparents are not entitled to visitation rights." *Id.*

In this case, like the donor in *Lamaritata,* T.M.H. signed a contract at the time of donation waiving any claims or rights to any potential child. And similar to the parties in *Lamaritata,* T.M.H. and D.M.T. agreed at some point to co-parent the child as evidenced by T.M.H. participating in parenting decisions for a period of time after the child's birth, although the parenting agreement in this case appears to have been oral and not formally executed. However, just as the Second District concluded in *Lamaritata,* I would hold that the donor in this case is a nonparent by operation of the waivers of rights she signed (as well as by operation of section 742.14). Because T.M.H. is not a legal parent, any agreement, oral or otherwise, that may have existed between the parties for T.M.H. to co-parent is unenforceable under Florida law. * * *

[Furthermore,] [p]roviding T.M.H. access to visitation and other incidents of a parental relationship over D.M.T.'s objection would violate D.M.T.'s due process and privacy rights as the child's legal parent. *See Wakeman,* 921 So.2d at 671 (holding that co-parenting agreement between same-sex couple was unenforceable and explaining that a non-legal parent "cannot be granted by statute the right to visitation with minor children, because, absent evidence of a demonstrable harm to the child, such a grant unconstitutionally interferes with a natural parent's privacy right to rear his or her child").

The majority skips any analysis of D.M.T.'s constitutional rights as the legal parent. Instead, the majority concludes as a matter of substantive due process and privacy that, because T.M.H. at some point established a relationship with the child, the promotion of stability and certainty in families employing assisted reproductive technology is an insufficient state interest to support the termination of that relationship. The majority's conclusion is based upon its argument that T.M.H. has a fundamental interest in her relationship with the child that is protected by the due process clauses of the United States and Florida Constitutions and the privacy clause of the Florida Constitution.

But contrary to the majority's description of the asserted interest as the elimination of an already established parental relationship, section 742.14 operates *at the time of donation* to eliminate any interests or obligations a sperm donor or egg donor may have with regard to a future, potential child. At the time of the donation of biological material, any interest in a potential parental relationship would have to be deemed an inchoate interest and not even possibly a fundamental interest protected by the due process and privacy clauses as there is indisputably no child or parental relationship with a child at that point.

Moreover, the majority's analysis ignores a vital aspect of substantive due process jurisprudence. The United States Supreme Court has recognized the temptation for members of a court to improperly constitutionalize their own preferences and thereby impose them upon the rest of the citizenry in perpetuity and, therefore, has "insisted not merely that the interest denominated as a 'liberty' be 'fundamental' (a concept that, in isolation, is hard to objectify), but also that it be an interest traditionally protected by our society." *Michael H. v. Gerald D.,* 491 U.S. 110, 122, 109 S.Ct. 2333, 105 L.Ed.2d 91 (1989). In other words, due process only affords protections to rights "so rooted in the traditions and conscience of our people as to be ranked as fundamental." *Snyder v. Massachusetts,* 291 U.S. 97, 105, 54 S.Ct. 330, 78 L.Ed. 674 (1934). . . .

Therefore, . . . the substantive due process issue in the present case really comes down to whether relationships like the one between T.M.H. and the child born to D.M.T. "ha[ve] been treated as a protected family unit under the historic practices of our society, or whether on any other basis [they have] been accorded special protection." [*Michael H.,* 491 U.S]. at 124, 109 S.Ct. 2333. Of course, it is impossible to conclude that such relationships have been treated in this manner. In fact, our history indicates that quite the opposite is true as our society has historically protected the legal rights of birth mothers and the traditional family.

. . . But not only does the majority's analysis skip the vital question of whether the alleged right is "so rooted in the traditions and conscience of our people as to be ranked as fundamental," it also suffers from the problem of having no seeming or logical end point. Does the majority's analysis now mean that section 742.14 is unconstitutional as applied to all sperm and egg donors since they are also denied the opportunity to develop parental relationships with children resulting from their biological material? Or perhaps the majority would limit its holding to those sperm and egg donors who may later develop relationships with resulting children despite the operation of the statute? However, does this mean that a child could have a constitutional right to two mothers and a father (or two fathers), perhaps where a married, heterosexual couple agrees to and then subsequently raises a child with the egg donor, an egg donor who is in a committed relationship with a man other than the genetic father? Or perhaps this new constitutional right to employ assisted reproductive technology without the relinquishment of any donor rights and obligations only applies to those in same-sex relationships? Additionally, does this newly created constitutional right now override all waivers of parental rights, including voluntary waivers leading to adoption?

... The majority also concludes that sections 742.14 and 742.13(2) violate the equal protection clauses of the United States and Florida Constitutions. . . . However, the Legislature had a legitimate state purpose in enacting these statutes. * * *

The rationale underlying sections 742.14 and 742.13(2) is the promotion of stability, certainty, and permanence in families employing assisted reproductive technology. And the State has a legitimate interest in regulating assisted reproductive technology and its social and economic effects. The statutes are rationally related to this legitimate interest since allowing claims of parentage by egg and sperm donors could disrupt the certainty, stability, and permanence that generally proves beneficial to families employing assisted reproductive technology, including the constitutionally protected parental rights of legal birth mothers "to make decisions concerning the care, custody, and control of their children." *Troxel,* 530 U.S. at 66, 120 S.Ct. 2054. Accordingly, because it pursues a legitimate purpose by rational means, Florida's decision to treat T.M.H. differently from a commissioning couple cannot be deemed a denial of equal protection.

Furthermore, as Judge Lawson aptly noted,

> the statute in question here is not directed just at men or women, heterosexuals or homosexuals, or any other narrow class. It places broad limits on the right of all citizens to make a parentage claim after donating genetic material to another. And . . . the statute does not bar [T.M.H.] (or any women, irrespective of sexual preference) from using assisted reproductive technology to conceive, bear and give birth to a child of her own, using her own body. This appears, at least on its face, to be a rational way to address this difficult social policy issue, irrespective of whether it reflects a policy choice that the majority or I would prefer.

T.M.H., 79 So.3d at 823 (Lawson, J., dissenting). Simply put, T.M.H. did not have to choose this way. The statute does not prohibit T.M.H. from engaging in any sexual activity, using assisted reproductive technology to pass along her genes to a child gestated by another, or parenting a child that she personally gave birth to or legally adopted. The statute does not stand in the way of T.M.H. having children.

ST. MARY V. DAMON

Supreme Court of Nevada, 2013
309 P.3d 1027

SAITTA, J.:

This appeal concerns the establishment of custodial rights over a minor child born to former female partners, appellant Sha'Kayla St. Mary and respondent Veronica Lynn Damon. The couple became romantically involved and decided to have a child. They drafted a co-parenting agreement, and eventually, St. Mary gave birth to a child through in vitro fertilization, using Damon's egg and an anonymous donor's sperm. Thereafter, their relationship ended, leading to the underlying dispute concerning the parties' custodial rights over the child. * * *

Approximately one year after entering into a romantic relationship with each other, St. Mary and Damon moved in together. They planned to have a child, deciding that Damon would have her egg fertilized by a sperm donor, and St. Mary would carry the fertilized egg and give birth to the child. In October 2007, Damon's eggs were implanted into St. Mary. Around the same time, Damon drafted a co-parenting agreement, which she and St. Mary signed. The agreement indicated that Damon and St. Mary sought to "jointly and equally share parental responsibility, with both of [them] providing support and guidance." In it, they stated that they would "make every effort to jointly share the responsibilities of raising [their] child," including paying for expenses and making major child-related decisions. The agreement provided that if their relationship ended, they would each work to ensure that the other maintained a close relationship with the child, share the duties of raising the child, and make a "good-faith effort to jointly make all major decisions affecting" the child.

St. Mary gave birth to a child in June 2008. The hospital birth confirmation report and certificate of live birth listed only St. Mary as the child's mother. The child was given both parties' last names, however, in the hyphenated form of St. Mary-Damon.

For several months, St. Mary primarily stayed home caring for the child during the day while Damon worked. But, nearly one year after the child's birth, their romantic relationship ended, St. Mary moved out of the home, and St. Mary and Damon disagreed about how to share their time with the child. St. Mary signed an affidavit declaring that Damon was the biological mother of the child, and in 2009, Damon filed an ex parte petition with the district court to establish maternity, seeking to have the child's birth certificate amended to add Damon as a mother. The district court issued an order stating that St. Mary gave birth to the child and that Damon "is the biological and legal mother of said child." The 2009 order also directed that the birth certificate be amended to add Damon's name as a mother.

Thereafter, St. Mary instituted the underlying case by filing a complaint and motion, in a separate district court case, to establish custody, visitation, and child support. In response, Damon contended that, due to her biological connection, she was entitled to sole custody of the child. Damon attached the 2009 order to her opposition.

During a hearing on St. Mary's complaint, the district court orally advised St. Mary that she had the burden of establishing her visitation rights as a surrogate, and the court scheduled an evidentiary hearing regarding her visitation. In a subsequent hearing, the district court ruled that the issues surrounding the parties' co-parenting agreement would be addressed at the evidentiary hearing.

Damon filed a motion to limit the scope of the evidentiary hearing to the issue of third-party visitation, excluding any parentage and custody issues. She asserted that the district court had already determined that St. Mary must establish her visitation rights as a surrogate and, as a result, there was no need to provide evidence to determine parentage. St. Mary opposed the motion, arguing that she was entitled to a full evidentiary hearing because limiting the hearing's scope to third-party visitation would, in effect, deny her parental rights without any opportunity to be heard on the matter.

The district court held the evidentiary hearing. Before taking evidence, the district court considered Damon's motion to limit the hearing's scope. Apparently looking to the 2009 birth certificate order and believing that Damon's status as the sole legal and biological mother had already been determined, the court decided that it would only consider the issue of third-party visitation. The limitation of the hearing's scope was significant. The district court barred consideration of St. Mary's assertion of custody rights, which concern a parent's legal basis to direct the upbringing of his or her child, and limited the hearing to a lesser right of third-party visitation.

The hearing moved forward with the parties focusing on the visitation issue. St. Mary and Damon gave conflicting testimonies regarding their relationship, the co-parenting agreement's purpose, and their intentions in using in vitro fertilization to produce the child. St. Mary testified that she and Damon intended to create the child together, wanted the child to be their child, and fertilized and implanted Damon's eggs into St. Mary so that both women would be "related" to the child. But Damon testified that she and St. Mary orally agreed that St. Mary would be a mere surrogate. St. Mary further testified that she and Damon created the co-parenting agreement together, believing that it would be required by the fertility clinic as a prerequisite for the performance of the reproductive procedure. St. Mary indicated that despite the fertility clinic not asking for the agreement before the procedure, she and Damon completed the agreement after the procedure. Damon asserted that she and St. Mary did not intend to create an enforceable co-parenting agreement but created the agreement to satisfy the fertility clinic's requirements and to seek insurance coverage for the pregnancy.

Following the hearing, in March 2011, the district court issued an order providing that St. Mary was entitled to third-party visitation but not custody. The court reiterated that the scope of the evidentiary hearing had been limited to the issue of third-party visitation and noted that St. Mary could not be awarded custody of the child because previous orders determined that she "has no biological or legal rights whatsoever under Nevada law." Relying on NRS 126.045, which was repealed by the 2013 Legislature, the court also concluded that the co-parenting agreement was null and void because under that statute "a surrogate agreement is only for married couples, which only include one man and one woman." *See* Nev. Stat., ch. 213, § 36, at 813 (repealing NRS 126.045). The 2011 order further provided that although St. Mary gave birth to the child, she "was simply a carrier for [the child]," and that she must "realize that [Damon] is the mother." As a result, St. Mary was granted third-party visitation rights and denied any rights as a legal mother. This appeal from the 2011 order followed.

St. Mary argues that the district court erred in determining that, legally, she was a surrogate and not the child's legal mother and in deeming the co-parenting agreement unenforceable as a matter of law. As a result of our de novo review of these legal questions, we agree.

St. Mary may be the child's legal mother

To determine parentage in Nevada, courts must look to the Nevada Parentage Act, which is modeled after the Uniform Parentage Act (UPA). As the Legislature's adoption of the UPA recognizes, the relationship between a parent and a child is of fundamental societal and constitutional dimension. In Nevada, all of the "rights, privileges, duties and obligations" accompanying parenthood are conferred on those persons who are deemed to have a parent-child relationship with the child, regardless of the parents' marital status. Surrogates who bear a child conceived through assisted conception for another, on the other hand, are often not entitled to claim parental rights. *See* NRS 126.045 (2009) (defining "[s]urrogate" as "an adult woman who enters into an agreement to bear a child conceived through assisted conception for the intended parents," who are treated as the natural parents); 2013 Nev. Stat., ch. 213, §§ 10, 23, 27 at 807–08, 810–11 (replacing the term "surrogate" with "[g]estational carrier" and defining such as a woman "who is not an intended parent and who enters into a gestational agreement," wherein she gives up "legal and physical custody" of the child to the intended parent or parents and may "relinquish all rights and duties as the parent[ ] of a child conceived through assisted reproduction"). Accordingly, whether St. Mary is treated as someone other than a legal mother, such as a surrogate, is of the upmost significance.

The multiple ways to prove maternity

Given the medical advances and changing family dynamics of the age, determining a child's parents today can be more complicated than it was in the past. To this end, although perhaps not encompassing every possibility, the Nevada Parentage Act provides several ways to determine a child's legal mother: a mother with a parent-child relationship with the child "incident to which the law confers or imposes rights, privileges, duties, and obligations." NRS 126.021(3). Under the pre-2013 and current versions of NRS 126.041(1), a woman's status as a legal mother can be established by "proof of her having given birth to the child." *See* NRS 126.041 (2009). In maternity actions under NRS Chapter 126, the statutes under which paternity may be determined apply "[i]nsofar as practicable." NRS 126.231. Paternity may be established in a variety of ways, including through presumptions based on marriage and cohabitation, NRS 126.051(1)(a)-(c), presumptions based on receiving the child into the home and openly holding oneself out as a parent, NRS 126.051(1)(d), genetic testing, NRS 126.051(2), and voluntary acknowledgment, NRS 126.053. Hence, a determination of parentage rests upon a wide array of considerations rather than genetics alone.

This case presents a situation where two women proffered evidence that could establish or generate a conclusive presumption of maternity to either woman. St. Mary testified that she gave birth to the child, thereby offering proof to establish that she is the child's legal mother. Damon showed that her egg was used to produce the child, demonstrating a genetic relationship to the child that may be a basis for concluding that she is the child's legal mother. By dividing the reproductive roles of conceiving a child, St. Mary and Damon each assumed functions traditionally used to evidence a legal maternal relationship. Hence, this matter raises the issue of whether the Nevada Parentage Act and its policies preclude a child from having two legal mothers where two women split the genetic and physical functions of creating a child.

The law does not preclude a child from having two legal mothers

When the district court apparently referenced the 2009 birth certificate order to conclude that Damon's status as the exclusive legal and biological mother was determined and that, as a result, it would not consider St. Mary's assertions of maternity or custody at the evidentiary hearing, it impliedly operated on the premise that a child, created by artificial insemination through an anonymous sperm donor, may not have two mothers under the law. However, contrary to this premise, the Nevada Parentage Act and its policies do not preclude such a child from having two legal mothers.

Although NRS 126.051(3) contains procedures for rebutting paternity presumptions by clear and convincing evidence or "a court decree establishing *paternity* . . . by another *man*," (emphases added), and while NRS 126.051(3) arguably applies in maternity cases, we decline to read this provision of the statute as conveying clear legislative intent to deprive a child conceived by artificial insemination of the emotional, financial, and physical support of an intended mother who "actively assisted in the decision and process of bringing [the child] into this world." *In re T.P.S.,* 365 Ill.Dec. 567, 978 N.E.2d 1070, 1077 (Ill.App.Ct.2012). In Nevada, as in other states, the best interest of the child is the paramount concern in determining the custody and care of children. Both the Legislature and this court have acknowledged that, generally, a child's best interest is served by maintaining two actively involved parents. Certainly, the Legislature has not instructed that children born to unregistered domestic partners bear any less rights to the best-interest considerations set forth in these statutes than children born to registered domestic partners, married persons, and unmarried persons. Ultimately, "the preservation and strengthening of family life is a part of the public policy of this State." NRS 128.005(1). * * *

Nonetheless, the district court determined that St. Mary was not the child's legal mother. The court appears to have grounded this conclusion on the 2009 order, which provided that Damon was the child's legal mother and required Damon's name to be added to the child's birth certificate. But while that order stated that Damon was "the biological and legal mother" of the child, it in no way purported to undo or deny St. Mary's parent-child relationship with the child. The order did not require the removal of St. Mary's name from the birth certificate or provide that St. Mary was not the child's legal mother. Rather, it acknowledged Damon's relationship with the child without denying the same of St. Mary. Moreover, whether St. Mary had rights to the child was not an issue that Damon's 2009 petition sought to resolve because it requested that "maternity be established" and "[t]hat the birth certificate be amended to add the biological mother's name of . . . D[amon]."

Further, the district court's finding that St. Mary was a mere surrogate went beyond the limited scope of the hearing, which the district court prefaced by confirming that it would not consider parentage. Because this argument was not resolved by the 2009 order or any other prior determination, and since the Nevada Parentage Act did not bar a consideration of the evidence regarding St. Mary's claims for maternity and custody rights, the district court erred in refusing to consider the parentage issue and limiting the scope of the evidentiary hearing based on its conclusion that St. Mary was a surrogate—which was a conclusion that was made without an evidentiary hearing on that issue.

. . . Although St. Mary's parentage can be established by virtue of her having given birth to the child, the parties dispute whether they intended for St. Mary to be the child's parent or simply a surrogate or gestational carrier who lacked a legal parent-child relationship to the child. Therefore, upon remand, the district court must hold an evidentiary hearing to determine whether St. Mary is the child's legal mother or if she is someone without a legal relationship to the child, during which the court may consider any relevant evidence for establishing maternity under the Nevada Parentage Act.

The co-parenting agreement was not a surrogacy agreement and was consistent with Nevada's public policy

St. Mary asserts that the co-parenting agreement demonstrates the parties' intent regarding parentage and custody of the child and that the district court erred in determining that the co-parenting agreement was an unenforceable surrogacy agreement under NRS 126.045. Damon responds that, because the agreement was between an unmarried intended parent and a surrogate and purported to resolve issues of parentage and child custody, the district court correctly deemed that the co-parenting agreement was prohibited by NRS 126.045 (2009).

At the time of the district court's determinations, NRS 126.045 (2009) governed contracts between two married persons and a gestational carrier, or surrogate, for assisted reproduction. It required such contracts to specify the parties' rights, including the "[p]arentage of the child," the "[c]ustody of the child in the event of a change of circumstances," and the "respective responsibilities and liabilities of the contracting parties." NRS 126.045(1)(a)–(c) (2009). Additionally, the statute defined a "[s]urrogate" as "an adult woman who enters into an agreement to bear a child conceived through assisted conception for the intended parents," and "[i]ntended parents" were defined as "a man and woman, married to each other," who agree to "be the parents of a child born to a surrogate through assisted conception." NRS 126.045(4)(b), (c) (2009). Here, St. Mary and Damon's co-parenting agreement was not within the scope of NRS 126.045. The agreement lacked any language intimating that St. Mary acted as a surrogate, such as language indicating that she surrendered custody of the child or relinquished her rights as a mother to the child. Rather, the agreement expressed that St. Mary would share the parental duties of raising the child and would jointly make major parenting decisions with Damon.

Nevertheless, Damon insists that, because the agreement covered issues of parentage and child custody, it necessarily addressed issues contemplated by NRS 126.045 and, as a result, is void for failing to meet the statute's other terms. In other words, Damon argues that outside of NRS 126.045, agreements (at least those with a non-parent) concerning parentage, custody, and responsibilities over a child are void. But, as explained above, parentage is governed by NRS Chapter 126. In the event that both parties are determined to be the child's parents, nothing in Nevada law prevents two parents from entering into agreements that demonstrate their intent concerning child custody.

"Parties are free to contract, and the courts will enforce their contracts if they are not unconscionable, illegal, or in violation of public policy." *Rivero v. Rivero,* 125 Nev. 410, 429, 216 P.3d 213, 226 (2009). It is presumed that fit parents act in the best interest of their children. *Troxel v. Granville,*530 U.S. 57, 68, 120 S.Ct. 2054, 147 L.Ed.2d 49 (2000). Thus, public policy favors fit parents entering agreements to resolve issues pertaining to their minor child's custody, care, and visitation.

When a child has the opportunity to be supported by two loving and fit parents pursuant to a co-parenting agreement, this opportunity is to be given due consideration and must not be foreclosed on account of the parents being of the same sex. . . . To bar the enforceability of a co-parenting agreement on the basis of the parents' genders conflicts with the Nevada Parentage Act's policies of promoting the child's best interest with the support of two parents.

St. Mary and Damon's co-parenting agreement was aligned with Nevada's policy of allowing parents to agree on how to best provide for their child. Within their co-parenting agreement, St. Mary and Damon sought to provide for their child's best interest by agreeing to share the responsibilities of raising the child, even if the relationship between St. Mary and Damon ended. The agreement's language provides the indicia of an effort by St. Mary and Damon to make the child's best interest their priority. Thus, in the event that St. Mary is found to be a legal mother, the district court must consider the parties' co-parenting agreement in making its child custody determination. * * *

[W]e reverse the 2011 order. We remand this matter to the district court for further proceedings to determine the child's parentage, custody, and visitation.

NOTES

1.   Notice that in *D.M.T. v. T.M.H.*, it was the woman who carried the child to term who contended that her former partner (who provided the egg) was not the child's legal parent. In contrast, in *St. Mary v. Damon,* it was the woman who contributed the egg who claimed that her former partner (who carried the child to term) was not the child's legal parent. As a general matter, should the law in these cases prioritize the genetic contribution over the gestational one (or vice-versa) or should the law treat women in both

categories as similarly situated for purposes of determining parenthood? Are there reasons to believe that the partner who carried the child to term in *St. Mary* was more of a "surrogate" than the partner who did so in *T.M.H.*? We continue the exploration of surrogacy issues in the next section.

2. As in *T.M.H.*, the petitioner in *K.M. v. E.G.*, 37 Cal.4th 130, 33 Cal.Rptr.3d 61, 117 P.3d 673 (2005), both provided her egg so that her female partner could become pregnant and signed an informed consent form seemingly waiving all parental rights. After the couple's relationship dissolved, the gestational mother tried to end all contact between her former partner and the twin children. The California Supreme Court, in siding with the former partner, rejected the analogy, accepted by the lower courts, between the petitioner and known sperm donors whose parental rights are legally terminated when they provide their sperm to licensed physicians. Sperm donors, the court noted, are not usually in relationships with the recipients and they rarely plan on living with them in the same home where the children will be raised. *See id.* 117 P.3d at 680–81. The genetic relationship between the petitioner and the children, when coupled with the inapplicability of the known sperm donor nonpaternity statute, meant that the children had two mothers. *Id.* The court also held that the signing of the informed consent form did not waive the genetic mother's rights because a "woman who supplies ova to be used to impregnate her lesbian partner, with the understanding that the resulting child will be raised in their joint home, cannot waive her responsibility to support that child. Nor can such a purported waiver effectively cause that woman to relinquish her parental rights." *Id.* at 682.

3. Surrogacy

THE RIGHT TO BE PARENTS: LGBT FAMILIES AND THE TRANSFORMATION OF PARENTHOOD*
Carlos A. Ball

It is not only lesbian women who have used alternative insemination and other forms of reproductive assistance to have children; so have gay men. But for the latter, of course, the process is complicated by the fact that they must rely not only on donated gametes (in their case eggs or ova), but also on the assistance of a surrogate to carry the fertilized embryo to term.

There are two different types of surrogacy. The first, known as "traditional surrogacy," involves the use of sperm—from either the intended father or a donor—to inseminate the surrogate mother. In these types of cases, the birth mother is linked to the child both genetically and through gestation.

---

* CARLOS A. BALL, THE RIGHT TO BE PARENTS: LGBT FAMILIES AND THE TRANSFORMATION OF PARENTHOOD (2012).

The second type of surrogacy, known as "gestational surrogacy," involves the retrieval of ova from either the intended mother or a donor. The ova is then fertilized in vitro (that is, outside of the womb) with the sperm of the intended father or of a donor, after which the embryo is placed in the surrogate's womb. In these situations, the birth mother is linked to the child through gestation but not through genetics.

When surrogacy pregnancies first began taking place in the United States with some frequency—around the mid-1980s—in vitro technology was not very advanced and was quite expensive, making traditional surrogacy the only realistic option for many individuals interested in pursuing surrogacy as a way of becoming parents. In 1986, the country became riveted by the story of Mary Beth Whitehead, a married woman who agreed to serve as a traditional surrogate by being inseminated with the sperm of a married man so that he and his wife could raise the resulting child. But the day after the baby was born, Whitehead changed her mind, and a protracted and highly visible lawsuit—known as the *Baby M.* case—ensued over who was the child's mother. Eventually, the New Jersey Supreme Court held that the surrogacy agreement entered into by Whitehead and the child's biological father violated public policy because it effectively called for the sale of a child. As a result, the court held that Whitehead—and not the father's wife—was the child's mother.[25]

Shortly after the *Baby M.* case, several states enacted laws prohibiting surrogacy agreements. With time, however, the political opposition to surrogacy diminished, in part because advances in reproductive technology made gestational surrogacy easier (and less costly) to achieve. The fact that gestational surrogates are not genetically related to the children has meant that they have generally not been viewed as either victims or as baby sellers. In fact, the media now routinely portray surrogate mothers in a positive light, highlighting their generosity in wanting to help prospective parents—both infertile heterosexuals and gay men—have children.

In addition, legislators these days seem less interested in discouraging surrogacy than they are, as one commentator has put it, in "providing certainty about parental status and protecting all participants, especially children." An example of this shift is a statute unanimously passed by the Illinois legislature in 2004 which creates a presumption that, in cases of gestational surrogacy, it is the intended parents and not the surrogate mothers who are the children's legal parents.[28] In other states, however, surrogacy of any kind remains strictly prohibited.

Although it is difficult to determine precise numbers, it appears that thousands of gay men have in recent years pursued the opportunity to

---

[25] *Matter of Baby M.*, 537 A.2d 1227 (N.J. 1988).

[28] 750 ILLINOIS COMP. ST. § 47/1–75 (2010).

have children with the assistance of surrogate mothers. While the majority of these surrogacy arrangements seem to have gone as planned with the mother relinquishing parental rights after birth, some have ended up in litigation.

Several of the surrogacy cases in which gay men are litigants have involved relatively rare instances of traditional surrogacy where the issue is usually not whether the surrogate mother should be deemed a parent (she usually is), but is instead who should have custody of the child. In one case, a New York trial court concluded that the biological gay father should have sole custody despite the objection of the surrogate mother, a former friend who had volunteered to help him have the child.[29] In another case, an Ohio appellate court ruled that a woman who was inseminated with the sperm of an anonymous donor did not have to share custody with her gay brother (and his male partner) even though there was evidence that she had agreed, prior to conception, that the brother could raise the child.[30]

There have also been some legal disputes between gay men and gestational surrogates. In 2009, a New Jersey trial court held that the *Baby M.* precedent also applied to gestational surrogacy. As a result, the court ruled that a gestational surrogate who had agreed to help a gay couple—one of whom was her brother—have children was a legal parent of the resulting twin girls.[31] But two years earlier, a Minnesota appellate court [in the case that follows] upheld the gestational surrogacy agreement between a gay man and his niece, holding that the former, and not the latter, was the child's legal parent.[32]

IN RE PATERNITY AND CUSTODY OF BABY BOY A.

Minnesota Court of Appeals, 2007
2007 WL 4304448

WILLIS, JUDGE.

Appellant, who served as the gestational surrogate for respondent's child, challenges the district court's determination of parentage and custody in favor of respondent, arguing that the district court . . . erred by enforcing the parties' gestational-surrogacy agreement . . . Because the record supports the district court's findings and it did not err in its application of the law, we affirm.

---

[29] *C. on Behalf of T. v. G. & E.*, Supreme Court of New York, New York County, *New York Law Journal*, Jan. 12, 2001, 29.

[30] *Decker v. Decker*, 2001 WL 1167475 (Ohio Ct.App. Sept. 28, 2001).

[31] *A.G.R. v. D.R.H. & S.H.*, Superior Court of New Jersey, Hudson County, No. FD–09–001838–07, December 23, 2009.

[32] *In Re Paternity and Custody of Baby Boy A.*, 2007 WL 4304448 (Minn.Ct.App. Dec. 11, 2007).

This case involves the disputed parentage and custody of a child born using in vitro fertilization and gestational surrogacy, which involves the fertilization in vitro of an egg (often from an anonymous donor) with the sperm of the intended father. Doctors then implant the fertilized egg into the womb of a woman who is the "gestational surrogate." Although the gestational surrogate carries and delivers the child, she is not genetically or biologically related to the child.

Respondent P.G.M. is a 38-year-old attorney, who lives in New York City. Raised in a large family, P.G.M. wanted to have a child. As a gay man with HIV,[1] he believed that the only method to produce a genetically related child was by using in vitro fertilization and a gestational surrogate. P.G.M. spent more than a year discussing the procedure with doctors, considering possible egg donors, and researching gestational surrogacy. After one of his doctors expressed a preference for a biologically related gestational surrogate, P.G.M. called his sister Mary during the spring of 2004 to ask if she would serve that function. Mary declined, but she told appellant J.M.A., Mary's daughter and a student in Minnesota, about her conversation with P.G.M. Although J.M.A. was pregnant at the time, she made an unsolicited call to P.G.M. and offered to act as his gestational surrogate. Aware that J.M.A. was then pregnant, P.G.M. declined J.M.A.'s offer.

Over the next several months, the parties exchanged correspondence about gestational surrogacy. After J.M.A. gave birth to her child in the fall of 2004, P.G.M. accepted J.M.A.'s oral offer to act as his gestational surrogate. On December 2, 2004, P.G.M. signed a gestational-surrogacy agreement (GSA) that he had drafted to memorialize the parties' agreement, using sample GSAs that he had found on the Internet as a guide. The GSA provides that it is to be governed by Illinois law and contains the core terms of the agreement, specifically, that J.M.A. would carry P.G.M.'s genetic child, give birth to the child, and disclaim any right to the child. It also contains P.G.M.'s agreement, in return, to pay all of J.M.A.'s unreimbursed and incidental expenses associated with the surrogacy. The GSA also included disclosures about P.G.M.'s HIV, the "sperm-washing" process,[2] and this declaration of intent:

> I, [J.M.A.] hereby acknowledge that I have agreed to carry and give birth to a child conceived via in vitro fertilization through the union of an anonymous donor's ovum/ova and [P.G.M.'s] sperm, so that [P.G.M.] may have a child genetically related to him. I have no intention of having physical or legal custody or

---

[1] The district court found that P.G.M.'s disease "is successfully controlled, that he is in excellent physical health, and that he has a normal life expectancy for a man his age."

[2] Sperm-washing cleanses the seminal fluid surrounding the donor's sperm and replaces it with a sterile solution. The district court found that sperm-washing minimizes the likelihood of the transmission of HIV to the gestational surrogate.

any parental rights, duties or obligations with respect to any child born of this gestational surrogacy process. Rather it is my intention that the genetic and intended parent, [P.G.M.], shall exclusively have such custody and all parental rights, duties and obligations.

In mid-December 2004, approximately a month after receiving a copy of the agreement, J.M.A. signed it after declining P.G.M.'s offer to have independent legal counsel review the document at P.G.M.'s expense. As part of an oral modification of the agreement, P.G.M. agreed to pay J.M.A. a $20,000 fee for her services as a gestational surrogate. P.G.M. delivered a check for $20,000 to J.M.A. at the end of December 2004.

In early 2005, the parties traveled to an Illinois medical facility specializing in sperm-washing and in-vitro fertilization, and they signed in Illinois numerous releases and disclosures that the facility required in order to perform the procedure. On April 12, 2005, in vitro fertilization specialists in Illinois fertilized an egg from an anonymous donor with P.G.M.'s sperm and implanted the fertilized egg into J.M.A.

During the summer of 2005, J.M.A. stayed for two months with P.G.M. in his New York City apartment. At some point during this stay, the parties had a falling out. Soon thereafter, J.M.A. demanded that P.G.M. pay her an additional $120,000, and threatened to abort the child if P.G.M. did not meet her demands.

In early December 2005, J.M.A. drafted a new GSA, which provided for additional compensation for transportation, medical, and psychological services. P.G.M. did not sign the revised GSA. On December 17, 2005, J.M.A. gave birth to the child in Minnesota. She named the child and did not tell P.G.M. about the child's birth, his name, or his whereabouts.

After learning about the child's birth from his sister, P.G.M. filed this paternity action on December 19, 2005. The district court immediately appointed an attorney for J.M.A. from the office of the Hennepin County Public Defender. At the direction of the district court, Hennepin County Court Services interviewed both parties and filed a report that recommended that P.G.M. have temporary custody of the child. That report also noted that P.G.M. had a strong emotional attachment to the child but that J.M.A. was motivated in large part by the prospect of financial gain.

A trial was held at which the district court heard extensive testimony and considered numerous exhibits. The district court issued its paternity findings of fact and conclusions of law on August 18, 2006, concluding that, under the Illinois Parentage Act, P.G.M. was the child's father and denying J.M.A. parental rights. The district court denied J.M.A.'s motion for a new trial, and she now appeals. * * *

The district court properly enforced the gestational-surrogacy agreement's choice-of-law provision. * * * The record contains no evidence that, by selecting Illinois law, the parties acted in bad faith or with the intent to evade Minnesota law. First, Minnesota law does not address— much less prohibit—GSAs. The parties, therefore, did not select Illinois law to avoid a Minnesota law. Illinois law, unlike Minnesota law, provides a clear statutory structure for interpreting GSAs.

We next review J.M.A.'s challenge to the district court's determination that the GSA is legally enforceable. She cites three reasons in support of her claim that it is unenforceable: (1) the GSA does not reflect the parties' actual agreement, (2) P.G.M. coerced J.M.A. to sign the GSA, and (3) the GSA contravenes the public policy of the state of Minnesota. We will address these arguments in turn.

The GSA is a valid contract and expresses the agreement of the parties.

J.M.A. argues first that the district court clearly erred because the "[GSA] does not express the true agreement of the parties." Specifically, she appears to claim that the district court erred by finding that the agreement does not include a provision that the parties agreed to a "joint living arrangement" and by finding that the parties orally modified their agreement to provide for additional compensation to J.M.A. . . .

Here, the record contains significant evidence to support the district court's finding that J.M.A. and P.G.M. entered into a written contract and orally modified that contract. The record supports the district court's finding that J.M.A. offered and P.G.M. accepted J.M.A.'s offer to serve as a gestational surrogate for P.G.M.'s child. P.G.M. then drafted—and J.M.A. signed—a GSA to memorialize the agreement. In consideration for acting as P.G.M.'s gestational surrogate, the GSA provides that P.G.M. will pay all of J.M.A.'s unreimbursed medical costs associated with the surrogacy. And the parties orally modified the GSA by agreeing that P.G.M. would pay J.M.A. an additional $20,000 fee. Although the GSA requires that all modifications be in writing, Illinois law permits oral modification of written agreements—even if the agreement requires that modifications be in writing. *See Tadros v. Kuzmak,* 660 N.E.2d 162, 170 (Ill.App.Ct.1995) * * *

To the extent that J.M.A. argues that the parties made additional agreements relating to living arrangements, we defer to the district court's finding that "there is insufficient credible evidence of such [other] agreement[s] in the trial exhibits or the testimony of any other witnesses at trial." We note that the district court also found that "[P.G.M.'s] story is credible, and [J.M.A.'s] is not." The record contains ample evidence to support the district court's finding that the parties have an enforceable agreement that expresses the "true agreement" of the parties.

J.M.A. was not coerced into signing the agreement.

J.M.A. argues next that the district court erred by enforcing the agreement because J.M.A. signed it under "psychological, emotional, and financial" coercion. * * * The record supports the district court's finding that J.M.A. was not coerced into serving as P.G.M.'s gestational surrogate . . . The district court found that three primary factors motivated J.M.A.: (1) her "attitudinal predisposition to help others"; (2) her "general desire to help" P.G.M.; and (3) the prospect "of receiving, what was to her, . . . a large sum of money."

At the time of J.M.A.'s initial offer, she was pregnant with her own child. P.G.M. knew that, declined J.M.A.'s offer, and "encouraged [J.M.A.] to focus on her own pregnancy before she committed to acting as his gestational surrogate." Throughout the summer of 2004, the parties discussed the process over the phone and by e-mail. And the district court found that P.G.M. invited J.M.A. to discuss the process with "the attending fertility physicians who were to perform the sperm washing and/or embryo transfer." In the fall of 2004, P.G.M. formally accepted J.M.A.'s offer to act as his gestational surrogate and drafted the GSA. After modifying a GSA he found on the Internet, P.G.M. sent the agreement to J.M.A. for her review and signature. An e-mail message accompanied the GSA, which provided, in relevant part:

> [A]nyway, I hope this is simple and very straightforward but of course I want you to feel free to talk to me or another lawyer (I'd be happy to pay the fee) if there is anything about this agreement which you want to discuss further. [A]s we've discussed, I would be happy to make the payment we've discussed at the outset, before you sign the agreement, rather than by the more traditional method of staggered payments.

Approximately a month after receiving the GSA, J.M.A. signed it and mailed it back to P.G.M. The district court found that J.M.A. did not "avail herself of the opportunity to consult separate counsel on her own behalf at [P.G.M.'s] expense." The district court also found that the parties did not meet face-to-face and that P.G.M. did not provide J.M.A. with legal advice. Finally, the district court cited family testimony and psychological evidence describing J.M.A. as "independent and strong willed" and having "no problem . . . protecting her rights." On the basis of these facts, the district court concluded that "[t]here was no fraud, misrepresentation, undue influence, or coercion by either party in the formation of the contract." Because the record supports the district court's findings, they are not manifestly contrary to the evidence.

The agreement does not violate the public policy of Minnesota.

J.M.A. contends next that the GSA is "void and unenforceable because it is in violation of public policy," and, therefore, the district court erred in enforcing the GSA. We disagree . . . Minnesota courts will not enforce an otherwise validly executed contract that contravenes public policy. Contracts violate public policy when they injure some established societal interest. The public policy of this state is found in various authorities, including legislation and judicial decisions.

J.M.A. argues that the district court erred by giving any effect to the GSA because there is "no statutory or case law authority under Minnesota law which sanctions the determination of a child's parentage and custody pursuant to a private contract." But as noted above, there is no Minnesota statute or caselaw that prohibits GSAs. And the legislature has expressly protected the rights of individuals who use assisted-reproduction technologies. *See, e.g.,* Minn.Stat. § 257.56 (2006) (providing a procedure to recognize the father of a child conceived by artificial insemination); Minn.Stat. § 62Q.14 (2006) (preventing health insurers from restricting policyholders' access to infertility services). * * *

To the extent that J.M.A. argues that proof of giving birth to the child is the exclusive manner by which to establish the maternity under § 257.54, J.M.A.'s argument also fails. Although that statute provides that maternity may be established by "proof of [the biological mother] having given birth to the child," Minn.Stat. § 257.54(a), it also provides other methods to establish the mother-child relationship. *See id.,* (b)–(c) (providing that the mother-child relationship may also be established by the Parentage Act, the voluntary recognition of the parties, or proof of adoption); *see also* Minn.Stat. § 257.34 (2006) (providing procedure for the declaration of parentage by the acknowledgement of unmarried parents).

J.M.A. also cites a statute that voids any transfer of a child from a parent to another individual, other than by the adoption process or by a consent decree, for the proposition that GSAs violate Minnesota's public policy. *See* Minn.Stat. § 257.02 (2006). That provision provides only that "no *parent* may assign or otherwise transfer to another parental rights or duties with respect to the permanent care and custody of a child under 14 years of age." *Id.* (emphasis added). But because that provision does not define "parent," the statute does not prohibit a gestational surrogate from carrying a genetically unrelated child and transferring the child to the child's biological parent upon birth.

Because there is no Minnesota legislative or judicial pronouncement that prohibits such agreements, we conclude that GSAs do not violate any articulated public policy of this state. By this opinion, however, we neither condemn nor condone gestational surrogacy. That is not our function. But a child has been born in this state as the result of the procedure, and the judiciary has been asked to determine the child's parentage and custody. That is our function.

We next address the district court's determination of the rights of the parties under Illinois law. [The court concluded that the Illinois Gestational Surrogacy Act of 2004, which calls for a presumption in cases of gestational surrogacy that it is the intended parents and not the surrogate mother who are the children's legal parents, applied only to surrogacy agreements entered into after January 1, 2005. The court then held that the relevant statute was the Illinois Parentage Act (IPA)]. The IPA sets forth a procedure to determine parentage by the voluntary consent of the parties. *See* 750 Ill. Comp. Stat. 45/6(a)(1) (2006) (authorizing consent agreements provided that the parties certify that they have met a series of requirements before the child's birth). The parties do not dispute that the GSA did not satisfy all of the statutory requirements for a consensual parentage determination. But failing to comply with the statutory provision does not invalidate the contract. *See* 750 Ill. Comp. Stat. 45/6(a)(2) (providing that a defective consent agreement raises only a presumption of a parent-child relationship between the gestational surrogate and child). Nor does it foreclose the district court from analyzing the child's parentage and custody in accordance with the law of the state chosen by the parties to govern those determinations, here, Illinois. Therefore, the district court correctly looked to the IPA's next subsection, which creates a rebuttable presumption of J.M.A.'s parentage. That subsection provides:

> Unless otherwise determined by order of the Circuit Court, the child shall be presumed to be the child of the gestational surrogate and of the gestational surrogate's husband, if any, if all requirements of subdivision (a)(1) are not met prior to the birth of the child. This presumption may be rebutted by clear and convincing evidence.

Thus, the district court properly determined that J.M.A. was the child's presumptive mother and that P.G.M. could rebut that presumption by showing that J.M.A. was not the child's mother by clear-and-convincing evidence.

We agree with the district court that there is clear-and-convincing evidence rebutting the presumption that J.M.A. is the child's mother. We agree with the district court that P.G.M. could overcome J.M.A.'s presumptive parentage by "meeting the substantive requirements of 750 Ill. Comp. Stat. 45/6(a)(1)(A–F) . . . [and by using] genetic testing to support his position." The evidence supports the district court's findings that (1) J.M.A. admitted, and genetic testing confirmed, that she is not the child's biological mother; (2) the child was conceived by using an anonymous egg donor; (3) DNA testing established that there is a 99.99% probability that P.G.M. is the child's biological father; (4) Dr. Seth Levrant performed the embryo transfer that resulted in J.M.A.'s gestational surrogacy; and (5) the parties intended to enter into an agreement that complied with the relevant Illinois statutes. Although the Illinois caselaw provides no guidance in this area, we conclude that the record evidence here satisfies the clear-and-convincing standard to rebut the statutory presumption of J.M.A.'s parentage. The district court did not err, therefore, when it analyzed the child's parentage under the IPA, and, in doing so, concluded that P.G.M. had rebutted J.M.A.'s presumptive parentage. . . . Affirmed.

NOTES

1.   In *Vogel v. Kirkbride*, a trial court in Connecticut ruled on the legality of a surrogacy contract between a gay male couple and a woman who agreed to carry and deliver an embryo from a donated egg fertilized by the sperm of one of the men. "In *Vogel*, the court found the two male plaintiffs to be the legal parents of the unborn child and ordered [the hospital] to place the names of the plaintiffs on the birth certificate as parents of the child. The *Vogel* court also found that 'the egg donor agreement and the gestational carrier agreement [were] valid, enforceable, irrevocable and of full legal effect" under the laws of the state of Connecticut.' " *Davis v. Kania*, 836 A.2d 480, 483, 48 Conn.Supp. 141, 145 (2003) (citing Vogel v. Kirkbride, New Haven, 2002 WL 34119315 (Conn. Super. Ct. 2002)).

2.   For an article surveying the surrogacy laws of all fifty states (most of which are silent on the enforceability of surrogacy agreements), see Darra L. Hofman, *"Mama's Baby, Daddy's Maybe:" A State-By-State Survey of Surrogacy Laws and Their Disparate Gender Impact*, 35 WM. MITCHELL L. REV. 449 (2009).

C. CUSTODY AND VISITATION

As lesbian or gay male couples together raise children, inevitably some of them will face problems and occasionally, like heterosexual families, dissolve. As we have already seen, when this happens, lesbians and gay men often turn to court and find themselves litigating against one another.

Given that the law has conventionally used sexual orientation as a reason for not awarding custody or visitation, and/or used biology as a reason for awarding it, lesbian and gay litigants have these arguments available to them. Should they use them? A gay advocacy group in Boston, the Gay & Lesbian Advocates & Defenders (GLAD) gathered community members and lawyers to address these questions and develop principles for the future. Consider their findings.

PROTECTING FAMILIES: STANDARDS FOR CHILD CUSTODY IN SAME-SEX RELATIONSHIPS*

Gay & Lesbian Advocates & Defenders

INTRODUCTION

A. Our Successes In Creating Families

For many years now, both lesbians and gay men have set out to create our own families with children, often with partners, and sometimes with a partner coming into a family after a child's birth. Many refer to our families as those "of intention and function." As we near the end of the second decade of the phenomenon known as the "lesbian baby boom" or "gayby boom," it is important to establish guideposts about how to protect our children when our families separate. Sometimes we form families with an adult who will not be a parent but is intended to have a special and important relationship with the child. This may be a sperm donor, surrogate mother, or some other person, and is referred to in this document as a "significant adult" or "family member." Our community has much to be proud of in its successes in creating families outside of conventional models. We want these lesbian and gay families to be treated as families in all contexts and by the law. Many of us have sought to obtain some kind of legal recognition for our families, whether through second parent adoption, coguardianship, domestic partnership benefits, or powers of attorney. To the nongay world, we have stressed that our relationships are those of a "family" rather than of "housemates" or "roommates." We assert that "if it looks like a family, if it holds itself out as a family, if it functions like a family, then it's a family." However, we know that except for second parent adoption, legal mechanisms do not confer equal parental status on all parents, much less do they allow for the nuances of other important roles we have created, such as the involved nonparent, donor, or other significant adult whose role is conceived of as stable and permanent, even if not "parental."

B. The Nightmare of Divorce Without Legal Process

As in non-gay families, our families sometimes separate. As in non-gay families, when our family relationships undergo changes or break-ups, we experience feelings ranging from sadness and betrayal to hostility and anger about the end of the relationship and about the former family member. In addition to the emotional issues that must be resolved, there may be property division issues and child custody and visitation disputes with which to contend. There is no divorce system in the background, poised as a default to help our families sort these issues out according to uniform and predictable rules.

---

* Gay & Lesbian Advocates & Defenders, *Protecting Families: Standards for Child Custody in Same–Sex Relationships*, 10 UCLA WOMEN'S L.J. 151, 152–62 (1999).

C. Preventing Harm to Children

The general lack of legal recognition for our important family relationships results in disrespect for our families and often can lead to the end of important family or parent-child relationships. After parents or families separate, some birth or adoptive parents terminate contact between the child and the other parent or family members immediately; others allow visitation for a period of time until they find the visitation too inconvenient or form a new relationship. Of course, some parents work hard to maintain their children's relationship with a parent or other significant adult. Some parents have even sought second parent adoptions of their children with their former partners.

D. Preventing Harm to Our Collective Interests

Some parents who are not legally recognized and other significant adults, when faced with a total loss of their relationship with their children, have turned to the courts to restore contact between themselves and their children. Often, although not always, courts interpret state law schemes to give authority to even bring a lawsuit only to those people that the law defines as "parents." Under these restrictive laws, "parents" are only persons related through birth, marriage, or adoption. In other words, in legal terms, the status of "parent" is an all or nothing proposition. Courts often wash their hands of considering the needs of the child when the family member lacks a biological or adoptive relationship, but may very well have been involved in everything from planning for the birth of the child to caring for the child virtually every day of the child's life. Legal cases are often very damaging to our collective interests in addition to threatening deep injury to the individual families and especially to the children. A focus solely on the legal rights of the biological or adoptive parent ignores the real relationships of many parents, significant adults, and children. It is extremely damaging to our community and our families when we disavow as insignificant the very relationships for which we are seeking legal and societal respect. Similarly, when an express agreement was entered into by the parties, it is very damaging later to turn around and claim that such an agreement has no validity simply because it has become inconvenient or feelings among the adults have changed.

As a legal matter, cases that go forward along these lines are likely to have the consequence of reinforcing narrow legal versions of what counts as a family and of what mechanisms are available to create security in establishing a family. We convey to the courts a disrespect for our own families when members of our own community insist that our relationships—of whatever duration and however intermingled—do not amount to a "family," or that the other parent was really nothing more than a babysitter. Obviously, this kind of argument also undercuts efforts in other contexts to win legal respect for our families—whether through domestic partnership, adoption, or resisting restrictions on a divorced parent's visitation when a same-sex partner is present. More cases stating that the biological parent is the winner in law, or that the only real family that merits court protection is one created by biology or marriage, and that agreements mean nothing, will come back to haunt our community in many contexts.

E.   Protect Our Children

These Standards are offered as an approach to the resolution of custody disputes upon the dissolution of a same-sex relationship or nonmarried family. These Standards are based on the belief that decisions about the care and custody of children whose same-sex parents, or other significant adults, share a commitment to and responsibility for those children should be based on the best interests of the children in the context of their actual relationships with each parent rather than on the relationship between the parents or on the existence of a legal relationship with one of those parents. The Standards are also grounded in the belief that our freedom to continue to create secure and stable families depends on respecting the methods we use to create them. Some individuals take on responsibility for children because they have entered into agreements that provide them some sense of security in their roles with those children. Thus, it is very harmful to our future ability to plan families when courts are encouraged (by some) to find the agreements invalid or legally unenforceable. By the same token, some individuals with a biological connection to a child (a birth parent, sperm donor, or egg donor) agree not to be involved in the child's life as parents and to forego the legal advantage that biology would otherwise give them. These individuals are encouraged not to use biology as a trump card that invalidates their agreements and to assert a superior or equal claim to those of the child's actual parents should disputes arise. These Standards may serve as a guide to individual families. More broadly, they may serve as the basis for a continued discussion within our community about how to establish an ethic that respects and protects the actual parent/child and other important relationships in our families. These Standards are intended to be aspirational and voluntary and are certainly not intended to generate disputes that may result in additional litigation. Nor should the Standards be cited as legal authority.

F.   Create Documents Supporting Your Family and Take Advantage of Legal Protections in States Where They Exist

People should be strongly encouraged to create legal and other documents articulating their intentions and expectations about the families they have and are creating. These may be coparenting agreements, estate planning documents, or other types of agreements used in their state. A secondary benefit of such agreements is that the process of reaching an agreement can uncover, and encourage resolution of, areas where the understanding among the parties is unclear or where there is outright disagreement. It is very important to identify and resolve as many potential disputes as possible. In the process, unexpected and undesired future scenarios should be considered, with special attention to the possibility of the family breaking up. When possible, it is important to take advantage of legal mechanisms that exist in some states to protect the relationship between the parents and the child. A number of states permit coparent adoption, a process by which non-biological parents become legal parents to the child. (Contact an attorney to find out if this is available in your area.) Even in states without second parent adoption, a legal parent may be able to name another parent as a coguardian or the nonlegal parent may be able to obtain a limited parental status under state law. It is important to utilize all of the protections which may exist unless there is some important reason why that is not practicable (e.g., a known sperm donor who will not waive his parental rights for a second parent adoption where such waiver is required).

G. Encourage Families in Distress to Review These Standards

As a community, we must remember to speak up, and use the power of our own voices when we encounter families in distress. Encourage those families to review and apply these Standards. The lack of legal recognition of our family relationships has an enormous impact on our community and on every family among us. As a community, we need to provide the support and incentive to behave reasonably even at very difficult times. All of us have a responsibility to educate others to the reality that litigating custody disputes in conventional courts of law may well lead to erosion of the societal and legal credibility our community has gained for our families. These Standards are offered in the spirit of community and in the hope of creating a community where our children are safe, loved, and protected. We encourage people to apply them to their own disputes and to help friends and loved ones who may benefit from them by providing them this document and support in following its principles.

STANDARDS

1. Be Honest About Existing Relationships Regardless of Legal Labels.

Individuals should be forthright and honest about the existence and nature of the relationships between and among the parents, other significant adults, and the children. Each situation is unique and there is no single approach that will work for all families. It is critical to recognize the actual relationships between the parties and the child. A focus on legal labels can easily obscure the actual relationships. Of course, not everyone who claims to be a "parent" or "significant adult" after a dispute is actually a person whose relation to the child is contemplated in the spirit of these standards. It may be that the relationship between the adult and child is of such a short duration, is so intermittent, or is so profoundly troubled in some way that no parent-child or other significant relationship exists. Agreements and documents, particularly when coupled with an ongoing course of conduct that establishes the intent of parent(s) to share parenting or allow an important relationship to develop with another parent or significant adult should be given great weight in determining the context in which the parties' relationships to the child developed.

2. *Consider the Dispute From the Perspective of the Child or Children.*

Separating parents or families experiencing conflict with a significant adult should consider the best interest of the children involved to be paramount and should consider the child(ren)'s perspective. Continuity of their relationships with significant adults is vital to children's well-being. While individuals may be critical of each other, to a child even a marginal parent is a parent. The abrupt termination of a relationship that was contemplated as permanent is very damaging. Sustaining the family members' present relationships with their children should be a primary goal of the resolution of the custody dispute.

3. *Try to Reach a Voluntary Resolution.*

At a minimum, this means that the persons involved should endeavor to reach a voluntary resolution about future care and support for the child. If the parties are at an impasse, consider involving family friends or relatives who know the family well or retaining the services of a mediator or arbitrator who can help the parties reach a voluntary agreement. It may be helpful to know that courts themselves increasingly utilize the services of alternative dispute resolution providers. Mediation, the most common form of alternative dispute resolution, involves a confidential and voluntary form of structured negotiation designed to help the participants reach an informed and agreed-upon resolution with the assistance of one impartial mediator. Other forms of dispute resolution include arbitration and agreements negotiated with lawyers or in couples' therapy. (Consult an attorney knowledgeable in this area of law for recommendations of mediators and arbitrators.)

4. *Try to Maintain Continuity For the Child.*

In arriving at a plan for the future, the parties should start with a presumption that an arrangement that most closely resembles the child's relationship with his or her family over the last two years (or for the life of the child when the child is under age two) is best from the child's perspective. Although it may be difficult, each person should allow and encourage a comparable level of involvement in the child's life and activities as each had before the dispute unless they agree otherwise. This applies to school and extracurricular activities, as well as to the need to share or alternate holidays and other special occasions. To the best of their ability, all family members should aim to continue to provide financial support for the child. Maintaining the status quo to the extent possible should be the goal for the family. Continuity of their relationships with significant adults is vital to our children. The abrupt departure of a loved adult simply because one parent has changed his or her view of that person can cause great harm to a child. Hand in hand with assuming the child's perspective in considering the rights of family members comes viewing responsibilities for support and caretaking that way too. Just as one who wishes to deny the relationship of the child and another family member must be urged to consider the impact on the child, a family member should do everything possible to maintain the status quo for the child in terms of support as well.

5. *Remember That Breaking Up Is Hard to Do.*

Individuals should be helped to understand that the end of a relationship is invariably difficult and disruptive to all involved. Even the most amicable divorces take months to process and many divorces are not entirely amicable. This is all the more reason to seek out the services of a trusted friend or professional mediator who can help the parents avoid impulsive and expedient decisions which are likely to be harmful to the child.

6. *Seriously Investigate Allegations Of Abuse In Determining What is Best for the Child.*

Abusive adult relationships and child abuse do occur in some of our families. If there are allegations of domestic violence, it is important to determine, based on a thorough history, whether or not the allegations are founded. If abuse is substantiated after investigation, whether it is physical or emotional abuse between the parties and/or between the parties and the child, then it should have a role in determining what is in the child's best interest. The focus should be on safety and treatment, not on using the fact of abuse to deny another person's status as a parent or other significant adult. When a parent or significant adult is abusive, the other family members should use legally available means to protect themselves as well as the child. In some cases, this may mean a suspension of visitation or supervised visitation. Research shows that children are often negatively affected by domestic violence even if they are not physically hurt or do not directly witness physical violence. The impact of any abuse on the children should be discussed and incorporated into all negotiations.

Allegations are different from substantiation. Allegations of abuse should be seriously explored in order to reach an honest determination as to whether there was abuse, or whether the feelings stated are those commonly associated with the break-up of a family relationship. A professional evaluator hired at the expense of the parents may be helpful.

7.   Honor Your Agreements.

Whether written or verbal, it is important to honor the agreements you have made. Of course circumstances can change from the time an agreement was formalized or a promise made. A commitment to a child involves significant emotional investment on both the child's and the adults' parts, so it is vital to be assured that important relationships are respected and permitted to remain stable by the child's other parent or caregivers.

8.   The Absence of Legal Documents Is Not Determinative of the Issues.

While it is important to take the available legal steps to protect our families, some cannot or do not pursue legal protections for their families. Some families do not fit the all or nothing definitions common in law. Money to obtain those protections may be an obstacle for some. Others may legitimately fear losing their jobs or homes by coming out in a court proceeding. Other obstacles may exist. For example, even in a state where second parent adoption is available, there may be another person (e.g., former spouse or sperm donor) whose non-consent to the adoption may prohibit the adoption under some states' laws. Thus, the failure of the parents and family members to take legal steps to secure their status as a family is only one factor in any evaluation of the child's best interests or of an agreement among the parties. In and of itself, the failure to take such legal steps cannot be a guiding or determining factor.

9.   Treat Litigation As A Last Resort.

Individuals need to understand that litigation is both a costly and time consuming process. In addition, court proceedings and files are often open to the public, thereby compromising the family's privacy. Lawsuits have a public dimension both for the family involved and, to some degree, for other same-sex families. Those lawsuits in which a parent asserts that another parent or family member who has no adoptive or biological relationship to the child cannot be heard from in court on the issues of visitation or custody run the risk of making bad legal precedent and signal very real disrespect for our own families. More particularly, litigation provides a highly structured forum in which the final decision remains with a judge. Mediation, as discussed in Standard 3, gives all parties input into the dispute-resolution process and the content of any voluntary resolution.

10. *Treat Homophobic Law and Sentiments as Off Limits.*

No one should reveal, or threaten to reveal, the sexual orientation of an opposing parent or other significant adult to employers or others in an attempt to harass or intimidate the opposing party. No one should use the fact of a person's transgendered identity to gain any advantage over another. When litigation occurs, it is improper and unethical to appeal to anti-gay laws or sentiments. Individuals should not use the fact that gay and lesbian relationships are not recognized under current law to gain some advantage. Specifically, we emphatically urge those who are confronted with lawsuits not to resort to arguing that a person who has had a parental or significant relationship with the child but who is not a biological or legal parent cannot ask for visitation or custody because of "standing." If there is a well-founded belief that the child's best interests compel limiting contact between the child and former family members, then the court case should proceed on those terms and not whether an agreement is enforceable or whether a non-legal parent can be in the court proceedings to begin with. Lawyers should consider: (1) limiting the terms of their representation to non-litigation options from the outset of the attorney-client relationship; (2) not relying upon laws or sentiments supporting the notion that parents have a more legitimate right to their children if they are biologically related to their children or related through adoption, than if they are not; and (3) after full discussion and disclosure to their clients, refusing to make arguments about lack of standing, refusing to disavow written agreements, and so limiting their representation at the outset.

CONCLUSION

We can all agree that our children deserve to be loved and protected. This means that we ourselves as well as others should respect our families and our children's relationships whether the legal system would do so or not. We hope these proposed standards will be the basis for fruitful discussion and bring all of us closer to our shared goals.

V.C. v. M.J.B.

Supreme Court of New Jersey, 2000
748 A.2d 539, 163 N.J. 200

LONG, J.

The following facts were established at trial. V.C. and M.J.B., who are lesbians, met in 1992 and began dating on July 4, 1993. On July 9, 1993, M.J.B. went to see a fertility specialist to begin artificial insemination procedures. She prepared for that appointment by recording her body temperature for eight to nine months prior for purposes of tracking her ovulation schedule. She had been planning to be artificially inseminated since late 1980. According to M.J.B., she made the final decision to become pregnant independently and before beginning her relationship with V.C. Two individuals who knew M.J.B. before she began dating V.C., confirmed that M.J.B. had been planning to become pregnant through artificial insemination for years prior to the beginning of the parties' relationship.

According to V.C., early in their relationship, the two discussed having children. However, V.C. did not become aware of M.J.B.'s visits with the specialist and her decision to have a baby by artificial insemination until September 1993. In fact, the doctor's records of M.J.B.'s first appointment indicate that M.J.B. was single and that she "desires children."

Nonetheless, V.C. claimed that the parties jointly decided to have children and that she and M.J.B. jointly researched and decided which sperm donor they should use. M.J.B. acknowledged that she consulted V.C. on the issue but maintained that she individually made the final choice about which sperm donor to use.

Between November 1993 and February 1994, M.J.B. underwent several insemination procedures. V.C. attended at least two of those sessions. In December 1993, V.C. moved into M.J.B.'s apartment. Two months later, on February 7, 1994, the doctor informed M.J.B. that she was pregnant. M.J.B. called V.C. at work to tell her the good news. Eventually, M.J.B. was informed that she was having twins.

During M.J.B.'s pregnancy, both M.J.B. and V.C. prepared for the birth of the twins by attending pre-natal and Lamaze classes. In April 1994, the parties moved to a larger apartment to accommodate the pending births. V.C. contended that during that time they jointly decided on the children's names. M.J.B. admitted consulting V.C., but maintained that she made the final decision regarding names.

The children were born on September 29, 1994. V.C. took M.J.B. to the hospital and she was present in the delivery room at the birth of the children. At the hospital, the nurses and staff treated V.C. as if she were a mother. Immediately following the birth, the nurses gave one child to M.J.B. to hold and the other to V.C., and took pictures of the four of them together. After the children were born, M.J.B. took a three-month maternity leave and V.C. took a three-week vacation.

The parties opened joint bank accounts for their household expenses, and prepared wills, powers of attorney, and named each other as the beneficiary for their respective life insurance policies. At some point, the parties also opened savings accounts for the children, and named V.C. as custodian for one account and M.J.B. as custodian for the other.

The parties also decided to have the children call M.J.B. "Mommy" and V.C. "Meema." M.J.B. conceded that she referred to V.C. as a "mother" of the children. In addition, M.J.B. supported the notion, both publicly and privately, that during the twenty-three months after the children were born, the parties and the children functioned as a family unit. M.J.B. sent cards and letters to V.C. that referred to V.C. as the children's mother, and indicated that the four of them were a family. The children also gave cards to V.C. that indicated that V.C. was their mother. M.J.B. encouraged a relationship between V.C. and the children and sought to create a "happy, cohesive environment for the children." M.J.B. admitted that, when the parties' relationship was intact, she sometimes thought of the four of them as a family. However, although M.J.B. sometimes considered the children "theirs," other times she considered them "hers".

M.J.B. agreed that both parties cared for the children but insisted that she made substantive decisions regarding their lives. For instance, M.J.B. maintained that she independently researched and made the final decisions regarding the children's pediatrician and day care center. V.C. countered that she was equally involved in all decision-making regarding the children. Specifically, V.C. claimed that she participated in choosing a day care center for the children, and it is clear that M.J.B. brought V.C. to visit the center she selected prior to making a final decision.

M.J.B. acknowledged that V.C. assumed substantial responsibility for the children, but maintained that V.C. was a mere helper and not a co-parent. However, according to V.C., she acted as a co-parent to the children and had equal parenting responsibility. Indeed, M.J.B. listed V.C. as the "other mother" on the children's pediatrician and day care registration forms. M.J.B. also gave V.C. medical power of attorney over the children. * * *

Together the parties purchased a home in February 1995. Later that year, V.C. asked M.J.B. to marry her, and M.J.B. accepted. In July 1995, the parties held a commitment ceremony where they were "married." At the ceremony, V.C., M.J.B. and the twins were blessed as a "family." * * *

. . . [I]n August 1996, M.J.B. ended the relationship. The parties then took turns living in the house with the children until November 1996. In December 1996, V.C. moved out. M.J.B. permitted V.C. to visit with the children until May 1997. During that time, V.C. spent approximately every other weekend with the children, and contributed money toward the household expenses.

In May 1997, M.J.B. went away on business and left the children with V.C. for two weeks. However, later that month, M.J.B. refused to continue V.C.'s visitation with the children, and at some point, M.J.B. stopped accepting V.C.'s money. M.J.B. asserted that she did not want to continue the children's contact with V.C. because she believed that V.C. was not properly caring for the children, and that the children were suffering distress from continued contact with V.C. Both parties became involved with new partners after the dissolution of their relationship. Eventually, V.C. filed this complaint for joint legal custody.

At trial, expert witnesses appeared for both parties. Dr. Allwyn J. Levine testified on behalf of V.C., and Dr. David Brodzinsky testified on behalf of M.J.B. Both experts arrived at similar conclusions after having examined the women individually and with the children, and after examining the children separately.

Dr. Levine concluded that both children view V.C. as a maternal figure and that V.C. regards herself as one of the children's mothers. "[B]ecause the children were basically parented from birth" by V.C. and M.J.B. "until they physically separated," Dr. Levine concluded that the children view the parties "as inter-changeable maternal mothering objects" and "have established a maternal bond with both of the women."

Dr. Levine likened the parties' relationship to a heterosexual marriage. Consequently, the children would be affected by the loss of V.C. just as if they had been denied contact with their father after a divorce. Dr. Levine explained that the children would benefit from continued contact with V.C. because they had a bonded relationship with her. Dr. Levine further noted that if the children felt abandoned by V.C., they might also feel unnecessary guilt and assume that they made V.C. angry or somehow caused the parties' separation. * * *

Likewise, Dr. Brodzinsky concluded that V.C. and the children enjoyed a bonded relationship that benefitted both children. Dr. Brodzinsky determined that the children regarded V.C. as a member of their family. . . . In contrast to Dr. Levine's opinion, Dr. Brodzinsky believed that the loss of V.C. was not akin to the loss of a parent in a heterosexual divorce. The doctor explained that societal views foster the expectation that a child and a parent will continue their relationship after a divorce, but that no similar expectation would exist for the children's relationship with V.C. . . .

The trial court denied V.C.'s applications for joint legal custody and visitation because it concluded that she failed to establish that the bonded relationship she enjoyed with the children had risen to the level of psychological or *de facto* parenthood. In so doing, the court gave significant weight to the fact that the decision to have children was M.J.B.'s, and not a joint decision between M.J.B. and V.C.

Finding that V.C. did not qualify as a psychological parent to the children, the trial court opined that it would "only be able to consider [V.C.'s] petition for custody if [she] was able [to] prove [M.J.B.] to be an unfit parent." Because V.C. did not allege that M.J.B. was an unfit parent, the trial court held that V.C. lacked standing to petition for joint legal custody. The court also denied V.C.'s application for visitation, determining that even a step-parent would not be granted such visitation except for equitable reasons, not present here. Further, it resolved that visitation was not in the children's best interests because M.J.B. harbored animosity toward V.C. that would "inevitably pass[ ] along to the children." According to the trial court, the case might have been different had V.C. "enjoyed a longer and more irreplaceable relationship with the children. . . ." Upon the entry of judgment, V.C. appealed. [The Appellate Division reversed the trial court's judgment.] * * *

There are no statutes explicitly addressing whether a former unmarried domestic partner has standing to seek custody and visitation with her former partner's biological children. That is not to say, however, that the current statutory scheme dealing with issues of custody and visitation does not provide some guiding principles. N.J.S.A. 9:2–3 prescribes:

> When the parents of a minor child live separately, or are about to do so, the Superior Court, in an action brought by either parent, shall have the same power to make judgments or orders concerning care, custody, education and maintenance as concerning a child whose parents are divorced. . . .

Further, N.J.S.A. 9:2–4 provides, in part, that

> [t]he Legislature finds and declares that it is in the public policy of this State to assure minor children of frequent and continuing contact with both parents after the parents have separated or dissolved their marriage and that it is in the public interest to encourage parents to share the rights and responsibilities of child rearing in order to effect this policy. In any proceeding involving the custody of a minor child, the rights of both parents shall be equal. . . .

By that scheme, the Legislature has expressed the view that children should not generally be denied continuing contact with parents after the relationship between the parties ends.

N.J.S.A. 9:2–13(f) provides that "[t]he word 'parent,' when not otherwise described by the context, means a natural parent or parent by previous adoption." M.J.B. argues that because V.C. is not a natural or adoptive parent, we lack jurisdiction to consider her claims. That is an incomplete interpretation of the Act. Although the statutory definition of parent focuses on natural and adoptive parents, it also includes the phrase, "when not otherwise described by the context." That language evinces a legislative intent to leave open the possibility that individuals other than natural or adoptive parents may qualify as "parents," depending on the circumstances.

By including the words "when not otherwise described by the context" in the statute, the Legislature obviously envisioned a case where the specific relationship between a child and a person not specifically denominated by the statute would qualify as "parental" under the scheme of Title 9. Although the Legislature may not have considered the precise case before us, it is hard to imagine what it could have had in mind in adding the "context" language other than a situation such as this, in which a person not related to a child by blood or adoption has stood in a parental role vis-a-vis the child. It is that contention by V.C. that brings this case before the court and affords us jurisdiction over V.C.'s complaint.

Separate and apart from the statute, M.J.B. contends that there is no legal precedent for this action by V.C. She asserts, correctly, that a legal parent has a fundamental right to the care, custody and nurturance of his or her child. Various constitutional provisions have been cited as the source of that right, which is deeply imbedded in our collective consciousness and traditions. In general, however, the right of a legal parent to the care and custody of his or her child derives from the notion of privacy. According to M.J.B., that right entitles her to absolute preference over V.C. in connection with custody and visitation of the twins. She argues that V.C., a stranger, has no standing to bring this action. We disagree.

The right of parents to the care and custody of their children is not absolute. For example, a legal parent's fundamental right to custody and control of a child may be infringed upon by the state if the parent endangers the health or safety of the child. Likewise, if there is a showing of unfitness, abandonment or gross misconduct, a parent's right to custody of her child may be usurped.

According to M.J.B., because there is no allegation by V.C. of unfitness, abandonment or gross misconduct, there is no reason advanced to interfere with any of her constitutional prerogatives. What she elides from consideration, however, is the "exceptional circumstances" category (occasionally denominated as extraordinary circumstances) that has been recognized as an alternative basis for a third party to seek custody and visitation of another person's child. The "exceptional circumstances" category contemplates the intervention of the Court in the exercise of its *parens patriae* power to protect a child.

Subsumed within that category is the subset known as the psychological parent cases in which a third party has stepped in to assume the role of the legal parent who has been unable or unwilling to undertake the obligations of parenthood. * * *

At the heart of the psychological parent cases is a recognition that children have a strong interest in maintaining the ties that connect them to adults who love and provide for them. That interest, for constitutional as well as social purposes, lies in the emotional bonds that develop between family members as a result of shared daily life. That point was emphasized in *Lehr v. Robertson*, 463 U.S. 248, 261 (1983), where the Supreme Court held that a stepfather's *actual* relationship with a child was the determining factor when considering the degree of protection that the parent-child link must be afforded. The Court stressed that "the importance of the familial relationship, to the individuals involved and to the society, stems from the emotional attachments that derive from the intimacy of daily association, and from the role it plays in 'promot[ing] a way of life' through the instruction of children as well as from the fact of blood relationship."

To be sure, prior cases in New Jersey have arisen in the context of a third party taking over the role of an unwilling, absent or incapacitated parent. The question presented here is different; V.C. did not step into M.J.B.'s shoes, but labored alongside her in their family. However, because we view this issue as falling broadly within the contours we have previously described, and because V.C. invokes the "exceptional circumstances" doctrine based on her claim to be a psychological parent to the twins, she has standing to maintain this action separate and apart from the statute.

The next issue we confront is how a party may establish that he or she has, in fact, become a psychological parent to the child of a fit and involved legal parent. That is a question which many of our sister states have attempted to answer. Some have enacted statutes to address the subject by deconstructing psychological parenthood to its fundamental elements, including: the substantial nature of the relationship between the third party and the child, *see, e.g.*, Ariz. Rev. Stat. Ann. § 25–415(G)(1) (West 2000); whether or not the third party and the child actually lived together, *see, e.g.*, Minn. Stat. Ann. § 257.022(2b) (West 1999); Tex. Fam. Code Ann. § 102.003(a)(9) (West 1999); and whether the unrelated third party had previously provided financial support for the child, *see, e.g.*, 1999 Nev. Stat. 125A.330(3)(I). * * *

The most thoughtful and inclusive definition of *de facto* parenthood is the test enunciated in *Custody of H.S.H.-K.*, 533 N.W.2d 419, 421 (Wisc. 1995), and adopted by the Appellate Division majority here. It addresses the main fears and concerns both legislatures and courts have advanced when addressing the notion of psychological parenthood. Under that test,

> [t]o demonstrate the existence of the petitioner's parent-like relationship with the child, the petitioner must prove four elements: (1) that the biological or adoptive parent consented to, and fostered, the petitioner's formation and establishment of a parent-like relationship with the child; (2) that the petitioner

and the child lived together in the same household; (3) that the petitioner assumed the obligations of parenthood by taking significant responsibility for the child's care, education and development, including contributing towards the child's support, without expectation of financial compensation [a petitioner's contribution to a child's support need not be monetary]; and (4) that the petitioner has been in a parental role for a length of time sufficient to have established with the child a bonded, dependent relationship parental in nature. * * *

Prong one is critical because it makes the biological or adoptive parent a participant in the creation of the psychological parent's relationship with the child. Without such a requirement, a paid nanny or babysitter could theoretically qualify for parental status. To avoid that result, in order for a third party to be deemed a psychological parent, the legal parent must have fostered the formation of the parental relationship between the third party and the child. By fostered is meant that the legal parent ceded over to the third party a measure of parental authority and autonomy and granted to that third party rights and duties vis-a-vis the child that the third party's status would not otherwise warrant. Ordinarily, a relationship based on payment by the legal parent to the third party will not qualify.

The requirement of cooperation by the legal parent is critical because it places control within his or her hands. That parent has the absolute ability to maintain a zone of autonomous privacy for herself and her child. However, if she wishes to maintain that zone of privacy she cannot invite a third party to function as a parent to her child and cannot cede over to that third party parental authority the exercise of which may create a profound bond with the child.

Two further points concerning the consent requirement need to be clarified. First, a psychological parent-child relationship that is voluntarily created by the legally recognized parent may not be unilaterally terminated after the relationship between the adults ends. Although the intent of the legally recognized parent is critical to the psychological parent analysis, the focus is on that party's intent during the formation and pendency of the parent-child relationship. The reason is that the ending of the relationship between the legal parent and the third party does not end the bond that the legal parent fostered and that actually developed between the child and the psychological parent. Thus, the right of the legal parent "[does] not extend to erasing a relationship between her partner and her child which she voluntarily created and actively fostered simply because after the party's separation she regretted having done so." *J.A.L. v. E.P.H.*, 682 A.2d 1314, 1322 (Pa. Super. Ct. 1996).

In practice, that may mean protecting those relationships despite the later, contrary wishes of the legal parent in order to advance the interests of the child. As long as the legal parent consents to the continuation of the relationship between another adult who is a psychological parent and the child after the termination of the adult parties' relationship, the courts need not be involved. Only when that consent is withdrawn are courts called on to protect the child's relationship with the psychological parent.

The second issue that needs to be clarified is that participation in the decision to have a child is not a prerequisite to a finding that one has become a psychological parent to the child. We make that point because the trial court appeared to view the fact that M.J.B. alone made the decision to have the twins as pivotal to the question of the existence of a psychological parent relationship between V.C. and the children. Although joint participation in the family's decision to have a child is probative evidence of the legally recognized parent's intentions, not having participated in the decision does not preclude a finding of the third party's psychological parenthood. Such circumstances parallel the situation in which a woman, already pregnant or a mother, becomes involved with or marries a man who is not the biological or adoptive father of the child, but thereafter fully functions in every respect as a father. There is nothing about that scenario that would justify precluding the possibility of denominating that person as a psychological parent. It goes without saying that adoption proceedings in these circumstances would eliminate the need for a psychological parent inquiry altogether and would be preferable to court intervention. However, the failure of the parties to pursue that option is not preclusive of a finding of psychological parenthood where all the other indicia of that status are present.

Concerning the remaining prongs of the *H.S.H.-K.* test, we accept Wisconsin's formulation with these additional comments. The third prong, a finding that a third party assumed the obligations of parenthood, is not contingent on financial contributions made by the third party. Financial contribution may be considered but should not be given inordinate weight when determining whether a third party has assumed the obligations of parenthood. Obviously, as we have indicated, the assumption of a parental role is much more complex than mere financial support. It is determined by the nature, quality, and extent of the functions undertaken by the third party and the response of the child to that nurturance.

Indeed, we can conceive of a case in which the third party is the stay-at-home mother or father who undertakes all of the daily domestic and child care activities in a household with preschool children while the legal parent is the breadwinner engaged in her occupation or profession. Although it is always possible to put a price on the contributions of the stay-at-home parent, *see* Martha M. Ertman, *Commercializing Marriage:*

A Proposal for Valuing Women's Work Through Premarital Security Agreements, 77 Tex. L. Rev. 17, 43 (1998) (outlining different economic models for placing value on homemaker's contribution), our point is that such an analysis is not necessary because it is the nature of what is done that will determine whether a parent-child bond has developed, not how much it is worth in dollars.

It bears repeating that the fourth prong is most important because it requires the existence of a parent-child bond. A necessary corollary is that the third party must have functioned as a parent for a long enough time that such a bond has developed. What is crucial here is not the amount of time but the nature of the relationship. How much time is necessary will turn on the facts of each case including an assessment of exactly what functions the putative parent performed, as well as at what period and stage of the child's life and development such actions were taken. Most importantly, a determination will have to be made about the actuality and strength of the parent-child bond. Generally, that will require expert testimony.

The standards to which we have referred will govern all cases in which a third party asserts psychological parent status as a basis for a custody or visitation action regarding the child of a legal parent, with whom the third party has lived in a familial setting.

This opinion should not be viewed as an incursion on the general right of a fit legal parent to raise his or her child without outside interference. What we have addressed here is a specific set of circumstances involving the volitional choice of a legal parent to cede a measure of parental authority to a third party; to allow that party to function as a parent in the day-to-day life of the child; and to foster the forging of a parental bond between the third party and the child. In such circumstances, the legal parent has created a family with the third party and the child, and has invited the third party into the otherwise inviolable realm of family privacy. By virtue of her own actions, the legal parent's expectation of autonomous privacy in her relationship with her child is necessarily reduced from that which would have been the case had she never invited the third party into their lives. Most important, where that invitation and its consequences have altered her child's life by essentially giving him or her another parent, the legal parent's options are constrained. It is the child's best interest that is preeminent as it would be if two legal parents were in a conflict over custody and visitation.

Once a third party has been determined to be a psychological parent to a child, under the previously described standards, he or she stands in parity with the legal parent. Custody and visitation issues between them are to be determined on a best interests standard giving weight to the factors set forth in N.J.S.A. 9:2–4. * * *

That is not to suggest that a person's status as a legal parent does not play a part in custody or visitation proceedings in those circumstances. Indeed, as the Appellate Division stated in *Todd v. Sheridan*, 633 A.2d 1009 (App. Div. 1993):

> No fair reading of [*Zack v. Fiebert*, 563 A.2d 58, 235 N.J.Super. 424 (App.Div.1989)] prohibits a judge from considering any aspect of either party's character or status in assessing the best interests of the child. N.J.S.A. 9:2–4. Obviously, as the trial judge recognized, he was not free to give an absolute preference to [the natural parent] because that would have undermined the salutary aims *Zack* was meant to accomplish. However, he was free to consider [the natural parent's] status as [the child's] biological father as one weight in the best interests balance.

We agree. The legal parent's status is a significant weight in the best interests balance because eventually, in the search for self-knowledge, the child's interest in his or her roots will emerge. Thus, under ordinary circumstances when the evidence concerning the child's best interests (as between a legal parent and psychological parent) is in equipoise, custody will be awarded to the legal parent.

Visitation, however, will be the presumptive rule, subject to the considerations set forth in N.J.S.A. 9:2–4, as would be the case if two natural parents were in conflict. As we said in *Beck v. Beck*, 86 N.J. 480, 495, 432 A.2d 63 (1981), visitation rights are almost "invariably" granted to the non-custodial parent. Indeed, "[t]he denial of visitation rights is such an extraordinary proscription that it should be invoked only in those exceptional cases where it clearly and convincingly appears that the granting of visitation will cause physical or emotional harm to the children or where it is demonstrated that the parent is unfit." *Barron v. Barron*, 184 N.J.Super. 297, 303, 445 A.2d 1182 (Ch. Div. 1982). Once the parent-child bond is forged, the rights and duties of the parties should be crafted to reflect that reality.

Ordinarily, when we announce a new standard, we remand the case to the trial court for reconsideration. That is not necessary here. This full record informs us that M.J.B. fostered and cultivated, in every way, the development of a parent-child bond between V.C. and the twins; that they all lived together in the same household as a family; that despite M.J.B.'s after-the-fact characterizations of V.C. as a "stranger" and a "nanny," V.C. assumed many of the day-to-day obligations of parenthood toward the twins, including financial support; and that a bonded relationship developed between V.C. and the twins that is parental in nature. In short, we agree with the Appellate Division that V.C. is a psychological parent to the twins.

That said, the issue is whether V.C. should be granted joint legal custody and visitation. As we have stated, the best interests standard applies and the factors set forth in N.J.S.A. 9:2–4 come into play. Under that statute V.C. and M.J.B. are essentially equal. Each appears to be a fully capable, loving parent committed to the safety and welfare of the twins. Although there is animosity between V.C. and M.J.B., that is not a determinant of whether V.C. can continue in the children's lives.

We note that V.C. is not seeking joint physical custody, but joint legal custody for decision making. However, due to the pendency of this case, V.C. has not been involved in the decision-making for the twins for nearly four years. To interject her into the decisional realm at this point would be unnecessarily disruptive for all involved. We will not, therefore, order joint legal custody in this case.

Visitation, however, is another matter. V.C. and the twins have been visiting during nearly all of the four years since V.C. parted company from M.J.B. Continued visitation in those circumstances is presumed. Nothing suggests that V.C. should be precluded from continuing to see the children on a regular basis. Indeed, it is clear that continued regular visitation is in the twins' best interests because V.C. is their psychological parent. We thus affirm the judgment of the Appellate Division.

[Concurring opinion by JUSTICE O'HERN is omitted.]

CHATTERJEE V. KING

Supreme Court of New Mexico, 2012
280 P.3d 283

CHÁVEZ, JUSTICE.

Bani Chatterjee (Chatterjee) and Taya King (King) are two women who were in a committed, long-term domestic relationship when they agreed to bring a child into their relationship. Chatterjee pleaded in the district court that during the course of their relationship, and with Chatterjee's active participation, King adopted a child (Child) from Russia. Chatterjee supported King and Child financially, lived in the family home, and co-parented Child for a number of years before their commitment to each other foundered and they dissolved their relationship. Chatterjee never adopted Child. After they ended their relationship, King moved to Colorado and sought to prevent Chatterjee from having any contact with Child.

Chatterjee filed a petition in the district court to establish parentage and determine custody and timesharing (Petition). Chatterjee alleged that she was a presumed natural parent under the . . . New Mexico

Uniform Parentage Act. She further claimed to be the equitable or de facto parent of Child, and as such, was entitled to relief.[2] In response to Chatterjee's Petition, King filed a motion to dismiss . . . argu[ing] that Chatterjee was a third party who was seeking custody and visitation of Child and that . . . third part[ies] are prohibited from receiving custody rights absent a showing of unfitness of the natural or adoptive parent. The district court dismissed the Petition for failure to state a claim upon which relief could be granted.

Chatterjee then appealed to the Court of Appeals, which . . . held that Chatterjee did not have standing to seek joint custody absent a showing of King's unfitness because she is neither the biological nor the adoptive mother of Child. The Court further held that presumptions establishing a father and child relationship cannot be applied to women, and a mother and child relationship can only be established through biology or adoption. . . . The Court of Appeals reversed the district court's dismissal concerning the opportunity for Chatterjee to seek standing for visitation and remanded to the district court, instructing the district court to determine whether visitation with Chatterjee would be in Child's best interests. On remand, the district court appointed a guardian ad litem for Child and accepted the guardian ad litem's recommendation that contact and visitation with Chatterjee would be in Child's best interests.

The question in this case is whether Chatterjee has pleaded sufficient facts in her Petition to give her standing to pursue joint custody of Child under the Dissolution of Marriage Act. Whether Chatterjee has standing to pursue joint custody depends on whether Chatterjee has pleaded facts sufficient to establish that she is an interested party under Section 40–11–21 of the New Mexico Uniform Parentage Act (UPA). Her pleading sets forth facts, which, if true, establish that she has a personal, financial, and custodial relationship with Child and has openly held Child out as her daughter, although she is neither Child's biological nor adoptive mother. * * *

Chatterjee argues that the Court of Appeals erred in holding that none of the UPA provisions relating to the father and child relationship may be applied to women. She claims that this holding directly contradicts the plain language of Section 40–11–21. King responds that the UPA provisions establishing paternity should not be applied to women because the UPA expressly provides the ways in which maternity can be established. We agree with Chatterjee. We find support for Chatterjee's argument not only in the plain language of the statute itself, but also in the purpose of the UPA, the application of paternity provisions to women in jurisdictions with similar UPA provisions, and in public

---

[2] Because we find that a plain reading of the Uniform Parentage Act gives Chatterjee standing to seek custody, we do not reach her arguments on extraordinary circumstances or constitutionality.

policy that encourages the love and support of children from able and willing parents. * * *

We begin our analysis with Section 40–11–2 of the UPA, which states that a " 'parent and child relationship' means the legal relationship existing between a child and his natural or adoptive parents incident to which the law confers or imposes rights, privileges, duties and obligations. It includes the mother and child relationship and the father and child relationship." For a mother, Section 40–11–4(A) provides that "the natural mother may be established by proof of her having given birth to the child, *or as provided by Section* [40–11–21 NMSA 1978]." (Emphasis added.) Section 40–11–21 states that "[a]ny interested party may bring an action to determine the existence or nonexistence of a mother and child relationship. Insofar as practicable, the provisions of the Uniform Parentage Act applicable to the father and child relationship apply."

The Court of Appeals held that reading Section 40–11–21 to allow Chatterjee to establish parentage through Section 40–11–5(A)(4) was impracticable. The Court also held that reading Section 40–11–5 to apply to women would render Section 40–11–4(A), which provides for how a woman may establish natural motherhood, "'surplusage or meaningless.'" It reasoned that the Legislature, in enacting Section 40–11–4(A), created separate sections for how a woman as opposed to a man can prove natural parenthood, implying that it intended each sex to have different means available for proving parenthood. The Court therefore concluded that applying the means for proving paternity to proving maternity would contravene the Legislature's intent. We disagree.

It is practicable to apply Section 40–11–5 to determine maternity in certain circumstances. "Practicable" is defined as "reasonably capable of being accomplished; feasible." *Black's Law Dictionary* 1291 (9th ed. 2009). Section 40–11–5(A)(4), which establishes a parental presumption, is reasonably capable of being accomplished by either a man or a woman. Section 40–11–5(A)(4) provides, in relevant part, that "[a] man is presumed to be the natural father of a child if . . . while the child is under the age of majority, he openly holds out the child as his natural child and has established a personal, financial or custodial relationship with the child." Because the presumption is based on a person's conduct, not a biological connection, a woman is capable of holding out a child as her natural child and establishing a personal, financial, or custodial relationship with that child. This is particularly true when, as is alleged in this case, the relationship between the child and both the presumptive and the adoptive parent occurred simultaneously.

In addition, by limiting proof of natural motherhood to biology under Section 40–11–4(A), the Court of Appeals renders meaningless the clear instruction in Section 40–11–4(A) that a "natural mother may [also] be established . . . as provided by Section 21 [40–11–21 NMSA 1978]." A straightforward reading of Section 40–11–4(A) is that motherhood may be established by giving birth, by adoption, and in any other way in which a father and child relationship may be established when it is practicable to do so. Because it is practicable for a woman to hold a child out as her own, the plain language instructs us to recognize that Section 40–11–5(A)(4) relating to the father and child relationship also applies to the mother and child relationship. * * *

Moreover, we seek to avoid an interpretation of a statute that would raise constitutional concerns. In *New Mexico Right to Choose/NARAL v. Johnson,* 126 N.M. 788, 975 P.2d 841, we held that classifications based on gender are presumptively unconstitutional. In this case, the Court of Appeals' reading would yield different results for a man than for a woman in precisely the same situation. If this Court interpreted Section 40–11–5(A)(4) as applying only to males, then a man in a same-sex relationship claiming to be a natural parent because he held out a child as his own would have standing simply by virtue of his gender, while a woman in the same position would not. In other words, if two men were in Chatterjee's and King's exact situation, Chatterjee's male counterpart would have standing under Section 40–11–5(A)(4) of the UPA to establish parentage, while Chatterjee would not. We avoid this disparate treatment, giving effect to the Legislature's intent, with a plain and simple application of Section 40–11–5(A)(4) to both men and women under Section 40–11–21. * * *

The Oregon Court of Appeals has also applied statutes establishing parentage presumptions based on marital status to women. *Shineovich & Kemp,* 229 Or.App. 670, 214 P.3d 29, 39–40 (2009). Although this case dealt with a parentage presumption arising from artificial insemination, it presented essentially the same issue facing this Court: whether a statute creating a presumption of parentage written in terms of paternity should be applied to similarly situated women.

In *Shineovich,* the Oregon Court of Appeals held that a statute recognizing a husband's parentage based on his consent to assisted reproduction was unconstitutional unless it was equally applied to women in same-sex relationships who consent to their partners' inseminations. . . . The court held that the statute was unconstitutional because it did not require that there be at least the possibility of a biological relationship with the child. In other words, all it required was conduct that indicated an intent to parent. The statute simply creates a presumption that the consenting husband of an artificially inseminated woman is the child's legal parent, regardless of biological connection. The court held that the Oregon statute that provided standing was unconstitutional as applied because there was no compelling justification to deny same-sex couples the right to enjoy that presumption. Therefore, the court extended the presumption to similarly situated women. * * *

. . . [T]he state has a strong interest in ensuring that a child will be cared for, financially and otherwise, by two parents. If that care is lacking, the state will ultimately assume the responsibility of caring for the child. This is one of the primary reasons that the original UPA was created, and it makes little sense to read the statute without keeping this overarching legislative goal in mind.

The original UPA was also written to address the interest that children have in their own support. The rationale underlying the original UPA is that every child should be treated equally, regardless of the marital status of the child's parents. In deciding illegitimacy cases, the United States Supreme Court recognized that it is "illogical and unjust" for a state to deny a child's essential right to be supported by two parents simply because the child's parents are not married. *Gomez v. Perez*, 409 U.S. 535, 538, 93 S.Ct. 872, 35 L.Ed.2d 56 (1973). The Court also noted, regarding irresponsible parenthood, that "no child is responsible for his [or her] birth and penalizing the illegitimate child is an ineffectual . . . way of deterring the parent." *Weber v. Aetna Cas. & Sur. Co.*, 406 U.S. 164, 175, 92 S.Ct. 1400, 31 L.Ed.2d 768 (1972). With this in mind, we see no reason for children to be penalized because of the decisions that their parents make, legal or otherwise.

Consistent with the underlying policy-based rationale of the New Mexico UPA that equality in child welfare requires laws that achieve equality in parentage, Child's need for love and support is no less critical simply because her second parent also happens to be a woman. Experts in child psychology recognize that sometimes the law is too limiting when it comes to actually addressing what is in the child's best interests. The attachment bonds that form between a child and a parent are formed regardless of a biological or legal connection. The law needs to address traditional expectations in light of current realities to keep up with the changing demographic of American families and to protect the children born into them. * * *

It is inappropriate to deny Chatterjee the opportunity to establish parentage, when denying Chatterjee this opportunity would only serve to harm both Child and the state. In our view, it is against public policy to deny parental rights and responsibilities based solely on the sex of either or both of the parents. The better view is to recognize that the child's best interests are served when intending parents physically, emotionally, and financially support the child from the time the child comes into their lives. This is especially true when both parents are able and willing to care for the child. Therefore, we hold that the Legislature intended that Section 40–11–5(A)(4) be applied to a woman who is seeking to establish a natural parent and child relationship with a child whom she has held out as her natural child from the moment the child came into the lives of both the adoptive mother and the presumptive mother. * * *

The fact that Chatterjee did not adopt Child does not impact our decision. Section 40–11–5 of the New Mexico UPA delineates the ways in which parentage can be presumed. Thus, our Legislature has recognized that there will be many situations in which someone is caring for a child but has not taken any steps to legalize that relationship. While taking legal action is the best way to ensure that both the alleged parent and the child have rights arising from that relationship, both our Legislature and this Court have indicated a willingness to confer rights to relationships that have not been legally established. This is so because parental rights are not automatically conferred when there is a biological relationship, but rather when an alleged parent has taken the responsibility of caring for a child. Considering the specific facts of this case, we hold that Chatterjee has alleged sufficient facts to attempt to establish that she is an interested party, and therefore she has standing to establish parentage under Section 40–11–21 of the New Mexico UPA.

BOSSON, JUSTICE (specially concurring).

I agree with the outcome reached by the majority, but on narrower grounds. I write out of concern that this Opinion might be interpreted to expand the population of presumed parents in a manner that would shake settled expectations of custody rights and child support responsibilities. If interpreted narrowly, the majority Opinion applies existing law to evolving, contemporary fact patterns, which is a good thing. If interpreted broadly, however, the majority Opinion could be read to impose seismic changes in custody and child support relationships that neither the New Mexico Uniform Parentage Act (UPA), nor sound policy authorizes, at least not in my judgment.

The majority Opinion holds that Chatterjee has standing to pursue shared custody of Child because the presumptions of paternity listed in Section 40–11–5 of the applicable UPA apply equally to women as presumptions of maternity when practicable. In order to reach this conclusion, I believe we need to address other questions that do not hinge upon Chatterjee's gender. *First, when is a nonadoptive, nonbiological individual a presumed parent under the holding-out provision of the UPA? Then, when does biology (the lack of a biological relationship) rebut such a presumption of parentage?*

Without answering these questions, the majority Opinion concludes that Chatterjee has standing to pursue custody because "[h]er pleading sets forth facts, which, if true, establish that she has a personal, financial, and custodial relationship with Child and has openly held Child out as her daughter, although she is neither Child's biological nor adoptive mother." But is concluding that Chatterjee has openly held out Child as her daughter the end of the inquiry? Not in my opinion.

Let me explain my concerns through a hypothetical. Suppose a hypothetical Mother has two children with men who are no longer involved in their lives for whatever reason, including death. Eventually, Mother begins a serious relationship with a hypothetical Man who moves in and lives happily with Mother and her two young children. Man assists in financial aspects of the household, which almost automatically includes expenses that support the children. At times he refers to himself as the children's father, for example in conversations with neighbors, perhaps on school documents and so forth, either for convenience purposes or perhaps because he truly does wish to become the children's father. Mother may or may not know that Man refers to himself in this way, but we will assume she does. Mother actively considers the possibility of marriage and that some day Man might adopt her two children.

After a few years, however, the relationship sours, and Mother asks Man to leave. It is over. But Man decides he does not want it to end entirely; he wants to share legal custody over the two children. Perhaps his motives are pure; perhaps he is just vindictive and extortionate. Whatever the motive, he alleges standing as a presumed father who has held out the children as his "own" and has established a financial, personal, and custodial relationship with them. He files in court and, as a presumed father, demands a full-blown custody hearing to prove his merits. The best interests of the children, he argues, require his presence in their lives, and Mother, whether out of spite or sincerity, is not acting in a manner consistent with those best interests. Mother finds herself in a custody battle to retain control over her own children.

A claim of presumed parenthood can be equally abused in the other direction. Perhaps Man chooses to end the relationship, never really interested in custody over the children. But it is the Mother who demands permanent child support from him, alleging that Man has become, however reluctantly, a presumed father by virtue of his holding out.

Neither of these scenarios strikes me as desirable from a policy point of view. They appear to run counter to conventional expectations among both professionals and the public at large. After all, the Mother in my hypothetical, completely fit as a parent, has never agreed to surrender her custodial rights to anyone. Should my hypothetical Man even have standing to pursue his claim? According to my reading of the UPA, such claims veer far outside the essential intent and structure of the statute. Yet we need to be careful, lest the majority Opinion be read to lay a legal basis for such claims.

The majority Opinion is not clear what facts Chatterjee has alleged sufficient to establish that she openly held out Child as her own.

Therefore, it is also not clear whether hypothetical Man, like Chatterjee, would have standing to pursue custody as a "presumed parent" under the holding-out provision. I believe Chatterjee's situation is distinct, and I write to explain why. Without this clarification and resulting narrowing of the Opinion, I fear the consequences of my hypothetical. As explained earlier, I fear that Man could force Mother to defend her sole custody rights in court, leaving the ultimate determination to a best-interests analysis by a judge, and only after prolonged, highly expensive, and totally unnecessary litigation. And, to make matters worse, if Man has deeper pockets than Mother, he might well win.

The majority states that "New Mexico courts have long recognized that children may form parent-child bonds with persons other than their legal parents." While I do not disagree, the point seems irrelevant, unless everything boils down to a "best interests" determination. For most of this Court's history, "the primary purpose of paternity suits [was] to insure the putative father meets his obligation to help support the child." *Aldridge ex rel. Aldridge v. Mims,* 118 N.M. 661, 665, 884 P.2d 817, 821 (Ct.App.1994). . . . In fact, there is only one prior New Mexico case in which a litigant cited the UPA as the basis for establishing parentage and thus, for standing to gain custody rights *for* a presumed father as opposed to child support *from* one. *See Lane v. Lane,* 121 N.M. 414, 912 P.2d 290. All other New Mexico cases apply the UPA to establish paternity in the child support context or in the context of paternal grandparents seeking visitation rights. And . . . the putative father in *Lane* was not successful under the holding-out provisions of the UPA. Given this limited history, this case poses questions of first impression regarding the UPA for which we truly do not have precedent. While it is self-evident that Chatterjee should have the same rights as a similarly-situated male, the more basic question asks whether and under what circumstances should such a male have standing to be considered a presumed natural parent under the Act.

We have certain traditional legal avenues for asserting parental rights over nonbiological children, primarily through adoption. Adoption can be complicated but, at the very least, it has a set legal protocol. It alerts everyone concerned, just like executing a will, of the solemnity of the occasion and its permanent consequences. . . .

We should be wary of interpreting statutes in a way that would dilute the need for such formality, relying instead upon the more ambiguous standard of "best interests." . . . The holding out provision under Section 40–11–5(A)(4) requires that "[a man] openly holds out the child as his natural child and has established a personal, financial or custodial relationship with the child." Although, "natural" in the context of "natural child," again, likely means biological in most cases, the provision does not require an assertion of, or an actual, biological relationship. It just requires that a presumed parent *hold a child out* as a natural child, meaning treating the child in the same way that a person would treat his or her biological child. Whether Chatterjee can allege that she has established a personal, financial, or custodial relationship with Child is not yet at issue. Whether Chatterjee "openly held out [Child] as [her] natural child," and exactly what that means, definitely is at issue. So too, is what my hypothetical Man should be required to allege by way of holding out before he could gain "presumed natural parent" status under the UPA and force hypothetical Mother to defend her sole custody status in court.

Cases from our own Court of Appeals as well as from California jurisprudence illustrate at least three common themes that define holding out a child as one's natural child. In each, the presumed parent (1) acted as a parent from the time the child was born or adopted; (2) assumed ongoing responsibilities to the child through legal and financial declarations; and (3) was recognized by the child's family, including another parent or the child, as the child's parent. This strikes me as a narrower class of presumed parents and significantly so, one that might just deter hypothetical Man from pursuit of custody. * * *

Under this high standard for "hold[ing] out," my hypothetical Man rightfully would have a difficult case to allege, much less prove, that he was a "presumed natural parent." In the hypothetical, Man was not involved in bringing Mother's children into the household, unlike Chatterjee who helped create the essential familial relationship. The children would not use or have Man's name. Man may or may not have listed the children formally on any legal documents as his own or as dependents in any formalized manner. It is not clear what role the children or the children's Mother would have considered hypothetical Man to have. To even come close to presumed parent status, Man must not just prove, but he must initially allege such facts. Hypothetical Man would have to make clear whether the children or Mother represented Man to others as the children's father, and in what context, or whether anyone else in the children's family would have believed Man to be the children's father. There would have to be evidence and allegations that hypothetical Man had assumed ongoing financial or legal obligations for the children.

Absent most of the foregoing, I do not believe that hypothetical Man could even allege that he has held himself out as a presumed natural parent. Thus, unlike Chatterjee, he would not have standing under the UPA, thereby avoiding the seismic shift in settled legal expectations that I outlined at the beginning of this discussion. Similarly, hypothetical Mother could not seek child support from hypothetical Man under the holding-out provision. All this follows, and justly so, as long as we take a disciplined view of what it really takes to become a presumed natural parent.

In re Marriage of Simmons

Appellate Court of Illinois, 2005
355 Ill.App.3d 942, 292 Ill.Dec. 47, 825 N.E.2d 303

Justice South.

Petitioner, Sterling Robert Simmons, and the minor child respondent, through his child-representative, Patrick T. Murphy, the Cook County Public Guardian, have filed these consolidated appeals arising from an order of the circuit court of Cook County which denied the petition for dissolution [of] marriage; declared that the marriage between petitioner and respondent, Jennifer Simmons, was invalid; awarded respondent sole care and custody of the minor child; held that petitioner lacked standing to seek custody of the child; terminated petitioner's parental rights; held that the minor child's constitutional rights were protected; and denied the minor child's motion for declaratory judgment.

Petitioner was born a female on March 31, 1959, and given the name of Bessie Cornelia Lewis. At a very young age, he[1] began experiencing a great discomfort with his female anatomy and became convinced that he was actually a boy who had been born into the body of a girl. This condition is commonly referred to in the psychiatric field as gender dysphoria or gender identity disorder. A person suffering from gender dysphoria is uncomfortable with his assigned or genetic sex and has a preoccupation with ridding himself of the physical characteristics of that assigned or genetic sex. To that end, petitioner began taking testosterone, the male hormone, to alter his appearance and started going by the name of Robert Sterling Simmons. He has been taking testosterone since he was 21 years old, and as a result thereof he now has the outward appearance of a man, which includes facial and body hair, male pattern baldness, a deep voice, a hypertrophied clitoris, and increased muscle and body mass.

Petitioner and respondent participated in a wedding ceremony on August 10, 1985, and a certificate of marriage was issued by the county clerk of Cook County on August 29, 1985. In 1991, they decided to have a child, and it was agreed that respondent would undergo artificial insemination. As a result of that procedure, respondent gave birth to the minor child on July 20, 1992, and petitioner is listed as the father on the child's birth certificate.

On July 31, 1991, petitioner underwent a total abdominal hysterectomy and a bilateral salpingo oophorectomy, which removed his uterus, fallopian tubes and ovaries. However, he still to this day retains all of his external female genitalia, which includes a vagina, labia, a hypertrophied clitoris, and breasts.

---

[1]   Throughout this opinion, we shall refer to petitioner as "He." This is done out of respect for petitioner and has no legal significance.

In 1994, petitioner sought to obtain a new birth certificate which would designate his sex as "male." In accordance with the Vital Records Act (410 ILCS 535/1 *et seq.* (West 2002)), Dr. Raymond McDermott, petitioner's treating physician who specializes in obstetrics and gynecology, submitted an "Affidavit by Physician as to Change of Sex Designation" to the Department of Public Health, attesting that he had performed "certain surgical operations" on petitioner "by reason of which the sex designation" should be changed from "female" to "male." The surgeries to which Dr. McDermott was alluding were the July 31, 1991, hysterectomy and oophorectomy. In October of 1994, the State Registrar issued petitioner a new birth certificate which bears the name of Sterling Robert Simmons and the gender designation of "male." The original birth certificate has been placed under seal and can only be opened by court order. Additionally, petitioner's name has been legally changed by court order to Sterling Robert Simmons.

The relationship between the parties was quite tumultuous and began to deteriorate throughout the years. On August 24, 1998, petitioner filed a petition for dissolution of marriage in which he sought, *inter alia,* temporary and permanent sole care and custody of the minor child. In her answer, respondent alleged that petitioner lacked standing to assert custody rights over the minor child because their same-sex marriage was invalid under Illinois law, and he was neither the biological nor adoptive parent. A trial was conducted on the petition, and the minor child was represented throughout the proceedings by a guardian *ad litem* and the office of the Public Guardian. At the conclusion of the trial, the court denied the petition for dissolution of marriage on the grounds that there was no marriage to dissolve since it was void *ab initio* as a same-sex marriage. The court also awarded sole custody of the minor child to respondent and declared that petitioner lacked parental rights or standing to seek custody. However, the court did grant petitioner visitation rights. While petitioner and the minor child appeal from the order, neither they nor respondent appeal that portion of the order which grants him visitation rights. * * *

Under the Illinois Marriage and Dissolution of Marriage Act (Marriage Act) (750 ILCS 5/101 *et seq.* (West 2002)), while a marriage between a man and a woman is valid (750 ILCS 5/201 (West 2002)), a marriage between two individuals of the same-sex is prohibited (750 ILCS 5/212(a)(5) (West 2002)). However, parties to a marriage prohibited under section 212 who cohabit after removal of the impediment are lawfully married as of the date of the removal of the impediment. 750 ILCS 5/212(b) (West 2002).

Petitioner challenges the trial court's conclusion that he is a female and not legally male. Petitioner was diagnosed as a transsexual male in his late teens and began undergoing sex reassignment treatments.

Petitioner maintains that he is male, that his marriage to respondent was valid, and that the trial court's conclusion that the marriage is invalid on the basis that he is a female was against the manifest weight of the evidence. * * *

Dr. Laurence Levin, respondent's expert in the field of gender reassignment, testified that while petitioner presents the physical appearance of a male, he has clear, normal female external genitalia and breast tissue. Dr. Frederic Ettner, petitioner's expert and a member of the Harry Benjamin International Gender Dysphoria Association, has treated hundreds of transsexuals during his medical career and described petitioner as a healthy male with male pattern baldness, the musculature of a male, facial and male body hair, and a male torso, but who still has female genitals, including atrophic or dysfunctional female breasts, atrophic labia, an enlarged clitoris, and a vagina. Dr. McDermott, while not an expert in the field of sexual or gender reassignment, testified that petitioner is still a female even after the hysterectomy and oophorectomy, and that those surgeries were never intended to be part of the sex-reassignment process. He admitted that the only reason he signed the physician's affidavit in connection with the issuance of the new birth certificate was to "help out" petitioner and make it easier for him to legally change his sex from female to male. All of the physicians testified that there were other surgeries which had to be done on petitioner before he could be considered completely sexually reassigned, which would include a vaginectomy, reduction mammoplasty, metoidoiplasty, scrotoplasty, urethroplasty, and phalloplasty.

Based upon the testimony of all of the expert witnesses who testified at trial that petitioner still possesses all of his female genitalia, we find that the judgment of the trial court that he is a female and not legally a male was not against the manifest weight of the evidence. Furthermore, once the trial court found that petitioner is a female who was "married" to another female, it had no choice but to deny the petition for dissolution of marriage on the grounds that the same-sex marriage was invalid under Illinois law.

Petitioner argues that even if the marriage was invalid at the time of the marriage ceremony in 1985, it subsequently became valid on July 31, 1991, when he underwent the hysterectomy and oophorectomy. He cites section 212(b) of the Marriage Act as support for his contention which provides that parties to a marriage prohibited under this section who cohabit after removal of the impediment are lawfully married as of the date of the removal of the impediment. 750 ILCS 5/212(b) (West 2002). Petitioner maintains that on July 31, 1991, the "impediment" was removed, and that he and respondent cohabited after removal of the impediment. However, contrary to petitioner's contention, the "impediment" has never been removed because while he has undergone surgeries to remove his internal female organs, he still possesses all of his external female genitalia and requires additional surgeries before sex reassignment can be considered completed. * * *

Petitioner maintains that even if we find his marriage is invalid, the artificial insemination agreement which he, respondent, and the physician signed pursuant to the Illinois Parentage Act (Parentage Act) (750 ILCS 40/1 *et seq.* (West 2002)) confers standing upon him to seek custody of the minor child.

The Parentage Act sets forth certain procedures for couples who wish to have children through artificial insemination:

> "If, under the supervision of a licensed physician and with the consent of her husband, a wife is inseminated artificially with semen donated by a man not her husband, the husband shall be treated in law as if he were the natural father of a child thereby conceived. The husband's consent must be in writing executed and acknowledged by both the husband and wife. The physician who is to perform the technique shall certify their signatures and the date of the insemination, and file the husband's consent in the medical record where it shall be kept confidential and held by the patient's physician. However, the physician's failure to do so shall not affect the legal relationship between father and child." 750 ILCS 40/3(a) (West 2002).

On April 18, 1991, the parties went to a fertility clinic and entered into a written artificial insemination agreement with a physician to perform "one or more, if necessary," artificial insemination procedures with sperm from a stranger-donor. That agreement stated, in relevant part:

> "It is further agreed that [at] the moment of conception the *husband* hereby accepts the act as his own, and agrees: 1. That such child or children so produced are his own legitimate child or children and are heirs of his body; and 2. That he hereby completely waives forever any right which he might have to disclaim such child or children as his own; and 3. That such child or children so procedure [*sic*] are, and shall be considered to be, in all respects including descent of property, child or children of his own body." (Emphasis added.)

That agreement was signed by petitioner as "husband," respondent as "wife," and the physician who performed the artificial insemination procedure.

This issue requires us to determine whether section 3 of the Parentage Act includes transsexual males who have signed artificial insemination agreements as husbands in an invalid same-sex marriage. We find that it does not. * * *

It is clear from reading the statute in question that the legislature intended that this statute apply to "husbands" and "wives" as those terms are ordinarily and popularly understood. Petitioner and respondent signed the agreement as "husband" and "wife." However, inasmuch as we have upheld the trial court's determination that petitioner was not a "husband" and respondent was not a "wife" due to the invalidity of their marriage, we are compelled to find that the agreement is also invalid. * * *

Petitioner further argues that even if the agreement is held to be invalid, section 5 of the Illinois Parentage Act of 1984 (Parentage Act of 1984) (750 ILCS 45/5 (West 2002)) grants a presumption of parenthood, and that a child born from artificial insemination to two married parents retains his right to parentage with both parents even if the marriage is subsequently held invalid.

Section 5 of the Parentage Act of 1984 states in relevant part:

"(a) A man is presumed to be the natural father of a child if:

(1) he and the child's natural mother are or have been married to each other, even though the marriage is or could be declared invalid, and the child is born or conceived during such marriage;

(2) after the child's birth, he and the child's natural mother have married each other, even though the marriage is or could be declared invalid, and he is named, with his written consent, as the child's father on the child birth certificate[.]" 750 ILCS 45/5(a)(1), (a)(2) (West 2002).

While we agree with petitioner's interpretation of the statute, we must conclude that it does not apply to him. That section, which confers a presumption on a "man" to be the natural father of a child even after a marriage has been declared invalid, is based on the premise that the parties who are involved are a man and a woman. As we have previously determined, petitioner is not a man within the meaning of the statute, and that, therefore, the statute does not apply. * * *

Petitioner also contends that he should be declared the *de facto* parent based upon his long, loving and close relationship with the minor child who has always known him as his "Daddy." In *In re Visitation With C.B.L.,* 309 Ill.App.3d 888, 243 Ill.Dec. 284, 723 N.E.2d 316 (1999), the petitioner, who had engaged in a long-term lesbian relationship with respondent, who had given birth to the minor as a result of artificial insemination, sought an order granting her visitation with the minor child pursuant to the Marriage Act. She argued that she had alleged facts in her petition sufficient to establish her standing as a common law *de facto* parent or as an individual *in loco parentis* to the minor child. On appeal, she abandoned her contention that the allegations within her petition were sufficient to establish her standing under the Marriage Act and contended only that they were sufficient to provide her standing as a common law *de facto* parent or as an individual *in loco parentis* to C.B.L. This court held that the Marriage Act superseded and supplanted the common law of visitation in Illinois and that, therefore, any standing for visitation must be found solely within that Act. Since petitioner conceded her lack of standing under the Act, her petition lacked merit.

The court in *C.B.L.* further stated:

"Finally, this court is not unmindful of the fact that our evolving social structures have created nontraditional relationships. This court, however, has no authority to ignore the manifest intent of our General Assembly. Who shall have standing to petition for visitation with a minor is an issue of complex social significance. Such an issue demands a comprehensive legislative solution. That solution is provided, by our General Assembly, within [the Marriage Act]." *C.B.L.,* 309 Ill.App.3d at 894–95, 243 Ill.Dec. 284, 723 N.E.2d 316.

Similarly, in the instant case, petitioner's standing to seek full care and custody of the minor child must be found solely within the Marriage Act, the Parentage Act, or the Parentage Act of 1984. Our determination that he lacks such standing under those acts is dispositive of the issue. . . . Affirmed.

NOTES

1. In all 50 states, either as a result of statutory or common law, a husband who consents to his wife's insemination with sperm donated by another man is considered to be the child's parent. *See* Courtney G. Joslin, *Protecting Children(?): Marriage, Gender, and Assisted Reproductive Technology,* 83 S. CAL. L. REV. 1177, 1184–85 (2010). But in most states, the same kind of explicit protection is not available to unmarried couples, including same-sex ones, who conceive through alternative insemination. *See id.* at 1186–87. This means that these couples' children "will have a legal parent-child relationship with only one of the intended parents." *Id.* at 1187 (footnote omitted).

2. Courts are divided on the question of whether the equitable doctrine of *de facto* parenthood (also sometimes referred to as *in loco parentis* or psychological parenthood) allows the unmarried partner of a legal parent to exercise rights over the child after the relationship between the adults ends. Some courts, like the New Jersey court in *V.C. v. M.J.B,* have ruled that it does. For other cases in which courts have ruled similarly in the context of dissolving same-sex relationships, *see, e.g., In re E.L.M.C.,* 100 P.3d 546, 555 (Colo. Ct. App. 2004); *King v. S.B.,* 837 N.E.2d 965, 967 (Ind. 2005); *C.E.W. v.*

D.E.W., 845 A.2d 1146, 1152, 2004 Me. 43 (2004); *E.N.O. v. L.M.M.*, 711 N.E.2d 886, 893, 429 Mass. 824, 832 (1999); *Latham v. Schwerdtfeger*, 802 N.W.2d 66, 74, 282 Neb. 121, 132 (2011); *Mason v. Dwinnell*, 660 S.E.2d 58, 65, 190 N.C.App. 209, 220 (2008); *T.B. v. L.R.M.*, 753 A.2d 873, 888, 2000 PA Super 168 (2000), *aff'd*, 786 A.2d 913, 567 Pa. 222 (2001); *Rubano v. Dicenzo*, 759 A.2d 959, 967 (R.I. 2000); *In re Parentage of L.B.*, 122 P.3d 161, 177, 155 Wash.2d 679, 708 (2005) (en banc); *Custody of H.S.H.-K*, 533 N.W.2d 419, 437, 193 Wis.2d 649, 699 (1995).

3.   Other courts, like the Illinois one in *In re Marriage of Simmons*, have rejected the equitable doctrine of *de facto* parenthood. For additional such rulings involving LGBT litigants, *see, e.g., Smith v. Gordon*, 968 A.2d 1, 2 (Del. 2009) (abrogated by DEL. CODE. ANN. TIT. 13, § 8–201(a)(4), (b)(6) (2009)); *Matter of Visitation with C.B.L.*, 309 Ill.App.3d 888, 895, 243 Ill.Dec. 284, 723 N.E.2d 316, 321 (1999); *Wakeman v. Dixon*, 921 So.2d 669, 671 (Fla. Dist. Ct. App. 2006) (en banc); *B.F. v. T.D.*, 194 S.W.3d 310, 312 (Ky. 2006); *Janice M. v. Margaret K.*, 948 A.2d 73, 75, 404 Md. 661, 664 (2008); *White v. White*, 293 S.W.3d 1, 15–16 (Mo.Ct.App. 2009); *Alison D. v. Virginia M.*, 77 N.Y.2d 651, 656, 569 N.Y.S.2d 586, 572 N.E.2d 27, 29 (1991); *In re Thompson*, 11 S.W.3d 913, 919 (Tenn.Ct.App. 1999); *Jones v. Barlow*, 154 P.3d 808, 815, 2007 UT 20 (2007); *Stadter v. Spirko*, 52 Va.App. 81, 91, 661 S.E.2d 494, 498–99 (2008). Several of these decisions were issued after the prestigious American Law Institute ("ALI") urged states to adopt equitable parenthood doctrines as part of their relationship dissolution laws. *See* PRINCIPLES OF THE LAW OF FAMILY DISSOLUTION: ANALYSIS AND RECOMMENDATIONS § 2.03 (American Law Institute ed., 2002). For example, despite the ALI's position on the issue, and the fact that several state supreme courts across the country have recognized the doctrine of *de facto* parenthood, the New York Court of Appeals reaffirmed its rejection of that doctrine. *See Debra H. v. Janice R.*, 14 N.Y.3d 576, 589, 904 N.Y.S.2d 263, 930 N.E.2d 184, 188 (2010).

4.   The Uniform Parentage Act, which was promulgated in 1973 and amended in 2002, has been adopted, often in modified form, by nineteen states. Note that the court in *Chatterjee* relied on the state's UPA, rather than on the equitable doctrine of de facto parenthood, to grant standing to the lesbian co-parent in the case. In particular, the court relied on the UPA's "holding out" provision, concluding that it applied to putative mothers, not just fathers. How would you characterize the concurring Justice's concerns about the potential application of the majority opinion? Do you think it was crucial for the outcome of the case that the petitioner in *Chatterjee* was involved in the decision to bring the child into the home from the very beginning? Is that the main difference between the facts in the case and the concurring Justice's hypothetical involving Mother and Man? Should parentage presumptions based on "holding out" apply to individuals who were not involved in the decision to bring the child into the home—that is, to individuals who became involved with the legal parent only after that parent had a child?

5. The transgender father in *In re Marriage of Simmons* lost in part because Illinois does not recognize the doctrine of de facto parenthood. But the court also concluded that because the father was legally a woman, his union with the child's mother was an invalid same-sex marriage. This, in turn, meant that the father could not seek custody of the child. In assessing the court's reasoning, try to determine why the court found it necessary to link the question of parenthood with that of the validity of the marriage. Does such a link make sense?

6. The Kansas Supreme Court, in *Frazier v. Goudschaal*, 296 Kan. 730, 751, 295 P.3d 542, 556 (2013), held that a parenting agreement entered into by a lesbian couple was enforceable, and that, as a result, the biological parent's former partner was entitled to a determination of whether granting her custody was in the child's best interests. In rejecting the biological mother's argument that the enforcement of the agreement violated her constitutional rights, the court explained that she

> overlooks . . . the fact that she exercised her due process right to decide upon the care, custody, and control of her children and asserted her preference as a parent when she entered into the coparenting agreement with Frazier. If a parent has a constitutional right to make the decisions regarding the care, custody, and control of his or her children, free of government interference, then that parent should have the right to enter into a coparenting agreement to share custody with another without having the government interfere by nullifying that agreement, so long as it is in the best interests of the children. Further, . . . parental preference can be waived and . . . the courts should not be required to assign to a mother any more rights than that mother has claimed for herself.

Id. at 557. Although some courts have held that parenting agreements are relevant to determining how custody should be arranged *after* there has been a determination that the party seeking to enforce the contract is a legal parent, see, e.g., *St. Mary v. Damon*, 309 P.3d 1027 (Nev. 2013), discussed in *supra* Section II.B.2, the *Frazier* court concluded that the agreement was strong evidence that the lesbian partner who was not biologically related to the child was a legal parent to begin with.

7. What role should the lack of a biological connection between a functional or *de facto* parent and the child play in determining whether the former can seek custody (rather than just visitation)? Notice that the New Jersey Supreme Court in *V.C. v. M.J.B.* ruled that a parent's biological connection should be given "*a significant weight* in the best interests balance because eventually, in the search for self-knowledge, the child's interest in his or her roots will emerge." 163 N.J. 200, 228, 748 A.2d 539, 554 (2000) (emphasis added). Do you agree with this type of presumption in favor of granting custody to the biological parent over the nonbiological one?

8. In *Jones v. Jones*, 884 A.2d 915, 919, 2005 PA Super 337 (2005), a Pennsylvania appellate court upheld the granting of custody to the

nonbiological mother rather than to the biological mother. The court, after reviewing Pennsylvania cases, concluded that the best interests analysis is weighted in favor of the biological parent over someone who is *in loco parentis* ("in the place of a parent") with the children. The court added that "[t]he burden of proof is not evenly balanced, as [biological] parents have a *prima facie* right to custody, which will be forfeited only if convincing reasons appear that the child's best interest will be served by an award to the third party." *Id.* It is not necessary, however, for a person who is *in loco parentis* with the children "to establish that the biological parent is unfit." *Id.* at 917. In reviewing the evidence presented below, the appellate court concluded that the trial judge did not err: "While the scale was tipped in favor of Boring [the biological mother], Jones [the nonbiological mother] produced clear and convincing reasons to even the scale and then tip it on her side. Jones did not establish that Boring was unfit, and was not required to do so, but Jones did clearly and convincingly establish that the children would be better off with her as the primary custodian and that the children's relationship with *both* parties would be better fostered if custody were awarded to Jones." 884 A.2d at 918.

9.   LGBT individuals who are deemed to be a child's parent under the equitable doctrine of *de facto* parenthood are sometimes required to pay child support. *See* L.S.K. v. H.A.N., 813 A.2d 872 (Pa. Super.Ct. 2002). *See also Elisa B. v. Superior Court*, 117 P.3d 660, 37 Cal.4th 108, 33 Cal.Rptr.3d 46 (2005) (holding that, under California Uniform Parentage Act, lesbian partner of biological mother who consented and participated in artificial insemination, with the understanding that she would help raise child, was liable for child support); *Karin T. v. Michael T.*, 484 N.Y.S.2d 780, 127 Misc.2d 14 (Fam. Ct. 1985) (male transgender individual who agreed to be child's co-parent is responsible for child support). For rulings in which courts have concluded that the LGBT individuals' degree of involvement in the child's life did not justify the imposition of child support obligations, see *T.F. v. B.L.*, 813 N.E.2d 1244, 1253, 442 Mass. 522, 533 (2004); *State ex rel. D.R.M.*, 34 P.3d 887, 898, 109 Wash.App. 182, 203 (Ct.App. 2001).

INDEX

References are to Pages